D0382493

MULTIPLE REGRESSION IN BEHAVIORAL RESEARCH

EXPLANATION AND PREDICTION

THIRD EDITION

ELAZAR J. PEDHAZUR

WADSWORTH

THOMSON LEARNING ™

Australia • Canada • Mexico • Singapore • Spain
United Kingdom • United States

WADSWORTH

THOMSON LEARNING

Publisher: Christopher P. Klein
Executive Editor: Earl McPeek
Project Editor: Kathryn Stewart
Production Managers: Jane Tyndall Ponceti,
 Serena Manning

Senior Product Manager: Susan Kindel
Art Director: Jeanette Barber
Cover Printer: Lehigh Press, Inc.
Compositor: TSI Graphics
Printer: R.R. Donnelley, Crawfordsville

COPYRIGHT © 1997, 1982, 1973
Thomson Learning, Inc. Thomson Learning™
is a trademark used herein under license.

ALL RIGHTS RESERVED. No part of this work
covered by the copyright hereon may be reproduced or used in any form or by any means—
graphic, electronic, or mechanical, including but
not limited to photocopying, recording, taping,
Web distribution, information networks, or information storage and retrieval systems—without the
written permission of the publisher.

Printed in the United States of America
 11 12 07

For more information about our products,
contact us at:
Thomson Learning Academic Resource Center
1-800-423-0563

For permission to use material from this
text, contact us by:
Phone: 1-800-730-2214
Fax: 1-800-730-2215
Web: http://www.thomsonrights.com

Library of Congress Catalog Card Number:
96-78486

ISBN-13: 978-0-03-072831-0
ISBN-10: 0-03-072831-2

Asia
Thomson Learning
60 Albert Street, #15-01
Albert Complex
Singapore 189969

Australia
Nelson Thomson Learning
102 Dodds Street
South Melbourne, Victoria 3205
Australia

Canada
Nelson Thomson Learning
1120 Birchmount Road
Toronto, Ontario M1K 5G4
Canada

Europe/Middle East/Africa
Thomson Learning
Berkshire House
168-173 High Holborn
London WC1 V7AA
United Kingdom

Latin America
Thomson Learning
Seneca, 53
Colonia Polanco
11560 Mexico D.F.
Mexico

Spain
Paraninfo Thomson Learning
Calle/Magallanes, 25
28015 Madrid, Spain

To Geula
Liora and Alan, Danielle and Andrew, and Alex
Hadar
Jonah, Chaya, Ziva and David

Preface to the Third Edition

Chapter 1 is an overview of the contents and general orientation of this edition. Here, I will mention briefly some major additions and extensions to topics presented in the Second Edition.

Regression Diagnostics. In addition to a new chapter in which I present current thinking and practice in regression diagnostics, I discuss aspects of this topic in several other chapters.

Logistic Regression. In view of the increased use of designs with categorical dependent variables (e.g., yes-no, agree-disagree responses), I have added a chapter on logistic regression.

Multilevel Analysis. Reflecting the shift from concerns about the "appropriate" unit of analysis (e.g., individuals, groups) to multilevel analysis, I introduce basic ideas and elements of this approach.

Computer Programs. Considering the prevalence and increased capacities of the personal computer, I introduce four popular statistical packages (BMDP, MINITAB, SAS, and SPSS) that can be run on a PC and use them in various chapters.

Research Examples. Because of widespread use (and abuse) of the type of analytic techniques I present, I expanded my critiques of research studies in the hope that this will help you read critically published research and avoid pitfalls in your research. Also, I commented on the peer review process.

Other Areas. While keeping the overall objectives and the nonmathematical approach of the Second Edition, I reorganized, edited, revised, expanded, and updated all chapters to reflect the most recent thinking on the topics presented, including references. Following are but some examples of topics I expanded: (1) factorial designs and the study and meaning of interaction in experimental and nonexperimental research, (2) cross-products of continuous variables in experimental and nonexperimental research, (3) treatment of measurement errors in path analysis, (4) indirect effects in structural equation models, and (5) the use of LISREL and EQS in the analysis of structural equation models.

I would like to thank several anonymous reviewers for their constructive comments on the proposed revision.

My deepest appreciation to Kathryn M. Stewart, project editor, for her efforts, responsiveness, attentiveness, and caring. Her contribution to the production of this book has been invaluable.

I am very grateful to Lawrence Erlbaum for lending his sensitive ears, caring heart, and sagacious mind, thereby making some ordeals almost bearable.

As always, I benefited greatly from my daughter's, Professor Liora Pedhazur Schmelkin, counsel and insights. Not only did we have an ongoing dialogue on every facet of this edition, but she read and commented on every aspect of the manuscript. Her contribution is immeasurable as is my love for her.

ELAZAR J. PEDHAZUR
Aventura, Florida

Preface to the Second Edition

This edition constitutes a major revision and expansion of the first. While the overall objectives and the nonmathematical approach of the first edition have been retained (see Preface to the First Edition), much that is new has been incorporated in the present edition. It is not possible to enumerate here all the changes and additions. An overview of the methods presented and the perspectives from which they are viewed will be found in Chapter 1. What follows is a partial listing of major expansions and additions.

Although, as in the first edition, Part 1 is devoted to the foundations of multiple regression analysis (MR), attempts have been made to delineate more clearly the role of theory, research goals, and research design in the application of MR and the interpretation of the results. Accordingly, chapters dealing exclusively with either prediction (Chapter 6) or explanation (Chapters 7 and 8) were added.

Among new or expanded topics in Part 1 are: the analysis of residuals (Chapter 2); specification and measurement errors (Chapters 2 and 8); multicollinearity (Chapter 8); variable-selection procedures (Chapter 6); variance partitioning (Chapter 7); and the interpretation of regression coefficients as indices of the effects of variables (Chapter 8).

Computer programs from three popular packages (SPSS, BMDP, and SAS), introduced in Chapter 4, are used repeatedly throughout the book. For each run, the control cards are listed and commented upon. This is followed by excerpts of the output and commentaries, which are designed not only to acquaint the reader with the output, but also for the purpose of elaborating upon and extending the discussion of specific methods dealt with in a given chapter.

Among notable expansions and additions in Part 2 are: A more detailed treatment of multiple comparisons among means, and the use of tests of significance among regression coefficients for the purpose of carrying out such comparisons (see, in particular, Chapters 9 and 13). An expanded discussion has been provided of nonorthogonal designs, and of distinctions in the use of such designs in experimental versus nonexperimental research (Chapter 10). There is a more detailed discussion of the concept of interaction, and tests of simple main effects (Chapter 10). A longer discussion has been given of designs with continuous and categorical variables, including multiple aptitudes in aptitude-treatment-interaction designs, and multiple covariates in the analysis of covariance (Chapters 12 and 13). There is a new chapter on repeated-measures designs (Chapter 14) and a discussion of issues regarding the unit of analysis and ecological inference (Chapter 13).

Part 3 constitutes an extended treatment of causal analysis. In addition to an enlarged discussion of path analysis (Chapter 15), a chapter devoted to an introduction to LInear Structural

RELations (LISREL) was added (Chapter 16). The chapter includes detailed discussions and illustrations of the application of LISREL IV to the solution of structural equation models.

Part 4 is an expanded treatment of discriminant analysis, multivariate analysis of variance, and canonical analysis. Among other things, the relations among these methods, on the one hand, and their relations to MR, on the other hand, are discussed and illustrated.

In the interest of space, it was decided to delete the separate chapters dealing with research applications. It will be noted, however, that research applications are discussed in various chapters in the context of discussions of specific analytic techniques.

I am grateful to Professors Ellis B. Page, Jum C. Nunnally, Charles W. McNichols, and Douglas E. Stone for reviewing various parts of the manuscript and for their constructive suggestions for its improvement.

Ellen Koenigsberg, Professor Liora Pedhazur Schmelkin, and Dr. Elizabeth Taleporos have not only read the entire manuscript and offered valuable suggestions, but have also been always ready to listen, willing to respond, eager to discuss, question, and challenge. For all this, my deepest appreciation.

My thanks to the administration of the School of Education, Health, Nursing, and Arts Professions of New York University for enabling me to work consistently on the book by granting me a sabbatical leave, and for the generous allocation of computer time for the analyses reported in the book.

To Bert Holland, of the Academic Computing Center, my thanks for expert assistance in matters concerning the use of the computing facilities at New York University.

My thanks to Brian Heald and Sara Boyajian of Holt, Rinehart and Winston for their painstaking work in preparing the manuscript for publication.

I am grateful to my friends Sheldon Kastner and Marvin Sontag for their wise counsel.

It has been my good fortune to be a student of Fred N. Kerlinger, who has stimulated and nourished my interest in scientific inquiry, research design and methodology. I was even more fortunate when as a colleague and friend he generously shared with me his knowledge, insights, and wit. For all this, and more, thank you, Fred, and may She . . .

My wife, Geula, has typed and retyped the entire manuscript—a difficult job for which I cannot thank her enough. And how can I thank her for her steadfast encouragement, for being a source of joy and happiness, for sharing? Dedicating this book to her is but a small token of my love and appreciation.

ELAZAR J. PEDHAZUR

Brooklyn, New York

Preface to the First Edition

Like many ventures, this book started in a small way: we wanted to write a brief manual for our students. And we started to do this. We soon realized, however, that it did not seem possible to write a brief exposition of multiple regression analysis that students would understand. The brevity we sought is possible only with a mathematical presentation relatively unadorned with numerical examples and verbal explanations. Moreover, the more we tried to work out a reasonably brief manual the clearer it became that it was not possible to do so. We then decided to write a book.

Why write a whole book on multiple regression analysis? There are three main reasons. One, multiple regression is a general data analytic system (Cohen, 1968) that is close to the theoretical and inferential preoccupations and methods of scientific behavioral research. If, as we believe, science's main job is to "explain" natural phenomena by discovering and studying the relations among variables, then multiple regression is a general and efficient method to help do this.

Two, multiple regression and its rationale underlie most other multivariate methods. Once multiple regression is well understood, other multivariate methods are easier to comprehend. More important, their use in actual research becomes clearer. Most behavioral research attempts to explain one dependent variable, one natural phenomenon, at a time. There is of course research in which there are two or more dependent variables. But such research can be more profitably viewed, we think, as an extension of the one dependent variable case. Although we have not entirely neglected other multivariate methods, we have concentrated on multiple regression. In the next decade and beyond, we think it will be seen as the cornerstone of modern data analysis in the behavioral sciences.

Our strongest motivation for devoting a whole book to multiple regression is that the behavioral sciences are at present in the midst of a conceptual and technical revolution. It must be remembered that the empirical behavioral sciences are young, not much more than fifty to seventy years old. Moreover, it is only recently that the empirical aspects of inquiry have been emphasized. Even after psychology, a relatively advanced behavioral science, became strongly empirical, its research operated in the univariate tradition. Now, however, the availability of multivariate methods and the modern computer makes possible theory and empirical research that better reflect the multivariate nature of psychological reality.

The effects of the revolution are becoming apparent, as we will show in the latter part of the book when we describe studies such as Frederiksen et al.'s (1968) study of organizational climate and administrative performance and the now well-known *Equality of Educational Opportunity* (Coleman et al., 1966). Within the decade we will probably see the virtual demise of one-variable thinking and the use of analysis of variance with data unsuited to the method. Instead, multivariate methods will be well-accepted tools in the behavioral scientist's and educator's armamentarium.

The structure of the book is fairly simple. There are five parts. Part 1 provides the theoretical foundations of correlation and simple and multiple regression. Basic calculations are illustrated and explained and the results of such calculations tied to rather simple research problems. The major purpose of Part 2 is to explore the relations between multiple regression analysis and analysis of variance and to show the student how to do analysis of variance and covariance with multiple regression. In achieving this purpose, certain technical problems are examined in detail: coding of categorical and experimental variables, interaction of variables, the relative contributions of independent variables to the dependent variable, the analysis of trends, commonality analysis, and path analysis. In addition, the general problems of explanation and prediction are attacked.

Part 3 extends the discussion, although not in depth, to other multivariate methods: discriminant analysis, canonical correlation, multivariate analysis of variance, and factor analysis. The basic emphasis on multiple regression as the core method, however, is maintained. The use of multiple regression analysis—and, to a lesser extent, other multivariate methods—in behavioral and educational research is the substance of Part 4. We think that the student will profit greatly by careful study of actual research uses of the method. One of our purposes, indeed, has been to expose the student to cogent uses of multiple regression. We believe strongly in the basic unity of methodology and research substance.

In Part 5, the emphasis on theory and substantive research reaches its climax with a direct attack on the relation between multiple regression and scientific research. To maximize the probability of success, we examine in some detail the logic of scientific inquiry, experimental and nonexperimental research, and, finally, theory and multivariate thinking in behavioral research. All these problems are linked to multiple regression analysis.

In addition to the five parts briefly characterized above, four appendices are included. The first three address themselves to matrix algebra and the computer. After explaining and illustrating elementary matrix algebra—an indispensable and, happily, not too complex a subject—we discuss the use of the computer in data analysis generally and we give one of our own computer programs in its entirety with instructions for its use. The fourth appendix is a table of the F distribution, 5 percent and 1 percent levels of significance.

Achieving an appropriate level of communication in a technical book is always a difficult problem. If one writes at too low a level, one cannot really explain many important points. Moreover, one may insult the background and intelligence of some readers, as well as bore them. If one writes at too advanced a level, then one loses most of one's audience. We have tried to write at a fairly elementary level, but have not hesitated to use certain advanced ideas. And we have gone rather deeply into a number of important, even indispensable, concepts and methods. To do this and still keep the discussion within the reach of students whose mathematical and statistical backgrounds are bounded, say, by correlation and analysis of variance, we have sometimes had to be what can be called excessively wordy, although we hope not verbose. To compensate, the assumptions behind multiple regression and related methods have not been emphasized. Indeed, critics may find the book wanting in its lack of discussion of mathematical and statistical assumptions and derivations. This is a price we had to pay, however, for what we hope is comprehensible exposition. In other words, understanding and intelligent practical use of multiple regression are more important in our estimation than rigid adherence to statistical assumptions. On the other hand, we have discussed in detail the weaknesses as well as the strengths of multiple regression.

The student who has had a basic course in statistics, including some work in inferential statistics, correlation, and, say, simple one-way analysis of variance should have little difficulty. The book should be useful as a text in an intermediate analysis or statistics course or in courses in research design and methodology. Or it can be useful as a supplementary text in such courses. Some instructors may wish to use only parts of the book to supplement their work in design and analysis. Such use is feasible because some parts of the books are almost self-sufficient. With instructor help, for example, Part 2 can be used alone. We suggest, however, sequential study since the force of certain points made in later chapters, particularly on theory and research, depends to some extent at least on earlier discussions.

We have an important suggestion to make. Our students in research design courses seem to have benefited greatly from exposure to computer analysis. We have found that students with little or no background in data processing, as well as those with background, develop facility in the use of packaged computer programs rather quickly. Moreover, most of them gain confidence and skill in handling data, and they become fascinated by the immense potential of analysis by computer. Not only has computer analysis helped to illustrate and enhance the subject matter of our courses; it has also relieved students of laborious calculations, thereby enabling them to concentrate on the interpretation and meaning of data. We therefore suggest that instructors with access to computing facilities have their students use the computer to analyze the examples given in the text as well as to do exercises and term projects that require computer analysis.

We wish to acknowledge the help of several individuals. Professors Richard Darlington and Ingram Olkin read the entire manuscript of the book and made many helpful suggestions, most of which we have followed. We are grateful for their help in improving the book. To Professor Ernest Nagel we express our thanks for giving us his time to discuss philosophical aspects of causality. We are indebted to Professor Jacob Cohen for first arousing our curiosity about multiple regression and its relation to analysis of variance and its application to data analysis.

The staff of the Computing Center of the Courant Institute of Mathematical Sciences, New York University, has been consistently cooperative and helpful. We acknowledge, particularly, the capable and kind help of Edward Friedman, Neil Smith, and Robert Malchie of the Center. We wish to thank Elizabeth Taleporos for valuable assistance in proofreading and in checking numerical examples. Geula Pedhazur has given fine typing service with ungrateful material. She knows how much we appreciate her help.

New York University's generous sabbatical leave policy enabled one of us to work consistently on the book. The Courant Institute Computing Center permitted us to use the Center's CDC-6600 computer to solve some of our analytic and computing problems. We are grateful to the university and to the computing center, and, in the latter case, especially to Professor Max Goldstein, associate director of the center.

Finally, but not too apologetically, we appreciate the understanding and tolerance of our wives who often had to undergo the hardships of talking and drinking while we discussed our plans, and who had to put up with, usually cheerfully, our obsession with the subject and the book.

This book has been a completely cooperative venture of its authors. It is not possible, therefore, to speak of a "senior" author. Yet our names must appear in some order on the cover and title page. We have solved the problem by listing the names alphabetically, but would like it understood that the order could just as well have been the other way around.

FRED N. KERLINGER
ELAZAR J. PEDHAZUR

Amsterdam, The Netherlands
Brooklyn, New York
March 1973

Contents

Overview

Remarkable advances in the analysis of educational, psychological, and sociological data have been made in recent decades. Much of this increased understanding and mastery of data analysis has come about through the wide propagation and study of statistics and statistical inference, and especially from the analysis of variance. The expression "analysis of variance" is well chosen. It epitomizes the basic nature of most data analysis: the partitioning, isolation, and identification of variation in a dependent variable due to different independent variables.

Other analytic statistical techniques, such as multiple regression analysis and multivariate analysis, have been applied less frequently until recently, not only because they are less well understood by behavioral researchers but also because they generally involve numerous and complex computations that in most instances require the aid of a computer for their execution. The recent widespread availability of computer facilities and package programs has not only liberated researchers from the drudgery of computations, but it has also put the most sophisticated and complex analytic techniques within the easy reach of anyone who has the rudimentary skills required to process data by computer. (In a later section, I comment on the use, and potential abuse, of the computer for data analysis.)

It is a truism that methods per se mean little unless they are integrated within a theoretical context and are applied to data obtained in an appropriately designed study. "It is sad that many investigations are carried out with no clear idea of the objective. This is a recipe for disaster or at least for an error of the third kind, namely 'giving the right answer to the wrong question' " (Chatfield, 1991, p. 241). Indeed, "The important question about methods is not 'how' but 'why' " (Tukey, 1954, p. 36).

Nevertheless, much of this book is about the "how" of methods, which is indispensable for appreciating their potentials, for keeping aware of their limitations, and for understanding their role in the overall research endeavor. Widespread misconceptions notwithstanding, data do *not* speak for themselves but through the medium of the analytic techniques applied to them. It is important to realize that analytic techniques not only set limits to the scope and nature of the answers one may obtain from data, but they also affect the type of questions a researcher asks and the manner in which the questions are formulated. "It comes as no particular surprise to discover that a scientist formulates problems in a way which requires for their solution just those techniques in which he himself is especially skilled" (Kaplan, 1964, p. 28).

Analytic techniques may be viewed from a variety of perspectives, among which are an analytic perspective and a research perspective. I use "analytic perspective" here to refer to such aspects as the mechanics of the calculations of a given technique, the meaning of its elements and the interrelations among them, and the statistical assumptions that underlie its valid application. Knowledge of these aspects is, needless to say, essential for the valid use of any analytic technique. Yet, the analytic perspective is narrow, and sole preoccupation with it poses the threat of losing sight of the role of analysis in scientific inquiry. It is one thing to know how to calculate a correlation coefficient or a *t* ratio, say, and quite another to know whether such techniques are applicable to the question(s) addressed in the study. Regrettably, while students can recite chapter and verse of a method, say a *t* ratio for the difference between means, they cannot frequently tell when it is validly applied and how to interpret the results it yields.

To fully appreciate the role and meaning of an analytic technique it is necessary to view it from the broader research perspective, which includes such aspects as the purpose of the study, its theoretical framework, and the type of research. In a book such as this one I cannot deal with the research perspective in the detail that it deserves, as this would require, among other things, detailed discussions of the philosophy of scientific inquiry, of theories in specific disciplines (e.g., psychology, sociology, and political science), and of research design. I do, however, attempt throughout the book to discuss the analytic techniques from a research perspective; to return to the question of why a given method is used and to comment on its role in the overall research setting. Thus I show, for instance, how certain elements of an analytic technique are applicable in one research setting but not in another, or that the interpretation of elements of a method depends on the research setting in which it is applied.[1]

I use the aforementioned perspectives in this chapter to organize the overview of the contents and major themes of this book. Obviously, however, no appreciable depth of understanding can be accomplished at this stage; nor is it intended. My purpose is rather to set the stage, to provide an orientation, for things to come. Therefore, do not be concerned if you do not understand some of the concepts and techniques I mention or comment on briefly. A certain degree of ambiguity is inevitable at this stage. I hope that it will be diminished when, in subsequent chapters, I discuss in detail topics I outline or allude to in the present chapter.

I conclude the chapter with some comments about my use of research examples in this book.

THE ANALYTIC PERSPECTIVE

The fundamental task of science is to explain phenomena. Its basic aim is to discover or invent general explanations of natural events (for a detailed explication of this point of view, see Braithwaite, 1953). Natural phenomena are complex. The phenomena and constructs of the behavioral sciences—learning, achievement, anxiety, conservatism, social class, aggression, reinforcement, authoritarianism, and so on—are especially complex. "Complex" in this context means that the phenomenon has many facets and many causes. In a research-analytic context, "complex" means that a phenomenon has several sources of variation. To study a construct or a variable scientifically we must be able to identify the sources of its variation. Broadly, a variable is any attribute on which objects or individuals vary. This means that when we apply an instrument that measures the variable to a sample of individuals, we obtain more or less different scores for each. We talk about the variance of college grade-point averages (as a measure of achievement) or the

---

[1]I recommend wholeheartedly Abelson's (1995) well-reasoned and engagingly written book on themes such as those briefly outlined here.

variability among individuals on a scale designed to measure locus of control, ego strength, learned helplessness, and so on.

Broadly speaking, the scientist is interested in explaining variance. In the behavioral sciences, variability is itself a phenomenon of great scientific curiosity and interest. The large differences in the intelligence and achievement of children, for instance, and the considerable differences among schools and socioeconomic groups in critical educational variables are phenomena of deep interest and concern to behavioral scientists.

In their attempts to explain the variability of a phenomenon of interest (often called the *dependent variable*), scientists study its relations or covariations with other variables (called the *independent variables*). In essence, information from the independent variables is brought to bear on the dependent variables. Educational researchers seek to explain the variance of school achievement by studying its relations with intelligence, aptitude, social class, race, home background, school atmosphere, teacher characteristics, and so on. Political scientists seek to explain voting behavior by studying variables presumed to influence it: sex, age, income, education, party affiliation, motivation, place of residence, and the like. Psychologists seek to explain aggressive behavior by searching for variables that may elicit it: frustration, noise, heat, crowding, exposure to acts of violence on television.

Various analytic techniques have been developed for studying relations between independent variables and dependent variables, or the effects of the former on the latter. In what follows I give a synopsis of techniques I present in this book. I conclude this section with some observations on the use of the computer for data analysis.

Simple Regression Analysis

Simple regression analysis, which I introduce in Chapter 2, is a method of analyzing the variability of a dependent variable by resorting to information available on an independent variable. Among other things, an answer is sought to the question: What are the expected changes in the dependent variable because of changes (observed or induced) in the independent variable?

In Chapter 3, I present current approaches for diagnosing, among other things, deviant or influential observations and their effects on results of regression analysis. In Chapter 4, I introduce computer packages that I will be using throughout most of the book, explain the manner in which I will be apply them, and use their regression programs to analyze a numerical example I analyzed by hand in earlier chapters.

Multiple Regression Analysis

When more than one independent variable is used, it is of course possible to apply simple regression analysis to each independent variable and the dependent variable. But doing this overlooks the possibility that the independent variables may be intercorrelated or that they may interact in their effects on the dependent variable. *Multiple regression* analysis (MR) is eminently suited for analyzing collective and separate effects of two or more independent variables on a dependent variable.

The bulk of this book deals with various aspects of applications and interpretations of MR in scientific research. In Chapter 5, I introduce the foundations of MR for the case of two independent variables. I then use matrix algebra to present generalization of MR to any number of independent variables (Chapter 6). Though most of the subject matter of this book can be mastered without resorting to matrix algebra, especially when the calculations are carried out by computer, I strongly recommend that you develop a working knowledge of matrix algebra, as it is extremely useful and general for conceptualization and analysis of diverse designs. To this end, I present an introduction to matrix algebra in Appendix A. In addition, to facilitate your acquisition of logic and skills in this very important subject, I present some topics twice: first in ordinary algebra (e.g., Chapter 5) and then in matrix algebra (e.g., Chapter 6).

Methods of statistical control useful in their own right (e.g., partial correlation) or that are important elements of MR (e.g., semipartial correlation) constitute the subject matter of Chapter 7. In Chapter 8, I address different aspects of using MR for prediction. In "The Research Perspective" section presented later in this chapter, I comment on analyses aimed solely at prediction and those aimed at explanation.

Multiple Regression Analysis in Explanatory Research

Part 2 of the book deals primarily with the use of MR in explanatory research. Chapters 9, 10, and 13 address the analyses of designs in which the independent variables are *continuous* or *quantitative*—that is, variables on which individuals or objects differ in degree. Examples of such variables are height, weight, age, drug dosage, intelligence, motivation, study time. In Chapter 9, I discuss various approaches aimed at partitioning the variance of the dependent variable and attributing specific portions of it to the independent variables. In Chapter 10, on the other hand, I show how MR is used to study the effects of the independent variables on the dependent variable. Whereas Chapters 9 and 10 are limited to linear regression analysis, Chapter 13 is devoted to curvilinear regression analysis.

There is another class of variables—*categorical* or qualitative—on which individuals differ in kind. Broadly, on such variables individuals are identified according to the category or group to which they belong. Race, sex, political party affiliation, and different experimental treatments are but some examples of categorical variables.

Conventionally, designs with categorical independent variables have been analyzed through the analysis of variance (ANOVA). Until recent years, ANOVA and MR have been treated by many as distinct analytic approaches. It is not uncommon to encounter students or researchers who have been trained exclusively in the use of ANOVA and who therefore cast their research questions in this mold even when it is inappropriate or undesirable to do so. In Part 2, I show that ANOVA can be treated as a special case of MR, and I elaborate on advantages of doing this. For now, I will make two points. (1) Conceptually, continuous and categorical variables are treated alike in MR—that is, both types of variables are viewed as providing information about the status of individuals, be it their measured aptitude, their income, the group to which they belong, or the type of treatment they have been administered. (2) MR is applicable to designs in which the independent variables are continuous, categorical, or combinations of both, thereby eschewing the inappropriate or undesirable practice of categorizing continuous variables (e.g., designating individuals above the mean as high and those below the mean as low) in order to fit them into what is considered, often erroneously, an ANOVA design.

Analytically, it is necessary to code categorical variables so that they may be used in MR. In Chapter 11, I describe different methods of coding categorical variables and show how to use them in the analysis of designs with a single categorical independent variable, what is often called simple ANOVA. Designs consisting of more than one categorical independent variable (factorial designs) are the subject of Chapter 12.

Combinations of continuous and categorical variables are used in various designs for different purposes. For instance, in an experiment with several treatments (a categorical variable), aptitudes of subjects (a continuous variable) may be used to study the interaction between these variables in their effect on a dependent variable. This is an example of an aptitude-treatments-interaction (ATI) design. Instead of using aptitudes to study their possible interactions with treatments, they may be used to control for individual differences, as in the analysis of covariance (ANCOVA). In Chapters 14 and 15, I show how to use MR to analyze ATI, ANCOVA, and related designs (e.g., comparing regression equations obtained from two or more groups).

In Chapter 16, I show, among other things, that when studying multiple groups, total, between-, and within-groups parameters may be obtained. In addition, I introduce some recent developments in multilevel analysis.

In all the designs I mentioned thus far, the dependent variable is continuous. In Chapter 17, I introduce logistic regression analysis—a method for the analysis of designs in which the dependent variable is categorical.

In sum, MR is versatile and useful for the analysis of diverse designs. To repeat: the overriding conception is that information from independent variables (continuous, categorical, or combinations of both types of variables) is brought to bear in attempts to explain the variability of a dependent variable.

Structural Equation Models

In recent years, social and behavioral scientists have shown a steadily growing interest in studying patterns of causation among variables. Various approaches to the analysis of causation, also called structural equation models (SEM), have been proposed. Part 3 serves as an introduction to this topic. In Chapter 18, I show how the analysis of causal models with observed variables, also called path analysis, can be accomplished by repeated applications of multiple regression analysis. In Chapter 19, I introduce the analysis of causal models with latent variables. In both chapters, I use two programs—EQS and LISREL—designed specifically for the analysis of SEM.

Multivariate Analysis

Because multiple regression analysis is applicable in designs consisting of a single dependent variable, it is considered a univariate analysis. I will note in passing that some authors view multiple regression analysis as a multivariate analytic technique whereas others reserve the term "multivariate analysis" for approaches in which multiple dependent variables are analyzed simultaneously. The specific nomenclature is not that important. One may view multivariate analytic techniques as extensions of multiple regression analysis or, alternatively, the latter may be viewed as a special case subsumed under the former.

Often, it is of interest to study effects of independent variables on more than one dependent variable simultaneously, or to study relations between sets of independent and dependent variables. Under such circumstances, multivariate analysis has to be applied. Part 4 is designed to serve as an introduction to different methods of multivariate analysis. In Chapter 20, I introduce discriminant analysis and multivariate analysis of variance for any number of groups. In addition, I show that for designs consisting of two groups with any number of dependent variables, the analysis may be carried out through multiple regression analysis. In Chapter 21, I present canonical analysis—an approach aimed at studying relations between sets of variables. I show, among other things, that discriminant analysis and multivariate analysis of variance can be viewed as special cases of this most general analytic approach.

Computer Programs

Earlier, I noted the widespread availability of computer programs for statistical analysis. It may be of interest to point out that when I worked on the second edition of this book the programs I used were available only for mainframe computers. To incorporate excerpts of output in the manuscript (1) I marked or copied them, depending on how much editing I did; (2) my wife then typed the excerpts; (3) we then proofread to minimize errors in copying and typing. For the current edition, I used only PC versions of the programs. Working in Windows, I ran programs as the need arose, without quitting my word processor, and cut and pasted relevant segments of the output. I believe the preceding would suffice for you to appreciate the great value of the recent developments. My wife surely does!

While the availability of user-friendly computer programs for statistical analysis has proved invaluable, it has not been free of drawbacks, as it has increased the frequency of blind or mindless application of methods. I urge you to select a computer program only after you have formulated your problems and hypotheses. Clearly, you have to be thoroughly familiar with a program so that you can tell whether it provides for an analysis that bears on your hypotheses.

In Chapter 4, I introduce four packages of computer programs, which I use repeatedly in various subsequent chapters. In addition, I introduce and use programs for SEM (EQS and LISREL) in Chapters 18 and 19. In all instances, I give the control statements and comment on them. I then present output, along with commentaries. My emphasis is on interpretation, the meaning of specific terms reported in the output, and on the overall meaning of the results. Consequently, I do not reproduce computer output in its entirety. Instead, I reproduce excerpts of output most pertinent for the topic under consideration.

I present more than one computer package so that you may become familiar with unique features of each, with its strengths and weaknesses, and with the specific format of its output. I hope that you will thereby develop flexibility in using any program that may be available to you, or one that you deem most suitable when seeking specific information in the results.

I suggest that you use computer programs from the early stages of learning the subject matter of this book. The savings in time and effort in calculations will enable you to pay greater attention to the meaning of the methods I present and to develop a better understanding and appreciation of them. Yet, there is no substitute for hand calculations to gain understanding of a method and a "feel" for what is going on when the data are analyzed by computer. I therefore strongly recommend that at the initial stages of learning a new topic you solve the numerical examples both by hand and by computer. Comparisons between the two solutions and the identification of specific aspects of the computer output can be a valuable part of the learning process. With this in mind, I present small, albeit unrealistic, numerical examples that can be solved by hand with little effort.

THE RESEARCH PERSPECTIVE

I said earlier that the role and meaning of an analytic technique can be fully understood and appreciated only when viewed from the broad research perspective. In this section I elaborate on some aspects of this topic. Although neither exhaustive nor detailed, I hope that the discussion will serve to underscore from the beginning the paramount role of the research perspective in determining how a specific method is applied and how the results it yields are interpreted. My presentation is limited to the following aspects: (1) the purpose of the study, (2) the type of research, and (3) the theoretical framework of the study. You will find detailed discussions of these and other topics in texts on research design and measurement (e.g., Cook & Campbell, 1979; Kerlinger, 1986; Nunnally, 1978; Pedhazur & Schmelkin, 1991).

Purpose of Study

In the broadest sense, a study may be designed for predicting or explaining phenomena. Although these purposes are not mutually exclusive, identifying studies, even broad research areas, in which the main concern is with either prediction or explanation is easy. For example, a college admissions officer may be interested in determining whether, and to what extent, a set of variables (mental ability, aptitudes, achievement in high school, socioeconomic status, interests, motivation) is useful in *predicting* academic achievement in college. Being interested solely in prediction, the admissions officer has a great deal of latitude in the selection of predictors. He or she may examine potentially useful predictors individually or in sets to ascertain the most useful ones. Various approaches aimed at selecting variables so that little, or nothing, of the predictive power of the entire set of variables under consideration is sacrificed are available. These I describe in Chapter 8, where I show, among other things, that different variable-selection procedures applied to the same data result in the retention of different variables. Nevertheless, this poses no problems in a predictive study. Any procedure that meets the specific needs and inclinations of the researcher (economy, ready availability of some variables, ease of obtaining specific measurements) will do.

The great liberty in the selection of variables in predictive research is countervailed by the constraint that no statement may be made about their meaningfulness and effectiveness from a theoretical frame of reference. Thus, for instance, I argue in Chapter 8 that when variable-selection procedures are used to optimize prediction of a criterion, regression coefficients should *not* be interpreted as indices of the effects of the predictors on the criterion. Furthermore, I show (see, in particular Chapters 8, 9, and 10) that a major source of confusion and misinterpretation of results obtained in some landmark studies in education is their reliance on variable-selection procedures although they were aimed at explaining phenomena. In sum, when variables are selected to optimize prediction, all one can say is, given a specific procedure and specific constraints placed by the researcher, which combination of variables best predicts the criterion.

Contrast the preceding example with a study aimed at *explaining* academic achievement in college. Under such circumstances, the choice of variables and the analytic approach are largely determined by the theoretical framework (discussed later in this chapter). Chapters 9 and 10 are devoted to detailed discussions of different approaches in the use of multiple regression analysis in explanatory research. For instance, in Chapter 9, I argue that popular approaches of incremental partitioning of variance and commonality analysis cannot yield answers to questions about the relative importance of independent variables or their relative effects on the dependent variable. As I point out in Chapter 9, I discuss these approaches in detail because they are often misapplied in various areas of social and behavioral research. In Chapter 10, I address the interpretation of regression coefficients as indices of effects of independent variables on the dependent variable. In this context, I discuss differences between standardized and unstandardized regression coefficients, and advantages and disadvantages of each. Other major issues I address in Chapter 10 are adverse effects of high correlations among independent variables, measurement errors, and errors in specifying the model that presumably reflects the process by which the independent variables affect the dependent variables.

Types of Research

Of various classifications of types of research, one of the most useful is that of experimental, quasi-experimental, and nonexperimental. Much has been written about these types of research, with special emphasis on issues concerning their internal and external validity (see, for example, Campbell & Stanley, 1963; Cook & Campbell, 1979; Kerlinger, 1986; Pedhazur & Schmelkin, 1991). As I pointed out earlier, I cannot discuss these issues in this book. I do, however, in various chapters, draw attention to the fact that the interpretation of results yielded by a given analytic technique depends, in part, on the type of research in which it is applied.

Contrasts between the different types of research recur in different contexts, among which are (1) the interpretation of regression coefficients (Chapter 10), (2) the potential for specification errors (Chapter 10), (3) designs with unequal sample sizes or unequal cell frequencies (Chapters 11 and 12), (4) the meaning of interactions among independent variables (Chapters 12 through 15), and (5) applications and interpretations of the analysis of covariance (Chapter 15).

Theoretical Framework

Explanation implies, first and foremost, a theoretical formulation about the nature of the relations among the variables under study. The theoretical framework determines, largely, the choice of the analytic technique, the manner in which it is to be applied, and the interpretation of the results. I demonstrate this in various parts of the book. In Chapter 7, for instance, I show that the calculation of a partial correlation coefficient is predicated on a specific theoretical statement regarding the patterns of relations among the variables. Similarly, I show (Chapter 9) that within certain theoretical frameworks it may be meaningful to calculate semipartial correlations, whereas in others such statistics are not meaningful. In Chapters 9, 10, and 18, I analyze the same data several times according to specific theoretical elaborations and show how elements obtained in each analysis are interpreted.

In sum, in explanatory research, data analysis is designed to shed light on theory. The potential of accomplishing this goal is predicated, among other things, on the use of analytic techniques that are commensurate with the theoretical framework.

RESEARCH EXAMPLES

In most chapters, I include research examples. *My aim is not to summarize studies I cite, nor to discuss all aspects of their design and analysis.* Instead, I focus on specific facets of a study insofar as they may shed light on a topic I present in the given chapter. I allude to other facets of the study only when they bear on the topic I am addressing. Therefore, *I urge you to read the original report of a study that arouses your interest before passing judgment on it.*

As you will soon discover, in most instances I focus on shortcomings, misapplications, and misinterpretations in the studies on which I comment. In what follows I detail some reasons for my stance, as it goes counter to strong norms of not criticizing works of other professionals, of tiptoeing when commenting on them. Following are but some manifestations of such norms.

In an editorial, Oberst (1995) deplored the reluctance of nursing professionals to express publicly their skepticism of unfounded claims for the effectiveness of a therapeutic approach, saying, "Like the citizens in the fairy tale, we seem curiously unwilling to go on record about the emperor's obvious nakedness" (p. 1).

Commenting on controversy surrounding the failure to replicate the results of an AIDS research project, Dr. David Ho, who heads an AIDS research center, was reported to have said, "The problem is that too many of us try to avoid the limelight for controversial issues and avoid pointing the finger at another colleague to say what you have published is wrong" (Altman, 1991, p. B6).

In a discussion of the "tone" to be used in papers submitted to journals published by the American Psychological Association, the *Publication Manual* (American Psychological Association, 1994) states, "Differences should be presented in a professional non-combative manner: For example, 'Fong and Nisbett did not consider . . . ' is acceptable, whereas 'Fong and Nisbett completely overlooked . . . ' is not" (pp. 6–7).

Beware of Learning Others' Errors

With other authors (e.g., Chatfield, 1991, pp. 248–251; Glenn, 1989, p. 137; King, 1986, p. 684; Swafford, 1980, p. 684), I believe that researchers are inclined to learn from, and emulate, articles published in refereed journals, not only because this appears less demanding than studying textbook presentations but also because it holds the promise of having one's work accepted for publication. This is particularly troubling, as wrong or seriously flawed research reports are prevalent even in ostensibly the most rigorously refereed and edited journals (see the "Peer Review" section presented later in this chapter).

Learn from Others' Errors

Although we may learn from our errors, we are more open, therefore more likely, to learn from errors committed by others. By exposing errors in research reports and commenting on them, I hope to contribute to the sharpening of your critical ability to scrutinize and evaluate your own research and that of others. In line with what I said earlier, I do not address overriding theoretical and research design issues. Instead, I focus on specific errors in analysis and/or interpretation of results of an analysis. I believe that this is bound to reduce the likelihood of you committing the same errors. Moreover, it is bound to heighten your general alertness to potential errors.

There Are Errors and There Are ERRORS

It is a truism that we all commit errors at one time or another. Also unassailable is the assertion that the quest for perfection is the enemy of the good; that concern with perfection may retard, even debilitate, research. Yet, clearly, errors vary in severity and the potentially deleterious consequences to which they may lead. I would like to stress that my concern is not with perfection, nor with minor, inconsequential, or esoteric errors, but with egregious errors that cast serious doubt about the validity of the findings of a study.

Recognizing full well that my critiques of specific studies are bound to hurt the feelings of their authors, I would like to apologize to them for singling out their work. If it is any consolation, I would point out that their errors are not unique, nor are they necessarily the worst that I have come across in research literature. I selected them because they seemed suited to illustrate common misconceptions or misapplications of a given approach I was presenting. True, I could have drawn attention to potential errors without citing studies. I use examples from actual studies for three reasons: (1) I believe this will have a greater impact in immunizing you against egregious errors in the research literature and in sensitizing you to avoid them in your research. (2) Some misapplications I discuss are so blatantly wrong that had I made them up, instead of taking them from the literature, I would have surely been accused of being concerned with the grotesque or of belaboring the obvious. (3) I felt it important to debunk claims about the effectiveness of the peer review process to weed out the poor studies—a topic to which I now turn.

PEER REVIEW

Budding researchers, policy makers, and the public at large seem to perceive publication in a refereed journal as a seal of approval as to its validity and scientific merit. This is reinforced by, among other things, the use of publication in refereed journals as a primary, if not the primary, criterion for (1) evaluating the work of professors and other professionals (for a recent "bizarre example," see Honan, 1995) and (2) admission as scientific evidence in litigation (for recent decisions by lower courts, rulings by the Supreme Court, and controversies surrounding them, see Angier, 1993a, 1993b; Greenhouse, 1993; Haberman, 1993; Marshall, 1993; *The New York Times,* National Edition, 1995, January 8, p. 12). It is noteworthy that in a brief to the Supreme Court, The American Association for the Advancement of Science and the National Academy of Sciences argued that the courts should regard scientific "claims 'skeptically' until they have been 'subject to some peer scrutiny.' Publication in a peer-reviewed journal is 'the best means' of identifying valid research" (Marshall, 1993, p. 590).

Clearly, I cannot review, even briefly, the peer review process here.[2] Nor will I attempt to present a balanced view of pro and con positions on this topic. Instead, I will draw attention to some major inadequacies of the review process, and to some unwarranted assumptions underlying it.

Failure to Detect Elementary Errors

Many errors to which I will draw attention are so elementary as to require little or no expertise to detect. Usually, a careful reading would suffice. Failure by editors and referees to detect such errors makes one wonder whether they even read the manuscripts. Lest I appear too harsh or unfair, I will give here a couple of examples of what I have in mind (see also the following discussion, "Editors and Referees").

---

[2]For some treatments of this topic, see *Behavioral and Brain Sciences* (1982, *5,* 187–255 and 1991, *14,* 119–186); Cummings and Frost (1985), *Journal of the American Medical Association* (1990, *263,* 1321–1441); Mahoney (1977); Spencer, Hartnett, and Mahoney (1985).

Reporting on an unpublished study by Stewart and Feder (scientists at the National Institutes of Health), Boffey (1986) wrote:

> Their study . . . concluded that the 18 full-length scientific papers reviewed had "an abundance of errors" and discrepancies—a dozen per paper on the average—that could have been detected by any competent scientist who read the papers carefully. Some errors were described as . . . "so glaring as to offend common sense." . . . [Data in one paper were] so "fantastic" that it ought to have been questioned by any scientist who read it carefully, the N.I.H. scientists said in an interview. The paper depicted a family with high incidence of an unusual heart disease; a family tree in the paper indicated that one male member supposedly had, by the age of 17, fathered four children, conceiving the first when he was 8 or 9. (p. C11)

Boffey's description of how Stewart and Feder's paper was "blocked from publication" (p. C11) is in itself a serious indictment of the review process.

Following is an example of an error that should have been detected by anyone with superficial knowledge of the analytic method used. Thomas (1978) candidly related what happened with a paper in archaeology he coauthored with White in which they used principal component analysis (PCA). For present purposes it is not necessary to go into the details of PCA (for an overview of PCA versus factor analysis, along with relevant references, see Pedhazur & Schmelkin, 1991, pp. 597–599). At the risk of oversimplifying, I will point out that PCA is aimed at extracting components underlying relations among variables (items and the like). Further, the results yielded by PCA variables (items and the like) have loadings on the components and the *loadings may be positive or negative.* Researchers use the high loadings to interpret the results of the analysis. Now, as Thomas pointed out, the paper he coauthored with White was very well received and praised by various authorities.

> One flaw, however, mars the entire performance: . . . the principal component analysis was incorrectly interpreted. We interpreted the major components based strictly on high positive values [loadings]. Principal components analysis is related to standard correlation analysis and, of course, both positive *and negative* values are significant. . . . The upshot of this statistical error is that our interpretation of the components must be reconsidered. (p. 234)

Referring to the paper by White and Thomas, Hodson (1973) stated, "These trivial but rather devastating slips could have been avoided by closer contact with relevant scientific colleagues" (350). Alas, as Thomas pointed out, "Some very prominent archaeologists—some of them known for their expertise in quantitative methods—examined the White-Thomas manuscript prior to publication, yet the error in interpreting the principal component analysis persisted into print" (p. 234).[3]

I am hardly alone in maintaining that many errors in published research are (should be) detectable through careful reading even by people with little knowledge of the methods being used. Following are but some instances.

In an insightful paper on "good statistical practice," Preece (1987) stated that "within British research journals, the quality ranges from the very good to the very bad, and this latter includes statistics so erroneous that *non*-statisticians should immediately be able to recognize it as rubbish" (p. 407).

Glantz (1980), who pointed out that "critical reviewers of the biomedical literature consistently found that about half the articles that used statistical methods did so incorrectly" (p. 1),

---

[3]Although Thomas (1978) addressed the "awful truth about statistics in archaeology," I strongly recommend that you read his paper, as what he said is applicable to other disciplines as well.

noted also "errors [that] rarely involve sophisticated issues that provoke debate among professional statisticians, but are simple mistakes" (p. 1).

Tuckman (1990) related that in a research-methods course he teaches, he asks each student to pick a published article and critique it before the class. "Despite the motivation to select perfect work (without yet knowing the criteria to make that judgment), each article selected, with rare exception, is torn apart on the basis of a multitude of serious deficiencies ranging from substance to procedures" (p. 22).

Editors and Referees

In an "Editor's Comment" entitled "Let's Train Reviewers," the editor of the *American Sociological Review* (October 1992, *57*, iii–iv) drew attention to the need to improve the system, saying, "The bad news is that in my judgment one-fourth or more of the reviews received by *ASR* (and I suspect by other journals) are not helpful to the Editor, and many of them are even misleading" (p. iii). Turning to his suggestions for improvement, the editor stated, "A good place to start might be by reconsidering a widely held assumption about reviewing—the notion that 'anyone with a Ph.D. is able to review scholarly work in his or her specialty' " (p. iii).[4]

Commenting on the peer review process, Crandall (1991) stated:

> I had to laugh when I saw the recent American Psychological Association announcements recruiting members of under represented groups to be reviewers for journals. The only qualification mentioned was that they must have published articles in peer reviewed journals, because *"the experience of publishing provides a reviewer with the basis for preparing a thorough, objective evaluative review"* [italics added]. (p. 143)

Unfortunately, problems with the review process are exacerbated by the appointment of editors unsuited to the task because of disposition and/or lack of knowledge to understand, let alone evaluate, the reviews they receive. For instance, in an interview upon his appointment as editor of *Psychological Bulletin* (an American Psychological Association journal concerned largely with methodological issues), John Masters is reported to have said, "I am consistently embarrassed that my statistical and methodological acumen became frozen in time when I left graduate school except for what my students have taught me" (Bales, 1986, p. 14). He may deserve an A+ for candor—but being appointed the editor of *Psychological Bulletin*? Could it be that Blalock's (1989, p. 458) experience of encountering "instances where potential journal editors were passed over because it was argued that their standards would be too demanding!" is not unique?

Commenting on editors' abdicating "responsibility for editorial decisions," Crandall (1991) stated, "I believe that many editors do not read the papers for which they are supposed to have editorial responsibility. If they don't read them closely, how can they be the editors?" (p. 143; see also, Tuckman, 1990).

In support of Crandall's assertions, I will give an example from my own experience. Following a review of a paper I submitted to a refereed journal, the editor informed me that he would like to publish it, but asked for some revisions and extensions. I was surprised when, in acknowledging receipt of the revised paper, the editor informed me that he had sent it out for another

---

[4]A similar, almost universally held, assumption is that the granting of a Ph.D. magically transforms a person into an all-knowing expert, qualified to guide doctoral students on their dissertations and to serve on examining committees for doctoral candidates defending their dissertations.

review. Anyway, some time later I received a letter from the editor, who informed me that though he "had all but promised publication," he regretted that he had to reject the paper *"given the fact that the technique has already been published"* [italics added]. Following is the *entire* review (with the misspellings of authors' names, underlining, and mistyping) that led to the editor's decision.

> The techniques the author discusses are treated in detail in the book *Introduction to Linear Models and the Design and Analysis of Experiments* by William Mendenhill [*sic.* Should be Mendenhall], Wadsworth Publishing Co. *1968,* Ch. 13, p. 384 and Ch. 4, p. 66, in detail and I may add are no longer in use with more sophisticated software statistical packages (e.g. Multivariance by Boik [*sic*] and Finn [should be Finn & Bock], FRULM by Timm and Carlson etc. etc. Under *no*/condition should this paper be published—not original and out of date.

I wrote the editor pointing out that I proposed my method as an alternative to a cumbersome one (presented by Mendenhall and others) that was then in use. In support of my assertion, I enclosed photocopies of the pages from Mendenhall cited by the reviewer and invited the editor to examine them.

In response, the editor phoned me, apologized for his decision, and informed me that he would be happy to publish the paper. In the course of our conversation, I expressed concern about the review process in general and specifically about (1) using new reviewers for a revised paper and (2) reliance on the kind of reviewer he had used. As to the latter, I suggested that the editor reprimand the reviewer and send him a copy of my letter. Shortly afterward, I received a copy of a letter the editor sent the reviewer. Parenthetically, the reviewer's name and address were removed from my copy, bringing to mind the question: "Why should the wish to publish a scientific paper expose one to an assassin more completely protected than members of the infamous society, the Mafia?" (R. D. Wright, quoted by Cicchetti, 1991, p. 131). Anyway, after telling the reviewer that he was writing concerning my paper, the editor stated:

> I enclose a copy of the response of the author. I have read the passage in Mendenhall and find that the author is indeed correct.
>
> On the basis of your advice, I made a serious error and have since apologized to the author. I would ask you to be more careful with your reviews in the future.

Why didn't the editor check Mendenhall's statements before deciding to reject my paper, especially when all this would have entailed is the reading of *two* pages pinpointed by the reviewer? And why would he deem the reviewer in question competent to review papers in the future? Your guesses are as good as mine.

Earlier I stated that detection of many egregious errors requires nothing more than careful reading. At the risk of sounding trite and superfluous, however, I would like to stress that to detect errors in the application of an analytic method, the reviewer ought to be familiar with it. As I amply show in my commentaries on research studies, their very publication leads to the inescapable conclusion that editors and referees have either not carefully read the manuscripts or have no knowledge of the analytic methods used. I will let you decide which is the worse offense.

As is well known, much scientific writing is suffused with jargon. This, however, should not serve as an excuse for not investing time and effort to learn the technical terminology required to understand scientific publications in specific disciplines. It is one thing to urge the authors of scientific papers to refrain from using jargon. It is quite something else to tell them, as does the *Publication Manual* of the American Psychological Association (1994), that "the technical terminology in a paper should be understood by psychologists *throughout the discipline"* [italics added] (p. 27). I believe that this orientation fosters, unwittingly, the perception that when one does not understand a scientific paper, the fault is with its author. Incalculable deleterious consequences of the widespread reporting of questionable scientific "findings" in the mass media have made the need to foster greater understanding of scientific research methodology and healthy skepticism of the peer review process more urgent than ever.

CHAPTER

2

Simple Linear Regression and Correlation

In this chapter, I address fundamentals of regression analysis. Following a brief review of variance and covariance, I present a detailed discussion of linear regression analysis with one independent variable. Among topics I present are the regression equation; partitioning the sum of squares of the dependent variable into regression and residual components; tests of statistical significance; and assumptions underlying regression analysis. I conclude the chapter with a brief presentation of the correlation model.

VARIANCE AND COVARIANCE

Variability tends to arouse curiosity, leading some to search for its origin and meaning. The study of variability, be it among individuals, groups, cultures, or within individuals across time and settings, plays a prominent role in behavioral research. When attempting to explain variability of a variable, researchers resort to, among other things, the study of its covariations with other variables. Among indices used in the study of variation and covariation are the variance and the covariance.

Variance

Recall that the sample variance is defined as follows:

$$s_x^2 = \frac{\Sigma(X - \overline{X})^2}{N - 1} = \frac{\Sigma x^2}{N - 1} \tag{2.1}$$

where s_x^2 = sample variance of X; Σx^2 = sum of the squared deviations of X from the mean of X; and N = sample size.

When the calculations are done by hand, or with the aid of a calculator, it is more convenient to obtain the deviation sum of squares by applying a formula in which only raw scores are used:

$$\Sigma x^2 = \Sigma X^2 - \frac{(\Sigma X)^2}{N} \tag{2.2}$$

where ΣX^2 = sum of the squared raw scores; and $(\Sigma X)^2$ = square of the sum of raw scores. Henceforth, I will use "sum of squares" to refer to deviation sum of squares unless there is ambiguity, in which case I will use "deviation sum of squares."

I will now use the data of Table 2.1 to illustrate calculations of the sums of squares and variances of X and Y.

Table 2.1   Illustrative Data for X and Y

X	X²	Y	Y²	XY
1	1	3	9	3
1	1	5	25	5
1	1	6	36	6
1	1	9	81	9
2	4	4	16	8
2	4	6	36	12
2	4	7	49	14
2	4	10	100	20
3	9	4	16	12
3	9	6	36	18
3	9	8	64	24
3	9	10	100	30
4	16	5	25	20
4	16	7	49	28
4	16	9	81	36
4	16	12	144	48
5	25	7	49	35
5	25	10	100	50
5	25	12	144	60
5	25	6	36	30
Σ: 60	220	146	1196	468
M: 3.00		7.30		

$$\Sigma x^2 = 220 - \frac{60^2}{20} = 40 \qquad \Sigma y^2 = 1196 - \frac{146^2}{20} = 130.2$$

$$s_x^2 = \frac{40}{19} = 2.11 \qquad s_y^2 = \frac{130.2}{19} = 6.85$$

The standard deviation (s) is, of course, the square root of the variance:

$$s_x = \sqrt{2.11} = 1.45 \qquad s_y = \sqrt{6.85} = 2.62$$

Covariance

The sample covariance is defined as follows:

$$s_{xy} = \frac{\Sigma(X - \bar{X})(Y - \bar{Y})}{N - 1} = \frac{\Sigma xy}{N - 1} \qquad (2.3)$$

where s_{xy} = covariance of X and Y; and Σxy = sum of the cross products deviations of pairs of X and Y scores from their respective means. Note the analogy between the variance and the covariance. The variance of a variable can be conceived of as its covariance with itself. For example,

$$s_x^2 = \frac{\Sigma(X - \overline{X})(X - \overline{X})}{N - 1}$$

In short, the variance indicates the variation of a set of scores from their mean, whereas the covariance indicates the covariation of two sets of scores from their respective means.

As in the case of sums of squares, it is convenient to calculate the sum of the cross products deviations (henceforth referred to as "sum of cross products") by using the following algebraic identity:

$$\Sigma xy = \Sigma XY - \frac{(\Sigma X)(\Sigma Y)}{N} \tag{2.4}$$

where ΣXY is the sum of the products of pairs of raw X and Y scores; and ΣX and ΣY are the sums of the raw scores of X and Y, respectively.

For the data of Table 2.1,

$$\Sigma xy = 468 - \frac{(60)(146)}{20} = 30$$

$$s_{xy} = \frac{30}{19} = 1.58$$

Sums of squares, sums of cross products, variances, and covariances are the staples of regression analysis; hence, it is essential that you understand them thoroughly and be able to calculate them routinely. If necessary, refer to statistics texts (e.g., Hays, 1988) for further study of these concepts.

SIMPLE LINEAR REGRESSION

I said earlier that among approaches used to explain variability of a variable is the study of its covariations with other variables. The least ambiguous setting in which this can be accomplished is the experiment, whose simplest form is one in which the effect of an independent variable, X, on a dependent variable, Y, is studied. In such a setting, the researcher attempts to ascertain how induced variation in X leads to variation in Y. In other words, the goal is to determine how, and to what extent, variability of the dependent variable depends upon manipulations of the independent variable. For example, one may wish to determine the effects of hours of study, X, on achievement in vocabulary, Y; or the effects of different dosages of a drug, X, on anxiety, Y. Obviously, performance on Y is usually affected also by factors other than X and by random errors. Hence, it is highly unlikely that all individuals exposed to the same level of X would exhibit identical performance on Y. But if X does affect Y, the means of the Y's at different levels of X would be expected to differ from each other. When the Y means for the different levels of X differ from each other and lie on a straight line, it is said that there is a simple linear regression of Y on X. By "simple" is meant that only one independent variable, X, is used. The preceding ideas can be expressed succinctly by the following linear model:

$$Y_i = \alpha + \beta X_i + \epsilon_i \tag{2.5}$$

where Y_i = score of individual i on the dependent variable; α(alpha) = mean of the population when the value of X is zero, or the Y intercept; β(beta) = regression coefficient in the population, or the slope of the regression line; X_i = value of independent variable to which individual i was exposed; ϵ(epsilon)$_i$ = random disturbance, or error, for individual i.[1] The regression coefficient (β) indicates the effect of the independent variable on the dependent variable. Specifically, for each unit change of the independent variable, X, there is an expected change equal to the size of β in the dependent variable, Y.

The foregoing shows that each person's score, Y_i, is conceived as being composed of two parts: (1) a fixed part indicated by $\alpha + \beta X$, that is, part of the Y score for an individual exposed to a given level of X is equal to $\alpha + \beta X$ (thus, all individuals exposed to the same level of X are said to have the same part of the Y score), and (2) A random part, ϵ_i, unique to each individual, i.

Linear regression analysis is not limited to experimental research. As I amply show in subsequent chapters, it is often applied in quasi-experimental and nonexperimental research to explain or predict phenomena. Although calculations of regression statistics are the same regardless of the type of research in which they are applied, interpretation of the results depends on the specific research design. I discuss these issues in detail later in the text (see, for example, Chapters 8 through 10). For now, my emphasis is on the general analytic approach.

Equation (2.5) was expressed in parameters. For a sample, the equation is

$$Y = a + bX + e \qquad (2.6)$$

where a is an estimator of α; b is an estimator of β; and e is an estimator of ϵ. For convenience, I did not use subscripts in (2.6). I follow this practice of omitting subscripts throughout the book, unless there is a danger of ambiguity. I will use subscripts for individuals when it is necessary to identify given individuals. In equations with more than one independent variable (see subsequent chapters), I will use subscripts to identify each variable.

I discuss the meaning of the statistics in (2.6) and illustrate the mechanics of their calculations in the context of a numerical example to which I now turn.

A Numerical Example

Assume that in an experiment on the effects of hours of study (X) on achievement in mathematics (Y), 20 subjects were randomly assigned to different levels of X. Specifically, there are five levels of X, ranging from one to five hours of study. Four subjects were *randomly* assigned to one hour of study, four other subjects were *randomly* assigned to two hours of study, and so on to five hours of study for the fifth group of subjects. A mathematics test serves as the measure of the dependent variable. Other examples may be the effect of the number of exposures to a list of words on the retention of the words or the effects of different dosages of a drug on reaction time or on blood pressure. Alternatively, X may be a nonmanipulated variable (e.g., age, grade in school), and Y may be height or verbal achievement. For illustrative purposes, I will treat the data of Table 2.1 as if they were obtained in a learning experiment, as described earlier.

Scientific inquiry is aimed at explaining or predicting phenomena of interest. The ideal is, of course, perfect explanation—that is, without error. Being unable to achieve this state, however,

---

[1]The term "linear" refers also to the fact that parameters such as those that appear in Equation (2.5) are expressed in linear form even though the regression of Y on X is nonlinear. For example, $Y = \alpha + \beta X + \beta X^2 + \beta X^3 + \epsilon$ describes the cubic regression of Y on X. Note, however, that it is X, not the β's, that is raised to second and third powers. I deal with such equations, which are subsumed under the general linear model, in Chapter 13.

scientists attempt to minimize errors. In the example under consideration, the purpose is to explain achievement in mathematics (*Y*) from hours of study (*X*). It is very unlikely that students studying the same number of hours will manifest the same level of achievement in mathematics. Obviously, many other variables (e.g., mental ability, motivation) as well as measurement errors will introduce variability in students' performance. All sources of variability of *Y*, other than *X*, are subsumed under *e* in Equation (2.6). In other words, *e* represents the part of the *Y* score that is not explained by, or predicted from, *X*.

The purpose, then, is to find a solution for the constants, *a* and *b* of (2.6), so that explanation or prediction of *Y* will be maximized. Stated differently, a solution is sought for *a* and *b* so that *e*—errors committed in using *X* to explain *Y*—will be at a minimum. The intuitive solution of minimizing the sum of the errors turns out to be unsatisfactory because positive errors will cancel negative ones, thereby possibly leading to the false impression that small errors have been committed when their sum is small, or that no errors have been committed when their sum turns out to be zero. Instead, it is the sum of the squared errors (Σe^2) that is minimized, hence the name *least squares* given to this solution.

Given certain assumptions, which I discuss later in this chapter, the least-squares solution leads to estimators that have the desirable properties of being best linear unbiased estimators (BLUE). An estimator is said to be unbiased if its average obtained from repeated samples of size *N* (i.e., expected value) is equal to the parameter. Thus *b*, for example, is an unbiased estimator of β if the average of the former in repeated samples is equal to the latter.

Unbiasedness is only one desirable property of an estimator. In addition, it is desirable that the variance of the distribution of such an estimator (i.e., its sampling distribution) be as small as possible. The smaller the variance of the sampling distribution, the smaller the error in estimating the parameter. Least-squares estimators are said to be "best" in the sense that the variance of their sampling distributions is the smallest from among linear unbiased estimators (see Hanushek & Jackson, 1977, pp. 46–56, for a discussion of BLUE; and Hays, 1988, Chapter 5, for discussions of sampling distributions and unbiasedness). Later in the chapter, I show how the variance of the sampling distribution of *b* is used in statistical tests of significance and for establishing confidence intervals. I turn now to the calculation of least-squares estimators and to a discussion of their meaning.

The two constants are calculated as follows:

$$b = \frac{\Sigma xy}{\Sigma x^2} \tag{2.7}$$

$$a = \overline{Y} - b\overline{X} \tag{2.8}$$

Using these constants, the equation for predicting *Y* from *X*, or the *regression equation,* is

$$Y' = a + bX \tag{2.9}$$

where Y' = predicted score on the dependent variable, *Y*. Note that (2.9) does not include *e* ($Y - Y'$), which is the error that results from employing the prediction equation, and is referred to as the residual. It is the $\Sigma(Y - Y')^2$, referred to as the sum of squared residuals (see the following), that is minimized in the least-squares solution for *a* and *b* of (2.9).

For the data in Table 2.1, $\Sigma xy = 30$ and $\Sigma x^2 = 40$ (see the previous calculations). $\overline{Y} = 7.3$ and $\overline{X} = 3.0$ (see Table 2.1). Therefore,

$$Y' = 5.05 + .75X$$

In order, then, to predict Y, for a given X, multiply the X by b (.75) and add the constant a (5.05). From the previous calculations it can be seen that b indicates the expected change in Y associated with a unit change in X. In other words, for each increment of one unit in X, an increment of .75 in Y is predicted. In our example, this means that for every additional hour of study, X, there is an expected gain of .75 units in mathematics achievement, Y. Knowledge of a and b is necessary and sufficient to predict Y from X so that squared errors of prediction are minimized.

A Closer Look at the Regression Equation

Substituting (2.8) in (2.9),

$$Y' = a + bX$$
$$= (\overline{Y} - b\overline{X}) + bX$$
$$= \overline{Y} + b(X - \overline{X})$$
$$= \overline{Y} + bx \tag{2.10}$$

Note that Y' can be expressed as composed of two components: the mean of Y and the product of the deviation of X from the mean of X (x) by the regression coefficient (b). Therefore, when the regression of Y on X is zero (i.e., $b = 0$), or when X does not affect Y, the regression equation would lead to a predicted Y being equal to the mean of Y for each value of X. This makes intuitive sense. When attempting to guess or predict scores of people on Y in the absence of information, except for the knowledge that they are members of the group being studied, the best prediction, in a statistical sense, for each individual is the mean of Y.

Such a prediction policy minimizes squared errors, inasmuch as the sum of the squared deviations from the mean is smaller than one taken from any other constant (see, for example, Edwards, 1964, pp. 5–6). Further, when more information about the people is available in the form of their status on another variable, X, but when variations in X are *not* associated with variations in Y, the best prediction for each individual is still the mean of Y, and the regression equation will lead to the same prediction. Note from (2.7) that when X and Y do not covary, Σxy is zero, resulting in $b = 0$. Applying (2.10) when $b = 0$ leads to $Y' = \overline{Y}$ regardless of the X values.

When, however, b is not zero (that is, when X and Y covary), application of the regression equation leads to a reduction in errors of prediction as compared with the errors resulting from predicting $\overline{Y}$ for each individual. The degree of reduction in errors of prediction is closely linked to the concept of partitioning the sum of squares of the dependent variable (Σy^2) to which I now turn.

Partitioning the Sum of Squares

Knowledge of the values of both X and Y for each individual makes it possible to ascertain how accurately each Y is predicted by using the regression equation. I will show this for the data of Table 2.1, which are repeated in Table 2.2. Applying the regression equation calculated earlier, $Y' = 5.05 + .75X$, to each person's X score yields the predicted Y's listed in Table 2.2 in the column labeled Y'. In addition, the following are reported for each person: $Y' - \overline{Y}$ (the deviation of the predicted Y from the mean of Y), referred to as deviation due to regression,

Table 2.2　Regression Analysis of a Learning Experiment

X	Y	Y'	$Y' - \bar{Y}$	$(Y' - \bar{Y})^2$	$Y - Y'$	$(Y - Y')^2$
1	3	5.80	−1.50	2.2500	−2.80	7.8400
1	5	5.80	−1.50	2.2500	−.80	.6400
1	6	5.80	−1.50	2.2500	.20	.0400
1	9	5.80	−1.50	2.2500	3.20	10.2400
2	4	6.55	−.75	.5625	−2.55	6.5025
2	6	6.55	−.75	.5625	−.55	.3025
2	7	6.55	−.75	.5625	.45	.2025
2	10	6.55	−.75	.5625	3.45	11.9025
3	4	7.30	.00	.0000	−3.30	10.8900
3	6	7.30	.00	.0000	−1.30	1.6900
3	8	7.30	.00	.0000	.70	.4900
3	10	7.30	.00	.0000	2.70	7.2900
4	5	8.05	.75	.5625	−3.05	9.3025
4	7	8.05	.75	.5625	−1.05	1.1025
4	9	8.05	.75	.5625	.95	.9025
4	12	8.05	.75	.5625	3.95	15.6025
5	7	8.80	1.50	2.2500	−1.80	3.2400
5	10	8.80	1.50	2.2500	1.20	1.4400
5	12	8.80	1.50	2.2500	3.20	10.2400
5	6	8.80	1.50	2.2500	−2.80	7.8400
Σ:　60	146	146	.00	22.50	.00	107.7

and its square $(Y' - \bar{Y})^2$; $Y - Y'$ (the deviation of observed Y from the predicted Y), referred to as the residual, and its square $(Y - Y')^2$.

Careful study of Table 2.2 will reveal important elements of regression analysis, two of which I will note here. The sum of predicted scores $(\Sigma Y')$ is equal to ΣY. Consequently, the mean of predicted scores is always equal to the mean of the dependent variable. The sum of the residuals $[\Sigma(Y - Y')]$ is always zero. These are consequences of the least-squares solution.

Consider the following identity:

$$Y = \bar{Y} + (Y' - \bar{Y}) + (Y - Y') \tag{2.11}$$

Each Y is expressed as composed of the mean of Y, the deviation of the predicted Y from the mean of Y (deviation due to regression), and the deviation of the observed Y from the predicted Y (residual). For the data of Table 2.2, $\bar{Y} = 7.30$. The first subject's score on $Y(3)$, for instance, can therefore be expressed thus:

$$3 = 7.30 + (5.80 - 7.30) + (3 - 5.80)$$

$$= 7.30 + \quad (-1.50) \quad + \quad (-2.80)$$

Similar statements can be made for each subject in Table 2.2.

Earlier, I pointed out that when no information about an independent variable is available, or when the information available is irrelevant, the best prediction for each individual is the mean of the dependent variable ($\bar{Y}$), and the sum of squared errors of prediction is Σy^2. When, however, the independent variable (X) is related to Y, the degree of reduction in errors of prediction that ensues from the application of the regression equation can be ascertained. Stated differently, it is possible to discern how much of the Σy^2 can be explained based on knowledge of the regression of Y on X.

Approach the solution to this problem by using the above-noted identity—see (2.11):

$$Y = \bar{Y} + (Y' - \bar{Y}) + (Y - Y')$$

Subtracting $\bar{Y}$ from each side,

$$Y - \bar{Y} = (Y' - \bar{Y}) + (Y - Y')$$

Squaring and summing,

$$\Sigma(Y - \bar{Y})^2 = \Sigma[(Y' - \bar{Y}) + (Y - Y')]^2$$
$$= \Sigma(Y' - \bar{Y})^2 + \Sigma(Y - Y')^2 + 2\Sigma(Y' - \bar{Y})(Y - Y')$$

It can be shown that the last term on the right equals zero. Therefore,

$$\Sigma y^2 = \Sigma(Y' - \bar{Y})^2 + \Sigma(Y - Y')^2 \tag{2.12}$$

or

$$\Sigma y^2 = ss_{\text{reg}} + ss_{\text{res}}$$

where ss_{reg} = regression sum of squares and ss_{res} = residual sum of squares.

This central principle in regression analysis states that the deviation sum of squares of the dependent variable, Σy^2, is partitioned into two components: the sum of squares due to regression, or the regression sum of squares, and the sum of squares due to residuals, or the residual sum of squares. When the regression sum of squares is equal to zero, it means that the residual sum of squares is equal to Σy^2, indicating that nothing has been gained by resorting to information from X. When, on the other hand, the residual sum of squares is equal to zero, all the variability in Y is explained by regression, or by the information X provides.

Dividing each of the elements in the previous equation by the total sum of squares (Σy^2),

$$\frac{\Sigma y^2}{\Sigma y^2} = \frac{ss_{\text{reg}}}{\Sigma y^2} + \frac{ss_{\text{res}}}{\Sigma y^2}$$

$$1 = \frac{ss_{\text{reg}}}{\Sigma y^2} + \frac{ss_{\text{res}}}{\Sigma y^2} \tag{2.13}$$

The first term on the right-hand side of the equal sign indicates the proportion of the sum of squares of the dependent variable due to regression. The second term indicates the proportion of the sum of squares due to error, or residual. For the present example, $ss_{\text{reg}} = 22.5$ and $ss_{\text{res}} = 107.7$ (see the bottom of Table 2.2). The sum of these two terms, 130.2, is the Σy^2 I calculated earlier. Applying (2.13),

$$\frac{22.5}{130.2} + \frac{107.7}{130.2} = .1728 + .8272 = 1$$

About 17% of the total sum of squares (Σy^2) is due to regression, and about 83% is left unexplained (i.e., attributed to error).

The calculations in Table 2.2 are rather lengthy, even with a small number of cases. I presented them in this form to illustrate what each element of the regression analysis means. Following are three equivalent formulas for the calculation of the regression sum of squares. I do not define the terms in the formulas, as they should be clear by now. I apply each formula to the data in Table 2.2.

$$ss_{reg} = \frac{(\Sigma xy)^2}{\Sigma x^2}$$

(2.14)

$$= \frac{(30)^2}{40} = 22.5$$

$$ss_{reg} = b\Sigma xy$$

(2.15)

$$= (.75)(30) = 22.5$$

$$ss_{reg} = b^2\Sigma x^2$$

(2.16)

$$= (.75)^2(40) = 22.5$$

I showed above that

$$\Sigma y^2 = ss_{reg} + ss_{res}$$

Therefore,

$$ss_{res} = \Sigma y^2 - ss_{reg}$$

(2.17)

$$= 130.2 - 22.5 = 107.7$$

Previously, I divided the regression sum of squares by the total sum of squares, thus obtaining the proportion of the latter that is due to regression. Using the right-hand term of (2.14) as an expression of the regression sum of squares, and dividing by the total sum of squares,

$$r_{xy}^2 = \frac{(\Sigma xy)^2}{\Sigma x^2 \Sigma y^2}$$

(2.18)

where r_{xy}^2 is the squared Pearson product moment coefficient of the correlation between X and Y. This important formulation, which I use repeatedly in the book, states that the squared correlation between X and Y indicates the proportion of the sum of squares of Y (Σy^2) that is due to regression. It follows that the proportion of Σy^2 that is due to errors, or residuals, is $1 - r_{xy}^2$.

Using these formulations, it is possible to arrive at the following expressions of the regression and residual sum of squares:

$$ss_{reg} = r_{xy}^2 \Sigma y^2$$

(2.19)

For the data in Table 2.2, $r_{xy}^2 = .1728$, and $\Sigma y^2 = 130.2$,

$$ss_{reg} = (.1728)(130.2) = 22.5$$

and

$$ss_{res} = (1 - r_{xy}^2)\Sigma y^2$$

(2.20)

$$ss_{res} = (1 - .1728)(130.2) = 107.7$$

Finally, instead of partitioning the sum of squares of the dependent variable, its *variance* may be partitioned:

$$s_y^2 = r_{xy}^2 s_y^2 + (1 - r_{xy}^2)s_y^2$$

(2.21)

where $r_{xy}^2 s_y^2 =$ portion of the variance of Y due to its regression on X; and $(1 - r_{xy}^2)s_y^2 =$ portion of the variance of Y due to residuals, or errors. r^2, then, is also interpreted as the proportion of the variance of the dependent variable that is accounted for by the independent variable, and $1 - r^2$ is the proportion of variance of the dependent variable that is not accounted for. In subsequent presentations, I partition sums of squares or variances, depending on the topic under discussion. Frequently, I use both approaches to underscore their equivalence.

Graphic Depiction of Regression Analysis

The data of Table 2.2 are plotted in Figure 2.1. Although the points are fairly scattered, they do depict a linear trend in which increments in X are associated with increments in Y. The line that best fits the regression of Y on X, in the sense of minimizing the sum of the squared deviations of the observed Y's from it, is referred to as the regression line. This line depicts the regression equation pictorially, where a represents the point on the ordinate, Y, intercepted by the regression

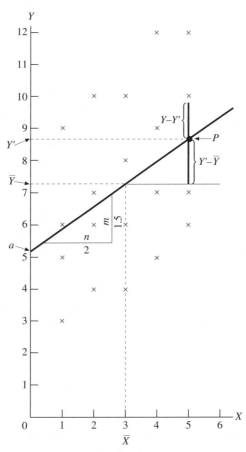

Figure 2.1

line, and b represents the slope of the line. Of various methods for graphing the regression line, the following is probably the easiest. Two points are necessary to draw a line. One of the points that may be used is the value of a (the intercept) calculated by using (2.8). I repeat (2.10) with a new number,

$$Y' = \overline{Y} + bx \tag{2.22}$$

from which it can be seen that, regardless of what the regression coefficient (b) is, $Y' = \overline{Y}$ when $x = 0$—that is, when $X = \overline{X}$. In other words, the means of X and Y are always on the regression line. Consequently, the intersection of lines drawn from the horizontal (abscissa) and the vertical (ordinate) axes at the means of X and Y provides the second point for graphing the regression line. See the intersection of the broken lines in Figure 2.1.

In Figure 2.1, I drew two lines, m and n, paralleling the Y and X axes, respectively, thus constructing a right triangle whose hypotenuse is a segment of the regression line. The slope of the regression line, b, can now be expressed trigonometrically: it is the length of the vertical line, m, divided by the horizontal line, n. In Figure 2.1, $m = 1.5$ and $n = 2.0$. Thus, $1.5/2.0 = .75$, which is equal to the value of b I calculated earlier. From the preceding it can be seen that b indicates the rate of change of Y associated with the rate of change of X. This holds true no matter where along the regression line the triangle is constructed, inasmuch as the regression is described by a straight line.

Since $b = m/n$, $m = bn$. This provides another approach to the graphing of the regression line. Draw a horizontal line of length n originating from the intercept (a). At the end of n draw a line m perpendicular to n. The endpoint of line m serves as one point and the intercept as the other point for graphing the regression line.

Two other concepts are illustrated graphically in Figure 2.1: the deviation due to residual ($Y - Y'$) and the deviation due to regression ($Y' - \overline{Y}$). For illustrative purposes, I use the individual whose scores are 5 and 10 on X and Y, respectively. This individual's predicted score (8.8) is found by drawing a line perpendicular to the ordinate (Y) from the point P on the regression line (see Figure 2.1 and Table 2.2 where I obtained the same Y' by using the regression equation). Now, this individual's Y score deviates 2.7 points from the mean of Y ($10 - 7.3 = 2.7$). It is the sum of the squares of all such deviations (Σy^2) that is partitioned into regression and residual sums of squares. For the individual under consideration, the residual: $Y - Y' = 10 - 8.8 = 1.2$. This is indicated by the vertical line drawn from the point depicting this individual's scores on X and Y to the regression line. The deviation due to regression, $Y' - \overline{Y} = 8.8 - 7.3 = 1.5$, is indicated by the extension of the same line until it meets the horizontal line originating from $\overline{Y}$ (see Figure 2.1 and Table 2.2). Note that $Y' = 8.8$ for all the individuals whose $X = 5$. It is their residuals that differ. Some points are closer to the regression line and thus their residuals are small (e.g., the individual whose $Y = 10$), and some are farther from the regression line, indicating larger residuals (e.g., the individual whose $Y = 12$).

Finally, note that the residual sum of squares is relatively large when the scatter of the points about the regression line is relatively large. Conversely, the closer the points are to the regression line, the smaller the residual sum of squares. When all the points are on the regression line, the residual sum of squares is zero, and explanation, or prediction, of Y using X is perfect. If, on the other hand, the regression of Y on X is zero, the regression line has no slope and will be drawn horizontally originating from $\overline{Y}$. Under such circumstances, $\Sigma y^2 = \Sigma(Y - Y')^2$, and all the deviations are due to error. Knowledge of X does not enhance prediction of Y.

TESTS OF SIGNIFICANCE

Sample statistics are most often used for making inferences about unknown parameters of a defined population. Recall that tests of statistical significance are used to decide whether the probability of obtaining a given estimate is small, say .05, so as to lead to the rejection of the null hypothesis that the population parameter is of a given value, say zero. Thus, for example, a small probability associated with an obtained *b* (the statistic) would lead to the rejection of the hypothesis that β (the parameter) is zero.

I assume that you are familiar with the logic and principles of statistical hypothesis testing (if necessary, review this topic in a statistics book, e.g., Hays, 1988, Chapter 7). As you are probably aware, statistical tests of significance are a major source of controversy among social scientists (for a compilation of articles on this topic, see Morrison & Henkel, 1970). The controversy is due, in part, to various misconceptions of the role and meaning of such tests in the context of scientific inquiry (for some good discussions of misconceptions and "fantasies" about, and misuse of, tests of significance, see Carver, 1978; Cohen, 1994; Dar, Serlin, & Omer, 1994; Guttman, 1985; Huberty, 1987; for recent exchanges on current practice in the use of statistical tests of significance, suggested alternatives, and responses from three journal editors, see Thompson, 1993).

It is very important to place statistical tests of significance, used repeatedly in this text, in a proper perspective of the overall research endeavor. Recall that all that is meant by a statistically significant finding is that the probability of its occurrence is small, assuming that the null hypothesis is true. But *it is the substantive meaning of the finding that is paramount*. Of what use is a statistically significant finding if it is deemed to be substantively not meaningful? Bemoaning the practice of exclusive reliance on tests of significance, Nunnally (1960) stated, "We should not feel proud when we see the psychologist smile and say 'the correlation is significant beyond the .01 level.' Perhaps that is the most he can say, but he has no reason to smile" (p. 649).

It is well known that given a sufficiently large sample, the likelihood of rejecting the null hypothesis is high. Thus, "if rejection of the null hypothesis were the real intention in psychological experiments, there usually would be no need to gather data" (Nunnally, 1960, p. 643; see also Rozeboom, 1960). Sound principles of research design dictate that the researcher first decide the effect size, or relation, deemed substantively meaningful in a given study. This is followed by decisions regarding the level of significance (Type I error) and the power of the statistical test (1 − Type II error). Based on the preceding decisions, the requisite sample size is calculated. Using this approach, the researcher can avoid arriving at findings that are substantively meaningful but statistically not significant or being beguiled by findings that are statistically significant but substantively not meaningful (for an overview of these and related issues, see Pedhazur & Schmelkin, 1991, Chapters 9 and 15; for a primer on statistical power analysis, see Cohen, 1992; for a thorough treatment of this topic, see Cohen, 1988).

In sum, the emphasis should be on the substantive meaning of findings (e.g., relations among variables, differences among means). Nevertheless, I do not discuss criteria for meaningfulness of findings, as what is deemed a meaningful finding depends on the characteristics of the study in question (e.g., domain, theoretical formulation, setting, duration, cost). For instance, a mean difference between two groups considered meaningful in one domain or in a relatively inexpensive study may be viewed as trivial in another domain or in a relatively costly study.

In short, criteria for substantive meaningfulness cannot be arrived at in a research vacuum. Admittedly, some authors (notably Cohen, 1988) provide guidelines for criteria of meaningfulness. But being guidelines in the abstract, they are, inevitably, bound to be viewed as unsatisfactory by some researchers when they examine their findings. Moreover, availability of such guidelines may have adverse effects in seeming to "absolve" researchers of the exceedingly important responsibility of assessing findings from the perspective of meaningfulness (for detailed discussions of these issues, along with relevant references, see Pedhazur & Schmelkin, 1991, Chapters 9 and 15). Although I will comment occasionally on the meaningfulness of findings, I will do so only as a reminder of the preceding remarks and as an admonition against exclusive reliance on tests of significance.

Testing the Regression of *Y* on *X*

Although formulas for tests of significance for simple regression analysis are available, I do not present them. Instead, I introduce general formulas that subsume simple regression analysis as a special case.

Earlier, I showed that the sum of squares of the dependent variable (Σy^2) can be partitioned into two components: regression sum of squares (ss_{reg}) and residual sum of squares (ss_{res}). Each of these sums of squares has associated with it a number of degrees of freedom (df). Dividing a sum of squares by its df yields a mean square. The ratio of the mean square regression to the mean square residual follows an F distribution with df_1 for the numerator and df_2 for the denominator (see the following). When the obtained F exceeds the tabled value of F at a preselected level of significance, the conclusion is to reject the null hypothesis (for a thorough discussion of the F distribution and the concept of df, see, for example, Hays, 1988; Keppel, 1991; Kirk, 1982; Walker, 1940; Winer, 1971). The formula for F, then, is

$$F = \frac{ss_{reg}/df_1}{ss_{res}/df_2} = \frac{ss_{reg}/k}{ss_{res}/(N-k-1)} \tag{2.23}$$

where df_1 associated with ss_{reg} are equal to the number of independent variables, k; and df_2 associated with ss_{res} are equal to N (sample size) minus k (number of independent variables) minus 1. In the case of simple linear regression, $k = 1$. Therefore, 1 df is associated with the numerator of the F ratio. The df for the denominator are $N - 1 - 1 = N - 2$.

For the numerical example in Table 2.2, $ss_{reg} = 22.5$; $ss_{res} = 107.7$; and $N = 20$.

$$F = \frac{22.5/1}{107.7/18} = 3.76$$

with 1 and 18 *df.*

Assuming that the researcher set α (significance level) $= .05$, it is found that the tabled F with 1 and 18 *df* is 4.41 (see Appendix B for a table of the F distribution). As the obtained F is smaller than the tabled value, it is concluded that the regression of Y on X is statistically not different from zero. Referring to the variables of the present example (recall that the data are illustrative), it would be concluded that the regression of achievement in mathematics on study time is statistically not significant at the .05 level or that study time does not significantly (at the .05 level) affect mathematics achievement. Recall, however, the important distinction between statistical significance and substantive meaningfulness, discussed previously.

Testing the Proportion of Variance Accounted for by Regression

Earlier, I said that r^2 indicates the proportion of variance of the dependent variable accounted for by the independent variable. Also, $1 - r^2$ is the proportion of variance of the dependent variable *not* accounted for by the independent variable or the proportion of error variance. The significance of r^2 is tested as follows:

$$F = \frac{r^2/k}{(1 - r^2)/(N - k - 1)} \tag{2.24}$$

where k is the number of independent variables.

For the data of Table 2.2, $r^2 = .1728$; hence,

$$F = \frac{.1728/1}{(1 - .1728)/(20 - 1 - 1)} = 3.76$$

with 1 and 18 *df*. Note that the same F ratio is obtained whether one uses sums of squares or r^2. The identity of the two formulas for the F ratio may be noted by substituting (2.19) and (2.20) in (2.23):

$$F = \frac{r^2 \Sigma y^2/k}{(1 - r^2)\Sigma y^2/(N - k - 1)} \tag{2.25}$$

where $r^2 \Sigma y^2 = ss_{reg}$ and $(1 - r^2)\Sigma y^2 = ss_{res}$. Canceling Σy^2 from the numerator and denominator of (2.25) yields (2.24). Clearly, it makes no difference whether sums of squares or proportions of variance are used for testing the significance of the regression of Y on X. In subsequent presentations I test one or both terms as a reminder that you may use whichever you prefer.

Testing the Regression Coefficient

Like other statistics, the regression coefficient, b, has a standard error associated with it. Before I present this standard error and show how to use it in testing the significance of b, I introduce the variance of estimate and the standard error of estimate.

Variance of Estimate.   The variance of scores about the regression line is referred to as the variance of estimate. The parameter is written as $\sigma_{y.x}^2$, which denotes the variance of Y given X. The sample unbiased estimator of $\sigma_{y.x}^2$ is $s_{y.x}^2$, and is calculated as follows:

$$s_{y.x}^2 = \frac{\Sigma(Y - Y')^2}{N - k - 1} = \frac{ss_{res}}{N - k - 1} \tag{2.26}$$

where Y = observed Y; Y' = predicted Y; N = sample size; and k = number of independent variables. The variance of estimate, then, is the variance of the residuals. It indicates the degree of variability of the points about the regression line. Note that the rightmost expression of $s_{y.x}^2$ is the same as the denominator of the F ratio presented earlier—see (2.23). The variance of estimate, then, is the mean square residual (*MSR*).

For the data in Table 2.2,

$$s_{y.x}^2 = MSR = \frac{107.7}{18} = 5.983$$

The *standard error of estimate* is the square root of the variance of estimate, that is, the standard deviation of the residuals:

$$s_{y.x} = \sqrt{\frac{\Sigma(Y - Y')^2}{N - k - 1}} = \sqrt{\frac{ss_{res}}{N - k - 1}} \tag{2.27}$$

For our data, $s_{y.x} = \sqrt{5.983} = 2.446$.

The standard error of b, the regression coefficient, is

$$s_b = \sqrt{\frac{s_{y.x}^2}{\Sigma x^2}} = \frac{s_{y.x}}{\sqrt{\Sigma x^2}} \tag{2.28}$$

where s_b = standard error of b; $s_{y.x}^2$ = variance of estimate; $s_{y.x}$ = standard error of estimate; and Σx^2 = sum of squares of the independent variable, X. s_b is the standard deviation of the sampling distribution of b and can therefore be used for testing the significance of b:

$$t = \frac{b}{s_b} \tag{2.29}$$

where t is the t ratio with df associated with $s_{y.x}^2$: $N - k - 1$ (N = sample size; k = number of independent variables).

For the data of Table 2.2, $b = .75$; $s_{y.x}^2 = 5.983$; and $\Sigma x^2 = 40$ (see the previous calculations). Hence,

$$t = \frac{.75}{\sqrt{\dfrac{5.983}{40}}} = \frac{.75}{\sqrt{.1496}} = 1.94$$

with 18 df $(20 - 1 - 1)$, $p > .05$. In simple linear regression, testing the significance of b is the same as testing the regression of Y on X by using sums of squares or proportions of variance. The conclusions are, of course, the same. Based on the previous test, you can conclude that the regression coefficient (b) is statistically not significantly different from zero (at the .05 level).

Recall that when, as in the present example, the numerator df for F is 1, $t^2 = F$. Thus, $1.94^2 = 3.76$, the F ratio I obtained earlier. There are, however, situations when the use of the t ratio is preferable to the use of the F ratio. First, although I used (2.29) to test whether b differs significantly from zero, it may be used to test whether b differs significantly from any hypothesized value. The formula takes the following form:

$$t = \frac{b - \beta}{s_b} \tag{2.30}$$

where β is the hypothesized regression coefficient.

Assume that in the numerical example under consideration I had reason to hypothesize that the regression coefficient in the population is .50. To test whether the obtained b differs significantly from the parameter, I would calculate

$$t = \frac{.75 - .50}{.3868} = .65$$

with 18 df. This is obviously statistically not significant at the .05 level. In other words, the obtained b is statistically not significantly different from the hypothesized regression coefficient.

Second, using a t ratio, confidence intervals can be set around the regression coefficient. The use of confidence intervals in preference to tests of statistical significance has been strongly advocated by various authors (e.g., Hays, 1988; Nunnally, 1960; Rozeboom, 1960). Because of space considerations, I will only sketch some arguments advanced in favor of the use of confidence intervals. Probably the most important argument is that a confidence interval provides more information than does a statement about rejecting (or failing to reject) a null hypothesis, which is almost always false anyway. Moreover, a confidence interval enables one to test simultaneously all possible null hypotheses. The narrower the confidence interval, the smaller the range of possible null hypotheses, and hence the greater the confidence in one's findings. In view of the preceding, confidence intervals should become an integral part of research reports, or standard errors of statistics should be reported so that interested readers may use them in assessing the findings.

The confidence interval for b is

$$b \pm t_{(\alpha/2,\ df)}s_b$$

where t is the tabled t ratio at $\alpha/2$ with df associated with standard error of estimate, and s_b is the standard error of b. Assuming that I wish to obtain the 95% confidence interval in the present example, the tabled t at .05/2 (0.025) with 18 df is 2.101 (see the table of t distribution in statistics books, or take $\sqrt{F}$ with 1 and 18 df from Appendix B), $b = .75$, and $s_b = .3868$. The 95% confidence interval is

$$.75 \pm (2.101)(.3868) = -.0627 \text{ and } 1.5627$$

or

$$-.0627 \le \beta \le 1.5627$$

As is pointed out in various statistics books (e.g., Hays, 1988; Li, J. C. R., 1964; Snedecor & Cochran, 1967), it is inappropriate to conclude that the parameter lies within the given confidence interval. Rather, the confidence interval is meant to serve as "*an estimated range of values with a given high probability of covering the true population value*" (Hays, 1988, p. 206). Stated differently, what is implied by the construction of a confidence interval is that, if many such intervals were to be constructed in like fashion, $1 - \alpha$ (95% in the present example) of them would contain the parameter (β in the present example). It is hoped that the interval being constructed is one of them. Note that in the present example the interval includes zero, thereby indicating that β is statistically not significantly different from zero at the .05 level.

Third, using a t ratio, instead of F, one may apply one-tailed tests of significance. Assume that I had reason to test the b at .05 using a one-tailed test, then the t I obtained previously (1.94 with 18 df) would have been declared statistically significant (a t of 1.73 is required for a one-tailed test at .05 level with 18 df). For discussions of one-tailed versus two-tailed tests of significance, see Burke (1953), Cohen (1965), Guilford and Fruchter (1978), Kaiser (1960), Pillemer (1991).

FACTORS AFFECTING PRECISION OF THE REGRESSION EQUATION

Careful study of the formulas for tests of significance in regression analysis reveals that three factors affect them: (1) sample size (N); (2) the scatter of points about the regression line, indicated by $\Sigma(Y - Y')^2$; and (3) the range of values selected for the X variable, reflected by Σx^2.

To demonstrate these points, I repeat formulas I used earlier with new numbers:

$$F = \frac{ss_{\text{reg}}/k}{ss_{\text{res}}/(N - k - 1)} \tag{2.31}$$

Other things equal, the larger N the smaller the denominator, and the larger the F ratio. Holding N constant, the smaller the scatter about the regression line (i.e., the smaller the ss_{res}), the larger ss_{reg}, and consequently the larger the F ratio:

$$t = \frac{b}{\sqrt{\dfrac{s_{y.x}^2}{\Sigma x^2}}} \tag{2.32}$$

Other things equal, the larger Σx^2, the smaller the s_b, and consequently, the larger the t ratio. Holding X constant, $s_{y.x}^2$ is a function of the scatter of points about the regression line. Therefore, the smaller $s_{y.x}^2$, the smaller the s_b, and the larger the t ratio. Similar reasoning applies also to formulas in which the proportion of variance accounted for is tested for significance.

I will illustrate the effects of the above-noted factors by selecting, in turn, different parts of the data of Table 2.2. These are reported in Table 2.3 and are plotted in Figure 2.2. Also given in Table 2.3, for easy reference, are some of the formulas I used in this chapter. I suggest that you repeat some of the calculations used in Table 2.3 as an exercise. Obtaining the same results by using one or more algebraic identities will help make the ideas of regression analysis part of your vocabulary.

Table 2.3   Four Sets of Illustrative Data

	(a)		*(b)*		*(c)*		*(d)*	
	X	Y	X	Y	X	Y	X	Y
	1	5	1	3	1	3	2	4
	1	6	1	9	1	5	2	6
	2	6	2	4	1	6	2	7
	2	7	2	10	1	9	2	10
	3	6	3	4	5	6	3	4
	3	8	3	10	5	7	3	6
	4	7	4	5	5	10	3	8
	4	9	4	12	5	12	3	10
	5	7	5	6			4	5
	5	10	5	12			4	7
							4	9
							4	12
N:	10		10		8		12	
ss:	20	20.9	20	108.5	32	59.5	8	70.67
a:		4.85		5.25		5.00		5.08
b:		.75		.75		.75		.75
r^2:		.54		.10		.30		.06
ss_{reg}:		11.25		11.25		18.00		4.50
ss_{res}:		9.65		97.25		41.50		66.17
$s_{y.x}$:		1.10		3.49		2.63		2.57
F:		9.33(1,8)		.93(1,8)		2.60(1,6)		.68(1,10)
t:		3.05(8)		.96(8)		1.61(6)		.82(10)

$$b = \frac{\Sigma xy}{\Sigma x^2} \qquad a = \overline{Y} - b\overline{X} \qquad ss_{reg} = b\Sigma xy = b^2\Sigma x^2 = r^2\Sigma y^2$$

$$ss_{res} = \Sigma y^2 - ss_{reg} = (1 - r^2)\Sigma y^2 \qquad F = \frac{ss_{reg}/k}{ss_{res}/(N - k - 1)} \qquad t = \frac{b}{s_b}$$

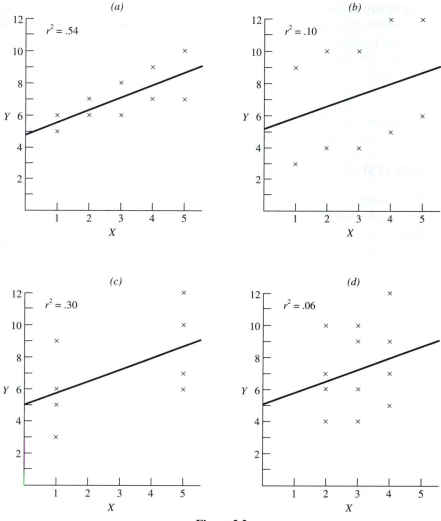

Figure 2.2

I will note several characteristics of Table 2.3 and Figure 2.2. The regression coefficient in the four sets of data is the same ($b = .75$). The F ratio associated with the b, however, is statistically significant only in (a). Compare and contrast (a) with (b): having an identical b and identical Σx^2 (20), the regression sum of squares ($b^2 \Sigma x^2$) is the same in both (11.25). N is also the same in both. They differ in the residual sum of squares—9.65 for (a) and 97.25 for (b)—which reflects the scatter of points about the regression line. Consequently, the standard error of estimate, which is the standard deviation of the residuals, of (a) is about one-third of what it is for (b), and similarly for the standard errors of the two b's. Note also that the proportion of variance (r^2) accounted for in (a) is .54, whereas in (b) it is .10.

Compare and contrast (c) and (d). The former consists of the extreme values of X (1 and 5), whereas the latter consists of the intermediate values of X (2, 3, and 4). Σx^2 in (c) is four times that of (d): 32 and 8, respectively. As the b's are the same in both sets, ss_{reg} in (c) is four times that of (d). Note also that the standard errors of estimate are very similar in both sets. Although the $s_{y.x}$ is slightly larger in (c), the standard error of b in (c) is .4649, as compared with .9086, which is the standard error of b in (d). This is directly a function of the different Σx^2's in the two sets, leading to a t of 1.61 in (c) and a t of .82 in (d). Also, the proportion of variance accounted for (r^2) in (c) is .30, whereas in (d) it is .06.

Study the example carefully to note the relations and principles I discussed and others I did not discuss.

ASSUMPTIONS

The intelligent and valid application of analytic methods requires knowledge of the rationale, hence the assumptions, behind them. Knowledge and understanding when violations of assumptions lead to serious biases, and when they are of little consequence, are essential to meaningful data analysis. Accordingly, I discuss the assumptions underlying simple linear regression and note some consequences of departures from them.

It is assumed that X, the independent variable, is a fixed variable. What this means is that if the experiment were to be replicated, the same values of X would have to be used. Referring to the numerical example used earlier, this means that the same values of hours of study would have to be used if the experiment were to be replicated.[2]

Inasmuch as the researcher is at liberty to fix the X values in an experimental study, or to select them in a nonexperimental study, the question arises: What are the considerations in determining the X values? Earlier, I showed that the larger Σx^2, the smaller the standard error of the regression coefficient. Therefore, selecting extreme X values optimizes tests of statistical significance. In the limiting case, selecting only two extreme X values maximizes the Σx^2. This, however, forces the regression to be linear even when it is curvilinear along the X continuum. Using only two X values thus precludes the possibility of determining whether the regression departs from linearity (Chapter 13). Decisions about the number of X values, their range, and spacing are to be made in light of substantive interests and theory regarding the process being modeled (Cox, 1958, pp. 138–142; Draper & Smith, 1981, pp. 51–55).

It is further assumed that X is measured without error.

The population means of the Y's at each level of X are assumed to be on a straight line. In other words, the regression of Y on X is assumed to be linear.

Unlike X, Y is a random variable, which means that Y has a range of possible values, each having an associated probability (for discussions of random variables, see Edwards, 1964, Chapter 4; Hays, 1988, pp. 92–106; Winer, 1971, Appendix A). Recall, however, that each Y score (Y_i) is assumed to be composed of a fixed component ($\alpha + \beta X$) and random error (ϵ_i).

The remaining assumptions, which are concerned with the errors, are (1) the mean of errors for each observation, Y_i, over many replications is zero; (2) errors associated with one observation, Y_i, are not correlated with errors associated with any other observation, Y_j; (3) the variance of errors at all values of X is constant, that is, the variance of errors is the same at all levels of X (this property is referred to as *homoscedasticity*, and when the variance of errors differs at

---

[2]Later in this chapter, I discuss linear regression analysis when X is a random variable.

different X values, *heteroscedasticity* is indicated); and (4) the errors are assumed to be not correlated with the independent variable, X.

The preceding assumptions are necessary to obtain best linear unbiased estimators (see the discussion earlier in the chapter). For tests of significance, an additional assumption is required, namely that the errors are normally distributed.

Violation of Assumptions

It has been demonstrated that regression analysis is generally robust in the face of departures from assumptions, except for measurement errors and specification errors (for detailed discussions see Bohrnstedt & Carter, 1971; Ezekiel & Fox, 1959; Fox, 1968; Hanushek & Jackson, 1977; Snedecor & Cochran, 1967). Therefore, I comment on these topics only.

Measurement Errors.   Measurement errors in the *dependent* variable do not lead to bias in the estimation of the regression coefficient, but they do lead to an increase in the standard error of estimate, thereby weakening tests of statistical significance.

Measurement errors in the *independent* variable lead to underestimation of the regression coefficient. It can be shown that the underestimation is related to the reliability of the measure of the independent variable. Reliability is a complex topic that I cannot discuss here (for different models of reliability and approaches to its estimation, see Nunnally, 1978, Chapters 6 and 7; Pedhazur & Schmelkin, 1991, Chapter 5). For present purposes I will only point out that, broadly speaking, reliability refers to the precision of measurement. Generally symbolized as r_{tt}, reliability can range from .00 to 1.00. The higher the r_{tt}, the more precise the measurement. Now,

$$b = \beta r_{tt} \tag{2.33}$$

where b = the statistic and β = the parameter. Equation (2.33) shows that with perfect reliability of the measure of X (i.e., $r_{tt} = 1.00$), $b = \beta$. When the reliability is less than 1.00, as it almost always is, b underestimates β. When $r_{tt} = .70$, say, there is a 30% underestimation of β. In experimental research, the independent variable is under the control of the experimenter. Consequently, it is reasonable to expect that, with proper care, high reliability of X may be realized.[3] In nonexperimental research, on the other hand, the reliability of the measure of the independent variable tends to be low to moderate (i.e., ranging from about .5 to about .8). This is particularly the case for certain attributes used in such research (e.g., cognitive styles, self–concept, ego strength, attitudes). Thus, bias in estimating the regression coefficient in nonexperimental research may be considerable.

Most researchers seem unaware of the biasing effects of measurement errors.[4] Among those who are aware of such effects, many are complacent about them, presuming their stance to be conservative as it leads to underestimation rather than overestimation of the regression

---

[3]Chatfield (1991) relates an example of an experimenter who faulted the computer program for regression analysis when, contrary to an expectation of an almost perfect fit, it indicated that 10% of the variance of the dependent variable was accounted for. It turned out that the fault was in the manner in which the observations were collected. Replication of the experiment with appropriate controls "resulted in a 99% fit!" (p. 243).

[4]A case in point are researchers who, adopting rules of thumb or "standards" of reliability proposed by various authors (notably Nunnally, 1967, 1978), contend that the reliabilities of their measures that hover around .70 are "acceptable." They then proceed to carry out regression analysis without the slightest hint that it is adversely affected by measurement errors. For a couple of recent examples, see Hobfoll, Shoham, and Ritter (1991, p. 334) and Thomas and Williams (1991, p. 305). For a discussion of "standards" of reliability, see Pedhazur and Schmelkin (1991, pp. 109–110).

coefficient. However, two things will be noted. First, when one wishes to test whether the regression of Y on X is the same in two groups, say, as in attribute-treatments-interaction (ATI) designs (Chapter 14), conclusions may be seriously in error if there is substantial variation in the reliabilities of the measure of X for the groups under consideration. The same is true for analysis of covariance designs (Chapter 15), and for some designs dealing with test bias (Chapter 14). Second, effects of measurement errors in designs with more than one independent variable (i.e., in multiple regression) are more complex, and the direction of the bias may be in overestimation or underestimation (Chapter 10).

The preceding remarks apply to the effects of random measurement errors. Effects of nonrandom errors are more complex and difficult to trace. In sum, it was no exaggeration on the part of Fleiss and Shrout (1977) when they stated that "effects of measurement errors can become devastating" (p. 1190).

Specification Errors.   Broadly, specification errors refer to any errors committed in specifying the model to be tested or to the violation of any of the assumptions that underlie the model. The term is generally used in a narrower sense to refer to errors in model specification (Hanushek & Jackson, 1977, pp. 79–86; Kmenta, 1971, pp. 391–405). The model used (i.e., the regression equation) represents a theoretical conception of the phenomenon under study. When the model is not tenable from a theoretical frame of reference, specification errors are indicated. Among such errors are (1) omission of relevant variables from the equation, (2) inclusion of irrelevant variables in the equation, and (3) specifying that the regression is linear when it is curvilinear.

I discuss specification errors in detail in Chapter 10. At this stage, I will only draw attention to serious biasing effects such errors may have. Earlier, I stated that under errors, e, are subsumed all variables, other than X, that affect the dependent variable, Y. I also stated that e is assumed to be not correlated with X. This situation is depicted in Figure 2.3.

Now, suppose that a relevant variable (or variables) not included in the equation is correlated with X. Since such a variable is subsumed under e, it follows that e and X are correlated, thus violating a crucial assumption (see preceding) and leading to bias in the estimation of the regression coefficient for X. I show the nature of the bias in Chapter 10. For now, suffice it to say that it may be very serious and lead to erroneous conclusions about the effect of X on Y.

The potential for specification errors of the kind just described stems in part from the type of research in which regression analysis is used. Particularly pertinent in this context is the distinction between experimental and nonexperimental research (see Pedhazur & Schmelkin, 1991, Chapters, 10, 12, and 14). In experimental research, subjects are randomly assigned to different levels of X, hence it is reasonable to assume that the effects of all variables, other than X, are

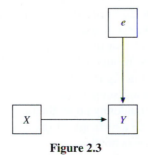

Figure 2.3

equally distributed in the various groups. In other words, the assumption about the absence of a relation between X and e is tenable, though not a certainty. The assumption may be highly questionable when the research is nonexperimental. In a very good discussion of the biasing effects of measurement and specification errors, Bohrnstedt and Carter (1971) pointed out that researchers often ignore such errors. "We can only come to the sobering conclusion, then, that many of the published results based on regression analysis . . . are possible distortions of whatever reality may exist" (p. 143). This indictment should serve to alert researchers to possible distortions in their analyses and the need to take steps to avoid them or to cope with them.

DIAGNOSTICS

Diagnostics aimed at affording a better understanding of one's results as well as the detection of possible violations of assumptions and influential observations have grown in sophistication and complexity in recent years. At this stage, I give only a rudimentary introduction to this topic. For more detailed treatments, see Chapters 3 and 10.

Data and Residual Plots

An indispensable approach for a better understanding of one's results and for discerning whether some of the assumptions (e.g., linearity, homoscedasticity) are tenable is the study of data plots (for very good discussions and instructive illustrations, see Anscombe, 1973; Atkinson, 1985; Cleveland & McGill, 1984; du Toit, Steyn, & Stumpf, 1986).

Another very useful approach is the study of residual plots. Probably the simplest and most useful plots are those of the standardized residuals against corresponding X's or predicted Y's (in raw or standardized form). You have, doubtless, encountered standard scores in introductory courses in statistics or measurement. Recall that

$$z = \frac{X - \overline{X}}{s} \tag{2.34}$$

where z = standard score; X = raw score; $\overline{X}$ = mean; and s = standard deviation. As I pointed out earlier, the mean of residuals is zero, and the standard deviation of residuals is the standard error of estimate ($s_{y.x}$). Therefore, to standardize residuals, divide each residual by $s_{y.x}$. Predicted scores (Y') are, of course, obtained through the application of the regression equation.

I use the data of Table 2.2 to illustrate residual plots and to discuss some approaches to studying them. In Table 2.2 the predicted Y's are reported in the column labeled Y', and the residuals are reported under $Y - Y'$. For these data, $s_{y.x} = 2.446$—see the calculations following (2.26) and (2.27). I divided the residuals by 2.446 to obtain standardized residuals, which I plotted against the predicted Y's in Figure 2.4.

Several things are being sought when studying plots like that of Figure 2.4. First, do the points appear to scatter randomly about the line originating from the mean of the residuals, depicting what appears to be a rectangle? Figure 2.5 illustrates departure from such a scatter, suggesting that the regression is nonlinear.

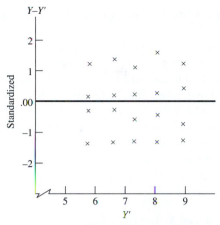

Figure 2.4

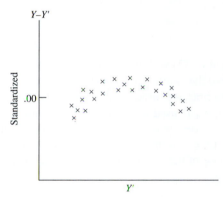

Figure 2.5

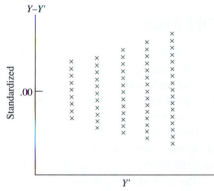

Figure 2.6

Second, are the points scattered evenly about the line originating from the mean of the residuals? If they are not, as exemplified in Figure 2.6, heteroscedasticity is indicated.

Third, are there outliers? I discuss outliers in Chapter 3. For now I will only point out that observations that are distinct or deviant from the rest of the data are referred to as outliers.

REGRESSION ANALYSIS WHEN *X* IS A RANDOM VARIABLE

Thus far, my discussion was limited to designs in which *X* is fixed. As is well known, however, in much of behavioral research, the researcher does not, or cannot, fix *X*. Instead, a sample is drawn from a defined population, and measures of *X* and *Y* are obtained. Thus, both *X* and *Y* are random variables. It was shown (e.g., Fox, 1984, pp. 61–63; Kmenta, 1971, pp. 297–304; Snedecor & Cochran, 1967, pp. 149–150) that when the other assumptions are reasonably met, particularly the assumption that *X* and *e* are not correlated, least-squares estimators and tests of significance presented earlier apply equally to the situation when both *X* and *Y* are random variables.

When both variables are random, the researcher may choose to study the regression of *Y* on *X*, or the regression of *X* on *Y*. The equation for the regression of *X* on *Y* is

$$X' = a + bY \tag{2.35}$$

where *X'* is the predicted *X*. The formulas for *a* and *b* are

$$b = \frac{\Sigma xy}{\Sigma y^2} \tag{2.36}$$

$$a = \overline{X} - b\overline{Y} \tag{2.37}$$

Compare (2.36) and (2.37) with the corresponding formulas for the regression of *Y* on *X*—(2.7) and (2.8)—and note the similarities and the differences.

Generally, subscripts are used to distinguish between the constants of the two equations. Thus, for example, b_{yx} is used to denote the regression coefficient for the regression of *Y* on *X*, whereas b_{xy} is used to denote the regression coefficient for the regression of *X* on *Y*. When there is no ambiguity about the designations of the independent variable and the dependent variable, it is convenient to dispose of the use of subscripts—a practice I followed in preceding sections of this chapter.

THE CORRELATION MODEL

Unlike the regression model, in the correlation model no distinction is made between an independent and a dependent variable. Instead, the nature (i.e., positive or negative) and degree of relation between two variables is sought.

Although the concept of covariance, which I discussed earlier in this chapter, is useful, it is difficult to interpret because its magnitude is affected by the specific scales used. For example, in studying the covariance between height and weight, one might express height in inches, say, and weight in ounces. If, instead, one were to express height in feet and weight in pounds, the underlying relation between the two variables would, of course, not change but the value of the covariance would change. This problem may be overcome by using the correlation coefficient:

$$\rho = \frac{\Sigma xy}{N\sigma_x\sigma_y} = \frac{\sigma_{xy}}{\sigma_x\sigma_y} \tag{2.38}$$

where ρ (rho) = population correlation coefficient; Σxy = sum of cross products; σ_{xy} = covariance of *X* and *Y*; and σ_x, σ_y = standard deviation of *X* and *Y*, respectively.

Earlier, I pointed out that dividing a deviation score by the standard deviation yields a standard score—see (2.34). Inspection of (2.38), particularly the first term on the right, reveals that the scores on X and Y are standardized. To make this more explicit, I express ρ in standard score form,

$$\rho = \frac{\Sigma z_x z_y}{N} \tag{2.39}$$

from which it can be seen clearly that the correlation coefficient is a covariance of standard scores, therefore not affected by the specific units used to measure X and Y. It can be shown that the maximum value of ρ is $|1.00|$. $\rho = +1.00$ indicates a perfect positive correlation, whereas $\rho = -1.00$ indicates a perfect negative correlation. $\rho = .00$ indicates no *linear* relation between X and Y. The closer ρ is to $|1.00|$, the stronger is the relation between X and Y. Also, the correlation coefficient is a symmetric index: $\rho_{xy} = \rho_{yx}$.

The sample correlation, r, is

$$r_{xy} = \frac{s_{xy}}{s_x s_y} \tag{2.40}$$

where s_{xy} = sample covariance; and s_x, s_y = sample standard deviations of X and Y, respectively. Of various formulas for the calculation of r, two that are particularly easy to use are

$$r_{xy} = \frac{\Sigma xy}{\sqrt{\Sigma x^2 \Sigma y^2}} \tag{2.41}$$

where Σxy = sum of the products; and Σx^2, Σy^2 = sums of squares of X and Y, respectively, and

$$r_{xy} = \frac{N\Sigma XY - (\Sigma X)(\Sigma Y)}{\sqrt{N\Sigma X^2 - (\Sigma X)^2}\ \sqrt{N\Sigma Y^2 - (\Sigma Y)^2}} \tag{2.42}$$

where all the terms are expressed in raw scores. Formula (2.42) is particularly useful for calculations by hand, or with the aid of a calculator.

Recall that in the regression model Y is a random variable assumed to be normally distributed, whereas X is fixed, its values being determined by the researcher. In the correlation model, both X and Y are random variables assumed to follow a bivariate normal distribution. That is, the joint distribution of the two variables is assumed to be normal. The assumptions about homoscedasticity and about the residuals, which I discussed earlier in this chapter, apply also to the correlation model.

Although r and r^2 enter regression calculations, r is irrelevant in the regression model. Therefore, interpreting r as indicating the linear relation between X and Y is inappropriate. Look back at Figure 2.2 and note that the b's are the same in the four sets of data, but the r's range from a low of .24 to a high of .73. Careful study of the figure and the calculations associated with it will reveal that r changes as a function of scatter of points about the regression line and the variability of X. The greater the scatter, other things equal, the lower r is. The smaller the variability of X, other things equal, the lower r is. As I said earlier, in regression analysis the researcher may increase the variability of X at will, thereby increasing r. There is nothing wrong in doing this provided one does not interpret r as the sample estimate of the linear correlation between two random variables.

Earlier, I showed that r^2 is a meaningful term in regression analysis, indicating the proportion of variance of Y accounted for by X. Moreover, $1 - r^2$ is closely related to the variance of estimate and the standard error of estimate. Also, I expressed the residual sum of squares as

$$ss_{\text{res}} = (1 - r^2)\Sigma y^2 \tag{2.43}$$

and the variance of estimate as

$$s_{\text{y.x}}^2 = \frac{(1 - r^2)\Sigma y^2}{N - 2} \tag{2.44}$$

From (2.43) and (2.44) it can be seen that when $1 - r^2$ is zero, ss_{res} and $s_{\text{y.x}}$ are zero. In other words, no error is committed. This, of course, happens when $r^2 = 1.00$, indicating that all the variance is due to regression. The larger r^2 is, the smaller is $1 - r^2$ (the proportion of variance due to error). It is this use of r^2 that is legitimate and meaningful in regression analysis, and not the use of its square root (i.e., r) as an indicator of the linear correlation between two random variables.

The regression model is most directly and intimately related to the primary goals of scientific inquiry: explanation and prediction of phenomena. When a scientist wishes, for instance, to state the expected changes in Y because of manipulations of, or changes in, X, it is the regression coefficient, b, that provides this information. Because of the greater potency of the regression model, some writers (e.g., Blalock, 1968; Tukey, 1954) argued that it be used whenever possible and that the correlation model be used only when the former cannot be applied. Tukey (1954), who referred to himself as a member of the "informal society for the suppression of the correlation coefficient" (p. 38), advanced strong arguments against its use. He maintained that "It is an enemy of generalization, a focuser on the 'here and now' to the exclusion of the 'there and then'" (Tukey, 1969, p. 89). Only bad reasons came to Tukey's mind when he pondered the appeal the correlation coefficient holds for behavioral researchers.

> Given two perfectly meaningless variables, one is reminded of their meaninglessness when a regression coefficient is given, since one wonders how to interpret its value. A correlation coefficient is less likely to bring up the unpleasant truth—we *think* we know what $r = .7$ means. *Do we?* How often? Sweeping things under the rug is the enemy of good data analysis. Often, using the correlation coefficient is "sweeping under the rug" with a vengeance.

Expressing the same point of view, though in a less impassioned tone, Fisher (1958) stated, "The regression coefficients are of interest and scientific importance in many classes of data where the correlation coefficient, if used at all, is an artificial concept of no real utility" (p. 129).

These are, admittedly, postures with which some writers may disagree. The important point, however, is that you keep in mind the differences between the regression and the correlation models and apply the one most suited for the given research problem.

For further discussions of the distinction between the two models, see Binder (1959), Ezekiel and Fox (1959, pp. 279–280), Fox (1968, pp. 167–190, 211–223), Kendall (1951), and Warren (1971). Although I deal occasionally with the correlation model, my primary concern in this book is with the regression model.

CONCLUDING REMARKS

In this chapter, I introduced elements of simple linear regression analysis. Along with the mechanics of the calculations, I discussed basic issues regarding the interpretation of the results.

In addition, I discussed assumptions underlying the regression model and pointed out that measurement errors in the independent variable and specification errors deserve special attention because they may lead to serious distortions of results of regression analysis. Finally, I discussed the distinction between the regression and correlation models.

STUDY SUGGESTIONS

1. You will do well to study simple regression analysis from a standard text. The following two sources are excellent—and quite different: Hays (1988, Chapter 13) and Snedecor and Cochran (1967, Chapter 6). Although these two chapters are somewhat more difficult than certain other treatments, they are both worth the effort.

2. Here are X and Y scores (the second, third, and fourth pairs of columns are continuations of the first pair of columns):

X	Y	X	Y	X	Y	X	Y
2	2	4	4	4	3	9	9
2	1	5	7	3	3	10	6
1	1	5	6	6	6	9	6
1	1	7	7	6	6	4	9
3	5	6	8	8	10	4	10

Calculate the following:

(a) Means, sums of squares and cross products, standard deviations, and the correlation between X and Y.
(b) Regression equation of Y on X.
(c) Regression and residual sum of squares.
(d) F ratio for the test of significance of the regression of Y on X, using the sums of squares (i.e., ss_{reg} and ss_{res}) and using r_{xy}^2.

(e) Variance of estimate and the standard error of estimate.
(f) Standard error of the regression coefficient.
(g) t ratio for the test of the regression coefficient. What should the square of the t equal? (That is, what statistic calculated above should it equal?)

Using the regression equation, calculate the following:
(h) Each person's predicted score, Y', on the basis of the X's.
(i) The sum of the predicted scores and their mean.
(j) The residuals, $(Y - Y')$; their sum, $\Sigma(Y - Y')$, and the sum of the squared residuals, $\Sigma(Y - Y')^2$.
(k) Plot the data, the regression line, and the standardized residuals against the predicted scores.

3. Following are summary data from a study: $N = 200$; $\overline{X} = 60$; $\overline{Y} = 100$; $s_x = 6$; $s_y = 9$; $r_{xy} = .7$. Calculate the following:
(a) Sum of squares for X and Y and the sum of products.
(b) Proportion of variance of Y accounted for by X.
(c) Regression of Y on X.
(d) Regression sum of squares.
(e) Residual sum of squares.
(f) F ratio for the test of significance of the regression of Y on X.

ANSWERS

2. (a) $\overline{X} = 4.95$; $\overline{Y} = 5.50$; $\Sigma x^2 = 134.95$; $\Sigma y^2 = 165.00$; $\Sigma xy = 100.50$; $s_x = 2.6651$; $s_y = 2.9469$; $r_{xy} = .6735$
(b) $Y' = 1.81363 + .74472X$
(c) $ss_{reg} = 74.84439$; $ss_{res} = 90.15561$
(d) $F = 14.94$, with 1 and 18 df
(e) $s_{y.x}^2 = 5.00865$; $s_{y.x} = 2.23800$
(f) $s_b = .19265$
(g) $t = 3.87$ with 18 df; $t^2 = F$ obtained in (d).
(h) $Y_1' = 3.30307 \ldots$; $Y_{20}' = 4.79251$
(i) $\Sigma Y' = 110.00 = \Sigma Y$; $\overline{Y}' = 5.50 = \overline{Y}$
(j) $Y_1 - Y_1' = -1.30307 \ldots$; $Y_{20} - Y_{20}' = 5.20749$; $\Sigma(Y - Y') = 0$; $\Sigma(Y - Y')^2 = 90.15561 = ss_{res}$

3. (a) $\Sigma x^2 = (N-1)s_x^2 = (199)(36) = 7164$;
      $\Sigma y^2 = (N-1)s_y^2 = 16119$;
      $\Sigma xy = (r_{xy}s_xs_y)(N-1) = 7522.2$;
   (b) $.49 = r_{xy}^2$
   (c) $Y' = 37 + 1.05X$
   (d) $ss_{reg} = 7898.31$
   (e) $ss_{res} = 8220.69$
   (f) $F = 190.24$ with 1 and 198 *df*

3

Regression Diagnostics

Merits of most regression diagnostics can be especially appreciated in multiple regression analysis (i.e., analysis with more than one independent variable). Some diagnostics are applicable only in this case. Further, familiarity with matrix algebra and analysis by computer are essential for the application and understanding of most diagnostics. Nevertheless, a rudimentary introduction in the context of simple regression analysis should prove helpful because the calculations involved are relatively simple, requiring neither matrix operations nor computer analysis. After introducing computer programs and basic notions of matrix algebra (Chapters 4 and 5), I elaborate and expand on some topics I introduce here.[1] The present introduction is organized under two main headings: "Outliers" and "Influence Analysis."[2]

OUTLIERS

As the name implies, an outlier is a data point distinct or deviant from the rest of the data. Of factors that may give rise to outliers, diverse errors come readily to mind. Thus, an outlier may be a result of a recording or an input error, measurement errors, the malfunctioning of an instrument, or inappropriate instructions in the administration of a treatment, to name but some. Detecting errors and correcting them, or discarding subjects when errors in their scores are not correctable, are the recommended strategies in such instances.

Outliers may occur in the absence of errors. In essence, these are "true" outliers, as contrasted with "false" ones arising from errors of the kind I discussed in the preceding paragraph. It is outliers not due to discernable errors that are of interest for what they may reveal, among other things, about (1) the model being tested, (2) the possible violation of assumptions, and (3) observations that have undue influence on the results.[3] This is probably what Kruskal (1988) had in mind when he asserted that "investigation of the mechanism for outlying may be far more important than the original study that led to the outlier" (p. 929).

---

[1] An advanced review of topics presented in this chapter is given by Chatterjee and Hadi (1986a) and is followed by comments by some leading authorities. See also Hoaglin (1992) for a very good explication of diagnostics.

[2] I do not present here diagnostic approaches addressed to issues of collinearity (see Chapter 10), as they are only relevant for the case of multiple regression analysis.

[3] As I explain in the next section, an influential observation is a special case of an outlier.

Individuals with a unique attribute, or a unique combination of attributes, may react uniquely to a treatment making them stand out from the rest of the group. Discovery of such occurrences may lead to new insights into the phenomenon under study and to the designing of research to explore and extend such insights.

DETECTION OF OUTLIERS

Procedures for the detection of outliers rely almost exclusively on the detection of extreme residuals, so much so that the two are used interchangeably by some authors and researchers. Using the outlier concept in a broader sense of a deviant case, it is possible for it to be associated with a small residual, even one equal to zero. Such outliers may become evident when studying influence analysis—a topic I present in the next section. In what follows, I present three approaches to the detection of outliers based on residual analysis: (1) standardized residuals, (2) studentized residuals, and (3) studentized deleted residuals.

Standardized Residuals (ZRESID)

I introduced standardized residuals in Chapter 2—see (2.34) and the discussion related to it. Various authors have suggested that standardized residuals greater than 2 in absolute value (i.e., $z > |2.0|$) be scrutinized. Notice that large standardized residuals serve to alert the researcher to study them; *not* to automatically designate the points in question as outliers. As in most other matters, what counts is informed judgment. The same is true of studentized and studentized deleted residuals, which I discuss later in the chapter.

To illustrate the calculation of the various indices presented here, I will use data from the numerical example I introduced in Chapter 2 (Table 2.1). For convenience, I repeat the data from Table 2.1 in the first two columns of Table 3.1. Also repeated in the table, in the column labeled RESID, are residuals I took from Table 2.2.

As an example, I will calculate the standardized residual for the last subject in Table 3.1. This subject's residual is −2.80. For the data under consideration, $s_{y.x} = 2.446$ (see Chapter 2, for calculations). Dividing the residual by 2.446 yields a standardized residual of −1.1447.

Standardized residuals for the rest of the subjects, reported in Table 3.1 in the column labeled ZRESID, were similarly calculated. As you can see, none of the standardized residuals is greater than $|2.0|$. Had standardized residuals been used for detection of outliers, it would have been plausible to conclude that there are no outliers in the data under consideration.

Studentized Residuals (SRESID)

Calculation of standardized residuals is based on the generally untenable assumption that all residuals have the same variance. To avoid making this assumption, it is suggested that SRESIDs be used instead. This is accomplished by dividing each residual by its estimated standard deviation, which for simple regression analysis is

$$s_{e_i} = s_{y.x} \sqrt{1 - \left[\frac{1}{N} + \frac{(X_i - \overline{X})^2}{\Sigma x^2} \right]} \tag{3.1}$$

Note that the standard deviation of a residual is obtained by multiplying the standard error of estimate ($s_{y.x}$)—used above as the denominator for standardized residuals—by the term under

Table 3.1   Residual Analysis for Data of Table 2.1

X	Y	RESID	ZRESID	SRESID	SDRESID
1	3	−2.80	−1.1447	−1.2416	−1.2618
1	5	−.80	−.3271	−.3547	−.3460
1	6	.20	.0818	.0887	.0862
1	9	3.20	1.3082	1.4190	1.4632
2	4	−2.55	−1.0425	−1.0839	−1.0895
2	6	−.55	−.2248	−.2338	−.2275
2	7	.45	.1840	.1913	.1861
2	10	3.45	1.4104	1.4665	1.5188
3	4	−3.30	−1.3491	−1.3841	−1.4230
3	6	−1.30	−.5315	−.5453	−.5343
3	8	.70	.2862	.2936	.2860
3	10	2.70	1.1038	1.1325	1.1420
4	5	−3.05	−1.2469	−1.2965	−1.3232
4	7	−1.05	−.4293	−.4463	−.4362
4	9	.95	.3884	.4038	.3942
4	12	3.95	1.6148	1.6790	1.7768
5	7	−1.80	−.7359	−.7982	−.7898
5	10	1.20	.4906	.5321	.5212
5	12	3.20	1.3082	1.4190	1.4633
5	6	−2.80	−1.1447	−1.2416	−1.2618

NOTE: *X* and *Y* were taken from Table 2.1.
RESID   = residual (taken from Table 2.2)
ZRESID   = standardized residual
SRESID   = studentized residual
SDRESID = studentized deleted residual
See text for explanations.

the radical. Examine the latter and notice that the more X_i deviates from the mean of X, the smaller the standard error of the residual; hence the larger the studentized residual. As I show in the "Influence Analysis" section of this chapter, the term in the brackets (i.e., that subtracted from 1) is referred to as *leverage* and is symbolized as h_i.[4]

For illustrative purposes, I will apply (3.1) to the last subject of Table 3.1. For the data of Table 3.1, $\overline{X} = 3.00$ and $\Sigma x^2 = 40$ (see Chapter 2 for calculations). Hence,

$$s_{e_i} = 2.446 \sqrt{1 - \left[\frac{1}{20} + \frac{(5 - 3.0)^2}{40} \right]} = 2.2551$$

Dividing the residual (−2.80) by its standard deviation (2.2551), SRESID for the last subject is −1.2416. Note that subjects having the same X have an identical standard error of residual. For example, the standard error of the residual for the last four subjects is 2.2551. Dividing these subjects' residuals by 2.2551 yields their SRESIDs. Studentized residuals for all the subjects in the example under consideration are reported in Table 3.1 under SRESID.

---

[4]The h stands for the so-called hat matrix, and i refers to the ith diagonal element of this matrix. If you are unfamiliar with matrix terminology, don't worry about it. I explain it in subsequent chapters (especially Chapter 6). I introduced the term here because it affords a simpler presentation of some subsequent formulas in this section and in the "Influence Analysis" section presented in this chapter.

When the assumptions of the model are reasonably met, SRESIDs follow a t distribution with $N - k - 1$ *df*, where N = sample size, k = number of independent variables. For the present example, $df = 18$ ($20 - 1 - 1$). It should be noted that the t's are not independent. This, however, is not a serious drawback, as the usefulness of the t's lies not so much in their use for tests of significance of residuals but as indicators of relatively large residuals whose associated observations deserve scrutiny.

The SRESIDs I discussed thus far are referred to by some authors (e.g., Cook & Weisberg, 1982, pp. 18–20) as "internally studentized residuals," to distinguish them from "externally studentized residuals." The distinction stems from the fact that $s_{y.x}$ used in the calculation of internally studentized residuals is based on the data for *all* the subjects, whereas in the case of externally studentized residuals $s_{y.x}$ is calculated after excluding the individual whose studentized residual is being sought (see the next section).

Studentized Deleted Residuals (SDRESID)

The standard error of SDRESID is calculated in a manner similar to (3.1), except that the standard error of estimate is based on data from which the subject whose studentized deleted residual is being sought was excluded. The reasoning behind this approach is that to the extent that a given point constitutes an outlier, its retention in the analysis would lead to upward bias in the standard error of estimate ($s_{y.x}$), thereby running the risk of failing to identify it as an outlier. Accordingly, the standard error of a deleted residual is defined as

$$s_{e(i)} = s_{y.x(i)} \sqrt{1 - \left[\frac{1}{N} + \frac{(X_i - \overline{X})^2}{\Sigma x^2}\right]} \tag{3.2}$$

where $s_{e(i)}$ = standard error of residual for individual i, who has been excluded from the analysis; and $s_{y.x(i)}$ = standard error of estimate based on data from which i was excluded. Dividing i's residual by this standard error yields a SDRESID, which, as I stated previously, is also called an externally studentized residual.

For illustrative purposes, I will calculate SDRESID for the last subject of Table 3.1. This requires that the subject in question be deleted and a regression analysis be done to obtain the standard error of estimate.[5] Without showing the calculations, the standard error of estimate based on the data from which the last subject was deleted (i.e., an analysis based on the first 19 subjects) is 2.407. Applying (3.2),

$$s_{e(1)} = 2.407 \sqrt{1 - \left[\frac{1}{20} + \frac{(5 - 3.0)^2}{40}\right]} = 2.2190$$

Dividing the last subject's residual (−2.80) by this standard error yields a SDRESID of −1.2618.

As you can see, application of (3.2) for all the subjects would entail 20 regression analyses, in each of which one subject is deleted. Fortunately, formulas obviating the need for such laboriously repetitious calculations are available.[6] Following are two alternative approaches to the calculation of SDRESID based on results of an analysis in which all the subjects were included.

$$SDRESID_{(i)} = e_i \sqrt{\frac{N - k - 2}{ss_{\text{res}}(1 - h_i) - e_i^2}} \tag{3.3}$$

---

[5]Later, I give formulas that obviate the need to do a regression analysis from which the subject in question was excluded.

[6]As I show in Chapter 4, current computer programs for regression analysis include extensive diagnostic procedures.

where $SDRESID_{(i)}$ = studentized deleted residual for subject i; e_i = residual for subject i; N = sample size; k = number of independent variables; ss_{res} = residual sum of squares from the analysis in which *all* the subjects were included; and $h_i = 1/N + (X_i - \overline{X})^2/\Sigma x^2$—see (3.1) and Footnote 4.

Using (3.3), I will calculate SDRESID for the last subject in the present example (using the data from Table 3.1). Recall that N = 20, and k = 1. From earlier calculations, $e_{20} = -2.80$; the mean of X = 3.0; ss_{res} = 107.70. Hence,

$$SDRESID_{(20)} = -2.80 \sqrt{\frac{20-1-2}{107.70\,(1-.15)-(-2.80)^2}} = -1.2618$$

which agrees with the value I obtained previously. Similarly, I calculated SDRESIDs for the rest of the subjects. I reported them in Table 3.1 under SDRESID.[7]

Having calculated studentized residuals—as I did earlier and reported under SRESID in Table 3.1—SDRESIDs can also be calculated as follows:

$$SDRESID_{(i)} = SRESID_i \sqrt{\frac{N-k-2}{N-k-1-SRESID_i^2}} \tag{3.4}$$

where all the terms were defined earlier.

Using (3.4), I will calculate SDRESID for the last subject of Table 3.1. From earlier calculations (see also Table 3.1), $SRESID_{20} = -1.2416$. Hence,

$$SDRESID_{(20)} = -1.2416 \sqrt{\frac{20-1-2}{20-1-1-(-1.2416)^2}} = -1.2619$$

which is, within rounding, the same value I obtained earlier.

The SDRESID is distributed as a t distribution with $N - k - 2$ *df.* As with ZRESID and SRESID, it is generally used not for tests of significance but for identifying large residuals, alerting the user to examine the observations associated with them.

INFLUENCE ANALYSIS

Although it has been recognized for some time that certain observations have greater influence on regression estimates than others, it is only in recent years that various procedures were developed for identifying influential observations. In their seminal work on influence analysis, Belsley, Kuh, and Welsch (1980) defined an influential observation as

> one which, either individually or together with several other observations, has a demonstrably larger impact on the calculated values of various estimates (coefficients, standard errors, *t*-values, etc.) than is the case for most of the other observations. (p. 11)

As I illustrate later in this chapter, an outlier (see the preceding section) is not necessarily an influential observation. Rather, "an influential case is a special kind of outlier" (Bollen & Jackman, 1985, p. 512). As with outliers, greater appreciation of the role played by influential observations can be gained in the context of multiple regression analysis. Nevertheless, I introduce this topic here for the same reasons I introduced outliers earlier, namely, in simple regression

---

[7]For the present data, SDRESIDs differ little from SRESIDs. In the next section, I give an example where the two differ considerably.

analysis the calculations are simple, requiring neither matrix operations nor computer analysis. Later in the text (especially Chapter 6), I show generalizations to multiple regression analysis of indices presented here.

LEVERAGE

As the name implies, an observation's undue influence may be likened to the action of a lever providing increased power to pull the regression line, say, in a certain direction. In simple regression analysis, leverage can be calculated as follows:

$$h_i = \frac{1}{N} + \frac{(X - \overline{X})^2}{\Sigma x^2} \tag{3.5}$$

As I pointed out earlier—see (3.1) and the discussion related to it—h_i refers to the ith diagonal element of the so-called hat matrix (see Chapter 6). Before applying (3.5) to the numerical example under consideration, I will list several of its properties.

1. Leverage is a function solely of scores on the independent variable(s). Thus, as I show in the next section, a case that may be influential by virtue of its status on the dependent variable will not be detected as such on the basis of its leverage.
2. Other things equal, the larger the deviation of X_i from the mean of X, the larger the leverage. Notice that leverage is at a minimum ($1/N$) when X_i is equal to the mean of X.
3. The maximum value of leverage is 1.
4. The average leverage for a set of scores is equal to $(k + 1)/N$, where k is the number of independent variables.

In light of these properties of leverage, Hoaglin and Welsch (1978, p. 18) suggested that, as a rule of thumb, $h_i > 2(k + 1)/N$ be considered high (but see Velleman & Welsch, 1981, pp. 234–235, for a revision of this rule of thumb in light of N and the number of independent variables). Later in this chapter, I comment on rules of thumb in general and specifically for the detection of outliers and influential observations and will therefore say no more about this topic here.

For illustrative purposes, I will calculate h_{20} (leverage for the last subject of the data in Table 3.1). Recalling that $N = 20$, $X_{20} = 5$, $\overline{X} = 3$, $\Sigma x^2 = 40$,

$$h_{20} = \frac{1}{20} + \frac{(5 - 3)^2}{40} = .15$$

Leverage for subjects having the same X is, of course, identical. Leverages for the data of Table 3.1 are given in column (1) of Table 3.2, from which you will note that all are relatively small, none exceeding the criterion suggested earlier.

To give you a feel for an observation with high leverage, and how such an observation might affect regression estimates, assume for the last case of the data in Table 3.1 that $X = 15$ instead of 5. This may be a consequence of a recording error or it may truly be this person's score on the independent variable. Be that as it may, after the change, the mean of X is 3.5, and $\Sigma x^2 = 175.00$ (you may wish to do these calculations as an exercise). Applying now (3.5), leverage for the changed case is .81 (recall that maximum leverage is 1.0).

Table 3.2   Influence Analysis for Data of Table 3.1

(1) h Leverage	(2) Cook's D	(3) a DFBETA	(4) b DFBETA	(5) a DFBETAS	(6) b DFBETAS
.15	.13602	−.65882	.16471	−.52199	.43281
.15	.01110	−.18824	.04706	−.14311	.11866
.15	.00069	.04706	−.01176	.03566	−.02957
.15	.17766	.75294	−.18824	.60530	−.50189
.07	.04763	−.34459	.06892	−.27003	.17912
.07	.00222	−.07432	.01486	−.05640	.03741
.07	.00148	.06081	−.01216	.04612	−.03059
.07	.08719	.46622	−.09324	.37642	−.24969
.05	.05042	−.17368	.00000	−.13920	.00000
.05	.00782	−.06842	.00000	−.05227	.00000
.05	.00227	.03684	.00000	.02798	.00000
.05	.03375	.14211	.00000	.11171	.00000
.07	.06814	.08243	−.08243	.06559	−.21754
.07	.00808	.02838	−.02838	.02162	−.07171
.07	.00661	−.02568	.02568	−.01954	.06481
.07	.11429	−.10676	.10676	−.08807	.29210
.15	.05621	.21176	−.10588	.16335	−.27089
.15	.02498	−.14118	.07059	−.10781	.17878
.15	.17766	−.37647	.18824	−.30265	.50189
.15	.13602	.32941	−.16471	.26099	−.43281

NOTE: The data, originally presented in Table 2.1, were repeated in Table 3.1. I discuss Column (2) under Cook's *D* and Columns (3) through (6) under DFBETA. *a* = intercept.

Using the data in Table 3.1, change *X* for the last case to 15, and do a regression analysis. You will find that

$$Y' = 6.96 + .10X$$

In Chapter 2—see the calculations following (2.9)—the regression equation for the original data was shown to be

$$Y' = 5.05 + .75X$$

Notice the considerable influence the change in one of the *X*'s has on both the intercept and the regression coefficient (incidentally, r^2 for these data is .013, as compared with .173 for the original data). Assuming one could rule out errors (e.g., of recording, measurement, see the earlier discussion of this point), one would have to come to grips with this finding. Issues concerning conclusions that might be reached, and actions that might be taken, are complex. At this stage, I will give only a couple of examples.

Recall that I introduced the numerical example under consideration in Chapter 2 in the context of an experiment. Assume that the researcher had intentionally exposed the last subject to $X = 15$ (though it is unlikely that only one subject would be used). A possible explanation for the undue influence of this case might be that the regression of *Y* on *X* is curvilinear rather than linear. That is, the last case seems to change a linear trend to a curvilinear one (*but see the caveats that follow;* note also that I present curvilinear regression analysis in Chapter 13).

Assume now that the data of Table 3.1 were collected in a nonexperimental study and that errors of recording, measurement, and the like were ruled out as an explanation for the last person's X score being so deviant (i.e., 15). One would scrutinize attributes of this person in an attempt to discern what it is that makes him or her different from the rest of the subjects. As an admittedly unrealistic example, suppose that it turns out that the last subject is male, whereas the rest are females. This would raise the possibility that the status of males on X is considerably higher than that of females. Further, that the regression of Y on X among females differs from that among males (I present comparison of regression equations for different groups in Chapter 14).

Caveats.   *Do not place too much faith in speculations such as the preceding.* Needless to say, one case does not a trend make. At best, influential observations should serve as clues. Whatever the circumstances of the study, and whatever the researcher's speculations about the findings, two things should be borne in mind.

1. Before accepting the findings, it is necessary to ascertain that they are replicable in newly designed studies. Referring to the first illustration given above, this would entail, among other things, exposure of more than one person to the condition of $X = 15$. Moreover, it would be worthwhile to also use intermediate values of X (i.e., between 5 and 15) so as to be in a position to ascertain not only whether the regression is curvilinear, but also the nature of the trend (e.g., quadratic or cubic; see Chapter 13). Similarly, the second illustration would entail, among other things, the use of more than one male.
2. Theoretical considerations should play the paramount role in attempts to explain the findings.

Although, as I stated previously, leverage is a property of the scores on the independent variable, the extent and nature of the influence a score with high leverage has on regression estimates depend also on the Y score with which it is linked. To illustrate this point, I will introduce a different change in the data under consideration. Instead of changing the last X to 15 (as I did previously), I will change the one before the last (i.e., the 19th subject) to 15.

Leverage for this score is, of course, the same as that I obtained above when I changed the last X to 15 (i.e., .81). However, the regression equation for these data differs from that I obtained when I changed the last X to 15. When I changed the last X to 15, the regression equation was

$$Y' = 6.96 + .10X$$

Changing the X for the 19th subject to 15 results in the following regression equation:

$$Y' = 5.76 + .44X$$

Thus, the impact of scores with the same leverage may differ, depending on the dependent-variable score with which they are paired. You may find it helpful to see why this is so by plotting the two data sets and drawing the regression line for each. Also, if you did the regression calculations, you would find that $r^2 = .260$ when the score for the 19th subject is changed to 15, as contrasted with $r^2 = .013$ when the score for the 20th subject is changed to 15. Finally, the residual and its associated transformations (e.g., standardized) are smaller for the second than for the first change:

	X	Y	Y'	Y − Y'	ZRESID	SRESID	SDRESID
20th subject	15	6	8.4171	−2.4171	−.9045	−2.0520	−2.2785
19th subject	15	12	12.3600	−.3600	−.1556	−.3531	−.3443

Based on residual analysis, the 20th case might be deemed an outlier, whereas the 19th would not be deemed thus.

COOK'S D

Earlier, I pointed out that leverage cannot detect an influential observation whose influence is due to its status on the dependent variable. By contrast, Cook's (1977, 1979) D (distance) measure is designed to identify an influential observation whose influence is due to its status on the independent variable(s), the dependent variable, or both.

$$D_i = \left[\frac{SRESID_i^2}{k+1} \right] \left[\frac{h_i}{1-h_i} \right] \tag{3.6}$$

where SRESID = studentized residual (see the "Outliers" section presented earlier in this chapter); h_i = leverage (see the preceding); and k = number of independent variables. Examine (3.6) and notice that D will be large when SRESID is large, leverage is large, or both.

For illustrative purposes, I will calculate D for the last case of Table 3.1. $SRESID_{20} = -1.2416$ (see Table 3.1); $h_{20} = .15$ (see Table 3.2); and $k = 1$. Hence,

$$D_{20} = \left[\frac{-1.2416^2}{1+1} \right] \left[\frac{.15}{1-.15} \right] = .1360$$

D's for the rest of the data of Table 3.1 are given in column (2) of Table 3.2.

Approximate tests of significance for Cook's D are given in Cook (1977, 1979) and Weisberg (1980, pp. 108–109). For diagnostic purposes, however, it would suffice to look for relatively large D values, that is, one would look for relatively large gaps between D for a given observation and D's for the rest of the data. Based on our knowledge about the residuals and leverage for the data of Table 3.1, it is not surprising that all the D's are relatively small, indicating the absence of influential observations.

It will be instructive to illustrate a situation in which leverage is relatively small, implying that the observation is not influential, whereas Cook's D is relatively large, implying that the converse is true. To this end, change the last observation so that $Y = 26$. As X is *unchanged* (i.e., 5), the leverage for the last case is .15, as I obtained earlier. Calculate the regression equation, SRESID, and Cook's D for the last case. Following are some of the results you will obtain:

$$Y' = 3.05 + 1.75X$$

$$SRESID_{20} = 3.5665; \quad h_{20} = .15; \quad k = 1$$

Notice the changes in the parameter estimates resulting from the change in the Y score for the 20th subject.[8] Applying (3.6),

$$D_{20} = \left[\frac{3.5665^2}{1+1} \right] \left[\frac{.15}{1-.15} \right] = 1.122$$

If you were to calculate D's for the rest of the data, you would find that they range from .000 to .128. Clearly, there is a considerable gap between D_{20} and the rest of the D's. To reiterate, sole reliance on leverage would lead to the conclusion that the 20th observation is not influential, whereas the converse conclusion would be reached based on the D.

---

[8]Earlier, I pointed out that SRESID (studentized residual) and SDRESID (studentized deleted residual) may differ considerably. The present example is a case in point, in that $SDRESID_{20} = 6.3994$.

I would like to make two points about my presentation of influence analysis thus far.

1. My presentation proceeded backward, so to speak. That is, I examined consequences of a change in an X or Y score on regression estimates. Consistent with the definition of an influential observation (see the preceding), a more meaningful approach would be to study changes in parameter estimates that would occur because of deleting a given observation.
2. Leverage and Cook's D are global indices, signifying that an observation may be influential, but not revealing the effects it may have on specific parameter estimates.

I now turn to an approach aimed at identifying effects on specific parameter estimates that would result from the deletion of a given observation.

DFBETA

$\text{DFBETA}_{j(i)}$ indicates the change in j (intercept or regression coefficient) as a consequence of deleting subject i.[9] As my concern here is with simple regression analysis—consisting of two parameter estimates—it will be convenient to use the following notation: $\text{DFBETA}_{a(i)}$ will refer to the change in the intercept (a) when subject i is deleted, whereas $\text{DFBETA}_{b(i)}$ will refer to the change in the regression coefficient (b) when subject i is deleted.

To calculate DFBETA for a given observation, then, delete it, recalculate the regression equation, and note changes in parameter estimates that have occurred. For illustrative purposes, delete the last observation in the data of Table 3.1 and calculate the regression equation. You will find it to be

$$Y' = 4.72 + .91X$$

Recall that the regression equation based on all the data is

$$Y' = 5.05 + .75X$$

Hence, $\text{DFBETA}_{a(20)} = .33$ ($5.05 - 4.72$), and $\text{DFBETA}_{b(20)} = -.16$ ($.75 - .91$). Later, I address the issue of what is to be considered a large DFBETA, hence identifying an influential observation.

The preceding approach to the calculation of DFBETAs is extremely laborious, requiring the calculation of as many regression analyses as there are subjects (20 for the example under consideration). Fortunately, an alternative approach based on results obtained from a single regression analysis in which all the data are used is available. The formula for DFBETA for a is

$$DFBETA_{a(i)} = a - a(i) = \left[\left(\frac{\Sigma X^2}{N\Sigma X^2 - (\Sigma X)^2} \right) + \left(\frac{-\Sigma X}{N\Sigma X^2 - (\Sigma X)^2} \right) X_i \right] \frac{e_i}{1 - h_i} \tag{3.7}$$

where N = number of cases; ΣX^2 = sum of squared raw scores; ΣX = sum of raw scores; $(\Sigma X)^2$ = square of the sum of raw scores; e_i = residual for subject i; and h_i = leverage for subject i. Earlier,

[9]DF is supposed to stand for the difference between the estimated statistic with and without a given case. I said "supposed," as initially the prefix for another statistic suggested by the originators of this approach (Belsley et al., 1980) was DI, as in DIFFITS, which was then changed to DFFITS and later to DFITS (see Welsch, 1986, p. 403). Chatterjee and Hadi (1986b) complained about the "computer-speak (à la Orwell)," saying, "We aesthetically rebel against DFFIT, DFBETA, etc., and have attempted to replace them by the last name of the authors according to a venerable statistical tradition" (p. 416). Their hope that "this approach proves attractive to the statistical community" (p. 416) has not materialized thus far.

I calculated all the preceding terms. The relevant sum and sum of squares (see Table 2.1 and the presentation related to it) are

$$\Sigma X = 60 \qquad \Sigma X^2 = 220$$

$N = 20$. Residuals are given in Table 3.1, and leverages in Table 3.2.

For illustrative purposes, I will apply (3.7) to the last (20th) case, to determine the change in a that would result from its deletion.

$$DFBETA_{a(20)} = a - a(20) = \left[\left(\frac{220}{(20)(220) - (60)^2} \right) + \left(\frac{-60}{(20)(220) - (60)^2} \right) 5 \right] \frac{-2.8}{1 - .15} = .32941$$

which agrees with the result I obtained earlier.

The formula for DFBETA for b is

$$DFBETA_{b(i)} = b - b(i) = \left[\left(\frac{-\Sigma X}{N\Sigma X^2 - (\Sigma X)^2} \right) + \left(\frac{N}{N\Sigma X^2 - (\Sigma X)^2} \right) X_i \right] \frac{e_i}{1 - h_i} \tag{3.8}$$

where the terms are as defined under (3.7). Using the results given in connection with the application of (3.7),

$$DFBETA_{b(20)} = b - b(20) = \left[\left(\frac{-60}{(20)(220) - (60)^2} \right) + \left(\frac{20}{(20)(220) - (60)^2} \right) 5 \right] \frac{-2.8}{1 - .15} = -.16471$$

which agrees with the value I obtained earlier.

To repeat, DFBETAs indicate the change in the intercept and the regression coefficient(s) resulting from the deletion of a given subject. Clearly, having calculated DFBETAs, calculation of the regression equation that would be obtained as a result of the deletion of a given subject is straightforward. Using, as an example, the DFBETAs I calculated for the last subject (.33 and −.16 for a and b, respectively), and recalling that the regression equation based on all the data is $Y' = 5.05 + .75X$,

$$a = 5.05 - .33 = 4.72$$

$$b = .75 - (-.16) = .91$$

Above, I obtained the same values when I did a regression analysis based on all subjects but the last one.

Using (3.7) and (3.8), I calculated DFBETAs for all the subjects. They are given in columns (3) and (4) of Table 3.2.

Standardized DFBETA

What constitutes a large DFBETA? There is no easy answer to this question, as it hinges on the interpretation of regression coefficients—a topic that will occupy us in several subsequent chapters. For now, I will only point out that the size of the regression coefficient (hence a change in it) is affected by the scale of measurement used. For example, using feet instead of inches to measure X will yield a regression coefficient 12 times larger than one obtained for inches, though the nature of the regression of Y on X will, of course, not change.[10]

In light of the preceding, it was suggested that DFBETA be standardized, which for a is accomplished as follows:

---

[10]It is for this reason that some researchers prefer to interpret standardized regression coefficients or beta weights—a topic I discuss in detail in Chapters 4 and 10.

$$DFBETAS_{a(i)} = \frac{DFBETA_{a(i)}}{\sqrt{MSR_{(i)}\left[\dfrac{\Sigma X^2}{N\Sigma X^2 - (\Sigma X)^2}\right]}} \tag{3.9}$$

where DFBETAS = standardized DFBETA;[11] and $MSR_{(i)}$ = mean square residual when subject i is deleted. The rest of the terms were defined earlier.

If, as I suggested earlier, you did a regression analysis in which the last subject was deleted, you would find that $MSR_{(20)}$ = 5.79273. Hence,

$$DFBETAS_{a(20)} = \frac{.32941}{\sqrt{5.79273\left[\dfrac{220}{(20)(220) - (60)^2}\right]}} = .26099$$

The formula for standardizing DFBETA for b is

$$DFBETAS_{b(i)} = \frac{DFBETA_{b(i)}}{\sqrt{MSR_{(i)}\left[\dfrac{N}{N\Sigma X^2 - (\Sigma X)^2}\right]}} \tag{3.10}$$

Applying (3.10) to the 20th case,

$$DFBETAS_{b(20)} = \frac{-.16471}{\sqrt{5.79273\left[\dfrac{20}{(20)(220) - (60)^2}\right]}} = -.43282$$

Notice that $MSR_{(i)}$ in the denominator of (3.9) and (3.10) is based on an analysis in which a given subject is deleted. Hence, as many regression analyses as there are subjects would be required to calculate DFBETAS for all of them. To avoid this, $MSR_{(i)}$ can be calculated as follows:

$$MSR_{(i)} = \frac{ss_{res} - \dfrac{(e_i)^2}{1 - h_i}}{N - k - 1 - 1} \tag{3.11}$$

For comparative purposes, I will apply (3.11) to the 20th subject. $e_{(20)} = -2.8$ (see Table 3.1); $h_{(20)} = .15$ (see Table 3.2); $ss_{res} = 107.70$ (see earlier calculations). $N = 20$ and $k = 1$. Therefore,

$$MSR_{(20)} = \frac{107.70 - \dfrac{(-2.8)^2}{1 - .15}}{20 - 1 - 1 - 1} = 5.79273$$

which agrees with the value I obtained earlier. Using (3.7) through (3.11), I calculated DFBETAS for all the subjects in the example under consideration (i.e., Table 3.1) and reported the results in columns (5) and (6) of Table 3.2.

In line with the recommendation that DFBETAS (standardized) be used instead of DFBETA (nonstandardized) for interpretive purposes (see preceding), criteria for what is to be considered a "large" DFBETAS have been proposed. Not surprisingly, there is no consensus on this point. Following are some examples of cutoffs that have been proposed.

Belsley et al. (1980) suggested, "as a first approximation," an "*absolute cutoff*" of 2 (p. 28). They went on to suggest that, because DFBETAS is affected by sample size, $2/\sqrt{n}$ serve as a

---

[11]For consistency with the literature on this topic, I use DFBETAS, although something like STDFBETA would be less prone to confuse.

"*size-adjusted cutoff*" (p. 28), when small samples are used. Neter, Wasserman, and Kutner (1989, p. 403), on the other hand, recommended that $2/\sqrt{n}$ serve as a cutoff for "large data sets," whereas 1 serve as a cutoff for "small to medium-size data sets." Finally, Mason, Gunst, and Hess (1989, p. 520) proposed $3/\sqrt{n}$ as a general cutoff.

Recalling that $N = 20$ for the example under consideration, following Belsley et al., the size-adjusted cutoff is .45, whereas following Mason et al. the cutoff is .67. Examine columns (5) and (6) of Table 3.2 and notice that a few of the DFBETASs are slightly larger than the size-adjusted cutoff proposed by Belsley et al. and that none meet the criteria proposed by Neter et al. or Mason et al. In sum, it is safe to assume that most researchers would conclude that none of the DFBETASs in the numerical example under consideration are "large."

Before I comment generally on criteria and rules of thumb, I will use an additional example to illustrate: (1) the value of DFBETA in pinpointing changes occurring as a result of the deletion of a subject and (2) that an outlier does *not* necessarily signify that the observation in question is influential. To this end, let us introduce yet another change in the data of Table 3.1. This time, change the Y for the first subject in the group whose $X = 3$ (i.e., the ninth subject) to 14 (instead of 4). Calculate the regression equation. In addition, for this subject, calculate (1) ZRESID, SRESID, and SDRESID; (2) leverage and Cook's D; (3) DFBETA (nonstandardized) and DFBETAS (standardized). Following are results you will obtain:

$$Y' = 5.55 + .75X$$

For the ninth subject,

(1)	ZRESID	SRESID	SDRESID
	2.2498	2.3082	2.6735

(2)	Leverage	Cook's D
	.050	.140

(3)	DFBETA	DFBETAS
	a: .32632	.26153
	b: .00000	.00000

Beginning with the residual, note that the observation under consideration would probably be identified as an outlier, especially when it is compared with those for the rest of the data. For example, the next largest SDRESID is -1.3718.

Turning to leverage, it is clear that it is small. The same is true of D. If you were to calculate the D's for the rest of the data, you would find that they range from .000 to .149. Clearly, the D for the ninth subject is not out of line from the rest of the D's, leading to the conclusion that the ninth observation is not influential. Here, then, is an example where an observation that might be identified as an outlier would not be deemed as influential.

Examine now the DFBETA and DFBETAS and note that the deletion of the ninth subject will result in an intercept change from 5.55 to 5.22 (i.e., $5.55 - .32632$). The regression coefficient will, however, *not* change as a result of the deletion of the ninth subject. Thus, the regression equation based on the data from which the ninth subject was deleted would be[12]

$$Y' = 5.22 + .75X$$

[12]If necessary, delete the ninth subject and do a regression analysis to convince yourself that this is the equation you would obtain.

It will be instructive to concentrate first on the interpretation of a change in *a*. Recall that *a* indicates the point at which the regression line intercepts the *Y* ordinate when $X = 0$. Stated differently, it is the predicted *Y* when $X = 0$. In many areas of behavioral sciences $X = 0$ is of little or no substantive meaning. Suffice it to think of *X* as a measure of mental ability, achievement, depression, and the like, to see why this is so. Therefore, even if the change in *a* was much larger than the one obtained earlier, and even if it was deemed to be large based on some criterion, it is conceivable that it would be judged not meaningful. This is not to say that one would ignore the extreme residual that would be associated with the observation in question. But this matter need not concern us here, as I addressed it earlier.

What is, however, most revealing in the present example—indeed my reason for presenting it—is the absence of change in the regression coefficient (*b*) as a result of deleting the ninth subject.[13] Thus, even if based on other indices (e.g., *D*), one was inclined to consider the ninth observation as influential, it is conceivable that focusing on the change in *b*, one would deem it not influential.

CRITERIA AND RULES OF THUMB

Dependence on criteria and rules of thumb in the conduct of behavioral research is so prevalent that it requires no documentation. The ubiquity of such practices is exemplified by conventions followed in connection with statistical tests of significance (e.g., Type I and Type II errors, effect size).[14]

Authors who propose criteria and rules of thumb do so, in my opinion, with the best of intentions to assist their readers to develop a "feel" for the indices in question. Notably, most stress the need for caution in resorting to criteria they propose and attempt to impress upon the reader that they are not meant to serve as substitutes for informed judgment. For instance, preceding their proposed criteria for influential observations, Belsley et al. (1980) cautioned:

> As with all empirical procedures, this question is ultimately answered by judgment and intuition in choosing reasonable cutoffs most suitable for the problem at hand, guided whenever possible by statistical theory. (p. 27)

Unfortunately, many researchers not only ignore the cautions, but also misinterpret, even misrepresent recommended guidelines.[15] Drawing attention to difficulties in interpreting outliers, Johnson (1985) bemoans the practice of treating methods for detecting them as a "technological fix," prompting "many investigators . . . to believe that statistical procedures will sort a data set into the 'good guys' and the 'bad guys'" (p. 958).

Perusal of published research reveals that many authors flaunt criteria with an air of finality and certainty. The allure of a criterion adorned by references to authorities in the field is apparently so potent as to dazzle even referees and editors of professional journals. Deleterious

---

[13]I suggest that you experiment by introducing other changes in *Y* for the same subject (e.g., make it 24, 30, or 40), and reanalyze the data. For the suggested changes, you will find the DFBETAS$_a$ becomes increasingly larger (.6623, .9027, and 1.3034, respectively), but the *b* is unchanged. Incidentally, the same will hold true if you changed any of the *Y*'s whose *X* scores are equal to the mean of *X*. The main point is that when *a* is not substantively meaningful, neither is a change in it, whatever its size.

[14]For examples relating to measurement models, see Bollen and Lennox (1991); for examples relating to adoption of "standards" of reliability of measures, see Pedhazur and Schmelkin (1991, pp. 109–110).

[15]For some examples relating to criteria for collinearity, see Chapter 10.

consequences of this practice cannot be overestimated. The most pernicious effect of this practice is that it seems to absolve the researcher of the responsibility of making an informed interpretation and decision—actions unimaginable without thorough knowledge of the research area, an understanding of statistical and design principles, and, above all, hard thinking.

The paramount role of knowledge and judgment in deciding what is an influential observation, say, may be discerned from the last example I gave earlier. Recall that it concerned a situation in which the deletion of an observation resulted in a change in *a* (intercept), but not in *b* (regression coefficient). Clearly, a researcher whose aim is to interpret *b* only would not deem an observation influential, regardless of the effect its deletion would have on *a*.

In sum, beware of being beguiled by criteria and rules of thumb. It is only in light of various aspects of the study (e.g., cost, duration, consequences, generalizability), as well as theoretical and analytic considerations, that you can hope to arrive at meaningful statements about its findings.

A Numerical Example

Before considering remedies, I present another numerical example designed to illustrate the potential hazards of neglecting to examine one's data and of failing to apply regression diagnostics. The example is reported in Part (*a*) of Table 3.3. Included in the table are summary statistics and results of tests of statistical significance.[16] As I used a similar format in Chapter 2 (see Table 2.3), I will not explain the terms.

Table 3.3   Two Data Sets

	(*a*)		(*b*)	
	X	Y	X	Y
	2	2	2	2
	3	3	3	3
	3	1	3	1
	4	1	4	1
	4	3	4	3
	5	2	5	2
	8	8		
N:	7		6	
M:	4.14	2.86	3.50	2.00
s:	1.95	2.41	1.05	.89
r_2:	.67		.00	
a:	−1.34		2.00	
b:	1.01		.00	
ss_{reg}:	23.43		.00	
ss_{res}:	11.42		4.00	
F:	10.25 (1,5)		.00 (1,4)	
t:	3.20 (5)		.00 (4)	
p:	.02		1.00	

[16]I discuss Part (*b*) of the table later on.

Examine Part (*a*) of Table 3.3 and note that, assuming $\alpha = .05$ was selected, the regression of *Y* on *X* is statistically significant. In the absence of diagnostics, one would be inclined to conclude, among other things, that (1) about 67% of the variance in *Y* is accounted for by *X* and (2) the expected change in *Y* associated with a unit change in *X* is 1.01.

In what follows, I will scrutinize the role of the last subject in these results. The residual and some of its transformations for this subject are as follows:

RESID	ZRESID	SRESID	SDRESID
1.2375	.8178	1.8026	2.7249

Inspection of ZRESID and SRESID would lead to the conclusion that there is nothing distinctive about this subject, although SDRESID might raise doubt about such a conclusion.

Here now are diagnostic indices associated with the last subject:

H_7	D_7	$DFBETA_{a(7)}$	$DFBETA_{b(7)}$	$DFBETAS_{a(7)}$	$DFBETAS_{b(7)}$
.79	6.25	−3.3375	1.0125	−3.5303	4.8407

Clearly, this is an influential observation. To appreciate how influential it is, I will use DFBETAs (unstandardized) to calculate the regression equation based on the first six subjects (i.e., deleting the seventh subject).

$$a = -1.34 - (-3.34) = 2.00$$

$$b = 1.01 - 1.01 = 0$$

These statistics are reported also in Part (*b*) of Table 3.3, which consists of results of a regression analysis based on the first six subjects of Part (*a*).

The most important thing to note is that in the absence of the seventh subject, the regression of *Y* on *X* is zero ($b = 0$). At the risk of being redundant, it is noteworthy that the statistically significant and, what appeared to be, the strong regression of *Y* on *X* was due to the inclusion of a single subject.

Note that, consistent with (2.10) and the discussion related to it, when $b = 0$, the intercept (*a*) is equal to the mean of the dependent variable.

REMEDIES

Awareness of the existence of a problem is, needless to say, a prerequisite for attempts to do something about it. More than a decade ago, Belsley et al. (1980) observed that "[i]t is increasingly the case that the data employed in regression analysis, and on which the results are conditioned, are given only the most cursory examination for their suitability" (p. 2). Remarkable increases in availability of computers and reliance on technicians (euphemistically referred to as "consultants") to analyze one's data have greatly exacerbated this predicament.

The larger the project, the greater the likelihood for data analysis "chores" to be relegated to assistants, and the lesser the likelihood for principal investigators to examine their data. Consequently, many a researcher is unaware that "dramatic" or "puzzling" findings may be due to one or more influential observations, or that a relation they treat as linear is curvilinear, to give but two examples of illusory or delusionary findings pervading social and behavioral research literature.

Suggested Remedies

Difficulties in selecting from among indices of influential observations, and of designating observations as influential, pale in comparison to those arising concerning action to be taken when influential observations are detected. Earlier, I pointed out that when it is determined that an observation in question is due to error, the action that needs to be taken is relatively uncomplicated. It is when errors are ruled out that complications abound, as the decision regarding action to be taken is predicated on a host of theoretical and analytic considerations (e.g., model, subjects, settings). What follows is not an exhaustive presentation of remedies but a broad sketch of some, along with relevant references.

Probably the first thing that comes to mind is to delete the influential observation(s) and reanalyze the data. Nevertheless, in light of norms against "fudging" data and "dishonesty" in data analysis, the tendency to refrain from doing this is strong. I concur strongly with Judd and McClelland's (1989) cogent argument that when an influential observation(s) affects the results, it is "misleading . . . to pretend" that this is not so.

> Somehow, however, in the social sciences the reporting of results with outliers included has come to be viewed as the "honest" thing to do and the reporting of results with outliers removed is sometimes unfortunately viewed as "cheating." Although there is no doubt that techniques for outlier identification and removal can be abused, we think it far more honest to omit outliers from the analysis with the explicit admission in the report that there are some observations which we do not understand and to report a good model for those observations which we do understand. If that is not acceptable, then separate analyses, with and without the outliers included, ought to be reported so that the reader can make his or her own decision about the adequacy of the models. *To ignore outliers by failing to detect and report them is dishonest and misleading.* (pp. 231–232; see also, Fox, 1991, p. 76)

I believe that, in addition to reporting results of analyses with and without influential observations, sufficient information ought to be given (or made available on request) so that readers who so desire may reanalyze the data.

Deletion of influential observations is by no means the only suggested course of action. Among others, a transformation of one or more variables may reduce the impact of influential observations (for discussions of transformations and their role in data analysis see, among others, Atkinson, 1985, Chapters 6–9; Fox, 1984, Chapter 3; Judd & McClelland, 1989, Chapter 16; Stoto & Emerson, 1983).

Another approach is to subject the data to a robust regression method (for a review of four such methods, see Huynh, 1982; see also, Neter et al., 1989, pp. 405–407; Rousseeuw & Leroy, 1987).

CONCLUDING REMARKS

I hope that this chapter served to alert you to the importance of scrutinizing data and using regression diagnostics. In subsequent chapters, I extend and elaborate on concepts I introduced in this chapter.

In Chapter 4, which is devoted to computers and computer programs, I will use several computer programs to reanalyze some of the numerical examples I presented in Chapter 2 and in the present chapter.

STUDY SUGGESTIONS

I presented the following data in Study Suggestion 2 of Chapter 2 (recall that the second, third, and fourth pairs of columns are continuations of the first pair of columns):

X	Y	X	Y	X	Y	X	Y
2	2	4	4	4	3	9	9
2	1	5	7	3	3	10	6
1	1	5	6	6	6	9	6
1	1	7	7	6	6	4	9
3	5	6	8	8	10	4	10

For all subjects, calculate the following:
(a) ZRESID, SRESID, and SDRESID.
(b) h_i, D, $DFBETA_a$, $DFBETA_b$, $DFBETAS_a$, and $DFBETAS_b$.

NOTE: Where applicable, use intermediate results you have obtained in Study Suggestion 2 of Chapter 2.

ANSWERS

(a) ZRESID	SRESID	SDRESID
−.5822	−.6187	−.6078
−1.0291	−1.0936	−1.0999
−.6963	−.7623	−.7531
−.6963	−.7623	−.7531
.4255	.4431	.4330
−.3541	−.3646	−.3556
.6536	.6706	.6600
.2068	.2121	.2064
−.0119	−.0124	−.0121
.7677	.7910	.7825
−.8009	−.8247	−.8170
−.4682	−.4876	−.4771
−.1260	−.1298	−.1262
−.1260	−.1298	−.1262
.9958	1.0609	1.0648
.2162	.2375	.2312
−1.4570	−1.6702	−1.7657
−1.1243	−1.2352	−1.2548
1.8800	1.9357	2.1140
2.3268	2.3957	2.8211

(b)	h	D	DFBETA$_a$	DFBETA$_b$	DFBETAS$_a$	DFBETAS$_b$
	.1145	.025	−.23281	.03217	−.21235	.16402
	.1145	.077	−.41147	.05685	−.38429	.29683
	.1656	.058	−.36399	.05467	−.33389	.28033
	.1656	.058	−.36399	.05467	−.33389	.28033
	.0782	.008	.12553	−.01493	.11390	−.07571
	.0567	.004	−.07128	.00591	−.06456	.02995
	.0500	.012	.07417	.00057	.06778	.00291
	.0500	.001	.02346	.00018	.02120	.00091
	.0811	.000	.00073	−.00044	.00066	−.00222
	.0582	.019	.02095	.01419	.01924	.07287
	.0567	.020	−.16123	.01338	−.14832	.06879
	.0782	.010	−.13813	.01642	−.12548	.08341
	.0582	.001	−.00344	−.00233	−.00310	−.01176
	.0582	.001	−.00344	−.00233	−.00310	−.01176
	.1189	.076	−.15651	.05717	−.14586	.29784
	.1715	.006	−.05756	.01753	−.05203	.08856
	.2390	.438	.57946	−.16034	.56882	−.87989
	.1715	.158	.29932	−.09115	.28233	−.48061
	.0567	.113	.37844	−.03140	.38377	−.17800
	.0567	.172	.46839	−.03886	.51213	−.23753

4

Computers and Computer Programs

The impact of computers on virtually every facet of our lives is so palpable as to require no documentation. Of the myriad uses computers have been put to, I address only that of data analysis. After some comments about potential benefits and drawbacks in using computers for data analysis, I present (1) my criteria for the selection of packages to be used in this book, (2) a listing of the selected packages and their documentation, (3) a brief discussion of computer manuals, (4) the format I will be using in displaying and commenting on input and output, and (5) some recommendations for the use of computer programs. I then apply regression procedures from the selected packages to a numerical example I analyzed in Chapters 2 and 3.

Potential Benefits

The most obvious benefit from the use of computers for data analysis is the ease of calculations at incredible speeds with low probability of errors. Analyses of large data sets or the application of methods involving complex or massive calculations were forbidding, even unthinkable, before the advent of the computer. Except for illustrative applications to small problems, methods such as multivariate analysis of variance and canonical correlation (see Part 4) lay dormant for decades until the advent of the computer. Further, development and application of approaches such as structural equation modeling (see Part 3), monte carlo, and bootstrapping (e.g., Bruce, 1991; Diaconis & Efron, 1983; Mooney & Duval, 1993; Noreen, 1989; Simon, 1991; Stine, 1990) are inconceivable without a computer.

Contrary to the notion that reliance on computers stifles thinking and creativity—not to mention the fear and awe with which computers are held by some (Markoff, 1991)—relegating the drudgery of calculations to the computer frees one to devote the time and energy saved to thinking about the meaning of the results. Of course, the meaningful interpretation of results is predicated on knowledge of the analytic methods and the properties of the computer programs used. I discuss these issues in the following sections.

Potential Drawbacks

The major drawback in using a computer for data analysis is that, in light of ready availability of "user-friendly" programs, one can carry out the most sophisticated and intricate analyses without having the slightest idea what they are about. Regrettably, some reviewers and software producers reinforce such behavior. For example, in a review of a statistical package, Petzold informed the reader that it "gives you an enormous number of canned procedures, so you don't actually need to know statistics to use it successfully" (quoted by Berk, 1987, p. 228). And a software company advertises its statistical package "for people who made it through statistics with their eyes closed." No wonder, "the ignorance of computer package users with respect to what is being computed is legion" (Searle, 1989, p. 189).

An additional potential drawback of relying on the computer for data analysis is the increased likelihood of becoming "detached from intimate knowledge" (Belsley et al., 1980, p. 2) of one's data. Worse yet is the penchant of not looking at all at the data entered into the computer (Preece, 1987).

Divergent Perspectives

In view of the foregoing, it is not surprising that some authors (e.g., Searle, 1989), statisticians, and educators view with disfavor, even alarm, the ready availability of computer programs for data analysis and the ease with which they can be used. In a review of SPSS (a package I use in this book), Pickles (1992) drew attention to its versatility and user-friendliness, saying, "This is why the package is so popular and also, since we believe that many users do not know what they are doing, why so many statisticians hate it" (p. 439). Although apprehension about potential misuse of computers for data analysis is well founded, attempts to discourage students and researchers from using computers for such purposes are, I believe, ill advised.

Of course, the meaningful and effective use of the computer requires learning and practice. It is for this reason that I introduce computer programs at this early stage and why they are an integral part of my presentation in subsequent chapters. I hope that this will contribute to the intelligent use of computer programs and to a better understanding of their output.

I believe it worthwhile to point out that some reviewers of my proposed revision of this book suggested that I relegate the computer to an appendix. Among other things, these reviewers asserted that because programs undergo frequent revisions, presentations of them are bound to become obsolete even before the book goes to press. The almost continuous change in computer software, as well as hardware, is undeniable. Nevertheless, this does not necessarily mean that learning to use a given program is worthless.

To begin with, learning to use any program is useful inasmuch as it orients one to general issues such as input, command structure, defaults, and output. Further, in the fiercely competitive field of statistical packages, many a revision is little more than window dressing. Sometimes, a new version of a computer package may include new procedures rather than modifications to existing ones. For example, regression analysis procedures, which I use extensively in this book, may undergo no modification in a new version of a statistical package.

Even when a given procedure is drastically revised, its output must consist of elements that a user of an earlier version would be familiar with, assuming, of course, that he or she is proficient in the method used. A case in point is output from programs I used in the second edition of this book. For instance, regression programs I used in the second edition have undergone considerable revisions and expansions. Nevertheless, the basic output (e.g., squared multiple correlation, regression equation, regression and residual sums of squares, standard errors, predicted scores, residuals) is necessarily the same.

It should be clear that programs written for different operating systems (e.g., MS-DOS, OS/2) yield identical core results. This is especially true of well-established procedures. Thus, regardless of the unique features of given computer programs, and regardless of the operating system for which they were written, means, standard deviations, correlations, and regression equations—to name but some aspects of output—generated by them better be, within rounding, the same.

In sum, I cannot agree more with Thisted and Velleman's (1992) assertion: "Because computers simultaneously are central to what statisticians do and the tools that make structured inquiry possible, we cannot imagine an up-to-date introductory or applied statistics course that does not give students substantial experience with computers" (p. 45).

PROGRAMS

I will use two types of programs: packages consisting of many procedures and special-purpose programs. In this chapter, I introduce and use four statistical packages. I will introduce and use special-purpose programs (e.g., LISREL, EQS, HLM) in the chapters where I present analytic approaches for which they were written.

I realize that my decision to use multiple packages will irritate some readers, especially those who are familiar with a given package and do not wish to be "bothered" to learn new ones. The obvious reason for my decision to present multiple packages is to address the potential needs and preferences of different readers. More important, however, is my belief that this is beneficial, as only by learning about unique features of different packages, and their strengths and weaknesses, is one in a position to ascertain which is best suited for a specific task. Actually, "no single package is best for every analysis, and sometimes no one program can beat an intelligent combination of analyses from various competitors" (Thisted, 1979, p. 29). Finally, "once the student learns to use one package, it is surprisingly easy to learn to use others and to evaluate their relative merits" (Thisted, 1979, p. 29). This is probably even more so when running packages under Windows. As I explain in the following, three of the four packages I use in this book run under Windows.

In sum, learning to use more than one package is not unlike learning more than one language. It provides a broader perspective, especially about the characteristics and properties of the program one is using. It has been aptly stated that fish are probably the last to discover the existence of water. In the same vein, being "shackled" to one program is bound to constrict one's view. I elaborate on this topic later, in the context of recommendations for use of statistical packages.

Criteria for Selection of Packages

Dramatic developments in computer hardware and software during the past decade have led to a blurring of distinctions among different types of computers (e.g., mainframe, mini). For present purposes, however, it will be useful to use the broad distinction between mainframe and personal computers. By a mainframe computer I mean one that serves multiple users and whose software is selected, maintained, and upgraded by a professional staff. Examples that come readily to mind are "large" computers or networks in academic, research, or corporate settings. By personal computer (PC) I mean a machine maintained and used by a single person, who is also generally the one selecting and/or upgrading the software.

As this book is addressed to students and researchers who are likely to have access to a mainframe at their place of study or work, and who are likely also to own a PC, I decided to introduce only programs that are available for both settings. By thus eliminating the need to learn new procedures and new commands when moving from one setting to another, I hope not only to ease the "burden" but also to foster the use of multiple packages.

The packages I selected are among the most comprehensive, widespread, and well established. They are frequently upgraded to expand given procedures and/or to add new ones. While it is probably true that no statistical software is error-free (Dallal, 1988), the packages I selected contain relatively few errors (I return to this topic later).

As a sign of the state of flux characteristic of statistical software, it is noteworthy that not only have the packages I selected undergone more than one revision since I began working on the third edition, but also Windows versions of three of them were issued recently. In trying to "keep up" with the most recent revisions, I found myself in the proverbial predicament of "trying to shovel the walk while it is still snowing" (Wainer & Thissen, 1986, p. 12). Accordingly, I decided to (1) limit my presentation to Windows versions, where available, in the hope that this will facilitate use of and experimentation with multiple packages (but see "Processing Mode," especially if you do not use Windows); (2) abandon certain practices I followed in the earlier stages of the writing (e.g., drawing attention to differences between, say, mainframe and PC versions of a program); and (3) minimize page references to manuals when commenting on specific aspects of a program.

If the version of a given package you are using is different from the one I am presenting, or if you prefer to work in a non-Windows environment, you will, I believe, have no difficulty using or adapting my input files. Anyway, as I explain in the "Content and Format of Input and Output" section, my emphasis is on output and commentaries related to it. These are, of course, relevant whatever the program version used to generate the results.

Before listing the packages I selected, I would like to make two points. One, student versions of various software packages (including three of the ones I introduce) are available (see Lock, 1993, for reviews and comparisons of student versions of five packages). Two, numerous statistical programs varying in comprehensiveness, quality, and cost are available on a variety of bulletin boards (notably on CompuServe and the Internet) and from authors who announce their programs in various journals (I later give a partial listing of such journals). Such programs are either free or shareware. As you probably know, the latter can be used for a trial period before you decide whether to register for a nominal fee (see Nash, 1992, for a review of some shareware programs for regression analysis). To give you a glimpse at what is available "out there," it will suffice to point out that Goldstein (1992) offered readers a free copy of "a 'data base' of [400] citations to software reviews from many academic and commercial publications" (p. 319). Not surprisingly, he added that the database will "probably contain more than 450 by the time you read this" (p. 319). If he keeps updating his database, it will certainly be much larger by the time you read my reference to it. Later, I stress the importance of testing any program before using it. This is true, with greater force, for the kind of programs I referred to previously.

Packages Selected

Following is a listing of the packages I will use, their version numbers, and documentation for procedures contained in them. I do not list documentation for related topics (e.g., data entry, guides to different operating systems). Nor do I give information about capacities, space requirements, speed of execution, pricing, and the like of the packages. You will find such information in reviews of statistical software (see "Some Recommendations" presented later in this chapter, for a listing of some sources of such reviews).

BMDP[1]

Release 7

Documentation: *BMDP statistical software manual* (Vols. 1–2) (Dixon, 1992). *BMDP/PC user's guide: Release 7* (BMDP Statistical Software, Inc., 1993). I am using version 7.01.

MINITAB[2]

Release 10Xtra, for Windows (Version 10.5)

Documentation: *MINITAB reference manual* (Minitab Inc., 1995a). *MINITAB user's guide for Windows* (Minitab Inc., 1995b).

SAS[3]

Version 6 for Windows

Documentation: *SAS companion for the Microsoft Windows environment: Version 6, First edition* (SAS Institute Inc., 1993).

Release 6.10 for Windows

Documentation: *SAS/STAT user's guide* (Vols. 1–2) (SAS Institute Inc., 1990a).

SPSS[4]

Release 6.1 for Windows

Documentation: *SPSS base system syntax reference guide: Release 6.0* (SPSS Inc., 1993). *SPSS for Windows base system user's guide: Release 6.0* (Norušis/SPSS Inc., 1993a). *SPSS for Windows advanced statistics: Release 6.0* (Norušis/SPSS Inc., 1993b). *SPSS for Windows professional statistics: Release 6.1* (Norušis/SPSS Inc., 1994).

Manuals

Commenting on a review of BMDP and SPSS, Andrews (1978) complained, "Both manuals are too big and heavy" (p. 85). Considering the flood of manuals, workbooks, technical reports,

---

[1]BMDP® is a registered trademark of BMDP Statistical Software, Inc., whom I would like to thank for furnishing me with a copy of the program.

[2]Minitab® is a registered trademark of Minitab Inc., whom I would like to thank for furnishing me with a copy of the program.

[3]SAS® is a registered trademark of SAS Institute Inc.

[4]SPSS® is a registered trademark of SPSS Inc., whom I would like to thank for furnishing me with a copy of the program.

newsletters, and the like associated with current packages, it is a safe bet that many a user yearns for the single-volume manual of yesteryear, no matter its size. The proliferation of manuals poses a threat that even conscientious users may refrain from using them. Exasperation with the current state of affairs is evident, among other things, from exchanges among professionals on various bulletin boards. In a posting on the Statistical Consulting mailing list (STAT-L@VM1.MCGILL.CA) (2/10/93), FACCOVEY@WSUVM1.BITNET weighed in with the following:

> Here's a few goodies from Dan Bloom I found in my files—
>
> If it can go wrong, it already has; you just haven't found it in the manual yet.
>
> You can lead a horse to a shelf of SAS Manuals . . . and with luck it will eat half.
>
> If you laid each page that SAS Institute publishes end to end, you'd get mighty tired.
>
> The SAS Manual test: Throw it in a bucket of water. It [*sic*] it floats the answer isn't there. If it sinks, the answer was there but will now be unreadable.

In addition to manuals, SAS publishes "Books by Users" and issues a newsletter (SAS Institute's *Authorline*) to keep authors and users abreast of what is being published. Under the banner "Finding Your Way with SAS Software Roadmaps," there appeared an interview with SherriJoyce [*sic*] King who, with Laurie Burch, coauthored *SAS software roadmaps*. When asked "What is the primary objective of *SAS Software Roadmaps?*" King answered:

> I have an entire bookshelf of SAS manuals, and I recently received Release 6.08 complete with two boxes of manuals. Laurie and I had mental images of someone standing in the middle of an office, knee-deep in manuals, and not knowing what to do or which part of the product to use to get the job done. We were compelled to write a book that would provide some guidance in that area. (First Quarter, 1994, p. 3)

About two decades ago, Muller (1978) observed that "there is no agreement on what constitutes adequate documentation, though there is considerable agreement on the need for better documentation" (p. 72). The need is even more urgent nowadays. As they say in the current health-care debate, "There's got to be a better way!"

Notwithstanding their limitations, it is important that you refer to the manuals for a program you are using. Yet, exclusive reliance on manuals would be imprudent. For a variety of reasons (e.g., space consideration, conceptions of the role of manuals), important topics are sometimes "covered" in a single sentence that is likely to baffle a novice user, assuming he or she would even notice it.

Attesting to the need for explications of manuals and/or supplementing them is the dizzying array of publications (e.g., books, special reports) devoted to specific packages. Following are but some examples of books devoted to one or more of the packages listed earlier: Afifi and Clark (1990); Barcikowski (1983a, 1983b, 1983c); Cody and Smith (1991); Levine, (1991); Ryan, Joiner, and Ryan (1985); and Snell (1987).[5] Some package publishers publish books, technical reports, or newsletters aimed at filling the gaps left by manuals and/or providing illustrative or novel applications of given procedures.

In light of the preceding, it should be clear that my discussions of computer programs are by no means exhaustive, nor are they meant to supplant the manuals. All I will attempt to do is explain specific aspects of programs as they relate to the topics I introduce. With the preceding in mind, I turn to a description of how I will use the packages listed previously, and what general format I will employ in presenting them.

---

[5]As you might have gathered from the dates, all the references are to non-Windows versions. Similar publications for Windows versions are bound to be available by the time this book is published.

Content and Format of Input and Output

Perhaps the best way to convey my orientation is to point out that even if I made no attempt to give guidance for the use of statistical packages, I would have relied heavily on output from such packages so as to not be distracted by tedious or complex calculations. As you will soon find out, although I comment briefly on input, I am almost solely concerned with the interpretation of output. Accordingly, if you are well versed in the use of a specific program I present, if you have no access to the program, or if you prefer to use another program, feel free to skip the listings of the control statements and my comments on them. *Do not, however, skip the output and the commentaries on it.* In subsequent chapters, I do most of the analyses by computer only and *introduce substantive issues in the context of commentaries on the output,* be it in connection with the specific analytic method I discuss or a specific problem I consider. *To reiterate: study the output and the substantive commentaries on it, even when the specific program that generated the output is of no interest, or is irrelevant, to you.*

Processing Mode.   In the remarks that follow, I ignore differences among the packages in formats, conventions, requirements, and the like. When I introduce and use a specific package, I comment on such matters as seems necessary.

Programs in the packages under consideration can be executed in interactive or noninteractive (also called batch) mode. Broadly, in interactive mode, commands are executed as they are issued. In noninteractive mode, on the other hand, all the commands are contained in a file that is submitted for execution. Interactive mode is particularly useful when a decision about an action at a given step in the analysis is to be made in light of results obtained in preceding steps—a practice characteristic of exploratory data analysis. Noninteractive mode is more useful and more efficient when using a well-established procedure(s) to test a model and estimate its parameters. Notwithstanding the advantages and disadvantages of each, I use noninteractive mode not only because it makes for a more efficient and less cumbersome presentation, but primarily because *the input files I thus present can be used with little or no change in non-Windows environments* (see "System Statements," below).

Because of my choice of processing mode, I do not show nor comment on the wide array of features available in Windows programs (e.g., extensive context-sensitive help; menu-driven choices and dialog boxes that facilitate preparation of input files and execution of analyses; the ease with which errors in an input file can be corrected, or an input file edited, and rerun). Of course, you can use my input files as guides while taking advantage of any or all the Windows facilities available in the packages you are using.

Finally, I will not use the elaborate facilities available in each package for creating and annotating high-resolution graphs. Instead, I will use so-called character graphs.

System Statements.   If you work under Windows, you are probably familiar with the various ways in which a package can be invoked (e.g., clicking on an icon, loading it when invoking Windows, issuing the RUN command). Invoking a package in other environments requires one or more statements referred to as system statements, job control language (JCL), and the like. System statements differ on different types of mainframes (e.g., IBM, VAX) and even on the same type of mainframe in different sites. On the PC, too, there are differences in the manner of execution, depending on the specific machine (e.g., DOS-based, Apple) or operating system (e.g., DOS, OS/2). In view of their specificity, I will not give system statements. When using a mainframe, check relevant documentation or consult personnel in charge of data processing. When using a PC, check relevant documentation.

Input Files and Editors.   Each of the aforementioned packages contains its own editor for creating and editing input files. In addition, each of the packages accepts ASCII[6] files. To avoid having to learn unique features of editors for different packages, I use an ASCII editor for creating and editing input files, and for editing output. Therefore, I will *not* comment on editors contained in the packages I present.

I do not address specific features and requirements of the packages unless they are directly related to a topic I discuss or to a numerical example I analyze. For example, in each package several formats may be used for reading data. Although I show the format I use to read the data, I generally do not comment on it. The format I use is not necessarily the "best" or the most efficient under all circumstances. "Best" and "efficient" are situation-specific, depending, among other things, on the amount of data, the type of facilities and support services available, and the overall analytic plan for a given data set. For instance, because I use small data sets, I usually include them as part of the input file. With larger data sets, it is more useful to place data in separate files. Further, under such circumstances, it is more efficient to convert data files into system files. For details, see the manual for the package you are using.

In short, my aim is to acquaint you with some programs or procedures in the selected packages and to help you identify and understand the meaning of different parts of the output. For each program, I list the control statements I used to analyze the numerical example under consideration. My choice of options for the analyses and output may not be the most suited for your specific problem. Thus, because I use small data sets, I need not worry about costs in central and peripheral processes or execution time. Consequently, I tend to use certain options even when I make no reference to results generated by them. For example, in SPSS, I tend to specify STATISTICS ALL even when I am not interested in some of the options and therefore do not report the output generated by them.

For convenience, I will refer to each package generically—BMDP, MINITAB, SAS, and SPSS—without the release or version number. Procedures may differ to a greater or lesser extent in different versions of the same package. Therefore, *it is very important that you become familiar with the version of the package you are using and with its special features.* Doing this will minimize the puzzlement and frustration that are likely to occur when the version you are using differs in important ways from the one I am using (see "Packages Selected" for a listing of the versions of the packages I am using).

Whenever possible, I display the input in a manner suitable for running on either a PC or a mainframe. For example, in all SPSS input files I include command terminators, required on a PC but ignored on a mainframe in batch processing. Similarly, except for the beginning of a command, I leave the first column blank—a requirement on a mainframe in batch processing but not on a PC.

When deemed useful, I comment briefly on the input. Often, I insert comments in the input file itself. Instead of using formats for comments unique to each package, I use a uniform format in which comments are italicized and placed in brackets (e.g., *[This is a comment]*). Such comments are *not* part of the input. If you wish to insert comments in your input, check the manual for the package you are using.

Although both lowercase and uppercase letters may be used as input, I use uppercase letters only. I do the same when referring to commands, subcommands, keywords, and the like, in the

---

[6]ASCII stands for American Standard Code for Information Interchange. Loosely, an ASCII file is one that does not contain unique formatting characters. Such files—also referred to as DOS text files—can be created with various word processing programs or text editors. Various software publishers publish text editors. In addition, freeware and shareware text editors are available on computer bulletin boards (e.g., CompuServe).

context of commentaries on input or output. For keywords that can be abbreviated, I sometimes use a combination of uppercase and lowercase letters to indicate the part that can be abbreviated.

Output and Commentaries.   Following input and commentaries, I present excerpts of output, accompanied by commentaries and explanations that, I hope, will help you understand the special features of each program so that you may use it to the best advantage. To enhance your understanding of the analytic methods as well as the output, I include in commentaries references to formulas and/or calculations presented in the current chapter or in others. When necessary and feasible, I show how parts of the output can be used to obtain results not reported by the program. Instead of reproducing output in its entirety, I present excerpts interspersed by commentaries, for the following reasons.

First, and foremost, this format is more flexible and efficient for focusing on specific pieces of information and for providing more or less elaboration as seems to be called for by a given topic. Thus, whereas a given piece of output may require a brief comment or no comment at all, another may require a detailed discussion.

Second, this format simplifies exclusion of output relevant to topics that I have not yet introduced, thereby avoiding confusion and frustration. For example, though the programs I use in this chapter report an adjusted R square, I do not reproduce it here, as I have not yet introduced this term. When I discuss adjusted R square in a subsequent chapter, I include it in the output that I reproduce.

Third, using this format, I can limit presentation of output to aspects unique to a given program, thereby avoiding duplication of information already presented as part of the output of another program. I frequently follow this practice to conserve space.

Although I edit the output, sometimes drastically, I attempt to preserve its basic format to facilitate comparisons with output from your runs (see the following section, "Some Recommendations"). It is for this reason that I also retain as many decimal places as are reported, even when rounding to two or three decimal places is warranted (Cohen & Cohen, 1983, pp. 19–20).

As I introduce here the packages for the first time, I will present a fair amount of their outputs to acquaint you with their relevant features. Thereafter, I will give detailed output of only one program and short excerpts of output from other programs when warranted. Although I will use SPSS more often than other packages, this is not meant to imply my preference for this package but rather my perception that it is more popular among behavioral researchers. To encourage you to use the other packages as well, I will include periodically input files for them, though I will give little or no output.

Some Recommendations

Following are some recommendations for the use of computer programs.

Study the Manual(s).   There is a Hebrew saying to the effect that there is a short road that is long and a long road that is short. Unfortunately, many people take the short road that turns out to be not only long but also fraught with potential mishaps, which in data analysis may be manifested in misapplications and misinterpretations. I have known students and colleagues who paid more attention to the manuals for their VCRs or CD players than to those for their calculators, computers, and software. Many admitted (sometimes boastfully) to not having even opened their manuals. Not surprisingly, they had little or no knowledge of the capacities of their hardware or software. For example, they had no idea about the storage capacities of their calculators, let alone how to use them for, say, the calculation of sums of squares and sums of products without having to write down intermediate results. Similarly, I have encountered students and colleagues who did not see the need to study the manual for a statistical package they were using. They seemed satisfied with whatever brief descriptions they were given by their instructors, friends, or computing center personnel.

Despite the shortcomings of software manuals (see the preceding discussion), it is essential that you study them and refer to them often to gain optimal use of the program(s) they accompany. In addition to studying instructions for such matters as data input, data manipulation, output, and the execution and options of a given procedure, it is very important that you pay attention to statements of limitations, qualifications, caveats, and the like. Following are a couple of examples.

In Chapter 3, I introduced the term *leverage*. Looking in the *SPSS base system syntax reference guide* (SPSS Inc., 1993, p. 641), the user will find the following: "**LEVER** *Centered leverage values*. (See Velleman & Welsch, 1981.)" It is a safe bet that many a user will not understand what this means. Having learned about leverage in Chapter 3, you are probably baffled by the meaning of "centered." I will not hazard a guess as to how many users, yourself included, would check in the reference given. Assuming the user, appropriately, does not limit himself or herself to the *syntax reference guide* and consults also Norušis/SPSS Inc. (1993a), he or she would find the following explanation:

> SPSS computes centered leverages. They range from 0 to $(N - 1)/N$, where N is the number of observations. The mean value of the centered leverage is p/N, where p is the number of independent variables in the equation. . . . It is a good idea to examine points of leverage values that exceed $2p/N$. (p. 353)

As I explain later, *leverage* reported in SPSS differs from that reported in the other three packages under consideration. Therefore, using leverage values reported in SPSS in the formulas I gave in Chapter 3 (e.g., calculating Cook's *D* with (3.6)) would yield incorrect results.

The foregoing quotation should also serve as a reminder of the inadvisability of resorting to rules of thumb (see Chapter 3). Thus, following the rule of thumb given here regarding leverage values deserving examination may lead to different conclusions than following that suggested by, say, Velleman and Welsch (1981; see Chapter 3).

The next example is meant to illustrate hazards of ignoring (perhaps not even noticing) cautions given in manuals. It concerns orthogonal (balanced) and nonorthogonal (unbalanced) factorial designs—a complex topic I discuss in detail in Chapter 12. For present purposes, I would like only to give a flavor of what the manuals for a couple of the packages under consideration tell the reader about this topic.

MINITAB

After describing what an orthogonal design is, the manual states:

> Minitab does not check to see if your design is orthogonal. It does check to see if it has equal cell numbers, and if not, prints a message to tell you. . . . You are then on your own. If your model is not orthogonal, you will almost certainly get answers that are wrong. (Minitab Inc., 1995a, p. 10-35)

SAS

> In general . . . the ANOVA procedure is recommended only for balanced data. **If you use ANOVA to analyze a design that is not balanced, you must assume responsibility for the validity of the output.** You are responsible for recognizing incorrect results, which may include negative values reported for the sums of squares. (SAS Institute, 1990, Vol. 1, p. 23)

I wonder how many users would grasp the meaning and implications of such admonitions, assuming they notice them and bother to read them in the first place. In Chapter 12, I discuss and illustrate the deleterious consequences of inappropriate analyses of nonorthogonal factorial designs.

Understand What the Program Does. By this I mean understanding how the results are determined. This, for many users, is easier said than done, as in many instances the manuals resort to matrix algebra when presenting the equations and the algorithms they use. Even if you are not conversant in matrix algebra,[7] there are several things you can do.

1. Run the procedure in question with data for which you calculated the results by hand or with the aid of a calculator. *It is with this in mind that I presented manual calculations first* (Chapters 2 and 3) *and why I use small,* albeit unrealistic, numerical examples throughout the book. I suggest that you *relegate your work to the computer only after having mastered a given method through manual calculations* (see Khamis, 1991, for a discussion of the benefits of doing this).
2. Read reviews of the program you are using. Various popular and professional publications publish reviews of statistical software. By and large, people writing in the former are ill equipped to evaluate statistical programs. Reviews in professional journals abound. Following is a listing of some journals that publish reviews of statistical software: *American Journal of Epidemiology; The American Statistician; Behavior Research Methods, Instruments and Computers; Educational and Psychological Measurement; Educational Statistician; Journal of the American Statistical Association; Journal of Marketing Research;* and *Multivariate Behavioral Research.* Some of these journals publish also (1) control statements for the solution of specific problems through one or more of the packages I present (I give examples of this in Chapter 14) and (2) authors' notices of availability of computer programs they have written.
3. Read general discussions of the use of statistical software. Earlier, I listed several books devoted to one or more of the packages under considerations. Following are some papers on the use of statistical software or on program manuals: Berk (1987), Berk and Francis (1978), Dallal (1988), Muller (1978), and Thisted (1979).[8]

Use More Than One Program. Earlier, I commented on the desirability of using more than one computer program. As I show later, different programs use different nomenclature to refer to the same results or the same nomenclature to refer to different results. Studying and comparing outputs of different programs will facilitate your understanding of the nomenclature used in any one of them. Another important reason for analyzing the same example by more than one program is that the likelihood of detecting bugs is thereby increased (see the next section).

---

[7]I introduce matrix algebra in Chapter 6 and in Appendix A.

[8]See also commentaries following Berk and Francis (1978), Muller (1978), and Thisted (1979), and their rejoinders.

Be on the Lookout for Bugs. Contrary to common misconceptions, computer programs can, and do, contain bugs or incorrect procedures. As Manes (1988) pointed out, the computer "presents itself as a veritable paragon of certainty, accuracy, and credibility. There's only one minor problem: What if it's wrong?" (p. 85). Even established programs are not free of bugs, particularly in new releases, when revisions or expansions may have unexpected or unintended effects.

A simple way to test a program is to use it with a "model" problem for which a complete solution is available. Many computer packages are supplied with ample input files for the analysis of examples taken from textbooks or from published research whose input and output are reproduced and explained in their manuals. This is true of BMDP, MINITAB, and SAS. SPSS is deficient in this regard. Although the manual uses examples from textbooks or research projects, the user has to key in the input file listed in the manual. Although this may be viewed as but a nuisance, there are, unfortunately, some notable instances where SPSS fails to list the data for the examples being discussed and commented on in the manuals. This diminishes the value of the discussion of the output, not to mention depriving the user of the opportunity to replicate the analysis or to do an alternative analysis aimed at a better understanding of the properties of the procedure(s) used, as well as the example in question.

You can enhance your understanding of the properties of a given procedure by running textbook or research examples in addition to those discussed in the manual of the package you are using. When necessary and/or feasible, calculate by hand as well as by computer so that you may determine whether you are getting what you are supposed to be getting, or discern what it is that you are getting. As I noted earlier, running the same problem on more than one program is also very useful in this regard.

In an insightful book, Norman (1988) drew attention to the phenomenon of blaming oneself for failure of mechanical devices.

> Invariably people feel guilty and either try to hide the error or blame themselves for "stupidity" or "clumsiness." . . . It is as if they take perverse pride in thinking of themselves as mechanically incompetent. (pp. 34–35)

Because of myths surrounding the computer, the tendency to blame oneself for something that has gone awry is particularly great.

I hasten to add that more often than not the fault is not with the computer program but with the person using it. It is possible, for instance, that the data were read in with the wrong format, or that some of the variables read in were not those relevant to the analysis, or that inappropriate options were called for in the analysis. Be always alert to the GIGO principle: Garbage In, Garbage Out.

Critically Evaluate the Results. Always attempt to answer the question: *DO THE RESULTS MAKE SENSE?* If you are unable to answer the question to your satisfaction, chances are that you are not well versed in the method you are applying. Of course, the sole remedy is more thorough study. Following are some obvious examples.

Under the heading "Court Computer Says All Hartford Is Dead," *The New York Times* (National Edition, September, 30, 1992, p. B6) reported that all residents of Hartford were excluded from jury duty:

> The computer that selected names thought every one in the city was dead. . . . The city's name had been listed in the wrong place on the computer records, forcing the "d" at the end of "Hartford" into the column used to describe the status of the prospective jurors. "D" stands for dead.

It is noteworthy that the error was not detected for three years. "The problem came to light in a lawsuit challenging the racial makeup of . . . [a] grand jury."

In a memoir on the evolution of the IEA (International Association for the Evaluation of Educational Achievement),[9] Purves (1987) reported that the University of Chicago computer presented the researchers "with many problems, the most famous of which was its finding that there were nine sexes in Sweden" (p. 15).

> A[nother] famous example occurred during the Six-Subject Survey when the data processing was done in New York and the analyses in Stockholm. The first correlations arrived in Stockholm, and all were surprised to find that interest in science and achievement in science were negatively correlated in every country. The same was true for interest in literature and achievement in literature. *Four of us spent a day and a half trying to find an adequate interpretation for the result* [italics added]. A telephone call to New York finally produced the reason: the scores on the interest measures were reversed so that a low score meant high interest. Other occasions have not been so humorous or so easily resolvable. (p. 26)

Clearly, gross errors are easier to detect than subtle ones that "appear to be correct" (Dallal, 1988, p. 212). Probably the most difficult errors to detect are ones that yield results too good to be true. This, because of the tendency to be less critical, even delusionary, when results support one's expectations (see Friedlander, 1964, for an interesting example). It takes a good deal of sophistication and discipline to question results that look too good.

You are probably familiar with the controversy surrounding the role of heredity and environment in mental abilities. It is not my aim to review the debate but rather to use it as an illustration of the beguiling nature of results that are too good to be true. Now, one of the leading exponents of the hereditary point of view was the prominent British psychologist Cyril Burt. While various authors took issue with or totally rejected Burt's position, none seemed to question his data on identical twins on which his position was allegedly based. In fact, many researchers (e.g., Jensen, 1972) cited Burt's data as the most comprehensive and representative available.

Scrutiny of Burt's reports, however, led some authors, notable among them Kamin (1974), to suspect the veracity of his data. Among other things, Kamin noticed that the results from what Burt claimed to be different studies were too good to be true (e.g., identical correlation coefficients to the third decimal place). For an analysis demonstrating the improbability of the results reported by Burt, see Dorfman (1978).

Another example comes from Shapiro and Charrow's (1985) report on the Food and Drug Administration's (FDA) practices in investigating scientific misconduct. Commenting on audits, they pointed out, "in some cases, audits are initiated by the FDA if the data in a study appear to be too 'clean'" (p. 732).

Scrutinize Error Messages. The quality of error messages in output has been improving steadily in recent years, though inexperienced users have difficulties in deciphering some messages. Perhaps this is why they tend to ignore them, especially when the program is not aborted and its output contains results. The tendency to ignore error messages is particularly great when they are contained in a separate log file (e.g., SAS). It is important that you pay attention to error messages, and that you not accept the results until you understand the meaning and implications of the messages (see Goldstein, 1991, for a discussion).

---

[9]I discuss IEA in Chapters 8 and 10, and reanalyze some of its data in the former (see Table 8.2 and the discussion related to it).

Report Only Relevant Results.   Inexperienced users have a tendency to "play it safe" by reproducing all or most of the output. You would do well to heed Glick's (1991) warning, "The more numbers are reported, the better the chances of including at least a few statistics that are inappropriate or misleading" (p. 262; see Preece, 1987, for some examples).

Before turning to the application of regression procedures from the different packages, I would like to point out that each contains more than one procedure for getting regression results. The choice of a given procedure depends on one's aims (e.g., diagnostics, regression by groups). In this chapter, I introduce the most comprehensive procedure for regression available in each of the packages under consideration.

BMDP

Input

```
/PROBLEM TITLE IS   'BMDP2R.     TABLES 2.1, 2.2, 3.1 AND 3.2'.
/INPUT VARIABLES ARE 2.    FORMAT IS FREE.
/VARIABLE NAMES ARE X,Y.
/REGRESS DEPEND=Y.   INDEP=X.   FORCE=1.
/PRINT LEVEL=MINIMAL.   DATA.   COVA.   CORR.   NO STEP.
 DIAGnostics=STRESID,   DSTRESID,   HATDIAG,   COOK.
/PLOT RESID.   VAR=X.
 SIZE=44,12.
/END
1    3
1    5    [first two subjects]
.    .
5    12    [last two subjects]
5    6
```

Commentary

As you can see from the title, the input file is for 2R. Notwithstanding its name Stepwise Regression,[10] 2R "is the primary general purpose multiple linear regression program" (Dixon, 1992, Vol. 2, p. 989), offering a wide variety of options. Following BMDP format (Dixon, 1992, Vol. 1, Chapter 10; BMDP Statistical Software, Inc., 1993, Chapter 9), I use the default extension INP for input files. Thus, I named the input file T21.INP. To run on the PC in batch mode, I typed at the DOS prompt:

BMDP 2R IN=T21

It is not necessary to type the extension (INP). By default, the output file is named T21.OUT

Consult the BMDP manual for details about the structure of input files and specific commands. For present purposes, I will only point out that the file is organized in paragraphs—each beginning with a slash (/)—dealing with different aspects (e.g., INPUT, REGRESS, PLOT; see Dixon, 1992, Vol. 1, pp. 4–5). "Each paragraph (except END) consists of at least one command

---

[10]I present stepwise regression analysis in Chapter 8.

ending with a period. . . . The END paragraph is required to terminate BMDP instructions" (Dixon, 1992, Vol. 1, p. 4).

REGRESS paragraph. I designated *Y* as the dependent variable and *X* as the independent variable. As I explain in Chapter 8, stepwise regression analysis is carried out in steps, entering and/or deleting variable(s) according to specific criteria. In 2R it is also possible to force variables into the equation and keep them there. This is accomplished through FORCE (see Dixon, 1992, Vol. 1, p. 416). As the present example consists of one independent variable, the notion of stepwise regression analysis is inapplicable. I use FORCE=1 here to specify that *X* be entered into the equation and not be removed.

PRINT paragraph is common to all procedures (see Dixon, 1992, Vol. 1, Chapter 7), though it may contain commands specific to a given procedure (e.g., DIAGnostics in the present example). LEVEL=MINIMAL is described in Dixon (1992, Vol. 1, p. 83). Note that I called for the printing of the covariance and correlation between *X* and *Y,* and for specific DIAGnostics (see commentary on the output). Following BMDP conventions, I indicated acceptable abbreviations by uppercase letters. Thus, DIAG is sufficient to call for diagnostics. As I stated earlier, both lowercase and uppercase letters may be used throughout.

In the PLOT paragraph I called for the plotting of the residuals against predicted scores and against *X*. By default, plot size is 50 columns wide and 35 lines high. For illustrative purposes, I specified a size of 44 columns by 12 lines.

Finally, I would like to point out that following the description of each program the manual provides a useful summary of commands specific to the program, along with indication of defaults and references to where in the manual each command is discussed. Also useful is *BMDP user's digest: Quick reference for the BMDP programs* (BMDP Statistical Software, Inc., 1992).

Output

VARIABLE NO.	NAME	MEAN	STANDARD DEV.	SMALLEST VALUE	LARGEST VALUE
1	X	3.0000	1.4510	1.0000	5.0000
2	Y	7.3000	2.6178	3.0000	12.0000

COVARIANCE MATRIX
- - - - - - - - - - - -

		X 1	Y 2
X	1	2.1052630	
Y	2	1.5789472	6.8526306

CORRELATION MATRIX
- - - - - - - - - - - -

		X 1	Y 2
X	1	1.0000	
Y	2	0.4157	1.0000

Commentary

The diagonal elements of the covariance matrix are variances. Thus, the variance of X is 2.105, and that of Y is 6.853. The square roots of the variances are the standard deviations (given in the preceding, alongside the means). As I explained in Chapter 2 (see "Correlation Model"), the correlation coefficient is a covariance of standard scores. Recall that the variance of standard scores is 1.0. Notice that the diagonal elements of the correlation matrix are 1's. For additional explanations of results such as the preceding, along with relevant formulas, see Chapter 2.

Output

STEP NO.   1

- - - - - - - - - - - - - -

VARIABLE ENTERED   1 X

MULTIPLE R	0.4157
MULTIPLE R-SQUARE	0.1728
STD. ERROR OF EST.	2.4461

ANALYSIS OF VARIANCE

	SUM OF SQUARES	DF	MEAN SQUARE	F RATIO
REGRESSION	22.499996	1	22.50000	3.76
RESIDUAL	107.69999	18	5.983333	

VARIABLES IN EQUATION FOR Y

VARIABLE	COEFFICIENT	STD. ERROR OF COEFF
(Y-INTERCEPT	5.05000)	
X	0.75000	0.3868

Commentary

The correlation between a dependent variable and more than one independent variables is referred to as a multiple correlation coefficient or multiple R (see Chapter 5). As the present example is comprised of one independent variable, MULTIPLE R refers to a bivariate correlation (Pearson r between X and Y; see the preceding correlation matrix).

STD. ERROR OF EST. is the square root of the variance of estimate—see Chapter 2, (2.26) and (2.27), and the discussion related to them.

In "Testing the Regression of Y on X" in Chapter 2, I discussed results such as those reported under ANALYSIS OF VARIANCE. The same is true for the output reported under VARIABLES IN EQUATION FOR Y (see Chapter 2, "The Regression Equation" and "Testing the Regression Coefficient"). Dividing the regression coefficient (.75) by its standard error (.3868) yields $t = 1.94$, with 18 *df*. As I discussed in Chapter 2, $t^2 = 3.76 = F$, with 1 and 18 *df* (look under ANALYSIS OF VARIANCE in the output).

Output

LIST OF PREDICTED VALUES, RESIDUALS, AND VARIABLES – ASTERISKS (UP TO 3) TO THE RIGHT OF A RESIDUAL INDICATE THAT THE RESIDUAL DEVIATES FROM THE MEAN BY MORE THAN THAT NUMBER OF STANDARD DEVIATIONS.

CASE NO.	PREDICTED	RESIDUAL	Y	X	STRESID	DSTRESID	HATDIAG	COOK
1	5.8000	−2.8000*	3.0000	1.0000	−1.2416	−1.2618	0.1500	0.1360
2	5.8000	−0.8000	5.0000	1.0000	−0.3547	−0.3460	0.1500	0.0111
3	5.8000	0.2000	6.0000	1.0000	0.0887	0.0862	0.1500	0.0007
4	5.8000	3.2000*	9.0000	1.0000	1.4190	1.4632	0.1500	0.1777
5	6.5500	−2.5500*	4.0000	2.0000	−1.0839	−1.0895	0.0750	0.0476
6	6.5500	−0.5500	6.0000	2.0000	−0.2338	−0.2275	0.0750	0.0022
7	6.5500	0.4500	7.0000	2.0000	0.1913	0.1861	0.0750	0.0015
8	6.5500	3.4500*	10.0000	2.0000	1.4665	1.5188	0.0750	0.0872
9	7.3000	−3.3000*	4.0000	3.0000	−1.3841	−1.4230	0.0500	0.0504
10	7.3000	−1.3000	6.0000	3.0000	−0.5453	−0.5343	0.0500	0.0078
11	7.3000	0.7000	8.0000	3.0000	0.2936	0.2860	0.0500	0.0023
12	7.3000	2.7000*	10.0000	3.0000	1.1325	1.1420	0.0500	0.0338
13	8.0500	−3.0500*	5.0000	4.0000	−1.2965	−1.3232	0.0750	0.0681
14	8.0500	−1.0500	7.0000	4.0000	−0.4463	−0.4362	0.0750	0.0081
15	8.0500	0.9500	9.0000	4.0000	0.4038	0.3942	0.0750	0.0066
16	8.0500	3.9500*	12.0000	4.0000	1.6790	1.7768	0.0750	0.1143
17	8.8000	−1.8000	7.0000	5.0000	−0.7982	−0.7898	0.1500	0.0562
18	8.8000	1.2000	10.0000	5.0000	0.5321	0.5212	0.1500	0.0250
19	8.8000	3.2000*	12.0000	5.0000	1.4190	1.4632	0.1500	0.1777
20	8.8000	−2.8000*	6.0000	5.0000	−1.2416	−1.2618	0.1500	0.1360

Commentary

Compare these results with those given in Tables 2.2, 3.1, and 3.2. What BMDP labels standardized residuals (STRESID), I labeled studentized residuals (SRESID) in Chapter 3. DSTRESID = *"deleted standardized residual"* (Dixon, 1992, Vol. 1, p. 402). In Chapter 3 (see Table 3.1 and the discussion related to it), I labeled this element studentized deleted residual (SDRESID). HATDIAG is the diagonal of the hat matrix, which is also called leverage—see the explanation following (3.1) in Chapter 3. COOK is Cook's *D*—see (3.6) and the explanation following it. You will find it instructive to compare the aforementioned formulas with those given in Dixon (1992, Vol. 1, pp. 402–403).

Output

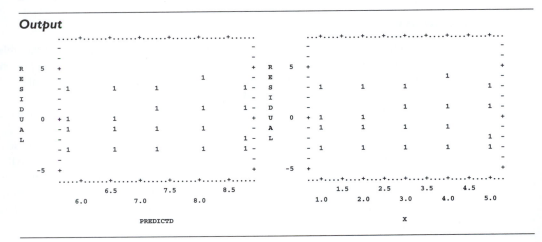

Commentary

In the plot on the left, residuals are plotted against the predicted scores, whereas in that on the right residuals are plotted against the independent variable (see Chapter 2 for explanations). For various other plot options, see Dixon, 1992, Vol. 1, pp. 419–421.

MINITAB

Input

GMACRO   *[global macro.   38-4]*
T21   *[template. macro name.   38-4]*
OUTFILE='T21.MIN';   *[name of output file.   2-15]*
   NOTERM.   *[subcommand.   no output displayed on monitor.   2-16]*
NOTE TABLES 2.1, 2.2, 3.1 AND 3.2   *[title.   43-2]*
READ C1-C2 *[data read into columns 1 and 2, free format. 1-29]*
1   3
1   5   *[first two subjects]*

.   .
5 12   *[last two subjects]*
5   6
END   *[advisable to use after READ, SET, INSERT. 1-39]*
ECHO   *[display the commands in the output file. 44-9]*
NAME C1 'X' C2 'Y'   *[1-39]*
DESCRIBE C1-C2   *[calculate descriptive statistics. 8-2]*
CORRELATION C1-C2 M1   *[put in M1 matrix. 8-19]*
COVARIANCE C1-C2 M2   *[put in M2 matrix. 8-21]*
PRINT M1 M2   *[2-9]*
BRIEF 3   *[maximum output; when issued before REGRESS. 9-29]*
REGRESS C2 1 C1 C3-C4;   *[SRESIDUALS & FITS in C3-C4.   9-2]*
   HI C5;   *[subcommand.   leverage in C5.   9-2]*
   COOKD C6;   *[subcommand.   Cook's D in C6.   9-2]*
   TRESIDUALS C7.   *[studentized deleted residuals in C7.   9-2]*
NAME C3 'SRESID' C4 'FIT' C5 'LEVER' C6 'COOKD' C7 'TRESID'
NOTE PRED IS FIT IN MINITAB   *[comment]*
PRINT C5-C7
GSTD   *[standard mode graphics.   28-2]*
PLOT 'Y' VERSUS 'X'; *[28-13]*
   XINCREMENT=1;   *[subcommand. 28-13]*
   XSTART=0;   *[subcommand. 28-13]*
   YINCREMENT=4;   *[subcommand. 28-13]*
   YSTART=0.   *[subcommand. 28-13]*
PLOT C3 C4
ENDMACRO   *[38-4]*

Commentary

As I stated earlier, brief comments in italics are *not* part of the input file. Numbers in comments are page numbers in Minitab Inc. (1995a).

Earlier, I pointed out that I present input files in a format suitable for batch processing. In MINITAB this is done through macros. Two kinds of macros can be used in MINITAB: GMACRO = global macro and MACRO = local macro (see Minitab Inc., 1995a, Chapters 38 through 41). The local macro is more complex than the global. For my purposes, global macros will suffice.[11] Examine the input and notice that a global macro is simple: it is a file containing MINITAB commands (which may also include data) that begins with GMACRO followed by a template (T21 in the previous input) and ends with ENDMACRO.

I named the macro T21.MAC, where MAC is the default extension. To execute, I typed in the SESSION window:

%t21

MINITAB looks for the macro in the current directory. If it does not find it there, it looks in the macros subdirectory. When the macro is in neither of the preceding, the path has to be supplied along with the macro name (see Minitab Inc., 1995a, p. 39-4).

I hope that the comments and page references I included in the input file will suffice to clarify the commands I used. Therefore, I comment briefly on a couple of topics only.

OUTFILE. When a name without an extension is specified, MINITAB adds the extension LIS. I use MIN because I use LIS for SPSS output (see the following).

SUBCOMMANDS. In the above input subcommands appear after OUTFILE, REGRESS, and PLOT commands. Note that each subcommand is terminated with a semicolon (;). A period (.) is used at the end the last subcommand.

Output

MTB > DESCRIBE C1-C2

	N	Mean	Median	StDev
X	20	3.000	3.000	1.451
Y	20	7.300	7.000	2.618

```
MTB > CORRELATION  C1-C2  M1
MTB > COVARIANCE  C1-C2  M2
MTB > PRINT  M1  M2
   Matrix  M1                    [correlation matrix]
      1.00000     0.41571
      0.41571     1.00000
   Matrix  M2                    [covariance matrix]
      2.10526     1.57895
      1.57895     6.85263
```

Commentary

Because I used ECHO (see input, after END), commands associated with a given piece of output are printed, thereby facilitating the understanding of elements of which it is comprised. Compare the preceding output with similar output from BMDP 2R.

---

[11]MINITAB is supplied with a number of macros to carry out tasks and analyses of varying complexity. In addition, macros appear frequently in *MUG: Minitab User's Group newsletter.*

Output

MTB > BRIEF 3
MTB > REGRESS C2 1 C1 C3-C4;
SUBC> HI C5;
SUBC> COOKD C6;
SUBC> TRESIDUALS C7.

The regression equation is
$Y = 5.05 + 0.750 \ X$

Predictor	Coef	Stdev	t-ratio	p
Constant	5.050	1.283	3.94	0.001
X	0.7500	0.3868	1.94	0.068

$s = 2.446$ $R\text{-sq} = 17.3\%$

Analysis of Variance

SOURCE	DF	SS	MS	F	p
Regression	1	22.500	22.500	3.76	0.068
Error	18	107.700	5.983		
Total	19	130.200			

Obs.	X	Y	Fit	Residual	St.Resid
1	1.00	3.000	5.800	−2.800	−1.24
2	1.00	5.000	5.800	−0.800	−0.35
3	1.00	6.000	5.800	0.200	0.09
4	1.00	9.000	5.800	3.200	1.42
5	2.00	4.000	6.550	−2.550	−1.08
6	2.00	6.000	6.550	−0.550	−0.23
7	2.00	7.000	6.550	0.450	0.19
8	2.00	10.000	6.550	3.450	1.47
9	3.00	4.000	7.300	−3.300	−1.38
10	3.00	6.000	7.300	−1.300	−0.55
11	3.00	8.000	7.300	0.700	0.29
12	3.00	10.000	7.300	2.700	1.13
13	4.00	5.000	8.050	−3.050	−1.30
14	4.00	7.000	8.050	−1.050	−0.45
15	4.00	9.000	8.050	0.950	0.40
16	4.00	12.000	8.050	3.950	1.68
17	5.00	7.000	8.800	−1.800	−0.80
18	5.00	10.000	8.800	1.200	0.53
19	5.00	12.000	8.800	3.200	1.42
20	5.00	6.000	8.800	−2.800	−1.24

Commentary

Compare the preceding output with relevant segments of BMDP given earlier and also with relevant sections in Chapters 2 and 3.

s = standard error of estimate, that is, the square root of the variance of estimate, which I discussed in Chapter 2—see (2.26) and (2.27).

Stdev is the standard error of the respective statistic. For example, Stdev for the regression coefficient (b) is .3868. Dividing b by its standard error (.75/.3868) yields a t ratio with *df* equal to those associated with the error or residual (18, in the present example). MINITAB reports the probability associated with a given t (or F). In the present case, it is .068. Thus, assuming α = .05 was selected, then it would be concluded that the null hypothesis that b = 0 cannot be rejected.

As I explained under the previous BMDP output, t^2 for the test of the regression coefficient (1.94^2) is equal to F (3.76) reported in the analysis of variance table.

MINITAB reports r^2 (R-sq) as percent ($r^2 \times 100$) of variance due to regression. In the present example, about 17% of the variance in Y is due to (or accounted by) X (see Chapter 2 for an explanation).

Predicted scores are labeled Fit in MINITAB. What I labeled studentized residuals (SRESID; see Chapter 3, Table 3.1, and the discussion accompanying it) is labeled here standardized residuals (St.Resid. See Minitab Inc., 1995a, p. 9-4). Recall that the same nomenclature is used in BMDP (see the previous output).

Output

```
MTB > NAME C5 'LEVER' C6 'COOKD' C7 'TRESID'
MTB > PRINT C5-C7
```

ROW	LEVER	COOKD	TRESID
1	0.150	0.136018	−1.26185
2	0.150	0.011104	−0.34596
3	0.150	0.000694	0.08620
4	0.150	0.177656	1.46324
5	0.075	0.047630	−1.08954
6	0.075	0.002216	−0.22755
7	0.075	0.001483	0.18608
8	0.075	0.087185	1.51878
9	0.050	0.050417	−1.42300
10	0.050	0.007824	−0.53434
11	0.050	0.002269	0.28602
12	0.050	0.033750	1.14201
13	0.075	0.068140	−1.32322
14	0.075	0.008076	−0.43617
15	0.075	0.006611	0.39423
16	0.075	0.114287	1.77677

17	0.150	0.056212	−0.78978
18	0.150	0.024983	0.52123
19	0.150	0.177656	1.46324
20	0.150	0.136018	−1.26185

Commentary

Lever = leverage, COOKD = Cook's *D*, TRESID = Studentized Deleted Residual (Minitab Inc., 1995a, p. 9-5). Compare with the previous BMDP output and with Tables 3.1 and 3.2. For explanations of these terms, see the text accompanying the aforementioned tables.

Output

```
MTB > PLOT 'Y' VERSUS 'X';
SUBC>  XINCREMENT 1;
SUBC>  XSTART 0;
SUBC>  YINCREMENT 4;
SUBC>  YSTART 0.
```

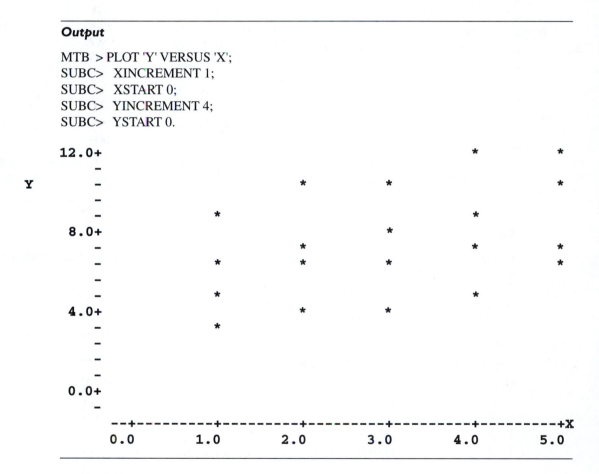

Commentary

The preceding is a plot of the raw data. For illustrative purposes, I specified 0 as the origin (see XSTART and YSTART) and noted that increments of 1 and 4, respectively, be used for *X* and *Y*. See Minitab Inc. (1995a, p. 28-13) for an explanation of these and other plot options.

Output

MTB > PLOT 'Y' VERSUS 'X';

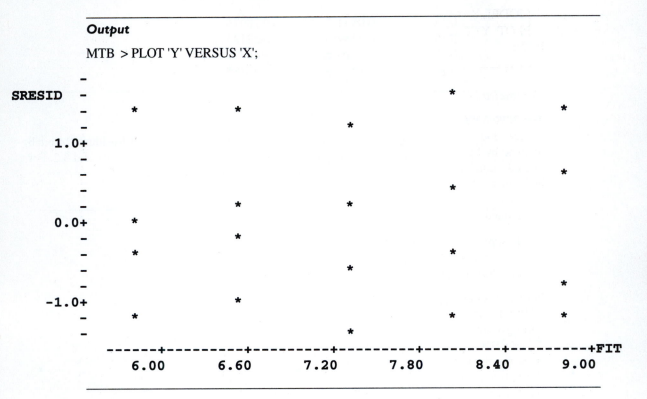

Commentary

In the preceding, I called for the plotting of the studentized residuals against the predicted scores, using the PLOT defaults.

SAS

Input

```
TITLE   'TABLES 2.1, 2.2, 3.1 AND 3.2';
DATA   T21;
   INPUT   X  Y;      [free format]
CARDS;
1  3
1  5                  [first two subjects]
.   .
5  12                 [last two subjects]
5  6
;
PROC PRINT;           [print the input data]
PROC MEANS N MEAN STD SUM CSS;  [CSS = corrected sum of squares]
PROC REG;
```

```
    MODEL Y=X/ALL R INFLUENCE;
    PLOT  Y*X  R.*P./SYMBOL='.'  HPLOTS=2 VPLOTS=2;
RUN;
```

Commentary

The SAS input files I give in this book can be used under Windows or in other environments (see "Processing Mode" and "System Statements," presented earlier in this chapter). Procedures are invoked by PROC and the procedure name (e.g., PROC PRINT). A semicolon (;) is used to terminate a command or a subcommand. When the file contains more than one PROC, RUN should be used as the last statement (see last line of input); otherwise only the first PROC will be executed.

I named the file T21.SAS. Following is, perhaps, the simplest way to run this file in Windows.

1. Open into the program editor.
2. In the OPEN dialog box, select the file you wish to run.
3. Click the RUN button.

For various other approaches, see SAS Institute Inc. (1993).

PROC "REG provides the most general analysis capabilities; the other [regression] procedures give more specialized analyses" (SAS Institute Inc., 1990a, Vol. 1, p. 1).

MODEL. The dependent variable is on the left of the equal sign; the independent variable(s) is on the right of the equal sign. Options appear after the slash (/). ALL = print all statistics; R = "print analysis of residuals"; INFLUENCE = "compute influence statistics" (SAS Institute Inc., 1990a, Vol. 2, p. 1363; see also, pp. 1366–1367).

PLOT. I called for a plot of the raw data (Y by X) and residuals (R) by predicted (P) scores. In the options, which appear after the slash (/), I specified that a period (.) be used as the symbol. Also, although I called for the printing of two plots only, I specified that two plots be printed across the page (HPLOTS) and two down the page (VPLOTS), thereby affecting their sizes. For explanations of the preceding, and other plot options, see SAS Institute Inc. (1990a, Vol. 2, pp. 1375–1378).

Output

Variable	N	Mean	Std Dev	Sum	CSS
X	20	3.0000000	1.4509525	60.0000000	40.0000000
Y	20	7.3000000	2.6177532	146.0000000	130.2000000

Commentary

The preceding was generated by PROC MEANS. As an illustration, I called for specific elements instead of specifying PROC MEANS only, in which case the defaults would have been generated.

Compare this output with Table 2.1 and with relevant output from BMDP and MINITAB. As I pointed out in the input file, CSS stands for corrected sum of squares or the deviation sum of squares I introduced in Chapter 2. Compare CSS with the deviation sums of squares I calculated through (2.2).

Output

Dependent Variable: Y

Analysis of Variance

Source	DF	Sum of Squares	Mean Square	F Value	Prob>F
Model	1	22.50000	22.50000	3.760	0.0683
Error	18	107.70000	5.98333		
C Total	19	130.20000			

Root MSE	2.44609	R-square	0.1728	

Parameter Estimates

Variable	DF	Parameter Estimate	Standard Error	T for H0: Parameter=0	Prob > |T|
INTERCEP	1	5.050000	1.28273796	3.937	0.0010
X	1	0.750000	0.38676005	1.939	0.0683

Commentary

Except for minor differences in nomenclature, this segment of the output is similar to outputs from BMDP and MINITAB given earlier. Therefore, I will not comment on it. If necessary, reread relevant sections of Chapters 2 and 3 and commentaries on output for the aforementioned programs. Note that what I labeled in Chapter 2, and earlier in this chapter, as standard error of estimate is labeled here Root MSE (Mean Square Error). This should serve to illustrate what I said earlier about the value of running more than one program as one means of becoming familiar with the nomenclature of each.

Output

Obs	Dep Var Y	Predict Value	Residual	Std Err Residual	Student Residual	–2–1 0 1 2	Cook's D	Rstudent	Hat Diag H	INTERCEP Dfbetas	X Dfbetas
1	3.0000	5.8000	–2.8000	2.255	–1.242	| **| |	0.136	–1.2618	0.1500	–0.5220	0.4328
2	5.0000	5.8000	–0.8000	2.255	–0.355	| | |	0.011	–0.3460	0.1500	–0.1431	0.1187
3	6.0000	5.8000	0.2000	2.255	0.089	| | |	0.001	0.0862	0.1500	0.0357	–0.0296
4	9.0000	5.8000	3.2000	2.255	1.419	| |** |	0.178	1.4632	0.1500	0.6053	–0.5019
5	4.0000	6.5500	–2.5500	2.353	–1.084	| **| |	0.048	–1.0895	0.0750	–0.2700	0.1791
6	6.0000	6.5500	–0.5500	2.353	–0.234	| | |	0.002	–0.2275	0.0750	–0.0564	0.0374
7	7.0000	6.5500	0.4500	2.353	0.191	| | |	0.001	0.1861	0.0750	0.0461	–0.0306
8	10.0000	6.5500	3.4500	2.353	1.466	| |** |	0.087	1.5188	0.0750	0.3764	–0.2497
9	4.0000	7.3000	–3.3000	2.384	–1.384	| **| |	0.050	–1.4230	0.0500	–0.1392	0.0000
10	6.0000	7.3000	–1.3000	2.384	–0.545	| *| |	0.008	–0.5343	0.0500	–0.0523	0.0000
11	8.0000	7.3000	0.7000	2.384	0.294	| | |	0.002	0.2860	0.0500	0.0280	0.0000
12	10.0000	7.3000	2.7000	2.384	1.132	| |** |	0.034	1.1420	0.0500	0.1117	0.0000
13	5.0000	8.0500	–3.0500	2.353	–1.296	| **| |	0.068	–1.3232	0.0750	0.0656	–0.2175
14	7.0000	8.0500	–1.0500	2.353	–0.446	| | |	0.008	–0.4362	0.0750	0.0216	–0.0717
15	9.0000	8.0500	0.9500	2.353	0.404	| | |	0.007	0.3942	0.0750	–0.0195	0.0648
16	12.0000	8.0500	3.9500	2.353	1.679	| |*** |	0.114	1.7768	0.0750	–0.0881	0.2921
17	7.0000	8.8000	–1.8000	2.255	–0.798	| *| |	0.056	–0.7898	0.1500	0.1634	–0.2709
18	10.0000	8.8000	1.2000	2.255	0.532	| |* |	0.025	0.5212	0.1500	–0.1078	0.1788
19	12.0000	8.8000	3.2000	2.255	1.419	| |** |	0.178	1.4632	0.1500	–0.3026	0.5019
20	6.0000	8.8000	–2.8000	2.255	–1.242	| **| |	0.136	–1.2618	0.1500	0.2610	–0.4328

Commentary

The preceding are selected output columns, which I rearranged. I trust that, in light of the outputs from BMDP and MINITAB given earlier and my comments on them, much of the preceding requires no comment. Therefore, I comment only on nomenclature and on aspects not reported in the outputs of programs given earlier. If necessary, compare also with Tables 3.1 and 3.2 and reread the discussions that accompany them.

Student Residual = Studentized Residual. Note that these are obtained by dividing each residual by its standard error (e.g., $-2.8000/2.255 = -1.242$, for the first value)—see (3.1) and the discussion related to it. Studentized residuals are plotted and Cook's D's are printed "as a result of requesting the R option" (SAS Institute Inc., 1990a, Vol. 2, p. 1404).

Rstudent = Studentized Deleted Residual (SDRESID). See Table 3.1 and the discussion related to it. See also the BMDP and MINITAB outputs given earlier.

I introduced DFBETA in Chapter 3—see (3.7) and (3.8) and the discussion related to them— where I pointed out that it indicates changes in the regression equation (intercept and regression coefficient) that would result from the deletion of a given subject. I also showed how to calculate standardized DFBETA—see (3.9) and (3.10). SAS reports standardized DFBETA only. Compare the results reported in the preceding with the last two columns of Table 3.2.

To get the results I used in Chapter 3 to illustrate calculations of DFBETA for the last subject, add the following statements to the end of the input file given earlier:

TITLE 'TABLE 2.1.   LAST SUBJECT OMITTED';
REWEIGHT OBS. = 20;
    PRINT;

See SAS Institute Inc. (1990, Vol. 2, pp. 1381–1384) for a discussion of the REWEIGHT statement.

Output

TABLES 2.1, 2.2, 3.1 AND 3.2

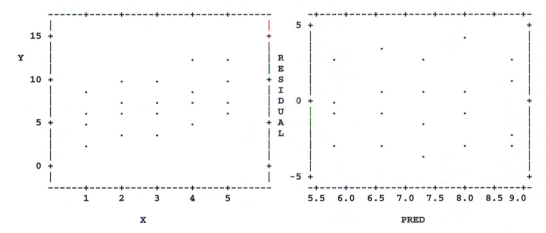

Commentary

Compare these plots with those from BMDP and MINITAB, which I reproduced here. See Chapter 2, Figures 2.4–2.6, and the discussion related to them for the use of such plots for diagnostic purposes.

SPSS

Input

```
TITLE  TABLES  2.1,  2.2,  3.1,  AND  3.2.
DATA  LIST  FREE/X  Y.          [free input format]
COMPUTE  X2=X**2.               [compute square of X]
COMPUTE  Y2=Y**2.               [compute square of Y]
COMPUTE  XY=X*Y.                [compute product of X and Y]
BEGIN  DATA
1   3
1   5          [first two subjects]
.   .
5   12         [last two subjects]
5   6
END  DATA
LIST  X  X2  Y  Y2  XY.
REGRESSION  VAR  Y,X/DES=ALL/STAT=ALL/DEP  Y/ENTER/
   RESIDUALS=ID(X)/CASEWISE=ALL  PRED   RESID   ZRESID   SRESID
   SDRESID  LEVER  COOK/
   SCATTERPLOT=(Y,X) (*RESID,*PRE)/
   SAVE  FITS.
LIST  VAR=DBE0_1   DBE1_1   SDB0_1   SDB1_1/FORMAT=NUMBERED.
```

Commentary

The input I present can be run noninteractively under Windows from a Syntax Window (see the following) or in other environments (see "Processing Mode" and "System Statements," presented earlier in this chapter). Under Windows, some commands "cannot be obtained through the dialog box interface and can be obtained only by typing command syntax in a syntax window" (Norušis/SPSS Inc., 1993a, p. 757; see pp. 757–758 for a listing of such commands).

Earlier, I indicated that noninteractive and batch processing are synonymous. However, SPSS uses the term batch processing in a special way (see SPSS Inc., 1993, pp. 13–14). *In the following presentation, I will cite page numbers only when referring to SPSS Inc. (1993).*

For a general orientation to SPSS, see pages 1–75. I suggest that you pay special attention to explanations of commands, subcommands, and keywords, as well as their syntax and order. For instance, whereas subcommands can be entered in any order for most commands, "some commands require a specific subcommand order. The description of each command includes a section on subcommand order" (p. 16).

The COMPUTE statements are not necessary for regression analysis. I included them so that you may compare the output obtained from listing the results they generate (i.e., through LIST X X2 Y Y2 XY) with calculations I carried out in Chapter 2 (see Table 2.1).

REGRESSION consists of a variety of subcommands (e.g., VARiables, DEScriptives, STATistics), some of which I use in the present run, and comment on in the following. The subcommand order for REGRESSION is given on page 623, following which the syntax rules for each subcommand are given.

DES = descriptive statistics. As I explained earlier, I call for ALL the statistics. "If the width is less than 132, some statistics may not be displayed" (p. 638).

RESIDUALS=ID(X): analyze residuals and use X for case identification. CASEWISE=ALL: print all cases. Standardized residuals (ZRESID) are plotted by default.

Instead of using the default printing, I called for the printing of predicted scores (PRED), residuals (RESID), standardized residuals (ZRESID), studentized residuals (SRESID), studentized deleted residuals (SDRESID), leverage (LEVER), and Cook's *D* (COOK).

"*The widest page allows a maximum of eight variables in a casewise plot*" [italics added] (p. 640). If you request more than eight, only the first eight will be printed. One way to print additional results is to save them first. As an example, I used SAVE FITS (p. 646) and then called for the listing of DFBETA raw (DBE0_1 = intercept; DBE1_1 = regression coefficient) and standardized (SDB0_1 and SDB1_1). To list the saved results, you can issue the LIST command without specifying variables to be listed, in which case all the variables (including the original data and vectors generated by, say, COMPUTE statements) will be listed. If they don't fit on a single line, they will be wrapped. Alternatively, you may list selected results. As far as I could tell, conventions for naming the information saved by SAVE FITS are not given in the manual. To learn how SPSS labels these results (I listed some of them in parentheses earlier; see also LIST in the input), you will have to examine the relevant output (see Name and Contents in the output given in the following) before issuing the LIST command.

FORMAT=NUMBERED on the LIST command results in the inclusion of sequential case numbering for ease of identification (p. 443).

SCATTERPLOT. For illustrative purposes, I called for two plots: (1) *Y* and *X* and (2) residuals and predicted scores. An asterisk (*) prefix indicates a temporary variable (p. 645). The default plot size is SMALL (p. 645). "All scatterplots are standardized in the character-based output" (p. 645). As I stated earlier, I use only character-based graphs. The choice between character-based or high-resolution graphs is made through the SET HIGHRES subcommand (p. 740), which can also be included in the Preference File (SPSSWIN.INI; see Norušis/SPSS Inc., 1993a, pp. 744–746).

The default extension for input files is SPS. The default extension for output files is LST. Earlier, I pointed out that I use LIS instead. I do this to distinguish the output from that of SAS, which also uses LST as the default extension for output files.

To run the input file, bring it into a syntax Window, select ALL, and click on the RUN button. Alternatively, (1) hold down the Ctrl key and press the letter A (select all), (2) hold down the Ctrl key and press the letter R (run).

Output

LIST X X2 Y Y2 XY.

X	X2	Y	Y2	XY	
1.00	1.00	3.00	9.00	3.00	*[first two subjects]*
1.00	1.00	5.00	25.00	5.00	
.	.	.	.	.	

| 5.00 | 25.00 | 12.00 | 144.00 | 60.00 | *[last two subjects]* |
| 5.00 | 25.00 | 6.00 | 36.00 | 30.00 | |

Number of cases read: 20 Number of cases listed: 20

Commentary

As I stated earlier, I use LIST to print the original data, as well as their squares and cross products (generated by the COMPUTE statements; see Input) so that you may compare these results with those reported in Table 2.1.

Output

	Mean	Std Dev	Variance
Y	7.300	2.618	6.853
X	3.000	1.451	2.105

N of Cases =   20
Correlation, Covariance, Cross-Product:

	Y	X
Y	1.000	.416
	6.853	1.579
	130.200	30.000
X	.416	1.000
	1.579	2.105
	30.000	40.000

Commentary

Note that the correlation of a variable with itself is 1.00. A covariance of a variable with itself is its variance. For example, the covariance of Y with Y is 6.853, which is the same as the value reported for the variance of Y. The cross product is expressed in deviation scores. Thus, 130.200 and 40.000 are the deviation sums of squares for Y and X, respectively, whereas 30.000 is the deviation sum of products for X and Y. If necessary, reread relevant sections of Chapter 2 and do the calculations by hand.

Output

Equation Number 1   Dependent Variable. .   Y

Multiple R	.41571
R Square	.17281
Standard Error	2.44609

Analysis of Variance

	DF	Sum of Squares	Mean Square
Regression	1	22.50000	22.50000
Residual	18	107.70000	5.98333

F = 3.76045   Signif F = .0683

- - - - - - - - - - - - - - - - Variables in the Equation - - - - - - - - - - - - - - - - -

Variable	B	SE B	95% Confdnce Intrvl B		T	Sig T
X	.750000	.386760	−.062553	1.562553	1.939	.0683
(Constant)	5.050000	1.282738	2.355067	7.744933	3.937	.0010

Commentary

The preceding is similar to outputs from BMDP, MINITAB, and SAS (see the preceding). Earlier, I pointed out that in the present example Multiple R is the Pearson correlation between X and Y. Standard Error = Standard Error of Estimate or the square root of the variance of estimate. Note that SPSS reports 95% confidence intervals of parameter estimates—see (2.30) and the discussion related to it.

Output

Casewise Plot of Standardized Residual

Case #	X	−3.0 0.0 3.0 O:.........:.........:O	*PRED	*RESID	*ZRESID	*SRESID	*SDRESID	*LEVER	*COOK D
1	1.00	. * . .	5.8000	−2.8000	−1.1447	−1.2416	−1.2618	.1000	.1360
2	1.00	. *. .	5.8000	−.8000	−.3271	−.3547	−.3460	.1000	.0111
3	1.00	. * .	5.8000	.2000	.0818	.0887	−.0862	.1000	.0007
4	1.00	. . * .	5.8000	3.2000	1.3082	1.4190	1.4632	.1000	.1777
5	2.00	. * . .	6.5500	−2.5500	−1.0425	−1.0839	−1.0895	.0250	.0476
6	2.00	. *. .	6.5500	−.5500	−.2248	−.2338	−.2275	.0250	.0022
7	2.00	. . * .	6.5500	.4500	.1840	.1913	.1861	.0250	.0015
8	2.00	. . * .	6.5500	3.4500	1.4104	1.4665	1.5188	.0250	.0872
9	3.00	. * . .	7.3000	−3.3000	−1.3491	−1.3841	−1.4230	.0000	.0504
10	3.00	. * . .	7.3000	−1.3000	−.5315	−.5453	−.5343	.0000	.0078
11	3.00	. .* .	7.3000	.7000	.2862	.2936	.2860	.0000	.0023
12	3.00	. . * .	7.3000	2.7000	1.1038	1.1325	1.1420	.0000	.0338
13	4.00	. * . .	8.0500	−3.0500	−1.2469	−1.2965	−1.3232	.0250	.0681
14	4.00	. *. .	8.0500	−1.0500	−.4293	−.4463	−.4362	.0250	.0081
15	4.00	. .* .	8.0500	.9500	.3884	.4038	.3942	.0250	.0066
16	4.00	. . * .	8.0500	3.9500	1.6148	1.6790	1.7768	.0250	.1143
17	5.00	. * . .	8.8000	−1.8000	−.7359	−.7982	−.7898	.1000	.0562
18	5.00	. .* .	8.8000	1.2000	.4906	.5321	.5212	.1000	.0250
19	5.00	. . * .	8.8000	3.2000	1.3082	1.4190	1.4632	.1000	.1777
20	5.00	. * . .	8.8000	−2.8000	−1.1447	−1.2416	−1.2618	.1000	.1360
Case #	X	O:.........:.........:O −3.0 0.0 3.0	*PRED	*RESID	*ZRESID	*SRESID	*SDRESID	*LEVER	*COOK D

Commentary

PRED = Predicted Score, ZRESID = Standardized Residual, SRESID = Studentized Residual, SDRESID = Studentized Deleted Residual, LEVER = Leverage, and COOK D = Cook's D. Compare the preceding excerpt with Tables 2.2, 3.1, 3.2, and with outputs from the other packages given earlier, and note that, differences in nomenclature aside, all the results are similar, *except for leverage.* Earlier, I stated that SPSS reports centered leverage, which is different from leverage reported in the other packages under consideration. Without going into details,[12] I will note that SPSS does not include $1/N$ when calculating leverage—see (3.5). Therefore, to transform the leverages reported in SPSS to those obtained when (3.5) is applied, or those reported in the other packages, add $1/N$ to the values SPSS reports. In the present example, $N = 20$. Adding .05 to the values reported under LEVER yields the values reported in Table 3.2 and in the outputs from the other packages given earlier. The same is true for transformation of SPSS leverage when more than one independent variable is used (see Chapter 5).

Output

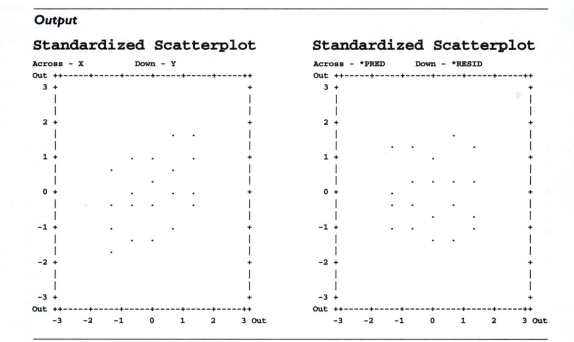

Commentary

As I pointed out earlier, all the scatterplots are standardized. To get plots of raw data, use PLOT.

---

[12]I discuss the notion of centering in Chapters 10, 13, and 16.

Output

From Equation   1:   7 new variables have been created.

Name	Contents
- - - -	- - - - - -
DBE0_1	Dfbeta for Intercept
DBE1_1	Dfbeta for X
SDB0_1	Sdfbeta for Intercept
SDB1_1	Sdfbeta for X

LIST VAR=DBE0_1 DBE1_1 SDB0_1 SDB1_1/FORMAT=NUMBERED.

	DBE0_1	DBE1_1	SDB0_1	SDB1_1
1	−.65882	.16471	−.52199	.43281
2	−.18824	.04706	−.14311	.11866
3	.04706	−.01176	.03566	−.02957
4	.75294	−.18824	.60530	−.50189
5	−.34459	.06892	−.27003	.17912
6	−.07432	.01486	−.05640	.03741
7	.06081	−.01216	.04612	−.03059
8	.46622	−.09324	.37642	−.24969
9	−.17368	.00000	−.13920	.00000
10	−.06842	.00000	−.05227	.00000
11	.03684	.00000	.02798	.00000
12	.14211	.00000	.11171	.00000
13	.08243	−.08243	.06559	−.21754
14	.02838	−.02838	.02162	−.07171
15	−.02568	.02568	−.01954	.06481
16	−.10676	.10676	−.08807	.29210
17	.21176	−.10588	.16335	−.27089
18	−.14118	.07059	−.10781	.17878
19	−.37647	.18824	−.30265	.50189
20	.32941	−.16471	.26099	−.43281

Commentary

I obtained the preceding through SAVE FITS. Unlike SAS, which reports standardized DFBETA only, SPSS reports both raw and standardized values—see Chapter 3 (3.7–3.10). To get terms I used in Chapter 3 to calculate DFBETA for the last subject, append the following statements to the end of the input file given earlier:

```
TITLE  TABLE  2.1  OR  TABLE  3.1.    LAST  CASE  DELETED.
N  19.
REGRESSION  VAR  Y,X/DES  ALL/STAT=ALL/DEP  Y/ENTER.
```

CONCLUDING REMARKS

Except for specialized programs (e.g., EQS, LISREL), which I use in specific chapters, I will use the packages I introduced in this chapter throughout the book. When using any of these packages, I will follow the format and conventions I presented in this chapter (e.g., commentaries on input and output). However, my commentaries on input and output will address primarily the topics under consideration. Consequently, if you have difficulties in running the examples given in subsequent chapters, or if you are puzzled by some aspects of the input, output, commentaries, and the like, you may find it useful to return to this chapter. To reiterate: study the manual(s) of the package(s) you are using, and refer to it when in doubt or at a loss.

In most instances, a single independent variable is probably not sufficient for a satisfactory, not to mention thorough, explanation of the complex phenomena that are the subject matter of behavioral and social sciences. As a rule, a dependent variable is affected by multiple independent variables. It is to the study of simultaneous effects of independent variables on a dependent variable that I now turn. In Chapter 5, I discuss analysis and interpretation with two independent variables, whereas in Chapter 6 I present a generalization to any number of independent variables.

5

Elements of Multiple Regression Analysis: Two Independent Variables

In this chapter, I extend regression theory and analysis to the case of two independent variables. Although the concepts I introduce apply equally to multiple regression analysis with any number of independent variables, the decided advantage of limiting this introduction to two independent variables is in the relative simplicity of the calculations entailed. Not having to engage in, or follow, complex calculations will, I hope, enable you to concentrate on the meaning of the concepts I present. Generalization to more than two independent variables is straightforward, although it involves complex calculations that are best handled through matrix algebra (see Chapter 6).

After introducing basic ideas of multiple regression, I present and analyze in detail a numerical example with two independent variables. As in Chapter 2, I carry out all the calculations by hand so that you may better grasp the meaning of the terms presented. Among topics I discuss in the context of the analysis are squared multiple correlation, regression coefficients, statistical tests of significance, and the relative importance of variables. I conclude the chapter with computer analyses of the numerical example I analyzed by hand, in the context of which I extend ideas of regression diagnostics to the case of multiple regression analysis.

BASIC IDEAS

In Chapter 2, I gave the sample linear regression equation for a design with one independent variable as (2.6). I repeat this equation with a new number. (For your convenience, I periodically resort to this practice of repeating equations with new numbers attached to them.)

$$Y = a + bX + e \tag{5.1}$$

where Y = raw score on the dependent variable; a = intercept; b = regression coefficient; X = raw score on the independent variable; and e = error, or residual.

Equation (5.1) can be extended to any number of independent variables or X's:

$$Y = a + b_1X_1 + b_2X_2 + \ldots + b_kX_k + e \tag{5.2}$$

where $b_1, b_2, \ldots, b_k$ are regression coefficients associated with the independent variables $X_1, X_2, \ldots, X_k$ and e is the error, or residual. As in simple linear regression (see Chapter 2), a solution is sought for the constants (a and the b's) such that the sum of the squared errors of prediction

(Σe^2) is minimized. This, it will be recalled, is referred to as the *principle of least squares*, according to which the independent variables are differentially weighted so that the sum of the squared errors of prediction is minimized or that prediction is optimized.

The prediction equation in multiple regression analysis is

$$Y' = a + b_1 X_1 + b_2 X_2 + \ldots + b_k X_k \tag{5.3}$$

where Y' = predicted Y score. All other terms are as defined under (5.2). One of the main calculation problems of multiple regression is to solve for the b's in (5.3). With only two independent variables, the problem is not difficult, as I show later in this chapter. With more than two X's, however, it is considerably more difficult, and reliance on matrix operations becomes essential. To reiterate: the principles and interpretations I present in connection with two independent variables apply equally to designs with any number of independent variables.

In Chapter 2, I presented and analyzed data from an experiment with one independent variable. Among other things, I pointed out that r^2 (squared correlation between the independent and the dependent variable) indicates the proportion of variance accounted for by the independent variable. Also, of course, $1 - r^2$ is the proportion of variance not accounted for, or error. To minimize errors, or optimize explanation, more than one independent variable may be used. Assuming two independent variables, X_1 and X_2, are used, one would calculate $R^2_{y.x_1 x_2}$ where R^2 = squared multiple correlation of Y (the dependent variable, which is placed before the dot) with X_1 and X_2 (the independent variables, which are placed after the dot). To avoid cumbersome subscript notation, I will identify the dependent variable as Y, and the independent variables by numbers only. Thus,

$$R^2_{y.x_1 x_2} = R^2_{y.12} \qquad r^2_{y.x_1} = r^2_{y.1} \qquad r^2_{x_1 x_2} = r^2_{12}$$

$R^2_{y.12}$ indicates the proportion of variance of Y accounted for by X_1 and X_2.

As I discussed in Chapter 2, regression analysis may be applied in different designs (e.g., experimental, quasi-experimental, and nonexperimental; see Pedhazur & Schmelkin, 1991, Chapters 12–14, for detailed discussions of such designs and references). In various subsequent chapters, I discuss application of regression analysis in specific designs. For present purposes, it will suffice to point out that an important property of a well-designed and well-executed experiment is that the independent variables are not correlated. For the case of two independent variables, this means that $r_{12} = .00$. Under such circumstances, calculation of R^2 is simple and straightforward:

$$R^2_{y.12} = r^2_{y1} + r^2_{y2} \qquad \text{(when } r_{12} = 0\text{)}$$

Each r^2 indicates the proportion of variance accounted for by a given independent variable.[1] Calculations of other regression statistics (e.g., the regression equation) are equally simple.

In quasi-experimental and nonexperimental designs, the independent variables are almost always correlated. For the case of two independent variables, or two predictors, this means that $r_{12} \neq .00$. The nonzero correlation indicates that the two independent variables, or predictors, provide a certain amount of redundant information, which has to be taken into account when calculating multiple regression statistics.

These ideas can perhaps be clarified by Figure 5.1, where each set of circles represents the variance of a Y variable and two X variables, X_1 and X_2. The set on the left, labeled (a), is a simple situation where $r_{y1} = .50$, $r_{y2} = .50$, and $r_{12} = 0$. Squaring the correlation of X_1 and X_2

---

[1]It is also possible, as I show in Chapter 12, to study the interaction between X_1 and X_2.

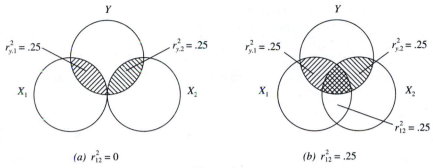

(a) $r_{12}^2 = 0$ $\qquad\qquad\qquad\qquad\qquad$ *(b)* $r_{12}^2 = .25$

Figure 5.1

with Y and adding them $[(.50)^2 + (.50)^2 = .50]$, the proportion of variance of Y accounted for by both X_1 and X_2 is obtained, or $R_{y.12}^2 = .50$.

But now study the situation in (b). The sum of r_{y1}^2 and r_{y2}^2 is *not* equal to $R_{y.12}^2$ because r_{12} is *not* equal to 0. (The degree of correlation between two variables is expressed by the amount of overlap of the circles.[2]) The hatched areas of overlap represent the variances common to pairs of depicted variables. The one doubly hatched area represents that part of the variance of Y that is common to the X_1 and X_2 variables. Or, it is part of r_{y1}^2, it is part of r_{y2}^2, and it is part of r_{12}^2. Therefore, to calculate that part of Y that is determined by X_1 *and* X_2, it is necessary to subtract this doubly hatched overlapping part so that it will not be counted twice.

Careful study of Figure 5.1 and the relations it depicts should help you grasp the principle I stated earlier. Look at the right-hand side of the figure. To explain or predict more of Y, so to speak, it is necessary to find other variables whose variance circles will intersect the Y circle and, at the same time, not intersect each other, or at least minimally intersect each other.

A Numerical Example

I purposely use an example in which the two independent variables are correlated, as it is the more general case under which the special case of $r_{12} = 0$ is subsumed. It is the case of correlated independent variables that poses so many of the interpretational problems that will occupy us not only in this chapter but also in subsequent chapters.

Suppose we have the reading achievement, verbal aptitude, and achievement motivation scores on 20 eighth-grade pupils. (There will, of course, usually be many more than 20 subjects.) We want to calculate the regression of Y, reading achievement, on both verbal aptitude and achievement motivation. But since verbal aptitude and achievement motivation are correlated, it is necessary to take the correlation into account when studying the regression of reading achievement on both variables.

Calculation of Basic Statistics

Assume that scores for the 20 pupils are as given in Table 5.1. To do a regression analysis, a number of statistics have to be calculated. The sums, means, and the sums of squares of raw scores on the three sets of scores are given in the three lines directly below the table. In addition,

[2]Although the figure is useful for pedagogical purposes, it is not always possible to depict complex relations among variables with such figures.

Table 5.1   Illustrative Data: Reading Achievement (Y), Verbal Aptitude (X_1), and Achievement Motivation (X_2)

Y	X_1	X_2	Y'	$Y - Y' = e$
2	1	3	2.0097	−.0097
4	2	5	3.8981	.1019
4	1	3	2.0097	1.9903
1	1	4	2.6016	−1.6016
5	3	6	5.1947	−.1947
4	4	5	5.3074	−1.3074
7	5	6	6.6040	.3960
9	5	7	7.1959	1.8041
7	7	8	9.1971	−2.1971
8	6	4	6.1248	1.8752
5	4	3	4.1236	.8764
2	3	4	4.0109	−2.0109
8	6	6	7.3086	.6914
6	6	7	7.9005	−1.9005
10	8	7	9.3098	.6902
9	9	6	9.4226	−.4226
3	2	6	4.4900	−1.4900
6	6	5	6.7167	−.7167
7	4	6	5.8993	1.1007
10	4	9	7.6750	2.3250
Σ: 117	87	110	117	0
M: 5.85	4.35	5.50		
SS: 825	481	658		$\Sigma e^2 = 38.9469$

NOTE: SS = sum of squared raw scores.

the following statistics will be needed: the deviation sums of squares for the three variables, their deviation cross products, and their standard deviations. They are calculated as follows:

$$\Sigma y^2 = \Sigma Y^2 - \frac{(\Sigma Y)^2}{N} = 825 - \frac{(117)^2}{20} = 825 - 684.45 = 140.55$$

$$\Sigma x_1^2 = \Sigma X_1^2 - \frac{(\Sigma X_1)^2}{N} = 481 - \frac{(87)^2}{20} = 481 - 378.45 = 102.55$$

$$\Sigma x_2^2 = \Sigma X_2^2 - \frac{(\Sigma X_2)^2}{N} = 658 - \frac{(110)^2}{20} = 658 - 605.00 = 53.00$$

$$\Sigma x_1 y = \Sigma X_1 Y - \frac{(\Sigma X_1)(\Sigma Y)}{N} = 604 - \frac{(87)(117)}{20} = 604 - 508.95 = 95.05$$

$$\Sigma x_2 y = \Sigma X_2 Y - \frac{(\Sigma X_2)(\Sigma Y)}{N} = 702 - \frac{(110)(117)}{20} = 702 - 643.50 = 58.50$$

$$\Sigma x_1 x_2 = \Sigma X_1 X_2 - \frac{(\Sigma X_1)(\Sigma X_2)}{N} = 517 - \frac{(87)(110)}{20} = 517 - 478.50 = 38.50$$

$$s_y = \sqrt{\frac{\Sigma y^2}{N-1}} = \sqrt{\frac{140.55}{20-1}} = 2.720$$

$$s_{x_1} = \sqrt{\frac{\Sigma x_1^2}{N-1}} = \sqrt{\frac{102.55}{20-1}} = 2.323$$

$$s_{x_2} = \sqrt{\frac{\Sigma x_2^2}{N-1}} = \sqrt{\frac{53.00}{20-1}} = 1.670$$

For visual convenience, I pulled together in Table 5.2 the results of the previous calculations. Below the principal diagonal of the matrix, I included the correlations between the variables (.792, .678, and .522), as I will need them later.

Table 5.2   Deviation Sums of Squares and Cross Products, Correlation Coefficients, and Standard Deviations for the Data in Table 5.1

	y	x_1	x_2
y	140.55	95.05	58.50
x_1	.792	102.55	38.50
x_2	.678	.522	53.00
s	2.720	2.323	1.670

NOTE: The tabled values are as follows: the first line is comprised, successively, of Σy^2, the deviation sum of squares of Y; the cross product of the deviations of X_1 and Y, or $\Sigma x_1 y$; and finally $\Sigma x_2 y$. The entries in the second and third lines, on the diagonal or above, are Σx_1^2, $\Sigma x_1 x_2$, and (in the lower right corner) Σx_2^2. The italicized entries *below* the diagonal are the correlation coefficients. The standard deviations are given in the last line.

There is more than one way to calculate the essential statistics of multiple regression analysis. Ultimately, I will cover several approaches. Now, however, I concentrate on calculations that use sums of squares, because they have the virtue of being additive and intuitively comprehensible.

Reasons for the Calculations

Before proceeding with the calculations, it will be useful to review why we are doing all this. First, we want to calculate the constants (a, b_1, and b_2) of the regression equation $Y' = a + b_1 X_1 + b_2 X_2$, so that we can, if we wish, use the X's of individuals and predict their Y's (Y'). This means, in the present example, that if we have scores of individuals on verbal aptitude and achievement motivation, we can insert them into the equation and obtain Y' values, or predicted reading achievement scores.

Second, we want to know the proportion of variance "accounted for," that is $R_{y.12}^2$. In other words, we want to know how much of the total variance of Y, reading achievement, is due to its regression on the X's, on verbal aptitude and achievement motivation.

Third, we wish to test the results for statistical significance so that we could state, for instance, whether the regression of Y on the X's is statistically significant, or whether each regression coefficient, b, in the regression equation is statistically different from zero.

Finally, we wish to determine the relative importance of the different X's in explaining Y. We wish to know, in this case, the relative importance of X_1 and X_2, verbal aptitude and achievement motivation, in explaining verbal achievement. As you will see, this is the most difficult question to answer. In this chapter, I deal briefly with the complexities attendant with such questions and some alternative approaches to answering them. A deeper knowledge of multiple regression analysis is necessary for fully comprehending the diverse approaches and the complexities of each. In succeeding chapters, I broaden and deepen the scope of the different uses and interpretations of multiple regression analysis.

Calculation of Regression Statistics

The calculation of the b's of the regression equation is done rather mechanically with formulas for two X variables. They are

$$b_1 = \frac{(\Sigma x_2^2)(\Sigma x_1 y) - (\Sigma x_1 x_2)(\Sigma x_2 y)}{(\Sigma x_1^2)(\Sigma x_2^2) - (\Sigma x_1 x_2)^2}$$

$$b_2 = \frac{(\Sigma x_1^2)(\Sigma x_2 y) - (\Sigma x_1 x_2)(\Sigma x_1 y)}{(\Sigma x_1^2)(\Sigma x_2^2) - (\Sigma x_1 x_2)^2}$$

(5.4)

Taking relevant values from Table 5.2 and substituting them in the formulas, I calculate the b's:

$$b_1 = \frac{(53.00)(95.05) - (38.50)(58.50)}{(102.55)(53.00) - (38.50)^2} = \frac{5037.65 - 2252.25}{5435.15 - 1482.25} = \frac{2785.40}{3952.90} = .7046$$

$$b_2 = \frac{(102.55)(58.50) - (38.50)(95.05)}{(102.55)(53.00) - (38.50)^2} = \frac{5999.175 - 3659.425}{5435.15 - 1482.25} = \frac{2339.75}{3952.90} = .5919$$

The formula for a is

$$a = \overline{Y} - b_1\overline{X}_1 - b_2\overline{X}_2$$

(5.5)

Substituting relevant values yields

$$a = 5.85 - (.7046)(4.35) - (.5919)(5.50) = -.4705$$

The regression equation can now be written with the calculated values of a and the b's

$$Y' = -.4705 + .7046X_1 + .5919X_2$$

As examples of the use of the equation in prediction, I calculate predicted Y's for the first and the last subjects of Table 5.1:

$$Y' = -.4705 + (.7046)(1) + (.5919)(3) = 2.0098$$

$$Y' = -.4705 + (.7046)(4) + (.5919)(9) = 7.6750$$

The *observed* Y's are $Y_1 = 2$ and $Y_{20} = 10$. The residuals, $e = Y - Y'$, are

$$e_1 = 2 - 2.0098 = -.0098$$

$$e_{20} = 10 - 7.6750 = 2.3250$$

The predicted Y's and the residuals are given in the last two columns of Table 5.1.[3] Recall that the a and the b's of the regression equation were calculated to satisfy the least-squares principle, that is, to minimize the squares of errors of prediction. Squaring each of the residuals and adding them, as I did in Chapter 2, $\Sigma e^2 = 38.9469$. (Note that $\Sigma e = 0$.) As I showed earlier, this can be symbolized Σy_{res}^2 or ss_{res}. In short, the residual sum of squares expresses that portion of the total Y sum of squares, Σy^2, that is *not* due to regression. In the following, I show that the residual

---

[3]The slight discrepancies between the results given here and those given in Table 5.1 are due to rounding.

sum of squares can be more readily calculated. I went through the lengthy calculations to show what this sum of squares consists of.

The regression sum of squares is calculated with the following general formula:

$$ss_{reg} = b_1\Sigma x_1 y + \ldots + b_k \Sigma x_k y \tag{5.6}$$

where k = the number of X, or independent variables. In the case of two X variables, $k = 2$, the formula reduces to

$$ss_{reg} = b_1 \Sigma x_1 y + b_2 \Sigma x_2 y \tag{5.7}$$

Taking the b values I calculated in the preceding and the deviation sums of cross products from Table 5.2, and substituting in (5.7),

$$ss_{reg} = (.7046)(95.05) + (.5919)(58.50) = 101.60$$

This is the portion of the total sum of squares of Y, or Σy^2, that is due to the regression of Y on the two X's. Note that the total sum of squares is 140.55 (from Table 5.2). In Chapter 2—see (2.17)—I showed that

$$ss_{res} = \Sigma y^2 - ss_{reg} \tag{5.8}$$

Therefore,

$$ss_{res} = 140.55 - 101.60 = 38.95$$

which is, within rounding, the same as the value I obtained through the lengthy calculations of Table 5.1.

Alternative Calculations

To reinforce and broaden your understanding of multiple regression analysis, I will calculate regression statistics by other methods, in which correlation coefficients are used. Before presenting the alternative calculations, it is necessary to digress briefly to discuss the distinction between standardized and unstandardized regression coefficients and how they are related to each other.

Regression Weights: *b* and β

Earlier, I used b as a symbol for the statistic and β as a symbol for the parameter. There is, however, another way in which these symbols are frequently used: b is the unstandardized regression coefficient, and β is the standardized regression coefficient (see the following). Unfortunately, there is no consistency in notation. For example, some authors use b^* as the symbol for the standardized regression coefficient, others use $\hat{\beta}$ as the symbol for the estimator of β (the unstandardized coefficient) and $\hat{\beta}^*$ as the symbol for the standardized coefficient. Although the use of the different symbols, as exemplified here, is meant to avoid confusion, I believe that they are unnecessarily cumbersome and may therefore lead to greater confusion. Adding to the potential confusion is another usage of β as a symbol for Type II error (see Hays, 1988, p. 261; Pedhazur & Schmelkin, 1991, p. 206). *Henceforth, I will use* b *as the symbol for the sample unstandardized regression coefficient and* β *as the symbol for the sample standardized coefficient.* Occasionally, it will be necessary to use β as a parameter. I will identify such usage when I resort to it.

When raw scores are used, as I did until now, b's are calculated and applied to the X's (raw scores) in the regression equation. If, however, the Y and X scores were standardized (i.e., converted to z scores), β's would be calculated and applied to z's in the regression equation. For simple regression, the regression equation in which standard scores are used is

$$z'_y = \beta z_x \qquad (5.9)$$

where z'_y = predicted standard score of Y; β = standardized regression coefficient; and z_x = standard score of X. As in the case of b, β is interpreted as the expected change in Y associated with a unit change in X. But because the standard deviation of z scores is equal to 1.00, a unit change in X, when it has been standardized, refers to a change of one standard deviation in X. Later in this chapter, I discuss distinctions in the use and interpretation of b's and β's.

With one independent variable, the formula for the calculation of β is

$$\beta = \frac{\Sigma z_x z_y}{\Sigma z_x^2} \qquad (5.10)$$

In Chapter 2, I showed that b is calculated as follows:

$$b = \frac{\Sigma xy}{\Sigma x^2} \qquad (5.11)$$

Note the similarity between (5.10) and (5.11). Whereas sum of cross products and sum of squares of standard scores are used in the former, the latter requires the deviation sum of cross products and sum of squares. It is, however, not necessary to carry out the calculations indicated in (5.10) as b and β are related as follows:

$$\beta = b\frac{s_x}{s_y}$$
$$b = \beta\frac{s_y}{s_x} \qquad (5.12)$$

where β = standardized regression coefficient; b = unstandardized regression coefficient; and s_x, s_y = standard deviations of X and Y, respectively. Substituting (5.11) and the formulas for the standard deviations of X and Y in (5.12), we obtain

$$\beta = b\frac{s_x}{s_y} = \frac{\Sigma xy\sqrt{\Sigma x^2}\sqrt{N-1}}{\Sigma x^2\sqrt{N-1}\sqrt{\Sigma y^2}} = \frac{\Sigma xy}{\sqrt{\Sigma x^2}\sqrt{\Sigma y^2}} = r_{xy} \qquad (5.13)$$

Note that with one independent variable $\beta = r_{xy}$. Also, when using standard scores, the intercept, a, is zero. The reason for this is readily seen when you recall that the mean of z scores is zero. Therefore,

$$a = \bar{Y} - \beta\bar{X} = 0 - \beta 0 = 0$$

For two independent variables, X_1 and X_2, the regression equation with standard scores is

$$z'_y = \beta_1 z_1 + \beta_2 z_2 \qquad (5.14)$$

where β_1 and β_2 are standardized regression coefficients; z_1 and z_2 are standard scores on X_1 and X_2, respectively. The formulas for calculating the β's when two independent variables are used are

$$\beta = \frac{r_{y1} - r_{y2}r_{12}}{1 - r_{12}^2} \qquad \beta_2 = \frac{r_{y2} - r_{y1}r_{12}}{1 - r_{12}^2} \qquad (5.15)$$

Note that when the independent variables are not correlated (i.e., $r_{12} = 0$), $\beta_1 = r_{y1}$ and $\beta_2 = r_{y2}$ as is the case in simple linear regression. This is true for any number of independent variables: when the independent variables are not intercorrelated, β for a given independent variable is equal to the correlation coefficient (r) of that variable with the dependent variable.

The correlations for the data of Table 5.1 (see Table 5.2) are $r_{y1} = .792; r_{y2} = .678;$ and $r_{12} = .522$.

$$\beta_1 = \frac{.792 - (.678)(.522)}{1 - .522^2} = .602$$

$$\beta_2 = \frac{.678 - (.792)(.522)}{1 - .522^2} = .364$$

The regression equation, in standard scores, for the data of Table 5.1 is

$$z'_y = .602z_1 + .364z_2$$

Having calculated the β's, the corresponding b's, the unstandardized regression coefficients, can be calculated as follows:

$$b_j = \beta_j \frac{s_y}{s_j} \tag{5.16}$$

where b = unstandardized regression coefficient; $j = 1, 2$; β = standardized regression coefficient; and s_y and s_j are, respectively, standard deviations of Y and X_j. For the data of Table 5.1,

$$s_y = 2.720 \qquad s_1 = 2.323 \qquad s_2 = 1.670$$

$$b_1 = .602 \frac{2.720}{2.323} = .705 \qquad b_2 = .364 \frac{2.720}{1.670} = .593$$

which are, within rounding errors, the same values I obtained earlier. Once the b's are calculated, a can be calculated by (5.5).

SQUARED MULTIPLE CORRELATION COEFFICIENT

In Chapter 2, I showed that the ratio of ss_{reg} to the total sum of squares, Σy^2, equals the squared correlation coefficient between the independent and the dependent variable. The same is true for the case of multiple independent variables, except that the ratio equals the squared multiple correlation:

$$R^2 = \frac{ss_{reg}}{\Sigma y^2} \tag{5.17}$$

R^2, then, indicates the proportion of variance of the dependent variable accounted for by the independent variables. Using the sums of squares I calculated earlier,

$$R^2 = \frac{101.60}{140.55} = .723$$

About 72% of the variance in reading achievement is accounted for by verbal aptitude and achievement motivation.

Another way of viewing R^2 is to note that it is the squared correlation of Y (observed Y's) and Y' (predicted Y's), which are of course a linear combination of the X's.

$$R^2_{y.12} = r^2_{yy'} = \frac{(\Sigma yy')^2}{\Sigma y^2 \Sigma y'^2} \tag{5.18}$$

The values of (5.18) can be calculated from the Y and Y' columns of Table 5.1. We already have $\Sigma y^2 = 140.55$. The comparable value of $\Sigma y'^2$ is calculated as follows:

$$\Sigma y'^2 = \Sigma Y'^2 - \frac{(\Sigma Y')^2}{N} = 786.0525 - \frac{(117)^2}{20} = 101.60$$

The sum of the deviation cross products is:

$$\Sigma yy' = \Sigma YY' - \frac{(\Sigma Y)(\Sigma Y')}{N} = 786.0528 - \frac{(117)(117)}{20} = 101.60$$

Note that $\Sigma y'^2 = \Sigma yy'$. Substituting in (5.18)

$$R^2 = \frac{(101.60)^2}{(140.55)(101.60)} = .723$$

The positive square root of R^2 gives R. Unlike r, which can take positive as well as negative values, R may vary from .00 to 1.00. For the data of Table 5.1

$$R_{y.12} = \sqrt{.723} = .85$$

or

$$R_{y.12} = r_{yy'} = \frac{\Sigma yy'}{\sqrt{\Sigma y^2}\ \sqrt{\Sigma y'^2}} = \frac{101.60}{\sqrt{140.55}\ \sqrt{101.60}} = .85$$

For completeness of presentation, I calculated R, even though it may be irrelevant in regression analysis. As I explained in the case of simple linear regression (see Chapter 2), r^2, not r, is the meaningful term in regression analysis; likewise R^2, not R, is the meaningful term in multiple regression analysis.

Calculation of Squared Multiple Correlation Coefficient

There are various formulas for the calculation of R^2. Following is one in which β's and r's are used:

$$R^2_{y.12} = \beta_1 r_{y1} + \beta_2 r_{y2} \tag{5.19}$$

For the present data,

$$R^2_{y.12} = (.602)(.792) + (.364)(.678) = .724$$

which is, within rounding, the same value I obtained in the lengthier calculations.

Yet another formula for the calculation of R^2 can be obtained by substituting (5.15) in (5.19):

$$R^2_{y.12} = \frac{r^2_{y1} + r^2_{y2} - 2r_{y1}r_{y2}r_{12}}{1 - r^2_{12}} \tag{5.20}$$

Formula (5.20) is very simple and very useful for the calculation of R^2 with two independent variables. All one needs are the three r's. Note that when the correlation between the independent variables is zero (i.e., $r_{12} = 0$), then (5.20) reduces to $R^2_{y.12} = r^2_{y1} + r^2_{y2}$, as was noted earlier.

For the data of Table 5.1,

$$R^2_{y.12} = \frac{.792^2 + .678^2 - 2(.792)(.678)(.522)}{1 - .522^2} = .723$$

Again, this is the same as the value I obtained earlier.

TESTS OF SIGNIFICANCE AND INTERPRETATIONS

I discussed the role of tests of significance and the assumptions underlying them in **Chapter 2** and will therefore not address these issues here. Of several tests of significance that may be applied to results of multiple regression analysis, I present three here: (1) test of R^2, (2) tests of regression coefficients, and (3) tests of increments in the proportion of variance accounted for by a given variable.

Test of R^2

The test of R^2 proceeds as the test of r^2, which I presented in Chapter 2.

$$F = \frac{R^2/k}{(1 - R^2)/(N - k - 1)} \tag{5.21}$$

with k and $N - k - 1$ *df.* k = number of independent variables and N = sample size. For the data of Table 5.1, $R^2_{y.12} = .723, N = 20$.

$$F = \frac{.723/2}{(1 - .723)/(20 - 2 - 1)} = \frac{.3615}{.0163} = 22.18$$

with 2 and 17 *df, p < .01.* One can, of course, calculate F using the appropriate sums of squares. The formula is

$$F = \frac{ss_{reg}/df_{reg}}{ss_{res}/df_{res}} \tag{5.22}$$

The degrees of freedom associated with ss_{reg} are $k = 2$, the number of independent variables. The degrees of freedom associated with ss_{res} are $N - k - 1 = 17$. Earlier I calculated $ss_{reg} = 101.60$ and $ss_{res} = 38.95$. Therefore,

$$F = \frac{101.60/2}{38.95/17} = \frac{50.80}{2.29} = 22.18$$

This agrees with the F I got when I tested R^2.

Whether one uses (5.21) or (5.22) is a matter of taste, as the same test is being performed. The identity of the two tests can be seen when it is noted that $ss_{reg} = R^2 \Sigma y^2$ and $ss_{res} = (1 - R^2) \Sigma y^2$. Substituting these equivalencies in (5.22), Σy^2 can be canceled from the numerator and the denominator, yielding (5.21).

Based on the R^2, one would conclude that verbal aptitude and achievement motivation account for about 72% of the variance in reading achievement and that this finding is statistically significant at the .01 level.

The test of R^2 indicates whether the regression of Y on the independent variables taken together is statistically significant. Stated differently, testing R^2 is tantamount to testing whether at least one regression coefficient differs from zero. Failure to reject the null hypothesis leads to the conclusion that all the regression coefficients do not differ significantly from zero (I discuss this point in the following section).

When, however, one wishes to determine whether the effect of a given variable is significantly different from zero, it is the regression coefficient, *b,* associated with it that is tested.

Tests of Regression Coefficients

Each b in a multiple regression equation indicates the expected change in Y associated with a unit change in the independent variable under consideration while controlling for, or holding constant, the effects of the other independent variables. Accordingly, the b's are called partial regression coefficients or partial slopes. To avoid cumbersome notation, I omitted certain subscripts from the multiple regression equations I presented thus far. Inserting the relevant subscripts, the regression equation with two independent variables, for example, is written thus:

$$Y' = a + b_{y1.2}X_1 + b_{y2.1}X_2 \qquad (5.23)$$

where $b_{y1.2}$ and $b_{y2.1}$ are partial regression coefficients. Each of these b's is referred to as a first-order partial regression coefficient, the order pertaining to the number of variables that are held constant, or partialed. With two independent variables, each b is of a first order because one variable is partialed in each case. With three independent variables, there are three second-order partial coefficients, as two variables are partialed in the calculation of each b. With k independent variables, the order of each b is $k - 1$. I will not use the notation of (5.23), as it is clear which variables are partialed.

In Chapter 2, I stated that dividing a b by its standard error yields a t ratio. The same is true in multiple regression analysis, where each b has a standard error associated with it. The standard error of b_1, for instance, when there are k independent variables, is

$$s_{b_{y1.2\ldots k}} = \sqrt{\frac{s^2_{y.12\ldots k}}{\Sigma x_1^2(1 - R^2_{1.2\ldots k})}} \qquad (5.24)$$

where $s_{b_{y1.2\ldots k}}$ = standard error of b_1; $s^2_{y.12\ldots k}$ = variance of estimate; Σx_1^2 = sum of squares of X_1; and $R^2_{1.2\ldots k}$ = squared multiple correlation of X_1, treated as a dependent variable, with X_2 to X_k as the independent variables. All other b's should be similarly treated. For the case of two independent variables,

$$s_{b_{y1.2}} = \sqrt{\frac{s^2_{y.12}}{\Sigma x_1^2(1 - r_{12}^2)}} \qquad s_{b_{y2.1}} = \sqrt{\frac{s^2_{y.12}}{\Sigma x_2^2(1 - r_{12}^2)}} \qquad (5.25)$$

The denominator of (5.24), or (5.25), reveals important aspects of tests of significance of b's, namely the effects of the correlations among the independent variables on the standard errors of the b's. I discuss the topic of high intercorrelations among independent variables in detail in Chapter 10 (see the "Collinearity" section). Here, I will only point out that the higher the intercorrelation among the independent variables, the larger the standard errors of the b's. It therefore follows that when the independent variables are highly intercorrelated, it may turn out that none of the b's is statistically significant when each is tested separately. Note, on the other hand, that when, for example, $r_{12} = 0$, the denominator of (5.25) reduces to Σx^2, as when a single independent variable is used—see (2.28) and the discussion related to it. These properties of s_b underscore the virtue of designing studies in which the independent variables are not correlated among themselves, as can be done in experimental research.

Test of R² versus Test of b.   Before illustrating calculations of standard errors of b's and their use in tests of significance, I elaborate on the distinction between the test of R^2 and the test of a given b in a multiple regression equation. I said earlier that the test of R^2 is tantamount to testing all the b's simultaneously. When testing a given b for significance, the question addressed is whether it differs from zero *while controlling for the effects of the other independent variables.* Clearly, the two tests are addressed to different questions.

Failure to distinguish between the purposes of the two tests has led some researchers to maintain that they might lead to contradictory or puzzling conclusions. For example, R^2 may be statistically significant, leading to the conclusion that at least one regression coefficient is statistically significant. Yet when each regression coefficient is tested separately, it may turn out that *none* is statistically significant. Earlier I alluded to a possible reason for such an occurrence—when the independent variables are highly intercorrelated the standard errors of the b's are relatively large. As long as the different questions addressed by the test of R^2 and by the test of a b are borne in mind, there should be no reason for puzzlement about seemingly contradictory results they may yield.[4]

Tests of b's for the Present Example.   Recall that

$$s_{y.12}^2 = \frac{ss_{res}}{N - k - 1} \tag{5.26}$$

where $s_{y.12}^2$ = variance of estimate; ss_{res} = residual sum of squares; N = sample size; and k = number of independent variables. For the present example (see calculations earlier in the chapter),

$$ss_{res} = 38.95$$

$$s_{y.12}^2 = \frac{38.95}{20 - 2 - 1} = 2.29$$

$$\Sigma x_1^2 = 102.55 \qquad \Sigma x_2^2 = 53.00$$

$$b_1 = .7046 \qquad b_2 = .5919 \qquad r_{12} = .522$$

$$s_{b_1} = \sqrt{\frac{2.29}{102.55(1 - .522^2)}} = .1752$$

$$t_{b_1} = \frac{b_1}{s_{b_1}} = \frac{.7046}{.1752} = 4.02$$

with 17 *df* (*df* associated with the variance of estimate: $N - k - 1$), $p < .05$.

$$s_{b_2} = \sqrt{\frac{2.29}{53.00(1 - .522^2)}} = .2437$$

$$t_{b_2} = \frac{b_2}{s_{b_2}} = \frac{.5919}{.2437} = 2.43$$

with 17 *df*, $p < .05$. Assuming that α (level of significance) = .05 was selected, it would be concluded that the effects of both independent variables on the dependent variable are statistically significant. *I remind you not to overlook the important distinction between statistically significant and substantively meaningful findings* (see Chapter 2).

Earlier in this chapter, I distinguished between b (unstandardized regression coefficient) and β (standardized regression coefficient) and pointed out that the former is applied to raw scores, whereas the latter is applied to standard scores. I do not show how to test β's inasmuch as the t (or F) for a given b is the same as the one that would be obtained when its corresponding β is tested (see formulas for getting β from b, and vice versa, earlier in this chapter). In short, testing a b is tantamount to testing its corresponding β.

---

[4]For a good discussion of the logic of tests of significance in multiple regression analysis, see Cramer (1972).

In Chapter 2, I discussed several factors that affect the precision of regression statistics. One of these factors is the variability of X as reflected by Σx^2. The effect of the variability of X in the present example may be noted from the two standard errors of the b's, given previously. Except for Σx^2, all other terms are identical in both standard errors. Since $\Sigma x_1^2 = 102.55$ and $\Sigma x_2^2 = 53.00$, the standard error of b_1 is smaller than the standard error of b_2. Other things equal, division by a smaller standard error will, of course, yield a larger t ratio.

Confidence Intervals.   In Chapter 2, I explained the idea and benefits of setting confidence intervals around the regression coefficient in simple regression analysis. The same approach is taken in multiple regression analysis, namely,

$$b \pm t_{(\alpha/2,\, df)} s_b$$

where t is the tabled t ratio at $\alpha/2$ with df associated with the variance of estimate, or the mean square residual; and s_b is the standard error of the b. For the present example, $df = 17$. Assuming it is desired to set the 95% confidence interval for the present example, the tabled t at .05/2 (.025) with 17 df is 2.11 (see table of t in statistics books, or take $\sqrt{F}$ with 1 and 17 df from Appendix B).

Using the results obtained in the preceding, 95% confidence intervals for the first and second regression coefficients, respectively, are

$$.7046 \pm (2.11)(.1752) = .3349 \text{ and } 1.0743$$

$$.5919 \pm (2.11)(.2437) = .0777 \text{ and } 1.1061$$

Note that, as expected based on the tests of significance of the two b's (see preceding), the confidence intervals do not include zero. Also, as expected based on the standard error of the b's, the confidence interval for b_1 is narrower than that for b_2.

Testing Increments in Proportion of Variance Accounted For.   In multiple regression analysis, an increment in the proportion of variance accounted for by a given variable, or a set of variables, can be tested. I discuss this approach in detail later in the text (notably Chapter 9). For now, I introduce some rudimentary ideas about this topic. The test for an increment in the proportion of variance accounted for is given by

$$F = \frac{(R_{y.12\ldots k_1}^2 - R_{y.12\ldots k_2}^2)/(k_1 - k_2)}{(1 - R_{y.12\ldots k_1}^2)/(N - k_1 - 1)} \tag{5.27}$$

where $R_{y.12\ldots k_1}^2$ = squared multiple correlation coefficient for the regression of Y on k_1 variables (the larger coefficient, referred to as the full model); $R_{y.12\ldots k_2}^2$ = squared multiple correlation for the regression of Y on k_2 variables, where k_2 = the smaller set of variables selected from among those of k_1 (referred to as the restricted model); and N = sample size. The F ratio has $k_1 - k_2\ df$ for the numerator and $N - k_1 - 1\ df$ for the denominator. Formula (5.27) could also be used to test increments in regression sum of squares. The test is, of course, identical, as a regression sum of squares is a product of a proportion of variance multiplied by the total sum of squares; for example,

$$ss_{\text{reg}(12\ldots k_1)} = (R_{y.12\ldots k_1}^2)\Sigma y^2$$

For the example under consideration, (5.27) can be used to test the increment due to X_2 (i.e., over and above what X_1 accounts for) and the increment due to X_1 (i.e., over and above X_2).

These are, respectively,

$$F = \frac{(R^2_{y.12} - R^2_{y.1})/(2-1)}{(1 - R^2_{y.12})/(N-2-1)}$$

and

$$F = \frac{(R^2_{y.12} - R^2_{y.2})/(2-1)}{(1 - R^2_{y.12})/(N-2-1)}$$

Earlier, I calculated $r_{y1} = R_{y.1} = .792$ and $r_{y2} = R_{y.2} = .678$. Thus, X_1 by itself accounts for about 63% ($.792^2$) of the variance of Y, and X_2 accounts for about 46% ($.678^2$) of the variance of Y. Together, the two variables account for about 72% of the variance ($R^2_{y.12} = .723$).

Testing the increment due to X_2,

$$F = \frac{(.723 - .6273)/(2-1)}{(1 - .723)/(20-2-1)} = \frac{.0957}{.0163} = 5.87$$

with 1 and 17 df, $p < .05$. Although, as I noted earlier, X_2 by itself accounts for about 46% of the variance of Y, its increment to the accounting of variance over X_1 is about 10% ($.0957$). This is to be expected, as some of the information X_1 and X_2 provide is redundant ($r_{12} = .522$). Clearly, the larger the correlation between the two variables, the smaller the increment in the proportion of variance accounted by either. Testing now the increment due to X_1,

$$F = \frac{(.723 - .4597)/(2-1)}{(1 - .723)/(20-2-1)} = \frac{.2633}{.0163} = 16.15$$

with 1 and 17 df, $p < .05$. Recall that by itself, X_1 accounted for about 62% of the variance of Y. Again, the reduction from 62% to 26% ($.2633$) reflects the correlation between X_1 and X_2.

For now, I will make two points about this procedure. One, testing the increment in proportion of variance accounted for by a single variable is equivalent to the test of the b associated with the variable. From earlier calculations, $b_1 = .7046$ with $t = 4.02$ (17 df) and $b_2 = .5919$ with $t = 2.43$ (17 df). Recall that $t = \sqrt{F}$, when F has one degree of freedom for the numerator. Using the above two F ratios, $\sqrt{16.15} = 4.01$ and $\sqrt{5.87} = 2.42$. To repeat, a test of a b is equivalent to a test of the increment in proportion of variance that is due to the variable with which it is associated. Two, the increment in the proportion of variance accounted for by a given variable (or by a set of variables) may be considerably different from the proportion of variance it accounts by itself, the difference being a function of the correlations of the variable with the other variables in the equation.

RELATIVE IMPORTANCE OF VARIABLES

Researchers use diverse approaches aimed at determining the relative importance of the independent variables under study. This is an extremely complex topic that I discuss later in the text (see, in particular, Chapters 9 and 10). Here, I comment briefly on the use of regression coefficients and increments in proportion of variance accounted for as indices of the relative importance of variables.

b's and β's

The magnitude of b is affected, in part, by the scale of measurement used to measure the variable with which the b is associated. Assume, for example, a simple linear regression in which X is length of objects measured in feet. Suppose that one were to express X in inches instead of feet. The nature of the regression of Y on X will, of course, not change, nor will the test of significance of the b. The magnitude of the b, however, will change considerably. In the present case, the b associated with X when measured in inches will be one-twelfth of the b when X is measured in feet. This should alert you to two things: (1) a relatively large b may be neither substantively meaningful nor statistically significant, whereas a relatively small b may be both meaningful and statistically significant, and (2) sizes of b's should *not* be used to infer the relative importance of the variables with which they are associated (see Chapter 10).

Incidentally, because b's are affected by the scales being used, it is necessary to carry out their calculations to several decimal places. For a given scale, the b may, for example, be .0003 and yet be substantively meaningful and statistically significant. Had one solved to two decimal places, this b would have been declared to equal zero (I give some such numerical examples in subsequent chapters). In general, it is suggested that calculations of regression analysis be carried out to as many decimal places as is feasible. Further rounding may be done at the end of the calculations.

Because of the incomparability of b's, researchers who wish to speak of the relative importance of variables resort to comparisons among β's, as they are based on standard scores. In the numerical example analyzed previously, $\beta_1 = .602$ and $\beta_2 = .364$. Thus one may wish to conclude that the effect of X_1 is more than 1.5 times as great as the effect of X_2. Broadly speaking, such an interpretation is legitimate, but it is not free of problems because the β's are affected, among other things, by the variability of the variable with which they are associated. Recall that $\beta = r$ in simple linear regression. In Chapter 2, I showed that while r, hence β, varied widely as a function of the variability of X, b remained constant (see Table 2.3 and the discussion related to it). The same principle operates in multiple regression analysis (for a discussion of this point, and numerical examples, see Chapter 10). My aim in the present discussion is only to alert you to the need for caution when comparing magnitudes of β's for the purpose of arriving at conclusions about the relative importance of variables. I postpone discussions of other issues regarding the interpretation of regression coefficients until after I give a more thorough presentation of multiple regression analysis.

Increment in Proportion of Variance Accounted For

I cannot discuss issues concerning the use of the increment in the proportion of variance accounted for by an independent variable as an indication of its relative importance without addressing the broader problem of variance partitioning—a topic to which I devote Chapter 9 in its entirety. All I will say here is that when the independent variables are intercorrelated, the proportion of variance incremented by a variable depends, among other things, on its point of entry into the regression analysis. Thus, when all the correlations among the variables are positive, the later the point of entry of a variable, the smaller the proportion of variance it is shown to account for in the dependent variable. Questions will undoubtedly come to your mind: How, then, does one determine the order of entry of the variables? Is there a "correct" order? As I show in Chapters 8 and 9, attempts to answer such questions are closely related to considerations of the theory that has generated the research and its focus—that is, explanation or prediction.

I can well imagine your sense of frustration at the lack of definitive answers to questions about the relative importance of variables. Yet, attempts to come to grips with such questions must be postponed until after multiple regression analysis has been explored in greater detail and depth. Only then will it become evident that there is more than one answer to such questions and that the ambiguity of some situations is not entirely resolvable.

COMPUTER ANALYSIS

Using computer packages I introduced in Chapter 4, I will analyze the numerical example I analyzed in preceding sections (Table 5.1).[5] First, I will present a detailed analysis through SPSS. Then, I will give listings of inputs for the other packages (BMDP, MINITAB, and SAS) and brief excerpts of output. Replicate my analysis using one or more of the computer programs available to you, and compare your output with mine. As I pointed out in Chapter 4, I introduce and discuss substantive issues in the context of commentaries on output. Therefore, *study the output and my commentaries on it, even when the specific program that generated the output is of no interest or is irrelevant to you.*

SPSS

Input

TITLE TABLE 5.1.   TWO INDEPENDENT VARIABLES.
DATA LIST FREE/Y,X1,X2.
BEGIN DATA
2 1 3
4 2 5   *[first two subjects]*
. . .
7 4 6   *[last two subjects]*
10 4 9
END DATA
LIST.
REGRESSION VAR Y,X1,X2/DES ALL/STAT ALL/DEP=Y/
    ENTER X1/ENTER X2/
    RESIDUALS OUTLIERS (COOK LEVER)/
    SCATTERPLOT (Y,X1)(Y,X2)(X1,X2)(*RES,*PRE)
    (*RES,X1)(*RES,X2)/
    SAVE COOK(COOK) LEVER(LEVER) DFBETA SDBETA/PARTIALPLOT/
    DEP Y/ENTER X2/ENTER X1.
PLOT /HSIZE=40/VSIZE=12/
    PLOT COOK LEVER WITH X1.
LIST COOK TO SDB2_1/FORMAT=NUMBERED.
TITLE TABLE 5.1. LAST CASE DELETED.
N 19.
REGRESSION VAR Y,X1,X2/DES ALL/STAT ALL/DEP=Y/
    ENTER X1/ENTER X2.

---

[5]If necessary, refer to Chapter 4 for a general orientation to the packages and to my practice in presenting and commenting on input and output.

Commentary

As I pointed out in Chapter 4, italicized comments in brackets (e.g., *[first two subjects]*), are *not* part of either the input or the output. As I gave an orientation to SPSS, with special emphasis on the use of REGRESSION, in Chapter 4, I will comment only on aspects of the input relevant to the analysis under consideration.

Examine the second line of the REGRESSION procedure and notice the two ENTER statements. Their effect is to enter the independent variables sequentially (X1 followed by X2), thereby enabling one to see how much of the variance of Y is accounted for by X1 and how much X2 adds over and above X1. Notice also that, several lines later, I reversed the order of entry of the variables (i.e., ENTER X2/ENTER X1). Entering variables, or blocks of variables, sequentially—often called hierarchical regression analysis—is probably the most misunderstood and abused approach in applications of multiple regression analysis. *Here, I use it solely to replicate my earlier analyses in this chapter.* In subsequent chapters (especially Chapters 9 and 10), I discuss hierarchical regression analysis in detail.

RESIDUALS Subcommand. Instead of specifying CASEWISE ALL, as in Chapter 4, I specified OUTLIERS for Cook's *D* and Leverage. As a result, the ten cases with the largest values for each of these indices will be listed. This approach, which I use here for illustrative purposes, is particularly useful when analyzing a large data set.

I will explain PARTIALPLOT when I reproduce output generated by it. For explanations of all other REGRESSION subcommands, see Chapter 4. The end of the REGRESSION procedure is signified by the period after X1 (see line preceding PLOT).

I then invoke two procedures: PLOT and LIST. In the former, I use HSIZE and VSIZE to specify the number of columns (horizontal) and number of rows (vertical) to be used in the plots. I call for the plotting of Cook's *D* and leverage against X1.

Following the LIST procedure, I invoke again the REGRESSION procedure. As I indicated in the TITLE, in this analysis I exclude the last subject. In my commentaries on the output generated by it, I explain why I do this analysis. Here it is convenient to exclude the last subject by specifying N 19. Various other approaches to subject selection (e.g., SELECT IF) are more useful in other circumstances.

Output

	Mean	Std Dev	Variance
Y	5.850	2.720	7.397
X1	4.350	2.323	5.397
X2	5.500	1.670	2.789

N of Cases =   20

Correlation, Covariance, Cross-Product:

	Y	X1	X2
Y	1.000	.792	.678
	7.397	5.003	3.079
	140.550	95.050	58.500
X1	.792	1.000	.522
	5.003	5.397	2.026
	95.050	102.550	38.500

X2	.678	.522	1.000
	3.079	2.026	2.789
	58.500	38.500	53.000

Commentary

I explained layout of this type of output in Chapter 4. To recapitulate briefly, though, each set of three rows in the second portion of the output is composed of correlations (first row), covariances or variances (second row), and deviation sum of cross products or sum of squares (third row). Following are some examples: (1) .792 (first row, second column) is the correlation between Y and X1; (2) 5.397 (fifth row, second column) is the variance of X1; (3) 38.500 (sixth row, third column) is the deviation sum of cross products of X1 and X2; and (4) 53.00 (ninth row, third column) is the deviation sum of squares of X2. Other terms are treated similarly.

Output

Equation Number 1   Dependent Variable. .   Y
Variable(s) Entered on Step Number 1. .   X1

					Analysis of Variance			
Multiple R	.79171					DF	Sum of Squares	Mean Square
R Square	.62681	R Square Change	.62681					
		F Change	30.23314	Regression		1	88.09851	88.09851
Standard Error	1.70704	Signif F Change	.0000	Residual		18	52.45149	2.91397

F =   30.23314   Signif F =   .0000

------------------------ Variables in the Equation ------------------------   ------------------ Variables not in the Equation ------------------

Variable	B	Beta	T	Sig T	Variable	Beta In	Partial	T	Sig T
X1	.926865	.791715	5.498	.0000	X2	.363476	.507417	2.428	.0266
(Constant)	1.818137		2.199	.0412					

Commentary

Notwithstanding some of the nomenclature (e.g., Multiple R), these results refer to a simple regression analysis, as only one independent variable (X1) was entered at this step. Thus, for example, .79171 is the Pearson correlation between Y and X1. I explained procedures for tests of significance in simple regression analysis in Chapter 2 and will therefore not comment on them here.

When only some of the independent variables are entered into the analysis, SPSS reports statistics for Variables in the Equation and Variables not in the Equation. I reproduced here *excerpts* from this output. Examine first the Variables in the Equation. B refers to the unstandardized regression coefficient (i.e., *b*). Constant refers to the intercept (*a*). Thus, the regression equation for Y on X1 is

$$Y' = 1.82 + .93X_1$$

Recall that dividing *b* by its standard error (not reproduced here) yields a *t* ratio: 5.498, with $N - k - 1$ *df* (18, in the present example) or *df* associated with the mean square residuals (*MSR*), as indicated in the output. As I explained earlier in this chapter, $t^2 = F$ with 1 *df* for the numerator and $N - k - 1$ *df* for the denominator. Accordingly, $5.498^2 = 30.228$, which is, within rounding, the same as the *F* reported under the Analysis of Variance portion of the output. Signif F refers to the probability of obtaining an *F* ratio of this size or larger, given that the null hypothesis is true. As SPSS reports this probability to four decimal places, one would conclude with $p < .0001$ that $b = 0$. Stated differently, the null hypothesis that $b = 0$ would be rejected at the indicated α level.

The foregoing should be not construed as an attempt to explain the logic of tests of significance. All I meant to do is give a rough explanation of the output. I assume that you are familiar with the major issues and controversies concerning statistical tests of significance (e.g., Type I and Type II errors, effect size, sample size). I reviewed briefly this topic in Chapter 2 (see "Tests of Significance"), where I also gave references for further study.

Beta in the preceding output refers to the standardized regression coefficient (β). Earlier in this chapter—see (5.10)–(5.13) and the discussion related to them—I pointed out, among other things, that in an equation with one independent variable, $\beta = r$. Examine the preceding output and notice that Beta for the variable in the equation is equal to Multiple R which, as I pointed out above, is *r* in the present case.

Look now at the variables *not* in the equation. "Beta In" means the Beta that would be obtained when X2 is added to the analysis. In addition, the *t* ratio (2.428) with its associated probability (.0266) for this Beta are reported (see also next excerpt of output). Again, my purpose here is solely to acquaint you with the output, *not to imply that a decision whether or not to add the variable, and how to interpret the results of such an addition, are simple and straightforward.* Earlier, I commented briefly on this topic and pointed out that I will discuss it in detail in Chapter 10.

Later, I explain the information reported under Partial.

Output

Variable(s) Entered on Step Number 2. . X2

				Analysis of Variance		
Multiple R	.85023					
R Square	.72290	R Square Change	.09609		DF	Sum of Squares	Mean Square
		F Change	5.89475	Regression	2	101.60329	50.80164
Standard Error	1.51360	Signif F Change	.0266	Residual	17	38.94671	2.29098

$F = 22.17461$ Signif F $= .0000$

------------ Variables in the Equation ------------

Variable	B	SE B	95% Confdnce Intrvl B		Beta	Correl	Part Cor	Partial	T	Sig T
X1	.704647	.175263	.334874	1.074420	.601900	.791715	.513306	.698143	4.021	.0009
X2	.591907	.243793	.077549	1.106265	.363476	.677801	.309976	.507417	2.428	.0266
(Constant)	−.470705	1.194154	−2.990149	2.048739					−.394	.6984

Commentary

I trust that you will have no difficulty identifying and interpreting most of this output, as I gave the same results earlier (see my hand calculations) and commented on them. Therefore, I limit my comments here to several specific issues.

R Square Change refers to the change in the squared multiple correlation as a result of adding X2 to the equation. As I showed earlier, it is the difference between $R^2_{y.12}$ and $R^2_{y.1}$ (i.e.,

.72290 − .62681); and the F Change (5.89475) is the F ratio for the test of significance of this increment—see (5.27) and the discussion related to it, where I obtained the same F, within rounding.

Earlier, I reported, and commented on, the regression equation, the confidence intervals of the b's, and the Beta coefficients. Note that Beta for X2 and its associated T ratio are the same as those reported in the preceding segment of output under Variables not in the Equation.

Correl is the Pearson correlation between the dependent variable and the independent variable on the given line. Compare with my earlier calculations and with the first segment of the output given in the preceding.

I discuss Part Cor(relation), also referred to as semipartial correlation, in Chapter 7. For now, I will only point out that the squared part correlation is equal to the proportion of variance that will be added (incremented) when the variable with which it is associated is entered last in the analysis. Thus, $.309976^2 = .09609$, which is the same as the R Square Change reported above when X2 is entered after X1. Earlier I showed that X1 by itself (first step of output) accounts for .62681 (or about 63%) of the variance of Y. The squared Part Cor for X1 ($.513306^2 = .26348$) indicates that if X1 were entered after X2 it would add about 26% to the variance accounted for (see output reported in the following). The marked difference between the proportion of variance X1 accounts for when it enters first or second is, of course, due to its correlation with X2. Had the correlation between the two variables been zero, X2 (and X1) would have accounted for the same proportion of variance (equal to the squared correlation with the dependent variable), re-gardless of their point of entry into the analysis. This important point is part of the general topic of variance partitioning, which I present in Chapter 9.

Partial is the partial correlation. In Chapter 7, I give a detailed discussion of partial correlation and its relation to part correlation.

Output

Summary table

Step	Variable	MultR	Rsq	F(Eqn)	SigF	RsqCh	FCh	SigCh
1	In: X1	.7917	.6268	30.233	.000	.6268	30.233	.000
2	In: X2	.8502	.7229	22.175	.000	.0961	5.895	.027

Commentary

The preceding is an excerpt from the summary table. As you can see, this is a handy summary from which the results of the analysis can be gleaned at a glance. This being a summary, it goes without saying that the information given has been reported earlier. I suggest that you examine elements of this table in conjunction with output given earlier or with output you obtained from your run.

At each step, the program reports which variable(s) was entered (In)[6] and its effect. F(Eqn) is the F ratio for the test of the b's for the variables that are in the equation up to and including the step in question (equivalently, it is the test of Rsq[uared] up to that point). Thus, 30.233 is the test of the b for X1, or the test of .6268 (Rsq), whereas 22.175 is the test of the b's for X1 *and* X2, or the test of .7229 (Rsq). In contrast, FCh(ange) is the F ratio for the increment in the proportion of variance accounted for by the variable(s) in question at the given point—Rsq(uared)Ch(ange). In

---

[6]SPSS places the information reported under Variable at the end of the lines. For convenience, I moved this information to its current position.

view of the fact that X1 is the first variable to enter, Rsq and RsqCh are equal, as are F(Eqn) and FCh. In contrast, at the second step F(Eqn) differs from FCh, as the former refers to the test of Rsq due to X1 *and* X2 and the latter refers to the increment in the proportion of variance due to X2 when it is entered after X1.

Output

Outliers -- Cook's Distance			Outliers -- Leverage	
Case #	*COOK D		Case #	*LEVER
20	.84038		20	.34331
9	.18391		16	.25111
3	.17941		3	.14947
10	.15172		1	.14947
4	.08533		11	.14674
17	.06915		10	.14309
12	.06682		15	.13035
14	.06225		9	.12725
8	.05496		4	.11096
11	.03408		17	.10342

Commentary

SPSS reports the indices in descending order of magnitude, making it easy to identify extreme cases. As I discussed Cook's D and leverage in Chapter 4, I will only point out that case #20 (the last subject) differs from the others, particularly on Cook's D.

Output

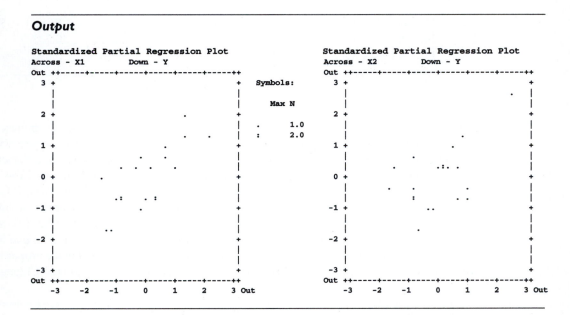

Commentary

Although I called for additional plots (see Input), in the interest of space I did not reproduce them. If, as I suggested earlier, you ran the data, then you may want to study the other plots. You will find that the data do not seem to contain serious irregularities.

My comments here are limited to the Partial Regression Plots, reproduced previously.[7] I will explain the meaning and benefits of such plots in the context of the current example. In partial regression plots, residuals, *not* original data, are plotted. For example, referring to the plot on the left, residuals of Y are plotted against residuals of X1. What this means is that the dependent variable and each independent variable are, in turn, regressed on all remaining variables (X2 in the present case) to obtain the residuals, which are then plotted (SPSS does this with standardized residuals).[8]

The reasoning behind this approach is that residuals of a given variable are *not* correlated with the independent variable(s), or predictor(s), used to obtain them.[9] Thus, residuals of Y are not correlated with the variable used to generate them (X2 in the example in question). Similarly, residuals of X1 are not correlated with X2. Another way of stating this is that X2 was partialed from Y and X1, hence the residuals of these two variables have nothing in common with X2. Now, if the residuals of X1 are shown to be correlated with the residuals of Y, then this correlation is independent of X2. In other words, Y and X1 are correlated after controlling for or partialing X2, thereby indicating that X1 would enhance the prediction of Y, after the contribution of X2 has been taken into account. This is why some authors (e.g., Cook & Weisberg, 1982, pp. 44–50) refer to the plots under consideration as "added variable plots." Others (e.g., Belsley et al., 1980, p. 30) prefer the term "partial-regression leverage plot." And, "at the risk of further confusion," Welsch (1986, p. 403) proposed "adjusted partial residual plot."

Examine now the two partial regression plots given earlier, and notice that after partialing X2 from Y and X1 (plot on the left) there is a fairly clear linear relation between the residuals, indicating that adding X1 after X2 would lead to a noticeable improvement in predicting Y. When, however, X1 is partialed from Y and X2 (plot on the right), the relation between the residuals seems to be primarily due to a single influential subject, namely case #20 (the point in the upper right-hand corner; recall that this case had a relatively large Cook's D; see also the following plots of Cook's D and leverage with X1). Notice that the scatter of remaining points appears almost random. I will return to this issue in my commentary of the analysis from which I removed the last subject.

Output

Equation Number 2   Dependent Variable. .   Y
Variable(s) Entered on Step Number 1. .   X2

						Analysis of Variance	
Multiple R	.67780						
R Square	.45941	R Square Change	.45941		DF	Sum of Squares	Mean Square
		F Change	15.29725	Regression	1	64.57075	64.57075
Standard Error	2.05452	Signif F Change	.0010	Residual	18	75.97925	4.22107

F =   15.29725   Signif F =   .0010

---

[7]For discussions of other diagnostic plots, see the references that follow.
[8]For comparative purposes, I use MINITAB, later on, to generate residuals (unstandardized) and plot them.
[9]For a detailed discussion of this topic, along with numerical examples, see Chapter 7.

---------------------------- Variables in the Equation ----------------------------   ------------- Variables not in the Equation -------------

Variable	B	Beta	T	Sig T	Variable	Beta In	T	Sig T
X2	1.103774	.677801	3.911	.0010	X1	.601900	4.021	.0009
(Constant)	−.220755		−.136	.8930				

Variable(s) Entered on Step Number 2. .   X1

					Analysis of Variance		
Multiple R	.85023						
R Square	.72290	R Square Change	.26348		DF	Sum of Squares	Mean Square
		F Change	16.16447	Regression	2	101.60329	50.80164
Standard Error	1.51360	Signif F Change	.0009	Residual	17	38.94671	2.29098
				F =	22.17461	Signif F =	.0000

--- Variables in the Equation ---

Variable	B	SE B	95% Confdnce Intrvl B		Beta	T	Sig T	Part Cor
X1	.704647	.175263	.334874	1.074420	.601900	4.021	.0009	.513306
X2	.591907	.243793	.077549	1.106265	.363476	2.428	.0266	.309976
(Constant)	−.470705	1.194154	−2.990149	2.048739		−.394	.6984	

Summary table

Step	Variable	MultR	Rsq	F(Eqn)	SigF	RsqCh	FCh	SigCh
2	In: X2	.6778	.4594	15.297	.001	.4594	15.297	.001
1	In: X1	.8502	.7229	22.175	.000	.2635	16.164	.001

Commentary

The preceding are excerpts from the second analysis in which I reversed the order of entry of the variables (see my commentary on the input). That is, I entered X2 first, and then I entered X1. As expected, when X2 enters first, the proportion of variance it accounts for is equal to the square of its correlation with Y (i.e., .46; see R Square at the first step or in the summary table). In contrast, when this variable entered second it accounted for only about 10% of the variance (see the earlier analysis). In the present analysis, the proportion of variance X1 accounts for, over and above that accounted by X2, is about 26% (see R Square Change in the second step or in the summary table). Contrast this with the 63% of the variance accounted for by this variable when it entered first. Note, however, that the overall proportion of variance accounted for, that is, R^2 of Y with all the independent variables (two, in the present example), is the same (.7229), regardless of the order in which the variables are entered. In other words, the order of entry of the variables in the analysis does *not* affect the overall R^2, but rather what portion of it is attributed to each variable.

Earlier I pointed out that the squared part correlation indicates the proportion of variance that the variable with which it is associated accounts for when the variable is entered last in the analysis. For X2, $.309976^2 = .09609$, the proportion of variance it accounted for when it entered second (compare with R Square Change in the second step of the first analysis). For X1, $.513306^2 = .26348$, the proportion of variance it accounted for when it entered second (compare with R Square Change in the second step of the current analysis).

To reiterate: when, as in the present example, the independent variables, or predictors, are correlated, the proportion of variance a given variable is shown to account for will vary, depending on its point of entry into the analysis. As I pointed out earlier, I discuss this topic in Chapter 9.

Earlier in this chapter, I discussed tests of regression coefficients and of increments in proportion of variance accounted for by a given variable. For present purposes, therefore, I will only remind you that each b indicates the expected change in the dependent variable associated with a unit change in the variable in question, while controlling for the remaining independent variables (this is why the b's are referred to as partial regression coefficients). It follows that a test of a b is equivalent to the test of the proportion of variance the variable with which it is associated accounts for when it is entered last in the analysis. Thus, T^2 for each b in the preceding output is equal to the F for the corresponding R Square Change. For the test of the b associated with X2, $2.428^2 = 5.895$, which is the same as the F ratio for R Square Change in the second step of the first analysis. For the test of the b associated with X1, $4.021^2 = 16.168$, which is the same as the F ratio for R Square Change in the second step of the current analysis. In light of the preceding it should come as no surprise that, when all the variables are in the equation, tests of the b's are the same regardless of the order in which the variables were entered. Compare the output given here with that given earlier, when X1 entered first. Lest you think that I am belaboring the obvious, I suggest that you peruse Chapter 10 where I give research examples of confusion and misconceptions about tests of regression coefficients.

Output

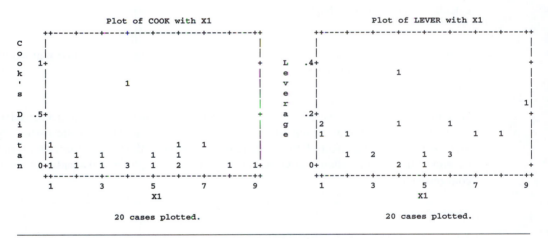

Commentary

I generated the preceding by the PLOT procedure (see Input). Examine the plots and notice that on both indices, but especially on Cook's D, one subject whose X1 = 4 is set apart from all the rest. If you looked back at the output for the outliers, you would see that it is Case #20—the last subject in the input file (see also, the next excerpt of output).

Output

Case#	COOK	LEVER	DFB0_1	DFB1_1	DFB2_1	SDB0_1	SDB1_1	SDB2_1
1	.00000	.14947	−.00382	.00025	.00039	−.00311	.00137	.00155
2	.00020	.05764	.01271	−.00304	.00113	.01033	−.01684	.00451
.	.	.	.	.	.	.	.	.
19	.01232	.01154	.00177	−.01122	.01921	.00146	−.06314	.07775
20	.84038	.34331	−1.14755	−.14862	.36103	−1.06158	−.93675	1.63591

Commentary

I introduced DFBETA and DFBETAS (standardized) in Chapter 3 for the case of simple linear regression. To recapitulate: $DFBETA_{j(i)}$ indicates the change in j (intercept or regression coefficient) as a consequence of deleting subject i. In Chapter 4, I reproduced, and commented on, computer output of such indices for simple linear regression. If necessary, review relevant sections in the aforementioned chapters.

In multiple regression analysis, DFBETAs are calculated for each independent variable, as well as for the intercept. In the above output, DFB refers to DFBETA whereas SDB refers to DFBETAS (standardized; see Chapter 3 for an explanation of the nomenclature used). For example, DFB1_1 is DFBETA associated with X1, whereas SDB2_1 is DEFBETAS associated with X2.

The results given earlier, notably Cook's D, led me to focus on the last subject (case #20). If I were inclined to delete this subject, then the output given above would tell me the nature of the changes that would ensue. For convenience, I repeat the regression equation for the entire group, calculated earlier in this chapter and also reported in the SPSS output:

$$Y' = -.470705 + .704647X_1 + .591907X_2$$

Using the DFBETAs associated with the last subject, the regression equation that would be obtained if this subject were deleted is

$$Y' = .67685 + .85327X_1 + .23088X_2$$

Note that deletion of the last subject would result in a slight increase in b_1 and a considerable decrease in b_2, reinforcing the notions gathered from the examination of the partial regression plots, namely that the effect of X_2 is largely due to a single influential subject (#20). In the next excerpt of the output, I show that when this subject is deleted, b_2 is statistically not significant at conventional levels.

Output

TABLE 5.1. LAST CASE DELETED
Equation Number 1   Dependent Variable. .   Y
Variable(s) Entered on Step Number 1. .   X1

					Analysis of Variance		
Multiple R	.86250						
R Square	.74391	R Square Change	.74391		DF	Sum of Squares	Mean Square
		F Change	49.38255	Regression	1	91.07008	91.07008
Standard Error	1.35800	Signif F Change	.0000	Residual	17	31.35098	1.84418
				F =	49.38255	Signif F =	.0000

```
----------------------------- Variables in the Equation -----------------------------
```

Variable	B	SE B	T	Sig T
X1	.942960	.134186	7.027	.0000
(Constant)	1.512333	.663829	2.278	.0359

Variable(s) Entered on Step Number 2. .   X2

						Analysis of Variance		
Multiple R	.86870							
R Square	.75464	R Square Change	.01073		DF	Sum of Squares	Mean Square	
		F Change	.69986	Regression	2	92.38394	46.19197	
Standard Error	1.37015	Signif F Change	.4152	Residual	16	30.03711	1.87732	
				F =	24.60528	Signif F =	.0000	

```
----------------------------- Variables in the Equation -----------------------------
```

Variable	B	SE B	T	Sig T
X1	.853265	.172699	4.941	.0001
X2	.230881	.275983	.837	.4152
(Constant)	.676841	1.202495	.563	.5813

Commentary

Except for the fact that the last case was deleted, the format of the output here is the same as that I reproduced earlier. Accordingly, I focus on the second step only. Notice that when entered after X1, X2 accounts for about 1% of the variance of Y and that this increment is statistically not significant at conventional levels of significance (see R Square Change, F Change, and Signif F Change). Examine now the Variables in the Equation and notice that (1) the regression equation is the same as I calculated above, using DFBETAs for the last case; and (2) the regression coefficient for X2 is statistically not significant. The latter piece of information is, of course, the same as obtained from R Square Change and the F Change (as I explained earlier, $T^2 = F$).

Incidentally, if you replicated this analysis and called also for a residual analysis, you would find that, for instance, all values of Cook's D are relatively small, the largest being .20 for subject #7. In sum, then, as expected from the diagnostic results based on the analysis of the data for all the subjects, the effect of X2 is drastically diminished when the last case is deleted.

Having found in this analysis that b_2 is statistically not significant, the idea of deleting X_2 from the analysis suggests itself. I discuss considerations in making such a decision in subsequent chapters (e.g., Chapter 10). Here, I will only point out that if I decided to delete X_2, then I would interpret the simple regression equation obtained in step 1 above.

Referring to the substantive example I used when I introduced these data (see the discussion of Table 5.1 presented earlier in this chapter), I would, for example, conclude that the expected change in reading achievement associated with a unit change in verbal aptitude is .85. Further, that achievement motivation seems to have no effect on reading achievement. *Recall, however, that the data are fictitious.*

Before turning to the other computer programs, I would like to suggest that you carry out additional analyses that will, I believe, help you better understand the material I presented thus far. In particular, I recommend that you use SPSS to (1) regress Y on X1 and save the residuals, labeling them Y.X1; (2) regress X2 on X1 and save the residuals, labeling them X2.X1; (3) regress

Y.X1 on X2.X1; and (4) plot Y.X1 against X2.X1. Following is an example of control statements to carry out the suggested analyses.

Input

```
REGRESSION VAR Y,X1,X2/DES ALL/STAT ALL/
   DEP Y/ENTER X1/SAVE RESID(Y.X1)/
   DEP X2/ENTER X1/SAVE RESID(X2.X1).
REGRESSION VAR Y.X1 X2.X1/DES ALL/
   DEP Y.X1/ENTER X2.X1.
PLOT VSIZE=15/HSIZE=50/VERTICAL='Y.X1'/
   HORIZONTAL='X2.X1'/
   PLOT Y.X1 WITH X2.X1.
```

Commentary

In the preceding, I did *not* include control statements for reading in the data, as they are the same as those I used earlier. Note that, with slight adjustments, the preceding can be incorporated in the input file I used earlier. Whichever way you run the preceding, study the results and compare them with those given earlier.[10] Among other things, you will find that b for the regression of Y.X1 on X2.X1 is .5919, which is the same as the b for X2 when Y was regressed on X1 and X2 earlier in this section. Also, the residual sum of squares in the suggested analysis is 38.9467, which is the same as that reported earlier when Y was regressed on X1 and X2. Finally, a comparison of the plot from the suggested analysis with the corresponding partial regression plot from the earlier analysis should also prove instructive, especially as standardized residuals were used in the earlier analysis.

BMDP

Input

```
/PROBLEM TITLE IS 'TABLE 5.1'.
/INPUT VARIABLES ARE 3. FORMAT IS FREE. FILE IS 'T51.DAT'.
/VARIABLE NAMES ARE Y,X1,X2.
/REGRESS DEPEND IS Y. INDEP=X1,X2. LEVEL=0,1,2.
/PRINT COVA. CORR. DATA.
 DIAG=HATDIAG,RESIDUAL,STRESID,DELRESID,DSTRESID,COOK.
/PLOT RESID. XVAR=X1,X1. YVAR=COOK,HATDIAG.
 SIZE=44,12.
/END
/END
/PROBLEM TITLE IS 'TABLE 5.1. LAST CASE OMITTED'.
/INPUT
/REGRESS SETNAMES=BOTH. BOTH=X1,X2.
/TRANSFORM OMIT=20.
/END
```

---

[10]You can also compare your results with excerpts from a similar MINITAB analysis I reproduce later.

Commentary

This input is for program 2R. See Chapter 4 for an orientation to BMDP and to basic elements of 2R.

INPUT. For illustrative purposes, I placed the data in an external file (see FILE IS 'T51.DAT'). This is particularly useful when, as in the present case, multiple problems are processed (see Dixon, 1992, Vol. 1, Chapter 9).

REGRESS. LEVEL is used to specify the order in which the variables are to enter into the equation. The zero is for the dependent variable, 1 is for X1, and 2 is for X2. Accordingly, X1 will enter first.

PLOT. I called for residual plots and plots of COOK (Cook's D) and HATDIAG (diagonal of the hat matrix; in Chapter 3, I pointed out that this is another term for leverage) against X1.

As I stated earlier, the present example is composed of two problems. For conventions for running multiple problems, see Dixon (1992, Vol. 1, Chapter 9). In the second problem, I reanalyzed the data after deleting the last subject. I used TRANSFORMATION OMIT=20 to omit case #20. To enter X1 and X2 together in the analysis, I used SETNAMES (see Dixon, 1992, Vol. 1, pp. 408–409).

Output

BMDP2R -- STEPWISE REGRESSION
TABLE 5.1
STEP NO.   1

VARIABLE ENTERED   2 X1

MULTIPLE R	0.7917
MULTIPLE R-SQUARE	0.6268
STD. ERROR OF EST.	1.7070

ANALYSIS OF VARIANCE

	SUM OF SQUARES	DF	MEAN SQUARE	F RATIO
REGRESSION	88.098540	1	88.09854	30.23
RESIDUAL	52.451460	18	2.913970	

VARIABLES IN EQUATION FOR Y

VARIABLE	COEFFICIENT	STD. ERROR OF COEFF	STD REG COEFF
(Y-INTERCEPT	1.81814)		
X1 2	0.92687	0.1686	0.792

STEP NO.   2

VARIABLE ENTERED   3 X2

MULTIPLE R	0.8502
MULTIPLE R-SQUARE	0.7229
STD. ERROR OF EST.	1.5136

ANALYSIS OF VARIANCE

	SUM OF SQUARES	DF	MEAN SQUARE	F RATIO
REGRESSION	101.60330	2	50.80165	22.17
RESIDUAL	38.946690	17	2.290982	

VARIABLES IN EQUATION FOR Y

VARIABLE		COEFFICIENT	STD. ERROR OF COEFF	STD REG COEFF	F TO REMOVE
(Y-INTERCEPT		−0.47071)			
X1	2	0.70465	0.1753	0.602	16.16
X2	3	0.59191	0.2438	0.363	5.89

SUMMARY TABLE

STEP NO.	VARIABLE ENTERED	MULTIPLE R	RSQ	CHANGE IN RSQ	F TO ENTER
1	2 X1	0.7917	0.6268	0.6268	30.23
2	3 X2	0.8502	0.7229	0.0961	5.89

```
    ...+....+....+....+....+....+....+....+...         ...+....+....+....+....+....+....+....+...
C   -                                   -   H   -                                          -
O   -                                   -   A   -                                          -
O  1.0 +                                +   T  .4 +            1                            +
K   -                                   -   D   -                                          -
    -             1                     -   I   -                                        1 -
    -                                   -   A   -                                          -
    -                                   -   G   -                                          -
  .50 +                                 +     .2 + 2            1        1        1         +
    -                                   -       - 1  1         1                 1         -
    -                                   -       -    1         1           1              -
    - 1                 1   1           -       -            2  1    1    2                 -
    - 1   1   1     1   1               -       -            1   1                          -
  0.0 + 1   1   1   3   1   2     1   1 +     0. +                                          +
    ...+....+....+....+....+....+....+....+...         ...+....+....+....+....+....+....+....+...
      1       3       5       7       9             1       3       5       7       9
          2       4       6       8                     2       4       6       8

                  X1                                            X1
```

2R TABLE 5.1.   LAST CASE OMITTED

NUMBER OF CASES READ   20
CASES WITH USE SET TO ZERO   1
REMAINING NUMBER OF CASES   19

VARIABLES IN EQUATION FOR Y

VARIABLE		COEFFICIENT	STD. ERROR OF COEFF	STD REG COEFF
(Y-INTERCEPT		0.67684)		
SET BOTH				
X1	2	0.85327	0.1727	0.780
X2	3	0.23088	0.2760	0.132

Commentary

In line with my earlier statement, I reproduced only brief excerpts of the output. If you are using this program, compare your output with the SPSS output I reproduced in the preceding section. When in doubt, reread my commentaries on the SPSS output and on my hand calculations. Here, I comment only on F TO REMOVE and F TO ENTER. These terms are used primarily in stepwise regression analysis—an approach I discuss in detail in Chapter 8. Although 2R was designed for stepwise regression analysis, it can be used for other types of analyses (see Chapter 4).

F TO REMOVE is essentially a test of the regression coefficient with which it is associated. Thus, 16.16 is for the test of b_1, and 5.89 is for the test of b_2. Each of these F ratios has 1 and $N - k - 1$ df (17, in the present example) or df for the mean square residuals (*MSR;* see output). Recall that when F has 1 df for the numerator, $t^2 = F$. For the present example, the corresponding t's are 4.02 and 2.43, respectively, which are the values I obtained earlier in this chapter (see "Tests of Regression Coefficients"; see also the SPSS output in the preceding section).

F TO ENTER is essentially a test of the R^2 change associated with a given variable. Thus, 30.23 is for the test of proportion of variance accounted for by X1 (.6268), whereas 5.89 is for the test of the proportion of variance incremented by X2 (0.0961). I obtained these values several times earlier. See, for example, RsqCh and FCh in the Summary Table of the SPSS output in the preceding section.

Finally, recall that the test of a b is equivalent to the test of the proportion of variance accounted for by a variable when it is entered last in the analysis. This is why F TO REMOVE and the F TO ENTER for X2 are identical (5.89).

MINITAB

Input

```
GMACRO
T51
OUTFILE='T51.MIN';
   NOTERM.
NOTE TABLE 5.1
READ C1-C3;
   FILE 'T51.DAT'.          [reading data from external file]
NAME C1 'Y' C2 'X1' C3 'X2'
ECHO
DESCRIBE C1-C3
CORRELATION C1-C3
COVARIANCE C1-C3 M1
PRINT M1
NOTE M1 IS A COVARIANCE MATRIX
BRIEF 3                   [maximum output]
REGRESS C1 2 C2-C3 C4-C5;
   RESIDUALS C6;
   HI C7;
   COOKD C8.
```

```
NAME C5 'FITS' C6 'RESIDS' C7 'LEVER' C8 'COOKD'
PRINT C4-C8
GSTD
WIDTH 50
PLOT C6 C5
PLOT C7 C2
PLOT C8 C2
REGRESS C1 1 C2;          [regress Y on X1]
   RESIDUALS C9.          [put residuals in C9]
REGRESS C3 1 C2;          [regress X2 on X1]
   RESIDUALS C10.         [put residuals in C10]
NAME C9 'Y.X1' C10 'X2.X1'
PRINT C9-C10
PLOT C9 C10               [partial regression plot]
DELETE 20 C1-C3           [delete case number 20. MINITAB, 1995a, p. 6–2]
PRINT C1-C3
NOTE CASE NUMBER 20 DELETED
REGRESS C1 2 C2-C3 C4-C5
ENDMACRO
```

Commentary

For an orientation to MINITAB, see Chapter 4, where I commented on many of the commands I use here. As MINITAB does not have an option for partial regression plots, I show how this can be accomplished with relative ease by generating the relevant residuals and plotting them.

Output

The regression equation is
Y = −0.47 + 0.705 X1 + 0.592 X2

Predictor	Coef	Stdev	t-ratio	p
Constant	−0.471	1.194	−0.39	0.698
X1	0.7046	0.1753	4.02	0.001
X2	0.5919	0.2438	2.43	0.027

s = 1.514   R-sq = 72.3%

Analysis of Variance

SOURCE	DF	SS	MS	F	p
Regression	2	101.603	50.802	22.17	0.000
Error	17	38.947	2.291		
Total	19	140.550			

SOURCE	DF	SEQ SS
X1	1	88.099
X2	1	13.505

Commentary

SEQ SS = sequential sum of squares, that is, the sum of squares incremented by a given variable at its point of entry into the analysis. Thus, 88.099 is the sum of squares of Y accounted for by X1, and 13.505 is the sum of squares *incremented* by X2 (i.e., what X2 accounts for over and above X1). Thus, SEQ SS constitute a hierarchical regression analysis.

To transform SEQ SS to proportions of variance accounted for, divide each by the total sum of squares: 140.550. Thus, 88.099/140.550 = .627 and 13.505/140.550 = .096. The sum of these two proportions is, of course, $R^2_{y.12}$. I obtained the preceding values several times earlier (see "Testing Increments in Proportion of Variance Accounted For," earlier in this chapter; see also relevant SPSS and BMDP output and commentaries).

Output

RESIDS	LEVER	COOKD	
−0.00966	0.199474	0.000004	
0.10187	0.107642	0.000204	*[first two subjects]*
.	.	.	
1.10067	0.061537	0.012316	*[last two subjects]*
2.32495	0.393306	0.840381	

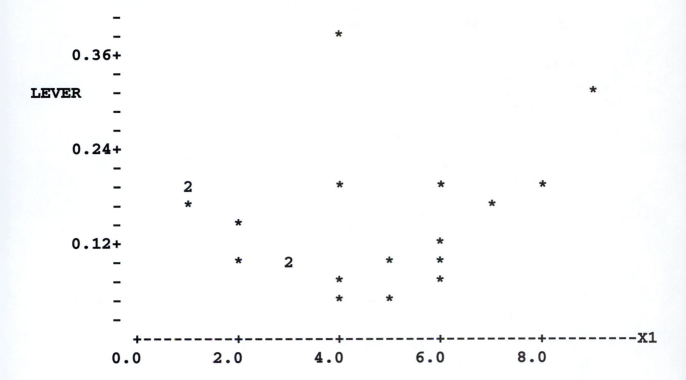

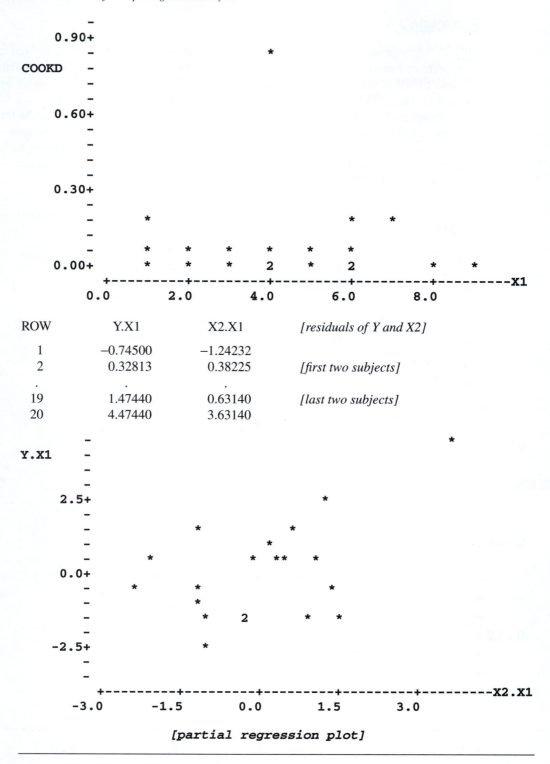

ROW	Y.X1	X2.X1	[residuals of Y and X2]
1	−0.74500	−1.24232	
2	0.32813	0.38225	[first two subjects]
.	.	.	
19	1.47440	0.63140	[last two subjects]
20	4.47440	3.63140	

[partial regression plot]

Commentary

Although the terminology and the layout of the preceding output differ somewhat from those of SPSS and BMDP, you should have no difficulties in understanding it. If necessary, reread relevant comments on output from the aforementioned programs, notably SPSS.

SAS

Input

```
TITLE 'TABLE 5.1';
DATA T51;
   INPUT Y X1 X2;
   CARDS;
2  1  3
4  2  5          [first two subjects]
 .   .   .
7  4  6          [last two subjects]
10  4  9
;
PROC PRINT;
PROC REG;
   MODEL Y=X1 X2/ALL R INFLUENCE PARTIAL;
RUN;
TITLE 'SECOND RUN AFTER DELETING CASES WITH COOK D >.5';
   REWEIGHT COOKD. >.5;
   PRINT;
RUN;
```

Commentary

For an orientation to SAS and its PROC REG, see Chapter 4. Here, I will only point out that for illustrative purposes I use the REWEIGHT command with the condition that cases whose Cook's D is greater than .5 be excluded from the analysis (see SAS Institute Inc., 1990a, Vol. 2, pp. 1381–1384, for a detailed discussion of REWEIGHT). Given the values of Cook's D for the present data, this will result in the exclusion of the last subject, thus yielding results similar to those I obtained from analyses with the other computer programs. PRINT calls for the printing of results of this second analysis.

Output

TABLE 5.1
Dependent Variable: Y

Analysis of Variance

Source	DF	Sum of Squares	Mean Square	F Value	Prob>F
Model	2	101.60329	50.80164	22.175	0.0001
Error	17	38.94671	2.29098		
C Total	19	140.55000			

[C Total = Corrected Total Sum of Squares]

Root MSE	1.51360	R-square	0.7229		
Dep Mean	5.85000				

Parameter Estimates

Variable	DF	Parameter Estimate	Standard Error	T for H0: Parameter=0	Prob > |T|	Type I SS	Type II SS	Standardized Estimate	Squared Semi-partial Corr Type I	Squared Semi-partial Corr Type II
INTERCEP	1	−0.470705	1.19415386	−0.394	0.6984				.	.
X1	1	0.704647	0.17526329	4.021	0.0009	88.098513	37.032535	0.60189973	0.62681261	0.26348300
X2	1	0.591907	0.24379278	2.428	0.0266	13.504777	13.504777	0.36347633	0.09608522	0.09608522

Commentary

You should have no difficulty with most of the preceding, especially if you compare it with output I presented earlier from other packages. Accordingly, I comment only on Type I and II SS and their corresponding squared semipartial correlations.

For a general discussion of the two types of sums of squares, see SAS Institute Inc. (1990a, Vol. 1, pp. 115–117). For present purposes I will point out that Type I SS are sequential sums of squares, which I explained earlier in connection with MINITAB output. To reiterate, however, the first value (88.0985) is the sum of squares accounted for by X1, whereas the second value (13.505) is the sum of squares incremented by X2. Squared Semi-partial Corr(elations) Type I are corresponding proportions accounted for sequentially, or in a hierarchical analysis. They are equal to each Type I SS divided by the total sum of squares (e.g., 88.0985/140.55 = .6268, for the value associated with X1). I calculated the same values in my commentaries on MINITAB output.

Type II SS is the sum of squares a variable accounts for when it enters last in the analysis, that is, after having been adjusted for the remaining independent variables. This is why some authors refer to this type of sum of squares as the unique sum of squares, and to the corresponding Squared Semi-partial correlation Type II as the unique proportion of variance accounted for by the variable in question. Thus, when X1 enters last, the increment in sum of squares due to it is 37.0325. Dividing this value by the total sum of squares yields the Squared Semi-partial Corr Type II (37.0325/140.55 = .2635; compare with the previous output). Similarly, the sum of squares accounted for uniquely by X2 (i.e., when it enters last) is 13.5048, and the corresponding Squared Semi-partial Corr Type II is 13.5048/140.55 = .0961 (compare with the previous output). What is labeled here Semi-partial Corr Type II is labeled Part Cor in SPSS (note that SAS reports the square of these indices). Clearly, *only when the independent variables, or predictors, are not correlated will the sum of the unique regression sums of squares be equal to the overall regression sum of squares. The same is true of the sum of the unique proportions of variance accounted for, which will be equal to the overall R^2 only when the independent variables, or predictors, are not correlated.*

You are probably wondering how one arrives at a decision when to use Type I SS and when to use Type II SS (or the corresponding Squared Semi-partial Correlations), and how they are interpreted substantively. I discuss this complex topic in detail in Chapter 9.

Output

Obs	Cook's D	Hat Diag H	INTERCEP Dfbetas	X1 Dfbetas	X2 Dfbetas
1	0.000	0.1995	−0.0031	0.0014	0.0015
2	0.000	0.1076	0.0103	−0.0168	0.0045
.	.	.	.	.	.
19	0.012	0.0615	0.0015	−0.0631	0.0777
20	0.840	0.3933	−1.0616	−0.9367	1.6359

Partial Regression Residual Plot

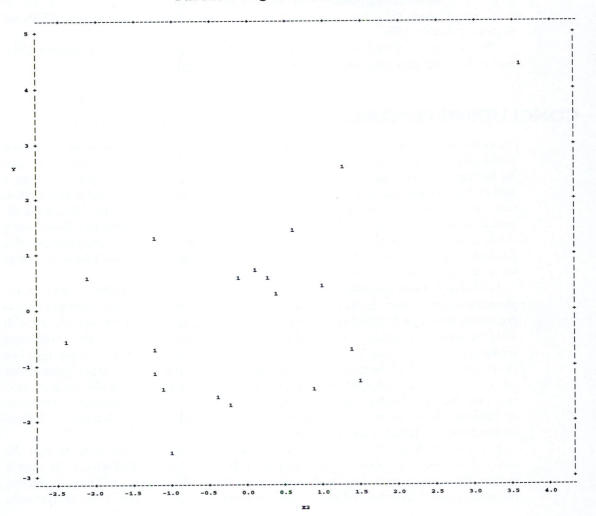

SECOND RUN AFTER DELETING CASES WITH COOK D > .5

Variable	DF	Parameter Estimate	Standard Error	T for H0: Parameter=0	Prob > |T|	Type I SS	Type II SS	Standardized Estimate	Squared Semi-partial Corr Type I	Squared Semi-partial Corr Type II
INTERCEP	1	0.676841	1.20249520	0.563	0.5813				.	.
X1	1	0.853265	0.17269862	4.941	0.0001	91.070076	45.827718	0.78045967	0.74390862	0.37434508
X2	1	0.230881	0.27598330	0.837	0.4152	1.313865	1.313865	0.13214835	0.01073235	0.01073235

Commentary

My comments on the preceding excerpts will be brief, as I obtained similar results several times earlier.

Hat Diag H. In Chapter 4, I explained that this is another term for leverage. I pointed out that SAS reports standardized DFBETAs only. By contrast, SPSS reports unstandardized as well as standardized values. What was labeled earlier partial regression plots, is labeled by SAS Partial Regression Residual Plots.

The last segment of the output is for the analysis in which the last subject was omitted. Compare with outputs from other packages for the same analysis (given earlier).

CONCLUDING REMARKS

I hope that by now you understand the basic principles of multiple regression analysis. Although I used only two independent variables, I presented enough of the subject to lay the foundations for the use of multiple regression analysis in scientific research. A severe danger in studying a subject like multiple regression, however, is that of becoming so preoccupied with formulas, numbers, and number manipulations that you lose sight of the larger purposes. Becoming engrossed in techniques, one runs the risk of ending up as their servant rather than their master. While it was necessary to go through a good deal of number and symbol manipulations, this poses the real threat of losing one's way. It is therefore important to pause and take stock of why we are doing what we are doing.

In Chapter 1, I said that multiple regression analysis may be used for two major purposes: explanation and prediction. To draw the lines clearly though crassly, if we were interested only in prediction, we might be satisfied with selecting a set of predictors that optimize R^2, and with using the regression equation for the predictors thus selected to predict individuals' performance on the criterion of interest. Success in high school or college as predicted by certain tests is a classic case. In much of the research on school success, the interest has been on prediction of this criterion, however defined. One need not probe too deeply into the whys of success in college; one wants mainly to be able to predict successfully, and this is, of course, no mean achievement. As I show in Chapter 8, which is devoted solely to the use of multiple regression analysis for prediction, various approaches are available to achieve this goal.

In much of behavioral research, however, prediction, successful or not, is not enough. We want to know why; we want to explain phenomena. This is the main goal of science. We want to explain, for instance, phenomena such as problem solving, achievement, creativity, aggression, prejudice, or job satisfaction. When the goal is explanation, the focus shifts to the interpretation of the regression equation. We want to know the magnitudes of the effects of independent variables on the dependent variable as they are reflected by the regression coefficients. But should we use unstandardized (b) or standardized (β) regression coefficients? In this chapter, I could offer only a glimpse at the answer to this question. In Part 2 of this book, I elaborate on applications of multiple regression analysis for explanatory purposes in various research designs. For example, in Chapters 9 and 10 I discuss applications of multiple regression in nonexperimental research, whereas in Chapters 11 and 12 I discuss such applications primarily in experimental research.

In sum, then, Chapters 2 through 5 were designed to set the stage for the study of analytic and technical problems encountered in the use of elements of multiple regression analysis in predictive and explanatory scientific research. Mastery of the technical aspects of an analytic approach is a prerequisite for its valid application and an important antidote against misapplications. Needless to say, the study and mastery of the technical aspects of research are necessary but not sufficient conditions for the solution of research problems.

Finally, recall that in the beginning of this chapter I said that the presentation was limited to two independent variables because of the ease this affords in calculating and discussing elements of multiple regression analysis. Although the meaning of elements of multiple regression analysis with more than two independent variables is the same as for the case of two independent variables, their calculations are best accomplished by the use of matrix algebra, a topic I present in Chapter 6.

STUDY SUGGESTIONS

1. Use the following illustrative data for the calculations indicated as follows. The second set of three columns is merely a continuation of the first set. I suggest that you do all the calculations by hand with the aid of a calculator. You may wish to set up tables like the ones I presented in this chapter to keep things orderly.

X_1	X_2	Y	X_1	X_2	Y
2	5	2	4	3	3
2	4	1	3	6	3
1	5	1	6	9	6
1	3	1	6	8	6
3	6	5	8	9	10
4	4	4	9	6	9
5	6	7	10	4	6
5	4	6	9	5	6
7	3	7	4	8	9
6	3	8	4	9	10

Calculate the following:
(a) Means, standard deviations, sums of squares and cross products, and the three r's.
(b) Regression equation of Y on X_1 and X_2.
(c) ss_{reg}, ss_{res}, $R^2_{y.12}$, F, $s^2_{y.12}$.

(d) t ratios for the two regression coefficients.
(e) Increment in the proportion of variance accounted for by X_2, over and above X_1, and the F ratio for the test of this increment. To what test statistic, calculated earlier, should this F be equal?
(f) Increment in the proportion of variance accounted for by X_1, over and above X_2, and the F ratio for the test of this increment. To what test statistic, calculated earlier, should this F be equal?
(g) Using the regression equation, calculate the predicted Y's, $Y - Y'$ (the residuals), $\Sigma(Y - Y')$, and $\Sigma(Y - Y')^2$.
(h) Calculate the squared correlation between Y' and Y. To what statistic, calculated earlier, should this correlation be equal?
2. Using a computer program, analyze the data given in the previous exercise. Compare results with those obtained in the previous exercise.
(a) For all subjects, obtain the following: standardized residuals (ZRESID), studentized residuals (SRESID), studentized deleted residuals (SDRESID), leverage (h), Cook's D, and DFBETAs (raw and standardized).

(b) Based on the DFBETAs obtained in (a), indicate what the regression equation would be if the first subject were deleted.

3. Consider the following correlation matrices:

	X_1	X_2	Y		X_1	X_2	Y
X_1	1.0	0	.7	X_1	1.0	.4	.7
X_2	0	1.0	.6	X_2	.4	1.0	.6
Y	.7	.6	1.0	Y	.7	.6	1.0
		A				**B**	

(a) For which matrix will $R^2_{y.12}$ be higher? Why?
(b) Calculate $R^2_{y.12}$ for each matrix.
(c) Calculate the regression equation for each matrix.
(d) Assume that each matrix is based on a sample of 100 people. Calculate the F ratio for each R^2 in (b).

ANSWERS

1. (a) $\bar{X}_1 = 4.95$; $\bar{X}_2 = 5.50$; $\bar{Y} = 5.50$; $s_1 = 2.6651$; $s_2 = 2.1151$; $s_y = 2.9469$; $\Sigma x_1^2 = 134.95$; $\Sigma x_2^2 = 85.00$; $\Sigma y^2 = 165.00$; $\Sigma x_1 x_2 = 15.50$; $\Sigma x_1 y = 100.50$; $\Sigma x_2 y = 63.00$; $r_{12} = .14472$; $r_{y1} = .67350$; $r_{y2} = .53197$

   (b) $Y' = -1.23561 + .67370X_1 + .61833X_2$

   (c) $ss_{reg} = 106.66144$; $ss_{res} = 58.33856$; $R^2_{y.12} = .64643$; $F = 15.54$, with 2 and 17 df; $s^2_{y.12} = 3.43168$

   (d) For b_1: $t = 4.18$, with 17 df; for b_2: $t = 3.04$, with 17 df

   (e) .1928; $F = 9.27$, with 1 and 17 df. F is equal to t^2 for b_2

   (f) .3634; $F = 17.47$, with 1 and 17 df. F is equal to t^2 for b_1

   (g) $\Sigma(Y - Y') = 0$; $\Sigma(Y - Y')^2 = 58.3386$

   (h) $r^2_{yy'} = R^2_{y.12} = .64643$

2. (a)

Excerpt from SPSS

Case #	*ZRESID	*SRESID	*SDRESID	*LEVER	*COOK D	DFB0_1	DFB1_1	DFB2_1	SDB0_1	SDB1_1	SDB2_1
1	−.6496	−.6905	−.6794	.0648	.0206	−.22806	.02942	.00263	−.16739	.17961	.01276
2	−.8557	−.9177	−.9132	.0807	.0422	−.41394	.03694	.02544	−.30723	.22807	.12467
3	−.8258	−.9040	−.8989	.1156	.0541	−.36234	.05355	.00102	−.26873	.33037	.00500
.	.										
18	−1.0361	−1.1461	−1.1575	.1327	.0979	.09713	−.07361	.02724	.07317	−.46128	.13546
19	1.4004	1.5088	1.5728	.0885	.1220	−.21008	−.03204	.09441	−.16334	−.20725	.48464
20	1.6064	1.8111	1.9558	.1632	.2963	−.48801	−.04547	.16403	−.39307	−.30466	.87231

Excerpt from SAS

Obs	Student Residual	Cook's D	Rstudent	Hat Diag H	INTERCEP Dfbetas	X1 Dfbetas	X2 Dfbetas
1	−0.690	0.021	−0.6794	0.1148	−0.1674	0.1796	0.0128
2	−0.918	0.042	−0.9132	0.1307	−0.3072	0.2281	0.1247
3	−0.904	0.054	−0.8989	0.1656	−0.2687	0.3304	0.0050
.	.	.	.	.	.	.	.
18	−1.146	0.098	−1.1575	0.1827	0.0732	−0.4613	0.1355
19	1.509	0.122	1.5728	0.1385	−0.1633	−0.2073	0.4846
20	1.811	0.296	1.9558	0.2132	−0.3931	−0.3047	0.8723

   Note. Recall that (1) leverage (*LEVER) in SPSS is centered (see the commentary on SPSS output in the chapter); and (2) SAS reports only standardized DFBETAs.

   (b) $Y' = -1.0075 + .64428X_1 + .61570X_2$

3. (a) Matrix **A**

   (b) For matrix **A**: $R^2_{y.12} = .85$; for matrix **B**: $R^2_{y.12} = .61$

   (c) For matrix **A**: $z'_y = .7z_1 + .6z_2$;

   for matrix **B**: $z'_y = .55z_1 + .38z_2$

   (d) For matrix **A**: $F = 274.83$, with 2 and 97 df;

   for matrix **B**: $F = 75.86$, with 2 and 97 df

6

General Method of Multiple Regression Analysis: Matrix Operations

My main objective in Chapter 5 was to introduce basic elements of multiple regression theory and analysis. Although I used only two independent variables, I pointed out that the same approach applies to any number of independent variables. I limited the presentation in Chapter 5 to two independent variables because algebraic formulas for analyses with more than two independent variables are intractable. The powerful and elegant techniques of matrix algebra are eminently suited for the solution of multivariable problems, of which multiple regression analysis is an important case.

In this chapter, I illustrate and discuss the use of matrix algebra in multiple regression analysis. Despite its generality, I limit here the application of matrix algebra to very simple examples, so as to enable you to concentrate on the meaning of the method instead of getting bogged down in numerous calculations.

Although matrix equations are elegant and succinct, some operations on matrices (particularly the calculation of inverses) are extremely laborious. This is why matrix solutions with more than two independent variables are almost always done by computer. To acquaint you with the rudiments of matrix operations, I begin with a numerical example with one independent variable, which I analyze first by hand and then by computer. I then turn to an example with two independent variables. The virtue of working through the matrix algebra with two independent variables is that it will give you an understanding of the matrix equations applicable to regression analysis with any number of independent variables.

To enhance your learning and understanding of the matrix approach, I purposely apply it to numerical examples I analyzed in preceding chapters. I suggest that you refer frequently to the analyses in relevant chapters when you are working through the matrix operations I present in this chapter. Compare the results I reported earlier with those I obtain in this chapter; study specific elements of the various matrices and see if you can identify them in the analyses I presented in preceding chapters. Above all, be patient and study the material systematically. It will pay off in better understanding.

If you have no knowledge of matrix algebra, I urge you to study Appendix A, which is a systematic elementary treatment of some fundamental elements of matrix algebra. My presentation is geared to the multiple regression needs of this book and should enable you to grasp the material I present in this chapter and in subsequent ones.

Study to the point of being familiar with the following elements of matrix algebra: matrix manipulations analogous to simple algebraic manipulations, particularly matrix multiplication; the notion of a determinant and an inverse of a matrix; and the ability to calculate them for a 2×2 matrix. I cover these topics in Appendix A.

REGRESSION ANALYSIS: MATRIX OPERATIONS

In earlier chapters, I presented equations in which a score on a dependent variable, Y, was expressed as a linear combination of independent variables, X's, plus a constant, a, and an error term, e.

For k independent variables, the equation is

$$Y = a + b_1 X_1 + b_2 X_2 + \ldots + b_k X_k + e \tag{6.1}$$

where a = intercept; b's = regression coefficients applied to the X's; and e = residual, or error. Recall that a solution is sought for the constants (a and the b's) so that the sum of the squared residuals (Σe^2) will be at a minimum.

As is indicated in Appendix A, matrices are presented by bold letters. Using matrix notation, (6.1) is expressed as follows:

$$\begin{array}{ccccc}
\mathbf{y} & = & \mathbf{X} & \mathbf{b} & + & \mathbf{e} \\
N \times 1 & & N \times (1+k) & (1+k) \times 1 & & N \times 1
\end{array} \tag{6.2}$$

where $\mathbf{y}$ is a column vector of raw scores on the dependent variable for N individuals (i.e., an N by 1 vector); $\mathbf{X}$ is an N by $1 + k$ matrix of raw scores for N individuals on k independent variables and a unit vector (a vector of 1's) for the intercept; $\mathbf{b}$ is a $1 + k$ by 1 column vector consisting of a, the intercept, and b_k regression coefficients;[1] and $\mathbf{e}$ is an N by 1 column vector of errors, or residuals. To make sure that you understand (6.2), I spell it out in the form of matrices:

$$
\begin{bmatrix} Y_1 \\ Y_2 \\ Y_3 \\ \cdot \\ \cdot \\ \cdot \\ Y_N \end{bmatrix} =
\begin{bmatrix}
1 & X_{11} & X_{12} & X_{13} & \cdots & X_{1k} \\
1 & X_{21} & X_{22} & X_{23} & \cdots & X_{2k} \\
1 & X_{31} & X_{32} & X_{33} & \cdots & X_{3k} \\
\cdot & \cdot & \cdot & \cdot & & \cdot \\
\cdot & \cdot & \cdot & \cdot & & \cdot \\
\cdot & \cdot & \cdot & \cdot & & \cdot \\
1_N & X_{N1} & X_{N2} & X_{N3} & \cdots & X_{Nk}
\end{bmatrix}
\begin{bmatrix} a \\ b_1 \\ b_2 \\ \cdot \\ \cdot \\ \cdot \\ b_k \end{bmatrix} +
\begin{bmatrix} e_1 \\ e_2 \\ e_3 \\ \cdot \\ \cdot \\ \cdot \\ e_N \end{bmatrix}
$$

where Y_1, for example, is the first person's score on the dependent variable, Y; X_{11} is the first person's score on X_1; X_{12} is the first person's score on X_2; and so on up to X_{1k}, the first person's score on X_k. In other words, each row of $\mathbf{X}$ represents the scores of a given person on the independent variables, X's, plus a constant (1) for the intercept (a). In the last column vector, e_1 is the residual for the first person, and so on for all the others in the group.

---

[1] In matrix presentations of multiple regression analysis, it is customary to use b_0, instead of a, as a symbol for the intercept. I retain a as the symbol for the intercept to clearly distinguish it from the regression coefficients, as in subsequent chapters I deal extensively with comparisons among intercepts from two or more regression equations.

Multiplying $\mathbf{X}$ by $\mathbf{b}$ and adding $\mathbf{e}$ yields N equations like (6.1), one for each person in the sample. Using the principle of least squares, a solution is sought for $\mathbf{b}$ so that $\mathbf{e'e}$ is minimized. ($\mathbf{e'}$ is the transpose of $\mathbf{e}$, or $\mathbf{e}$ expressed as a row vector. Multiplying $\mathbf{e'}$ by $\mathbf{e}$ is the same as squaring each e and summing them, i.e., Σe^2.)

The solution for $\mathbf{b}$ that minimizes $\mathbf{e'e}$ is

$$\mathbf{b} = (\mathbf{X'X})^{-1}\mathbf{X'y} \tag{6.3}$$

where $\mathbf{b}$ is a column vector of a (intercept) plus b_k regression coefficients. $\mathbf{X'}$ is the transpose of $\mathbf{X}$, the latter being an N by $1 + k$ matrix composed of a unit vector and k column vectors of scores on the independent variables. $(\mathbf{X'X})^{-1}$ is the inverse of $(\mathbf{X'X})$. $\mathbf{y}$ is an N by one column of dependent variable scores.

AN EXAMPLE WITH ONE INDEPENDENT VARIABLE

I turn now to the analysis of a numerical example with one independent variable using matrix operations. I use the example I introduced and analyzed in earlier chapters (see Table 2.1 or Table 3.1). To make sure that you follow what I am doing, I write the matrices in their entirety. For the data of Table 2.1,

$$\mathbf{b} = \left\{ \begin{bmatrix} 11111111111111111111 \\ 11112222333344445555 \end{bmatrix} \begin{bmatrix} 1 & 1 \\ 1 & 1 \\ 1 & 1 \\ 1 & 1 \\ 1 & 2 \\ 1 & 2 \\ 1 & 2 \\ 1 & 2 \\ 1 & 3 \\ 1 & 3 \\ 1 & 3 \\ 1 & 3 \\ 1 & 4 \\ 1 & 4 \\ 1 & 4 \\ 1 & 4 \\ 1 & 5 \\ 1 & 5 \\ 1 & 5 \\ 1 & 5 \end{bmatrix}^{-1} \begin{bmatrix} 11111111111111111111 \\ 11112222333344445555 \end{bmatrix} \begin{bmatrix} 3 \\ 5 \\ 6 \\ 9 \\ 4 \\ 6 \\ 7 \\ 10 \\ 4 \\ 6 \\ 8 \\ 10 \\ 5 \\ 7 \\ 9 \\ 12 \\ 7 \\ 10 \\ 12 \\ 6 \end{bmatrix} \right\}$$

$$\mathbf{X'} \qquad\qquad \mathbf{X} \qquad\qquad \mathbf{X'} \qquad\qquad \mathbf{y}$$

Multiplying $\mathbf{X'}$ by $\mathbf{X}$,

$$\mathbf{X'X} = \begin{bmatrix} 20 & 60 \\ N & \Sigma X \\ 60 & 220 \\ \Sigma X & \Sigma X^2 \end{bmatrix}$$

Under each number, I inserted the term that it represents. Thus, $N = 20$, $\Sigma X = 60$, and $\Sigma X^2 = 220$. Compare these calculations with the calculations in Chapter 2.

$$\mathbf{X'y} = \begin{bmatrix} 146 \\ \Sigma Y \\ \\ 468 \\ \Sigma XY \end{bmatrix}$$

Again, compare this calculation with the calculation in Chapter 2.

Calculating the Inverse of a 2 × 2 Matrix

To calculate the inverse of a 2×2 **X**, where

$$\mathbf{X} = \begin{bmatrix} a & b \\ c & d \end{bmatrix}$$

$$\mathbf{X}^{-1} = \begin{bmatrix} \dfrac{d}{ad - bc} & \dfrac{-b}{ad - bc} \\ \\ \dfrac{-c}{ad - bc} & \dfrac{a}{ad - bc} \end{bmatrix}$$

Note that the denominator is the determinant of **X**—that is, $|\mathbf{X}|$ (see the next paragraph). Also, the elements of the principal diagonal (a and d) are interchanged and the signs of the other two elements (b and c) are reversed.

For our data, calculate first the determinant of $(\mathbf{X'X})$:

$$|\mathbf{X'X}| = \begin{vmatrix} 20 & 60 \\ 60 & 220 \end{vmatrix} = (20)(220) - (60)(60) = 800$$

Now calculate the inverse of $(\mathbf{X'X})$:

$$(\mathbf{X'X})^{-1} = \begin{bmatrix} \dfrac{220}{800} & \dfrac{-60}{800} \\ \\ \dfrac{-60}{800} & \dfrac{20}{800} \end{bmatrix} = \begin{bmatrix} .275 & -.075 \\ -.075 & .025 \end{bmatrix}$$

We are now ready to calculate the following:

$$\mathbf{b} = (\mathbf{X'X})^{-1}\mathbf{X'y} = \begin{bmatrix} .275 & -.075 \\ -.075 & .025 \end{bmatrix} \begin{bmatrix} 146 \\ 468 \end{bmatrix} = \begin{bmatrix} 5.05 \\ .75 \end{bmatrix}$$

$$a = 5.05 \quad \text{and} \quad b_1 = .75$$

or

$$Y' = 5.05 + .75X$$

which is the regression equation I calculated in Chapter 2.

Regression and Residual Sums of Squares

The regression sum of squares in matrix form is

$$ss_{reg} = \mathbf{b'X'y} - \frac{(\Sigma Y)^2}{N} \tag{6.4}$$

where $\mathbf{b'}$ is the row vector of b's; $\mathbf{X'}$ is the transpose of $\mathbf{X}$ matrix of scores on independent variables plus a unit vector; $\mathbf{y}$ is a column vector of dependent variable scores; and $(\Sigma Y)^2/N$ is a correction term—see (2.2) in Chapter 2.

As calculated above,

$$\mathbf{X'y} = \begin{bmatrix} 146 \\ 468 \end{bmatrix} \qquad \mathbf{b'} = [5.05 \quad .75] \qquad \Sigma Y = 146$$

$$ss_{reg} = [5.05 \quad .75] \begin{bmatrix} 146 \\ 468 \end{bmatrix} - \frac{(146)^2}{20} = 1088.3 - 1065.8 = 22.5$$

I calculated the same value in Chapter 2.

The residual sum of squares is

$$\mathbf{e'e} = \mathbf{y'y} - \mathbf{b'X'y} \tag{6.5}$$

where $\mathbf{e'}$ and $\mathbf{e}$ are row and column vectors of the residuals, respectively. As I stated earlier, premultiplying a column by its transpose is the same as squaring and summing the elements of the column. In other words, $\mathbf{e'e} = \Sigma e^2$. Similarly $\mathbf{y'y} = \Sigma Y^2$, the sum of raw scores squared.

$$\mathbf{y'y} = 1196 \qquad \mathbf{b'X'y} = 1088.3$$

$$ss_{res} = \mathbf{e'e} = 1196 - 1088.3 = 107.7$$

Squared Multiple Correlation Coefficient

Recall that the squared multiple correlation coefficient (R^2, or r^2 with a single independent variable) indicates the proportion of variance, or sum of squares, of the dependent variable accounted for by the independent variable. In matrix form,

$$R^2 = \frac{\mathbf{b'X'y} - (\Sigma Y)^2/N}{\mathbf{y'y} - (\Sigma Y)^2/N} = \frac{ss_{reg}}{\Sigma y^2} \tag{6.6}$$

where $(\Sigma Y)^2/N$ in the numerator and the denominator is the correction term.

$$R^2 = \frac{1088.3 - (146)^2/20}{1196 - (146)^2/20} = \frac{22.5}{130.2} = .1728$$

Also,

$$R^2 = 1 - \frac{\mathbf{e'e}}{\mathbf{y'y} - (\Sigma Y)^2/N} = 1 - \frac{ss_{res}}{\Sigma y^2}$$

I could, of course, test the regression sum of squares, or the proportion of variance accounted for (R^2), for significance. Because the tests are the same as those I used frequently in Chapters 2 and 3, I do not repeat them here.

Having applied matrix algebra to simple linear regression analysis, I can well sympathize with readers unfamiliar with matrix algebra who wonder why all these matrix operations were necessary when I could have used the methods presented in Chapter 2. Had regression analysis in the social sciences been limited to one or two independent variables, there would have been no need to resort to matrix algebra. The methods I presented in Chapters 2 and 5 would have sufficed. As you know, however, more than two independent variables are used in much, if not all, of social science research. For such analyses, matrix algebra is essential. As I said earlier, it is easy to demonstrate the application of matrix algebra with one and two independent variables. Study the analyses in this chapter until you understand them well and feel comfortable with them. After that, you can let the computer do the matrix operations for you. But you will know what is being done and will therefore understand better how to use and interpret the results of your analyses. It is with this in mind that I turn to a presentation of computer analysis of the numerical example I analyzed earlier.

COMPUTER PROGRAMS

Of the four computer packages I introduced in Chapter 4, BMDP does not contain a matrix procedure. In what follows, I will use matrix operations from MINITAB, SAS, and SPSS to analyze the numerical example I analyzed in the preceding section. Although I could have given more succinct input statements (especially for SAS and SPSS), I chose to include control statements for intermediate calculations paralleling my hand calculations used earlier in this chapter. For illustrative purposes, I will give, sometimes, both succinct and more detailed control statements.

MINITAB

In Chapter 4, I gave a general orientation to this package and to the conventions I use in presenting input, output, and commentaries. Here, I limit the presentation to the application of MINITAB matrix operations (Minitab Inc., 1995a, Chapter 17).

Input

```
GMACRO                        [global macro]
T61
OUTFILE='T61.MIN';
   NOTERM.
NOTE SIMPLE REGRESSION ANALYSIS. DATA FROM TABLE 2.1
READ 'T61.DAT' C1–C3
END
NOTE STATEMENTS BEGINNING WITH "--" ARE NOT PART OF INPUT.
NOTE SEE COMMENTARY FOR EXPLANATION.
ECHO
COPY C1 C2 M1              --   M1=X
TRANSPOSE M1 M2           --   M2=X′
MULTIPLY M2 M1 M3         --   M3=X′X
PRINT M3
```

```
MULTIPLY M2 C3 C4              --    C4=X'y
PRINT C4
INVERT M3 M4                   --    M4=(X'X)⁻¹
PRINT M4
MULTIPLY M4 M2 M5              --    M5=(X'X)⁻¹X'
MULTIPLY M5 C3 C5              --    C5=(X'X)⁻¹X'y=b
PRINT C5
MULTIPLY M1 C5 C6              --    C6=X(X'X)⁻¹X'y=PREDICTED
SUBTRACT C6 C3 C7              --    C7=y−[X(X'X)⁻¹X'y]=RESIDUALS
MULTIPLY M1 M5 M6              --    M6=X(X'X)⁻¹X'=HAT MATRIX
DIAGONAL M6 C8                 --    DIAGONAL VALUES OF HAT MATRIX IN C8
NAME C3 'Y' C6 'PRED' C7 'RESID' C8 'LEVERAGE'
PRINT C3 C6-C8
ENDMACRO
```

Commentary

READ. Raw data are read from a separate file (T61.DAT), where X_1 (a column of 1's or a unit vector) and X_2 (scores on X) occupy C(column)1 and C2, respectively, and Y occupies C3. As I stated in the first NOTE, I carry out simple regression analysis, using the data from Table 2.1. Incidentally, most computer programs for regression analysis add a unit vector (for the intercept) by default. This is why it is not part of my input files in other chapters (e.g., Chapter 4).

In my brief comments on the input, I departed from the format I am using throughout the book because I wanted to include matrix notation (e.g., bold-faced letters, superscripts). As I stated in the NOTES, comments begin with "--". I refrained from using MINITAB's symbol for a comment (#), lest this would lead you to believe, erroneously, that it is possible to use bold-faced letters and superscripts in the input file.

Unlike most matrix programs, MINITAB does *not* resort to matrix notation. It is a safe bet that MINITAB's syntax would appeal to people who are not familiar, or who are uncomfortable, with matrix notation and operations. Yet, the ease with which one can learn MINITAB's syntax is countervailed by the limitation that commands are composed of single operations (e.g., add two matrices, multiply a matrix by a constant, calculate the inverse of a matrix). As a result, compound operations have to be broken down into simple ones. I will illustrate this with reference to the solution for **b** (intercept and regression coefficients). Look at my matrix notation on C5 (column 5) in the input and notice that **b** (C5) is calculated as a result of the following: (1) **X** is transposed, (2) the transposed **X** is multiplied by **X**, (3) the resulting matrix is inverted, (4) the inverse is multiplied by the transpose of **X**, and (5) the result thus obtained is multiplied by **y**. Programs accepting matrix notation (e.g., SAS, SPSS; see below) can carry out these operations as a result of a single statement, as in my comment on C5 in the input.

Whenever a matrix operation yielded a column vector, I assigned it to a column instead of a matrix (see, e.g., C4 in the input). Doing this is particularly useful when working with a version of MINITAB (*not* the Windows version) that is limited to a relatively small number of matrices. For pedagogical purposes, I retained the results of each command in a separate matrix, instead of overwriting contents of intermediate matrices.

Output

MATRIX M3

20	60	--	$20=N$, $60=\Sigma X$
60	220	--	$220=\Sigma X^2$

C4

146	468	--	$146=\Sigma Y$, $468=\Sigma XY$

MATRIX M4   --   INVERSE OF $\mathbf{X'X}$

0.275	−0.075
−0.075	0.025

C5

5.05	0.75	--	$5.05=a$, $.75=b$

Row	Y	PRED	RESID	LEVERAGE		
1	3	5.80	−2.80000	0.150		
2	5	5.80	−0.80000	0.150	--	first two subjects
.	.	.	.	.		
19	12	8.80	3.20000	0.150	--	last two subjects
20	6	8.80	−2.80000	0.150		

Commentary

As in the input, comments beginning with "--" are *not* part of the output. I trust that the identification of elements of the output would suffice for you to follow it, especially if you do this in conjunction with earlier sections in this chapter. You may also find it instructive to study this output in conjunction with computer outputs for the same example, which I reported and commented on in Chapter 4.

SAS

Input

```
TITLE 'SIMPLE REGRESSION ANALYSIS. DATA FROM TABLE 2.1';
PROC IML;
RESET PRINT;                          -- print all the results
COMB={1 1 3,1 1 5,1 1 6,1 1 9,1 2 4,1 2 6,1 2 7,1 2 10,1 3 4,1 3 6,
    1 3 8,1 3 10,1 4 5,1 4 7,1 4 9,1 4 12,1 5 7,1 5 10,1 5 12,1 5 6};
X=COMB[,1:2];                         -- create X from columns 1 and 2 of COMB
Y=COMB[,3];                           -- create y from column 3 of COMB
XTX=X`*X;                             -- X'X
XTY=X`*Y;                             -- X'y
DETX=DET(X`*X);                       -- Determinant of X'X
INVX=INV(XTX);                        -- Inverse of X'X
B=INVX*X`*Y;                          -- b=(X'X)-1X'y
```

```
PREDICT = X*B;                      --   y'=Xb=PREDICTED SCORES
RESID = Y-PREDICT;                  --   RESIDUALS
HAT=X*INVX*X`;                      --   HAT matrix
HATDIAG = VECDIAG(HAT);            --   put diagonal of HAT in HATDIAG
PRINT Y PREDICT RESID HATDIAG;
```

Commentary

My comments beginning with "--" are *not* part of the input. For an explanation, see commentary on the previous MINITAB input.

See Chapter 4 for a general orientation to SAS and the conventions I follow in presenting input, output, and commentaries. Here, I limit the presentation to the application of PROC IML (Interactive Matrix Language, SAS Institute Inc., 1990b)—one of the most comprehensive and sophisticated programs for matrix operations. It is not possible, nor is it necessary, to describe here the versatility and power of IML. Suffice it to point out that a person conversant in matrix algebra could use IML to carry out virtually any statistical analysis (see *SAS/IML: Usage and reference,* SAS Institute, 1990b, for illustrative applications; see also, sample input files supplied with the program).

Various formats for data input, including from external files, can be used. Here, I use free format, with commas serving as separators among rows (subjects). I named the matrix COMB(ined), as it includes the data for *X* and *Y.* I used this format, instead of reading two matrices, to illustrate how to extract matrices from a larger matrix. Thus, **X** is a 20 by 2 matrix, where the first column consists of 1's (for the intercept) and the second column consists of scores on the independent variable (*X*). **y** is a 20 by 1 column vector of scores on the dependent variable (*Y*).

Examine the input statements and notice that terms on the left-hand side are names or labels assigned by the user (e.g., I use XTX to stand for X transpose X and INVX to stand for the inverse of XTX). The terms on the right-hand side are matrix operations "patterned after linear algebra notation" (SAS Institute Inc., 1990b, p. 19). For example, **X'X** is expressed as X`*X, where "`" signifies transpose, and "*" signifies multiplication. As another example, $(\mathbf{X'X})^{-1}$ is expressed as INV(XTX), where INV stands for inverse, and XTX is **X'X** obtained earlier.

Unlike MINITAB, whose statements are limited to a single operation (see the explanation in the preceding section), IML expressions can be composed of multiple operations. As a simple example, the two preceding expressions can be combined into a compound statement. That is, instead of first obtaining XTX and then inverting the result, I could have stated INVX = INV (X`*X). As I stated earlier, I could have used more succinct statements in the input file. For instance, assuming I was interested only in results of regression analysis, then the control statements following the data in the Input file could be replaced by:

```
B=INV(X`*X)*X`*Y;
PREDICT=X*B;
RESID=Y-PREDICT;
HAT=X*INV(X`*X)*X`;
HATDIAG=VECDIAG(HAT);
PRINT Y PREDICT RESID HATDIAG;
```

You may find it instructive to run both versions of the input statements and compare the outputs. Or, you may wish to experiment with other control statements to accomplish the same tasks.

Output

1	TITLE 'SIMPLE REGRESSION ANALYSIS. DATA FROM TABLE 2.1';		
2	PROC IML;		
IML Ready			
3	RESET PRINT;		*[print all the results]*

X	20 rows	2 cols	*[IML reports dimensions of matrix]*
	1	1	
	1	1	*[first two subjects]*
	.	.	
	1	5	*[last two subjects]*
	1	5	

Y	20 rows	1 cols	*[dimensions of column vector]*
	3		
	5		*[first two subjects]*
	.		
	12		*[last two subjects]*
	6		

8   XTX=X`*X;

XTX	2 rows	2 cols	
	20	60	*[20=N, 60=ΣX]*
	60	220	*[220=ΣX²]*

9   XTY=X`*Y;

XTY	2 rows	1 col	
	146		*[ΣY]*
	468		*[ΣXY]*

10   DETX=DET(X`*X);

DETX	1 rows	1 col
	800	

11   INVX=INV(XTX);

INVX	2 rows	2 cols
	0.275	−0.075
	−0.075	0.025

B	2 rows	1 col	
	5.05		*[a]*
	0.75		*[b]*

17   PRINT Y PREDICT RESID HATDIAG;

Y	PREDICT	RESID	HATDIAG	*[HATDIAG=Leverage]*
3	5.8	−2.8	0.15	
5	5.8	−0.8	0.15	*[first two subjects]*

Here $XTX = X'X$, $DETX = DET(X'X)$, with $20 = N$, $60 = \Sigma X$, $220 = \Sigma X^2$, $146 = \Sigma Y$, $468 = \Sigma XY$.

.	.	.	.	
12	8.8	3.2	0.15	*[last two subjects]*
6	8.8	−2.8	0.15	

Commentary

The numbered statements are from the LOG file. See Chapter 4 for my discussion of the importance of always examining LOG files.

I believe you will have no problems understanding these results, particularly if you compare them to those I got through hand calculations and through MINITAB earlier in this chapter. When in doubt, see also the relevant sections in Chapter 4.

SPSS

Input

TITLE LINEAR REGRESSION. DATA FROM TABLE 2.1.
MATRIX.
COMPUTE COMB={1,1,3;1,1,5;1,1,6;1,1,9;1,2,4;1,2,6;1,2,7;1,2,10;1,3,4;1,3,6;
    1,3,8;1,3,10;1,4,5;1,4,7;1,4,9;1,4,12;1,5,7;1,5,10;1,5,12;1,5,6}.
COMPUTE X=COMB(:,1:2).   --   create **X** from columns 1 and 2 of COMB
COMPUTE Y=COMB(:,3).   --   create **y** from column 3 of COMB
PRINT X.
PRINT Y.
COMPUTE XTX=T(X)*X.   --   **X'X**
COMPUTE XTY=T(X)*Y.   --   **X'y**
COMPUTE SPCOMB=SSCP(COMB).   --   sums of squares and cross products
COMPUTE DETX=DET(XTX).   --   Determinant of **X'X**
COMPUTE INVX=INV(XTX).   --   Inverse of **X'X**
COMPUTE B=INVX*T(X)*Y.   -- $b=(X'X)^{-1}X'y$
COMPUTE PREDICT=X*B.   -- $y'=Xb$=PREDICTED SCORES
COMPUTE RESID=Y-PREDICT.   --   RESIDUALS
COMPUTE HAT=X*INVX*T(X).   --   HAT matrix
COMPUTE HATDIAG=DIAG(HAT).   --   put diagonal of HAT in HATDIAG
PRINT XTX.
PRINT XTY.
PRINT SPCOMB.
PRINT DETX.
PRINT INVX.
PRINT B.
PRINT PREDICT.
PRINT RESID.
PRINT HATDIAG.
END MATRIX.

Commentary

Note that all elements of the MATRIX procedure have to be placed between MATRIX and END MATRIX. Thus, my title is *not* part of the MATRIX procedure statements. To include a title as part of the MATRIX input, it would have to be part of the PRINT subcommand and adhere to its format (i.e., begin with a slash (/) and be enclosed in quotation marks).

As in MINITAB and SAS inputs, I begin comments in the input with "--". For an explanation, see my commentary on MINITAB input.

With few exceptions (e.g., beginning commands with COMPUTE, using T for Transpose, different command terminators), the control statements in SPSS are very similar to those of SAS. This is not surprising as both procedures resort to matrix notations.

As I indicated in the input, SPCOMB = sums of squares and cross products for all the vectors of COMB. Hence, it includes $X'X$ and $X'y$—the two matrices generated through the statements preceding SPCOMB in the input. I included the redundant statements as another example of a succinct statement that accomplishes what two or more detailed statements do.

Output

XTX
20	60	$[20=N, 60=\Sigma X]$
60	220	$[220=\Sigma X^2]$

XTY
146	$[\Sigma Y]$
468	$[\Sigma XY]$

SPCOMB   *[see commentary on input]*
20	60	146
60	220	468
146	468	1196

DETX   *[Determinant of XTX]*
    800.0000000

INVX   *[Inverse of XTX]*
.2750000000	−.0750000000
−.0750000000	.0250000000

B
5.050000000	*[a]*
.750000000	*[b]*

PREDICT	RESID	HATDIAG	*[HATDIAG = Leverage]*
5.800000000	−2.800000000	.1500000000	
5.800000000	−.800000000	.1500000000	*[first two subjects]*
.	.	.	
8.800000000	3.200000000	.1500000000	
8.800000000	−2.800000000	.1500000000	*[last two subjects]*

Commentary

As I suggested in connection with MINITAB and SAS outputs, study this output in conjunction with my hand calculations earlier in this chapter and with computer outputs and commentaries for the same data in Chapter 4.

AN EXAMPLE WITH TWO INDEPENDENT VARIABLES: DEVIATION SCORES

In this section, I will use matrix operations to analyze the data in Table 5.1. Unlike the preceding section, where the matrices consisted of raw scores, the matrices I will use in this section consist of deviation scores. Subsequently, I will do the same analysis using correlation matrices. You will thus become familiar with three variations on the same theme. The equation for the b's using deviation scores is

$$\mathbf{b} = (\mathbf{X}_d'\mathbf{X}_d)^{-1}\mathbf{X}_d'\mathbf{y}_d \tag{6.7}$$

where $\mathbf{b}$ is a column of regression coefficients; $\mathbf{X}_d$ is an $N \times k$ matrix of deviation scores on k independent variables; $\mathbf{X}_d'$ is the transpose of $\mathbf{X}_d$; and $\mathbf{y}_d$ is a column of deviation scores on the dependent variable (Y). Unlike the raw-scores matrix ($\mathbf{X}$ in the preceding section), $\mathbf{X}_d$ does *not* include a unit vector. When (6.7) is applied, a solution is obtained for the b's only. The intercept, a, is calculated separately (see the following).

$(\mathbf{X}_d'\mathbf{X}_d)$ is a $k \times k$ matrix of deviation sums of squares and cross products. For k independent variables,

$$\mathbf{X}_d'\mathbf{X}_d = \begin{bmatrix} \Sigma x_1^2 & \Sigma x_1 x_2 & \cdots & \Sigma x_1 x_k \\ \Sigma x_2 x_1 & \Sigma x_2^2 & \cdots & \Sigma x_2 x_k \\ \cdot & & \cdot & \cdot \\ \cdot & & \cdot & \cdot \\ \cdot & & \cdot & \cdot \\ \Sigma x_k x_1 & \Sigma x_k x_2 & \cdots & \Sigma x_k^2 \end{bmatrix}$$

Note that the diagonal consists of sums of squares, and that the off-diagonals are sums of cross products. $\mathbf{X}_d'\mathbf{y}_d$ is a $k \times 1$ column of cross products of x_k variables with y, the dependent variable.

$$\mathbf{X}_d'\mathbf{y}_d = \begin{bmatrix} \Sigma x_1 y \\ \Sigma x_2 y \\ \cdot \\ \cdot \\ \cdot \\ \Sigma x_k y \end{bmatrix}$$

Before I apply (6.7) to the data in Table 5.1, it will be instructive to spell out the equation for the case of two independent variables using symbols.

$$\mathbf{b} = \underbrace{\begin{bmatrix} \Sigma x_1^2 & \Sigma x_1 x_2 \\ \Sigma x_2 x_1 & \Sigma x_2^2 \end{bmatrix}}_{\mathbf{X}_d'\mathbf{X}_d}^{-1} \underbrace{\begin{bmatrix} \Sigma x_1 y \\ \Sigma x_2 y \end{bmatrix}}_{\mathbf{X}_d'\mathbf{y}_d}$$

First, calculate the determinant of $(\mathbf{X}_d'\mathbf{X}_d)$:

$$\left|\mathbf{X}_d'\mathbf{X}_d\right| = \begin{vmatrix} \Sigma x_1^2 & \Sigma x_1 x_2 \\ \\ \Sigma x_2 x_1 & \Sigma x_2^2 \end{vmatrix} = (\Sigma x_1^2)(\Sigma x_2^2) - (\Sigma x_1 x_2)^2$$

Second, calculate the inverse of $(\mathbf{X}_d'\mathbf{X}_d)$:

$$(\mathbf{X}_d'\mathbf{X}_d)^{-1} = \begin{bmatrix} \dfrac{\Sigma x_2^2}{(\Sigma x_1^2)(\Sigma x_2^2) - (\Sigma x_1 x_2)^2} & \dfrac{-\Sigma x_1 x_2}{(\Sigma x_1^2)(\Sigma x_2^2) - (\Sigma x_1 x_2)^2} \\ \\ \dfrac{-\Sigma x_2 x_1}{(\Sigma x_1^2)(\Sigma x_2^2) - (\Sigma x_1 x_2)^2} & \dfrac{\Sigma x_1^2}{(\Sigma x_1^2)(\Sigma x_2^2) - (\Sigma x_1 x_2)^2} \end{bmatrix}$$

Note that (1) the denominator for each term in the inverse is the determinant of $(\mathbf{X}_d'\mathbf{X}_d)$: $\left|\mathbf{X}_d'\mathbf{X}_d\right|$, (2) the sums of squares ($\Sigma x_1^2, \Sigma x_2^2$) were interchanged, and (3) the signs for the sum of the cross products were reversed. Now solve for **b**:

$$\mathbf{b} = \begin{bmatrix} \dfrac{\Sigma x_2^2}{(\Sigma x_1^2)(\Sigma x_2^2) - (\Sigma x_1 x_2)^2} & \dfrac{-\Sigma x_1 x_2}{(\Sigma x_1^2)(\Sigma x_2^2) - (\Sigma x_1 x_2)^2} \\ \\ \dfrac{-\Sigma x_2 x_1}{(\Sigma x_1^2)(\Sigma x_2^2) - (\Sigma x_1 x_2)^2} & \dfrac{\Sigma x_1^2}{(\Sigma x_1^2)(\Sigma x_2^2) - (\Sigma x_1 x_2)^2} \end{bmatrix} \begin{bmatrix} \Sigma x_1 y \\ \\ \Sigma x_2 y \end{bmatrix}$$

$$\qquad\qquad\qquad (\mathbf{X}_d'\mathbf{X}_d)^{-1} \qquad\qquad\qquad\qquad \mathbf{X}_d'\mathbf{y}_d$$

$$= \begin{bmatrix} \dfrac{(\Sigma x_2^2)(\Sigma x_1 y) - (\Sigma x_1 x_2)(\Sigma x_2 y)}{(\Sigma x_1^2)(\Sigma x_2^2) - (\Sigma x_1 x_2)^2} \\ \\ \dfrac{(\Sigma x_1^2)(\Sigma x_2 y) - (\Sigma x_1 x_2)(\Sigma x_1 y)}{(\Sigma x_1^2)(\Sigma x_2^2) - (\Sigma x_1 x_2)^2} \end{bmatrix}$$

Note that the solution is identical to the algebraic formula for the *b*'s in Chapter 5—see (5.4). I presented these matrix operations not only to show the identity of the two approaches, but also to give you an idea how unwieldy algebraic formulas would become had one attempted to develop them for more than two independent variables. Again, this is why we resort to matrix algebra.

I will now use matrix algebra to analyze the data in Table 5.1. In Chapter 5, I calculated the following:

$$\Sigma x_1^2 = 102.55 \qquad \Sigma x_2^2 = 53.00 \qquad \Sigma x_1 x_2 = 38.50$$

$$\Sigma x_1 y = 95.05 \qquad \Sigma x_2 y = 58.50$$

Therefore,

$$\mathbf{b} = \begin{bmatrix} 102.55 & 38.50 \\ \\ 38.50 & 53.00 \end{bmatrix}^{-1} \begin{bmatrix} 95.05 \\ \\ 58.50 \end{bmatrix}$$

$$\qquad\qquad \mathbf{X}_d'\mathbf{X}_d \qquad\qquad \mathbf{X}_d'\mathbf{y}_d$$

First find the determinant of $\mathbf{X}_d'\mathbf{X}_d$:

$$\left|\mathbf{X}_d'\mathbf{X}_d\right| = \begin{vmatrix} 102.55 & 38.50 \\ \\ 38.50 & 53.00 \end{vmatrix} = (102.55)(53.00) - (38.50)^2 = 3952.90$$

Now invert $(\mathbf{X}_d'\mathbf{X}_d)$:

$$(\mathbf{X}_d'\mathbf{X}_d)^{-1} = \begin{bmatrix} \dfrac{53.00}{3952.90} & \dfrac{-38.50}{3952.90} \\[2ex] \dfrac{-38.50}{3952.90} & \dfrac{102.55}{3952.90} \end{bmatrix} = \begin{bmatrix} .01341 & -.00974 \\[1ex] -.00974 & .02594 \end{bmatrix}$$

$$\mathbf{b} = \begin{bmatrix} .01341 & -.00974 \\[1ex] -.00974 & .02594 \end{bmatrix} \begin{bmatrix} 95.05 \\[1ex] 58.50 \end{bmatrix} = \begin{bmatrix} .7046 \\[1ex] .5919 \end{bmatrix}$$

The b's are identical to those I calculated in Chapter 5. The intercept can now be calculated using the following formula:

$$a = \overline{Y} - b_1\overline{X}_1 - b_2\overline{X}_2 \tag{6.8}$$

Using the means reported in Table 5.1,

$$a = 5.85 - (.7046)(4.35) - (.5919)(5.50) = -.4705$$

The regression equation is

$$Y' = -.4705 + .7046X_1 + .5919X_2$$

Regression and Residual Sums of Squares

The regression sum of squares when using matrices of deviation scores is

$$ss_{reg} = \mathbf{b}'\mathbf{X}_d'\mathbf{y}_d \tag{6.9}$$

$$= [.7046 \quad .5919] \begin{bmatrix} 90.05 \\[1ex] 58.50 \end{bmatrix} = 101.60$$

$$\qquad\quad \mathbf{b}' \qquad\qquad \mathbf{X}_d'\mathbf{y}_d$$

and the residual sum of squares is

$$ss_{res} = \mathbf{y}_d'\mathbf{y}_d - \mathbf{b}'\mathbf{X}_d'\mathbf{y}_d \tag{6.10}$$

$$= 140.55 - 101.60 = 38.95$$

which agree with the values I obtained in Chapter 5.

I could, of course, calculate R^2 now and do tests of significance. However, as these calculations would be identical to those I presented in Chapter 5, I do not present them here. Instead, I introduce the variance/covariance matrix of the b's.

Variance/Covariance Matrix of the b's

As I discussed earlier in the text (e.g., Chapters 2 and 5), each b has a variance associated with it (i.e., the variance of its sampling distribution; the square root of the variance of a b is the standard error of the b). It is also possible to calculate the covariance of two b's. The variance/covariance matrix of the b's is

$$\mathbf{C} = \frac{\mathbf{e}'\mathbf{e}}{N-k-1}\,(\mathbf{X}_d'\mathbf{X}_d)^{-1} = s^2_{y.12\ldots k}(\mathbf{X}_d'\mathbf{X}_d)^{-1} \tag{6.11}$$

where $\mathbf{C}$ = the variance/covariance matrix of the b's; $\mathbf{e}'\mathbf{e}$ = residual sum of squares; N = sample size; k = number of independent variables; and $(\mathbf{X}_d'\mathbf{X}_d)^{-1}$ = inverse of the matrix of deviation scores on the independent variables, $\mathbf{X}_d$, premultiplied by its transpose, $\mathbf{X}_d'$, that is, the inverse of the matrix of the sums of squares and cross products. As indicated in the right-hand term of (6.11), $(\mathbf{e}'\mathbf{e})/(N - k - 1) = s_{y.12...k}^2$ is the variance of estimate, or the mean square residual, which I used repeatedly in earlier chapters (e.g., Chapters 2 and 5). The matrix $\mathbf{C}$ plays an important role in tests of statistical significance. I use it extensively in subsequent chapters (see Chapters 11 through 14). At this point I explain its elements and show how they are used in tests of statistical significance.

Each diagonal element of $\mathbf{C}$ is the variance of the b with which it is associated. Thus c_{11}—the first element of the principal diagonal—is the variance of b_1, c_{22} is the variance of b_2, and so on. $\sqrt{c_{11}}$ is the standard error of b_1, $\sqrt{c_{22}}$ is the standard error of b_2. The off-diagonal elements are the covariances of the b's with which they are associated. Thus, $c_{12} = c_{21}$ is the covariance of b_1 and b_2, and similarly for the other off-diagonal elements. Since there is no danger of confusion—diagonal elements are variances, off-diagonal elements are covariances—it is more convenient to refer to $\mathbf{C}$ as the covariance matrix of the b's.

I now calculate $\mathbf{C}$ for the present example, and use its elements in statistical tests to illustrate and clarify what I said previously. Earlier, I calculated $\mathbf{e}'\mathbf{e} = ss_{res} = 38.95$; $N = 20$; and $k = 2$. Using these values and $(\mathbf{X}_d'\mathbf{X}_d)^{-1}$, which I also calculated earlier,

$$\mathbf{C} = \frac{38.95}{20 - 2 - 1} \begin{bmatrix} .01341 & -.00974 \\ -.00974 & .02594 \end{bmatrix} = \begin{bmatrix} .03072 & -.02232 \\ -.02232 & .05943 \end{bmatrix}$$

As I pointed out in the preceding, the first term on the right is the variance of estimate $(s_{y.12}^2 = 2.29)$ which is, of course, the same value I got in Chapter 5—see the calculations following (5.22). The diagonal elements of $\mathbf{C}$ are the variances of the b's. Therefore, the standard errors of b_1 and b_2 are, respectively, $\sqrt{.03072} = .1753$ and $\sqrt{.05943} = .2438$. These agree with the values I got in Chapter 5. Testing the two b's,

$$t = \frac{b_1}{s_{b_1}} = \frac{.7046}{.1753} = 4.02$$

$$t = \frac{b_2}{s_{b_2}} = \frac{.5919}{.2438} = 2.43$$

Again, the values agree with those I got in Chapter 5. Each has 17 df associated with it (i.e., $N - k - 1$).

I said previously that the off-diagonal elements of $\mathbf{C}$ are the covariances of their respective b's. The standard error of the difference between b_1 and b_2 is

$$s_{b_1 - b_2} = \sqrt{c_{11} + c_{22} - 2c_{12}} \tag{6.12}$$

where c_{11} and c_{22} are the diagonal elements of $\mathbf{C}$ and $c_{12} = c_{21}$ is the off-diagonal element of $\mathbf{C}$. It is worth noting that extensions of (6.12) to designs with more than two independent variables would become unwieldy. But, as I show in subsequent chapters, such designs can be handled with relative ease by matrix algebra.

Applying (6.12) to the present numerical example,

$$s_{b_1 - b_2} = \sqrt{.03072 + .05943 - 2(-.02232)} = \sqrt{.13479} = .3671$$

$$t = \frac{b_1 - b_2}{s_{b_1 - b_2}} = \frac{.7046 - .5919}{.3671} = \frac{.1127}{.3671} = 3.26$$

with 17 df $(N - k - 1)$.

Such a test is meaningful and useful only when the two b*'s are associated with variables that are of the same kind and that are measured by the same type of scale. In the present example, this test is not meaningful.* I introduced it here to acquaint you with this approach that I use frequently in some subsequent chapters, where I test not only differences between two b's, but also linear combinations of more than two b's.

Increments in Regression Sum of Squares

In Chapter 5, I discussed and illustrated the notion of increments in regression sum of squares, or proportion of variance, due to a given variable. That is, the portion of the sum of squares attributed to a given variable, over and above the other variables already in the equation. Such increments can be easily calculated when using matrix operations. An increment in the regression sum of squares due to variable j is

$$ss_{\text{reg}(j)} = \frac{b_j^2}{x^{jj}} \tag{6.13}$$

where $ss_{\text{reg}(j)}$ = increment in regression sum of squares attributed to variable j; b_j = regression coefficient for variable j; and x^{jj} = diagonal element of the inverse of $(\mathbf{X_d'X_d})$ associated with variable j. As calculated in the preceding, $b_1 = .7046$, $b_2 = .5919$, and

$$(\mathbf{X_d'X_d})^{-1} = \begin{bmatrix} .01341 & -.00974 \\ -.00974 & .02594 \end{bmatrix}$$

The increment in the regression sum of squares due to X_1 is

$$ss_{\text{reg}(1)} = \frac{.7046^2}{.01341} = 37.02$$

and due to X_2,

$$ss_{\text{reg}(2)} = \frac{.5919^2}{.02594} = 13.51$$

Compare these results with the same results I got in Chapter 5 (e.g., Type II SS in SAS output for the same data).

If, instead, I wanted to express the increments as proportions of variance, all I would have to do is to divide each increment by the sum of squares of the dependent variable (Σy^2). For the present example, $\Sigma y^2 = 140.55$. Therefore, the increment in proportion of variance accounted for due to X_1 is

$$37.02/140.55 = .263$$

and due to X_2,

$$13.51/140.55 = .096$$

Compare these results with those I calculated in Chapter 5, where I also showed how to test such increments for significance.

My aim in this section was to show how easily terms such as increments in regression sum of squares can be obtained through matrix algebra. In subsequent chapters, I discuss this approach in detail.

AN EXAMPLE WITH TWO INDEPENDENT VARIABLES: CORRELATION COEFFICIENTS

As I explained in Chapter 5, when all the variables are expressed in standard scores (z), regression statistics are calculated using correlation coefficients. For two variables, the regression equation is

$$z'_y = \beta_1 z_1 + \beta_2 z_2 \tag{6.14}$$

where z'_y is the predicted Y in standard scores; β_1 and β_2 are standardized regression coefficients; and z_1 and z_2 are standard scores on X_1 and X_2, respectively.

The matrix equation for the solution of the standardized coefficients is

$$\beta = \mathbf{R}^{-1}\mathbf{r} \tag{6.15}$$

where β is a column vector of standardized coefficients; $\mathbf{R}^{-1}$ is the inverse of the correlation matrix of the independent variables; and $\mathbf{r}$ is a column vector of correlations between each independent variable and the dependent variable. I now apply (6.15) to the data of Table 5.1. In Chapter 5 (see Table 5.2), I calculated

$$r_{12} = .522 \qquad r_{y1} = .792 \qquad r_{y2} = .678$$

Therefore,

$$\mathbf{R} = \begin{bmatrix} 1.000 & .522 \\ .522 & 1.000 \end{bmatrix}$$

r_{11} and r_{22} are, of course, equal to 1.000.

The determinant of $\mathbf{R}$ is

$$|\mathbf{R}| = \begin{vmatrix} 1.000 & .522 \\ .522 & 1.000 \end{vmatrix} = (1.000)^2 - (.522)^2 = .72752$$

The inverse of $\mathbf{R}$ is

$$\mathbf{R}^{-1} = \begin{bmatrix} \dfrac{1.000}{.72752} & \dfrac{-.522}{.72752} \\ \dfrac{-.522}{.72752} & \dfrac{1.000}{.72752} \end{bmatrix} = \begin{bmatrix} 1.37454 & -.71751 \\ -.71751 & 1.37454 \end{bmatrix}$$

Applying (6.15),

$$\beta = \begin{bmatrix} 1.37454 & -.71751 \\ -.71751 & 1.37454 \end{bmatrix} \begin{bmatrix} .792 \\ .678 \end{bmatrix} = \begin{bmatrix} .602 \\ .364 \end{bmatrix}$$

The regression equation is $z'_y = .602z_1 + .364z_2$. Compare with the β's I calculated in Chapter 5. Having calculated β's, b's (unstandardized regression coefficients) can be calculated as follows:

$$b_j = \beta_j \frac{s_y}{s_j} \tag{6.16}$$

where b_j = unstandardized regression coefficient for variable j; β_j = standardized regression coefficient for variable j; s_y = standard deviation of the dependent variable, Y; and s_j = standard deviation of variable *j*. I do not apply (6.16) here, as I applied the same formula in Chapter 5—see (5.16).

Squared Multiple Correlation

The squared multiple correlation can be calculated as follows:

$$R^2 = \boldsymbol{\beta}'\mathbf{r} \tag{6.17}$$

where $\boldsymbol{\beta}'$ is a row vector of β's (the transpose of $\boldsymbol{\beta}$), and $\mathbf{r}$ is a column of correlations of each independent variable with the dependent variable. For our data,

$$[.602 \quad .364]\begin{bmatrix} .792 \\ .678 \end{bmatrix} = .72$$

I calculated the same value in Chapter 5.

It is, of course, possible to test the significance of R^2, as I showed in Chapter 5.

Increment in Proportion of Variance

In the preceding, I showed how to calculate the increment in regression sum of squares due to a given variable. Using correlation matrices, the proportion of variance incremented by a given variable can be calculated as follows:

$$prop_{(j)} = \frac{\beta_j^2}{r^{jj}} \tag{6.18}$$

where $prop_{(j)}$ = increment in proportion of variance due to variable *j*; and r^{jj} = diagonal element of the inverse of $\mathbf{R}$ (i.e., $\mathbf{R}^{-1}$) associated with variable *j*. As calculated previously,

$$\beta_1 = .602 \qquad \beta_2 = .364$$

$$\mathbf{R}^{-1} = \begin{bmatrix} 1.37454 & -.71751 \\ -.71751 & 1.37454 \end{bmatrix}$$

The increment in proportion of variance due to X_1 is

$$prop_{(1)} = \frac{.602^2}{1.37454} = .264$$

The increment due to X_2 is

$$prop_{(2)} = \frac{.364^2}{1.37454} = .096$$

Compare with the corresponding values I calculated earlier, as well as with those I calculated in Chapter 5.

Finally, just as one may obtain increments in proportions of variance from increments in regression sums of squares (see the previous calculations), so can one do the reverse operation. That is, having increments in proportions of variance, increments in regression sums of squares can be calculated. All one need do is multiply each increment by the sum of squares of the dependent variable (Σy^2). For the present example, $\Sigma y^2 = 140.55$. Therefore,

$$ss_{reg(1)} = (.264)(140.55) = 37.11$$

$$ss_{reg(2)} = (.096)(140.55) = 13.49$$

These values agree (within rounding) with those I calculated earlier.

CONCLUDING REMARKS

In this chapter, I introduced and illustrated matrix algebra for the calculation of regression statistics. Despite the fact that it cannot begin to convey the generality, power, and elegance of the matrix approach, I used a small numerical example with one independent variable to enable you to concentrate on understanding the properties of the matrices used and on the matrix operations. Whatever the number of variables, the matrix equations are the same. For instance, (6.3) for the solution of a and the b's, $\mathbf{b} = (\mathbf{X'X})^{-1}\mathbf{X'y}$, could refer to one, two, three, or any number of independent variables. Therefore, what is important is to understand the meaning of this equation, the properties of its elements, and the matrix operations that are required. In any case, with large data sets the calculations are best done by computers. With this in mind, I have shown how to use MINITAB, SAS, and SPSS to analyze the same example. I then applied matrix operations to an example with two independent variables.

At this stage, you probably don't appreciate, or are unimpressed by, the properties of matrices used in multiple regression analysis. If this is true, rest assured that in subsequent chapters I demonstrate the usefulness of matrix operations. Following are but a couple of instances. In Chapter 11, I show how to use the variance/covariance matrix of the b's ($\mathbf{C}$), I introduced in this chapter, to test multiple comparisons among means; in Chapter 15, I show how to use it to test multiple comparisons among adjusted means in the analysis of covariance. In Chapters 9 and 10, I use properties of the inverse of the correlation matrix of the independent variables, $\mathbf{R}^{-1}$, which I introduced earlier, to enhance your understanding of elements of multiple regression analysis or to facilitate the calculation of such elements.

In sum, greater appreciation of the matrix approach is bound to occur when I use it in more advanced treatments of multiple regression analysis, not to mention the topics I introduce in Parts 3 and 4 of this book. Whenever you experience problems with the matrix notation or matrix operations I present in subsequent chapters, I urge you to return to this chapter and to Appendix A.

STUDY SUGGESTIONS

1. I used the following correlation matrices, **A** and **B,** in Study Suggestion 3 in Chapter 5. This time, do the following calculations using matrix algebra. Compare the results with those calculated in Chapter 5.

	X_1	X_2	Y		X_1	X_2	Y
X_1	1.0	0	.7	X_1	1.0	.4	.7
X_2	0	1.0	.6	X_2	.4	1.0	.6
Y	.7	.6	1.0	Y	.7	.6	1.0
		A				**B**	

(a) Calculate the inverse of the correlation matrix of the independent variables, X_1 and X_2, for **A** and **B**.

(b) Multiply each of the inverses calculated under (a) by the column of the zero-order correlations of the X's with Y. What is the meaning of the resulting values?

(c) Multiply each row obtained under (b) by the column of the zero-order correlations of the X's with Y. What is the meaning of the resulting values?

2. The following summary statistics, which I took from Study Suggestion 1 in Chapter 5, are presented in the

format I used in Table 5.2. That is, diagonal elements are sums of squares, elements above the diagonal are sums of cross products, and elements below the diagonal are correlations. The last line contains standard deviations.

	y	x_1	x_2
y	165.00	100.50	63.00
x_1	.6735	134.95	15.50
x_2	.5320	.1447	85.00
s	2.9469	2.6651	2.1151

Use matrix algebra to do the calculations indicated, and compare your results with those I obtained in Chapter 5. Calculate the following:

(a) The inverse of the matrix of the sums of squares and cross products of the X's: $(X'_dX_d)^{-1}$.

(b) $(X'_dX_d)^{-1}X'_dy_d$, where X'_dy_d is a column of the cross products of the X's with Y. What is the meaning of the resulting values?

(c) The standardized regression coefficients (β's), using the b's obtained in the preceding and the standard deviations of the variables.

(d) $b'X'_dy_d$, where b' is a row vector of the b's obtained previously. What is the meaning of the obtained result?

(e) The residual sum of squares, and $s^2_{y.12}$.

(f) $s^2_{y.12}(X'_dX_d)^{-1}$. What is the resulting matrix?

(g) The t ratios for the b's, using relevant values from the matrix obtained under (f).

(h) (1) the increment in the regression sum of squares due to X_1, over and above X_2, and (2) the increment in the regression sum of squares due to X_2, over and above X_1. For the preceding, use the b's and relevant values from $(X'_dX_d)^{-1}$.

(i) $R^2_{y.12}$ and the F ratio for the test of R^2. ($N = 20$.) If you have access to a matrix procedure, replicate the previous analyses and compare the results with those you got through hand calculations.

ANSWERS

1. (a)

$$\begin{bmatrix} 1.0 & 0 \\ 0 & 1.0 \end{bmatrix} \quad \begin{bmatrix} 1.19048 & -.47619 \\ -.47619 & 1.19048 \end{bmatrix}$$
$$\quad\quad A \quad\quad\quad\quad\quad\quad B$$

(b) **A**: [.7 .6]; **B**: [.54762 .38096]. These are the standardized regression coefficients, β's, for each of the matrices. Note that the β's for **A** are equal to the zero-order correlations of the X's with the Y's. Why?

(c) **A**: .85; **B**: .61. These are the R^2's of Y on X_1 and X_2 in **A** and **B**, respectively.

2. (a)

$$(X'_dX_d)^{-1} = \begin{bmatrix} .0075687 & -.0013802 \\ -.0013802 & .0120164 \end{bmatrix}$$

(b) [.67370 .61833]. These are the unstandardized regression coefficients: b's.

(c) $\beta_1 = .60928$; $\beta_2 = .44380$

(d) $106.66164 = ss_{reg}$

(e) $ss_{res} = 58.33836$; $s^2_{y.12} = 3.43167$

(f)

$$\begin{bmatrix} .0259733 & -.0047364 \\ -.0047364 & .0412363 \end{bmatrix}$$

This is the variance/covariance matrix of the b's: **C**.

(g) t for $b_1 = 4.18$, with 17 df; t for $b_2 = 3.04$, with 17 df

(h) (1) 59.96693; (2) 31.81752

(i) $R^2_{y.12} = .6464$; $F = 15.54$, with 2 and 17 df

7

Statistical Control: Partial and Semipartial Correlation

In this chapter, I introduce partial and semipartial correlations, both because these are meaning-ful techniques in their own right and because they are integral parts of multiple regression analy-sis. Understanding these techniques is bound to lead to a better understanding of multiple regression analysis.

I begin with a brief discussion of the idea of control in scientific research, followed by a presentation of partial correlation as a means of exercising statistical control. I then outline and illustrate causal assumptions underlying the application and interpretation of partial correla-tion. Among other things, I discuss effects of measurement errors on the partial correlation. Following that, I introduce the idea of semipartial correlation and explicate its role in multi-ple regression analysis. Throughout, I use numerical examples, which I analyze by hand and/or by computer, to illustrate the concepts I present. I conclude the chapter with a comment on suppressor variables and a brief discussion of generalizations of partial and semipartial correlations.

CONTROL IN SCIENTIFIC RESEARCH

Studying relations among variables is not easy. The most severe problem is expressed in the question: Is the relation I am studying what I think it is? This can be called the problem of the va-lidity of relations. Science is basically preoccupied with formulating and verifying statements of the form of "if p then q"—if dogmatism, then ethnocentrism, for example. The problem of validity of relations boils down essentially to the question of whether it is *this p* that is re-lated to q or, in other words, whether the discovered relation between *this* independent vari-able and the dependent variable is "truly" the relation we think it is. To have some confidence in the validity of any particular "if p then q" statement, we have to have some confidence that it is "really" p that is related to q and not r or s or t. To attain such confidence, scientists in-voke techniques of control.

Reflecting the complexity and difficulty of studying relations, control is itself a complex subject. Yet, the technical analytic notions I present in this chapter are best understood when discussed in the context of control. A discussion of control, albeit brief, is therefore essential (for more detailed discussions, see, e.g., Kish, 1959, 1975; Pedhazur & Schmelkin, 1991, Chapter 10).

In scientific research, control means control of variance. Among various ways of exercising control, the best known is to set up an experiment, whose most elementary form is an experimental group and a so-called control group. The scientist tries to increase the difference between the two groups by experimental manipulation. To set up a research design is itself a form of control. One designs a study, in part, to maximize systematic variance, minimize error variance, and control extraneous variance.

Other well-known forms of control are subject matching and subject selection. To control the variable sex, for instance, one can select as subjects only males or only females. This of course reduces sex variability to zero.

Potentially the most powerful form of control in research is the random assignment of subjects to treatment groups (or treatments and controls). Other things being equal, when people are randomly assigned to different groups, it is reasonable to assume that the groups are equal in all characteristics. Therefore, when groups thus composed are exposed to different treatments, it is plausible to conclude that observed differences among them on the phenomenon of interest (the dependent variable) are due to the treatments (the independent variable).

Unfortunately, in much behavioral research random assignment is not possible on ethical and/or practical grounds. Hence, much of the research is either quasi-experimental or nonexperimental. Without going into the details,[1] I will point out that although one or more variables are manipulated in both experimental and quasi-experimental research, random assignment to treatments is absent in the latter. Consequently, statements about the effects of manipulations are necessarily much more tenuous in quasi-experimental research. In nonexperimental research, the presumed independent variable is beyond the manipulative control of the researcher. All the researcher can do is observe the phenomenon of interest (dependent variable) and attempt to discern the variable(s) that might have led to it, that might have affected it (presumed independent variable).

Testing alternative hypotheses to the hypothesis under study is a form of control, although different in kind from those I already discussed and will discuss later. The point of this discussion is that different forms of control are similar in function. They are different expressions of the same principle: control is control of variance. So it is with *statistical control,* which means the use of statistical methods to identify, isolate, or nullify variance in a dependent variable that is presumably "caused" by one or more independent variables that are extraneous to the particular relation or relations under study. Statistical control is particularly important when one is interested in the joint or mutual effects of more than one independent variable on a dependent variable, because one has to be able to sort out and control the effects of some variables while studying the effects of other variables. Multiple regression and related forms of analysis provide ways to achieve such control.

---

[1]For a discussion of different types of designs, see Pedhazur and Schmelkin (1991, Chapters 12–14).

Some Examples

In his preface to *The Doctor's Dilemma,* Shaw (1930) gave some interesting examples of the pitfalls to interpreting relations among variables as being "real" because other relevant variables were not controlled.

> [C]omparisons which are really comparisons between two social classes with different standards of nutrition and education are palmed off as comparisons between the results of a certain medical treatment and its neglect. Thus it is easy to prove that the wearing of tall hats and the carrying of umbrellas enlarges the chest, prolongs life and confers comparative immunity from disease; for the statistics shew that the classes which use these articles are bigger, healthier, and live longer than the class which never dreams of possessing such things. It does not take much perspicacity to see that what really makes this difference is not the tall hat and the umbrella, but the wealth and nourishment of which they are evidence, and that a gold watch or membership of a club in Pall Mall might be proved in the same way to have the like sovereign virtues. A university degree, a daily bath, the owning of thirty pairs of trousers, a knowledge of Wagner's music, a pew in the church, anything, in short, that implies more means and better nurture than the mass of laborers enjoy, can be statistically palmed off as a magic-spell conferring all sort of privileges. (p. 55)

Shaw's examples illustrate what are called spurious correlations. When two variables are correlated solely because they are both affected by the same cause, the correlation is said to be spurious. Once the effects of the common cause are controlled, or removed from the two variables, the correlation between them vanishes. A spurious correlation between variables Z and Y is depicted in Figure 7.1. Removing the effects of the common cause, X, from both Z and Y results in a zero correlation between them. As I show in the following, this can be accomplished by the calculation of the partial correlation between Z and Y, when X is partialed out.

Here is another example of what is probably a spurious correlation. Under the heading "Prof Fired after Finding Sex Great for Scholars," Goodwin (1971) reported, "Active sex contributes to academic success, says a sociologist who conducted a survey of undergraduates at the University of Puerto Rico." Basically, Dr. Martin Sagrera found a positive correlation between the reported frequency of sexual intercourse and grade-point average (GPA). The finding was taken seriously not only by the university's administration, who fired Sagrera, but also by Sagrera himself, who was quoted as saying, "These findings appear to contradict the Freudian view that sublimation of sex is a powerful factor in intellectual achievement." Problems of research based on self-reports notwithstanding, it requires little imagination to formulate hypotheses about the factor, or factors, that might be responsible for the observed correlation between frequency of sexual intercourse and GPA.

An example of what some medical researchers believe is a spurious correlation was reported by Brody (1973) under the heading "New Heart Study Absolves Coffee." The researchers were

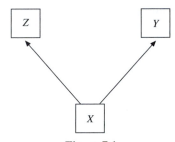

Figure 7.1

reported to have challenged the view held by other medical researchers that there is a causal rela-tion between the consumption of coffee and heart attacks. While they did not deny that the two variables are correlated, they claimed that the correlation is spurious. "Rather than coffee drink-ing itself, other traits associated with coffee drinking habits—such as personality, national ori-gin, occupation and climate of residence—may be the real heart-disease risk factors, the California researchers suggested."

Casti (1990) drew attention to the "familiar example" of "a high positive correlation between the number of storks seen nesting in English villages and the number of children born in these same villages" (p. 36). He then referred the reader to the section "To Dig Deeper," where he explained:

> It turns out that the community involved was one of mostly new houses with young couples living in them. Moreover, storks don't like to nest beside chimneys that other storks have used in the past. Thus, there is a *common cause* [italics added]: new houses occupied on the inside by young couples and oc-cupied on the outside by storks. (p. 412)

A variable that, when left uncontrolled in behavioral research, often leads to spurious correla-tions is chronological age. Using a group of children varying in age, say from 4 to 15, it can be shown that there is a very high positive correlation between, say, the size of the right-hand palm and mental ability, or between shoe size and intelligence. In short, there is bound to be a high correlation between any two variables that are affected by age, when the latter is not controlled for. Age may be controlled for by using a sample of children of the same age. Alternatively, age may be controlled statistically by calculating the partial correlation coefficient between two vari-ables, with age partialed out. Terman (1926, p. 168), for example, reported correlations of .835 and .876 between mental age and standing height for groups of heterogeneous boys and girls, re-spectively. After partialing out age, these correlations dropped to .219 and .211 for boys and girls, respectively. Control for an additional variable(s) may have conceivably led to a further re-duction in the correlation between intelligence and height. In the following I discuss assump-tions that need to be met when exercising such statistical controls. At this stage, my aim is only to introduce the meaning of statistical control.

The examples I presented thus far illustrate the potential use of partial correlations for detect-ing spurious correlations. Another use of partial correlations is in the study of the effects of a variable as it is mediated by another variable. Assume, for example, that it is hypothesized that socioeconomic status (SES) does not affect achievement (ACH) directly but only indirectly through the mediation of achievement motivation (AM). In other words, it is hypothesized that SES affects AM, which in turn affects ACH. This hypothesis, which is depicted in Figure 7.2, may be tested by calculating the correlation between SES and ACH while controlling for, or par-tialing out, AM. A zero, or close to zero, partial correlation between SES and ACH would lend support to this hypothesis. Carroll (1975), for instance, reported that "Student socioeconomic background tended not to be associated with performance when other variables, such as student interest, etc., were controlled" (p. 29). Such a statement should, of course, not be construed that socioeconomic background is not an important variable, but that its effects on performances may be mediated by other variables, such as student interest.

Figure 7.2

THE NATURE OF CONTROL BY PARTIALING

Formulas for calculating partial correlation coefficients are comparatively simple. What they accomplish, however, is not so simple. To help you understand what is being accomplished, I present a detailed analysis of what is behind the statistical operations. I suggest that you work through the calculations and the reasoning I present.

The symbol for the correlation between two variables with a third variable partialed out is $r_{12.3}$, which means the correlation between variables 1 and 2, partialing out variable 3. Similarly, $r_{xy.z}$ is the partial correlation between X and Y when Z is partialed out. The two variables whose partial correlation is sought are generally called the primary variables, whereas variables that are partialed out are generally called control variables. In the previous examples, variables 1 and 2 are primary, whereas 3 is a control variable. Similarly, X and Y are primary variables, whereas Z is a control variable.

Though it is customary to speak of the variable being partialed out as being controlled or held constant, such expressions should not be taken literally. *A partial correlation is a correlation between two variables from which the linear relations, or effects, of another variable(s) have been removed.* Stated differently, a partial correlation is an estimate of the correlation between two variables in a population that is homogeneous on the variable(s) that is being partialed out. Assume, for example, that we are interested in the correlation between height and intelligence and that the sample consists of a heterogeneous group of children ranging in age from 4 to 10. To control for age, we can calculate the correlation between height and intelligence within each age group. That is, we can calculate the correlation among, say, children of age 4, 5, 6, and so on. A partial correlation between height and intelligence, with age partialed out, is a weighted average of the correlations between the two variables when calculated within each age group in the range of ages under consideration. To see how this is accomplished, I turn to a discussion of some elements of regression analysis.

Partial Correlation and Regression Analysis

Suppose that we have data on three variables, X_1, X_2, and X_3 as reported in Table 7.1. Using the methods presented in Chapter 2, calculate the regression equation for predicting X_1 from X_3, and verify that it is[2]

$$X_1' = 1.2 + .6X_3$$

Similarly, calculate the regression equation for predicting X_2 from X_3:

$$X_2' = .3 + .9X_3$$

Having calculated the two regression equations, calculate for each subject predicted values for X_1 and X_2, as well as the residuals for each variable; that is, $e_1 = X_1 - X_1'$ and $e_2 = X_2 - X_2'$. I reported these residuals in Table 7.1 in columns e_1 and e_2, respectively.

It is useful to pursue some of the relations among the variables reported in Table 7.1. To facilitate the calculations and provide a succinct summary of them, Table 7.2 presents summary statistics for Table 7.1. The diagonal of Table 7.2 comprises deviation sums of squares, whereas the

---

[2]I suggest that you do these and the other calculations I do in this chapter. Also, do not be misled by the simplicity and the uniformity of the numbers and variables in this example. I chose these very simple numbers so that you could follow the discussion easily.

Table 7.1   Illustrative Data for Three Variables and Residuals for Two

	X_1	X_2	X_3	e_1	e_2
	1	3	3	−2.0	0
	2	1	2	−.4	−1.1
	3	2	1	1.2	.8
	4	4	4	.4	.1
	5	5	5	.8	.2
Σ:	15	15	15	0	0

NOTE: e_1 are the residuals when X_1 is predicted from X_3; e_2 are the residuals when X_2 is predicted from X_3.

values above the diagonal are sums of cross product deviations. The values below the diagonal are correlations.

I repeat a formula for the correlation coefficient, which I introduced in Chapter 2, (2.41):

$$r_{x_1 x_2} = \frac{\Sigma x_1 x_2}{\sqrt{\Sigma x_1^2 \, \Sigma x_2^2}} \tag{7.1}$$

Using the appropriate sum of cross products and sums of squares from Table 7.2, calculate

$$r_{x_3 e_1} = \frac{0}{\sqrt{(10)(6.4)}} = .0 \qquad r_{x_3 e_2} = \frac{0}{\sqrt{(10)(1.9)}} = .0$$

As the sum of cross products in each case is zero, the correlation is necessarily zero. This illustrates an important principle: The correlation between a predictor and the residuals of another variable, calculated from the predictor, is always zero. This makes sense as the residual is that part of the criterion that is not predictable by the predictor—that is, the error. When we generate a set of residuals for X_1 by regressing it on X_3, we say that we residualize X_1 with respect to X_3. In Table 7.1, e_1 and e_2 were obtained by residualizing X_1 and X_2 with respect to X_3. Consequently, e_1 and e_2 represent those parts of X_1 and X_2 that are not shared with X_3, or those parts that are left over after the effects of X_3 are taken out from X_1 and X_2. Calculating the correlation between e_1 and e_2 is therefore tantamount to determining the relation between two residualized variables. Stated differently, it is the correlation between X_1 and X_2 after the effects of X_3 were taken out, or partialed, from both of them. This, then, is the meaning of a partial correlation coefficient. Using relevant values from Table 7.2,

$$r_{12.3} = r_{e_1 e_2} = \frac{1.6}{\sqrt{(6.4)(1.9)}} = .46$$

Table 7.2   Deviation Sums of Squares and Cross Products and Correlations Based on Data in Table 7.1

	X_1	X_2	X_3	e_1	e_2
X_1	10.0	7.0	6.0	6.4	1.6
X_2	.7	10.0	9.0	1.6	1.9
X_3	.6	.9	10.0	0	0
e_1			.0	6.4	1.6
e_2			.0	.46	1.9

NOTE: The sums of squares are on the diagonal, the cross products are above the diagonal. Correlations, shown italicized, are below the diagonal.

I have gone through these rather lengthy calculations to convey the meaning of the partial correlation. However, calculating the residuals is not necessary to obtain the partial correlation coefficient. Instead, it may be obtained by applying a simple formula in which the correlations among the three variables are used:

$$r_{12.3} = \frac{r_{12} - r_{13}r_{23}}{\sqrt{1 - r_{13}^2} \sqrt{1 - r_{23}^2}} \tag{7.2}$$

Before applying (7.2), I will explain its terms. To this end, it will be instructive to examine another version of the formula for the bivariate correlation coefficient. In (7.1) I used a formula composed of sums of squares to calculate correlation coefficients. Dividing the terms of (7.1) by $N - 1$ yields

$$r_{x_1 x_2} = \frac{s_{x_1 x_2}}{s_{x_1} s_{x_2}} \tag{7.3}$$

where the numerator is the covariance of X_1 and X_2 and the denominator is the product of the standard deviations of X_1 and X_2—see (2.40) in Chapter 2. It can be shown (see Nunnally, 1978, p. 169) that the numerator of (7.2) is the covariance of standardized residualized variables and that each term under the radical in the denominator is the standard deviation of a standardized residualized variable (see Nunnally, 1978, p. 129). In other words, though the notation of (7.2) may seem strange, it is a special case of (7.3) for standardized residualized variables.[3]

Turning to the application of (7.2), calculate first the necessary bivariate correlations, using sums of products and sums of squares from Table 7.2.

$$r_{12} = \frac{7}{\sqrt{(10)(10)}} = .7 \qquad r_{13} = \frac{6}{\sqrt{(10)(10)}} = .6 \qquad r_{23} = \frac{9}{\sqrt{(10)(10)}} = .9$$

Accordingly,

$$r_{12.3} = \frac{(.7) - (.6)(.9)}{\sqrt{1 - .6^2} \sqrt{1 - .9^2}} = \frac{.7 - .54}{\sqrt{.64} \sqrt{.19}} = \frac{.16}{.3487} = .46$$

I got the same value when I calculated the correlation between the residuals, e_1 and e_2. From the foregoing discussion and illustrations, it should be evident that the partial correlation is symmetric: $r_{12.3} = r_{21.3}$.

The partial correlation between two variables when one variable is partialed out is called a first-order partial correlation. As I will show, it is possible to partial out, or hold constant, more than one variable. For example, $r_{12.34}$ is the second-order partial correlation between variables 1 and 2 from which 3 and 4 were partialed out. And $r_{12.345}$ is a third-order partial correlation. The order of the partial correlation coefficient is indicated by the number of variables that are controlled—that is, the number of variables that appear after the dot. Consistent with this terminology, the correlation between two variables from which no other variables are partialed out is called a zero-order correlation. Thus, r_{12}, r_{13}, and r_{23}, which I used in (7.2), are zero-order correlations.

In the previous example, the zero-order correlation between variables 1 and 2 (r_{12}) is .7, whereas the first-order partial correlation between 1 and 2 when 3 is partialed out ($r_{12.3}$) is .46.

---

[3]In the event that you are puzzled by the explanation, I suggest that you carry out the following calculations: (1) standardize the variables of Table 7.1 (i.e., transform them to z_1, z_2, and z_3); (2) regress z_1 on z_3; (3) predict z_1 from z_3, and calculate the residuals; (4) regress z_2 on z_3; (5) predict z_2 from z_3, and calculate the residuals; (6) calculate the covariance of the residuals obtained in steps 3 and 5, as well as the standard deviations of these residuals. Compare your results with the values I use in the application of (7.2) in the next paragraph.

Careful study of (7.2) indicates that the sign and the size of the partial correlation coefficient are determined by the signs and the sizes of the zero-order correlations among the variables. It is possible, for instance, for the sign of the partial correlation to differ from the sign of the zero-order correlation coefficient between the same variables. Also, the partial correlation coefficient may be larger or smaller than the zero-order correlation coefficient between the variables.

Higher-Order Partials

I said previously that one may partial, or control for, more than one variable. The basic idea and analytic approach are the same as those I presented in relation to first-order partial correlations. For example, to calculate $r_{12.34}$ (second-order partial correlation between X_1 and X_2, partialing X_3 and X_4), I could (1) residualize X_1 and X_2 with respect to X_3 and X_4, thereby creating two sets of residuals, e_1 (residuals of X_1) and e_2 (residuals of X_2), and (2) correlate e_1 and e_2. This process is, however, quite laborious. To get e_1, for instance, it is necessary to (1) regress X_1 on X_3 and X_4 (i.e., do a multiple regression analysis); (2) calculate the regression equation: $X_1' = a + b_3X_3 + b_4X_4$; (3) use this equation to get predicted scores (X_1'); and (4) calculate the residuals (i.e., $e_1 = X_1 - X_1'$). A similar set of operations is necessary to residualize X_2 with respect to X_3 and X_4 to obtain e_2.

As in the case of a first-order partial correlation, however, it is not necessary to go through the calculations just outlined. I outlined them to indicate what in effect is accomplished when a second-order partial correlation is calculated. The formula for a second-order partial correlation, say, $r_{12.34}$ is

$$r_{12.34} = \frac{r_{12.3} - r_{14.3}r_{24.3}}{\sqrt{1 - r_{14.3}^2}\sqrt{1 - r_{24.3}^2}} \tag{7.4}$$

The format of (7.4) is the same as (7.2), except that the terms in the former are first-order partials, whereas those in the latter are zero-order correlations.

I will now calculate $r_{12.34}$, using the zero-order correlations reported in Table 7.3. First, it is necessary to calculate three first-order partial correlations:

$$r_{12.3} = \frac{r_{12} - r_{13}r_{23}}{\sqrt{1 - r_{13}^2}\sqrt{1 - r_{23}^2}} = \frac{.6735 - (.5320)(.1447)}{\sqrt{1 - .5320^2}\sqrt{1 - .1447^2}} = .7120$$

$$r_{14.3} = \frac{r_{14} - r_{13}r_{34}}{\sqrt{1 - r_{13}^2}\sqrt{1 - r_{34}^2}} = \frac{.3475 - (.5320)(.0225)}{\sqrt{1 - .5320^2}\sqrt{1 - .0225^2}} = .3964$$

$$r_{24.3} = \frac{r_{24} - r_{23}r_{34}}{\sqrt{1 - r_{23}^2}\sqrt{1 - r_{34}^2}} = \frac{.3521 - (.1447)(.0225)}{\sqrt{1 - .1447^2}\sqrt{1 - .0225^2}} = .3526$$

Table 7.3 Correlation Matrix for Four Variables

	X_1	X_2	X_3	X_4
X_1	1.0000	.6735	.5320	.3475
X_2	.6735	1.0000	.1447	.3521
X_3	.5320	.1447	1.0000	.0225
X_4	.3475	.3521	.0225	1.0000

Applying (7.4),

$$r_{12.34} = \frac{r_{12.3} - r_{14.3}r_{24.3}}{\sqrt{1 - r_{14.3}^2}\sqrt{1 - r_{24.3}^2}} = \frac{.7120 - (.3964)(.3526)}{\sqrt{1 - .3964^2}\sqrt{1 - .3526^2}} = \frac{.5722}{.8591} = .6660$$

In this particular example, the zero-order correlation does not differ much from the second-order partial correlation: .6735 and .6660, respectively.

Formula (7.4) can be extended to calculate partial correlations of any order. The higher the order of the partial correlation, however, the larger the number of lower-order partials one would have to calculate. For a systematic approach to successive partialing, see Nunnally (1978, pp. 168–175).

Computer Programs.   Although some software packages (e.g., BMDP and SPSS) have special procedures for partial correlation, I will limit my presentation to the use of multiple regression programs for the calculation of partial and semipartial correlations. In the next section, I show how to calculate partial correlations of any order through multiple correlations. Such an approach is not only more straightforward and does not require specialized computer programs for the calculation of partial correlations, but also shows the relation between partial and multiple correlation.

Partial Correlations via Multiple Correlations

Partial correlation can be viewed as a relation between residual variances in a somewhat different way than described in the preceding discussion. $R_{1.23}^2$ expresses the variance in X_1 accounted for by X_2 and X_3. Recall that $1 - R_{1.23}^2$ expresses the variance in X_1 *not* accounted for by the regression of X_1 on X_2 and X_3. Similarly, $1 - R_{1.3}^2$ expresses the variance *not* accounted for by the regression of X_1 on X_3. The squared partial correlation of X_1 with X_2 partialing X_3 is expressed as follows:

$$r_{12.3}^2 = \frac{R_{1.23}^2 - R_{1.3}^2}{1 - R_{1.3}^2} \tag{7.5}$$

The numerator of (7.5) indicates the proportion of variance incremented by variable 2, that is, the proportion of variance accounted for by X_2 after the effects of X_3 have been taken into account.[4] The denominator of (7.5) indicates the residual variance, that is, the variance left after what X_3 is able to account for. Thus, the squared partial correlation coefficient is a ratio of variance incremented to residual variance.

To apply (7.5) to the data of Table 7.1, it is necessary to calculate first $R_{1.23}^2$. From Table 7.2, $r_{12} = .7$, $r_{13} = .6$, and $r_{23} = .9$. Using (5.20),

$$R_{1.23}^2 = \frac{r_{12}^2 + r_{13}^2 - 2r_{12}r_{13}r_{23}}{1 - r_{23}^2} = \frac{.7^2 + .6^2 - 2(.7)(.6)(.9)}{1 - .9^2} = \frac{.094}{.19} = .4947$$

Applying (7.5),

$$r_{12.3}^2 = \frac{.4947 - .6^2}{1 - .6^2} = \frac{.1347}{.64} = .2105$$

---

[4]In Chapter 5, I pointed out that this is a squared semipartial correlation—a topic I discuss later in this chapter.

$r_{12.3} = \sqrt{r_{12.3}^2} = \sqrt{.2105} = .46$, which is the same as the value I obtained earlier, when I used (7.2).

An alternative formula for the calculation of the squared partial correlation via the multiple correlation is

$$r_{12.3}^2 = \frac{R_{2.13}^2 - R_{2.3}^2}{1 - R_{2.3}^2} \tag{7.6}$$

Note the pattern in the numerators of (7.5) and (7.6): the first term is the squared multiple correlation of one of the primary variables (X_1 or X_2) with the remaining variables; the second term is the squared zero-order correlation of the same primary variable with the control variable—that is, variable 3.[5] In (7.5) and (7.6), the denominator is one minus the right-hand term of the numerator. I apply now (7.6) to the numerical example I analyzed earlier.

$$R_{2.13}^2 = \frac{r_{21}^2 + r_{23}^2 - 2r_{21}r_{23}r_{13}}{1 - r_{13}^2} = \frac{.7^2 + .9^2 - 2(.7)(.9)(.6)}{1 - .6^2} = \frac{.544}{.64} = .85$$

$$r_{12.3}^2 = \frac{.85 - .81}{1 - .81} = \frac{.04}{.19} = .2105$$

which is the same value as the one I obtained when I used (7.5). As I stated earlier, the partial correlation is symmetric; that is, $r_{12.3} = r_{21.3}$.

Because (7.5) or (7.6) yields a squared partial correlation coefficient, it is not possible to tell whether the sign of the partial correlation coefficient is positive or negative. The sign of the partial correlation coefficient is the same as the sign of the regression coefficient (b or β) in which any control variables are partialed out. Thus, if (7.5) is used to calculate $r_{12.3}^2$, the sign of $r_{12.3}$ is the same as the sign of $\beta_{12.3}$ (or $b_{12.3}$) in the equation in which X_1 is regressed on X_2 and X_3. Similarly, if (7.6) is used, the sign of $r_{12.3}$ is the same as that of $\beta_{21.3}$ (or $b_{21.3}$) in the equation in which X_2 is regressed on X_1 and X_3.

Generalization of (7.5) or (7.6) to higher-order partial correlations is straightforward. Thus the formula for a squared second-order partial correlation via multiple correlations is

$$r_{12.34}^2 = \frac{R_{1.234}^2 - R_{1.34}^2}{1 - R_{1.34}^2} \tag{7.7}$$

or

$$r_{12.34}^2 = \frac{R_{2.134}^2 - R_{2.34}^2}{1 - R_{2.34}^2} \tag{7.8}$$

The formula for a squared third-order partial correlation is

$$r_{12.345}^2 = \frac{R_{1.2345}^2 - R_{1.345}^2}{1 - R_{1.345}^2} = \frac{R_{2.1345}^2 - R_{2.345}^2}{1 - R_{2.345}^2} \tag{7.9}$$

COMPUTER ANALYSES

To apply the approach I outlined in the preceding section, relevant R^2's have to be calculated. This can be best accomplished by a computer program. In what follows, I show first how to use SPSS REGRESSION to calculate R^2's necessary for the application of (7.7) and (7.8) to the data

---

[5]For more than one control variable, see (7.7) and (7.8).

of Table 7.3. Following that, I give input listing for SAS, along with minimal output, to show that partial correlations are part of the output.

In earlier applications of the aforementioned packages, I used raw data as input. In the present section, I illustrate the use of summary data (e.g., correlation matrix) as input.

SPSS

Input

```
TITLE TABLE 7.3, FOR PARTIALS.
MATRIX DATA VARIABLES=X1 TO X4
   /CONTENTS=CORR N.      [reading correlation matrix and N]
BEGIN DATA
1
   .6735   1
   .5320   .1447   1
   .3475   .3521   .0225   1
100   100   100   100
END DATA
REGRESSION MATRIX=IN(*)/      [data are part of input file]
   VAR=X1 TO X4/STAT ALL/
   DEP X1/ENTER X3 X4/ENTER X2/
   DEP X2/ENTER X3 X4/ENTER X1.
```

Commentary

For a general orientation to SPSS, see Chapter 4. In the present application, I am reading in a correlation matrix and N (number of cases) as input. For an orientation to matrix data input, see SPSS Inc. (1993, pp. 462–480). Here, I use CONTENTS to specify that the file consists of a CORRelation matrix and N. I use the default format for the correlation matrix (i.e., lower triangle with free format).

Table 7.3 consists of correlations only (recall that they are fictitious). Therefore, an equation with standardized regression coefficients and zero intercept is obtained (see the following output). This, for present purposes, is inconsequential as the sole interest is in squared multiple correlations. Had the aim been to obtain also regression equations for raw scores, then means and standard deviations would have had to be supplied.

SPSS requires that N be specified. I used $N = 100$ for illustrative purposes.

Output

Equation Number 1   Dependent Variable..   X1
Block Number   1.   Method: Enter   X3   X4

Multiple R   .62902
R Square   .39566

Block Number   2.   Method: Enter   X2

Multiple R   .81471
R Square   .66375

- - - - - - - - - - - - - - - Variables in the Equation - - - - - - - - - - - - - - - - - -

Variable	B	Beta	Part Cor	Partial
X2	.559207	.559207	.517775	.666041
X3	.447921	.447921	.442998	.607077
X4	.140525	.140525	.131464	.221102
(Constant)	.000000			

Summary table
- - - - - - - -

Step	Variable	MultR	Rsq	RsqCh
1	In: X4			
2	In: X3	.6290	.3957	.3957
3	In: X2	.8147	.6638	.2681

Commentary

I reproduced only excerpts of output necessary for present purposes. Before drawing attention to the values necessary for the application of (7.7), I will make a couple of comments about other aspects of the output.

I pointed out above that when a correlation matrix is used as input, only standardized regression coefficients can be calculated. Hence, values under B are equal to those under Beta. Also, under such circumstances, a (Constant) is zero. If necessary, review the section entitled "Regression Weights: b and β" in Chapter 5.

Examine now the column labeled Partial. It refers to the partial correlation of the dependent variable with the variable in question, while partialing out the remaining variables. For example, .666 (the value associated with X2) = $r_{12.34}$, which is the same as the value I calculated earlier. As another example, .221 = $r_{14.23}$. This, then, is an example of a computer program for regression analysis that also reports partial correlations. In addition, Part Cor(relation) or semipartial correlation is reported. I discuss this topic later.

In light of the foregoing, it is clear that when using a procedure such as REGRESSION of SPSS, it is not necessary to apply (7.7). Nevertheless, I will now apply (7.7) to demonstrate that as long as the relevant squared multiple correlations are available (values included in the output of any program for multiple regression analysis), partial correlations can be calculated.

Examine the input and notice that in each of the regression equations I entered the variables in two steps. For example, in the first equation, I entered X_3 and X_4 at the first step. At the second step, I entered X_2. Consequently, at Block Number 1, R Square = .39566 = $R^2_{1.34}$. At Block Number 2, R Square = .66375 = $R^2_{1.234}$.

The values necessary for the application of (7.7) are readily available in the Summary table, given in the output. Thus, Rsq(uare)Ch(ange) associated with X2 (.2681) is the value for the numerator of (7.7), whereas 1 − .3957—Rsq(uare) for X3 and X4—is the value for the denominator. Thus,

$$r_{12.34}^2 = .2681/(1 - .3957) = .44. \qquad \sqrt{.44} = .66$$

Compare this with the value given under Variables in the Equation and with my hand calculations, given earlier.

Output

Summary table

- - - - - - - -

Step	Variable	MultR	Rsq	RsqCh
1	In: X4			
2	In: X3	.3777	.1427	.1427
3	In: X1	.7232	.5230	.3803

Commentary

In light of my commentary on the output given in the preceding, I reproduced only excerpts of the Summary table for the second regression analysis. The two relevant values for the application of (7.8) are .3803 and .1427. Thus, $r_{12.34}^2 = .3803/(1 - .1427) = .44$. Compare this with the result I obtained in the preceding and with that I obtained earlier by hand calculations.

SAS

Input

```
TITLE 'TABLE 7.3.   FOR PARTIAL CORRELATION';
DATA T73(TYPE=CORR);
  INPUT _TYPE_ $ _NAME_ $ X1 X2 X3 X4;
  CARDS;
N             .       100       100       100       100
CORR      X1    1.0000    .6735    .5320    .3475
CORR      X2    .6735    1.0000    .1447    .3521
CORR      X3    .5320    .1447    1.0000    .0225
CORR      X4    .3475    .3521    .0225    1.0000
;
PROC PRINT;
PROC REG;
  M1: MODEL X1=X2 X3 X4/ALL;
  M2: MODEL X1=X3 X4/ALL;
RUN;
```

Commentary

For a general orientation to SAS, see Chapter 4. In the present example, I am reading in N and a correlation matrix. On the INPUT statement, TYPE is used to identify the type of information. Thus, for the first line of data, TYPE refers to N, whereas for the remaining lines it refers to CORRelation coefficients. NAME refers to variable names (e.g., X1). I am using free format. If necessary, see the SAS manual for detailed explanations of input. I explained PROC REG in Chapters 4 and 5. Notice that I am calling for the analysis of two models. In the first model (M1), X1 is regressed on X2, X3, and X4. In the second model (M2), X1 is regressed on X3 and X4.

Output

NOTE: The means of one or more variables in the input data set WORK.T73 are missing and are assumed to be 0.
NOTE: The standard deviations of one or more variables in the input data set WORK.T73 are missing and are assumed to be 1.
NOTE: No raw data are available. Some options are ignored.

Commentary

In earlier chapters, I stressed the importance of examining the LOG file. The preceding is an excerpt from the LOG file to illustrate a message SAS gives about the input data.

Output

Parameter Estimates

Variable	DF	Parameter Estimate	Standardized Estimate	Squared Partial Corr Type II
INTERCEP	1	0	0.00000000	.
X2	1	0.559207	0.55920699	0.44361039
X3	1	0.447921	0.44792094	0.36854254
X4	1	0.140525	0.14052500	0.04888629

Commentary

As I pointed out in my commentaries on SPSS output, only standardized regression coefficients can be calculated when a correlation matrix is read in as input. Hence, Parameter Estimate (i.e., unstandardized regression coefficient) is the same as Standardized Estimate (i.e., standardized regression coefficient).

In Chapter 5, I explained two types of Sums of Squares and two types of Squared Semipartial correlations reported in SAS. Also reported in SAS are two corresponding types of Squared Partial Correlation coefficients. Without repeating my explanations in Chapter 5, I will point out that for present purposes, Type II Squared Partial Correlations are of interest. Thus, the value corresponding to X2 (.444) is $r^2_{12.34}$, which is the same value I calculated earlier and also the one

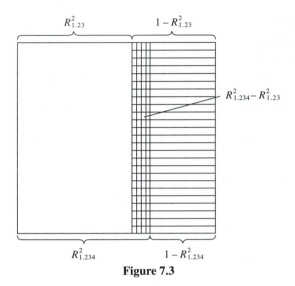

Figure 7.3

reported in SPSS output. Similarly, the value corresponding to X4 (.049) is $r^2_{14.23}$. Compare with the preceding SPSS output, where $r_{14.23}$ = .221.

Instead of reproducing results from the analysis of the second model, I will point out that the relevant information for the application of (7.7) is .3957 ($R^2_{1.34}$), which is the same as the value reported in SPSS output. Earlier, I used this value in my application of (7.7).

A Graphic Depiction

Before turning to the next topic, I will use Figure 7.3 in an attempt to clarify the meaning of the previous calculations. I drew the figure to depict the situation in calculating $r^2_{14.23}$. The area of the whole square represents the total variance of X_1: it equals 1. The horizontally hatched area represents $1 - R^2_{1.23} = 1 - .64647 = .35353$. The vertically hatched area (it is doubly hatched due to the overlap with the horizontally hatched area) represents $R^2_{1.234} - R^2_{1.23} = .66375 - .64647 = .01728$. (The areas $R^2_{1.23}$ and $R^2_{1.234}$ are labeled in the figure.) The squared partial correlation coefficient is the ratio of the doubly hatched area to the horizontally hatched area, or $(.66375 - .64647)/.35353 = .01728/.35353 = .0489$

CAUSAL ASSUMPTIONS[6]

Partial correlation is not an all-purpose method of control. Its valid application is predicated on a sound theoretical model. Controlling variables without regard to the theoretical considerations about the pattern of relations among them may yield misleading or meaningless results. Emphasizing the need for a causal model when calculating partial correlations, Fisher (1958) contended:

[6]In this chapter, I do *not* discuss the concept of causation and the controversies surrounding it. For a discussion of these issues, see Chapter 18.

> If . . . we choose a group of social phenomena with no antecedent knowledge of the causation or the absence of causation among them, then the calculation of correlation coefficients, total or partial, will not advance us a step towards evaluating the importance of the causes at work. . . . In no case, however, can we judge whether or not it is profitable to eliminate a certain variate unless we know, or are willing to assume, a qualitative scheme of causation. (pp. 190–191)

In an excellent discussion of what he called the partialing fallacy, Gordon (1968) maintained that the routine presentation of all higher-order partial correlations in a set of data is a sure sign that the researcher has not formulated a theory about the relations among the variables under consideration. Even for only three variables, various causal models may be postulated, two of which are depicted in Figure 7.4. Note that $r_{xz.y} = .00$ is consistent with the two radically different models of Figure 7.4. In (a), Y is conceived as mediating the effects of X on Z, whereas in (b), Y is conceived as the common cause that leads to a spurious correlation between X and Z. $r_{xz.y} = .00$, which is expected for both models, does not reveal which of them is tenable. It is theory that dictates the appropriate analytic method to be used, *not* the other way around.

(a)   (b)

Figure 7.4

Two additional patterns of possible causation among three variables are depicted in Figure 7.5, where in (a), X affects Z directly as well as through Y, whereas in (b), X and Y are correlated causes of Z. In either of these situations, partial correlation is inappropriate, as it may result in partialing too much of the relation. Burks (1928) gave a good example of partialing too much. Assume that X = parent's intelligence, Y = child's intelligence, Z = child's academic achievement, and the interest is in assessing the effect of the child's intelligence on achievement when parent's intelligence is controlled for.

> If we follow the obvious procedure of partialing out parental intelligence, we indeed succeed in eliminating all effect of parental intelligence. But . . . we have partialed out more than we should, for the *whole* of the child's intelligence, including that part which can be predicted from parents' intelligence as well as the parts that are due to all other conditioning factors, properly belongs to our problem. We are interested in the contribution made to school achievement by intelligence of a normal range of variability rather than by the narrow band of intelligence that would be represented by children whose parents' intelligence was a constant. The partial-correlation technique has made a clean sweep of parental intelligence. But the influence of parental intelligence that affects achievement indirectly *via*

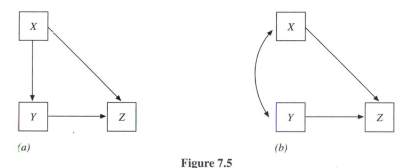

(a)   (b)

Figure 7.5

heredity (i.e., *via* the child's intelligence) should stay; only the direct influence should go. Thus, the partial-correlation technique is inadequate to this situation. Obviously, it is inadequate to any other situation of this type. (p. 14)

In sum, calculation of partial correlations is inappropriate when one assumes causal models like those depicted in Figure 7.5. I present methods for the analysis of such models in Chapter 18.

Another potential pitfall in the application of partial correlation without regard to theory is what Gordon (1968) referred to as partialing the relation out of itself. This happens when, for example, two measures of a given variable are available and one of the measures is partialed out in order to study the relation of the other measure with a given criterion. It makes no sense to control for one measure of mental ability, say, while correlating another measure of mental ability with academic achievement when the aim is to study the relation between mental ability and academic achievement. As I pointed out earlier, this is tantamount to partialing a relation out of itself and may lead to the fallacious conclusion that mental ability and academic achievement are not correlated.

Good discussions of causal assumptions and the conditions necessary for appropriate applications of partial correlation technique will be found in Blalock (1964), Burks (1926a, 1926b), Duncan (1970), Linn and Werts (1969).

MEASUREMENT ERRORS

I discussed effects of errors of measurement on regression statistics in Chapter 2. Measurement errors also lead to biased estimates of zero-order and partial correlation coefficients. Although my concern here is with effects of measurement errors on partial correlation coefficients, it will be instructive to discuss briefly the effects of such errors on zero-order correlations.

When errors are present in the measurement of either X_1, X_2, or both, the correlation between the two variables is attenuated—that is, it is lower than it would have been had true scores on X_1 and X_2 been used. In other words, when the reliability of either or both measures of the variables is less than perfect, the correlation between the variables is attenuated. The presence of measurement errors in behavioral research is the rule rather than the exception. Moreover, reliabilities of many measures used in the behavioral sciences are, at best, moderate (i.e., .7–.8).

To estimate what the correlation between two variables would have been had they been measured without error, the so-called correction for attenuation formula may be used:

$$r_{12}^* = \frac{r_{12}}{\sqrt{r_{11}} \sqrt{r_{22}}} \tag{7.10}$$

where r_{12}^* = the correlation between X_1 and X_2, corrected for attenuation; r_{12} = the observed correlation; and r_{11} and r_{22} are reliability coefficients of X_1 and X_2, respectively (see Nunnally, 1978, pp. 219–220; Pedhazur & Schmelkin, 1991, pp. 113–114). From the denominator of (7.10) it is evident that $r_{12}^* = r_{12}$ only when $r_{11} = r_{22} = 1.00$—that is when the reliabilities of both measures are perfect. With less than perfect reliabilities, r_{12} will always underestimate r_{12}^*. Assume that $r_{12} = .7$, and $r_{11} = r_{22} = .8$. Applying (7.10),

$$r_{12}^* = \frac{r_{12}}{\sqrt{r_{11}} \sqrt{r_{22}}} = \frac{.7}{\sqrt{.8} \sqrt{.8}} = \frac{.7}{.8} = .875$$

The estimated correlation between X_1 and X_2, had both variables been measured without error, is .875. One may choose to correct for the unreliability of either the measure of X_1 only or that of X_2 only. For a discussion of this and related issues, see Nunnally (1978, pp. 237–239).

Using the preceding conceptions, formulas for the estimation of partial correlation coefficients corrected for one or more than one of the measures in question may be derived. Probably most important is the correction for the unreliability of the measure of the variable that is controlled, or partialed out, in the calculation of the partial correlation coefficient. The formula is

$$r_{12.3}{}^* = \frac{r_{33}r_{12} - r_{13}r_{23}}{\sqrt{r_{33} - r_{13}^2}\,\sqrt{r_{33} - r_{23}^2}} \tag{7.11}$$

where $r_{12.3}{}^*$ is the estimated partial correlation coefficient when the measure of X_3 is corrected for unreliability, and r_{33} is the reliability coefficient of the measure of X_3. Note that when X_3 is measured without error (i.e., $r_{33} = 1.00$), (7.11) reduces to (7.2), the formula for the first-order partial correlation I introduced earlier in this chapter. Unlike the zero-order correlation, which underestimates the correlation in the presence of measurement errors (see the preceding), the partial correlation coefficient uncorrected for measurement errors may result in either overestimation or underestimation.

For illustrative purposes, assume that

$$r_{12} = .7 \qquad r_{13} = .5 \qquad r_{23} = .6$$

Applying first (7.2),

$$r_{12.3} = \frac{r_{12} - r_{13}r_{23}}{\sqrt{1 - r_{13}^2}\,\sqrt{1 - r_{23}^2}} = \frac{.7 - (.5)(.6)}{\sqrt{1 - .5^2}\,\sqrt{1 - .6^2}} = \frac{.4}{.6928} = .58$$

Assuming now that the reliability of the measure of the variable being controlled for, X_3, is .8 (i.e., $r_{33} = .8$), and applying (7.11),

$$r_{12.3}{}^* = \frac{r_{33}r_{12} - r_{13}r_{23}}{\sqrt{r_{33} - r_{13}^2}\,\sqrt{r_{33} - r_{23}^2}} = \frac{(.8)(.7) - (.5)(.6)}{\sqrt{.8 - .5^2}\,\sqrt{.8 - .6^2}} = \frac{.26}{.4919} = .53$$

In the present case, $r_{12.3}$ overestimated $r_{12.3}{}^*$.

Here is another example:

$$r_{12} = .7 \qquad r_{13} = .8 \qquad r_{23} = .7 \qquad r_{33} = .8$$

Applying (7.2),

$$r_{12.3} = \frac{r_{12} - r_{13}r_{23}}{\sqrt{1 - r_{13}^2}\,\sqrt{1 - r_{23}^2}} = \frac{.7 - (.8)(.7)}{\sqrt{1 - .8^2}\,\sqrt{1 - .7^2}} = \frac{.14}{.4285} = .33$$

Applying now (7.11),

$$r_{12.3}{}^* = \frac{r_{33}r_{12} - r_{13}r_{23}}{\sqrt{r_{33} - r_{13}^2}\,\sqrt{r_{33} - r_{23}^2}} = \frac{(.8)(.7) - (.8)(.7)}{\sqrt{.8 - .8^2}\,\sqrt{.8 - .7^2}} = .00$$

When the measure of X_3 is corrected for unreliability, the correlation between X_1 and X_2 appears to be spurious; or it may be that X_3 mediates the effect of X_1 on X_2. (For a discussion of this point, see earlier sections of this chapter.) A quite different conclusion is reached when no correction is made for the unreliability of the measure of X_3.

Assume now that the correlations among the three variables are the same as in the preceding but that $r_{33} = .75$ instead of .8. $r_{12.3}$ is the same as it was earlier (i.e., .33). Applying (7.11),

$$r_{12.3}{}^* = \frac{r_{33}r_{12} - r_{13}r_{23}}{\sqrt{r_{33} - r_{13}^2} \sqrt{r_{33} - r_{23}^2}} = \frac{(.75)(.7) - (.8)(.7)}{\sqrt{.75 - .8^2} \sqrt{.75 - .7^2}} = \frac{-.035}{.1691} = -.21$$

This time, the two estimates differ not only in size but also in sign (i.e., $r_{12.3} = .33$ and $r_{12.3}{}^* = -.21$). The above illustrations suffice to show the importance of correcting for the unreliability of the measure of the partialed variable. For further discussions, see Blalock (1964, pp. 146–150), Cohen and Cohen (1983, pp. 406–412), Kahneman (1965), Linn and Werts (1973), Liu (1988), and Lord (1963, 1974).

As I pointed out earlier, it is possible to correct for the unreliability of more than one of the measures used in the calculation of a partial correlation coefficient. The estimated partial correlation when all three measures are corrected for unreliability is

$$r_{12.3}^* = \frac{r_{33}r_{12} - r_{13}r_{23}}{\sqrt{r_{11}r_{33} - r_{13}^2} \sqrt{r_{22}r_{33} - r_{23}^2}} \tag{7.12}$$

where $r_{12.3}^*$ is the corrected partial correlation coefficient; and r_{11}, r_{22}, and r_{33} are the reliability coefficients for measures of X_1, X_2, and X_3, respectively (see Bohrnstedt, 1983, pp. 74–76; Bohrnstedt & Carter, 1971, pp. 136–137; Cohen & Cohen, 1983, pp. 406–412). Note that when the three variables are measured with perfect reliability (i.e., $r_{11} = r_{22} = r_{33} = 1.00$), (7.12) reduces to (7.2). Also, the numerators of (7.12) and (7.11) are identical. Only the denominator changes when, in addition to the correction for the unreliability of the measure of the control variable, corrections for the unreliability of the measures of the primary variables are introduced.

For illustrative purposes, I will first apply (7.2) to the following data:

$$r_{12} = .7 \qquad r_{13} = .5 \qquad r_{23} = .6$$

$$r_{12.3} = \frac{r_{12} - r_{13}r_{23}}{\sqrt{1 - r_{13}^2} \sqrt{1 - r_{23}^2}} = \frac{.7 - (.5)(.6)}{\sqrt{1 - .5^2} \sqrt{1 - .6^2}} = \frac{.4}{.6928} = .58$$

Assume now, for the sake of simplicity, that $r_{11} = r_{22} = r_{33} = .8$. Applying (7.12),

$$r_{12.3}^* = \frac{r_{33}r_{12} - r_{13}r_{23}}{\sqrt{r_{11}r_{33} - r_{13}^2} \sqrt{r_{22}r_{33} - r_{23}^2}} = \frac{(.8)(.7) - (.5)(.6)}{\sqrt{(.8)(.8) - .5^2} \sqrt{(.8)(.8) - .6^2}} = \frac{.26}{.3305} = .79$$

In the present example, $r_{12.3}$ underestimated $r_{12.3}^*$. Depending on the pattern of intercorrelations among the variables, and the reliabilities of the measures used, $r_{12.3}$ may either underestimate or overestimate $r_{12.3}^*$.

In conclusion, I will note again that the most important correction is the one applied to the variable that is being controlled, or partialed out. In other words, the application of (7.11) may serve as a minimum safeguard against erroneous interpretations of partial correlation coefficients. For a good discussion and illustrations of adverse effects of measurement error on the use of partial correlations in hypothesis testing, see Brewer, Campbell, and Crano (1970).

SEMIPARTIAL CORRELATION

Thus far, my concern has been with the situation in which a variable (or several variables) is partialed out from *both* variables whose correlation is being sought. There are, however, situations in which one may wish to partial out a variable from only one of the variables that are being correlated. For example, suppose that a college admissions officer is dealing with the following three variables: X_1 = grade-point average, X_2 = entrance examination, and X_3 = intelligence. One would expect intelligence and the entrance examination to be positively correlated. If the admissions officer is interested in the relation between the entrance examination and grade-point average, while controlling for intelligence, $r_{12.3}$ will provide this information. Similarly, $r_{13.2}$ will indicate the correlation between intelligence and grade-point average, while controlling for performance on the entrance examination. It is possible, however, that of greater interest to the admissions officer is the predictive power of the entrance examination after that of intelligence has been taken into account. Stated differently, the interest is in the increment in the proportion of variance in grade-point average accounted for by the entrance examination, over and above the proportion of variance accounted for by intelligence. In such a situation, intelligence should be partialed out from the entrance examination, but not from grade-point average where it belongs. This can be accomplished by calculating the squared *semipartial* correlation. Some authors (e.g., DuBois, 1957, pp. 60–62; McNemar, 1962, pp. 167–168) use the term *part* correlation.

Recall that a partial correlation is a correlation between two variables that were residualized on a third variable. A semipartial correlation is a correlation between an unmodified variable and a variable that was residualized. The symbol for a first-order semipartial correlation is $r_{1(2.3)}$, which means the correlation between X_1 (unmodified) and X_2, after it was residualized on X_3, or after X_3 was partialed out from X_2. Referring to the variables I used earlier, $r_{1(2.3)}$ is the semipartial correlation between grade-point average and an entrance examination, after intelligence was partialed out from the latter. Similarly, $r_{1(3.2)}$ is the semipartial correlation of grade-point average and intelligence, after an entrance examination was partialed out from the latter.

To demonstrate concretely the meaning of a semipartial correlation, I return to the numerical example in Table 7.1. Recall that e_1 and e_2 in Table 7.1 are the residuals of X_1 and X_2, respectively, when X_3 was used to predict each of these variables. Earlier, I demonstrated that $r_{x_3e_1} = r_{x_3e_2} = .00$, and that therefore the correlation between e_1 and e_2 is the relation between those two parts of X_1 and X_2 that are not shared with X_3, that is, the partial correlation between X_1 and X_2, after X_3 was partialed out from both variables. To calculate, instead, the semipartial correlation between X_1 (unmodified) and X_2, after X_3 was partialed out from it, I will correlate X_1 with e_2. From Table 7.2, I obtained the following:

$$\Sigma x_1^2 = 10 \qquad \Sigma e_2^2 = 1.9 \qquad \Sigma x_1 e_2 = 1.6$$

Therefore,

$$r_{x_1e_2} = r_{1(2.3)} = \frac{\Sigma x_1 e_2}{\sqrt{\Sigma x_1^2 \Sigma e_2^2}} = \frac{1.6}{\sqrt{(10)(1.9)}} = \frac{1.6}{4.359} = .37$$

I can, similarly, calculate $r_{2(1.3)}$—that is, the semipartial correlation between X_2 (unmodified) and X_1, after X_3 was partialed out from it. This is tantamount to correlating X_2 with e_1. Again, taking the appropriate values from Table 7.2,

$$\Sigma x_1^2 = 10 \qquad \Sigma e_1^2 = 6.4 \qquad \Sigma x_2 e_1 = 1.6$$

and

$$r_{x_2e_1} = r_{2(1.3)} = \frac{\Sigma x_2 e_1}{\sqrt{\Sigma x_2^2 \Sigma e_1^2}} = \frac{1.6}{\sqrt{(10)(6.4)}} = \frac{1.6}{8} = .2$$

I presented the preceding calculations to show the meaning of the semipartial correlation. But, as in the case of partial correlations, there are simple formulas for the calculation of semipartial correlations. For comparative purposes, I repeat (7.2)—the formula for a first-order partial correlation—with a new number:

$$r_{12.3} = \frac{r_{12} - r_{13}r_{23}}{\sqrt{1 - r_{13}^2}\sqrt{1 - r_{23}^2}} \tag{7.13}$$

The formula for $r_{1(2.3)}$ is

$$r_{1(2.3)} = \frac{r_{12} - r_{13}r_{23}}{\sqrt{1 - r_{23}^2}} \tag{7.14}$$

and

$$r_{2(1.3)} = \frac{r_{12} - r_{13}r_{23}}{\sqrt{1 - r_{13}^2}} \tag{7.15}$$

Probably the easiest way to grasp the difference between (7.14) and (7.15) is to interpret their squared values. Recall that a squared semipartial correlation indicates the proportion of variance incremented by the variable in question, after controlling for the other independent variables or predictors. Accordingly, the square of (7.14) indicates the proportion of variance in X_1 that X_2 accounts for, over and above what is accounted for by X_3. In contrast, the square of (7.15) indicates the proportion of variance in X_2 that X_1 accounts for, over and above what is accounted for by X_3.

Examine (7.13)–(7.15) and notice that the numerators for the semipartial correlations are identical to that of the partial correlation corresponding to them. The denominator in the formula for the partial correlation (7.13) is composed of two standard deviations of standardized residualized variables, whereas the denominators in the formulas for the semipartial correlation, (7.14) and (7.15), are composed of the standard deviation of the standardized residualized variable in question—X_2 in (7.14) and X_1 in (7.15). In both instances, the standard deviation for the unmodified variable is 1.00 (i.e., the standard deviation of standard scores); hence it is not explicitly stated, though it could, of course, be stated.

From the foregoing it follows that $r_{12.3}$ will be larger than either $r_{1(2.3)}$ or $r_{2(1.3)}$, except when r_{13} or r_{23} equals zero, in which case the partial correlation will be equal to the semipartial correlation.

To demonstrate the application of (7.14) and (7.15) I return once more to the data in Table 7.1. The correlations among the variables of Table 7.1 (see the calculations accompanying the table and a summary of the calculations in Table 7.2) are as follows:

$$r_{12} = .7 \qquad r_{13} = .6 \qquad r_{23} = .9$$

Applying (7.14),

$$r_{1(2.3)} = \frac{r_{12} - r_{13}r_{23}}{\sqrt{1 - r_{23}^2}} = \frac{(.7) - (.6)(.9)}{\sqrt{1 - .9^2}} = \frac{.16}{.4359} = .37$$

I obtained the same value previously when I correlated X_1 with e_2.

Applying (7.15),

$$r_{2(1.3)} = \frac{r_{12} - r_{13}r_{23}}{\sqrt{1 - r_{13}^2}} = \frac{(.7) - (.6)(.9)}{\sqrt{1 - .6^2}} = \frac{.16}{.8} = .20$$

Again, this is the same as the value I obtained when I correlated X_2 with e_1.

Earlier I calculated $r_{12.3} = .46$, which, as I noted in the preceding, is larger than either of the semipartial correlations.

Having gone through the mechanics of the calculations, it is necessary to address the question of when to use a partial correlation and when a semipartial correlation would be more appropriate. Moreover, assuming that a semipartial correlation is called for, it is still necessary to decide which of two semipartial correlations should be calculated. Answers to such questions depend on the theory and causal assumptions that underlie the research (see Werts & Linn, 1969). As I discuss in greater detail later and in Chapter 9, some researchers use squared semipartial correlations in their attempts to partition the variance of the dependent variable. Several times earlier, I pointed out that the validity of any analytic approach is predicated on the purpose of the study and on the soundness of the theoretical model that underlies it. For now, though, an example of the meaning and implications of a choice between two semipartial correlations may help show some of the complexities and serve to underscore the paramount role that theory plays in the choice and valid interpretation of an analytic method.[7]

Suppose, for the sake of illustration, that in research on the effects of schooling one is dealing with three variables only: I = a student input variable (e.g., aptitude, home background); S = a school quality variable (e.g., teachers' verbal ability or attitudes); and C = a criterion variable (e.g., achievement or graduation). Most researchers who study the effects of schooling in the context of the previously noted variables are inclined to calculate the following squared semipartial correlation:

$$r_{C(S.I)}^2 = \frac{(r_{CS} - r_{CI}r_{SI})^2}{1 - r_{SI}^2} \tag{7.16}$$

In (7.16), the student variable is partialed out from the school variable. Thus, (7.16) yields the proportion of variance of the criterion variable that the school variable accounts for over and above the variance accounted for by the student input variable.

Some researchers, notably Astin and his associates (see, for example, Astin, 1968, 1970; Astin & Panos, 1969) take a different analytic approach to the same problem. In an attempt to control for the student input variable, they residualize the criterion variable on it. They then correlate the residualized criterion with the school variable to determine the effect of the latter on the former. For the example under consideration, this approach amounts to calculating the following squared semipartial correlation:

$$r_{S(C.I)}^2 = \frac{(r_{CS} - r_{CI}r_{SI})^2}{1 - r_{CI}^2} \tag{7.17}$$

Equations (7.16) and (7.17) have the same numerators, hence the size of the proportion of variance attributed to the school variable under each approach depends on the relative magnitudes of r_{SI} and r_{CI}. When $r_{SI} = r_{CI}$, the two approaches yield the same results. When $|r_{SI}| > |r_{CI}|$, then $r_{C(S.I)}^2 > r_{S(C.I)}^2$. The converse is, of course, true when $|r_{SI}| < |r_{CI}|$. Which approach should be followed? Werts and Linn (1969) answer facetiously that it depends on the kind of hypothesis one wishes to support. After presenting four approaches (two of which are the ones I discussed earlier), Werts and Linn provide the reader with a flow diagram for selecting the approach that holds the greatest promise for supporting one's hypothesis. Barring inspection of the intercorrelations among the variables prior to a commitment to an approach, the choice between the

---

[7]The remainder of this section is adapted from Pedhazur (1975), by permission from the American Educational Research Association.

two I discussed depends on whether one wishes to show a greater or a lesser effect of the school variable. A hereditarian, for example, would choose the approach in which the school variable is residualized on the student input (7.16). The reason is that in educational research, correlations of student input variables with the criterion tend to be greater than correlations of student input variables with school variables. Consequently, the application of the approach exemplified by (7.16) will result in a smaller proportion of variance attributed to the school variable than will the approach exemplified by (7.17). An environmentalist, on the other hand, may be able to squeeze a little more variance for the school by applying (7.17). Needless to say, this advice is not meant to be taken seriously. It does, however, underscore the complex nature of the choice between the different approaches.

The important point to bear in mind is that the complexities arise, among other things, because the student input variable is correlated with the school quality variable. As long as the researcher is unwilling, or unable, to explain how this correlation comes about, it is not possible to determine whether (7.16) or (7.17) is more appropriate. As I discuss in Chapter 9, in certain instances neither of them leads to a valid answer about the effects of schooling.

Thus far, I presented only first-order semipartial correlations. Instead of presenting special formulas for the calculation of higher-order semipartial correlations, I will show how you may obtain semipartial correlations of any order via multiple correlations.

Semipartial Correlations via Multiple Correlations

I said previously that a squared semipartial correlation indicates the proportion of variance in the dependent variable accounted for by a given independent variable after another independent variable(s) was partialed out from it. The same idea may be stated somewhat differently: a squared semipartial correlation indicates the proportion of variance of the dependent variable accounted for by a given independent variable after another variable(s) has already been taken into account. Stated thus, a squared semipartial correlation is indicated by the difference between two squared multiple correlations. It is this approach that affords the straightforward calculation of squared semipartial correlations of any order. For example,

$$r^2_{1(2.3)} = R^2_{1.23} - R^2_{1.3}$$
(7.18)

where $r^2_{1(2.3)}$ = squared semipartial correlation of X_1 with X_2 after X_3 was partialed out from X_2. Note that the first term to the right of the equal sign is the proportion of variance in X_1 accounted for by X_2 *and* X_3, whereas the second term is the proportion of variance in X_1 accounted for by X_3 alone. Therefore, the difference between the two terms is the proportion of variance due to X_2 after X_3 has already been taken into account. Also, the right-hand side of (7.18) is the same as the numerator in the formula for the square of the partial correlation of the same order—see (7.5) and the discussion related to it. The difference between (7.18) and (7.5) is that the latter has a denominator (i.e., $1 - R^2_{1.3}$), whereas the former has no denominator. Since $1 - R^2_{1.3}$ is a fraction (except when $R^2_{1.3}$ is zero) and both formulas have the same numerator, it follows, as I stated earlier, that the partial correlation is larger than its corresponding semipartial correlations.

Analogous to (7.18), $r^2_{1(3.2)}$ is calculated as follows:

$$r^2_{1(3.2)} = R^2_{1.23} - R^2_{1.2}$$
(7.19)

This time the increment in proportion of variance accounted for by X_3, after X_2 is already in the equation, is obtained.

The present approach may be used to obtain semipartial correlations of any order. Following are some examples:

$$r^2_{1(2.34)} = R^2_{1.234} - R^2_{1.34} \qquad (7.20)$$

which is the squared second-order semipartial correlation of X_1 with X_2, when X_3 and X_4 are partialed out from X_2.

Similarly,

$$r^2_{1(3.24)} = R^2_{1.234} - R^2_{1.24} \qquad (7.21)$$

which is the squared second-order semipartial correlation of X_1 with X_3, after X_2 and X_4 were partialed out from X_3.

The squared third-order semipartial of X_3 with X_1, after X_2, X_4, and X_5 are partialed out from X_1 is

$$r^2_{3(1.245)} = R^2_{3.1245} - R^2_{3.245} \qquad (7.22)$$

From the preceding examples it should be clear that to calculate a squared semipartial correlation of any order it is necessary to (1) calculate the squared multiple correlation of the dependent variable with all the independent variables, (2) calculate the squared multiple correlation of the dependent variable with the variables that are being partialed out, and (3) subtract the R^2 of step 2 from the R^2 of step 1.

The semipartial correlation is, of course, equal to the square root of the squared semipartial correlation. As I stated earlier in connection with the partial correlation, the sign of the semipartial correlation is the same as the sign of the regression coefficient (b or β) that corresponds to it.

Numerical Examples

To show the application of the approach I outlined previously, and to provide for comparisons with the calculations of partial correlations, I will use the correlation matrix I introduced in Table 7.3, which I repeat here for convenience as Table 7.4. Using data from Table 7.4, I will calculate several squared semipartial correlations and comment on them briefly.

$$r^2_{1(2.3)} = R^2_{1.23} - R^2_{1.3}$$

$$= .64647 - .28302 = .36345$$

By itself, X_2 can account for about .45, or 45%, of the variance in X_1 (i.e., $r^2_{12} = .6735^2 = .4536$). However, after partialing X_3 from X_2, or after allowing X_3 to enter first into the regression equation, it accounts for about 36% of the variance.

$$r^2_{1(3.2)} = R^2_{1.23} - R^2_{1.2}$$

$$= .64647 - .45360 = .19287$$

Table 7.4   Correlation Matrix for Four Variables

	X_1	X_2	X_3	X_4
X_1	1.0000	.6735	.5320	.3475
X_2	.6735	1.0000	.1447	.3521
X_3	.5320	.1447	1.0000	.0225
X_4	.3475	.3521	.0225	1.0000

X_3 by itself can account for about 28% of the variance in X_1 (i.e., $r_{13}^2 \times 100$). But it accounts for about 19% of the variance after X_2 is partialed out from it.

$$r_{1(2.34)}^2 = R_{1.234}^2 - R_{1.34}^2$$

$$= .66375 - .39566 = .26809$$

Having partialed out X_3 and X_4 from X_2, the latter accounts for about 27% of the variance in X_1. Compare with the variance accounted for by the zero-order correlation (45%) and by the first-order semipartial correlation (36%). Compare also with the squared partial correlation of the same order: $r_{12.34}^2 = .4436$ (see the calculations presented earlier in this chapter).

$$r_{1(4.23)}^2 = R_{1.234}^2 - R_{1.23}^2$$

$$= .66375 - .64647 = .01728$$

Variable X_4 by itself accounts for about 12% of the variance in X_1 (i.e., $r_{14}^2 \times 100$). But when X_2 and X_3 are partialed out from X_4, the latter accounts for about 2% of the variance in X_1. In an earlier section, I calculated the squared partial correlation corresponding to this squared semipartial correlation: $r_{14.23}^2 = .0489$.

The successive reductions in the proportions of variance accounted for by a given variable as one goes from a zero-order correlation to a first-order semipartial, and then to a second-order semipartial, is due to the fact that the correlations among the variables under consideration are of the same sign (positive in the present case). Successive partialing takes out information redundant with that provided by the variables that are being controlled. However, similar to a partial correlation, a semipartial correlation may be larger than its corresponding zero-order correlation. Also, a semipartial correlation may have a different sign than the zero-order correlation to which it corresponds. The size and the sign of the semipartial correlation are determined by the sizes and the pattern of the correlations among the variables under consideration.

I will illustrate what I said in the preceding paragraph by assuming that $r_{12} = .6735$ and $r_{13} = .5320$ (these are the same values as in Table 7.4), but that $r_{23} = -.1447$ (this is the same correlation as the one reported in Table 7.4, but with a change in its sign). Applying (7.14),

$$r_{1(2.3)} = \frac{r_{12} - r_{13}r_{23}}{\sqrt{1 - r_{23}^2}} = \frac{(.6735) - (.5320)(-.1447)}{\sqrt{1 - (-.1447)^2}} = \frac{.75048}{.98948} = .75846$$

Note that X_2 by itself accounts for about 45% of the variance in X_1. But when X_3 is partialed out from X_2, the latter accounts for about 58% of the variance in X_1 (i.e., $.75846^2 \times 100$).

Of course, I could have demonstrated the preceding through the application of (7.18). I used (7.14) instead, because it is possible to see clearly what is taking place. Examine the numerator first. Because r_{13} and r_{23} are of different signs, their product is added to r_{12}, resulting, of course, in a value larger than r_{12}. Moreover, the denominator is a fraction. Consequently, $r_{1(2.3)}$ must, in the present case, be larger than r_{12}. What I said, and showed, in the preceding applies also to semipartial correlations of higher orders, although the pattern is more complex and therefore not as easily discernable as in a first-order semipartial correlation.

TESTS OF SIGNIFICANCE

In Chapter 5, I introduced a formula for testing the significance of an increment in the proportion of variance of the dependent variable accounted for by any number of independent variables—see (5.27) and the discussion related to it. I repeat this formula here:

$$F = \frac{(R^2_{y.12\ldots k_1}) - (R^2_{y.12\ldots k_2})/(k_1 - k_2)}{(1 - R^2_{y.12\ldots k_1})/(N - k_1 - 1)} \qquad (7.23)$$

where $R^2_{y.12\ldots k1}$ = squared multiple correlation coefficient for the regression of Y on k_1 variables (the larger coefficient); $R^2_{y.12\ldots k_2}$ = squared multiple correlation for the regression of Y on k_2 variables; k_2 = the smaller set of variables selected from among those of k_1; and N = sample size. The F ratio has $(k_1 - k_2)$ df for the numerator and $(N - k_1 - 1)$ df for the denominator.

Recall that the squared semipartial correlation indicates the increment in proportion of variance of the dependent variable accounted for by a given independent variable, after controlling for the other independent variables. It follows that the formula for testing the statistical significance of a squared semipartial correlation is a special case of (7.23). Specifically, for a squared semipartial correlation, k_1 is the total number of independent variables, whereas k_2 is the total number of independent variables minus one, that being the variable whose semipartial correlation with the dependent variable is being sought. Consequently, the numerator of the F ratio will always have one df.

Assuming that the correlation matrix of Table 7.4 is based on $N = 100$, I show now how squared semipartial correlations calculated in the preceding section are tested for significance.

For $r^2_{1(2.3)}$,

$$F = \frac{R^2_{1.23} - R^2_{1.3}}{(1 - R^2_{1.23})/(N - k_1 - 1)} = \frac{.64647 - .28302}{(1 - .64647)/(100 - 2 - 1)} = \frac{.36345}{.00364} = 99.85$$

with 1 and 97 df.

For $r^2_{1(3.2)}$,

$$F = \frac{R^2_{1.23} - R^2_{1.2}}{(1 - R^2_{1.23})/(N - k_1 - 1)} = \frac{.64647 - .45360}{(1 - .64647)/(100 - 2 - 1)} = \frac{.19287}{.00364} = 52.992$$

with 1 and 97 df.

For $r^2_{1(2.34)}$,

$$F = \frac{R^2_{1.234} - R^2_{1.34}}{(1 - R^2_{1.234})/(N - k_1 - 1)} = \frac{.66375 - .39566}{(1 - .66375)/(100 - 3 - 1)} = \frac{.26809}{.00350} = 76.60$$

with 1 and 96 df.

For $r^2_{1(4.23)}$,

$$F = \frac{R^2_{1.234} - R^2_{1.23}}{(1 - R^2_{1.234})/(N - k_1 - 1)} = \frac{.66375 - .64647}{(1 - .66375)/(100 - 3 - 1)} = \frac{.01728}{.00350} = 4.94$$

with 1 and 96 df.

Testing the significance of a squared semipartial correlation is identical to testing the significance of the regression coefficient (b or β) associated with it. Thus, testing $r^2_{1(2.3)}$ for significance is the same as testing the significance of $b_{12.3}$ in an equation in which X_1 was regressed on X_2 and X_3. Similarly, testing $r^2_{1(2.34)}$ for significance is the same as testing $b_{12.34}$ in an equation in which X_1 was regressed on X_2, X_3, and X_4. In short, testing the significance of any regression coefficient (b or β) is tantamount to testing the increment in the proportion of variance that the independent variable associated with the b (or β) in question accounts for in the dependent variable when it is entered last into the regression equation (see the SPSS output and commentaries that follow).

Finally, specialized formulas for testing the significance of partial correlations are available (see, for example, Blalock, 1972, pp. 466–467). These are not necessary, however, because testing the significance of a partial correlation coefficient is tantamount to testing the significance of the semipartial correlation, or the regression coefficient, corresponding to it. Thus, to test $r_{12.3}$ for significance, test $r_{1(2.3)}$ or $b_{12.3}$.

MULTIPLE REGRESSION AND SEMIPARTIAL CORRELATIONS

Conceptual and computational complexities and difficulties of multiple regression analysis stem from the intercorrelations among the independent variables. *When the correlations among the independent variables are all zero*, the solution and interpretation of results are simple. Under such circumstances, the squared multiple correlation is simply the sum of the squared zero-order correlations of each independent variable with the dependent variable:

$$R^2_{y.12...k} = r^2_{y1} + r^2_{y2} + \ldots + r^2_{yk} \tag{7.24}$$

Furthermore, it is possible to state unambiguously that the proportion of variance of the dependent variable accounted for by each independent variable is equal to the square of its correlation with the dependent variable. The simplicity of the case in which the correlations among the independent variables are zero is easily explained: each independent variable furnishes information not shared with any of the other independent variables.

One of the advantages of experimental research is that, when appropriately planned and executed, the independent variables are not correlated. Consequently, the researcher can speak unambiguously of the effects of each independent variable, as well as of the interactions among them. Much, if not most, of behavioral research is, however, nonexperimental. In this type of research the independent variables are usually correlated, sometimes substantially.

Multiple regression analysis may be viewed as a method of adjusting a set of correlated variables so that they become uncorrelated. This may be accomplished by using, successively, semipartial correlations. Equation (7.24) can be altered to express this viewpoint. For four independent variables,

$$R^2_{y.1234} = r^2_{y1} + r^2_{y(2.1)} + r^2_{y(3.12)} + r^2_{y(4.123)} \tag{7.25}$$

(For simplicity, I use four independent variables rather than the general equation. Once the idea is grasped, the equation can be extended to accommodate as many independent variables as is necessary or feasible.)

Equation (7.24) is a special case of (7.25) (except for the number of variables). If the correlations among the independent variables are all zero, then (7.25) reduces to (7.24). Scrutinize (7.25) and note what it includes. The first term is the squared zero-order correlation between the dependent variable, Y, and the first independent variable to enter into the equation, 1. The second term is the squared first-order semipartial correlation between the dependent variable and second variable to enter, 2, partialing out from variable 2 what it shares with variable 1. The third term is the squared second-order semipartial correlation between the dependent variable and the third variable to enter, 3, partialing out from it variables 1 and 2. The last term is the squared third-order semipartial correlation between the dependent variable and the last variable to enter, 4, partialing out from it variables 1, 2, and 3. In short, the equation spells out a procedure that residualizes each successive independent variable on the independent variables that preceded it. This is tantamount to creating new variables (i.e., residualized variables) that are not correlated with each other.

Earlier, I showed that a squared semipartial correlation can be expressed as a difference between two squared multiple correlations. It will be instructive to restate (7.25) accordingly:

$$R^2_{y.1234} = R^2_{y.1} + (R^2_{y.12} - R^2_{y.1}) + (R^2_{y.123} - R^2_{y.12}) + (R^2_{y.1234} - R^2_{y.123})$$

$$= r^2_{y1} + r^2_{y(2.1)} + r^2_{y(3.12)} + r^2_{y(4.123)}$$

(7.26)

(For uniformity, I express the zero-order correlation between X_1 and Y, r_{y1}, as $R_{y.1}$.) Removing the parentheses in (7.26) and doing the indicated operations results in the following identity: $R^2_{y.1234} = R^2_{y.1234}$.

As far as the calculation of R^2 is concerned, it makes no difference in what order the independent variables enter the equation and the calculations. For instance, $R^2_{y.123} = R^2_{y.213} = R^2_{y.312}$. But the order in which the independent variables are entered into the equation may make a great deal of difference in the amount of variance incremented by each. When entered first, a variable will almost always account for a larger proportion of the variance than when it is entered second or third. In general, when the independent variables are positively correlated, the later a variable is entered in the regression equation, the less of the variance it accounts for.

With four independent variables, there are 24 (4!) different orders in which the variables may be entered into the equation. In other words, it is possible to generate 24 equations like (7.25) or (7.26), each of which will be equal to $R^2_{y.1234}$. But the proportion of variance of the dependent variable attributed to a given independent variable depends on its specific point of entry into the equation. Is the choice of the order of entry of variables, then, arbitrary, or are there criteria for its determination? I postpone attempts to answer this question to Chapter 9, in which I address the present approach in the context of methods of variance partitioning. For now, I will only point out that criteria for a valid choice of a given order of entry for the variables depend on whether the research is designed solely for prediction or whether the goal is explanation. The choice in predictive research relates to such issues as economy and feasibility, whereas the choice in explanatory research is predicated on the theory and hypotheses being tested (see Chapters 8 and 9).

Numerical Examples

I will now use the correlation matrix reported in Table 7.4 to illustrate the effect of the order of entry of independent variables into the equation on the proportion of variance of the dependent variable attributed to given independent variables. I will carry out the analyses through the REGRESSION procedure of SPSS.

SPSS

Input

TITLE TABLE 7.4.   ORDER OF ENTRY OF VARIABLES.
MATRIX DATA VARIABLES=X1 TO X4
   /CONTENTS=CORR N.
BEGIN DATA
1
   .6735 1

```
 .5320   .1447  1
 .3475   .3521   .0225 1
100  100  100  100
END DATA
REGRESSION MATRIX=IN(*)/
  VAR=X1 TO X4/STAT ALL/
  DEP X1/ENTER X2/ENTER X3/ENTER X4/
  DEP X1/ENTER X4/ENTER X3/ENTER X2/
  DEP X1/ENTER X3/ENTER X2/ENTER X4.
```

Commentary

Earlier, I used similar input and commented on it. Therefore all I will note here is that I called for three regression analyses in which the same three independent variables are entered in different orders.

Output

Variable(s) Entered on Step Number   2..   X3

Multiple R	.80403	R Square Change	.19287
R Square	.64647	F Change	52.91798
		Signif F Change	.0000

- - - - - - - - - - - - - - - Variables in the Equation - - - - - - - - - - - - - - - -

Variable	B	T	Sig T
X2	.609277	9.986	.0000
X3	.443838	7.274	.0000
(Constant)	.000000		

Commentary

In the interest of space, I reproduce minimal output here and in subsequent sections. I suggest that you run the same problem, using SPSS or another program(s) to which you have access or which you prefer, so that you can compare your output with excerpts I report.

   This is the second step of Equation Number 1, when X3 is entered. As I explained in Chapter 5, R Square Change is the proportion of variance incremented by the variable(s) entered at this step. Thus, the proportion of variance accounted by X3, over and above what X2 accounts, is .19287. F Change for this increment is 52.92. Earlier, I got the same values, within rounding, when I applied (7.23).

   Examine now the column labeled B. Because I analyze a correlation matrix, these are standardized regression coefficients. Earlier, I said that testing the significance of a regression coefficient (b or β) is tantamount to testing the increment in the proportion of variance that the independent variable associated with the b (or β) accounts for in the dependent variable when it is entered last into the regression equation. That this is so can now be seen from the tests of the two B's. Examine first the T ratio for the test of the B for X3. Recall that $t^2 = F$, when the F ratio has 1 df for the numerator. Thus, $7.274^2 = 52.91$, which is, within rounding, the same as the value reported in the preceding and the one I obtained earlier through the application of (7.23). Similarly, for the test of B for X2: $9.986^2 = 99.72$, which is the same as the F ratio I obtained earlier for the test of the proportion of variance X2 increments, when it enters last (i.e., the test of $r_{1(2.3)}^2$).

Output

Variable(s) Entered on Step Number   3..   X4

Multiple R	.81471	R Square Change	.01728
R Square	.66375	F Change	4.93430
		Signif F Change	.0287

- - - - - - - - - - - - - - - Variables in the Equation - - - - - - - - - - - - - - - -

Variable	B	T	Sig T
X2	.559207	8.749	.0000
X3	.447921	7.485	.0000
X4	.140525	2.221	.0287
(Constant)	.000000		

Commentary

This is the last step of Equation Number 1, when X4 is entered. Earlier, I obtained, through the application of (7.23), the same R Square Change and the F Change reported here.

Again, the test of each of these B's is tantamount to testing the proportion of variance the variable associated with the B in question accounts for when it enters last in the equation. For example, the T ratio for the test of B for X2 is also the test of the proportion of variance X2 accounts for when it enters last in the equation. Equivalently, it is a test of the corresponding semipartial or partial correlation. Earlier, through the application of (7.23), I found that $F = 76.60$ for the test of $r_{1(2.34)}^2$, which is, within rounding, the same as T^2 (8.749^2) for the test of the B for X2. Tests of the other B's are similarly interpreted.

Output

		Equation Number 1 Summary table				Equation Number 2 Summary table				Equation Number 3 Summary table		
Step	Variable	Rsq	RsqCh	FCh	Variable	Rsq	RsqCh	FCh	Variable	Rsq	RsqCh	FCh
1	In: X2	.4536	.4536	81.357	In: X4	.1208	.1208	13.459	In: X3	.2830	.2830	38.685
2	In: X3	.6465	.1929	52.918	In: X3	.3957	.2749	44.124	In: X2	.6465	.3634	99.720
3	In: X4	.6638	.0173	4.934	In: X2	.6638	.2681	76.541	In: X4	.6638	.0173	4.934

Commentary

Recall that I called for estimation of three regression equations. In this segment, I placed excerpts of the three summary tables alongside each other to facilitate comparisons among them. The information directly relevant for present purposes is contained in the columns labeled Rsq(uared)Ch(ange). Thus, for example, when X2 enters first (first line of Equation Number 1), it accounts for .4536 of the variance in X1. When X2 enters second (second line of Equation Number 3), it accounts for .3634 of the variance of X1. When X2 enters last (last line of Equation Number 2), it accounts for .2681 of the variance of X1.

The values reported under RsqCh are squared semipartial correlations (except for the first, which is a squared zero-order correlation) of successive orders as expressed by (7.25) or (7.26). I illustrate this with the values reported for Equation Number 1:

$$.4536 = r_{12}^2 \qquad .1929 = r_{1(3.2)}^2 \qquad .0173 = r_{1(4.23)}^2$$

FCh(ange) are F ratios for tests of RsqCh. Compare these with the same values I calculated earlier.

Earlier, I showed that squared partial correlations can be calculated using relevant squared multiple correlations—see, for example, (7.5) and (7.7). The following examples show how values reported in the summary table of Equation Number 1 can be used for this purpose:

$$r_{13.2}^2 = (.1929)/(1 - .4536) = .3530$$

$$r_{14.23}^2 = (.0173)/(1 - .6465) = .0489$$

SUPPRESSOR VARIABLE: A COMMENT

Horst (1941) drew attention to a counterintuitive occurrence of a variable that has a zero, or close to zero, correlation with the criterion leads to improvement in prediction when it is included in a multiple regression analysis. This takes place when the variable in question is correlated with one or more than one of the predictor variables. Horst reasoned that the inclusion in the equation of a seemingly useless variable, so far as prediction of the criterion is concerned, suppresses, or controls for, irrelevant variance, that is, variance that it shares with the predictors and not with the criterion, thereby ridding the analysis of irrelevant variation, or noise—hence, the name *suppressor variable*. For example, assume the following zero-order correlations:

$$r_{12} = .3 \qquad r_{13} = .0 \qquad r_{23} = .5$$

If variable 1 is the criterion, it is obvious that variable 3 shares nothing with it and would appear to be useless in predicting it. But variable 3 is related to variable 2, and whatever these two variables share is evidently different from what 1 and 2 share.

Probably the most direct way to show the effect of using variable 3, under such circumstances, is to calculate the following semipartial correlation:

$$r_{1(2.3)} = \frac{.3 - (.0)(.5)}{\sqrt{1 - .5^2}} = \frac{.3}{\sqrt{.75}} = \frac{.3}{.866} = .35$$

Note that the semipartial correlation is larger than its corresponding zero-order correlation because a certain amount of irrelevant variance was suppressed, thereby purifying, so to speak, the relation between variables 1 and 2.

The same can be demonstrated by calculating the squared multiple correlation using (5.20):

$$R^2_{1.23} = \frac{r^2_{12} + r^2_{13} - 2r_{12}r_{13}r_{23}}{1 - r^2_{23}} = \frac{.3^2 + .0^2 - 2(.3)(.0)(.5)}{1 - .5^2} = \frac{.09}{.75} = .12$$

While variable 2 accounts for 9% of the variance of variable 1 ($r^2_{12} = .3^2 = .09$), adding variable 3, whose correlation with variable 1 is zero, results in an increase of 3% in the variance accounted for in variable 1. This should serve as a reminder that inspection of the zero-order correlations is not sufficient to reveal the potential usefulness of variables when they are used simultaneously to predict or explain a dependent variable. Using (5.15), I calculate the β's for variables 2 and 3:

$$\beta_2 = \frac{r_{12} - r_{13}r_{23}}{1 - r^2_{23}} = \frac{.3 - (.0)(.5)}{1 - .5^2} = \frac{.3}{.75} = .4$$

$$\beta_3 = \frac{r_{13} - r_{12}r_{23}}{1 - r^2_{23}} = \frac{.0 - (.3)(.5)}{1 - .5^2} = \frac{-.15}{.75} = -.2$$

Note that the suppressor variable gets a negative regression coefficient. As we are dealing here with standard scores, the manner in which the suppressor variable operates in the regression equation can be seen clearly. People whose scores are above the mean on the suppressor variable (3) have positive z scores; those whose scores are below the mean have negative z scores. Consequently, when the regression equation is applied, predicted scores for people who score above the mean on the suppressor variable are lowered as a result of multiplying a negative regression coefficient by a positive score. Conversely, predicted scores of those below the mean on the suppressor variable are raised as a result of multiplying a negative regression coefficient by a negative score. In other words, people who are high on the suppressor variable are penalized, so to speak, for being high, whereas those who are low on the suppressor variable are compensated for being low.

Horst (1966) gave a good research example of this phenomenon. In a study to predict the success of pilot training during World War II, it was found that tests of mechanical, numerical, and spatial abilities had positive correlations with the criterion, but that verbal ability had a very low positive correlation with the criterion. Verbal ability did, however, have relatively high correlations with the three predictors. This was not surprising as all the abilities were measured by paper-and-pencil tests and therefore, "Some verbal ability was necessary in order to understand the instructions and the items used to measure the other three abilities" (Horst, 1966, p. 355). Verbal ability, therefore, served as a suppressor variable. "To include the verbal score with a negative weight served to suppress or subtract irrelevant ability, and to discount the scores of those who did well on the test simply because of their verbal ability rather than because of abilities required for success in pilot training."

Elaborations and Extensions

The conception of the suppressor variable as I have discussed it thus far has come to be known as classical or traditional suppression, to distinguish it from two extensions labeled negative and reciprocal suppression. As implied by the title of this section, it is not my intention to discuss this topic in detail. Instead, I will make some general observations.

"The definition and interpretation of the suppressor-concept within the context of multiple regression remains a controversial issue" (Holling, 1983, p. 1). Indeed, it "is frequently a source of dismay and/or confusion among researchers using some form of regression analysis to analyze their data" (McFatter, 1979, p. 123). Broadly, two definitions were advanced—one is expressed with reference to regression coefficients (e.g., Conger, 1974), whereas the other is expressed with reference to squared semipartial correlations (e.g., Velicer, 1978).

Consistent with either definition, a variable may act as a suppressor even when it is correlated with the criterion. Essentially, the argument is that a variable qualifies as a suppressor when its inclusion in a multiple regression analysis leads to a standardized regression coefficient of a predictor to be larger than it is in the absence of the suppressor variable (according to Conger's definition) or when the semipartial correlation of the criterion and a predictor is larger than the corresponding zero-order correlation (according to Velicer's definition). For a comparison of the two definitions, see Tzelgov and Henik (1981). For a recent statement in support of Conger's definition, see Tzelgov and Henik (1991). For one supporting Velicer's definition, see Smith, Ager, and Williams (1992).

Without going far afield, I will note that, by and large, conceptions of suppressor variables were formulated from the perspective of prediction, rather than explanation. Accordingly, most, if not all, discussions of suppressor effects appeared in the psychometric literature in the context of validation of measures, notably criterion-related validation (for an introduction to validation of measures, see Pedhazur & Schmelkin, 1991, Chapters 3–4). It is noteworthy that the notion of suppression is hardly alluded to in the literature of some disciplines (e.g., sociology, political science).

I discuss the distinction between predictive and explanatory research later in the text (especially, Chapters 8–10). For now, I will only point out that prediction may be carried out in the absence of theory, whereas explanation is what theory is about. What is overlooked when attempting to identify suppressor variables solely from a predictive frame of reference is that "differing structural equation (causal) models can generate the same multiple regression equation and that the interpretation of the regression equation depends critically upon which model is believed to be appropriate" (McFatter, 1979, p. 125. See also, Bollen, 1989, pp. 47–54). Indeed, McFatter offers some examples of what he terms "*enhancers*" (p. 124), but what may be deemed *suppressors* by researchers whose work is devoid of a theoretical framework. Absence of theory in discussions of suppressor variables is particularly evident when Velicer (1978) notes that the designation of which variable is the suppressor is arbitrary (p. 955) and that his definition is consistent with "stepwise regression procedures" (p. 957; see Chapter 8, for a discussion of the atheoretical nature of stepwise regression analysis).

In sum, the introduction of the notion of suppressor variable served a useful purpose in alerting researchers to the hazards of relying on zero-order correlations for judging the worth of variables. However, it also increased the potential for ignoring the paramount role of theory in interpreting results of multiple regression analysis.

MULTIPLE PARTIAL AND SEMIPARTIAL CORRELATIONS

My presentation thus far has been limited to a correlation between two variables while partialing out other variables from *both* of them (partial correlation) or from only *one* of them (semipartial correlation). Logical extensions of such correlations are the multiple partial and the multiple semipartial correlations.

Multiple Partial Correlation

A multiple partial correlation may be used to calculate the squared multiple correlation of a dependent variable with a set of independent variables after controlling, or partialing out, the effects of another variable, or variables, from the dependent as well as the independent variables. The difference, then, between a partial and a multiple partial correlation is that in the former, one independent variable is used, whereas in the latter, more than one independent variable is used. For example, suppose that a researcher is interested in the squared multiple correlation of academic achievement with mental ability and motivation. Since, however, the sample is heterogeneous in age, the researcher wishes to control for this variable while studying the relations among the other variables. This can be accomplished by calculating a multiple partial correlation. Note that had only one independent variable been involved (i.e., either mental ability or motivation) a partial correlation would be required.

Conceptually and analytically, the multiple partial correlation and the partial correlation are designed to accomplish the same goal. In the preceding example this means that academic achievement, mental ability, and motivation are residualized on age. The residualized variables may then be used as ordinary variables in a multiple regression analysis. As with partial correlations, one may partial out more than one variable. In the previous example, one may partial out age and, say, socioeconomic status.

I use the following notation: $R^2_{1.23(4)}$, which means the squared multiple correlation of X_1 with X_2 and X_3, after X_4 was partialed out from the other variables. Note that the variable that is partialed out is placed in parentheses. Similarly, $R^2_{1.23(45)}$ is the squared multiple correlation of X_1 with X_2 and X_3, after X_4 and X_5 were partialed out from the other three variables.

The calculation of squared multiple partial correlations is similar to the calculation of squared partial correlations:

$$R^2_{1.23(4)} = \frac{R^2_{1.234} - R^2_{1.4}}{1 - R^2_{1.4}} \tag{7.27}$$

Note the similarity between (7.27) and (7.5), the formula for the squared partial correlation. Had there been only one independent variable (i.e., X_2 or X_3), (7.27) would have been reduced to (7.5). To calculate a squared multiple partial correlation, then, (1) calculate the squared multiple correlation of the dependent variable with the remaining variables (i.e., the independent and the control variables); (2) calculate the squared multiple correlation of the dependent variable with the control variables only; (3) subtract the R^2 obtained in step 2 from the R^2 obtained in step 1; and (4) divide the value obtained in step 3 by one minus the R^2 obtained in step 2.

The formula for the calculation of the squared multiple partial correlation with two control variables is

$$R^2_{1.23(45)} = \frac{R^2_{1.2345} - R^2_{1.45}}{1 - R^2_{1.45}} \tag{7.28}$$

Extensions of (7.27) or (7.28) to any number of independent variables and any number of control variables are straightforward.

Numerical Examples

A correlation matrix for five variables is reported in Table 7.5. Assume first that you wish to calculate the squared multiple partial correlation of achievement (X_1) with mental ability (X_2) and

Table 7.5   Correlation Matrix for Five Variables; N = 300 (Illustrative Data)

	1 Achievement	2 Mental Ability	3 Motivation	4 Age	5 SES
1	1.00	.80	.60	.70	.30
2	.80	1.00	.40	.80	.40
3	.60	.40	1.00	.30	.35
4	.70	.80	.30	1.00	.04
5	.30	.40	.35	.04	1.00

motivation (X_3), while controlling for age (X_4). In what follows, I use REGRESSION of SPSS to calculate the R^2's necessary for the application of (7.27). I suggest that you replicate my analysis using a program of your choice.

SPSS

Input

TITLE TABLE 7.5. MULTIPLE PARTIALS AND SEMIPARTIALS.
MATRIX DATA VARIABLES=ACHIEVE ABILITY MOTIVE AGE SES/
   CONTENTS=CORR N.
BEGIN DATA
1
 .80 1
 .60 .40 1
 .70 .80   .30 1
 .30 .40   .35   .04 1
300 300 300 300 300
END DATA
REGRESSION MATRIX=IN(*)/
  VAR=ACHIEVE TO SES/STAT ALL/
  DEP ACHIEVE/ENTER AGE/ENTER ABILITY MOTIVE/
  DEP ACHIEVE/ENTER AGE SES/ENTER ABILITY MOTIVE.

Commentary

I used and commented on input such as the preceding several times earlier in this chapter. Therefore, I will make only a couple of brief comments. For illustrative purposes, I assigned substantive names to the variables. I called for two regression equations in anticipation of calculating two multiple partials.

Output

TITLE TABLE 7.5. MULTIPLE PARTIALS AND SEMIPARTIALS.

Summary table

- - - - - - - -

Step	Variable	Rsq	RsqCh	FCh	SigCh
1	In: AGE	.4900	.4900	286.314	.000
2	In: MOTIVE				
3	In: ABILITY	.7457	.2557	148.809	.000

Commentary

To avoid cumbersome subscript notation, I will identify the variables as follows: 1 = achievement, 2 = mental ability, 3 = motivation, 4 = age, and 5 = SES. I now use relevant values from the summary table to calculate $R^2_{1.23(4)}$:

$$R^2_{1.23(4)} = \frac{R^2_{1.234} - R^2_{1.4}}{1 - R^2_{1.4}} = \frac{.7457 - .4900}{1 - .4900} = \frac{.2557}{.51} = .5014$$

Note that the value for the numerator is available directly from the second entry in the RsqCh column. The denominator is 1 minus the first entry in the same column (equivalently, it is Rsq of age with achievement). If you calculated the squared multiple correlation of achievement with motivation and mental ability you would find that it is equal to .7333. Controlling for age reduced by about .23 (.7333 − .5014) the proportion of variance of achievement that is attributed to mental ability and motivation.

Output

Summary table

- - - - - - - -

Step	Variable	Rsq	RsqCh	FCh	SigCh
1	In: SES				
2	In: AGE	.5641	.5641	192.176	.000
3	In: MOTIVE				
4	In: ABILITY	.7475	.1834	107.103	.000

Commentary

Assume that you wish to control for both age and SES, that is, to calculate $R^2_{1.23(45)}$.

$$R^2_{1.23(45)} = \frac{R^2_{1.2345} - R^2_{1.45}}{1 - R^2_{1.45}} = \frac{.7475 - .5641}{1 - .5641} = \frac{.1834}{.4359} = .4207$$

Again, the value for the numerator is available in the form of RsqCh, and the denominator is 1 minus Rsq with the control variables (age and SES). Controlling for both age and SES, the squared multiple correlation of achievement with mental ability and motivation is .4207. Compare with $R^2_{1.23(4)} = .5014$ and $R^2_{1.23} = .7333$.

Multiple Semipartial Correlation

Instead of partialing out variables from both the dependent and the independent variables, variables can be partialed out from the independent variables only. For example, one may wish to calculate the squared multiple correlation of X_1 with X_2 and X_3, after X_4 was partialed out from X_2 and X_3. This, then is an example of a squared multiple semipartial correlation. The notation is $R^2_{1(23.4)}$. Note the analogy between this notation and the squared semipartial correlation. The dependent variable is outside the parentheses. The control variable (or variables) is placed after the dot. Similarly, $R^2_{1(23.45)}$ is the squared multiple semipartial correlation of X_1 with X_2 and X_3, after X_4 and X_5 were partialed out from X_2 and X_3.

Analogous to the squared semipartial correlation, the squared multiple semipartial correlation indicates the increment in the proportion of variance of the dependent variable that is accounted for by more than one independent variable. In other words, in the case of the squared semipartial correlation, the increment is due to one independent variable, whereas in the case of the squared multiple semipartial correlation, the increment is due to more than one independent variable. Accordingly, the squared multiple semipartial correlation is calculated as one would calculate a squared semipartial correlation, except that more than one independent variable is used for the former. For example,

$$R^2_{1(23.4)} = R^2_{1.234} - R^2_{1.4} \tag{7.29}$$

where $R^2_{1(23.4)}$ indicates the proportion of variance in X_1 accounted for by X_2 and X_3, after the contribution of X_4 was taken into account. Note that the right-hand side of (7.29) is the same as the numerator of (7.27), the equation for the squared multiple partial correlation. Earlier, I showed that a similar relation holds between equations for the squared semipartial and the squared partial correlations.

For the data in Table 7.5, I use the previous output to calculate the following:

$$R^2_{1(23.4)} = R^2_{1.234} - R^2_{1.4} = .7457 - .4900 = .2557$$

After partialing out age from mental ability and motivation, these two variables account for about 26% of the variance in achievement. Stated differently, the increment in the percent of variance in achievement (X_1) accounted for by mental ability (X_2) and motivation (X_3), over and above what age (X_4) accounts for, is 26%.

I calculate now as follows:

$$R^2_{1(23.45)} = R^2_{1.2345} - R^2_{1.45} = .7475 - .5641 = .1834$$

After controlling for both age and SES, mental ability and motivation account for about 18% of the variance in achievement.

Tests of Significance

Tests of significance for squared multiple partial and squared multiple semipartial correlations yield identical results. Basically, the increment in the proportion of variance of the dependent variable accounted for by a set of independent variables is tested. Consequently, I use (7.23) for this purpose. Recalling that I assumed that $N = 300$ for the illustrative data of Table 7.5, the test of $R^2_{1(23.4)}$ is

$$F = \frac{(R^2_{y.12...k_1} - R^2_{y.12...k_2})/(k_1 - k_2)}{(1 - R^2_{y.12...k_1})/(N - k_1 - 1)} = \frac{(.7457 - .4900)/(3 - 1)}{(1 - .7457)/(300 - 3 - 1)} = \frac{.12785}{.00086} = 148.81$$

with 2 and 296 *df*. This is also a test of $R^2_{1.23(4)}$.

The F ratio calculated here can be obtained directly from the output as the FCh. Look back at the first summary table in the previous output and notice that the FCh for the test of the increment is 148.809.

The test of $R^2_{1(23.45)}$ is

$$F = \frac{(R^2_{y.12...k_1} - R^2_{y.12...k_2})/(k_1 - k_2)}{(1 - R^2_{y.12...k_1})/(N - k_1 - 1)} = \frac{(.7475 - .5641)/(4 - 2)}{(1 - .7475)/(300 - 4 - 1)} = \frac{.09170}{.00086} = 107.13$$

with 2 and 295 *df*. This is also a test of $R^2_{1.23(45)}$.

Again, the F ratio calculated here is, within rounding, the same as the FCh for the increment in the second summary table of the output given earlier.

CONCLUDING REMARKS

The main ideas of this chapter are the control and explication of variables through partial and semipartial correlations. I showed that a partial correlation is a correlation between two variables that were residualized on one or more control variables. Also, a semipartial correlation is a correlation between an unmodified variable and a variable that was residualized on one or more control variables.

I argued that meaningful control of variables is precluded without a theory about the causes of the relations among the variables under consideration. When, for instance, one wishes to study the relation between two variables after the effects of their common causes were removed, a partial correlation is required. When, on the other hand, one wishes to study the relation between an independent variable and a dependent variable after removing the effects of other independent variables from the former only, a semipartial correlation is necessary. Clearly, the preceding statements imply different theoretical formulations regarding the relations among the variables being studied.

I showed that the squared semipartial correlation indicates the proportion of variance that a given independent variable accounts for in the dependent variable, after taking into account the effects of other independent variables. Consequently, I stated, and demonstrated, that the order in which independent variables are entered into the analysis is crucial when one wishes to determine the proportion of variance incremented by each. I stated that in Chapter 9 I discuss issues concerning the order of entry of variables into the analysis.

I then discussed and illustrated adverse effects of measurement errors on attempts to study the relation between two variables while controlling for other variables. After commenting on the idea of suppressor variable, I concluded the chapter with a presentation of extensions of partial and semipartial correlations to multiple partial and multiple semipartial correlations.

STUDY SUGGESTIONS

1. Suppose that the correlation between palm size and verbal ability is .55, between palm size and age is .70, and between age and verbal ability is .80. What is the correlation between palm size and verbal ability after partialing out age? How might one label the zero-order correlation between palm size and verbal ability?

2. Assume that the following correlations were obtained in a study: .51 between level of aspiration and academic achievement; .40 between social class and academic achievement; .30 between level of aspiration and social class.

(a) Suppose you wish to determine the correlation between level of aspiration and academic achievement after controlling for social class. What is the correlation?

(b) Assume that the reliability of the measurement of social class is .82. What is the correlation between level of aspiration and academic achievement after controlling for social class and correcting for the unreliability of its measurement? Interpret the results.

3. How does a semipartial-correlation coefficient differ from a partial-correlation coefficient?

4. Express the following as differences between R^2's:
   (a) $r^2_{1(3.2)}$; (b) $r^2_{1(3.24)}$; (c) $r^2_{5(1.234)}$.

5. Express $R^2_{2.1435}$ as the following:
   (a) One squared zero-order correlation and a set of squared semipartial correlations.
   (b) One squared zero-order correlation and a set of terms composed of differences between R^2's.

6. Read the following correlation matrix in a program for multiple regression analysis. Call for the necessary R^2's, entering variables in appropriate hierarchies, so that you may use the relevant output to calculate the following terms ($N = 500$):

	1	2	3	4	5
1	1.00	.35	.40	.52	.48
2	.35	1.00	.15	.37	.40
3	.40	.15	1.00	.31	.50
4	.52	.37	.31	1.00	.46
5	.48	.40	.50	.46	1.00

(a) (1) $r^2_{13.2}$ and $r^2_{1(3.2)}$
    (2) $r^2_{14.23}$ and $r^2_{1(4.23)}$
    (3) $r^2_{15.234}$ and $r^2_{1(5.234)}$

(b) (1) $r^2_{32.4}$ and $r^2_{3(2.4)}$
    (2) $r^2_{35.24}$ and $r^2_{3(5.24)}$
    (3) $r^2_{31.245}$ and $r^2_{3(1.245)}$

ANSWERS

1. $-.02$; spurious

2. (a) The partial correlation between level of aspiration and academic achievement is .45.
   (b) After correcting for the unreliability of the measurement of social class, the partial correlation between level of aspiration and academic achievement is .43.

4. (a) $R^2_{1.23} - R^2_{1.2}$; (b) $R^2_{1.234} - R^2_{1.24}$; (c) $R^2_{5.1234} - R^2_{5.234}$

5. (a) $r^2_{21} + r^2_{2(4.1)} + r^2_{2(3.14)} + r^2_{2(5.134)}$
   (b) $r^2_{21} + (R^2_{2.14} - R^2_{2.1}) + (R^2_{2.134} - R^2_{2.14}) + (R^2_{2.1345} - R^2_{2.134})$

6. (a) (1) .14078 and .12354; (2) .14983 and .11297; (3) .03139 and .02012
   (b) (1) .00160 and .00144; (2) .18453 and .16653; (3) .03957 and .02912

8

PREDICTION

Regression analysis can be applied for predictive as well as explanatory purposes. In this chapter, I elaborate on the fundamental idea that the validity of applying specific regression procedures and the interpretation of results is predicated on the purpose for which the analysis is undertaken. Accordingly, I begin with a discussion of prediction and explanation in scientific research. I then discuss the use of regression analysis for prediction, with special emphasis on various approaches to predictor selection. While doing this, I show deleterious consequences of using predictive approaches for explanatory purposes. Issues in the application and interpretation of regression analysis for explanation constitute much of Part 2 of this book, beginning with Chapter 9.

PREDICTION AND EXPLANATION

Prediction and explanation are central concepts in scientific research, as indeed they are in human action and thought. It is probably because of their preeminence that these concepts have acquired a variety of meanings and usages, resulting in ambiguities and controversies. Philosophers of science have devoted a great deal of effort to explicating prediction and explanation, some viewing them as structurally and logically identical, others considering them distinct and predicated on different logical structures. Advancing the former view, Hempel (1965) argued:

> Thus, the logical structure of a scientific prediction is the same as that of a scientific explanation. . . . The customary distinction between explanation and prediction rests mainly on a pragmatic difference between the two: While in the case of an explanation, the final event is known to have happened, and its determining conditions have to be sought, the situation is reversed in the case of a prediction: here, the initial conditions are given, and their "effect"—which, in the typical case, has not yet taken place—is to be determined. (p. 234)

DeGroot (1969) equated knowledge with the ability to predict, "The criterion *par excellence* of true knowledge is to be found in the ability to predict the results of a testing procedure. *If one knows something to be true, he is in a position to predict; where prediction is impossible, there is no knowledge*" (p. 20).

Scriven (1959), on the other hand, asserted that there is "a gross difference" (p. 480) between prediction and explanation. He pointed out, among other things, that in certain situations it is possible to predict phenomena without being able to explain them, and vice versa.

> Roughly speaking, the prediction requires only a correlation, the explanation requires more. This difference has as one consequence the possibility of making predictions from indicators of causes—for example, predicting a storm from a sudden drop in the barometric pressure. Clearly we could not say that the drop in pressure in our house caused the storm: it merely presaged it. (p. 480)

Kaplan (1964) maintained that from the standpoint of a philosopher of science the ideal explanation is probably one that allows prediction.

> The converse, however, is surely questionable; predictions can be and often are made even though we are not in a position to explain what is being predicted. This capacity is characteristic of well-established empirical generalizations that have not yet been transformed into theoretical laws. . . . In short, explanations provide understanding, but we can predict without being able to understand, and we can understand without necessarily being able to predict. It remains true that if we can predict successfully on the basis of certain explanations we have good reason, and perhaps the best sort of reason, for accepting the explanation. (pp. 349–350)

Focusing on psychological research, Anderson and Shanteau (1977) stated:

> Two quite different goals can be sought in psychological research. These are the goal of prediction and the goal of understanding. These two goals are often incompatible, a fact of importance for the conduct of inquiry. Each goal imposes its own constraints on design and procedure. . . . The difference between the goals of prediction and understanding can be highlighted by noting that an incorrect model, one that misrepresents the psychological process, may actually be preferable to the correct model for predictive purposes. Linear models, for example, are easier to use than nonlinear models. The gain in simplicity may be worth the loss in predictive power. (p. 1155)

I trust that the foregoing statements give you a glimpse at the complex problems attendant with attempts to delineate the status and role of prediction and explanation in scientific research. In addition to the preceding sources, you will find discussions of prediction and explanation in Brodbeck (1968, Part Five), Doby (1967, Chapter 4), Feigl and Brodbeck (1953, Part IV), Scheffler (1957), and Sjoberg and Nett (1968, Chapter 11).

Regardless of one's philosophical orientation concerning prediction and explanation, it is necessary to distinguish between research designed primarily for predictive purposes and that designed primarily for explanatory purposes. In predictive research the main emphasis is on practical applications, whereas in explanatory research the main emphasis is on understanding phenomena. This is not to say that the two research activities are unrelated or that they have no bearing on each other. Predictive research may, for example, serve as a source of hunches and insights leading to theoretical formulations. This state of affairs is probably most characteristic of the initial stages of the development of a science. Explanatory research may serve as the most powerful means for prediction. Yet the importance of distinguishing between the two types of research activities cannot be overemphasized.

The distinction between predictive and explanatory research is particularly germane to the valid use of regression analysis and to the interpretation of results. In predictive research, the goal is to optimize prediction of criteria (e.g., income, social adjustment, election results, academic achievement, delinquency, disease). Consequently, the choice of variables in research of this kind is primarily determined by their contribution to the prediction of the criterion. "If the correlation is high, no other standards are necessary. Thus if it were found that accuracy in horseshoe pitching correlated highly with success in college, horseshoe pitching would be a valid means of predicting success in college" (Nunnally, 1978, p. 88). Cook and Campbell (1979) made the same point:

For purely forecasting purposes, it does not matter whether a predictor works because it is a symptom or a cause. For example, your goal may be simply to predict who will finish high school. In that case, entering the Head Start experience into a predictive equation as a negative predictor which reduces the likelihood of graduation may be efficient even if the Head Start experience improved the chances of high school graduation. This is because receiving Head Start training is also evidence of massive environmental disadvantages which work against completing high school and which may be only slightly offset by the training received in Head Start. In the same vein, while psychotherapy probably reduces a depressed person's likelihood of suicide, for forecasting purposes it is probably the case that the more psychotherapy one has received the greater is the likelihood of suicide. (p. 296)

In a reanalysis of data from the Coleman Report, Armor (1972) found that an index of nine household items (e.g., having a television set, telephone, refrigerator, dictionary) had the highest correlation with verbal achievement: .80 and .72 for black and white sixth-grade students, respectively. It is valid to treat such an index as a useful predictor of verbal achievement. But would one venture to use it as a cause of verbal achievement? Would even a naive researcher be tempted to recommend that the government scrap the very costly and controversial compensatory educational programs in favor of a less costly program, that of supplying all families who do not have them with the nine household items, thereby leading to the enhancement of verbal achievement? Yet, as I show in this and in the next chapter, behavioral researchers frequently fall into such traps when they use purely predictive studies for the purpose of explaining phenomena.

You are probably familiar with the controversy surrounding the relation between IQ and race, which was rekindled recently as a result of the publication of *The Bell Curve* by R. Herrnstein and C. Murray. In a review of this book Passell (1994b) stated:

> But whatever the [IQ] tests measure, Mr. Herrnstein . . . and Mr. Murray correctly remind us that the scores predict success in school for ethnic minorities as well as for whites.
>
> What works in predicting school performance apparently also works for predicting success on the job. . . . It seems that the growing role of intelligence in *determining* [italics added] economic productivity largely accounts for the widening gap between rich and poor. (p. B3)

Notice how from the harmless idea of the role of IQ tests in prediction, Passell slips into the role of IQ in determining economic productivity. As I have not read the book, I cannot tell whether it is Passell or the book's authors who blurred the distinction between prediction and explanation. Be that as it may, the deleterious consequences of pronouncements such as the preceding are incalculable, particularly when they are disseminated in the mass media (*The New York Times*, in the present instance). I will say no more here, as I discuss social sciences and social policy in Chapter 10.

Theory as Guide

The fact that the usefulness of variables in a predictive study is empirically determined should not be taken to mean that theory plays no role, or is irrelevant, in the choice of such variables. On the contrary, theory is the best guide in selecting criteria and predictors, as well as in developing measures of such variables. The chances of attaining substantial predictability while minimizing cost, in the broadest sense of these terms, are enhanced when predictor variables are selected as a result of theoretical considerations. Discussions of criterion-related validation are largely devoted to issues related to the selection and measurement of criterion and predictor variables (see, for example, Cronbach, 1971; Nunnally, 1978, Chapter 3; Pedhazur & Schmelkin, 1991, Chapter 3; Thorndike, 1949).

Nomenclature

As a safeguard against confusing the two types of research, some writers have proposed different terminologies for each. Thus, Wold and Juréen (1953) proposed that in predictive research the predictors be called *regressors* and the criterion be called *regressand*. In explanatory research, on the other hand, they proposed the label *cause* (or *explanatory*) for what is generally referred to as an independent variable, and the label *effect* for the dependent variable.[1] In this book, I use *predictor* and *criterion* in predictive research, and *independent* and *dependent* variables in explanatory research.

Responding to the need to distinguish between predictive and explanatory research, Tukey (1954) suggested that regression analysis be called "predictive regression" in the former and "structural regression" in the latter. In predictive research, the researcher is at liberty to interchange the roles of the predictor and the criterion variables. From a predictive frame of reference, it is just as tenable to use mental ability, say, to predict motivation as it is to use motivation to predict mental ability. Similarly, a researcher may use self-concept to predict achievement, or reverse the role of these variables and use achievement to predict self-concept. Examples of the arbitrary designation of variables as predictors and criteria abound in the social sciences. There is nothing wrong with this, provided the variables are not accorded the status of independent and dependent variables, and the results are not interpreted as if they were obtained in explanatory research.

Finally, when appropriately used, regression analysis in predictive research poses few difficulties in interpretation. It is the use and interpretation of regression analysis in explanatory research that is fraught with ambiguities and potential misinterpretations.

REGRESSION ANALYSIS IN SELECTION

A primary application of regression analysis in predictive research is for the selection of applicants for a job, a training program, college, or the armed forces, to name but some examples. To this end, a regression equation is developed for use with applicants' scores on a set of predictors to predict their performance on a criterion. Although my concern here is exclusively with the development of prediction equations, it is necessary to recognize that various other factors (e.g., the ratio of available positions to the number of applicants, cost, utility) play a role in the selection process. For an introductory presentation of such issues see Pedhazur and Schmelkin (1991, Chapter 3). For more advanced expositions see, for example, Cronbach and Gleser (1965), Thorndike (1949).

Before developing a prediction equation, it is necessary to select a criterion (e.g., success on the job, academic achievement), define it, and have valid and reliable measures to assess it. This is a most complex topic that I cannot address here (for extensive discussions, see Cronbach, 1971; Cureton, 1951; Nunnally, 1978; Pedhazur & Schmelkin, 1991, Part 1). Assuming one has a valid and reliable measure of the criterion, predictor variables are selected, preferably based on theoretical considerations and previous research evidence. Using a representative sample of

---

[1] Wold and Juréen's (1953, Chapter 2) discussion of the distinction between predictive and explanatory research in the context of regression analysis is probably the best available on this topic. See also Blalock (1964) for a very good discussion of these issues.

potential applicants for whom scores on the predictors and on the criterion are available, a regression equation is developed. This equation is then used to predict criterion scores for future applicants.

A Numerical Example

Assume that for the selection of applicants for graduate study, a psychology department uses grade-point average (GPA) as a criterion. Four predictors are used. Of these, three are measures administered to each student at the time of application. They are (1) the Graduate Record Examination—Quantitative (GREQ), (2) the Graduate Record Examination—Verbal (GREV), and (3) the Miller Analogies Test (MAT). In addition, each applicant is interviewed by three professors, each of whom rate the applicant on a five-point scale—the higher the rating the more promising the applicant is perceived to be. The fourth predictor is the average of the ratings (AR) by the three professors. Illustrative data for 30 subjects on the five variables are given in Table 8.1. I will carry out the analysis through PROC REG of SAS.

SAS

Input

```
TITLE    'TABLE 8.1.    A SELECTION EXAMPLE';
DATA T81;
   INPUT GPA 1-2 .1 GREQ 3-5 GREV 6-8 MAT 9-10 AR 11-12 .1;
CARDS;
326255406527
415756807545     [first two subjects]

.  .  .  .  .  .
305857106527     [last two subjects]
336006108550
;
PROC PRINT;
PROC REG;
   MODEL GPA=GREQ GREV MAT AR/P CLI CLM;
   LABEL  GPA='GRADE POINT AVERAGE'
          GREQ='GRADUATE RECORD EXAM: QUANTITATIVE'
          GREV='GRADUATE RECORD EXAM: VERBAL'
          MAT='MILLER ANALOGIES TEST'
          AR='AVERAGE RATINGS';
RUN;
```

Commentary

INPUT. In earlier SAS runs (Chapters 4 and 5), I used a free format. Here, I use a fixed format that specifies the column location of variables and the number of digits to the right of the decimal

Table 8.1 Illustrative Data for a Selection Problem; N = 30

	GPA	GREQ	GREV	MAT	AR
	3.2	625	540	65	2.7
	4.1	575	680	75	4.5
	3.0	520	480	65	2.5
	2.6	545	520	55	3.1
	3.7	520	490	75	3.6
	4.0	655	535	65	4.3
	4.3	630	720	75	4.6
	2.7	500	500	75	3.0
	3.6	605	575	65	4.7
	4.1	555	690	75	3.4
	2.7	505	545	55	3.7
	2.9	540	515	55	2.6
	2.5	520	520	55	3.1
	3.0	585	710	65	2.7
	3.3	600	610	85	5.0
	3.2	625	540	65	2.7
	4.1	575	680	75	4.5
	3.0	520	480	65	2.5
	2.6	545	520	55	3.1
	3.7	520	490	75	3.6
	4.0	655	535	65	4.3
	4.3	630	720	75	4.6
	2.7	500	500	75	3.0
	3.6	605	575	65	4.7
	4.1	555	690	75	3.4
	2.7	505	545	55	3.7
	2.9	540	515	55	2.6
	2.5	520	520	55	3.1
	3.0	585	710	65	2.7
	3.3	600	610	85	5.0
M:	3.31	565.33	575.33	67.00	3.57
s:	.60	48.62	83.03	9.25	.84

NOTE: GPA = Grade-Point Average
GREQ = Graduate Record Examination—Quantitative
GREV = Graduate Record Examination—Verbal
MAT = Miller Analogies Test
AR = Average Rating

point. For example, GPA is in columns 1 and 2, with one digit to the right of the decimal point (e.g., 3.2 for the first subject; compare it with the data in Table 8.1).

MODEL. The options are P = predicted scores, CLI = confidence limits individual, and CLM = confidence limits mean. I explain the latter two in my commentary on the relevant excerpt of the output.

Output

Dependent Variable: GPA   GRADE POINT AVERAGE

Analysis of Variance

Source	DF	Sum of Squares	Mean Square	F Value	Prob>F
Model	4	6.68313	1.67078	11.134	0.0001
Error	25	3.75153	0.15006		
C Total	29	10.43467			

Root MSE	0.38738	R-square	0.6405
Dep Mean	3.31333	Adj R-sq	0.5829

Commentary

The four predictors account for about 64% of the variance of GPA ($R^2 = .6405$). I discuss Adj R-sq (adjusted R^2) under "Shrinkage." To obtain the F Value, the Mean Square Model (i.e., regression) is divided by the Mean Square Error (i.e., residual, called Mean Square Residual or *MSR* in this book; $1.67078/.15006 = 11.13$), with 4 and 25 *df*, p < .0001. This F ratio is, of course, also a test of R^2. To show this, I use (5.21) to calculate

$$F = \frac{R^2/k}{(1 - R^2)/(N - k - 1)} = \frac{.6405/4}{(1 - .6405)/(30 - 4 - 1)} = \frac{.1601}{.0144} = 11.12$$

with 4 and 25 *df*.

Root MSE is what I called standard error of estimate in Chapter 2—see (2.27) and the discussion related to it. It is equal to the square root of the mean square error (.15006) or the variance of estimate—see (2.26).

Output

Parameter Estimates

Variable	DF	Parameter Estimate	Standard Error	T for H0: Parameter=0	Prob > |T|	Variable Label
INTERCEP	1	−1.738107	0.95073990	−1.828	0.0795	Intercept
GREQ	1	0.003998	0.00183065	2.184	0.0385	GRADUATE RECORD EXAM: QUANTITATIVE
GREV	1	0.001524	0.00105016	1.451	0.1593	GRADUATE RECORD EXAM: VERBAL
MAT	1	0.020896	0.00954884	2.188	0.0382	MILLER ANALOGIES TEST
AR	1	0.144234	0.11300126	1.276	0.2135	AVERAGE RATINGS

Commentary

The regression equation, reported under parameter estimate, is

GPA′ = −1.738107 + .003998 GREQ + .001524 GREV + .020896 MAT + .144234 AR

By dividing each regression coefficient by its standard error, *t* ratios are obtained. Each *t* has 25 *df* (the degrees of freedom associated with the *MSR*).

Using $\alpha = .05$, it is evident from the probabilities associated with the *t* ratios (see the Prob column) that the regression coefficients for GREV and AR are statistically not different from zero. This is due, in part, to the small sample size I use here for illustrative purposes only. Normally, a much larger sample size is called for (see the following discussion). Assume, for the sake of illustration, that the sample size is adequate. Note that the largest regression coefficient (.144234 for AR) has the smallest *t* ratio (1.276). As I pointed out in Chapter 5 (see "Relative Importance of Variables"), the size of the *b* is affected by, among other things, the units of the scale used to measure the variable with which the *b* is associated. AR is measured on a scale that may range from 1 to 5, whereas GREV and GREQ are based on scales with much larger ranges, hence the larger coefficient for AR. Also, because the range of scores for the criterion is relatively small, all the *b*'s are relatively small. I suggested earlier that calculations be carried out to as many decimal places as is feasible. Note that had the *b*'s for the present example been calculated to two decimal places only, the *b* for GREQ, which is statistically significant, would have been incorrectly reported as equal to .00.

Deleting Variables from the Equation

Based on the statistical tests of significance, it appears that GREV and AR may be deleted from the equation without substantial loss in predictability. Recall that the test of a *b* is tantamount to testing the proportion of variance incremented by the variable with which the *b* is associated when the variable is entered last in the equation (see "Testing Increments in Proportion of Variance Accounted For" in Chapter 5 and "Increments in Regression Sum of Squares and Proportion of Variance" in Chapter 6). Depending on the pattern of the intercorrelations among the variables, it is possible that a variable that was shown to have a statistically nonsignificant *b* will turn out to have a statistically significant *b* when another variable(s) is deleted from the equation. In the present example, it is possible for the *b* associated with GREV to be statistically significant when AR is deleted, or for the *b* associated with AR to be statistically significant when GREV is deleted. Deleting both variables simultaneously will, of course, not provide this type of information. It is therefore recommended that variables be deleted one at a time so that the effect of the deletion on the sizes and tests of significance of the *b*'s for the remaining variables may be noted. For the present example, it is necessary to calculate two regression analyses: one in which AR is deleted, and one in which GREV is deleted. Following are the two regression equations I obtained from such analyses for the data in Table 8.1.[2] *t* ratios (each with 26 *df*) are given in parentheses underneath the regression coefficients.

$$\text{GPA}' = -2.148770 + .004926 \text{ GREQ} + .026119 \text{ MAT} + .001612 \text{ GREV}$$

$$(2.90) \qquad (2.99) \qquad (1.52)$$

$$\text{GPA}' = -1.689019 + .004917 \text{ GREQ} + .024915 \text{ MAT} + .155065 \text{ AR}$$

$$(2.80) \qquad (2.67) \qquad (1.35)$$

---

[2]If you are using SAS, you may wish to run these analyses by adding two model statements in Input, in the preceding. If you are using another program, make the necessary changes to get the same results.

Examine the *t* ratios for GREV and AR in these equations and notice that the *b* associated with each is statistically not significant. Accordingly, I delete both predictors from the equation. The final regression equation is

$$\text{GPA}' = -2.12938 + .00598\ \text{GREQ} + .03081\ \text{MAT}$$

$$(3.76) \qquad\qquad (3.68)$$

I suggest that you calculate R^2 for GPA with GREQ and MAT. You will find it to be .5830, as compared with $R^2 = .6405$ when the four predictors are used. Thus, adding GREV and AR, after GREQ and MAT, would result in an additional 6% $(.6405 - .5830 = .0575)$ of the variance of GPA accounted for. Such an increment would not be viewed as trivial in most social science research. (Later in this chapter, I further analyze this example.)

Although my discussion thus far, and the numerical example, dealt with a selection problem, the same approach is applicable whenever one's aim is to predict a criterion. Thus, the analysis will proceed as stated if, for instance, one were interested in predicting delinquency by using family size, socioeconomic status, health, sex, race, and academic achievement as predictors. In short, the analytic approach is the same, whatever the specific criterion and predictors, and whatever the predictive use to which the analysis is put.

Finally, note carefully that I did *not* interpret the *b*'s as indices of the effects of the variables on the criterion. This, because such an interpretation is inappropriate in predictive research. I discuss this topic in detail in Chapter 10.

CONFIDENCE LIMITS

A predicted *Y* for a given *X* can be viewed as either an estimate of the mean of *Y* at the *X* value in question or as an estimate of *Y* for any given individual with such an *X*. As with other statistics, it is possible to calculate the standard error of a predicted score and use it to set confidence limits around the predicted score. To avoid confusion between the two aforementioned views of the predicted *Y*, I will use different notations for their standard errors. I will use $s_{\mu'}$ for the standard error of the mean predicted scores, and $s_{y'}$ for the standard error of an individual score. I present these standard errors and their use in confidence limits in turn, beginning with the former.

In the hope of facilitating your understanding of this topic, I introduce it in the context of simple regression (i.e., one predictor). I then comment on the case of multiple predictors in the context of the numerical example under consideration (i.e., Table 8.1).

Standard Error of Mean Predicted Scores: Single Predictor

The standard error of mean predicted scores is

$$s_{\mu'} = \sqrt{s_{y.x}^2\left[\frac{1}{N} + \frac{(X_i - \overline{X})^2}{\Sigma x^2}\right]} \tag{8.1}$$

where $s_{y.x}^2$ = variance of estimate or *MSR*—see (2.26) and the discussion related to it; *N* = sample size; X_i = score of person *i* on the predictor; $\overline{X}$ = mean of the predictor; and Σx^2 = deviation sum of squares of the predictor. Examine the numerator of the second term in the brackets and note that $s_{\mu'}$ has the smallest possible value when X_i is equal to the mean of X. Further, the more X deviates from the mean of X, the larger $s_{\mu'}$. It makes sense intuitively that the more deviant, or extreme, a score, the more prone it is to error. Other things equal, the smaller the variance of estimate $(s_{y.x}^2)$, the smaller $s_{\mu'}$. Also, the larger the variability of the predictor (X), the smaller the $s_{\mu'}$. Further insight into (8.1) can be gained when you recognize that the term in the brackets is leverage—a concept introduced in Chapter 3.[3]

To illustrate calculations of $s_{\mu'}$, I will use data from the numerical example I introduced in Chapter 2 (Table 2.1), where I calculated the following:

$$s_{y.x}^2 = 5.983 \qquad \overline{X} = 3.00 \qquad \Sigma x^2 = 40$$

$$Y' = 5.05 + .75X$$

For $X = 1$,

$$Y' = 5.05 + .75(1) = 5.8$$

Recalling that $N = 20$,

$$s_{\mu'} = \sqrt{5.983\left[\frac{1}{20} + \frac{(1-3)^2}{40}\right]} = .947$$

For $X = 2$,

$$Y' = 5.05 + .75(2) = 6.55$$

$$s_{\mu'} = \sqrt{5.983\left[\frac{1}{20} + \frac{(2-3)^2}{40}\right]} = .670$$

For $X = 3$,

$$Y' = 5.05 + .75(3) = 7.3$$

$$s_{\mu'} = \sqrt{5.983\left[\frac{1}{20} + \frac{(3-3)^2}{40}\right]} = .547$$

The preceding illustrate what I said earlier, namely, the closer X is to the mean of X, the smaller is the standard error.

Confidence Intervals

The confidence interval for Y' is

$$Y' \pm t_{(\alpha/2,\ df)}s_{\mu'} \tag{8.2}$$

where α = level of significance; df = degrees of freedom associated with the variance of estimate, $s_{y.x}^2$, or with the residual sum of squares. In the present example, $N = 20$ and k (number of predictors) $= 1$. Therefore, df for (8.2) are $N - k - 1 = 20 - 1 - 1 = 18$. Assume, for example, that one wishes the 95% confidence interval. The t ratio (.025, 18) $= 2.101$ (see a t table in statistics books, or take $\sqrt{F}$ with 1 and 18 df from Appendix B).

---

[3]I believe that you will benefit from rereading the discussion of leverage.

For $X = 1$: $Y' = 5.8$ and $s_{\mu'} = .947$ (see the previous calculations). The 95% confidence interval for the mean predicted scores is

$$5.8 \pm (2.101)(.947) = 3.81 \text{ and } 7.79$$

For $X = 2$: $Y' = 6.55$ and $s_{\mu'} = .670$. The 95% confidence interval is

$$6.55 \pm (2.101)(.670) = 5.14 \text{ and } 7.96$$

For $X = 3$: $Y' = 7.3$ and $s_{\mu'} = .547$. The 95% confidence interval is

$$7.3 \pm (2.101)(.547) = 6.15 \text{ and } 8.45$$

Standard Error of Predicted Score: Single Predictor

The standard error of a predicted score is

$$s_{y'} = \sqrt{s_{y.x}^2 \left[1 + \frac{1}{N} + \frac{(X_i - \bar{X})^2}{\Sigma x^2} \right]} \tag{8.3}$$

Note that (8.3) is similar to (8.1), except that it contains an additional term in the brackets (1) to take account of the deviation of a predicted score from the mean predicted scores. Accordingly, $s_{y'} > s_{\mu'}$.

I now calculate standard errors of predicted scores for the same values of X that I used in the preceding section.

For $X = 1$,

$$s_{y'} = \sqrt{5.983 \left[1 + \frac{1}{20} + \frac{(1 - 3)^2}{40} \right]} = 2.623$$

Compare this with .947, which is the corresponding value for the standard error of mean predicted scores for the same X value.

Apply (8.3) for the case of $X = 2$ and $X = 3$ and verify that $s_{y'}$ for the former is 2.536 and for the latter is 2.506.

Prediction Interval: Single Predictor

I now use the standard errors of predicted scores calculated in the preceding section to calculate prediction intervals for the predicted values for the same X values I used in the preceding in connection with confidence intervals for mean predicted scores.

Recalling that for $X = 1$, $Y' = 5.8$, the prediction interval is

$$5.8 \pm (2.101)(2.623) = .29 \text{ and } 11.31$$

As expected, this interval is considerably wider than the corresponding one for the mean predicted scores (3.81 and 7.79; see the previous calculations).

For $X = 2$, $Y' = 6.55$, the prediction interval is

$$6.55 \pm (2.101)(2.536) = 1.22 \text{ and } 11.88$$

For $X = 3$, $Y' = 7.3$, the prediction interval is

$$7.3 \pm (2.101)(2.506) = 2.03 \text{ and } 12.57$$

Multiple Predictors

Confidence limits for the case of multiple predictors are direct generalizations of the case of a single predictor, presented in the preceding sections, except that algebraic formulas become unwieldy. Therefore matrix algebra is used. Instead of using matrix algebra,[4] however, I will reproduce SAS output from the analysis of the data of Table 8.1.

Output

Obs	Dep Var GPA	Predict Value	Std Err Predict	Lower95% Mean	Upper95% Mean	Lower95% Predict	Upper95% Predict	Residual
1	3.2000	3.3313	0.191	2.9370	3.7255	2.4413	4.2212	−0.1313
2	4.1000	3.8132	0.136	3.5332	4.0933	2.9677	4.6588	0.2868
.	.	.	.	.	.	.	.	.
29	3.0000	3.4304	0.193	3.0332	3.8275	2.5392	4.3216	−0.4304
30	3.3000	4.0876	0.174	3.7292	4.4460	3.2130	4.9622	−0.7876

Commentary

I comment only on confidence limits. To get output such as the preceding, I used the following options on the MODEL statement: P (predicted), CLI (confidence limit individual), and CLM (confidence limit mean).

Std Err Predict is the standard error for mean predicted scores ($s_{\mu'}$). To get the standard error for a predicted score ($s_{y'}$), (1) square the corresponding $s_{\mu'}$, (2) add to it the *MSR* (variance of estimate), and (3) take the square root of the value found under (2). For the example under consideration $MSR = .15006$ (see the output given earlier). Thus, for subject number 1, for example,

$$s_{y'} = \sqrt{.191^2 + .15006} = .4319$$

The *t* ratio for $\alpha = .05$ with 25 *df* is 2.059. The prediction interval for this subject is

$$3.3313 \pm (2.059)(.4319) = 2.44 \text{ and } 4.22$$

Compare this with the output given above.

Obviously, with output like the preceding it is not necessary to go through the calculations of the $s_{y'}$. I presented the calculations to show what you would have to do if you wanted to set confidence limits other than those reported by PROC REG (i.e., 95%).

From the foregoing it should be clear that having the standard error of mean predicted scores or of a predicted score, and using the relevant *t* value (or taking the square root of the relevant *F* value) confidence limits, can be constructed at whatever α level you deem useful.

In the event that you are using a computer program that does not report confidence limits or the relevant standard errors, you can still obtain them with relative ease, provided the program reports leverage. As I pointed out earlier, (8.1) is comprised of two terms: variance of estimate and leverage. The former is necessarily part of the output of any multiple regression program. The latter is reported in many such programs.

---

[4]For a presentation using matrix algebra, see Pedhazur (1982, pp. 145–146).

Finally, *the predicted scores and the confidence intervals reported in the previous output are based on the regression equation with the four predictors.* When predictors are deleted because they do not contribute meaningfully, or significantly, to prediction (see the discussion in the preceding section), the predicted scores and the confidence intervals are, of course, calculated using regression estimates for the retained predictors. Using PROC REG from SAS, for example, this would necessitate a MODEL statement in which only the retained predictors appear.

SHRINKAGE

The choice of coefficients in regression analysis is aimed at maximizing the correlation between the predictors (or independent variables) and the criterion (or dependent variable). Recall that the multiple correlation can be expressed as the correlation between the predicted scores and the observed criterion scores—see (5.18) and the discussion related to it. If a set of coefficients derived in one sample were to be applied to predictor scores of another sample and the predicted scores were then correlated with the observed criterion scores, the resulting R would almost always be smaller than R calculated in the sample for which the coefficients were calculated. This phenomenon—called the shrinkage of the multiple correlation—occurs because the zero-order correlations are treated as if they were error-free when coefficients are calculated to maximize R. Of course, this is never the case. Consequently, there is a certain amount of capitalization on chance, and the resulting R is biased upward.

The degree of overestimation of R is affected by, among other things, the ratio of the number of predictors to the size of the sample. Other things equal, the larger this ratio, the greater the overestimation of R. Some authors recommend that the ratio of predictors to sample size be at least 1:15, that is, at least 15 subjects per predictor. Others recommend smaller ratios (e.g., 1:30). Still others recommend that samples be comprised of at least 400 subjects. Instead of resorting to rules of thumb, however, it is preferable to employ statistical power analysis for the determination of sample size. Instead of attempting to address this important topic briefly, hence inadequately, I refer you to Cohen's (1988) detailed treatment (see also, Cohen & Cohen, 1983; Gatsonis & Sampson, 1989; Green, 1991).

The importance of having a small ratio of number of predictors to number of subjects may be appreciated when one considers the expectation of R^2. Even when R^2 in the population is zero, the expectation of the sample R^2 is $k/(N - 1)$, where k is the number of predictors, and N is the sample size. What this means is that when the number of predictors is equal to the number of subjects minus one, the correlation will be perfect even when it is zero in the population.

Consider, for example, the case of one predictor and two subjects. Since the scores of the two subjects are represented by two points, a straight line may be drawn between them, no matter what the variables are—hence a perfect correlation. The preceding is based on the assumption that the two subjects have different scores on the two variables. When their scores on one of the variables are equal to each other, the correlation coefficient is undefinable. Although admittedly extreme, this example should serve to alert you to the hazards of overfitting, which occur when the number of predictors approaches the sample size. Lauter (1984) gives a notable real life example of this:

> Professor Goetz cites as an example a major recent civil case in which a jury awarded hundreds of thousands of dollars in damages based on a statistical model presented by an economist testifying as an expert witness. The record in the case shows, he says, that the economist's model was extrapolated on the basis of only *six observations* [italics added]. (p. 10)

ESTIMATION PROCEDURES

Although it is not possible to determine exactly the shrinkage of R, various approaches were proposed for estimating the population squared multiple correlation or the squared cross-validity coefficient (i.e., the coefficient that would be obtained when doing a cross validation; see the following). I will not review the various approaches that were proposed (for some discussions, comparisons, and recommendations, see Cattin, 1980; Cotter & Raju, 1982; Darlington, 1968; Drasgow & Dorans, 1982; Drasgow, Dorans, & Tucker, 1979; Herzberg 1969; Huberty & Mourad, 1980; Rozeboom, 1978; Schmitt, Coyle, & Rauschenberger, 1977; Stevens, 1996, pp. 96–100). Instead, I will first give an example of an approach to the estimation of the squared multiple correlation. Then I will discuss cross validation and give an example of formula-based estimation of the cross-validation coefficient.

Adjusted R^2

Following is probably the most frequently used formula for estimating the population squared multiple correlation. It is also the one used in most computer packages, including those I use in this book.

$$\hat{R}^2 = 1 - (1 - R^2)\frac{N - 1}{N - k - 1} \tag{8.4}$$

where $\hat{R}^2$ = adjusted (or shrunken) squared multiple correlation; R^2 = obtained squared multiple correlation; N = sample size; and k = number of predictors.

I now apply (8.4) to the data of Table 8.1, which I analyzed earlier. Recall that $N = 30$ and $k = 4$. From the SAS output given earlier, $R^2 = .6405$. Hence,

$$\hat{R}^2 = 1 - (1 - .6405)\frac{30 - 1}{30 - 4 - 1} = .583$$

See the SAS output, where Adj R-sq = 0.5829.

To illustrate the effect of the ratio of the number of predictors to sample size on shrinkage of the squared multiple correlation, I will assume that the R^2 obtained earlier with four predictors was based on a sample of 100, instead of 30. Applying (8.4),

$$\hat{R}^2 = 1 - (1 - .6405)\frac{100 - 1}{100 - 4 - 1} = .625$$

If, on the other hand, the sample size was 15,

$$\hat{R}^2 = 1 - (1 - .6405)\frac{15 - 1}{15 - 4 - 1} = .497$$

From (8.4) you may also note that, other things equal, the smaller R^2, the larger the estimated shrinkage. Assume that $R^2 = .30$. Using the same number of predictors (4) and the same sample sizes as in the previous demonstration, the application of (8.4) yields the following:

$$\hat{R}^2 = .020 \text{ for } N = 15$$

$$\hat{R}^2 = .188 \text{ for } N = 30$$

$$\hat{R}^2 = .271 \text{ for } N = 100$$

Formula (8.4) is applicable to the situation when all the predictors are retained in the equation. When a selection procedure is used to retain only some of the predictors (see the following), capitalization on chance is even greater, resulting in greater shrinkage. The use of large samples (about 500) is therefore particularly crucial when a number of predictors is to be selected from a larger pool of predictors.

Cross-Validation

Instead of estimating the population squared multiple correlation, as I did in the preceding section, the researcher's aim may be to determine how well a regression equation obtained in one sample performs in another sample from the same population. To this end, a cross-validation study is carried out as follows (for more detailed discussions, see Herzberg, 1969; Lord & Novick, 1968, pp. 285 ff.; Mosier, 1951).

Two samples from the same population are used. For the first sample—called the *screening sample* (Lord & Novick, 1968, p. 285)—a regression analysis is done. The regression equation from this sample is then applied to the predictors of the second sample—called the *calibration sample* (Lord & Novick, 1968, p. 285)—thus yielding a Y' for each subject. (If a selection of predictors is used in the screening sample, the regression equation is applied to the same predictors in the calibration sample.) A Pearson r is then calculated between the observed criterion scores (Y) in the calibration sample and the predicted criterion scores (Y'). This $r_{yy'}$ is referred to a cross-validity coefficient.

If the difference between the R^2 of the screening sample and the squared cross-validity coefficient of the calibration is small, the regression equation obtained in the screening sample may be applied for future predictions, assuming, of course, that the conditions under which the regression equation was developed remain unchanged. Changes in the situation may diminish the usefulness of the regression equation or even render it useless. If, for example, the criterion is grade-point average in college, and drastic changes in grading policies have occurred, a regression equation derived before such changes may no longer apply. A similar problem would occur if there has been a radical change in the type of applicants.

As Mosier (1951) pointed out, a regression equation based on the combined samples (the screening and calibration samples) is more stable due to the larger number of subjects on which it is based. It is therefore recommended that after deciding that shrinkage is small, the two samples be combined and the regression equation for the combined samples be used in future predictions.

Double Cross-Validation

Some researchers are not satisfied with cross-validation and insist on double cross-validation (Mosier, 1951), in which the procedure outlined in the preceding is applied twice. For each sample the regression equation is calculated. Each regression equation obtained in one sample is then applied to the predictors of the other sample, and $r_{yy'}$ is calculated. If the results are close, it is suggested that a regression equation calculated for the combined samples be used for prediction.

Data Splitting

Cross-validation is a costly process. Moreover, long delays in assessing the findings may occur due to difficulties in obtaining a second sample. As an alternative, it is recommended that a large sample (say 500) be randomly split into two subsamples, and that one subsample be used as the screening sample, and the other be used for calibration. Green (1978, pp. 84–86) and Stevens (1996, p. 98) give examples of data splitting using BMDP programs.

Formula-Based Estimation of the Cross-Validity Coefficient

Several authors proposed formulas for the estimation of cross-validity coefficients, thereby obviating the need to carry out costly cross-validation studies. Detailed discussions of such approaches will be found in the references cited earlier. See, in particular, Cotter and Raju (1982) who concluded, based on Monte Carlo investigations, that "formula-based estimation of population squared cross-validity is satisfactory, and there is no real advantage in conducting a separate, expensive, and time consuming cross-validation study" (p. 516; see also Drasgow et al., 1979).

There is no consensus as to the "best" formula for the estimation of cross-validity coefficients. From a practical viewpoint, though, when based on samples of moderate size, numerical differences among various estimates are relatively small. In what follows, I present formulas that some authors (e.g., Darlington, 1968, p. 174; Tatsuoka, 1988, p. 52) attribute to Stine, whereas others (e.g., Drasgow et al., 1979, p. 388; Stevens, 1996, p. 99) attribute to Herzberg.

In Chapter 2, I distinguished between the regression model where the values of the predictors are fixed, and the correlation model where the values of the predictors are random. For the regression model, the formula for the squared cross-validity coefficient is

$$\hat{R}_{cv}^2 = 1 - \left(\frac{N-1}{N}\right)\left(\frac{N+k+1}{N-k-1}\right)(1-R^2) \tag{8.5}$$

where $\hat{R}_{cv}^2$ = estimated squared cross-validity coefficient; N = sample size; k = number of predictors; and R^2 = observed squared multiple correlation.

For the correlation model, the formula for the squared cross-validity coefficient is

$$\hat{R}_{cv}^2 = 1 - \left(\frac{N-1}{N-k-1}\right)\left(\frac{N-2}{N-k-2}\right)\left(\frac{N+1}{N}\right)(1-R^2) \tag{8.6}$$

where the terms are as defined under (8.5).

For comparative purposes, I will apply (8.5) and (8.6) to results from the analysis of the data in Table 8.1, which I used to illustrate the application of (8.4). For the data of Table 8.1: $R^2 = .6405$; $N = 30$; and $k = 4$. Assuming a regression model, and applying (8.5),

$$\hat{R}_{cv}^2 = 1 - \left(\frac{30-1}{30}\right)\left(\frac{30+4+1}{30-4-1}\right)(1-.6405) = .513$$

Assuming a correlation model, and applying (8.6),

$$\hat{R}_{cv}^2 = 1 - \left(\frac{30-1}{30-4-1}\right)\left(\frac{30-2}{30-4-2}\right)\left(\frac{30+1}{30}\right)(1-.6405) = .497$$

As an exercise, you may wish to apply (8.5) and (8.6) to other values I used earlier in connection with the application of (8.4).

Computer-Intensive Approaches

In recent years, alternative approaches to cross-validation, subsumed under the general heading of computer-intensive methods, were developed. Notable among such approaches are Monte Carlo methods and bootstrapping. For some introductions, illustrative applications, and computer programs, see Bruce (1991), Diaconis and Efron (1983), Efron and Gong (1983), Hanushek and Jackson (1977, e.g., pp. 60–65, 78–79, 83–84), Lunneborg (1985, 1987), Mooney and Duval (1993), Noreen (1989), Picard and Berk (1990), Simon (1991), and Stine (1990).

PREDICTOR SELECTION

Because many of the variables used in the behavioral sciences are intercorrelated, it is often possible and useful to select from a pool of predictors a smaller set that will be as efficient, or almost as efficient, as the entire set for predictive purposes. Generally, the aim is the selection of the minimum number of variables necessary to account for almost as much of the variance as is accounted for by the total set. However, because of practical considerations (e.g., relative costs in obtaining given predictors, ease of administration of measures), a larger number of variables than the minimum necessary may be selected. A researcher may select, say, five predictors instead of three others that would yield about the same R^2 but at greater cost.

Practical considerations in the selection of specific predictors may vary, depending on the circumstances of the study, the researcher's specific aims, resources, and frame of reference, to name but some. Clearly, it is not possible to develop a systematic selection method that would take such considerations into account. When, however, the sole aim is the selection of variables that would yield the "best" regression equation, various selection procedures may be used. I placed best in quotation marks to signify that there is no consensus as to its meaning. Using different criteria for what is deemed best may result in the selection of different sets of variables (see Draper & Smith, 1981, Chapter 6).

An Initial Cautionary Note

Predictor-selection procedures may be useful in predictive research only. Although you will grasp the importance of this statement only after gaining an understanding of variable selection procedures, I felt it imperative to begin with this cautionary note to alert you to the potential for misusing the procedures I will present.

Misapplications of predictor-selection procedures are rooted in a disregard of the distinction between explanatory and predictive research. When I discussed this distinction earlier in this chapter, I suggested that different terminologies be used as a safeguard against overlooking it. Regrettably, terminology apt for explanatory research is often used in connection with misapplications of predictor-selection procedures. Probably contributing to this state of affairs are references to "model building" in presentations of predictor-selection methods in textbooks and computer manuals.

Admittedly, in some instances, readers are also cautioned against relying on such procedures for model construction and are urged that theory be their guide. I am afraid, however, that readers most in need of such admonitions are the least likely to heed them, perhaps even notice them. Be that as it may, the pairing of model construction, whose very essence is a theoretical framework (see Chapter 10), with predictor-selection procedures that are utterly atheoretical is deplorable. I return to these issues later in this chapter.

SELECTION PROCEDURES

Of various predictor-selection procedures, I will present all possible regressions, forward selection, backward elimination, stepwise selection, and blockwise selection. For a thorough review of selection methods, see Hocking (1976). See also, Daniel and Wood (1980), Darlington (1968), and Draper and Smith (1981, Chapter 6).

All Possible Regressions

The search for the "best" subset of predictors may proceed by calculating all possible regression equations, beginning with an equation in which only the intercept is used, followed by all one-predictor equations, two-predictor equations, and so on until all the predictors are used in a single equation. A serious shortcoming of this approach is that one must examine a very large number of equations, even when the number of predictors is relatively small. The number of all possible regressions with k predictors is 2^k. Thus, with three predictors, for example, eight equations are calculated: one equation in which none of the predictors is used, three one-predictor equations, three two-predictor equations, and one three-predictor equation. This can, of course, be done with relative ease. Suppose, however, that the number of predictors is 12. Then, 4096 (or 2^{12}) regression equations have to be calculated. With 20 predictors, 1,048,576 (or 2^{20}) regression equations are called for.

In view of the foregoing, it is imprudent to use the method of all possible regressions when the number of predictors is relatively large. Not only are computer resources wasted under such circumstances, but also the output consists of numerous equations that a researcher has to plod through in an effort to decide which of them is the "best." I will note in passing that an alternative approach, namely all possible subset regressions (referred to as regression by leaps and bounds) can be used when the number of predictors is large (see Daniel & Wood, 1980, Chapter 6; Draper & Smith, 1981, Chapter 6; Hocking, 1976).

Criteria for the Selection of a Subset.   No single criterion is available for determining how many, and which, predictors are to comprise the "best" subset. One may use a criterion of meaningfulness, statistical significance, or a combination of both. For example, you may decide to select an equation from all possible four-predictor equations because in the next stage (i.e., all possible five-predictor equations) no equation leads to a meaningful increment in R^2. Meaningfulness is largely situation-specific. Moreover, different researchers may use different criteria of meaningfulness even in the same situation.

A seemingly less problematic criterion is whether the increment in R^2 is statistically significant. Setting aside for now difficulties attendant with this criterion (I comment on them later), it should be noted that, with large samples, even a minute increment in R^2 may be declared statistically significant. Since the use of large samples is mandatory in regression analysis, particularly when a subset of predictors is to be selected, it is imprudent to rely solely on tests of statistical significance. Of what good is a statistically significant increment in R^2 if it is deemed not substantively meaningful? Accordingly, it is recommended that meaningfulness be the primary consideration in deciding what is the "best" equation and that tests of statistical significance be used loosely as broad adjuncts in such decisions.

Even after the number of predictors to be selected has been decided, further complications may arise. For example, several equations with the same number of predictors may yield virtually the same R^2. If so, which one is to be chosen? One factor in the choice among the competing equations may be economy. Assuming that some of the predictors are costlier to obtain than others, the choice would then appear obvious. Yet, other factors (e.g., stability of regression coefficients) need to be considered. For further discussions of criteria for selecting the "best" from among all possible regressions, see Daniel and Wood (1980, Chapter 6) and Draper and Smith (1981, Chapter 6).

A Numerical Example

I will use the numerical example I introduced earlier in this chapter (Table 8.1) to illustrate the application of the method of all possible regressions, as well as the other predictor-selection procedures that I present subsequently. I hope comparing the results from the different methods applied to the same data will help you to better understand the unique features of each.

Again, I will use PROC REG of SAS. Except for a SELECTION option on the model statement (see the following), the input is the same as the one I gave earlier in this chapter. For the present analysis, the model statement is

MODEL GPA=GREQ GREV MAT AR/SELECTION=RSQUARE;

Multiple model statements may be specified in PROC REG. Hence, to carry out the analysis presented earlier as well as the present one, add the preceding model statement to the input file given earlier. Actually, this is what I did to obtain the results I reported earlier and those I report in the output that follows.

Output

TABLE 8.1. VARIABLE SELECTION

N = 30   Regression Models for Dependent Variable: GPA

Number in Model	R-square	Variables in Model
1	0.38529398	AR
1	0.37350131	GREQ
1	0.36509196	MAT
1	0.33808659	GREV
2	0.58300302	GREQ MAT
2	0.51549156	GREV AR
2	0.50329629	GREQ AR
2	0.49347870	GREV MAT
2	0.49232208	MAT AR
2	0.48524079	GREQ GREV
3	0.61704497	GREQ GREV MAT
3	0.61020192	GREQ MAT AR
3	0.57187378	GREV MAT AR
3	0.57160608	GREQ GREV AR
4	0.64047409	GREQ GREV MAT AR

Commentary

As you can see, the results are printed in ascending order, beginning with one-predictor equations and concluding with a four-predictor equation. At each stage, R^2's are presented in descending order. Thus, at the first stage, AR is listed first because it has the highest R^2 with GPA, whereas GREV is listed last because its correlation with GPA is the lowest. As single predictors are used at this stage, the R^2's are, of course, the squared zero-order correlations of each predictor with the criterion.

Note that AR alone accounts for about 38% of the variance in GPA. Had the aim been to use a single predictor, AR would appear to be the best choice. Recall, however, that various factors may affect the choice of a predictor. AR is the average rating of an applicant by three professors who interview him or her. This is a time-consuming process. Assuming that the sole purpose of the interview is to obtain the AR for predictive purposes (admittedly, an unrealistic assumption), it is conceivable that one would choose GREQ instead of AR because it is less costly and it yields about the same level of predictability. For that matter, MAT is an equally likely candidate for selection instead of AR. This, then, is an example of what I said earlier about decisions regarding what is the "best" equation.[5]

Moving on to the results with two predictors, the combination of GREQ and MAT appears to be the best. The next best (i.e., GREV and AR) accounts for about 7% less of the variance as compared with that accounted by GREQ and MAT. Note that the best variable at the first stage (i.e., AR) is not included in the best equation at the second stage. This is due to the pattern of intercorrelations among the variables. Note also that I retained the same two variables when I used tests of significance of b's for deletion of variables (see "Deleting Variables from the Equation," presented earlier in this chapter). This, however, will not always happen.

Of the three-variable equations, the best combination is GREQ, GREV, and MAT, together accounting for about 62% of the variance. The increment from the best subset of two predictors to the best subset of three is about 4%. In line with what I said earlier, I will note that a decision as to whether an increment of 4% in the variance accounted for is meaningful depends on the researcher's goal and his or her view regarding various factors having to do with adding GREV (e.g., cost).

Although the increment in question can be tested for statistical significance, tabled F values corresponding to a prespecified α (e.g., .05) are not valid (see the following for a comment on statistical tests of significance).

Forward Selection

This solution proceeds in the following manner. The predictor that has the highest zero-order correlation with the criterion is entered first into the analysis. The next predictor to enter is the one that produces the greatest increment to R^2, after taking into account the predictor already in the equation. In other words, it is the predictor that has the highest squared semipartial correlation with the criterion, after having partialed out the predictor already in the equation (for

---

[5]For convenience, henceforth I will use best without quotation marks.

detailed discussions of semipartial and partial correlations, see Chapter 7). The third predictor to enter is the one that has the highest squared semipartial correlation with the criterion, after having partialed out the first two predictors already in the equation, and so forth. Some programs use partial rather than semipartial correlations. The results are the same, as semipartial correlations are proportional to partial correlations (see Chapter 7).

Earlier, I discussed criteria for determining the best equation (see "All Possible Regressions"), and I will therefore not address this topic here. I will now use the REGRESSION procedure of SPSS to do a Forward Selection on the data in Table 8.1.

SPSS

Input

```
TITLE PEDHAZUR, TABLE 8.1, FORWARD SELECTION.
DATA LIST/GPA 1-2(1),GREQ,GREV 3-8,MAT 9-10,AR 11-12(1).
VARIABLE LABELS GPA 'GRADE POINT AVERAGE'
   /GREQ 'GRADUATE RECORD EXAM: QUANTITATIVE'
   /GREV 'GRADUATE RECORD EXAM: VERBAL'
   /MAT 'MILLER ANALOGIES TEST'
   /AR 'AVERAGE RATINGS'.
BEGIN DATA
326255406527
415756807545        [first two subjects]

. . . . . .
305857106527        [last two subjects]
336006108550
END DATA
LIST.
REGRESSION VAR=GPA TO AR/DESCRIPTIVES/STAT DEFAULTS CHA/
   DEP=GPA/FORWARD.
```

Commentary

As I discussed SPSS input in some detail earlier in the text (e.g., Chapter 4), my comments here will be brief.

DATA LIST. As with SAS, which I used earlier in this chapter, I am using a fixed format here. Notice that each variable name is followed by a specification of the columns in which it is located. A number, in parentheses, following the column location, specifies the number of digits to the right of the decimal point. For example, GPA is said to occupy the first two columns, and there is one digit to the right of the decimal point. As GREQ and GREV have the same format, I specify their locations in a block of six columns, which SPSS interprets as comprising two blocks of three columns each.

REGRESSION. For illustrative purposes, I am calling for selected statistics: DEFAULTS and CHA $= R^2$ change.

Output

	Mean	Std Dev	Label
GPA	3.313	.600	GRADE POINT AVERAGE
GREQ	565.333	48.618	GRADUATE RECORD EXAM: QUANTITATIVE
GREV	575.333	83.034	GRADUATE RECORD EXAM: VERBAL
MAT	67.000	9.248	MILLER ANALOGIES TEST
AR	3.567	.838	AVERAGE RATINGS

N of Cases =   30

Correlation:

	GPA	GREQ	GREV	MAT	AR
GPA	1.000	.611	.581	.604	.621
GREQ	.611	1.000	.468	.267	.508
GREV	.581	.468	1.000	.426	.405
MAT	.604	.267	.426	1.000	.525
AR	.621	.508	.405	.525	1.000

Dependent Variable..   GPA   GRADE POINT AVERAGE
Block Number   1.   Method: Forward   Criterion   PIN   .0500

Variable(s) Entered on Step Number   1.. AR   AVERAGE RATINGS

R Square	.38529	R Square Change	.38529
Adjusted R Square	.36334	F Change	17.55023

----------------------- Variables in the Equation -----------------------   ------------ Variables not in the Equation ------------

Variable	B	SE B	Beta	T	Sig T	Variable	Beta In	Partial	T	Sig T
AR	.444081	.106004	.620721	4.189	.0003	GREQ	.398762	.438139	2.533	.0174
(Constant)	1.729444	.388047		4.457	.0001	GREV	.394705	.460222	2.694	.0120
						MAT	.384326	.417268	2.386	.0243

Variable(s) Entered on Step Number 2.. GREV GRADUATE RECORD EXAM: VERBAL

R Square	.51549	R Square Change	.13020
Adjusted R Square	.47960	F Change	7.25547

----------------------- Variables in the Equation -----------------------   ------------ Variables not in the Equation ------------

Variable	B	SE B	Beta	T	Sig T	Variable	Beta In	Partial	T	Sig T
AR	.329625	.104835	.460738	3.144	.0040	GREQ	.291625	.340320	1.845	.0764
GREV	.002851	.001059	.394705	2.694	.0120	MAT	.290025	.341130	1.850	.0756
(Constant)	.497178	.576516		.862	.3961					

End Block Number   1   PIN =   .050 Limits reached.

Commentary

Although I *edited* the output, I kept the basic layout to facilitate comparisons with output you may have from SPSS or from other programs you may be using.

One of two criteria for entering predictors can be specified: (1) *F*-to-enter (see "Stepwise Selection," later in this chapter) and (2) Probability of F-to-enter (keyword PIN), whose default value is 0.05. When a criterion is not specified, PIN = .05 is used. To enter into the equation, a predictor must also pass a criterion of tolerance—a topic I explain in Chapter 10.

Examine the correlation matrix given in the beginning of the output and notice that AR has the highest zero-order correlation with GPA. Accordingly, it is selected to enter first into the regression equation. Note, however, that the correlation of AR with GPA is only slightly higher than the correlations of the other predictors with GPA. Even though the slight differences in the correlations of the predictors with the criterion may be due to random fluctuations and/or measurement errors, the forward method selects the predictor with the highest correlation, be it ever so slightly larger than correlations of other predictors with the criterion.

As only one predictor is entered at Step Number 1, R Square is, of course, the squared zero-order correlation of AR with GPA ($.621^2$). The same is true for R Square Change.

Examine now the section labeled Variables in the Equation and notice that T = 4.189 for the test of the B associated with AR. As I explained several times earlier, the test of a regression coefficient is tantamount to a test of the proportion of variance incremented by the variable with which it is associated when it enters last. At this stage, only one variable is in the equation. Hence, T^2 = F Change (4.189^2 = 17.55).

Look now at the section labeled Variables not in the Equation (Step Number 1). For each predictor a partial correlation is reported. As I explained in Chapter 7, this is the partial correlation of the criterion with the predictor in question, after partialing out the predictor that is already in the equation (i.e., AR). For example, the partial correlation of GPA with GREQ, controlling for AR, is .438139. Examine Sig T for the predictors not in the equation and notice that the probabilities associated with them are less than .05 (but see the comment on statistical tests of significance, which follows). Recall t^2 = F, when *df* for the numerator of F is 1. Hence, the three predictors meet the criterion for entry (see the previous comment on PIN). Of the three, GREV has the highest partial correlation with GPA (.460222). Equivalently, it has the largest T ratio. Consequently, it is the one selected to enter in Step Number 2.

Examine now Step Number 2 and notice that the increment in the proportion of variance due to GREV is .13020. Recall that this is the squared semipartial correlation of GPA with GREV, after partialing out AR from the latter. In line with what I said earlier, the T^2 for the B associated with GREV is equal to F Change (2.694^2 = 7.26). Note that the T ratio for the partial correlation associated with GREV in Step Number 1 (Variables not in the Equation) is identical to the T ratio for the B associated with GREV in Step Number 2, where it is in the equation (see earlier chapters, particularly Chapter 7, for discussions of the equivalence of tests of *b*'s, β's, partial, and semipartial correlations).

Turning now to the column Sig T for the Variables *not* in the Equation at Step Number 2, note that the values reported exceed the default PIN (.05). Hence, the analysis is terminated. See message: PIN = .050 Limits reached.

Thus AR and GREV are the only two predictors selected by the forward method. Recall that the best two-predictor equation obtained by All Possible Regressions consisted of GREQ and

MAT. Thus the two methods led to the selection of different predictors, demonstrating what I said earlier—namely, what emerges as the best equation depends on the selection method used. In the analysis of all possible regressions, the best set of two predictors accounted for about 58% of the variance in GPA. In contrast, the predictors selected by the forward method account for about 52% (see R Square at Step Number 2). Incidentally, even if MAT were also brought into the equation, R^2 would still be (slightly) smaller (.57187) than the one obtained for two-predictors in the analysis of all possible regressions, underscoring once more that what is best under one procedure may not be best under another.

A serious shortcoming of the Forward Selection procedure is that no allowance is made for studying the effect the introduction of new predictors may have on the usefulness of the predictors already in the equation. Depending on the combined contribution of predictors introduced at a later stage, and on the relations of those predictors with the ones in the equation, it is possible for a predictor(s) introduced at an earlier stage to be rendered of little or no use for prediction (see "Backward Elimination," later in this chapter). In short, in Forward Selection the predictors are "locked" in the order in which they were introduced into the equation.

Statistical Tests of Significance in Predictor-Selection Procedures

Even if your statistical background is elementary, you probably know that carrying out multiple tests (e.g., multiple t tests, multiple comparisons among means) on the same data set affects Type I Error (α) adversely. You may even be familiar with different approaches to control Type I Error, depending on whether such tests are planned or carried out in the course of data snooping (I discuss these topics in Chapter 11). If so, you have surely noticed that predictor-selection procedures constitute data snooping in the extreme. Suffice it to note, for example, that at the first step of a Forward Selection all the predictors are, in effect, tested to see which of them has, say, the largest F ratio. Clearly, the probability associated with the F ratio thus selected is considerably larger than the ostensible criterion for entry of variables, say, .05. The same is true of other tests (e.g., of R^2).

Addressing problems of "data-dredging procedures," Selvin and Stuart (1966) pointed out that when variables are discarded upon examining the data, "we cannot validly apply standard statistical procedures to the retained variables in the relation as though nothing had happened" (p. 21). Using a fishing analogy they aptly reasoned, "the fish which don't fall through the net are bound to be bigger than those which do, and it is quite fruitless to test whether they are of average size" (p. 21).

Writing on this topic almost two decades ago, Wilkinson (1979) stated, "Unfortunately, the most widely used computer programs print this statistic without any warning that it does not have the F distribution under automated stepwise selection" (p. 168). More recently, Cliff (1987a) asserted, "most computer programs for multiple regression are positively satanic in their temptation toward Type I errors in this context" (p. 185). Attempts to alert users to the problem at hand have been made in recent versions of packages used in this book, as is evidenced by the following statements.

> The usual tabled F values (percentiles of the F distribution) should not be used to test the need to include a variable in the model. The distribution of the largest F-to-enter is affected by the number of variables available for selection, their correlation structure, and the sample size. When the independent

variables are correlated, the critical value for the largest F can be much larger than that for testing one preselected variable. (Dixon, 1992, Vol. 1, p. 395)

When many significance tests are performed, each at a level of, say 5 percent, the overall probability of rejecting at least one true null hypothesis is much larger than the 5 percent. If you want to guard against including any variables that do not contribute to the predictive power of the model in the population, you should specify a very small significance level. (SAS Institute Inc., 1990a, Vol. 2, p. 1400)

The actual significance level associated with the F-to-enter statistic is not the one usually obtained from the F distribution, since many variables are being examined and the largest F value is selected. Unfortunately, the true significance level is difficult to compute, since it depends not only on the number of cases and variables but also on the correlations between independent variables. (Norušis/SPSS Inc., 1993a, p. 347)

Yet, even a cursory examination of the research literature reveals that most researchers pay no attention to such admonitions. In light of the fact that the preceding statements constitute all the manuals say about this topic, it is safe to assume that many users even fail to notice them. Unfortunately, referees and editors seem equally oblivious to the problem under consideration.

There is no single recommended or agreed upon approach for tests of significance in predictor-selection procedures. Whatever approach is followed, it is important that its use be limited to the case of prediction. Adverse effects of biased Type I errors pale in comparison with the deleterious consequences of using predictor-selection procedures for explanatory purposes. Unfortunately, commendable attempts to alert users to the need to control Type I errors, and recommended approaches for accomplishing it, are often marred by references to the use of predictor-selection approaches for model building and explanation. A notable case in point is the work of McIntyre et al. (1983) who, while proposing a useful approach for testing the adjusted squared multiple correlation when predictor-selection procedures are used, couch their presentation with references to model building, as is evidenced by the title of their paper: "Evaluating the Statistical Significance of Models Developed by Stepwise Regression." Following are some illustrative statements from their paper: "a subset of the independent variables to include in the model" (p. 2); "maximization of *explanatory* [italics added] power" (p. 2); "these criteria are based on the typical procedures researchers use in developing a model" (p. 3).

For a very good discussion of issues concerning the control of Type I errors when using predictor-selection procedures, and some alternative recommendations, see Cliff (1987a, pp. 185–189; among the approaches he recommends is Bonferonni's—a topic I present in Chapter 11). See also, Huberty (1989), for a very good discussion of the topic under consideration and the broader topic of stepwise methods.

Backward Elimination

The backward elimination solution starts with the squared multiple correlation of the criterion with all the predictors. Predictors are then scrutinized one at a time to ascertain the reduction in R^2 that will result from the deletion of each from the equation. In other words, each predictor is treated, in turn, as if it were entered last in the analysis. The predictor whose deletion from the equation would lead to the smallest reduction in R^2 is the candidate for deletion at the first step. Whether or not it is deleted depends on the criterion used. As I stated earlier, the most important criterion is that of meaningfulness.

If no variable is deleted, the analysis is terminated. Evidently, based on the criterion used, all the predictors are deemed to be contributing meaningfully to the prediction of the criterion. If, on the other hand, a predictor is deleted, the process just described is repeated for the remaining predictors. That is, each of the remaining predictors is examined to ascertain which would lead to the smallest reduction in R^2 as a result of its deletion from the equation. Again, based on the criterion used, it may be deleted or retained. If the predictor is deleted, the process I described is repeated to determine whether an additional predictor may be deleted. The analysis continues as long as predictors whose deletion would result in a loss in predictability deemed not meaningful are identified. The analysis is terminated when the deletion of a predictor is judged to produce a meaningful reduction in R^2.

I will now use REGRESSION of SPSS to illustrate backward elimination. The input file is identical to the one I used earlier for the forward solution, except that the option BACKWARD is specified (instead of FORWARD). As I stated earlier, multiple analyses can be carried out in a single run. If you wish to do so, add the following to the REGRESSION command:

    DEP=GPA/BACKWARD

Output

Dependent Variable..   GPA   GRADE POINT AVERAGE
Block Number   1.   Method: Enter
Variable(s) Entered 1..   AR   AVERAGE RATINGS
                    2..   GREV   GRADUATE RECORD EXAM: VERBAL
                    3..   MAT   MILLER ANALOGIES TEST
                    4..   GREQ   GRADUATE RECORD EXAM: QUANTITATIVE

R Square   .64047   Adjusted R Square   .58295

-- Variables in the Equation --

Variable	B	SE B	Beta	T	Sig T
AR	.144234	.113001	.201604	1.276	.2135
GREV	.001524	.001050	.210912	1.451	.1593
MAT	.020896	.009549	.322145	2.188	.0382
GREQ	.003998	.001831	.324062	2.184	.0385
(Constant)	−1.738107	.950740		−1.828	.0795

End Block Number   1   All requested variables entered.

Block Number   2.   Method: Backward   Criterion POUT   .1000
Variable(s) Removed on Step Number   5..   AR   AVERAGE RATINGS

R Square   .61704   R Square Change   −.02343
Adjusted R Square   .57286   F Change   1.62917

----------------------- Variables in the Equation ------------------------   ------------ Variables not in the Equation -----------

Variable	B	SE B	Beta	T	Sig T	Variable	Beta In	Partial	T	Sig T
GREV	.001612	.001060	.223171	1.520	.1405	AR	.201604	.247346	1.276	.2135
MAT	.026119	.008731	.402666	2.991	.0060					
GREQ	.004926	.001701	.399215	2.896	.0076					
(Constant)	−2.148770	.905406		−2.373	.0253					

Variable(s) Removed on Step Number   6..   GREV   GRADUATE RECORD EXAM: VERBAL

R Square	.58300	R Square Change	−.03404
Adjusted R Square	.55211	F Change	2.31121

----------------------- Variables in the Equation ------------------------   ------------ Variables not in the Equation ----------

Variable	B	SE B	Beta	T	Sig T	Variable	Beta In	Partial	T	Sig T
MAT	.030807	.008365	.474943	3.683	.0010	GREV	.223171	.285720	1.520	.1405
GREQ	.005976	.001591	.484382	3.756	.0008	AR	.216744	.255393	1.347	.1896
(Constant)	−2.129377	.927038		−2.297	.0296					

End Block Number   2   POUT =   .100 Limits reached.

Commentary

Notice that at Block Number 1, ENTER is used, thereby entering all the predictors into the equation. I will not comment on this type of output, as I did so in earlier chapters. Anyway, you may want to compare it with the SAS output I reproduced, and commented on, earlier in this chapter.

Examine now the segment labeled Block Number 2 and notice that the method is backward and that the default criterion for removing a predictor is a *p* of .10 or greater (see Criterion POUT .1000). Look now at the values of Sig T in the preceding segment (i.e., when all the predictors are in the equation), and notice that the one associated with AR is > .10. Moreover, it is the largest. Hence, AR is removed first.

As I have stated, each T ratio is a test of the regression coefficient with which it is associated and equivalently a test of the proportion of variance accounted for by the predictor in question if it were to be entered last in the equation. In the present context, the T test can be viewed as a test of the reduction in R^2 that will result from the removal of a predictor from the equation. Removing AR will result in the smallest reduction in R^2, as compared with the removal of any of the other predictors. As indicated by R Square Change, the deletion of AR results in a reduction of about 2% ($-.02343 \times 100$) in the variance accounted for. Thus, in Forward Selection AR was entered first and was shown to account for about 38% of the variance (see the preceding Forward Selection), but when the other predictors are in the equation it loses almost all of its usefulness.

GREV is removed next as the *p* associated with its *T* ratio is .1405. The two remaining predictors have T ratios with probabilities < .05. Therefore neither is removed, and the analysis is terminated.

Selecting two predictors only, Forward Selection led to the selection of AR and GREV ($R^2 = .51549$), whereas Backward Elimination led to the selection of GREQ and MAT ($R^2 = .58300$). To repeat: what is the best regression equation depends, in part, on the selection method used.

Finally, recall that *the probability statements should not be taken literally, but rather used as rough guides, when predictor-selection procedures are implemented* (see "Statistical Tests of Significance," earlier in this chapter). Bear this in mind whenever I allude to tests of significance in this chapter.

Stepwise Selection

Stepwise Selection is a variation on Forward Selection. Earlier, I pointed out that a serious short-coming of Forward Selection is that predictors entered into the analysis are retained, even if they have lost their usefulness upon inclusion of additional predictors. In Stepwise Selection, tests are done at each step to determine the contribution of each predictor already in the equation if it were to enter last. It is thus possible to identify predictors that were considered useful at an ear-lier stage but have lost their usefulness when additional predictors were brought into the equa-tion. Such predictors become candidates for removal. As before, the most important criterion for removal is meaningfulness.

Using REGRESSION of SPSS, I will now subject the data of Table 8.1 to Stepwise Selection. As in the case of Backward Selection, all that is necessary is to add the following subcommands in the input file I presented earlier in this chapter.

CRITERIA=FIN(3.0) FOUT(2.0)/DEP=GPA/STEPWISE

Commentary

FIN = F-to-enter a predictor, whose default value is 3.84. FOUT = F-to-remove a predictor, whose default value is 2.71. The smaller the FIN, the greater the likelihood for a predictor to enter. The smaller FOUT, the smaller the likelihood for a predictor to be removed. The decision about the magnitudes of FIN and FOUT is largely "a matter of personal preference" (Draper & Smith, 1981, p. 309). It is advisable to select F-to-enter on the "lenient" side, say 2.00, so that the analysis would not be terminated prematurely. Using a small F-to-enter will generally result in entering several more variables than one would wish to finally use. But this has the advantage of providing the option of backing up from the last step in the output to a step in which the set of variables included is deemed most useful.

Whatever the choice, to avoid a loop (i.e., the same predictor being entered and removed con-tinuously), FIN should be larger than FOUT. When PIN (probability of F-to-enter) is used in-stead, it should be smaller than POUT (probability of F-to-remove). For illustrative purposes, I specified FIN = 3.0 and FOUT = 2.0. Accordingly, at any given step, predictors not in the equation whose F ratios are equal to or larger than 3.00 are candidates for entry in the subse-quent step. The predictor entered is the one that has the largest F from among those having F ra-tios equal to or larger than 3.00. At each step, predictors already in the equation, and whose F ratios are equal to or less than 2.00 (F-to-remove), are candidates for removal. The predictor with the smallest F ratio from among those having $F \leq 2.0$ is removed.

Output

Dependent Variable..   GPA   GRADE POINT AVERAGE
Block Number 1.   Method: Stepwise   Criteria   FIN   3.000   FOUT   2.000
Variable(s) Entered on Step Number   1.. AR   AVERAGE RATINGS

R Square   .38529   R Square Change   .38529
Adjusted R Square   .36334   F Change   17.55023

----------------------- Variables in the Equation ----------------------   ------------ Variables not in the Equation ------------

Variable	B	SE B	Beta	T	Sig T	Variable	Beta In	Partial	T	Sig T
AR	.444081	.106004	.620721	4.189	.0003	GREQ	.398762	.438139	2.533	.0174
(Constant)	1.729444	.388047		4.457	.0001	GREV	.394705	.460222	2.694	.0120
						MAT	.384326	.417268	2.386	.0243

Variable(s) Entered on Step Number   2..   GREV   GRADUATE RECORD EXAM: VERBAL

R Square   .51549   R Square Change   .13020
Adjusted R Square   .47960   F Change   7.25547

----------------------- Variables in the Equation ----------------------   ------------ Variables not in the Equation ------------

Variable	B	SE B	Beta	T	Sig T	Variable	Beta In	Partial	T	Sig T
AR	.329625	.104835	.460738	3.144	.0040	GREQ	.291625	.340320	1.845	.0764
GREV	.002851	.001059	.394705	2.694	.0120	MAT	.290025	.341130	1.850	.0756
(Constant)	.497178	.576516		.862	.3961					

Variable(s) Entered on Step Number   3..   MAT MILLER ANALOGIES TEST

R Square   .57187   R Square Change   .05638
Adjusted R Square   .52247   F Change   3.42408

----------------------- Variables in the Equation ----------------------   ------------ Variables not in the Equation ------------

Variable	B	SE B	Beta	T	Sig T	Variable	Beta In	Partial	T	Sig T
AR	.242172	.110989	.338500	2.182	.0383	GREQ	.324062	.400292	2.184	.0385
GREV	.002317	.001054	.320781	2.198	.0371					
MAT	.018813	.010167	.290025	1.850	.0756					
(Constant)	−.144105	.651990		−.221	.8268					

Variable(s) Entered on Step Number   4..   GREQ   GRADUATE RECORD EXAM: QUANTITATIVE

R Square   .64047   R Square Change   .06860
Adjusted R Square   .58295   F Change   4.77019

--- Variables in the Equation ---

Variable	B	SE B	Beta	T	Sig T
AR	.144234	.113001	.201604	1.276	.2135
GREV	.001524	.001050	.210912	1.451	.1593
MAT	.020896	.009549	.322145	2.188	.0382
GREQ	.003998	.001831	.324062	2.184	.0385
(Constant)	−1.738107	.950740		−1.828	.0795

Variable(s) Removed on Step Number   5..   AR   AVERAGE RATINGS

R Square	.61704	R Square Change	−.02343
Adjusted R Square	.57286	F Change	1.62917

------------------------ Variables in the Equation ------------------------ ----------- Variables not in the Equation -----------

Variable	B	SE B	Beta	T	Sig T	Variable	Beta In	Partial	T	Sig T
GREV	.001612	.001060	.223171	1.520	.1405	AR	.201604	.247346	1.276	.2135
MAT	.026119	.008731	.402666	2.991	.0060					
GREQ	.004926	.001701	.399215	2.896	.0076					
(Constant)	−2.148770	.905406		−2.373	.0253					

Commentary

The first two steps are the same as those I obtained previously through Forward Selection. Look now at Step Number 2, Variables not in the Equation. Squaring the T's for the two predictors (GREQ and MAT), note that both are greater than 3.0 (F-to-enter), and are therefore both candidates for entry in Step Number 3. A point deserving special attention, however, is that the F ratios for these predictors are almost identical (3.40 and 3.42). This is because both predictors have almost identical partial correlations with GPA, after GREV and AR are controlled for (.340 and .341). A difference this small is almost certainly due to random fluctuations. Yet the predictor with the slightest edge (MAT) is given preference and is entered next. Had the correlation between GREQ and MAT been higher than what it is in the present fictitious example (.267; see the output earlier in this chapter) it is conceivable that, after entering MAT, GREQ may have not met the criterion of F-to-enter and would have therefore not been entered at all. Thus it is possible that of two equally "good" predictors, one may be selected and the other not, just because of a slight difference between their correlations with the criterion. I return to this point later (see also "Collinearity" in Chapter 10). In the present example, GREQ qualifies for entry in Step Number 4.

Thus far a Forward Selection was obtained because at no step has the F-to-remove for any predictor fallen below 2.00. At Step Number 4, however, AR has an F-to-remove of 1.63 (square the T for AR, or see F Change at Step Number 5), and it is therefore removed. Here, again, is a point worth special attention: a predictor that was shown as the best when no other predictors are in the equation turns out to be the worst when the other predictors are in the equation. Recall that AR is the average rating given an applicant by three professors who interview him or her.

In view of the previous results, is one to conclude that AR is not a "good" variable and that interviewing applicants for graduate study is worthless? Not at all! At least, not based on the previous evidence. All one may conclude is that if the sole purpose of interviewing candidates is to obtain AR in order to use it as one of the predictors of GPA, the effort and the time expended may not be warranted, as after GREQ, GREV, and MAT are taken into account, AR adds about 2% to the accounting of the variance in the criterion.

As Step Number 5 shows, the regression coefficient associated with GREV is statistically not significant at the .05 level. When entered last, GREV accounts for about 3% of the variance in GPA. Assuming that the *t* ratio associated with GREV were statistically significant, one would still have to decide whether it is worthwhile to retain it in the equation. Unlike AR, GREV is relatively inexpensive to obtain. It is therefore conceivable that, had the previous results all been statistically significant, a decision would have been made to remove AR but to retain GREV. In sum, the final decision rests with the researcher whose responsibility it is to assess the usefulness of a predictor, taking into account such factors as cost and benefits.

OTHER COMPUTER PROGRAMS

In this section, I give BMDP and MINITAB input files for stepwise regression analysis of the data in Table 8.1. Following each input file, I reproduce summary output for comparative purposes with the SPSS output I gave in the preceding section. I do not comment on the BMDP and MINITAB outputs. If necessary, see commentary on similar output from SPSS.

BMDP

Input

```
/PROBLEM TITLE IS 'STEPWISE SELECTION.    TABLE 8.1'.
/INPUT VARIABLES ARE 5 FORMAT IS '(F2.1,2F3.0,F2.0,F2.1)'.
/VARIABLE NAMES ARE  GPA,  GREQ,  GREV,  MAT,  AR.
/REGRESS DEPENDENT IS GPA.  ENTER=3.0.  REMOVE=2.0.
/END
326255406527
415756807545    [first two subjects]

.   .   .   .   .   .

305857106527    [last two subjects]
336006108550
```

Commentary

This input is for 2R. For a general orientation to BMDP, see Chapter 4. I gave examples of 2R runs in Chapters 4 and 5. For comparative purposes with the SPSS run, I am using the same *F*-to-enter (ENTER) and *F*-to-remove (REMOVE).

Output

STEPWISE REGRESSION COEFFICIENTS

VARIABLES STEP	0 Y-INTCPT	2 GREQ	3 GREV	4 MAT	5 AR
0	3.3133*	0.0075	0.0042	0.0392	0.4441
1	1.7294*	0.0049	0.0029	0.0249	0.4441*
2	0.4972*	0.0036	0.0029*	0.0188	0.3296*
3	−0.1441*	0.0040	0.0023*	0.0188*	0.2422*
4	−1.7381*	0.0040*	0.0015*	0.0209*	0.1442*
5	−2.1488*	0.0049*	0.0016*	0.0261*	0.1442

*** NOTE *** 1) REGRESSION COEFFICIENTS FOR VARIABLES IN
THE EQUATION ARE INDICATED BY AN ASTERISK.
2) THE REMAINING COEFFICIENTS ARE THOSE WHICH WOULD
BE OBTAINED IF THAT VARIABLE WERE TO ENTER IN
THE NEXT STEP.

SUMMARY TABLE

STEP NO.	VARIABLE ENTERED	REMOVED	RSQ	CHANGE IN RSQ	F TO ENTER	F TO REMOVE
1	5 AR		0.3853	0.3853	17.55	
2	3 GREV		0.5155	0.1302	7.26	
3	4 MAT		0.5719	0.0564	3.42	
4	2 GREQ		0.6405	0.0686	4.77	
5		5 AR	0.6170	−0.0234		1.63

MINITAB

Input

```
GMACRO
T81
OUTFILE='T81MIN.OUT';
  NOTERM.
NOTE TABLE 8.1.   STEPWISE REGRESSION ANALYSIS
READ C1-C5;
  FORMAT (F2.1,2F3.0,F2.0,F2.1).
326255406527
415756807545    [first two subjects]
 .  .  .  .  .  .
305857106527    [last two subjects]
336006108550
END
ECHO
```

```
NAME C1 'GPA' C2 'GREQ' C3 'GREV' C4 'MAT' C5 'AR'
DESCRIBE C1-C5
CORRELATION C1-C5
BRIEF 3
STEPWISE C1 C2-C5;
    FENTER=3.0;
    FREMOVE=2.0.
ENDMACRO
```

Commentary

For a general orientation to MINITAB, see Chapter 4. For illustrative applications, see Chapters 4 and 5. I remind you that I am running MINITAB through global macros. See the relevant sections for explanations of how to run such files.

Output

Response is	GPA	on	4 predictors,	with N =	30
Step	1	2	3	4	5
Constant	1.7294	0.4972	−0.1441	−1.7381	−2.1488
AR	0.44	0.33	0.24	0.14	
T-Ratio	4.19	3.14	2.18	1.28	
GREV		0.0029	0.0023	0.0015	0.0016
T-Ratio		2.69	2.20	1.45	1.52
MAT			0.0188	0.0209	0.0261
T-Ratio			1.85	2.19	2.99
GREQ				0.0040	0.0049
T-Ratio				2.18	2.90
R-Sq	38.53	51.55	57.19	64.05	61.70

Blockwise Selection

In Blockwise Selection, Forward Selection is applied to *blocks*, or sets, of predictors, while using any of the predictor-selection methods, or combination of such methods, to select predictors from each block. As there are various variations on this theme, I will describe first one such variation and then comment on other possibilities.

Basically, the predictors are grouped in blocks, based on theoretical and psychometric considerations (e.g., different measures of socioeconomic status may comprise a block). Beginning with the first block, a Stepwise Selection is applied. At this stage, predictors in other blocks are ignored, while those of the first block compete for entry into the equation, based on specified criteria for entry (e.g., F-to-enter, increment in R^2). Since Stepwise Selection is used, predictors that entered at an earlier step may be deleted, based on criteria for removal (e.g., F-to-remove).

Upon completion of the first stage, the analysis proceeds to a second stage in which a Stepwise Selection is applied to the predictors of the second block, with the restriction that predictors selected at the first stage remain in the equation. In other words, although the predictors of the second block compete for entry, their usefulness is assessed in light of the presence of first-block predictors in the equation. Thus, for example, a predictor in the second block, which in relation to the other variables in the block may be considered useful, will not be selected if it is correlated highly with one, or more than one, of the predictors from the first block that are already in the equation.

The second stage having been completed, a Stepwise Selection is applied to the predictors of the third block. The usefulness of predictors from the third block is assessed in view of the presence of predictors from the first two blocks in the equation. The procedure is repeated sequentially until predictors from the last block are considered.

A substantive example may further clarify the meaning of Blockwise Selection. Assume that for predicting academic achievement predictors are grouped in the following four blocks: (1) home background variables, (2) student aptitudes, (3) student interests and attitudes, and (4) school variables.[6] Using Blockwise Selection, the researcher may specify, for example, that the order of entry of the blocks be the one in which I presented them. This means that home background variables will be considered first, and that those that meet the criterion for entry and survive the criterion for removal will be retained in the equation. Next, a Stepwise Selection will be applied to the student aptitude measures, while locking in the predictors retained during the first stage of the analysis (i.e., home background predictors). Having completed the second stage, student interests and attitudes will be considered as candidates for entry into the equation that already includes the predictors retained in the first two stages of the analysis. Finally, school variables that meet the criterion for entry, in the presence of predictors selected at preceding stages, will compete among themselves.

Because the predictors in the various blocks tend to be intercorrelated, it is clear that whether or not a predictor is entered depends, in part, on the order of entry assigned to the block to which it belongs. Generally speaking, variables belonging to blocks assigned an earlier order of entry stand a better chance to be selected than those belonging to blocks assigned a later order of entry. Depending on the pattern of the intercorrelations among all the variables, it is conceivable for all the predictors in a block assigned a late order of entry to fail to meet the criterion for entry.

I trust that by now you recognize that in predictive research the "correct" order assigned to blocks is the one that meets the specific needs of the researcher. *There is nothing wrong with any ordering of blocks as long as the researcher does not use the results for explanatory purposes.* Referring to the previous example, a researcher may validly state, say, that after considering the first two blocks (home background and student aptitudes) the remaining blocks add little or nothing to the prediction of achievement. *It would, however, be incorrect to conclude that student interests and attitudes, and school variables are not important determiners of achievement.* A change in the order of the blocks could lead to the opposite conclusion.

Anticipating my discussion of the cross-national studies conducted under the auspices of the International Association for the Evaluation of Educational Achievement (IEA) in Chapter 10, I

---

[6]For present purposes, I ignore the matter of the unit of analysis. That is, I ignore the fact that some data are from individuals whereas others are from schools. For a treatment of this important topic, see Chapter 16.

will note here that, despite the fact that results of these studies were used for explanatory purposes, their analyses were almost exclusively based on Blockwise Selection. Moreover, an extremely lenient criterion for the entry of variables into the equation was used, namely, a predictor qualified for entry if the increment in the proportion of variance due to its inclusion was .00025 or more (see, for example, Peaker, 1975, p. 79). Peaker's remark on the reason for this decision is worth quoting: "It was clear that the probable result of taking anything but a lenient value for the cut-off would be to fill . . . [the tables] mainly with blanks" (p. 82). I discuss this and other issues relating to the analyses and interpretation of results in the IEA studies in Chapter 10.

Earlier, I stated that there are variations on the theme of Blockwise Selection. For example, instead of doing Stepwise Selection for each block, other selection methods (e.g., Forward Selection, Backward Elimination) may be used. Furthermore, one may choose to do what is essentially a Forward Selection of blocks. In other words, one may do a hierarchical regression analysis in which blocks of predictors are forced into the equation, regardless of whether individual predictors within a block meet the criterion for entry, for the sole purpose of noting whether blocks entered at later stages add meaningfully to the prediction of the criterion. Note that in this case no selection is applied to the predictors within a block.

A combination of forcing some blocks into the equation and doing Blockwise Selection on others is particularly useful in applied settings. For example, a personnel selection officer may have demographic information about applicants, their performance on several inexpensive paper-and-pencil tests, and their scores on a test battery that is individually administered by a psychologist. Being interested in predicting a specific criterion, the selection officer may decide to do the following hierarchical analysis: (1) force into the equation the demographic information; (2) force into the equation the results of the paper-and-pencil test; (3) do a Stepwise Selection on the results of the individually administered test battery. Such a scheme is entirely reasonable from a predictive frame of reference, as it makes it possible to see whether, after having used the less expensive information, using more expensive information is worthwhile.

The importance of forcing certain predictors into the equation and then noting whether additional predictors increase predictability is brought out forcefully in discussions of incremental validity (see, for example, Sechrest, 1963). Discussing test validity, Conrad (1950) stated, "we ought to know what is the contribution of this test over and beyond what is available from other, easier sources. For example, it is very easy to find out the person's chronological age; will our measure of aptitude tell us something that chronological age does not already tell us?" (p. 65). Similarly, Cronbach and Gleser (1965) maintained, "Tests should be judged on the basis of their contribution over and above the best strategy available that makes use of prior information" (p. 34).

In their attempts to predict criteria of achievement and creativity, Cattell and Butcher (1968) used measures of abilities and personality. In one set of analyses, they first forced the ability measures into the equation and then noted whether the personality measures increased the predictive power. The increments in proportions of variance due to the personality measures were statistically not significant in about half of these analyses. Cattell and Butcher (1968) correctly noted, "In this instance, each test of significance involved the addition of fourteen new variables. . . . If for each criterion one compared not abilities alone and abilities plus fourteen personality factors, but abilities alone and abilities plus three or four factors most predictive of that particular criterion, there is little doubt that one could obtain statistically significant improvement in almost every case" (p. 192). Here, then, is an example in which one would force the ability measures into the equation and then apply a Stepwise Selection, say, to the 14 personality measures.

The main thing to bear in mind when applying any of the predictor-selection procedures I have outlined is that *they are designed to provide information for predictive, not explanatory, purposes.* Finding, for example, that intelligence does not enhance the prediction of achievement over and above, say, age, does not mean that intelligence is not an important determiner of achievement. This point was made most forcefully by Meehl (1956), who is one of the central figures in the debate about clinical versus statistical prediction. Commenting on studies in which statistical prediction was shown to be superior to clinical prediction, Meehl said:

> After reading these studies, it almost looks as if the first rule to follow in trying to predict the subsequent course of a student's or a patient' behavior is carefully to avoid talking to him, and that the second rule is to avoid thinking about him! (p. 263)

RESEARCH EXAMPLES

I began this chapter with an examination of the important distinction between predictive and explanatory research. Unfortunately, studies aimed solely at prediction, or ones in which analytic approaches suitable only for prediction were employed, are often used for explanatory purposes. Potential deleterious consequences of such practices are grave. Therefore, vigilance is imperative when reading research reports in which they were followed. Signs that results of a research study should *not* be used for explanatory purposes include the absence of a theoretical rationale for the choice of variables; the absence of hypotheses or a model of the phenomena studied; the selection of a "model" from many that were generated empirically; and the use of predictor-selection procedures. In what follows, I give some research examples of one or more of the preceding. My comments are addressed primarily to issues related to the topics presented in this chapter, though other aspects of the papers I cite may merit comment.

VARIABLES IN SEARCH OF A "MODEL"

The Philadelphia school district and the federal reserve bank of Philadelphia conducted a study aimed at ascertaining "What works in reading?" (Kean, Summers, Raivetz, & Farber, 1979). Describing how they arrived at their "model," the authors stated:

> In this study, which examined the determinants of reading achievement growth, there is no agreed-upon body of theory to test. What has been done, then, in its absence, is to *substitute an alternative way of arriving at a theoretical model and a procedure for testing it* [italics added]. More specifically, the following steps were taken:
> 1. The data . . . were looked at to see what they said—i.e., through a series of multiple regression equations they were mined extensively in an experimental sample.
> 2. *The final equation was regarded as The Theory—the hypothesized relationship between growth in reading achievement . . . and many inputs.* [italics added]. (p. 37)

What the authors referred to as a "series" of multiple regression equations, turns out to be "over 500" (p. 7). As to the number of variables used, the authors stated that they started with "162 separate variables" (p. 33), but that their use of "dummy *variables* [italics added] and interaction *variables* [italics added] eventually increased this number to 245" (p. 33). I discuss the use of dummy vectors to represent categorical variables and the products of such vectors to represent interactions in Chapters 11 and 12, respectively, where I show that treating such vectors as distinct variables is wrong.

Although the authors characterized their study as "explanatory observational" (p. 21), I trust that the foregoing will suffice for you to conclude that the study was anything but explanatory. The tortuous way in which the final equation was arrived at casts serious doubts on its usefulness, even for predictive purposes.

The following news item from *The New York Times* (1988, June 21, p. 41) illustrates the adverse effects of subjecting data to myriad analyses in search for an equation to predict a criterion.

> Using 900 equations and 1,450 variables, a new computer program analyzed New York City's economy and predicted in January 1980 that 97,000 jobs would be wiped out in a recession before the year was out. That would be about 3.5 percent of all the city's jobs.

As it turned out, there was an *increase* of about 20,000 jobs. Commenting on the 1980 prediction, Samuel M. Ehrenhalt, the regional commissioner of the Federal Bureau of Labor Statistics, is reported to have said, "It's one of the things that econometricians fall into when they become mesmerized by the computer."

Teaching a summer course in statistical methods for judges, Professor Charles J. Goetz of the University of Virginia School of Law is reported to have told them that they

> always should ask statistical experts what other models they tried before finding one that produced the results the client liked. Almost always the statistical model presented in court was not the first one tried, he says. A law school colleague, he notes, passed that suggestion along to a judge who popped the question on an expert witness during a bench trial. The jurist later called Professor Goetz's colleague to report what happened. "It was wonderful," the judge reported. "The expert looked like he was going to fall off his chair." (Lauter, 1984, p. 10)

Judging by the frequency with which articles published in refereed journals contain descriptions of how a "model" was arrived at in the course of examining numerous equations, in a manner similar to those described earlier, it is clear that editors and referees do not even have to "pop the question." A question that inevitably "pops up" is this: Why are such papers accepted for publication?

PREDICTOR-SELECTION PROCEDURES

When I reviewed various predictor-selection procedures earlier in this chapter, I tried to show why they should not be used in explanatory research. Before giving some research examples, it will be instructive to pursue some aspects of data that lead to complications, when results yielded by predictor-selection procedures are used for explanatory purposes.

For convenience, I do this in the context of Forward Selection. Actually, although the authors of some of the studies I describe later state that they used stepwise regression analysis, it appears that they used Forward Selection. The use of the term stepwise regression analysis generically is fairly common (see Huberty, 1989, p. 44). For convenience, I will use their terminology in my commentaries on the studies, as this does not alter the point I am trying to make. I hope you recognize that had the authors indeed applied stepwise regression analysis as I described earlier (i.e., allowing also for removal of variables from the equation), my argument that the results should *not* be used for explanatory purposes would only be strengthened.

Consider a situation in which one of several highly intercorrelated predictors has a slightly higher correlation with the criterion than do the rest of them. Not only will this predictor be selected first in Forward Selection, but also it is highly likely that none of the remaining predictors will meet the criterion for entry into the equation. Recall that an increment in the proportion of variance accounted for is a squared semipartial correlation (see Chapter 7). Partialing out from one predictor another predictor with which it is highly correlated will generally result in a small, even meaningless, semipartial correlation. Situations of this kind are particularly prone to occur when several indicators of the same variable are used, *erroneously,* by intent or otherwise, as distinct variables. I now illustrate the preceding ideas through an examination of several research studies.

Teaching of French as a Foreign Language

I took this example from one of the International Evaluation of Educational Achievement (IEA) studies, which concerned the study of French as a foreign language in eight countries. The correlation matrix reported in Table 8.2 is from Carroll (1975, p. 268). The criteria are a French reading test (reading) and a French listening test (listening). The predictors "have been selected to represent the major types of factors that have been identified as being important *influences* [italics added] on a student's proficiency in French" (Carroll, 1975, p. 267). For present purposes, I focus on two predictors: the student's aspiration to understand spoken French and the student's aspiration to be able to read French. Issues of validity and reliability notwithstanding, it is not surprising that the correlation between the two measures is relatively high (.762; see Table 8.2), as they seem to be indicators of the same construct: aspirations to acquire skills in French.

For illustrative purposes, I applied Forward Selection twice, using REGRESSION of SPSS. In the first analysis, reading was the criterion; in the second analysis listening was the criterion. In both analyses, I used the seven remaining measures listed in Table 8.2 as predictors. I do not give an input file here, as I gave an example of such an analysis earlier in this chapter. I suggest that you run the example and compare your results with those given in the following. For present purposes, I wanted to make sure that all the predictors enter into the equation. Therefore, I used a high PIN (.90). Alternatively, I could have used a small FIN. See earlier in this chapter for a discussion of PIN and FIN.

Output

Summary table READING				Summary table LISTENING		
Step	Rsq	RsqCh	Variable	Rsq	RsqCh	Variable
1	.4007	.4007	AMOUNT OF INSTRUCTION	.3994	.3994	AMOUNT OF INSTRUCTION
2	.4740	.0733	ASPIRATIONS ABLE TO READ FRENCH	.4509	.0515	ASPIRATIONS UNDERSTAND SPOKEN
3	.4897	.0156	STUDENT EFFORT	.4671	.0162	TEACHER COMPETENCE IN FRENCH
4	.5028	.0131	STUDENT APTITUDE FOR FOREIGN	.4809	.0138	TEACHING PROCEDURES
5	.5054	.0026	TEACHER COMPETENCE IN FRENCH	.4900	.0091	STUDENT APTITUDE FOR FOREIGN
6	.5059	.0004	ASPIRATIONS UNDERSTAND SPOKEN	.4936	.0035	STUDENT EFFORT
7	.5062	.0003	TEACHING PROCEDURES	.4949	.0014	ASPIRATIONS ABLE TO READ FRENCH

Table 8.2   Correlation Matrix of Seven Predictors and Two Criteria

	1	2	3	4	5	6	7	8	9
1 Teacher's competence in French	1.000	.076	.269	−.004	−.017	.077	.050	.207	.299
2 Teaching procedures	.076	1.000	.014	.095	.107	.205	.174	.092	.179
3 Amount of instruction	.269	.014	1.000	.181	.107	.180	.188	.633	.632
4 Student effort	−.004	.095	.181	1.000	.108	.185	.198	.281	.210
5 Student aptitude for a foreign language	−.017	.107	.107	.108	1.000	.376	.383	.277	.235
6 Aspirations to understand spoken French	.077	.205	.180	.185	.376	1.000	.762	.344	.337
7 Aspirations to be able to read French	.050	.174	.188	.198	.383	.762	1.000	.385	.322
8 Reading test	.207	.092	.633	.281	.277	.344	.385	1.000	
9 Listening test	.299	.179	.632	.210	.235	.337	.322		1.000

NOTE: Data taken from J. B. Carroll, *The teaching of French as a foreign language in eight countries*, p. 268. Copyright 1975 by John Wiley & Sons. Reprinted by permission.

Commentary

These are excerpts from the summary tables for the two analyses, which I placed alongside each other for ease of comparison.[7] Also, I inserted the lines to highlight the results for the aspiration indicators.

Turning first to the results relating to the prediction of reading, it will be noted from Table 8.2 that student's "aspiration to understand spoken French" and student's "aspiration to be able to read French" have almost identical correlations (.180 and .188, respectively) with the predictor that enters first into the equation: "Amount of instruction." Because "aspiration to be able to read French" has a slightly higher correlation with reading than does "aspiration to understand spoken French" (.385 and .344, respectively), it is selected to enter at Step 2 and is shown to account for about 7% of the variance in reading, after the contribution of "amount of instruction" is taken into account. Recall that the correlation between the indicators under consideration is .762. Consequently, after "aspiration to be able to read French" enters into the equation, "aspiration to understand spoken French" cannot add much to the prediction of Reading. In fact, it enters at Step 6 and is shown to account for an increment of only .04% of the variance in reading.

The situation is reversed for the analysis in which the criterion is listening. In this case, the correlation of "aspiration to understand spoken French" with listening is ever so slightly higher than the correlation of "aspiration to be able to read French" with listening (.337 and .322, respectively; see Table 8.2). This time, therefore, "aspiration to understand spoken French" is the preferred indicator. It is entered at Step 2 and is shown to account for an increment of 5% of the variance in listening. "Aspiration to be able to read French," on the other hand, enters last and is shown to account for an increment of about .14% of the variance in listening.

[7]Specifying DEP=READING,LISTENING as a subcommand in REGRESSION will result in two analyses: one in which READING is the criterion; the other in which LISTENING is the criterion.

I carried out the preceding analyses to show that variable-selection procedures are blind to the substantive aspects of the measures used. Each vector is treated as if it were a distinct variable.[8] The moral is that, as in any other research activity, it is the researcher, not the method, that should be preeminent. It is the researcher's theory, specific goals, and knowledge about the measures used that should serve as guides in the selection of analytic methods and the interpretation of the results. Had one (erroneously) used the previous results for the purpose of explanation instead of prediction, the inescapable conclusions would have been that, of the two aspiration "variables," only the "aspiration to be able to read French" is an important determiner of reading and that only "aspiration to understand spoken French" is an important determiner of listening. The temptation to accept such conclusions as meaningful and valid would have been particularly compelling in the present case because they appear to be consistent with "commonsense" expectations.[9]

Coping in Families of Children with Disabilities

A study by Failla and Jones (1991) serves as another example of the difficulties I discussed earlier. "The purpose of this study was to examine relationships between family hardiness and family stressors, family appraisal, social support, parental coping, and family adaptation in families of children with developmental disabilities" (p. 42). In the interest of space, I will not comment on this amorphous statement.

Failla and Jones collected data on 15 variables or indicators of variables from 57 mothers of children with disabilities (note the ratio of the number of variables to the "sample" size). An examination of the correlation matrix (their Table 2, p. 46) reveals a correlation of .94[!] between two variables (indicators of the same variable?). Correlations among some other indicators range from .52 to .57.

Failla and Jones stated, "Multiple regression analysis was conducted to determine which variables were predictive of satisfaction with family functioning" (p. 45). Notwithstanding their use of the term "predictive," it is clear from their discussion and conclusions that they were interested in explanation. Here is but one example: "The results highlight the potential value of extending the theoretical development and investigation of individual hardiness to the family system" (p. 48).

Failla and Jones reported that about 42% of the variance "in predicting satisfaction with family functioning was accounted for by four variables," and that "the addition of other variables did not significantly increase the amount of variance accounted for" (p. 45). Although they do not say so, Failla and Jones used Forward Selection. Therefore, their discussion of the results with reference to theoretical considerations are inappropriate, as are their comparisons of the results with those of other studies. In addition, I will note two things.

One, the column of standardized regression coefficients (β's) in their Table 3 (p. 47) is a hodgepodge in that each reported β is from the step at which the predictor with which it is associated was entered. The authors thus ignored the fact that the β's surely changed in subsequent

---

[8]A degenerate case is the use of variable-selection procedures when categorical predictors are represented by sets of coded vectors. For a discussion of this topic, see Chapter 12.

[9]Carroll (1975) did *not* use variable-selection procedures for this particular example. Instead, he interpreted the standardized regression coefficients as "the relative degree to which each of the seven *variables* [italics added] contribute independently to the criterion" (p. 289). In Chapter 10, I deal with this approach to the interpretation of the results.

steps when predictors correlated with the ones already in the equation were added (for a discussion of this point, see Chapter 10). The preceding statement should not be construed as implying that had Failla and Jones reported the β's from the last step in their analysis it would have been appropriate to interpret them as indices of the effects of the variables with which they are associated. I remind you that earlier in this chapter I refrained from interpreting b's in my numerical examples and referred you to Chapter 10 for a discussion of this topic.

Two, the F ratios reported in their Table 3 (p. 47) are *not* of the β's or R^2 change but rather of R^2 obtained at a given step (e.g., the F at step 2 is for R^2 associated with the first two predictors). Such tests can, of course, be carried out,[10] but readers should be informed what they represent. As reported in the table, readers may be led to believe that the F's are tests of R^2 change at each step.

Kinship Density and Conjugal Role Segregation

Hill (1988) stated that his aim was to "determine whether kinship density affected conjugal role segregation" (p. 731). "A stepwise regression procedure in which the order of variable inclusion was based on an item's contribution to explained variance" (p. 736) was used.[11] Based on the results of his analysis, Hill concluded that "although involvement in dense kinship networks is associated with conjugal role segregation, the effect is not pronounced" (p. 731).

As in the preceding example, some of Hill's reporting is unintelligible. To see what I have in mind, I suggest that you examine the F ratios in his Table 2 (p. 738). According to Hill, five of them are statistically significant. Problems with the use of tests of statistical significance in predictor-selection procedures aside, I draw your attention to the fact that three of the first five F ratios are statistically *not* significant at the .05 level, as they are smaller than 3.84 (the largest is 2.67). To understand the preceding statement, I suggest that you examine the table of F distribution in Appendix B and notice that when the df for the numerator of F is 1, an $F = 3.84$ is statistically significant at .05 when the df for the denominator are infinite. Clearly, $F < 3.84$ with whatever df for the denominator cannot be statistically significant at the .05 level of significance. Accordingly, the F ratios cannot be tests of the betas as each would then have 1 df for the numerator. Yet, Hill attached asterisks to the first five betas, and indicated in a footnote that they are statistically significant at the .05 level. Using values from the R^2 column of Table 2, I did some recalculations in an attempt to discern what is being tested by the F ratios. For instance, I tried to see whether they are tests of R^2 at each step. My attempts to come up with Hill's results were unsuccessful.

Psychological Correlates of Hardiness

Hannah and Morrissey (1987) stated, "The purpose of the present study was to determine some of the psychosocial correlates of hardiness . . . in order to illuminate some of the factors possibly important in the development of hardiness" (p. 340). The authors then pointed out that they used

---

[10]See, however, my earlier discussion of tests of statistical significance when predictor-selection procedures are applied.

[11]I remind you of my comment that, notwithstanding the nomenclature, the authors of the studies I review in this section appear to have applied Forward Selection. As you can see, Hill speaks only of inclusion of items. Hereafter, I will not repeat this reminder.

"stepwise multiple regression analysis" (p. 341). That this is a questionable approach is evident not only in light of their stated aim, but also in light of their subsequent use of path analysis "in order to determine possible paths of causality" (p. 341. I present path analysis in Chapter 18).

Discussing the results of their stepwise regression analysis, the authors said, "All five variables were *successfully* [italics added] entered into the equation, which was highly reliable, $F(5,311)$ 13.05, $p < .001$" (p. 341). The reference to all the variables having entered "successfully" into the equation makes it sound as if this is a desired result when applying stepwise regression analysis. Being a predictor-selection procedure, stepwise regression analysis is used for the purpose of selecting a subset of predictors that will be as efficient, or almost as efficient, as the entire set for predictive purposes (see the introduction to "Predictor Selection," earlier in this chapter). I do not mean to imply that there is something wrong when all the predictors enter into the equation. I do, however, want to stress that this in no way means that the results are meritorious.

As Hannah and Morrissey do not give the correlations among the predictors, nor the criteria they used for entry and removal of predictors, it is only possible to speculate as to why all the variables were entered into the equation. Instead of speculating, it would suffice to recall that when, earlier in this section, I used a Forward Selection in my reanalysis of data from a study of the teaching of French as a foreign language, I said that to make sure that all the predictors enter into the equation I used a high PIN (.90). Further, I said that alternatively I could have used a small FIN. Similarly, choosing certain criteria for entry and removal of variables in Stepwise Selection, it is possible to ensure that all the predictors enter into the equation and that none is removed.

Finally, the authors' statement about the equation being "highly reliable" (see the preceding) is erroneous. Though they don't state this, the F ratio on which they based this conclusion is for the test of the overall R^2, which they do not report. As I explained in Chapter 5, a test of R^2 is tantamount to a test that all the regression coefficients are equal to zero. Further, rejection of the null hypothesis means that at least one of the regression coefficients is statistically significant. Clearly, this test does not provide information about the reliability of the regression equation.

Racial Identity, Gender-Role Attitudes, and Psychological Well-Being

Using black female student ($N = 78$) and nonstudent ($N = 65$) groups, Pyant and Yanico (1991) used racial identity and gender-role attitudes as predictors and three indicators of psychological well-being as separate criteria. The authors stated, "We . . . chose to use stepwise rather than simultaneous regression analyses because stepwise analyses had the potential to increase our power somewhat by reducing the number of predictor variables" (p. 318). I trust that, in light of my earlier discussion of statistical tests of significance in predictor-selection procedures, you recognize that the assertion that stepwise regression analysis can be used to increase the power of statistical tests of significance is, to say the least, erroneous. Moreover, contrary to what may be surmised from the authors' statement, stepwise and simultaneous regression analyses are *not* interchangeable. As I explained earlier, stepwise regression analysis is appropriate for predictive purposes. A simultaneous regression analysis, on the other hand, is used primarily for explanatory purposes (see Chapter 10). Without going far afield, I will make a couple of additional comments.

One, an examination of Pyant and Yanico's Table 3 (p. 319) reveals that the wrong *df* for the numerator of the *F* ratios were used in some instances. For example, in the second step of the first analysis, four predictors are entered. Hence, the *df* = 4, *not* 5, for the numerator of the *F* ratio for the test of the increment in proportion of variance accounted for. Notice that when, on the next line, the authors reported a test of what they called the "overall model," they used, correctly, 5 *df* for the numerator of the *F* ratio. This, by itself, should have alerted referees and editors that something is amiss. As but one other example, in the analysis of well-being for the nonstudent sample, when the first predictor was entered, the authors reported, erroneously, 2 *df* for the numerator of the *F* ratio. When the second predictor was entered, the numerator *df* were reported, erroneously, to be 2. Then, when the "overall model" (comprised of the first two predictors entered) was tested the numerator *df* were, correctly, reported to be 2. Incidentally, in some instances the authors reported the wrong number of *df* though they seem to have used the correct number in the calculations. In other cases, it appears that the wrong number of *df* was also used in the calculations. I say "appear" because I could not replicate their results. To see what I am driving at, I suggest that you recalculate some values using (5.21) and (5.27). Though some discrepancies may occur because of the denominator *df*—an issue I will not go into here—my recalculations with adjustments to denominator *df* did not suffice to resolve the discrepancies.

Two, although Pyant and Yanico spoke of prediction, they were clearly interested in explanation, as is evidenced, for example, by the following: "Our findings indicate that racial identity attitudes are related to psychological health in Black women, although not entirely in ways consistent with theory or earlier findings" (pp. 319–320).

Career Decision Making

Luzzo (1993) was interested in effects of (1) career decision-making (CDM) *skills*, CDM self-efficacy, age, gender, and grade-point average (GPA) on CDM *attitudes* and (2) CDM *attitudes*, CDM self-efficacy, age, gender, and grade point average (GPA) on CDM *skills*. Luzzo stated that he used "Stepwise multiple regression analysis . . . because of the lack of any clearly logical hierarchical ordering of the predictor variables and the exploratory nature of the investigation" (p. 197).

Note that the first named measure in each set, which I italicized, serves as a predictor in one analysis and a criterion in the other analysis. In the beginning of this chapter, I pointed out, among other things, that in predictive research the researcher is at liberty to interchange the roles of predictors and criteria. I will not comment on the usefulness of Luzzo's approach from a predictive perspective, as it is clear from his interpretation and discussion of the results that he was interested in explanations. For example, "the results provide important information regarding the utility of Bandura's . . . self-efficacy theory to the CDM domain and raise several additional questions that warrant further research" (p. 198).

As in some of the studies I commented on earlier, Luzzo reported some puzzling results. I suggest that you examine the *F* columns in his Tables 2 and 3 (p. 197) and ponder the following questions. Given that $N = 233$ (see note to Table 1, p. 196), and the regression equation in Tables 2 and 3 is composed of five predictors, how come the *df* for the denominator of the *F* ratios reported in these tables are 191? How can an $F = 3.07$ with 1 and 191 *df* be statistically significant at the .01 level (see the preceding, where I pointed out that even for the .05 level the *F* ratio would have to exceed 3.84). Similarly, how can the two *F*'s of 2.27 (each with 1 and 191 *df*) in Table 2 be statistically significant at the .05 level?

Finally, in Table 4 (p. 198) Luzzo reported that there were statistically significant differences between the means of CDM skills and GPA for women and men. Think of how this might have affected the results of his analyses, which were based on the combined data from women *and* the men. See Chapter 16 for a discussion of this topic and a numerical example (Table 16.1).

CONCLUDING REMARKS

Unfortunately, due to a lack of appreciation of the distinction between explanatory and predictive research, and a lack of understanding of the properties of variable-selection procedures, social science research is replete with examples of misapplications and misinterpretations of such methods. Doubtless, the ready availability of computer programs to carry out such analyses has contributed to the proliferation of such abuses. Writing in the pre–personal computer era, Maxwell (1975) noted, "The routine procedure today is to feed into a computer all the independent variates that are available and to hope for the best" (p. 53). Is it necessary to point out that, as a result of the widespread availability of personal computers, matters have gotten much worse?

A meaningful analysis applied to complex problems is never routine. It is the unwary researcher who applies routinely all sorts of analytic methods and then compounds the problem by selecting the results that are consistent with his or her expectations and preconceptions. From the perspective of theory formulation and testing, "the most vulgar approach is built into stepwise regression procedures, which essentially automate mindless empiricism" (Berk, 1988, p. 164). No wonder, Leamer (1985, p. 312) branded it "unwise regression," and King (1986) suggested that it may be characterized as "Minimum Logic Estimator" (p. 669; see also Thompson, 1989).

Speaking on the occasion of his retirement, Wherry (1975) told his audience:

> Models are fine and statistics are dandy
> But don't choose too quickly just 'cause they're handy
>
> . . .
>
> Too many variables and too few cases
> Is too much like duelling at ten paces
> What's fit may be error rather than trend
> And shrinkage will get you in the end. (pp. 16–17)

STUDY SUGGESTIONS

1. Distinguish between explanation and prediction. Give examples of studies in which the emphasis is on one or the other.

2. In Study Suggestion 2 of Chapter 2, I suggested that you analyze a set of 20 observations on X and Y. The following results are from the suggested analysis (see Answers to Chapter 2): $\overline{X} = 4.95$; $\Sigma x^2 = 134.95$; $s_{y.x} = 2.23800$; Y'_1 (predicted score for the first person whose $X = 2$) = 3.30307; Y'_{20} (predicted score for the last person whose $X = 4$) = 4.79251. Use the preceding to calculate the following:

   (a) The standard error of mean predicted scores (i.e., $s_{\mu'}$) for $X = 2$ and for $X = 4$, and the 95% confidence interval for the mean predicted scores.

   (b) The standard error of predicted Y'_1 and Y'_{20}, and 95% prediction interval for the predicted scores.

3. What is meant by "shrinkage" of the multiple correlation? What is the relation between shrinkage and sample size?

4. Calculate the adjusted R^2 ($\hat{R}^2$), and squared cross-validity coefficient ($\hat{R}^2_{cv}$; regression model) for the following:

(a) $R^2_{y.12} = .40; N = 30$

(b) $R^2_{y.123} = .55; N = 100$

(c) $R^2_{y.1234} = .30; N = 200$

5. Here is an illustrative correlation matrix ($N = 150$). The criterion is verbal achievement. The predictors are race, IQ, school quality, self-concept, and level of aspiration.

1	2	3	4	5	6
Race	*IQ*	*School Quality*	*Self-Concept*	*Level of Aspiration*	*Verbal Achievement*
1.00	.30	.25	.30	.30	.25
.30	1.00	.20	.20	.30	.60
.25	.20	1.00	.20	.30	.30
.30	.20	.20	1.00	.40	.30
.30	.30	.30	.40	1.00	.40
.25	.60	.30	.30	.40	1.00

Use a computer program to do a Forward Selection. Use the program defaults for entry of variables.

ANSWERS

2.

(a) For $X = 2, s_{\mu'} = .757$; 95% confidence interval: 1.71 and 4.89

For $X = 4, s_{\mu'} = .533$; 95% confidence interval: 3.67 and 5.91

(b) for $X = 2, s_{y'} = 2.363$; 95% prediction interval: -1.66 and 8.27

for $X = 4, s_{y'} = 2.301$; 95% prediction interval: $-.04$ and 9.63

4.

(a) $\hat{R}^2 = .36; \hat{R}^2_{cv} = .29$

(b) $\hat{R}^2 = .54; \hat{R}^2_{cv} = .52$

(c) $\hat{R}^2 = .29; \hat{R}^2_{cv} = .27$

5.

SPSS

Output

PIN = .050 Limits reached.

Summary table

Step	Variable		Rsq	RsqCh
1	In:	IQ	.3600	.3600
2	In:	ASPIRATION	.4132	.0532
3	In:	QUALITY	.4298	.0166

Commentary

Note that race and self-concept did not meet the default criterion for variable entry (.05).

SAS

Output

No other variable met the 0.5000 significance level for entry into the model.

Summary of Forward Selection Procedure for Dependent Variable ACHIEVEMENT

Step	Variable Entered	Number In	Model $R^{**}2$
1	IQ	1	0.3600
2	ASPIRATION	2	0.4132
3	QUALITY	3	0.4298
4	SELF-CONCEPT	4	0.4392

Commentary

I suggested that you use program defaults for entry of variables so as to alert you to the need to be attentive to them. As illustrated in the present example, because SPSS and SAS use different default values (.05 and .50, respectively), the latter enters one more predictor than the former.

VARIANCE PARTITIONING

Chapter 8 was devoted to the use of multiple regression analysis in predictive research. In this and subsequent chapters, I address the use and interpretation of multiple regression analysis in explanatory research. Unlike prediction, which is relatively straightforward and may be accomplished even without theory, explanation is inconceivable without it. Some authors equate scientific explanation with theory, whereas others maintain that it is theory that enables one to arrive at explanation.[1]

Explanation is probably the ultimate goal of scientific inquiry, not only because it satisfies the need to understand phenomena, but also because it is the key for creating the requisite conditions for the achievement of specific objectives. Only by identifying variables and understanding the processes by which they lead to learning, mental health, social mobility, personality development, intergroup conflicts, international conflicts, drug addiction, inflation, recession, and unemployment, to name but a few, is there promise of creating conditions conducive to the eradication of social and individual ills and the achievement of goals deemed desirable and beneficial.

In their search to explain phenomena, behavioral scientists attempt not only to identify variables that affect them but also to determine their relative importance. Of various methods and analytic techniques used in the pursuit of such explanations, I address only those subsumed under multiple regression analysis. These can be grouped under two broad categories: (1) variance partitioning, which is the topic of this chapter, and (2) analysis of effects, which is the topic of Chapter 10.

As I pointed out in earlier chapters, multiple regression analysis may be used in experimental, quasi-experimental, and nonexperimental research. However, interpreting the results is by far simpler and more straightforward in experimental research because of the random assignment of subjects to treatments (independent variable) whose effects on a dependent variable are then studied. Moreover, in balanced factorial experimental designs (see Chapter 12), the independent variables are not correlated. Consequently, it is possible to identify the distinct effects of each independent variable as well as their joint effects (i.e., interactions). What distinguishes quasi-experimental from experimental research is the absence of random assignment in the former, rendering the results much more difficult to interpret. Nonexperimental research is characterized

---

[1]For discussions of scientific explanation, see Brodbeck (1968, Part Five), Feigl and Brodbeck (1953, Part IV), Kaplan (1964, Chapter IX), Pedhazur and Schmelkin (1991, Chapter 9, and the references therein), and Sjoberg and Nett (1968, Chapter 11).

by the absence of both random assignment and variable manipulation. In such research, the independent variables tend to be correlated, sometimes substantially, making it difficult, if not impossible, to untangle the effects of each. In addition, some of the variables may serve as proxies for the "true" variables—a situation that when overlooked may lead to useless or nonsensical conclusions.[2]

I consider applications of multiple regression analysis in nonexperimental research in this and the next chapter. Later in the text (e.g., Chapters 11 and 12), I address issues and procedures concerning the application of multiple regression analysis in experimental and quasi-experimental research. Extra care and caution are imperative when interpreting results from multiple regression analysis in nonexperimental research. *Sound thinking within a theoretical frame of reference and a clear understanding of the analytic methods used are probably the best safeguards against drawing unwarranted, illogical, or nonsensical conclusions.*

THE NOTION OF VARIANCE PARTITIONING

Variance partitioning refers to attempts to partition R^2 into portions attributable to different independent variables, or to different sets of independent variables. In Chapter 7, I showed that R^2 can be expressed as the sum of the squared zero-order correlation of the dependent variable with the first independent variable entered into the analysis, and squared semipartial correlations, of successive orders, for additional variables entered—see, for example, (7.26) and the discussion related to it. Among other things, I pointed out, and illustrated numerically, that R^2 is invariant regardless of the order in which the independent variables are entered into the analysis, but that the proportion of variance incremented by a given variable depends on its point of entry, except when the independent variables are *not* intercorrelated.

Partitioning of R^2 is but one of several approaches, which were probably inspired and sustained by the existence of different but algebraically equivalent formulas for R^2. Apparently intrigued by the different formulas for R^2, various authors and researchers attempted to invest individual elements of such formulas with substantive meaning. Deriding such attempts in a witty statement, Ward (1969) proposed two laws that characterize them:

> If a *meaningful number* can be computed as the sum of several numbers, then each term of the sum must be as *meaningful* or more *meaningful than the sum.*

> If results of a meaningful analysis do not agree with expectations, then a more meaningful analysis must be performed. (pp. 473-474)

Various other authors have argued against attempts to partition R^2 for the purpose of ascertaining the relative importance or unique effects of independent variables when they are intercorrelated. 'Thus, Darlington (1968) stated, "It would be better to simply concede that the notion of 'independent contribution to variance' has no meaning when predictor variables are intercorrelated" (p. 169). And according to Duncan:

> the "problem" of partitioning R^2 bears no essential relationship to estimating or testing a model, and it really does not add anything to our understanding of how the model works. The simplest recommen-

---

[2]For an introduction to the three types of research designs, see Pedhazur and Schmelkin (1991, Chapters 12–14, and the references therein).

dation—one which saves both work and worry—is to eschew altogether the task of dividing up R^2 into unique causal components. In a strict sense, it just cannot be done, even though many sociologists, psychologists, and other quixotic persons cannot be persuaded to forego the attempt. (1975, p. 65)

A question that undoubtedly comes to mind is: *If the preceding statements are valid, why devote an entire chapter to variance partitioning?* The answer is that variance partitioning is widely used, mostly abused, in the social sciences for determining the relative importance of independent variables. Therefore, I felt that it deserves a thorough examination. In particular, I felt it essential to discuss conditions under which it may be validly applied, questions that it may be used to answer, and the nature of the answers obtained. In short, as with any analytic approach, a thorough understanding of its properties is an important requisite for its valid use or for evaluating the research studies in which it was used.

Since the time I enunciated the preceding view in the second edition of this book, abuses of variance partitioning have not abated but rather increased. Admittedly, the presentation of such approaches is not without risks, as researchers lacking in knowledge tend to ignore admonitions against their use for purposes for which they are ill suited. As a case in point, I will note that when applying commonality analysis (see the following) for explanatory purposes, various authors refer the reader to the second edition of this book, without the slightest hint that I argued (strongly, I believe) against its use for this very purpose.

In recent years, various authors have elaborated on the limitations of variance partitioning and have urged that it not be used. Thus, Lieberson (1985) declared, "Evaluating research in terms of variance explained may be as invalid as demanding social research to determine whether or not there is a deity" (p. 11). Lieberson deplored social scientists' "obsession with 'explaining' variation" (p. 91), and what he viewed as their motto: "HAPPINESS IS VARIANCE EXPLAINED" (p. 91).

Berk (1983) similarly argued, "it is not at all clear why models that explain more variance are necessarily better, especially since the same causal effects may explain differing amounts of variance" (p. 526).

Commenting in a letter to the editor on recent attempts to come to grips with the problems of variance partitioning, Ehrenberg (1990) asserted that "only unsophisticated people try to make . . . statements" (p. 260) about the relative importance of independent variables.[3]

Before turning to specific approaches of variance partitioning, it is important to note that R^2—the portion that is partitioned—is sample specific. That is, R^2 may vary from sample to sample even when the effects of the independent variables on the dependent variable are identical in all the samples. The reason is that R^2 is affected, among other things, by the variability of a given sample on (1) variables under study, (2) variables not under study, and (3) errors in the measurement of the dependent variable. Recall that (2) and (3) are subsumed under the error term, or the residual. Other things equal, the larger the variability of a given sample on variables not included in the study, or on measurement errors, the smaller the R^2. Also, other things equal, the larger the variability of a given sample on the independent variables, the larger the R^2.

Although limited to simple linear regression, I demonstrated in Chapter 2 (see Table 2.3 and the discussion related to it) that while the regression coefficient (*b*) was identical for four sets of data, r^2 ranged from a low of .06 to a high of .54. The same phenomenon may occur in multiple

---

[3]You are probably familiar with the idea of effect size and the various attempts to define it (see, in particular, Cohen, 1988). You may also know that some authors use the proportion of variance accounted for as an index of effect size. I address this topic in Chapter 11.

regression analysis (for further discussions, see Blalock, 1964; Ezekiel & Fox, 1959; Fox, 1968; Hanushek & Jackson, 1977).

The properties of R^2, noted in the preceding, limit its generalizability, thereby casting further doubts about the usefulness of methods designed to partition it. Thus, Tukey (1954) asserted, "Since we know that the question [of variance partitioning] arises in connection with specific populations, and that in general determination is a complex thing, we see that we do not lose much by failing to answer the question" (p. 45).

Writing from the perspective of econometrics, Goldberger (1991) asserted that R^2

> has a very modest role . . . [A] high R^2 is not evidence in favor of the model, and a low R^2 is not evidence against it. Nevertheless in empirical research reports, one often reads statements to the effect "I have a high R^2, so my theory is good," or "My R^2 is higher than yours, so my theory is better than yours." (p. 177)

Lest I leave you with the impression that there is consensus on this topic, here is a statement, written from the perspective of causal modeling that diametrically opposes the preceding:

> For good quality data an R^2 of approximately .90 should be required. This target is much higher than one finds in most empirical studies in the social sciences. However, a high threshold is necessary in order to avoid unjustified causal inferences. If the explained variance is lower, it becomes more likely that important variables have been omitted . . . Only if the unexplained variance is rather small (<10%), one can trust the estimates of the causal effects. (Saris & Stronkhorst, 1984, p. 271)

Finally, it is noteworthy that even Lewis-Beck and Skalaban (1991), who attempted to renew interest in the use of R^2, stated that "when the researcher wants to know 'the effect of X,' the R^2 has little utility. In that case, he or she should consult the relevant slope estimate (b) and its standard error (SE$_b$)" (p. 169).[4]

With the previous remarks in mind, I turn to an examination of two approaches to variance partitioning: incremental partitioning of variance, and commonality analysis.

INCREMENTAL PARTITIONING OF VARIANCE

Incremental partitioning of variance—popularized by Cohen and Cohen (1983, e.g., pp. 120–123) under the name of hierarchical regression analysis—is by far the most popular variance partitioning approach. Whatever the nomenclature, according to this approach the proportion of variance accounted by all the independent variables (i.e., R^2) is partitioned incrementally, noting the increment in the proportion of variance accounted for by each independent variable (or by a set of independent variables) at the point at which it is entered into a regression analysis. As I pointed out in the preceding, I introduced this type of variance partitioning, which is accomplished by a process of successive partialing, in Chapter 7 (see, in particular, "Multiple Regression and Semipartial Correlations").

Since the order of the entry of variables into the analysis is crucial in the incremental partitioning approach, the question is: How is the order determined? When answering this question it is necessary to distinguish between two major purposes for which this approach is used, which are to study the (1) effect of an independent variable(s) on the dependent variable after having

---

[4]For comments on Lewis-Beck and Skalaban's call for greater utilization of R^2, see Achen (1991) and King (1991a). See also King (1991b) and Luskin (1991).

controlled for another variable(s) and (2) relative effects of a set of independent variables on the dependent variable. The first purpose, that of control, is valid and useful in various designs. For example, the analysis of covariance (see Chapter 15) can be viewed as an incremental partitioning of variance in which the covariate(s) is entered first into the analysis, thereby controlling for it while studying the effects of treatments on the dependent variable. The important thing to remember is that *such an analysis is not intended to provide information about the relative importance of variables, but rather about the effect of a variable(s) after having controlled for another variable(s).*

My major aim in this chapter is to show why the incremental partitioning of variance is *not* a valid approach for determining the relative importance of variables. Before doing this, however, I will make some general observations about the use of incremental partitioning of variance for the purpose of controlling for a variable(s) while studying the effect(s) of another variable(s).

Incremental Partitioning for Control

The decision to control for a variable(s) is not at all arbitrary. Unless one has formulated a theory about the pattern of relations among the variables under study, there is no logical way to decide which variables should be controlled.[5] Unfortunately, variables are often controlled without theoretical justification or with what appears to be dubious justification. Probably the justification advanced most often for the need to control for a variable is that its effect has occurred earlier in a time sequence. Merely because one independent variable preceded another independent variable in time does not justify controlling the one while studying the effect of the other. To repeat: the meaning and validity of controlling certain variables while studying the effects of others depend on the theoretical formulations about the pattern of relations among the variables under study. Suppose, for the sake of illustration, that one is dealing with three variables only: B = student background characteristics; S = school quality; and A = academic achievement. Figure 9.1 illustrates some possible models relevant to variance partitioning.

To understand the differences among the models in Figure 9.1 and others that I present later, I need to digress briefly to comment on the distinction made in causal models between exogenous and endogenous variables.[6] An *exogenous* variable is one whose variability is assumed to be determined by causes outside the causal model under consideration. Stated differently, no

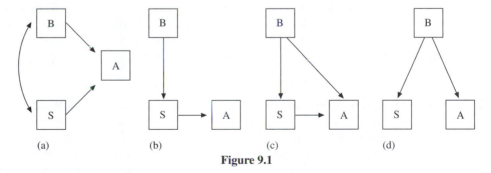

(a)   (b)   (c)   (d)

Figure 9.1

[5]See Chapter 7 for a discussion of the logic of control.

[6]Some of the terminology and methods I use in this chapter are closely related to those of path analysis. Studying introductory presentations of path analysis (e.g., Chapter 18) will enhance your understanding of the present discussion.

attempt is made to explain the variability of an exogenous variable or its relations with other exogenous variables. An *endogenous* variable, on the other hand, is one whose variation is to be explained by exogenous and other endogenous variables in the causal model.

I will use models in Figure 9.1 to give examples of exogenous and endogenous variables. In (a), B and S are treated as exogenous variables, whereas A is treated as an endogenous variable. In (b), on the other hand, only B is treated as an exogenous variable, whereas S and A are treated as endogenous variables.

Returning to the topic under consideration, whether or not a variable can be meaningfully controlled while studying the effects of another variable depends, among other things, on the causal model postulated and on the specific questions addressed. I will illustrate this for the models of Figure 9.1. Turning first to (a), note that the two exogenous variables (B and S) are correlated. This is indicated by the curved line, with arrowheads at both ends, connecting these variables. This means that the correlation between B and S is treated as "given." In other words, the model does not question why these variables are correlated. (This is always the case when correlated exogenous variables are used in a causal model.) Attempts to explain the correlation between B and S would require a model revision, an example of which would be treating one of these variables as endogenous (e.g., model (c)).

To reiterate: the choice of a model is not arbitrary. Nor is it determined by considerations regarding the analytic approach one wishes to use. A model reflects one's theory about the interrelations among the variables being studied and the process by which the independent variables affect the dependent variable.

When exogenous variables are correlated, as in (a), there is no sound basis for incremental partitioning of variance aimed at controlling for one variable while studying the effect of the other, even if the one precedes the other in time. The reason is that the researcher is unable, or unwilling, to state why the variables are correlated. They may, for example, be correlated because one of them affects the other, or because they are affected by a common cause(s). Whatever the reason for the correlation between B and S, if B is entered first into the analysis because it precedes S in time, the variance in A attributed to it will include also the explanatory power it has by virtue of its correlation with S. In other words, the shared explanatory power of B and S is allocated exclusively to B when it is entered first into the regression analysis.

Suppose, however, that the theoretical considerations indicate that the pattern of relations among the three variables is due to a process as depicted in (b), Figure 9.1, according to which the school (S) mediates the effects of the background characteristics (B) on achievement (A). Note that, according to this model, B does not affect A directly (there is no arrow from the former to the latter; I discuss direct and indirect effects later). In such a model it is valid to study the effect of S after controlling for B. This is accomplished by calculating

$$R^2_{A.BS} - R^2_{A.B}$$

where $R^2_{A.BS}$ is the proportion of variance of A accounted for by *both* B and S, and $R^2_{A.B}$ is the proportion of variance of A accounted for by B alone. The difference between these two terms, then, is the proportion of variance accounted for by S over and above what is accounted for by B.

As can be seen from model (b), S transmits the effect of B on A. In addition, S by itself may affect A, that is apart from the effect of B that it transmits. The increment in the proportion of variance accounted for that is attributed to S reflects the part of the effect of this variable on A that is independent of B. In other words, the increment in the proportion of variance attributed to S does *not* include the effect of B on A that S transmits. Clearly, then, one may choose to control for B in model (b) if one wishes to address the question of the effect of S on A that is independent of B. As I explain later, however, this should not be construed as an answer to the question which of the two variables (B or S) has a greater effect on A or which of the two variables is more important.

What I said earlier about model (b) applies also to (c). The difference between these models is that in the former B is hypothesized to affect A only indirectly, via S, whereas in the latter it is hypothesized that B affects A directly as well as indirectly (I analyze such alternative models in Chapter 18).

Turning to (d) in Figure 9.1, you will note that, according to this model, it is hypothesized that the correlation between school quality (S) and achievement (A) is due to a common cause—student background characteristics (B). This, then, is an instance in which B would be controlled by partialing it out from both S and A in order to determine whether the correlation between S and A is spurious (see Chapter 7).

My brief discussion of the four alternative models in Figure 9.1 was designed to underscore the point that it is not possible to decide whether and how to control for a variable without first formulating a causal model about the process by which the independent variables affect the dependent variable. To reiterate, however, even when variables are controlled according to a causal model *it is not valid to compare proportions of variance accounted for by the different variables for the purpose of ascertaining their relative effects on the dependent variable, or their relative importance.* It is to this issue that I now turn by examining the properties of elements obtained in an incremental partitioning of variance.

The Meaning of Incremental Partitioning of Variance

I will examine the meaning of elements obtained in an incremental partitioning of variance, first in a three-variable model and then in several four-variable models. In the course of the presentation I will resort to some concepts used in the analysis of causal models—a topic to which Chapters 18 and 19 are devoted. I introduce these concepts here on an intuitive level, and hope that this will suffice for the present purpose (for a deeper understanding of topics I discuss here, see the relevant sections of Chapter 18).

In the analysis of causal models, a distinction is made between the direct and indirect effects of independent variables on dependent variables. A *direct effect* of an independent variable on a dependent variable is defined as the part of its effect that is not mediated, or transmitted, by other variables. An *indirect effect*, on the other hand, is the part of the effect of the independent variable that is mediated, or transmitted, by another variable or other variables.

I will illustrate these concepts with reference to the three-variable models I presented earlier in Figure 9.1. In (a), B and S are said to have direct effects on A, as indicated by the arrows emanating from B and S to A. In this model, there are no indirect effects, that is, no variables mediate the effects of B and S on A. As I pointed out earlier, the curved line with arrowheads at both ends indicates that the two exogenous variables are correlated.

Turning to model (b) in Figure 9.1, note that B has a direct effect on S, as indicated by the arrow from the former to the latter. B does not affect A directly (there is no arrow connecting the two variables). B does, however, affect A indirectly, via S. The indirect effect of B on A is indicated by B → S → A. Finally, no variable mediates the effect of S and A. Thus, the former has only a direct effect on the latter.

Contrast model (b) with model (c) in Figure 9.1. The difference between the two models is that the former hypothesizes that B has only an indirect effect on A, whereas the latter hypothesizes that B has both a direct and an indirect effect on A.

One additional term I will introduce here is that of a *total effect*. A total effect of an independent variable on a dependent variable is defined as the sum of its direct and indirect effect(s). Depending on the causal model, a variable may or may not have a direct effect on another variable. Moreover, a variable may have more than one indirect effect on another variable (see the four-variable models that follow). In Chapter 18, I show how to calculate direct and indirect effects. For present purposes one need only to know that a total effect of a variable is the sum of its direct and indirect effect(s). When a variable has only a direct effect on another variable, this is its total effect. Similarly, the total effect of a variable that has no direct effect on another variable is equal to its indirect effect, or the sum of its indirect effects. We are ready now to examine the meaning of elements obtained in incremental partitioning of variance.

A Three-Variable Model

Assume that the model of Figure 9.2 is hypothesized to reflect the process of academic achievement.[7] That is, it is hypothesized that student background (B) affects achievement (A) directly as well as indirectly, via school quality (S). Note also that in this model B has a direct effect on S, and S has a direct effect on A.

For illustrative purposes, assume that the correlations among the three variables are

$$r_{BS} = .5 \qquad r_{AB} = .4 \qquad r_{AS} = .65$$

Using (5.20), I calculate $R^2_{A.BS}$

$$R^2_{A.BS} = \frac{r^2_{AB} + r^2_{AS} - 2r_{AB}r_{AS}r_{BS}}{1 - r^2_{BS}} = \frac{.4^2 + .65^2 - 2\,(.4)(.65)(.5)}{1 - .5^2} = .43$$

B and S account for 43% of the variance of A. To do an incremental partitioning of variance according to the model depicted in Figure 9.2, it is necessary to calculate the proportion of variance in A accounted for by B, and the proportion of variance in A accounted for by S after B has been taken into account, or the increment in the proportion of variance accounted for that is due to S. Symbolically this may be stated as

$$R^2_{A.BS} = r^2_{AB} + r^2_{A(S.B)} = R^2_{A.B} + (R^2_{A.BS} - R^2_{A.B})$$

where the first term is the squared zero-order correlation of A with B and the second term is the squared semipartial correlation of A with S, after B has been partialed out from the latter.

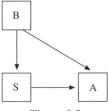

Figure 9.2

---

[7]This oversimplified model is, of course, inadequate to explain academic achievement. I use it for illustrative purposes only.

For the present data, the proportion of variance accounted for by B is .16 (r^2_{AB}), and the increment in the proportion of variance accounted for due to S is

$$R^2_{A.BS} - R^2_{A.B} = .43 - .16 = .27$$

Thus, student background accounts for 16% of the variance in achievement, and school quality accounts for an additional 27% of the variance in achievement, that is, over and above what is accounted for by student background.

The main question for present purposes is: *What do these two elements represent?* It can be shown[8] that the proportion of variance accounted for by B (.16) is equal to the square of its total effect on A. In other words, it is equal to the square of the sum of the direct effect of B on A and its indirect effect on A, via S. The increment in the proportion of variance due to S, on the other hand, is *not* equal to the square of its total effect. It can be shown that the square of the total effect of S on A is .36. But the increment in the proportion of variance due to S (.27) represents only that part of the effect of S on A that is independent of B. That is, the effect of B on A that is transmitted by S is not included in this quantity.

I could have avoided the preceding discussion by simply noting that the increment in the proportion of variance accounted for by S is equal to the squared semipartial correlation, $r^2_{A(S.B)}$, thereby indicating that it is the proportion of variance S accounts for after B was partialed out from it. I presented the previous argument to show that the two elements represent different types of effects and that it is therefore inappropriate to compare them for the purpose of ascertaining the relative importance of the variables with which they are associated.

Finally, I will note that it is appropriate, and sometimes useful, to compare the total effects of different variables in an effort to ascertain their relative effects on the dependent variable. I discuss this approach in Chapter 18, where I point out that the total effect is also referred to as the effect coefficient.

Four-Variable Models

Assume that one wishes to explain the grade-point average (GPA) of college students by resorting to the following independent variables: socioeconomic status (SES), intelligence (IQ), and achievement motivation (AM).[9] An illustrative correlation matrix for these variables is reported in Table 9.1.

Obviously, different theoretical formulations may be advanced regarding the relations among the variables under consideration. Without attempting to justify them on theoretical grounds, I will examine three possible models for the sole purpose of noting what type of variance partitioning, if any, is appropriate for each and what effects the partitioned elements represent.

Model A. I begin with the model depicted in Figure 9.3, according to which SES affects IQ; SES and IQ affect AM; and SES, IQ, and AM affect GPA. To avoid cumbersome subscript notation, I use Y to represent GPA, and numbers to identify the independent variables. Specifically, 1 = SES, 2 = IQ, and 3 = AM.

---

[8]See Chapter 18, where I reanalyze some of the models in this chapter.

[9]I will not attempt to justify the choice of these variables or the omission of other important variables. I feel that the use of substantive variables, instead of labeling them X_1, X_2, and so on, will enhance the understanding of the illustrations.

Table 9.1   Correlation Matrix for Three Independent Variables and a Dependent Variable; N = 300

	1 SES	2 IQ	3 AM	Y GPA
1	1.00	.30	.41	.33
2	.30	1.00	.16	.57
3	.41	.16	1.00	.50
Y	.33	.57	.50	1.00

Doing an incremental partitioning of variance, beginning with SES, determines that it accounts for about 11% of the variance in GPA:

$$r_{y1}^2 = .33 = .1089$$

Without presenting the calculations, I will note that $R_{y.12}^2 = .35268$ and $R_{y.123}^2 = .49647$.[10] To obtain the increment in the proportion of variance of GPA accounted for by IQ, calculate

$$R_{y.12}^2 - R_{y.1}^2 = .35268 - .1089 = .24378$$

IQ adds about 24% to the variance accounted for in GPA.

The proportion of variance of GPA that AM accounts for, over and above SES and IQ, is

$$R_{y.123}^2 - R_{y.12}^2 = .49647 - .35268 = .14379$$

In sum, the three variables combined account for about 50% of the variance of GPA ($R_{y.123}^2 = .49647$), of which SES accounts for about 11%, IQ adds 24%, and AM adds another 14%.

According to the model depicted in Figure 9.3, SES has a direct effect on GPA as well as the following three indirect effects: (1) SES → AM → GPA, (2) SES → IQ → GPA, and (3) SES → IQ → AM → GPA. The total effect of SES on GPA, then, is equal to its direct effect and the three

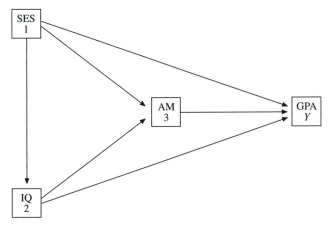

Figure 9.3

---

[10]As an exercise, you may wish to calculate these values, using a computer program. In Chapter 7, I gave examples of matrix input for SPSS and SAS.

indirect effects. Now, it can be shown that the proportion of variance of GPA accounted for by SES (.1089) is equal to the square of its total effect.

Notice that according to the model depicted in Figure 9.3, IQ has a direct effect on GPA as well as an indirect effect: IQ → AM → GPA. It can be shown that the total effect (direct plus the indirect effect) of IQ on GPA is .52. The proportion of variance incremented by IQ (.24) is *not* equal to the square of its total effect on GPA. Rather it reflects the part of the effect of IQ on GPA that is independent of SES.

Finally, according to the model depicted in Figure 9.3, the total effect of AM on GPA is equal to its direct effect, as no variables mediate the effect of the former on the latter. It can be shown that the total effect of AM on GPA is .42. The proportion of variance of GPA accounted for by AM, over and above SES and IQ (.14), is *not* equal to the square of its total effect, but rather to the square of its effect that is independent of SES and IQ.

From the preceding discussion it is clear that the proportions of variance attributed to the three variables reflect different types of effects: for SES it is the square of its total effect; for IQ it is the square of its effect that is independent of SES; and for AM it is the square of its effect that is independent of SES and IQ. Thus, based on the previous analysis, it is valid to make statements about the proportion of variance accounted for by IQ after controlling for SES and about the proportion of variance accounted for by AM after controlling for SES and IQ (assuming, of course, that the model that led to this partitioning of the variance is valid and sound from a theoretical frame of reference; I later present alternative models for the four variables). But it is not valid to make comparisons among such components to determine the relative effects of the variables with which they are associated on GPA, or the relative importance of the three independent variables.

Model B.   Assume now that the model related to the data of Table 9.1 is as depicted in Figure 9.4. The difference between Model A (Figure 9.3) and Model B (Figure 9.4) is that in the former only SES is treated as an exogenous variable, whereas in the latter SES and IQ are treated as exogenous variables. In Model A, the correlation between SES and IQ is conceived of as a consequence of the former affecting the latter. In Model B, on the other hand, the correlation between SES and IQ is left unexplained. The two variables are treated as correlated causes of AM and GPA.

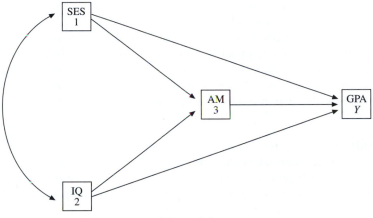

Figure 9.4

Some authors (e.g., Duncan, 1975, p. 41; MacDonald, 1979, p. 295) maintain that when exogenous variables are correlated, the concept of a total effect is inapplicable to any of them. Other authors (e.g., Alwin & Hauser, 1975, pp. 38–39) use the term total effect to indicate the direct and indirect effect(s) of an exogenous variable, even when it is correlated with other exogenous variables. Thus, following Alwin and Hauser, and referring to Model B, one would consider the total effect of SES, say, on GPA to be equal to its direct effect plus its indirect effect: SES → AM → GPA.

Whether or not one applies the concept of total effect to correlated exogenous variables, the important thing to note is that under such circumstances it is not possible to detect parts of their (probable) effects on a given endogenous variable. Thus, from Figure 9.4 one can discern that part of the correlation between SES and GPA is due to the correlation of SES with another cause of GPA, IQ. As I show in Chapter 18 (see the section entitled "The Decomposition of Correlations"), this part of the correlation between SES and GPA remains unanalyzed (as is the part of the correlation between IQ and GPA that is due to the correlation between IQ and SES).

The implication of the preceding discussion for the topic under consideration is that when exogenous variables are correlated it is not possible to untangle some of their relations with a given endogenous variable, hence to partition the variance of the latter into distinct portions attributable to each of the former. As MacDonald (1979) put it, "Since then we cannot (whilst retaining our model as specified) assign 'total effects' to our exogenous variables, we equally cannot produce any decomposition of variance amongst them" (p. 295). MacDonald brands attempts to partition variance among exogenous variables as "nonsense" (p. 295).

All one can do when variance is partitioned in the presence of correlated exogenous variables is to determine the proportion of variance they account for simultaneously. Referring to Model B, Figure 9.4, this means that one may calculate the proportion of variance of GPA accounted for by SES and IQ taken together, and the proportion of variance incremented by AM over and above what is accounted for by SES and IQ. Using the correlations reported in Table 9.1, such a partitioning of variance is

1. Due to SES and IQ: $R^2_{y.12}$ $= .35268$
2. Increment due to AM: $R^2_{y.123} - R^2_{y.12} = \underline{.14379}$
$$R^2_{y.123} = .49647$$

SES and IQ together account for about 35% of the variance of GPA. AM accounts for an additional 14% of the variance of GPA.

Note two things about the preceding analysis. First, had a researcher erroneously applied an incremental partitioning of variance beginning with SES only, the implication would have been that Model A, *not* B, reflects the pattern of causal relations among the variables under study. Second, as in the analysis of Model A, the increment in the proportion of variance accounted for by AM reflects that part of its effect that is independent of SES and IQ.

Model C.   This time, I assume that the model related to the data in Table 9.1 is as in Figure 9.5. The three independent variables are treated as exogenous. In this model it is still possible to determine the direct effects of each of the exogenous variables on GPA (I do this in Chapters 10 and 18). But there is no meaningful way to partition the variance of GPA and to attribute distinct portions to each of the independent variables. All one can do is determine the proportion of variance accounted for by the three variables simultaneously: $R^2_{y.123} = .49647$.

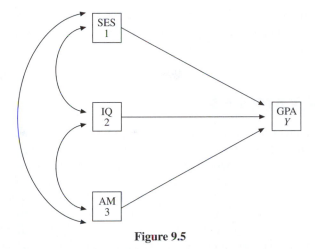

Figure 9.5

These three models differ in the degree of their theoretical elaboration: Model A being the most elaborate, and Model C the least elaborate. The more elaborate the model, the more explicit are the statements about the causal relations among the variables, the greater the freedom in partitioning the variance. When no causal statement is made about the relations among the independent variables (i.e., they are treated as exogenous variables, as in Model C), the researcher is in effect professing ignorance, or unwillingness to make a statement, about the reasons for the correlations among the independent variables. Be that as it may, the absence of a statement that explains the correlations among the independent variables precludes the possibility of partitioning the variance of the dependent variable.

RECAPITULATION

I believe it worthwhile to recapitulate the major points of the preceding sections. First, I pointed out that one may use incremental partitioning of variance to control for a variable(s) while studying the effect(s) of another variable(s) on a given dependent variable. Second, I stressed that, to be meaningful, controls should be applied in accordance with a specific causal model. Third, I stated that the increment in the proportion of variance accounted for by a given variable reflects that part of its effect that is independent of the variables that have been controlled. Finally, I argued that because the elements obtained in incremental partitioning of variance reflect different types of effects, it is not valid to compare them for the purpose of determining their relative effects on a dependent variable (for further discussions of these points, see Coleman, 1975a, 1976; MacDonald, 1979).

In the beginning of this chapter, I expressed reservations regarding the use of variance partitioning for the purpose of determining the relative importance of independent variables. I said that because of their popularity such approaches deserve a thorough examination to better understand what can and cannot be accomplished by their application. More appropriate and more powerful methods for the analysis of models than those I presented in the preceding sections exist. In Chapter 18, I use path analysis to reanalyze the models I presented in this chapter, and I draw comparisons between the two approaches. I turn now to an examination of some studies in which incremental partitioning of variance was used (erroneously) to determine the relative importance of variables.

RESEARCH EXAMPLES

Incremental partitioning of variance is used frequently in behavioral research, often inappropriately. In what follows, I examine first in some detail a set of international studies, and then comment briefly on some other studies. My sole aim is to illustrate some applications of incremental partitioning of variance, to scrutinize the rationale (if any) in support of the analysis, and to examine the validity of some of the conclusions in light of the unique properties of the analytic method used. I do not comment on research design issues that are not directly related to variance partitioning (e.g., sampling, measurement, unit of analysis), although it is, of course, crucial to evaluate them whenever one evaluates substantive findings of a study. When I allude to substantive issues, I do so only to convey the purpose of a study, *not* to summarize it. If you are interested in a specific study, you should read the source cited rather than rely on my sketchy comments.

The International Evaluation of Educational Achievement (IEA)

A set of cross-national studies of achievement in various subjects (e.g., reading, science, literature, civic education) was conducted under the auspices of the International Association for Evaluation of Educational Achievement (for some summaries and reviews, see Härnqvist, 1975; Inkeles, 1977; Purves & Levine, 1975). Although the studies differ in the application of some specific analyses, they share a major theme and a major analytic approach (for a technical report and some summaries, see Peaker, 1975). The major theme is explanation of achievement by resorting to blocks of independent variables. The major analytic technique used for this purpose is incremental partitioning of variance. My discussion is limited to this aspect of the analysis in the IEA studies.[11] Because my concern here is exclusively with the validity of the analyses and the conclusions drawn from them, I will not attempt to summarize the findings or to distinguish between specific studies. I will use illustrations and statements from the various studies eclectically for the sole purpose of shedding light on the analytic approach. Consequently, some of my comments may be more or less applicable to some studies.

The Variables.   The large number of variables was reduced to a smaller and more manageable one by combining some into composite indices and by deleting others. The variables were then grouped in the following blocks:

1. Home and student background, including father's education, mother's education, number of books in the home, and family size. In some studies this block included also the age and sex of the student.
2. Type of school and type of program in which the student was enrolled.

[11]Later in this chapter and in Chapter 10, I discuss other methods used in some IEA studies.

3. Learning conditions, including variables that reflect school practices and teachers' characteristics and training. In some studies this block also included the amount of prior instruction.
4. Kindred variables, including students' attitudes toward school life and learning, current reading habits, leisure activities, expected occupation, parental expectations, and parental involvement in students' work.
5. School achievement, including one or more measures of achievement in the specific area under study (e.g., science, French, literature).

Outline of the Analysis.   The dependent variable, school achievement, was regressed on the blocks of the independent variables in the order in which I presented them. That is, home background was entered first into the analysis, followed by school type, learning conditions, and kindred variables. When each block was entered, a stepwise regression analysis was done on the variables included in it. Variables that met a prespecified criterion were retained, whereas those that did not meet the criterion were discarded. At the conclusion of the stepwise regression analysis within a given block, the proportion of variance incremented by it was noted. In short, the analysis was based on blockwise incremental partitioning of variance, with the added restriction that variables that did not meet a prespecified criterion at the stepwise regression stage of the analysis were deleted (see section entitled "Blockwise Selection" in Chapter 8).

Rationale for the Analysis.   The authors of the various studies used almost identical language in support of the incremental partitioning of variance. Basically, they maintained that the analysis reflected a causal model in which variables entered at an earlier stage of the analysis are assumed to affect those entered at later stages. Thus, for example, reporting on the study of Science Education, Comber and Keeves (1973) stated:

> The basic proposition underlying the development of this causal model was that earlier events in the life of an individual student have influenced later events in the student's life and schooling. It seemed reasonable to use this proposition rather than any other to guide the order in which the variables were entered into the regression equation. (p. 191; see also Purves, 1973, pp. 117–119; Torney, Oppenheim, & Farnen, l975, pp. 127–129)

Critique.   The most important criticism that may be leveled against the causal model advanced in the IEA studies is that its sole justification appears to be a presumed time sequence, or temporal priority, in the occurrence of the variables under study. "Time provided the rationale for the ordering of the blocks to be entered into the regression equation" (Purves, 1973, p. 118). This is a fallacious approach in that it treats temporal priority as a sufficient condition for a causal relation between two variables. On logical grounds we are not willing to accept the notion that an event that occurred later in time caused one that preceded it. Some authors have, however, argued that a temporal sequence is not necessary for causal statements (see Marini & Singer, 1988, pp. 358–359, and the references therein).[12] Be that as it may, a temporal sequence of events is not in and of itself evidence of a causal process. Further, the temporal sequence of variables in the IEA studies is itself questionable. For example, are learning conditions temporally prior

---

[12]I discuss causation in Chapter 18.

to kindred variables (see the preceding), or is it the other way around? The most plausible assumption is that their occurrence is cyclical.

The situation is even more problematic when one considers the presumed causal status of the variables, including the dependent variable. That such problems existed was conceded to by authors of the IEA studies in their discussions of the status of the kindred variables in relation to school achievement. Thus Purves (1973), for example, stated:

> The fourth set of variables is not perhaps part of a model of causation, since it consists of concomitants of achievement. . . . In addition there are some variables related to the home and the attitude of the parents toward learning and school. *All these variables influence achievement or are influenced by it . . . , but they can hardly be termed causative* [italics added]. (p. 118)

Or as Schwille (1975) put it, "Kindred variables, that is, variables which, though expected to correlate with test scores, did not fit in other blocks, usually because they might be considered *either cause or effect of achievement* [italics added]" (p. 127). Similar doubts, though not expressed by authors of IEA studies, may be raised about the causal relations among the other blocks of variables. Do, for example, learning conditions affect school achievement, or does the latter affect the former? There is probably a reciprocal causation between them.

Attempts to depict graphically the causal model of the IEA studies further highlight its dubious nature. Setting aside the questions I raised about the validity of the temporal sequence and about the causal status of the blocks of variables, it is still not possible to tell from IEA reports whether a given block is assumed to affect subsequent ones directly, indirectly, or both. To clarify this point, I depict two of various possible models in Figure 9.6. Note that according to Model (a) all the possible direct and indirect effects are posited, whereas Model (b) describes a strict chain of causation. I do not make any claims for the plausibility of either of the models of

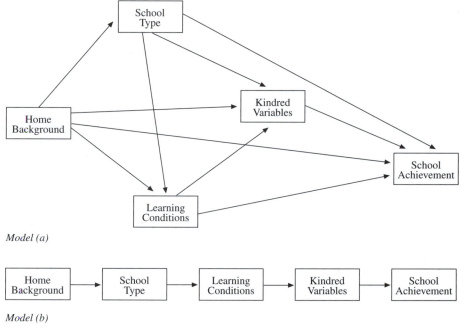

Model (a)

Model (b)

Figure 9.6

Figure 9.6. Note, however, that both (and others) reflect the temporal sequence assumed by authors of IEA studies.

While there are methods for testing whether a causal model is consistent with a given set of data,[13] incremental partitioning of variance (the method used in the IEA studies) is not one of them. In other words, knowledge about the proportion of variance incremented by blocks of variables entered in a given sequence sheds no light on the specific causal model. Consider, for example, the squared correlation between home background and school achievement. From earlier discussions in this chapter, we know that it reflects the total effect of the former on the latter. The total effect may, however, at one extreme, reflect the direct effect and all possible indirect effects, as depicted in Model (a) of Figure 9.6. At the other extreme, the total effect of home background on school achievement may be due only to indirect effects, as depicted in Model (b) of Figure 9.6. Intermediate statements between these extremes are also possible. For example, home background may affect school achievement directly, and in addition indirectly through the mediation of some, but not all the remaining blocks. In other words, one may hypothesize that some of the indirect effects are zero, or close to zero. The main point is that merely knowing the proportion of achievement variance accounted for by home background is insufficient for even a conjecture as to which of several possible models of causation is more tenable. Incidentally, the inclusion of age and sex as part of the home background block in some IEA studies is an additional hindrance to attempts to unravel the process of school achievement.

The main purpose of doing incremental partitioning of variance in IEA studies was to determine the relative importance of the various blocks of variables. Peaker (1975), for example, stated, "Our concern is to assess the *differential effects* [italics added] of those recent conditions that we have measured, and in doing this we must do our best to make a due discount for the effects of earlier conditions, whether at home or at school" (p. 53). Earlier in this chapter, I reasoned that incremental partitioning of variance is inappropriate for ascertaining the relative importance of variables.[14]

That the authors of IEA studies were somewhat ambivalent about their use of incremental partitioning of variance to explain the process of school achievement is evident, among other things, from their attempts to note the changes in the proportion of variance attributed to given blocks as a result of changes in the order of their entry into the analysis. Schwille (1975), in particular, reported the percentage of variance accounted for by each block at different points of entry into the analysis. Thus, for example, the median percentage of variance accounted for by home background when it was entered first (the usual position for this block) was 18. When entered in the third or fourth position, home background accounted for 2% of the variance. The median percentage of variance accounted for by learning conditions when it was entered in its usual third position was 12. But when it was entered first it accounted for 32% of the variance. When learning conditions was entered fourth, it accounted for 9% of the variance (see Schwille, 1975, p. 138).

Had the percent of variance accounted for in an incremental partitioning of variance been a valid indicator of the relative importance of a variable, the inevitable conclusion from the previous results would have been that learning conditions are more important than home background because in the three entry positions they accounted for a greater proportion of variance than did the latter. Such a conclusion would run counter to the one drawn by authors of IEA studies,

---

[13]See Chapters 18 and 19.

[14]For further discussions of this point, with special reference to the IEA studies, see Coleman (1975a, 1976).

namely that home background is the most important block of variables. To repeat, however, *neither of the above conclusions is supportable by incremental partitioning of variance.*[15] Furthermore, the attempts to note how changes in the order in which the blocks are entered affect the manner in which the variance is partitioned evidence an absence of a clearly stated theoretical model about the relations among the variables under study.

Another interesting example of the ambiguity of the theoretical frame of reference in IEA studies comes from the manner in which measures that may be construed as indices of verbal ability were treated in some of them. For example, in the study of *Literature Education in Ten Countries* (Purves, 1973), two such measures were word knowledge and reading comprehension. Discussing these measures, and the decision at what point to enter them into the analysis, Purves (1973) stated:

> The critical reading of Literature is certainly a specialized aspect of reading, and reading ability is a form of a general verbal strength. . . . One might expect therefore, that reading ability as measured by the Reading test would be the most powerful predictor of cognitive ability in Literature. For that reason it must be considered in the analysis, *but to consider it first would deny any of the other predictors a chance to show their contribution to achievement in Literature. Word knowledge and Reading ability are therefore considered last* [italics added]. (p. 156)

The considerable differences in the proportion of variance attributed to the measures of verbal ability when they were entered first or last into the equation are evident in the various tables reported by Purves (1973). For example, in Table 6.1 (p. 160), the mean correlation of word knowledge with literature achievement score was .51, and that for reading comprehension with literature achievement was .67. Consequently, when word knowledge was entered first, it accounted for about 26% of the variance ($.51^2 \times 100$). When reading comprehension was entered first, it accounted for about 45% of the variance ($.67^2 \times 100$). From Table 6.4 (p. 163), note that word knowledge was entered as the fifth block, accounting for an average of about 7% of the variance. Reading comprehension, which was entered last, accounted for an average of about 11% of the variance (see Table 6.4, p. 163). Together, then, the verbal ability measures accounted for about 18% of the variance when they are entered last into the analysis.

It is more important, however, to note what would have happened to the proportion of variance attributed to the other blocks had the verbal ability measures been entered first. Table 6.4 (p. 163) shows that the mean percentage of variance accounted for by the six blocks together was about 55. Earlier I pointed out that, on the average, reading comprehension alone accounted for 45%, leaving 10% of the variance to the remaining blocks. If word knowledge and reading comprehension were used as the first block, virtually nothing of the variance in literature achievement scores would have been accounted by remaining blocks.

Another example of the same problem comes from the study of *Teaching of French as a Foreign Language in Eight Countries* (Carroll, 1975). Speaking of a measure of word knowledge, Carroll stated:

> Probably because this block occurred at the end of the blockwise regression analysis, its variances are relatively small. The Word Knowledge test presumably measures a general verbal ability dimension that is highly associated with school performance. *The reason for extracting its variance late in the analysis was that it was desired to allow all other types of variables to "show their colors" independently even if they happened to be correlated with verbal ability* [italics added]. (p. 207)

---

[15]Other examples of the effects of changes in the order of entry of the blocks into the regression equation abound. See, for example, Peaker (1975, pp. 90–91).

To say that one wishes to allow the other types of variables to show what they contribute independently of verbal ability even if they happen(!) to be correlated with it is questionable reasoning particularly when considering the nature of the variables (some of which are multiple indicators of variables[16]) and the analytic method used. Be that as it may, determination of the order of entry of verbal ability into the regression equation should be based not on how this might affect the proportion of variance attributed to the other variables, but on theoretical considerations. In the absence of a model about the relations among the variables, no meaningful decision about the order of entry of variables into the analysis can be made. Even when variables are entered according to a model, my major objections to the use of incremental partitioning of variance for the determination of the relative importance of variables persist.

Finally, in the various IEA studies incremental partitioning of variance was done separately for each of the participating countries. The authors then proceeded to compare the proportions of variance accounted for by a given block across countries to determine in which of them the block was more or less important. As I pointed out several times earlier, this is inappropriate inasmuch as variance partitioning is sample-specific and depends largely on the variability of the variables within the sample.[17]

Effects of Parental Authoritarianism and Authoritativeness on Self-Esteem

Buri et al. (1988), who were interested in the effects of *perceived* parental authoritarianism and authoritativeness on college students' self-esteem, reported that they used hierarchical regression analysis as follows: "Sex was entered . . . first, and *since there were no theoretical determinants for the order of entry of the independent variables, they were entered based upon the strength of the bivariate correlations* [italics added]" (p. 275) of the independent variables with self-esteem.

In light of my earlier discussion of the pivotal role of theory in incremental partitioning of variance, I trust that you realize the fallacy of the authors' approach. I hope you also recall that, even when guided by theory, incremental partitioning of variance should not be used to assess the relative contributions of independent variables. Therefore, I could have stopped here, except that I would like to draw your attention to a couple of other steps that the authors took, which made matters worse.

One, the authors reported that "the order in which the authoritativeness variables were entered into the regression models was rotated in order to evaluate their relative contributions to the total variance" (p. 275). Not surprisingly, the proportion of variance accounted for by a given variable varied, depending on its point of entry.[18] The use of the different orders of entry of variables appeared to serve no purpose, as the authors ended up interpreting the results obtained when the order of entry of variables was determined based on the zero-order correlations (see the preceding).

Two, the authors first did an analysis on data from *both* males and females. They then did separate analyses for males and females. Based on the latter they concluded, among other things,

---

[16]In my comments on studies in this section I am ignoring the very serious problem of treating multiple indicators of a variable as if they were distinct variables. What I say about this topic in subsequent chapters (e.g., Chapters 10, 18, and 19) applies also to the current topic. Also, I will note in passing that when stepwise regression analysis was applied within each block (see previous), multiple indicators of variables have, in effect, been treated as if they were distinct variables.

[17]In later chapters (e.g., Chapters 14 and 15), I present methods of cross-sample comparisons.

[18]Earlier, in the context of comments on the IEA studies, I questioned the validity of such an approach.

that "another striking finding of the present study is that over twice as much of the variance in the females' self-esteem is associated with these parental authority variables than is the variance in the males' self-esteem" (p. 281).

Earlier, I pointed out that R^2 is sample specific. Therefore comparisons such as the preceding are, to say the least, not meaningful (for a similar comment, see my earlier discussion of IEA studies). Later in the text (e.g., Chapter 14), I present methods for comparing regression equations or more complex models across groups.

Relative Effects of Procedural and Distributive Justice on Employee Attitudes

Following is the abstract of a paper by Konovsky, Folger, and Cropanzano (1987):

> This study investigated the relative influence of two aspects of fairness, procedural and distributive justice, on two employee attitudes: organizational commitment and satisfaction with pay. Hierarchical regression analysis of data from 36[!] employees from one organization indicated that the variance in organizational commitment was uniquely associated with procedural factors, whereas the variance in satisfaction with pay was uniquely associated with distributive factors. (p. 15)

Referring the reader to Table 2, the authors stated that it contained results of hierarchical regression analysis. Soon afterward, however, they stated, "The data are presented in the form of a usefulness analysis (Darlington, 1978) [the correct date, 1968, is given in the references] which examines the relative abilities of procedural and distributive justice to explain the variance in the criterion variables depending on which predictor is entered first into the regression equation" (pp. 20–21).

The vagueness of the foregoing statement aside, what the authors reported (and what Darlington defined as usefulness) were the proportions of variance accounted for by each variable when it entered *last* into the analysis. As I explain in the section on commonality analysis later in this chapter, such components are also labeled uniqueness. Whatever the nomenclature, what Konovsky et al. reported goes counter to the idea of hierarchical analysis. Further, as I elaborate under commonality analysis, determination of usefulness or uniqueness is not affected by theoretical considerations, nor do such components have any bearing on theory.

Parental Bonds in Childhood, Social Competencies, and Social Support

Mallinckrodt (1992) hypothesized that

> (a) early developmental experiences, especially the emotional responsiveness of primary caregivers, are critical for the development of (b) social competencies, which include a sense of self-efficacy for social skills and the belief that practicing these skills will produce desired outcomes, outcomes that include (c) a satisfying sense of connection with a supportive social network. (p. 453)

Essentially, Mallinckrodt grouped measures he administered to college students into the following clusters:

> Parental bonds [referred to under (a) above]: Mother Care, Mother Overprotection, Father Care, Father Overprotection

Self-efficacy [referred to under (b) above]: General, Social
Attribution style [referred to under (b) above]: Internal, External
Social support [referred to under (c) above]

I focus here on one of his analyses, which he introduced as follows:

> The third research question involved comparison of the relative amount of variance in social support accounted for by parental bond variables and social competency variables. Two hierarchical multiple regressions were performed to investigate this question. In the first regression, the block of the four social competency variables [the self-efficacy and attribution style; see above] was entered in the first step, followed in the second step by the block of four parental bond variables. In the second regression, this order of entry was reversed, with parental bonds entered first and social competencies entered second. (pp. 458–459)

The merits of incremental partitioning of variance aside, I trust that you can see that the analysis as described in the preceding statement is not consistent with theory stated earlier, according to which parental bonds affect social competencies, which in turn affect social support. Therefore, only the second analysis should have been carried out and its results interpreted (again, I am overlooking the limitations of incremental partitioning of variance).

Carrying out both analyses to determine the proportion of variance incremented by the block that is entered second yields what is referred to as uniqueness of the block (or the variable) in question. As I indicated earlier in my comment on Konovsky et al.'s study, calculating and interpreting uniqueness, as Mallinckrodt did, goes counter to the notion of hierarchical analysis. Moreover, as I elaborate in the next section, theoretical formulation has no bearing on the calculation of uniqueness, and vice versa.

Factors Affecting Memory for Spatial Location

A study by Cherry and Park (1993) serves as an example of the lack of appreciation of the questions addressed by a hierarchical regression analysis. I will not go into substantive details of Cherry and Park's study, nor will I comment on whether their analytic approach was addressed to the questions they raised. Instead, I will point out that after reporting on their hierarchical regression analyses, they stated,

> In addition, a fourth regression analysis was computed where the order of entry of the variables was reversed. The purpose of the final analysis was to determine whether the working memory, spatial context, and age variables were still predictive of spatial memory when entered in reversed order, *because the order of entry is known to influence the outcome of regression analysis* [italics added]. (p. 522)

Assuming that the order of entry of variables was determined by theoretical considerations (see introductory discussions in this chapter), then the fact that another order of entry might yield different results is irrelevant.

COMMONALITY ANALYSIS

Commonality analysis is a method of variance partitioning designed to identify the proportions of variance in the dependent variable that may be attributed uniquely to each of the independent variables, and the proportions of variance that are attributed to various combinations of independent variables. Mood (1969, 1971) and Mayeske et al. (1969), who developed this approach, applied it to data of the Coleman Report (see "Research Examples" later in the chapter). Two researchers in England, Newton and Spurrell (1967a, 1967b), independently developed the same approach, which they labeled elements analysis, and applied it to problems in industrial settings. For comments on some earlier and related approaches, see Creager (1971).

The unique contribution of an independent variable is defined as the proportion of variance of the dependent variable attributed to it when it is entered last in the analysis. Thus defined, the unique contribution is actually a squared semipartial correlation between the dependent variable and the variable of interest, after partialing all the other independent variables from it. With two independent variables, 1 and 2, the unique contribution of variable 1 is defined as

$$U(1) = R^2_{y.12} - R^2_{y.2} \tag{9.1}$$

where $U(1)$ = unique contribution of variable 1; $R^2_{y.12}$ = squared multiple correlation of Y with variables 1 and 2; and $R^2_{y.2}$ = squared correlation of Y with variable 2. Similarly, the unique contribution of variable 2 is defined as

$$U(2) = R^2_{y.12} - R^2_{y.1} \tag{9.2}$$

where $U(2)$ = unique contribution of variable 2. The definition of the commonality of variables 1 and 2 is

$$C(12) = R^2_{y.12} - U(1) - U(2) \tag{9.3}$$

where $C(12)$ = commonality of variables 1 and 2. Substituting the right-hand sides of (9.1) and (9.2) for $U(1)$ and $U(2)$ in (9.3),

$$\begin{aligned}
C(12) &= R^2_{y.12} - (R^2_{y.12} - R^2_{y.2}) - (R^2_{y.12} - R^2_{y.1}) \\
&= R^2_{y.12} - R^2_{y.12} + R^2_{y.2} - R^2_{y.12} + R^2_{y.1} \\
&= R^2_{y.2} + R^2_{y.1} - R^2_{y.12}
\end{aligned} \tag{9.4}$$

As a result of determining unique and common contribution of variables, it is possible to express the correlation of any independent variable with the dependent variable as a composite of the unique contribution of the variable of interest plus its commonalities with other independent variables. Thus $R^2_{y.1}$ in the previous example can be expressed as

$$R^2_{y.1} = U(1) + C(12) \tag{9.5}$$

That this is so can be shown by restating (9.5), using the right-hand sides of (9.1) and (9.4):

$$R^2_{y.1} = (R^2_{y.12} - R^2_{y.2}) + (R^2_{y.2} + R^2_{y.1} - R^2_{y.12})$$

Similarly,

$$R^2_{y.2} = U(2) + C(12) \tag{9.6}$$

The commonality of variables 1 and 2 is referred to as a second-order commonality. With more than two independent variables, second-order commonalities are determined for all pairs of variables. In addition, third-order commonalities are determined for all sets of three variables, fourth-order commonalities for all sets of four variables, and so forth up to one commonality whose order is equal to the total number of independent variables. Thus, for example, with three independent variables, A, B, and C, there are three unique components, namely $U(A)$, $U(B)$, and $U(C)$; three second-order commonalities, namely $C(AB)$, $C(AC)$, and $C(BC)$, and one third-order commonality, namely $C(ABC)$. Altogether, there are seven components in a three-variable problem. In general, the number of components is equal to $2^k - 1$, where k is the number of

independent variables. Thus, with four independent variables there are $2^4 - 1 = 15$ components, four of which are unique, six are second-order, four are third-order, and one is a fourth-
order commonality. With five independent variables there are $2^5 - 1 = 31$ components. Note
that with each addition of an independent variable there is a considerable increase in the number
of components, a point I discuss later.

Writing Commonality Formulas

Mood (1969) and Wisler (1969) proposed a rule for writing formulas for unique and commonality components in a commonality analysis, which I will explain by an example. Suppose that we
have three independent variables, X_1, X_2, and X_3, and a dependent variable, Y. To write the formula for the unique contribution of X_2, say, construct first the product,

$$-(1 - X_2)X_1X_3$$

where the variable of interest, X_2, is subtracted from one, and this term is multiplied by the remaining independent variables, which in the present example are X_1 and X_3. Expanding this
product

$$-(1 - X_2)X_1X_3 = -(X_1X_3 - X_1X_2X_3) = -X_1X_3 + X_1X_2X_3$$

After expanding the product, each term is replaced by R^2 of the dependent variable with the variables indicated in the given term. Thus, using the previous expansion, the unique contribution of
X_2 is

$$U(X_2) = -R^2_{y.x_1x_3} + R^2_{y.x_1x_2x_3}$$

or, written more succinctly,

$$U(2) = -R^2_{y.13} + R^2_{y.123}$$

I will now illustrate how the rule is applied to writing the formula for the commonality of two
variables. First, the product is constructed. This time, however, there are two terms in which each
of the variables of interest is subtracted from one. The product of these terms is multiplied by the
remaining independent variable(s). The product to be expanded for the commonality of, say, X_2
and X_3 is

$$-(1 - X_2)(1 - X_3)X_1$$

After expansion

$$-(1 - X_2)(1 - X_3)X_1 = -X_1 + X_1X_2 + X_1X_3 - X_1X_2X_3$$

Replacing each term in the right-hand side of this equation by R^2,

$$C(23) = -R^2_{y.1} + R^2_{y.12} + R^2_{y.13} - R^2_{y.123}$$

To write the formula for the commonality of X_1 and X_3, expand the product $-(1 - X_1)(1 - X_3)X_2$
and then replace each term by the appropriate R^2.

For the commonality of all the independent variables in the previous example, it is necessary
to expand the following product:

$$-(1 - X_1)(1 - X_2)(1 - X_3)$$

After expansion, this product is equal to

$$-1 + X_1 + X_2 - X_1X_2 + X_3 - X_1X_3 - X_2X_3 + X_1X_2X_3$$

When the rule is applied to writing the formula for the commonality of all the independent variables, the expanded product has one term equal to -1. This term is deleted and the remaining terms are replaced by R^2's in the manner I illustrated in the preceding. Accordingly, using the expansion for the product terms of X_1, X_2, and X_3, the formula for the commonality of these variables is

$$C(123) = R^2_{y.1} + R^2_{y.2} - R^2_{y.12} + R^2_{y.3} - R^2_{y.13} - R^2_{y.23} + R^2_{y.123}$$

The rule I introduced earlier applies to any number of independent variables. I illustrate this for some components in a problem with k independent variables. To obtain, say, the unique contribution of variable X_1, the following product is constructed:

$$-(1 - X_1)X_2X_3 \ldots X_k$$

After expanding this product, each term is replaced by R^2 of the dependent variable with the independent variables indicated in the given term. To write the formula for the commonality of variables X_1, X_2, X_3, and X_4, for example, the following product is expanded:

$$-(1 - X_1)(1 - X_2)(1 - X_3)(1 - X_4)X_5X_6 \ldots X_k$$

Again, after expanding this product, each term is replaced by the appropriate R^2. The formula for the commonality of all k independent variables is obtained by expanding the following product:

$$-(1 - X_1)(1 - X_2) \ldots (1 - X_k)$$

As I pointed out above, after expanding the product with all the independent variables there is one term equal to -1. This term is deleted, and all other terms are replaced by R^2's in the manner shown above.

A Numerical Example

Before discussing problems in interpreting results from commonality analysis, I apply the method to the numerical example I used earlier in this chapter to illustrate incremental partitioning of variance. Briefly, the example consisted of three independent variables: socioeconomic status (SES), intelligence (IQ), and achievement motivation (AM). The dependent variable was the grade-point average (GPA) of college students. I repeat the intercorrelations among these variables in Part I of Table 9.2. Part II of the table gives the various R^2's necessary for a commonality analysis.

I will now apply to the present example the rule for writing the formulas for the various components. To avoid cumbersome notation, however, I will use the following: X_1 = SES; X_2 = IQ; X_3 = AM; and Y = GPA. For the unique contribution of X_1, I expand the following product:

$$-(1 - X_1)X_2X_3 = -X_2X_3 + X_1X_2X_3$$

I now replace each term in this expansion with relevant R^2's from Table 9.2:

$$U(1) = -R^2_{y.23} + R^2_{y.123} = -.49641 + .49647 = .00006$$

Similarly, I calculated the unique contributions of X_2 and X_3. They are

$$U(2) = -R^2_{y.13} + R^2_{y.123} = -.26878 + .49647 = .22769$$

$$U(3) = -R^2_{y.12} + R^2_{y.123} = -.35268 + .49647 = .14379$$

Table 9.2   Illustrative Data for a Commonality Analysis

	Correlation Matrix			
	1 *SES*	*2* *IQ*	*3* *AM*	*Y* *GPA*
1	1.0000	.3000	.4100	.3300
2	.0900	1.0000	.1600	.5700
3	.1681	.0256	1.0000	.5000
Y	.1089	.3249	.2500	1.0000

Squared Multiple Correlations

$R^2_{y.123} = .49647$	$R^2_{y.12} = .35268$
$R^2_{y.13} = .26878$	$R^2_{y.23} = .49641$

NOTE: Entries above the principal diagonal of the correlation matrix are zero-order correlations, whereas those below the diagonal are squared zero-order correlations. For example, $r_{12} = .3000$, $r^2_{12} = .0900$.

For the commonality of X_1 and X_2, I expand the following product:

$$-(1 - X_1)(1 - X_2)X_3 = -X_3 + X_1X_3 + X_2X_3 - X_1X_2X_3$$

Replacing each term in the expansion with the relevant R^2's from Table 9.2,

$$C(12) = -R^2_{y.3} + R^2_{y.13} + R^2_{y.23} - R^2_{y.123}$$

$$= -.25000 + .26878 + .49641 - .49647 = .01872$$

The commonality of X_1 and X_3, and that of X_2 and X_3, are similarly obtained. They are

$$C(13) = -R^2_{y.2} + R^2_{y.12} + R^2_{y.23} - R^2_{y.123}$$

$$= -.3249 + .35268 + .49641 - .49647 = .02772$$

$$C(23) = -R^2_{y.1} + R^2_{y.12} + R^2_{y.13} - R^2_{y.123}$$

$$= -.1089 + .35268 + .26878 - .49647 = .01609$$

The commonality of X_1, X_2, and X_3 is obtained through the following expansion

$$-(1 - X_1)(1 - X_2)(1 - X_3) = -1 + X_1 + X_2 - X_1X_2 + X_3 - X_1X_3 - X_2X_3 + X_1X_2X_3$$

Deleting the -1 and replacing the remaining terms with the R^2's from Table 9.2,

$$C(123) = R^2_{y.1} + R^2_{y.2} - R^2_{y.12} + R^2_{y.3} - R^2_{y.13} - R^2_{y.23} + R^2_{y.123}$$

$$= .1089 + .3249 - .35268 + .2500 - .26878 - .49641 + .49647 = .0624$$

Following Mayeske et al. (1969), I summarize the analysis in Table 9.3. Note that each term in the last line (labeled Σ) is equal to the squared zero-order correlation of the variable with which it is associated and the dependent variable. Thus, for example, in the last line under SES .1089 is equal to the squared zero-order correlation between SES and GPA ($.3300^2$; see Table 9.2).

Reading down each column of Table 9.3, it is possible to note how the proportion of variance accounted for by a given variable is partitioned into various components. For instance, the proportion of variance accounted for by SES is partitioned as follows: .00006 unique to SES, .01872 common to SES and IQ, .02772 common to SES and AM, and .06240 common to SES, IQ, and AM. From this analysis it is evident that SES makes practically no unique contribution. Most of the variance accounted for by SES (.1089) is due to its commonalities with the other independent

Table 9.3   Summary of Commonality Analysis of Table 9.2 Data

	Variables		
	1 *SES*	*2* *IQ*	*3* *AM*
Unique to 1, SES	.00006		
Unique to 2, IQ		.22769	
Unique to 3, AM			.14379
Common to 1 and 2	.01872	.01872	
Common to 1 and 3	.02772		.02772
Common to 2 and 3		.01609	.01609
Common to 1, 2, and 3	.06240	.06240	.06240
Σ:	.1089	.3249	.2500

variables. In contrast, IQ and AM show relatively large unique contributions, about 23% and 14%, respectively.

The squared multiple correlation can be written as a composite of all the unique and common components. Thus, for the present problem,

$$R^2_{y.123} = U(1) + U(2) + U(3) + C(12) + C(13) + C(23) + C(123)$$

$$.49647 = .00006 + .22769 + .14379 + .01872 + .02772 + .01609 + .06240$$

From this form of partitioning of the variance, it appears that the unique contributions of IQ and AM account for about 37% of the variance, and all the commonalities account for the remaining 13%.

A Closer Look at Uniqueness

In the preceding, I defined the unique contribution of a variable as the increment in the proportion of variance it accounts for when it is entered last into the regression equation. When the independent variables are not correlated, the uniqueness of each is equal to the squared zero-order correlation between it and the dependent variable. Under such circumstances, there are no commonalities. Consequently, there is no ambiguity about the partitioned variance. In nonexperimental research, the independent variables are almost always correlated. Under such circumstances, uniqueness and commonality elements are affected by the magnitudes and the signs of the correlations among the variables. Assuming, for example, that all the variables are positively correlated, the higher the correlations among the independent variables, the smaller the uniqueness and the larger the relative proportions of variance attributed to the commonality of variables.

I noted earlier that the uniqueness of a variable is equal to its squared semipartial correlation with the dependent variable when all the other independent variables are partialed out from the one under consideration. An equivalent way of expressing uniqueness of a variable, say X_1, is $\beta^2_{y1.23\ldots k}(1 - R^2_{1.23\ldots k})$, where $\beta^2_{y1.23\ldots k}$ is the squared standardized coefficient of X_1 in the regression equation of Y on all the X's, and $R^2_{1.23\ldots k}$ is the squared multiple correlation of X_1 with the remaining independent variables. Consequently, $1 - R^2_{1.23\ldots k}$ is what X_1 *does not* share with the other X's, or the residual variance. Now, β is a partial regression coefficient, and its magnitude is affected, among other things, by the correlations among the independent variables. In addition, other things being equal, the smaller the residual variance of a given variable (i.e., the higher the squared multiple correlation between it and the other independent variables), the smaller the uniqueness associated with it. I now illustrate this formulation of uniqueness with the numerical example in Table 9.2. Regressing Y on the three X's, the following regression equation is obtained

$$z'_y = .00919z_1 + .50066z_2 + .41613z_3$$

Calculate the following:

$$R^2_{1.23} = .22449 \qquad R^2_{2.13} = .09165 \qquad R^2_{3.12} = .16960$$

Using these results, the unique contributions of the three variables are

$$U(1) = (.00919^2)(1 - .22449) = .00006$$

$$U(2) = (.50066^2)(1 - .09165) = .22769$$

$$U(3) = (.41613^2)(1 - .16960) = .14379$$

The same values are reported in Table 9.3.

Before turning to a simpler method for calculating uniqueness, I will note that some authors (e.g., Purves, 1973, p. 134) use the previous terminology in their discussions of the uniqueness of variables. Similarly, Coleman (1968, pp. 241–242; 1972, p. 156) expresses the same ideas using the notation $b^2(1 - C^2)$, where b^2 is the squared standardized regression coefficient, β^2, associated with the variable whose uniqueness is being calculated, and $1 - C^2$ is the residual variance of this variable, as defined earlier.

Darlington (1968, pp. 168–169) uses the term *usefulness* for what I labeled here *uniqueness* and shows how it may be calculated from the overall regression of the dependent variable on all the independent variables.

In Chapter 7, I said that tests of significance of a partial correlation, a semipartial, a b, and a β are all equivalent. Computer programs for multiple regression analysis routinely report F ratios for tests of significance of the regression coefficients (some programs report t ratios instead, but in the present case $t^2 = F$, as each F ratio has one degree of freedom for the numerator). The uniqueness of a variable, say X_1, can be calculated as follows:

$$U(1) = \frac{F_1(1 - R^2_{y.12...k})}{N - k - 1} \tag{9.7}$$

where F_1 is the F ratio for test of significance of the regression coefficient for X_1; $R^2_{y.12...k}$ is squared multiple correlation of Y with all the independent variables; N is sample size; and k is the number of independent variables.

To illustrate the application of (9.7) to the data in Table 9.2, I assumed that $N = 300$. The three F ratios associated with the β's reported in the preceding are F_1 (for SES) = .038; F_2 (for IQ) = 133.849; and F_3 (for AM) = 84.529. The df for each of these F's are 1 and 296. $R^2_{y.12...k} = .49647$. Applying (9.7),

$$U(1) = \frac{(.038)(1 - .49647)}{300 - 3 - 1} = \frac{.019134}{296} = .00006$$

$$U(2) = \frac{(133.849)(1 - .49647)}{296} = \frac{67.39699}{296} = .22769$$

$$U(3) = \frac{(84.529)(1 - .49647)}{296} = \frac{42.56289}{296} = .14379$$

Earlier, I calculated the same values.

Yet another way of observing the effect of correlations among independent variables on the uniqueness of each is to note the manner in which the uniqueness of a variable is related to the inverse of the correlation matrix of the independent variables. In Chapter 6—see (6.18) and the discussion related to it—I introduced the following formula for the calculation of the increment in the proportion of variance accounted for by a given variable:

$$prop_{(j)} = \frac{\beta_j^2}{r^{jj}} \tag{9.8}$$

where $prop_{(j)}$ = increment in the proportion of variance accounted for by variable j; and r^{jj} = the diagonal element of the inverse of $\mathbf{R}$ (i.e., $\mathbf{R}^{-1}$) associated with variable j. When the correlations among all the independent variables are zero, the inverse of the correlation matrix ($\mathbf{R}^{-1}$) is an identity matrix—that is, a matrix whose diagonal elements are 1's and the off-diagonal elements are 0's (see Appendix A). Under such circumstances, the application of (9.8) for the calculation of uniqueness leads to the conclusion that the uniqueness of each variable is equal to the squared β associated with it. But when independent variables are not correlated, each β is equal to the zero-order correlation of the variable with which it is associated and the dependent variable. Therefore, squaring the β to obtain uniqueness is tantamount to squaring the zero-order correlation.

When the independent variables are correlated, the diagonal elements of $\mathbf{R}^{-1}$ are larger than unity. They become relatively large when the correlations among the independent variables are relatively large (see the discussion of collinearity in Chapter 10). Consequently, when the independent variables are intercorrelated, the uniqueness of a variable will always be smaller than its squared β, approaching the vanishing point as the diagonal elements of $\mathbf{R}^{-1}$ become increasingly larger.

The inverse of the correlation matrix of the independent variables for the data of Table 9.2 is:

$$\mathbf{R}^{-1} = \begin{bmatrix} 1.28947 & -.310192 & -.479051 \\ -.310192 & 1.10089 & -.0489638 \\ -.479051 & -.0489638 & 1.20425 \end{bmatrix}$$

Note that the diagonal elements of $\mathbf{R}^{-1}$ exceed unity, but not by very much. The reason is that the correlations among the independent variables are relatively low (see Table 9.2). Having the $\mathbf{R}^{-1}$, it is now possible to apply (9.8) to obtain the unique contributions of each variable. Recall that the regression equation for the data in Table 9.2 is

$$z_y' = .00919z_1 + .50066z_2 + .41613z_3$$

Using, in turn, each element of the diagonal of $\mathbf{R}^{-1}$ reported above and applying (9.8),

$$U(1) = \frac{.00919^2}{1.28947} = .00006$$

$$U(2) = \frac{.50066^2}{1.10089} = .22769$$

$$U(3) = \frac{.41613^2}{1.20425} = .14379$$

I obtained these values several times earlier.

My discussion in this section was limited to an examination of the effects of the intercorrelations among the independent variables on the uniqueness of each. It is possible also to show the parts that make up the commonality of variables. This, however, becomes unwieldy for higher-order commonalities (i.e., beyond the second and the third). More important, such terms elude straightforward interpretations. Therefore, I do not present them.[19]

Problems in the Interpretation of Commonality Analysis

As with any analytic method, it is imperative to understand the meaning of the results from commonality analysis. Referring to the analysis of the illustrative data in Table 9.2, several questions come immediately to mind. Do the results answer the question of relative importance of independent variables? May one conclude that SES is not an important variable, as it makes almost no unique contribution to GPA (.00006; see Table 9.3)? Does the larger proportion of variance attributed uniquely to IQ, as compared with AM, indicate that it is the more important variable of the two? And what do the commonality elements mean?

The key to answering these and other questions is in the realization that *commonality analysis is useful and meaningful in predictive but not in explanatory research.* By its very nature, commonality analysis evades the problem of explanation, or fails to address it. This becomes evident when one realizes that, *given a set of independent variables and a dependent variable, commonality analysis is applied in exactly the same way, and of course yields identical results, regardless of one's causal model concerning the variables under study or in the absence of any such model.*

Advocates of commonality analysis extolled its virtues as being safe. Cooley and Lohnes (1976), for example, said:

> The commonality method of partitioning of variance in multivariate regression is an informative, conservatively safe method for most situations likely to arise in evaluations, and it is therefore strongly recommended as the usual style of analysis for evaluative researches. (p. 219)

There is no denying that the method is conservative and safe, but its safety stems from the fact that it does not address questions relating to attempts at explaining phenomena. It is informative only for predictive research, where it can be used for decisions about which variables may be eliminated while sacrificing little in overall predictability. In short, commonality analysis can be used as an alternative to other variable-selection procedures (e.g., stepwise selection; see Chapter 8). Newton and Spurrell (1967a, 1967b) maintained that commonality analysis is superior to other selection methods currently used, and they gave empirical evidence in support of this claim. They suggested, among other things, that when selecting variables from a larger pool, those with small commonalities and large unique components are preferable. This makes good sense in a predictive framework. Doing this in an explanatory framework, however, may be highly misleading.

Beaton, who played a major role in developing methodological approaches for the extensive reanalyses of the data from the Coleman Report (Mayeske & Beaton, 1975; Mayeske et al., 1972, 1973a, 1973b), distinguished between the use of regression analysis for predictive purposes and for the estimation of parameters in a causal model. He then stated, "Commonality analysis is an attempt to understand the relative *predictive* [italics added] power of the regressor

---

[19]See Wisler (1969) for a mathematical development in which commonality analysis is expressed as squared semipartial correlations. See also Beaton (1973).

variables, both individually and in combination. [It] may be used as a procedure to guide a step-wise regression" (Beaton, 1973, p. 2).

In their response to criticism of commonality analysis, Lohnes and Cooley (1978) urged researchers to revert to Darlington's term *usefulness* instead of *uniqueness.* This is probably a good idea as it may serve as a safeguard against misinterpretations of such elements, provided that one is mindful of what Darlington (1968) said about usefulness: "When the focus is on the *prediction* [italics added] of X_o, *rather than causal analysis* [italics added], usefulness is clearly the measure of greatest interest" (p. 168). Even Lohnes and Cooley (1978) ended up saying, "In this context 'useful' refers to the *utility of the predictor in estimating* [italics added] the dependent variable after all the predictors have been introduced" (p. 7).

Uniqueness, then, is useful in a predictive framework, but not in an explanatory one. This, however, is not how the measure was interpreted by leading exponents of commonality analysis. Mayeske et al. (1972), for example, stated, "It does not seem unreasonable to assume that some degree of proportionality exists between the percent of variance of a dependent variable that can be uniquely associated with a set of variables and its *causal influence* [italics added]" (p. 52). I fail to see the justification for this statement.

Discussing the difficulties that arise when commonalities are large and the unique components are small, Mood (1971) attributed them not to the analytic method used, but to "our state of ignorance about educational variables" (p. 197). He further asserted that commonality analysis helps us "identify indicators which are failing badly with respect to specificity" (p. 197). While it is true that large commonalities are a consequence of high correlations among variables, it does not necessarily follow that a high correlation reflects lack of specificity of variables. "Correlations between sets may be of substantive importance and not solely artifacts of the inadequacy of the proxy variables" (Creager, 1971, p. 675). It is possible, for instance, that two variables are highly correlated because one is a cause of the other. Commonality analysis, however, does not distinguish between situations in which variables lack specificity and those in which causal relations exist. Applying commonality analysis in the latter situation may lead to the erroneous conclusion that a presumed cause lacks specificity or is unimportant because it has little or no uniqueness, on the one hand, and large commonalities with other variables on the other hand. For example, in a reanalysis of the Coleman Report data, Mayeske et al. (1972) used student's racial-ethnic group membership as a student variable and teacher's racial-ethnic group membership as a school variable. Not surprisingly, these variables were found to be highly correlated, thus contributing to high commonalities for school and student variables when attempting to explain dependent variables such as achievement. It is obvious, however, that the high correlation between student and teacher racial composition does not reflect a lack of specificity of these variables but is primarily a consequence of a policy of segregation.

Finally, it is important to note that there is nothing absolute about the uniqueness of a variable, as it depends on the relations among the specific variables under study. Addition or deletion of variables may change drastically the uniqueness attributed to some or all of them.

Problems of interpreting unique elements in an explanatory framework pale in comparison with the difficulties encountered in the interpretation of commonality elements in such a framework. Witness, for example, the statement about the commonality between two sets of variables by a leading exponent of commonality analysis. "In its strictest sense this common portion represents an intermediate situation. That is to say, we cannot tell to which of the two sets . . . all or some part of this common portion should be attributed" (Mayeske, 1970, p. 105). This statement refers to a second-order commonality, that is, between two variables or two sets of variables.

With more than two independent variables, the difficulty increases: one obtains higher-order commonalities that will almost always elude explanation. Yet one encounters interpretations of commonalities even as indications of interactions between variables (e.g., Hanushek & Kain, 1972, p. 125; Purves, 1973, p. 135). Such interpretations are wrong in the sense in which the term is used in experimental research. An interaction between, say, two independent variables means that there is dependent-variable variance that neither variable alone accounts for; both variables operate jointly to produce it. Commonality, on the other hand, being a result of a correlation between, say, two predictors, reflects variation in the criterion that would be accounted for by either predictor alone.[20]

Another problem with commonality elements is that they may have negative signs.[21] Negative commonalities may be obtained in situations where some of the variables act as suppressors, or when some of the correlations among the independent variables are positive and others are negative. It does not seem necessary to elaborate on the logical problem posed by a negative proportion of variance attributed to the commonality of a set of variables. And the problem is not solved by saying, as Mayeske et al. (1972) did: "Negative commonalities will be regarded as equivalent to zero" (p. 49).

Still another problem with commonality analysis, alluded to earlier, is the proliferation of higher-order commonalities that results from the addition of independent variables. Even with only five independent variables, there are 31 components, 26 of which are commonalities. Although it may be possible, but by no means always easy, to explain a second- or a third-order commonality, it is extremely difficult, even impossible, to explain commonalities of higher orders. Recognizing this difficulty, Mood and Mayeske suggested that independent variables be grouped and that commonality analysis be done on the grouped variables. And Wisler (1969) maintained that "It is by grouping variables and performing commonality analyses that one can begin to discern the structure in nonexperimental, multivariate data" (p. 359). While admittedly simpler, commonality analysis with grouped variables may still yield results that are difficult to interpret. One can find examples of such difficulties in the reanalysis of data from the Coleman Report by Mayeske et al. (1969). For instance, Mood (1971) reproduced one such analysis from Mayeske, in which peer quality and school quality, each comprising about 30 indicators, were used. An analysis of achievement in grades 3, 6, 9, and 12 found that the unique contributions of each of the aforementioned grouped indicators ranged from .04 to .11, while their commonalities ranged from .45 to .75. Mood (1971) concluded, "The overlap between peer quality and school quality is so large that there seems hardly any point in referring to them as different factors; or perhaps the problem is that we are so ignorant about specificity of indicators that ours have almost no specificity at all" (p. 198).

In view of the previously noted difficulties with the interpretation of commonality elements it is not surprising that some researchers (e.g., Cooley & Lohnes, 1976; Purves, 1973) report the uniqueness of each variable, or set of variables, and lump together all the commonalities. Although Cooley and Lohnes (1976, pp. 224–227) label the combined commonalities as the "Jointly Explained" proportion of variance, their characterization, in parentheses, of this quantity as "confounded" more appropriately reflects its ambiguous status. Authors who do report separate commonalities either confess their inability to explain them or make some general comments about them (e.g., that they tend to be large compared with the unique elements).

---

[20]See Chapter 12 for a detailed discussion of interaction.

[21]Unique elements are always positive. They may, however, be equal to zero.

RESEARCH EXAMPLES

"[E]nthusiasm for commonality partitioning of variance is running high" (Cooley & Lohnes, 1976, p. 220), especially among researchers engaged in evaluation studies in general, and studies on the effect of schooling in particular. Most studies in which commonality analysis was used were aimed at explaining phenomena (e.g., school achievement). If my assertion about the inappropriateness of commonality analysis in explanatory research is valid, then conclusions of explanatory studies in which it was applied would have to be rejected. On these grounds, I could have refrained from commenting on specific studies. I felt, however, that such an omission would be unwise because some of the studies have had, and will probably continue to have, a strong impact not only on educational researchers but also on educational policy makers, educators, and the general public. Additionally, I hope that my comments will illustrate and highlight some of the problems in the application of commonality analysis in explanatory research.

The brief statements that follow cannot begin to do justice to the broad scope and extensive efforts that have gone into some of the studies on which I comment. Furthermore, I focus only on commonality analysis, which is one of several methods used in some of these studies. In short, the following presentations are neither summaries nor reviews of the studies. You are encouraged to read the original reports and judge whether, and to what degree, they help explain the phenomena under consideration.

Reanalyses of the Coleman Report Data

Probably the most extensive use of commonality analysis is to be found in a set of studies conducted by personnel of the United States Office of Education under the leadership of Mayeske (e.g., Mayeske et al., 1972, 1973a, 1973b, 1975). A major goal of these studies was to determine the relative effects of student background characteristics and schooling on student cognitive and noncognitive functioning. For example, in the preface to *A Study of Our Nation's Schools* (Mayeske et al., 1972), Mayeske stated that one of its major purposes was "to show the extent to which the structural properties of the data will permit answers to be obtained about possible influences that schools may have on their students" (p. vii).

In this study, approximately 400 questionnaire items from the Coleman Report were initially reduced to about 70 variables. These were subsequently grouped in blocks, the two major ones being background (B) and school (S) variables. The most pervasive finding that emerged from repeated applications of commonality analysis was that nearly all of the achievement variance was attributable to commonality elements. For example, for the twelfth grade, $U(B) = .08$, $U(S) = .04$, and $C(BS) = .75$. While $C(BS)$ was considerably larger than $U(S)$ and $U(B)$ at all grade levels, there were some differences in the relative magnitudes of these elements across grade levels. The authors commented on these differences, saying, for example, "A reversal in the unique portion of B and S occurs at the third grade, and this trend persists at the higher grades. The second-order commonality coefficient shows a progressive increase from the first to the 12th grades" (Mayeske et al., 1972, p. 46). Such comparisons are unwarranted because unique and commonality elements are sample-specific.

The precarious nature of such cross-sample comparisons was even more striking when the authors attempted to study the effects of different aspects of schooling by partitioning S into three subsets: school personnel and personnel expenditure variables (T), pupil programs and policies variables (P), and facilities variables (F). At all grade levels the unique elements were small, though they differed across grades. For example, U(T) was .06 at the first-grade level; .03 at the third- and sixth-grade levels; and .02 at the ninth- and twelfth-grade levels. Of all the commonalities, C(BT) was the largest, ranging from .28 in the first grade to .55 in the sixth (see Table 5.4.2.5 in Mayeske et al., 1972, p. 51). Here is what the authors had to say about this:

> A diminishing role is played by T at the higher grade levels. The fact that the unique portion is so high at the lower grade levels is somewhat puzzling until one observes that the second-order commonality coefficient, C(BT), increases for higher grade levels. This suggests that T comes to share more of the predictable variance in Achievement at the higher grade levels instead of making an independent contribution. . . . The variables we have called F, with P and B, share an increasing amount of variance at the ninth and 12th grades. . . . The relative ordering, however, is for B to be slightly to appreciably larger than T, and for T to be larger than F—until the 12th grade. These results suggest that B and T may play an important role in the development of Achievement. If P and F play a role, it would be by virtue of their shared variances with B and T. (Mayeske et al., 1972, p. 51)

The preceding amounts to a statement that the patterns and magnitudes of the correlations among the variables differ in the different grades. This may, in part, be due to differences in the variabilities of the variables at the different grade levels. Be that as it may, the use of uniqueness of variables as indicators of their effects on achievement is, to say the least, questionable. To compare such indices across samples is even more questionable. The foregoing comments apply also to comparisons of unique and common elements across different dependent variables (e.g., achievement, motivation, attitudes).

Reservations about specific aspects of the analyses and specific conclusions notwithstanding, the overall findings reflect a situation in which commonality analysis cannot help untangle the highly correlated variables, nor does it help determine whether, how, and to what extent each of them produces an effect. The authors of the report also reached this inevitable conclusion, and said, "The principal findings were as follows. On the whole, the influence of the school cannot be separated from that of the student's social background—and vice versa. Moreover, the common influence of the school and the student's social background exceeds either of their distinguishable influences" (Mayeske et al., 1972, p. ix).

Because my aim in the preceding presentation was to illustrate some difficulties in applying commonality analysis to the Coleman Report data, it was convenient to use illustrations from only one of the studies. It should be noted, however, that my comments apply equally to those sections of the other studies in which commonality analysis was used. Although other analytic approaches were also used (see, in particular, Mayeske et al., 1975), all the studies relied primarily on commonality analysis. In response to criticisms of their reliance on commonality analysis, Mayeske et al. (1975) tried alternative approaches to variance partitioning and concluded, "We tested several of these alternative models, and found them unproductive. The most promising approach, it seemed to us, lay in further refinements of the commonality model" (p. 130). The crucial point is that none of the variance-partitioning approaches can provide answers to the questions raised by Mayeske and his associates. Moreover, without a theory of the process of achievement, it is not possible to tell which analytic method is potentially useful. It is noteworthy that Mood, who wrote forewords to the various Mayeske studies, defended their use of commonality analysis on the grounds that no theory of education exists:

> When it comes to quantitative models, education . . . is still in the Stone Age: true theoretical models are still lacking, as are reproducible conceptual connections that might give us a few clues

on constructing even a simple model. . . . We shall eventually develop some believable theory. As we proceed along that path *we shall abandon partitions of variance as soon as possible and move to calculation of regression coefficients and path coefficients* [italics added]. (Mood, 1973, p. iv)

While Mood's contention about the absence of a theory of education may be accurate, using an analytic technique in a theoretical vacuum is not only the least promising route for arriving at a theory, but may also deflect attention from the need to develop one. Furthermore, the seemingly valid answers obtained by relying solely on analytic methods may result in deleterious consequences for educational practices and policies (see "Social Sciences and Social Policy" in Chapter 10).

The International Evaluation of Educational Achievement (IEA)

Earlier in this chapter, I described the IEA studies along with a detailed discussion of the major type of analysis used in them—namely, incremental partitioning of variance. Commonality analysis was also used in some of the studies. I comment on findings from the study of *Literature Education in Ten Countries* (Purves, 1973) because commonality analysis was used extensively in it. Additional examples may be found in other IEA studies and also in a technical report (Peaker, 1975) that includes a general discussion of the methodology of the IEA studies and some summaries of their findings.

In the Literature study, the following six blocks of variables were used: (1) home background, (2) type of school, (3) learning conditions, (4) kindred variables, (5) word knowledge, and (6) reading comprehension.[22] In a commonality analysis with six blocks, 63 elements (i.e., $2^6 - 1$) may be obtained (see the discussion of commonality analysis earlier in this chapter). Of the 63 elements, 6 are unique and 57 are commonalities (15 second-order, 20 third-order, 15 fourth-order, 6 fifth-order, and 1 sixth-order). Purves (1973) did not report the proportion of variance attributed to the separate elements. Instead, he reported the sum of the unique elements, and the sum of all the commonalities, which he labeled "joint contribution of the variables."

Overall, the finding in the different populations was that most of the variance of achievement in Literature was due to commonalities. For example, in Population II, the total percent of variance accounted for in the ten countries ranged from 66.6 to 93.2. The sum of the unique elements ranged from 7% to 44.3%, whereas the sum of the commonalities ranged from 40.7% to 82.2% (see Purves, 1973, Table 5.3, p. 133).

The higher the intercorrelations among the blocks within a given country, the smaller the sum of the unique elements and the larger the sum of the commonalities. This is demonstrated dramatically for Population II in England and in Finland. In England, the variance accounted for by the six blocks was 89.5%, of which 7.3% was the sum of the unique elements and 82.2% was the sum of the commonalities. In Finland, the six blocks accounted for 92.8% percent of the variance, of which 7.0% was the sum of the unique elements and 85.9% was the sum of the commonalities. Clearly, results such as these afford little insight into the process of achievement in Literature, except for the obvious conclusion that the blocks are highly intercorrelated. Purves was prudent in not reporting the separate commonalities, as they would have certainly eluded meaningful interpretation. It will be noted, however, that Purves' occasional reference to commonalities as interactions is potentially misleading. Thus, he stated, "That so much of the variance is accounted for not

---

[22]For a description of these blocks, see "Incremental Partitioning of Variance" earlier in this chapter.

only by the unique contribution of the variables but by their *interactions* [italics added] also reflects the tight relationship between them" (Purves, 1973, pp. 133–134).[23]

An additional point regarding the previously cited results is noteworthy. As I discussed earlier in this chapter, the major analytic approach in the IEA studies was incremental partitioning of variance in which the six blocks were entered in a fixed order, beginning with home background. For Population II, home background accounted for 68.4% of the variance in England and 79.1% in Finland (see Purves, 1973, Table 5.3, p. 133). But, as I reported previously, the sum of the unique contributions, *including home background*, was 7.3 and 7.0 in England and Finland, respectively. Is, then, home background an important block? Obviously, the answer depends on which of the two analyses one interprets. In the incremental partitioning of variance, home background appears to have the overwhelming effect, as it accounts for about 80% of the variance accounted for by the six blocks together. In the commonality analysis, on the other hand, it accounts for a fraction of 7% of the total variance. The crucial point is that, as I discussed earlier, *neither incremental partitioning of variance nor commonality analysis is a valid approach for ascertaining relative importance of variables.*

Purves reported a large number of analyses that are not only of dubious explanatory value but are also potentially misleading. In these analyses the unique contribution of each variable was assessed when only the variables of the block in which it appeared were used in a commonality analysis. Thus, for example, using only the variables that comprise Block I, in Population II, age of the student in school was reported to have a uniqueness of 1.0% in the United States, 1.5% in Finland, and none in Sweden and England (see Purves, 1973, Table 5.5, p. 136). Or, using only the block of student attitudes and interests (Table 5.6), reading books about art made a unique contribution in Sweden only (3.6%), and reading travel and mystery made a unique contribution only in Chile (2.1%). Similar findings were reported in various other tables that, except for sprinklings of small unique elements, were mostly blank (see, for example, Purves, 1973, pp. 138, 146–149, 166–167, 176–178). There is, of course, nothing absolute about the uniqueness of these values that would certainly change in the presence of other blocks in the analysis. Furthermore, to the extent that the logic and the method of grouping variables were valid in the first place, one would expect the variables within a block to be intercorrelated. Consequently, the sum of the unique elements within a block would be expected to be small relative to the sum of their commonalities. Most important, however, is that one fails to see the validity of such analyses for explanatory purposes.

Measures of School Effectiveness

Madaus, Kellaghan, Rakow, and King (1979) argued that failure to detect differential effects of schooling was due primarily to the exclusive reliance on standardized achievement tests as measures of the dependent variable. They maintained that curriculum-based tests are more sensitive and therefore more appropriate as measures of the dependent variable in studies of the effect of schooling. In support of their premise, Madaus and associates offered results of a study conducted in secondary schools in the Republic of Ireland. I review this study here because it affords an opportunity to illustrate some serious conceptual and methodological problems in using commonality analysis in explanatory research.

[23]See the discussion of this point earlier in this chapter.

Beginning with 82 predictors, Madaus et al. grouped them in five blocks. I will point out in passing that little or no justification was given in support of the clustering of disparate variables into a block. Thus, for example, the authors stated, "Variables describing the student, such as sex, age, attitude to education, and academic self-concept, were assigned to an *individual* block" (Madaus et al., p. 212). The situation was further confounded by the fact that the unit of analysis was the classroom, not the individual. That is, class means, or class indices, presumably described the individual.

After grouping the predictors in blocks, a two-stage process was undertaken in order to reduce their number. In the first stage, "eight 'key' dependent variables [of a total of 18] were selected. . . . Each selected dependent variable was regressed separately in a stepwise fashion on the variables in each block. To be retained within a block, a regressor variable had to be a significant predictor (.05 level) of any four or more of the 'key' variables" (Madaus et al., p. 213). Of the original 82 variables, 42 survived this stage of the analysis.

> In the second stage of the screening of variables, a single set of predictor variables was selected for each dependent variable by a step-wise regression on all the predictor variables, regardless of block, that were retained from the first stage of analysis. Variables were eliminated *as predictors of a specific dependent variable* [italics added] if they did not contribute significantly to the prediction of that dependent variable. *At this stage a unique set of predictor variables was associated with each dependent variable. These were the variables used in subsequent analyses to estimate the shares of variance attributable to each block* [italics added]. (p. 213)

I will make several points. In Chapter 8, I argued that stepwise regression analysis is useful in predictive research only. In this chapter I showed that the uniqueness of a variable is directly related to the test of significance of the regression coefficient associated with the variable. Therefore, the stepwise regression analysis, coupled with the criterion of significant b's, favored predictors whose unique contributions were relatively large. As the uniqueness of a variable is larger the less it is correlated with the other predictors, the predictor-selection process at the first stage of the analysis necessarily resulted in blocks composed of relatively heterogeneous predictors (i.e., predictors whose intercorrelations are relatively small). This may be useful in predictive but not in explanatory research, where the substantive meaning of each block is paramount. In short, beginning with a grouping of variables that was questionable in the first place (see my earlier comment), Madaus and coworkers ended up with an even more questionable grouping.

In the second stage of the analysis, each of 18 measures was regressed on the 42 predictors that survived the first-stage selection process. Again, a stepwise regression analysis was used, and predictors whose b's were statistically significant were retained. Thus, at this stage, too, the analysis favored predictors with relatively large unique contributions. This time, however, different combinations of predictors were selected for each dependent variable. It is not known how many variables from each block were retained in each of the 18 analyses, nor is one told of the degree of redundancy with which each predictor was selected. For instance, 13 predictors of the first block survived the first stage of the variable-selection process. How many of these predictors survived in each of the 18 analyses of the second stage? How many times was a given predictor selected? In principle, it is possible that two different subsets of the 13 predictors included in the first block were retained in two separate analyses in the second stage of the variable-selection process. Yet both subsets would be treated as representing an *individual* block.

Treating each of 18 measures of achievement as a separate dependent variable is, to say the least, questionable. Moreover, in the second stage of the variable-selection process, stepwise analyses were done with 42 predictors for classes whose numbers ranged from a low of 51 to a high of 101. Hazards of capitalization on chance and the resulting shrinkage (see Chapter 8) loom large indeed. They are magnified by the two-stage process in the selection of predictors.

At the conclusion of the second stage of the variable selection, the specific variables that were retained in each of the 18 analyses were grouped into their original blocks. These were then used in commonality analyses for each of the 18 measures of achievement. Earlier, I argued at length that commonality analysis is not useful for the purpose of determining the relative importance of variables. Also, I stated that comparisons of proportions of variance accounted for in different measures are not valid indicators of the relative importance of independent variables. On these grounds alone, one would have to question the analyses done by Madaus et al., not to mention their interpretations of the results. The two-stage process of variable selection that preceded the commonality analysis exacerbated the difficulties that arise when attempting to use it in explanatory research.

Federal Medicaid Program

Unlike the originators of commonality analysis (see the preceding sections), who acknowledged some of its limitations, particularly problems attendant with high commonalities,[24] Chen (1984) advocated its use with almost boundless enthusiasm, as the following exemplifies:

> The regression analysis based on individual coefficients [*sic*] suffers the usual deficiency: high degree of multicollinearity, at least among some of the regressor variables. Depending on which variables are included, the regression coefficients of the remaining variables may change somewhat; in some cases, their signs may even be reversed. In addition, we have chosen some indicators to represent theoretical variables that could not be measured with the available data. *Clearly, a complete partition of the variance is called for* [italics added]. (p. 31)

Even a modicum of knowledge of regression and commonality analysis would suffice to recognize various misconceptions in the preceding statement. To begin with, I will point out that, loosely speaking, high multicollinearity means high intercorrelations among the independent variables. As I discuss in detail in Chapter 10 (see "Collinearity"), high multicollinearity does have the kind of adverse effects alluded to by Chen. It is, however, important to recognize that multicollinearity is not inherent in the regression approach. For present purposes, I will give a couple of examples to clarify this point.

One, in appropriately planned and executed experiments, the independent variables are not correlated at all, posing none of the difficulties about which Chen was concerned.

Two, when multiple indicators of a variable are used (e.g., several measures of mental ability), correlations among them tend to be high. Hence, their use as distinct variables in a regression analysis aimed at explanation is bound to create very serious problems. As but one example, it may turn out that none of the regression coefficients is statistically significant.[25]

Chen used multiple indicators of variables. Though he did not report the correlation matrix, he did provide information about correlations between some of the indicators (e.g., .95 between

---

[24]As I pointed out earlier, Mood even expressed the hope that commonality analysis would be abandoned in favor of regression analysis.

[25]Later in the text (particularly Chapters 10 and 19), I discuss analytic approaches in which such difficulties are avoided.

DOCTOR and HOSPITAL and .75 between PARTY and GINI; see pp. 30–31). Not surprisingly, when he subjected his data to a regression analysis, Chen found that most of the regression coefficients were statistically not significant (see his Table 1, p. 30). This is not to say that it is clear, as Chen asserted, that variance partitioning was necessary.

My reason for saying this will, I hope, be easier to grasp after a brief description of Chen's illustrative study and some excerpts in which he described what he did and how he interpreted the results. Chen studied the federal Medicaid program. In particular, he wanted to "assess the impact of the policy variable—differential federal matching ratio—on the per capita expenditures from state and local sources" (p. 25). Using data for 48 states, Chen grouped 15 indicators "into five categories . . . somewhat arbitrarily as several variables might be placed in more than one category" (p. 28) and used the five categories in a commonality analysis.

Chen asserted that commonality analysis "permits us to focus on the variables which make the greatest unique contributions, as well as to identify those variables which in combination contribute particularly to explaining dependent variable variation" (p. 33). More specifically,

> The usual regression analysis in the policy impact model needs to be extended to include the partition of variance to examine the secondary and higher order impact of the policy variables. It is possible that a policy variable may exhibit a small unique contribution to R^2 but contribute significantly when in combination with others. Such a policy variable may be effective when other factors are present. . . . Most importantly, in the structural (or operational) analysis of a policy impact model, the purpose of a statistical study frequently involves the assessment of the impact of the policy variable to aid in the redesign of the system for better planning and control. We would need to determine whether a given policy variable exhibits higher order contributions in conjunction with other regressor variables or not for a fuller understanding of the impact. The effect of a policy variable may be much greater than the first order contribution would indicate, depending on the magnitude of the higher order contribution. (pp. 25–26)

Unlike the originators of commonality analysis, who grappled with difficulties attendant with high commonalities (see the earlier discussion in this chapter), Chen seems to extol them as a virtue. This, I believe, stems from his misconstruing commonalities as if they were interactions in the sense in which this term is used in experimental research. As I pointed out earlier (see Chapter 12 for detailed discussions), an interaction is defined as the joint effect of variables that are *not* correlated. Accordingly, it is possible to ascertain the independent effects of each variable (referred to as the main effects), as well as their joint effect (referred to as interactions). In contrast, large commonalities are a consequence of high correlations among the variables in question. Without repeating earlier discussions, recall that substantive interpretations of commonalities are, to say the least, difficult because of the correlations among the variables involved.

Discussing his commonality analysis results, Chen asserted, "By looking at sets of variables which, in various combinations, contributed significantly to explaining [the dependent variable] . . . we can compare the relative importance of the different factors comprising several variables" (p. 33). Chen's use of the term "significance" (e.g., "No significant contribution exists for the fourth order component," p. 33) is not clear. It should be noted, however, that while unique contributions can be tested (when single variables are used, such tests are equivalent to tests of b's), F tests cannot be used to test commonalities (see Mood, 1971, pp. 196–197).

I will not repeat my earlier arguments against the use of variance partitioning for the purpose of ascertaining the relative importance of variables. Instead, I will point out that in the next section I argue that proportions of variance accounted for are of little or no use as policy guides.

Finally, in case you are wondering why I devoted that much space to Chen's paper, I would like to point out that I did so for two reasons. One, it was presented as a methodological paper (the Medicaid study was used for illustrative purposes only). Two, I was hoping that it would underscore the importance of critically evaluating published papers.

Speed Mediation of Adult Age Differences in Cognition

I comment on a study by Salthouse (1993) because it illustrates a common error: the application of multiple analytic approaches whose aims may be contradictory, and the results that some or all of them yield may have no bearing on the questions raised or hypotheses formulated by the researcher. Among the analytic approaches Salthouse used are hierarchical regression analysis, path analysis, and commonality analysis.

Without going far afield, I will point out that Salthouse used an exogenous variable (age) and four endogenous variables[26] (see the following) in a path analysis model (his Figure 3, p. 732). According to his model, (1) age affects motor speed (MSPD), perceptual speed (PSPD), and memory; (2) MSPD affects PSPD and cognition; (3) PSPD affects memory and cognition; and (4) memory affects cognition. Assuming that Salthouse's theoretical rationale for this model is valid (an issue I will not address), then the inescapable conclusion is that his other analyses go counter to this conception. Following are some comments in support of this assertion.

In several hierarchical regression analyses, Salthouse was interested in studying the effect of age on one of the endogenous variables after controlling for one or more of the remaining endogenous variables. For example, in one such analysis, he showed that when age was entered first in the analysis, it accounted for .202 of the variance in cognition. But when it was entered last (after motor speed, perceptual speed, and memory), it accounted for an increment of .001 of the proportion of variance in cognition (see the last analysis in his Table 6, p. 732). I suggest that you ponder the meaning of such hierarchical analyses, bearing in mind that in his path model Salthouse hypothesized that age affects the variables he controlled for. You may find it helpful to review relevant sections of Chapter 7, where I discussed the logic of control (e.g., "Causal Assumptions").

Assuming now that the hierarchical regression analyses served a meaningful purpose, then this casts doubt on the use of commonality analysis. Salthouse stated:

> As applied in the present context, the goal of this technique is to decompose the total effects of age on either the cognition or memory composite variable into a unique contribution of age and into contributions in common with motor speed, perceptual speed, or both. (p. 733)

I will not repeat my discussion of commonality analysis, which you may want to review at this point. Anyway, I suggest that you think of the meaning of attributing variance not uniquely accounted for by age to commonality with variables that, according to the path model (see the preceding), it is said to affect. Further, assuming it was meaningful to do the hierarchical analyses, is it meaningful to also do an analysis in which components of variance are attributed to the commonality of age with the variables that were controlled in the hierarchical analyses?

I believe that the dubious nature of the hierarchical and commonality analyses becomes compelling when one recognizes that, *unlike path analysis*, they cannot be used to estimate direct and

---

[26]For definitions of exogenous and endogenous variables, see "Incremental Partitioning for Control," earlier in this chapter.

indirect effects of independent variables on dependent variables. Earlier in this chapter, I discussed briefly direct and indirect effects (e.g., in connection with Figures 9.1 and 9.6), and I pointed out that in Chapter 18 I show how to estimate such effects. In the context of the present comment I will only point out that an application of path analysis may show that the direct effect of a variable (e.g., age on cognition in the present example) is small or even zero, whereas its indirect effect is large and substantively meaningful. If you are puzzled by this statement, I suggest that you read some sections of Chapter 18.

In sum, the use of an analytic approach can be meaningful only to the extent that it is appropriate for testing the model under consideration.

VARIANCE PARTITIONING: RETROSPECT

I devoted an entire chapter to variance partitioning because it is frequently used *inappropriately* to study the relative importance of the effects of independent variables on a dependent variable. I scrutinized several major studies that relied heavily on some form of variance partitioning to illustrate some of the problems and difficulties attendant with the application of such methods.

In the beginning of this chapter, I said that incremental partitioning of variance may be used when one wishes to control for a variable(s) while studying the effect of another variable(s), provided that this is done in accordance with a causal model. I stressed, however, that the results from such an analysis should not be construed as shedding light on the question of the relative importance of the effects of independent variables on the dependent variable.

Finally, it is important to recognize that, even when appropriately applied, the results from an incremental partitioning of variance are of dubious value, if not useless, as guides for policy and decision making (for a discussion, see Cain & Watts, 1968, p. 170). What are the policy implications of a finding that a given variable accounts for, say, 10% of the variance of the dependent variable? What should be done to increase, or decrease, its effect on the dependent variable? Assuming that the variable can be manipulated, by how much should it be changed? What will a specific change cost? What will be its measurable consequences? Such questions are unanswerable in the context of variance partitioning.

The predicament is particularly grave when, as is done in virtually all major studies, the partitioned variance is attributed to blocks of variables (or indicators) instead of to single ones. Assume, for example, that a researcher finds that a block of variables describing the teacher (e.g., years of experience, salary, level of education, attitudes toward education) accounts for a certain proportion of the variance in student achievement. How can such a finding be translated into policy? Even if all the variables were under the control of the decision maker (an admittedly unrealistic assumption), by how much should each be changed to achieve a desired effect? What is a desired effect when the proportion of variance accounted for is used as the index? As complex as these problems are, they pale compared with those arising when most or all the variables constituting a block are nonmanipulable, not to mention the use of multiple indicators or proxies of variables. If the situation appears hopeless, it is because it is indeed so in the context of variance partitioning. Other approaches, which I present in subsequent chapters, are more appropriate and hold promise for attempts to explain the complex phenomena with which behavioral scientists are concerned.[27]

---

[27]For some general observations about the use of variance partitioning in explanatory research and about the possible effects of the results of such research on policy makers and the general public, see the concluding section of Chapter 10.

STUDY SUGGESTIONS

1. I introduced the following correlation matrix ($N = 150$) in Study Suggestion 5 of Chapter 8.

1	2	3	4	5	6
		School	Self-	Level of	Verbal
Race	IQ	Quality	Concept	Aspiration	Achievement
1.00	.30	.25	.30	.30	.25
.30	1.00	.20	.20	.30	.60
.25	.20	1.00	.20	.30	.30
.30	.20	.20	1.00	.40	.30
.30	.30	.30	.40	1.00	.40
.25	.60	.30	.30	.40	1.00

Assume that the causal model depicted in the figure below reflects the theoretical framework about the relations among the variables under consideration.

    (a) Which variables are treated as exogenous?

    (b) Which variables are treated as endogenous?

    (c) What proportion of variance of verbal achievement is accounted for by the five independent variables?

    (d) Assuming you wish to partition the variance obtained in (c) in a manner that is consistent with the causal model depicted in the figure, outline the necessary steps to accomplish this.

    (e) Do the variance partitioning as indicated in (d). Determine the different components and explain what each of them means.

    (f) Can the results obtained in (e) be used to assess the relative importance of variables under consideration? Explain.

2. Assume that one wishes to do a commonality analysis, using the variables of Study Suggestion 1 and treating verbal achievement as the dependent variable.

    (a) How many components will be obtained in such an analysis?

    (b) Indicate the number of components of each type (i.e., how many unique, second-order, etc.) that would be obtained.

    (c) Using the correlation matrix of Study Suggestion 1, apply (9.7) to calculate the uniqueness of the five independent variables.

    (d) Use R^2's to indicate how you would go about calculating the following: C(12), C(235).

3. How does the causal model depicted in the figure under Study Suggestion 1 affect the manner in which commonality analysis would be applied to the variables under consideration?

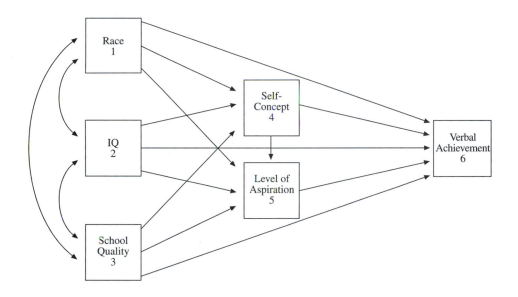

ANSWERS

1.

(a) Race, IQ, and school quality.

(b) Self-concept, level of aspiration, and verbal achievement.

(c) $.43947 = R^2_{6.12345}$

(d) (1) Proportion of variance accounted for by 1, 2, and 3: $R^2_{6.123}$

(2) Proportion of variance incremented by 4: $R^2_{6.1234} - R^2_{6.123}$

(3) Proportion of variance incremented by 5: $R^2_{6.12345} - R^2_{6.1234}$

(e) (1) Proportion of variance accounted for by 1, 2, and 3: .39510

(2) Proportion of variance incremented by 4: .02275

(3) Proportion of variance incremented by 5: .02161

(f) No. For an explanation, see beginning of this chapter.

2.

(a) $31 = 2^5 - 1$

(b) 5 unique, 10 second-order, 10 third-order, 5 fourth-order, 1 fifth-order

(c) $U(1) = .0003, U(2) = .2190, U(3) = .0148, U(4) = .0097, U(5) = .0216$

(d) $C(12) = -R^2_{6.345} + R^2_{6.1345} + R^2_{6.2345} - R^2_{6.12345}$

$C(235) = -R^2_{6.14} + R^2_{6.124} + R^2_{6.134} - R^2_{6.1234} + R^2_{6.145} - R^2_{6.1245} - R^2_{6.1345} + R^2_{6.12345}$

3. The causal model does not affect the manner in which commonality analysis is carried out. Given a set of independent variables and a dependent variable, commonality analysis is carried out in exactly the same manner, regardless of the specific causal model advanced by the researcher or in the absence of any causal model.

CHAPTER

10

ANALYSIS OF EFFECTS

In Chapter 9, I presented methods of variance partitioning, paying special attention to difficulties that arise when such methods are used for explaining phenomena. Also, I commented on the dubious value of variance partitioning as a guide for policy making. In this chapter, I turn to the use of the regression equation for explaining phenomena, particularly to the interpretation of regression coefficients as indices of the effects of independent variables on the dependent variable.

Earlier in the text (e.g., Chapter 5), I pointed out that the partial regression coefficient (i.e., a regression coefficient obtained in the regression of a dependent variable on a set of interrelated independent variables) indicates the expected change in the dependent variable associated with a unit change in a given independent variable while controlling for the other independent variables. This interpretation of the regression coefficient has great appeal for many theoreticians and research workers because it holds the promise for unraveling complex phenomena and for effecting desired changes in them. It is necessary, however, to take a closer look at the properties of regression coefficients, paying particular attention to factors that may lead to their biased estimation or instability, as well as to the restrictive conditions under which they can be validly interpreted as indices of the effects of the variables with which they are associated.

A sober examination of the properties of the regression equation is particularly pressing because its apparent simplicity is deceptive and can lead an unwary user to serious misconceptions, misinterpretations, and misapplications. I focus on major sources of error, on most serious pitfalls to be avoided, when interpreting regression coefficients as indices of the effects of the variables with which they are associated.

I begin with a discussion of the distinction between experimental and nonexperimental research as it relates to the interpretation of regression coefficients. I then address the following major topics: (1) specification errors, (2) measurement errors, (3) collinearity, (4) standardized versus unstandardized regression coefficients, and (5) the role of theory. In the context of some of the preceding topics, I present and comment on research examples that illustrate specific issues. I then discuss and illustrate contrasts between hierarchical analysis (presented in Chapter 9) and simultaneous analysis (presented in this chapter). I conclude the chapter with some observations about social sciences and social policy.

EFFECTS IN EXPERIMENTAL AND NONEXPERIMENTAL RESEARCH

Several times earlier (see, in particular, Chapters 7 through 9), I discussed the important distinction between experimental and nonexperimental research. Among other things, I noted that in experimental research the researcher not only manipulates the independent variables but is also better able to control extraneous variables directly or by randomization. Under such circumstances, the researcher may feel reasonably confident in interpreting regression coefficients as indices of the effects of the independent variables on the dependent variable. The policy maker can note the investment necessary to change a unit of an independent variable and the returns expected to accrue from the change, thus being in a position to make informed decisions about resource allocation.

The situation is considerably more complex and more ambiguous when the regression equation is obtained in nonexperimental research. Cook and Campbell (1979, Chapter 7), Michelson (1970), Mood (1970), Smith, M. S. (1972), and Snedecor and Cochran (1967, pp. 393–397), among other authors, address problems concerning the interpretation of regression equations estimated from data obtained in nonexperimental research. The most important thing to note is that such equations reflect average relations between a dependent and a set of independent variables, not necessarily the process by which the latter produce the former. For example, in their discussion of the findings of the Coleman Report, Mosteller and Moynihan (1972) noted:

> [W]e can estimate the difference in achievement between schools not having and those having a language laboratory, say. But we cannot tell whether actually adding or removing a language laboratory would produce nearly the same difference. Through the years, regression forecasts made in this manner in other fields have often failed in their predictions. (p. 35)

Concluding his excellent discussion of use and abuse of regression analysis, Box (1966) stated, "To find out what happens to a system when you interfere with it you have to interfere with it (not just passively observe it)" (p. 629). Although one cannot take issue with Box's dictum, following it to the letter will result in the exclusion of much, if not most, of human behavior from the realm of scientific inquiry. Because of ethical considerations, or because manipulations of variables are infeasible, or because one wishes to study behavior in complex field settings, nonexperimental research is frequently the only mode of research available to the behavioral researcher. Such research can and does lead to meaningful findings, provided it is designed with forethought, executed with care, and its results are interpreted with circumspection. Referring to data obtained in nonexperimental research, Finney (1982) cautioned:

> To analyse such data uncritically as though they come from a planned experiment invites fallacious argument and misleading conclusions. Although the same types of calculation may be required, more intensive examination of non-experimental data is commonly needed; the inferential problems contain many additional difficulties. (p. 6)

Used wisely, regression analysis can play an important role in nonexperimental research. Unfortunately, all too often one encounters almost mindless interpretations of regression analysis in nonexperimental research.

RESEARCH EXAMPLES

Earlier in the text (particularly, Chapters 7 through 9), I gave several examples of erroneous, or potentially erroneous, conclusions based on the interpretations of results obtained in nonexperimental research. Some additional examples follow.

Mental Ability

A striking example of misinterpretation of regression coefficients comes from Burt's work in the area of mental ability. Burt (1921) collected data on the following four variables: (1) mental age as measured by a modification of the Binet-Simon Scale (Binet); (2) school attainment expressed as educational age (School Work); (3) Burt's reasoning test, which he viewed as a measure of intelligence (Intelligence); and (4) chronological age (Age).

Using the Binet score as a criterion, and the remaining variables as predictors, Burt (1921, p. 183) obtained the following regression equation:

$$\text{Binet}' = .54 \text{ School Work} + .33 \text{ Intelligence} + .11 \text{ Age}$$

As the regression coefficients happen to sum to about one (their sum is .98), Burt interpreted each coefficient as a percent of the variance of the Binet attributable to the effect of the variable with which the given coefficient is associated. Thus, Burt (1921) argued:

> Of the gross result, then, one-ninth is attributable to age, one-third to intellectual development, and over one-half to school attainment. School attainment is thus the preponderant contributor to the Binet-Simon tests. To school the weight assigned is nearly double that of intelligence alone, and distinctly more than that of intelligence and age combined. *In determining the child's performance in the Binet-Simon Scale, intelligence can bestow but little more than half the share of the school, and age but one-third of intelligence.* (p. 183)

To bolster his argument, Burt used as evidence results he obtained from calculating all the possible first- and second-order partial correlations for the four variables (see Chapter 7 for admonitions against such practices). Burt stated:

> With both age and intelligence constant, the partial correlation between school attainments and Binet results remains at .61. Of all the partial coefficients of the second order this is the largest. There can therefore be little doubt that *with the Binet-Simon Scale a child's mental age is a measure not only of the amount of intelligence with which he is congenitally endowed, not only of the plane of intelligence at which in the course of life and growth he has eventually arrived: it is also an index, largely if not mainly, of the mass of scholastic information and skill which in virtue of attendance more or less regular, by dint of instructions more or less effective, he has progressively accumulated in school.* (p. 182)

Holzinger and Freeman (1925), who correctly criticized Burt's interpretation of the regression equation, used his results to calculate three additional regression equations, treating in turn each of the variables as the criterion. Their equation in which they used age as the criterion follows:

$$\text{Age}' = .15 \text{ Binet} + .51 \text{ School Work} + .03 \text{ Intelligence}$$

To highlight the fallacies in Burt's interpretation, Holzinger and Freeman (1925) interpreted this equation in a manner done by Burt, using some of the very same expressions he used.

It appears at once that over half of a child's age is "attributable" to school attainment. This is truly alarming. We had always supposed that age was a comparatively simple thing, when it could be discovered, but now we find that there can be little doubt that age is a measure not only of the amount of age with which a child is congenitally endowed—but it is also an index, largely, if not mainly, of the mass of scholastic information and skill which in virtue of attendance more or less regular, by dint of instruction more or less effective, he has accumulated in school. Isolated from scholastic progress and from development in mental age, intelligence subscribes but a paltry portion. Indeed, if the child were removed from school and his mental age taken away from him, he would probably not get old at all. The secret of eternal youth has at last been discovered! (pp. 581–582)

One might be tempted to attribute Burt's wrong interpretations to the fact that they were committed at a time when regression theory was clearly understood by relatively few researchers, except that in the fourth edition of his book Burt (1962) repeated the interpretation without as much as changing a single word (Burt commented on Holzinger and Freeman's critique in Appendix VI).

Outlandish application and interpretation of regression analysis are, regrettably, not uncommon. Following are two additional examples.

Climate and SAT Scores

Pederson and DeGuire (1982) stated that "A glance at the 1980 average Scholastic Aptitude Test (SAT) scores by state reveals a curious pattern" (p. 68): states with colder climates rank high on the SAT, and those with hotter climates rank low on it. Accordingly, they raised the question, "To what extent does living in a cold climate *correlate* [italics added] with scholastic aptitude,[1] as measured by such standardized tests as the SAT?" (p. 69).

The authors were not content to stop at the descriptive level implied by their question.[2] Instead, in the very next sentence they stated that to answer the question they decided to use "multiple regression analysis, with the states' total SAT scores as the dependent variable" (p. 69). They designated the average high temperature in January for each state as the "principal independent variable" (p. 69). But "*to increase the breadth of the study* [italics added]" (p. 69), they included three additional variables: per pupil expenditure, the year in which the compulsory school attendance law was passed, and the date when the first state normal school was established.

It is not clear to me what the authors meant by "principal independent variable," especially as all the variables seem to have been treated alike in the analysis. Further, although it may have a nice ring to it, I do not know what to make of the statement that additional variables were included to increase the breadth of the study. Be that as it may, starting with what is probably an innocuous question, the authors drifted into an explanatory context.

Without going into all the details, I will point out that Pederson and DeGuire reported that temperature was "the only variable significantly correlated" (p. 69) with SAT. They then pro-

---

[1]Parenthetically, this is an inappropriate statement, as a correlation refers to a relation between *variables*. Reference should therefore be made to living in all kinds of climates, *not* only cold. Thus, one may wish to speak of the correlation between, say, climate (temperature, or something along such lines) and scholastic aptitude.

[2]I am not concerned here with the important question of whether or not a descriptive statement based on a correlation coefficient, say, would have been useful or meaningful. Nor will I address the very important issue of the unit of analysis used in this paper (i.e., the state) and the fallacies that may ensue when generalizing from states to families within the states. For issues concerning the unit of analysis, see Chapter 16.

ceeded to search for an explanation for their "finding," and concluded that severe winters in states with colder climates force children to stay home after school and on weekends and that this leads to greater interaction with their parents, which, in turn, leads to greater academic achievement.

Stating that they "may have stumbled" (p. 69) on a way to increase children's performance on standardized tests, the authors recommended, "Adopt programs that promote increased interaction between parents and children. Another solution, of course, is simply to move north" (p. 69).

I confess that while reading this piece I wondered whether it was meant as a spoof on this kind of abuse so prevalent in behavioral research. I am afraid, however, that the authors were dead serious. All I can say is: Read their statement and judge for yourself.

Lest you be inclined to think that educational researchers have a monopoly on "stumbling on" theories by "glancing" at data, consider the next example.

Lawyers and the GNP

Econometricians Datta and Nugent (1986) report that they "simply"[!] regressed "the rate of growth of per capita GNP . . . on the share of lawyers in the labor force" (p. 1458) in 52 countries. Having found the regression coefficient for the share of lawyers to be negative even after the inclusion of other variables in the regression equation, they concluded that the results "provide at least very tentative support for the hypothesis that, the higher are the percentages of the labor force induced to enter the legal profession . . . the lower may be the overall rate of per capita income growth" (p. 1459).

Rest assured that the authors *did not* propose to heed Dick's urging: "The first thing we do, let's kill all the lawyers" (Shakespeare, *Henry VI, Part II,* Act IV, Scene ii). Actually, doing this would go counter to their "theory," which I will not go into but whose essence you may discern from their concluding statement:

> The results of this paper suggest that societies which find ways of reducing the number of highly qualified people that are needed for resolving conflicts, thereby allowing people to concentrate on economically productive activities, may be better able to enjoy more rapid economic growth than societies which are not able to do so. (p. 1460)

Proxies and Intercorrelated Variables

As the major sources of errors in interpreting the results of regression analysis in nonexperimental research constitute the body of this chapter, I will not enumerate them here. Instead, I will make two points as a broad frame of reference.

One, variables used in nonexperimental research may be, and often are, proxies for causal variables not included in the regression equation (e.g., the number of books in the house as a proxy for home background). The size and sign of a regression coefficient associated with a proxy variable notwithstanding, obviously manipulating such a variable will not produce the presumed effect. Yet, one frequently encounters not only interpretation of proxies as if they were causal variables but also recommendations for policy decisions based on such interpretations. Thus, for example, in a nonexperimental study of reading achievement, Heim and Perl (1974) spoke of the cost effectiveness of different "inputs" and concluded, among other things, the following:

> Using the additional $100 per pupil available to upgrade the degree status of principals seemed most cost effective, suggesting an astounding 14 percentile gain. Use of these resources to upgrade teacher-degree-status levels is associated with a 9 percentile point gain, making this strategy the second most cost effective. (p. 26)

It requires little imagination to come up with a variety of variables for which the previous indices may serve as proxies.

Two, variables in nonexperimental research tend to be intercorrelated. Since more often than not researchers neither understand the causes of the interrelations nor attempt to study them, implications of regression coefficients for policy decisions are questionable. Specifically, statements about achieving a desired effect by changing a given independent variable while holding all others constant tend to have an air of fantasy about them, as is illustrated by the following example.

A researcher wishes to study the effects of a set of independent variables on academic achievement. Assume that among these are self-concept, locus of control, and motivation. It is known that these variables are intercorrelated, though the causes of the correlations are not clear, or are debatable, depending on one's theoretical formulations and assuming that such were attempted in the first place. Be that as it may, the notion of varying one of the variables while holding the others constant may be tenable from a statistical frame of reference (i.e., effecting a partialing process), but it is much more problematic from a theoretical or a practical frame of reference. Assuming that one can arrive at a clear explication of the relations among the variables, it is conceivable that varying one while holding the others constant is neither theoretically meaningful nor practically feasible. Hence, the air of fantasy. (See Smith, M. S., 1972, on this and related issues.)

With the preceding remarks in mind, I now present major sources of errors in the interpretation of regression coefficients as indices of effects.

SPECIFICATION ERRORS

I introduced the concept of specification errors in Chapter 2, where I stated that such errors refer to the use of a wrong or inappropriate model. Examples of such errors are: omitting relevant variables from the regression equation, including irrelevant variables in the regression equation, and postulating a linear model when a nonlinear model is more appropriate.

The most important thing to note about the foregoing is that it refers to a situation in which the researcher enunciated a model that describes the manner in which the independent variables affect the dependent variable. The regression equation, whose coefficients are to be estimated, is meant to reflect this model. The absence of a model precludes a meaningful interpretation of the estimated coefficients. In short, specification errors refer to a misspecified model, not to its absence. Following are some major aspects and consequences of specification errors.[3]

Omission of Relevant Variables

When relevant variables omitted from the regression equation are correlated with variables in the equation, estimation of the coefficients for the latter is biased. I show this for the case of two independent variables. Assume that the "true" model is

---

[3]For further discussions, see Bohrnstedt and Carter (1971), Deegan (1974), Duncan (1975, Chapter 8), Hanushek and Jackson (1977, pp. 79–86), Hocking (1974), and Kmenta (1971, pp. 391–405).

$$Y = a + b_1X_1 + b_2X_2 + e \tag{10.1}$$

but instead the researcher postulates the following:

$$Y = a + b_1X_1 + e' \tag{10.2}$$

In Chapter 2 I pointed out that one of the assumptions underlying regression analysis is that the variables not included in the model, and subsumed under the error term, are not correlated with the variables in the model. That is, in (10.1) it is assumed the e is not correlated with X_1 or X_2. Under such circumstances, the estimation of regression coefficients for the variables in the model is not biased. If, however, in the preceding example, the researcher uses (10.2) instead, and if X_1 and X_2 are correlated, it is obvious that the e', under which X_2 is subsumed, is correlated with X_1, thereby leading to bias in the estimation of the regression coefficient for X_1. It can be shown that[4]

$$b_{y1} = b_{y1.2} + b_{y2.1}b_{21} \tag{10.3}$$

where b_{y1} is the regression coefficient for the regression of Y on X_1 only; $b_{y1.2}$ and $b_{y2.1}$ are partial regression coefficients for the regression of Y on X_1 and X_2; and b_{21} is the regression coefficient for the regression of X_2 (the omitted variable) on X_1. b_{21} may be calculated as follows:

$$b_{21} = r_{21}\left(\frac{s_2}{s_1}\right) \tag{10.4}$$

where r_{21} is the correlation between X_2 and X_1; and s_2 and s_1 are standard deviations of X_2 and X_1, respectively. Substituting (10.4) in (10.3),

$$b_{y1} = b_{y1.2} + b_{y2.1}r_{21}\left(\frac{s_2}{s_1}\right) \tag{10.5}$$

Clearly, the source of bias in estimating b_{y1} is r_{21}. When $r_{21} = .00$, the second term on the right in (10.5) vanishes, and the estimation of b_{y1} is not biased. The size and the direction of the bias, when X_2 is omitted, depend on the sizes and signs of r_{21} and $b_{y2.1}$.

Numerical Examples

I now apply (10.3) to two sets of data, one in which the two independent variables are correlated and one in which they are not correlated. I use the illustrative data in Table 10.1 for this purpose.

Table 10.1   Illustrative Correlation Matrix, Means, and Standard Deviations; N = 100

	Y	X_1	X_2	X_3
Y	1.0	.7	.5	.5
X_1	.7	1.0	.6	.0
X_2	.5	.6	1.0	.4
X_3	.5	.0	.4	1.0
M:	50	30	40	40
s:	6	4	5	5

[4]For proofs, see references cited in Footnote 3. Although the estimation of a is also biased, I will not address this issue here.

Assume, first, that the researcher regresses Y on X_1 only and that the omitted variable is X_2. Using (10.4), I calculate the following:

$$b_{y1} = r_{y1}\left(\frac{s_y}{s_1}\right) = .7\left(\frac{6}{4}\right) = 1.05$$

$$b_{21} = r_{21}\left(\frac{s_2}{s_1}\right) = .6\left(\frac{5}{4}\right) = .75$$

Using (5.15) and (5.16) from Chapter 5, I calculate the following:

$$b_{y1.2} = \frac{r_{y1} - r_{y2}r_{12}}{1 - r_{12}^2}\left(\frac{s_y}{s_1}\right) = \frac{.7 - (.5)(.6)}{1 - .6^2}\left(\frac{6}{4}\right) = .9375$$

$$b_{y2.1} = \frac{r_{y2} - r_{y1}r_{12}}{1 - r_{12}^2}\left(\frac{s_y}{s_2}\right) = \frac{.5 - (.7)(.6)}{1 - .6^2}\left(\frac{6}{5}\right) = .15$$

Because the wrong model was used—(10.2) instead of (10.1)—the estimation of the regression coefficient for X_1, with the present data, is biased upward (from .9375 to 1.05).

Using the above results in (10.3),

$$b_{y1} = .9375 + (.15)(.75) = 1.05$$

Assume now that the researcher regresses Y on X_1, but that the omitted variable this time is X_3. Using the data of Table 10.1, I calculate the following:

$$b_{y1} = 1.05 \text{ (as in the preceding)}$$

$$b_{31} = r_{31}\left(\frac{s_3}{s_1}\right) = .00\left(\frac{5}{4}\right) = .00$$

$$b_{y1.3} = \frac{r_{y1} - r_{y3}r_{13}}{1 - r_{13}^2}\left(\frac{s_y}{s_1}\right) = \frac{.7 - (.5)(.0)}{1 - .0^2}\left(\frac{6}{4}\right) = 1.05$$

$$b_{y3.1} = \frac{r_{y3} - r_{y1}r_{13}}{1 - r_{13}^2}\left(\frac{s_y}{s_3}\right) = \frac{.5 - (.7)(.0)}{1 - .0^2}\left(\frac{6}{5}\right) = .6$$

Obviously, the estimation of b_{y1} is not biased (i.e., $b_{y1} = b_{y1.3}$). Applying (10.3),

$$b_{y1} = 1.05 + (.6)(.0) = 1.05$$

Of course, this is because $r_{31} = .00$; hence $b_{31} = .00$.

Extensions of the previous formulation to more than two independent variables are straightforward (see the references cited in Footnote 3).

In view of the fact that no estimation bias occurs when the omitted variables are not correlated with those of the model, one may be inclined to conclude that no harm is done by omitting such variables. Note, however, that when relevant variables not correlated with those in the equation are omitted, the standard errors of the latter are biased upward, thereby reducing the sensitivity of their statistical tests of significance and increasing the magnitudes of their confidence intervals. This is because the omitted variables are treated as error, resulting in a larger standard error of estimate, hence in larger standard errors for the b's.

I illustrate this by using the data for variables Y, X_1, and X_3 in Table 10.1. I will state the results without showing the calculations (you may wish to do the calculations as an exercise using formulas from either Chapter 5 or 6 or a computer program).

Previously, I showed that because the correlation between X_1 and X_3 is zero, the regression coefficient for X_1 is the same regardless of whether Y is regressed on X_1 only or on X_1 and X_3:

$$b_{y1} = b_{y1.3} = 1.05$$

When Y is regressed on X_1 only, the standard error of estimate $(s_{y.1})$ is 4.30666, and the standard error of b_{y1} is .10821. Consequently, the t ratio for this b is 9.70, with 98 df. But when Y is regressed on X_1 and X_3, the standard error of estimate $(s_{y.12})$ is 3.09079, and the standard error of $b_{y1.3} = .07766$. Therefore, the t ratio for this regression coefficient is 13.52, with 97 df.

The reduction in the standard error of the b for X_1 in the second analysis is a function of reducing the standard error of estimate due to the inclusion in the analysis of a variable (X_3) that is not correlated with X_1.

Inclusion of Irrelevant Variables

In an attempt to offset deleterious consequences of omitting relevant variables, some researchers are tempted to "play it safe" by including variables regarding whose effects they have no theoretical expectations. Sometimes, a researcher will include irrelevant variables in order to "see what will happen." Kmenta (1971) labeled such approaches as "kitchen sink models" (p. 397).

When irrelevant variables are included in the equation, the estimation of the regression coefficients is not biased. The inclusion of irrelevant variables has, however, two consequences. One, there is a loss in degrees of freedom, resulting in a larger standard error of estimate. This is not a serious problem when the sample size is relatively large, as it should always be. Two, to the extent that the irrelevant variables are correlated with relevant ones, the standard errors of the regression coefficients for the latter will be larger than when the irrelevant variables are not included in the equation.

In sum, then, although the inclusion of irrelevant variables is not nearly as serious as the omission of relevant ones, it should not be resorted to routinely and thoughtlessly. While the estimates of the regression coefficients are not biased in the presence of irrelevant variables, the efficiency of the tests of significance of the coefficients of the relevant variables may be decreased (see Rao, 1971, for a more detailed discussion; see also Mauro, 1990, for a method for estimating the effects of omitted variables).

Nonlinearity and Nonadditivity

The application of a linear additive model when a nonlinear or nonadditive one is called for is another instance of specification errors. Some forms of nonlinear relations may be handled in the context of multiple regression analysis by using powered vectors of variables, as is indicated in the following for the case of a single independent variable:

$$Y' = a + b_1X + b_2X^2 + \ldots b_kX^k \tag{10.6}$$

I discuss such models in Chapter 13.

Nonadditivity is generally treated under the heading of interaction, or joint, effects of independent variables on the dependent variable. In a two-variable model, for example, this approach takes the following form:

$$Y' = a + b_1X_1 + b_2X_2 + b_3X_1X_2 \tag{10.7}$$

where the product of X_1 and X_2 is meant to reflect the interaction between these variables. I discuss interaction in subsequent chapters (e.g., Chapter 12).

Detecting and Minimizing Specification Errors

Earlier, I illustrated some consequences of specification errors by contrasting parameter estimation in "true" and in misspecified models. The rub, however, is that the true model is seldom, if ever, known. "Indeed it would require no elaborate sophistry to show that we will never have the 'right' model in any absolute sense. Hence, we shall never be able to compare one of our many wrong models with a definitely right one" (Duncan, 1975, p. 101). The researcher is therefore faced with the most difficult task of detecting specification errors and minimizing them while not knowing what the true model is. Obviously, there is neither a simple nor an entirely satisfactory solution to this predicament.

Some specification errors are easier to detect and to eliminate or minimize than others. The simplest error to detect is probably the inclusion of irrelevant variables (see Kmenta, 1971, pp. 402–404, for testing procedures). Some forms of nonlinearities can be detected by, for example, comparing models with and without powered vectors of the variables (see Chapter 13). The need for fitting a nonlinear model can also be ascertained from the study of data and residual plots. (See Chapter 2 for a general discussion and the references therein for more advanced treatments of the topic. Figure 2.5 illustrates a residual plot that indicates the need for curvilinear analysis.)

The most pernicious specification errors are also the most difficult to detect. These are errors of omitting relevant variables. One possible approach is to plot residuals against a variable suspected to have been erroneously omitted. A nonrandom pattern in such a plot would suggest the need to include the variable in the model. The absence of a specific pattern in the residual plot, however, does not ensure that a specification error was not committed by not including the variable in the model (see Rao & Miller, 1971, p. 115).

The most important safeguard against committing specification errors is theory. The role of theory is aptly captured in the following anecdote related by Ulam (1976): "Once someone asked, 'Professor Whitehead, which is more important: ideas or things?' 'Why, I would say ideas about things,' was his instant reply" (pp. 118–119). It is the ideas about the data that count; it is they that provide the cement, the integration. Nothing can substitute for a theoretical model, which, as I stated earlier, the regression equation is meant to reflect. No amount of fancy statistical acrobatics will undo the harm that may result by using an ill-conceived theory or a caricature of a theory.[5]

MEASUREMENT ERRORS

In Chapter 2, I stated that one assumption of regression analysis is that the independent variables are measured without error. Various types of errors are subsumed under the generic term *measurement errors*. Jencks and coworkers (1979, pp. 34–36) classified such errors into three broad categories: conceptual, consistent, and random (see also Cochran, 1968, pp. 637–639).

Conceptual errors are committed when a proxy is used instead of the variable of interest either because of a lack of knowledge as to how to measure the latter or because the measure-

---

[5]See "The Role of Theory," later in this chapter.

ment of the former is more convenient and/or less expensive. For example, sometimes a measure of vocabulary is used as a proxy for mental ability. Clearly, an inference about the effect of mental ability based on a regression coefficient associated with a measure of vocabulary will be biased. The nature and size of the bias is generally not discernible because it depends, among other things, on the relation between the proxy and the variable of interest, which is rarely known.

Consistent, or systematic, errors occur for a variety of reasons. Respondents may, for example, provide systematically erroneous information (e.g., about income, age, years of education). Reporting errors may be conscious or unconscious.

Respondents are not the only source of systematic errors. Such errors may emanate from measuring instruments, research settings, interviewers, raters, and researchers, to name but some. The presence of systematic errors introduces bias in the estimation of regression coefficients. The direction and magnitude of the bias cannot be determined without knowing the direction and magnitude of the errors—an elusive task in most instances.

Random, or nonsystematic, errors occur, among other things, as a result of temporary fluctuations in respondents, raters, interviewers, settings, and the like. Much of psychometric theory is concerned with the effects of such errors on the reliability of measurement instruments (see Guilford, 1954; Nunnally, 1978; Pedhazur & Schmelkin, 1991, Part 1).

Most of the work on the effects of measurement errors on regression statistics was done with reference to random errors. Even in this area the work is limited to rudimentary, hence largely unrealistic, models. Yet what is known about effects of measurement errors should be of serious concern to researchers using multiple regression analysis. Unfortunately, most researchers do not seem to be bothered by measurement errors—either because they are unaware of their effects or because they do not know what to do about them. Jencks et al. (1972) characterized this general attitude, saying, "The most frequent approach to measurement error is indifference" (p. 330). Much of the inconsistencies and untrustworthiness of findings in social science research may be attributed to this indifference.

Following is a summary of what is known about effects of measurement errors on regression statistics, and some proposed remedies. I suggest that you study the references cited below to gain a better understanding of this topic.

In Chapter 2, I discussed effects of measurement errors in simple regression analysis. Briefly, I pointed out that measurement errors in the dependent variable are absorbed in the residual term and do not lead to bias in the estimation of the unstandardized regression coefficient (b). The standardized regression coefficient is attenuated by measurement errors in the dependent variable. Further, I pointed out that measurement errors in the independent variable lead to a downward bias in the estimation of both the b and the β.

Turning to multiple regression analysis, note that measurement errors in the dependent and/or the independent variables lead to a downward bias in the estimation of R^2. Cochran (1970), who discussed this point in detail, maintained that measurement errors are largely responsible for the disappointingly low R^2 values in much of the research in the social sciences. Commenting on studies in which complex human behavior was measured, Cochran (1970) stated, "The data were obtained by questionnaires filled out in a hurry by apparently disinterested graduate students. The proposal to consign this material at once to the circular file (except that my current wastebasket is rectangular) has some appeal" (p. 33).

As in simple regression analysis, measurement errors in the dependent variable do not lead to bias in the estimation of the b's, but they do lead to a downward bias in the estimation of the β's.

Unlike simple regression analysis, measurement errors in the independent variables in a multiple regression analysis may lead to either upward or downward bias in the estimation of regression coefficients. The effects of the errors are "complicated" (Cochran, 1968, p. 655).

In general, the lower the reliabilities of the measures or the higher the correlations among the variables (see the next section, "Collinearity"), the greater the distortions in the estimation of regression coefficients that result from measurement errors. Also, even if some of the independent variables are measured without error, the estimation of their regression coefficients may not be bias free because of the relations of such variables with others that are measured with errors.

Because of the complicated effects of measurement errors, it is possible, for example, that while $\beta_1 > \beta_2$ (where the β's are standardized regression coefficients that would be obtained if X_1 and X_2 were measured without error), $\beta'_1 < \beta'_2$ (where the β''s are standardized coefficients obtained when errors are present in the measurement of X_1 or X_2). "Thus, interpretation of the relative sizes of different regression coefficients may be severely distorted by errors of measurement" (Cochran, 1968, p. 656). (See the discussion, "Standardized or Unstandardized Coefficients?" offered later in this chapter.)

Measurement errors also bias the results of commonality analysis. For instance, since the uniqueness of a variable is related, among other things, to the size of the β associated with it (see Chapter 9), it follows that a biased β will lead to a biased estimation of uniqueness. Estimation of commonality elements, too, will be biased as a result of measurement errors (see Cochran, 1970, p. 33, for some examples).

Clearly, the presence of measurement errors may be very damaging to results of multiple regression analysis. Being indifferent to problems arising from the use of imperfect measures will not make go away. What, then, can one do about them? Various remedies and approaches were suggested. When the reliabilities of the measures are relatively high and one is willing to make the rather restrictive assumption that the errors are random, it is possible to introduce conventional corrections for attenuation prior to calculating the regression statistics (Lord & Novick, 1968; Nunnally, 1978). The use of corrections for attenuation, however, precludes tests of significance of regression coefficients in the usual way (Kenny, 1979, p. 83). Corrections for attenuation create other problems, particularly when there are high correlations among the variables or when there is a fair amount of variability in the reliabilities of the measures used (see Jencks et al., 1972, pp. 332–336; 1979, pp. 34–37).

Other approaches designed to detect and offset the biasing effects of measurement errors are discussed and illustrated in the following references: Bibby (1977); Blalock, Wells, and Carter (1970); Duncan (1975, Chapter 9); Johnston (1972, pp. 278–281); Kenny (1979, Chapter 5); and Zeller and Carmines (1980). In Chapter 19, I discuss, among other things, treatment of measurement errors in the context of structural equation models (SEM).

In conclusion, although various proposals to deal with measurement errors are important and useful, the goal of bridging the gap between theory and observed behavior by constructing highly valid and reliable measures deserves greater attention, sophistication, and expertise on the part of behavioral scientists.

COLLINEARITY

As will become evident directly, collinearity relates to the potential adverse effects of correlated independent variables on the estimation of regression statistics. In view of the fact that I devoted major portions of preceding chapters to this topic in the form of procedures for adjusting for correlations among independent variables (e.g., calculating partial regression coefficients, partitioning variance), you may wonder why I now devote a special section to it. The reason is that adverse effects may be particularly grave when correlations among independent variables are high, though there is, understandably, no agreement as to what "high" means.

Literally, *collinearity* refers to the case of data vectors representing two variables falling on the same line. This means that the two variables are perfectly correlated. However, most authors use the term to refer also to *near collinearity*. Until recently, the term multicollinearity was used to refer to collinear relations among more than two variables. In recent years, collinearity has come to be used generically to refer to near collinearity among a set of variables, and it is in this sense that I use it here. Whatever the term used, it refers to correlations among independent variables.

Collinearity may have devastating effects on regression statistics to the extent of rendering them useless, even highly misleading. Notably, this is manifested in imprecise estimates of regression coefficients. In the presence of collinearity, slight fluctuations in the data (e.g., due to sampling, measurement error, random error) may lead to substantial fluctuations in the sizes of such estimates or even to changes in their signs. Not surprisingly, Mandel (1982) asserted, "Undoubtedly, the greatest source of difficulties in using least squares is the existence of 'collinearity' in many sets of data" (p. 15).

In what follows, I present first approaches to the diagnosis of collinearity, in the context of which I discuss and illustrate some of its adverse effects. I then present some proposed remedies and alternative estimation procedures.

DIAGNOSTICS

Of the various procedures proposed for diagnosing collinearity, I will introduce the following: variance inflation factor (VIF), condition indices, and variance-decomposition proportions. For a much more thorough treatment of these procedures, as well as critical evaluations of others, see Belsley's (1991) authoritative book.

Variance Inflation Factor (VIF)

Collinearity has extremely adverse effects on the standard errors of regression coefficients. This can be readily seen by examining the formula for the standard error of a regression coefficient for the case of two independent variables. In Chapter 5—see (5.25) and the discussion related to it—I showed that the standard error for b_1, say, is

$$s_{b_{y1.2}} = \sqrt{\frac{s_{y.12}^2}{\Sigma x_1^2 (1 - r_{12}^2)}} \tag{10.8}$$

where $s_{y.12}^2$ = variance of estimate; Σx_1^2 = sum of squares of X_1; and r_{12}^2 = squared correlation between independent variables X_1 and X_2.

Note that, other things equal, the standard error is at a minimum when $r_{12} = .00$. The larger r_{12}, the larger the standard error. When $r_{12} = |1.00|$, the denominator is zero, and the standard error is indeterminate. In Chapter 5 (see "Tests of Regression Coefficients"), I showed that the t ratio for the test of a b is obtained by dividing the latter by its standard error. It follows that the t ratio becomes increasingly smaller, and the confidence interval for the b increasingly wider, as the standard error of the b becomes increasingly larger.

In the diagnosis of collinearity, the focus is on the variance of b, which is, of course, the square of (10.8):

$$s^2_{b_{y1.2}} = \frac{s^2_{y.12}}{\Sigma x_1^2(1 - r_{12}^2)} = \frac{s^2_{y.12}}{\Sigma x_1^2}\left[\frac{1}{1 - r_{12}^2}\right] \tag{10.9}$$

The term in the brackets is labeled the variance inflation factor (VIF), as it indicates the inflation of the variance of b as a consequence of the correlation between the independent variables. Note that when $r_{12}^2 = .00$, VIF $= 1.00$. The higher the correlation between the independent variables, the greater the inflation of the variance of the b.

What I said about the case of two independent variables is true for any number of independent variables. This can be seen from the formula for the standard error of a regression coefficient when $k > 2$. The standard error of b_1, say, as given in Chapter 5, is

$$s_{b_{y1.2...k}} = \sqrt{\frac{s^2_{y.12...k}}{\Sigma x_1^2(1 - R_{1.2...k}^2)}} \tag{10.10}$$

where the terms are as defined under (10.8), except that $s^2_{y.12}$ is replaced by $s^2_{y.12...k}$, and r_{12}^2 is replaced by $R_{1.2...k}^2 = $ the squared multiple correlation between X_1, used as a dependent variable, and X_2 to X_k as the independent variables. Obviously, (10.8) is a special case of (10.10).

The variance of b when $k > 2$ is, of course, the square of (10.10), from which it follows that

$$\text{VIF}_1 = \frac{1}{1 - R_{1.2...k}^2}$$

Or, more generally,

$$\text{VIF}_i = \frac{1}{1 - R_i^2} \tag{10.11}$$

where $1 - R_i^2$ is the squared multiple correlation of independent variable i with the remaining independent variables.

From (10.10) or (10.11) it should be clear that in designs with more than two independent variables it is insufficient to diagnose collinearity solely based on zero-order correlations—a practice prevalent in the research literature (see "Collinearity Diagnosis in Practice," presented later in the chapter). Clearly, the zero-order correlations may be low, and yet a given R_i^2 may be high, even perfect.

Matrix Operations

Returning to the case of two independent variables, I will use matrix algebra to elaborate on VIF and related concepts. In Chapter 6, I presented and illustrated the use of matrix algebra for the calculation of regression statistics. For the case of standardized variables (i.e., when correlations are used), I presented the following equation—see (6.15) and the discussion related to it:

$$\beta = \mathbf{R}^{-1}\mathbf{r} \tag{10.12}$$

where β is a column vector of standardized coefficients; $\mathbf{R}^{-1}$ is the inverse of the correlation matrix of the independent variables; and $\mathbf{r}$ is a column vector of correlations between each independent variable and the dependent variable.[6]

---

[6]When necessary, refer to Appendix A for a discussion of the matrix terminology and operations I use here.

In Chapter 6, I showed how to invert a 2×2 matrix (see also Appendix A). Briefly, given

$$\mathbf{R} = \begin{bmatrix} a & b \\ c & d \end{bmatrix}$$

then to invert $\mathbf{R}$, find its determinant: $|\mathbf{R}| = ad - bc$; interchange the elements of the main diagonal (i.e., a with d); change the signs of b and c; and divide each element by $|\mathbf{R}|$. The resulting matrix is the inverse of $\mathbf{R}$. When the matrix is one of correlations (i.e., $\mathbf{R}$), its main diagonal consists of 1's and its off-diagonal elements of correlation coefficients. For two independent variables,

$$\mathbf{R} = \begin{bmatrix} 1.00 & r_{12} \\ r_{21} & 1.00 \end{bmatrix}$$

$$|\mathbf{R}| = (1)(1) - (r_{12})(r_{21}) = 1 - r_{12}^2$$

and

$$\mathbf{R}^{-1} = \begin{bmatrix} \dfrac{1.00}{1 - r_{12}^2} & \dfrac{-r_{12}}{1 - r_{12}^2} \\ \dfrac{-r_{21}}{1 - r_{12}^2} & \dfrac{1.00}{1 - r_{12}^2} \end{bmatrix}$$

Note that the principal diagonal of $\mathbf{R}^{-1}$ (i.e., from the upper left corner to the lower right) consists of VIFs (the same is true when $\mathbf{R}$ is composed of more than two independent variables). As I showed earlier, the larger r_{12}, the larger the VIF. Also, when $r_{12} = .00$, $\mathbf{R}$ is an identity matrix:

$$\mathbf{R} = \begin{bmatrix} 1.00 & 0 \\ 0 & 1.00 \end{bmatrix}$$

The determinant of an identity matrix of any size is 1.00. Under such circumstances, $\mathbf{R}^{-1} = \mathbf{R}$.

Two variables are said to be *orthogonal* when they are at right angles (90°). The correlation between orthogonal variables is zero. A matrix consisting of orthogonal independent variables is referred to as an orthogonal matrix. An orthogonal *correlation matrix* is an identity matrix.

Consider now what happens when, for the case of two independent variables, $|r_{12}| > 0$. When this occurs, the determinant of $\mathbf{R}$ is a fraction that becomes increasingly smaller as the correlation between X_1 and X_2 increases. When r_{12} reaches its maximum (i.e., $|1.00|$), $|\mathbf{R}| = .00$. Recall that in the process of inverting $\mathbf{R}$, each of its elements is divided by the determinant of $\mathbf{R}$. Obviously, $\mathbf{R}$ cannot be inverted when its determinant is zero. A matrix that cannot be inverted is said to be *singular*. Exact collinearity results in a singular matrix. Under such circumstances, the regression coefficients are indeterminate.

A matrix is singular when it contains at least one linear dependency. *Linear dependency* means that one vector in the matrix may be derived from another vector or, when dealing with more than two variables, from a linear combination of more than one of the other vectors in the matrix. Some examples of linear dependencies are: $X_2 = 3X_1$, that is, each element in vector X_2 is three times its corresponding element in X_1; $X_1 = X_2 + X_3$; $X_3 = .5X_1 + 1.7X_2 - .3X_4$. Although linear dependencies do not generally occur in behavioral research, they may be introduced by an unwary researcher. For example, assume that one is using a test battery consisting of four subtests as part of the matrix of the independent variables. If, in addition to the scores on the subtests, their sum is used as a total score, a linear dependency is introduced, causing the matrix to be singular. Other examples of linear dependencies that may be introduced inadvertently by a researcher are when (1) a categorical variable is coded for use in multiple regression analysis and the number of coded vectors is equal to the number of categories (see Chapter 11) and (2) an ipsative measure (e.g., a rank-order scale) is used in multiple regression analysis (see Clemans, 1965).

When a matrix contains linear dependencies, information from some variables is completely redundant with that available from other variables and is therefore useless for regression analysis. In the case of two independent variables, the existence of a linear dependency is evident when the correlation between them is perfect. Under such circumstances, either variable, but not both, may be used in a regression analysis. When more than two independent variables are used, inspecting the zero-order correlations among them does not suffice to ascertain whether linear dependencies exist in the matrix. When the determinant of the matrix is zero, at least one linear dependency is indicated.

To reiterate: the larger the VIF, the larger the standard error of the regression coefficient in question. Accordingly, it has been proposed that large VIFs be used as indicators of regression coefficients adversely affected by collinearity. While useful, VIF is not without shortcomings. Belsley (1984b), who discussed this topic in detail, pointed out, among other things, that

> no diagnostic threshold has yet been systematically established for them [VIFs]—the value of 10 frequently offered is without meaningful foundation, and . . . they are unable to determine the number of coexisting near-dependencies. (p. 92)

Arguing cogently in favor of the diagnostics presented in the next section, Belsley nevertheless stated that when not having access to them he "would consider the VIFs simple, useful, and second best" (p. 92; see also Belsley, 1991, e.g., pp. 27–30).

It is instructive to note the relation between the diagonal elements of $\mathbf{R}^{-1}$ and the squared multiple correlation of each of the independent variables with the remaining ones.

$$R_i^2 = 1 - \frac{1}{r^{ii}} = 1 - \frac{1}{\text{VIF}_i} \tag{10.13}$$

where R_i^2 is the squared multiple correlation of X_i with the remaining independent variables; and r^{ii} is the diagonal element of the inverse of the correlation matrix for variable i. From (10.13) it is evident that the larger r^{ii}, or VIF, the higher the squared multiple correlation of X_i with the remaining X's.

Applying (10.13) to the 2×2 matrix given earlier,

$$R_1^2 = 1 - \frac{1}{\left(\dfrac{1}{1 - r_{12}^2}\right)} = 1 - (1 - r_{12}^2) = r_{12}^2$$

and similarly for R_2^2 because only two independent variables are used.

Tolerance

Collinearity has adverse effects not only on the standard errors of regression coefficients, but also on the accuracy of computations due to rounding errors. To guard against such occurrences, most computer programs resort to the concept of *tolerance,* which is defined as $1 - R_i^2$. From (10.13) it follows that

$$\text{Tolerance} = 1 - R_i^2 = \frac{1}{\text{VIF}_i} \tag{10.14}$$

The smaller the tolerance, the greater the computational problems arising from rounding errors.

Not unexpectedly, there is no agreement on what constitutes "small" tolerance. For example, BMDP (Dixon, 1992, Vol. 1, p. 413) uses a tolerance of .01 as a default cutoff for entering variables into the analysis. That is, variables with tolerance < .01 are not entered. MINITAB (Minitab Inc., 1995a, p. 9–9) and SPSS (SPSS Inc., 1993, p. 630) use a default value of .0001. Generally, the user can override the default value. When this is done, the program issues a warning. Whether or not one overrides the default tolerance value depends on one's aims. Thus, in Chapter 13, I override the default tolerance value and explain why I do so.

Condition Indices and Variance-Decomposition Proportions

An operation on a data matrix—one that plays an important role in much of multivariate analysis—is to decompose it to its basic structure. The process by which this is accomplished is called singular value decomposition (SVD). I will not explain the process of calculating SVD, but rather I will show how results obtained from it are used for diagnosing collinearity. Following are references to some very good introductions to SVD: Belsley (1991, pp. 42–50; Belsley's book is the most thorough treatment of the utilization of SVD for diagnosing collinearity), Green (1976, pp. 230–240; 1978, pp. 348–351), and Mandel (1982). For more advanced treatments, see Horst (1963, Chapters 17 and 18) and Lunneborg and Abbott (1983, Chapter 4).

Numerical Examples[7]

I will use several numerical examples to illustrate the concepts I have presented thus far (e.g., VIF, tolerance), utilization of the results derived from SVD, and some related issues. Of the four packages I use in this book (see Chapter 4), SAS and SPSS provide thorough collinearity diagnostics. As the procedures I will be using from these packages report virtually the same type of collinearity diagnostics, I will use them alternately. In the interest of space, I will give input to either of the programs only once, and I will limit the output and my commentaries to issues relevant to the topic under consideration. Though I will edit the output drastically, I will retain its basic layout to facilitate your comparisons with output of these or other programs you may be using.

Examples in Which Correlations of the Independent Variables with the Dependent Variable Are Identical

Table 10.2 presents two illustrative summary data sets, (a) and (b), composed of correlation matrices, means, and standard deviations. Note that the two data sets are identical in all respects, except for the correlation between X_2 and X_3, which is low (.10) in (a) and high (.85) in (b).

---

[7]The numerical examples in this and the next section are patterned after those in Gordon's (1968) excellent paper, which deserves careful study.

Table 10.2   Two Illustrative Data Sets with Three Independent Variables; N = 100

| | (a) | | | | (b) | | | |
	X_1	X_2	X_3	Y	X_1	X_2	X_3	Y
X_1	1.00	.20	.20	.50	1.00	.20	.20	.50
X_2	.20	1.00	.10	.50	.20	1.00	.85	.50
X_3	.20	.10	1.00	.50	.20	.85	1.00	.50
Y	.50	.50	.50	1.00	.50	.50	.50	1.00
M:	7.60	7.70	7.14	32.31	7.60	7.70	7.14	32.31
s:	2.57	2.59	2.76	6.85	2.57	2.59	2.76	6.85

SPSS

Input

```
TITLE TABLE 10.2 (A).
MATRIX DATA VARIABLES ROWTYPE_ X1 X2 X3 Y.
BEGIN DATA
MEAN 7.60   7.70   7.14   32.31
STDDEV 2.57   2.59   2.76   6.85
N 100 100 100 100
CORR 1.00
CORR .20   1.00
CORR .20   .10   1.00
CORR .50   .50   .50   1.00
END DATA
REGRESSION MATRIX=IN(*)/VAR X1 TO Y/DES/STAT ALL/
    DEP Y/ENTER.
```

Commentary

In Chapter 7, I gave an example of reading summary data (a correlation matrix and *N*) in SPSS, using CONTENTS to specify the type of data read. Here I use instead ROWTYPE, where the data of each row are identified (e.g., MEAN for row of means). To use CONTENTS with these data, specify CONTENTS=MEAN SD N CORR. If you do this, delete the labels I attached to each row.

As I explained in Chapter 4, I use STAT ALL. To limit your output, use the keyword COLLIN in the STAT subcommand. Note that I used the subcommand ENTER without specifying any independent variables. Consequently, all the independent variables (X1, X2, and X3 in the present example) will be entered.

The input file is for the data in (a) of Table 10.2. To run the analysis for the data in (b), all you need to do is change the correlation between X2 and X3 from .10 to .85.

Output

| TITLE TABLE 10.2 (A). | | | TITLE TABLE 10.2 (B). | |

	Mean	Std Dev
X1	7.600	2.570
X2	7.700	2.590
X3	7.140	2.760
Y	32.310	6.850

N of Cases = 100

Correlation:

	X1	X2	X3	Y
X1	1.000	.200	.200	.500
X2	.200	1.000	.100	.500
X3	.200	.100	1.000	.500
Y	.500	.500	.500	1.000

Dependent Variable.. Y

Variable(s) Entered on Step Number 1.. X1
2.. X2
3.. X3

Multiple R	.75082
R Square	.56373
Adjusted R Square	.55009
Standard Error	4.59465

------------------------ Variables in the Equation ------------------------

Variable	B	SE B	Beta	Tol.	VIF	T	Sig T
X1	.91459	.18659	.34314	.92727	1.08	4.90	.000
X2	1.03717	.18233	.39216	.95625	1.05	5.69	.000
X3	.97329	.17110	.39216	.95625	1.05	5.69	.000
(Constant)	10.42364	2.02391				5.15	.000

TITLE TABLE 10.2 (B).

	Mean	Std Dev
X1	7.600	2.570
X2	7.700	2.590
X3	7.140	2.760
Y	32.310	6.850

N of Cases = 100

Correlation:

	X1	X2	X3	Y
X1	1.000	.200	.200	.500
X2	.200	1.000	.850	.500
X3	.200	.850	1.000	.500
Y	.500	.500	.500	1.000

Dependent Variable.. Y

Variable(s) Entered on Step Number 1.. X1
2.. X2
3.. X3

Multiple R	.65635
R Square	.43079
Adjusted R Square	.41300
Standard Error	5.24818

------------------------ Variables in the Equation ------------------------

Variable	B	SE B	Beta	Tol.	VIF	T	Sig T
X1	1.09175	.20983	.40961	.95676	1.05	5.20	.000
X2	.59769	.38725	.22599	.27656	3.62	1.54	.126
X3	.56088	.36340	.22599	.27656	3.62	1.54	.126
(Constant)	15.40582	2.08622				7.39	.000

Commentary

I placed excerpts of output from analyses of (a) *and* (b) of Table 10.2 alongside each other to facilitate comparisons. As I stated earlier, my comments will be limited to the topic under consideration.

Earlier in this chapter—see (10.14)—I defined tolerance as $1 - R_i^2$, where R_i^2 is the squared multiple correlation of independent variable i with the remaining independent variables. Recall that tolerance of 1.00 means that the independent variable in question is not correlated with the remaining independent variables, hence all the information it provides is unique. In contrast, .00 tolerance means that the variable in question is perfectly correlated with the remaining independent variables, hence the information it provides is completely redundant with that provided by the remaining independent variables. Examine now Tol(erance) for the two data sets and notice that in (a) it is > .9 for all the variables, whereas in (b) it is .96 for X1 but .28 for X2 and X3. Hence, $R_2^2 = R_3^2 = .72$. In the present example, it is easy to see that the source of the redundancy in X2 and X3 is due primarily to the correlation between them. With larger matrices, and with a more complex pattern of correlations among the variables, inspection of the zero-order correlations would not suffice to reveal sources of redundancies. Also, being a global index, R_i^2 does not provide information about the sources of redundancy of the independent variable in question with the remaining independent variables.

Earlier, I defined VIF as $1/(1 - R_i^2)$—see (10.11), where I pointed out that it is at a minimum (1.00) when the correlation between the independent variable in question with the remaining independent variables is zero. Note that all the VIFs in (a) are close to the minimum, whereas those for X2 and X3 in (b) are 3.62. Recall that a relatively large VIF indicates that the estimation of the regression coefficient with which it is associated is adversely affected.

Examine and compare the B's for the respective variables in the two regression equations and note that whereas the B for X1 is about the same in the two analyses, the B's for X2 and X3 in (b) are about half the sizes of their counterparts in (a). Recalling that the B's are partial regression coefficients, it follows that when, as in (b), variables that are highly correlated are partialed, the B's are smaller. As expected from the VIFs, the standard errors of the B's for X2 and X3 in (b) are about twice those for the same variables in (a). Taken together, the preceding explains why the B's for X2 and X3 in (a) are statistically significant at conventional levels (e.g., .05), whereas those in (b) are not.

Because of the nature of the present data (e.g., equal standard deviations), it was relatively easy to compare B's across regression equations. In more realistic situations, such comparisons could not be carried out as easily. Instead, the effect of collinearity could be readily seen from comparisons of Betas (standardized regression coefficients). For convenience, I focus on Betas (β) in the discussion that follows.

In connection with the present discussion, it is useful to introduce a distinction Gordon (1968) made between *redundancy* (or *high correlation* between independent variables, no matter what the number of variables) and *repetitiveness* (or the *number* of redundant variables, regardless of the degree of redundancy among them). An example of repetitiveness would be the use of more than one measure of a variable (e.g., two or more measures of intelligence). Gordon gave dramatic examples of how repetitiveness leads to a reduction in the size of the β's associated with the variables comprising the repeated set. To clarify the point, consider an analysis in which intelligence is one of the independent variables and a single measure of this variable is used. The β associated with intelligence would presumably reflect its effect on the dependent variable, while partialing out all the other independent variables. Assume now that the researcher regards intelligence to be the more important variable and therefore decides to use two measures of it, while using single measures of the other independent variables. In a regression analysis with the two measures of intelligence, the β that was originally obtained for the single measure would split between the two measures, leading to a conclusion that intelligence is less effective than it appeared to have been when it was represented by a single measure. Using three measures for the same variable would split the β among the three of them. In sum, then, increasing repetitiveness leads to increasingly smaller β's.

For the sake of illustration, assume that X_2 and X_3 of data (b) in Table 10.2 are measures of the same variable. Had Y been regressed on X_1 and X_2 only (or on X_1 and X_3 only)—that is, had only one measure of the variable been used—$\beta_{y2.1}$ (or $\beta_{y3.1}$) would have been .41667.[8] When both measures are used, $\beta_{y1.23} = .4096$, but $\beta_{y2.13} = \beta_{y3.12} = .22599$ (see the preceding). Note also that, with the present sample size (100), $\beta_{y2.1}$ (or $\beta_{y3.1}$) would be declared statistically significant at, say, .05 level ($t = 5.26$, with 97 df). Recall, however, that the $\beta_{y2.13}$ and $\beta_{y3.12}$ are statistically not significant at the .05 level (see the previous output). Thus, using one measure for the variable under consideration, one would conclude that it has a statistically significant effect on the dependent variable. Using two measures of the same variable, however, would lead one to conclude that neither has a statistically significant effect on the dependent variable (see the following discussion).

Researchers frequently introduce collinearity by using multiple indicators for variables in which they have greater interest or which they deem more important from a theoretical point of view. This is not to say that multiple indicators are not useful or that they should be avoided. On the contrary, they are of utmost importance (see Chapter 19). But it is necessary to recognize that when multiple indicators are used in a regression analysis, they are treated as if they were distinct variables. As I stated earlier, the β that would have been obtained for an indicator of a variable had it been the only one used in the equation would split when several indicators of the variable are used, resulting in relatively small β's for each. Under such circumstances, a researcher using β's as indices of effects may end up concluding that what was initially considered a tangential variable, and therefore represented in the regression equation by a single indicator, is more important, or has a stronger effect, than a variable that was considered important and was therefore represented by several indicators.

Recall that collinearity leads not only to a reduction in the size of β's for the variables with low tolerance (or large VIFs), but also to inflation of the standard errors. Because of such effects, the presence of collinearity may lead to seemingly puzzling results, as when the squared multiple correlation of the dependent variable with a set of independent variables is statistically significant but *none* of the regression coefficients is statistically significant. While some view such results as contradictory, there is nothing contradictory about them, as each of the tests addresses a different question. The test of R^2 addresses the question of whether one or more of the regression coefficients are statistically significant (i.e., different from zero) against the hypothesis that all are equal to zero. The test of a single regression coefficient, on the other hand, addresses the question whether it differs from zero, while partialing out all the other variables.[9]

Output

Collinearity Diagnostics (a)

Number	Eigenval	Cond Index	Variance Constant	Proportions X1	X2	X3
1	3.77653	1.000	.00351	.00624	.00633	.00799
2	.10598	5.969	.00346	.02918	.26750	.77411
3	.07931	6.900	.00025	.74946	.39691	.06589
4	.03817	9.946	.99278	.21512	.32926	.15201

Collinearity Diagnostics (b)

Number	Eigenval	Cond Index	Variance Constant	Proportions X1	X2	X3
1	3.81916	1.000	.00416	.00622	.00185	.00234
2	.11726	5.707	.04263	.38382	.04076	.08719
3	.04689	9.025	.87644	.60810	.00075	.04275
4	.01669	15.128	.07677	.00187	.95664	.86772

[8]You may find it useful to run this analysis and compare your output with what I am reporting. Incidentally, you can get the results from both analyses by specifying ENTER X1 X2/ENTER X3. The output for the first step will correspond to what I am reporting here, whereas the output for the second step will correspond to what I reported earlier.

[9]See "Tests of Significance and Interpretations" in Chapter 5.

Commentary

The preceding results were obtained from the application of singular value decomposition (SVD). I explain Eigenval(ue), symbolized as λ, in Chapter 20. For present purposes, I will only point out that an eigenvalue equal to zero indicates a linear dependency (see the preceding section) in the data. Small eigenvalues indicate near linear dependencies. Instead of examining eigenvalues for near linear dependencies, indices based on them are used.

Condition Indices

Two indices were proposed: *condition number (CN)* and *condition index (CI)*. The former is defined as follows:

$$CN = \sqrt{\frac{\lambda_{max}}{\lambda_{min}}} \qquad (10.15)$$

where CN = condition number; λ_{max} = largest eigenvalue; and λ_{min} = smallest eigenvalue. CN "provides summary information on the potential difficulties to be encountered in various calculations . . . the larger the condition number, the more ill conditioned the given matrix" (Belsley, 1991, p. 50).

Condition index is defined as follows:

$$CI_i = \sqrt{\frac{\lambda_{max}}{\lambda_i}} \qquad (10.16)$$

where CI = condition index; λ_{max} = largest eigenvalue; and λ_i = the ith eigenvalue.

Examine now the column labeled Cond(ition) Index in the output for the (a) data set (the left segment) and notice that it is obtained, in accordance with (10.16), by taking the square root of the ratio of the first eigenvalue to succeeding ones. Thus, for instance, the second condition index is obtained as follows:

$$CI_2 = \sqrt{\frac{3.77653}{.10598}} = 5.969$$

Similarly, this is true for the other values. Note that the last value (9.946) is the condition number to which I referred earlier. The condition number, then, is the largest of the condition indices.

There is no consensus as to what constitutes a large condition number. Moreover, some deem the condition number of "limited value as a collinearity diagnostic" (Snee & Marquardt, 1984, p. 87) and prefer VIF for such purposes. Responding to his critics, Belsley (1984b) pointed out that he did not recommend the use of the condition number by itself, but rather the utilization of the "full set of condition indexes" (p. 92) in conjunction with the variance-decomposition proportions, a topic to which I now turn.

Variance-Decomposition Proportions

Examine the excerpt of output given earlier and notice the Variance Proportions section, which is composed of a column for the intercept and one for each of the independent variables. *Variance proportions* refers to the proportion of variance of the intercept (*a*) and each of the regression coefficients (*b*) associated with each of the condition indices. Accordingly, each column sums to 1.0.

I will attempt to clarify the meaning of the preceding by using, as an example, the values in column X1 for data set (a)—the left segment of the preceding output. Multiplying each value by 100 shows that about .6% of the variance of b_1 is associated with the first condition index, about 3% with the second, about 75% with the third, and about 22% with the fourth. Similarly, this is true for the other columns.

For diagnosing collinearity, it was suggested (e.g., Belsley, 1991; Belsley et al., 1980) that large condition indices be scrutinized to identify those associated with large variance proportions for two or more coefficients. Specifically, collinearity is indicated for the variables whose coefficients have large variances associated with a given large condition index.

As you probably surmised by now, the issue of what constitute "large" in the preceding statements is addressed through rules of thumb. For example, Belsley (1991) stated that "weak dependencies are associated with condition indexes around 5–10, whereas moderate to strong relations are associated with condition indexes of 30–100" (p. 56). Most authors deem a variance proportion of .5 or greater as large.

With the foregoing in mind, examine the Variance Proportions for data sets (a) and (b) in Table 10.2, given in the previous output. Turning first to (a), notice that none of the b's has a large variance proportion associated with the largest condition index. Even for the smaller condition indices, no more than one b has a variance proportion > .5 associated with it. Taken together, this is evidence of the absence of collinearity in (a).

The situation is quite different in (b). First, the largest condition index is 15.128. Second, both b_2 and b_3 have large variance proportions associated with it (.95664 and .86772, respectively). This is not surprising when you recall that $r_{23} = .85$. You may even wonder about the value of going through complex calculations and interpretations when an examination of the correlation would have sufficed. Recall, however, that I purposely used this simple example to illustrate how collinearity is diagnosed. Further, as I stated earlier, with more variables and/or more complex patterns of correlations, an examination of zero-order correlations would not suffice to diagnose collinearities.

A valuable aspect of using condition indices with variance-decomposition proportions is that, in contrast to global indices (e.g., a small determinant of the matrix of the independent variables), it enables one to determine the number of near linear dependencies and to identify the variables involved in each.

Before turning to some comments about collinearity diagnosis in practice, I will address two additional topics: scaling and centering.

Scaling

The units in which the measures of the independent variables are expressed affect the size of condition indices as well as variance-decomposition proportions. Thus, for example, age expressed in years, and height expressed in feet would result in different indices and different variance proportions than age expressed in months, and height expressed in inches. To avoid this undesirable state of affairs, it is recommended that one "scale each column to have equal length—column equilibration" (Belsley, 1991, p. 66). An approach for doing this that probably comes readily to mind is to standardize the variables (i.e., transform the scores to z scores, having a mean of zero and a standard deviation of one). This, however, is not a viable approach (see the next section).

As Belsley (1991) pointed out, "the exact length to which the columns are scaled is unimportant, just so long as they are equal, since the condition indexes are readily seen to be invariant to scale changes that affect columns equally" (p. 66). Nonetheless, Belsley recommended that the variables be scaled to have unit length. What this means is that the sum of the squares of each variable is equal to 1.00 (another term used for such scaling is *normalization*). This is accomplished by dividing each score by the square root of the sum of the squares of the variable in question. Thus, to scale variable X to unit length, divide each X by $\sqrt{\Sigma X^2}$. For the sake of illustration, assume that X is composed of four scores as follows: 2, 4, 4, and 8. To normalize X, divide each score by $\sqrt{2^2 + 4^2 + 4^2 + 8^2} = 10$. The sum of the squares of the scaled X is

$$(2/10)^2 + (4/10)^2 + (4/10)^2 + (8/10)^2 = 1.00$$

Centering

When the mean of a variable is subtracted from each score, the variable is said to be centered. Various authors have recommended that variables be centered to minimize collinearity. In this connection it is useful to make note of a distinction between "*essential*" and "*nonessential*" collinearity (Marquardt, 1980, p. 87). Essential collinearity refers to the type of collinearity I discussed thus far. An example of nonessential collinearity is when, say, X and X^2 are used to study whether there is a quadratic relation between X and Y. I present this topic in Chapter 13. For present purposes, I will only point out that the correlation between X and X^2 tends to be high and it is this nonessential collinearity that can be minimized by centering X. In contrast, centering X in the case of essential collinearity does not reduce it, though it may mask it by affecting some of the indices used to diagnose it. It is for this reason that Belsley (1984a) argued cogently, I believe, against centering when attempting to diagnose collinearity.

A Numerical Example

I will use a numerical example to illustrate the imprudence of centering variables when attempting to diagnose collinearity. For this purpose, I will reanalyze data set (b) in Table 10.2, using as input the correlation matrix only. Recall that a correlation is a covariance of standard scores—see (2.39) and the discussion related to it. Hence, using the correlation matrix only is tantamount to scaling as well as centering the variables.

I will not give input statements, as they are very similar to those I gave earlier in connection with the analysis of data set (a) in Table 10.2. Recall that in the analyses of (a) and (b) in Table 10.2, I included means and standard deviations in addition to the correlation matrix. For present purposes, then, I removed the two lines comprising the means and the standard deviations.

Output

-- Variables in the Equation --

Variable	Beta	SE Beta	Part Cor	Partial	Tolerance	VIF	T	Sig T
X1	.409605	.078723	.400650	.469013	.956757	1.045	5.203	.0000
X2	.225989	.146421	.118846	.155606	.276563	3.616	1.543	.1260
X3	.225989	.146421	.118846	.155606	.276563	3.616	1.543	.1260

Number	Eigenval	Cond Index	Variance Constant	Proportions X1	X2	X3
1	1.93551	1.000	.00000	.04140	.06546	.06546
2	1.00000	1.391	1.00000	.00000	.00000	.00000
3	.91449	1.455	.00000	.95860	.01266	.01266
4	.15000	3.592	.00000	.00000	.92187	.92188

Commentary

I reproduced only output relevant for present concerns. Recall that when correlations are analyzed, only standardized regression coefficients (Betas) are obtained. Although the program reports both B's (not reproduced in the preceding) and Betas, the former are the same as the latter. Also, the intercept is equal to zero. As expected, Betas reported here are identical to those reported in the preceding where I included also means and standard deviations in the input. The same is, of course, true for Tolerance, VIF, and the T ratios. In other words, the effects of collinearity, whatever they are, are manifested in the same way here as they were in the earlier analysis. Based of either analysis, one would conclude that the regression coefficients for X_2 and X_3 are statistically not significant at, say, the .05 level, and that this is primarily due to the high correlation between the variables in question.

Examine now the column labeled Cond(ition) Index and notice that the largest (i.e., the condition number; see Condition Indices in the preceding) is considerably smaller than the one I obtained earlier (15.128) when I also included means and standard deviations. Thus, examining the condition indices in the present analysis would lead to a conclusion at variance with the one arrived at based on the condition indices obtained in the earlier analysis. True, the variance proportions for the coefficients of X_2 and X_3 associated with the condition number are large, but they are associated with what is deemed a small condition index.

In sum, the earlier analysis, when the data were not centered, would lead to the conclusion that collinearity poses a problem, whereas the analysis of the centered data might lead to the opposite conclusion.

Lest you be inclined to think that there is a consensus on centering variables, I will point out that various authors have taken issue with Belsley's (1984a) position (see the comments following his paper). It is noteworthy that in his reply, Belsley (1984b) expressed his concern that "rather than clearing the air," the comments on his paper "serve[d] only to muddy the waters" (p. 90). To reiterate: I believe that Belsley makes a strong case against centering.

In concluding this section, I will use the results of the present analysis to illustrate and underscore some points I made earlier about the adverse effects of using multiple indicators of a variable in multiple regression analysis.

As in the earlier discussion, assume that X_2 and X_3 are indicators of the same variable (e.g., two measures of mental ability, socioeconomic status). With this in mind, examine the part and partial correlations associated with these measures in the previous output (.118846 and .155606, respectively). Recall that the correlation of each of these measures with the dependent variable is .50 (see Table 10.2). But primarily because of the high correlation between X_2 and X_3 (.85), the part and partial correlations are very low. In essence, the variable is partialed out from itself. As a result, adding X_3 after X_2 is already in the equation would increment the proportion of variance accounted for (i.e., R^2) by a negligible amount: .014 (the square of the part correlation). The same would be true if X_2 were entered after X_3 is already in the equation.

Earlier, I pointed out that when multiple indicators are used, the betas associated with them are attenuated. To see this in connection with the present example, run an additional analysis in which only X_1 and X_2 (or X_3) are the independent variables. You will find that X_1 and X_2 (or X_1 and X_3) have the same betas (.4167) and the same t ratios (5.26, with 97 df). Assuming $\alpha = .05$ was prespecified, one would conclude that both betas are statistically significant. Contrast these results with those given earlier (i.e., when I included both X_2 and X_3). Note that because X_1 has a low correlation with X_2 and X_3 (.20), the beta for X_1 hardly changed as a result of the inclusion of the additional measure (i.e., X_2 or X_3). In contrast, the betas for X_2 and X_3 split (they are now .225989), and neither is statistically significant at $\alpha = .05$.

To repeat: when one indicator of, say, mental ability is used, its effect, expressed as a standardized regression coefficient (beta), is .4167 and it is statistically significant at, say, the .05 level. When two indicators of the same variable are used, they are treated as distinct variables, resulting in betas that are about half the size of the one obtained for the single indicator. Moreover, these betas would be declared statistically not significant at the .05 level. The validity of the preceding statement is predicated on the assumption that the correlation between the two indicators is relatively high. When this is not so, one would have to question the validity of regarding them as indicators of the same variable.

Collinearity Diagnosis in Practice

Unfortunately, there is a chasm between proposed approaches to diagnosing collinearity (or multicollinearity), as outlined in preceding sections, and the generally perfunctory approach to diagnosis of collinearity as presented in the research literature. Many, if not most, attempts to diagnose collinearity are based on an examination of the zero-order correlations among the independent variables. Using some rule of thumb for a threshold, it is generally concluded that collinearity poses no problem. For example, MacEwen and Barling (1991) declared, "Multicollinearity was not a problem in the data (all correlations were less than .8; Lewis-Beck, 1980)" (p. 639).

Except for the reference to Lewis-Beck, to which I turn presently, this typifies statements encountered in the research literature. At the very least, referees and journal editors should be familiar with, if not thoroughly knowledgeable of, current approaches to diagnosis of collinearity, and therefore they should be in a position to reject statements such as the one I quoted above as woefully inadequate. Regrettably, referees and editors seem inclined not to question methodological assertions, especially when they are buttressed by a reference(s). I submit that it is the responsibility of referees and editors to make a judgment on the merit of the case being presented, regardless of what an authority has said, or is alleged to have said, about it. I said "alleged" because views that are diametrically opposed to those expressed by an author are often attributed to him or her. As a case in point, here is what Lewis-Beck (1980) said about the topic under consideration:

> A frequent practice is to examine the bivariate correlations among the independent variables, looking for coefficients of about .8, or larger. Then, if none is found, one goes on to conclude that multicollinearity is not a problem. While suggestive, *this approach is unsatisfactory* [italics added], for it fails to take into account the relationship of an independent variable with *all* the other independent variables. It is possible, for instance, to find no large bivariate correlations, although one of the independent variables is a nearly perfect linear combination of the remaining independent variables. (p. 60)

I believe it is not expecting too much of referees and editors to check the accuracy of a citation, especially since the author of the paper under review can be asked to supply a page location and perhaps even a photocopy of the section cited or quoted. Whatever your opinion on this matter, I hope this example serves to show once more the importance of checking the sources cited, especially when the topic under consideration is complex or controversial.

Before presenting some additional examples, I would like to remind you of my comments about the dubious value of rules of thumb (see "Criteria and Rules of Thumb" in Chapter 3). The inadequacy of examining only zero-order correlations aside, different authors use different threshold values for what is deemed a high correlation. Consistency is even lacking in papers published in the same journal. A case in point is a statement by Schumm, Southerly, and Figley (1980) published in the same journal in which MacEwen and Barling's (1991; see the earlier reference) was published to the effect that $r > .75$ constitutes "severe multicollinearity" (p. 254). Recall that for MacEwen and Barling, a correlation of .8 posed no problem regarding collinearity.

Here are a few additional, almost random, examples of diagnoses of collinearity based solely on the zero-order correlations among the independent variables, using varying threshold values.

> As can be seen in the table, the correlations ranged from .01 to .61. There were a number of moderate, theoretically expected correlations between the various predictors, but none were so high for multicollinearity to be a serious problem. (Smith, Arnkoff, & Wright, 1990, p. 316)

> Pearson correlational analysis was used to examine collinearity of variables . . . Coefficients . . . did not exceed .60. Therefore, all variables . . . were free to enter regression equations. (Pridham, Lytton, Chang, & Rutledge, 1991, p. 25)

> Since all correlations among variables were below .65 (with the exception of correlations of trait anger subscales with the total trait anger), multicollinearity was not anticipated. Nonetheless, collinearity diagnostics were performed. (Thomas & Williams, 1991, p. 306)

Thomas and Williams did not state what kind of diagnostics they performed, nor did they report any results of such. Unfortunately, this kind of statement is common not only in this area. Thus, one often encounters statements to the effect that, say, the reliability, validity, or what have you of a measure is satisfactory, robust, and the like, without providing any evidence. One cannot but wonder why referees and editors do not question such vacuous statements.

Finally, the following is an example with a twist on the theme of examination of zero-order correlations that the referees and the editors should not have let stand:

> Although there is multicollinearity between the foci and bases of commitment measures, there also appears to be evidence for the discriminant validity of the two sets of variables [measures?]. The mean across the 28 correlations of the foci and the bases measures is .435, which leaves an average 81 percent of the variance in the foci and bases unaccounted for by their intercorrelation. (Becker, 1992, p. 238, footnote 2)

I will not comment on this statement, as I trust that, in light of the preceding presentation, you recognize that it is fallacious.

Examples in Which Correlations with the Dependent Variable Differ

In the preceding two examples, the independent variables have identical correlations with the dependent variable (.50). The examples in this section are designed to show the effects of

Table 10.3   Two Illustrative Data Sets with Three Independent Variables; N = 100

| | (a) | | | | (b) | | | |
	X_1	X_2	X_3	Y	X_1	X_2	X_3	Y
X_1	1.00	.20	.20	.50	1.00	.20	.20	.50
X_2	.20	1.00	.10	.50	.20	1.00	.85	.50
X_3	.20	.10	1.00	.52	.20	.85	1.00	.52
Y	.50	.50	.52	1.00	.50	.50	.52	1.00
M:	7.60	7.70	7.14	32.31	7.60	7.70	7.14	32.31
s:	2.57	2.59	2.76	6.85	2.57	2.59	2.76	6.85

NOTE: Except for r_{y3}, the data in this table are the same as in Table 10.2.

collinearity when there are slight differences in correlations between independent variables with the dependent variable. I will use the two data sets given in Table 10.3. Note that the statistics for the independent variables in (a) and (b) of Table 10.3 are identical, respectively, with those of (a) and (b) of Table 10.2. Accordingly, collinearity diagnostics are the same for both tables. As I discussed collinearity diagnostics in detail in the preceding section in connection with the analysis of the data of Table 10.2, I will not comment on them here, though I will reproduce relevant SAS output for comparative purposes with the SPSS output given in the preceding section. Here, I focus on the correlations of independent variables with the dependent variable, specifically on the difference between r_{y2} (.50) and r_{y3} (.52) in both data sets and how it affects estimates of regression coefficients in the two data sets.

SAS

Input

```
TITLE 'TABLE 10.3 (A)';
DATA T103(TYPE=CORR);
   INPUT _TYPE_ $  _NAME_ $   X1 X2 X3 Y;
   CARDS;
MEAN  .    7.60   7.70   7.14   32.31
STD   .    2.57   2.59   2.76   6.85
N     .    100    100    100    100
CORR X1    1.00   .20    .20    .50
CORR X2    .20    1.00   .10    .50
CORR X3    .20    .10    1.00   .52
CORR Y     .50    .50    .52    1.00
;
PROC PRINT;
PROC REG;
   MODEL Y=X1 X2 X3/ALL COLLIN;
RUN;
```

Commentary

DATA. TYPE=CORR indicates that a correlation matrix will be read as input.

INPUT. Data are entered in free format, where $ indicates a character (as opposed to numeric) value. TYPE serves to identify the type of information contained in each line. As you can see, the first line is composed of means, the second of standard deviations, the third of the number of cases, and succeeding lines are composed of correlations. I use NAME to name the rows of the correlation matrix (i.e., X1, X2, and so forth). The dots in the first three rows serve as placeholders.

I commented on PROC REG earlier in the text (e.g., Chapters 4 and 8). As you have surely gathered, COLLIN calls for collinearity diagnostics.

As in the SPSS run for the data of Table 10.2, I give an input file for (a) only. To run (b), change the correlation between X2 and X3 from .10 to .85. Be sure to do this both above and below the diagonal. Actually, SAS uses the values below the diagonal. Thus, if you happen to change only the value below the diagonal, you would get results from an analysis of data set (b) of Table 10.3. If, on the other hand, you happen to change only the value above the diagonal, you would get results from an analysis of data set (a) (i.e., identical to those you would obtain from the input given previously).[10]

SAS issues a warning when the matrix is not symmetric, but it does this in the LOG file. For illustrative purposes, I changed only the value below the diagonal. The LOG file contained the following message:

WARNING: CORR matrix read from the input data set WORK.T103 is not symmetric.
Values in the lower triangle will be used.

I guess that many users do not bother reading the LOG, especially when they get output. I hope that the present example serves to alert you to the importance of *always* reading the log.

Output

TABLE 10.3 (A)

R-square   0.5798
Adj R-sq   0.5667

Parameter Estimates

Variable	DF	Parameter Estimate	Standard Error	T for H0: Parameter=0	Prob > $|T|$	Standardized Estimate
INTERCEP	1	10.159068	1.98619900	5.115	0.0001	0.00000000
X1	1	0.904135	0.18311781	4.937	0.0001	0.33921569
X2	1	1.033714	0.17892950	5.777	0.0001	0.39084967
X3	1	1.025197	0.16790848	6.106	0.0001	0.41307190

---

[10]You can enter a lower triangular matrix in SAS, provided it contains dots as placeholders for the values above the diagonal.

TABLE 10.3 (B)

R-square   0.4413
Adj R-sq   0.4238

Parameter Estimates

Variable	DF	Parameter Estimate	Standard Error	T for H0: Parameter=0	Prob > |T|	Standardized Estimate
INTERCEP	1	15.412709	2.06691983	7.457	0.0001	0.00000000
X1	1	1.085724	0.20788320	5.223	0.0001	0.40734463
X2	1	0.436315	0.38366915	1.137	0.2583	0.16497175
X3	1	0.740359	0.36003736	2.056	0.0425	0.29830508

Commentary

Examine R^2 in the two excerpts and notice that, because of the high correlation between X_2 and X_3 in (b), R^2 for these data is considerably smaller than for (a), although the correlations of the independent variables with Y are identical in both data sets.

Turning now to the regression equations, it will be convenient, for present purposes, to focus on the β's (standardized regression coefficients, labeled Standardized Estimate in SAS output). In (a), where the correlation between X_2 and X_3 is low (.10), β_3 is slightly greater than β_2. But in (b), the high correlation between X_2 and X_3 (.85) tips the scales in favor of the variable that has the slight edge, making β_3 about twice the size of β_2. The discrepancy between the two coefficients in (b) is counterintuitive considering that there is only a slight difference between r_{y2} and r_{y3} (.02), which could plausibly be due to sampling or measurement errors. Moreover, β_3 is statistically significant (at the .05 level), whereas β_2 is not. One would therefore have to arrive at the paradoxical conclusion that although X_2 and X_3 are highly correlated, and may even be measures of the same variable, the latter has a statistically significant effect on Y but the former does not. Even if β_2 were statistically significant, the difference in the sizes of β_2 and β_3 would lead some to conclude that the latter is about twice as effective as the former (see the next section, "Research Examples").

Output

TABLE 10.3 (A)
Collinearity Diagnostics

Number	Eigenvalue	Condition Index	Var Prop INTERCEP	Var Prop X1	Var Prop X2	Var Prop X3
1	3.77653	1.00000	0.0035	0.0062	0.0063	0.0080
2	0.10598	5.96944	0.0035	0.0292	0.2675	0.7741
3	0.07931	6.90038	0.0003	0.7495	0.3969	0.0659
4	0.03817	9.94641	0.9928	0.2151	0.3293	0.1520

TABLE 10.3 (B)
Collinearity Diagnostics

Number	Eigenvalue	Condition Index	Var Prop INTERCEP	Var Prop X1	Var Prop X2	Var Prop X3
1	3.81916	1.00000	0.0042	0.0062	0.0019	0.0023
2	0.11726	5.70698	0.0426	0.3838	0.0408	0.0872
3	0.04689	9.02473	0.8764	0.6081	0.0007	0.0428
4	0.01669	15.12759	0.0768	0.0019	0.9566	0.8677

Commentary

As I stated earlier, for comparative purposes with the results from SPSS, I reproduced the collinearity diagnostics but will not comment on them.

RESEARCH EXAMPLES

Unfortunately, the practice of treating multiple indicators as if they were distinct variables is prevalent in the research literature. I trust that by now you recognize that this practice engenders the kind of problems I discussed and illustrated in this section, namely collinearity among independent variables (actually indicators erroneously treated as variables) whose correlations with the dependent variable tend to be similar to each other. Not surprisingly, researchers often face results they find puzzling and about which they strain to come up with explanations. I believe it instructive to give a couple of research examples in the hope that they will further clarify the difficulties arising from collinearity and alert you again to the importance of reading research reports critically.

As I stated in Chapter 1, I use research examples with a very limited goal in mind, namely, to illustrate or highlight issues under consideration. Accordingly, I generally refrain from commenting on various crucial aspects (e.g., theoretical rationale, research design, measurement). Again, I caution you not to pass judgment on any of the studies solely on the basis of my discussion. There is no substitute for reading the original reports, which I strongly urge you to do.

Teaching of French as a Foreign Language

I introduced and discussed this example, which I took from Carroll's (1975) study of the teaching of French in eight countries, in Chapter 8 in connection with stepwise regression analysis (see Table 8.2 and the discussion related to it). For convenience, I repeat Table 8.2 here as Table 10.4.

Briefly, I regressed, in turn, a reading test and a listening test in French (columns 8 and 9 of Table 10.4) on the first seven "variables" listed in Table 10.4. For present purposes, I focus on "variables" 6 and 7 (aspirations to understand spoken French and aspirations to be able to read French). Not surprisingly, the correlation between them is relatively high (.762). As I stated in Chapter 8, it would be more appropriate to treat them as indicators of aspirations to learn French

Table 10.4   Correlation Matrix of Seven Predictors and Two Criteria

	1	2	3	4	5	6	7	8	9
1 Teacher's competence in French	1.000	.076	.269	−.004	−.017	.077	.050	.207	.299
2 Teaching procedures	.076	1.000	.014	.095	.107	.205	.174	.092	.179
3 Amount of instruction	.269	.014	1.000	.181	.107	.180	.188	.633	.632
4 Student effort	−.004	.095	.181	1.000	.108	.185	.198	.281	.210
5 Student aptitude for foreign language	−.017	.107	.107	.108	1.000	.376	.383	.277	.235
6 Aspirations to understand spoken French	.077	.205	.180	.185	.376	1.000	.762	.344	.337
7 Aspirations to be able to read French	.050	.174	.188	.198	.383	.762	1.000	.385	.322
8 Reading test	.207	.092	.633	.281	.277	.344	.385	1.000	
9 Listening test	.299	.179	.632	.210	.235	.337	.322		1.000

NOTE: Data taken from J. B. Carroll, *The teaching of French as a foreign language in eight countries*, p. 268. Copyright 1975 by John Wiley & Sons. Reprinted by permission.

than as distinct variables. (For convenience, I will continue to refer to these indicators as variables and will refrain from using quotation marks.)

Examine the correlation matrix and notice that variables 6 and 7 have very similar correlations with the remaining independent variables. Therefore, it is possible, for present purposes, to focus only on the correlations of 6 and 7 with the dependent variables (columns 8 and 9). The validity of treating reading and listening as two distinct variables is also dubious.

Regressing variables 8 and 9 in Table 10.4 on the remaining seven variables, the following equations are obtained:

$$z'_8 = .0506z_1 + .0175z_2 + .5434z_3 + .1262z_4 + .1231z_5 + .0304z_6 + .1819z_7$$

$$z'_9 = .1349z_1 + .1116z_2 + .5416z_3 + .0588z_4 + .0955z_5 + .1153z_6 + .0579z_7$$

As I analyzed the correlation matrix, the regression equations consist of standardized regression coefficients. I comment only on the coefficients for variables 6 and 7, as my purpose is to illustrate what I said in the preceding section about the scale being tipped in favor of the variable whose correlation with the dependent variable is larger.

Note that variable 7 has a slightly higher correlation with variable 8 (.385) than does variable 6 (.344). Yet, because of the high correlation between 6 and 7 (.762), the size of β_7 (.1819) is about six times that of β_6 (.0304). The situation is reversed when 9 is treated as the dependent variable. This time the discrepancy between the correlations of 6 and 7 with the dependent variable is even smaller ($r_{96} = .337$ and $r_{97} = .322$). But because variable 6 has the slightly higher correlation with dependent variable, its β (.1153) is about twice as large as the β for variable 7 (.0579).

The discrepancies between the correlations of 6 and 7 with 8, and of 6 and 7 with 9, can plausibly be attributed to measurement errors and/or sampling fluctuations. Therefore, an interpretation of the highly discrepant β's as indicating important differences in the effects of the two variables is highly questionable. More important, as I suggested earlier, 6 and 7 are not distinct variables but appear to be indicators of the same variable.

Carroll (1975) did not interpret the β's as indices of effects but did use them as indices of "the relative degree to which each of the seven variables contribute independently to the prediction of the criterion" (p. 269). Moreover, he compared the β's across the two equations, saying the following:

> *Student Aspirations:* Of interest is the fact that aspirations to learn to understand spoken French makes *much more contribution* [italics added] to Listening scores than to Reading, and conversely, aspirations to learn to read French makes *much more contribution* [italics added] to Reading scores than to Listening scores. (p. 274)

Such statements may lead to misconceptions among researchers and the general public who do not distinguish between explanatory and predictive research. Furthermore, in view of what I said about the behavior of the β's in the presence of collinearity and small discrepancies between the correlations of predictors with the criterion, one would have to question Carroll's interpretations, even in a predictive framework.

Interviewers' Perceptions of Applicant Qualifications

Parsons and Liden (1984) studied "interviewer perceptions of applicant nonverbal cues" (p. 557). Briefly, each of 251 subjects was interviewed by one of eight interviewers for about 10 minutes, and rated on eight nonverbal cues.

> The correlations among the perceptions of nonverbal cues were very high, ranging from .54 to .90. . . . One possible explanation is the sheer number of applicants seen per day by each interviewer in the current study may have caused them to adopt some simple response-bias halo rating. (pp. 560–561)

While this explanation is plausible, it is also necessary to recognize that the cues the interviewers were asked to rate (e.g., poise, posture, articulation, voice intensity) cannot be construed as representing different variables. Yet, the authors carried out a "forward stepwise regression procedure" (p. 561).[11]

As would be expected, based on the high correlations among the independent "variables," after three were entered, the remaining ones added virtually nothing to the proportion of variance accounted for. The authors made the following observation about their results:

> Voice Intensity did not enter the equation under the stepwise criteria. This is curious because "Articulation" was the first variable [*sic*] entered into the equation, and it would be *logically related to Voice Intensity* [italics added]. Looking back to Table 1, it is seen that the correlation between Articulation and Voice Intensity is .87, which means that there is almost complete redundancy between the variables [*sic*]. (p. 561)

In the context of my concerns in this section, I will note that tolerance values for articulation and for voice intensity were about the same (.20 and .19, respectively). The correlation between articulation and the criterion was .81, and that between voice intensity and the criterion was .77. This explains why the former was given preference in the variable selection process. Even more relevant to present concerns is that Parsons and Liden reported a standardized regression coefficient of .42 for articulation and one of .00 for voice intensity.

---

[11]When I presented variable selection procedures in Chapter 9, I distinguished between *forward* and *stepwise*. Parsons and Liden did a forward selection.

Finally, I would like to point out that Parsons and Liden admitted that "Due to the high degree of multicollinearity, the use of the stepwise regression procedure could be misleading because of the sampling error of the partial correlation, which determines the order of entry" (p. 561). They therefore carried out another analysis meant to "confirm or disconfirm the multiple regression results" (p. 561). I cannot comment on their other analysis without going far afield. Instead, I would like to state that, in my opinion, their multiple regression analysis was, at best, an exercise in futility.

Hope and Psychological Adjustment to Disability

A study by Elliott, Witty, Herrick, and Hoffman (1991) "was conducted to examine the relationship of two components of hope to the psychological adjustment of people with traumatically acquired physical disabilities" (p. 609). To this end, Elliott et al. regressed, in turn, an inventory to diagnose depression (IDD) and a sickness impact profile (SIP) on the two hope components (pathways and agency) and on time since injury (TSI). For present purposes, I will point out that the correlation between pathway and agency was .64, and that the former correlated higher with the two criteria (−.36 with IDD, and −.47 with SIP) than the latter (−.19 with IDD, and −.31 with SIP). Further, the correlations of pathway and agency with TSI were negligible (−.13 and −.01, respectively). In short, the pattern of the correlations is similar to that in my example of Table 10.3 (b).

In light of my discussion of the results of the analysis of Table 10.3 (b), the results reported by Elliott et al. should come as no surprise. When they used IDD as the criterion, "the following beta weights resulted for the two Hope subscales: agency, $\beta = .09$, $t(53) = .55$, *ns,* and pathways, $\beta = −.44$, $t(53) = −2.72$, $p < .01$." Similarly, when they used SIP as the criterion: "agency, $\beta = −.01$, $t(53) = −.08$, *ns,* and pathways, $\beta = −.46$, $t(53) = −2.90$, $p < .01$" (610).

White Racial Identity and Self-Actualization

"The purpose of this study was to test the validity of Helms's (1984) model of White racial identity development by exploring the relationship between White racial identity attitudes and dimensions of self-actualization" (Tokar & Swanson, 1991, p. 297). Briefly, Tokar and Swanson regressed, in turn, components of self-actualization on five subscales of a measure of racial identity. Thus, subscales of both measures (of the independent and the dependent variable) were treated as distinct variables.

Even a cursory glance at the correlation matrix (their Table 1, p. 298) should suffice to cast doubt about Tokar and Swanson's analytic approach. Correlations among the subscales of racial identity ranged from −.29 to .81, and those among the components of self-actualization ranged from .50 to .81. You may find it instructive to reanalyze the data reported in their Table 1 and study, among other things, collinearity diagnostics. Anyhow, it is not surprising that, because of slight differences in correlations between independent and the dependent "variables" (actually indicators of both), in each of the three regression equations two of the five subscales have statistically significant standardized regression coefficients that are also larger than the remaining three (see their Table 2, p. 299).

Remarkably, the authors themselves stated:

The strong relationships between predictors suggest that WRIAS subscales may not be measuring independent constructs. Likewise, high intercorrelations among criterion variables indicate that there was considerable overlap between variables for which POI subscales were intended to measure independently. (p. 298)

The authors even pointed out that, in view of the reliabilities, correlations among some "variables" "were essentially as high as they could have been" (p. 299). Further, they stated, "Wampold and Freund (1987) warned that if two predictors correlate highly, none (or at best one) of them will demonstrate a significant unique contribution to the prediction of the criterion variable" (p. 300).

In light of the foregoing, one cannot but wonder why they not only proceeded with the analysis, but even concluded that "despite methodological issues [?], the results of this study have important implications for cross-cultural counseling and counselor training" (p. 300). Even more puzzling is that the referees and editors were apparently satisfied with the validity of the analysis and the conclusion drawn.

This phenomenon, though disturbing, should not surprise readers of the research literature, as it appears that an author(s) admission of deficiencies in his or her study (often presented in the guise of limitations) seems to serve as immunization against criticism or even questioning. Earlier, I speculated that the inclusion of references, regardless of their relevance, seems to have a similar effect in dispelling doubts about the validity of the analytic approach, interpretations of results, implications, and the like.

Stress, Tolerance of Ambiguity, and Magical Thinking

"The present study investigated the relationship between psychological stress and magical thinking and the extent to which such a relationship may be moderated by individuals' tolerance of ambiguity" (Keinan, 1994, p. 48). Keinan measured "four categories" (p. 50) of magical thinking. Referring to the correlation matrix of "the independent and the dependent variables" (p. 51), he stated, "the correlations among the different types of magical thinking were relatively high, indicating that they belong to the same family. At the same time, it is evident that each type can be viewed as a separate entity" (p. 51). Considering that the correlations among the four types of magical thinking ranged from .73 to .93 (see Keinan's Table 3, p. 53), I suggest that you reflect on the plausibility of his statement and the validity of his treating each type as a distinct dependent variable in separate regression analyses. I will return to this study in Chapter 15.

SOME PROPOSED REMEDIES

It should be clear by now that collinearity poses serious threats to valid interpretation of regression coefficients as indices of effects. Having detected collinearity, what can be done about it? Are there remedies? A solution that probably comes readily to mind is to delete "culprit" variables. However, recognize that when attempting to ascertain whether collinearity exists in a set of independent variables it is assumed that the model is correctly specified. Consequently, deleting variables to reduce collinearity may lead to specification errors (Chatterjee & Price, 1977).

Before turning to proposed remedies, I will remind you that collinearity is preventable when it is introduced by unwary researchers in the first place. A notable case in point, amply demonstrated in the preceding section, is the use of multiple indicators in a regression analysis. To reiterate: this is not to say that multiple indicators should be avoided. On the contrary, their use is almost mandatory in many areas of behavioral research, where the state of measuring constructs is in its infancy. However, one should avoid treating multiple indicators as if they were distinct variables. The use of multiple indicators in regression analysis is a form of model misspecification.

Another situation where collinearity may be introduced by unwary researchers is the use of a single-stage regression analysis, when the model requires a multistage analysis. Recall that in a single-stage analysis, all the independent variables are treated alike as if they were exogenous, having only direct effects on the dependent variable (see the discussion related to Figures 9.3 through 9.5 in Chapter 9; see also "The Role of Theory," presented later in the chapter). High correlations among exogenous and endogenous variables may indicate the strong effects of the former on the latter. Including such variables in a single-stage analysis would manifest itself in collinearity, whereas using a multistage analysis commensurate with the model may not manifest itself as such.

Turning to proposed remedies, one is that additional data be collected in the hope that this may ameliorate the condition of collinearity. Another set of remedies relates to the grouping of variables in blocks, based on a priori judgment or by using such methods as principal components analysis and factor analysis (Chatterjee & Price, 1977, Chapter 7; Gorsuch, 1983; Harman, 1976; Mulaik, 1972; Pedhazur & Schmelkin, 1991, Chapters 22 and 23). These approaches are not free of problems. When blocks of variables are used in a regression analysis, it is not possible to obtain a regression coefficient for a block unless one has first arrived at combinations of variables so that each block is represented by a single vector. Coleman (1975a, 1976) proposed a method of arriving at a summary coefficient for each block of variables used in the regression analysis (see also Igra, 1979). Referring as they do to blocks of variables, such summary statistics are of dubious value when one wishes to make statements about the effect of a variable, not to mention policy implications.

What I said in the preceding paragraph also applies to situations in which the correlation matrix is orthogonalized by subjecting it to, say, a principal components analysis. Regression coefficients based on the orthogonalized matrix may not lend themselves to meaningful interpretations as indices of effects because the components with which they are associated may lack substantive meaning.

Another set of proposals for dealing with collinearity is to abandon ordinary least-squares analysis and use instead other methods of estimation. One such method is ridge regression (see Chatterjee & Price, 1977, Chapter 8; Horel & Kennard, 1970a, 1970b; Marquardt & Snee, 1975; Mason & Brown, 1975; Myers, 1990, Chapter 8; Neter et al., 1989, Chapter 11; Price, 1977; Schmidt & Muller, 1978; for critiques of ridge regression, see Pagel & Lunneborg, 1985; Rozeboom, 1979).

In conclusion, it is important to note that none of the proposed methods of dealing with collinearity constitutes a cure. High collinearity is symptomatic of insufficient, or deficient, information, which no amount of data manipulation can rectify. As thorough an understanding as is possible of the causes of collinearity in a given set of data is the best guide for determining which action should be taken.

STANDARDIZED OR UNSTANDARDIZED COEFFICIENTS?

In Chapter 5, I introduced and discussed briefly the distinction between standardized (β) and unstandardized (b) regression coefficients. I pointed out that the interpretation of β is analogous to the interpretation of b, except that β is interpreted as indicating the expected change in the dependent variable, expressed in standard scores, associated with a standard deviation change in an independent variable, while holding the remaining variables constant. Many researchers use the relative magnitudes of β's to indicate the relative importance of variables with which they are associated. To assess the validity of this approach, I begin by examining properties of β's, as contrasted with those of b's. I then address the crucial question of the interpretability of β's, particularly in the context of the relative importance of variables.

Some Properties of β's and b's

The size of a β reflects not only the presumed effect of the variable with which it is associated but also the variances and the covariances of the variables in the model (including the dependent variable), as well as the variance of the variables not in the model and subsumed under the error term. In contrast, b remains fairly stable despite differences in the variances and the covariances of the variables in different settings or populations. I gave examples of this contrast early in the book in connection with the discussion of simple linear regression. In Chapter 2, Table 2.3, I showed that $b_{yx} = .75$ for four sets of fictitious data, but that because of differences in the variances of X, Y, or both, in these data sets, r_{yx} varied from a low of .24 to a high of .73. I also showed—see Chapter 5, (5.13)—that $\beta = r$ when one independent variable is used. Thus, interpreting β as an index of the effect of X on Y, one would conclude that it varies greatly in the four data sets of Table 2.3. Interpreting b as an index of the effect of X on Y, on the other hand, one would conclude that the effect is identical in these four data sets.

I will use now the two illustrative sets of data reported in Table 10.5 to show that the same phenomenon may occur in designs with more than one independent variable. Using methods presented in Chapter 5 or 6, or a computer program, regress Y on X_1 and X_2 for both sets of data of Table 10.5. You will find that the regression equation for raw scores in both data sets is

$$Y' = 10 + 1.0X_1 + .8X_2$$

The regression equations in standard score form are

$$z_y' = .6z_1 + .4z_2 \quad \text{for set (a)}$$

$$z_y' = .5z_1 + .25z_2 \quad \text{for set (b)}$$

In Chapter 5, I gave the relation between β and b as

$$\beta_j = b_j \frac{s_j}{s_y} \tag{10.17}$$

where β_j and b_j are, respectively, standardized and unstandardized regression coefficients associated with independent variable j; and s_j and s_y are, respectively, standard deviations of independent variable j and the dependent variable, Y. From (10.17) it is evident that the size of β is affected by the ratio of the standard deviation of the variable with which it is associated to the standard deviation of the dependent variable. For data set (a) in Table 10.5,

Table 10.5   Two Sets of Illustrative Data with Two Independent Variables in Each

	1	2	Y			1	2	Y
1	1.00	.50	.80		1	1.00	.40	.60
2	.50	1.00	.70		2	.40	1.00	.45
Y	.80	.70	1.00		Y	.60	.45	1.00
s:	12	10	20		s:	8	5	16
M:	50	50	100		M:	50	50	100
		(a)					(b)	

$$\beta_1 = 1.0\left(\frac{12}{20}\right) = .6$$

$$\beta_2 = .8\left(\frac{10}{20}\right) = .4$$

and for data set (b),

$$\beta_1 = 1.0\left(\frac{8}{16}\right) = .5$$

$$\beta_2 = .8\left(\frac{5}{16}\right) = .25$$

Assume that the two data sets of Table 10.5 were obtained in the same experimental setup, except that in (a) the researcher used values of X_1 and X_2 that were more variable than those used in (b). Interpreting the unstandardized regression coefficients as indices of the effects of the X's on Y, one would conclude that they are identical in both data sets. One would conclude that the X's have stronger effects in (a) than in (b) if one interpreted the β's as indices of their effects.

The same reasoning applies when one assumes that the data in Table 10.5 were obtained in nonexperimental research.[12] For example, data set (a) may have been obtained from a sample of males or a sample of Whites, and data set (b) may have been obtained from a sample of females or a sample of Blacks. When there are relatively large differences in variances in the two groups, their b's may be identical or very similar to each other, whereas their β's may differ considerably from each other. To repeat: assuming that the model is valid, one would reach different conclusions about the effects of X_1 and X_2, depending on whether b's or β's are interpreted as indices of their effects. Smith, M. S. (1972), who reanalyzed the Coleman Report data, gave numerous examples in which comparisons based on b's or β's for different groups (e.g., Blacks and Whites, different grade levels, different regions of the country) led to contradictory conclusions about the relative importance of the same variables.

In light of considerations such as the foregoing and in light of interpretability problems (see the following), most authors advocate the use of b's over β's as indices of the effects of the variables with which they are associated. As Luskin (1991) put it: "standardized coefficients

---

[12]This is a more tenable assumption, as $r_{12} \neq .00$ in the examples in Table 10.5—a condition less likely to occur in an experiment that has been appropriately designed and executed.

have been in bad odor for some time . . . and for at least one very good reason, which simply put is that they are not the unstandardized ones" (p. 1033). Incidentally, Luskin argued that, under certain circumstances, β's may provide additional useful information. For a response, see King (1991b).

Among general discussions advocating the use of b's are Achen (1982), Blalock (1964, 1968), Kim and Mueller (1976), King (1986); Schoenberg (1972), Tukey (1954), Turner and Stevens (1959), and Wright (1976). For discussions of this issue in the context of research on educational effects, see Bowles and Levin (1968); Cain and Watts (1968, 1970); Hanushek and Kain (1972); Linn, Werts, and Tucker (1971); Smith, M. S. (1972); and Werts and Watley (1968). The common theme in these papers is that b's come closest to statements of scientific laws. For a dissenting view, see Hargens (1976), who argued that the choice between b's and β's should be made on the basis of theoretical considerations that relate to the scale representation of the variable. Thus, Hargens maintained that when the theoretical model refers to one's standing on a variable not in an absolute sense but relative to others in the group to which one belongs, β's are the appropriate indices of the effects of the variables in the model.

Not unexpectedly, reservations regarding the use of standardized regression coefficients were expressed in various textbooks. For example, Darlington (1990) asserted that standardized regression coefficients "should rarely if ever be used" (p. 217). Similarly, Judd and McClelland (1989) "seldom find standardized regression coefficients to be useful" (p. 202). Some authors do not even allude to standardized regression coefficients. After noting the absence of an entry for standardized regression coefficients in the index and after perusing relevant sections of the text, it appears to me that among such authors are Draper and Smith (1981) and Myers (1990).

Though I, too, deem standardized regression coefficients of limited value (see the discussion that follows), I recommend that they be reported along with the unstandardized regression coefficients, or that the standard deviations of all the variables be reported so that a reader could derive one set of coefficients from the other. Of course, information provided by the standard deviations is important in and of itself and should therefore always be part of the report of a research study. Unfortunately, many researchers report only correlation matrices, thereby not only precluding the possibility of calculating the unstandardized coefficients but also omitting important information about their sample or samples.

Finally, there seems to be agreement that b's should be used when comparing regression equations across groups. I present methods for comparing b's across groups in Chapter 14. For now, I will only note that frequently data from two or more groups are analyzed together without determining first whether this is warranted. For example, data from males and females are analyzed together without determining first whether the regression equations in the two groups are similar to each other. Sometimes the analysis includes one or more than one coded vectors to represent group membership (see Chapter 11). As I demonstrate in Chapter 14, when data from two or more groups are used in a single regression analysis in which no coded vectors are included to represent group membership, it is assumed that the regression equations (intercepts and regression coefficients) are not different from each other in the groups under study. When coded vectors representing group membership are included, it is assumed that the intercepts of the regression equations for the different groups differ from each other but that the regression coefficients do not differ across groups. Neither the question of the equality of intercepts nor that of the equality of regression coefficients should be relegated to assumptions. Both should be studied and tested before deciding whether the data from different groups may be combined (see Chapters 14 and 15).

Interpretability of *b*'s and β's

In addition to their relative stability, unstandardized regression coefficients (*b*'s) are recommended on the grounds that, unlike the standardized regression coefficients (β's), they are potentially translatable into guides for policy decisions. I said potentially, as their interpretation is not free of problems, among which are the following.

First, the sizes of *b*'s depend on the units used to measure the variables with which they are associated. Changing units from dollars to cents, say, will change the coefficient associated with the variable. Clearly, *b*'s in a given equation cannot be compared for the purpose of assessing the relative importance of the variables with which they are associated, unless the variables are measured on the same scale (e.g., dollars).

Second, many measures used in behavioral research are not on an interval level. Hence, statements about a unit change at different points of such scales are questionable. A corollary of the preceding is that the meaning of a unit change on many scales used in social sciences is substantively unknown or ambiguous. What, for example, is the substantive meaning of a unit change on a specific measure of teacher attitudes or warmth? Or what is the substantive meaning of a unit change on a specific scale measuring a student's locus of control or educational aspirations?

Third, when the reliabilities of the measures of independent variables differ across groups, comparisons of the *b*'s associated with such variables may lead to erroneous conclusions.

In conclusion, two points are noteworthy. One, reliance on and interpretation of β's is deceptively simple. What is being overlooked is that when β's are interpreted, problems attendant with the substantive meaning of the units of measurement are evaded. The tendency to speak glibly of the expected change in the dependent variable associated with a change of a standard deviation in the independent variable borders on the delusive.

Two, the major argument in favor of β's is that they can be used to determine the relative importance of variables. Recalling that the size of β's is affected by variances and covariances of the variables in the study, as well as by those not included in the study (see the preceding section), should suffice to cast doubts about their worth as indicators of relative importance.

In sum, not only is there no simple answer to the question of the relative importance of variables, the validity or usefulness of the question itself is questioned by some (e.g., King, 1986). Considering the complexity of the phenomena one is trying to explain and the relatively primitive tools (notably the measurement instruments) available, this state of affairs is to be expected. As always, there is no substitute for clear thinking and theory. To underscore the fact that at times questions about relative importance of variables may degenerate into vacuousness, consider the following. Referring to an example from Ezekiel and Fox (1959, p. 181), Gordon (1968) stated:

> Cows, acres, and men were employed as independent variables in a study of dairy farm income. The regression coefficients showed them to be important in the order listed. Nonetheless, it is absolutely clear that *no matter what* the rank order of cows in this problem, and *no matter how small* its regression coefficient turned out to be, no one would claim that cows are irrelevant to dairy farm income. One would as soon conceive of a hog farm without hogs. Although men turned out to be the factor of production that was least important in this problem, no one would claim either that men are not in fact essential. (p. 614)

In another interesting example, Goldberger (1991) described a situation in which a physician is using the regression equation of weight on height and exercise to advise an overweight patient. "Would either the physician or the patient be edified to learn that height is 'more important' than exercise in explaining variation in weight?" (p. 241).

THE ROLE OF THEORY

Confusion about the meaning of regression coefficients (b's and β's) is bound to persist so long as the paramount role of theory is ignored. Reservations about the use of β's aside (see the preceding), it will be convenient to use them to demonstrate the pivotal role of theory in the context of attempts to determine effects of independent variables on dependent variables. I will do this in the context of a miniature example.

In Chapter 7, I introduced a simple example of an attempt to explain grade-point average (GPA) by using socioeconomic status (SES), intelligence (IQ), and achievement motivation (AM) as the independent variables. For the sake of illustration, I will consider here the two alternative models depicted in Figure 10.1. In model (a), the three independent variables are treated as exogenous variables (see Chapters 9 and 18 for definitions of exogenous and endogenous variables). For present purposes, I will only point out that this means that no theory exists, or that none is advanced, about the relations among the independent variables. The equation (in standard scores) that reflects this model is

$$z_y = \beta_{y1}z_1 + \beta_{y2}z_2 + \beta_{y3}z_3 + e_y$$

where the subscripts refer to the variables given in Figure 10.1. This type of model is the most prevalent in the application of multiple regression analysis in the social sciences either because a theory of causal relations among the independent variables is not formulated or because it is not recognized that the regression equation reflects a specific theoretical model. Whatever the reason, *when a single regression equation is used to study the effects of a set of independent variables on a dependent variable, a model such as (a) of Figure 10.1 is used, by design or by default.*

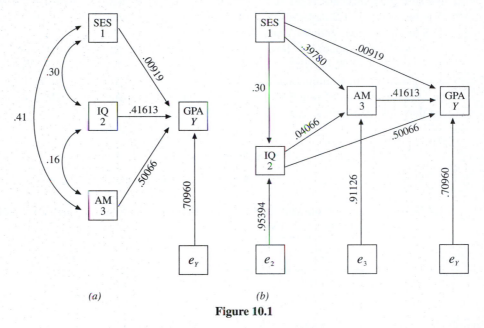

(a)   (b)

Figure 10.1

Turning now to model (b) of Figure 10.1, note that only SES (variable number 1) is treated as an exogenous variable, whereas the remaining variables are treated as endogenous variables. The equations that reflect this model are

$$z_1 = e_1$$

$$z_2 = \beta_{21}z_1 + e_2$$

$$z_3 = \beta_{31}z_1 + \beta_{32}z_2 + e_3$$

$$z_y = \beta_{y1}z_1 + \beta_{y2}z_2 + \beta_{y3}z_3 + e_y$$

Note that the last equation is the same as the single equation given earlier for model (a). The difference, then, between the two models is that in model (a) relations among SES, IQ, and AM (variables 1, 2, and 3) are left unanalyzed, whereas model (b) specifies the causes for the relations among these variables. For example, in model (a) it is noted that SES is correlated with AM, but no attempt is made to determine the cause of this relation. In model (b), on the other hand, it is hypothesized that the correlation between SES and AM is due to (1) the direct effect of the former on the latter, as indicated by SES → AM, and (2) the indirect effect of the former on the latter, as indicated by SES → IQ → AM.

To show the implications of the two models for the study of the effects of independent variables on a dependent variable, I will use the correlation matrix reported in Table 10.6 (I introduced this matrix in Chapter 9 as Table 9.1). For illustrative purposes, I will scrutinize the effect of SES on GPA in the two models.

The effects of SES, IQ, and AM on GPA for model (a) are calculated by regressing the latter on the former variables. Without showing the calculations (you may wish to do them as an exercise), the regression equation is

$$z'_y = .00919z_1 + .50066z_2 + .41613z_3$$

Because the effects are expressed as standardized coefficients (β's), one would have to conclude that the effect of SES on GPA (.00919) is virtually zero. In other words, one would conclude that SES has no meaningful effect on GPA.

According to model (b), however, SES affects GPA indirectly via the following paths: (1) SES → AM → GPA, (2) SES → IQ → GPA, and (3) SES → IQ → AM → GPA. It can be shown that, given certain assumptions, the effects for model (b) can be calculated by regressing: (1) IQ on SES; (2) AM on SES and IQ; and (3) GPA on SES, IQ, and AM.[13] The three equations that are thus obtained for the data of Table 10.6 are

$$z'_2 = .30z_1$$

$$z'_3 = .39780z_1 + .04066z_2$$

$$z'_4 = .00919z_1 + .50066z_2 + .41613z_3$$

Table 10.6 Correlation Matrix for Three Independent Variables and a Dependent Variable; N = 300

	1 SES	2 IQ	3 AM	Y GPA
1	1.00	.30	.41	.33
2	.30	1.00	.16	.57
3	.41	.16	1.00	.50
Y	.33	.57	.50	1.00

[13]I introduce methods for analyzing causal models in Chapter 18, where I reanalyze the models I discuss here.

In Chapter 7, I introduced the concepts of direct, indirect, and total effects of a variable (see also Chapter 18). Note that in the results for model (b), the direct effect of SES on GPA is .00919, which is the same as the effect of SES on GPA obtained in model (a). But, as I said earlier, according to model (b) SES has also indirect effects on GPA. It can be shown (I do this in Chapter 18) that the sum of the indirect effects of SES on GPA is .32081. Since the total effect of a variable is equal to the sum of its direct effect and its indirect effects (see Chapters 7 and 18), it follows that the total effect of SES on GPA in model (b) is .33 (.00919 + .32081).

Clearly, radically different conclusions would be reached about the effect of SES on GPA, depending on whether model (a) or model (b) is used. Specifically, if model (a) is used, the researcher would conclude that SES has practically no effect on GPA. If, on the other hand, model (b) is used, the researcher would conclude that whereas SES has practically no direct effect on GPA, it has meaningful indirect effects whose sum is .32081.

The choice between models (a) and (b), needless to say, is not arbitrary. On the contrary, it is predicated on one's theoretical formulations. As I pointed out earlier, in model (a) the researcher is unwilling, or unable, to make statements about the causes of the relations among SES, IQ, and AM (they are treated as exogenous variables). In model (b), on the other hand, a pattern of causation among these variables is specified, thereby enabling one to study indirect effects in addition to direct effects.

In conclusion, my sole purpose in the preceding demonstration was to show that different theoretical models dictate different approaches to the analysis and may lead to different conclusions about effects of independent variables. I treat the analysis of causal models in Chapters 18 and 19.

RESEARCH EXAMPLES

In this section, I present selected research examples to illustrate some topics of the preceding sections. At the risk of repetitiveness, I urge you to read the original report of a study before passing judgment on it.

International Evaluation of Educational Achievement (IEA)

I described this set of cross-national studies in some detail in Chapter 9, where I pointed out that the primary analytic approach used in them was variance partitioning.[14] In some of the studies, regression equations were also used for explanatory purposes. I begin with several general comments about the use and interpretation of regression equations in the IEA studies. Overall, my comments apply to all the studies in which regression coefficients were interpreted as indices of effects. But because the studies vary in their reliance on such interpretations, the relevance of my comments varies accordingly.

The most important point, from which several others follow, is that the valid interpretation of regression coefficients as indices of effects is predicated on the notion that the regression equation validly reflects the process by which the independent variables affect the dependent variable. In other words, it is necessary to assume that there are no specification errors, or at least that they are minimal (see the discussion earlier in this chapter). Peaker (1975), who was largely

---

[14]Earlier in this chapter, I analyzed data from an IEA study (see "Teaching of French as a Foreign Language").

responsible for the methodology used in the IEA studies, aptly stated, "Underlying any interpretation is the general proviso '*If* this is how the thing works *these* equations are the most relevant. But if not, not'" (p. 29). Do, then, the regression equations used in the IEA studies reflect "how the thing works"? Regrettably, the answer is no! Even the authors of the IEA studies acknowledged that their models were deficient not only regarding omitted variables, possible nonlinearities, and the like, but also because of the questionable status of variables included in the models (see, for example, my discussion of the status of kindred variables in Chapter 9). The editors of a symposium on the IEA studies (Purves & Levine, 1975) stated that there was agreement among the participants, some of whom were authors of IEA studies, that multiple regression analysis "would not suffice" (p. ix) to deal with the complexity of the relations among the variables.

Even if one were to overlook the preceding reservations, it must be noted that the routine use of stepwise regression analysis in the IEA studies rendered their results useless for the purpose of explanation (see Chapter 8 for a discussion of this point). This may explain, in part, some of the puzzling, inconsistent, and contradictory results in the various studies, of which the following are but a few examples.

> *Total Science Homework per Week in Hours.* In four countries the time spent in hours per week on Science homework was positively related to the level of achievement in Science. . . . However, in three other countries . . . a negative relationship was noted. The nature of this relationship is indicated by the signs of the regression coefficients. (Comber & Keeves, 1973, p. 231)

> *Teacher's University Training in French.* Seven of the *t*-values reach the critical level of significance, some favoring larger amounts of training and others lesser amounts. (Carroll, 1975, pp. 217–218)

> *Teacher's Time in Marking Students' Papers.* The results for this variable are highly inconsistent, with 5 strong positive values, and 7 strong negative values, the remaining 10 being nonsignificant. (Carroll, 1975, pp. 217–218)

> Students in schools where the civics teachers were specialized generally did better in three countries, but worse in one. Students who reported stress on facts in Civic Education classes were generally less successful in Italy, New Zealand and Ireland, but in Finland they did better than other students. (Torney, Oppenheim, & Farnen, 1975, p. 147)

Without going far afield, I will point out that one explanation for inconsistent and counterintuitive results such as the preceding may be collinearity, probably due to the use of multiple indicators (see the explanation of results from analysis of data from the teaching of French as a foreign language, earlier in this chapter).

Another explanation may be the manner in which one arrives at the final equations. In their discussions of the blocks of variables, authors of IEA studies put forward a multistage causal model, which they have used as the rationale for incremental partitioning of variance (see Chapter 9). Assuming that the multistage model is valid (see, however, Chapter 9 for a critique, including the use of stepwise regression analysis for variable selection), one would have to question the usefulness of regression coefficients as indices of effects when these were arrived at in an analysis in which the dependent variable was regressed on all the independent variables simultaneously. In the preceding section, I showed that in such an analysis the regression coefficients indicate direct effects only. Conclusions about importance of variables based on direct effects overlook the possibility that the effects of variables may be mostly, or solely, indirect. In sum, the simultaneous analysis goes counter to the hierarchical model. I return to this topic later.

I will make two final general comments regarding the use of regression equations in the IEA studies. First, standardized regression coefficients were compared across samples and countries to determine the relative importance of variables associated with them (for a discussion of the inappropriateness of such an approach, see earlier sections of this chapter). Second, the authors of some of the studies (e.g., Carroll, 1975, p. 213; Comber & Keeves, 1973, pp. 291–292) reported considerable differences between boys and girls on certain variables. Nevertheless, they used only a coded vector to represent sex, thereby assuming that the difference between boys and girls is limited to the intercepts of the regression equations (see my explanation earlier in this chapter).

In conclusion, I would like to point out that more sophisticated analytic approaches have been used in more recent IEA studies. For discussions and some examples, see Cheung et al. (1990).

Philadelphia School District Studies

In this section, I scrutinize two related studies. The first, which was conducted under the auspices of the Federal Reserve Bank of Philadelphia (FRB), was designed to identify factors that affect student achievement. Its "findings" and recommendations probably received wide publicity in the form of a booklet that the FRB provided free of charge to the general public (Summers & Wolfe, 1975). A notice about the availability of this booklet was included in a report of the study's findings and recommendations in *The New York Times* (Maeroff, 1975). A more technical report was also published (Summers & Wolfe, 1977). Henceforth, I will refer to this study as Study I.

When "it became evident that the School District had no intention of utilizing this study for policy development or decision making purposes" (Kean et al., 1979, p. 14), a second study was designed as a result of cooperation and agreement between FRB and the Philadelphia school district. While the second study (henceforth referred to as Study II) was concerned with the identification of factors affecting reading, it not only utilized the same analytic techniques as in Study I but also included the authors of Study I among the people who planned and executed it. A report of Study II (Kean et al., 1979) was made available, free of charge, from the Office of Research and Evaluation, the School District of Philadelphia.[15]

As with the IEA studies (see the preceding discussion), my comments about these studies are limited to analytic approaches and interpretations purported to indicate the effects of the independent variables on the dependent variable. Unless otherwise stated, my comments apply equally to both studies.

To begin with, I will point out that the dependent variable was a measure of growth obtained by subtracting a premeasure from a postmeasure. I will not comment on problems in the use and interpretation of difference scores, as there is an extensive literature on these topics (e.g., Bohrnstedt, 1969; Cronbach & Furby, 1970; Harris, 1963; and Willett, 1988; for an elementary exposition, see Pedhazur & Schmelkin, 1991, pp. 291–294). I will note, however, that the problems in Study I were compounded by the use of the differences between grade equivalents as a measure of growth. Among major shortcomings of grade equivalents is that they are not expressed on an equal-intervals scale (Coleman & Karweit, 1972, Chapter Five; Thorndike, Cunningham, Thorndike, & Hagen, 1991, pp. 57–60). This in itself renders them of dubious value as a measure of the dependent variable, not to mention the further complication of using differences between such measures. Evidently, the authors of Study I had second thoughts about the use of grade

---

[15]I commented on this study in Chapter 8, under the heading "Variables in Search of a Model."

equivalents, as is evidenced by their use of other types of measures in Study II, "thereby *avoiding the problems of subtracting grade equivalents* [italics added] or percentile ranks" (Kean et al., 1979, pp. 32–33).

The most important criticism of the Philadelphia studies is that they are devoid of theory, as is evidenced from the following statement by the authors of Study I:

> In winnowing down the original list of variables to get the equation of "best fit," *many regressions have been run* [italics added]. The data have been mined, of course. One starts with so few hypotheses convincingly turned up by theory that classical hypothesis testing is in this application sterile. The data are there to be looked at for what they can reveal. (Summers & Wolfe, 1977, p. 642)

The approach taken in Study II was similar to that of Study I. Because I described the former in Chapter 8, I will only remind you that the authors reported that they carried out more than 500 regression analyses and deemed the equation they settled on as their theory.

The authors of both studies stressed that an important aspect of their analytic approach was the study of interactions between variables by means of cross-product vectors. In Chapter 12, I discuss problems in the use and interpretation of cross-product vectors in regression analysis of data obtained in nonexperimental research. Here, I will only point out that even strong advocates of such an approach warned that the simultaneous analysis of vectors and their cross products "results in general in the distortion of the partial coefficients" (Cohen, 1978, p. 861) associated with the vectors from which the cross products were generated. This occurs because there is generally a high correlation between the original vectors and their cross products, thereby resulting in the latter appropriating some (often much) of the variance of the former. Cohen (1978) pointed out that when the original vectors and their cross products are included in a simultaneous analysis, the coefficients associated with the former are, "in general, arbitrary nonsense" (p. 861). The solution, according to Cohen (1978), "is the use of a hierarchical model in which IVS [independent variables] are entered in a predetermined sequence so that earlier entering variables are partialed from later ones and *not* vice versa" (p. 861).

The merits of Cohen's solution aside, it appears that the equations reported in the Philadelphia studies were obtained by using the variables and their cross products in simultaneous analyses. Some examples of the deleterious consequences of this approach are noted from Study I, in which the regression equations with and without the cross-product vectors are reported (Summers & Wolfe, 1977, Table 1, p. 643). Thus, for example, the *b* for race when cross-product vectors were *not* included in the regression equation was −3.34 (t = −2.58), as compared with a *b* of −.23 (t = −.10) when the cross-product vectors *were included* in the regression equation.

The most glaring consequence occurred in connection with third-grade score, which appeared four times in the equation in the form of cross products with other variables (i.e., presumably reflecting interactions), but did not appear by itself in the regression equation (i.e., presumably implying that it has no main effect). In the absence of additional information, it is not possible to tell why this occurred, except to point out that, among other things, "variables which had coefficients whose significance were very sensitive to the introduction and discarding of other variables were not retained" (Summers & Wolfe, 1977, p. 642). The preceding is a clear indication of collinearity in their data.

In view of the tortuous route that led to the final equations in both studies it is not surprising that not only are some results puzzling but also that results for specific variables in Study I are at odds with those for the same variables in Study II. Following are but a few examples.

Class Size.   The authors of Study I claimed to have found that "Low-achieving students . . . did worse in classes with more than 28 students; high-achieving students . . . did better . . . ; those around grade level appeared unaffected" (Summers & Wolfe, 1977, p. 645). Interestingly, in a booklet designed for the general public, the results were reported as follows:

> Elementary students in our sample who are below grade level *gain* [italics added] in classes with less than 28 students, but *the rest of the students* [italics added], can, without any negative effects on achievement, be in classes up to 33. *For all elementary students, in the sample, being in a class of 34 or more has a negative effect, and increasingly so as the size of the class increases* [italics added]. (Summers & Wolfe, 1975, p. 12)

Incidentally, the latter version was used also in a paper presented to the Econometric Society (Summers & Wolfe, 1974, pp. 10–11). Whatever the version, and other issues notwithstanding, note that the conclusions about the differential effects of class size were based on the regression coefficient associated with the cross product of one of the dummy vectors representing class size and third-grade score—a variable on whose questionable status in the regression equation I commented earlier.

The findings of Study II were purported to indicate that "students do better in larger classes" (Kean et al., 1979, p. 46). The authors attempted to explain the contradictory findings about the effect of class size. Thus, when they presumably found that classes of 34 or more have a negative effect, they gave the following explanation: "It is possible that the negative relationship may arise from a teacher's hostile reaction to a class size larger than mandated by the union contract, rather than from largeness itself" (Summers & Wolfe, 1975, p. 12). But when class size seemed to have a positive effect, the authors said:

> In interpreting the finding, however, it is important to emphasize that it is a finding which emerges when many other variables are controlled—that is, what the positive coefficients are saying is that larger classes are better, *after* controlling for such instructional characteristics as the degree of individualization in teaching reading. (Kean et al., 1979, pp. 46–47)

One of the authors is reported to have come up with another explanation of the positive effect of class size. A publication of Division H (School Evaluation and Program Development) of the American Educational Research Association reported the following:

> A Federal Reserve Bank economist, Anita Summers, . . . one of the authors of the study, had a possible explanation for this interesting finding. She felt that the reason why the larger classes seem to show greater growth could be tied to the fact that teachers with larger classes may be forced to instill more discipline and therefore prescribe more silent reading (which appears to positively affect reading achievement). (*Pre Post Press,* September 1979, *1*, p. 1)

There are, of course, many other alternative explanations, the simplest and most plausible being that the model reflected by the regression equation has little or nothing to do with a theory of the process of achievement in reading. It is understandable that authors are reluctant to question their own work, let alone find fault with it. But it is unfortunate that a publication of a division of the American Educational Research Association prints a front-page feature on the study, entitled "Philadelphia Study Pinpoints Factors in Improving Reading Achievement," listing all sorts of presumed findings without the slightest hint that the study may be flawed.

Disruptive Incidents.   When they found that "for students who are at or below grade level, more Disruptive Incidents . . . are associated with greater achievement growth" (Summers &

Wolfe, 1977, p. 647), the authors strained to explain this result. Mercifully, they concluded, "In any case, it would seem a bit premature to engage in a policy of encouraging disruptive incidents to increase learning!" (Summers & Wolfe, 1977, p. 647). I hope that, in light of earlier discussions in this chapter, you can see that collinearity is probably the most plausible explanation of these so-called findings.

Ratings of Teachers Colleges.　The colleges from which the teachers graduated were rated on the Gourman Scale, which the authors described as follows:

> The areas rated include (1) individual departments, (2) administrations, (3) faculty (including student/ staff ratio and research), (4) student services (including financial and honor programs), and (5) general areas such as facilities and alumni support. The Gourman rating is a *simple average* [italics added] of all of these. (Summers & Wolfe, 1975, p. 14)

One cannot help but question whether a score derived as described in the foregoing has any meaning. In any case, the authors dichotomized the ratings so that colleges with ratings of 525 or higher were considered high, whereas those with ratings below 525 were considered low. Their finding: "Teachers who received B.A.'s from higher rated colleges . . . were associated with students whose learning rate was greater" (Summers & Wolfe, 1977, p. 644). Even if one were to give credence to this finding, it would at least be necessary to entertain the notion that the Gourman Scale may serve as a proxy for a variety of variables (teachers' ability or motivation to name but two). It is noteworthy that when the Ratings of Teachers Colleges were found not to contribute significantly to the results of Study II, this fact was mentioned, almost in passing (see Kean et al., 1979, p. 45), without the slightest hint that it was at odds with what was considered a major finding in Study I.

Lest you feel that I unduly belabor these points, note that not only did the authors reject any questioning of their findings, but they also advocated that their findings be used as guides for policy changes in the educational system. The following are but two instances in support of my assertion.

In response to criticisms of their work, the authors of Study I are reported to have "*implied that it's about time educators stopped using technicalities as excuses for not seeking change*" (*Education U.S.A.*, 1975, *17*, p. 179). Further, they are quoted as having said that "The broad findings . . . are firm enough in this study and supported enough by other studies to warrant confidence. We think that this study provides useful information for policy decisions."

The same tone of confidence by the authors of Study I about the implications of their findings is evidenced in the following excerpts from a report of their study in *The New York Times* (Maeroff, 1975, p. 27B).

> On the basis of their findings, the authors advocated not only a reordering of priorities to support those factors that make the most difference in achievement, but also "making teacher salary scales more reflective of productivity."
>
> "For example," they wrote, "graduating from a higher-rated college seems to be a 'productive' characteristic of teachers in terms of achievement growth, though currently this is not rewarded or even used as a basis for hiring."

HIERARCHICAL VERSUS SIMULTANEOUS ANALYSES

Judging by the research literature, it seems that the difference between a hierarchical analysis (Chapter 9) and a simultaneous analysis (present chapter) is not well understood. In many instances, it is ignored altogether. Therefore, I believe it worthwhile to summarize salient points of differences between the two approaches. As most researchers who apply hierarchical analysis refer to Cohen and Cohen (1983), though many of them pay little or no attention to what they say about it (see "Research Examples," later in this chapter), it is only fitting that I begin by quoting Cohen and Cohen.

> When the variables *can* be fully sequenced—that is, when a full causal model can be specified that does not include any reciprocal causation, feedback loops, or unmeasured common causes, the hierarchical procedure becomes a tool for estimating the effects associated with each cause. Indeed, this type of causal model is sometimes called a hierarchical causal model. *Of course, formal causal models use regression coefficients rather than variance proportions to indicate the magnitude of causal effects* [italics added]. (p. 121)

I am concerned by the reference to "formal causal models," as it seems to imply that hierarchical analysis is appropriate for "informal" causal models, whose meaning is left unexplained. Nonetheless, the important point, for present purposes, is that according to Cohen and Cohen a special type of causal model (i.e., variables being "fully sequenced," no "reciprocal causation," etc.) is requisite for the application of hierarchical analysis.

Addressing the same topic, Darlington (1990) stated, "a hierarchical analysis may be either *complete* or *partial,* depending on whether the regressors are placed in a complete causal sequence" (p. 179). He went on to elaborate that when a complete causal sequence is not specified, some effects cannot be estimated.

In Chapter 9 (see Figure 9.6 and the discussion related to it), I argued that even when a complete causal sequence is specified it is not possible to tell what effects are reflected in hierarchical analysis. (For example, does it reflect direct as well as indirect effects? Does it reflect some or all of the latter?). I also pointed out that even if one were to overlook the dubious value of proportions of variance accounted for as indices of effects, it is not valid to use them to determine the relative effects of the variables with which they are associated.

Current practice of statistical tests of significance in hierarchical analysis is to test the proportion of variance incremented at each step and to report whether it is statistically significant at a given alpha level (see Cliff, 1987a, pp. 181–182, for a good discussion of the effect of such an approach on Type I error). Setting aside the crucial problem of what model is reflected in a hierarchical analysis (see the preceding paragraph), such statistical tests of significance do not constitute a test of the model. Cliff (1987a) argued cogently that when "sets of variables are tested according to a strictly defined a priori order, and as soon as a set is found to be nonsignificant, *no further tests are made*" (p. 181). As far as I can tell, this restriction is rarely, if ever, adhered to in the research literature.

I hope that by now you recognize that a simultaneous analysis implies a model contradictory to that implied by a hierarchical analysis. Nevertheless, to make sure that you appreciate the distinction, I will contrast a single-stage simultaneous analysis with a hierarchical analysis applied to the same variables. As I explained earlier (see "The Role of Theory"), when all the independent variables are included in a single-stage simultaneous analysis they are treated, wittingly or unwittingly, as exogenous variables. As a result, it is assumed that they have only direct effects on the dependent variable. Recall that each direct effect, in the form of a partial regression coefficient, is obtained by controlling for the other independent variables. In contrast, in hierarchical analysis, as it is routinely applied, only the variable (or set of variables) entered in the first step is treated as exogenous. Moreover, at each step an adjustment is made only for the variables entered in steps preceding it. Thus, the variable entered at the second step is adjusted for the one entered at the first step; the variable entered at the third step is adjusted for those entered at the first and second step; and so forth.

Recall also that a test of a regression coefficient is tantamount to a test of the variance incremented by the variable with which it is associated when it is entered last into the analysis. Accordingly, a test of the regression coefficient associated with, say, the *first variable* entered in a hierarchical analysis is in effect a test of the proportion of variance the variable in question increments when it is entered *last* in the analysis. Clearly, the two approaches are equivalent only when testing the proportion of variance incremented by the variable that is entered last in a hierarchical analysis and the test of the regression coefficient associated with this variable.

RESEARCH EXAMPLES

The research examples that follow are meant to illustrate lack of appreciation of some of the problems I discussed in the preceding section. In particular they are meant to illustrate lack of appreciation of the (1) requirement of a causal model in hierarchical analysis, and/or (2) difference between hierarchical and simultaneous analysis.

Intellectual Functioning in Adolescents

Simpson and Buckhalt (1988, p. 1097) stated that they used multiple regression analysis "to determine the combination of predictor variables that would optimize prediction of" general intellectual functioning among adolescents. From the foregoing one would conclude that Simpson and Buckhalt were interested solely in prediction. That this is not so is evident from their description of the analytic approach:

> *Based on the recommendation of Cohen and Cohen (1983) to use hierarchical rather than stepwise analysis whenever possible* [italics added], a hierarchical model for entering the predictor variables was developed. Since no predictor variable entering later should be a presumptive cause of a variable entering earlier, the predictor variables were entered in the following order: race, sex, age, PVVT-R, and PIAT. (p. 1099)

True, Cohen and Cohen (1983) stated that "no IV [independent variable] entering later should be a presumptive cause of an IV that has been entered earlier" (p. 120). But, as you can see from the quotation from their book in the beginning of the preceding section, this is not all they said about the requirements for hierarchical analysis. In any event, the requirement stated by Simpson and Buckhalt is a far cry from what is entailed in causal modeling—a topic I present in Chapters 18 and 19. Here, I will comment briefly on the variables and their hierarchy.

Turning first to the variables race, sex, and age, I am certain that the authors did not mean to imply that race affects sex, and that sex (perhaps also race) affects age. Yet, the hierarchy that they established implies this causal chain. The merits of hierarchical analysis aside, I would like to remind you that earlier in this chapter I pointed out that when variables are treated as exogenous (which the aforementioned surely are), they should be entered as a set (see Figures 9.3–9.5 and the discussion related to them). Cohen and Cohen (1983) advocated the same course of action as, for example, when "we are unable to specify the causal interrelationships among the demographic variables" (p. 362).

What about the other two variables? PPVT-R is the "Peabody Picture Vocabulary Test—Revised," and PIAT is the "Peabody Individual Achievement Test" (p. 1097). In view of the hierarchy specified by Simpson and Buckhalt (see the preceding), is one to infer that vocabulary causes achievement? In a broader sense, are these distinct variables? And do these "variables" affect general intellectual functioning? If anything, a case can be made for the latter affecting the former.

I will make three additional comments. One, considering that the correlation between PPVT-R and PAT. was .71, it is not surprising that, because the former was entered first, it was said to account for a considerably larger proportion of variance in general intellectual functioning than the latter.

Two, Simpson and Buckhalt reported also regression coefficients (see their Table 2, p. 1101). As I pointed out in the preceding section, this goes counter to a hierarchical analysis. Incidentally, in the present case, it turns out that judging by the standardized regression coefficients (see the beta weights in their Table 2), PIAT has a greater impact than PPVT-R. As indicated in the preceding paragraph, however, the opposite conclusion would be reached (i.e., that PPVT-R is more important than PIAT) if one were *erroneously* to use proportions of variance incremented by variables entered hierarchically as indices of their relative importance.

Three, Simpson and Buckhalt reported results from an additional analysis aimed at assessing the "unique contributions of the PIAT and PPVT-R" (p. 1101). I suggest that you review my discussion of the unique contribution of a variable in Chapter 9, paying special attention to the argument that it is irrelevant to model testing. Also, notice that Simpson and Buckhalt's analysis to detect uniqueness was superfluous, as the same information could be discerned from their other analyses.

Unique Effects of Print Exposure

Cunningham and Stanovich (1991) were interested in studying the effects of children's exposure to print on what they referred to as "dependent variables" (e.g., spelling, word checklist, verbal fluency). In a "series of analyses" they "examined the question whether print exposure . . . is an independent predictor of these criterion variables" (p. 268). The reference to "independent predictor" notwithstanding, the authors where interested in explanation, as is attested to, among other things, by their statement that their study was "designed to empirically isolate the unique cognitive *effects* [italics added] of exposure to print" (p. 264).

Essentially, Cunningham and Stanovich did a relatively large number of hierarchical analyses, entering a measure of print exposure (Title Recognition Test, TRT) last. Referring to the results in their Table 3, the authors stated, "The beta weight of each variable in the final (simultaneous) regression is also presented" (p. 268). After indicating that TRT added to the proportion of variance accounted for over and above age and Raven Standard Progressive Matrices they stated, "the beta weight for the TRT in the final regression equation is larger than that of the Raven" (p. 268). As you can see, results of hierarchical and simultaneous analyses were used alongside each other. Referring to the aforementioned variables, in the hierarchical analysis Raven was partialed out from TRT, but *not* vice versa. In contrast, when the betas were compared and interpreted, Raven was partialed from TRT, *and* vice versa.

Even more questionable is the authors' practice of switching the roles of variables in the process of carrying out various analyses. For instance, in the first set of analyses (Table 3, p. 268), phonological coding was treated as a dependent variable, and TRT as one of the independent variables. In subsequent analyses (Tables 4–6, pp. 269–271), phonological coding was treated as an independent variable *preceding* TRT in the hierarchical analysis (implying that the former affects the latter?). As another example, word checklist was treated as a dependent variable in two sets of analyses (Tables 3 and 4), as an independent variable in another set of analyses (Table 5), and then again as a dependent variable (Table 6). In all these analyses, TRT was treated as an independent variable entered last into the analysis.

It is analyses such as the preceding that were extolled by the authors as being "quite conservative" (p. 265). Thus they said, "we have partialed out variance in abilities that were likely to be developed by print exposure itself. . . . Yet even when print exposure was robbed of some of its rightful variance, it remained a unique predictor" (p. 265). Or, "our conservative regression strategy goes further than most investigations to stack the deck against our favored variable" (p. 272). As I explained in Chapter 8, in predictive research variables may be designated arbitrarily as either predictors or criteria. In explanatory research, which is what the study under consideration was about, theory should dictate the selection and role of variables.

SOCIAL SCIENCES AND SOCIAL POLICY

In the course of reading this and the preceding chapter you were probably troubled by the state of behavioral research in general and educational research in particular. You were undoubtedly nagged by questions concerning the researchers whose studies I discussed and perhaps about others with whose work you are familiar. Some of the authors whose studies I reviewed in these chapters are prominent researchers. Is it possible, then, that they were unaware of the shortcomings and limitations of the methods they used? Of course they were aware of them, as is attested to by their own writings and caveats. Why, then, do they seem to have ignored the limitations of the methods they were using? There is no simple answer. Actually, more than one answer may be conjectured.

Some researchers (e.g., Coleman, 1970) justified the use of crude analytic approaches on the grounds that the state of theory in the social sciences is rudimentary, at best, and does not warrant the use of more sophisticated analytic approaches. In response to his critics, Coleman (1970) argued that neither he nor anyone else can formulate a theoretical model of achievement, and maintained that "As with any problem, one must start where he is, not where he would like to be" (p. 243).

Similarly, Lohnes and Cooley (1978) defended the use of commonality analysis by saying, "We favor weak over strong interpretations of regressions. This stems from our sense that Congress and other policy agents can better wait for converging evidence of the effects of schooling initiatives than they can recover from confident advisements on what to do which turn out to be wrong" (p. 4).

The authors of the IEA studies expressed reservations and cautions about the analytic methods they were using. Some authors even illustrated how incremental partitioning of variance yielded dramatically different results when the order of the entry of the blocks into the analysis was varied.

Yet the reservations, the cautions, and the caveats seem to have a way of being swept under the rug. Despite the desire to make weak and qualified statements, strong and absolute pronouncements and prescriptions emerge and seem to develop a life of their own. Perhaps this is "because the indices produced by this method [commonality analysis], being pure numbers (proportions or percentages), are especially prone to float clear of their data bases and achieve transcendental quotability and memorableness" (Cooley & Lohnes, 1976, p. 220). Perhaps it is because of a need to make a conclusive statement after having expended large sums of money and a great deal of energy designing, executing, and analyzing large-scale research studies. One may sense the feeling of frustration that accompanies inconclusive findings in the following statement by one of the authors of the IEA studies: "As one views the results on school factors related to reading achievement *it is hard not to feel somewhat disappointed and let down* [italics added]. There is so little that provides a basis for any positive or constructive action on the part of teachers or administrators" (Thorndike, 1973, p. 122).

Perhaps it is the sincere desire to reform society and its institutions that leads to a blurring of the important distinction between the role of the social scientist qua scientist and his or her role as advocate of social policies to which he or she is committed. It is perhaps this process that leads researchers to overlook or mute their own reservations about their research findings and to forget their own exhortations about the necessary caution in interpreting them and in translating them into policy decisions (see Young & Bress, 1975, for a critique of Coleman's role as a social policy advocate, and see Coleman's, 1975b, reply).

One can come up with other explanations for the schism between researchers' knowledge about their research design and methods, and their findings, or what they allege them to be. Whatever the explanations, whatever the motives, which are best left to the psychology and the sociology of scientific research, the unintended damage of conclusions and actions based on questionable research designs and the inappropriate use of analytic methods is incalculable.

Few policy makers, politicians, judges, or journalists, not to mention the public at large, are versed in methodology well enough to assess the validity of conclusions based on voluminous research reports chock-full of tables and bristling with formulas and tests of statistical significance. Fewer still probably even attempt to read the reports. Most seem to get their information from summaries or reports of such summaries in the news media. Often, the summaries do not faithfully reflect the findings of the study, not to mention the caveats with which they were presented in the report itself. Summaries of government-sponsored research may be prepared under the direction of, or even exclusively by, government officials who may be not only poorly versed in methodology but also more concerned with the potential political repercussions of the summary than with its veracity. A case in point is the summary of the Coleman Report, whose tortuous route to publication is detailed by Grant (1973). No fewer than three different versions were being written by different teams, while policy makers at the U.S. Office of Education bickered about what the public should and should not be told in the summary. When it was finally published, there was general agreement among those who studied the report that its summary was misleading. Yet, it is the summary, or news reports about it, that has had the greatest impact on the courts, Congress, and other policy makers.

The gap between what the findings of the Coleman Report were and what policy makers knew about them is perhaps best captured by the candid statement of Howard Howe, then U.S. commissioner of education, whom Grant (1973) quoted as saying:

> I think the reason I was nervous was because I was dealing with something I didn't fully understand. I was not on top of it. You couldn't read the summary and get on top of it. You couldn't read the whole damn thing so you were stuck with trying to explain publicly something that maybe had all sorts of implications, but you didn't want to say the wrong thing, yet you didn't know what the hell to say so it was a very difficult situation for me. (p. 29)

This from a person who was supposed to draw policy implications from the report (see Howe, 1976, for general observations regarding the promise and problem of educational research). Is there any wonder that other, perhaps less candid policy makers have drawn from the report whatever conclusions they found compatible with their preconceptions?[16]

Often, policy makers and the general public learn about findings of a major study from reports of news conferences held by one or more of the researchers who participated in the study or from news releases prepared by the researchers and/or the sponsoring agency. It is, admittedly, not possible or useful to provide reporters with intricate information about analyses and other research issues because, lacking the necessary training, they could not be expected to follow them or even to be interested in them. It is noteworthy that in his presidential address to the American Statistical Association (ASA), Zellner (1992) suggested that there was "a need for a new ASA section which would develop methods for measuring and monitoring accuracy of news reported in the media. *Certainly, schools of journalism need good statistics courses* [italics added]" (p. 2).

It is time that social scientists rethink their role when it comes to disseminating the results of their studies to the general public. It is time they realize that current practices are bound to lead to oversimplification, misunderstanding, selectivity, and even outright distortion consistent with one's preconceived notions, beliefs, or prejudices.

In connection with my critique of the Philadelphia School District studies earlier in this chapter, I showed, through excerpts from a report in *The New York Times,* what the public was told about the "findings" of these studies and the recommendations that were presumably based on them. Following are a couple of examples of what the public was told about the IEA studies. Reporting on a news conference regarding the IEA studies, *The New York Times* (May 27, 1973) ran the story titled "Home Is a Crucial Factor," with the lead sentence being, "The home is more important than the school to a child's overall achievement." The findings were said to support earlier findings of the Coleman Report. On November 18, 1973, *The New York Times* (Reinhold, 1973) reported on another news conference regarding the IEA studies. This time the banner proclaimed, "Study Questions Belief That Home Is More Vital to Pupil Achievement Than the School." Among other things, the article noted:

> Perhaps the most intriguing result of the study was that while home background did seem to play an important role in reading, literature and civics, school conditions were generally more important when it came to science and foreign languages. . . . Home background was found to account for 11.5 percent of the variation on the average for all subjects in all countries, and learning conditions amounted to 10 percent on the average.

Is there any wonder that readers are bewildered about what it is that the IEA studies have found? Moreover, faced with conflicting reports, are policy makers to be blamed for selecting the so-called findings that appear to them more reasonable or more socially just?

Hechinger (1979), who was education editor of *The New York Times,* reacted to contradictory findings about the effects of schooling. In an article titled "Frail Sociology," he suggested that "The Surgeon General should consider labeling all sociological studies: 'Keep out of reach of politicians and judges.' Indiscriminate use of these suggestive works can be dangerous to the nation's health." He went on to draw attention to contradictory findings being offered even by the same researchers.

> For example, take the pronouncement in 1966 by James S. Coleman that school integration helps black children learn more. The Coleman report became a manual for political and court actions involving

---

[16]Examples of such behavior by politicians in Sweden, Germany, and Britain regarding "findings" from some of the IEA studies will be found in Husén (1987, p. 34).

busing and other desegregation strategies. But in 1975 Mr. Coleman proclaimed that busing was a failure. "What once appeared to be fact is now known to be fiction," Coleman II said, reversing Coleman I.

After pointing out contradictions in works of other authors, Hechinger concluded that in matters of social policy we should do what we believe is right and eschew seeking support for such policies in results from frail studies.

Clearly, the dissemination of findings based on questionable research designs and analyses may lead policy makers and the public either to select results to suit specific goals or to heed suggestions such as Hechinger's to ignore social scientific research altogether. Either course of action is, of course, undesirable and may further erode support for social-science research as a means of studying social phenomena and destroy what little credibility it has as a guide for social policy.

Commenting on the technical complexities of the Coleman Report, Mosteller and Moynihan (1972) stated:

> We have noted that the material is difficult to master, even for those who had the time, facilities, and technical equipment to try. As a result, in these technical areas society must depend upon the judgment of experts. (Thus does science recreate an age of faith!) Increasingly the most relevant findings concerning the state of society are the work of elites, and must simply be taken—or rejected—by the public at large, at times even by the professional public involved, on such faith. Since the specialists often disagree, however, the public is frequently at liberty to choose which side it will, or, for that matter, to choose neither and continue comfortable in the old myths. (p. 32)

Of course, the solution is to become knowledgeable to a degree that would enable one to read research reports intelligently and to make informed judgments about their findings and the claims made for them. Commendably, professionals in some areas have begun to take steps in this direction. As but one example, I will point out that when in the legal profession "statistics have become . . . the hottest new way to prove a complicated case" (Lauter, 1984, p. 10), lawyers, prosecutors, and judges have found it necessary to acquire a basic understanding of statistical terminology and methodology. In the preface to the sixth edition of his popular book, Zeisel (1985) stated that he had been wondering whether adding a presentation of uses and abuses of regression analysis would serve a useful purpose, but that "all doubts were removed when my revered friend Judge Marvin Frankel, learning that I was revising the book said to me, 'Be sure that after I have read it I will know what regression analysis is'" (p. ix).

And Professor Henry G. Mann—director of the Law and Economic Center at Emory University—is reported to have said:

> Ten years ago if you had used the word "regression-equation", [*sic*] there would have not been more than five judges in the country who would have known what you are talking about. It is all around now. I think it has become a part of most sophisticated people's intellectual baggage. (Lauter, 1984, p. 10)

Presiding over a case of discrimination in employment, Judge Patrick E. Higginbotham found it necessary not only to become familiar with the intricacies of multiple regression analysis but also to render a lengthy opinion regarding its appropriate use and interpretation! (Vuyanich v. Republic National Bank, 505 Federal Supplement. 224–394 (N.D. Texas, 1980).

Following are a couple of excerpts from Judge Higginbotham's opinion:

> Central to the validity of any multiple regression model and resulting statistical inferences is the use of a proper procedure for determining what explanatory variables should be included and what mathematical form the equation should follow. The model devised must be based on theory, *prior to* looking

at the data and running the model on the data. If one does the reverse, the usual tests of statistical inference do not apply. And proceeding in the direction of data to model is perceived as illegitimate. Indeed it is important in reviewing the final numerical product of the regression studies that we recall the model's dependence upon this relatively intuitive step. (p. 269)

"There are problems, however, associated with the use of R^2. A high R^2 does not necessarily indicate model quality" (p. 273).[17]

Regrettably, many behavioral researchers and practitioners fail to recognize the need to become knowledgeable in the very methods they apply, not to mention those who reject quantitative methods altogether and seek refuge in qualitative ones. For good discussions of misconceptions regarding a quantitative-qualitative divide, see Brodbeck (1968), Cizek (1995), Erickson (1986), Kaplan (1964), and Rist (1980).

STUDY SUGGESTIONS

1. I repeat here the illustrative correlation matrix ($N = 150$) that I used in the Study Suggestions for Chapters 8 and 9.

1	*2*	*3* School Quality	*4* Self- Concept	*5* Level of Aspiration	*6* Verbal Achievement
Race	IQ				
1.00	.30	.25	.30	.30	.25
.30	1.00	.20	.20	.30	.60
.25	.20	1.00	.20	.30	.30
.30	.20	.20	1.00	.40	.30
.30	.30	.30	.40	1.00	.40
.25	.60	.30	.30	.40	1.00

Using a computer program, regress verbal achievement on the five independent variables.
(a) What is R^2?
(b) What is the regression equation?
(c) What information would you need to convert the β's obtained in (b) to b's?
(d) Assuming you were to use magnitude of the β's as indices of the effects of the variables with which they are associated, interpret the results.
(e) The validity of the preceding interpretation is predicated, among other things, on the assumptions that the model is correctly specified and that the measures of the independent variables are perfectly reliable. Discuss the implications of this statement.
(f) Using relevant information from the computer output, what is $1 - R_i^2$, where R_i^2 is the squared

multiple correlation of each independent variable with the remaining independent variables. What is this value called? How is it used in computer programs for regression analysis?
(g) What is $1/(1 - R_i^2)$ for each of the independent variables? What is it called? What is it used for?

2. Use a computer program that enables you to do matrix operations (e.g., MINITAB, SAS, SPSS).
(a) Calculate the determinant of the correlation matrix of the five independent variables in Study Suggestion 1.
(b) What would the determinant be if the matrix was orthogonal?
(c) What would the determinant be if the matrix contained a linear dependency?
(d) If the determinant was equal to 1.00, what would the regression equation be?
(e) Calculate the inverse of the correlation matrix of the five independent variables.
(f) Using relevant values from the inverse and a formula given in this chapter, calculate $1 - R_i^2$, where R_i^2 is the squared multiple correlation of each independent variable with the remaining independent variables. Compare the results with those obtained under Study Suggestion 1(f). If you do not have access to a computer program for matrix operations, use the inverse given in the answers to this chapter to solve for $1 - R_i^2$.
(g) What would the inverse of the correlation matrix among the independent variables be if all the correlations among them were equal to zero?

[17]For a review of the use of results of multiple regression analyses in legal proceedings, see Fisher (1980).

ANSWERS

1. (a) .43947
   (b) $z'_6 = -.01865z_1 + .50637z_2 + .13020z_3 + .11004z_4 + .17061z_5$
   (c) The standard deviations
   (d) IQ has the largest effect on verbal achievement. Assuming $\alpha = .05$ was selected, the effects of race, school quality, and self-concept are statistically not significant.
   (f) $1 - R^2_{1.2345} = .81378; 1 - R^2_{2.1345} = .85400; 1 - R^2_{3.1245} = .87314; 1 - R^2_{4.1235} = .80036; 1 - R^2_{5.1234} = .74252.$ Tolerance. See the explanation in chapter.
   (g) 1.229; 1.171; 1.145; 1.249; 1.347. VIF. See the explanation in chapter.
2. (a) .54947
   (b) 1.00
   (c) .00
   (d) $z'_6 = .25z_1 + .60z_2 + .30z_3 + .30z_4 + .40z_5.$ That is, each β would equal the zero-order correlation of a given independent variable with the dependent variable.
   (e)

1.22883	−.24369	−.16689	−.22422	−.15579
−.24369	1.17096	−.09427	−.05032	−.22977
−.16689	−.09427	1.14530	−.06433	−.23951
−.22422	−.05032	−.06433	1.24944	−.39811
−.15579	−.22977	−.23951	−.39811	1.34676

   (f) .81378; .85400; .87313; .80036; .74252. By (10.13).
   (g) An identity matrix

A Categorical Independent Variable: Dummy, Effect, and Orthogonal Coding

My presentation of regression analysis in preceding chapters was limited to designs in which the independent variables or the predictors are continuous. A continuous variable is one on which subjects differ in amount or degree. Some examples of continuous variables are weight, height, study time, dosages of a drug, motivation, and mental ability. Note that a continuous variable expresses gradations; that is, a person is more or less motivated, say, or has studied more or less.[1]

Another type of variable is one composed of mutually exclusive categories, hence the name categorical variable.[2] Sex, race, religious affiliation, occupation, and marital status are some examples of categorical variables. On categorical variables, subjects differ in type or kind; not in degree. In contrast to a continuous variable, which reflects a condition of "more or less," a categorical variable reflects a condition of "either/or." On a categorical variable, a person either belongs to a given category or does not belong to it. For example, when in experimental research subjects are randomly assigned to different treatments such as different teaching methods, different modes of communication, or different kinds of rewards, the treatments constitute a set of mutually exclusive categories that differ from each other in kind. Similarly, when people are classified into groups or categories based on attributes such as race, occupation, political party affiliation, or marital status, the classification constitutes a set of mutually exclusive categories.

Information from a categorical variable can be used to explain or predict phenomena. Indeed, a major reason for creating classifications is to study how they relate to, or help explain, other variables (for discussions of the role of classification in scientific inquiry, see Hempel, 1952, pp. 50–54; 1965, pp. 137–145).

Categorical variables can be used in regression analysis, provided they are coded first. In this chapter, I describe procedures for coding a categorical independent variable, or a predictor, and

---

[1]Strictly speaking, a continuous variable has infinite gradations. When measuring height, for example, ever finer gradations may be used. The choice of gradations on such a scale depends on the degree of accuracy called for in the given situation. Certain variables can take only discrete values (e.g., number of children, number of arrests). In this book, I refer to such variables, too, as *continuous*. Some authors use the term *numerical variable* instead of continuous.

[2]Some authors use the terms *qualitative* and *quantitative* for categorical and continuous, respectively.

show how to use the coded vectors in regression analysis. In Chapter 12, I extend these ideas to multiple categorical variables, and in Chapter 14, I show how to apply regression analysis to designs consisting of both continuous and categorical independent variables or predictors.

I present three coding methods and show that overall results (e.g., R^2) from their application are identical, but that intermediate results (e.g., regression equation) differ. Further, I show that some intermediate results from the application of different coding methods are useful for specific purposes, especially for specific types of comparisons among means.

In the first part of the chapter, I discuss and illustrate the analysis of data from designs with equal sample sizes. I then examine the analysis of data from designs with unequal sample sizes. I conclude the chapter with some general observations about multiple regression analysis versus the analysis of variance.

RESEARCH DESIGNS

Before I turn to the substance of this chapter, I would like to point out that, as with continuous variables, categorical variables may be used in different research designs (e.g., experimental, quasi-experimental, nonexperimental) for explanatory and predictive purposes. Consequently, what I said about these topics in connection with continuous independent variables (see, in particular, Chapters 8 through 10) applies equally to categorical variables.

For example, a categorical variable such as occupation may be used to predict or explain attitudes toward the use of nuclear power plants or voting behavior. When the goal is explanation, it is essential that the researcher formulate a theoretical model and stay alert to potential threats to a valid interpretation of the results, particularly to specification and measurement errors. It is necessary, for instance, to keep in mind that occupation is correlated with a variety of variables or that it may serve as a proxy for a variable not included in the model. Depending on the specific occupations used, occupation may be strongly related to education. Is it, then, occupation or education that determines attitudes or voting behavior, or do both affect such phenomena? Some occupations are held primarily by women; others are held primarily by men. Assuming that such occupations are used in explanatory research, is sex or occupation (or are both) the "cause" (or "causes") of the phenomenon studied? Moreover, it is possible that neither sex nor occupation affects the phenomenon under study, but that they appear to affect it because they are related to variables that do affect it.

In earlier chapters, I said that experimental research has the potential of providing less ambiguous answers to research questions than quasi-experimental and nonexperimental research. This is true whether the independent variables are continuous or categorical. One should recognize, however, that experimental research does not always lead to less ambiguous answers than other types of research (see the discussion of the definition of variables in the next section).

The method of coding categorical variables and the manner in which they are used in regression analysis is the same, regardless of the type of design and regardless of whether the aim is explanation or prediction. Occasionally, I will remind you of, or comment briefly about, the importance of distinguishing between these types of designs. For detailed discussions of such distinctions, see books on research design (e.g., Kerlinger, 1986, Part Seven; Pedhazur & Schmelkin, 1991, Part 2). I urge you to pay special attention to discussions concerning the internal and external validity of different designs (Campbell & Stanley, 1963; Cook & Campbell, 1979).

CODING AND METHODS OF CODING

A *code* is a set of symbols to which meanings can be assigned. For example, a set of symbols {A, B, C} can be assigned to three different treatments or to three groups of people, such as Protestants, Catholics, and Jews. Or the set {0, 1} can be assigned to a control and an experimental group, or to males and females. Whatever the symbols, they are assigned to objects of mutually exclusive subsets of a defined universe to indicate subset or group membership.

The assignment of symbols follows a rule or a set of rules determined by the definition of the variable used. For some variables, the rule may be obvious and may require little or no explanation, as in the assignment of 1's and 0's to males and females, respectively. However, some variables require elaborate definitions and explication of rules, about which there may not be agreement among all or most observers. For example, the definition of a variable such as occupation may involve a complex set of rules about which there may not be universal agreement. An example of even greater complexity is the explication of rules for the classification of mentally ill patients according to their diseases, as what is called for is a complex process of diagnosis about which psychiatrists may not agree or may strongly disagree. The validity of findings of research in which categorical nonmanipulated variables are used depends, among other things, on the validity and reliability of their definitions (i.e., the classification rules). Indeed, "the establishment of a suitable system of classification in a given domain of investigation may be considered as a special kind of scientific concept formation" (Hempel, 1965, p. 139).

What I said about the definition of nonmanipulated categorical variables applies equally to manipulated categorical variables. Some manipulated variables are relatively easy to define theoretically and operationally, whereas the definition of others may be very difficult, as is evidenced by attempts to define, through manipulations, anxiety, motivation, prejudice, and the like. For example, do different instructions to subjects or exposure to different films lead to different kinds of aggression? Assuming they do, are exposures to different instructions the same as exposures to different films in inducing aggression? What other variables might be affected by such treatments? The preceding are but some questions the answers to which have important implications for the valid interpretation of results. In short, as in nonexperimental research, the validity of conclusions drawn from experimental research is predicated, among other things, on the validity and reliability of the definitions of the variables.

Whatever the definition of a categorical variable and whatever the coding, subjects classified in a given category are treated as being alike on it. Thus, if one defines rules of classification into political parties, then people classified as Democrats, say, are considered equal, regardless of their devotion, activity, and commitment to the Democratic party and no matter how different they may be on other variables.

For analytic purposes, numbers are used as symbols (codes) and therefore do not reflect quantities or a rank ordering of the categories to which they are assigned. Any set of numbers may be used: {1, 0}, {−99, 123}, {1, 0, −1}, {24, 5, −7}, and so on. However, some coding methods have properties that make them more useful than others. This is especially so when the symbols are used in statistical analysis. In this book, I use three coding methods: *dummy, effect,* and *orthogonal.* As I pointed out earlier, the overall analysis and results are identical no matter which of the three methods is used in regression analysis. As I will show, however, some intermediate results and the statistical tests of significance associated with the three methods are different. Therefore, a given coding method may be more useful in one situation than in another. I turn now to a detailed treatment of each of the methods of coding categorical variables.

DUMMY CODING

The simplest method of coding a categorical variable is dummy coding. In this method, one generates a number of vectors (columns) such that, in any given vector, membership in a given group or category is assigned 1, whereas nonmembership in the category is assigned 0. I begin with the simplest case: a categorical variable consisting of two categories, as in a design with an experimental and a control group or one with males and females.

A VARIABLE WITH TWO CATEGORIES

Assume that the data reported in Table 11.1 were obtained in an experiment in which E represents an experimental group and C represents a control group. Alternatively, the data under E may have been obtained from males and those under C from females, or those under E from people who own homes and those under C from people who rent (recall, however, the importance of distinguishing between different types of designs).

t Test

As is well known, a t test may be used to determine whether there is a statistically significant difference between the mean of the experimental group and the mean of the control group. I do this here for comparison with a regression analysis of the same data (see the following). The formula for a test of the difference between two means is

$$t = \frac{\bar{Y}_1 - \bar{Y}_2}{\sqrt{\frac{\Sigma y_1^2 + \Sigma y_2^2}{n_1 + n_2 - 2}\left(\frac{1}{n_1} + \frac{1}{n_2}\right)}} \tag{11.1}$$

where $\bar{Y}_1$ and $\bar{Y}_2$ are the means of groups 1 and 2, respectively (for the data of Table 11.1, consider $\bar{Y}_1 = \bar{Y}_E$ and $\bar{Y}_2 = \bar{Y}_C$); Σy_1^2 and Σy_2^2 are the sums of squares for E and C, respectively; n_1 is the number of people in E; and n_2 is the number of people in C. The t ratio has $n_1 + n_2 - 2$ degrees of freedom. (For detailed discussions of the test, see Edwards, 1985, Chapter 4; Hays, 1988, Chapter 8). Recalling that for the numerical example under consideration, the number of

Table 11.1   Illustrative Data for an Experimental (E) and a Control (C) Group

	E	C
	20	10
	18	12
	17	11
	17	15
	13	17
Σ:	85	65
$\bar{Y}$:	17	13
Σy^2:	26	34

people in each group is 5, and using the means and sums of squares reported at the bottom of Table 11.1,

$$t = \frac{17 - 13}{\sqrt{\frac{26 + 34}{5 + 5 - 2}\left(\frac{1}{5} + \frac{1}{5}\right)}} = \frac{4}{\sqrt{3}} = 2.31$$

with 8 *df, p* < .05. Using the .05 level of significance, one will conclude that the difference between the experimental group mean and the control group mean is statistically significant.

Simple Regression Analysis

I now use the data in Table 11.1 to illustrate the application of dummy coding and regression analysis. Table 11.2 displays the scores on the measure of the dependent variable for both groups in a single vector, *Y.* Three additional vectors are displayed in Table 11.2: X_1 is a unit vector (i.e., all subjects are assigned 1's in this vector). In X_2, subjects in *E* are assigned 1's, whereas those in *C* are assigned 0's. Conversely, in X_3, subjects in *C* are assigned 1's and those in *E* are assigned 0's. X_2 and X_3, then, are dummy vectors in which a categorical variable with two categories (e.g., *E* and *C,* male and female) was coded.

One could now regress *Y* on the *X*'s to note whether the latter help explain, or predict, some of the variance of the former. In other words, one would seek to determine whether information about membership in different groups, which exist naturally or are created for the purpose of an experiment, helps explain some of the variability of the subjects on the dependent variable, *Y.*

In Chapter 6, I showed how matrix algebra can be used to solve the equation,

$$\mathbf{b} = (\mathbf{X'X})^{-1}\mathbf{X'y} \tag{11.2}$$

where **b** is a column vector of *a* (intercept) plus b_k regression coefficients. $\mathbf{X'}$ is the transpose of **X,** the latter being an *N* by $1 + k$ matrix composed of a unit vector and *k* column vectors of scores on the independent variables. $(\mathbf{X'X})^{-1}$ is the inverse of $(\mathbf{X'X})$. **y** is an *N* by 1 column of dependent

Table 11.2   Dummy Coding for Experimental and Control Groups, Based on Data from Table 11.1

	Y	X_1	X_2	X_3
	20	1	1	0
	18	1	1	0
	17	1	1	0
	17	1	1	0
	13	1	1	0
	10	1	0	1
	12	1	0	1
	11	1	0	1
	15	1	0	1
	17	1	0	1
M:	15	1	.5	.5
ss:	100	0	2.5	2.5
	$\Sigma yx_2 = 10$		$\Sigma yx_3 = -10$	

NOTE: *M* = mean; *ss* = deviation sum of squares.

variable scores. Equation (11.2) applies equally when **X** is a matrix of scores on continuous variables or when it is, as in the present example, composed of coded vectors. In Table 11.2, **X** is composed of a unit vector and two dummy vectors. Inspecting this matrix reveals that it contains a linear dependency: $X_2 + X_3 = X_1$. Therefore $(\mathbf{X'X})$ is singular and cannot be inverted, thus precluding a solution for (11.2). To show clearly that $(\mathbf{X'X})$ is singular, I carry out the matrix operations with the three X vectors of Table 11.2 to obtain the following:

$$(\mathbf{X'X}) = \begin{bmatrix} 10 & 5 & 5 \\ 5 & 5 & 0 \\ 5 & 0 & 5 \end{bmatrix}$$

Notice that the first row, or column, of the matrix is equal to the sum of the two other rows, or columns. The determinant of $(\mathbf{X'X})$ is zero. (If you are encountering difficulties with this presentation, I suggest that you review the relevant sections in Chapter 6, where I introduced these topics.)

The linear dependency in **X** can be eliminated, as either X_2 or X_3 of Table 11.2 is necessary and sufficient to represent membership in two categories of a variable. That is, X_2, or X_3, alone contains all the information about group membership. Therefore, it is sufficient to use X_1 and X_2, or X_1 and X_3, as **X** in (11.2). The overall results are the same regardless of which set of vectors is used. However, as I will show, the regression equations for the two sets differ.

I presented procedures for calculating regression statistics with a single independent variable in Chapter 2 (using algebraic formulas) and in Chapter 6 (using matrix operations). Therefore, there appears no need to repeat them here. Instead, Table 11.3 summarizes results for the regression

Table 11.3   Calculation of Statistics for the Regression of Y on X_2 and Y on X_3, based on Data from Table 11.2

	(a) Y on X_2	(b) Y on X_3
$b = \dfrac{\Sigma xy}{\Sigma x^2}$	$\dfrac{10}{2.5} = 4$	$\dfrac{-10}{2.5} = -4$
$a = \bar{Y} - b\bar{X}$	$15 - (4)(.5) = 13$	$15 - (-4)(.5) = 17$
$Y' = a + bX$	$13 + 4X$	$17 - 4X$
$ss_{reg} = b\Sigma xy$	$(4)(10) = 40$	$(-4)(-10) = 40$
$ss_{res} = \Sigma y^2 - ss_{reg}$	$100 - 40 = 60$	$100 - 40 = 60$
$s^2_{y.x} = \dfrac{ss_{res}}{N - k - 1}$	$\dfrac{60}{10 - 1 - 1} = 7.5$	$\dfrac{60}{10 - 1 - 1} = 7.5$
$s_b = \sqrt{\dfrac{s^2_{y.x}}{\Sigma x^2}}$	$\sqrt{\dfrac{7.5}{2.5}} = 1.732$	$\sqrt{\dfrac{7.5}{2.5}} = 1.732$
$t = \dfrac{b}{s_b}$	$\dfrac{4}{1.732} = 2.31$	$\dfrac{-4}{1.732} = -2.31$
$r^2 = \dfrac{ss_{reg}}{\Sigma y^2}$	$\dfrac{40}{100} = .4$	$\dfrac{40}{100} = .4$
$F = \dfrac{r^2/k}{(1 - r^2)/(N - k - 1)}$	$\dfrac{.4/1}{(1 - .4)/8} = 5.33$	$\dfrac{.4/1}{(1 - .4)/8} = 5.33$

of Y on X_2 and Y on X_3. For your convenience, I included in the table the algebraic formulas I used. If necessary, refer to Chapter 2 for detailed discussions of each. I turn now to a discussion of relevant results reported in Table 11.3.

The Regression Equation.   Consider first the regression of Y on X_2:

$$Y' = a + bX_2 = 13 + 4X_2$$

Since X_2 is a dummy vector, the predicted Y for each person assigned 1 (members of the experimental group) is

$$Y' = a + bX_2 = 13 + 4(1) = 17$$

and the predicted Y for each person assigned 0 (members of the control group) is

$$Y' = a + bX_2 = 13 + 4(0) = 13$$

Thus, the regression equation leads to a predicted score that is equal to the mean of the group to which an individual belongs (see Table 11.1, where $\bar{Y}_E = 17$ and $\bar{Y}_C = 13$).

Note that the intercept (a) is equal to the mean of the group assigned 0 in X_2 (the control group):

$$Y'_C = \bar{Y}_C = a + b(0) = a = 13$$

Also, the regression coefficient (b) is equal to the deviation of the mean of the group assigned 1 in X_2 from the mean of the group assigned 0 in the same vector:

$$Y'_E = \bar{Y}_E = a + b(1) = a + b = 17$$

$$\bar{Y}_E - \bar{Y}_C = 17 - 13 = 4 = (a + b) - a = b$$

From Table 11.3, the equation for the regression of Y on X_3 is

$$Y' = a + bX_3 = 17 - 4X_3$$

Applying this equation to the scores on X_3,

$$Y'_E = 17 - 4(0) = 17$$

$$Y'_C = 17 - 4(1) = 13$$

In X_3, members of the control group were assigned 1's, whereas those in the experimental group were assigned 0's. Although this regression equation [part (b) of Table 11.3] differs from the equation for the first analysis [part (a) of Table 11.3], both lead to the same predicted Y: the mean of the group to which the individual belongs.

Note that, as in (a), the intercept for the regression equation in (b) is equal to the mean of the group assigned 0 in X_3 (the experimental group). Again, as in (a), the regression coefficient in (b) is equal to the deviation of the mean of the group assigned 1 in X_3 (the control group) from the mean of the group assigned 0 (the experimental group): $\bar{Y}_C - \bar{Y}_E = 13 - 17 = -4 = b$.

In sum, the properties of the regression equations in (a) and (b) of Table 11.3 are the same, although the specific values of the intercept and the regression coefficient differ depending on which group is assigned 1 and which is assigned 0. The predicted scores are the same (i.e., the mean of the group in question), regardless of which of the two regression equations is used.

Test of the Regression Coefficient.   I pointed out earlier that the regression coefficient (b) is equal to the deviation of the mean of the group assigned 1 from the mean of the group assigned 0. In other words, b is equal to the difference between the two means. The same value is, of course, obtained in (a) and (b) of Table 11.3, except that in the former it is positive (i.e., $\overline{Y}_E - \overline{Y}_C$) whereas in the latter it is negative (i.e., $\overline{Y}_C - \overline{Y}_E$). Therefore, testing the b for significance is tantamount to testing the difference between the two means. Not surprisingly, then, the t ratio of 2.31 with 8 df $(N - k - 1)$ is the same as the one I obtained earlier when I applied (11.1) to the test of the difference between the means of the experimental and control groups.

Regression and Residual Sums of Squares.   Note that these two sums of squares are identical in (a) and (b) of Table 11.3 inasmuch as they reflect the same information about group membership, regardless of the specific symbols assigned to members of a given group.

Squared Correlation.   The squared correlation, r^2, between the independent variable (i.e., the coded vector) and the dependent variable, Y, is also the same in (a) and (b) of Table 11.3: .4, indicating that 40% of Σy^2, or of the variance of Y, is due to its regression on X_2 or on X_3. Testing r^2 for significance, $F = 5.33$ with 1 and 8 df. Since the numerator for the F ratio has one degree of freedom, $t^2 = F$ $(2.31^2 = 5.33$; see Table 11.3). Of course, the same F ratio would be obtained if ss_{reg} were tested for significance (see Chapter 2).

A VARIABLE WITH MULTIPLE CATEGORIES

In this section, I present an example in which the categorical independent variable, or predictor, consists of more than two categories. Although I use a variable with three categories, extensions to variables with any number of categories are straightforward. As in the numerical example I analyzed in the preceding, I first analyze this example using the more conventional approach of the analysis of variance (ANOVA).

As is well known, a one-way, or simple, ANOVA is the appropriate analytic method to test differences among more than two means. As I show in the following, the same can be accomplished through multiple regression analysis. The reason I present ANOVA here is to show the equivalence of the two approaches. If you are not familiar with ANOVA you may skip the next section without loss of continuity, or you may choose to study an introductory treatment of one-way ANOVA (e.g., Edwards, 1985, Chapter 6; Keppel, 1991, Chapter 3; Keppel & Zedeck, 1989, Chapter 6; Kirk, 1982, Chapter 4).

One-Way Analysis of Variance

In Table 11.4, I present illustrative data for three groups. You may think of these data as having been obtained in an experiment in which A_1 and A_2 are, say, two treatments for weight reduction whereas A_3 is a placebo. Or, A_1, A_2, and A_3 may represent three different methods of teaching reading. Alternatively, the data may be viewed as having been obtained in nonexperimental research. For example, one might be interested in studying the relation between marital status of adult males and their attitudes to the awarding of child custody to the father after a divorce. A_1 may be married males, A_2 may be single males, and A_3 may be divorced males. Scores on Y would indicate their attitudes. The three groups can, of course, represent three other kinds of categories, say, religious groups, countries of origin, professions, political parties, and so on.

Table 11.4   Illustrative Data for Three Groups and Analysis of Variance Calculations

A_1	A_2	A_3	
4	7	1	
5	8	2	
6	9	3	
7	10	4	
8	11	5	
ΣY: 30	45	15	$\Sigma Y_t = 90$
$\bar{Y}$: 6	9	3	$(\Sigma Y_t)^2 = 8100$
			$\Sigma Y^2 = 660$

$$C = \frac{8100}{15} = 540$$

$$\text{Total} = 660 - 540 = 120$$

$$\text{Between} = \frac{30^2 + 45^2 + 15^2}{5} - 540 = 90$$

Source	df	ss	ms	F
Between	2	90	45.00	18.00
Within	12	30	2.50	
Total	14	120		

Data such as those reported in Table 11.4 may be analyzed by what is called a one-way analysis of variance (ANOVA), *one-way* referring to the fact that only one independent variable is used. I will not comment on the ANOVA calculations, which are given in Table 11.4, except to note that the $F(2, 12) = 18, p < .01$ indicates that there are statistically significant differences among the three means. I comment on specific elements of Table 11.4 after I analyze the same data by multiple regression methods.

Multiple Regression Analysis

I now use the data in Table 11.4 to illustrate the application of dummy coding to a variable with multiple categories. In Table 11.5, I combined the scores on the dependent variable, *Y,* in a single vector. *This procedure of combining the scores on the dependent variable in a single vector is always followed, regardless of the number of categories of the independent variable and regardless of the number of independent variables* (see Chapter 12). This is done to cast the data in a format appropriate for multiple regression analysis in which a dependent variable is regressed on two or more independent variables. That in the present case there is only one categorical independent variable consisting of three categories does not alter the basic conception of bringing information from a set of vectors to bear on a dependent variable. The information may consist of (1) continuous independent variables (as in earlier chapters), (2) a categorical variable (as in the present chapter), (3) multiple categorical variables (Chapter 12), or (4) a combination of continuous and categorical variables (Chapter 14). The overall approach and conception are the same, although the interpretation of specific aspects of the results depends on the type of variables

Table 11.5   Dummy Coding for Illustrative Data from Three Groups

Group	Y	D1	D2
A_1	4	1	0
	5	1	0
	6	1	0
	7	1	0
	8	1	0
A_2	7	0	1
	8	0	1
	9	0	1
	10	0	1
	11	0	1
A_3	1	0	0
	2	0	0
	3	0	0
	4	0	0
	5	0	0

NOTE: I analyzed the same data by ANOVA in Table 11.4.

used. Furthermore, as I show later in this chapter, specific methods of coding categorical variables yield results that lend themselves to specific interpretations.

For the example under consideration, we know that the scores on the dependent variable, *Y*, of Table 11.5 were obtained from three groups, and it is this information about group membership that is coded to represent the independent variable in the regression analysis. Using dummy coding, I created two vectors, D1 and D2, in Table 11.5. In D1, I assigned 1's to subjects in group A_1 and 0's to subjects *not* in A_1. In D2, I assigned 1's to subjects in group A_2 and 0's to those *not* in A_2. Note that I am using the letter D to stand for dummy coding and a number to indicate the group assigned 1's in the given vector. Thus, assuming a design with five categories, D4 would mean the dummy vector in which group 4 is assigned 1's.

I could create also a vector in which subjects of group A_3 would be assigned 1's and those *not* in this group would be assigned 0's. This, however, is not necessary as the information about group membership is exhausted by the two vectors I created. A third vector will not add any information to that contained in the first two vectors—see the previous discussion about the linear dependency in **X** when the number of coded vectors is equal to the number of groups and about (**X'X**) therefore being singular.

Stated another way, knowing an individual's status on the first two coded vectors is sufficient information about his or her group membership. Thus, an individual who has a 1 in D1 and a 0 in D2 belongs to group A_1; one who has a 0 in D1 and a 1 in D2 is a member of group A_2; and an individual who has 0's in both vectors is a member of group A_3. In general, to code a categorical variable with *g* categories or groups it is necessary to create $g - 1$ vectors, each of which will have 1's for the members of a given group and 0's for those not belonging to the group. Because only $g - 1$ vectors are created, it follows that members of one group will have 0's in all the vectors. In the present example there are three categories and therefore I created two vectors. Members of group A_3 are assigned 0's in both vectors.

Instead of assigning 1's to groups A_1 and A_2, I could have created two different vectors (I do this in the computer analyses that follow). Thus, I could have assigned 1's to members of groups A_2 and A_3, respectively, in the two vectors. In this case, members of group A_1 would be assigned 0's in both vectors. In the following I discuss considerations in the choice of the group assigned 0's. Note, however, that regardless of which groups are assigned 1's, the number of vectors necessary and sufficient for information about group membership in the present example is two.

Nomenclature

Hereafter, *I will refer to members of the group assigned 1's in a given vector as being identified in that vector.* Thus, members of A_1 are identified in D1, and members of A_2 are identified in D2 (see Table 11.5). This terminology generalizes to designs with any number of groups or categories, as each group (except for the one assigned 0's throughout) is assigned 1's (i.e., identified) in one vector only and is assigned 0's in the rest of the vectors.

Analysis

Since the data in Table 11.5 consist of two coded vectors, the regression statistics can be easily done by hand using the formulas I presented in Chapter 5 or the matrix operations I presented in Chapter 6. The calculations are particularly easy as correlations between dummy vectors are obtained by a simplified formula (see Cohen, 1968):

$$r_{ij} = -\sqrt{\frac{n_i n_j}{(n - n_i)(n - n_j)}} \tag{11.3}$$

where n_i = sample size in group i; n_j = sample size in group j; and n = total sample in the g groups. When the groups are of equal size (in the present example, $n_1 = n_2 = n_3 = 5$), (11.3) reduces to

$$r_{ij} = -\frac{1}{g - 1} \tag{11.4}$$

where g is the number of groups. In the present example $g = 3$. Therefore the correlation between D1 and D2 of Table 11.5 is

$$r_{12} = -\frac{1}{3 - 1} = -.5$$

Formulas (11.3) and (11.4) are applicable to any number of dummy vectors. Thus for five groups or categories, say, four dummy vectors have to be created. Assuming that the groups are of equal size, then the correlation between any two of the dummy vectors is

$$r_{ij} = -\frac{1}{5 - 1} = -.25$$

Calculation of the correlation between any dummy vector and the dependent variable can also be simplified. Using, for example, (2.42) for the correlation between dummy vector D1 and Y,

$$r_{yD_1} = \frac{N\Sigma YD_1 - (\Sigma Y)(\Sigma D_1)}{\sqrt{N\Sigma Y^2 - (\Sigma Y)^2} \sqrt{N\Sigma D_1^2 - (\Sigma D_1)^2}}$$

Note that ΣYD_1 is equal to ΣY for the group identified in D1, $\Sigma D_1 = \Sigma D_1^2$ is the number of people in the group identified in D1, and similarly for the correlation of any dummy vector with the dependent variable.

Despite the ease of the calculations for the present example, I do not present them here (you may wish to do them as an exercise). Instead, I will use REGRESSION of SPSS. Following that, I will give sample input and output for MINITAB.

SPSS

Input

```
TITLE TABLE 11.5, DUMMY CODING.
DATA LIST FREE/T Y.
COMPUTE D1=0.
COMPUTE D2=0.
COMPUTE D3=0.
IF (T EQ 1) D1 = 1.
IF (T EQ 2) D2 = 1.
IF (T EQ 3) D3 = 1.
BEGIN DATA
1  4
1  5
1  6
1  7
1  8
2  7
2  8
2  9
2  10
2  11
3  1
3  2
3  3
3  4
3  5
END DATA
LIST.
REGRESSION VAR Y TO D3/DES/STAT ALL/
    DEP Y/ENTER D1 D2/
    DEP Y/ENTER D1 D3/
    DEP Y/ENTER D2 D3.
```

Commentary

As I introduced SPSS in Chapter 4, where I also explained the REGRESSION procedure, my commentaries here will be limited to the topic under consideration, beginning with the input data.

Notice that instead of reading in the data as displayed in Table 11.5 (Y and the coded vectors), I am reading in two vectors, the second being Y. The first is a category identification vector, consisting of consecutive integers. Thus, 1 identifies subjects in the first category or group (A_1 in the present example), 2 identifies subjects in the second category or group (A_2 in the present example), and so on. For illustrative purposes, I labeled this vector T, to stand for treatments. Of course, any relevant name can be used (e.g., RACE, RELIGION), as long as it conforms with SPSS format (e.g., not exceeding eight characters).

I prefer this input mode for three reasons. One, whatever the number of groups, or categories, a single vector is sufficient. This saves labor and is also less prone to typing errors. Two, as I show in the following and in subsequent sections, any coding method can be produced by relevant operations on the category identification vector. Three, most computer packages require a category or group identification vector for some of their procedures (e.g., ONEWAY in SPSS, ONEWAY in MINITAB, 7D in BMDP, ANOVA in SAS). This input mode obviates the need of adding a category identification vector when using a program that requires it. In sum, using a category identification vector saves labor, is less prone to typing errors, and affords the greatest flexibility.

Parenthetically, if you prefer to enter data as in Table 11.5, you should *not* include a unit vector for the intercept. Most programs for regression analysis add such a vector automatically.

The packages I use in this book have extensive facilities for data manipulation and transformations. Here I use COMPUTE and IF statements to generate dummy coding.

COMPUTE Statements. I use three COMPUTE statements to generate three vectors consisting of 0's.

IF Statements. I use three IF statements to insert, in turn, 1's for a given category in a given vector. For example, as a result of the first IF statement, 1's will be inserted in D1 for members of A_1 [see T EQ(ual) 1 in the first IF statement]. Members *not* in A_1 have 0's by virtue of the COMPUTE statements. Similarly, for the other IF statements. Thus, members of group 1 are identified in D1 (see "Nomenclature," presented earlier in this chapter). Members of group 2 are identified in D2, and those of group 3 are identified in D3. Clearly, other approaches to the creation of the dummy vectors are possible.

As I explained earlier, only two dummy vectors are necessary in the present example. I am creating three dummy vectors for two reasons. One, for comparative purposes, I analyze the data using the three possible sets of dummy vectors for the case of three categories (see "REGRESSION," discussed next). Two, later in this chapter, I show how to use the dummy vectors I generated here to produce other coding methods.

REGRESSION. Notice that I did not mention T, as I used it solely in the creation of the dummy vectors.

VAR(iables) Y TO D3. This discussion calls for a general comment about the use of the term *variables* in the present context. Understandably, computer programs do not distinguish between a variable and a coded vector that may be one of several representing a variable. As far as the program is concerned, each vector is a "variable."[3] Thus, if you are using a computer program that requires a statement about the number of variables, you would have to count each coded vector as a variable. For the data in Table 11.5 this would mean three variables (Y, and two dummy vectors), although only *two* variables are involved (i.e., Y and two dummy vectors representing the independent variable). Or, assuming that a single independent variable with six categories is

---

[3]For convenience, I will henceforth refrain from using quotation marks.

used, then five dummy vectors would be required. The number of variables (including the dependent variable) would therefore be six. To repeat: *the computer program does not distinguish between a coded vector and a variable. It is the user who must keep the distinction in mind when interpreting the results.*[4] Consequently, as I show in the following and in Chapter 12, some parts of the output may be irrelevant for a given solution, or parts of the output may have to be combined to get the relevant information.

SPSS does not require a statement about the number of variables read in, but it does require a variable list. Such a list must include the dependent variable and all the coded vectors that one contemplates using.

Finally, notice that I am calling for three regression analyses, in each case specifying two dummy vectors as the independent variables.[5] Had I mistakenly specified three vectors, the program would have entered only two of them, and it would have given a message to the effect that there is high collinearity and that tolerance (see Chapter 10) is zero. Some programs may abort the run when such a mistake is made.

Output

T	Y	D1	D2	D3	
1.00	4.00	1.00	.00	.00	
1.00	5.00	1.00	.00	.00	*[first two subjects in A_1]*
.	.	.	.	.	
2.00	7.00	.00	1.00	.00	
2.00	8.00	.00	1.00	.00	*[first two subjects in A_2]*
.	.	.	.	.	
3.00	1.00	.00	.00	1.00	
3.00	2.00	.00	.00	1.00	*[first two subjects in A_3]*

Commentary

The preceding is an excerpt of the listing generated by the LIST command (see Input). Examine the listing and note the dummy vectors created by the COMPUTE and IF statements. I remind you that comments in italics are *not* part of the input or output (see Chapter 4 for an explanation).

Output

	Mean	Std Dev
Y	6.000	2.928
D1	.333	.488
D2	.333	.488
D3	.333	.488

N of Cases = 15

---

[4]In Chapter 12, I give some research examples of the deleterious consequences of failing to pay attention to this distinction.

[5]Keep in mind what I said earlier about variables and dummy vectors.

Correlation:

	Y	D1	D2	D3
Y	1.000	.000	.750	−.750
D1	.000	1.000	−.500	−.500
D2	.750	−.500	1.000	−.500
D3	−.750	−.500	−.500	1.000

Commentary

Because a dummy vector consists of 1's and 0's, its mean is equal to the proportion of 1's (i.e., the sum of the scores, which is equal to the number of 1's, divided by the total number of people). Consequently, it is useful to examine the means of dummy vectors for clues of wrong data entry or typing errors (e.g., means equal to or greater than 1, unequal means when equal sample sizes are used).

Examine the correlation matrix and notice that, as expected, the correlation between any two dummy vectors is −.5—see (11.3) and (11.4) and the discussion related to them.

Output

Multiple R	.86603	Analysis of Variance			
R Square	.75000		DF	Sum of Squares	Mean Square
Adjusted R Square	.70833	Regression	2	90.00000	45.00000
Standard Error	1.58114	Residual	12	30.00000	2.50000

$$F = \quad 18.00000 \qquad \text{Signif } F = \quad .0002$$

Commentary

The preceding results are obtained for any two dummy vectors representing the three groups under consideration. $R^2_{y.12} = .75$; that is, 75% of the variance of Y is explained by (or predicted from) the independent variable. The F ratio of 18.00 with 2 and 12 *df* is a test of this R^2:

$$F = \frac{R^2/k}{(1 - R^2)/(N - k - 1)} = \frac{.75/2}{(1 - .75)/(15 - 2 - 1)} = 18.00$$

When I introduced this formula as (5.21), I defined k as the number of independent variables. When, however, coded vectors are used to represent a categorical variable, k is the number of coded vectors, which is equal to the number of groups minus one ($g - 1$). Stated differently, k is the number of degrees of freedom associated with treatments, groups, or categories (see the previous commentary on Input).

Alternatively, the F ratio is a ratio of the mean square regression to the mean square residuals: $45.00/2.50 = 18.00$. Compare the above results with those I obtained when I subjected the same data to a one-way analysis of variance (Table 11.4). Note that the Regression Sum of Squares (90.00) is the same as the Between-Groups Sum of Squares reported in Table 11.4, and that the Residual Sum of Squares (30.00) is the same as the Within-Groups Sum of Squares. The degrees of freedom are, of course, also the same in both tables. Consequently, the mean squares and the

F ratio are identical in both analyses. The total sum of squares (120) is the sum of the Regression and Residual Sums of Squares or the sum of the Between-Groups and the Within-Groups Sums of Squares.

When ANOVA is calculated one may obtain the proportion of the total sum of squares accounted for by the independent variable by calculating η^2 (eta squared; see Hays, 1988, p. 369; Kerlinger, 1986, pp. 216–217):

$$\eta^2 = \frac{ss \text{ between groups}}{ss \text{ total}} \tag{11.5}$$

Using the results from ANOVA of Table 11.4:

$$\eta^2 = \frac{90}{120} = .75$$

Thus, $\eta^2 = R^2$.

The equivalence of ANOVA and multiple regression analysis with coded vectors should now be evident. If you are more familiar and more comfortable with ANOVA, you are probably wondering what, if any, are the advantages of using multiple regression analysis in preference to ANOVA. You are probably questioning whether anything can be gained by learning what seems a more complicated analysis. In subsequent sections, I show some advantages of using multiple regression analysis instead of ANOVA. At the end of this chapter, I give a summary statement contrasting the two approaches.

Output

--- Variables in the Equation --

Variable	B	SE B	T	Sig T	Variable	B	T	Sig T	Variable	B	T	Sig T
D1	3.000000	1.000000	3.000	.0111	D1	−3.000000	−3.000	.0111	D2	3.000000	3.000	.0111
D2	6.000000	1.000000	6.000	.0001	D3	−6.000000	−6.000	.0001	D3	−3.000000	−3.000	.0111
(Constant)	3.000000				(Constant)	9.000000			(Constant)	6.000000		

Commentary

The preceding are excerpts from the three regression analyses, which I placed alongside each other for comparative purposes. Before turning to the specific equations, I will comment generally on the properties of regression equations with dummy coding. Examine the dummy vectors in Table 11.5 and notice that members of A_1 are identified in D1, and members of A_2 are identified in D2. For individuals in either group, only two elements of the regression equation are relevant: (1) the intercept and (2) the regression coefficient associated with the vector in which their group was identified. For individuals assigned 0's in all the vectors (A_3), only the intercept is relevant. For reasons I explain later, the group assigned 0's in all vectors will be referred to as the comparison or control group (Darlington, 1990, p. 236, uses also the term *base cell* to refer to this group or category).

As individuals in a given category have identical "scores" (a 1 in the dummy vector identifying the category in question and 0's in all the other dummy vectors), it follows that their predicted scores are also identical. Further, consistent with a least-squares solution, each individual's predicted score is equal to the mean of his or her group (see Chapter 2).

Referring to the coding scheme I used in Table 11.5, the preceding can be stated succinctly as follows:

$$Y'_{A_3} = a = \overline{Y}_{A_3}$$

$$Y'_{A_1} = a + b_{D1} = \overline{Y}_{A_1}$$

$$Y'_{A_2} = a + b_{D2} = \overline{Y}_{A_2}$$

According to the first equation, a (intercept) is equal to the mean of the comparison group (group assigned 0's throughout. See the preceding). Examine now the second and third equations and notice that b (regression coefficient) for a given dummy vector can be expressed as the mean of the group identified in the vector minus a. As a is equal to the mean of the comparison group, the preceding can be stated as follows: each b is equal to the deviation of the mean of the group identified in the dummy vector in question from the mean of the group assigned 0's throughout, hence the label comparison or control (see the next section) used for the latter.

As I stated earlier, regardless which groups are identified in the dummy vectors, the overall results (i.e., R^2, F ratio) are identical. The regression equation, however, reflects the specific pattern of dummy coding used. This can be seen by comparing the three regression equations reported in the previous excerpts of the output, under Variables in the Equation. Beginning with the left panel, for the regression of Y on D1 and D2, the equation is

$$Y' = 3.00 + 3.00D1 + 6.00D2$$

The means of the three groups (see Table 11.4) are

$$\overline{Y}_{A_1} = 6.00 \qquad \overline{Y}_{A_2} = 9.00 \qquad \overline{Y}_{A_3} = 3.00$$

As I explained earlier, $a = 3.00$ (CONSTANT in the previous output) is equal to the mean of the comparison group (A_3 in the case under consideration). The mean of the group identified in D1 (A_1) is 6.00. Therefore,

$$\overline{Y}_{A_1} - \overline{Y}_{A_3} = 6.00 - 3.00 = 3.00 = b_{D1}$$

Similarly, the mean of the group identified in D2 (A_2) is 9.00. Therefore,

$$\overline{Y}_{A_2} - \overline{Y}_{A_3} = 9.00 - 3.00 = 6.00 = b_{D2}$$

Examine now the center panel of the output and notice that the regression equation is

$$Y' = 9.00 - 3.00D1 - 6.00D3$$

where A_1 was identified in D1 and A_3 was identified in D3. Consequently, A_2 serves as the comparison group.

In line with what I said earlier, a is equal to the mean of A_2 (9.00). Each b is equal to the deviation of the mean of the group identified in the vector with which it is associated from the mean of the comparison group:

$$6.00 - 9.00 = -3.00 = b_{D1}; \quad 3.00 - 9.00 = -6.00 = b_{D3}.$$

Examine now the regression equation in the right panel and confirm that its properties are analogous to those I delineated for the first two panels.

Tests of Regression Coefficients. Earlier in the text (see, in particular, Chapters 5 and 6), I showed that dividing a b by its standard error yields a t ratio with *df* equal to those for the residual sum of squares. For the first regression equation (left panel), $t = 3.00$ for b_{D1}, and $t = 6.00$ for b_{D2}.[6] Each t ratio has 12 df (see the previous output).

From what I said earlier about the b's in a regression equation with dummy coding it should be evident that the test of a b is tantamount to a test of the difference between the mean of the group identified in the vector with which the b is associated and the mean of the comparison group. Tests of the b's are therefore relevant when one wishes to test, in turn, the difference between the mean of each group identified in a given vector and that of the comparison group. An example of such a design is when there are several treatments and a control group, and the researcher wishes to compare each treatment with the control (see, for example, Edwards, 1985, pp. 148–150; Keppel, 1991, pp. 175–177; Winer, 1971, pp. 201–204).

The t ratios associated with the b's are identical to the t ratios obtained when, following Dunnett (1955), one calculates t ratios between each treatment mean and the control group mean. Such tests are done subsequent to a one-way analysis of variance in the following manner:

$$t = \frac{\bar{Y}_1 - \bar{Y}_C}{\sqrt{MS_W\left(\dfrac{1}{n_1} + \dfrac{1}{n_C}\right)}} \tag{11.6}$$

where $\bar{Y}_1$ = mean of treatment 1; $\bar{Y}_C$ = mean of control group; MS_W = mean square within groups from the analysis of variance; n_1, n_C = number of subjects in treatment 1 and the control group, respectively. Incidentally, (11.6) is a special case of a t test between any two means subsequent to an analysis of variance. For the general case, the numerator of (11.6) is $\bar{Y}_i - \bar{Y}_j$ (i.e., the difference between the means of groups or categories i and j). The denominator is similarly altered only with respect to the subscripts. When $n_1 = n_C$, (11.6) can be stated as follows:

$$t = \frac{\bar{Y}_1 - \bar{Y}_C}{\sqrt{\dfrac{2MS_W}{n}}} \tag{11.7}$$

where n = number of subjects in one of the groups. All other terms are as defined for (11.6).

For the sake of illustration, assume that group A_3 of Table 11.4 is a control group, whereas A_1 and A_2 are two treatment groups. From Table 11.4,

$$\bar{Y}_{A_1} = 6.00 \qquad \bar{Y}_{A_2} = 9.00 \qquad \bar{Y}_{A_3} = 3.00$$

$$n_1 = n_2 = n_3 = 5$$

$$MS_W = 2.50$$

Comparing the mean of A_1 with A_3 (the control group):

$$t = \frac{6.00 - 3.00}{\sqrt{\dfrac{2(2.5)}{5}}} = \frac{3.00}{\sqrt{1}} = \frac{3}{1} = 3.00$$

Comparing A_2 with A_3:

$$t = \frac{9.00 - 3.00}{\sqrt{\dfrac{2(2.5)}{5}}} = \frac{6.00}{\sqrt{1}} = \frac{6}{1} = 6.00$$

[6]I omitted the standard errors of the b's in the next two panels, as they are all equal to 1.00.

The two t ratios are identical to the ones obtained for the two b's associated with the dummy vectors of Table 11.5, where A_3 was assigned 0's in both vectors and therefore served as a comparison, or control group to which the means of the other groups were compared.

To determine whether a given t ratio for the comparison of a treatment mean with the control mean is statistically significant at a prespecified α, one may check a special table prepared by Dunnett. This table is reproduced in various statistics books, including Edwards (1985), Keppel (1991), and Winer (1971). For the present case, where the analysis was performed as if there were two treatments and a control group, the tabled values for a one-tailed t with 12 df are 2.11 (.05 level), 3.01 (.01 level), and for a two-tailed test they are 2.50 (.05 level), 3.39 (.01 level).

To recapitulate, when dummy coding is used to code a categorical variable, the F ratio associated with the R^2 of the dependent variable with the dummy vectors is a test of the null hypothesis that the group means are equal to each other. This is equivalent to the overall F ratio of the analysis of variance. The t ratio for each b is equivalent to the t ratio for the test of the difference between the mean of the group identified in the vector with which it is associated and the mean of the comparison group. The comparison group need not be a control group. In nonexperimental research, for example, one may wish to compare the mean of each of several groups with that of some base group (e.g., mean income of each minority group with that of the white majority).

Dummy coding is *not* restricted to designs with a comparison or control group. It can be used to code any categorical variable. When the design does not include a comparison group, the designation of the group to be assigned 0's in all the vectors is arbitrary. Under such circumstances, the t ratios for the b's are irrelevant. Instead, the overall F ratio for the R^2 is interpreted. To test whether there are statistically significant differences between specific means, or between combinations of means, it is necessary to apply one of the methods for multiple comparisons between means—a topic I discuss in a subsequent section.

If, on the other hand, the design is one in which several treatment means are to be compared with a control mean, the control group is the one assigned 0's in all vectors. Doing this, all one needs to determine which treatment means differ significantly from the control group mean is to note which of the t ratios associated with the b's exceed the critical value in Dunnett's table.

Before turning to the next topic, I give an input file for the analysis of the data of Table 11.5 through MINITAB, followed by brief excerpts of output.

MINITAB

Input

```
GMACRO
T115
ECHO
OUTFILE='T115.MIN';
   NOTERM.
NOTE TABLE 11.5
READ C1-C2;
   FILE 'T115.DAT'.            [read data from external file]
INDICATOR C1 C3-C5     [create dummy vectors using C1. Put in C3-C5]
NAME C1 'T' C2 'Y' C3 'D1' C4 'D2' C5 'D3'
PRINT C1-C5
```

DESCRIBE C2-C5   *[calculate descriptive statistics for C2-C5]*
CORRELATION C2-C5   *[calculate correlation matrix for C2-C5]*
REGRESS C2 2 C3-C4
REGRESS C2 2 C3 C5
REGRESS C2 2 C4-C5
ENDMACRO

Commentary

For an introduction to MINITAB, see Chapter 4. As I pointed out in Chapter 4, comments in italics are *not* part of input files. I also pointed out that all MINITAB input files in this book are set up for batch processing. Thus, I named this input file T115.MAC, and at the prompt (MTB >) I typed the following: %T115

READ. For illustrative purposes, I am reading the data from an external file (T115.DAT) instead of as part of the input file.

INDICATOR. MINITAB creates dummy vectors corresponding to the codes in C1 (see Minitab Inc., 1995a, p. 7-13). In the present case, three dummy vectors are created (see the following output) and are placed in columns 3 through 5, as I specified in the command.

Output

ROW	T	Y	D1	D2	D3	
1	1	4	1	0	0	
2	1	5	1	0	0	*[first two subjects in A_1]*
.	.	.	.	.	.	
6	2	7	0	1	0	
7	2	8	0	1	0	*[first two subjects in A_2]*
.	.	.	.	.	.	
11	3	1	0	0	1	
12	3	2	0	0	1	*[first two subjects in A_3]*

MTB > DESCRIBE C2-C5

	N	Mean	StDev
Y	15	6.000	2.928
D1	15	0.333	0.488
D2	15	0.333	0.488
D3	15	0.333	0.488

MTB > CORRELATION C2-C5

	Y	D1	D2
D1	0.000		
D2	0.750	−0.500	
D3	−0.750	−0.500	−0.500

MTB > REGRESS C2 2 C3-C4	MTB > REGRESS C2 2 C3 C5	MTB > REGRESS C2 2 C4-C5
The regression equation is	The regression equation is	The regression equation is
Y = 3.00 + 3.00 D1 + 6.00 D2	Y = 9.00 − 3.00 D1 − 6.00 D3	Y = 6.00 + 3.00 D2 − 3.00 D3

Predictor	Coef	Stdev	t-ratio	p	Predictor	Coef	t-ratio	p	Predictor	Coef	t-ratio	p
Constant	3.0000	0.7071	4.24	0.001	Constant	9.0000	12.73	0.000	Constant	6.0000	8.49	0.000
D1	3.000	1.000	3.00	0.011	D1	−3.000	−3.00	0.011	D2	3.000	3.00	0.011
D2	6.000	1.000	6.00	0.000	D3	−6.000	−6.00	0.000	D3	−3.000	−3.00	0.011

Commentary

As with SPSS output, I placed the results of the three regression analyses alongside each other. I trust that you will encounter no difficulties in interpreting this output. If necessary, review commentaries on similar SPSS output.

EFFECT CODING

Effect coding is so named because, as I will show, the regression coefficients associated with the coded vectors reflect treatment effects. The code numbers used are 1's, 0's, and −1's. Effect coding is thus similar to dummy coding. The difference is that in dummy coding one group or category is assigned 0's in all the vectors, whereas in effect coding one group is assigned −1's in all the vectors. (See the −1's assigned to A_3, in Table 11.6.) Although it makes no difference which group is assigned −1's, it is convenient to do this for the last group. As in dummy coding, k (the number of groups minus one) coded vectors are generated. In each vector, members of one group are identified (i.e., assigned 1's); all other subjects are assigned 0's except for members of the last group, who are assigned −1's.

Table 11.6 displays effect coding for the data I analyzed earlier by dummy coding. Analogous to my notation in dummy coding, I use E to stand for effect coding along with a number indicating the group identified in the given vector. Thus, in vector E1 of Table 11.6 I assigned 1's to members of group A_1, 0's to members of group A_2, and −1's to members of group A_3. In vector E2, I assigned 0's to members of A_1, 1's to those of A_2, and −1's to those of A_3. As in the case of dummy coding, I use REGRESSION of SPSS to analyze the data of Table 11.6.

SPSS

Input

```
. . . . . . . . . . . . . . . . . . . . .   [see commentary]
COMPUTE E1=D1−D3.
COMPUTE E2=D2−D3.
. . . . . . . . . . . . . . . . . . . . .   [see commentary]
REGRESSION VAR Y TO E2/DES/STAT ALL/
. . . . . . . . . . . . . . . . . . . . .   [see commentary]
   DEP Y/ENTER E1 E2.
```

Table 11.6   Effect Coding for Illustrative Data from Three Groups

Group	Y	E1	E2
	4	1	0
	5	1	0
A_1	6	1	0
	7	1	0
	8	1	0
	7	0	1
	8	0	1
A_2	9	0	1
	10	0	1
	11	0	1
	1	−1	−1
	2	−1	−1
A_3	3	−1	−1
	4	−1	−1
	5	−1	−1
M:	6	0	0

NOTE: Vector *Y* is repeated from Table 11.5. *M* = mean.

Commentary

Although I did not mention it, I ran the present analysis concurrently with that of dummy coding I reported earlier in this chapter.[7] The preceding statements are only those that I omitted from the dummy coding input file I presented earlier. Thus, to replicate the present analysis, you can edit the dummy coding input file as follows: (1) Add the COMPUTE statements after the IF statements. (2) On the REGRESSION statement change D3 to E2, thus declaring that the variables to be considered would be from *Y* to E2. (3) On the last DEP statement in the dummy input file, change the period (.) to a slash (/). (4) Add the DEP statement given here.

Of course, you could create a new input file for this analysis. Moreover, you may prefer to use IF statements to create the effect coding vectors. Analogous to dummy vectors, I will, henceforth, use the term *effect vectors*. As you can see, I am subtracting in turn D3 from D1 and D2 (using COMPUTE statements), thereby creating effect vectors (see the following output).

Output

T	Y	D1	D2	D3	E1	E2	
1.00	4.00	1.00	.00	.00	1.00	.00	
1.00	5.00	1.00	.00	.00	1.00	.00	*[first two subjects in A_1]*
.	.	.	.	.	.	.	
2.00	7.00	.00	1.00	.00	.00	1.00	
2.00	8.00	.00	1.00	.00	.00	1.00	*[first two subjects in A_2]*

[7]I included also in this run the analysis with orthogonal coding, which I present later in this chapter.

3.00	1.00	.00	.00	1.00	−1.00	−1.00	
3.00	2.00	.00	.00	1.00	−1.00	−1.00	*[first two subjects in A_3]*

Commentary

Although in the remainder of this section I include only output relevant to effect coding, I also included in the listing the dummy vectors so that you may see clearly how the subtraction carried out by the COMPUTE statements resulted in effect vectors.

Output

	Mean	Std Dev
Y	6.000	2.928
E1	.000	.845
E2	.000	.845

N of Cases =   15

Correlation:

	Y	E1	E2
Y	1.000	.433	.866
E1	.433	1.000	.500
E2	.866	.500	1.000

Commentary

As with dummy coding (see the commentary on relevant output presented earlier in this chapter), the means and correlations of effect vectors have special properties. Notice that the mean of effect vectors is .00. This is so when *sample sizes are equal,* as in each vector the number of 1's is equal the number of −1's. The correlation between any two effect vectors is .5, *when sample sizes are equal.* Accordingly, it is useful to examine the means of effect vectors and the correlations among such vectors for clues to incorrect input, errors in data manipulations aimed at generating effect coding (e.g., COMPUTE, IF) or typing errors.

Output

Dependent Variable..   Y
Variable(s) Entered on Step Number 1..   E1
                                     2..   E2

		Analysis of Variance			
Multiple R	.86603		DF	Sum of Squares	Mean Square
R Square	.75000				
Adjusted R Square	.70833	Regression	2	90.00000	45.00000
Standard Error	1.58114	Residual	12	30.00000	2.50000
		F = 18.00000		Signif F = .0002	

Commentary

As I pointed out earlier, the overall results are the same, no matter what method was used to code the categorical variable. I reproduced the preceding segment to show that it is identical to the one I obtained earlier with dummy coding. The difference between the two coding methods is in the properties of the regression equations that result from their application. Earlier, I explained the properties of the regression equation for dummy coding. I will now examine the regression equation for effect coding.

Output

Variables in the Equation

Variable	B	SE B
E1	.000000	.57735
E2	3.000000	.57735
(Constant)	6.000000	

Commentary

Other information reported under Variables in the Equation (e.g., tests of the regression coefficients) is immaterial for present purposes.

The *regression equation* is

$$Y' = 6 + 0E1 + 3E2$$

Note that a (the intercept) is equal to the grand mean of the dependent variable, $\bar{Y}$. Each b is equal to the deviation of the mean of the group identified in the vector with which it is associated from the grand mean. Thus,

$$b_{E1} = \bar{Y}_{A_1} - \bar{Y} = 6.00 - 6.00 = 0$$

$$b_{E2} = \bar{Y}_{A_2} - \bar{Y} = 9.00 - 6.00 = 3.00$$

As I explain in the following discussion, the deviation of a given treatment mean from the grand mean is defined as its effect. It is evident, then, that *each b reflects a treatment effect*: b_{E1} reflects the effect of A_1 (the treatment identified in E1), whereas b_{E2} reflects the effect of A_2 (the treatment identified in E2). Hence the name *effect coding*. To better appreciate the properties of the regression equation for effect coding, it is necessary to digress for a brief presentation of the linear model. After this presentation, I resume the discussion of the regression equation.

The Fixed Effects Linear Model

The fixed effects one-way analysis of variance is presented by some authors (for example, Graybill, 1961; Scheffé, 1959; Searle, 1971) in the form of the linear model:

$$Y_{ij} = \mu + \beta_j + \varepsilon_{ij} \tag{11.8}$$

where Y_{ij} = the score of individual i in group or treatment j; μ = population mean; β_j = effect of treatment j; and ε_{ij} = error associated with the score of individual i in group, or treatment, j. *Linear model* means that an individual's score is conceived as a linear composite of several components. In (11.8) it is a composite of three parts: the grand mean, a treatment effect, and an error term. As a restatement of (11.8) shows, the error is the part of Y_{ij} not explained by the grand mean and the treatment effect:

$$\varepsilon_{ij} = Y_{ij} - \mu - \beta_j \tag{11.9}$$

The method of least squares is used to minimize the sum of squared errors ($\Sigma\varepsilon_{ij}^2$). In other words, an attempt is made to explain as much of Y_{ij} as possible by the grand mean and a treatment effect. To obtain a unique solution to the problem, the constraint that $\Sigma\beta_g = 0$ is imposed (g = number of groups). This condition simply means that the sum of the treatment effects is zero. I show later that such a constraint results in expressing each treatment effect as the deviation of the mean of the treatment whose effect is studied from the grand mean.

Equation (11.8) is expressed in parameters, or population values. In actual analyses, statistics are used as estimates of these parameters:

$$Y_{ij} = \overline{Y} + b_j + e_{ij} \tag{11.10}$$

where $\overline{Y}$ = the grand mean; b_j = effect of treatment j; and e_{ij} = error associated with individual i under treatment j.

The deviation sum of squares, $\Sigma(Y - \overline{Y})^2$, can be expressed in the context of the regression equation. Recall from (2.10) that $Y' = \overline{Y} + bx$. Therefore,[8]

$$Y = \overline{Y} + bx + e$$

A deviation of a score from the mean of the dependent variable can be expressed thus:

$$Y - \overline{Y} = \overline{Y} + bx + e - \overline{Y}$$

Substituting $Y - \overline{Y} - bx$ for e in the previous equation,

$$Y - \overline{Y} = \overline{Y} + bx + Y - \overline{Y} - bx - \overline{Y}$$

Now, $\overline{Y} + bx = Y'$ and $Y - \overline{Y} - bx = Y - Y'$. By substitution,

$$Y - \overline{Y} = Y' + Y - Y' - \overline{Y}$$

Rearranging the terms on the right,

$$Y - \overline{Y} = (Y' - \overline{Y}) + (Y - Y') \tag{11.11}$$

As we are interested in explaining the sum of squares,

$$\Sigma y^2 = \Sigma[(Y' - \overline{Y}) + (Y - Y')]^2$$

$$= \Sigma(Y' - \overline{Y})^2 + \Sigma(Y - Y')^2 + 2\Sigma(Y' - \overline{Y})(Y - Y')$$

The last term on the right can be shown to equal zero. Therefore,

$$\Sigma y^2 = \Sigma(Y' - \overline{Y})^2 + \Sigma(Y - Y')^2 \tag{11.12}$$

The first term on the right, $\Sigma(Y' - \overline{Y})^2$, is the sum of squares due to regression. It is analogous to the between-groups sum of squares of the analysis of variance. $\Sigma(Y - Y')^2$ is the residual sum of squares, or what is called within-groups sum of squares in ANOVA. $\Sigma(Y' - \overline{Y})^2 = 0$ means that Σy^2 is all due to residuals, and thus nothing is explained by resorting to X. If, on the other hand, $\Sigma(Y - Y')^2 = 0$, all the variability is explained by regression or by the information X provides. I now return to the regression equation that resulted from the analysis with effect coding.

---

[8]See Chapter 2 for a presentation that parallels the present one.

The Meaning of the Regression Equation

The foregoing discussion shows that the use of effect coding results in a regression equation that reflects the linear model. I illustrate this by applying the regression equation I obtained earlier ($Y' = 6 + 0E1 + 3E2$) to some subjects in Table 11.6. For subject number 1,

$$Y'_1 = 6 + 0(1) + 3(0) = 6$$

This, of course, is the mean of the group to which this subject belongs, namely the mean of A_1. The residual for subject 1 is

$$e_1 = Y_1 - Y'_1 = 4 - 6 = -2$$

Expressing the score of subject 1 in components of the linear model,

$$Y_1 = a + b_{E1} + e_1$$

$$4 = 6 + 0 + (-2)$$

Because a is equal to the grand mean ($\overline{Y}$), and for each group (except the one assigned -1's) there is only one vector in which it is assigned 1's, the predicted score for each subject is a composite of a and the b for the vector in which the subject is assigned 1. In other words, *a predicted score is a composite of the grand mean and the treatment effect of the group to which the subject belongs.* Thus, for subjects in group A_1, the application of the regression equation results in $Y' = 6 + 0(1) = 6$, because subjects in this group are assigned 1's in the first vector only, and 0's in all others, regardless of the number of groups involved in the analysis.

For subjects of group A_2, the regression equation is, in effect, $Y' = 6 + 3(1) = 9$, where $6 = a$ and $3 = b_{E2}$, the vector in which this group was identified. Thus, because the predicted score for any subject is the mean of his or her group expressed as a composite of $a + b$, and because a is equal to the grand mean, it follows that b is the deviation of the group mean from the grand mean. As I stated earlier, b is equal to the treatment effect for the group identified in the vector with which it is associated. For group A_1, the treatment effect is $b_{E1} = 0$, and for group A_2 the treatment effect is $b_{E2} = 3$.

Applying the regression equation to subject number 6 (the first subject in A_2),

$$Y'_6 = 6 + (0)(0) + 3(1) = 9$$

$$e_6 = Y_6 - Y'_6 = 7 - 9 = -2$$

Expressing the score of subject 6 in components of the linear model:

$$Y_6 = a + b_{E2} + e_6$$

$$7 = 6 + 3 + (-2)$$

The treatment effect for the group assigned -1 is easily obtained when considering the constraint $\Sigma b_g = 0$. In the present problem this means

$$b_{E1} + b_{E2} + b_3 = 0$$

Substituting the values for b_{E1} and b_{E2} I obtained in the preceding,

$$0 + 3 + b_3 = 0$$

$$b_3 = -3$$

In general, the treatment effect for the group assigned -1's is equal to minus the sum of the coefficients for the effect vectors.

$$b_3 = -(0 + 3) = -3$$

Note that b_3 is *not* part of the regression equation, which consists of two b's only because there are only two coded vectors. For convenience, I use b_{k+1} to represent the treatment effect of the group assigned -1's in all the vectors. For example, in a design consisting of five treatments or categories, four effect vectors are necessary. To identify the treatment effect of the category assigned -1's in all the vectors, I will use b_5. The fact that, unlike the other b's, whose subscripts consist of the letter E plus a number, this b has a number subscript only, should serve as a reminder that it is *not* part of the equation.

Applying the regression equation to subject 11 (the first subject in A_3),

$$Y'_{11} = 6 + 0(-1) + 3(-1)$$

$$= 6 - 3 = 3$$

As expected, this is the mean of A_3. Of course, all other subjects in A_3 have the same predicted Y.

$$e_{11} = Y_{11} - Y'_{11} = 1 - 3 = -2$$

$$Y_{11} = a + b_3 + e_{11}$$

$$1 = 6 + (-3) + (-2)$$

The foregoing discussion can perhaps be best summarized and illustrated by examining Table 11.7. Several points about this table will be noted.

Each person's score is expressed as composed of three components: (1) $\bar{Y}$—the grand mean of the dependent variable, which in the regression equation with effect coding is equal to the intercept (a). (2) b_j—effect of treatment j, defined as the deviation of the mean of the group

Table 11.7 Data for Three Groups Expressed as Components of the Linear Model

Group	Ss	Y	$\bar{Y}$	b_j	Y'	$e_{ij} = Y - Y'$
A_1	1	4	6	0	6	-2
	2	5	6	0	6	-1
	3	6	6	0	6	0
	4	7	6	0	6	1
	5	8	6	0	6	2
A_2	6	7	6	3	9	-2
	7	8	6	3	9	-1
	8	9	6	3	9	0
	9	10	6	3	9	1
	10	11	6	3	9	2
A_3	11	1	6	-3	3	-2
	12	2	6	-3	3	-1
	13	3	6	-3	3	0
	14	4	6	-3	3	1
	15	5	6	-3	3	2
Σ:		90	90	0	90	0
SS:		660	540	90	630	30

NOTE: Vector Y is repeated from Table 11.6. SS = sum of squared elements in a given column. Thus, $SS_y = \Sigma Y^2$, $SS_{\bar{Y}} = \Sigma \bar{Y}^2$, and so forth.

administered treatment j from the grand mean. In the regression equation with effect coding, this is equal to b for the vector in which a given treatment was identified (assigned 1's). For the treatment assigned −1's in all the vectors, it is equal to minus the sum of the regression coefficients. (3) e_{ij}—the residual for person i in treatment j.

Squaring and summing the treatment effects (column b_j of Table 11.7), the regression sum of squares is obtained: 90 (see the last line of Table 11.7). Clearly, then, the regression sum of squares reflects the differential effects of the treatments.

Squaring and summing the residuals (column e_{ij} in Table 11.7), the residual sum of squares is obtained: 30 (see the last line of Table 11.7). Clearly, this is the sum of the squared errors of prediction.

In Chapter 2, Equation (2.2), I showed that a deviation sum of squares may be obtained as follows:

$$\Sigma y^2 = \Sigma Y^2 - \frac{(\Sigma Y)^2}{N}$$

From Table 11.7,

$$\Sigma y^2 = 660 - \frac{(90)^2}{15} = 120$$

which is the sum of squares that is partitioned into ss_{reg} (90) and ss_{res} (30).

An alternative formula for the calculation of Σy^2 is

$$\Sigma y^2 = \Sigma(Y - \overline{Y})^2 = \Sigma Y^2 - \Sigma \overline{Y}^2$$

$$= 660 - 540 = 120 \text{ (from last line of Table 11.7)}$$

Similarly,

$$ss_{reg} = \Sigma(Y' - \overline{Y})^2 = \Sigma Y'^2 - \Sigma \overline{Y}^2$$

$$= 630 - 540 = 90 \text{ (from last line of Table 11.7)}$$

$$ss_{res} = \Sigma(Y - Y')^2 = \Sigma Y^2 - \Sigma Y'^2$$

$$= 660 - 630 = 30 \text{ (from last line of Table 11.7)}$$

Pooling this together,

$$\Sigma y^2 = ss_{reg} + ss_{res}$$

$$\Sigma Y^2 - \Sigma \overline{Y}^2 = (\Sigma Y'^2 - \Sigma \overline{Y}^2) + (\Sigma Y^2 - \Sigma Y'^2)$$

$$660 - 540 = (630 - 540) + (660 - 630)$$

$$120 = 90 + 30$$

The second line is an algebraic equivalent of (11.12). The third and fourth lines are numeric expressions of this equation for the data in Table 11.7.

Although b's of the regression equation with effect coding can be tested for significance (computer programs report such tests routinely), these tests are generally not used in the present context, as the interest is not in whether a mean for a given treatment or category differs significantly from the grand mean (which is what b reflects) but rather whether there are statistically significant differences among the treatment or category means. It is for this reason that I did not reproduce tests of the b's in the earlier output.

MULTIPLE COMPARISONS AMONG MEANS

A statistically significant F ratio for R^2 leads to the rejection of the null hypothesis that there is no relation between group membership or treatments and performance on the dependent variable. For a categorical independent variable, a statistically significant R^2 in effect means that the null hypothesis $\mu_1 = \mu_2 = \ldots \mu_g$ (g = number of groups or categories) is rejected. Rejection of the null hypothesis, however, does not necessarily mean that all the means show a statistically significant difference from each other. To determine which means differ significantly from each other, one of the procedures for multiple comparisons of means has to be applied.

The topic of multiple comparisons is complex and controversial. As but one example, consider the following. After discussing shortcomings of the Newman-Keuls procedure, Toothaker (1991) stated that "it is not recommended for use" (p. 54). He went on to say that "in spite of all of its bad publicity . . . this method is available on SAS and SPSS and is even popularly used in some applied journals" (pp. 75–76). It is noteworthy that when this procedure is illustrated in SAS PROC ANOVA, the reader is referred to PROC GLM for a discussion of multiple comparisons. After a brief discussion of this approach in PROC GLM, the reader is told that "the method cannot be recommended" (SAS Institute, 1990, Vol. 2, p. 947). By contrast, Darlington (1990) concluded "that the Newman-Keuls method seems acceptable more often than not" (p. 267).

Controversy regarding the relative merits of the relatively large number of multiple comparison procedures stems not only from statistical considerations (e.g., which error rate is controlled, how the power of the statistical test is affected), but also from "difficult philosophical questions" (Darlington, 1990, p. 263).

In light of the preceding, "there may be a tendency toward despair" (Toothaker, 1991, p. 68) when faced with the decision which procedure to use. I do not intend to address the controversy, nor to make recommendations as to which procedure is preferable for what purpose. (Following are but some references where you will find good discussions of this topic: Darlington, 1990, Chapter 11; Games, 1971; Hochberg & Tamhane, 1987; Keppel, 1991, Chapters 6 and 8; Kirk, 1982, Chapter 3; Maxwell & Delaney, 1990, Chapters 4 and 5; Toothaker, 1991.) All I will do is give a rudimentary introduction to some procedures and show how they may be carried out in the context of multiple regression analysis.

A *comparison* or a *contrast* is a linear combination of the form

$$L = C_1\bar{Y}_1 + C_2\bar{Y}_2 + \ldots + C_g\bar{Y}_g \qquad (11.13)$$

where C = coefficient by which a given mean, $\bar{Y}$, is multiplied. It is required that $\Sigma C_j = 0$. That is, the sum of the coefficients in any given comparison must equal zero. Thus, to contrast $\bar{Y}_1$ with $\bar{Y}_2$ one can set $C_1 = 1$ and $C_2 = -1$. Accordingly,

$$L = (1)(\bar{Y}_1) + (-1)(\bar{Y}_2) = \bar{Y}_1 - \bar{Y}_2$$

When the direction of the contrast is of interest, the coefficients are assigned accordingly. Thus, to test whether $\bar{Y}_2$ is greater than $\bar{Y}_1$, the former would be multiplied by 1 and the latter by -1, yielding $\bar{Y}_2 - \bar{Y}_1$.

As indicated in (11.13), a contrast is not limited to one between two means. One may, for example, contrast the average of $\bar{Y}_1$ and $\bar{Y}_2$ with that of $\bar{Y}_3$. Accordingly,

$$L = \left(\frac{1}{2}\right)(\bar{Y}_1) + \left(\frac{1}{2}\right)(\bar{Y}_2) + (-1)(\bar{Y}_3)$$

$$= \frac{\bar{Y}_1 + \bar{Y}_2}{2} - \bar{Y}_3$$

To avoid working with fractions, the coefficients may be multiplied by the lowest common denominator. For the previous comparison, for example, the coefficients may be multiplied by 2, yielding: $C_1 = 1, C_2 = 1, C_3 = -2$. This will result in testing $(\bar{Y}_1 + \bar{Y}_2) - 2\bar{Y}_3$, which is equivalent to testing the previous comparison. What I said earlier about the signs of the coefficients when the interest is in the direction of the contrast applies also to linear combinations of more than two means. Thus, if in the present case it is hypothesized that mean A_3 is larger than the average of A_1 and A_2, then the former would be multiplied by 2 and the latter two means by -1.

Broadly, two types of comparisons are distinguished: planned and post hoc. *Planned,* or *a priori,* comparisons are hypothesized by the researcher prior to the overall analysis. *Post hoc,* or *a posteriori,* comparisons are done following the rejection of the overall null hypothesis. At the risk of belaboring the issue of lack of agreement, I will point out that some authors question the merits of this distinction. For example, Toothaker (1991) maintained that "the issues of planned versus post hoc . . . are secondary for most situations, and unimportant in others" (p. 25).

As will, I hope, become clear from the presentation that follows, I believe the distinction between the two types of comparisons is important. I present post hoc comparisons first and then a priori ones.

POST HOC COMPARISONS

I limit my presentation to a method developed by Scheffé (1959), which is most general in that it is applicable to all possible comparisons between individual means (i.e., pairwise comparisons) as well as combinations of means. In addition, it is applicable when the groups, or categories of the variable, consist of equal or unequal frequencies. Its versatility, however, comes at the price of making it the most conservative. That is, it is less likely than other procedures to show differences as being statistically significant. For this reason, many authors recommend that it not be used for pairwise comparisons, for which more powerful procedures are available (see Levin, Serlin, & Seaman, 1994; Seaman, Levin, & Serlin, 1991; see also the references given earlier).

A comparison is considered statistically significant, by the Scheffé method, if $|L|$ (the absolute value of L) exceeds a value S, which is defined as follows:

$$S = \sqrt{kF_{\alpha;\, k,\, N-k-1}} \ \sqrt{MSR\left[\Sigma \frac{(C_j)^2}{n_j}\right]} \tag{11.14}$$

where k = number of coded vectors, or the number of groups minus one; $F_{\alpha;\, k,\, N-k-1}$ = tabled value of F with k and $N - k - 1$ degrees of freedom at a prespecified α level; MSR = mean square residuals or, equivalently, the mean square error from ANOVA; C_j = coefficient by which the mean of treatment or category j is multiplied; and n_j = number of subjects in category j.

For illustrative purposes, I will apply this method to some comparisons for the data in Table 11.7. For this example,

$$\bar{Y}_{A_1} = 6.00 \qquad \bar{Y}_{A_2} = 9.00 \qquad \bar{Y}_{A_3} = 3.00$$

where $MSR = 2.50$; $k = 2$; and $N - k - 1 = 12$ (see Table 11.4 or the previous SPSS output). The tabled F ratio for 2 and 12 *df* for the .05 level is 3.88 (see Appendix B). Contrasting $\bar{Y}_{A_1}$ with $\bar{Y}_{A_2}$,

$$L = (1)(\overline{Y}_{A_1}) + (-1)(\overline{Y}_{A_2}) = 6.00 - 9.00 = -3.00$$

$$S = \sqrt{(2)(3.88)}\sqrt{2.50\left[\frac{(1)^2}{5} + \frac{(-1)^2}{5}\right]} = \sqrt{7.76}\sqrt{2.50\left(\frac{2}{5}\right)} = 2.79$$

Since $|L|$ exceeds S, one can conclude that there is a statistically significant difference (at .05 level) between $\overline{Y}_{A_1}$ and $\overline{Y}_{A_2}$. Because $n_1 = n_2 = n_3 = 5$, S is the same for any comparison between two means. One can therefore conclude that the differences between $\overline{Y}_{A_1}$ and $\overline{Y}_{A_3}$ (6.00 − 3.00) and that between $\overline{Y}_{A_2}$ and $\overline{Y}_{A_3}$ (9.00 − 3.00) are also statistically significant. In the present example, all the possible pairwise comparisons of means are statistically significant.[9]

Suppose that one also wanted to compare the average of the means for groups A_1 and A_3 with the mean of group A_2. This can be done as follows:

$$L = \left(\frac{1}{2}\right)(\overline{Y}_{A_1}) + \left(\frac{1}{2}\right)(\overline{Y}_{A_3}) + (-1)(\overline{Y}_{A_2})$$

$$= \left(\frac{1}{2}\right)(6.00) + \left(\frac{1}{2}\right)(3.00) + (-1)(9.00) = -4.50$$

$$S = \sqrt{(2)(3.88)}\sqrt{(2.50)\left[\frac{(.5)^2}{5} + \frac{(.5)^2}{5} + \frac{(-1)^2}{5}\right]}$$

$$= \sqrt{7.76}\sqrt{(2.50)\frac{1.50}{5}} = 2.41$$

As $|L|$ (4.50) is larger than S (2.41), one can conclude that there is a statistically significant difference between $\overline{Y}_{A_2}$ and $(\overline{Y}_{A_1} + \overline{Y}_{A_3})/2$.

As I pointed out earlier, to avoid working with fractions the coefficients may be multiplied by a constant (2, in the present example). Accordingly,

$$L = (1)(6.00) + (1)(3.00) + (-2)(9.00) = -9.00$$

$$S = \sqrt{(2)(3.88)}\sqrt{(2.50)\left[\frac{(1)^2}{5} + \frac{(1)^2}{5} + \frac{(-2)^2}{5}\right]}$$

$$= \sqrt{7.76}\sqrt{(2.50)\frac{6}{5}} = 4.82$$

The second $|L|$ is twice as large as the first $|L|$. But, then, the second S is twice as large as the first S. Therefore, the conclusion from either test is the same.

Any number of means and any combination of means can be similarly compared. The only constraint is that the sum of the coefficients of each comparison be zero.

An Alternative Approach

Following is an alternative approach for performing the Scheffé test:

$$F = \frac{[C_1(\overline{Y}_1) + C_2(\overline{Y}_2) + \ldots + C_j(\overline{Y}_j)]^2}{MSR\left[\Sigma\frac{(C_j)^2}{n_j}\right]} \tag{11.15}$$

---

[9]As I pointed out earlier, there are more powerful tests for pairwise comparisons of means.

where the numerator is the square of the comparison as defined in (11.13). In the denominator, MSR = mean square residuals, C_j = coefficient by which the mean of group j is multiplied, and n_j = number of subjects in group j. The F ratio has 1 and $N - k - 1$ df.

As I show throughout the remainder of this chapter, *(11.15) is most general in that it is applicable to any comparison among means* (e.g., planned). When it is used in conjunction with Scheffé comparisons, the F ratio has to exceed $kF_{\alpha; k, N - k - 1}$, where k is the number of coded vectors, or the number of groups minus one; and $F_{\alpha; k, N - k - 1}$ is the tabled value of F with k and $N - k - 1$ df at a prespecified α.

For the data of Table 11.7, $\overline{Y}_{A_1} = 6.00$; $\overline{Y}_{A_2} = 9.00$; $\overline{Y}_{A_3} = 3.00$; $MSR = 2.50$; $k = 2$; $N - k - 1 = 12$.

I now apply (11.15) to the same comparisons I carried out earlier where I used (11.14). Testing the difference between $\overline{Y}_{A_1}$ and $\overline{Y}_{A_2}$,

$$F = \frac{[(1)(6.00) + (-1)(9.00)]^2}{2.5 \left[\frac{(1)^2}{5} + \frac{(-1)^2}{5} \right]} = \frac{9}{1} = 9$$

The tabled F ratio for 2 and 12 df for .05 level is 3.88. The obtained F exceeds $(2)(3.88) = 7.76$ ($kF_{\alpha; k, N - k - 1}$ as described earlier), and one can therefore conclude that the comparison is statistically significant at $\alpha = .05$.

Contrasting the means of A_1 and A_3 with that of A_2,

$$F = \frac{[(1)(6.00) + (-2)(9.00) + (1)(3.00)]^2}{2.5 \left[\frac{(1)^2}{5} + \frac{(-2)^2}{5} + \frac{(1)^2}{5} \right]} = \frac{81}{3} = 27$$

This F ratio exceeds 7.76 ($kF_{\alpha; k, N - k - 1}$), and one can therefore conclude that the contrast is statistically significant at $\alpha = .05$. Conclusions based on the use of (11.15) are, of course, identical to those arrived at when (11.14) is applied.

Multiple Comparisons via *b*'s

Earlier, I showed that the mean of a group is a composite of the grand mean and the treatment effect for the group. For effect coding, I expressed this as $\overline{Y}_j = a + b_j$, where $\overline{Y}_j$ = mean of group j; a = intercept, or grand mean, $\overline{Y}$; and b_j = effect of treatment j, or $\overline{Y}_j - \overline{Y}$. Accordingly, when contrasting, for example, $\overline{Y}_{A_1}$ with $\overline{Y}_{A_2}$,

$$L = (1)(\overline{Y}_{A_1}) + (-1)(\overline{Y}_{A_2}) = (1)(a + b_{E1}) + (-1)(a + b_{E2})$$

$$= a + b_{E1} - a - b_{E2}$$

$$= b_{E1} - b_{E2}$$

Similarly,

$$L = (1)(\overline{Y}_{A_1}) + (-2)(\overline{Y}_{A_2}) + (1)(\overline{Y}_{A_3}) = (1)(a + b_{E1}) + (-2)(a + b_{E2}) + (1)(a + b_3)$$

$$= a + b_{E1} - 2a - 2b_{E2} + a + b_3$$

$$= b_{E1} + b_3 - 2b_{E2}$$

Therefore, testing differences among *b*'s is tantamount to testing differences among means. I introduced the notion of testing the difference between two *b*'s in Chapter 6—see (6.11) and the presentation related to it—in connection with the covariance matrix of the b's ($\mathbf{C}$).[10] One can, of course, calculate $\mathbf{C}$ using a matrix algebra program (see Chapter 6 for descriptions and applications of such programs). This, however, is not necessary, as $\mathbf{C}$ can be obtained from many computer programs for statistical analysis. Of the four packages I introduced in Chapter 4, SAS and SPSS provide for an option to print $\mathbf{C}$ (labeled COVB in SAS and BCOV in SPSS). BMDP provides instead for the printing of the correlation matrix of the b's (labeled RREG).[11] To obtain $\mathbf{C}$ from RREG, (1) replace each diagonal element of RREG by the square of the standard error of the b associated with it (the standard errors are reported routinely in most computer programs for regression analysis), and (2) multiply each off-diagonal element by the product of the standard errors of the b's corresponding to it (see illustration in my commentary on the Var-Covar matrix obtained from SPSS, reproduced in the following). MINITAB provides for the printing of $(\mathbf{X'X})^{-1}$ (labeled XPXINV), which when multiplied by the MSR yields $\mathbf{C}$—see (6.11)[12]. For illustrative purposes, I use output from SPSS.

SPSS

Output

Var-Covar Matrix of Regression Coefficients (B)
Below Diagonal: Covariance   Above: Correlation

	E1	E2
E1	.33333	−.50000
E2	−.16667	.33333

Commentary

When STAT=ALL is specified in the REGRESSION procedure (as I explained in Chapter 4, I do this routinely with the small examples in this book), Var-Covar Matrix is also printed. Alternatively, specify BCOV as an option on the STAT subcommand. I took this excerpt from the output for my analysis of the data of Table 11.6, earlier in this chapter.

As explained in the caption, Var-Covar Matrix is a hybrid: the values below the diagonal are covariances of b's, whereas those above the diagonal are correlations. The diagonal values are variances of b's (i.e., squared standard errors of the b's; see the output for effect coding presented earlier in this chapter).

Before proceeding with the matter at hand, I take the opportunity to illustrate how to convert the correlation between b_{E1} and b_{E2} (−.5) into a covariance between them (I said I would do this when I pointed out that BMDP reports the correlation matrix of the b's). As I stated earlier, to convert the correlation into a covariance, multiply the correlation by the product of the standard errors of the b's in question. For the case under consideration,

$$-.50000\sqrt{(.33333)(.33333)} = -.16667$$

which agrees with the value reported below the diagonal.

---

[10]If you are experiencing difficulties with the presentation in this section, I suggest that you review the relevant discussions of $\mathbf{C}$ and its properties in Chapter 6.

[11]In Chapter 14 (see "Regions of Significance: Alternative Calculations"), I give BMDP output that includes RREG.

[12]In Chapter 14 (see "Regions of Significance: Alternative Calculations"), I show how to obtain $\mathbf{C}$ from MINITAB output.

For present purposes, we need the covariance matrix of the b's ($\mathbf{C}$). With output such as given in the preceding, one need only to replace elements above the diagonal with their respective elements below the diagonal. In the present case, there is only one such element ($-.50000$), which is replaced with $-.16667$ to yield

$$\mathbf{C} = \begin{bmatrix} .33333 & -.16667 \\ -.16667 & .33333 \end{bmatrix}$$

Before showing how to use elements of $\mathbf{C}$ in tests of differences among b's in the present context, it is necessary to augment $\mathbf{C}$. I explain the meaning and purpose of this operation in the next section.

Augmented C: C*

For the present example, $\mathbf{C}$ is a 2×2 matrix corresponding to the two b's associated with the two coded vectors of Table 11.6. Consequently, information is available for contrasts between treatments A_1 and A_2 (recall that b_{E1} indicates the effect of treatment A_1 and b_{E2} indicates the effect of treatment A_2). To test contrasts that involve treatment A_3, it is necessary to obtain the variance for b_3 as well as its covariances with the remaining b's. This can be easily accomplished analogously to the calculation of b_3 (i.e., the effect of the treatment assigned -1's in all the coded vectors). As I explained earlier, to obtain b_3, sum the b's of the regression equation and reverse the sign. Take the same approach to augment $\mathbf{C}$ so that it includes the missing elements for b_3. A missing element in a row (or column) of $\mathbf{C}$ is equal to $-\Sigma c_i$ (or $-\Sigma c_j$), where i is row i of $\mathbf{C}$ and j is column j of $\mathbf{C}$. Note that what this means is that the sum of each row (and column) of the augmented matrix ($\mathbf{C}^*$) is equal to zero. For the present example,

$$\mathbf{C}^* = \begin{bmatrix} .33333 & -.16667 & \vdots & -.16667 \\ -.16667 & .33333 & \vdots & -.16667 \\ \hline -.16667 & -.16667 & & .33333 \end{bmatrix}$$

where I inserted dashes so that elements I added to $\mathbf{C}$, given in the output, could be seen clearly.

Note that the diagonal elements are equal to each other, and the off-diagonal elements are equal to each other. This is so in designs with equal cell frequencies. Therefore, in such designs it is not necessary to go through the procedure I outlined earlier to obtain the missing elements. To augment $\mathbf{C}$ in designs with equal cell frequencies, add to it a diagonal element equal to those of its diagonal, and similarly for the off-diagonal elements.

In designs with unequal cell frequencies, or ones consisting of both categorical and continuous independent variables, the diagonal elements of $\mathbf{C}$ will generally not be equal to each other, nor will the off-diagonal elements be equal to each other. It is for such designs that the procedure I outlined previously would be used to augment $\mathbf{C}$. We are ready now to test differences among b's.

Test of Differences among b's

The variance of estimate of the difference between two b's is

$$s^2_{b_i - b_j} = c_{ii} + c_{jj} - 2c_{ij} \tag{11.16}$$

where $s^2_{b_i - b_j}$ = variance of estimate of the difference between b_i and b_j; c_{ii} = diagonal element of $\mathbf{C}^*$ for i, and similarly for c_{jj}; and c_{ij} = off-diagonal elements of $\mathbf{C}^*$ corresponding to ij—see also (6.12). The test of a contrast between b_i and b_j is

$$F = \frac{[(1)(b_i) + (-1)(b_j)]^2}{s^2_{b_i - b_j}} \tag{11.17}$$

with 1 *df* for the numerator and $N - k - 1$ *df* for the denominator (i.e., *df* associated with the mean square residual).

For the data of Table 11.6, the regression equation is

$$Y' = 6.00 + 0E1 + 3E2$$

and

$$b_3 = -\Sigma(0 + 3) = -3$$

Taking the appropriate elements from $\mathbf{C}^*$ (reported earlier), calculate F for the difference between b_{E1} and b_{E2}:

$$F = \frac{[(1)(0) + (-1)(3)]^2}{.33333 + .33333 - 2(-.16667)} = \frac{9}{1} = 9$$

I obtained the same value when I applied (11.15) to test the difference between $\bar{Y}_{A_1}$ and $\bar{Y}_{A_2}$ (see the preceding). My sole purpose here was to show that (11.15) and (11.17) yield identical results. As I stated earlier, when the Scheffé procedure is used, F has to exceed $kF_{\alpha;\, k,\, N-k-1}$ for the contrast to be declared statistically significant.

As in the case of (11.15), (11.17) can be expanded to accommodate comparisons between combinations of b's. For this purpose, the numerator of the F ratio consists of the squared linear combination of b's and the denominator consists of the variance of estimate of this linear combination. Although it is possible to express the variance of estimate of a linear combination of b's in a form analogous to (11.16), this becomes unwieldy when several b's are involved. Therefore, it is more convenient and more efficient to use matrix notation. Thus, for a linear combination of b's,

$$F = \frac{[a_1(b_1) + a_2(b_2) + \ldots + a_j(b_j)]^2}{\mathbf{a'C^*a}} \tag{11.18}$$

where $a_1, a_2, \ldots, a_j$ are coefficients by which the b's are multiplied (I used a's instead of c's so as not to confuse them with elements of $\mathbf{C}^*$, the augmented matrix); $\mathbf{a'}$ and $\mathbf{a}$ are, respectively, row and column vectors of the coefficients of the linear combination; and $\mathbf{C}^*$ is the augmented covariance matrix of the b's.

Some a's of a given linear combination may be 0's, thereby excluding the b's associated with them from consideration. Accordingly, it is convenient to exclude such terms from the numerator and the denominator of (11.18). Thus, only that part of $\mathbf{C}^*$ whose elements correspond to nonzero a's is used in the denominator of (11.18). I illustrate this now by applying (11.18) to the b's of the numerical example under consideration. First, I calculate F for the contrast between b_{E1} and b_{E2}—the same contrast that I tested through (11.17). Recall that $b_{E1} = 0$ and $b_{E2} = 3$. From $\mathbf{C}^*$, I took the values corresponding to the variances and covariances of these b's.

$$F = \frac{[(1)(0) + (-1)(3)]^2}{[1 \quad -1]\begin{bmatrix} .33333 & -.16667 \\ -.16667 & .33333 \end{bmatrix}\begin{bmatrix} 1 \\ -1 \end{bmatrix}} = \frac{9}{1} = 9$$

I obtained the same value previously when I applied (11.17). Earlier, I contrasted $\overline{Y}_{A_1}$ and $\overline{Y}_{A_3}$ with $\overline{Y}_{A_2}$ using (11.15). I show now that the same F ratio (27) is obtained when contrasting b_{E1} and b_3 with b_{E2} by applying (11.18). Recall that $b_{E1} = 0$, $b_{E2} = 3$, $b_3 = -3$.

$$F = \frac{[(1)(0) + (-2)(3) + (1)(-3)]^2}{[1 \quad -2 \quad 1]\begin{bmatrix} .33333 & -.16667 & -.16667 \\ -.16667 & .33333 & -.16667 \\ -.16667 & -.16667 & .33333 \end{bmatrix}\begin{bmatrix} 1 \\ -2 \\ 1 \end{bmatrix}} = \frac{81}{3} = 27$$

Any other linear combination of b's can be similarly tested. For example, contrasting b_{E2} with b_3:

$$F = \frac{[(1)(3) + (-1)(-3)]^2}{[1 \quad -1]\begin{bmatrix} .33333 & -.16667 \\ -.16667 & .33333 \end{bmatrix}\begin{bmatrix} 1 \\ -1 \end{bmatrix}} = \frac{36}{1} = 36$$

The same F ratio would be obtained if one were to use (11.15) to test the difference between $\overline{Y}_{A_2}$ and $\overline{Y}_{A_3}$.

Before turning to the next topic, I will make several remarks about tests of linear combinations of b's. The approach, which is applicable whenever a test of a linear combination of means is appropriate, yields an F ratio with 1 and $N - k - 1$ df. How this F ratio is used depends on the type of comparison in question. Earlier I showed that in a Scheffé test F has to exceed $kF_{\alpha; k, N - k - 1}$ for the comparison to be declared statistically significant. But several other multiple comparison procedures involve an F ratio of the type previously obtained, sometimes requiring only that it be checked against specially prepared tables for the given procedure (see references cited in connection with multiple comparisons). Also, some multiple comparison procedures require a t ratio instead. As the F obtained with the present procedure has 1 df for the numerator, all that is necessary is to take $\sqrt{F}$ (see "Planned Nonorthogonal Comparisons" later in this chapter).

It is worthwhile to amplify and illustrate some of the preceding remarks. Earlier I showed that dummy coding is particularly suited for comparing one or more treatments to a control group. Suppose, however, that effect coding was used instead. Using the approach previously outlined, the same purpose can be accomplished. Assume that for the data in Table 11.6, the researcher wishes to treat A_3 as a control group (i.e., the group I treated as a control when I used dummy coding; see Table 11.5 and the calculations related to it). To do this via tests of differences between b's, do the following: (1) Calculate two F ratios, one for the difference between b_{E1} and b_3 and one for the difference between b_{E2} and b_3. (2) Take the square root of each F to obtain t's. (3) Refer to a Dunnett table. In fact, I did one such contrast earlier. For the contrast between b_{E2} with b_3, I obtained $F = 36$. Therefore, $t = 6.00$, which is the same value I obtained for this comparison when I used dummy coding.

If, instead, A_2 were to be treated as a control group and effect coding was used, then by applying the above procedure one would test the differences between b_{E1} and b_{E2} and that between b_3 and b_{E2}, obtain t's from the F's, and refer to a Dunnett table. (The decision as to which group is assigned -1's in all the vectors is, of course, immaterial.)

Suppose now that effect coding was used but one wished to do orthogonal or planned nonorthogonal comparisons. The previous approach still applies (see the following).

Finally, the procedure for augmenting **C** and using it in tests of linear combinations of b's applies equally in designs with equal and unequal sample sizes (see the following), as well as in those consisting of categorical and continuous independent variables (e.g., analysis of covariance). It is in the latter design that this approach is most useful (e.g., Chapters 14 and 17).

A PRIORI COMPARISONS

In the preceding section, I illustrated post hoc comparisons among means using the Scheffé procedure. I pointed out that such comparisons are done subsequent to a statistically significant R^2 to determine which means, or treatment effects, differ significantly from each other. Post hoc comparisons were aptly characterized as data snooping as they afford any or all conceivable comparisons among means.

As the name implies, a priori, or planned, comparisons are hypothesized prior to the analysis of the data. Clearly, such comparisons are preferable as they are focused on tests of hypotheses derived from theory or ones concerned with the relative effectiveness of treatments, programs, practices, and the like.

Statistical tests of significance for post hoc comparisons are more conservative than those for a priori comparisons, as they should be. Therefore, it is possible for a specific comparison to be statistically not significant when tested by post hoc methods but statistically significant when tested by a priori methods. Nevertheless, the choice between the two approaches depends on the state of knowledge in the area under study or on the researcher's goals. The greater the knowledge, or the more articulated and specific the goals, the lesser the dependence on omnibus tests and data snooping, and greater the opportunity to formulate and test a priori comparisons.

There are two types of a priori comparisons: orthogonal and nonorthogonal. I begin with a detailed presentation of orthogonal comparisons, following which I comment briefly on nonorthogonal ones.

Orthogonal Comparisons

Two comparisons are orthogonal when the sum of the products of the coefficients for their respective elements is zero. As a result, the correlation between such comparisons is zero. Consider the following comparisons:

$$L_1 = (-1)(\overline{Y}_1) + (1)(\overline{Y}_2) + (0)(\overline{Y}_3)$$

$$L_2 = \left(\frac{1}{2}\right)(\overline{Y}_1) + \left(\frac{1}{2}\right)(\overline{Y}_2) + (-1)(\overline{Y}_3)$$

In the first comparison, L_1, $\overline{Y}_1$ is contrasted with $\overline{Y}_2$. In L_2 the average of $\overline{Y}_1$ and $\overline{Y}_2$ is contrasted with $\overline{Y}_3$. To ascertain whether these comparisons are orthogonal, multiply the coefficients for each element in the two comparisons and sum. Accordingly,

$$1: (-1) + (1) + (0)$$

$$2: (1/2) + (1/2) + (-1)$$

$$1 \times 2: (-1)(1/2) + (1)(1/2) + (0)(-1) = 0$$

L_1 and L_2 are orthogonal.

Consider now the following comparisons:

$$L_3 = (1)(\overline{Y}_1) + (-1)(\overline{Y}_2) + (0)(\overline{Y}_3)$$

$$L_4 = (-1)(\overline{Y}_1) + (0)(\overline{Y}_2) + (1)(\overline{Y}_3)$$

The sum of the products of the coefficients of these comparisons is

$$(1)(-1) + (-1)(0) + (0)(1) = -1$$

Comparisons L_3 and L_4 are *not* orthogonal.

Table 11.8   Some Possible Comparisons among Means of Three Groups

Comparison	Groups		
	A_1	A_2	A_3
1	−1	1	0
2	1/2	1/2	−1
3	1	−1/2	−1/2
4	0	1	−1
5	1	0	−1
6	−1/2	1	−1/2

The maximum number of orthogonal comparisons possible in a given design is equal to the number of groups minus one, or the number of coded vectors necessary to depict group membership. For three groups, for example, two orthogonal comparisons can be done. Table 11.8 lists several possible comparisons for three groups. Comparison 1, for instance, contrasts the mean of A_1 with the mean of A_2, whereas comparison 2 contrasts the mean of A_3 with the average of the means of A_1 and A_2. Previously I showed that these comparisons are orthogonal.

Other sets of two orthogonal comparisons listed in Table 11.8 are 3 and 4, 5 and 6. Of course, the orthogonal comparisons tested are determined by the hypotheses one advances. If, for example, A_1 and A_2 are two experimental treatments whereas A_3 is a control group, one may wish, on the one hand, to contrast means A_1 and A_2, and, on the other hand, to contrast the average of means A_1 and A_2 with the mean of A_3 (comparisons 1 and 2 of Table 11.8 will accomplish this). Or, referring to nonexperimental research, one may have samples from three populations (e.g., married, single, and divorced males; Blacks, Whites, and Hispanics) and formulate two hypotheses about the differences among their means. For example, one hypothesis may refer to the difference between married and single males in their attitudes toward the awarding of child custody to the father after a divorce. A second hypothesis may refer to the difference between these two groups and divorced males.

A Numerical Example

Before showing how orthogonal comparisons can be carried out through the use of orthogonal coding in regression analysis, it will be instructive to show how (11.15) can be used to carry out such comparisons. For illustrative purposes, I will do this for the numerical example I introduced in Table 11.4 and analyzed subsequently through regression analysis, using dummy and effect coding.

The example in question consisted of three categories: A_1, A_2, and A_3, with five subjects in each. Assume that you wish to test whether (1) mean A_2 is larger than mean A_1 and (2) the average of means A_1 and A_2 is larger than mean A_3. Accordingly, you would use the following coefficients:

Comparison	A_1	A_2	A_3
1	−1	1	0
2	1	1	−2

Verify that, as required for orthogonal comparisons, the sum of the products of the coefficients is equal to zero.

To apply (11.15), we need the group means and the mean square residual (*MSR*) or the mean square within-groups from an ANOVA. From Table 11.4,

$$\overline{Y}_{A_1} = 6; \quad \overline{Y}_{A_2} = 9; \quad \overline{Y}_{A_3} = 3; \quad MSR = 2.5$$

For the first comparison,

$$F = \frac{[(-1)(6) + (1)(9)]^2}{2.5\left[\dfrac{(-1)^2}{5} + \dfrac{(1)^2}{5}\right]} = \frac{9}{1} = 9$$

with 1 and 12 *df.* Assuming that $\alpha = .05$ was selected, then the tabled value is 4.75 (see Appendix B, table of distribution of F). Accordingly, one would conclude that the difference between the two means is statistically significant. If, in view of the fact that a directional hypothesis was advanced, one decides to carry out a one-tailed test, all that is necessary is to look up the tabled value of F at $2(\alpha)$—.10 for the present example. Various statistics books include tables with such values (e.g., Edwards, 1985; Keppel, 1991; Kirk, 1982; Maxwell & Delaney, 1990). If you looked up such a table you would find that $F = 3.178$. Alternatively, take $\sqrt{F}$ to obtain a t ratio with 12 *df,* and look up in a table of t, available in virtually any statistics book. For the case under consideration, the tabled values for a two- and one-tailed t, respectively, are 2.179 and 1.782.

For the second comparison,

$$F = \frac{[(1)(6) + (1)(9) + (-2)(3)]^2}{2.5\left[\dfrac{(1)^2}{5} + \dfrac{(1)^2}{5} + \dfrac{(-2)^2}{5}\right]} = \frac{81}{3} = 27$$

with 1 and 12 *df, p < .05.*

Parenthetically, the topic of one- versus two-tailed tests is controversial. The following statements capture the spirit of the controversy. Cohen (1965) asked, "How many tails hath the beast?" (p. 106). Commenting on the confusion and the contradictory advice given regarding the use of one-tailed tests, Wainer (1972) reported an exchange that took place during a question-and-answer session following a lecture by John Tukey:

> Tukey: "Don't ever make up a test. If you do, someone is sure to write and ask you for the one-tailed values. In fact, if there was such a thing as a half-tailed test they would want those values as well."
>
> A voice from the audience: "Do you mean to say that one should *never* do a one-tailed test?"
>
> Tukey: "Not at all. It depends upon to whom you are speaking. Some people will believe anything." (p. 776)

Kaiser (1960) concluded his discussion of the traditional two-tailed tests with the statement that "[i]t seems obvious that . . . [it] should almost never be used" (p. 164). For a recent consideration of this topic, see Pillemer (1991).

ORTHOGONAL CODING

In orthogonal coding, coefficients from orthogonal comparisons are used as codes in the coded vectors. As I show, the use of this coding method in regression analysis yields results directly interpretable with respect to the contrasts contained in the coded vectors. In addition, it simplifies calculations of regression analysis.

Regression Analysis with Orthogonal Coding

I will now use orthogonal coding to analyze the data I analyzed earlier with dummy and effect coding. I hope that using the three coding methods with the same illustrative data will facilitate understanding the unique properties of each.

Table 11.9 repeats the Y vector of Table 11.5 (also Table 11.6). Recall that this vector consists of scores on a dependent variable for three groups: A_1, A_2, and A_3. Vectors O1 and O2 of Table 11.9 represent two orthogonal comparisons between: mean A_1 and mean A_2 (O1); the average of means A_1 and A_2 with the mean of A_3 (O2).

These two comparisons, which I tested in the preceding section, are the same as the first two comparisons in Table 11.8. Note, however, that in comparison 2 of Table 11.8, two of the coefficients are fractions. As in earlier sections, I transformed the coefficients by multiplying them by the lowest common denominator (2), yielding the coefficients of 1, 1, and −2, which I use as the codes of O2 of Table 11.9. Such a transformation for the convenience of hand calculation or data

Table 11.9 Orthogonal Coding for Illustrative Data from Three Groups

Group	Y	O1	O2
	4	−1	1
	5	−1	1
A_1	6	−1	1
	7	−1	1
	8	−1	1
	7	1	1
	8	1	1
A_2	9	1	1
	10	1	1
	11	1	1
	1	0	−2
	2	0	−2
A_3	3	0	−2
	4	0	−2
	5	0	−2
Σ:	90	0	0
M:	6	0	0
ss:	120	10	30

$$\Sigma o_1 y = 15 \qquad \Sigma o_2 y = 45 \qquad \Sigma o_1 o_2 = 0$$
$$r_{y.O1} = .4330 \qquad r_{y.O2} = .7500 \qquad r_{O1,O2} = 0$$
$$r^2_{y.O1} = .1875 \qquad r^2_{y.O2} = .5625$$

NOTE: Vector Y is repeated from Table 11.5.

entry in computer analysis may be done for any comparison. Thus, in a design with four groups, A_1, A_2, A_3, and A_4, if one wanted to compare the average of groups A_1, A_2, A_3 with that of A_4, the comparison would be

$$\frac{\overline{Y}_{A_1} + \overline{Y}_{A_2} + \overline{Y}_{A_3}}{3} - \overline{Y}_{A_4}$$

or

$$\frac{1}{3}(\overline{Y}_{A_1}) + \frac{1}{3}(\overline{Y}_{A_2}) + \frac{1}{3}(\overline{Y}_{A_3}) + (-1)(\overline{Y}_{A_4})$$

To convert the coefficients to integers, multiply each by 3, obtaining

$$(1)(\overline{Y}_{A_1}) + (1)(\overline{Y}_{A_2}) + (1)(\overline{Y}_{A_3}) + (-3)(\overline{Y}_{A_4})$$

As another example, assume that in a design with five groups one wanted to make the following comparison:

$$\frac{\overline{Y}_{A_1} + \overline{Y}_{A_2} + \overline{Y}_{A_3}}{3} - \frac{\overline{Y}_{A_4} + \overline{Y}_{A_5}}{2}$$

or

$$\frac{1}{3}(\overline{Y}_{A_1}) + \frac{1}{3}(\overline{Y}_{A_2}) + \frac{1}{3}(\overline{Y}_{A_3}) + \left(-\frac{1}{2}\right)(\overline{Y}_{A_4}) + \left(-\frac{1}{2}\right)(\overline{Y}_{A_5})$$

To convert the coefficients to integers, multiply by 6, obtaining

$$(2)(\overline{Y}_{A_1}) + (2)(\overline{Y}_{A_2}) + (2)(\overline{Y}_{A_3}) + (-3)(\overline{Y}_{A_4}) + (-3)(\overline{Y}_{A_5})$$

The results of the regression analysis and the tests of significance will be the same, whether the fractional coefficients or the integers to which they were converted are used (however, see the following comments about the effects of such transformations on the magnitudes of the regression coefficients).

I will analyze the data of Table 11.9 by hand, using algebraic formulas I presented in Chapter 5.[13] The main reason I am doing this is that it affords an opportunity to review and illustrate numerically some ideas I discussed in earlier chapters, particularly those regarding the absence of ambiguity in the interpretation of results when the independent variables are not correlated. *Note carefully that in the present example there is only one independent variable* (group membership in *A,* whatever the grouping). However, because the two coded vectors representing this variable are not correlated, the example affords an illustration of ideas relevant to situations in which the independent variables are not correlated.

A secondary purpose for doing the calculations by hand is to demonstrate the ease with which this can be done when the independent variables are not correlated (again, *in the present example there is only one independent variable, but it is represented by two vectors that are not correlated*).[14]

---

[13]The simplest and most efficient method is the use of matrix operations. Recall that a solution is sought for $\mathbf{b} = (\mathbf{X'X})^{-1}\mathbf{X'y}$ (see Chapter 6). With orthogonal coding, $(\mathbf{X'X})$ is a diagonal matrix; that is, all the off-diagonal elements are 0. The inverse of a diagonal matrix is a diagonal matrix whose elements are reciprocals of the diagonal elements of the matrix to be inverted. You may wish to analyze the present example by matrix operations to appreciate the ease with which this can be done when orthogonal coding is used. For guidance in doing this, see Chapter 6.

[14]Later in this chapter, I show how to revise the input file I used earlier for the analysis of the same example with dummy and effect coding to do also an analysis with orthogonal coding. For comparative purposes, I give excerpts of the output.

I will not comment on the formulas I will be using, as I did this in earlier chapters. If you have difficulties with the presentation that follows, review earlier chapters, particularly Chapter 5.

To begin with, some aspects of the statistics reported at the bottom of Table 11.9 are noteworthy. The sums, hence the means, of O1 and O2 are 0. This will always be so with this type of coding. As a result, ss (deviation sum of squares) for a coded vector is equal to the sum of its squared elements (i.e., 10 for O1 and 30 for O2). Also, because ΣX ($\Sigma O1$ and $\Sigma O2$, in the present example) $= 0$, Σxy (deviation sum of products) is the sum of the products of the two vectors. For the present example, then, $\Sigma o_1 y = \Sigma O_1 Y$; $\Sigma o_2 y = \Sigma O_2 Y$. Note the properties of these sums of products. To obtain $\Sigma o_1 y$, values of O1 are multiplied by values of Y and added. But examine these two columns in Table 11.9 and note that each Y of A_1 is multiplied by -1, and each Y of A_2 is multiplied by 1. Consequently, $\Sigma O_1 Y = \Sigma Y_{A_2} - \Sigma Y_{A_1}$, showing clearly that O1, which was designed to contrast $\bar{Y}_{A_1}$ with $\bar{Y}_{A_2}$, does this, except that total scores are used instead of means.

Examine now $\Sigma O_2 Y$ and notice that Y scores in A_1 and A_2 are multiplied by 1, whereas scores in A_3 are multiplied by -2. Consequently, $\Sigma O_2 Y = (\Sigma Y_{A_1} + \Sigma Y_{A_2}) - 2\Sigma Y_{A_3}$, which is what the second comparison was designed to accomplish, except that sums, instead of means, are contrasted. Finally, $\Sigma o_1 o_2 = 0$ indicates that O1 and O2 are orthogonal. Of course, $r_{o1,o2} = 0$. With these observations in mind, I turn to the regression analysis of Y on O1 and O2, beginning with the calculation of R^2.

R^2

As I pointed out in Chapter 5, when the independent variables are not correlated, R^2 is equal to the sum of the squared zero-order correlations of the dependent variable with each of the independent variables. The same is true for coded vectors, as long as they are orthogonal. For the data of Table 11.9,

$$R^2_{y.12} = r^2_{y1} + r^2_{y2} \quad \text{(because } r_{12} = 0)$$

From the last line of Table 11.9,

$$R^2_{y.12} = .1875 + .5625 = .75$$

Of course, R^2 is the same as those I obtained earlier when I analyzed these data with dummy and effect coding. Together, the two comparisons account for 75% of the variance of Y. The first comparison accounts for about 19% of the variance of Y, and the second comparison accounts for about 56% of the variance of Y. Following procedures I presented in Chapter 5—see (5.27) and the discussion related to it—each of these proportions can be tested for statistical significance. Recall, however, that the same can be accomplished by testing the regression sum of squares, which is what I will do in here.

Partitioning the Sum of Squares

From Table 11.9, $\Sigma y^2 = 120$. Therefore,

$$ss_{\text{reg(O1)}} = (.1875)(120) = 22.5$$

$$ss_{\text{reg(O2)}} = (.5625)(120) = 67.5$$

As expected, the regression sum of squares due to the two comparisons (90.00) is the same as that I obtained in earlier analyses of these data with dummy and effect coding. This overall regression sum of squares can, of course, be tested for significance. From earlier analyses, $F = 18$, with 2 and 12 *df* for the test of the overall regression sum of squares, which is also a test of the overall R^2.

When using orthogonal comparisons, however, the interest is in tests of each. To do this, it is necessary first to calculate the mean square residuals (*MSR*).

$$ss_{res} = \Sigma y^2 - ss_{reg}$$

$$= 120 - 90 = 30$$

Equivalently,

$$ss_{res} = (1 - R^2_{y.12})(\Sigma y^2) = (1 - .75)(120) = 30$$

and

$$MSR = \frac{ss_{res}}{N - k - 1} = \frac{30}{15 - 2 - 1} = \frac{30}{12} = 2.5$$

Testing each ss_{reg},

$$F_1 = \frac{ss_{reg(O1)}}{MSR} = \frac{22.5}{2.5} = 9$$

$$F_2 = \frac{ss_{reg(O2)}}{MSR} = \frac{67.5}{2.5} = 27$$

Earlier in this chapter, I obtained these *F* ratios, each with 1 and 12 *df,* through the application of (11.15).

Note the relation between the *F* ratios for the individual degrees of freedom and the overall *F* ratio. The latter is an average of the *F* ratios for all the orthogonal comparisons. In the present case, $(9 + 27)/2 = 18$, which is the value of the overall *F* ratio (see the preceding). This shows an advantage of orthogonal comparisons. Unless the treatment effects are equal, some orthogonal comparisons will have *F* ratios larger than the overall *F* ratio. Accordingly, even when the overall *F* ratio is statistically not significant, some orthogonal comparisons may have statistically significant *F* ratios. Furthermore, whereas a statistically significant overall *F* ratio is a necessary condition for the application of post hoc comparisons between means, this is not so for tests of orthogonal comparisons, where the interest is in the *F* ratios for the individual degrees of freedom corresponding to the specific differences hypothesized prior to the analysis.[15]

The foregoing analysis is summarized in Table 11.10, where you can see how the total sum of squares is partitioned into the various components. As the *F* ratio for each component has one degree of freedom for the numerator, $\sqrt{F} = t$ with *df* equal to those associated with the denominator of the *F* ratio, or with the *MSR*. Such *t*'s are equivalent to those obtained from testing the *b*'s (see the following).

The Regression Equation.   Because $r_{o1,o2} = 0$, the calculation of each regression coefficient is, as in the case of simple linear regression (see Chapter 2), $\Sigma xy/\Sigma x^2$. Taking relevant values from the bottom of Table 11.9,

---

[15]Although the sums of squares of each comparison are independent, the *F* ratios associated with them are not, because the same mean square error is used for all the comparisons. When the number of degrees of freedom for the mean square error is large, the comparisons may be viewed as independent. For a discussion of this point, see Hays (1988, p. 396) and Kirk (1982, pp. 96–97). For a different perspective, see Darlington (1990, p. 268).

Table 11.10   Summary of the Analysis with Orthogonal Coding, Based on Data of Table 11.9.

Source	df	ss		ms	F
Total regression	2	90.00		45.00	18.00
Regression due to O1	1		22.50	22.50	9.00
Regression due to O2	1		67.50	67.50	27.00
Residual	12	30.00		2.50	
Total	14	120.00			

$$b_{O1} = \Sigma o_1 y / \Sigma o_1^2 = 15/10 = 1.5$$

$$b_{O2} = \Sigma o_2 y / \Sigma o_2^2 = 45/30 = 1.5$$

Recall that

$$a = \overline{Y} - b_{O1}\overline{O}_1 - b_{O2}\overline{O}_2$$

But since the means of the coded vectors are equal to zero, $a = \overline{Y} = 6.00$. With orthogonal coding, as with effect coding, a is equal to $\overline{Y}$, the grand mean of the dependent variable. The regression equation for the data of Table 11.9 is therefore

$$Y' = 6.00 + 1.5(O_1) + 1.5(O_2)$$

Applying this equation to the scores (i.e., codes) of a subject on O1 and O2 will, of course, yield a predicted score equal to the mean of the group to which the subject belongs. For example, for the first subject of Table 11.9,

$$Y' = 6.0 + 1.5(-1) + 1.5(1) = 6.0$$

which is equal to the mean of A_1—the group to which this subject belongs.

Similarly, for the last subject of Table 11.9,

$$Y' = 6.0 + 1.5(0) + 1.5(-2) = 3.0$$

which is equal to the mean of A_3. I turn now to an examination of the b's.

As I explained, each sum of cross products (i.e., $\Sigma o_1 y$ and $\Sigma o_2 y$) reflects the contrast contained in the coded vector with which it is associated. Examine O1 in Table 11.9 and note that the "score" for any subject in group A_1 is -1, whereas that for any subject in A_2 is 1. If I used $-1/2$ and $1/2$ instead (i.e., coefficients half the size of those I used), the results would have been: $\Sigma o_1^2 = 2.5$, and $\Sigma o_1 y = 7.5$, leading to $b = 3.00$, which is twice the size of the one I obtained above.

Differences in b's for the same comparison, when different codes are used, reflect the scaling factor by which the codes differ. This can be seen when considering another method of calculating b's; that is, $b_j = \beta_j s_y / s_j$—see (5.12). Recall that when the independent variables are not correlated, each β (standardized regression coefficient) is equal to the zero-order correlation between the variable with which it is associated and the dependent variable. For the example under consideration, $\beta_{y1} = r_{y1}$, $\beta_{y2} = r_{y2}$. Now, multiplying or dividing O1 by a constant does not change its correlation with Y. Consequently, the corresponding β will not change either. What will change is the standard deviation of O1, which will be equal to the constant times the original standard deviation. Concretely, then, when O1 is multiplied by 2, for example, $b_{O1} = \beta_{O1} s_y / (2) s_{O1}$, it results in a b that is half the size of the one I originally obtained. The main point, however, is that the b reflects the contrast, whatever the factor by which the codes were scaled, and that the test of significance of the b (see the following) is the test of the significance of the comparison that it reflects.

Testing the Regression Coefficients. In Chapter 5—see (5.24)—I showed that the standard error of a b is

$$s_{b_{y1.2...k}} = \sqrt{\frac{s^2_{y.12...k}}{\Sigma x^2_1 (1 - R^2_{1.2...k})}}$$

where $s_{b_{y1.2...k}}$ = standard error of b_1; $s^2_{y.12...k}$ = variance of estimate; Σx^2_1 = sum of squares of X_1; and $R^2_{1.2...k}$ = squared multiple correlation of independent variable 1 with the remaining independent variables. Because orthogonal vectors representing the independent variable(s) are not correlated, the formula for the standard error of a b reduces to

$$s_{b_1} = \sqrt{\frac{s^2_{y.12...k}}{\Sigma x^2_1}}$$

Note carefully that this formula *applies only when the independent variables (or coded vectors representing an independent variable) are orthogonal.* $s^2_{y.12} = MSR = 2.5$ (see Table 11.10). From Table 11.9, $\Sigma o^2_1 = 10$, $\Sigma o^2_2 = 30$.

$$s_{b_{O1}} = \sqrt{\frac{2.5}{10}} = \sqrt{.25} = .5$$

Recalling that $b_{O1} = 1.50$.

$$t_{b_{O1}} = \frac{b_{O1}}{s_{b_{O1}}} = \frac{1.50}{.5} = 3$$

Note that $t^2_{b_{O1}} = 9.00$, which is equal to the F ratio for the test of $ss_{reg(O1)}$ (see the preceding).

An examination of the test of the b confirms what I said earlier: multiplying (or dividing) a coded vector by a constant affects the magnitude of the b associated with it but does not affect its test of significance. Assume, for the sake of illustration, that a coded vector is multiplied by a constant of 2. Earlier I showed that this will result in a b half the size of the one that would be obtained for the same vector prior to the transformation. But note that when each value of the coded vector is multiplied by 2, the sum of squares of the vector, Σx^2, will be multiplied by 2^2. Since $s^2_{y.12...k}$ will not change, and since Σx^2 is quadrupled, the square root of the ratio of the former to the latter will be half its original size. In other words, the standard error of b will be half its original size. Clearly, when the coded vector is multiplied by 2, the b as well as its standard error are half their original size, thus leaving the t ratio invariant.

Calculate now the standard error of b_{O2}:

$$s_{b_{O2}} = \sqrt{\frac{2.5}{30}} = \sqrt{.08333} = .28868$$

Recalling that $b_{O2} = 1.5$,

$$t_{b_{O2}} = \frac{b_{O2}}{s_{b_{O2}}} = \frac{1.50}{.28868} = 5.19615$$

$t^2_{b_{O2}} = 27.00$, which is the same as the F ratio for the test of $ss_{reg(O2)}$ (see the preceding).

The degrees of freedom for a t ratio for the test of a b equal those associated with the residual sum of squares: $(N - k - 1)$. For the present example, $N = 15$, $k = 2$ (coded vectors). Hence, each t ratio has 12 df.

Not to lose sight of the main purpose of orthogonal coding, I will give a brief summary. When a priori orthogonal comparisons among a set of means are hypothesized, it is necessary to generate orthogonally coded vectors, each of which reflects one of the hypotheses. Regressing Y on the coded vectors, proportions of variance (or ss) due to each comparison may be obtained. These may be tested separately for significance. But the tests of the b's provide the same information; that is, each t ratio is a test of the comparison reflected in the vector with which the b is associated. Thus, when a computer program is used for multiple regression analysis, one need only to inspect the t ratios for the b's to note which hypotheses were supported.

Recall that the number of possible orthogonal comparisons among g groups is $g - 1$. Assume that a researcher is working with five groups. Four orthogonal comparisons are therefore possible. Suppose, however, that the researcher has only two a priori hypotheses that are orthogonal. These can still be tested in the manner I outlined previously provided that, in addition to the two orthogonal vectors representing these hypotheses, two additional orthogonal vectors are included in the analysis. This is necessary to exhaust the information about group membership (recall that for g groups $g - 1 = k$ coded vectors are necessary; this is true regardless of the coding method). Having done this, the researcher will examine only the t ratios associated with the b's that reflect the a priori hypotheses. In addition, post hoc comparisons among means (e.g., Scheffé) may be pursued.

In the beginning of this section I said that planned nonorthogonal comparisons may also be hypothesized. I turn now to a brief treatment of this topic.

Planned Nonorthogonal Comparisons

Some authors, notably Ryan (1959a, 1959b), argued that there are neither logical nor statistical reasons for the distinction between planned and post hoc comparisons, that all comparisons may be treated by a uniform approach and from a common frame of reference. The topic is too complex to discuss here. Instead, I will point out that the recommended approach was variously referred to as *Bonferroni t statistics* (Miller, 1966) or the Dunn (1961) procedure. Basically, this procedure involves the calculation of F or t ratios for the hypothesized comparisons (any given comparison may refer to differences between pairs of means or combinations of means) and the adjustment of the overall α level for the number of comparisons done. A couple of examples follow. Suppose that in a design with seven groups, five planned nonorthogonal comparisons are hypothesized and that overall $\alpha = .05$. One would calculate F or t ratios for each comparison in the manner shown earlier. But for a given comparison to be declared statistically significant, its associated t or F would have to exceed the critical value at the .01 ($\alpha/5 = .05/5$) level instead of the .05. Suppose now that for the same number of groups (7) and the same α (.05), one wanted to do all 21—(7)(6)/2—pairwise comparisons between means; then for a comparison to be declared statistically significant the t ratio would have to exceed the critical value at .002 ($\alpha/21 = .05/21$).

In general, then, given c (number of comparisons), and α (overall level of significance), a t or F for a comparison has to exceed the critical value at α/c for a comparison to be declared statistically significant. Degrees of freedom for t ratio are those associated with the mean square residual (MSR), $N - k - 1$, and those for F ratio are 1 and $N - k - 1$.

The procedure I outlined earlier frequently requires critical values at α levels not found in conventional tables of t or F. Tabled values for what are either referred to as Bonferroni test statistics or the Dunn Multiple Comparison Test may be found in various statistics books (e.g., Kirk, 1982; Maxwell & Delaney, 1990; Myers, 1979). Such tables are entered with the number of comparisons (c) and $N - k - 1$ (df for MSR). For example, suppose that for the data of Table 11.9 pairwise comparisons between the means were hypothesized (i.e., $\overline{Y}_{A_1} - \overline{Y}_{A_2}$; $\overline{Y}_{A_1} - \overline{Y}_{A_3}$; $\overline{Y}_{A_2} - \overline{Y}_{A_3}$), and that the overall $\alpha = .05$. There are three comparisons, and df for MSR are 12 (see the preceding analysis). Entering the Dunn table with these values shows that the critical t ratio is 2.78. Thus, a t ratio for a comparison has to exceed 2.78 for it to be declared statistically significant. Alternatively, having access to a computer program that reports exact p values for tests of significance (most do), obviates the need to resort to the aforementioned tables (see "Computer Analysis" later in the chapter).

The Bonferroni, or Dunn, procedure is very versatile. For further discussions and applications, comparisons with other procedures, error rates controlled by each, and recommendations for use, see Bielby and Kluegel (1977), Darlington (1990), Davis (1969), Keppel (1991), Kirk (1982), Maxwell and Delaney (1990), Myers (1979), and Perlmutter and Myers (1973).

Using C*

Earlier, I showed how to use elements of $\mathbf{C}^*$ (augmented covariance matrix of the b's) for testing differences among b's. This approach may be applied for post hoc, planned orthogonal, and planned nonorthogonal comparisons. Basically, a t or F ratio is obtained for a contrast among b's. How it is then used depends on the specific multiple comparison procedure used. If, for instance, the Scheffé procedure is used, the F is checked against $kF_{\alpha; k, N - k - 1}$ (see the discussion of the Scheffé procedure earlier in this chapter). If, on the other hand, the Bonferroni approach is applied, then the obtained t is checked against t with α/c, where c is the number of comparisons.

Using orthogonal coefficients for tests among b's obtained from effect coding, the same F's or t's would be obtained as from a regression analysis with orthogonal coding. Of the two orthogonal comparisons I used in Table 11.9, I obtained the first earlier (see "Multiple Comparison via b's"), though I used it to illustrate the calculation of post hoc comparisons. Note that the F ratio associated with this comparison (9.00) is the same as the one I obtained in this section.

In sum, when effect coding is used one may still test planned orthogonal or nonorthogonal comparisons by testing linear combinations of b's. When, however, the planned comparisons are orthogonal, it is more efficient to use orthogonal coding, as doing this obviates the need for additional tests subsequent to the overall analysis. All the necessary information is available from the tests of the b's in the overall analysis.

Computer Analysis

As I did earlier for the case of effect coding, I will show here how to edit the SPSS input file with dummy coding (see the analysis of Table 11.5 offered earlier in this chapter) so that an analysis with orthogonal coding will also be carried out. In addition, I will include input statements for ONEWAY of SPSS, primarily to show how this procedure can be used to carry out the contrasts I obtained earlier in this chapter through the application of (11.15). Subsequently, I present analyses of the same example using SAS procedures.

SPSS

Input

```
. . . . . . . . . . . . . . . . . . . . . . . . .    [see commentary]
COMPUTE O1=D2–D1.
COMPUTE O2=(D1+D2)–2*D3.
. . . . . . . . . . . . . . . . . . . . . . . . .    [see commentary]
REGRESSION DES/VAR Y TO O2/STAT ALL/
. . . . . . . . . . . . . . . . . . . . . . . . .    [see commentary]
  DEP Y/ENTER O1 O2.
ONEWAY Y BY T(1,3)/STAT=ALL/
   CONTRAST –1  1   0/
   CONTRAST  1  1  –2/
   CONTRAST  1  0  –1/
   CONTRAST  0  1  –1.
```

Commentary

Earlier, when I showed how to edit the input file to incorporate also effect coding, I pointed out that I also incorporated orthogonal coding in the same run. Thus, if you wish to use the three coding procedures in a single run, incorporate the statements given here, as well as analogous statements given earlier for effect coding, in the SPSS input file to analyze the data in Table 11.5 (i.e., analysis with dummy coding) given earlier in this chapter. If necessary, see the commentaries on the analysis with effect coding concerning the editing of the input file.

COMPUTE. The preceding two statements are designed to generate vectors O1 and O2 containing the orthogonal codes I used when I analyzed the data of Table 11.9 by hand. The asterisk (*) in the second statement means multiplication.

ONEWAY. As I pointed out earlier, I am also including input statements for this procedure. Notice that I am using T as the (required) group identification vector, specifying that it ranges from 1 to 3. Although ONEWAY has options for several multiple comparisons (e.g., Scheffé), I call only for the calculation of contrasts. Note that the first two contrasts are the same as the orthogonal contrasts I used in Table 11.9 and analyzed by hand in an earlier section. In the third statement, the mean of group 1 is contrasted with the mean of group 3. In the last statement, the mean of group 2 is contrasted with the mean of group 3. For explanations, see the commentary on the output generated by these comparisons.

Output

T	Y	D1	D2	D3	O1	O2	
1.00	4.00	1.00	.00	.00	–1.00	1.00	
1.00	5.00	1.00	.00	.00	–1.00	1.00	*[first two subjects in A_1]*
.	.	.	.	.	.	.	
2.00	7.00	.00	1.00	.00	1.00	1.00	
2.00	8.00	.00	1.00	.00	1.00	1.00	*[first two subjects in A_2]*
.	.	.	.	.	.	.	
3.00	1.00	.00	.00	1.00	.00	–2.00	
3.00	2.00	.00	.00	1.00	.00	–2.00	*[first two subjects in A_3]*

Commentary

Although in the remainder of this section I include output relevant only to orthogonal coding, I included the dummy coding in the listing so that you may see how the COMPUTE statements yielded the orthogonal vectors.

Output

	Mean	Std Dev
Y	6.000	2.928
O1	.000	.845
O2	.000	1.464

N of Cases =   15
Correlation:

	Y	O1	O2
Y	1.000	.433	.750
O1	.433	1.000	.000
O2	.750	.000	1.000

Commentary

I included the preceding excerpts so that you may compare them with the summary statistics given at the bottom of Table 11.9. Note that the means of orthogonally coded vectors equal zero, as does the correlation between orthogonally coded vectors (O1 and O2).

Output

Dependent Variable..   Y
Variable(s) Entered on Step Number 1..   O1
                                     2..   O2

Multiple R	.86603	Analysis of Variance			
R Square	.75000		DF	Sum of Squares	Mean Square
Adjusted R Square	.70833	Regression	2	90.00000	45.00000
Standard Error	1.58114	Residual	12	30.00000	2.50000

F =   18.00000   Signif F =   .0002

------------------------------------ Variables in the Equation --

Variable	B	SE B	Beta	Tolerance	T	Sig T
O1	1.500000	.500000	.433013	1.000000	3.000	.0111
O2	1.500000	.288675	.750000	1.000000	5.196	.0002
(Constant)	6.000000					

Commentary

I believe that most of the preceding requires no comment, as I commented on the same results when I did the calculations by hand.

As I explained earlier, when independent variables (or coded vectors) are not correlated, each Beta is equal to the zero-order correlation between the vector with which it is associated and the dependent variable.

As the coded vectors are not correlated, Tolerance = 1.0 (see Chapter 10 for an explanation).

Output

Analysis of Variance

Source	D.F.	Sum of Squares	Mean Squares	F Ratio	F Prob.
Between Groups	2	90.0000	45.0000	18.0000	.0002
Within Groups	12	30.0000	2.5000		
Total	14	120.0000			

Group	Count	Mean	Standard Deviation
Grp 1	5	6.0000	1.5811
Grp 2	5	9.0000	1.5811
Grp 3	5	3.0000	1.5811
Total	15	6.0000	2.9277

Variable Y
By Variable T

Contrast Coefficient Matrix

	Grp 1	Grp 2	Grp 3
Contrast 1	−1.0	1.0	.0
Contrast 2	1.0	1.0	−2.0
Contrast 3	1.0	.0	−1.0
Contrast 4	.0	1.0	−1.0

Pooled Variance Estimate

	Value	S. Error	T Value	D.F.	T Prob.
Contrast 1	3.0000	1.0000	3.000	12.0	.011
Contrast 2	9.0000	1.7321	5.196	12.0	.000
Contrast 3	3.0000	1.0000	3.000	12.0	.011
Contrast 4	6.0000	1.0000	6.000	12.0	.000

Commentary

The preceding are excerpts from the ONEWAY output. Compare the first couple of segments with the results of the same analysis summarized in Table 11.4.

As I said earlier, my main aim in running ONEWAY was to show how it can be used to test contrasts. Given in the preceding are the contrasts I specified and their tests. Squaring each *t* yields the corresponding *F* (with 1 and 12 *df*) I obtained earlier through the application of (11.15).

Earlier, in my discussion of Bonferroni *t* statistics, I pointed out that when the output contains exact *p* values for each test, it is not necessary to use specialized tables for Bonferroni tests. Such *p*'s are reported above under T Prob(ability). To illustrate how they are used in Bonferroni tests, assume that in the present case only comparisons 1 and 3 were hypothesized. Verify that these comparisons are *not* orthogonal. Assuming overall $\alpha = .05$, each *t* has to be tested at the .025 level ($\alpha/2 = .025$). As the probability associated with each of the *t*'s under consideration (.011) is smaller than .025, one can conclude that both comparisons are statistically significant.

SAS

In what follows I give an input file for the analysis of the example under consideration through both PROC REG and PROC GLM. I used the former several times in earlier chapters, whereas I use the latter for the first time here.

Input

```
TITLE 'TABLES 11.4-11.6, AND 11.9. PROC REG & GLM';
DATA T115;
INPUT T Y;
IF T=1 THEN D1=1; ELSE D1=0;        [generate dummy vector D1]
IF T=2 THEN D2=1; ELSE D2=0;        [generate dummy vector D2]
IF T=3 THEN D3=1; ELSE D3=0;        [generate dummy vector D3]
E1=D1–D3;                           [generate effect vector E1]
E2=D2–D3;                           [generate effect vector E2]
O1=D2–D1;                           [generate orthogonal vector O1]
O2=(D1+D2)–2*D3;                    [generate orthogonal vector O2]
CARDS;
1   4
1   5
1   6
1   7
1   8
2   7
2   8
2   9
2   10
2   11
3   1
3   2
3   3
3   4
3   5
;
PROC PRINT;
```

```
PROC REG;
MODEL Y=D1 D2;
MODEL Y=E1 E2/COVB;          [option: print covariance matrix of b's]
MODEL Y=O1 O2;
PROC GLM;
CLASS T;
MODEL Y=T;
MEANS T;
CONTRAST 'T1 VS. T2' T -1 1 0;
CONTRAST 'T1+T2 VS. T3' T 1 1 -2;
CONTRAST 'T1 VS. T3' T 1 0 -1;
CONTRAST 'T2 VS. T3' T 0 1 -1;
ESTIMATE 'T1 VS. T2' T -1 1 0;
ESTIMATE 'T1+T2 VS. T3' T 1 1 -2;
ESTIMATE 'T1 VS. T3' T 1 0 -1;
ESTIMATE 'T2 VS. T3' T 0 1 -1;
PROC GLM;
MODEL Y=O1 O2;
RUN;
```

Commentary

For an introduction to SAS as well as an application of PROC REG, see Chapter 4 (see also Chapters 8 and 10). As I stated earlier, I use PROC GLM (General Linear Model)—one of the most powerful and versatile procedures available in any of the packages I introduced in Chapter 4—for the first time in this book. For an overview of GLM see SAS Institute (1990a, Vol. 1, Chapter 2). For a detailed discussion of GLM input and output, along with examples, see SAS Institute (1990a, Vol. 2, Chapter 24). Here, I comment only on aspects pertinent to the topic under consideration.

PROC REG. Notice that I am using three model statements, thus generating results for the three coding schemes. As indicated in the italicized comment in the input,[16] for one of the models I am calling for the printing of the covariance matrix of the *b*'s.

PROC GLM:

CLASS. Identifies T as the categorical variable.

MODEL. Identifies Y as the dependent variable and T as the independent variable. Unlike PROC REG, PROC GLM allows for only one model statement. See the comment on the next PROC GLM.

CONTRAST. Calls for tests of contrasts (see SAS Institute Inc., 1990a, Vol. 2, pp. 905-906). For comparative purposes, I use the same contrasts as those I used earlier in SPSS.

ESTIMATE. Can be used to estimate parameters of the model or linear combinations of parameters (see SAS Institute Inc., 1990a, Vol. 2, p. 907 and pp. 939–941). I use it here to show how the same tests are carried out as through the CONTRAST statement, except that the results are reported in a somewhat different format.

---

[16]I remind you that italicized comments are *not* part of the input.

Output

OBS	T	Y	D1	D2	D3	E1	E2	O1	O2
1	1	4	1	0	0	1	0	−1	1
2	1	5	1	0	0	1	0	−1	1
.	.	.	.	.	.	.	.	.	.
6	2	7	0	1	0	0	1	1	1
7	2	8	0	1	0	0	1	1	1
.	.	.	.	.	.	.	.	.	.
11	3	1	0	0	1	−1	−1	0	−2
12	3	2	0	0	1	−1	−1	0	−2

Commentary

The preceding is an excerpt generated by PROC PRINT. Examine E1 through O2 in conjunction with the input statements designed to generate them.

Output

Dependent Variable: Y

Analysis of Variance

Source	DF	Sum of Squares	Mean Square	F Value	Prob>F
Model	2	90.00000	45.00000	18.000	0.0002
Error	12	30.00000	2.50000		
C Total	14	120.00000			

Root MSE	1.58114	R-square	0.7500	
Dep Mean	6.00000	Adj R-sq	0.7083	

Variable	DF	Parameter Estimate
INTERCEP	1	6.000000
E1	1	0
E2	1	3.000000

Covariance of Estimates

COVB	INTERCEP	E1	E2
INTERCEP	0.1666666667	0	0
E1	0	0.3333333333	−0.166666667
E2	0	−0.166666667	0.3333333333

Commentary

Notwithstanding differences in format and labeling, I obtained results such as those reported here earlier through hand calculations and through SPSS. Accordingly, my comments will be brief.

For illustrative purposes, I included excerpts from the analysis with effect coding only (see E1 and E2). As I explained earlier in this chapter, the Analysis of Variance Table is identical for the three models. What differ are the regression equations. Reported here is the equation for effect coding (compare with SPSS output).

The 2×2 matrix corresponding to E1 and E2 (Under Covariance of Estimates) is **C** = covariance matrix of the b's. See earlier in this chapter for explanations and illustrations as to how **C** is augmented and how the augmented matrix is used for tests of comparisons among b's.

Output

General Linear Models Procedure
Class Level Information

Class	Levels	Values
T	3	1 2 3

Number of observations in data set = 15

Dependent Variable: Y

Source	DF	Sum of Squares	Mean Square	F Value	Pr > F
Model	2	90.00000000	45.00000000	18.00	0.0002
Error	12	30.00000000	2.50000000		
Corrected Total	14	120.00000000			

R-Square	Root MSE	Y Mean
0.750000	1.58113883	6.00000000

Commentary

The preceding excerpts from PROC GLM should pose no difficulties, especially if you study them in conjunction with SPSS output and/or with the results I obtained earlier in this chapter through hand calculations.

Output

Level of T	N	Mean	SD
		------------------Y--------------------	
1	5	6.00000000	1.58113883
2	5	9.00000000	1.58113883
3	5	3.00000000	1.58113883

Commentary

The preceding was generated by the MEANS T statement (see the preceding input).

Output

Dependent Variable: Y

Contrast	DF	Contrast SS	Mean Square	F Value	Pr > F
T1 VS. T2	1	22.50000000	22.50000000	9.00	0.0111
T1+T2 VS. T3	1	67.50000000	67.50000000	27.00	0.0002
T1 VS. T3	1	22.50000000	22.50000000	9.00	0.0111
T2 VS. T3	1	90.00000000	90.00000000	36.00	0.0001

Parameter	Estimate	T for H0: Parameter=0	Pr > |T|	Std Error of Estimate
T1 VS. T2	3.00000000	3.00	0.0111	1.00000000
T1+T2 VS. T3	9.00000000	5.20	0.0002	1.73205081
T1 VS. T3	3.00000000	3.00	0.0111	1.00000000
T2 VS. T3	6.00000000	6.00	0.0001	1.00000000

Commentary

As I pointed out earlier, although CONTRAST and ESTIMATE present somewhat different information, it amounts to the same thing. Notice, for example, that the squared T's reported under estimate are equal to their respective F's under contrast. Compare these results with the SPSS output given earlier or with results I obtained through hand calculations.

Output

Parameter	Estimate	T for H0: Parameter=0	Pr > |T|	Std Error of Estimate
INTERCEPT	6.000000000	14.70	0.0001	0.40824829
O1	1.500000000	3.00	0.0111	0.50000000
O2	1.500000000	5.20	0.0002	0.28867513

Commentary

As I pointed out earlier, only one MODEL statement can be used in PROC GLM. The preceding is an excerpt generated by MODEL in the second PROC GLM and its associated MODEL statement. I did this to show, albeit in a very limited form, the versatility of PROC GLM. Notice that it yields here results identical to ones I obtained from a regression analysis. I reproduced only the regression equation and some related statistics. Compare the results with those I gave earlier for the analysis with orthogonal coding.

UNEQUAL SAMPLE SIZES

Among major reasons for having equal sample sizes, or equal n's, in experimental designs, are that (1) statistical tests presented in this chapter are more sensitive and (2) distortions that may occur because of departures from certain assumptions underlying these tests are minimized (see Li, J. C. R., 1964, Vol. I, pp. 147–148 and 197–198, for a discussion of the advantages of equal sample sizes). The preceding issues aside, it is necessary to examine briefly other matters relevant to the use of unequal n's as they may have serious implications for valid interpretation of results.

Unequal n's may occur by design or because of loss of subjects in the course of an investigation, frequently referred to as subject mortality or subject attrition. I examine, in turn, these two types of occurrences in the context of experimental and nonexperimental research.

In *experimental research,* a researcher may find it necessary or desirable to randomly assign subjects in varying numbers to treatments differing in, say, cost. Other reasons for designing experiments with unequal n's come readily to mind. The use of unequal n's by design does not pose threats to the internal validity of the experiment, that is, to valid conclusions about treatment effects.[17]

Subject mortality may pose very serious threats to internal validity. The degree of bias introduced by subject mortality is often difficult, if not impossible, to assess, as it requires a thorough knowledge of the reasons for the loss of subjects. Assume that an experiment was begun with equal n's but that in the course of its implementation subjects were lost. This may have occurred for myriad reasons, from simple and tractable ones such as errors in the recording of scores or the malfunctioning of equipment, to very complex and intractable ones that may relate to the subjects' motivations or reactions to specific treatments. Threats to internal validity are not diminished when subject attrition results in groups of equal n's, though such an occurrence may generally be more reasonably attributed to a random process. Clearly, subject mortality may reflect a process of self-selection leading to groups composed of different kinds of people, thereby raising questions as to whether the results are due to treatment effects or to differences among subjects in the different treatment conditions. The less one is able to discern the reasons for subject mortality, the greater is its potential threat to the internal validity of the experiment.

In *nonexperimental research,* too, unequal n's may be used by design or they may be a consequence of subject mortality. The use of equal or unequal n's by design is directly related to the sampling plan and to the questions the study is designed to answer. Thus, when the aim is to study the relation between a categorical and a continuous variable in a defined population, it is imperative that the categories, or subgroups, that make up the categorical variable be represented according to their proportions in the population. For example, if the purpose is to study the relation between race and income in the United States, it is necessary that the sample include all racial groups in the same proportions as such groups are represented in the population, thereby resulting in a categorical variable with unequal n's.

Probably more often, researchers are interested in making comparisons among subgroups, or strata in sampling terminology. Thus, the main interest may be in comparing the incomes of different racial groups. For such purposes it is desirable to have equal n's in the subgroups. This is accomplished by disproportionate, or unequal probabilities, sampling. Disproportionate sampling of racial or ethnic groups is often used in studies on the effects of schooling.

---

[17]For discussions of internal validity of experiments, see Campbell and Stanley (1963), Cook and Campbell (1979, pp. 50–58), Pedhazur and Schmelkin (1991, pp. 224–229).

Obviously, the aforementioned sampling plans are not interchangeable; the choice of each depends on the research question (see Pedhazur & Schmelkin, 1991, Chapter 15, for an introduction to sampling and relevant references). Whatever the sampling plan, subject mortality may occur for a variety of reasons and affect the validity of results to a greater or lesser extent. Probably one of the most serious threats to the validity of results stems from what could broadly be characterized as nonresponse and undercoverage. Sampling experts developed various techniques aimed at adjusting the results for such occurrences (see, for example, Namboodiri, 1978, Part IV). The main thing to keep in mind is that nonresponse reflects a process of self-selection, thus casting doubts about the representativeness of the subgroups being compared.

The preceding brief review of situations that may lead to unequal n's and the potential threats some of them pose to the validity of the results should alert you to the hazards of not being attentive to these issues. I will now consider the regression analysis of a continuous variable on a categorical variable whose categories are composed of unequal n's. First, I present dummy and effect coding together. Then, I address the case of orthogonal coding.

Dummy and Effect Coding for Unequal *N*'s

Dummy or effect coding of a categorical variable with unequal n's proceeds as with equal n's. I illustrate this with part of the data I used earlier in this chapter. Recall that the example I analyzed with the three coding methods consisted of three groups, each composed of five subjects. For the present analysis, I deleted the scores of the fourth and the fifth subjects from group A_1 and the score of the fifth subject from group A_2. Accordingly, there are three, four, and five subjects, respectively, in A_1, A_2, and A_3. The scores for these groups, along with dummy and effect coding, are reported in Table 11.11. Note that the approaches are identical to those I used with equal n's (see Tables 11.5 and 11.6). Following the practice I established earlier, the dummy vector in which subjects in A_1 are identified is labeled D1; the dummy vector in which subjects in A_2 are identified is labeled D2. The corresponding effect coded vectors are labeled E1 and E2.

Table 11.11 Dummy and Effect Coding for Unequal *n*'s

		Dummy Coding		Effect Coding	
Group	*Y*	*D1*	*D2*	*E1*	*E2*
A_1	4	1	0	1	0
	5	1	0	1	0
	6	1	0	1	0
A_2	7	0	1	0	1
	8	0	1	0	1
	9	0	1	0	1
	10	0	1	0	1
A_3	1	0	0	−1	−1
	2	0	0	−1	−1
	3	0	0	−1	−1
	4	0	0	−1	−1
	5	0	0	−1	−1

SPSS

I analyzed the data in Table 11.11 through SPSS. Except for the deletion of three subjects to which I referred in the preceding paragraph, the input file is identical to the one I used in the earlier analyses. Therefore, I will not repeat it. Instead, I will give excerpts of output and comment on them.

Output

		Analysis of Variance			
Multiple R	.89399		DF	Sum of Squares	Mean Square
R Square	.79921				
Adjusted R Square	.75459	Regression	2	67.66667	33.83333
Standard Error	1.37437	Residual	9	17.00000	1.88889
		$F = $ 17.91176		Signif $F = $ .0007	

Commentary

This output is identical for dummy and effect coding. The total sum of squares, which SPSS does not report, can be readily obtained by adding the regression and residual sum of squares $(67.66667 + 17.00000 = 77.66667)$. The categorical variable accounts for about 80% of the variance of Y (R^2). The F ratio with 2 $(k = 2$ coded vectors) and 9 $(N - k - 1 = 12 - 2 - 1)$ df is $17.91, p < .01$.

Output (for Dummy Coding)

-------------------------------------- Variables in the Equation --------------------------------------

Variable	B	SE B	T	Sig T
D1	2.000000	1.003697	1.993	.0775
D2	5.500000	.921954	5.966	.0002
(Constant)	3.000000	.614636	4.881	.0009

Commentary

The *regression equation for dummy coding* is

$$Y' = 3.0 + 2.0D1 + 5.5D2$$

Applying this equation to the codes of a subject yields a predicted score equal to the mean of the group to which the subject belongs.

For subjects in group A_1,

$$Y' = 3.0 + 2.0(1) + 5.5(0) = 5.00 = \overline{Y}_{A_1}$$

for those in A_2,

$$Y' = 3.0 + 2.0(0) + 5.5(1) = 8.5 = \overline{Y}_{A_2}$$

and for those in A_3,

$$Y' = 3.0 + 2.0(0) + 5.5(0) = 3.0 = \overline{Y}_{A_3}$$

Note that the properties of this equation are the same as those of the regression equation for dummy coding with equal n's: a (CONSTANT) is equal to the mean of the group assigned 0's throughout (A_3), b_{D1} is equal to the deviation of the mean of A_1 from the mean of A_3 ($5.0 - 3.0 = 2.0$), and b_{D2} is equal to the deviation of the mean of A_2 from the mean of A_3 ($8.5 - 3.0 = 5.5$).

Earlier, I stated that with dummy coding the group assigned 0's throughout acts as a control group and that testing each b for significance is tantamount to testing the difference between the mean of the group with which the given b is associated and the mean of the control group. The same is true for designs with unequal n's. Assuming that A_3 is indeed a control group, and that a two-tailed test at $\alpha = .05$ was selected, the critical t value reported in the Dunnett table for two treatments and a control, with 9 *df*, is 2.61. Based on the T ratios reported in the previous output (1.99 and 5.97 for D1 and D2, respectively), one would conclude that the difference between the means of A_1 and A_3 is statistically not significant, whereas that between the means of A_2 and A_3 is statistically significant.

When there is no control group and dummy coding is used for convenience, tests of the b's are ignored. Instead, multiple comparisons among means are done—a topic I discuss later under effect coding.

Output (for Effect Coding)

Variables in the Equation

Variable	B
E1	−.500000
E2	3.000000
(Constant)	5.500000

Commentary

I did not reproduce the standard errors of b's and their associated t ratios as they are generally not used in this context. Instead, multiple comparisons among means are done (see the following).

The *regression equation with effect coding* is

$$Y' = 5.5 - .5E1 + 3.0E2$$

Though this equation has properties analogous to the equation for effect coding with equal n's, it differs in specifics. When the categorical variable is composed of unequal n's, a (CONSTANT) is *not* equal to the grand mean of the dependent variable (i.e., the mean of the Y vector in Table 11.11), but rather it is equal to its unweighted mean, that is, the average of the group means. In the present example, the weighted (i.e., weighted by the number of people in each group) mean of the dependent variable is

$$\bar{Y} = \frac{(3)(5.0) + (4)(8.5) + (5)(3.0)}{3 + 4 + 5} = 5.33$$

which is the same as adding all the Y scores and dividing by the number of scores.

The unweighted mean of Y is

$$\frac{5.0 + 8.5 + 3.0}{3} = 5.5$$

When sample sizes are equal, the average of the means is the same as the weighted mean, as all the means are weighted by a constant (the sample size).

To repeat: the intercept, *a*, of the regression equation for effect coding with unequal *n*'s is equal to the unweighted mean or the average of the *Y* means.

Recall that in the case of equal *n*'s, each *b* indicates the effect of the treatment with which it is associated or the deviation of the group mean with which the *b* is associated from the grand mean. In the case of unequal *n*'s, on the other hand, each *b* indicates the deviation of the mean of the group with which the *b* is associated from the *unweighted* mean. In the present example:

$$\text{Effect of } A_1 = b_{E1} = 5.0 - 5.5 = -.5$$

$$\text{Effect of } A_2 = b_{E2} = 8.5 - 5.5 = 3.0$$

The effect of A_3 is, as always in effect coding, equal to minus the sum of the *b*'s: $-(-.5 + 3.0) = -2.5$, which is equal to the deviations of the mean of A_3 from the unweighted mean $(3.0 - 5.5 = -2.5)$.

As always, applying the regression equation to the codes of a subject on E1 and E2 yields the mean of the group to which the subject belongs. Thus, for subjects in A_1,

$$Y' = 5.5 - .5(1) + 3.0(0) = 5.0 = \bar{Y}_{A_1}$$

for those in A_2,

$$Y' = 5.5 - .5(0) + 3.0(1) = 8.5 = \bar{Y}_{A_2}$$

and for those in A_3,

$$Y' = 5.5 - .5(-1) + 3.0(-1) = 3.0 = \bar{Y}_{A_3}$$

Multiple Comparisons among Means

As with equal *n*'s, multiple comparisons among means can be done when *n*'s are unequal. Also, the comparisons may be post hoc, planned nonorthogonal, and planned orthogonal. Assume that in the present example no planned comparisons were hypothesized. Because the overall *F* ratio is statistically significant, one may proceed with post hoc comparisons, say, the Scheffé procedure.

For illustrative purposes, I will test the following two comparisons:

$$\bar{Y}_{A_1} - \bar{Y}_{A_2} \quad \text{and} \quad \frac{\bar{Y}_{A_1} + \bar{Y}_{A_2}}{2} - \bar{Y}_{A_3}$$

Applying, in turn, (11.15) to each comparison,

$$F = \frac{[C_1(\bar{Y}_1) + C_2(\bar{Y}_2)]^2}{MSR\left[\sum \frac{(C_j)^2}{n_j}\right]} = \frac{[(1)(5.0) + (-1)(8.5)]^2}{1.88889\left[\frac{(1)^2}{3} + \frac{(-1)^2}{4}\right]} = \frac{(-3.5)^2}{1.10185} = 11.12$$

for the first comparison. And

$$F = \frac{[(1)(5.0) + (1)(8.5) + (-2)(3.0)]^2}{1.88889\left[\frac{(1)^2}{3} + \frac{(1)^2}{4} + \frac{(-2)^2}{5}\right]} = \frac{(7.5)^2}{2.61296} = 21.53$$

for the second comparison. Using the Scheffé procedure, a comparison is declared statistically significant if its *F* ratio exceeds $kF_{\alpha;\ k,\ N-k-1}$, which for the present example is $(2)(4.26) = 8.52$, where 4.26 is the tabled *F* ratio with 2 and 9 *df* at the .05 level. Both comparisons are statistically significant at the .05 level.

Comparisons Using b's

I now show how the same tests can be carried out by using relevant b's and elements of $\mathbf{C}^*$ (augmented covariance matrix of the b's).

Output

$$\mathbf{C}^* = \begin{bmatrix} .37428 & -.20288 & \vdots & -.17140 \\ -.20288 & .32181 & \vdots & -.11893 \\ \hdashline & & & \\ -.17140 & -.11893 & & .29033 \end{bmatrix}$$

The values enclosed by the dashed lines are reported in the output. When I discussed $\mathbf{C}^*$ for equal n's, I said that for unequal n's the diagonal elements are not equal to each other and that neither are the off-diagonal elements equal to each other. Yet, the manner of obtaining the missing elements is the same as for equal n's. That is, a missing element in a row is equal to $-\Sigma c_i$, and the same is true for a missing element in a column.

Recalling that the regression equation is

$$Y' = 5.5 - .5E1 + 3.0E2$$

and that the b for the groups assigned -1's, A_3, is -2.5, I turn to multiple comparisons among means via tests of differences among b's.

Applying (11.18) to the difference between corresponding b's is the same as a test of the difference between the means of A_1 and A_2:

$$F = \frac{[(1)(-.5) + (-1)(3)]^2}{[1 \quad -1]\begin{bmatrix} .37428 & -.20288 \\ -.20288 & .32181 \end{bmatrix}\begin{bmatrix} 1 \\ -1 \end{bmatrix}} = \frac{(-3.5)^2}{1.10185} = 11.12$$

which is the same as the F ratio I obtained earlier.

Using b's to test the difference between the average of the means of A_1 and A_2 and the mean of A_3,

$$F = \frac{[(1)(-.5) + (1)(3) + (-2)(-2.5)]^2}{[1 \quad 1 \quad -2]\begin{bmatrix} .37428 & -.20288 & -.17140 \\ -.20288 & .32181 & -.11893 \\ -.17140 & -.11893 & .29033 \end{bmatrix}\begin{bmatrix} 1 \\ 1 \\ -2 \end{bmatrix}} = \frac{(7.5)^2}{2.61297} = 21.53$$

Again, I obtained the same F ratio previously.

It is important to note that when n's are unequal, tests of linear combinations of means (or b's) are done on *unweighted* means. In the second comparison it was the *average* of the means of A_1 and A_2 that was contrasted with the mean of A_3. That the means of A_1 and A_2 were based on different numbers of people was not taken into account. Each group was given equal weight.

I will show the meaning of this through a concrete example. Suppose that A_1 represents a group of Blacks, A_2 a group of Hispanics, and A_3 a group of Whites. When the average of the means of the Blacks and Hispanics is contrasted with the mean of the Whites (as in the second comparison), the fact that Blacks may outnumber Hispanics, or vice versa, is ignored.

Whether or not comparisons among unweighted means are meaningful depends on the questions one wishes to answer. Assume that A_1, A_2, and A_3 were three treatments in an experiment and that the researcher used unequal n's by design (i.e., they are not a consequence of subject mortality). It makes sense for the researcher to compare unweighted means, thus ignoring the unequal n's. Or, in the example I used earlier, the researcher may wish to contrast minority group members with those of the majority, ignoring the fact that one minority group is larger than the other.

It is conceivable for one to be interested in contrasting weighted means (i.e., weighting each mean by the number of people in the group). For the second comparison in the numerical example under consideration, this would mean

$$\frac{(3)(5.0) + (4)(8.5)}{3 + 4} - 3 = 7 - 3 = 4$$

as compared with the contrast between unweighted means: $(5.0 + 8.5)/2 - 3 = 3.75$. I discuss comparisons among weighted means in the following section on orthogonal coding.

ORTHOGONAL CODING WITH UNEQUAL *n*'s

For samples with unequal n's, a comparison or a linear combination of means is defined as

$$L = n_1 C_1 + n_2 C_2 + \ldots + n_j C_j \tag{11.19}$$

where $n_1, n_2, \ldots n_j$ = number of subjects in groups $1, 2, \ldots, j$, respectively; C = coefficient. (For convenience, I did not include the symbols for the means in the preceding.) When (11.19) is applied in designs with equal n's, $L = 0$ (e.g., there is an equal number of 1's and -1's in a coded vector meant to contrast two means), thus satisfying the requirement I stated earlier in this chapter that $\Sigma C_j = 0$. This, however, is generally not true when n's are unequal. Consider the example with unequal n's I analyzed with dummy and effect coding, where the number of subjects in groups A_1, A_2, and A_3, respectively, is 3, 4, and 5. Suppose I wanted to create a coded vector (to be used in regression analysis) in which the mean of A_1 is contrasted with that of A_2, and assigned -1's to members of the former group, 1's to members of the latter, and 0 to members of A_3. By (11.19),

$$L = (3)(-1) + (4)(1) + (5)(0) = 1$$

The coefficients I used are inappropriate, as $L \neq 0$.

The simplest way to satisfy the condition that $L = 0$ is to use $-n_2$ (-4, in the present example) as the coefficient for the first group and n_1 (3, in the present example) as the coefficient for the second group. Accordingly,

$$L_1 = (3)(-4) + (4)(3) + (5)(0) = 0$$

Suppose I now wished to contrast groups A_1 and A_2 with group A_3, and used n_3(i.e., 5) as the coefficients for groups A_1 and A_2, and $-(n_1 + n_2)$(i.e., -7) as the coefficient for group A_3. Accordingly,

$$L_2 = (3)(5) + (4)(5) + (5)(-7) = 0$$

Are L_1 and L_2 orthogonal? With unequal n's, comparisons are orthogonal if

$$n_1 C_{11} C_{21} + n_2 C_{12} C_{22} + n_3 C_{13} C_{23} = 0 \tag{11.20}$$

where the first subscript for each C refers to the comparison number, and the second subscript refers to the group number. For example, C_{11} means the coefficient of the first comparison for group 1, and C_{21} is the coefficient of the second comparison for group 1, and the same is true for the other coefficients. For the two comparisons under consideration,

$$L_1 = (3)(-4) + (4)(3) + (5)(0)$$

$$L_2 = (3)(5) + (4)(5) + (5)(-7)$$

$$(L_1)(L_2) = (3)(-4)(5) + (4)(3)(5) + (5)(0)(-7) = (3)(-20) + (4)(15) + 0 = 0$$

These comparisons are orthogonal.

As in designs with equal n's, the coefficients for comparisons in designs with unequal n's can be incorporated in vectors representing the independent variable. Table 11.12 shows the illustrative data for the three groups, where O1 reflects the contrast between the mean of A_1 and that of A_2, and O2 reflects the contrast of the weighted average of A_1 and A_2 and the mean of A_3.

Table 11.12   Orthogonal Coding for Unequal n's

Group	Y	O1	O2
	4	−4	5
A_1	5	−4	5
	6	−4	5
	7	3	5
	8	3	5
A_2	9	3	5
	10	3	5
	1	0	−7
	2	0	−7
A_3	3	0	−7
	4	0	−7
	5	0	−7
Σ:	64	0	0
M:	5.33	0	0
ss:	84.67	84.00	420.00

$\Sigma o_1 y = 42$ $\Sigma o_2 y = 140$ $\Sigma o_1 o_2 = 0$

$r_{y.O1} = .498$ $r_{y.O2} = .742$ $r_{o1.o2} = 0$

$r_{y.O1}^2 = .248$ $r_{y.O2}^2 = .551$

I analyzed the data of Table 11.12 by REGRESSION of SPSS. Following are excerpts of input, output, and commentaries.

SPSS

Input

. . . .   *[see commentary]*

IF (T EQ 1) O1=−4.
IF (T EQ 2) O1=3.
IF (T EQ 3) O1=0.

IF (T LT 3) O2=5.
IF (T EQ 3) O2=−7.

. . . .

Commentary

Except for the IF statements, which I use to generate the orthogonal vectors, the input file is identical to the one I used for the analysis of Table 11.11. For illustrative purposes, I used LT (less than; see SPSS Inc., 1993, p. 413) 3 in the fourth IF statement. Accordingly, groups 1 and 2 will be assigned a code of 5 in O2.

Output

	Mean	Std Dev
Y	5.333	2.774
O1	.000	2.763
O2	.000	6.179

	Y	O1	O2
Y	1.000	.498	.742
O1	.498	1.000	.000
O2	.742	.000	1.000

Commentary

As expected, the means of the coded vectors equal to zero, as does the correlation between the coded vectors. Compare these results with those given at the bottom of Table 11.12.

Output

Multiple R	.89399	Analysis of Variance			
R Square	.79921		DF	Sum of Squares	Mean Square
Adjusted R Square	.75459	Regression	2	67.66667	33.83333
Standard Error	1.37437	Residual	9	17.00000	1.88889

$$F = \ 17.91176 \qquad \text{Signif } F = \ .0007$$

Commentary

The above output is identical to that I obtained for the same data when I used dummy or effect coding. I will therefore not comment on it, except to note that, because the coded vectors are not correlated, R^2 is equal to the sum of the squared zero-order correlations of the coded vectors with the dependent variable ($.498^2 + .742^2$). The first contrast accounts for about 25% of the variance of Y, and the second accounts for about 55% of the variance of Y.

Output

```
------------------------------------------- Variables in the Equation -------------------------------------------
```

Variable	B	SE B	T	Sig T
O1	.500000	.149956	3.334	.0087
O2	.333333	.067062	4.971	.0008
(Constant)	5.333333	.396746	13.443	.0000

Commentary

The *regression equation* is

$$Y' = 5.33 + .50(O1) + .33(O2)$$

Applying the regression equation to the codes of a subject on O1 and O2 yields a predicted score equal to the mean of the group to which the subject belongs.

As in the analysis with orthogonal coding when n's are equal, a (CONSTANT) is equal to the grand mean of the dependent variable ($\overline{Y}$; see Table 11.12). In other words, when orthogonal coding is used with unequal n's, a is equal to the weighted mean of Y.

Although the size of the b's is affected by the specific codes used (see the discussion of this point in the section on "Orthogonal Coding with Equal n's"), each b reflects the specific planned comparison with which it is associated. Thus b_{O1} reflects the contrast between the means of groups A_1 and A_2, and b_{O2} reflects the contrast between the weighted mean of A_1 and A_2 with the mean of A_3. Consequently, a test of a b is tantamount to a test of the comparison it reflects. Thus, for the first comparison, $t = 3.334$ with 9 *df*. For the second comparison, $t = 4.971$ with 9 *df*.

Partitioning the Regression Sum of Squares

Recall that (see Chapter 5)

$$ss_{reg} = b_1 \Sigma x_1 y + b_2 \Sigma x_2 y$$

From Table 11.12, $\Sigma o_1 y = 42$ and $\Sigma o_2 y = 140$. Hence,

$$ss_{reg} = (.50)(42) + (.33333)(140)$$

$$= 21.00 + 46.6662 = 67.6662$$

The regression sum of squares was partitioned into two independent components, which together are equal to the regression sum of squares (see the previous output). Dividing each ss_{reg} by the mean square residual (*MSR*) yields an F ratio with 1 and 9 *df* (*df* for *MSR*). From the output, $MSR = 1.88889$. Hence,

$$F_{O1} = 21/1.88889 = 11.12$$

$$F_{O2} = 46.6662/1.88889 = 24.71$$

The square roots of these F ratios (3.33 and 4.97) are equal to the t ratios for the b's (see the previous output).

Alternatively, because $r_{12} = 0$,

$$ss_{reg} = r_{y1}^2 \Sigma y^2 + r_{y2}^2 \Sigma y^2$$

Table 11.13 **Summary of the Analysis with Orthogonal Coding for Unequal n's. Data of Table 11.12**

Source	df	ss		ms		F
Total regression	2	67.6662		33.8331		17.91
Regression due to O1	1		21.0000		21.0000	11.12
Regression due to O2	1		46.6662		46.6662	24.71
Residual	9	17.0005		1.8889		
Total	11	84.6667				

From Table 11.12, $r_{y.O1} = .498$, $r_{y.O2} = .742$, and $\Sigma y^2 = 84.67$. Therefore,

$$ss_{reg} = (.498)^2(84.67) + (.742)^2(84.67)$$

$$= 21.00 + 46.62 = 67.62$$

Earlier, I obtained the same values (within rounding). Of course, each r^2 can be tested for significance. If you did this, you would find that the F ratios are the same as in the preceding.

I summarize the foregoing analysis in Table 11.13, where you can see clearly the partitioning of the total sum of squares to the various components. (Slight discrepancies between some values of Table 11.13 and corresponding ones in the previous computer output are due to rounding.)

Earlier, I discussed the question of whether to do multiple comparisons among weighted or unweighted means. I showed that when effect coding is used, tests of linear combinations of means (or b's) are done on unweighted means. In this section, I showed that by using orthogonal coding, linear combinations of weighted means are tested. It is also possible to test linear combinations of weighted means when applying post hoc or planned nonorthogonal comparisons. Basically, it is necessary to select coefficients for each desired contrast such that (11.19) is satisfied: that is, the sum of the products of the coefficients by their respective n's will be equal to zero in each comparison. When a set of such comparisons is not orthogonal, procedures outlined earlier for planned nonorthogonal or post hoc comparisons may be applied.

MULTIPLE REGRESSION VERSUS ANALYSIS OF VARIANCE

Early in this chapter, I showed that when the independent variable is categorical, multiple regression analysis (MR) and the analysis of variance (ANOVA) are equivalent. At that juncture, I raised the question of whether there are any advantages to using MR in preference to ANOVA. The contents of this chapter provides a partial answer to this question. Thus, I showed that the use of the pertinent coding method for the categorical independent variable in MR obviates the need for additional calculations required following ANOVA (e.g., using dummy coding when contrasting each of several treatments with a control group, using orthogonal coding when testing orthogonal comparisons). Had a reduction in some calculations been the only advantage, it would understandably not have sufficed to convince one to abandon ANOVA in favor of MR, particularly when one is more familiar and comfortable with the former, not to mention the wide availability of computer programs for either approach.

Although the superiority of MR will become clearer as I present additional topics in subsequent chapters, some general comments about it are in order here. The most important reason for preferring MR to ANOVA is that it is a more comprehensive and general approach on the conceptual as well as the analytic level. On the conceptual level, all variables, be they categorical or continuous, are viewed from the same frame of reference: information available when attempting to explain or predict a dependent variable. On the analytic level, too, different types of variables (i.e., categorical and continuous) can be dealt with in MR. On the other hand, ANOVA is limited to categorical independent variables (except for manipulated continuous variables).

The following partial list identifies situations in which MR is the superior or the only appropriate method of analysis: (1) when the independent variables are continuous; (2) when some of the independent variables are continuous and some are categorical, as in analysis of covariance, aptitude-treatment interactions, or treatments by levels designs; (3) when cell frequencies in a factorial design are unequal and disproportionate; and (4) when studying trends in the data—linear, quadratic, and so on. I present these and other related topics in subsequent chapters.

CONCLUDING REMARKS

In this chapter, I presented three methods of coding a categorical variable: dummy, effect, and orthogonal. Whatever the coding method used, results of the overall analysis are the same. When a regression analysis is done with Y as the dependent variable and k coded vectors (k = number of groups minus one) reflecting group membership as the independent variables, the overall R^2, regression sum of squares, residual sum of squares, and the F ratio are the same with any coding method. Predictions based on the regression equations resulting from the different coding methods are also identical. In each case, the predicted score is equal to the mean of the group to which the subject belongs. The coding methods do differ in the properties of their regression equations. A brief summary of the major properties of each method follows.

With *dummy coding,* k coded vectors consisting of 1's and 0's are generated. In each vector, in turn, subjects of one group are assigned 1's and all others are assigned 0's. As k is equal to the number of groups minus one, it follows that members of one of the groups are assigned 0's in all the vectors. This group is treated as a control group in the analysis. In the regression equation, the intercept, $a,$ is equal to the mean of the control group. Each regression coefficient, $b,$ is equal to the deviation of the mean of the group identified in the vector with which it is associated from the mean of the control group. Hence, the test of significance of a given b is a test of significance between the mean of the group associated with the b and the mean of the control group. Although dummy coding is particularly useful when the design consists of several experimental groups and a control group, it may also be used in situations in which no particular group serves as a control for all others. The properties of dummy coding are the same for equal or unequal sample sizes.

Effect coding is similar to dummy coding, except that in dummy coding one group is assigned 0's in all the coded vectors, whereas in effect coding one group is assigned −1's in all the vectors. As a result, the regression equation reflects the linear model. That is, the intercept, $a,$ is equal to the grand mean of the dependent variable, $\overline{Y},$ and each b is equal to the treatment effect for the group with which it is associated, or the deviation of the mean of the group from the grand mean. When effect coding is used with unequal sample sizes, the intercept of the regression equation is equal to the unweighted mean of the group means. Each b is equal to the deviation of the mean of the group with which it is associated from the unweighted mean.

Orthogonal coding consists of k coded vectors of orthogonal coefficients. I discussed and illustrated the selection of orthogonal coefficients for equal and unequal sample sizes. In the regression equation, a is equal to the grand mean, $\overline{Y}$, for equal and unequal sample sizes. Each b reflects the specific comparison with which it is related. Testing a given b for significance is tantamount to testing the specific hypothesis that the comparison reflects.

The choice of a coding method depends on one's purpose and interest. When one wishes to compare several treatment groups with a control group, dummy coding is the preferred method. Orthogonal coding is most efficient when one's sole interest is in orthogonal comparisons among means. As I showed, however, the different types of multiple comparisons—orthogonal, planned nonorthogonal, and post hoc—can be easily done by testing the differences among regression coefficients obtained from effect coding. Consequently, effect coding is generally the preferred method of coding categorical variables.

STUDY SUGGESTIONS

1. Distinguish between categorical and continuous variables. Give examples of each.
2. The regression of moral judgment on religious affiliation (e.g., Catholic, Jewish, Protestant) was studied.
   (a) Which is the independent variable?
   (b) Which is the dependent variable?
   (c) What kind of variable is religious affiliation?
3. In a study with six different groups, how many coded vectors are necessary to exhaust the information about group membership? Explain.
4. Under what conditions is dummy coding particularly useful?
5. In a study with three treatments, A_1, A_2, and A_3, and a control group, C, dummy vectors were constructed as follows: subjects in A_1 were identified in D1, those in A_2 were identified in D2, and those in A_3 were identified in D3. A multiple regression analysis was done in which the dependent variable was regressed on the three coded vectors. The following regression equation was obtained:

   $$Y' = 8 + 6D1 + 5D2 - 2D3$$

   (a) What are the means of the four groups on the dependent variable?
   (b) What is the zero-order correlation between each pair of coded vectors, assuming equal n's in the groups?
6. In a study of problem solving, subjects were randomly assigned to two different treatments, A_1 and A_2, and a control group, C. At the conclusion of the experiment, the subjects were given a set of problems to solve. The problem-solving scores for the three groups were as follows:

A_1	A_2	C
7	2	3
6	3	3
4	2	4
7	5	4
8	3	2
4	5	2

Using dummy coding, do a multiple regression analysis in which the problem-solving scores are regressed on the coded vectors. I suggest that you do the calculations by hand as well as by a computer program. Calculate the following:
   (a) R^2
   (b) Regression sum of squares.
   (c) Residual sum of squares.
   (d) The regression equation.
   (e) The overall F ratio.
   (f) t ratios for the test of the difference of each treatment mean from the control mean.
   (g) What table would you use to check whether the t's obtained in (f) are statistically significant?
   (h) Interpret the results.
7. The following regression equation was obtained from an analysis with effect coding for four groups with equal n's:

   $$Y' = 102.5 + 2.5E1 - 2.5E2 - 4.5E3$$

   (a) What is the grand mean of the four groups?
   (b) What are the means of the four groups, assuming that the fourth group was assigned -1's?
   (c) What is the effect of each treatment?

8. In a study consisting of four groups, each with ten subjects, the following results were obtained:
$\bar{Y}_1 = 16.5$ $\bar{Y}_2 = 12.0$ $\bar{Y}_3 = 16.0$ $\bar{Y}_4 = 11.5$ $MSR = 7.15$

   (a) Write the regression equation that will be obtained if effect coding is used. Assume that subjects in the fourth group are assigned -1's.
   (b) What are the effects of the four treatments?
   (c) What is the residual sum of squares?
   (d) What is the regression sum of squares? [*Hint:* Use the treatment effect in (b).]
   (e) What is R^2?
   (f) What is the overall F ratio?
   (g) Do Scheffé tests for the following comparisons, using $\alpha = .05$: (1) between $\bar{Y}_1$ and $\bar{Y}_2$; (2) between the mean of $\bar{Y}_1$ and $\bar{Y}_2$, and $\bar{Y}_3$; (3) between the mean of $\bar{Y}_1$, $\bar{Y}_2$, $\bar{Y}_4$, and $\bar{Y}_3$.

9. A researcher studied the regression of attitudes toward school busing on political party affiliation. She administered an attitude scale to samples of Conservatives, Republicans, Liberals, and Democrats, and obtained the following scores. The higher the score, the more favorable the attitude. (The scores are illustrative.)

Conservatives	Republicans	Liberals	Democrats
2	3	5	4
3	3	6	5
4	4	6	5
4	4	7	7
6	5	7	7
6	6	9	7
7	8	10	9
7	8	10	9
8	9	11	10
8	10	12	10

   (a) Using dummy coding, do a regression analysis of these data. Calculate (1) R^2; (2) ss_{reg}; (3) ss_{res}; (4) the regression equation; (5) the overall F ratio.
   (b) Using effect coding, do a regression analysis of these data. Calculate the same statistics as in (a).

   (c) Using the regression equations obtained under (a) and (b), calculate the means of the four groups.
   (d) Calculate F ratios for the following comparisons: (1) between Conservatives and Republicans; (2) between Liberals and Democrats; (3) between the mean of Conservatives and Republicans, and that of Liberals and Democrats; (4) between the mean of Conservatives, Republicans, and Democrats, and the mean of Liberals.
   (e) Taken together, what type of comparisons are 1, 2, and 3 in (d)?
   (f) Assuming that the researcher wished to use the Scheffé test at $\alpha = .05$ for the comparisons under (d), what F ratio must be exceeded so that a comparison would be declared statistically significant?
   (g) Using the regression coefficients obtained from the analysis with effect coding under (d), and $\mathbf{C}^*$ [if you don't have access to a computer program that reports $\mathbf{C}$, use $\mathbf{C}^*$ given in the answers, under (g)] calculate F ratios for the same comparisons as those done under (d). In addition, calculate F ratios for the following comparisons: (1) between Republicans and Democrats; (2) between Liberals and Democrats, against the Conservatives.
   (h) Assume that the researcher advanced the following a priori hypotheses: that Republicans have more favorable attitudes toward school busing than do Conservatives; that Liberals are more favorable than Democrats; that Liberals and Democrats are more favorable toward school busing than Conservatives and Republicans.

   Use orthogonal coding to express these hypotheses and do a regression analysis. Calculate the following: (1) R^2; (2) the regression equation; (3) the overall F ratio; (4) t ratios for each of the b's; (5) regression sum of squares due to each hypothesis; (6) residual sum of squares; (7) F ratios for each hypothesis; (8) What should each of these F ratios be equal to? (9) What should the average of these F ratios be equal to?

   Interpret the results obtained under (a)–(h).

ANSWERS

2. (a) Religious affiliation
   (b) Moral judgment
   (c) Categorical

3. 5
4. When one wishes to test the difference between the mean of each experimental group and the mean of a control group.
5. (a) $\overline{Y}_{A_1} = 14$, $\overline{Y}_{A_2} = 13$, $\overline{Y}_{A_3} = 6$, $\overline{Y}_C = 8$
   (b) $-.33$
6. (a) .54275
   (b) 32.44444
   (c) 27.33333
   (d) $Y' = 3.00 + 3.00D1 + .33D2$
   (e) $F = 8.90$, with 2 and 15 df
   (f) t for b_{D1} (i.e., the difference between $\overline{Y}_{A_1}$ and $\overline{Y}_C$) is 3.85, with 15 df, $p < .01$; t for b_{D2} (i.e., between $\overline{Y}_{A_2}$ and $\overline{Y}_C$) is .43, with 15 df, $p > .05$
   (g) Dunnett.
7. (a) 102.5
   (b) $\overline{Y}_1 = 105$; $\overline{Y}_2 = 100$; $\overline{Y}_3 = 98$; $\overline{Y}_4 = 107$
   (c) $T_1 = 2.5$; $T_2 = -2.5$; $T_3 = -4.5$; $T_4 = 4.5$
8. (a) $Y' = 14.0 + 2.5E1 - 2.0E2 + 2.0E3$
   (b) $T_1 = 2.5$; $T_2 = -2.0$; $T_3 = 2.0$; $T_4 = -2.5$
   (c) 257.4 ($MSR \times df$).
   (d) $205 = [(2.5)^2 + (-2.0)^2 + (2.0)^2 + (-2.5)^2](10)$
   (e) $.44334 = ss_{reg}/\Sigma y^2$, where $\Sigma y^2 = 257.4 + 205.0 = 462.4$
   (f) 9.56, with 3 and 36 df
   (g) (1) $|D| = 4.5$; $S = 3.5$; statistically significant
       (2) $|D| = 3.5$; $S = 6.1$; statistically not significant
       (3) $|D| = 8.0$; $S = 8.6$; statistically not significant
9. (a) (1) $R^2 = .19868$
       (2) $ss_{reg} = 48.275$
       (3) $ss_{res} = 194.700$
       (4) $Y' = 7.3 - 1.8D1 - 1.3D2 + 1.0D3$
       (5) $F = 2.98$, with 3 and 36 df
   (b) All the results are the same as under (a), except for the regression equation:
$$Y' = 6.775 - 1.275E1 - .775E2 + 1.525E3$$
   (c) Conservatives = 5.5; Republicans = 6.0; Liberals = 8.3; Democrats = 7.3
   (d) (1) .23; (2) .92; (3) 7.77; (4) 5.73. Each of these F ratios has 1 and 36 df.
   (e) Orthogonal
   (f) 8.58 ($kF_{\alpha; k, N-k-1}$)
   (g) The F ratios for the comparisons under (d) are the same as those obtained earlier. For the two additional comparisons, the F ratios are (1) 1.56; (2) 6.52
$$\mathbf{C^*} = \begin{bmatrix} .40563 & -.13521 & -.13521 & -.13521 \\ -.13521 & .40563 & -.13521 & -.13521 \\ -.13521 & -.13521 & .40563 & -.13521 \\ -.13521 & -.13521 & -.13521 & .40563 \end{bmatrix}$$
   (h) (1) $R^2 = .19868$
       (2) $Y' = 6.775 + .250(O1) + .500(O2) + 1.025(O3)$
       (3) $F = 2.98$, with 3 and 36 df
       (4) t for $b_{O1} = .48$; t for $b_{O2} = .96$; t for $b_{O3} = 2.79$. Each t has 36 df.
       (5) $ss_{reg(1)} = 1.250$; $ss_{reg(2)} = 5.000$; $ss_{reg(3)} = 42.025$
       (6) $ss_{res} = 194.70$
       (7) $F_1 = .23$; $F_2 = .92$; $F_3 = 7.77$. Each F has 1 and 36 df. Note that the same results were obtained when the regression equation from effect coding and $\mathbf{C^*}$ were used. See (d) and (g).
       (8) Each F in (7) is equal to the square of its corresponding t in (4).
       (9) The average of the three F's in (7) should equal the overall F (i.e., 2.97).

CHAPTER

12

Multiple Categorical Independent Variables and Factorial Designs

As with continuous variables, regression analysis is not limited to a single categorical independent variable or predictor. Complex phenomena almost always require the use of more than one independent variable if substantial explanation or prediction is to be achieved. Multiple categorical variables may be used in predictive or explanatory research; in experimental, quasi-experimental, or nonexperimental designs. The context of the research and the design type should always be borne in mind to reduce the risks of arriving at erroneous interpretations and conclusions.

As I show in this chapter, the major advantage of designs with multiple independent variables is that they afford opportunities to study, in addition to the effect of each independent variable, their joint effects or interactions. Earlier in the text (e.g., Chapter 11), I maintained that the results of experimental research are generally easier to interpret than those of nonexperimental research. In the first part of this chapter, I deal exclusively with experimental research with equal cell frequencies or orthogonal designs. Following that, I discuss nonorthogonal designs in experimental and nonexperimental research.

In this chapter, I generalize methods of coding categorical variables, which I introduced in Chapter 11, to designs with multiple categorical independent variables. In addition, I introduce another approach—criterion scaling—that may be useful for certain purposes. I conclude the chapter with a comment on the use of variance accounted for as an index of effect size.

FACTORIAL DESIGNS

In the context of the analysis of variance, independent variables are also called *factors*. A factor is a variable; for example, teaching methods, sex, ethnicity. The two or more subdivisions or categories of a factor are, in set theory language, *partitions* (Kemeny, Snell, & Thompson, 1966, Chapter 3). The subdivisions in a partition are subsets and are called cells. If a sample is divided into male and female, there are two cells, A_1 and A_2, with males in one cell and females in the other. In a factorial design, two or more partitions are combined to form a *cross partition* consisting of all subsets formed by the intersections of the original partitions. For instance, the intersection of two partitions or sets, $A_i \cap B_j$ is a cross partition. (The cells must be disjoint and they

	B_1	B_2	B_3
A_1	A_1B_1	A_1B_2	A_1B_3
A_2	A_2B_1	A_2B_2	A_2B_3

Figure 12.1

must exhaust all the cases.) It is possible to have 2×2, 2×3, 3×3, 4×5, and in fact, $p \times q$ factorial designs. Three or more factors with two or more subsets per factor are also possible: $2 \times 2 \times 2$, $2 \times 3 \times 3$, $3 \times 3 \times 5$, $2 \times 2 \times 3 \times 3$, $2 \times 3 \times 3 \times 4$, and so on.

A factorial design is customarily displayed as in Figure 12.1, which comprises two independent variables, *A* and *B,* with two subsets of A: A_1 and A_2, and three subsets of B: B_1, B_2, and B_3. The cells obtained by the cross partitioning are indicated by A_1B_1, A_1B_2, and so on.

Advantages of Factorial Designs

There are several advantages to studying simultaneously the effects of two or more independent variables on a dependent variable. First, and most important, is the possibility of learning whether the independent variables interact in their effect on the dependent variable. An interaction between two variables refers to their joint effect on the dependent variable. It is possible, for instance, for two independent variables to have little or no effect on the dependent variable and for their joint effect to be substantial. In essence, each variable may enhance the effect of the other. By contrast, it is possible for two independent variables to operate at cross purposes, diminishing their individual effects. This, too, is an interaction. Stated another way, two variables interact when the effect of one of them depends on the categories of the other with which it is combined. Clearly, studying the effect of each variable in isolation, as in Chapter 11, cannot reveal whether there is an interaction between them.

Fisher (1926), who invented the ANOVA approach, probably had the notion of interaction uppermost in mind when he stated:

> No aphorism is more frequently repeated in connection with field trials, than that we ask Nature few questions, or ideally, one question at a time. The writer is convinced that this view is wholly mistaken. Nature, he suggests, will best respond to a logical and carefully thought out questionnaire; indeed, if we ask her a single question, she will often refuse to answer until some other topic has been discussed. (p. 511)

Second, factorial designs afford greater control, and consequently more sensitive statistical tests, than designs with a single independent variable. When a single independent variable is used, the variance not explained by it is relegated to the error term. The larger the error term, the less sensitive the statistical test. One method of reducing the size of the error term is to identify as many sources of systematic variance of the dependent variable as is possible, feasible, and meaningful under a given set of circumstances. Assume, for example, a design in which leadership styles is the independent variable and group productivity is the dependent variable. Clearly, all the variance not explained by leadership styles is relegated to the error term. Suppose, however, that the sample consists of an equal number of males and females and that there is a relation between sex and the type of productivity under study. In other words, some of the variance of productivity is due to sex. Under such circumstances, the introduction of sex as another independent variable leads to a reduction in the error estimate by reclaiming that part of the dependent variable variance due to it. Note that the proportion of variance due to leadership styles will remain unchanged. But since the error term will be decreased, the test of significance for the effect of leadership styles will be more sensitive. Of course, the same reasoning applies to the test of the effect of sex. In addition, as I noted earlier, it would be possible to learn whether there is an interaction between the two factors. For instance, one style of leadership may lead to greater productivity among males, whereas another style may lead to greater productivity among females.

Third, factorial designs are efficient. The separate and joint effects of several variables can be studied using the same subjects.

Fourth, in factorial experiments, the effect of a treatment is studied across different conditions of other treatments, settings, subject attributes, and the like. Consequently, generalizations from factorial experiments are broader than from single-variable experiments.

In sum, factorial designs are examples of efficiency, power, and elegance.

Manipulated and Classificatory Variables

A factorial design may consist of either manipulated variables only or of manipulated and classificatory variables. A classificatory, or grouping, variable is one in which subjects either come from naturally existing groups or are classified by the researcher into two or more classes for research purposes. Examples of the former are sex and marital status. Examples of the latter are extrovert, introvert; psychotic, neurotic, normal; learning disabled, mentally retarded. The inclusion of classificatory variables, in addition to the manipulated variables, has no bearing on the mechanics of the analysis. It does, however, as I explain later, have implications for the interpretation of the results.

In experiments consisting of manipulated independent variables only, subjects are randomly assigned to different treatment combinations. The analysis in such designs is aimed at studying the separate effects of each variable (main effects) and their joint effects (interactions). For example, one may study the effects of three methods of teaching and three types of reinforcement. This, then, would be a 3×3 design in which both variables are manipulated. Subjects would be randomly assigned to the nine cells (treatment combinations), and the researcher would then study the effects of teaching methods, reinforcement, and their interaction on the dependent variable, say, reading achievement. Assuming the research is well designed and executed, interpretation of results is relatively straightforward, depending, among other things, on the soundness and complexity of the theory from which the hypotheses were derived and on the knowledge, abilities, and sophistication of the researcher.

Consider now designs in which classificatory variables are used in combination with manipulated variables. As I explained, one purpose of such designs is to control extraneous variables. For example, sex (religion, ethnicity) may be introduced as a factor to isolate variance due to it, thereby increasing the sensitivity of the analysis. Another purpose for introducing classificatory variables in experimental research is explanation: to test hypotheses about the effects of such variables and/or interactions among themselves and with manipulated variables. It is this use of classificatory variables that may lead to serious problems in the interpretation of the results.

An example with one manipulated and one classificatory variable will, I hope, help clarify this point. Assume, again, that one wishes to study the effects of three methods of teaching but hypothesizes that the methods interact with the regions in which the schools are located. That is, it is hypothesized that given methods have differential effects depending on whether they are used in urban, suburban, or rural schools. This, then, is also a 3×3 design, except that this time it consists of one manipulated and one classificatory variable.

To validly execute such a study, students from each region (urban, suburban, and rural) have to be randomly assigned to the teaching methods. The analysis then proceeds in the same manner as in a study in which both variables are manipulated. But what about the interpretation of the results? Suppose that the example under consideration reveals that region has a substantively meaningful and statistically significant effect on the dependent variable or that there is an interaction between region and teaching methods. Such results would not be easily interpretable because region is related to many other variables whose effects it may be reflecting. For example, it is well known that in some parts of the country urban schools are attended mostly by minority group children, whereas all or most students in suburban and rural schools are white. Should the findings regarding the classificatory variable be attributed to region, to race, to both? To complicate matters further, it is known that race is correlated with many variables. Is it race, then, or variables correlated with it that interact with teaching methods? There is no easy answer to such questions. All one can say is that when using classificatory variables in experimental research it is necessary to consider variables associated with them as possible alternative explanations regarding findings about their effects or interactions with the manipulated variables. The greater one's knowledge of the area under study, the greater the potential for arriving at a valid interpretation of the results, although the inherent ambiguity of the situation cannot be resolved entirely. As my sole purpose in the following presentation is to show how to analyze data from factorial designs by multiple regression methods, I will make no further comments about the distinction between designs consisting of only manipulated variables and ones that also include classificatory variables. You should, however, keep this distinction in mind when designing a study or when reading research reports.

Analysis

As with a single categorical independent variable (see Chapter 11), designs with multiple categorical variables can be analyzed through analysis of variance (ANOVA) or multiple regression (MR). The superiority of MR, about which I have commented in Chapter 11, becomes even more evident in this chapter, especially when dealing with nonorthogonal designs. By and large, I use MR for the analyses in this chapter, although occasionally I use the ANOVA approach to illustrate a specific point or to show how to obtain specific results from a computer procedure.

Throughout this chapter, I will assume that the researcher is interested in making inferences only about the categories included in the design being analyzed. In other words, my concern will be with fixed effects models (see Hays, 1988; Keppel, 1991; Kirk, 1982; Winer, 1971, for discussions of fixed and random effects models).

I begin with an example of the smallest factorial design possible: a 2×2. I then turn to a 3×3 design in which I incorporate the data of the 2×2 design. I explain why I do this when I analyze the 3×3 design.

ANALYSIS OF A TWO-BY-TWO DESIGN

In Table 12.1, I give illustrative data for two factors (*A* and *B*), each consisting of two categories. In line with what I said in the preceding section, you may think of this design as consisting of

Table 12.1   Illustrative Data for a Two-by-Two Design

	B_1	B_2	$\overline{Y}_A$
A_1	12	10	
	10	8	10
A_2	7	17	
	7	13	11
$\overline{Y}_B$	9	12	$\overline{Y} = 10.5$

NOTE: $\overline{Y}_A$ = means for the two A categories; $\overline{Y}_B$ = means for the two B categories; and $\overline{Y}$ = grand mean.

two manipulated variables or of one manipulated and one classificatory variable. As will become evident, and consistent with my concluding remarks in Chapter 11, I mainly use effect coding. I use dummy coding for the sole purpose of showing why I recommend that it *not* be used in factorial designs, and orthogonal coding to show how it may be used to test specific contrasts.

EFFECT CODING

The scores on the dependent variable are placed in a single vector, *Y,* representing the dependent variable. This is always done, whatever the design type and number of factors of which it is composed. Coded vectors are then generated to represent the independent variables or factors of the design. Each factor is coded separately as if it were the only one in the design. In other words, when one independent variable or factor is coded, all other independent variables or factors are ignored. As with a single categorical independent variable (Chapter 11), the number of coded vectors necessary and sufficient to represent a variable in a factorial design equals the number of its categories minus one or the number of degrees of freedom associated with it. Thus, each set of coded vectors identifies one independent variable, be it manipulated or classificatory. In the present example it is necessary to generate one coded vector for each of the categorical variables.

The procedure outlined in the preceding paragraph is followed whatever the coding method (effect, orthogonal, dummy). I introduced effect coding in Chapter 11, where I pointed out that in each coded vector, members of one category are assigned 1's (i.e., identified) and all others are assigned 0's, except for the members of one category (for convenience, I use the last category of the variable) who are assigned −1's. In the special case of variables that comprise two categories, only 1's and −1's are used. As a result, effect coding and orthogonal coding are indistinguishable for this type of design (I present orthogonal coding for factorial designs later in this chapter).

In Table 12.2, I repeat the scores of Table 12.1, this time in the form of a single vector, *Y.* In Chapter 11, I found it useful to label coded vectors according to the type of coding used, along with a number for the category identified in the vector (e.g., E2 for effect coding in which category 2 was identified). In factorial designs it will be more convenient to use the factor label, along with a number indicating the category of the factor being identified. Accordingly, I labeled the first coded vector of Table 12.2 A1, meaning that members of category A_1 are identified in it (i.e., assigned 1's). As I said earlier, when one factor or independent variable is coded, the other factors are ignored. Thus, in A1, subjects in category A_1 are assigned 1's, regardless of what categories of *B* they belong to. This is also true for those assigned −1's in this vector. I could now

Table 12.2   Effect Coding for a 2 × 2 Design: Data in Table 12.1

Cell	Y	A1	B1	A1B1
A_1B_1	12	1	1	1
	10	1	1	1
	10	1	−1	−1
A_1B_2	8	1	−1	−1
	7	−1	1	−1
A_2B_1	7	−1	1	−1
	17	−1	−1	1
A_2B_2	13	−1	−1	1

NOTE: *Y* is dependent variable; A1, in which subjects in A_1 are identified, represents factor *A*; B1, in which subjects in B_1 are identified, represents factor *B*; and A1B1 represents the interaction between *A* and *B*. See the text for explanation.

regress *Y* on only A1, and such an analysis would be legitimate. However, it would defeat the very purpose for which factorial designs are used, as the effects of *B* and the interaction between *A* and *B* would be ignored. In fact, they would be relegated to the error term, or the residual.

As I did when I coded factor *A,* I coded factor *B* as if *A* does not exist. Examine B1 of Table 12.2 and notice that subjects of B_1 are identified. To repeat, A1 represents factor *A* and B1 represents factor *B*. These two vectors represent what are called main effects of factors *A* and *B*. Before proceeding with the analysis it is necessary to generate coded vectors that represent the interaction between *A* and *B*.

To understand how many vectors are needed to represent an interaction, it is necessary to consider the degrees of freedom (*df*) associated with it. The *df* for an interaction between two variables equal the product of *df* associated with each of the variables in question. In the present example, *A* has 1 *df* and *B* has 1 *df*, hence 1 *df* for the interaction (*A* × *B*). Had the design consisted of, say, four categories of *A* and five categories of *B,* then *df* would be 3 for the former and 4 for the latter. Therefore, *df* for interaction would be 12.

In light of the foregoing, vectors representing the interaction are generated by cross multiplying, in turn, vectors representing one factor with those representing the other factor. For the 2 × 2 design under consideration this amounts to the product of A1 and B1, which I labeled A1B1. Later, I show that the same approach is applicable to variables with any number of categories.

When a computer program that allows for manipulation of vectors is used (most do), it is not necessary to enter the cross-product vectors, as this can be accomplished by an appropriate command (e.g., COMPUTE in SPSS; see the following "Input"). As I will show, I do *not* enter the coded vectors for the main effects either. I displayed them in Table 12.2 to show what I am after. But, as I did in Chapter 11, in addition to *Y*, I enter vectors identifying the cell to which each subject belongs. The number of such vectors necessary equals the number of factors in the design. In Chapter 11, I used only one categorical independent variable, hence only one identification vector was required. Two identification vectors are necessary for a two-factor design, no matter the number of categories in each variable. Much as I did in Chapter 11, I use the identification vectors to generate the necessary coded vectors. I hope this will become clearer when I show the input file. I begin with an analysis using REGRESSION of SPSS. Subsequently, I use also other computer programs.

SPSS

Input

```
TITLE TABLE 12.1, A 2 BY 2.
DATA LIST/A 1 B 2 Y 3-4.        [fixed format, see commentary]
IF (A EQ 1) A1=1.
IF (A EQ 2) A1=−1.
IF (B EQ 1) B1=1.
IF (B EQ 2) B1=−1.
COMPUTE A1B1=A1*B1.
BEGIN DATA
1112
1110
1210
12 8
21 7
21 7
2217
2213
END DATA
LIST.
REGRESSION VAR=Y TO A1B1/DES/STAT ALL/DEP=Y/
  ENTER A1/ENTER B1/ENTER A1B1/
  TEST (A1) (B1) (A1B1).
```

Commentary

I introduced SPSS and its REGRESSION procedure in Chapter 4 and used it in subsequent chapters. Here I comment briefly on some specific issues.

DATA LIST. I use a fixed input format, specifying that *A* occupies column 1, *B* column 2, and *Y* columns 3 and 4.

IF. I introduced the use of IF statements to generate coded vectors in Chapter 11.

COMPUTE. I use this command to multiply A1 by B1 to represent the interaction between A and B. Note the pattern: the name of the new vector (or variable) is on the left-hand side of the equal sign; the specified operation is on the right-hand side. The '*' refers to multiplication (see SPSS Inc., 1993, pp. 143–154, for varied uses of this command).

ENTER. As I will show and explain, the coded vectors are not correlated. Nevertheless, I enter them in three steps, beginning with A1, followed by B1, and then A1B1. As a result, the analysis will be carried out in three steps, regressing Y on (1) A1, (2) A1 and B1, and (3) A1, B1, and A1B1. I do this to acquaint you with some aspects of the output.

TEST. I explain this command in connection with the output it generates.

A	B	Y	A1	B1	A1B1
1	1	12	1.00	1.00	1.00
1	1	10	1.00	1.00	1.00
1	2	10	1.00	−1.00	−1.00
1	2	8	1.00	−1.00	−1.00
2	1	7	−1.00	1.00	−1.00
2	1	7	−1.00	1.00	−1.00
2	2	17	−1.00	−1.00	1.00
2	2	13	−1.00	−1.00	1.00

Commentary

The preceding output was generated by LIST. Examine the listing in conjunction with the input and the IF and COMPUTE statements. Also, compare vectors Y through A1B1 with those in Table 12.2.

Output

	Mean	Std Dev
Y	10.500	3.423
A1	.000	1.069
B1	.000	1.069
A1B1	.000	1.069

N of Cases = 8

Correlation:

	Y	A1	B1	A1B1
Y	1.000	−.156	−.469	.781
A1	−.156	1.000	.000	.000
B1	−.469	.000	1.000	.000
A1B1	.781	.000	.000	1.000

Commentary

As I explained in Chapter 11, when sample sizes are equal, means of effect (and orthogonal) coding are equal to zero. Earlier, I pointed out that when a categorical variable is composed of two categories, effect and orthogonal coding are indistinguishable. Examine the correlation matrix and notice that correlations among the coded vectors are zero. Therefore, R^2 is readily calculated as the sum of the squared zero-order correlations of the coded vectors with the dependent variable:

$$R^2_{Y.A,B,AB} = (-.156)^2 + (-.469)^2 + (.781)^2 = .024 + .220 + .610 = .854$$

Notice the subscript notation: I use factor names (e.g., A) rather than names of coded vectors that represent them (e.g., A1). Also, I use AB for the interaction. Commas serve as separators between components. Thus, assuming the same factor labels, I use the same subscripts for any two-factor design, whatever the number of categories of each factor (e.g., 3×5; 4×3).

As you can see, the two factors and their interaction account for about 85% of the variance in Y. Because the coded vectors are not correlated, it is possible to state unambiguously the proportion of variance of Y accounted for by each component: A accounts for about 2%, B for about 22%, and AB (interaction) for about 61%.

In Chapter 5—see (5.27)—I showed how to test the proportion of variance incremented by a variable (or a set of variables). Because in the present case the various components are not correlated, the increment due to each is equal to the proportion of variance it accounts for. As a result, each can be tested for significance, using a special version of (5.27). For example, to test the proportion of variance accounted by A:

$$F = \frac{R^2_{Y.A}/k_A}{(1 - R^2_{Y.A,B,AB})/(N - k_A - k_B - k_{AB} - 1)} \tag{12.1}$$

Notice the pattern of (12.1), the numerator is composed of the proportion of variance accounted for by the component in question (A, in the present case) divided by the number of coded vectors representing it or its *df* (1, in the present case). The denominator is composed of 1 minus the overall R^2, that is, the squared multiple correlation of Y with *all* the components (A, B, and AB) divided by its *df*: N (total number of subjects in the design) minus the sum of the coded vectors representing all the components (3, in the present case) minus 1. In other words, the denominator is composed of the overall error divided by its *df*.

Before applying (12.1) to the present results, I would like to point out that it is applicable to any factorial design with equal cell frequencies when effect or orthogonal coding is used. Thus, for example, had A consisted of four categories, then it would have required three coded vectors. Consequently, the numerator would be divided by 3. The denominator *df* would, of course, also be adjusted accordingly (I give examples of such tests later in this chapter).

Turning now to tests of the components for the present example:

$$F_A = \frac{.024/1}{(1 - .854)/(8 - 3 - 1)} = .66$$

with 1 and 4 *df*, $p > .05$.

$$F_B = \frac{.220/1}{(1 - .854)/(8 - 3 - 1)} = 6.03$$

with 1 and 4 *df*, $p > .05$.

$$F_{AB} = \frac{.610/1}{(1 - .854)/(8 - 3 - 1)} = 16.71$$

with 1 and 4 *df*, $p < .05$.

Assuming that $\alpha = .05$ was specified in advance of the analysis, one would conclude that only the interaction is statistically significant. Recall, however, that *not only am I using small numerical examples* (notice that there are only 4 *df* for the error term), *but also that the data are fictitious.*

I am certain that you will not be surprised when I show that the preceding tests are available in the output. Nevertheless, I did the calculations in the hope of enhancing your understanding of the analysis, as well as the output. Thus, you will see, for example, that certain F ratios reported in the output are irrelevant to the present analysis.

Output

Equation Number 1 Dependent Variable. . Y
Block Number 1. Method: Enter A1
Variable(s) Entered on Step Number 1. . A1

				Analysis of Variance			
					DF	Sum of Squares	Mean Square
R Square	.02439	R Square Change	.02439	Regression	1	2.00000	2.00000
		F Change	.15000	Residual	6	80.00000	13.33333
		Signif F Change	.7119				
				F =	.15000	Signif F =	.7119

Commentary

At this first step, only A1 entered (see ENTER keyword in the Input). Although I deleted some portions of the output (e.g., Adjusted R Square), I kept its basic format to facilitate comparisons with output you may generate.

R Square is, of course, the squared zero-order correlation of Y with A1. Because A1 is the only "variable" in the equation, R Square Change is, of course, the same as R Square, as are their tests of significance. In subsequent steps, R Square Change is useful.

It is important to note that I reproduced the F ratios to alert you to the fact that they are *not* relevant here. The reason is that at this stage the data are treated as if they were obtained in a design consisting of factor A only. Whatever is due to B and $A \times B$ is relegated to residual (error). This is why the residual term is also irrelevant. The following information is relevant: R Square (.02439); regression sum of squares (2.0), which is, of course, the product of R Square and the total sum of squares (82.0);[1] and *df* for regression.

Output

Block Number 2. Method: Enter B1
Variable(s) Entered on Step Number 2. . B1

				Analysis of Variance		
					DF	Sum of Squares
R Square	.24390	R Square Change	.21951	Regression	2	20.00000

[1] SPSS does not report the total sum of squares. To obtain it, add the regression and residual sums of squares.

Commentary

In light of my commentary on the preceding step, I did *not* reproduce here irrelevant information. Notice that the R Square reported here is cumulative, that is, for preceding step(s) and the
current one (i.e., *both* A1 and B1). R Square Change (.21951) is the proportion of variance incremented by B1 (over what A1 accounted for). Recall, however, that because B1 is not correlated
with A1, R Square Change is equal to the squared zero-order correlation of Y with B1 (see the
previous correlation matrix).

Output

Block Number   3.   Method: Enter   A1B1
Variable(s) Entered on Step Number   3. .   A1B1

				Analysis of Variance			
R Square	.85366	R Square Change	.60976		DF	Sum of Squares	Mean Square
Adjusted R Square	.74390	F Change	16.66667	Regression	3	70.00000	23.33333
Standard Error	1.73205	Signif F Change	.0151	Residual	4	12.00000	3.00000
				F =	7.77778	Signif F =	.0381

Commentary

Unlike preceding steps, information about the test of R Square Change at the *last step* in the sequential analysis *is* relevant. Compare with the result I obtained earlier when I applied (12.1).
The same is true of the test of regression sum of squares due to the main effects A and B and their
interaction (70.00). This $F = 7.78$ (23.33/3.00), with 3 and 4 *df, p < .05*, is equivalent to the test
of R^2, which by (5.21) is

$$F = \frac{(.85366)/3}{(1 - .85366)/(8 - 3 - 1)} = 7.78$$

Overall, then, the main effects and the interaction account for about 85% of the variance,
$F(3, 4) = 7.78, p < .05$. It is instructive to examine the meaning of R^2 in the present context.
With two independent variables, each consisting of two categories, there are four distinct combinations that can be treated as four separate groups. For instance, one group exists under conditions A_1B_1, another under conditions A_1B_2, and so forth for the rest of the combinations. If one
were to do a multiple regression analysis of Y with four distinct groups (or a one-way analysis of
variance for four groups) one would obtain the same R^2 as that reported above. Of course, the
F ratio associated with the R^2 would be the same as that reported in the output for the last step of
the analysis. In other words, the overall R^2 indicates the proportion of the variance of Y explained by (or predicted from) all the available information.

In what way, then, is the previous output useful when it is obtained from an analysis of a factorial design? It is useful only for learning whether overall a meaningful proportion of variance
is explained. Later in this chapter, I address the question of meaningfulness as reflected by the
proportion of variance accounted for. For now, I will only point out that what is deemed meaningful depends on the state of knowledge in the area under study, cost, and the consequences of
implementing whatever it is the factors represent, to name but some issues. (Do not be misled by
the very high R^2 in the example under consideration. I contrived the data so that even with small
n's some results would be statistically significant. R^2's as large as the one obtained here are rare
in social science research.)

An overall R^2 that is considered meaningful may be associated with a nonsignificant F ratio. Considerations of sample size and statistical power (see, for example, Cohen, 1988) aside, this may happen because when testing the overall R^2, the variance accounted for by all the components (i.e., main effects and the interactions) are lumped together, as are the degrees of freedom associated with them. When, for example, only one factor accounts for a meaningful proportion of the variance of Y, the numerator of the overall F ratio tends to be relatively small, possibly leading one to conclude that the overall R^2 is statistically not significant.

I believe it worthwhile to illustrate this phenomenon with a numerical example. Assume that in the analysis I carried out above B accounted for .02195 of the variance, instead of the .21951 reported earlier. Accordingly, R^2 would be .65610 (.02439 + .02195 + .60976). Applying (5.21),

$$F = \frac{(.65610)/3}{(1 - .65610)/(8 - 3 - 1)} = 2.54$$

with 3 and 4 df, $p > .05$.

Assuming that $\alpha = .05$ was preselected, one would conclude that the null hypothesis that R^2 is zero cannot be rejected. Again, issues of sample size aside, this happened because the numerator, which is mostly due to the interaction $(A \times B)$, is divided by 3 df. But test now the proportion of variance accounted for by A1B1 alone:

$$F = \frac{(.60976)/1}{(1 - .65610)/(8 - 3 - 1)} = 7.09$$

with 1 and 4 df, $p < .05$.

Note that the denominator is the same for both F ratios, as it should be because it reflects the error, the portion of Y *not* accounted for by A, B, and $A \times B$. But because in the numerator of the second F ratio 1 df is used (that associated with A1B1), the mean square regression is considerably larger than the one for the first F ratio (.60976 as compared with .21870). What took place when everything was lumped together (i.e., overall R^2) is that a proportion of .044634 (accounted for by A and B) brought with it, so to speak, 2 df leading to an overall relatively smaller mean square regression. In sum, a statistically nonsignificant overall R^2 should not be construed as evidence that all the components are statistically not significant.

What I said about the overall R^2 applies equally to the test of the overall regression sum of squares. For the data in Table 12.1 (see the preceding output), $ss_{reg} = 70.00$ and $ss_{res} = 12.00$. Of course, $\Sigma y^2 = 82.00$. $R^2 = ss_{reg}/\Sigma y^2 = 70.00/82.00 = .85366$. Thus, it makes no difference whether the overall R^2 or the overall regression sum of squares is tested for significance.

Partitioning the Regression Sum of Squares

When analyzing a factorial design, the objective is to partition and test the regression sum of squares or the proportion of variance accounted for by each factor and by the interaction. Earlier, I showed how to use SPSS output to determine the proportion of variance due to each component. Of course, each proportion of variance accounted for can be multiplied by the total sum of squares to yield the regression sum of squares. Instead, I will show how SPSS output like the one reported earlier can be readily used to accomplish the same.

Look back at the output for the first step of the analysis when only the vector representing A (i.e., A1) was entered and notice that the regression sum of squares is 2.00. Examine now the second step, where B1 was entered, and notice that the regression sum of squares is 20.00. As in the case of R^2 (see the previous explanation) the regression sum of squares is cumulative. Thus,

20.00 is for *A and B*. Therefore, the regression sum of squares due to *B* is 18.00 (20.00 − 2.00). Similarly, the regression sum of squares at the third, and last, step (70.00) is due to *A, B,* and $A \times B$. Therefore, the regression sum of squares due to the interaction is 50.00 (70.00 − 20.00).

When working with output like the preceding, the easiest approach is to obtain the regression sum of squares due to each component in the manner I described in the preceding paragraph. Dividing the regression mean square for each component (because in the present example each has 1 *df,* it is the same as the regression sum of squares) by the *MSR from the last step of the output* (3.00) yields the respective *F* ratios:

$$F_A = 2.00/3.00 = .67$$

$$F_B = 18.00/3.00 = 6.00$$

$$F_{AB} = 50.00/3.00 = 16.67$$

each with 1 and 4 *df* (compare with the results of my hand calculations, presented earlier).

I summarized the preceding results in Table 12.3. I could have used proportions of variance in addition to, or in lieu of, sums of squares. The choice what to report is determined by, among other things, personal preferences, the format required by a journal to which a paper is to be submitted, or the dissertation format required by a given school. For example, the *Publication Manual* of the American Psychological Association (1994) stipulates, "Do not include columns of data that can be calculated easily from other columns" (p. 130). For Table 12.3 this would mean that either *ss* or *ms* be deleted. The format followed in APA journals is to report *ms* only.

Output

--- Variables in the Equation ---

Variable	B	Beta	Part Cor	Tolerance	VIF
A1	−.500000	−.156174	−.156174	1.000000	1.000
B1	−1.500000	−.468521	−.468521	1.000000	1.000
A1B1	2.500000	.780869	.780869	1.000000	1.000
(Constant)	10.500000				

Commentary

Except for the regression equation, which I discuss later, the preceding excerpt of the output is *not* relevant for present purposes. Nevertheless, I reproduced it so that I may use it to illustrate special properties of the least-squares solution when the independent variables are not correlated. Remember that the three coded vectors representing the two independent variables and

Table 12.3   Summary of Multiple Regression Analysis for Data in Table 12.1

Source	ss	df	ms	F
A	2.00	1	2.00	.67
B	18.00	1	18.00	6.00
$A \times B$	50.00	1	50.00	16.67*
Residual	12.00	4	3.00	
Total	92.00	7		

*$p < .05$.

their interaction are not correlated. *For illustrative purposes only,* think of the three vectors as if they were three uncorrelated variables.

Beta (standardized regression coefficient). As expected—see (5.15) and the discussion related to it—each beta is equal to the zero-order correlation of the dependent variable (Y) with the "variable" (vector) with which it is associated. For example, the beta for A1 (−.156) is equal to correlation of Y with A1 (compare the betas with the correlations reported under Y in the correlation matrix given earlier in this chapter).

Part Cor(relation). In Chapter 7, I referred to this as semipartial correlation. Examine, for example, (7.14) or (7.19) to see why, for the case under consideration, the semipartial correlations are equal to their corresponding zero-order correlations.

I discussed Tolerance and VIF (variance inflation factor) in Chapter 10 under "Diagnostics" for "Collinearity." Read the discussion related to (10.9) to see why VIF $=$ 1.0 when the independent variables are not correlated. Also examine (10.14) to see why tolerance is equal to 1.0 when the independent variables are not correlated.

Output

Block Number   4.   Method: Test   A1   B1   A1B1

Hypothesis Tests

DF	Sum of Squares	Rsq Chg	F	Sig F	Source
1	2.00000	.02439	.66667	.4601	A1
1	18.00000	.21951	6.00000	.0705	B1
1	50.00000	.60976	16.66667	.0151	A1B1
3	70.00000		7.77778	.0381	Regression
4	12.00000				Residual
7	82.00000				Total

Commentary

The preceding was generated by the TEST keyword (e.g., SPSS Inc., 1993, p. 627). Differences in format and layout aside, this segment contains the same information as that I summarized in Table 12.3 based on the sequential analysis (see the earlier output and commentaries). In light of that, you are probably wondering what was the point of doing the sequential analysis. Indeed, having the type of output generated by TEST obviates the need for a sequential analysis of the kind I presented earlier. I did it to show what you may have to do when you use a computer program for regression analysis that does not contain a command or facility analogous to TEST of SPSS. Also, as you will recall, I wanted to use the opportunity to explain why some intermediate results are not relevant in an analysis of this type.[2]

---

[2]The use of TEST is straightforward when, as in the present example, the vectors (or variables) are not correlated. Later in this chapter (see "Nonorthogonal Designs"), I explain TEST in greater detail and show circumstances under which the results generated by it are *not* relevant and others under which they *are* relevant. At this point, I just want to caution you against using TEST indiscriminately.

The Regression Equation

In Chapter 11, I showed that the regression equation for effect coding with one categorical independent variable reflects the linear model. The same is true for the regression equation for effect coding in factorial designs. For two categorical independent variables, the linear model is

$$Y_{ijk} = \mu + \alpha_i + \beta_j + (\alpha\beta)_{ij} + \varepsilon_{ijk} \tag{12.2}$$

where Y_{ijk} = score of subject k in row i and column j, or the treatment combination α_i and β_j; μ = population mean; α_i = effect of treatment i of factor A; β_j = effect of treatment j of factor B; $(\alpha\beta)_{ij}$ = interaction term for treatment combination A_i and B_j; and ε_{ijk} = error associated with the score of individual k under treatment combination A_i and B_j.

Equation (12.2) is expressed in parameters. In statistics the linear model for two categorical independent variables is

$$Y_{ijk} = \overline{Y} + a_i + b_j + (ab)_{ij} + e_{ijk} \tag{12.3}$$

where the terms on the right are estimates of the respective parameters of (12.2). Thus, for example, $\overline{Y}$ = the grand mean of the dependent variable and is an estimate μ of (12.2), and similarly for the remaining terms. The score of a subject is conceived as composed of five components: the grand mean, the effect of treatment a_i, the effect of treatment b_j, the interaction of a_i and b_j, and error.

From the computer output given above (see Variables in the Equation), the regression equation for the 2×2 design I analyzed with effect coding (the original data are given in Table 12.1) is

$$Y' = 10.5 - .5A1 - 1.5B1 + 2.5A1B1$$

Note that a is equal to the grand mean of the dependent variable, $\overline{Y}$. I discuss separately the regression coefficients for the main effects and the one for the interaction, beginning with the former.

Regression Coefficients for Main Effects

To facilitate understanding of the regression coefficients for the main effects, Table 12.4 reports cell and marginal means, as well as treatment effects, from which you can see that each b is equal to the treatment effect with which it is associated. Thus, in vector A1, subjects belonging to category A_1 were identified (i.e., assigned 1's; see Table 12.2, the input, or the listing of the data in the output). Accordingly, the coefficient for A1, $-.5$, is equal to the effect of category or treatment, A_1. That is,

$$b_{A1} = \overline{Y}_{A_1} - \overline{Y} = 10.0 - 10.5 = -.5$$

Similarly, the coefficient for B1, -1.5, indicates the effect of treatment B_1:

$$b_{B1} = \overline{Y}_{B_1} - \overline{Y} = 9.0 - 10.5 = -1.5$$

The remaining treatment effects—that is, those associated with the categories that were assigned -1's (in the present example these are A_2 and B_2) can be readily obtained in view of the constraint that the sum of the treatment effects for any factor equals zero. In the case under consideration (i.e., factors composed of two categories), all that is necessary to obtain the effect of a treatment assigned -1 is to reverse the sign of the coefficient for the category identified in the vector in question (later in this chapter, I give examples for factors composed of more than two categories). Thus, the effect of $A_2 = .5$, and that of $B_2 = 1.5$. Compare these results with the values reported in Table 12.4.

Table 12.4   Cell and Treatment Means, and Treatment Effects for Data in Table 12.1

	B_1	B_2	$\overline{Y}_A$	$\overline{Y}_A - \overline{Y}$
A_1	11	9	10	−.5
A_2	7	15	11	.5
$\overline{Y}_B$	9	12		$\overline{Y} = 10.5$
$\overline{Y}_B - \overline{Y}$	−1.5	1.5		

NOTE: $\overline{Y}_A$ = marginal means for A; $\overline{Y}_B$ = marginal means for B; $\overline{Y}$ = grand mean; and $\overline{Y}_B - \overline{Y}$ and $\overline{Y}_A - \overline{Y}$ are treatment effects for a category of factor A and a category of factor B, respectively.

THE MEANING OF INTERACTION

In the preceding section, I showed how to determine the main effects of each independent variable. I showed, for instance, that the effects of factor A for the data in Table 12.2 are $A_1 = -.5$ and $A_2 = .5$ (see Table 12.4). This means that when considering scores of subjects administered treatment A_1, one part of their scores (i.e., −.5) is attributed to the fact that they have received this treatment. Note that in the preceding statement I made no reference to the fact that subjects under A_1 received different B treatments, hence the term *main effect*. The effects of the other category of A, and those of B, are similarly interpreted.

In short, when main effects are studied, each factor's independent effects are considered separately. It is, however, possible for factors to have joint effects. That is, a given combination of treatments (one from each factor) may be particularly effective because they enhance the effects of each other, or particularly ineffective because they operate at cross purposes, so to speak. Referring to examples I gave earlier, it is possible for a combination of a given teaching method (A) with a certain type of reinforcement (B) to be particularly advantageous in producing achievement that is higher than what would be expected based on their combined separate effects. Conversely, a combination of a teaching method and a type of reinforcement may be particularly disadvantageous, leading to achievement that is lower than would be expected based on their combined separate effects. Or, to take another example, a given teaching method may be particularly effective in, say, urban schools, whereas another teaching method may be particularly effective in, say, rural schools.

When no effects are observed over and above the separate effects of the various factors, it is said that the variables do not interact or that they have no joint effects. When, on the other hand, in addition to the separate effects of the factors, they have joint effects as a consequence of specific treatment combination, it is said that the factors interact with each other. Formally, an interaction for two factors is defined as follows:

$$(AB)_{ij} = (\overline{Y}_{ij} - \overline{Y}) - (\overline{Y}_{A_i} - \overline{Y}) - (\overline{Y}_{B_j} - \overline{Y}) \tag{12.4}$$

where $(AB)_{ij}$ = interaction of treatments A_i and B_j; $\overline{Y}_{ij}$ = mean of treatment combination A_i and B_j, or the mean of cell ij; $\overline{Y}_{A_i}$ = mean of category, or treatment, i of factor A; $\overline{Y}_{B_j}$ = mean of category, or treatment, j of factor B; and $\overline{Y}$ = grand mean. Note that $\overline{Y}_{A_i} - \overline{Y}$ in (12.4) is the effect of treatment A_i and that $\overline{Y}_{B_j} - \overline{Y}$ is the effect of treatment B_j. From (12.4) it follows that when the deviation of a cell mean from the grand mean is equal to the sum of the treatment effects related to the given cell, then the interaction term for the cell is zero. Stated differently, to predict the mean of such a cell it is sufficient to know the grand mean and the treatment effects.

Using (12.4), I calculated interaction terms for each combination of treatments and report them in Table 12.5. For instance, I obtained the term for cell A_1B_1 as follows:

$$A_1 \times B_1 = (\overline{Y}_{A_1B_1} - \overline{Y}) - (\overline{Y}_{A_1} - \overline{Y}) - (\overline{Y}_{B_1} - \overline{Y})$$
$$= (11 - 10.5) - (10 - 10.5) - (9 - 10.5)$$
$$= .5 - (-.5) - (-1.5) = 2.5$$

The other terms of Table 12.5 are similarly calculated.

Another way of determining whether an interaction exists is to examine, in turn, the differences between the cell means of two treatment levels of one factor across all the levels of the other factor. This can perhaps be best understood by referring to the numerical example under consideration. Look back at Table 12.4 and consider first rows A_1 and A_2. Row A_1 displays the means of groups that were administered treatment A_1, and row A_2 displays the means of groups that were administered treatment A_2. If the effects of these two treatments are independent of the effects of factor B (i.e., if there is no interaction), it follows that the difference between any two means under a given level of B should be equal to a constant, that being the difference between the effect of treatment A_1 and that of A_2. In Table 12.4 the effect of A_1 is $-.5$ and that of A_2 is .5. Therefore, if there is no interaction, the difference between any two cell means under the separate B's should be equal to -1 (i.e., $-.5 - .5$). Stated another way, if there is no interaction, $A_1 - A_2$ under B_1, and $A_1 - A_2$ under B_2 should be equal to each other because for each difference between the A's B is constant. This can be further clarified by noting that when A and B do not interact, each cell mean can be expressed as a composite of three elements: the grand mean $(\overline{Y})$, the effect of treatment A administered to the given group (a_i), and the effect of treatment B (b_j) administered to the group. For cell means in rows A_1 and A_2, under B_1, in Table 12.4, this translates into

$$A_1B_1 = \overline{Y} + a_1 + b_1$$
$$A_2B_1 = \overline{Y} + a_2 + b_1$$

Subtracting the second row from the first obtains $a_1 - a_2$: the difference between the effects of treatments A_1 and A_2. Similarly,

$$A_1B_2 = \overline{Y} + a_1 + b_2$$
$$A_2B_2 = \overline{Y} + a_2 + b_2$$

Again, the difference between these two cell means is equal to $a_1 - a_2$.

Consider now the numerical example in Table 12.4:

$$A_1B_1 - A_2B_1 = 11 - 7 = 4$$
$$A_1B_2 - A_2B_2 = 9 - 15 = -6$$

The differences between the cell means are *not* equal, indicating that there is an interaction between A and B. Thus, the grand mean and the main effects are not sufficient to express the mean

Table 12.5   Interaction Effects for Data in Table 12.4

	B_1	B_2	Σ
A_1	2.5	-2.5	0
A_2	-2.5	2.5	0
Σ	0	0	

of a given cell; a term for the interaction is also necessary. In Table 12.5, I report the interaction terms for each cell for the example under consideration. Consider, for instance, the difference between cell means of A_1B_1 and A_2B_1 when each is expressed as a composite of the grand mean, main effects, and an interaction term:

$$A_1B_1 = 10.5(\overline{Y}) + (-.5)(a_1) + (-1.5)(b_1) + (2.5)(a_1b_1) = 11$$

$$A_2B_1 = 10.5(\overline{Y}) + (.5)(a_2) + (-1.5)(b_1) + (-2.5)(a_2b_1) = 7$$

Subtracting the second row from the first obtains the difference between the two-cell means, (4). Had I ignored the interaction terms in the previous calculations, I would have erroneously predicted the mean for cell A_1B_1 as 8.5 and that for cell A_2B_1 as 9.5, leading to a difference of -1 between the means—that is, a difference equal to that between treatments A_1 and A_2 ($-.5 - .5$). Clearly, only when there is no interaction will all the elements in tables such as Table 12.5 be equal to zero.

Instead of doing the comparisons by rows, they may be done by columns. That is, differences between cell means of columns B_1 and B_2 across the levels of A may be compared. The same condition holds: an interaction is indicated when the differences between the means for the two comparisons are not equal. Note, however, that it is *not* necessary to do the comparisons for both columns and rows, because the same information is contained in either comparison.

What I said about the detection and meaning of an interaction for the case of a 2×2 design generalizes to any two-factor design, whatever the number of categories that compose each. I show this later for a 3×3 design.

Graphic Depiction

The ideas I expressed in the preceding can be clearly seen in a graphic depiction. Assigning one of the factors (it does not matter which one) to the abscissa, its cell means are plotted across the levels of the other factor. The points representing a set of cell means at a given level of a factor are then connected. I give examples of such plots in Figure 12.2.

When there is no interaction between the factors, the lines connecting respective cell means at the levels of one of the factors would be parallel. I depict this hypothetical case in (a) of Figure 12.2, where the means associated with B_1 are equally larger than those associated with B_2, regardless of the levels of A. Under such circumstances, it is meaningful to interpret the main effects of A and B.

Disordinal and Ordinal Interactions

Without a substantive research example it is difficult to convey the meaning of graphs like the ones depicted in Figure 12.2. To impart at least some of their meaning, I assume in the following discussion that the higher the mean of the dependent variable, whatever it is, the more desirable the outcome.

In (b) of Figure 12.2, I plotted the means of the 2×2 numerical example I analyzed earlier (see Table 12.4). Examine this graph and notice that references to the main effects of A or B are not meaningful because the effect of a given treatment of one factor depends largely on the type of treatment of the other factor with which it is paired. Consider, for instance, B_2. In combination with A_2 it leads to the best results, the cell mean being the highest (15). But when combined with

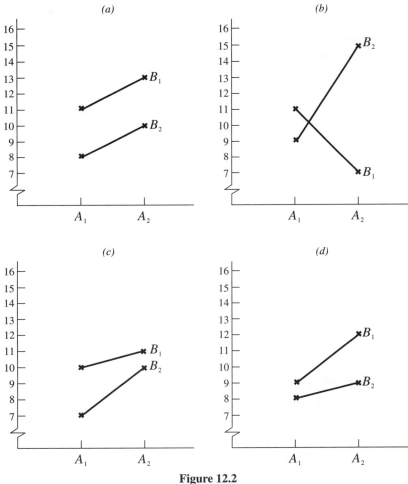

Figure 12.2

A_1 it leads to a cell mean of 9. Actually, the second best combination is B_1 with A_1, yielding a mean of 11. The weakest effect is obtained when B_1 is combined with A_2 (7).

To repeat: it is not meaningful to speak of main effects in (b) as no treatment leads consistently to higher means than does the other treatment, but rather the rank order of effects of the treatments changes depending on their specific pairings. Thus, under A_1 the rank order of effectiveness of the B treatments is B_1, B_2. But under A_2 the rank order of the B's is reversed (i.e., B_2, B_1). When the rank order of treatment effects changes, the interaction is said to be *disordinal* (Lubin, 1961).

In (c) and (d) of Figure 12.2, I give two other examples of an interaction between A and B. Unlike the situation in (b), the interactions in (c) and (d) are *ordinal*. That is, the rank order of the treatment effects is constant: B_1 is consistently superior to B_2. But the differences between the treatments is *not* constant. They vary, depending on the specific combination of B's and A's, therefore reflecting ordinal interaction. In (c), when combined with A_1 the difference between the B's is larger than when combined with A_2. The converse is true in (d), where the difference between the B's is larger when they are combined with A_2.

When the interaction is ordinal, one may speak of the main effects of the treatments, although such statements are generally of dubious value because they ignore the fact that treatments of a factor differ in their effectiveness, depending on their pairing with the treatments of another factor. Thus, while B_1 is more effective than B_2 in both (c) and (d), it is important to consider its differential effectiveness. Assume that B_1 is a very expensive treatment to administer. Based on results like those in (c) of Figure 12.2, it is conceivable for a researcher to decide that the investment involved in using B_1 is worthwhile only when it can be administered in combination with A_1. If, for whatever reason, A_2 is to be used, the researcher may decide to select the less expensive B treatment (B_2). In fact, when tests of statistical significance are done pursuant to a statistically significant interaction (see the following), it may turn out that the difference between the B's at A_2 is statistically not significant.

The situation in (d) is reversed. Assuming, again, that B_1 is a much more expensive treatment, and that A_1 is to be used, the researcher may decide to use B_2, despite the fact that B_1 is superior to it.

Finally, what may appear as interactions in a given set of data may be due to random fluctuations or measurement errors. Whether nonzero interactions are to be attributed to other than random fluctuations is determined by statistical tests of significance. In the absence of a statistically significant interaction it is sufficient to speak of main effects only. When an interaction is statistically significant, it is possible to pursue it with tests of simple effects (see the following).

I return now to the regression equation to examine the properties of the regression coefficient for the interaction.

Regression Coefficient for Interaction

I repeat the regression equation for the 2×2 design of the data given in Table 12.2:

$$Y' = 10.5 - .5A1 - 1.5B1 + 2.5A1B1$$

Earlier, I showed that the first two b's of this equation refer to the effect of the treatments with which they are associated ($-.5$ for A_1 and -1.5 for B_1). The remaining b refers to an interaction effect. Specifically, it refers to the interaction term for the cell with which it is associated. Look back at Table 12.2 and note that I generated A1B1 by multiplying A1 and B1—the vectors identifying A_1 and B_1. Hence, the regression coefficient for A1B1 indicates the interaction term for cell A_1B_1. Examine Table 12.5 and note that the interaction term for this cell is 2.5, which is the same as b for A1B1.

Earlier, I pointed out that in the present example there is 1 df for the interaction. Hence, one term in the regression equation. As with main effects, the remaining terms for the interaction are obtained in view of the constraint that the sum of interaction terms for each row and each column equals zero. Thus, for instance, the interaction term for A_2B_1 is -2.5. Compare this term with the value of Table 12.5, and verify that the other terms may be similarly obtained.

Applying the Regression Equation

The properties of the regression equation for effect coding, as well as the overall analysis of the data of Table 12.2, can be further clarified by examining properties of predicted scores. Applying the regression equation given earlier to the "scores" (codes) of the first subject of Table 12.2, that is, the first row,

$$Y' = 10.5 - .5(1) - 1.5(1) + 2.5(1)$$
$$= 10.5 - .5 \quad - 1.5 \quad + 2.5 \quad = 11$$

As expected, the predicted score (11) is equal to the mean of the cell to which the first subject belongs (see A_1B_1 of Table 12.4).

The residual, or error, for the first subject is $Y - Y' = 12 - 11 = 1$. It is now possible to express the first subject's observed score as a composite of the five components of the linear model. To show this, I repeat (12.3) with a new number:

$$Y_{ijk} = \overline{Y} + a_i + b_j + (ab)_{ij} + e_{ijk} \tag{12.5}$$

where Y_{ijk} = score of subject k in row i and column j, or the treatment combination A_i and B_j; $\overline{Y}$ = population mean; a_i = effect of treatment i of factor A; b_j = effect of treatment j of factor B; $(ab)_{ij}$ = interaction term for treatment combinations A_i and B_j; and e_{ijk} = error associated with the score of individual k under treatment combination A_i and B_j.

Using (12.5) to express the score of the first subject in cell A_1B_1,

$$12 = 10.5 - .5 - 1.5 + 2.5 + 1$$

where 10.5 = grand mean; $-.5$ = effect of treatment A_1; -1.5 = effect of treatment B_1; 2.5 = interaction term for cell A_1B_1; and 1 = residual, $Y - Y'$.

As another example, I apply the regression equation to the last subject of Table 12.2:

$$Y' = 10.5 - .5(-1) - 1.5(-1) + 2.5(1)$$
$$= 10.5 + .5 \quad + 1.5 \quad + 2.5 \quad = 15$$

Again, the predicted score is equal to the mean of the cell to which this subject belongs (see Table 12.4). The residual for this subject is $Y - Y' = 13 - 15 = -2$. Expressing this subject's score in the components of the linear model,

$$13 = 10.5 + .5 + 1.5 + 2.5 + (-2)$$

In Table 12.6, I use this format to express the scores of all the subjects of Table 12.2. A close study of Table 12.6 will enhance your understanding of the analysis of these data. Notice that squaring and summing the elements in the column for the main effects of factor A (a_i) yields a sum of squares of 2. This is the same sum of squares I obtained earlier for factor A (see, for instance, Table 12.3). The sums of the squared elements for the remaining terms are factor B (b_j) = 18; interaction, $A \times B$ (ab_{ij}) = 50; and residuals ($Y - Y'$) = 12. I obtained the same values in earlier calculations. Adding the four sums of squares of Table 12.6, the total sum of squares of Y is

$$\Sigma y^2 = 2 + 18 + 50 + 12 = 82$$

MULTIPLE COMPARISONS

Multiple comparisons among main effect means are meaningful once one concludes that the interaction is statistically not significant. Recall that in the numerical example I analyzed earlier, the interaction is statistically significant. Even if this were not so, it would not have been necessary to do multiple comparisons, as the F ratio for each main effect in a 2×2 design refers to a

Table 12.6 Data for a 2 × 2 Design Expressed as Components of the Linear Model

Cell	Y	$\overline{Y}$	a_i	b_j	ab_{ij}	Y'	$Y - Y'$
	12	10.5	−.5	−1.5	2.5	11	1
A_1B_1	10	10.5	−.5	−1.5	2.5	11	−1
	10	10.5	−.5	1.5	−2.5	9	1
A_1B_2	8	10.5	−.5	1.5	−2.5	9	−1
	7	10.5	.5	−1.5	−2.5	7	0
A_2B_1	7	10.5	.5	−1.5	−2.5	7	0
	17	10.5	.5	1.5	2.5	15	2
A_2B_2	13	10.5	.5	1.5	2.5	15	−2
ss:			2	18	50		12

NOTE: Y = observed score; $\overline{Y}$ = grand mean; a_i = effect of treatment i of factor A; b_j = effect of treatment j of factor B; ab_{ij} = interaction between a_i and b_j; Y' = predicted score, where in each case it is equal to the sum of the elements in the four columns preceding it; $Y - Y'$ = residual, or error; and ss = sum of squares.

test between two means. Later in this chapter, when I analyze a 3 × 3 design, I show that multiple comparisons among main effect means are done much as in a design with a single categorical independent variable (see Chapter 11).

When the interaction is statistically significant, it is not meaningful to compare main effect means inasmuch as it is not meaningful to interpret such effects in the first place (see earlier discussion of this point). Instead, one may analyze simple effects or interaction contrasts. As the latter are relevant in designs in which at least one of the factors consists of more than two categories, I present them later in this chapter.

Simple Effects

The idea behind the analysis of simple effects is that differential effects of treatments of one factor are studied, in turn, at each treatment (or level) of the other factor. Referring to the 2 × 2 design I analyzed earlier, this means that one would study the difference between B_1 and B_2 separately at A_1 and at A_2. It is as if the research is composed of two separate studies each consisting of the same categorical variable B, except that each is conducted in the context of a different A category. If this does not matter, then the differences between the B's across the two "studies" should be equal, within random fluctuations. This, of course, would occur when there is no interaction between A and B. When, however, A and B interact it means that the pattern of the differences between the B's at the two separate levels of A differ. Thus, for example, it may turn out that under A_1 the effects of B_1 and B_2 are equal to each other, whereas under A_2 the effect of B_1 is greater than that of B_2. Other patterns are, of course, possible.

From the foregoing it should be clear that when studying simple effects, the 2 × 2 design I have been considering is sliced into two slabs—each consisting of one category of A and two categories of B—which are analyzed separately. The 2 × 2 design can also be sliced by columns. Thus one would have one slab for the two A categories under condition B_1 and another slab under condition B_2. Slicing the table this way allows one to study separately the differential effects of the A treatments under each level of B. This, then, is the idea of studying simple effects.

To test simple effects for B, say, the dependent variable, Y, is regressed, separately for each A category, on a coded vector representing the B's. Referring to the example under consideration, each separate regression analysis would consist of four subjects (there are two subjects in each cell and two cells of *B* are used in each analysis). The regression sum of squares obtained from each such analysis is divided, as usual, by its degrees of freedom to obtain a mean square regression. But instead of using the mean square residual (*MSR*) from the separate analyses as the denominator of each of the *F* ratios, the *MSR* from the overall analysis of the factorial design is used. In sum, the separate regression analyses are done for the sole purpose of obtaining the mean square regression from each.

What I said about testing simple effects for *B* applies equally to such tests for *A*. Doing both for a two-factor design would therefore require four separate analyses. In the course of the presentation, I will show how this can be accomplished in several different ways so that you may choose the one you prefer or deem most suitable in light of the software you are using. Among other approaches, I will show how you can obtain the required regression sum of squares for simple effects from the results of an overall regression analysis with effect coding of the kind I presented in preceding sections.

Calculations via Multiple Regression Analysis

In what follows, I present SPSS input statements for separate analyses to get regression sums of squares for tests of simple effects.

SPSS

Input

. . . .   *[see commentary]*
SPLIT FILE BY A.
LIST VAR=A B Y B1.
REGRESSION VAR=Y B1/DES/DEP=Y/ENTER.
SORT CASES BY B.
SPLIT FILE BY B.
LIST VAR=A B Y A1.
REGRESSION VAR=Y A1/DES/DEP=Y/ENTER.

Commentary

The dotted line is meant to signify that other input statements should precede the ones I give here. The specific statements to be included depend on the purpose of the analysis. If you wish to run the analyses for the simple effects simultaneously with the overall analysis I presented earlier, attach the preceding statements to the end of the input file I gave earlier. If, on the other hand, you wish to run simple effects analyses only, include the following: (1) TITLE, (2) DATA LIST, (3) IF statements, (4) BEGIN DATA, (5) the data, (6) END DATA. Note that when doing analyses for simple effects only, it is not necessary to include the COMPUTE statement, which I used earlier to generate the vector representing the interaction (see the input file for the earlier analysis).

"SPLIT FILE splits the working file into subgroups that can be analyzed separately" (SPSS Inc., 1993, p. 762). Before invoking SPLIT FILE, make sure that the cases are sorted appropriately (see SPSS Inc., 1993, pp. 762–764). The data I read in are sorted appropriately for an analysis of the simple effects of B. It is, however, necessary to sort the cases by B when analyzing for the simple effects of A (see the following output and commentaries on the listed data).

SPLIT FILE is in effect throughout the session, unless it is (1) preceded by a TEMPORARY command, (2) turned off (i.e., SPLIT FILE OFF), or (3) overridden by SORT CASES or a new SPLIT FILE command.

Output

SPLIT FILE BY A.
LIST VAR=A B Y B1.

A: 1

A	B	Y	B1
1	1	12	1.00
1	1	10	1.00
1	2	10	−1.00
1	2	8	−1.00

Number of cases read: 4   Number of cases listed: 4

A: 2

A	B	Y	B1
2	1	7	1.00
2	1	7	1.00
2	2	17	−1.00
2	2	13	−1.00

Number of cases read: 4   Number of cases listed: 4

Commentary

I listed the cases to show how the file was split. Examine column A and notice that it consists of 1's in subset A: 1, and 2's in subset A: 2. When Y is regressed on B1 (see the following) the regression sum of squares for the simple effects of B (B_1 versus B_2) under A_1 and under A_2 is obtained.

Output

REGRESSION VAR=Y B1/DES/DEP=Y/ENTER.
A: 1
Analysis of Variance   *[B at A_1]*

	DF	Sum of Squares	Mean Square
Regression	1	4.00000	4.00000

A: 2
Analysis of Variance   *[B at A₂]*

	DF	Sum of Squares	Mean Square
Regression	1	64.00000	64.00000

SORT CASES BY B.
SPLIT FILE BY B.
LIST VAR=A B Y A1.

B: 1

A	B	Y		A1
1	1	12		1.00
1	1	10		1.00
2	1	7		−1.00
2	1	7		−1.00

Number of cases read: 4   Number of cases listed: 4

B: 2

A	B	Y		A1
1	2	10		1.00
1	2	8		1.00
2	2	17		−1.00
2	2	13		−1.00

Number of cases read: 4   Number of cases listed: 4

REGRESSION VAR=Y A1/DES/DEP=Y/ENTER.

B: 1
Analysis of Variance   *[A at B₁]*

	DF	Sum of Squares	Mean Square
Regression	1	16.00000	16.00000

B: 2
Analysis of Variance   *[A at B₂]*

	DF	Sum of Squares	Mean Square
Regression	1	36.00000	36.00000

Commentary

I reproduced only the output relevant for the present purposes. In the present example, the Mean Square is equal to the Sum of Squares because it is associated with 1 DF. When a factor comprises more than two categories, the Mean Square will, of course, be the relevant statistic. In the italicized comments I indicated the specific analysis to which the results refer.

The sum of the regression sums of squares of simple effects for a given factor is equal to the regression sum of squares for the factor in question plus the regression sum of squares for the interaction. For simple effects of B,

$$ss_B + ss_{A \times B} = ss_{\text{reg}} \text{ of } B \text{ at } A_1 + ss_{\text{reg}} \text{ of } B \text{ at } A_2$$

$$18.00 + 50.00 = \quad 4.00 \quad + \quad 64.00$$

And for A,

$$ss_A + ss_{A \times B} = ss_{\text{reg}} \text{ of } A \text{ at } B_1 + ss_{\text{reg}} \text{ of } A \text{ at } B_2$$

$$2.00 + 50.00 = \quad 16.00 \quad + \quad 36.00$$

When I calculate regression sums of squares for simple effects from results of an overall analysis (see the following), I show that effects of a given factor and the interaction enter into the calculations.

Tests of Significance

Each Mean Square is divided by the *MSR* from the overall analysis (3.00, in the present example; see the output given earlier) to yield an F ratio with 1 and 4 *df* (i.e., *df* associated with *MSR*). I summarized these tests in Table 12.7.

To control α when doing multiple tests, it is recommended that it be divided by the number of simple effects tests for a given factor. In the present case, I did two tests for each factor. Assuming that I selected $\alpha = .05$ for the overall analysis, then I would use $\alpha = .025$ for each F ratio. As it happens, critical values of F for $\alpha = .025$ are given in some statistics books (e.g., Edwards, 1985; Maxwell & Delaney, 1990), which show that the critical value of F with 1 and 4 *df* at $\alpha = .025$ is 12.22.[3] Accordingly, only the test for the simple effect of B at A_2 is statistically significant (see Table 12.7). In other words, only the difference between B_1 and B_2 at A_2 is statistically significant.

I remind you, again, *that the data are fictitious. Moreover, the cell frequencies are extremely small.* Nevertheless, the preceding analysis illustrates how tests of simple effects pursuant to a statistically significant interaction help pinpoint specific differences. I return to this topic later, when I comment on the controversy surrounding the use of tests of simple effects and interaction contrasts.

Table 12.7   Summary of Tests of Simple Main Effects for Data in Table 12.1

Source	ss	df	ms	F
A at B_1	16.00	1	16.00	5.33
A at B_2	36.00	1	36.00	12.00
B at A_1	4.00	1	4.00	1.33
B at A_2	64.00	1	64.00	21.33*
Residual	12.00	4	3.00	

*$p < .025$. See the text for explanation.

[3]Later I explain how you may obtain α values not reported in statistics books.

Simple Effects from Overall Regression Equation

To facilitate the presentation, I use a 2×2 format to display in Table 12.8 the effects I obtained earlier from the regression analysis of all the data. I placed the main effects of A and B in the margins of the table and identified two of them—one for A and one for B—by a b with a subscript corresponding to the coded vector associated with the given effect (see Table 12.2). I did not attach b's to the other two effects—one for A and one for B—as they are *not* part of the regression equation. Recall that I obtained them based on the constraint that the sum of the effects of a given factor is zero. The entries in the body of Table 12.8 are the interaction terms for each cell, which I reported earlier in Table 12.5, except that here I added the b for the term I obtained from the regression equation. Again, entries that have no b's attached to them are *not* part of the regression equation. I obtained them based on the constraint that the sum of interaction terms in rows or columns equals zero.[4]

To get a feel for how I will use elements of Table 12.8, look at the marginals for factor A. The first marginal ($-.5$) is, of course, the effect of A_1. Four subjects received this treatment (two subjects are in each cell). In other words, part of the Y score for each of these subjects is $-.5$, and the same is true for the other A marginal, which belongs to the other four subjects. Recall that each marginal represents a deviation of the mean of the treatment to which it refers from the grand mean (this is the definition of an effect). Therefore, to calculate the regression sum of squares due to A, square each A effect, multiply by the number of subjects to whom the effect refers, and sum the results. As the number of subjects for each effect is the same, this reduces to

$$ss_{reg}(A) = 4[(-.5)^2 + (.5)^2] = 2.0$$

which is, of course, the same as the value I obtained earlier. Actually what I did here with the information from Table 12.8, I did earlier in Table 12.6, except that in the latter I spelled out the effects for each person in the design.

To calculate the regression sum of squares due to B, use the marginals of B in Table 12.8:

$$ss_{reg}(B) = 4[(-1.5)^2 + (1.5)^2] = 18.0$$

which is the same as the value I obtained earlier.

Now, for the interaction. As each cell is based on 2 subjects,

$$ss_{reg}(A \times B) = 2[(2.5)^2 + (-2.5)^2 + (-2.5)^2 + (2.5)^2] = 50.0$$

which is the same as the value I obtained earlier.

As I said, I obtained all the foregoing values from the overall regression analysis. I recalculated them here to give you a better understanding of the approach I will use to calculate the sum of squares for simple effects.

Table 12.8   Main Effects and Interaction for Data in Table 12.2

	B_1	B_2	A Effects
A_1	$2.5 = b_{A1B1}$	-2.5	$-.5 = b_{A1}$
A_2	-2.5	2.5	$.5$
B Effects:	$-1.5 = b_{B1}$	1.5	

[4]If you are having difficulties with the preceding, I suggest that you reread the following sections in the present chapter: (1) "The Regression Equation" and (2) "Regression Coefficient for Interaction."

I begin with the calculations for simple effects for A. Look at Table 12.8 and consider only the first column (B_1). As the effect of B_1 is a constant, the differences between A_1 and A_2 under B_1 may be expressed as a composite of the effects of A and the interaction. Thus for cell A_1B_1, this translates into $-.5 + 2.5$, and for A_2B_1 it is $.5 + (-2.5)$. Each of these elements is relevant for two subjects. Following the approach outlined earlier, the regression sums of squares for simple effects for A are

$$\text{For } A \text{ at } B_1: 2[(-.5 + 2.5)^2 + (.5 - 2.5)^2] = 16$$
$$\text{For } A \text{ at } B_2: 2[(-.5 - 2.5)^2 + (.5 + 2.5)^2] = \underline{36}$$
$$\Sigma: 52$$

These are the same as the values I obtained earlier (see Table 12.7; also see the output given earlier). Earlier, I pointed out that the sum of the regression sums of squares for simple effects for A is equal to $ss_A + ss_{A \times B}$, which for the present example is $2 + 50 = 52$. Why this is so should be clear from my preceding calculations of the simple effects for which I used the effects of A and the interaction between A and B.

The sums of squares for simple effects for B are calculated in a similar manner:

$$\text{For } B \text{ at } A_1: 2[(-1.5 + 2.5)^2 + (1.5 - 2.5)^2] = 4$$
$$\text{For } B \text{ at } A_2: 2[(-1.5 - 2.5)^2 + (1.5 + 2.5)^2] = \underline{64}$$
$$\Sigma: 68$$

Again, these are equal to the values I obtained earlier (see Table 12.7; also see the output given earlier). The sum of the regression sums of squares for the simple effects of B is equal to the $ss_B + ss_{A \times B} = 18 + 50 = 68$.

My aim in this section was limited to showing how to use relevant main effects and interaction terms to calculate the regression sums of squares for simple effects. Later in this chapter, I show that this approach generalizes to two factors with any number of categories. Also, although I do not show this, the approach I presented here generalizes to higher-order designs for the calculations of terms such as simple interactions and simple-simple effects.[5] I presented tests of significance of simple effects earlier (see Table 12.7 and the discussion related to it) and will therefore not repeat them here.

Analysis via MANOVA

MANOVA (Multivariate Analysis of Variance) is probably the most versatile procedure in SPSS. I use some of this procedure's varied options in later chapters (especially in Part 4). Here, I limit its use to tests of simple effects, though I take this opportunity to also show how to obtain an overall factorial analysis.

SPSS

Input

. . . .   *[see commentary]*
MANOVA Y BY A,B(1,2)/ERROR=WITHIN/
  PRINT=CELLINFO(MEANS)PARAMETERS/

---

[5]Later in this chapter, I comment briefly on higher-order designs.

DESIGN/
DESIGN=A WITHIN B(1), A WITHIN B(2)/
DESIGN=B WITHIN A(1), B WITHIN A(2).

Commentary

As in the previous example, here I only give statements necessary for running MANOVA. You can incorporate these statements in the earlier run (as I did) or you can use them in a separate run. The dotted line preceding the MANOVA statements is meant to signify omitted statements. If you choose to run MANOVA separately, add the following: (1) TITLE, (2) DATA LIST, (3) BEGIN DATA, (4) the data, and (5) END DATA.

MANOVA. The dependent variable(s), Y, must come first and be separated from the factor names by the keyword BY. Minimum and maximum values for each factor are specified in parentheses. Factors having the same minimum and maximum values may be grouped together, as I did here.

ERROR. One can choose from several error terms (see Norušis/SPSS Inc., 1993b, pp. 397–398). Without going far afield, I will point out that for present purposes we need the within-cells error term. If you followed my frequent reminders to study the manuals for the software you are using, you may be puzzled by my inclusion of ERROR=WITHIN, as the manual states that it is the *default* (see Norušis/SPSS Inc., 1993b, p. 397). *That this is no longer true* can be seen from the following message in the output, *when no error term is specified:*

> The default error term in MANOVA has been changed from WITHIN CELLS to WITHIN+RESIDUAL. Note that these are the same for all full factorial designs.

In Chapter 4, and in subsequent chapters, I stressed the importance of being thoroughly familiar with the software you are using and of paying attention to messages in the output and/or separate log files (e.g., for SAS). The present example is a case in point. If you omitted the specification ERROR=WITHIN on the assumption that it is the default, you would get the correct sums of squares for the simple effects. However, the error term and its degrees of freedom would not be relevant, as they would also include values of one of the main effects. For example, for the analysis of A within B_1 and B_2, the error term would be 30.00, with 5 *df*. This represents values of both B ($ss = 18.00$, with 1 *df*) and within cells ($ss = 12.00$, with 4 *df*).

From the preceding it follows that instead of specifying ERROR=WITHIN, the following design statements can be used:

DESIGN=B, A WITHIN B(1), A WITHIN B(2)/

DESIGN=A, B WITHIN A(1), B WITHIN A(2).

Notice that in each case I added the factor within which the simple effects are studied. Therefore, its sum of squares and *df* would *not* be relegated to the error term.

PRINT. MANOVA has extensive print options. For each keyword, options are placed in parentheses. For illustrative purposes, I show how to print cell information: means, standard deviations, and confidence intervals. Stating PARAMETERS (without options) results in the printing of the same information as when ESTIM is placed in parentheses (see the following commentary on the output).

DESIGN. This must be the last subcommand. When stated without specifications, a full factorial analysis of variance is carried out (i.e., all main effects and interactions). More than one

DESIGN statement may be used. Here I am using two additional DESIGN statements for tests of simple effects (see the following commentary on the output).

Output

* * * * * ANALYSIS OF VARIANCE -- DESIGN 1 * * * * *

Tests of Significance for Y using UNIQUE sums of squares

Source of Variation	SS	DF	MS	F	Sig of F
WITHIN CELLS	12.00	4	3.00		
A	2.00	1	2.00	.67	.460
B	18.00	1	18.00	6.00	.070
A BY B	50.00	1	50.00	16.67	.015

Commentary

In the interest of space, I did not include the output for the means. Except for a difference in nomenclature for the error term (WITHIN CELLS here, *MSR* in regression analysis), the preceding is the same as the results I reported earlier (compare it with Table 12.3). Most computer programs report the probability of an *F* given that the null hypothesis is true, thereby obviating the need to resort to a table. Assuming $\alpha = .05$, Sig of F shows that only the interaction is statistically significant. Earlier, I pointed out that there are times when probabilities not reported in statistical tables are necessary (e.g., when dividing α by the number of comparisons). Under such circumstances, output such as that reported under Sig of F is very useful.

Output

A

Parameter	Coeff.	Std. Err.	t-Value	Sig. t
2	−.50000000	.61237	−.81650	.460

B

Parameter	Coeff.	Std. Err.	t-Value	Sig. t
3	−1.5000000	.61237	−2.44949	.070

A BY B

Parameter	Coeff.	Std. Err.	t-Value	Sig. t
4	2.50000000	.61237	4.08248	.015

Commentary

The Coeff(icients) reported here are the same as those I obtained earlier in the regression analysis with effect coding. As I explained earlier, each coefficient indicates the effect of the term with which it is associated. For example, −.5 is the effect of the first level of A. If necessary, reread the following sections: (1) "The Regression Equation" and (2) "Regression Coefficient for Interaction."

As in regression analysis, dividing a coefficient by its standard error (Std. Err.) obtains a *t* ratio with *df* equal to those for the error term. Earlier, I stated that such tests are, in general, not of interest in designs with categorical independent variables, and I therefore did not include them in the regression output. However, when a factor consists of two levels only, the test of the coefficient is equivalent to the test of the factor. This is the case in the present example, where each *t* ratio is equal to the square root of its corresponding *F* ratio reported earlier.

Output

* * * * * ANALYSIS OF VARIANCE -- DESIGN 2 * * * * *

Tests of Significance for Y using UNIQUE sums of squares

Source of Variation	SS	DF	MS	F	Sig of F
WITHIN CELLS	12.00	4	3.00		
A WITHIN B(1)	16.00	1	16.00	5.33	.082
A WITHIN B(2)	36.00	1	36.00	12.00	.026

Commentary

Earlier I obtained the same results from regression analyses by hand and by computer (see Table 12.7 for a summary). Assuming that $\alpha = .05$, you could conclude that both simple effects are statistically not significant, as the probabilities of their *F* ratios are greater than .025. If necessary, reread the earlier discussion of this topic.

Output

A WITHIN B(1)

Parameter	Coeff.	Std. Err.	t-Value	Sig. t
2	2.00000000	.86603	2.30940	.082

A WITHIN B(2)

Parameter	Coeff.	Std. Err.	t-Value	Sig. t
3	−3.0000000	.86603	−3.46410	.026

Commentary

The coefficients reported here are the same as those I obtained previously in the hand calculations, where I showed that each such term is a composite of the main effect and the interaction term under consideration. Notice that the *t* ratios are equal to the square roots of the *F* ratios reported above.

Output

* * * * * ANALYSIS OF VARIANCE -- DESIGN 3 * * * * *

Tests of Significance for Y using UNIQUE sums of squares

Source of Variation	SS	DF	MS	F	Sig of F
WITHIN CELLS	12.00	4	3.00		
B WITHIN A(1)	4.00	1	4.00	1.33	.313
B WITHIN A(2)	64.00	1	64.00	21.33	.010

Commentary

Compare these results with those reported in Table 12.7. As I concluded earlier, only the effect of B within A_2 is statistically significant at the .05 level ($p < .025$). That is, there is a statistically significant difference between B_1 and B_2 at A_2. In the interest of space, I did not reproduce the parameter estimates for DESIGN 3.

DUMMY CODING

In my regression analyses of the 2×2 design in the preceding sections, I used effect coding.[6] It is of course possible to do the analysis with dummy coding, although I recommend that you refrain from doing so. In fact, *my sole purpose in this section is to show the inadvisability of using dummy coding in factorial designs.*

Turning first to mechanics, coding main effects with dummy coding is the same as with effect coding, except that instead of assigning -1's to the last category of each factor, 0's are assigned. As in the previous analyses, the vectors for the interaction are generated by cross multiplying the vectors for the main effects.

The overall results (e.g., R^2, F ratio) from an analysis with dummy coding are the same as those with effect coding. Like effect coding, the dummy vectors for main effects are not correlated. However, unlike effect coding, the *product vector representing the interaction is correlated with the dummy vectors representing the main effects.* Therefore, unlike effect coding, with dummy coding

$$R^2_{Y.A,B,AB} \neq R^2_{Y.A} + R^2_{Y.B} + R^2_{Y.AB}$$

The preceding should not be construed as implying that getting the correct results with dummy coding is not possible, but rather that an adjustment for the intercorrelations between the coded vectors is necessary. What this amounts to is that the proportion of variance (or the regression sum of squares) due to the interaction has to be calculated as the increment due to the product vector *after the main effects have been taken into account.* For the design under consideration, this means

$$R^2_{Y.A,B,AB} - (R^2_{Y.A} + R^2_{Y.B})$$

Stated differently, the proportion of variance due to the interaction is the squared semipartial correlation of Y with the interaction vector, while partialing the main effects from the latter (see Chapter 7, especially "Multiple Regression and Semipartial Correlations").

When doing the analysis by computer, you can accomplish this by entering the interaction vector last. To demonstrate this as well as to highlight hazards of overlooking the special properties of dummy coding in factorial designs, I will analyze the data in Table 12.1, using REGRESSION of SPSS.

SPSS

Input

TITLE TABLE 12.1, USING DUMMY CODING.
DATA LIST/A 1 B 2 Y 3-4.
IF (A EQ 1) A1=1.

[6]As I pointed out earlier, in a 2×2 design, effect and orthogonal coding are indistinguishable.

```
IF (B EQ 1) B1=1.
IF (A EQ 2) A1=0.
IF (B EQ 2) B1=0.
COMPUTE  A1B1=A1*B1.
BEGIN DATA
1112
1110
1210
12 8
21 7
21 7
2217
2213
END DATA
LIST.
REGRESSION VAR=Y TO A1B1/DES/STAT ALL/DEP=Y/
   ENTER A1/ENTER B1/ENTER A1B1/
   TEST (A1) (B1) (A1B1).
```

Commentary

This layout is virtually the same as the one I used for effect coding, except that I use the IF statements to generate dummy vectors. I enter the three coded vectors sequentially, with the product vector being the last. The order of entry of the main effects vectors is immaterial, as they are not correlated.

Output

A	B	Y	A1	B1	A1B1
1	1	12	1.00	1.00	1.00
1	1	10	1.00	1.00	1.00
1	2	10	1.00	.00	.00
1	2	8	1.00	.00	.00
2	1	7	.00	1.00	.00
2	1	7	.00	1.00	.00
2	2	17	.00	.00	.00
2	2	13	.00	.00	.00

Correlation:

	Y	A1	B1	A1B1
Y	1.000	−.156	−.469	.090
A1	−.156	1.000	.000	.577
B1	−.469	.000	1.000	.577
A1B1	.090	.577	.577	1.000

Commentary

I reproduced the listing of the data so that you may see the dummy vectors generated by the IF statements.

Examine the correlation matrix and notice that whereas the correlation between A1 and B1 is zero, the correlation between these two vectors and A1B1 is .577. It is because of these correlations that A1B1 has to be entered last so as to obtain the correct proportion of variance (and regression sum of squares) accounted by the interaction.

Output

Equation Number 1   Dependent Variable..   Y

Variable(s) Entered on Step Number 1..   A1

					DF	Sum of Squares
R Square	.02439	R Square Change	.02439	Regression	1	2.00000

Variable(s) Entered on Step Number 2..   B1

					DF	Sum of Squares
R Square	.24390	R Square Change	.21951	Regression	2	20.00000

Variable(s) Entered on Step Number 3..   A1B1

				Analysis of Variance			
Multiple R	.92394				DF	Sum of Squares	Mean Square
R Square	.85366	R Square Change	.60976	Regression	3	70.00000	23.33333
Adjusted R Square	.74390	F Change	16.66667	Residual	4	12.00000	3.00000
Standard Error	1.73205	Signif F Change	.0151	F = 7.77778		Signif F = .0381	

Commentary

I reproduced only information relevant for present purposes. As I explained in connection with the earlier analysis, the regression sum of squares at each step is cumulative. Thus, when B1 is entered (the second step), the regression sum of squares (20.0) is for A1 *and* B1 (as is R Square). Therefore, the regression sum of squares due to B1 is 18.0 (20.0 − 2.0). Similarly, the regression sum of squares due to the interaction is 50.0 (70.0 − 20.0). Compare the values reported in the preceding with those given earlier for the analysis with effect coding and you will find that they are identical (compare them also with Table 12.3). Thus, a judicious order of entry of the dummy vectors yields correct results.

Output

-- Variables in the Equation --

Variable	B	SE B	Part Cor	Tolerance	VIF	T	Sig T
A1	−6.000000	1.732051	−.662589	.500000	2.000	−3.464	.0257
B1	−8.000000	1.732051	−.883452	.500000	2.000	−4.619	.0099
A1B1	10.000000	2.449490	.780869	.333333	3.000	4.082	.0151
(Constant)	15.000000	1.224745					

Commentary

I will not comment on the properties of the regression equation for dummy coding, except to note that they are determined in relation to the mean of the cell assigned 0's in all the vectors (A_2B_2 in the present example. See the preceding listing of data). For example, the intercept (Constant) is equal to the mean of the aforementioned cell. Nevertheless, application of the regression equation to "scores" on the coded vectors yields predicted scores equal to the means of the cells to which the individuals belong (you may wish to verify this, using the data listing in the previous output).

Specific properties of the regression coefficients aside, it will be instructive to examine the meaning of tests of significance applied to them. In Chapter 5 (see "Testing Increments in Proportion of Variance Accounted For"), I showed that a test of a regression coefficient (b) is tantamount to a test of the proportion of variance accounted for by the variable with which it is associated when it is entered last in the analysis (see also Chapter 10). Accordingly, a test of the b associated with the interaction (A1B1) is the same as a test of the proportion of variance it increments when it is entered last. Notice that $T^2 = 4.082^2 = 16.66 = F$ for the R Square change at the last step (see the preceding).

In light of the specific order of entry of coded vectors required for dummy vectors, it should be clear that *only the test of the b for the interaction is valid.* Testing the other b's (i.e., for the main effects) would go counter to the required order of entry of the coded vectors. Note that had I, *erroneously,* interpreted tests of b for main effects, the conclusions would have gone counter to those I arrived at earlier, where I found that only the interaction is statistically significant at the .05 level (see Table 12.3 and the discussion related to it). In case you are wondering why I discussed what may appear obvious to you, I would like to point out that tests of all the b's when only the one for the variable (or coded vector) entered last is valid are relatively common in the research literature (I give some examples in Chapters 13 and 14). I believe that this is due, in part, to the fact that the tests are available in computer output. This should remind you that not all computer output is relevant and/or valid for a given research question. In fact, it is for this reason that I reproduced the Part Cor(relations), which I introduced in Chapter 7 under the synonym semipartial correlation. As was true for tests of the b's (see the preceding paragraph), only the semipartial correlation of Y with A1B1 (partialing A1 and B1 from the latter) is relevant for present purposes. Notice that $.780869^2 = .61$ is the proportion of variance incremented by the interaction vector when it is entered last in the analysis (see the previous output as well as earlier sections, where I obtained the same value). Finally, I reproduced Tolerance and VIF to illustrate what I said about these topics in Chapter 10. Specifically, neither Tolerance nor VIF is 1.0 because the vectors are correlated.

Output

Equation Number 1	Dependent Variable..	Y		
Block Number 4.	Method: Test	A1	B1	A1B1

Hypothesis Tests

DF	Sum of Squares	Rsq Chg	F	Sig F	Source
1	36.00000	.43902	12.00000	.0257	A1
1	64.00000	.78049	21.33333	.0099	B1
1	50.00000	.60976	16.66667	.0151	A1B1

3	70.00000	7.77778	.0381	Regression
4	12.00000			Residual
7	82.00000			Total

Commentary

Earlier in this chapter, I introduced this type of output to show its usefulness for the analysis of factorial designs. I reproduced the preceding output to show that it would be *wrong* to use it to analyze factorial designs with dummy coding. Even a glance at the sums of squares and the Rsq Chg should reveal that something is amiss. Suffice to point out that the sum of the regression sums of squares reported above ($36 + 64 + 50 = 150$) far exceeds the overall regression sum of squares (70). Actually, it even exceeds the total sum of squares (82). Similarly, the sum of Rsq Chg (1.82927) not only far exceeds the overall R^2, but is also greater than 1. If you took the square roots of the values reported under Rsq Chg, you would find that they are equal to the values reported under Part Cor in the previous output. Accordingly, only values associated with the interaction term are relevant.

To repeat, I carried out the analysis of a factorial design with dummy coding to show why you should refrain from using this coding scheme in such designs, and why you should be particularly alert when reading reports in which it was used (see "A Research Example," later in this chapter. For additional discussion of pitfalls in using dummy coding for factorial designs, see O'Grady & Medoff, 1988).

OTHER COMPUTER PROGRAMS

Having analyzed the data in Table 12.1 in detail through SPSS in preceding sections, I show now how to analyze the same example with program 4V of BMDP (Dixon, 1992, Vol. 2, pp. 1259–1310). In line with what I said in Chapter 4, I give only brief excerpts of the output and brief commentaries. If you run 4V, compare your output with that of SPSS I gave earlier. When necessary, reread my commentaries on the SPSS output.

BMDP

Input

```
/PROBLEM TITLE IS 'TABLE 12.1. 2 × 2. PROGRAM 4V'.
/INPUT VARIABLES=3. FORMAT IS '(2F1.0,F2.0)'.
/VARIABLE NAMES ARE A,B,Y.
/BETWEEN FACTORS=A,B.
 CODES(A)=1,2. CODES(B)=1,2.
 NAME (A)=A1,A2. NAME(B)=B1,B2.
/WEIGHT BETWEEN=EQUAL.
/PRINT CELLS. MARGINALS=ALL.
/END
1112
1110
1210
```

```
12 8
21 7
21 7
2217
2213
/END
ANALYSIS PROC=FACT. EST. UNISUM./
ANALYSIS PROC=SIMPLE./
END/
```

Commentary

For an introduction to BMDP, see Chapter 4. The versatility of 4V is evident even from its name: "Univariate and Multivariate Analysis of Variance and Covariance, Including Repeated Measures." The user is aptly cautioned: "Effective use of the advanced features of this program requires more than a casual background in analysis of variance" (Dixon, 1992, Vol. 2, p. 1259). Here, I am using the program in a very limited sense to do tests of simple effects. Later in this chapter, I show how to use it to test interaction contrasts.

VARIABLES. Of the three "variables" read as input, the first two are for identification of the two factors and the third is the dependent variable. See NAMES in the subsequent statement.

FORMAT. For illustrative purposes, I use a fixed format, according to which the first two variables occupy one column each, whereas the dependent variable occupies two columns.

BETWEEN. This refers to between subjects or grouping factors, in contrast to WITHIN subjects factors in repeated measures designs.

CODES. The categories of each factor are listed. They are named in the subsequent statement.

WEIGHT. I specify equal cell weights. For a description and other options, see Dixon (1992, Vol. 2, p. 1301).

When, as in the present example, the data are part of the input file, they "must come between the first /END paragraph and the first ANALYSIS paragraph" (Dixon, 1992, Vol. 2, p. 1266).

For illustrative purposes, I call for two analyses (1) a full FACT(orial) and (2) SIMPLE effects. EST(imate) "prints parameter estimates for specified linear-model components" (Dixon, 1992, Vol. 2, p. 1303) and yields the same estimates I obtained in the preceding sections through SPSS. UNISUM "prints compact summary table . . . in a classical ANOVA format" (Dixon, 1992, Vol. 2, p. 1302). It is these tables that I reproduce as follows.

Note that the ANALYSIS paragraph and the final END paragraph are terminated by slashes.

Output

SOURCE	SUM OF SQUARES	DF	MEAN SQUARE	F	TAIL PROB.
A	2.00000	1	2.00000	0.67	0.46
B	18.00000	1	18.00000	6.00	0.07
AB	50.00000	1	50.00000	16.67	0.02
ERROR	12.00000	4	3.00000		

Commentary

This summary table is part of the output from the first ANALYSIS statement. Compare these results with those of SPSS REGRESSION given earlier as well as with Table 12.3.

Output

SOURCE	SUM OF SQUARES	DF	MEAN SQUARE	F	TAIL PROB.
B.C: B AT A1	4.00000	1	4.00000	1.33	0.31
ERROR	12.00000	4	3.00000		

SOURCE	SUM OF SQUARES	DF	MEAN SQUARE	F	TAIL PROB.
B.C: B AT A2	64.00000	1	64.00000	21.33	0.01
ERROR	12.00000	4	3.00000		

SOURCE	SUM OF SQUARES	DF	MEAN SQUARE	F	TAIL PROB.
A.C: A AT B1	16.00000	1	16.00000	5.33	0.08
ERROR	12.00000	4	3.00000		

SOURCE	SUM OF SQUARES	DF	MEAN SQUARE	F	TAIL PROB.
A.C: A AT B2	36.00000	1	36.00000	12.00	0.03
ERROR	12.00000	4	3.00000		

Commentary

The preceding are excerpts from results of simple effects analyses generated by the second ANALYSIS statement. Compare them with the results I obtained earlier through SPSS and also with Table 12.7.

MULTICATEGORY FACTORS

The approaches I introduced in the preceding sections for the case of a 2×2 design generalize to two-factor designs of any dimensions. For illustrative purposes, I will analyze a 3×3 design in this section. In the context of the analysis, I will introduce, among other topics, multiple comparisons among main effects and interaction contrasts.

A Numerical Example

I present illustrative data for a 3×3 design in Table 12.9. The data in the first two columns and the first two rows are the same as those of Table 12.1, that is, the data I used in the preceding sections to illustrate analyses of a 2×2 design.

Table 12.9   Illustrative Data for a Three-by-Three Design

	B_1	B_2	B_3	$\overline{Y}_A$
A_1	12 10	10 8	8 6	9
A_2	7 7	17 13	10 6	10
A_3	16 14	14 10	17 13	14
$\overline{Y}_B$	11	12	10	$\overline{Y} = 11$

NOTE: $\overline{Y}_A$ = means for the three *A* categories; $\overline{Y}_B$ = means for the three *B* categories; and $\overline{Y}$ = grand mean.

Graphic Depiction

Following procedures I outlined earlier in this chapter (see Figure 12.2 and the discussion related to it), I plotted the cell means for the data of Table 12.9 in Figure 12.3, from which it is evident that there is an interaction between *A* and *B* (the line segments are *not* parallel). Assuming that the higher the score the greater the effectiveness of the treatment, then it can be seen, for instance, that at A_2, B_2 is the most effective treatment, and it is quite disparate from B_1 and B_3. At A_3, however, B_2 is the least effective treatment, and the effects of B_1 and B_3 are alike. Examine the figure for other patterns.

Coding the Independent Variables

Following the approach I explained and used in earlier sections, I placed the dependent variable scores in a single vector, *Y*, to be regressed on coded vectors representing the main effects and the interaction. Recall that each factor is coded as if it is the only one in the design. As always, the number of coded vectors necessary to represent a factor equals the number of its categories minus one (i.e., number of *df*). In the present example, two coded vectors are necessary to

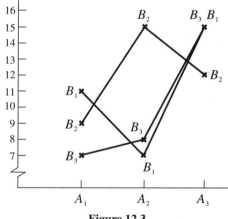

Figure 12.3

represent each factor.[7] As I explained earlier in this chapter, the vectors representing the interaction are generated by multiplying, in turn, the vectors representing one factor by the vectors representing the other factor. For the present example, I will generate four vectors (equal to the number of *df*) to represent the interaction.

In this section, I use effect coding. Subsequently, I analyze the same data using orthogonal coding. In both instances, I generate the coded vectors by the computer program (instead of making them part of the input file). As in the preceding sections, I present first a detailed analysis through SPSS, and then I give sample input and output for other packages.

SPSS

Input

```
TITLE TABLE 12.9. A 3 BY 3 DESIGN.
DATA LIST/A 1 B 2 Y 3-4.
COMPUTE A1=0.
COMPUTE A2=0.
COMPUTE B1=0.
COMPUTE B2=0.
IF (A EQ 1) A1=1.
IF (A EQ 3) A1=−1.
IF (A EQ 2) A2=1.
IF (A EQ 3) A2=−1.
IF (B EQ 1) B1=1.
IF (B EQ 3) B1=−1.
IF (B EQ 2) B2=1.
IF (B EQ 3) B2=−1.
COMPUTE A1B1=A1*B1.
COMPUTE A1B2=A1*B2.
COMPUTE A2B1=A2*B1.
COMPUTE A2B2=A2*B2.
BEGIN DATA
1112
1110
1210
12 8
13 8
13 6
21 7
21 7
2217
2213
```

[7]As another example, assume that *A* consisted of four categories and *B* of five, then it would be necessary to use three coded vectors to represent the former and four coded vectors to represent the latter. Later in this chapter, I show that this approach generalizes to higher-order designs.

```
2310
23 6
3116
3114
3214
3210
3317
3313
END DATA
LIST VAR=A TO A2B2.
REGRESSION VAR Y TO A2B2/DES/STAT ALL/
   DEP Y/ENTER A1 A2/ENTER B1 B2/ENTER A1B1 TO A2B2/
   TEST (A1 A2)(B1 B2)(A1B1 TO A2B2).
MANOVA Y BY A(1,3) B(1,3)/ERROR=WITHIN/
   PRINT=CELLINFO(MEANS)PARAMETERS(ALL) SIGNIF(SINGLEDF)/
   DESIGN/
   DESIGN=A WITHIN B(1), A WITHIN B(2), A WITHIN B(3)/
   DESIGN=B WITHIN A(1), B WITHIN A(2), B WITHIN A(3).
```

Commentary

As in Chapter 11, I use COMPUTE statements to generate vectors comprised of 0's, which I then use in the IF statements. I will not comment on the rest of the input as it follows the same pattern as that for the 2×2 design I analyzed in the preceding section. If necessary, refer to my commentaries on the input file for the 2×2 design.

As in the earlier analysis, I omitted from this input file statements I used for other analyses (e.g., an analysis with orthogonal coding). Later, when I present results of analyses generated by statements omitted from the input file given in the preceding, I follow the practice of listing only the relevant omitted statements.

Output

A	B	Y	A1	A2	B1	B2	A1B1	A1B2	A2B1	A2B2
1	1	12	1.00	.00	1.00	.00	1.00	.00	.00	.00
1	1	10	1.00	.00	1.00	.00	1.00	.00	.00	.00
1	2	10	1.00	.00	.00	1.00	.00	1.00	.00	.00
1	2	8	1.00	.00	.00	1.00	.00	1.00	.00	.00
1	3	8	1.00	.00	−1.00	−1.00	−1.00	−1.00	.00	.00
1	3	6	1.00	.00	−1.00	−1.00	−1.00	−1.00	.00	.00
2	1	7	.00	1.00	1.00	.00	.00	.00	1.00	.00
2	1	7	.00	1.00	1.00	.00	.00	.00	1.00	.00
2	2	17	.00	1.00	.00	1.00	.00	.00	.00	1.00
2	2	13	.00	1.00	.00	1.00	.00	.00	.00	1.00
2	3	10	.00	1.00	−1.00	−1.00	.00	.00	−1.00	−1.00
2	3	6	.00	1.00	−1.00	−1.00	.00	.00	−1.00	−1.00
3	1	16	−1.00	−1.00	1.00	.00	−1.00	.00	−1.00	.00

3	1	14	−1.00	−1.00	1.00	.00	−1.00	.00	−1.00	.00
3	2	14	−1.00	−1.00	.00	1.00	.00	−1.00	.00	−1.00
3	2	10	−1.00	−1.00	.00	1.00	.00	−1.00	.00	−1.00
3	3	17	−1.00	−1.00	−1.00	−1.00	1.00	1.00	1.00	1.00
3	3	13	−1.00	−1.00	−1.00	−1.00	1.00	1.00	1.00	1.00

Commentary

Examine this listing to see how the COMPUTE and IF statements generated the effect coded vectors.

Output

	Mean	Std Dev
Y	11.000	3.662
A1	.000	.840
A2	.000	.840
B1	.000	.840
B2	.000	.840
A1B1	.000	.686
A1B2	.000	.686
A2B1	.000	.686
A2B2	.000	.686

N of Cases =   18

Correlation:

	Y	A1	A2	B1	B2	A1B1	A1B2	A2B1	A2B2
Y	1.000	−.574	−.459	.115	.229	.187	.234	−.047	.468
A1	−.574	1.000	.500	.000	.000	.000	.000	.000	.000
A2	−.459	.500	1.000	.000	.000	.000	.000	.000	.000
B1	.115	.000	.000	1.000	.500	.000	.000	.000	.000
B2	.229	.000	.000	.500	1.000	.000	.000	.000	.000
A1B1	.187	.000	.000	.000	.000	1.000	.500	.500	.250
A1B2	.234	.000	.000	.000	.000	.500	1.000	.250	.500
A2B1	−.047	.000	.000	.000	.000	.500	.250	1.000	.500
A2B2	.468	.000	.000	.000	.000	.250	.500	.500	1.000

Commentary

Recall that when cell frequencies are equal, the means of effect coded vectors are equal to zero. Further, effect coded vectors representing main effects and interactions are mutually orthogonal. In other words, coded vectors of one factor are not correlated with coded vectors of other factors, nor are they correlated with coded vectors representing interactions.[8] Always examine the means and the correlation matrix to verify that they have the aforementioned properties. When this is not true of either the means or the correlation matrix, it serves as a clue that there is an error(s) in the input file (e.g., incorrect: category identifications, input format, IF statements).

Because of the absence of correlations among effect coded vectors representing different components of the model (see the preceding), each set of vectors representing a given component provides unique information. As a result, the overall R^2 for the present model can be expressed as follows:

$$R^2_{Y.A,B,AB} = R^2_{Y.A} + R^2_{Y.B} + R^2_{Y.AB}$$

where the subscripts A and B stand for factors, whatever the number of coded vectors representing them, and AB stands for the interaction between *A* and *B,* whatever the number of coded vectors representing it. Clearly, then, the regression of *Y* on a set of coded vectors representing a given main effect or an interaction yields an independent component of the variance accounted for and, equivalently, an independent component of the regression sum of squares (see the following).

As you can see from the correlation matrix, vectors representing a given component (main effect or interaction) *are* correlated. This, however, poses no difficulty, as vectors representing a given component should be treated as a set; *not* as separate variables (see Chapter 11 for a discussion of this point). In fact, depending on how the codes are assigned, a given vector may be shown to account for a smaller or a larger proportion of variance. But, taken together, the set of coded vectors representing a given component will always account for the same proportion of variance, regardless of the specific codes assigned to a given category.

In view of the foregoing, when a factorial design is analyzed with effect coding it is necessary to group the contributions made by the vectors that represent a given component. This can be done whatever the order in which the individual vectors are entered into the analysis (i.e., even when vectors are entered in a mixed order). It is, however, more convenient and more efficient to group each set of vectors representing a factor or an interaction term and enter the sets sequentially. The sequence itself is immaterial because, as I pointed out earlier, the sets of coded vectors are mutually orthogonal. In the previous input file, I specified the following order of entry for vectors representing the different components of the design: (1) *A,* (2) *B,* and (3) *A × B.*

Output

Equation Number 1	Dependent Variable..	Y			
Block Number 1.	Method: Enter	A1	A2		

				DF	Sum of Squares	Mean Square
R Square	.36842	R Square Change	.36842	Regression	2	84.00000	42.00000

Block Number 2.	Method: Enter	B1	B2

				DF	Sum of Squares
R Square	.42105	R Square Change	.05263	Regression	4	96.00000

---

[8]Earlier, I showed that this is not true for dummy coding, and I therefore recommended that it not be used to analyze factorial designs.

Block Number 3.		Method: Enter	A1B1	A1B2	A2B1	A2B2
Multiple R	.90805			Analysis of Variance		
R Square	.82456	R Square Change	.40351		DF	Sum of Squares	Mean Square
Adjusted R Square	.66862	F Change	5.17500	Regression	8	188.00000	23.50000
Standard Error	2.10819	Signif F Change	.0192	Residual	9	40.00000	4.44444
				F =	5.28750	Signif F =	.0112

Commentary

As I explained earlier, I reproduce only relevant output from each step. For example, for Block 1 the Mean Square regression is relevant. This, however, is not true of the Mean Square regression for Block 2, as it refers to both A and B. What we want is the mean square regression for the latter only (see below). All the information for Block 3 is relevant, albeit from different perspectives. For instance, the regression sum of squares for this block refers to what all the terms in the model account for (i.e., main effects and interaction). Thus, the Mean Square is relevant if one wishes to test this overall term, which is equivalent to testing the overall R Square (.82456), to which $F = 5.28750$, with 8 and 9 df, refers. Earlier in this chapter, I pointed out that in factorial designs such tests are generally not revealing. Yet, from a statistical perspective they are correct. As another example, R Square Change for each block is relevant, though the F Change associated with it is relevant only for the last block, as only for this block is the appropriate error term used in the denominator of the F ratio (i.e., the error after all the terms of the model have been taken into account). Compare the F Change for the last term with the F ratio for the interaction calculations that follow.

Probably the simplest approach with output such as the preceding is to (1) determine the regression sum of squares for each term and its df, (2) divide the regression sum of squares by its df to obtain a mean square, and (3) divide each mean square by the overall mean square reported in the output. I do this now for the present example.

From Block 1: mean square for $A = 42.00$. Dividing this term by the Mean Square Residuals: $F = 42.00/4.44 = 9.46$, with 2 and 9 df, $p < .05$ (see the table of F distribution in Appendix B).

Subtracting the regression sum of squares of Block 1 from that of Block 2, the regression sum of squares for $B = 12.00$ (96 − 84). Similarly, subtracting df of Block 1 from those of Block 2, df for $B = 2 (4 − 2)$.[9] The mean square for $B = 6.00$ (12.00/2), and $F = 1.35$ (6.00/4.44), with 2 and 9 df, $p > .05$.

Following the same procedure, the regression sum of squares for the interaction is 92 (188 − 96), with 4 (8 − 4) df. The mean square for the interaction is 23 (92/4), and $F = 5.18$ (23/4.44), with 4 and 9 df, $p < .05$ (compare this F ratio with the F Change for R Square Change for Block 3). I summarized the results of the analysis in Table 12.10, using a format similar to that I used in Table 12.3.

In case you have been wondering why I bothered to carry out the above calculations when they are available in the output as a result of using the TEST subcommand (see the discussion that follows), I did it (1) in the hope of further enhancing your understanding of SPSS output, and (2) to show what you may have to do if you are using a computer program for regression analysis that does not have a feature similar to that of TEST.

---

[9]Though we know that df for a given component equal the number of coded vectors representing it, I wanted to show that the df can be obtained in a manner analogous to that of obtaining the regression sum of squares, that is, by subtracting df of a preceding step from those of the step under consideration.

Table 12.10   Summary of Multiple Regression Analysis for Data in Table 12.9

Source	prop.	ss	df	ms	F
A	.36842	84.00	2	42.00	9.46*
B	.05263	12.00	2	6.00	1.35
A × B	.40351	92.00	4	23.00	5.18*
Residual		40.00	9	4.44	
Total		228.00	17		

NOTE: *prop.* = proportion of variance accounted for. For example, 84.00/228.00 = .36842. These values are reported at each step of the output, under R Square Change. Of course, their sum is equal to the overall R Square.
*$p < .05$.

Output

Block Number 4.   Method: Test   A1   A2   B1   B2   A1B1   A1B2   A2B1   A2B2

Hypothesis Tests

DF	Sum of Squares	Rsq Chg	F	Sig F	Source			
2	84.00000	.36842	9.45000	.0061	A1	A2		
2	12.00000	.05263	1.35000	.3071	B1	B2		
4	92.00000	.40351	5.17500	.0192	A1B1	A1B2	A2B1	A2B2
8	188.00000		5.28750	.0112	Regression			
9	40.00000				Residual			
17	228.00000				Total			

Commentary

I reproduced this output to show that when using SPSS you can get the same information as in Table 12.10 without going through the calculations. Also, as I explained earlier, having this type of output obviates the need to refer to a table of the *F* distribution. Values in the Sig F column equal to or less than α are statistically significant.

Output

Variable	B
A1	−2.000000
A2	−1.000000
B1	0.000000
B2	1.000000
A1B1	2.000000
A1B2	−1.000000
A2B1	−3.000000
A2B2	4.000000
(Constant)	11.000000

Table 12.11   Main Effects and Interaction Terms for Data in Table 12.9

	B_1	B_2	B_3	A Effects
A_1	$2 = b_{A1B1}$	$-1 = b_{A1B2}$	-1	$-2 = b_{A1}$
A_2	$-3 = b_{A2B1}$	$4 = b_{A2B2}$	-1	$-1 = b_{A2}$
A_3	1	-3	2	3
B Effects:	$0 = b_{B1}$	$1 = b_{B2}$	-1	

NOTE: The values I obtained from the regression equation are identified by subscripted b's. Other values are *not* part of the regression equation. I obtained them considering the constraint that effects of a factor sum to zero, as is the sum of a row or column of interaction terms. For explanation, see earlier sections in this chapter.

Commentary

Earlier in this chapter, I explained the properties of the regression equation for effect coding. To recapitulate: a (intercept, Constant) is equal to the grand mean of the dependent variable. Each b represents an effect of either a treatment identified in the vector with which it is associated or an interaction term for a cell identified in the vector. I summarized the preceding in Table 12.11, using a format similar to the one I used in Table 12.8. Although various statistics are reported in the output alongside B (e.g., t ratios), they are not relevant for present purposes. Therefore I did not reproduce them.

Simple Effects

Recall that pursuant to a statistically significant interaction, the analysis of simple effects can shed light on its nature. Earlier, I showed how to use MANOVA of SPSS for this purpose. I used similar statements in the input file given earlier. Following are excerpts of the output generated by these statements.

Output

* * * * * ANALYSIS OF VARIANCE -- DESIGN 2 * * * * * *

Tests of Significance for Y using UNIQUE sums of squares

Source of Variation	SS	DF	MS	F	Sig of F
WITHIN CELLS	40.00	9	4.44		
A WITHIN B(1)	64.00	2	32.00	7.20	.014
A WITHIN B(2)	36.00	2	18.00	4.05	.056
A WITHIN B(3)	76.00	2	38.00	8.55	.008

* * * * * ANALYSIS OF VARIANCE -- DESIGN 3 * * * * * *

Tests of Significance for Y using UNIQUE sums of squares

Source of Variation	SS	DF	MS	F	Sig of F
WITHIN CELLS	40.00	9	4.44		
B WITHIN A(1)	16.00	2	8.00	1.80	.220
B WITHIN A(2)	76.00	2	38.00	8.55	.008
B WITHIN A(3)	12.00	2	6.00	1.35	.307

Commentary

Verify that the sum of the sum of squares for simple effects for a given factor is equal to the sum of squares for the factor in question plus the sum of squares for the interaction. If necessary, see "Simple Effects from Overall Regression Equation," earlier in this chapter, for an explanation.

Assuming that the .05 level was selected, then $.05/3 = .017$ would be used for these comparisons. Based on the p values reported under Sig of F, one would conclude that the following are statistically significant: A WITHIN B(1), A WITHIN B(3), B WITHIN A(2).

When, as in the present example, a statistically significant F ratio for a simple effect has more than one df for its numerator, simple comparisons (Keppel, 1991, p. 245) may be carried out so that statistically significant differences between treatments, or treatment combinations, at a given level of another factor may be pinpointed. I later show how this is done.

Before turning to the next topic, I show, again, how information such as that reported in Table 12.11 may be used to calculate sums of squares for simple effects. I do this to enhance your understanding of this approach so that you may employ it when a program you use does not provide information in the form obtained above from MANOVA.

For illustrative purposes, I will calculate the sum of squares for A WITHIN B(1). Examine Table 12.11 and notice that for cell A_1B_1 the relevant values are -2 (the effect of A_1) and 2 (this cell's interaction term). For cell A_2B_1 the analogous terms are -1 (effect of A_2) and -3 (the interaction term). For cell A_3B_1 the relevant terms are 3 (main effect of A_3) and 1 (the interaction term). Recalling that there are two subjects in each cell, the sum of squares for A at B_1 is

$$2[(-2+2)^2 + (-1-3)^2 + (3+1)^2] = 64$$

Compare with the value reported in the output above.[10]

This sum of squares is divided by its df (2, in the present case) to obtain a mean square, which is then divided by the *MSR* from the overall analysis (4.44, in the present example) to yield an F ratio. I suggest that you use the relevant terms from Table 12.11 to replicate the MANOVA results reported in the preceding. If necessary, see the earlier explanation of the approach I outlined here.

MULTIPLE COMPARISONS

Earlier, I pointed out that when, as in the present analysis, the interaction is statistically significant, it is not meaningful to do multiple comparisons among main effects. Instead, tests of simple effects are carried out, as I did in the preceding section, or interaction contrasts are tested, as I show later on. Nevertheless, I take this opportunity to show how to do multiple comparisons among main effects.

Main Effects Comparisons

A statistically nonsignificant interaction means that the treatment effects of one factor are *not* dependent on levels of the other factor with which they are combined. Under such circumstances, it makes sense to do multiple comparisons among main effects. Such comparisons are carried out

---

[10]Earlier in this chapter (see the input file for the 2×2 design), I showed an alternative approach for obtaining sums of squares for simple effects through the use of SPLIT FILE.

in the same manner as I did in Chapter 11 for comparisons among means in a single-factor design, except that the mean square residuals (*MSR*) from the overall analysis of the factorial design is used in the denominator. Because my discussion of multiple comparisons among means for a single categorical independent variable (i.e., post hoc, planned orthogonal and nonorthogonal) in Chapter 11 applies equally to multiple comparisons among main effects in factorial designs, I will not repeat it. Instead, using the data in Table 12.9 and *assuming, for illustrative purposes, that the interaction is statistically not significant,* I will show how to carry out multiple comparisons of main effects.

In Chapter 11, I gave a formula for the test of a comparison—see (11.15) and the discussion related to it. When applied to comparisons among main effects of a given factor, say *A,* this formula takes the following form:

$$F = \frac{[C_1(\overline{Y}_{A_1}) + C_2(\overline{Y}_{A_2}) + \ldots + C_i(\overline{Y}_{A_i})]^2}{MSR\left[\Sigma\dfrac{(C_i)^2}{n_i}\right]} \tag{12.6}$$

where *C* is a coefficient applied to the mean of a given treatment (recall from Chapter 11 that the sum of the coefficients for a given comparison is zero); *MSR* is the mean square residual from the overall analysis of the factorial design; n_i is the number of subjects in treatment *i*—that is, all the subjects administered treatment A_i whatever treatment *B* they were administered. The *F* ratio has 1 and $N - k - 1$ *df,* where *k* is the number of coded vectors in the factorial design (i.e., for the main effects and the interaction). In other words, the denominator *df* are those for the *MSR.* An expression similar to (12.6) is used for a comparison among main effects of *B,* except that $\overline{Y}_{A_i}$ and n_i are replaced by $\overline{Y}_{B_j}$ and n_j.

I now apply (12.6) to two comparisons: (1) between A_1 and A_2 and (2) between the average of A_1 and A_2 and that of A_3. From Table 12.9, $\overline{Y}_{A_1} = 9$, $\overline{Y}_{A_2} = 10$, $\overline{Y}_{A_3} = 14$, and from Table 12.10, *MSR* = 4.44. For the first comparison,

$$F = \frac{[(1)(9) + (-1)(10)]^2}{4.44\left[\dfrac{1^2}{6} + \dfrac{(-1)^2}{6}\right]} = \frac{1}{1.48} = .68$$

with 1 and 9 *df.*

For the second comparison,

$$F = \frac{[(-1)(9) + (-1)(10) + (2)(14)]^2}{4.44\left[\dfrac{(-1)^2}{6} + \dfrac{(-1)^2}{6} + \dfrac{2^2}{6}\right]} = \frac{81}{4.44} = 18.24$$

with 1 and 9 *df.*

The critical value of *F* for such comparisons depends on what type they are (i.e., planned orthogonal or nonorthogonal, post hoc). Note that the preceding comparisons are orthogonal. If the comparisons were planned, the preselected α would be used for each *F.* If the comparisons were planned but not orthogonal, then $\alpha/2$ would be used.

Finally, if the comparisons were done post hoc, then one would have to select from among various post hoc multiple comparisons approaches. In Chapter 11, I presented the Scheffé method only. Assuming that one were to use it for the preceding comparisons then to be declared statistically significant, the *F* ratio would have to exceed $k_A F_{\alpha; kA, N-k-1}$, where k_A = number of coded vectors used to represent factor *A* or the number of *df* associated with factor *A*. $F_{\alpha; kA, N-k-1}$ is the tabled value of F at α with k_A df for the numerator and $N - k - 1$ df for the denominator, where k is the total number of coded vectors for the factorial design. In other words, $N - k - 1$ are the df for the MSR. For comparisons for factor B, replace k_A with k_B, where the latter is the number of coded vectors used to represent factor B. As $k_A = k_B$ in the present example, the same critical value of F would apply to comparisons for either factor.

Assuming that I selected $\alpha = .05$, the tabled value of F with 2 and 9 df is 4.26 (see Appendix B). Therefore, the critical value of F for the present example is 8.52 (2×4.26). The F ratio for the second comparison exceeds this critical value and would therefore be declared statistically significant.

Simple Comparisons

Earlier I pointed out that when the numerator df for an F ratio for a test of simple effects is greater than 1, tests of simple comparisons can be carried out to pinpoint statistically significant differences between treatments, or treatment combinations, at a given level of another factor. The procedure for carrying out such tests is the same as that shown for tests of multiple comparisons—that is, by applying (12.6)—except that n_i in the denominator is replaced by n_{ij} (the number of subjects within the cell in question).

In the example under consideration, each test of simple effects has 2 df for the numerator of the F ratio (see, e.g., the MANOVA output). For illustrative purposes, I will show how to carry out simple comparisons between A treatments within B_1. Specifically, I will test the difference between (1) A_1 and A_2 and (2) A_2 and A_3.

The cell means for A_1, A_2, and A_3 under B_1 are 11, 7, and 15, respectively; $MSR = 4.44$, with 9 df; $n_{ij} = 2$. Applying (12.6) to test the simple comparison between A_1 and A_2 at B_1:

$$F = \frac{[(1)(11) + (-1)(7)]^2}{4.44 \left[\frac{1^2}{2} + \frac{(-1)^2}{2} \right]} = \frac{16}{4.44} = 3.60$$

with 1 and 9 df.

Testing the simple comparison between A_2 and A_3 at B_1:

$$F = \frac{[(1)(7) + (-1)(15)]^2}{4.44 \left[\frac{1^2}{2} + \frac{(-1)^2}{2} \right]} = \frac{64}{4.44} = 14.41$$

with 1 and 9 df. As in the case of tests of simple effects, the critical value of F depends on whether the comparison is planned (orthogonal or nonorthogonal) or post hoc.

When I introduced multiple comparisons in Chapter 11, I pointed out that it is complex and controversial. This is even more so for the case of tests of simple effects and simple comparisons. For instance, there is no agreement on how and under what circumstances α ought to be controlled. For some views on these topics, see Keppel (1991, pp. 245–248), Kirk (1982, pp. 367–370), Maxwell and Delaney (1990, pp. 265–266), and Toothaker (1991, pp. 122–126).

OTHER COMPUTER PROGRAMS

Later in this chapter, I present input files and excerpts of output for BMDP and SAS programs. Here, I give an input file for MINITAB to analyze the 3×3 design (Table 12.9), which I analyzed earlier through SPSS. Subsequent to commentaries on the input, I reproduce brief excerpts of the output and comment on them. If you are running MINITAB, compare your output with SPSS output given in preceding sections.

MINITAB

Input

```
GMACRO
T129
OUTFILE='T129.MIN';
  NOTERM.
NOTE TABLE 12.9.   3 × 3.   USING REGRESSION.
READ C1-C3;
  FORMAT (2F1,F2).          [fixed format]
1112
1110
1210
12 8
13 8
13 6
21 7
21 7
2217
2213
2310
23 6
3116
3114
3214
3210
3317
3313
END
ECHO
NAME C1='A' C2='B' C3='Y'
INDICATOR C1 C4-C6       [create dummy vectors using C1. Put in C4-C6]
INDICATOR C2 C7-C9       [create dummy vectors using C2. Put in C7-C9]
LET C10=C4-C6            [I use the LET commands to generate
LET C11=C5-C6            four effect coded vectors. For example,
LET C12=C7-C9            in the first, C6 is subtracted from C4
LET C13=C8-C9            to create A1. See NAME for vectors created]
NAME C10='A1' C11='A2' C12='B1' C13='B2'
PRINT C1-C3 C10-C13
LET C14=C10*C12          [generate product vectors for the interaction.
LET C15=C10*C13          See NAME command]
LET C16=C11*C12
```

```
LET C17=C11*C13
NAME C14='A1B1' C15='A1B2' C16='A2B1' C17='A2B2'
PRINT C14-C17
DESCRIBE C10-C17          [calculate descriptive statistics for C10-C17]
CORRELATION C10-C17       [calculate correlation matrix for C10-C17]
REGRESS C3 8 C10-C17      [regress Y on the effect coded vectors]
NOTE TABLE 12.9.   3 × 3.  USING GLM.
GLM Y=A│B;                [Y is dependent. Generate full factorial]
BRIEF 3;
XMATRIX M1.               [put the design matrix in M1]
PRINT M1                  [print the design matrix]
ENDMACRO
```

Commentary

For an introduction to MINITAB, see Chapter 4, where I explained, among other things, that I am running in batch mode, using *.MAC input files. Instead of placing the data in the input file, as I did here, I could have placed them in an external file (for an example, see the MINITAB input file for the analysis of Table 11.5 in Chapter 11). I remind you that the italicized comments are *not* part of the input file. For a more detailed explanation of the INDICATOR command, see the MINITAB input file in Chapter 11 for the analysis of Table 11.5.

I show how the analysis can be carried out using (1) REGRESS (Minitab Inc., 1995a, Chapter 9) and (2) GLM (Minitab Inc., 1995a, pp. 10-40 to 10-50).

Output

MTB > REGRESS C3 8 C10-C17

The regression equation is
$Y = 11.0 - 2.00\,A1 - 1.00\,A2 + 0.000\,B1 + 1.00\,B2 + 2.00\,A1B1$
$- 1.00\,A1B2 - 3.00\,A2B1 + 4.00\,A2B2$

$s = 2.108$ R-sq $= 82.5\%$ R-sq(adj) $= 66.9\%$

Analysis of Variance

SOURCE	DF	SS	MS	F	p
Regression	8	188.000	23.500	5.29	0.011
Error	9	40.000	4.444		
Total	17	228.000			

Commentary

The preceding are excerpts from the overall regression analysis. As I explained earlier, $F = 5.29$, with 8 and 9 *df*, is for the overall regression sum of squares (i.e., for the main effects and the interaction) or, equivalently, for the overall R-sq(uare) $= .825$.

Output

SOURCE	DF	SEQ SS
A1	1	75.000
A2	1	9.000
B1	1	3.000
B2	1	9.000
A1B1	1	8.000
A1B2	1	6.000
A2B1	1	6.000
A2B2	1	72.000

Commentary

Seq SS = sequential sum of squares, that is, the regression sum of squares accounted for by the listed vectors in their order of entry. In my commentaries on the input and output of SPSS for the same example earlier in this chapter, I pointed out that (1) the effect coded vectors are mutually orthogonal and (2) vectors representing a given factor or the interaction have to be treated as a set. Using output such as the preceding, the latter is easily accomplished: simply add the Seq SS associated with vectors representing a given component. Thus, $ss_{reg}(A) = 84$ (75 + 9), with 2 *df*; $ss_{reg}(B) = 12$ (3 + 9), with 2 *df*; and $ss_{reg}(AB) = 92$ (8 + 6 + 6 + 72), with 4 *df*. Compare this with GLM output below and with the SPSS output given earlier, or compare this with Table 12.10.

To obtain intermediate results analogous to those given in SPSS output, replace the single REGRESS statement with the following three:

```
REGRESS C3 2 C10-C11
REGRESS C3 4 C10-C13
REGRESS C3 8 C10-C17
```

Output

```
MTB  > GLM Y=A|B;
SUBC> BRIEF 3;
SUBC> XMATRIX M1.
```

Analysis of Variance for Y

Source	DF	Seq SS	Adj SS	Adj MS	F	P
A	2	84.000	84.000	42.000	9.45	0.006
B	2	12.000	12.000	6.000	1.35	0.307
A*B	4	92.000	92.000	23.000	5.17	0.019
Error	9	40.000	40.000	4.444		
Total	17	228.000				

Term	Coeff
Constant	11.0000
A	
1	−2.0000
2	−1.0000
B	
1	0.0000
2	1.0000
A*B	
1 1	2.0000
1 2	−1.0000
2 1	−3.0000
2 2	4.0000

Commentary

GLM reports Seq(uential) and Adj(usted) sums of squares (see Minitab Inc., 1995a, p. 10-40). In REGRESS output (see the preceding), sequential sums of squares were reported for each vector.[11] GLM reports sequential sums of squares for each factor and their interactions. Compare the values reported here with my summations of the sequential sums of squares for the separate components of this design.

Adjusted sums of squares refer to sums of squares incremented by each component when it is entered last into the analysis (hence the term adjusted). In factorial designs with equal cell frequencies (balanced designs), the adjusted sums of squares equal the corresponding sequential sums of squares. See my earlier discussion of vectors representing different components being mutually orthogonal.

Compare the preceding output with the SPSS output given earlier or with Tables 12.10 and 12.11.

If you ran MINITAB with an input file such as the one I gave earlier, you would find that, except for a vector of 1's for the intercept, M1—the design matrix—consists of effect coded vectors identical to those I generated by the LET statements and used in the regression analysis. For a discussion of the design matrix, see Minitab Inc. (1995a, pp. 10-48 to 10-49).

ORTHOGONAL CODING

I introduced orthogonal coding in Chapter 11, where I applied it in a single-factor design. The same approach is applicable in factorial designs. As with effect coding, each factor is coded separately. Interaction vectors are generated by multiplying each vector of one factor by each vector of the other factor. The dependent variable is then regressed on the orthogonally coded vectors. For illustrative purposes, I apply orthogonal coding to the 3×3 design (Table 12.9) I analyzed earlier with effect coding.

---

[11]As I explained in Chapter 11, coded vectors are treated as distinct variables in multiple regression programs. It is the user's responsibility to treat vectors representing a given variable as a set.

As a substantive example, assume that (1) A_1 and A_2 are two different drugs for the treatment of hypertension and that A_3 is a placebo; (2) B_1 is a low-sodium diet, B_2 is exercise, and B_3 is a control (i.e., neither diet nor exercise).[12] Without going into theoretical considerations, and bearing in mind that the fictitious data are *not* meant to reflect any measure (e.g., the numbers do not reflect hypertension), I will assume that a researcher is interested in testing the following hypotheses: (1) A_1 is more effective than A_2, (2) the average effect of A_1 and A_2 is greater than the effect of A_3, (3) B_1 is more effective than B_2, and (4) the average effect of B_1 and B_2 is greater than the effect of B_3. Construct four coded vectors to reflect these hypotheses and verify that they are orthogonal. If you are having difficulties, refer to Chapter 11 (the section on orthogonal coding). Also see the following input and commentaries.

When I presented the input file for the analysis of the data in Table 12.9 with effect coding earlier in this chapter, I pointed out that I omitted from it some statements that I would give later, along with output generated by them. In the following input file, I give the omitted statements. You can use them to run the analyses separately by adding relevant statements (i.e., TITLE, DATA LIST, BEGIN DATA, the data, END DATA). Alternatively, you can run simultaneously the analyses shown here and those done earlier, in which case some statements in the original input file would have to be edited to accommodate the additional analyses. Having run the analyses simultaneously, I show a statement from the earlier analyses that I edited. I identify it in the input file by an italicized comment, and I comment on it in the commentary on the input, where I also discuss the need to edit command terminators.

SPSS

Input

```
. . . . . . . . . . . .                              [see commentary]
IF (A EQ 1)A1O=1.
IF (A EQ 2)A1O=-1.
IF (A EQ 3)A1O=0.
IF (A EQ 1)A2O=1.
IF (A EQ 2)A2O=1.
IF (A EQ 3)A2O=-2.
IF (B EQ 1)B1O=1.
IF (B EQ 2)B1O=-1.
IF (B EQ 3)B1O=0.
IF (B EQ 1)B2O=1.
IF (B EQ 2)B2O=1.
IF (B EQ 3)B2O=-2.
COMPUTE A1OB1O=A1O*B1O.
COMPUTE A1OB2O=A1O*B2O.
```

---

[12]Among other examples that come readily to mind are (1) A_1 and A_2 are two types of "innovative" teaching methods, whereas A_3 is the "traditional" method. B_1 and B_2 are two kinds of rewards, whereas B_3 is no reward. (2) *A* consists of three therapies, and *B* of three diagnostic groups. (3) *A* consists of three leadership styles, and *B* consists of three settings.

```
COMPUTE A2OB1O=A2O*B1O.
COMPUTE A2OB2O=A2O*B2O.
. . . . . . . . . . . . . . . . . . .        [see commentary]
LIST VAR=A B Y A1O TO A2OB2O.
REGRESSION VAR Y TO A2OB2O/DES/STAT ALL/      [edit]
. . . . . . . . . . . . . . . . . . .        [see commentary]
 DEP Y/ENTER A1O TO A2OB2O/
 TEST (A1O A2O)(B1O B2O)(A1OB1O TO A2OB2O).
. . . . . . . . . . . . . . . . . . .
 SIGNIF(SINGLEDF)/     [place after MANOVA line from earlier input]
 CONTRAST(A)=SPECIAL(1   1   1
                     1  -1   0
                     1   1  -2)/
 CONTRAST(B)=SPECIAL(1  1 1 1  -1  0 1 1  -2).
```

Commentary

Dotted lines are meant to stand for statements from the input file I used earlier for the analysis with effect coding that should be included in the present input file (e.g., TITLE, DATA LIST). I remind you that italicized comments are *not* part of the input file.

To distinguish between effect and orthogonal vectors, I labeled the latter A1O, A2O, and so forth.

REGRESSION. Replace A2B2 with A2OB2O so that both types of coded vectors would be available for analysis.

ENTER A1O TO A2OB2O. Unlike the analysis with effect coding, I enter all the coded vectors simultaneously. I discuss this point in the following commentary on Variables in the Equation.

TEST. As I pointed out in Chapter 4, the SPSS input files I give are for the PC version in which command terminators (a period by default) are required. (Command terminators are not required on the mainframe version. Instead, all subcommands have to be indented at least one space.) Notice the period at the end of TEST. In the input file given earlier, the period was at the end of TEST for effect coding. If you want to run simultaneously the analysis described here and the one with effect coding done earlier in this chapter, and if you place the subcommands for the analysis with orthogonal coding after those with effect coding, then delete the period after the first TEST subcommand. Alternatively, you can delete the period at the end of TEST in the statements given here, and place the subcommands for the analysis with orthogonal coding before those for the analysis with effect coding.

SIGNIF. This is one of the keywords on the print subcommand in MANOVA. Among its options is SINGLEDF, that is, print results for single *df*. In the commentary on the output generated by this keyword, I explain why I use it in the present analysis.

CONTRAST. For an explanation of this MANOVA subcommand, see Norušis/SPSS Inc. (1993b, pp. 398–400). When specifying SPECIAL, as I did, it is necessary to enter "a square matrix in parentheses with as many rows and columns as there are levels in the factor. The first row represents the mean effect of the factor and is generally a vector of 1's" (Norušis/SPSS Inc., 1993b, p. 400). Although the matrix can be stated on a single line (see CONTRAST for B), I stated the one for A in matrix format to show more clearly the contrasts I specified. As you can see, the second and third lines of the matrix contain the orthogonal contrasts for A, as I discussed earlier and generated by the IF statements (see the following output). This is also true for the B contrasts, where the fourth, fifth, and sixth codes constitute the first contrast and the seventh, eighth, and ninth constitute the second contrast.

Output

A	B	Y	A1O	A2O	B1O	B2O	A1OB1O	A1OB2O	A2OB1O	A2OB2O
1	1	12	1.00	1.00	1.00	1.00	1.00	1.00	1.00	1.00
1	1	10	1.00	1.00	1.00	1.00	1.00	1.00	1.00	1.00
1	2	10	1.00	1.00	−1.00	1.00	−1.00	1.00	−1.00	1.00
1	2	8	1.00	1.00	−1.00	1.00	−1.00	1.00	−1.00	1.00
1	3	8	1.00	1.00	.00	−2.00	.00	−2.00	.00	−2.00
1	3	6	1.00	1.00	.00	−2.00	.00	−2.00	.00	−2.00
2	1	7	−1.00	1.00	1.00	1.00	−1.00	−1.00	1.00	1.00
2	1	7	−1.00	1.00	1.00	1.00	−1.00	−1.00	1.00	1.00
2	2	17	−1.00	1.00	−1.00	1.00	1.00	−1.00	−1.00	1.00
2	2	13	−1.00	1.00	−1.00	1.00	1.00	−1.00	−1.00	1.00
2	3	10	−1.00	1.00	.00	−2.00	.00	2.00	.00	−2.00
2	3	6	−1.00	1.00	.00	−2.00	.00	2.00	.00	−2.00
3	1	16	.00	−2.00	1.00	1.00	.00	.00	−2.00	−2.00
3	1	14	.00	−2.00	1.00	1.00	.00	.00	−2.00	−2.00
3	2	14	.00	−2.00	−1.00	1.00	.00	.00	2.00	−2.00
3	2	10	.00	−2.00	−1.00	1.00	.00	.00	2.00	−2.00
3	3	17	.00	−2.00	.00	−2.00	.00	.00	.00	4.00
3	3	13	.00	−2.00	.00	−2.00	.00	.00	.00	4.00

Commentary

I reproduced the preceding so that you may see the orthogonally coded vectors generated by the IF and COMPUTE statements.

In the interest of space, I did not reproduce the means and the correlation matrix. I trust that, in light of my discussion of orthogonal coding in Chapter 11, you know that the means of and the correlations among the coded vectors are equal to zero. I return to these issues in the commentary on Variables in the Equation next.

The overall results of the analysis (not reproduced here) are the same as those I obtained in the earlier analysis with effect coding.

Output

-- Variables in the Equation --

Variable	B	SE B	Beta	Correl	Part Cor	T	Sig T
A1O	−.500000	.608581	−.114708	−.114708	−.114708	−.822	.4325
A2O	−1.500000	.351364	−.596040	−.596040	−.596040	−4.269	.0021

B1O	−.500000	.608581	−.114708	−.114708	−.114708	−.822	.4325
B2O	.500000	.351364	.198680	.198680	.198680	1.423	.1885
A1OB1O	2.500000	.745356	.468293	.468293	.468293	3.354	.0085
A1OB2O	.000000	.430331	.000000	.000000	.000000	.000	1.0000
A2OB1O	−1.000000	.430331	−.324443	−.324443	−.324443	−2.324	.0452
A2OB2O	.500000	.248452	.280976	.280976	.280976	2.012	.0750
(Constant)	11.000000	.496904					

Commentary

As with effect coding, a (Constant) is equal to the mean of the dependent variable. The properties of the orthogonally coded vectors render regression statistics (e.g., R^2, regression sum of squares, regression equation) and tests of significance easily obtainable by hand calculations. For instance, the square of the zero-order correlation of any coded vector with Y (Correl, in the preceding output) indicates the proportion of variance accounted for by the comparison reflected in the vector. And, of course, the sum of the squared zero-order correlations of the coded vectors with Y is equal to the overall R^2 (.82456, in the present example).

Examine the columns labeled Beta and Part Cor(relation) and notice that, as expected, they are identical to Correl. Parenthetically, all the tolerance and VIF values (not reproduced here) equal 1.00. If you are experiencing difficulty with any of the preceding statements, I suggest that you reread relevant sections in Chapters 5, 7, 9, and 11.

In Chapter 11, I showed that though the sizes of unstandardized regression coefficients (B in the previous output) for orthogonally coded vectors are affected by the values of the codes used, tests of significance of the B's are *not* affected by them. As always, the test of a B is also a test of the associated beta and the semipartial correlation. With orthogonal coding, a test of a B is also a test of the associated zero-order correlation. To clarify this point, I repeat (5.27) with a new number.

$$F = \frac{(R^2_{y.12...k_1} - R^2_{y.12...k_2})/(k_1 - k_2)}{(1 - R^2_{y.12...k_1})/(N - k_1 - 1)} \tag{12.7}$$

where $R^2_{y.12...k_1}$ = squared multiple correlation for the regression of Y on k_1 coded vectors (the larger coefficient); and $R^2_{y.12...k_2}$ = squared multiple correlation for the regression of Y on k_2 coded vectors. When (12.7) is applied to the special case under consideration, $k_2 = k_1 - 1$ coded vectors, that is, all the coded vectors but one whose contribution to the R^2 is being tested. N = sample size. The F ratio has $k_1 - k_2$ (1, in the case under consideration) *df* for the numerator and $N - k_1 - 1$ *df* for the denominator. I will note two things about (12.7).

One, in Chapter 5 and subsequent chapters I applied (5.27) in designs where k_1 and k_2 were variables. By contrast, in defining the terms of (12.7) I was careful to refer to k_1 and k_2 as coded vectors. This may strike some as nitpicking, especially in light of the tendency of many authors and researchers to refer to coded vectors as variables (e.g., as when speaking of "dummy variables"). It is because of such usage, which may lead unwary researchers astray, that I stress this distinction. Of course, (5.27) and (12.7) are indistinguishable in the mechanics of their application.

Two, as I stated earlier, for the special case under consideration, *df* = 1 for numerator of (12.7). Further, recalling that in the design under consideration the coded vectors are orthogonal, it follows that the numerator of (12.7) is the squared zero-order correlation of a coded vector with the dependent variable. As always, the error term (the denominator) is from the overall analysis.

I will illustrate this application of (12.7) to the testing of the first two of the orthogonal comparisons I specified earlier. From the previous output (Variables in the Equation), the correlation of Y with A1O (the first orthogonal contrast) is $-.11471$. In my earlier analyses of these data I found overall $R^2 = .82456$. Hence,

$$F = \frac{(-.11471)^2}{(1 - .82456^2)/(18 - 8 - 1)} = .675$$

with 1 and 9 *df*. In the preceding, the *t* ratio for b_{A1O} is reported as $-.822$. Recall that $t^2 = F$, when the numerator *df* for the latter is 1. Thus, $(-.822)^2 = .676$ is, within rounding, the same as the *F* ratio for the test of the squared zero-order correlation.

Turning to the second comparison, the previous output shows that the correlation of Y with A2O is $-.59604$. Hence,

$$F = \frac{(-.59604)^2}{(1 - .82456^2)/(18 - 8 - 1)} = 18.225$$

with 1 and 9 *df*. The *t* ratio for the test of b_{A2O} (the *b* for the second contrast) is -4.269 (see the previous output), and $t^2 = 18.224$ is, within rounding, the same as the *F* ratio. I suggest that, as an exercise, you calculate the *F* ratio for the squared correlation of Y with each of the other coded vectors and verify that it is equal to the squared *t* for the corresponding *b*.

Output

* * * * * ANALYSIS OF VARIANCE -- DESIGN 1 * * * * * *

Tests of Significance for Y using UNIQUE sums of squares

Source of Variation	SS	DF	MS	F	Sig of F
WITHIN CELLS	40.00	9	4.44		
A	84.00	2	42.00	9.45	.006
1ST Parameter	3.00	1	3.00	.67	.433
2ND Parameter	81.00	1	81.00	18.23	.002
B	12.00	2	6.00	1.35	.307
1ST Parameter	3.00	1	3.00	.67	.433
2ND Parameter	9.00	1	9.00	2.03	.188
A BY B	92.00	4	23.00	5.17	.019
1ST Parameter	50.00	1	50.00	11.25	.008
2ND Parameter	.00	1	.00	.00	1.000
3RD Parameter	24.00	1	24.00	5.40	.045
4TH Parameter	18.00	1	18.00	4.05	.075

Commentary

The preceding is an excerpt from the MANOVA run. Notice the legend about the UNIQUE sums of squares used in tests of significance. I introduced the notion of uniqueness in Chapter 9 (see "Commonality Analysis"), where I defined it as the proportion of variance incremented by a variable when it is entered last in the analysis. Recall also that the test of a regression coefficient is tantamount to testing the uniqueness of the variable with which it is associated. Thus, the tests of single parameters (see explanation that follows) are analogous to tests of b's.

Notice the organization of the table: for each component (i.e., A, B, A BY B) are reported the sum of squares, *df,* and F ratio, which are the same as the values I obtained through the regression analyses and summarized in Table 12.10. The single parameters under each component are reported because I used the SINGLEDF option (see the input file). As I pointed out, the test of each parameter is analogous to the test of the b corresponding to it. Thus each F ratio reported here for a single parameter is equal to the square of the t ratio associated with the corresponding b of the regression equation for orthogonal coding given earlier. For example, for the first parameter under A, $\sqrt{.67} = .82$, which is the same value as the t ratio for b_{A1O}. For the second parameter under A, $\sqrt{18.23} = 4.27$, which is equal to the t ratio for b_{A2O}. Verify that the same is true for the other parameters.

When I discussed tests of orthogonal comparisons in Chapter 11, I pointed out that the average of the F ratios for such comparisons is equal to the overall F ratio. If you were to average the 8 F ratios for the single parameters you would find it to be 5.287, which is the same as the F ratio for the overall R^2 calculated earlier. As another example, the average of the F ratios for the two parameters under A is 9.45 [(.67 + 18.23)/2], which is the same as the F ratio for A.

In the previous output, sums of squares are reported. As always, to convert a regression sum of squares to a proportion of variance accounted for, divide it by the total sum of squares. For the example under consideration, the total sum of squares is 228.00 (see, for example, Table 12.10). Thus, the proportion of variance accounted for by the first comparison under A is 3.00/228.00 = .013, which is the square of the zero-order correlation of Y with A1O. This is also true for the other terms, which you may want to calculate and compare with the squared zero-order correlations of respective coded vectors with the dependent variable.

In the preceding analyses, I found that the interaction between A and B is statistically significant. Therefore, following my earlier recommendation, one would refrain from testing and interpreting the results of main effects. Instead, one would carry out tests of simple effects in a manner I showed earlier or via interaction contrasts (see the following). *For illustrative purposes, I will pretend here that the interaction is statistically not significant.* Accordingly, from the tests of the b's for the orthogonal comparisons for the main effects or, equivalently, from the tests of the single parameters under A and B, it would be concluded (based on Sig T for the former or Sig of F for the latter) that only comparison A2O is statistically significant. Recall that A2O reflects the contrast between the average of A_1 and A_2 with that of A_3. Notice that the sign of b_{A2O} is negative. Thus, assuming that the lower the score on the dependent variable the "better," one would conclude that the hypothesis was supported. Referring to one of the substantive examples I introduced in connection with the illustrative data, one would conclude that the average effect of two drugs on hypertension is greater than that of a placebo.

Remember, however, that the interaction is statistically significant. As I presented earlier tests of simple effects following a statistically significant interaction, I will not discuss them here. Instead, I turn to a presentation of interaction contrasts.

INTERACTION CONTRASTS

Most authors, I believe, recommend that a statistically significant interaction be followed by tests of simple effects (see the preceding sections). Some authors, notably Levin and Marascuilo

(Levin & Marascuilo, 1972, 1973; Marascuilo & Levin, 1970, 1976; see also Rosenthal & Rosnow, 1985; Rosnow & Rosenthal, 1989, 1991), assert that this is the wrong thing to do and advocate instead the use of interaction contrasts. Before I address the controversy surrounding the choice between the two approaches, I will show what interaction contrasts are and how they are calculated.

Calculating Interaction Contrasts

In designs greater than a 2×2, interaction contrasts may be used to pinpoint origins of an overall interaction.[13] Interaction contrasts can be planned (i.e., hypothesized) or post hoc (i.e., following a statistically significant interaction). Either way, they constitute a partitioning of the overall design into sets of 2×2 designs whose elements may be single cells or combinations of cells. To clarify how this is done, I begin by showing, with the aid of Figure 12.4, that such a partitioning was effected through the product vectors in the 3×3 design I analyzed earlier.

Examine the top portion of Figure 12.4 and notice, in the left margin, the nine cell identifications of the 3×3 design under consideration. Alongside the cell identifications are the codes of

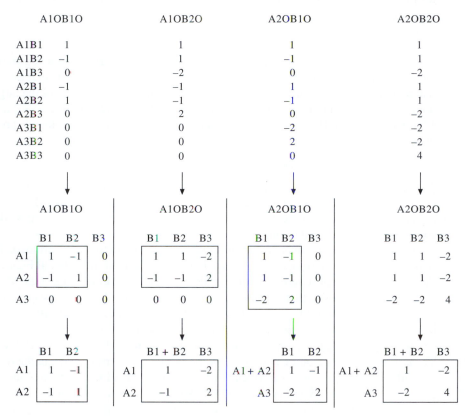

Figure 12.4

[13]See Boik (1979), for other types of contrasts, which he refers to as partial interactions. See also Keppel (1991, Chapter 12) and Kirk (1982, Chapter 8).

the interaction vectors I obtained as a result of cross multiplying the orthogonally coded vectors for the main effects. I took these codes from the data listing in the output given earlier and labeled them accordingly.

In the bottom portion of Figure 12.4, I display the same information in a factorial design format. Keep in mind that *the values in the cells are codes taken from the top portion of the figure.* From the bottom portion it is clear that each interaction vector generates a 2×2 design. In the segment on the left, labeled A1OB1O, four cells are used; the rest of the cells are ignored (they have 0 codes). In the other segments, some cells from the original design are combined to form single cells. For example, in the second segment from the left, labeled A1OB2O, B1 and B2 are combined to form single cells.

Earlier in this chapter (see "The Meaning of Interaction"), I showed that one way to determine whether two factors interact is to compare differences between cell means of one of the factors across all the levels of the other factor. For the 2×2 design formed by product vector A1OB1O (see the bottom portion of Figure 12.4), this translates into

$$\mu_{11} - \mu_{12} = \mu_{21} - \mu_{22} \tag{12.8}$$

where μ_{11} = population mean of cell A_1B_1, μ_{12} = population mean of cell A_1B_2, and so forth. Equation (12.8) implies that

$$\mu_{11} - \mu_{12} - \mu_{21} + \mu_{22} = 0 \tag{12.9}$$

Tests of contrasts such as the one depicted in (12.9) are carried out using statistics (i.e., cell means). When a contrast is not statistically significant one can conclude that the null hypothesis that there is no interaction in the population represented in the segment of the larger design cannot be rejected. Examine now the codes in the cells of the aforementioned 2×2 design in Figure 12.4, labeled A1OB1O, and notice that when applied to the cell means they express the contrast given by (12.9):

$$(1)(\overline{Y}_{A_1B_1}) + (-1)(\overline{Y}_{A_1B_2}) + (-1)(\overline{Y}_{A_2B_1}) + (1)(\overline{Y}_{A_2B_2})$$

Thus, the test of this contrast constitutes a test as to whether in this segment of the original 3×3 design there is an interaction between factors A and B (each at two levels). The same is true of the other 2×2 designs at the bottom of Figure 12.4, except that they were formed by combining some cells of the original design.

As I stated earlier, product vectors generated by cross multiplying the orthogonal vectors of the main effects are also orthogonal. As a result, the four contrasts depicted in Figure 12.4 partition the interaction sum of squares into independent components. Look back at the MANOVA output given earlier and notice that the sums of squares (SS) for the four contrasts are A1OB1O = 50, A1OB2O = 0, A2OB1O = 24, A2OB2O = 18. Each of these SS has 1 *df*, hence, each is also a mean square. Dividing each mean square by the within cells mean square (or the mean square residuals) yields the F ratio listed alongside it. Each F thus obtained has 1 *df* for the numerator. The *df* for the denominator equal those for the mean square error, which in the regression analysis with coded vectors was shown earlier to be $N - k - 1$. In the example under consideration, error *df* = 9 (see the MANOVA or REGRESSION output given earlier).

Look back at the output for the regression analysis with orthogonal coding, under Variables in the Equation, and notice that each *t* ratio associated with a *b* for an interaction vector (A1OB1O through A2OB2O) is equal to the square root of the corresponding F ratio reported in the MANOVA output. For example, the square of the *t* ratio for A1OB1O ($3.354^2 = 11.25$) is equal to the F ratio for the first parameter reported under MANOVA. Verify that the same is true for the other test statistics. Thus, as I explained earlier, the same results are obtained whether one uses multiple regression analysis with orthogonal coding or MANOVA with the same contrasts declared by the user (see SPECIAL CONTRASTS in the input file, and my commentary on them, earlier in this chapter).

The decision as to which of the interaction contrasts are declared statistically significant depends on whether they were planned or post hoc. In the case of the former, there is no agreement as to when α should be adjusted (e.g., divided by the number of contrasts, as in the Bonferroni approach; see Chapter 11). Some authors maintain that an adjustment is necessary only when the planned interaction contrasts are not orthogonal, whereas others maintain that an adjustment should be made even when the contrasts are orthogonal. For approaches to the testing of post hoc interaction contrasts, see Marascuilo and Levin (1970).

Assuming that I selected $\alpha = .05$, and that I planned the present orthogonal interaction, then, concurring with those asserting that no adjustment of α is necessary, the p values associated with each of the F or t ratios would be examined to see which of them is $\leq .05$. Based on such an examination in the REGRESSION or the MANOVA output for the present example, one would conclude that the first and the third interaction contrasts are statistically significant.

I address the paramount matter of interpretation of significant interaction contrasts later. For now, I comment briefly on the two statistically significant contrasts. Turning first to the contrast generated by A1OB1O (see the first 2×2 design at the bottom of Figure 12.4), one would conclude that A_1 and A_2 interact with B_1 and B_2. For this segment, the two lowest cell means are $A_2B_1 = 7$ and $A_1B_2 = 9$ (see Table 12.4).[14] Earlier, I used a substantive example where the dependent variable was hypertension, A_1 and A_2 two drugs, B_1 low sodium diet, and B_2 exercise. Also, I assumed that the lower the score the better. Accordingly, I would conclude that the pairing of drug A_2 with a low sodium diet (B_1) yields the best results, whereas the second best results are yielded when drug A_1 is paired with exercise (B_2).

Turning now to the second statistically significant interaction contrast, labeled A2OB1O in Figure 12.4, notice that it was generated by combining A_1 and A_2 into a single category, and crossing it and A_3 with B_1 and B_2. The substantive example in the preceding paragraph should show that this contrast is probably of dubious value. Without speculating about the effect of administering a combination of two unidentified drugs, it is necessary, at the very least, to acknowledge that medical researchers may view such combinations undesirable, if not downright dangerous. Be that as it may, I purposely used this example to demonstrate that *interaction contrasts generated by product vectors are not necessarily meaningful from a substantive perspective.*

Before I turn to the controversy surrounding the use and interpretation of interaction contrasts, I will show how you can calculate interaction contrasts using information obtained from a regression analysis with effect coding. I would like to stress that I am doing this *not* to show yet another analytic approach but rather because I believe that it will lead to a better understanding of what tests of interaction contrasts entail, thereby laying the ground for a better understanding of the controversy surrounding the choice between tests of simple effects and interaction contrasts.

---

[14]This interaction should come as no surprise when you recognize that it refers to data from the four cells I introduced as a 2×2 design in the beginning of this chapter (see Table 12.1). Recall that only the interaction was statistically significant in this design (see, for example, Table 12.3 and the discussion related to it).

Testing Interaction Contrasts Using Results from Effect Coding

In the preceding section, interaction contrasts were generated by default, so to speak, inasmuch as they were obtained as products of orthogonally coded vectors, regardless of whether or not they were substantively meaningful. My aim in this section is to show how to test interaction contrasts of interest by using results from a regression analysis with effect coding. Essentially, the approach is identical to the one I introduced in Chapter 11 for testing comparisons in a single-factor design and also used earlier in this chapter to test main-effects comparisons—see (12.6) and the discussion related to it. For comparative purposes, I will show how to apply (12.6) to test the same interaction contrasts generated in the preceding through the products of the orthogonally coded vectors.

The first step is to construct a 2×2 design, which you can test by selecting either four cells of interest or by combining relevant cells. Beginning with the former, assume that one wants to test the interaction contrast obtained from the crossing of A_1 and A_2 with B_1 and B_2 of the 3×3 design analyzed earlier (i.e., the data in Table 12.9). Recall that two people are in each of the cells under consideration. The cell means are $A_1B_1 = 11$, $A_1B_2 = 9$, $A_2B_1 = 7$, $A_2B_2 = 15$. From the output for the analysis of the 3×3 design with effect coding given earlier in this chapter, $MSR = 4.44444$. Formulating the contrast of interest in the format of (12.9) and using it as the numerator in (12.6),

$$F = \frac{[(1)(11) + (-1)(9) + (-1)(7) + (1)(15)]^2}{4.44444 \left[\frac{(1)^2}{2} + \frac{(-1)^2}{2} + \frac{(-1)^2}{2} + \frac{(1)^2}{2} \right]} = \frac{10^2}{(4.44444)(2)} = \frac{100}{8.88888} = 11.25$$

with 1 and 9 *df*. Compare this with t^2 for this comparison in the regression analysis with orthogonal coding or with the F ratio I obtained earlier when I tested this comparison through MANOVA with special contrasts.

Instead of using cell means in tests of interaction contrasts as in the preceding, seeing how the same can be accomplished by using interaction terms for the cells in question will be instructive. I turn now to this approach.

Tests of Interaction Contrasts via *b*'s

In Chapter 11, I showed how to use *b*'s from the equation with effect coding, instead of means, to test multiple comparisons among means. I show now, beginning with the contrast I analyzed earlier, that the same approach is applicable to tests of interaction contrasts. For convenience, in Table 12.12 I repeat the interaction terms I gave earlier in Table 12.11.

Recall that I obtained the elements identified by subscripts in Table 12.12 from the regression equation with effect coding and that the other elements I calculated considering the constraints

Table 12.12   Interaction Terms for Data in Table 12.9

	B_1	B_2	B_3
A_1	$2 = b_{A1B1}$	$-1 = b_{A1B2}$	-1
A_2	$-3 = b_{A2B1}$	$4 = b_{A2B2}$	-1
A_3	1	-3	2

NOTE: I took the values in this table from Table 12.11.

that the sums of rows and columns equal zero (if you are having problems with the preceding, see discussion related to Table 12.11). For the contrast I tested in the preceding, the interaction terms are $2 = b_{A1B1}, -1 = b_{A1B2}, -3 = b_{A2B1},$ and $4 = b_{A2B2}$. Applying (12.6),

$$F = \frac{[(1)(2) + (-1)(-1) + (-1)(-3) + (1)(4)]^2}{4.44444\left[\frac{(1)^2}{2} + \frac{(-1)^2}{2} + \frac{(-1)^2}{2} + \frac{(1)^2}{2}\right]} = \frac{10^2}{(4.44444)(2)} = 11.25$$

which is the same as the value I obtained when I used the corresponding means in the contrast.

Using the same approach, I show now the calculations of the remaining three interaction contrasts indicated at the bottom of Figure 12.4, which I tested earlier through regression analysis with orthogonal coding and through MANOVA with analogous special contrasts.

The second interaction contrast, labeled A1OB2O in Figure 12.4, was formed by combining B_1 and B_2 and crossing it and B_3 with A_1 and A_2. Using relevant interaction terms from Table 12.12,

$$F = \frac{[(1)(2) + (1)(-1) + (-2)(-1) + (-1)(-3) + (-1)(4) + (2)(-1)]^2}{4.44444\left[\frac{(1)^2}{2} + \frac{(1)^2}{2} + \frac{(-2)^2}{2} + \frac{(-1)^2}{2} + \frac{(-1)^2}{2} + \frac{(2)^2}{2}\right]} = \frac{0}{(4.44444)(6)} = 0$$

The third interaction contrast, labeled A2OB1O in Figure 12.4, was formed by combining A_1 and A_2 and crossing it and A_3 with B_1 and B_2. Using relevant interaction terms from Table 12.12,

$$F = \frac{[(1)(2) + (-1)(-1) + (1)(-3) + (-1)(4) + (-2)(1) + (2)(-3)]^2}{4.44444\left[\frac{(1)^2}{2} + \frac{(-1)^2}{2} + \frac{(1)^2}{2} + \frac{(-1)^2}{2} + \frac{(-2)^2}{2} + \frac{(2)^2}{2}\right]} = \frac{(-12)^2}{(4.44444)(6)} = 5.40$$

The fourth interaction contrast, labeled A2OB2O in Figure 12.4, was formed by crossing the combined A_1 and A_2, and A_3 with the combined B_1 and B_2, and B_3. Using the relevant interaction terms from Table 12.12,

$$F = \frac{[(1)(2) + (1)(-1) + (-2)(-1) + (1)(-3) + (1)(4) + (-2)(-1) + (-2)(1) + (-2)(-3) + (4)(2)]^2}{4.44444\left[\frac{(1)^2}{2} + \frac{(1)^2}{2} + \frac{(-2)^2}{2} + \frac{(1)^2}{2} + \frac{(1)^2}{2} + \frac{(-2)^2}{2} + \frac{(-2)^2}{2} + \frac{(-2)^2}{2} + \frac{(4)^2}{2}\right]} = \frac{(18)^2}{(4.44444)(18)} = 4.05$$

As you can see, using results from regression analysis with effect coding, any interaction contrast of interest may be tested with relative ease. The application of (12.9) to such contrasts is the same whether they are planned (orthogonal or nonorthogonal) or post hoc. The type of contrast tested determines whether and how α is adjusted (see the preceding).

Using interaction terms, instead of means, in tests of interaction contrasts, shows clearly that only these terms play a role. Moreover, the specific elements entering in any given contrast are evident.

Effect versus Orthogonal Coding: A Comment

The foregoing calculations demonstrate once more that the results from an analysis with effect coding can be used to test linear combinations of b's for any type of comparison (e.g., orthogonal, post hoc). What, then, is the advantage of using orthogonal instead of effect coding? The only advantage of orthogonal coding is that the tests of the orthogonal comparisons they reflect are obtained directly from the output (i.e., the tests of the b's). On the other hand, effect coding is simpler and yields a regression equation that reflects the general linear model. Moreover, multiple comparisons subsequent to an analysis with effect coding involve very simple calculations. In view of the preceding, effect coding appears to be the preferred method even when orthogonal comparisons are hypothesized, except when the calculations are to be done by hand.

Simple versus Interaction Contrasts: Interpretations and Controversies

Earlier, I drew attention to the controversy surrounding the choice between tests of simple effects and interaction contrasts. Authors who argue in favor of tests of interaction contrasts and against tests of simple effects (e.g., Marascuilo & Levin, 1970; see the preceding, for additional references) focus on the ambiguity of the latter inasmuch as they are addressed to main effects and interaction components. That this is indeed so can be seen from my earlier presentation of the analysis of simple effects (see, e.g., Table 12.7 and the discussion related to it).

Authors who reject arguments favoring interaction contrasts (e.g., Games, 1973; Meyer, 1991; Toothaker, 1991, pp. 119–121) do so on the grounds that they do not lend themselves to substantive interpretations and may even lead to substantively erroneous conclusions. This can, perhaps, be best understood when you recognize that a correct expression derived from a statistical model does not necessarily lend itself to a substantive interpretation. I dealt with such situations in Chapter 9, where I was critical of what were, in my opinion, futile attempts to invest elements obtained in a partitioning of variance of the dependent variables with substantive meanings (see, in particular, my discussion of commonality analysis).

Attempts to interpret interaction terms substantively imply that they are separate entities; not elements identified after taking into account the effects of treatment combinations. It would be well to remember that one administers treatments—*not* what is left after adjusting for treatment effects, which is what the interaction terms represent. This should not be construed to imply that the study of interactions is not meaningful or useless. Rather, the study of interactions is meant to shed light on the operation of main effects. That is, whether or not the effects of treatments of one factor depend on treatments or levels of another factor with which they are combined.

To clarify what I have in mind, I return to the 2×2 example, which I analyzed in the beginning of this chapter (introduced in Table 12.1). Recall that the interaction was statistically significant and that when I carried out tests of simple effects I found that only the difference between B_1 and B_2 at A_2 was statistically significant. Setting aside issues of statistical power analysis and various other considerations (e.g., costs), and assuming that the higher the score the better, one can conclude that the combination of B_2 with A_2 leads to the best results. But examine Table 12.5, where I listed the interaction terms for these data, and notice that, except for differences in sign, they are all the same (i.e., $|2.5|$). This, of course, is a consequence of the constraint that the sum of rows and columns equal zero. Therefore, regardless of the nature of the interaction (e.g., ordinal, disordinal), this pattern of interaction terms will always be found in a 2×2 design. Interpreting substantively such interaction terms, which are the ones I tested in interaction contrasts, may lead one to conclusions at variance with findings regarding the optimal combinations of treatments from two or more factors. In a similar vein, Meyer (1991) and Toothaker (1991, pp. 119–121) used Rosnow and Rosenthal's (1989) example, who advanced it to support their preference for interaction contrasts, to show that a treatment deemed beneficial based on an examination of simple effects is deemed harmful based on an examination of the interaction terms.

I do not mean to suggest that interaction contrasts should not be tested. As I showed in the 3×3 design I analyzed earlier (see Table 12.9), they are useful in pinpointing the origins of an overall interaction. Moreover, interaction contrasts may reflect a researcher's hypothesis. I am suggesting that, for substantive interpretations and practical considerations (e.g., decisions regarding combinations of treatments for optimal effects), statistically significant interaction contrasts be followed by tests of simple effects. For similar recommendations and good examples, see Keppel (1991, Chapter 12) and Keppel and Zedeck (1989, Chapter 15).

OTHER COMPUTER PROGRAMS

Before turning to the next topic, I present input files and excerpts of output for BMDP and SAS programs for the analysis of the 3×3 design (Table 12.9), which I analyzed thoroughly in preceding sections through SPSS. Instead of showing how to use coded vectors in the regression procedures from the aforementioned packages (I believe that, following earlier examples, you will have no difficulty in doing this), I use 4V of BMDP and GLM of SAS to acquaint you with some of their special features. Following my practice in presenting other computer programs, I give only brief excerpts of their output and, when necessary, make brief comments. If you are using either of these programs, study your output in conjunction with SPSS output given earlier.

BMDP

Input

```
/PROBLEM TITLE IS 'TABLE 12.9.   PROGRAM 4V.'.
/INPUT VARIABLES=3.   FORMAT IS   '(2F1.0,F2.0)'.
/VARIABLE NAMES ARE A,B,Y.
/BETWEEN FACTORS=A,B.
 CODES(A)=1 TO 3.   CODES(B)=1 TO 3.
 NAME (A)=A1,A2,A3.   NAME(B)=B1,B2,B3.
/WEIGHT BETWEEN=EQUAL.
/PRINT CELLS. MARGINALS=ALL.
/END
1112
1110
1210
12 8
13 8
13 6
21 7
21 7
2217
2213
2310
23 6
3116
3114
```

```
3214
3210
3317
3313
/END
ANALYSIS PROC=FACT.EST. UNISUM./
ANALYSIS PROC=SIMPLE./
DESIGN  FACTOR=A.  TYPE=BETWEEN, REGRESSION.
  CODE=READ.
  NAME='A12:  A1 VERSUS A2'.
  VALUES= 1,  −1,  0./
DESIGN FACTOR=A.
  NAME='A123:  A1+A2 VERSUS A3'.
  VALUES= 1,  1,  −2./
DESIGN FACTOR=B.
  NAME='B12:  B1 VERSUS B2'.
  VALUES= 1,  −1,  0./
DESIGN FACTOR=B.
  NAME= 'B123:  B1+B2 VERSUS B3'.
  VALUES= 1,  1,  −2./
PRINT ALL./
ANALYSIS PROCEDURE=STRUCTURE.
  BFORM= '(A12 + A123)*(B12 + B123)'./
END/
```

Commentary

The preceding input is for program 4V of BMDP (Dixon, 1992, Vol. 2, pp. 1259–1310). I used 4V earlier in this chapter to analyze the 2×2 design of Table 12.1. Except for the fact that here I use 4V to analyze a 3×3 design, the statements up to and including ANALYSIS PROC= SIMPLE./ are the same as those I used and commented on when I analyzed the data of Table 12.1. Therefore, I comment only on the statements beginning with DESIGN.

DESIGN.

> Specifies one customized hypothesis to be tested for parameters in the model. The hypothesis, which may be one or a set of simultaneous linear combinations of parameters set equal to zero, is defined by stating the names of the factors to be used in the linear combination. Coefficients for the linear combination(s) must also be specified . . . The design paragraph may be repeated and must precede the corresponding ANALYSIS paragraph. (Dixon, 1992, Vol. 2, p. 1304)

CONTRAST or REGRESSION. One has to be specified in the DESIGN paragraph. Although for present purposes, I could have used CONTRAST, I chose not to because it "consist [s] only of 1's, −1's, and 0's" (Dixon, 1992, Vol. 2, p. 1305). The program then "determines the proper coefficients (based on the weights used). For example, the contrast (1,−1,−1) becomes (1,−1/2,−1/2)" (Dixon, 1992, Vol. 2, p. 1305). I use REGRESSION so that I may specify the same coefficients I used in SPSS and will use in SAS (see the following).

NAME. As you can see, I use the same main-effects orthogonal comparisons I used earlier in SPSS.

ANALYSIS. "The STRUCTURE procedure is discussed in detail in BMDP Technical Report #67" (Dixon, 1992, Vol. 2, p. 1293). For present purposes, I will only point out that I use BFORM (BetweenFORMula) to generate the same interaction contrasts I calculated earlier through SPSS.

Output

4V TABLE 12.9
UNIVARIATE SUMMARY TABLE FOR DEPENDENT VARIATE Y

SOURCE	SUM OF SQUARES	DF	MEAN SQUARE	F	TAIL PROB.
A	84.00000	2	42.00000	9.45	0.01
B	12.00000	2	6.00000	1.35	0.31
AB	92.00000	4	23.00000	5.18	0.02
ERROR	40.00000	9	4.44444		

UNIVARIATE SUMMARY TABLE FOR DEPENDENT VARIATE Y

SOURCE	SUM OF SQUARES	DF	MEAN SQUARE	F	TAIL PROB.
A12: A1 VERSUS A2	3.00000	1	3.00000	0.68	0.43
A123: A1+A2 VERSUS A3	81.00000	1	81.00000	18.23	0.00
B12: B1 VERSUS B2	3.00000	1	3.00000	0.68	0.43
B123: B1+B2 VERSUS B3	9.00000	1	9.00000	2.03	0.19
A12B12	50.00000	1	50.00000	11.25	0.01
A123B12	24.00000	1	24.00000	5.40	0.05
A12B123	0.00000	1	0.00000	0.00	1.00
A123B123	18.00000	1	18.00000	4.05	0.08
ERROR	40.00000	9	4.44444		

Commentary

For comparative purposes with earlier analyses of the same example, I reproduced only the overall summary table and results of the orthogonal comparisons and the interaction contrasts. As I suggested, if you are running BMDP, compare your output with the SPSS output I gave earlier.

SAS

Input

```
TITLE 'TABLE 12.9.   FACTORIAL 3 BY 3';
DATA T129;
INPUT A 1 B 2 Y 3-4;
CARDS;
1112
1110
1210
```

```
12  8
13  8
13  6
21  7
21  7
2217
2213
2310
23  6
3116
3114
3214
3210
3317
3313
;
PROC PRINT;
PROC GLM;
CLASS A B;
MODEL Y=A|B/SOLUTION;
MEANS A B A*B;
CONTRAST 'A1 VS. A2' A 1 –1 0;
CONTRAST 'A1+A2 VS. A3' A 1 1 –2;
CONTRAST 'B1 VS. B2' B 1 –1 0;
CONTRAST 'B1+B2 VS. B3' B 1 1 –2;
CONTRAST 'A1B1' A*B 1 –1 0 –1 1 0 0 0 0;
CONTRAST 'A1B2' A*B 1 1 –2 –1 –1 2 0 0 0;
CONTRAST 'A2B1' A*B 1 –1 0 1 –1 0 –2 2 0;
CONTRAST 'A2B2' A*B 1 1 –2 1 1 –2 –2 –2 4;
ESTIMATE 'A1 VS. A2' A 1 –1 0;
ESTIMATE 'A1+A2 VS. A3' A 1 1 –2;
ESTIMATE 'B1 VS B2' B 1 –1 0;
ESTIMATE 'B1+B2 VS. B3' B 1 1 –2;
ESTIMATE 'A1B1' A*B 1 –1 0 –1 1 0 0 0 0;
ESTIMATE 'A1B2' A*B 1 1 –2 –1 –1 2 0 0 0;
ESTIMATE 'A2B1' A*B 1 –1 0 1 –1 0 –2 2 0;
ESTIMATE 'A2B2' A*B 1 1 –2 1 1 –2 –2 –2 4;
RUN;
```

Commentary

When I introduced PROC GLM in Chapter 11, I commented on an input file very much like the one I use here, except that here in MODEL I specify a full factorial (A|B is equivalent to A, B, A*B; see SAS Institute Inc., 1990a, Vol. 2, p. 897), whereas in Chapter 11 I analyzed a single-factor design. The same is true of the CONTRAST and ESTIMATE statements. Therefore, I will not comment on the input file. If necessary, see Chapter 11 for commentaries.

Output

TABLE 12.9.   FACTORIAL 3 BY 3
General Linear Models Procedure

Source	DF	Type I SS	Mean Square	F Value	Pr > F
A	2	84.00000000	42.00000000	9.45	0.0061
B	2	12.00000000	6.00000000	1.35	0.3071
A*B	4	92.00000000	23.00000000	5.18	0.0192

Contrast	DF	Contrast SS	Mean Square	F Value	Pr > F
A1 VS. A2	1	3.00000000	3.00000000	0.68	0.4325
A1+A2 VS. A3	1	81.00000000	81.00000000	18.23	0.0021
B1 VS. B2	1	3.00000000	3.00000000	0.67	0.4325
B1+B2 VS. B3	1	9.00000000	9.00000000	2.03	0.1885
A1B1	1	50.00000000	50.00000000	11.25	0.0085
A1B2	1	0.00000000	0.00000000	0.00	1.0000
A2B1	1	24.00000000	24.00000000	5.40	0.0452
A2B2	1	18.00000000	18.00000000	4.05	0.0750

Parameter	Estimate	T for H0: Parameter=0	Pr > |T|
A1 VS A2	−1.0000000	−0.82	0.4325
A1+A2 VS A3	−9.0000000	−4.27	0.0021
B1 VS B2	−1.0000000	−0.82	0.4325
B1+B2 VS B3	3.0000000	1.42	0.1885
A1B1	10.0000000	3.35	0.0085
A1B2	0.0000000	0.00	1.0000
A2B1	−12.0000000	−2.32	0.0452
A2B2	18.0000000	2.01	0.0750

Commentary

For an explanation of output very similar to the one given here, see commentaries on the analysis of data of Table 11.4 in Chapter 11. Compare the results reported here with those from BMDP and from SPSS, given earlier. Also, compare the estimates with my application of (12.9) for the same contrasts.

HIGHER-ORDER DESIGNS: COMMENT

In the preceding sections, I showed how to code categorical independent variables in two-factor designs and use the coded vectors in multiple regression analysis with a continuous dependent variable. The same approach may be extended to any number of independent variables with any number of categories. As in two-factor designs, each categorical variable is coded as if it were the only one in the design. Cross-product vectors are then generated to represent interactions, including ones involving more than two variables (i.e., higher-order interactions).

To clarify what I said, I will use an example of a design with three categorical independent variables as follows: *A* with two categories, represented by one coded vector (say number 1); *B* with three categories, represented by two coded vectors (2 and 3); and *C* with four categories, represented by three coded vectors (4, 5, and 6). Vectors representing the two-factor interactions, also called first-order interactions, are generated in the manner I described in earlier sections: by multiplying, in turn, vectors of one factor by those of another factor. For instance, vectors to represent $A \times B$ are generated by multiplying: 1 by 2, and 1 by 3.

A three-factor design may have a three-factor or a second-order interaction. Vectors representing such an interaction are generated by multiplying the vectors associated with the three variables. Referring to the example under consideration, the second-order interaction ($A \times B \times C$) is generated by multiplying the vectors representing these variables as follows: $1 \times 2 \times 4$; $1 \times 3 \times 4$; $1 \times 2 \times 5$; $1 \times 3 \times 5$; $1 \times 2 \times 6$; $1 \times 3 \times 6$. Altogether, six vectors are generated to represent the 6 degrees of freedom associated with this second-order interaction (*df* for *A, B,* and *C,* respectively, are 1, 2, and 3; *df* for the interaction, $A \times B \times C$, are therefore $1 \times 2 \times 3$). Having generated the necessary vectors, the dependent variable is regressed on them.

I hope that the foregoing helps you to better understand the flexibility of the coding approach. Used judiciously, you can also extend it to other types of designs. For instance, sometimes one wishes to use one or more control groups, even when they do not fit into the factorial design being contemplated. Under such circumstances, the control groups are attached to the factorial design (see Himmelfarb, 1975; Hornbeck, 1973; Winer, 1971, pp. 468–473). You can easily accommodate such designs by using the coding methods I presented in this chapter and by subjecting them to a multiple regression analysis. The same is true for other designs (e.g., Hierarchical, Latin Squares). In Chapters 20 and 21, I use coded vectors in multivariate analysis.

Thus far, I addressed the mechanics of analyzing higher-order designs with coded vectors. More important, of course, is the logic of the analysis and the interpretation of results. Without going into detail, I will point out that when analyzing a higher-order design, examine the highest-order interaction first to determine the next step to take. If the highest-order interaction is statistically significant, then calculate simple interactions for the factors involved in it. If in the design considered above $A \times B \times C$ is statistically significant, then one would study, for instance, $A \times B$ within each level of *C*. Such components are called simple interactions. When a simple interaction is statistically significant, it is followed by an analysis of simple-simple effects.

A statistically nonsignificant highest-order interaction means that lower-order interactions are not dependent on other factors and can therefore be interpreted without having to take other factors into account. Thus, if $A \times B \times C$ is statistically not significant, then $A \times B$, say, would be interpreted without considering the presence of *C*. This is also true for the other first-order interactions.

To repeat: the approach I outlined in the preceding paragraphs can be generalized to designs of any order. Among texts giving detailed discussions of higher-order designs, along with numerical examples, are Keppel (1991), Kirk (1982), Maxwell and Delaney (1990), Winer (1971). I believe that, in addition to studying such sources, you will benefit from analyzing the examples they contain in a manner analogous to that I used in this chapter for two-factor designs.

NONORTHOGONAL DESIGNS

I discussed unequal *n*'s in single-factor designs in Chapter 11, where I noted special issues concerning their use in experimental and nonexperimental research. In addition, I drew attention to the important distinction between situations in which unequal *n*'s are used by design and those in which they are a consequence of subject attrition. For convenience, I used the term *attrition* to cover all contingencies leading to a loss of subjects, though some (e.g., errors in the recording of some scores) do not pose nearly as great a threat to the internal validity of the study as others (e.g., subjects unwilling to continue to participate because of what appear to be characteristics of the treatment to which they were assigned). As an example of the latter, consider the following:

> It would be embarrassing to conclude that some form of therapy led to shorter stays in your hypothetical hospital when further investigation revealed that it was really because patients who received that therapy decided that your hospital was bad for their health and, if they survived, escaped as soon as possible! (Cliff, 1987a, p. 260)

Difficulties attendant with nonorthogonal designs arise when, as often happens, it is not possible to discern the reasons for subject attrition.

While showing that the analysis for a single-factor design with unequal *n*'s is straightforward, I noted that the researcher is faced with choices (e.g., whether to compare unweighted or weighted means) and with ambiguities in the interpretation of the results, depending on the specific design and the specific causes that have given rise to the unequal *n*'s.

In factorial designs, too, unequal cell frequencies may occur in experimental and nonexperimental research, either by design or because of subject attrition. The analysis and interpretation of results in factorial designs with unequal cell frequencies are, however, considerably more complex and more ambiguous than in a single-factor design. The reason is that when the frequencies in the cells of a factorial design are unequal, the treatment effects and their interactions are correlated, thereby rendering attribution of a portion of the sum of squares to each main effect and to the interaction ambiguous. In short, the design is not orthogonal and it is therefore not possible to partition the regression sum of squares into independent components in the manner I showed earlier in this chapter for orthogonal designs (i.e., designs with equal cell frequencies).

There is no agreed-upon approach to the analysis of designs with unequal cell frequencies, which are also called nonorthogonal, unbalanced, with disproportional frequencies. In fact, this topic has generated lively debate and controversy among social scientists, as is evidenced by published arguments and counterarguments, comments, replies to comments, and comments on replies to comments. I do not reference most of these as instead of clarifying the problems they further obfuscate them, bearing witness to Appelbaum and Cramer's (1974) apt observation that "The nonorthogonal multifactor analysis of variance is perhaps the most misunderstood analytic technique available to the behavioral scientist, save factor analysis" (p. 335). In a more recent statement, Cliff (1987a) expressed the same sentiment:

> Probably no issue of analysis of variance causes more head-scratching, nail-biting, dog-kicking, wrist-slashing, name-calling, and finger-pointing than nonorthogonality. For decades, almost no one knew what to do in a factorial anova when the cell frequencies were unequal. . . . Today, many investigators *know* what to do in such cases, although they may end up doing different things in the same situation. (p. 253)

Because issues concerning the analysis and interpretation of nonorthogonal designs in experimental research are largely distinct from those relevant to nonexperimental research, I treat the two research settings separately, beginning with the former.

Nonorthogonal Designs in Experimental Research

Unequal cell frequencies in experimental research may occur either by design or because of subject attrition. A researcher may, for example, decide to assign different numbers of subjects to different treatments because some are costlier than others. Under such circumstances, it is highly likely that the researcher will design a study in which the cell frequencies, though unequal, are proportional. A factorial design is said to have proportional cell frequencies when the ratio of cell frequencies in the rows is constant across columns or, equivalently, when the ratio of cell frequencies in columns is constant across rows. Consider the following 2×3 design in which the numbers refer to frequencies:

	B_1	B_2	B_3	
A_1	10	20	30	60
A_2	20	40	60	120
	30	60	90	180

You may note that the ratio of row frequencies is 1:2:3 and that of column frequencies is 1:2. In general, proportionality of cell frequencies is indicated when

$$n_{ij} = \frac{n_{i.}n_{.j}}{n_{..}}$$

where n_{ij} = frequency in cell of row i and column j; $n_{i.}$ = frequency in row i; $n_{.j}$ = frequency in column j; and $n_{..}$ = total frequency in the table. Basically, then, when each cell frequency is equal to the product of its marginal frequencies divided by the total frequency, the design is proportional. For the 2×3 given in the preceding, $(30)(60)/180 = 10$, $(30)(120)/180 = 20$, and so forth.

Designs with proportional cell frequencies are analyzed and interpreted in the same manner as are those with equal cell frequencies. That is, in such designs it is still possible to partition the regression sum of squares into orthogonal components due to main effects and interaction. Consequently, all I said about designs with equal cell frequencies applies also to designs with proportional cell frequencies.

The absence of orthogonality and the resultant ambiguity occur in designs in which the cell frequencies are disproportionate. In experimental research this happens most often because of subject attrition. Under such circumstances, the validity of the analysis and the interpretation of the results are predicated on the assumption that the loss of subjects is due to a random process. In other words, one can assume that subject attrition is not related in a systematic manner to the treatment combinations. When this assumption is not tenable, "there would seem to be no remedy short of pretending that the missing observations are random" (Appelbaum & Cramer, 1974, p. 336).

I patterned the following presentation after those by Appelbaum and Cramer (1974) and Cramer and Appelbaum (1980) as they are, in my opinion, lucid and logical treatments of the topic of nonorthogonal designs. Basically, they argued that on logical and conceptual grounds there is no difference between orthogonal and nonorthogonal designs. In both cases the method of least squares is applied, and tests of significance are used to compare different linear models in an attempt to determine which of them appears to be most consistent with the data at hand.

Parenthetically, prior to the widespread availability of computer facilities, researchers used analytic approaches that were generally less satisfactory than least-squares solutions (e.g., unweighted-means analysis; see Kirk, 1982, Chapter 8; Maxwell & Delaney, 1990, Chapter 7; Snedecor & Cochran, 1967, Chapter 16; Winer, 1971, Chapter 16). Interestingly, although Snedecor and Cochran presented the least-squares solution, they did so after presenting the other methods: "*Unfortunately* [italics added], with unequal cell numbers the exact test of the null hypothesis that interactions are absent requires the solution of a set of linear equations like those in a multiple regression" (1967, pp. 473–474). Fortunately, conditions have changed drastically since the time the preceding statement was made. The ready availability of computer facilities and programs for multiple regression analysis render the use of the less satisfactory approaches unnecessary. Here, then, is yet another example of the superiority of multiple regression over the analysis of variance approach.

Appelbaum and Cramer (1974) pointed out that in a two-factor design one of the following five models may be the most consistent with the data:

1. $Y_{ijk} = \mu + \alpha_i + \beta_j + (\alpha\beta)_{ij} + \varepsilon_{ijk}$
2. $Y_{ijk} = \mu + \alpha_i + \beta_j + \varepsilon_{ijk}$
3. $Y_{ijk} = \mu + \alpha_i + \varepsilon_{ijk}$
4. $Y_{ijk} = \mu + \beta_j + \varepsilon_{ijk}$
5. $Y_{ijk} = \mu + \varepsilon_{ijk}$

Model 1, which I introduced earlier as (12.2), is the most comprehensive. According to this model, an individual's (k) score under treatment combination ij is conceived as composed of the grand mean, μ; two main effects, α_i and β_j; an interaction effect, $(\alpha\beta)_{ij}$; and a residual ε_{ijk}. Model 1 is appropriate and sufficient for estimates and tests of the effects in an orthogonal design. Based on the tests, it is possible to determine whether some components may be deleted from the model, thereby leading to a more parsimonious one. For example, if the interaction is statistically not significant, but the two main effects are, then Model 2 would be plausible.

In nonorthogonal designs, on the other hand, the validity of estimates of effects depends on the tenability of the model used. To clarify this point, consider, for example, Models 2 and 3. Model 2 requires estimates of α and β, whereas Model 3 requires an estimate of α only. Unlike the orthogonal design, estimates of α will differ depending on whether this is done in the context of Model 2 or Model 3. How, then, does one decide which model to retain? Doing a sequence of tests, beginning with the most comprehensive model, may provide the answer.

Test of the Interaction

The first test addresses the question of whether Model 1 or Model 2 is more plausible. The contrast between these two models is designed to determine whether an interaction term is necessary or whether a model composed of main effects only would suffice. The interaction is tested by using the difference between two R^2's—one in which the interaction is included (usually referred to as the full model) and one in which it is excluded (the restricted model). For a two-factor design (A and B), this is expressed as

$$R^2_{Y.A,B,AB} - R^2_{Y.A,B}$$

where A stands for one or more coded vectors representing A; B stands for one or more coded vectors representing B; and AB stands for the interaction.

It is instructive to note that in an orthogonal design,

$$R^2_{Y.A,B,AB} - R^2_{Y.A,B} = R^2_{Y.AB}$$

In a nonorthogonal design, the difference between the two R^2's is a squared multiple semipartial correlation: $R^2_{Y(AB.A,B)}$, that is, the squared multiple correlation of Y with the interaction vectors after partialing from the latter what they share with A and B.[15]

When the interaction is statistically significant, one proceeds as in the case of an orthogonal design. Recall that earlier in the chapter I maintained that when the interaction is statistically significant it is not meaningful to test main effects, although such tests are not wrong from a statistical point of view. Instead, perform tests of simple effects or interaction contrasts to gain insight into the differential effects of treatments of one factor depending on their combinations with treatments of the other factor. The same is true for nonorthogonal designs. As my concern here is solely with the problem of unequal cell frequencies, I will not show these tests, which are done in the same manner as I presented earlier for the case of orthogonal designs.

Tests of the Main Effects

When the interaction is not statistically significant, one proceeds with tests of main effects, as in orthogonal designs, except that each main effect is tested after it has been adjusted for its correlation with the other main effect. Appelbaum and Cramer (1974) prefer to refer to this test as a test of a main effect after eliminating the other main effect. Searle (1971) prefers to speak of a test of a main effect after another main effect. The specific terminology notwithstanding, the reference is to the same thing: a test of a squared multiple semipartial correlation or a test of the increment in the proportion of variance due to one main effect after the contribution of the other main effect was taken into account. Referring to the five models listed in the preceding, the B main effect is tested by contrasting Model 2 (in which B is included) with Model 3 (in which B is not included). Expressed as a test of the difference between two R^2's, the test of B after adjusting for its correlation with A is

$$R^2_{Y.A,B} - R^2_{Y.A}$$

A statistically significant F ratio would indicate that B has to be retained in Model 2.

Similarly, the A main effect is tested after adjusting for its correlation with B:

$$R^2_{Y.A,B} - R^2_{Y.B}$$

If this test, too, is statistically significant, Model 2 is retained.

If only one of the main effects is statistically significant, the model containing it is retained. When neither of the main effects is statistically significant, Appelbaum and Cramer (1974) suggested two additional tests: one in which A is tested while ignoring B, and one in which B is tested while ignoring A. Note carefully that these tests do not take into account the correlation between A and B. When A is tested, Model 3, which includes A, is compared with Model 5, which includes only the grand mean. Similarly, when B is tested, Model 4 is compared with Model 5. Several patterns of results may emerge from such tests:

---

[15]For a discussion of the squared multiple semipartial correlation, see Chapter 7.

1. The effects of both *A* and *B* are statistically significant, which would, of course, be evidence of serious confounding between the two variables. Recall that these tests are done when both *A* and *B* are statistically *not* significant after adjusting each for its correlation with the other. Appelbaum and Cramer suggested that when the effects of both *A* and *B* are statistically significant, only one factor should be retained in the final model—"the choice is indeterminate" (p. 341).
2. The effect of only one of the factors is statistically significant, in which case it is retained in the final model.
3. Neither of the factors have statistically significant effects, in which case a model consisting of only the grand mean is retained. In other words, there are no main and interaction effects.

Appelbaum and Cramer (1974) urge caution in interpreting the results of tests of main effects when the other factors are ignored. Since the statistical significance of such tests serves to underscore the fact that the factors are seriously confounded due to relatively extreme disproportionality, I suggest that they *not* be carried out, as the potential of misinterpreting the results based on such tests far outweighs whatever benefits arise from using them. Moreover, extreme disproportionality of cell frequencies should be a cause of grave concern because it raises serious doubts about the assumption that subject attrition is due to a random process, thereby casting serious doubts on the internal validity of the experiment. Retaining, under such circumstances, a factor that was shown to be statistically significant only when the other factor was ignored is, to say the least, hazardous. If, despite the foregoing, you choose to follow Appelbaum and Cramer's suggestion to carry out tests of each main effect while ignoring the other factor (after it was established that neither is statistically significant when adjusted for the other), you would also be well advised to heed their call for caution in interpreting results of such tests.

Finally, note that only in the case of nonorthogonal designs is it possible to encounter patterns of results in which main effects are statistically not significant when adjusted for one another, but one or both are statistically significant when each is tested without taking the other into account. In orthogonal designs, the regression sum of squares due to a given main effect will not change when it is adjusted for other main effects because the main effects (and interactions) are not correlated. This, of course, is the meaning of orthogonality.

Summary of Testing Sequence

The following list summarizes the testing sequence in nonorthogonal designs:

1. Test whether the interaction is statistically significant. If it is, do tests of simple effects. If it is not, go to step 2.
2. Test each factor while adjusting it for the other factor. That is, test *A* after *B,* and *B* after *A*. Retain one or both, depending on whether they are statistically significant. If neither is statistically significant, you would conclude that Model 5 is tenable, that is, that there are no main effects and interactions.

To reiterate: there is no agreement about the analysis of nonorthogonal designs. As but one example, I will point out that some authors, notably Overall, Spiegel, and Cohen (1975), argued that the main effects should be adjusted also for the interaction (see also Carlson & Timm, 1974; Edwards, 1979, Chapter 13; Keppel & Zedeck, 1989, Chapter 24). For a critique of this approach, see Cramer and Appelbaum (1980). On the other hand, Keppel and Zedeck (1989) were critical of the approach suggested by Appelbaum and Cramer: "What is disturbing about this approach is that it is *data-dependent* and is clearly not based on theory or on independent empirical information" (p. 545). Although being cold comfort to the researcher facing the problem of unequal cell frequencies, I believe it worthwhile to conclude by quoting Cochran and Cox (1950): "The only complete solution of the 'missing data' problem is not to have them" (p. 74).

A Numerical Example

For convenience, I will use a 2×2 design to illustrate the application of the approach I outlined earlier for the analysis of nonorthogonal designs. Assume an experiment on attitude change toward the use of cocaine. The experiment consists of two factors, each with two treatments, as follows. Factor A refers to source of information, where A_1 = a former addict and A_2 = a nonaddict. Factor B refers to fear arousal, where B_1 = mild fear arousal and B_2 = intense fear arousal. Without going into the details of the design, assume further, for the sake of illustration, that five subjects were randomly assigned to each treatment combination, that the experiment has been in progress for several sessions, and that subject attrition has occurred. During the final session, measures of attitude change were available for only 14 of the 20 original subjects. The scores for these subjects, the cell means, and the unweighted treatment means are given in Table 12.13. I will use REGRESSION of SPSS to analyze the data in Table 12.13.

Table 12.13   Illustrative Data from an Experiment on Attitude Change

	B_1	B_2	*Unweighted Means*
A_1	4 3 2 $\overline{Y} = 3.00$	8 10 $\overline{Y} = 9.00$	 6.00
A_2	3 2 5 6 4 $\overline{Y} = 4.00$	5 4 5 6 $\overline{Y} = 5.00$	 4.50
Unweighted Means	3.50	7.00	5.25

SPSS

Input

TITLE TABLE 12.13.   2 BY 2 NONORTHOGONAL.   EFFECT CODING.
DATA LIST/A 1 B 2 Y 3-4.
IF (A EQ 1) A1=1.
IF (A EQ 2) A1=−1.
IF (B EQ 1) B1=1.
IF (B EQ 2) B1=−1.
COMPUTE A1B1=A1*B1.

```
BEGIN DATA
11  4
11  3
11  2
12  8
1210
21  3
21  2
21  5
21  6
21  4
22  5
22  4
22  5
22  6
END DATA
LIST.
REGRESSION VAR=Y TO A1B1/DES/STAT ALL/
   DEP=Y/ENTER A1/ENTER B1/ENTER A1B1/
   DEP=Y/ENTER B1/ENTER A1/ENTER A1B1/
   TEST (A1)(B1)(A1B1).
```

Commentary

As you can see, I generated effect coded vectors for the main effects and the interaction in exactly the same manner as I did in orthogonal designs. As it may be necessary to adjust one main effect for the other, I specified two regression analyses in which I entered the vectors representing the three components sequentially. In both analyses, I entered the interaction last. In the first analysis, I entered A1 first, followed by B1. I used the reverse order of entry in the second analysis.

Output

	Mean	Std Dev
Y	4.786	2.225
A1	−.286	.994
B1	.143	1.027
A1B1	.000	1.038

N of Cases =   14
Correlation:

	Y	A1	B1	A1B1
Y	1.000	.214	−.625	−.300
A1	.214	1.000	.043	.149
B1	−.625	.043	1.000	−.289
A1B1	−.300	.149	−.289	1.000

Commentary

Examine the previous output and note that the means of the coded vectors are *not* equal to zero. Nor are the correlations among the coded vectors equal to zero. This, of course, is a consequence of the design being nonorthogonal.

Output

Step	Variable	Summary table Rsq	RsqCh	FCh	SigCh	Step	Variable	Summary table Rsq	RsqCh	FCh	SigCh
1	In: A1	.0456	.0456	.573	.464	1	In: B1	.3908	.3908	7.697	.017
2	In: B1	.4487	.4031	8.043	.016	2	In: A1	.4487	.0579	1.156	.305
3	In: A1B1	.7514	.3027	12.175	.006	3	In: A1B1	.7514	.3027	12.175	.006

Commentary

The preceding are excerpts from the summary tables for the *two* regression analyses, which I placed alongside each other. The box surrounding results of Step 2 is *not* part of the output. I inserted it to highlight results I will discuss later.

Recall that the first step in the analytic approach outlined here is a test of the interaction. This test is readily available in the last step of the summary table. As you can see, the increment in the proportion of variance due to the interaction (A1B1) is .3027 (RsqCh). In Chapter 5, I introduced a formula for testing an increment in the proportion of variance accounted for—see (5.27) and the discussion related to it—and used it repeatedly in subsequent chapters including the present one. The application of such a formula to R Square Change associated with the interaction yields $F = 12.175$, with 1 and 10 ($N - k - 1 = 14 - 3 - 1$) *df*, $p < .05$.

Having entered the interaction last in both analyses, the proportion of variance it increments is, of course, the same in both. For present purposes, then, it would have sufficed to enter the interaction in only one of the analyses. I entered it in both for completeness of the presentation.

In line with what I said earlier, one would follow the statistically significant interaction with tests of simple effects. Although I do not carry out such tests here, it is instructive to note by inspecting Table 12.13 that the difference between B_1 and B_2 at A_1 is 6 ($9 - 3$), as compared with 1 ($5 - 4$) at A_2. Also, the difference between A_1 and A_2 at B_1 is 1 ($4 - 3$), as compared with 4 ($9 - 5$) at B_2. All this, of course, is what interaction is about.

Tests of Main Effects

To illustrate tests of main effects in a nonorthogonal design, *I will pretend that the interaction in the present analysis is statistically not significant.* Recall that, under such circumstances, each factor's contribution is adjusted for its correlation with the other factor. As I showed earlier, this is done by determining the proportion of variance incremented by the factor in question when it is entered after the other factor. *The RsqCh and its associated* F *ratio at the second step of the summary table provides this information.* Examine the boxed line in the preceding summary tables and notice that the proportion of variance incremented by *B* when it is entered after *A* (the left segment) is .4031; $F = 8.043$, with 1 and 11 *df*, $p < .05$. Notice that when *B* is entered first it accounts for .3908 of the variance (the right segment). The reason is, of course, due to the nonorthogonality of the design.

Turning now to the contribution of A after it is adjusted for B (the right segment), it will be noted that it accounts for .0579, over and above of what is accounted for by B; $F = 1.156$, with 1 and 11 *df, p* > .05. Again, because of the nonorthogonality of the design, the proportion of variance accounted for by A when it is entered first (the left segment) is not equal to the proportion of variance it increments when it is entered second (i.e., after B).

Recalling that, for illustrative purposes, *I pretended that the interaction is statistically not significant,* and following my outline of the analysis above, a model consisting of only B effects would be tested (see model 4 of the five potential models listed earlier). For the present example, this would entail an examination of the line in which B is entered first (the right segment). Accordingly, one would conclude that B accounts for .3908 of the variance; $F = 7.697$, with 1 and 12 *df.* In essence, this is a test of the squared zero-order correlation of Y with the coded vector representing B (B1 of the input).

Before turning to the next topic, I would like to stress that in actual research, you would be well advised to refrain from firm conclusions, not to mention actions, before replicating the results. Doing this may also shed light on the tenability of the assumption that subject attrition in the original study was random. If, for example, attrition takes place again, and if its pattern is similar to that of the original study, serious doubt would be cast on the assumption that it was random and thereby on the validity of the analysis.

Output

```
------------------------------- Variables in the Equation -------------------------------
```

Variable	B	Part Cor	T	Sig T
A1	.750000	.330106	2.094	.0627
B1	−1.750000	−.770247	−4.885	.0006
A1B1	−1.250000	−.550176	−3.489	.0058
(Constant)	5.250000			

Commentary

Before commenting on the regression equation, I would like to point out that I reproduced Part Cor because I intend to refer to it in the next section, when I discuss output generated by the TEST subcommand.

The regression equation for effect coding has the same properties as in orthogonal designs, except that in nonorthogonal designs the estimates are based on unweighted means (this is similar to the case of unequal *n*'s in a single-factor design; see Chapter 11). Thus, the intercept, 5.25, is equal to the unweighted grand mean, or the mean of the cell means (see Table 12.13). The weighted grand mean ($\overline{Y}$) for the present data is 4.786 (see the earlier excerpt of the output). $b_{A_1} = .75$ is equal to the difference between the unweighted mean of A_1 (6.00) and the unweighted grand mean. Recall that in vector A1, subjects in A_1 were identified (i.e., assigned 1's; see the IF statements in the input file). Accordingly, b_{A_1} is equal to the effect of treatment A_1. If the assumption about the missing data being due to a random process is reasonable, it makes sense to arrive at statements of treatment effects in this manner. If, on the other hand, subject attrition is not due to a random process, the validity of the analysis is dubious.

As usual, the effect of the treatment assigned -1 is equal to $-\Sigma b_i$, which in the present example is $-.75$. Examine Table 12.13 and notice that the deviation of the unweighted mean of A_2 from the unweighted grand mean is $-.75$ $(4.50 - 5.25)$. Similarly, b_{B1} (-1.75) is equal to the effect of B_1, and the effect of B_2 is 1.75.

b_{A1B1} (-1.25) is the interaction effect for cell A_1B_1. Again, this is the same as in an orthogonal design (see the discussion in earlier parts of this chapter), except that in a nonorthogonal design the estimate is based on unweighted means. To show this, I repeat values from Table 12.13:

$$\overline{Y}_{A_1 B_1} = 3.00 \qquad \overline{Y}_{A_1} = 6.00 \qquad \overline{Y}_{B_1} = 3.50 \qquad \overline{Y} = 5.25$$

(Note that the last three are unweighted means.) Applying (12.4) the interaction term for cell A_1B_1 is

$$(3.00 - 5.25) - (6.00 - 5.25) - (3.5 - 5.25) = -1.25$$

In view of the constraint that the sum of interaction terms for each row and each column equals zero, the other interaction terms are readily obtained. Thus, for A_1B_2 the interaction term is 1.25, and so forth.

Applying the regression equation to the codes of a subject on the three vectors yields a predicted score equal to the mean of the cell to which the subject belongs. This is always so, as long as all the coded vectors (i.e., for main effects and interaction) are included in the analysis.

Because in the present example each vector represents a different component, it will be useful to examine the meaning of the tests of the b's. Beginning with the test of b_{A1B1} note that the square of the t ratio associated with it is equal to the F ratio for the interaction reported in the summary table, $(-3.489^2 = 12.17)$ in the preceding. This illustrates what I stated earlier—namely, that in a 2×2 design the test of the b associated with the vector representing the interaction is the same as the test of the proportion of variance incremented by the interaction term when it is entered last (i.e., after the main effects). Note that in designs with more than two categories per factor, the interaction has to be tested in the manner I showed earlier (i.e., by testing the difference between two R^2's).

Turning now to the tests of the b's associated with the main effects, it should be evident that the test of each b is tantamount to a test of the effect of the factor with which it is associated after adjusting for the other factor *and* for the interaction. This, of course, is the meaning of a test of a partial regression coefficient. But this is *not* what we wish to do in a nonorthogonal design. Recall that if the interaction is statistically not significant, we adjust each main effect for the other main effect. If, on the other hand, the interaction is statistically significant, no adjustments are made. Instead, we do tests of simple main effects. In sum, the tests of the b's for the main effects reported earlier are irrelevant, even though we are dealing with a 2×2 design and therefore each b is associated with one of the main effects.

Output

Block Number   4.   Method: Test   A1   B1   A1B1

Hypothesis Tests

DF	Sum of Squares	Rsq Chg	F	Sig F	Source
1	7.01299	.10897	4.38312	.0627	A1
1	38.18182	.59328	23.86364	.0006	B1
1	19.48052	.30269	12.17532	.0058	A1B1

3	48.35714		10.07440	.0023	Regression
10	16.00000				Residual
13	64.35714				Total

Commentary

Earlier, I showed the usefulness of output such as the preceding—generated by the TEST sub-command—in orthogonal designs. *Here, I reproduce it to demonstrate once again the importance of understanding output, thereby knowing whether it is relevant for the purpose at hand.*

To begin with, I would like to point out that each F ratio reported here is equal to the squared t ratio for the test of a b corresponding to it. For example, t ratio for $b_{A1} = 2.094$ (see the t's reported in the preceding under Variables in the Equation), whose square (4.38) is equal to the F ratio for A1 reported here. I suggest that you verify that the same is true for the other F's reported here. Recalling that a test of a b is tantamount to a test of the proportion of variance incremented by the variable with which it is associated when it is entered last in the analysis should suffice to alert you that only the F for the interaction is relevant for present purposes.

Compare now Rsq Chg reported here and the corresponding ones reported in the summary tables given earlier and notice that only the one for the interaction is the same. Moreover, notice that, unlike the summary tables reported earlier, the sum of Rsq Chg is *not* equal to the overall R^2 (.75139). In fact, the sum of Rsq Chg in this excerpt is > 1 (1.005)! The reason is that Rsq Chg reported here represents a squared semipartial correlation of Y with the term in question (i.e., a main effect or an interaction) while partialing the other terms from the latter. That this is so can be easily verified from the Part Cor given above under Variables in the Equation. For example, squaring Part Cor for A1 (.330106) yields the corresponding Rsq Chg (.10897) reported earlier. This serves to show, again, that the F ratios reported here are equivalent to tests of the corresponding b's.

I hope that you realize that my statement in the foregoing—that only the F ratio for the interaction is relevant for present purposes—is predicated on the assumption that the approach for the analysis of nonorthogonal designs outlined earlier is followed. But, as I pointed out, various other approaches were recommended (see the references given earlier). Probably the predominant approach is to adjust each term for all other terms, that is, to adjust each main effect for the other main effects *as well as* for the interaction. For obvious reasons, this approach has also been referred to as testing unique sums of squares (see the discussion of uniqueness in Chapter 9). Some computer programs (e.g., SAS) use the label Type III sum of squares.

Computer Programs: Caveat

I hope that the foregoing discussion served to remind you of the importance of understanding computer output so as to be in a position to select elements relevant to the problem at hand. The risk of carrying out the wrong analysis is particularly great when, as in the case under consideration, computer programs provide for various options. Failure to pay attention to the options, to what is being done by default, and to cautions in the manual may result in an inappropriate analysis. In Chapter 4 (see "Some Recommendations"), I quoted brief warnings by MINITAB and SAS concerning the use of their programs for the analysis of nonorthogonal designs, and I expressed doubts whether users would even notice them.

The problems are compounded by the lack of uniform terminology and by poor labeling of output (for a good discussion, with special reference to nonorthogonal designs, see Preece, 1987, pp. 404–405). After discussing various errors and deficiencies in computer programs, Dallal (1988) advised the reader: "Trust no one, and do everything yourself. Until a particular option has proven itself trustworthy, treat all output as if it were in error" (pp. 214–215).

Uncritical reliance on computer program options in situations such as the one I dealt with in this section is particularly prone to error. For this reason I strongly recommend that you use a multiple regression program with coded vectors (instead of ANOVA programs), thereby taking an active part in specifying the models to be tested.

Nonorthogonal Designs in Nonexperimental Research

In earlier chapters (e.g., Chapters 9–11), I drew attention to the importance of distinguishing between experimental and nonexperimental research and pointed out that whereas the mechanics of multiple regression analysis are the same in both, the interpretation of results is not. Regrettably, some textbooks and manuals for computer programs pay little or no attention to the distinction between experimental and nonexperimental research. A notable case in point is the lack of attention to this distinction in SPSS manuals. For example, the detailed discussion and illustrative applications of multivariate analysis of variance (Norušis/SPSS Inc., 1993b, Chapter 3) is devoted solely to the study of "the relationship between field dependence, sex, and various motor abilities" (p. 57). Following a description of the study from which the data were taken, it is stated:

> The *experiment* [italics added][16] described above is fairly typical of many investigations. There are several classification or independent variables—sex and field independence in this case—and a dependent variable. The goal of the *experiment* [italics added] is to examine the relationship between the classification variables and the dependent variable. For example, is motor ability related to field dependence? Does the relationship differ for men and women? Analysis-of-variance techniques are usually used to answer these questions. (pp. 57–58)[17]

When faced with unequal cell frequencies, the importance of the distinction between experimental and nonexperimental designs is (or should be) evident. As I showed earlier, unequal cell frequencies in experimental research result in correlations among the coded vectors that represent the independent variables. *The converse is true in nonexperimental research, where unequal cell frequencies are generally a consequence of correlations among independent variables or predictors.* Consider, for example, a 2×2 design in which one variable (*A*) is race (A_1 = Black, A_2 = White) and the other variable (*B*) is education (B_1 = high school, B_2 = college). Assume that the dependent variable is income. As this appears to be similar to a 2×2 experimental design, researchers are often inclined to treat it as such. That is, they seek answers to questions

---

[16]I believe that most authors and researchers would agree that two conditions have to be met for a study to qualify as an experiment: (1) at least one variable has to be manipulated and (2) subjects have to be randomly assigned to treatments or treatment combinations (for detailed discussions of research designs, see Pedhazur & Schmelkin, 1991, Chapters 12–14). Neither of these conditions was met in this study.

[17]In Chapter 14, I return to this topic and argue that ANOVA is inappropriate in designs of this kind. For now, I will point out that no allusion was made in the SPSS manual to the fact that the design is nonorthogonal. In a brief section entitled "Different Types of Sums of Squares" (pp. 89–90) mention is made of unbalanced designs and of two options in SPSS: unique or sequential sums of squares.

about main effects and interactions. In the present example this would mean that one may be tempted to determine the effects of race and education as well as their interaction on income. It is necessary, however, to recognize that race and education are correlated. Consequently, when drawing representative samples of Blacks and Whites from defined populations, there are bound to be more college-educated Whites than Blacks. Assuming that one finds that Whites earn significantly more money than Blacks (i.e., a main effect for race), it is necessary to realize that the difference may be partly, or entirely, due to differences in education, not to mention a host of other variables that are related to race and education. A statement about the effect of education is equally questionable. Furthermore, the notion of an interaction between race and education is, as I discuss later, inherently ambiguous.

As another example, assume that one is interested in studying the educational attitudes of elementary school personnel and that one variable (A) is status (A_1 = administrator, A_2 = teacher) and the other variable (B) is sex (B_1 = male, B_2 = female). It is well known that these variables are correlated: most school administrators are males, whereas the majority of teachers are females. Is, then, an observed difference in educational attitudes between administrators and teachers due to status or due to sex? Conversely, does a difference between males and females reflect a difference due to sex or due to status? And what, if any, is the meaning of an interaction between status and sex? Again, the situation is further complicated because status and sex are correlated with many other variables that are not included in the design.[18]

In view of the foregoing, it should be evident that what I said earlier about the analysis of nonorthogonal designs in experimental research is *not* applicable to such designs in nonexperimental research. Indeed,

> To analyse such data uncritically as though they come from a planned experiment invites fallacious argument and misleading conclusions. Although the same types of calculation may be required, more intensive examination of non-experimental data is commonly needed; the inferential problems contain many additional difficulties. (Finney, 1982, p. 6)

When I introduced the topic of unequal n's in nonexperimental research for the case of one categorical independent variable (Chapter 11), I pointed out that for certain purposes one may sample disproportionately from the different strata to arrive at a design with equal n's. The temptation to use a similar approach in designs with multiple categorical variables should be resisted as the use of equal cell frequencies when the variables are correlated is tantamount to pretending that they are *not* correlated. Artificial orthogonalization of what are inherently nonorthogonal designs is (borrowing a phrase from Hoffmann, 1960) "*quite literally a dismemberment of reality*" [italics added] (p. 45). Humphreys and Fleishman (1974) aptly characterized designs that have been artificially orthogonalized as "pseudo-orthogonal."

How, then, are nonorthogonal designs in nonexperimental research to be treated? Except for consisting of categorical variables, such designs are conceptually and analytically not different from designs with continuous independent variables. Therefore, all I said in earlier chapters about analytic approaches in nonexperimental research with continuous independent variables also applies to designs with categorical variables. But because categorical variables that are composed of more than two categories are represented by more than one coded vector, analyses with such variables must take this into account. For example, assume that multiple categorical

---

[18]For additional examples and a very good discussion of problems relevant to factorial designs in nonexperimental research, see McNemar (1969, pp. 444–449).

variables are used in a predictive study and that one wishes to apply a variable-selection procedure (e.g., stepwise regression analysis; see Chapter 8). Unless each variable consists of two categories only, it is inappropriate to apply the variable-selection method to the coded vectors
because each will be treated as a distinct variable. Instead, selection needs to be applied to sets of
coded vectors, each representing a given variable.[19]

The analysis with categorical independent variables in explanatory research is, as in the case
of continuous independent variables, predicated on the theoretical model the researcher advances and on the questions he or she wishes to answer. Thus, if one wishes to partition the variance of the dependent variable, it is necessary to formulate a causal model about the correlations
among the independent variables. Recall that if all the independent variables are treated as exogenous (i.e., no explanation is advanced about the correlations among them), then there is no
meaningful way to partition the variance of the dependent variable (see Chapter 9 for a detailed
discussion of this and related topics). If, on the other hand, some of the independent variables are
treated as endogenous (i.e., as being affected by other independent variables), then the analysis
proceeds in the same manner as for the case of continuous independent variables (Chapter 9), except that coded vectors are used to represent the categorical variables.

Consider the first hypothetical example I introduced earlier. One may argue that race (A) affects to some extent one's level of education (B). The converse is, obviously, not true. Consequently, one may decide to determine first the proportion of the variance in income (Y) that may
be attributed to race and then the proportion of variance incremented by education. This is done
in the usual manner: $R^2_{Y.A}$ is the proportion of variance attributed to race, and $R^2_{Y.AB} - R^2_{Y.A}$ is the
proportion of variance incremented by education. Each proportion of variance accounted for is
tested for significance in the usual manner. A and B in the preceding represent factors, or categorical variables, whatever the number of categories that compose them. Thus whereas in the example under consideration each factor consists of only two categories, the same approach is
taken when factors consist of more than two categories, except that more than one coded vector
is necessary to represent each. In other words, each factor is coded in the usual manner and then
an incremental, or hierarchical, partitioning of variance is done to reflect the pattern of causality
among the independent variables. When testing each proportion, the degrees of freedom for the
numerator of a given F ratio are, of course, the number of coded vectors used to represent the
factor under consideration. The error term is, as always, 1 minus the overall R^2 (i.e., R^2 for all
the factors) divided by the degrees of freedom associated with the residual (i.e., $N - k - 1$, where
k is the total number of coded vectors in the design).

Finally, recall that an incremental, or hierarchical, partitioning of variance does not provide
answers to questions about the relative importance of the independent variables. Further, the proportion of variance incremented by a variable is of dubious value for policy decisions (see Chapter 9 for a detailed discussion of these topics).

Assume now that instead of partitioning the variance of the dependent variable, one wishes to
study the effects of categorical independent variables in a manner analogous to the study of regression coefficients for continuous independent variables (see Chapter 10). Obviously, when
each of the categorical variables consists of two categories only, the b's would be tested in the
same manner as is done for the case of continuous independent variables. Thus, in the previous
hypothetical example, the test of the b associated with the vector representing race tests this

---

[19]I will discuss this point in the section titled "Criterion Scaling."

factor after adjusting for its correlation with education. This is also true for the test of the *b* associated with the vector that represents education.

When the categorical independent variables consist of more than two categories, it is necessary to test, in turn, the proportion of variance accounted for by a given categorical variable after adjusting for the other categorical independent variables. Stated differently, one would test, in turn, the proportion of variance due to a given categorical independent variable when it is entered last into the equation. For illustrative purposes, assume a design with three categorical independent variables as follows: *A* with three categories, *B* with four categories, and *C* with five categories. *A* would therefore require two coded vectors; *B*, three coded vectors; and *C*, four coded vectors. The proportion of variance attributed to *A*, for instance, is $R^2_{Y.ABC} - R^2_{Y.BC}$. The same is true for the other factors. The test of the proportion of variance attributed to *A* is

$$F = \frac{(R^2_{Y.ABC} - R^2_{Y.BC})/(k_1 - k_2)}{(1 - R^2_{Y.ABC})/(N - k_1 - 1)}$$

where k_1 = *df* associated with the overall R^2 (i.e., the one in which *A*, *B*, and *C* are included). In the present example, $k_1 = 9$. k_2 = *df* associated with the R^2 for *B* and *C* (7, in the present example). Therefore the degrees of freedom for the numerator of the above *F* ratio are 2 (i.e., $9 - 7$) or the number of coded vectors representing the factor under consideration—namely, factor *A*. Tests for the other factors are carried out in a similar manner.

Multiplicative or Joint Relations

In the previous presentation, I purposely refrained from mentioning interactions among the categorical independent variables, as my aim was to show first that analyses with categorical independent variables in nonexperimental research parallel analyses with continuous independent variables in similar settings. Recall that in factorial designs in experimental research, the interaction terms are generated by cross multiplying the coded vectors for the main effects. The same procedure can be followed in designs with multiple categorical variables in nonexperimental research. I suggest, however, that in such settings the term *multiplicative,* or *joint, relations* be used to refer to the relations of combinations of categorical independent variables with the dependent variable. I hope that you will not view my use of different labels as an exercise in semantics, but rather see it as a constant reminder of the important differences between experimental and nonexperimental research.

In experimental research, the administration of combinations of treatments is under the control of the researcher. Moreover, the random assignment of subjects to treatment combinations minimizes specification errors. Consequently, one may assume that variables not included in the design are not correlated with variables whose effects are being studied. Under such circumstances, statements about main effects and interactions are straightforward and unambiguous. This is not to say that the substantive meaning of specific findings, particularly of higher-order interactions, is always clear-cut. Whether or not the interpretation of results is simple or complex, clear-cut or ambiguous, depends not on the analysis per se but, among other things, on the (1) substantive meaning of the variables used and their operational definitions (see Chapter 11), (2) theory, and (3) overall validity of the research design.

In nonexperimental research, on the other hand, the variables are almost always intercorrelated. Frequently, it is not possible to unravel the reasons for the correlations among the variables. Moreover, in such designs it is highly likely that variables being studied are correlated with variables that are not considered in the design. Often, variables included in the design serve as proxies for variables that affect the dependent variable but are not included in the study. Under such circumstances, references to the main effects of variables, not to mention interactions, are misleading. References to interactions are equally misleading when one postulates a pattern of causal relations among the variables that are treated as the independent variables.

Yet, cross-product vectors in nonexperimental research may be associated with a meaningful increment in the proportion of variance accounted for, although the interpretation of such increments will generally pose serious difficulties. Some of the difficulties may, perhaps, be best understood in the context of a concrete example. Let us return to the hypothetical study in which race and education are used to explain income. It is known that race and education are correlated. As I pointed out earlier, it is plausible to assume that race affects education to some extent. It is a fact that when, in addition to the coded vectors that represent race and education, cross products of these vectors are used, the cell means of the combinations of the two variables are predictable from the regression equation. In other words, errors of prediction are minimized when cross-product vectors are used in addition to the vectors that represent the variables. Assuming that in the example under consideration the multiplicative term accounts for a meaningful increment in the proportion of variance accounted for, how is one to interpret such a finding? Using the terminology of experimental research, one may be tempted to conclude that race and education interact in their effects on income. Stated differently, one may be tempted to conclude, for example, that the effect of race on income depends on the level of education. But such a conclusion would not be tenable if the assumption that race affects education is tenable.

Even if the possibility of a causal relation between race and education were excluded, it is necessary to recognize that other variables may be operating. Consider, for instance, the combinations of Blacks with a college education and that of Whites with a high school education only. Both of these may be, in part, a consequence of mental ability, motivation, and socioeconomic status, to name but three variables. These variables, too, tend to be intercorrelated, and the causes of the correlations are, to say the least, not clear. In view of the foregoing, it is evident that although it is valid to state that predicted income varies depending on specific combinations of categories of race and education, the conclusion that there is an interaction between race and education is clearly not valid.

Whether or not my distinction between interactions and multiplicative relations is accepted, there appears to be general agreement that the analysis should be carried out hierarchically.[20] That is, the cross-product vectors are adjusted for their correlations with the vectors representing the variables, but not the other way around. In other words, the purpose is to note whether the multiplicative, or joint, relations add meaningfully and significantly to the proportion of variance accounted for by the variables themselves. In the context of the example under consideration, this means a test of the increment in the proportion of variance of income (Y) attributed to the product of race (A) and education (B), over and above the proportion of variance attributed to race and education alone—that is, a test of $R^2_{Y.A,B,AB} - R^2_{Y.A,B}$, where AB stands for the cross product of the A and B vectors. If this increment is statistically not significant, the multiplicative term is deleted and the analysis proceeds as I outlined in the preceding section: each variable's contribution is studied after adjusting for its correlations with the other variables. Thus, for the

---

[20]I discuss this point in detail in Chapter 13 in connection with attempts to interpret products of continuous variables as interactions.

proportion of variance incremented by *A*, test $R^2_{Y.A,B} - R^2_{Y.B}$. For the proportion of variance incremented by *B*, test $R^2_{Y.A,B} - R^2_{Y.A}$.

When the multiplicative term is statistically significant, it is necessary to study the joint relations and attempt to unravel their causes. Although the analytic procedure is not unlike the study of simple effects in experimental research, the interpretation is much more complex in view of the correlation among the variables and the high risk of specification errors.

I can well imagine your sense of frustration while reading this section. I cannot, however, relieve the frustration by providing simple solutions because there are none. It is very simple to construct coded vectors to represent categorical variables. It is also very simple to generate cross-product vectors and label them interactions. But having done this, the interpretational problems do not vanish. Consider, for example, a study in which race, religion, political party affiliation, and sex are used to explain attitudes toward the Equal Rights Amendment. Sounds simple! And it is simple, so far as the mechanics of coding the variables and generating cross-product vectors is concerned. But what about interpreting the results? What does an interaction between, say, race, religion, and political party affiliation mean, particularly when these variables not only are intercorrelated but also are correlated with variables not included in the design and that may even serve as proxies for some? This does not just sound complicated; *it is complicated.*

The best antidote against erroneously interpreting the results from complex studies is clear thinking and sound theory. It is first and foremost important not to be trapped by the mechanics of the analysis. Second, the more one knows about the causes for the patterns of relations among the variables under study, the sounder the theoretical formulation, the better will one be able not only to select the most appropriate analytic approach but also to interpret the results thus obtained.

A RESEARCH EXAMPLE

In this section, I focus on a phenomenon that often leads me to suspect that, in some instances, editors of professional journals do not even read some of the stuff published in their journals, to say nothing of making an informed decision about what is to be published. What I have in mind is the publication of contradictory statements by a critic of a study and the author's reply, when it is clear that both cannot be correct. I would like to stress that I am *not* concerned with acceptable differences of opinion about what might be viewed as philosophical or ideological treatises, think pieces, and the like. Nor am I concerned with complex methodological issues about which one might expect differences of opinion, but rather with rudimentary matters about which there can be no disagreement among knowledgeable people.

While it is understandable that errors may slip by referees and editors when reviewing a manuscript, the publication of egregious errors and misconceptions made in the context of a response to a critique is inexcusable.[21] I trust that after reading the presentation that follows you will agree that the publication of the statement in question constitutes a dereliction of duty (I would like to think that it is not sheer ignorance) on the part of the editors and the referees involved.

---

[21]In Chapters 13 and 14, I show other examples of errors that should have been detected during the review process.

Minority Status, Ethnic Culture, and Distress

Mirowsky and Ross (1980) were interested in studying the effects of a number of variables on "psychological and psychophysiological distress" (p. 487). Among the variables they used were minority status, ethnicity, race, place of residence, sex, age, social class, and marital status. As my concern is exclusively with issues of design and analysis, I will not describe the theoretical considerations that led to the authors' choices of the independent variables, nor to the hypotheses they formulated. In fact, so far as the study itself is concerned, all that is necessary for my purposes is to point out that the authors reported analyses and tests based on the regression of distress on what they maintained were dummy coded vectors representing the independent variables and interactions among them.

More relevant for my purposes is the authors' response to criticisms of their analytic approach. Briefly, Johnson and Benin (1984) correctly pointed out that Mirowsky and Ross used "An unorthodox approach to coding dummy variables" (p. 1189), resulting in misinterpretations of the regression coefficients associated with what are presumably main effects and interactions. Johnson and Benin dealt with this issue, and others, in some detail, but the preceding would suffice to set the stage for the authors' response, which is what I focus on.

Mirowsky and Ross's (1984) response to the criticism of their use of dummy coded vectors begins thus: "Johnson and Benin's major criticism is that the set of dummy variables [*sic*] we use is not a set of orthogonal contrasts" (p. 1197). They then went on to reject this criticism. Before I quote what they said and comment on it, I would like to point out that I believe that Mirowsky and Ross misconstrued Johnson and Benin's criticism. In any event, here is how Mirowsky and Ross (1984) countered what they perceived the criticism to be:[22]

> *Orthogonal coding is used in experimental research* [1], where subjects can be assigned [randomly, of course] to groups and, more important [?], where the relationship between groups and their characteristics (treatments) [?] are under the control of the researcher. An experimental researcher has no problem assigning treatments to groups in such a way that orthogonal coding of the relevant contrasts is possible. If each group contains exactly the same number of respondents, *orthogonal coding produces a set of dichotomous [?] independent variables that are uncorrelated with each other* (Kerlinger and Pedhazur, 1973) [2]. This is useful because it makes the [standardized] multiple regression coefficients equal to the bivariate [correlation] coefficients (thus simplifying computations) and *allows the explained variance to be partitioned into segments uniquely attributable to each treatment* [3]. *Survey researchers rarely use orthogonal coding* [4] (we cannot think of a single instance), possibly because they prefer to treat the distribution of respondents across categories as given and to *allow multiple regression to handle the problem of nonindependent explanatory variables* [5]. (p. 1197)

In a footnote to the preceding, the authors stated, " 'Regression calculations are greatly simplified when orthogonal coding is used,' say Kerlinger and Pedhazur. 'When a computer program is available, of course, this is not much of an advantage' (1973, p. 139)" (p. 1197) [6].

I quoted the first paragraph of Mirowsky and Ross's response about the use of dummy coding in its entirety, as it exemplifies the failure to distinguish between the mechanics of coding categorical variables and the characteristics of the design. Moreover, it contains some very serious misconceptions.

For simplicity, I begin by discussing some of the misconceptions in the context of a one-way design (i.e., a design with a single categorical independent variable consisting of more than two

---

[22]For convenience of reference, I attached numbers in brackets to statements I will comment on later. In addition, all other statements in brackets (including question marks meant to indicate questionable or ambiguous expressions) are mine, as are all the italics.

categories), thereby enabling you to view my comments in the context of relevant sections of Chapter 11. Subsequently, I address the misconceptions in the context of designs with multiple categorical independent variables, presented in this chapter.

The first sentence [1] reflects a failure to distinguish between *orthogonal comparisons* and *orthogonal coding.* When I introduced three coding schemes (dummy, effect, and orthogonal) in Chapter 11, I pointed out, and illustrated with the aid of detailed analyses of a numerical example, that the overall results are the same regardless of the method of coding used. In addition, I discussed intermediate aspects of the analysis (e.g., tests of *b*'s, partitioning of variance) whose relevance is predicated on the given design and coding scheme used. Thus, I showed that certain coding methods may facilitate the calculation of specific elements in a specific type of design (e.g., dummy coding for a design consisting of several treatments and a control group; orthogonal coding for orthogonal comparisons). But I also pointed out that, *whatever the coding method used, any type of comparisons (including orthogonal) can be carried out.* For instance, while using dummy or effect coding, a researcher may still hypothesize and test orthogonal comparisons. The difference between using orthogonal coding in contrast to dummy or effect coding under such circumstances is that with orthogonal coding tests of the corresponding orthogonal comparisons are obtained as part of the regression analysis output (i.e., in the form of tests of the *b*'s), whereas additional calculations subsequent to the regression analysis are required when dummy or effect coding is used—see (11.15) and the discussion related to it.

In view of the preceding it should be clear that survey researchers *may be, and often are,* interested in orthogonal comparisons between groups (see examples in Chapter 11). Whether or not they use orthogonal coding, [1] and [4], or no coding at all, but rather the ANOVA approach, is entirely a matter of the mechanics of the analysis or even taste. Contrary to the impression one might form on the basis of [1], experimenters are not necessarily interested in testing orthogonal comparisons. My discussion of multiple comparisons in Chapter 11 shows that an experimenter may be interested in planned nonorthogonal comparisons. Moreover, depending on the stage of knowledge in the field in which the experiment is conducted, an experimenter may refrain altogether from advancing hypotheses regarding specific contrasts. Instead, he or she may do post hoc comparisons subsequent to a rejection of the overall null hypothesis.

To underscore the distinction I have been discussing, I will point out that it is conceivable for a researcher to use orthogonal coding for ease of hand calculations [6]. But, then it would be *wrong* to test such comparisons, or to interpret the proportions of variance uniquely attributed to each, as this would be tantamount to claiming that the orthogonally coded vectors reflect a priori hypotheses. It is in such a context, and with reference to a one-way design, that Kerlinger and Pedhazur's statement [6] was made. The context in which it is cited by Mirowsky and Ross makes it sound as if the difficulties arising in designs with correlated independent variables are taken care of by the use of a computer program, as is evidenced by their puzzling statement that the survey researcher prefers to "allow multiple regression to handle the problem of nonindependent explanatory variables." [5]

Further, it is *not* true that orthogonal coding results in a set of uncorrelated variables [2]. Kerlinger and Pedhazur said nothing of the kind.[23] What they did say is that the *vectors representing the comparisons are not correlated.* It is also *not* true that orthogonal coding allows the partitioning of variance explained into segments uniquely attributable to *each treatment* [3]. The variance explained uniquely by each vector is that due to the *contrast* between treatments, or combination of treatments (more generally, between groups), that it reflects.

---

[23]This illustrates the importance of checking the context in which a quoted statement was made. See also the discussion of orthogonality of contrasts that follows.

Mirowsky and Ross asserted, "What is crucial is the meaning of a contrast, not its orthogonality to other contrasts" (p. 1198). This, of course, is true, as is evidenced by the use of other types of comparisons (e.g., planned nonorthogonal). But in their attempt to demonstrate why this is so they misconstrued the notion of a contrast and, hence, of orthogonal contrasts. I believe it worthwhile to briefly elaborate on this point, as this would also enable me to lead into the distinction between an orthogonal design and the coded vectors used to analyze such a design.

Mirowsky and Ross constructed an example of two variables (race and marital status), each consisting of two levels (Black and White; married and unmarried), and showed how these variables would be coded using dummy coding. They then stated:

> Under the assumption that the number of persons in each category is the same . . . these two contrasts are orthogonal if the minor product of their coding vectors is zero (Kerlinger and Pedhazur, 1973). Since $(1 \times 1) + (1 \times 0) + (0 \times 1) + (0 \times 0) = 1 \neq 0$, the contrast [*sic*] is not orthogonal. Of course, this does not invalidate all the studies that have measured marital status and race in this way, since the two contrasts represent exactly what they are meant to represent even though they are not orthogonal. (p. 1198)

Here, then, is an example of a confusion between a coding scheme and the definition of a contrast. Recall that an aspect of the definition of a contrast is that the sum of its coefficients be zero—see (11.3) and the discussion related to it. It is this type of contrast that most authors resort to when they are interested in multiple comparisons between means (for references, see Chapter 11, under "Multiple Comparisons among Means"). On these grounds, Mirowsky and Ross's coded vectors do not qualify as contrasts in the sense used by most researchers. Hence, their attempt to demonstrate that the contrasts are not orthogonal is inappropriate.

Further, note that Mirowsky and Ross's first two coded vectors represent *two variables,* and the third vector is meant to represent the interaction between them. This brings us to another misconception in the previous example, one that underlies the general reasoning in Mirowsky and Ross's response. What I have in mind is the distinction between an orthogonal design and the coding scheme used to represent it. As I explained earlier in this chapter, a design with multiple categorical variables is orthogonal when the cell frequencies are equal. Among other things, I pointed out that effect coding may be used to obtain the proportion of variance, or sum of squares, due to each term in the design (i.e., main effects and interactions) because vectors representing a given term, while correlated among themselves, are not correlated with vectors representing other terms.

Further, I showed that this is *not* true of dummy coding. Specifically, I showed that when dummy coding is used in an orthogonal design, the vectors representing main effects are *not* correlated with each other. But, unlike effect coding, dummy coded vectors representing main effects *are* correlated with vectors representing interactions. It is very important to recognize that this is *not* a property of the design, which is still orthogonal, but of the coding scheme used. As you will recall, I showed that even with dummy coding, one may obtain the same proportions of variance, or sums of squares, uniquely attributed to each term in the design, except that appropriate adjustments for the correlations between the coded vectors of the main effects and those of the interaction have to be made in the course of the analysis.

In light of the preceding, it is to be expected that for Mirowsky and Ross's example, the dummy coded vectors representing the two variables would *not* be correlated. But the product of these vectors would be correlated with both of them, even though the design is orthogonal.

After a couple of other questionable statements that I will not comment on, Mirowsky and Ross stated:

One must then choose between the convenience of uncorrelated independent variables and the useful-ness of meaningful ones. . . . If orthogonal factors make less sense than correlated ones, it is probably because the assumption of orthogonality is unrealistic. In general we do not choose to purchase a sta-tistically independent subset of explanatory variables at the cost of less meaningful results. (p. 1198)

This statement, especially the last sentence, may have a nice ring to it. Alas . . .

In conclusion, I would like to stress that I discussed Mirowsky and Ross's response in detail in the hope that it will serve as a reminder of my exhortation in Chapter 1 that you should not as-sume that a paper is valid and meaningful just because it has undergone a review process and was published in a prestigious journal. I dare say that, even if your background is no more than one based on the reading of this and the preceding chapter, you have recognized the major errors in Mirowsky and Ross's statement. Surely, referees and editors should have.

CRITERION SCALING

Although the method of coding categorical independent variables or predictors is straightfor-ward and is generalizable to any number of variables with any number of categories, it becomes unwieldy when the number of variables and/or the number of categories is large. For example, Beaton (1969a) estimated that about 600 vectors would be required to code the variables for the ninth-grade students in the Coleman Report. This number pales when compared with the poten-tial number of cross-product vectors, which Beaton (1969a) estimated as 10^{75}.

To handle the problem, Beaton (1969a, 1969b) proposed a coding method that he called *crite-rion scaling*. The idea of criterion scaling is simple. Recall that the regression equation for a set of coded vectors yields predicted scores that are equal to the means of the groups or categories on the dependent variable. A categorical variable is said to be criterion scaled when it is trans-formed into a single vector in which each individual's score is equal to the criterion mean of the group to which he or she belongs. In other words, a criterion-scaled variable is one consisting of the predicted scores of the individuals under consideration.

Recall that $R^2_{y.12...k} = r^2_{yy'}$, where $R^2_{y.12...k}$ is the squared multiple correlation of Y with k in-dependent variables or coded vectors; and $r^2_{yy'}$ is the squared correlation of Y with the predicted Y's—see (5.18) and the discussion related to it. Thus, when a categorical variable is criterion scaled, a multiple regression analysis with coded vectors is replaced by a bivariate regression analysis in which the dependent variable is regressed on the criterion-scaled variable. This is true regardless of the number of categories of the categorical variable, for equal and unequal n's.

A Numerical Example

To show that a regression analysis with a criterion-scaled variable yields an R^2 identical to that obtained in an analysis with coded vectors representing the same variable, I will use the data from Table 11.11. In Table 12.14, I repeat the criterion, Y, from Table 11.11. Instead of using two coded vectors (as in Table 11.11), I use a criterion-scaled variable, Y', that is, a vector consisting of predicted scores or means on the criterion to which the subjects belong. Thus, for the first three subjects $Y' = 5.0$, which is the mean of the group ($\overline{Y}_{A_1}$) to which they belong. This is also true for subjects in the other groups.

Table 12.14 Criterion Scaling of an Independent Variable Consisting of Three Categories

Group	Y	Y^2	Y'	Y'^2	YY'
	4	16	5.0	25.00	20.0
A_1	5	25	5.0	25.00	25.0
	6	36	5.0	25.00	30.0
	7	49	8.5	72.25	59.5
	8	64	8.5	72.25	68.0
A_2	9	81	8.5	72.25	76.5
	10	100	8.5	72.25	85.0
	1	1	3.0	9.00	3.0
	2	4	3.0	9.00	6.0
A_3	3	9	3.0	9.00	9.0
	4	16	3.0	9.00	12.0
	5	25	3.0	9.00	15.0
Σ:	64	426	64	409	409
M:	5.33		5.33		

NOTE: Y scores were taken from Table 11.11.

I calculate the regression of Y on Y' without commenting on the mechanics, as these should be clear by now.[24] Using values reported at the bottom of Table 12.14,

$$\Sigma y^2 = \Sigma Y^2 - \frac{(\Sigma Y)^2}{N} = 426 - \frac{(64)^2}{12} = 84.66667$$

$$\Sigma y'^2 = \Sigma Y'^2 - \frac{(\Sigma Y')^2}{N} = 409 - \frac{(64)^2}{12} = 67.66667$$

$$\Sigma yy' = \Sigma YY' - \frac{(\Sigma Y)(\Sigma Y')}{N} = 409 - \frac{(64)(64)}{12} = 67.66667$$

$$r_{yy'}^2 = \frac{(\Sigma yy')^2}{(\Sigma y^2)(\Sigma y'^2)} = \frac{67.66667^2}{(84.66667)(67.66667)} = .79921$$

Compare $r_{yy'}^2$ with $R_{y.12}^2$ I obtained when I analyzed the same data with coded vectors and note that they are identical (see the analyses of Table 11.11 in Chapter 11). Thus, using either coded vectors or criterion scaling, the proportion of variance accounted for by the categorical variable is the same. Note, however, that it would be wrong to test $r_{yy'}^2$ as if it were a squared zero-order correlation. Instead, the appropriate degrees of freedom for the numerator and the denominator of the F ratio have to be used when testing $r_{yy'}^2$. For the present example, the numerator degrees of freedom are 2 (there are three categories). Therefore,

$$F = \frac{.79921/2}{(1 - .79921)/(12 - 2 - 1)} = \frac{.39961}{.02231} = 17.91$$

with 2 and 9 *df*. Not surprisingly, I got the same F ratio when I analyzed these data with coded vectors representing the categorical independent variable (see Chapter 11).

---

[24]For an analysis identical to the one I am doing here, except that the independent variables were continuous, see Chapter 5.

If the data in Table 12.14 were analyzed by a computer program for regression analysis, the proportion of variance accounted for, the regression and residual sums of squares reported in the output would be correct. However, the reported F ratio would be *incorrect,* as it would be calculated as if the proportion of variance accounted for (or the regression sum of squares) is associated with one degree of freedom. This will always be so, as a categorical variable, whatever the number of its categories, is embodied in a single vector when it is criterion scaled.

Regression Equation

$$b = \frac{\Sigma yy'}{\Sigma y'^2} = \frac{67.66667}{67.66667} = 1.00$$

$$a = \overline{Y} - b\overline{Y}' = 5.33 - (1.0)(5.33) = 0$$

Notice the properties of the regression equation with criterion scaling: (1) as $\Sigma yy' = \Sigma y'^2$, the regression coefficient is always 1.0. This makes sense as values on the predictor (i.e., the criterion-scaled variable) are actually the predicted scores. (2) The intercept is equal to zero. This will always be so, as $\overline{Y} = \overline{Y}'$ (see Chapter 2) and b is always 1.0.

Regression Sum of Squares.   In the preceding I calculated the regression sum of squares as $\Sigma y'^2 = 67.66667$. Alternatively, using one of the formulas I introduced in Chapter 2,

$$ss_{reg} = b\Sigma yy' = (1.0)(67.66667) = 67.66667$$

Compare this with the results of analyses of the same data in Chapter 11.

An Alternative Coding Scheme.   When n's are equal, the total scores for each group on the dependent variable may be used for criterion scaling, instead of the means. This is so as the multiplication of the criterion-scaled variable by a constant (n) does not affect $r_{yy'}^2$. The use of total scores is preferable as possible rounding errors in the use of means are thereby avoided. Note carefully that with unequal n's, *means* must be used for criterion scaling.

Concluding Comments

Before turning to criterion scaling in designs with multiple categorical independent variables, I will make several comments.

For convenience, I illustrated criterion scaling of a categorical variable with only three categories. Of course, criterion scaling is particularly advantageous when a variable consists of many categories, therefore requiring many coded vectors. There are two additional advantages to criterion scaling.

One, when data are missing for subjects on the categorical variable, these subjects are treated as another category. That is, their mean on the dependent variable is used as the score on the criterion-scaled variable. This amounts to using "the information that we have no information on X to assist us in the estimation of Y" (Beaton, 1969b, p. 342).

Two, criterion scaling can be used to scale variables that are expressed on an ordinal level. Doing this will accomplish the same results as using a set of coded vectors to represent the ordinal variable. Because researchers try to avoid the proliferation of coded vectors when they use ordinal variables, they resort to scaling schemes (mostly judgmental) for the assignment of scale values to the different levels of the variable. The authors of the Coleman Report, for example, resorted to such schemes. In a reanalysis of data from the Coleman Report, Beaton (1969a) demonstrated that using criterion scaling for ordinal variables resulted in accounting for larger proportions of criterion variance as compared with those accounted for when researchers assigned arbitrary values to such variables.

Multiple Categorical Variables

In designs with multiple categorical independent variables each variable is criterion scaled separately. The dependent variable is then regressed on the criterion-scaled variables. Only when the categorical variables are not correlated (i.e., when the cell frequencies are equal) will this approach yield the same results as when coded vectors are used to represent the categorical variables. Criterion scaling for correlated categorical variables yields results that are discrepant from those in which coded vectors are used. The degree of the discrepancy cannot be exactly determined, although it generally appears to be small (Beaton, 1969a, 1969b; Gocka, 1973).

Although a solution with criterion-scaled variables is not exact when the categorical variables are correlated, it may still be a useful or even the only feasible approach when the number of coded vectors required is prohibitively large. Terms representing interactions may also be criterion scaled by using cell means as a criterion-scaled variable, in addition to the criterion-scaled vectors that represent the main effects (see Beaton, 1969a, 1969b).

A situation in which criterion scaling is particularly useful occurs when one wishes to apply a variable-selection procedure (e.g., stepwise regression; see Chapter 6) to a set of categorical variables. Using such a procedure when the variables are represented by coded vectors treats each vector as a separate variable. Consequently, the results will almost always consist of parts of variables (i.e., only some of the coded vectors representing a variable are selected) in a mixed order. Such results are not only difficult to interpret but may have little or no bearing on the questions posed by the researcher. When, for instance, one wishes to make a statement about increments in the proportions of variance accounted for by predictors as they are entered successively into the analysis, it is not possible to do so when vectors representing different variables are entered in a mixed order and only parts of variables are retained in the final analysis.

Examples of stepwise regression analysis applied to independent variables represented by coded vectors occur in research on college effects by Astin and his associates. Astin and Panos (1969), for example, reported on a large number of such analyses in which they treated coded vectors as if each represented an independent variable or a distinct predictor. Thus, when predicting persistence in college, 19 out of 90 coded vectors were retained as a result of the application of a stepwise regression analysis. Of the 19 vectors, 5 represented high school grade average (out of 9 categories), 3 were career choices (out of 30 categories), 2 were father's education (out of 6 categories), and so on. Moreover, the vectors that represented fragments of variables were entered in a mixed order. Yet Astin and Panos reported (and tested) the increment in the proportion of variance due to each vector as it entered into the analysis. Needless to say such results are not meaningful.

Clearly, criterion scaling can be used to avoid the difficulties encountered when applying variable-selection procedures to coded vectors representing independent variables. Further, this approach may also be applied in what Gocka (1973) referred to as mixed-mode variables, namely, interval as well as categorical or ordinal variables that have been criterion scaled. While the analysis proceeds in the usual manner, it is necessary to adjust the degrees of freedom for the categorical variables, as each is represented in the analysis by a single vector, regardless of the number of degrees of freedom associated with it. It is probably preferable to follow Gocka's (1973) suggestion to do the analysis in two stages. First, apply the variable selection procedure to the criterion-scaled variables (and the interval variables if there are such in the design). Second, having decided which variables are to be retained, based on the results of the first analysis, enter the categorical variables that were retained in the form of coded vectors (along with any interval variables that were retained) and do the analysis in the usual manner. The virtue of this two-stage process is that chances are that a relatively small number of variables will be retained as a result of the application of the first stage of the analysis. Consequently, the use of coded vectors to represent the categorical variables in the second stage of the analysis would be feasible.

In conclusion, Beaton's words should be borne in mind: "Criterion scaling does not attempt to produce an absolute scale for a factor but instead to scale the factor with reference to an external criterion" (Beaton, 1969b, p. 343). Therefore, the categories of a variable may be assigned different scale values, and even change in their rank order, when different criterion variables are used in the process of criterion scaling. Examples of criterion scaling applied to data from the Coleman Report may be found in Beaton (1969a) and Mayeske et al. (1969).[25]

VARIANCE ACCOUNTED FOR AS EFFECT SIZE: CAVEAT

In earlier chapters (especially Chapter 9), I drew attention to difficulties and ambiguities attendant with attempts to interpret, substantively and practically, the proportion of variance accounted for in the form of R^2. Further, I discussed in detail the dubious value of partitioning R^2 for the purpose of determining the relative importance of variables. I return briefly to this topic to alert you that similar problems arise in the context of experimental designs with categorical independent variables.

Eta-Squared

In the beginning of Chapter 11, I showed the equivalence of R^2 of a dependent variable with a set of coded vectors representing a categorical variable and η^2 (eta-squared) calculated in a one-way analysis of variance as the ratio of the between groups sum of squares to the total sum of squares—see (11.5) and the discussion related to it. The same is true for factorial designs, where for each R^2 associated with a given component (factor or interaction) a parallel η^2 may be calculated by dividing the sum of squares associated with the component in question by the total sum of squares.

In earlier chapters I pointed out that many authors deplore the sole reliance on tests of statistical significance and recommend that indices of effect size, or magnitude-of-effect, accompany them (for an exhaustive treatment of this topic and its relation to sample size and the power of the statistical test of significance, see Cohen, 1988, 1992). η^2 is among the indices recommended for use in factorial designs to ascertain effect size for each component (for discussions of these

---

[25]In the second edition of this book (Pedhazur, 1982, Chapter 14), I showed how criterion scaling can be used to facilitate analyses of repeated-measures designs.

and other indices, see, e.g., Hays, 1988, pp. 453–454; Keppel, 1991, pp. 221–224; Maxwell, Camp, & Arvey, 1981; also "Partial Eta-Squared," in the following section). In addition to using η^2 as an index of the effect of the component with which it is associated, authors and researchers compare η^2's within and/or across studies. Comparisons of η^2's within a study are done primarily to identify factors having stronger effects than others. Comparisons of η^2's across studies are done primarily to determine whether effects of the "same" factor are similar.

Arguments against the use of η^2 as an index of effect size were advanced from methodological and substantive perspectives. Some of the issues addressed by the critics follow.

"As a general proposition it can be stated that *all measures of variance accounted for are specific to characteristics of the experiments from which the estimates were obtained,* and therefore the ultimate interpretation of proportion of variance accounted for is a dubious prospect at best" (Sechrest & Yeaton, 1982, p. 592; for a general discussion of the dubious value of measures of explained variance, see O'Grady, 1982).

η^2 is affected by the size of the design as well as the total sample. Thus, for example, other things equal, the larger the total sample, the smaller η^2 tends to be. On the other hand, the greater the number of treatments, the larger η^2 tends to be (see, e.g., Murray & Dosser, 1987; Strube, 1988).

Even if factors in a study consist of the same number of treatments, statements about relative strength of their effects based on, say, magnitudes of η^2 associated with them, are generally not meaningful. Ronis (1981), who discussed this and related issues, stressed that "to draw clear conclusions about the relative impact of two independent variables, we must have some assurance that the manipulations of the two variables are of comparable magnitudes" (p. 998). But how is one to determine that two manipulations are of comparable magnitudes when, in light of the state of theory and measurement in many areas of social-science research, it is virtually impossible to assess the strength of a manipulation in the first place (see, e.g., Pedhazur & Schmelkin, 1991, pp. 258–265; Sechrest & Yeaton, 1982)? This is probably why reports of manipulation checks are rare in the research literature.

Pedhazur and Schmelkin (1991) point out that the assessment of manipulation strength is especially problematic for categorical variables, as they tend to be global, hence vaguely defined. Frequently it is not possible to tell what is being manipulated, to say nothing of the strength of the manipulation. Following are some of the examples they give.

> Consider the standard teacher-centered versus student-centered teaching styles. What do these actually mean? Even a cursory glance at the research literature will show that many different treatments go under these names. The converse is also true—treatments called by different names may refer to the same variable. For example, are student-centered and teacher-centered teaching styles the same as democratic and autocratic teaching styles, respectively, or as Progressivism and Traditionalism (Conservatism?) respectively? It depends on whose research one is looking at. Other examples of treatments of categorical variables that tend to be global are leadership styles (e.g., democratic, authoritarian, laissez-faire), psychotherapies (e.g., cognitive, behavior). (Pedhazur & Schmelkin, 1991, p. 255)

The same proportion of variance accounted for may be deemed important in one area and trivial in another (e.g., LaTour, 1981a, 1981b). Further, what is deemed a small effect, based on the proportion of variance accounted for, is deemed an important effect, based on other criteria (e.g., Abelson, 1985; Rosenthal, 1990;[26] Rosenthal & Rubin, 1979; Rosnow & Rosenthal, 1988; Wolf & Cornell, 1986).

---

[26]For comments on Rosenthal, see Crow (1991), McGraw (1991), and Strahan (1991). See Rosenthal (1991) for a reply.

> It seems generally and naively to be assumed by those who favor calculations of proportion of variance explained that the actual variance to be explained is 100%. This assumption is unwarranted, since it requires the additional assumption that the dependent measure is measured without error. . . . By definition, unreliable variance cannot be accounted for. (Sechrest & Yeaton, 1982, p. 591)

Finally, some researchers seem to assume, erroneously, that all indices of the proportion of variance accounted for have a maximum of 1.00. When, for example, the shape of the distributions of two variables differ, the correlation between them cannot reach 1.00. Thus, the correlation between a categorical variable (e.g., coded vector identifying two groups) and a continuous variable (referred to as a point-biserial correlation) cannot reach 1.00. "The maximum size of r_{pb} [point-biserial] between a dichotomous variable and a normally distributed variable is about .80, which occurs when the p value of the dichotomous variable is .50. The further the p value deviates from .50 in either direction, the lower the ceiling on r_{pb}" (Nunnally, 1978, p. 145).

Partial Eta-Squared

Before commenting on the use of partial η^2, I will show how it is calculated and discuss some of its properties. Cohen (1973, p. 108) stated that "*partial η^2 of a research factor A with a dependent variable Y from which all other nonerror sources of variance (main effects, interactions, trend components, etc.) in the experiment (B,C, . . . J) have been removed*" is

$$\eta^2_{YA.BC...J} = \frac{df_A F_A}{df_A F_A + df_E} = \frac{ss_A}{ss_A + ss_E} \tag{12.10}$$

where df_A = degrees of freedom for the numerator of the F ratio for factor A; F_A = F ratio for factor A; df_E = degrees of freedom associated with the error term; ss_A = sum of squares for factor A; and ss_E = sum of squares for error. An examination of (12.10) reveals that in a single-factor design partial η^2 is equal to η^2. This is to be expected, as there are no components to be partialed. In multifactor designs the magnitude of partial eta-squared is determined by the size of the error term. The smaller the error term, the larger the partial eta-squared.

I will now apply (12.10) to the 3×3 design I analyzed earlier in this chapter. For this purpose, it will be easiest to use information I summarized in Table 12.10. Examine the table and notice that the values reported under *prop*(ortion) are actually η^2's associated with each component of the model. As I indicated in the note to the table, the sum of the η^2's is equal to the overall R Square.

Using relevant sums of squares from Table 12.10, I calculated the corresponding partial η^2's, and report them, for comparative purposes, alongside the η^2's in Table 12.15. As an exercise, I

Table 12.15   Eta-Squared and Partial Eta-Squared for Data in Table 12.9

Source	ss	η^2	Partial η^2
A	84.00	.36842	.67742
B	12.00	.05263	.23077
$A \times B$	92.00	.40351	.69697
Residual	40.00		
Total	228.00		

NOTE: I took the values under η^2 from Table 12.10 from the column labeled *prop*. As I illustrated in the footnote to Table 12.10, proportion of variance accounted for by A = 84.00/228.00 = .36842. Partial η^2 for A = (84.00)/(84.00 + 40.00) = .67742.

suggest that you verify that the same partial η^2's are obtained when relevant F ratios and df are used in (12.10).

Two things are notable about the results in Table 12.15. One, partial η^2 tends to be larger (sometimes considerably) than η^2. Two, unlike η^2's, partial η^2's are *not* additive. Notice that the sum of the partial η^2's is not equal to the overall R Square. Further, as in the present example, it can exceed 1.00.

Some authors, notably Cohen (1973), argued that in many instances, especially when comparing effect sizes of a factor in designs that differ in, say, the number of factors, partial η^2 is more appropriate than η^2 (for a critique of this point of view, see Kennedy, 1970).

My reservations concerning the interpretation of proportion of variance as effect size (see the preceding) apply also to situations when partial η^2 is used for comparisons across studies. Further, such comparisons introduce additional elements that are bound to complicate matters. Suffice it to mention how differences in subjects may affect the results. As is well known, in most experiments, subjects who happen to be available (euphemistically referred to as samples of convenience) are used. Therefore, it is not surprising when such "samples" differ in variability, thereby casting serious doubt about comparisons of proportions of variance accounted for, be they in the form of η^2 or partial η^2. Clearly, other aspects (e.g., settings, researchers) may also render comparisons across studies questionable. In a broader sense, it is necessary to keep in mind that various artifacts and pitfalls in research (e.g., experimenter expectations, subjects' response styles) may masquerade as effects of manipulated variables (see Pedhazur & Schmelkin, 1991, Chapters 11 and 12, and references therein).

According to Cohen (1973), "In general, one wishes to partial out variables which are not properly considered 'error' in one's conception of the background against which a factor A is to be appraised" (p. 110). Cohen mentioned "two kinds of variables that are obvious candidates for partialing" (p. 110):

1. "*Manipulated variables,* . . . since by definition the manipulated variable accounts for none of the SS_E in the reference experiment" (p. 111). I believe it would suffice to mention my earlier comments about ambiguities regarding definition of treatments and artifacts in research to raise doubts about manipulated variables having no effect on the error term.

2. "*Variables controlled by being held constant*" (p. 111). This, I believe, is even more questionable, as it is open to widely different interpretation. A case in point is the example Cohen gave. Briefly, he described an experiment in which the experimenter studied the effect of teaching methods, and stated, "Good craftsmanship in experimentation would dictate that the teachers used would be of comparable level of experience and the pupils would be relatively homogeneous in demographic background (socioeconomic status, ethnicity)" (p. 109). It is a safe bet that researchers would differ in their interpretation of the meaning of "comparable level" of teaching experience or "relative homogeneity" on demographic background, not to mention the manner in which they are to be measured.

Cohen then posited that another researcher "performs an experiment which uses the same teaching methods" but also studies the "amount of teaching experience" and the interaction between the two variables. It is under such circumstances, Cohen asserted, that teaching experience and the interaction have to be partialed when comparing the teaching methods. Without going far afield, I would like to point out that even with the best of intentions what may be deemed the same teaching methods may turn out to be not so, and controlling for teaching experience may not be the same as having teachers with "comparable experience," not to mention a host of other variables that may be operating (e.g., "samples," settings).

I believe the following example to be more characteristic of what might take place when attempting a replication. Sechrest and Yeaton (1982) cited a study whose authors claimed that, except for a slight increase in the number of subjects, they were unaware of any deviation from a study they tried to replicate. Yet, while in the original study a statistically significant interaction was found, this was not true of the replication study. Sechrest and Yeaton stated that "for whatever reason . . . [there was] a considerably larger amount of unexplained variation in the within-subjects part" (p. 594) in the replication experiment (19.88 as compared to 2.40 in the original study). Recall that it is this error term that plays a crucial role in the calculation of partial η^2.

Notwithstanding my reservations regarding the usefulness of the proportion of variance accounted for as an index of effect size, I would like to stress that Cohen was careful to caution the reader: "The proportions of variance defined by η^2 and partial η^2 refer to different *bases,* and the choice between them and their interpretation demands an understanding of the sources which have contributed to the base, and particularly to SS_E" (p. 112). I submit that this is a tall order even for sophisticated and knowledgeable researchers.

Because partial η^2 tends to be larger than η^2, I am afraid that novices will be inclined to use it as an index of effect size within a single study. The likelihood of this happening has, I think, increased with the inclusion of partial η^2 as an option in SPSS (see EFSIZE in MANOVA) as an index of effect size. So far as I could tell, brief descriptions of partial eta-squared are given in the manual (Norušis/SPSS Inc., 1993b, pp. 41, 409). Following is the latter description:

> For univariate F tests and t-tests, MANOVA computes a measure of effect size based on partial η^2:
> partial $\eta^2 = (ssh)/(ssh+sse)$
> where *ssh* is hypothesis sum of squares and *sse* is error sum of squares. The measure is an overestimate of the actual effect size. However, it is consistent and is applicable to all F and t-tests. For a discussion of effect size measures, see Cohen (1977) and Hays (1981).

It is a safe bet that the less knowledgeable users will not bother to go to the references, assuming they even noticed the quoted statement.

Finally, what I said about partial η^2 applies in a general sense to partial ω^2 (omega-squared). It is noteworthy that in their detailed discussion of ω^2, Keren and Lewis (1979) had this to say: "Thus, an effect which is highly significant but accounts for only a small proportion of the variance is not of interest since its explanatory power is rather weak and its usefulness for understanding the phenomenon under study is limited" (p. 122).

CONCLUDING REMARKS

In this chapter, I extended the idea of coding categorical independent variables to factorial designs. As in the case of one categorical independent variable, the scores on the dependent variable measure are regressed on a set of coded vectors. Factorial designs have subsets of coded vectors, each subset representing a factor or an interaction between factors. Each factor is coded separately as if it were the only one in the design. Vectors to represent interaction between factors, or independent variables, are generated by cross multiplying each vector of one factor by each vector of the other factor. Vectors for higher-order interactions are similarly obtained. That is, each vector of one factor is multiplied by each vector of the factors whose higher-order interaction is being considered. Although the three coding methods I introduced in Chapter 11 (effect, orthogonal, and dummy) may be used in factorial designs, effect coding is the most useful and straightforward and has therefore received the most detailed treatment in the chapter.

Main effects and interactions can be tested by using either the proportions of variance accounted for by each subset of coded vectors or the regression sums of squares attributable to each subset of coded vectors. Multiple comparisons among main effects may take the form of planned orthogonal or nonorthogonal, and post hoc, depending on the specific hypotheses the researcher formulated. I contended that when the interaction is statistically significant, it is more meaningful to test simple effects. In addition, I showed how to test interaction contrasts, when a statistically significant interaction is associated with more than one degree of freedom, and I commented on the assertion by some authors that such contrasts be used in lieu of tests of simple effects.

In presenting the analysis and interpreting nonorthogonal designs, I stressed the importance of distinguishing between experimental and nonexperimental research. Among other things, I recommended that the concept of interaction be used in the former only. I suggested that cross-product vectors in nonexperimental research be referred to as multiplicative, or joint, relations.

I concluded the chapter with two brief sections. In the first, I presented criterion scaling as a method of representing a categorical variable composed of any number of categories in a single vector, and I pointed out that this approach is particularly useful when a variable-selection procedure is to be applied to a set of categorical independent variables or to one composed of a mixture of categorical and continuous variables. In the second, I sounded cautionary notes about the use of η^2 and partial η^2 as indices of effect size.

STUDY SUGGESTIONS

1. Discuss the advantages of a factorial experiment over a single-factor experiment.
2. In a factorial experiment, factors *A, B,* and *C* have, respectively, three, three, and five categories. Indicate the number of coded vectors necessary to represent each main effect, and each interaction term.
3. In an experiment with two factors, *A* with three categories and *B* with six categories, there are ten subjects per cell or treatment combination. What are the degrees of freedom associated with the *F* ratio for each main effect and for the interaction?
4. In a factorial design with orthogonal coding, there are three coded vectors, 1, 2, and 3, for factor *A*. The zero-order correlations of the dependent variable, *Y,* with each of these vectors are $r_{y1} = .36$; $r_{y2} = .41$; and $r_{y3} = .09$. The total sum of squares, Σy^2, is 436.00. What is(are) the following?
   (a) β's (standardized coefficients) associated with each coded vector for factor *A*.
   (b) Proportion of variance accounted for by factor *A*.

(c) Regression sum of squares for factor *A*.
(d) Mean square regression for factor *A*.
(e) Additional information you need to test the main effects of *A*.

5. In an analysis of a factorial design, effect coding was used. Factor *B* consisted of four categories. In the regression equation obtained from the analysis, *a* (intercept) = 8.5. The three *b*'s associated with the coded vectors for *B* are $b_{B1} = .5$, $b_{B2} = -1.5$, $b_{B3} = 2.5$. What are the means of the four levels of factor *B?*

6. In an analysis of a factorial design with three factors, the following coded vectors were used: 1 and 2 for factor *A;* 3, 4, and 5 for factor *B;* 6, 7, and 8 for factor *C.* There are five subjects per cell. The proportion of variance accounted for by all the factors and their interactions is .37541. The proportion of variance accounted for by factor *B* is .23452. What is the *F* ratio for factor *B?*

7. Using effect coding, analyze the following 2 × 3 factorial experiment:

	B_1	B_2	B_3
	5	4	9
A_1	6	5	10
	7	6	11
	3	7	5
A_2	4	8	6
	5	9	7

What is(are) the following?

(a) Proportion of variance accounted for by each factor and by their interaction.

(b) Regression sum of squares due to each factor and the interaction.

(c) Mean square residuals.

(d) Regression equation.

(e) F ratio for each factor and for the interaction.

(f) Construct a 2×3 table. In the marginals of the table show the main effects of A and B. In each cell show the interaction term (for an example of such a table, see Table 12.11).

(g) Using relevant values from the table under (f) and the relevant n's, show how the regression sums of squares for A, B, and $A \times B$ may be obtained.

(h) Since the F ratio for the interaction is statistically significant [see (e)], what type of tests are indicated?

(i) Using values from the table under (f) and relevant n's, calculate sums of squares for simple effects for A and for B. Calculate the F ratios for the simple effects and display the results in a table, using a format as in Table 12.7.

(j) What should the sum of the sums of squares for the simple effects for A be equal to?

(k) What should the sum of the sums of squares for the simple effects for B be equal to?

(l) Show how by using relevant values from the table under (f) and the intercept (a) from the regression equation obtained under (d) one can calculate the mean of each cell.

(m) Test interaction contrasts for the following:

(1) B1   B2   (2) B1 + B2   B3

A1	
A2	

A1	
A2	

8. Discuss the importance of distinguishing between nonorthogonal designs in experimental and nonexperimental research.

ANSWERS

2. $A = 2$; $B = 2$; $C = 4$; $A \times B = 4$; $A \times C = 8$; $B \times C = 8$; $A \times B \times C = 16$

3. For A: 2 and 162; for B: 5 and 162; for $A \times B$: 10 and 162.

4. (a) $\beta_1 = .36$; $\beta_2 = .41$; $\beta_3 = .09$
   (b) .3058
   (c) 133.3288
   (d) 44.44293
   (e) The mean square residual

5. $\overline{Y}_{B_1} = 9$, $\overline{Y}_{B_2} = 7$, $\overline{Y}_{B_3} = 11$, $\overline{Y}_{B_4} = 7$

6. $F = 24.03$, with 3 and 192 *df*. (*df* for total = 239. *df* for $A = 2$, $B = 3$, $C = 3$, $AB = 6$, $AC = 6$, $BC = 9$, $ABC = 18$. Therefore, *df* for main effects and interaction are 47. *df* for error are $239 - 47 = 192$.)

7. (a) $A = .05455$, $B = .32727$; $A \times B = .47272$
   (b) $A = 4.50$; $B = 27.00$; $A \times B = 39.00$
   (c) $MSR = 1.00$
   (d) $Y' = 6.5 + .5A1 - 1.5B1 + 0B2 + .5A1B1 - 2.0A1B2$
   (e) $F(1,12) = 4.50$ for A
   $F(2,12) = 13.50$ for B
   $F(2,12) = 19.50$ for $A \times B$

(f)

	B_1	B_2	B_3	A Effects
A_1	$.5 = b_{A1B1}$	$-2.0 = b_{A1B2}$	1.5	$.5 = b_{A1}$
A_2	$-.5$	2.0	-1.5	$-.5$
B Effects:	$-1.5 = b_{B1}$	$0 = b_{B2}$	1.5	

(g) $ss_A = [(.5)^2 + (-.5)^2](9) = 4.5$
$ss_B = [(-1.5)^2 + (0)^2 + (1.5)^2](6) = 27.0$
$ss_{AB} = [(.5)^2 + (-2.0)^2 + (1.5)^2 + (-.5)^2 + (2.0)^2 + (1.5)^2](3) = 39.0$

(h) Simple effects

(i) For example, A at $B_1 = (3)[(.5 + .5)^2 + (-.5 + -.5)^2] = 6.0$. The remaining terms are treated similarly. If you are having problems, see the text.

Source	ss	df	ms	F
A at B_1	6.0	1	6.0	6.0
A at B_2	13.5	1	13.5	13.5
A at B_3	24.0	1	24.0	24.0
B at A_1	42.0	2	21.0	21.0
B at A_2	24.0	2	12.0	12.0
Residual	12.0	12	1.0	

(j) $ss_A + ss_{AB} = 4.5 + 39.0 = 43.5 = 6.0 + 13.5 + 24.0$

(k) $ss_B + ss_{AB} = 27.0 + 39.0 = 66.0 = 42.0 + 24.0$

(l) For example, the mean for cell A_1B_1 is
$$6.5 + .5 + (-1.5) + (.5) = 6.0$$
$$a \quad A_1 \quad B_1 \quad A_1B_1$$
The other cells are treated similarly.

(m) (1) $F(1,12) = 18.75$
(2) $F(1,12) = 20.25$
If you are having problems, see the text.

13

Curvilinear Regression Analysis

In Chapters 11 and 12, I demonstrated that multiple regression analysis with coded vectors representing categorical independent variables yields overall results identical to those from an analysis of variance of the same data. For such designs, one may choose between regression analysis and analysis of variance based on a greater familiarity with one or the other, the availability of or preference for a specific computer program, and the like.[1]

When the independent variable is continuous, the choice between analysis of variance and regression analysis is not arbitrary. Although either approach may be used with a continuous independent variable that consists of a limited number of levels (e.g., hours of practice, dosages of a drug, years of education), each addresses a different question. Applying analysis of variance, or multiple regression analysis with coded vectors, with such an independent variable amounts to treating it as if it were a categorical variable. Under such circumstances, the answer being sought, wittingly or unwittingly, is whether one may infer that the population means for the different levels differ from each other. When regression analysis is applied with a continuous independent variable, the answer being sought is about the nature of the relation between the independent and the dependent variable. Thus, one may determine whether the regression of the dependent variable on the independent variable is linear or curvilinear. Moreover, when the relation is curvilinear, one may determine its specific form.

In the first section of the chapter, I discuss the study of linear regression and departures therefrom. I then turn to a treatment of curvilinear regression analysis. As in preceding chapters, I present first such analyses in experimental research and then in nonexperimental research.

ANALYSIS OF VARIANCE WITH A CONTINUOUS INDEPENDENT VARIABLE

Assume that in an experiment on the learning of paired associates, the independent variable is the number of exposures to a list. Specifically, 15 subjects are randomly assigned, in equal numbers, to five levels of exposure to a list, so that one group is given one exposure, a second group

---

[1]Being more flexible, the multiple regression approach is preferable even in such designs. More important, as I showed in Chapter 12, under certain circumstances (e.g., nonorthogonal designs) the multiple regression approach is called for even when the independent variables are categorical. In designs consisting of both categorical and continuous variables (see Chapter 14 and 15), the multiple regression approach must be used.

Table 13.1   Illustrative Data for a Learning Experiment and Analysis of Variance Calculations

	Number of Exposures					
	1	2	3	4	5	
	2	3	3	4	4	
	3	4	4	5	5	
	4	5	5	6	6	
ΣY:	9	12	12	15	15	$\Sigma Y_t = 63$
$\bar{Y}$:	3	4	4	5	5	$(\Sigma Y_t)^2 = 3969$
						$\Sigma Y_t^2 = 283$

$$C = (3969)/15 = 264.60$$
$$\text{Total} = 283 - 264.60 = 18.40$$
$$\text{Between} = (9^2 + 12^2 + 12^2 + 15^2 + 15^2)/3 - 264.60 = 8.40$$

Source	df	ss	ms	F
Between	4	8.40	2.10	2.10
Within	10	10.00	1.00	
Total	14	18.40		

is given two exposures, and so on to five exposures for the fifth group. The dependent variable measure is the number of correct responses on a subsequent test.

Illustrative data for five groups and analysis of variance calculations are given in Table 13.1. As $F(4, 10) = 2.10$, $p > .05$, one can conclude that the hypothesis $\mu_1 = \mu_2 = \mu_3 = \mu_4 = \mu_5$ cannot be rejected.[2] In this analysis, I treated the continuous independent variable as if it were categorical, that is, as if it consisted of five distinct treatments.

Linear Regression Analysis of the Learning Experiment

I now apply regression analysis to the data in Table 13.1, taking account of the fact that the independent variable is continuous. For linear regression to be applicable, the means of the arrays (the five treatments in the present case) should fall on the regression line. It is possible, however, that though the population means fall on the regression line, the sample means do not fall exactly on it but are sufficiently close to describe a linear trend. Whether the trend is linear is generally decided based on a test of the deviation from linearity (see the following). When the deviation from linearity is statistically not significant, one can conclude that the trend is linear. When the deviation from linearity is statistically significant, one may still apply analysis of variance, bearing in mind that the continuous independent variable is treated as if it were categorical.[3] In what follows, I apply the methods of regression and analysis of variance to the data in Table 13.1.

In Table 13.2, I present the data in Table 13.1 in a format suitable for regression analysis. Following procedures outlined in Chapter 2,

[2]I am not concerned here with the important distinction between statistical significance and meaningfulness, but with two analyses applied to the same data. It is possible that based on meaningfulness one would decide to repeat the experiment with larger *n*'s to increase the power of the test. More appropriately, considerations of effect size and power of the statistical test should be an integral part of the study's design (see, e.g., Cohen, 1988, for a detailed treatment of these and related topics).

[3]Later, I present the alternative of applying curvilinear regression analysis.

Table 13.2 Data from the Learning Experiment (Table 13.1), Laid Out for Regression Analysis

	X	Y	XY
	1	2	2
	1	3	3
	1	4	4
	2	3	6
	2	4	8
	2	5	10
	3	3	9
	3	4	12
	3	5	15
	4	4	16
	4	5	20
	4	6	24
	5	4	20
	5	5	25
	5	6	30
Σ:	45	63	204
SS:	165	283	

$$\Sigma y^2 = \Sigma Y^2 - \frac{(\Sigma Y)^2}{N} = 283 - \frac{(63)^2}{15} = 18.40$$

$$\Sigma x^2 = \Sigma X^2 - \frac{(\Sigma X)^2}{N} = 165 - \frac{(45)^2}{15} = 30.00$$

$$\Sigma xy = \Sigma XY - \frac{(\Sigma X)(\Sigma Y)}{N} = 204 - \frac{(45)(63)}{15} = 15.00$$

$$ss_{\text{reg}} = \frac{(\Sigma xy)^2}{\Sigma x^2} = \frac{(15.00)^2}{30.00} = 7.50$$

$$b = \frac{\Sigma xy}{\Sigma x^2} = \frac{15.00}{30.00} = .50$$

$$a = \bar{Y} - b\bar{X} = 4.20 - (.50)(3.00) = 2.70$$

Look back at Table 13.1 and notice that the between-treatments sum of squares is 8.40. The sum of squares due to deviation from linearity is calculated by subtracting the regression sum of squares from the between-treatments sum of squares.

$$ss_{\text{dev}} = ss_{\text{treat}} - ss_{\text{reg}}$$

$$ss_{\text{dev}} = 8.40 - 7.50 = .90$$

The Meaning of the Deviation Sum of Squares

Before interpreting the results, I will explain the meaning of the sum of squares due to deviation from linearity with the aid of a figure as well as by direct calculation. In Figure 13.1, I plotted the

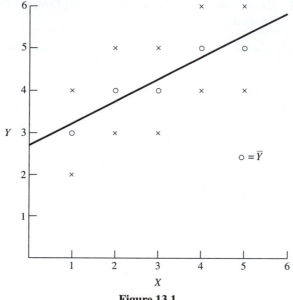

Figure 13.1

15 scores from Table 13.2. Following procedures I presented in Chapter 2, I drew the regression line. In addition, I used circles to present the mean of each of the five arrays. Note that the circles are close to the regression line, but none is actually on it. The vertical distance between the mean of an array and the regression line is the deviation of that mean from linear regression.

Now, $Y' = 2.7 + .5X$, which is an expression of the regression line, can be used to calculate the predicted Y's for each of the X's:

$$Y'_1 = 2.7 + .5X_1 = (2.7) + (.5)(1) = 3.2$$

$$Y'_2 = 2.7 + .5X_2 = (2.7) + (.5)(2) = 3.7$$

$$Y'_3 = 2.7 + .5X_3 = (2.7) + (.5)(3) = 4.2$$

$$Y'_4 = 2.7 + .5X_4 = (2.7) + (.5)(4) = 4.7$$

$$Y'_5 = 2.7 + .5X_5 = (2.7) + (.5)(5) = 5.2$$

As expected, the five predicted Y's fall on the regression line. Deviation from linearity is indicated by the deviation of the mean of each array from its Y'. Thus,

$$3.00 - 3.2 = -.2$$

$$4.00 - 3.7 = +.3$$

$$4.00 - 4.2 = -.2$$

$$5.00 - 4.7 = +.3$$

$$5.00 - 5.2 = -.2$$

Notice that in each case the predicted Y of a given array is subtracted from the mean of the Y's of that array. For example, the predicted Y for the array of X's with the value of 1 is 3.2, whereas the mean of the Y's of that array is 3.00 $[(2 + 3 + 4)/3]$. Squaring each deviation listed, weighting the result by the number of scores in its array, and summing all the values yields the sum of squares due to deviation from regression:

$$(3)(-.2^2) + (3)(.3^2) + (3)(-.2^2) + (3)(.3^2) + (3)(-.2^2) = .90$$

I obtained the same value (.90) by subtracting the regression sum of squares from the between-treatments sum of squares. When calculating the sum of squares due to deviation from linearity, one is asking the following question: What is the difference between restricting the data to conform to a linear trend and placing no such restriction? When the between-treatments sum of squares is calculated, there is no restriction on the trend of the treatment means. If the means are in fact on a straight line, the between-treatments sum of squares will be equal to the regression sum of squares. With departures from linearity, the between-treatments sum of squares will always be larger than the regression sum of squares. A method is necessary that enables one to decide when the difference between the two sums of squares is sufficiently small to warrant the use of linear regression analysis.

Test of the Deviation Sum of Squares

The method of testing the significance of deviation from linearity is straightforward. Instead of the one F ratio (for the between-treatments sum of squares), two F ratios are obtained: one for the sum of squares due to linear regression and one for the sum of squares due to deviation from linearity. As I have shown, these two sums of squares are components of the between-treatments sum of squares. The sum of squares due to linear regression has 1 degree of freedom, whereas the sum of squares due to deviation from linearity has $g - 2$ df (g = number of treatments). Dividing each sum of squares by its df yields a mean square. Each mean square is divided by the mean square error from the analysis of variance, thus yielding two F ratios. If the F ratio for the sum of squares due to deviation from linearity is statistically not significant, one may conclude that the data describe a linear trend and that the application of linear regression analysis is appropriate. If, on the other hand, the F ratio for the sum of squares due to deviation from linearity is statistically significant, a nonlinear trend is indicated. In Table 13.3, I summarize the application of this procedure to the data of the learning experiment (originally presented in Table 13.1).

Note how the between-treatments sum of squares is partitioned into two components, as are the df associated with the treatments sum of squares. The mean square for deviation from linearity (.30) is divided by the mean square error (1.00) to yield an F ratio of .30, which is statistically not significant. Therefore, one can conclude that linear regression analysis is appropriate. The F ratio associated with the linear trend is 7.50(1, 10), $p < .01$, indicating that the linear trend is

Table 13.3   Analysis of Variance Table: Test for Linearity for Learning Experiment Data

Source	df	ss		ms	F
Between Treatments	4	8.40			
Linearity	1		7.50	7.50	7.50*
Deviation from Linearity	3		.90	.30	<1
Within Treatments	10	10.00		1.00	
Total	14	18.40			

*$p < .05$

statistically significant. In effect, this means that the regression coefficient (b_{yx}) is statistically different from zero. For each unit increment in the independent variable (number of exposures), there is an expected .50 (b) unit increment in the dependent variable (number of correct responses).

MULTIPLE REGRESSION ANALYSIS OF THE LEARNING EXPERIMENT

In the preceding section, I presented analysis of variance and regression analysis of the same data in detail to show the process and meaning of testing deviation from linearity. I show now how you may obtain the same results in the context of multiple regression analysis. I display the basic approach in Table 13.4. Look first at vectors Y and X. These are the same as the Y and X vectors of Table 13.2. Consequently, we know (see the calculations following Table 13.2) that $\Sigma xy = 15.00$; $\Sigma x^2 = 30.00$; $\Sigma y^2 = 18.40$. Therefore,

$$r_{xy}^2 = \frac{(15.00)^2}{(30.00)(18.40)} = \frac{225}{552} = .40761$$

The linear regression of Y on X accounts for about 41% of the variance in the Y scores.

Suppose you decide not to restrict the data to a linear regression. In other words, suppose a multiple regression analysis is calculated in which Y is the dependent variable and group membership in the various treatments levels is the independent variable. Recall from Chapter 11 that any method of coding group membership will yield the same overall results. Look now at Table 13.4 in which vectors D1 through D4 represent group membership using dummy coding. When these vectors are used, the independent variable is treated as if it were a categorical variable. It is now possible to calculate the squared multiple correlation of Y with the four dummy

Table 13.4   Data for Learning Experiment (Table 13.1), Laid Out for Multiple Regression Analysis

Treatment	Y	X	D1	D2	D3	D4
	2	1	1	0	0	0
1	3	1	1	0	0	0
	4	1	1	0	0	0
	3	2	0	1	0	0
2	4	2	0	1	0	0
	5	2	0	1	0	0
	3	3	0	0	1	0
3	4	3	0	0	1	0
	5	3	0	0	1	0
	4	4	0	0	0	1
4	5	4	0	0	0	1
	6	4	0	0	0	1
	4	5	0	0	0	0
5	5	5	0	0	0	0
	6	5	0	0	0	0

vectors.[4] Recall, however, that doing this is equivalent to doing a one-way analysis of variance, and that $R^2_{y.1234} = \eta^2_{yx}$, or the ratio of the between-treatments sum of squares to the total sum of squares (see Chapter 11). Using relevant values from Table 13.3, $\eta^2_{yx} = (8.40)/(18.40) = .45652 = R^2_{y.1234}$ (where the subscript numbers stand for the dummy coded vectors of Table 13.4). Thus, when I placed a restriction of linearity on the data, I found that the proportion of variance accounted for is .40761 (r^2_{yx}). When I placed no trend restriction on the data, the proportion of variance accounted for by X is .45652 $(R^2_{y.1234})$. It is now possible to test whether the increment in the proportion of variance accounted for, when no restriction is placed on the data, is statistically significant. For this purpose, I adapt a formula I used frequently in earlier chapters:

$$F = \frac{(R^2_{y.1234} - R^2_{y.x})/(k_1 - k_2)}{(1 - R^2_{y.1234})/(N - k_1 - 1)} \tag{13.1}$$

where $R^2_{y.1234}$ = squared multiple correlation of the dependent variable, Y, with vectors D1 through D4 of Table 13.4; $R^2_{y.x}$ = squared correlation of Y with the X vector of Table 13.4, in which the independent variable is treated as continuous; k_1 = number of vectors associated with the first R^2; k_2 = number of vectors associated with the second R^2; and N = number of subjects. The degrees of freedom for the F ratio are $k_1 - k_2$ and $N - k_1 - 1$ for the numerator and the denominator, respectively.

Note that $R^2_{y.1234}$ is larger or equal to $R^2_{y.x}$. When the regression of Y on X is exactly linear, that is, when the Y means for all X values are on a straight line, $R^2_{y.1234} = R^2_{y.x}$. When, on the other hand, there is a deviation from linearity, $R^2_{y.1234} > R^2_{y.x}$. It is this deviation from linearity that (13.1) tests. For the data in Table 13.4,

$$F = \frac{(.45652 - .40761)/(4 - 1)}{(1 - .45652)/(15 - 4 - 1)} = \frac{.01630}{.05435} = .30$$

$F(3, 10) = .30$ is the same as the value I calculated earlier (see Table 13.3). Of course, the same conclusion is reached, namely the deviation from linearity is statistically not significant.

The test of the linear trend is $F = .40761/.05435 = 7.50$, with 1 and 10 *df*. The numerator is r^2_{yx} and the denominator is the same as the error term I used in calculating the F ratio for the deviation from linearity. Again, this F ratio is the same as the one given in Table 13.3.

For completeness, I show now how the various sums of squares are calculated.

$$\text{Overall regression} = (R^2_{y.1234})(\Sigma y^2) = (.45652)(18.40) = 8.40$$

$R^2_{y.1234}$ indicates the proportion of variance accounted for by the overall regression when no restriction for trend is placed on the data. Σy^2 = total sum of squares of the dependent variable. The sum of squares due to overall regression, 8.40, is equal to the between-treatments sum of squares, which I calculated in the analysis of variance (see Table 13.1).

$$\text{Linear regression} = (r^2_{yx})(\Sigma y^2) = (.40761)(18.40) = 7.50$$

One can, of course, obtain the sum of squares due to deviation from linearity by subtracting the regression sum of squares due to linearity from the overall regression sum of squares. Symbolically the sum of squares due to deviation from linearity is

$$(R^2_{y.1234})(\Sigma y^2) - (r^2_{yx})(\Sigma y^2) = (R^2_{y.1234} - r^2_{yx})(\Sigma y^2)$$

For the present data,

$$\text{Deviation from linearity} = (.45642 - .40761)(18.40) = .90$$

---

[4]As an exercise, you may wish to use a computer program to do this. If necessary, see Chapter 11 for examples of input files.

The sum of squares due to error is, as always, $(1 - R^2)(\Sigma y^2)$: that is, the proportion of variance not accounted for multiplied by the total sum of squares. For the present data,

$$\text{Error} = (1 - R^2_{y.1234})(\Sigma y^2) = (1 - .45652)(18.40) = 10.00$$

All of these sums of squares are identical to those reported in Table 13.3.

CURVILINEAR REGRESSION ANALYSIS

Until now, my presentation was restricted to linear regression analysis. I showed that when the data depart from linearity, one can do a multiple regression analysis in which the continuous variable is treated as a categorical variable. All that such an analysis can tell, however, is whether there is some trend in the data. When one wishes to study the nature of the trend, it is necessary to resort to nonlinear models. Such models may be classified into two categories: (1) intrinsically linear models and (2) intrinsically nonlinear models. An intrinsically linear model is one that is linear in its parameters but nonlinear in the variables. By an appropriate transformation, a model that is nonlinear in the variables may be reduced to a linear model, hence the name intrinsically linear model. Examples of transformations are raising variables to powers (see the following), expressing variables as logarithms, or taking square roots of variables. Intrinsically linear models may be analyzed by the method of ordinary least squares. In effect, the nonlinear variables are replaced by their transformations, and the latter are used in a multiple regression analysis. Intrinsically nonlinear models, on the other hand, are nonlinear in the parameters. The use of ordinary least squares is generally not appropriate for such models. My presentation is limited to intrinsically linear models. Specifically, I discuss and illustrate only polynomial regression. For other transformations in intrinsically linear models, see Cohen and Cohen (1983, Chapter 6), Draper and Smith (1981, Chapter 5), and Kmenta (1971, pp. 451–460). For good introductions to analyses of intrinsically nonlinear models, see Draper and Smith (1981, Chapter 10), Kmenta (1971, pp. 461–472), Myers (1990, Chapter 9), and Williams (1959, Chapter 4).

The Polynomial Equation

The method of curvilinear regression analysis is similar to linear regression analysis. The difference between the two is in the regression equation used. Curvilinear regression analysis uses a polynomial regression equation. This means that the independent variable is raised to a certain power. The highest power to which the independent variable is raised indicates the degree of the polynomial. The equation

$$Y' = a + b_1 X + b_2 X^2$$

is a second-degree polynomial, since X is raised to the second power.

$$Y' = a + b_1 X + b_2 X^2 + b_3 X^3$$

is a third-degree polynomial equation.

The order of the equation indicates the number of bends in the regression curve. A first-degree polynomial, like $Y' = a + bX$, describes a straight line. A second-degree polynomial describes a single bend in the regression curve and is referred to as a quadratic equation. A third-degree polynomial has two bends and is referred to as a cubic equation. The highest order that a given equation may take is equal to $g - 1$, where g is the number of distinct values of the independent variable. If, for example, a continuous independent variable consists of seven distinct values, then it may be raised to the sixth power. When this is done, the regression equation yields predicted Y's that are equal to the means of the different Y arrays, thus resulting in the smallest possible value for the residual sum of squares. When the highest-degree polynomial is used with any set of data, the resulting $R^2 = \eta^2_{yx}$, as both analyses permit as many bends in the curve as there are degrees of freedom minus one for the between-treatments sum of squares.

One goal of scientific research, however, is parsimony. Our interest is not in the predictive power of the highest-degree polynomial equation possible, but rather in the highest-degree polynomial equation necessary to describe a set of data.[5]

Polynomial regression analysis is carried out as an ordinary multiple regression analysis, except that powered vectors are included and the analysis is done *hierarchically*. That is, the analysis is carried out in a sequence of steps, beginning with the first-degree polynomial and followed by successively higher-degree polynomials. At each step, the proportion of variance of the dependent variable incremented by a higher-degree polynomial is tested for statistical significance.

Assume, for example, a continuous variable with five distinct values. The increments in the proportion of variance accounted for at each step are calculated as follows:

Linear: $R^2_{y.x}$

Quadratic: $R^2_{y.x, x^2} - R^2_{y.x}$

Cubic: $R^2_{y.x, x^2, x^3} - R^2_{y.x, x^2}$

Quartic: $R^2_{y.x, x^2, x^3, x^4} - R^2_{y.x, x^2, x^3}$

At each step, the increment in the proportion of variance accounted is tested with an F ratio. For the quartic element in the previous example, the F ratio is

$$F = \frac{(R^2_{y.x, x^2, x^3, x^4} - R^2_{y.x, x^2, x^3})/(k_1 - k_2)}{(1 - R^2_{y.x, x^2, x^3, x^4})/(N - k_1 - 1)} \tag{13.2}$$

where N = number of subjects; $k_1 = df$ for the larger R^2 (4, in the present case); and $k_2 = df$ for the smaller R^2 (3, in the present case). I used this type of F ratio extensively in earlier chapters. Note, however, that the R^2's in the present example are based on *one* independent variable raised to certain powers, whereas in earlier uses of the formula R^2 was based on several independent variables.

Caution on Nomenclature

Many authors refer to different degrees of the polynomial as variables. Later in this chapter, I discuss equations containing products of variables, as in

$$Y' = a + bX + bZ + bXZ$$

where XZ is the product of variables X and Z (notice the analogy between X^2, which is the product of X and X, and XZ). In such cases, too, many authors refer to XZ as a variable.

This imprudent practice is, in part, to blame for misinterpretations and misapplications, as evidenced by the use of stepwise regression analysis when products of variables are treated as if

---

[5]In the first part of this chapter, I demonstrated that a linear equation was sufficient to describe a set of data. Using higher-degree polynomials on such data will not appreciably enhance the description of the data and the predictions based on regression equations derived from the data.

they were distinct variables (see "Research Examples," later in this chapter). As you may recall, I made a similar point in Chapter 12 (see "Nonorthogonal Designs in Nonexperimental Research," and "Criterion Scaling"), where I cautioned against treating coded vectors representing a given variable as if they were distinct variables.

A Numerical Example

Suppose that we are interested in the effect of time spent in practice on the performance of a visual discrimination task. Subjects are randomly assigned to different levels of practice, following which a test of visual discrimination is administered, and the number of correct responses is recorded for each subject. Table 13.5 contains illustrative data for three subjects at each of six levels of practice. As there are six levels, the highest-degree polynomial possible for these data is the fifth. Our aim, however, is to determine the lowest-degree polynomial that best fits the data.

Some computer packages have special procedures for polynomial regression (e.g., BMDP 5R, Dixon, 1992, Vol. 2, pp. 1063–1072). Nevertheless, I will use a multiple regression procedure to (1) show how to do a polynomial regression analysis with any program for multiple regression analysis and (2) elaborate on some topics I discussed in earlier chapters (e.g., simultaneous versus hierarchical regression analysis, collinearity, tolerance). First, I do the analysis through REGRESSION of SPSS, and then I give an input file for PROC REG of SAS along with brief excerpts of the output.

Table 13.5   Illustrative Data from a Study of Visual Discrimination

	Practice Time (in Minutes)					
	2	4	6	8	10	12
	4	7	13	16	18	19
	6	10	14	17	19	20
	5	10	15	21	20	21
Σ:	15	27	42	54	57	60
$\bar{Y}$:	5	9	14	18	19	20

NOTE: The dependent variable measure is the number of correct responses.

SPSS

Input

```
TITLE TABLE 13.5.      POLYNOMIAL REGRESSION.
DATA LIST/Y X 1-4.     [Fixed format: Two columns for each variable]
COMPUTE X2=X**2.       [raise X to second power]
COMPUTE X3=X**3.       [raise X to third power]
COMPUTE X4=X**4.       [raise X to fourth power]
COMPUTE X5=X**5.       [raise X to fifth power]
BEGIN DATA
 4 2
 6 2
 5 2
 7 4
```

```
10  4
10  4
13  6
14  6
15  6
16  8
17  8
21  8
1810
1910
2010
1912
2012
2112
END DATA
LIST.
REGRESSION VAR=Y TO X5/DES/STAT ALL/CRITERIA TOLERANCE(.0000001)/
  DEP=Y/ENTER X/ENTER X2/ENTER X3/ENTER X4/ENTER X5/
  DEP=Y/ENTER X X2/SAVE=PRED(PREDICT).
LIST Y X PREDICT.
PLOT HSIZE=40/VSIZE=20/
  TITLE='TABLE 13.5'/HORIZONTAL='PRACTICE TIME'/
  VERTICAL='PREDICTED SCORES'/
  PLOT=PREDICT WITH X.
```

Commentary

For an introduction to SPSS, see Chapter 4, where I also explain the format I use for presenting input and output files and comment on them. Here, I comment only on statements relevant to the analysis under consideration. First, though, I remind you that italicized comments in brackets are *not* part of either input or output files (see Chapter 4).

I call for two regression analyses (see two DEP=Y statements). In the first, I enter the vectors sequentially, beginning with X and ending with X5. In light of the fact that vectors raised to successive powers tend to be highly correlated (see the following output), I specify very low tolerance so as to force entry of all the vectors in the first analysis. In Chapter 10 (see "Tolerance"), I pointed out that in the present chapter I would override the default tolerance (.0001; see SPSS Inc., 1993, p. 631). Had I not done this, only the linear and the quadratic terms would have entered.

I included the second DEP=Y statement so that I could use the quadratic equation to generate predicted scores, save them (see SAVE), and plot them against X. See the relevant output and commentaries.[6]

---

[6]This setup worked fine with earlier versions of the program. When I used it with Version 6.1.2, however, the program terminated with an unintelligible error message. When informed of this, SPSS acknowledged that it is a bug. If you are using 6.1.2 you can avoid the problem by running two REGRESSION commands, instead of one. Specifically, place a period after the first run (i.e., after ENTER X5). Call REGRESSION again for the second run. Of course, you can delete irrelevant elements I used for the first run (e.g., TOLERANCE). All you need for the second run is REGRESSION DEP=Y/ENTER X X2/SAVE=PRED(PREDICT).

Output

Y	X	X2	X3	X4	X5	
4	2	4.00	8.00	16.00	32.00	*[first subject]*
.	.	.	.	.	.	
21	12	144.00	1728.00	20736.00	248832.0	*[last subject]*

Commentary

I included the listing of scores for the first and last subject to show (1) how X was raised to successive powers as a result of the COMPUTE STATEMENTS and (2) that even with relatively small values of X, the values of powered vectors become increasingly large (e.g., values for last subject).

Output

	Mean	Std Dev
Y	14.167	5.823
X	7.000	3.515
X2	60.667	50.265
X3	588.000	626.542
X4	6066.667	7604.306
X5	65072.000	91696.203

N of Cases = 18

Correlation:

	Y	X	X2	X3	X4	X5
Y	1.000	.940	.870	.795	.731	.679
X	.940	1.000	.979	.938	.896	.857
X2	.870	.979	1.000	.988	.965	.940
X3	.795	.938	.988	1.000	.993	.980
X4	.731	.896	.965	.993	1.000	.996
X5	.679	.857	.940	.980	.996	1.000

Commentary

In the preceding I drew attention to the fact that scores on powered vectors become increasingly large. As you can see, this leads to increasingly large means and standard deviations. In the following I comment on the effects of standard deviations on the size of regression coefficients.

In my discussion of collinearity (Chapter 10), I pointed out, among other things, that examination of zero-order correlations is not sufficient to determine whether high collinearity exists in a set of data. Yet, when dealing with powered vectors, the zero-order correlations tend to be so high as to hit one between the eyes, so to speak. In the present example, correlations between vectors range from .857 (between X and X^5) to .996 (between X^4 and X^5). In what follows, I briefly explain some implications of the very high correlations. I hope that these will become clearer from my comments on the results of the analysis.

As an example, notice that the correlation between X and X^2 is .979. Not surprisingly, the correlation of Y with X is fairly similar to that of Y with X^2 (.940 and .870, respectively). Two implications follow from this.

One, using X^2 only, one would conclude, *erroneously,* that the quadratic term accounts for a substantial proportion of the Y variance. What we want is the proportion of variance X^2 increments over and above that accounted for by X. Stated differently, we want the squared semipartial correlation of Y with X^2 when X is partialed from it (i.e., $r^2_{y(x2.x)}$). The same is true for the other terms. Recall that such squared semipartial correlations can be expressed as a difference between two R^2's (see Chapters 7 and 9), hence, the *hierarchical* approach taken in the analysis.

Two, although I discuss tests of significance later, I will note at this stage that, in view of the foregoing, when a given degree polynomial is retained, lower-order ones should be retained as well, even when they are statistically not significant. In other words, all vectors up to and including the highest-degree polynomial that is determined to best fit the data should be retained.

Output

Equation Number 1   Dependent Variable..   Y
Block Number 5.   Method: Enter   X5

* * * * * * * *** WARNING *** * * * * * * *

The following variables in the equation have low tolerances:

Variable	Tolerance
X	.00001
X2	5.24980E–07
X3	1.24224E–07
X4	1.45444E–07
X5	1.22809E–06

* * * * * * *** END OF WARNING *** * * * * * * *

Multiple R	.97541			Analysis of Variance			
R Square	.95143	R Square Change	.00052		DF	Sum of Squares	Mean Square
Adjusted R Square	.93119	F Change	.12755	Regression	5	548.50000	109.70000
Standard Error	1.52753	Signif F Change	.7272	Residual	12	28.00000	2.33333

F = 47.01429   Signif F = .0000

Commentary

I reproduced the warning concerning variables having low tolerance to illustrate that in the present context it may be ignored. Incidentally, SPSS uses scientific notation here. For example, tolerance for X2 is .00000052.

This being the last step in the analysis, you can see that about 95% of the variance is accounted for by a fifth-degree polynomial, $F(5, 12) = 47.01, p < .01$. As I explained and demonstrated in connection with the analysis of the data in Table 13.1, testing the highest-degree polynomial possible in a set of data is tantamount to testing whether the means of the arrays are equal, which is equivalent to testing whether the means of the treatments differ from each other when a one-way analysis of variance is applied.[7] Recall also that $\eta_{yx}^2 = R^2$ of the highest-degree polynomial possible—that is, .95143.

At this stage, all we can tell from the analysis is that the data show a statistically significant trend. To see what degree polynomial best fits these data, it is necessary to turn our attention to the hierarchical analysis in which increments due to each degree of the polynomial are tested successively. Of course, we could do this by examining the results at each step. However, it can be done more efficiently by examining the summary table, excerpts of which I now reproduce.

Output

Summary table

Step	Variable	Rsq	RsqCh	FCh	SigCh
1	In: X	.8832	.8832	121.029	.000
2	In: X2	.9428	.0595	15.604	.001
3	In: X3	.9463	.0035	.911	.356
4	In: X4	.9509	.0046	1.231	.287
5	In: X5	.9514	.0005	.128	.727

Commentary

As the experiment is fictitious, I cannot address the paramount issue of meaningfulness of the results. Instead, I limit my comments to tests of statistical significance. As you can see from FCh (*F* Change), the increment due to the quadratic term is statistically significant, whereas all the terms beyond the quadratic are statistically not significant. I therefore conclude that a quadratic equation best fits the data. Examine RsqCh (R squared Change) and notice that the linear term accounts for about 88% of the variance and that the increment in the proportion of variance accounted for by the quadratic term (X2) is about 6%. Altogether, about 94% of the variance of the dependent variable is accounted for by a second-degree polynomial, as compared with about 95% accounted for by the highest-degree polynomial possible.

Output

-- Variables in the Equation --

Variable	B	SE B	Beta	Part Cor	Tolerance	VIF	T	Sig T
X	5.125000	27.888065	3.093171	.011691	1.429E−05	69996.976	.184	.8573
X2	−1.718750	10.172449	−14.835588	−.010749	5.250E−07	1904836.07	−.169	.8686
X3	.401042	1.677687	43.148402	.015208	1.242E−07	8049981.82	.239	.8151

[7]For a discussion of this point, see Li, J. C. R. (1964, Vol. II, pp. 171–174).

X4	−.039062	.127749	−51.008719	−.019453	1.454E−07	6875506.32	−.306	.7650
X5	.001302	.003646	20.502883	.022721	1.228E−06	814270.056	.357	.7272
(Constant)	−1.000000	26.793449					

Commentary

Before reproducing and examining the quadratic equation, I comment on some other aspects of the output from the present analysis. Recall from Chapter 10 that tolerance and VIF are used for diagnosis of collinearity. The extremely low tolerance values and the extremely high VIF values should come as no surprise when you recall the high correlations among the vectors representing the independent variable. If you ran these data you would also find that some of the condition indices (not reproduced here) are very high. All this, of course, confirms what we know already, namely that there is high collinearity in the data. In Chapters 5 and 10, I pointed out that when collinearity is high, standard errors of b's tend to be large. Examine SE B and notice that this is indeed the case in the present example. As a result, *all* the b's are statistically not significant (see the T and Sig T columns). Recall, however, that the b's are partial coefficients and that a test of a b is tantamount to a test of the increment in the proportion of variance due to the variable with which it is associated (*a vector representing a polynomial term,* in the present case) when it is entered last in the analysis. In other words, it is the test of the squared semipartial correlation of Y with the vector in question, while partialing from it all the other vectors. As you might have expected, all the semipartial correlations (see Part Cor) are very small.

It is important to recognize that in polynomial regression the only information relevant in the above output is that associated with the vector that entered last (X5), as it addresses the question of the increment in the proportion of variance due to the last vector. *The information associated with the other vectors goes counter to the requirement that the analysis be done hierarchically.*

Later, I discuss interpretation of b's. For now, I would like to draw your attention to the fact that the standardized regression coefficients (beta) are all considerably larger than 1.00. Although this is, admittedly, an extreme example, it nevertheless should dispel the mistaken notion held by some researchers and authors that the standardized regression coefficient cannot exceed 1.00. Only for the case of a single independent variable, where beta is equal to the zero-order correlation between the independent and the dependent variable, is the upper limit of beta 1.00 (I discussed standardized and unstandardized regression coefficients in detail in Chapters 5 and 10).

Having decided on the degree of the polynomial that best fits the data, it is necessary to calculate the regression equation with the terms that are to be retained. In the present example it is necessary to calculate the quadratic equation. Actually, this equation is available as Step 2 of the output (not reproduced here). Nevertheless, I called for a second regression analysis in which I included only the linear and quadratic terms (see the second DEP=Y statement in the input file given earlier) to show, among other things, how to generate predicted scores, save them, and then use them in the PLOT procedure (see the following).

Output

Equation Number 2   Dependent Variable..   Y
Block Number 1.   Method: Enter   X   X2
Variable(s) Entered on Step Number 1..   X2
2..   X

					Analysis of Variance			
Multiple R	.97096					DF	Sum of Squares	Mean Square
R Square	.94277	R Square Change	.94277		Regression	2	543.50714	271.75357
Adjusted R Square	.93514	F Change	123.55109		Residual	15	32.99286	2.19952
Standard Error	1.48308	Signif F Change	.0000					

$F = 123.55109 \quad$ Signif F = .0000

--- Variables in the Equation ---

Variable	B	SE B	Beta	Part Cor	Tolerance	VIF	T	Sig T
X	3.494643	.501046	2.109176	.430814	.041721	23.969	6.975	.0000
X2	−.138393	.035034	−1.194554	−.243996	.041721	23.969	−3.950	.0013
(Constant)	−1.900000							

Commentary

As I stated earlier, the results reported here are the same as those reported at Step 2 of the first analysis in which the highest-degree polynomial was included. Whatever output is examined, note that when the regression analysis is done with only the terms to be retained (linear and quadratic, in the present example), higher-order polynomials are relegated to the error term, as are the *df* associated with them.

As I explained earlier, only the test of the *b* for the quadratic term—$t(15) = -3.950$—is relevant in this analysis; $t^2 = 15.60 = F(1, 15)$, which is the FCh reported at Step 2 of the Summary table for the earlier analysis (see the preceding).

In sum, when a polynomial regression analysis is done, tests of trend components are done hierarchically. Once you determine the highest-degree polynomial that fits the data, you can calculate the regression equation with the terms that are to be retained. Only the test of the *b* associated with the highest-degree polynomial in the equation is meaningful. As I pointed out, even when *t* ratios for *b*'s of lower-order polynomials are statistically not significant, the vectors associated with such *b*'s should be retained.

In his presidential address to the Royal Statistical Society, Yates (1968) was critical of an author who failed to pay attention to the hierarchy in the polynomial model:

> Those familiar with multiple regression will doubtless be horrified at this maltreatment of the data. But is the author to blame? He is a plant physiologist, not a statistician. He was merely using a ready-made all purpose statistical tool provided by the computer. The biggest crime, of course, is the failure to recognize that there is a hierarchy of terms in his original equation; consequently, in an empirical model of this kind, if the quadratic term is included the corresponding linear term should also be included . . . Had he adopted an exploratory approach, and worked forwards, not backwards, he might well have found that few if any of the quadratic terms . . . were significant, or if formally significant, of any consequence. (p. 470)

The considerably greater availability of computers and software nowadays has contributed to a manifold increase in misapplications of statistical analysis. Surely, you will not be surprised when I say that users are to blame. Misapplications abound not because researchers are not statisticians, but because many *merely* use computer programs without understanding the method in question, how and when it is applicable, and how to interpret results it yields.

Predicted Scores

Having the regression equation one can, of course, calculate predicted scores. For the present data,

$$Y' = -1.90000 + 3.49464X - .13839X^2$$

For example, for subjects practicing for two minutes,

$$Y' = -1.90000 + (3.49464)(2) + (-.13839)(4) = 4.54$$

That is, for subjects practicing for two minutes, the prediction is 4.54 correct responses on the visual discrimination test. As you may recall, I called for predicted scores, saved them and called for a plot of the predicted scores against X. Following are excerpts of the output.

Output

Y	X	PREDICT	
4	2	4.53571	*[first subject]*
.	.	.	
16	8	17.20000	*[tenth subject]*
.	.	.	
21	12	20.10714	*[last subject]*

TABLE 13.5

```
          ++----+----+----+----+----+----+----+----++
            30+                                        +
        P      |                                       |
        R      |                                       |
        E      |                                       |
        D    20+                           3     3     +
        I      |                      3                |
        C      |                                       |
        T      |                 3                     |
        E      |                                       |
        D    10+            3                          +
               |                                       |
        S      |                                       |
        C      |       3                               |
        O      |                                       |
        R     0+                                       +
        E      |                                       |
        S      |                                       |
               |                                       |
           -10+                                        +
          ++----+----+----+----+----+----+----+----++
            -2        2         6        10        14
```

PRACTICE TIME
18 cases plotted.

Commentary

"VSIZE and HSIZE control length and width of the plot, respectively" (SPSS Inc., 1993, p. 571). They "are applicable only if SET HIGHRES is OFF" (p. 571). See SPSSWIN.INI file in your Windows directory for your settings.

While being very versatile, PLOT does not provide for specifying the increments to be used for X and/or Y. If you don't like the increments used, experiment with different MIN(imum) and/or MAX(imum) values.

Interpolation

It is generally acceptable to use the regression equation to predict performance on the dependent variable for values not used in the study, provided they are within the range of those originally used. In other words, interpolation is generally acceptable. If one wanted, for instance, to make a prediction for five minutes of practice (a condition not used in the study),

$$Y' = -1.90000 + (3.49464)(5) + (-.13839)(25) = 12.11$$

For five minutes of practice, the prediction is a score of 12.11 on the visual discrimination test.

Extrapolation

Extrapolation beyond the original range of X values is hazardous and should be avoided. In other words, one should *not* engage in predictions for values of the independent variable that are outside the range used in the study. To show the potential danger of extrapolation, I plotted the scores of the present example in Figure 13.2, where the circles indicate the means of the arrays. Note that for the values 2, 4, 6, and 8 of the independent variable, the trend is virtually linear. Had only these values been used in the study, one might have been led to believe that the trend is generally linear. As you can see from Figure 13.2, and as I concluded based on the analysis of these data, the curve is quadratic. There is no way of telling what shape the curve would take if one increased practice time beyond 12 minutes (the maximum time in the present study). If one

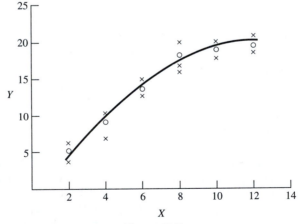

Figure 13.2

is interested in the effects of values outside the range of those under consideration, they should be included in the study or in a subsequent study.

Following are some examples of what may be unleashed by extrapolation.

> In the space of one hundred and seventy-six years the Lower Mississippi has shortened itself two hundred and forty-two miles. That is an average of a trifle over one mile and a third per year. Therefore, any calm person, who is not blind or idiotic, can see that in the Old Oölistic Silurian Period, just a million years ago next November, the Lower Mississippi River was upward of one million three hundred thousand miles long, and stuck out over the Gulf of Mexico like a fishing-rod. And by the same token any person can see that seven hundred and forty-two years from now the Lower Mississippi River will be only a mile and three-quarters long, and Cairo and New Orleans will have joined streets together, and be plodding comfortably along under a single mayor and a mutual board of aldermen. There is something fascinating about science. One gets such wholesale returns on conjecture out of such a trifling investment of fact. (Mark Twain, 1911, pp. 151–152)

Based on annual growth rates, it has been projected that "the lawyers would outnumber the people in 2188. At that point, America would have 840 million lawyers and 820 million people, and there would be probable cause for certifying numerous lawyers as not human" (Seligman, 1992, p. 159).

Commenting on a study that predicted "that female runners may one day run faster then the best of male runners," Chang (1992, p. A14) pointed out that the study is

> limited by its reliance on linear extrapolation in the prediction of future performance. While the rate of improvement in women's performance has exceeded that of men since the 1920's, little evidence suggests that this trend would continue to the point where women overtake men.

Indeed,

> A trend is a trend is a trend.
> The question is, will it bend?
> Will it alter its course
> Through some unforeseen cause
> And come to a premature end?
> (Cairncross, A. Quoted by Chatfield, 1988, p. 227)

Interpretation of Regression Coefficients

Generally, the b's do not lend themselves to easy interpretation. Some of the reasons are as follows.

First, in polynomial regression an independent variable is represented by more than one vector. Therefore the usual interpretation of a b as the expected change in Y associated with a unit change in the variable under consideration while holding the other variables constant makes no sense in polynomial regression. In the present example, it makes no sense to interpret the b associated with X^2 as the effect of this "variable" while holding X constant, because when the latter does not vary the former cannot vary either. Referring to the example under consideration, visual discrimination does not depend on practice time and on practice time squared as if these were distinct variables. Instead, the analysis indicates that the regression of visual discrimination on practice time is quadratic.

Second, the relative magnitudes of b's cannot be compared because, as I showed earlier, the standard deviations of higher-order terms become increasingly larger, thereby leading to increasingly smaller b's. In the present example (see the output given earlier), $s_x = 3.515$, $s_{x^2} = 50.265$, $s_{x^3} = 626.542$, and increasingly larger standard deviations for higher-order terms.

Third, a linear transformation of X will, of course, not affect its standard deviation, but the standard deviations of the powered vectors will change, as will the correlations among the vectors.

Centering. Suppose, that for the present example instead of using X, one were to use deviations from the mean of X [i.e., $x = (X - \overline{X})$]—a transformation referred to as centering (see, e.g., Cohen & Cohen, 1983, pp. 237–238; Marquardt, 1980). The standard deviation of x would, of course, be the same as that of X. But the standard deviation of x^2, would be 10.267, as compared with 50.265 for X^2. The correlation between x and x^2 would be zero, as compared with .979 (the correlation between X and X^2). Incidentally, whenever the X's are distributed symmetrically around the mean of X (as is the case in the present example), the correlation between x and x^2 is zero.

As a result of centering, the quadratic equation for the example under consideration would be

$$Y' = 15.78125 + 1.55714x - .13839x^2$$

As I pointed out, the regression equation for the original scores is

$$Y' = -1.90000 + 3.49464X - .13839X^2$$

Notice that the b for the linear component in the equation for the centered X is less than half the size of the b for the linear component in the equation for the original data. The b for the quadratic term, on the other hand, is identical in both equations. In general, the last term in both equations will be the same (for further details of the effects of linear transformations of X on the regression equation and other regression statistics, see Allison, 1977; and Cohen, 1978).

The foregoing should suffice to illustrate the difficulties attendant with attempting to interpret b's in a polynomial regression as if they were associated with distinct variables. For an approach to the interpretation of the b's in polynomial regression in terms of partial derivatives, see Stimson, Carmines, and Zeller (1978), and Stolzenberg (1979).

It is important to note that whatever the linear transformation of X, the hierarchical regression analysis is invariant. That is, proportions of variance accounted for by higher-order polynomials entered sequentially are not affected by a linear transformation of X.

Nevertheless, in view of the high collinearity among powered vectors, various authors (e.g., Bradley & Srivastava, 1979; Cohen & Cohen, 1983, pp. 237–238; Marquardt, 1980; Smith & Sasaki, 1979) recommend that X be transformed (the most common recommendations being centering or standardization) to reduce the likelihood of inaccuracies due to computational problems. With the kind of computers currently in use, transformations appear unnecessary, though, of course, they can do no harm. A special kind of transformation of X is the use of orthogonal polynomials. Before I turn to this topic, I give an example of an input file for PROC REG of SAS, followed by brief excerpts of the output.

SAS

Input

TITLE 'TABLE 13.5.   POLYNOMIAL REGRESSION';
DATA T135;
  INPUT Y X;   *[free format]*
  X2=X**2;   *[raise X to second power]*

```
   X3=X**3;        [raise X to third power]
   X4=X**4;        [raise X to fourth power]
   X5=X**5;        [raise X to fifth power]
CARDS;
  4   2
  6   2
  5   2
  7   4
 10   4
 10   4
 13   6
 14   6
 15   6
 16   8
 17   8
 21   8
 18  10
 19  10
 20  10
 19  12
 20  12
 21  12
;
PROC PRINT;
PROC REG ALL;
   MODEL Y=X X2 X3 X4 X5/ALL P R COLLIN SEQB;
RUN;
```

Commentary

For an introduction to SAS, see Chapter 4, where I also introduced PROC REG. In addition, I used PROC REG in several subsequent chapters. Therefore, I will not comment on the input. Instead, I will quote the manual on the only option I did not use earlier: "SEQB prints a sequence of parameter estimates as each variable is entered into the model. This is printed as a matrix where each row is a set of parameter estimates" (SAS Institute Inc., 1990a, Vol. 2, p. 1367).

Output

Dependent Variable: Y

Analysis of Variance

Source	DF	Sum of Squares	Mean Square	F Value	Prob>F
Model	5	548.50000	109.70000	47.014	0.0001
Error	12	28.00000	2.33333		
C Total	17	576.50000			

| | Root MSE | 1.52753 | R-square | 0.9514 |
| | Dep Mean | 14.16667 | Adj R-sq | 0.9312 |

Parameter Estimates

Variable	DF	Parameter Estimate	Standard Error	T for H0: Parameter=0	Prob > |T|	Type I SS	Squared Semi-partial Corr Type I
INTERCEP	1	−1.000000	26.79344862	−0.037	0.9708	3612.500000	
X	1	5.125000	27.88806523	0.184	0.8573	509.185714	0.88323628
X2	1	−1.718750	10.17244850	−0.169	0.8686	34.321429	0.05953413
X3	1	0.401042	1.67768709	0.239	0.8151	2.016667	0.00349812
X4	1	−0.039063	0.12774876	−0.306	0.7650	2.678571	0.00464626
X5	1	0.001302	0.00364583	0.357	0.7272	0.297619	0.00051625

Commentary

Except for the last two columns under parameter estimates, the preceding excerpts are, by and large, similar to SPSS output given earlier. Therefore, I limit my comments to the last two columns. PROC REG reports, by default, two types of sums of squares, which I explained in Chapter 5 in connection with my analysis of Table 5.1 through SAS (see also SAS Institute Inc., 1990a, Vol. 1, Chapter 9). For present purposes, I will point out that Type I is a sequential sum of squares and is the kind used in a hierarchical analysis. Thus, for example, 509.186 is the sum of squares associated with the linear term, 34.321 is the sum of squares incremented by the quadratic term, and so on. If you wanted to calculate an F ratio for each term, you would divide each sum of squares by the mean square error (2.33333, see the preceding). For example, F for the linear term is $509.186/2.333 = 218.25$, with 1 and 12 *df*.

Being sequential, the squared Semi-partial Corr Type I is analogous to R Squared Change reported in SPSS (see, for example, Summary table of SPSS output in the preceding section). Of course, one can use the squared semipartial correlations to calculate the F ratios reported in the Summary table of SPSS. I suggest you do this as an exercise.

Output

Sequential Parameter Estimates

INTERCEP	X	X2	X3	X4	X5
14.166666667	0	0	0	0	0
3.2666666667	1.5571428571	0	0	0	0
−1.9	3.4946428571	−0.138392857	0	0	0
0.6666666667	1.8802910053	0.128968254	−0.012731481	0	0
8.1666666667	−4.578042328	1.8663194444	−0.195023148	0.0065104167	0
−1.000000001	5.125000001	−1.71875	0.4010416667	−0.0390625	0.0013020833

Commentary

From this output, which is printed when the SEQB option is specified, you can see at a glance the regression equation for each step. For example,

$$Y' = 3.267 + 1.557X \qquad \text{(Linear)}$$

$$Y' = -1.9 + 3.495X - .138X^2 \quad \text{(Quadratic)}$$

and so forth for the remaining terms. Compare this with SPSS output.

REGRESSION ANALYSIS WITH ORTHOGONAL POLYNOMIALS

Polynomial regression analysis may be done by using a set of orthogonal vectors coded to reflect various degrees of polynomials, thereby reducing and simplifying considerably the calculations. The coefficients in such vectors are called *orthogonal polynomials.* The underlying principle of orthogonal polynomials is the same as that of orthogonal coefficients coding method (see Chapter 11). But whereas in orthogonal coding, coefficients are used to contrast groups, in orthogonal polynomials they are used to describe different degrees of polynomials.

When the levels of the continuous independent variable are equally spaced, and there is an equal number of subjects at each level, the construction of orthogonal polynomials is simple (see, for example, Myers, 1979, pp. 441–443). Rather than constructing them, however, one may find the necessary coefficients in tables of orthogonal polynomials, such as the one given in Appendix B. More extensive tables are available (e.g., Fisher & Yates, 1963). The size of the difference between the levels of the continuous independent variable is immaterial, provided it is the same between all levels. Thus, it makes no difference whether one is dealing with levels such as 2, 4, 6, and 8; 5, 10, 15, and 20; 7, 14, 21, and 28; or any other set of equally spaced levels. The orthogonal polynomial coefficients obtained from the tables apply equally to any set, provided they are equally spaced and there is an equal number of subjects at each level. Since the experimenter is interested in studying a trend, the levels of the continuous independent variable can be equally spaced, and an equal number of subjects can be assigned randomly to each level.

It is possible, though somewhat complicated, to construct orthogonal polynomial coefficients for unequally spaced levels or when *n*'s are unequal. For a treatment of this topic see Kirk (1982, Appendix C). Alternatively, tabled coefficients of orthogonal polynomials may be used when *n*'s are unequal. Although the coded vectors are not orthogonal under such circumstances, hierarchical regression analysis with such vectors will yield the same results as the ones obtained from an analysis with powered vectors. Coefficients of orthogonal polynomials may also be adapted for the case of unequally spaced values (see Cohen & Cohen, 1983, pp. 248–249). Finally, some computer procedures (e.g., MANOVA of SPSS) allow for the specification of unequal spacing.

Analysis of Visual Discrimination Data

For illustrative purposes, I will reanalyze the example of the preceding section (Table 13.5) using orthogonal polynomials. Examine the table of orthogonal polynomials in Appendix B and notice that in most instances values are *not* given for the highest-degree polynomial possible. This is because in behavioral research polynomials beyond the cubic are rarely used (I discuss this topic later). For the present example, though, I wanted to use coefficients for the highest-degree polynomial possible so that I could compare the results with those I obtained in the earlier analyses. Accordingly, I took the necessary coefficients from Fisher and Yates (1963).

SPSS

Input

TITLE TABLE 13.5.   ORTHOGONAL POLYNOMIALS.
DATA LIST FREE/Y O1 TO O5.
BEGIN DATA

4	−5	5	−5	1	−1
6	−5	5	−5	1	−1
5	−5	5	−5	1	−1
7	−3	−1	7	−3	5
10	−3	−1	7	−3	5
10	−3	−1	7	−3	5
13	−1	−4	4	2	−10
14	−1	−4	4	2	−10
15	−1	−4	4	2	−10
16	1	−4	−4	2	10
17	1	−4	−4	2	10
21	1	−4	−4	2	10
18	3	−1	−7	−3	−5
19	3	−1	−7	−3	−5
20	3	−1	−7	−3	−5
19	5	5	5	1	1
20	5	5	5	1	1
21	5	5	5	1	1

END DATA
LIST.
REGRESSION DES/VAR=Y TO O5/STAT ALL/
   DEP=Y/ENTER O1/ENTER O2/ENTER O3/ENTER O4/ENTER O5.

Commentary

Notice that I named the orthogonal vectors O1, O2, and so on. Of course, this analysis can be incorporated in the input file I gave in the preceding section. I trust that by now you do not need guidance on this matter.

Notice the pattern of the signs of the coefficients in each column of the orthogonal polynomials. In first column (O1) they change once (− to +). In the second column (O2) they change twice (+ to − to +). In the third column (O3) they change three times (− to + to − to +). These changes in signs correspond to the degree of the polynomial. O1 has one sign change; it describes the linear trend. O2 has two sign changes; it describes the quadratic trend. The other vectors are handled similarly.

As the orthogonal polynomials are not correlated (see the following output), I could have entered them simultaneously. I entered them hierarchically because I wanted to use some of the results in my discussion of tests of the *b*'s.

Output

	Mean	Std Dev
Y	14.167	5.823
O1	.000	3.515
O2	.000	3.850
O3	.000	5.636
O4	.000	2.223
O5	.000	6.669

N of Cases = 18

Correlation:

	Y	O1	O2	O3	O4	O5
Y	1.000	.940	−.244	−.059	.068	.023
O1	.940	1.000	.000	.000	.000	.000
O2	−.244	.000	1.000	.000	.000	.000
O3	−.059	.000	.000	1.000	.000	.000
O4	.068	.000	.000	.000	1.000	.000
O5	.023	.000	.000	.000	.000	1.000

Commentary

Notice that the means of the orthogonal polynomial vectors are equal to zero, as are the correlations among the vectors. Recall that these conditions simplify considerably regression calculations. All that is necessary to determine the proportion of variance due to any component is to square the zero-order correlation of Y with the vector in question. For example, the proportion of variance due to the linear component is .8836 ($.940^2$); that due to the quadratic is .05954 ($−.244^2$), and so on for the remaining components. Also, the proportion of variance due to the highest-degree polynomial (i.e., overall R^2) is equal to the sum of the squared zero-order correlations of Y with each of the orthogonal polynomial vectors.

Output

Dependent Variable..   Y

Block Number 5.   Method: Enter   O5

		Analysis of Variance			
Multiple R	.97541		DF	Sum of Squares	Mean Square
R Square	.95143	Regression	5	548.50000	109.70000
Adjusted R Square	.93119	Residual	12	28.00000	2.33333
Standard Error	1.52753				

F = 47.01429   Signif F = .0000

Commentary

This is the last step (see Block Number 5) in which the fifth-degree polynomial was entered. These results are identical to those I obtained earlier for the fifth-degree polynomial, where I used powered vectors. Also, $R^2 = \eta^2_{yx}$ that would be obtained if the data were subjected to a one-way analysis of variance.

Output

```
---------------------------------------- Variables in the Equation ----------------------------------------
```

Variable	B	SE B	Beta	Correl	Part Cor	T	Sig T
O1	1.557143	.105409	.939807	.939807	.939807	14.772	.0000
O2	−.369048	.096225	−.243996	−.243996	−.243996	−3.835	.0024
O3	−.061111	.065734	−.059145	−.059145	−.059145	−.930	.3709
O4	.178571	.166667	.068164	.068164	.068164	1.071	.3051
O5	.019841	.055556	.022721	.022721	.022721	.357	.7272
(Constant)	14.166667	.360041					

Commentary

Recalling that the vectors are orthogonal, it follows that Beta = Correl(ation) = Part Cor(relation). For the same reason, Tolerance and VIF (not reproduced here) for all the vectors equal 1.00 (I discussed tolerance and VIF in Chapter 10). A test of each B is, of course, a test of the component with which it is associated. Thus, for the linear component T = 14.772, with 12 df (df for the *MSR*; see the output above). For the quadratic component T(12) = −3.835; the same is true for the other terms.

An examination of the column labeled Sig T reveals that the quadratic term is statistically significant at conventional levels and that terms beyond the quadratic are statistically not significant. I reached the same conclusions in the earlier analysis when I used powered vectors. The two analyses differ, however, with respect to the tests of the individual components. Look back at the Summary table of the analysis with the powered vectors and notice, for example, that the proportion of variance accounted for by the linear component is .8832, which is equal to the squared Correl (or squared Beta, or squared Part Cor.) associated with O1. Yet the FCh reported in the previous analysis (121.029) is *not* equal to the squared T reported here (218.21 = 14.772^2). The difference is due to the different error terms used in the two analyses. The earlier analysis was hierarchical, whereas the present one is simultaneous. Thus, in the previous analysis the proportions of variance due to higher-order terms were part of the error term, whereas in the present analysis they are not.

I trust that a numerical demonstration will facilitate your understanding of the difference between the two approaches to tests of significance. Let us test the proportion of variance due to the linear component. From the previous output, the proportion of variance due to the linear term is .88324 (.939807^2). Recalling that $N = 18$,

$$F = \frac{(.88324)/1}{(1 - .88324)/(18 - 1 - 1)} = 121.03$$

which is, within rounding, the same value reported in the Summary table of the previous analysis. Note that $df = 16$ for the denominator of this F ratio.

Turning to the test of the linear term in the present analysis, note that the error term used is that from the overall analysis based on the highest-degree polynomial. From the previous output, $R^2 = .95143$ for the highest-degree polynomial. Testing the linear term,

$$F = \frac{(.88324)/1}{(1 - .95143)/(18 - 5 - 1)} = 218.22$$

which is, within rounding, equal to the squared T (14.772) reported earlier. Note that $df = 12$ for the denominator of this F ratio. The loss of df in the latter test was offset by a smaller proportion of variance due to error. As a result, the error term in the first test (the hierarchical analysis) is .00730, whereas that of the second (the simultaneous analysis) is .00405.

Output

Summary table

Step	Variable	Rsq	RsqCh	FCh	SigCh
1	In: O1	.8832	.8832	121.029	.000
2	In: O2	.9428	.0595	15.604	.001
3	In: O3	.9463	.0035	.911	.356
4	In: O4	.9509	.0046	1.231	.287
5	In: O5	.9514	.0005	.128	.727

Commentary

Compare this Summary table with the one for the earlier analysis and notice that they are identical, demonstrating again the difference between the hierarchical and simultaneous analyses.

As a final aspect of this demonstration, I reproduce an excerpt of Step 1 from the present analysis.

Output

Block Number 1.   Method: Enter   O1

		Analysis of Variance			
Multiple R	.93981				
R Square	.88324		DF	Sum of Squares	Mean Square
Adjusted R Square	.87594	Regression	1	509.18571	509.18571
Standard Error	2.05113	Residual	16	67.31429	4.20714

F =   121.02886   Signif F =   .0000

------------------------ Variables in the Equation ------------------------

Variable	B	SE B	T	Sig T
O1	1.557143	.141542	11.001	.0000
(Constant)	14.166667	.483456		

Commentary

Notice that the B reported here is the same as the one reported for O1 in the simultaneous analysis presented earlier. Yet, the T's are different: 11.001 here versus 14.772 in the simultaneous analysis. The difference is due to the different error terms for the B's: .141542 here versus .105409 in the last step (see the preceding output). Examine the formula for the standard error of a regression coefficient—see (5.24) and the discussion related to it—and notice that the different *t*'s for the test of the same *b* at Step 1 and Step 5 are due to the difference in the variance of estimate, which is 4.20714 at Step 1 versus 2.33333 at Step 5 (see Mean Square in the two segments of the output).

I discussed the tests of the *b*'s in some detail because I felt that this will not only enhance your understanding of the results of the present analysis, but it will also contribute to a better understanding of regression analysis. In sum, the differences in the results of tests of significance boil down to different error models used. For a good discussion of different error models and recommendations based on, among other things, considerations of sample size and power of the statistical test of significance, see Cohen and Cohen (1983, pp. 245–248). For present purposes it will suffice to point out that the analysis with orthogonal polynomials parallels the trend analysis carried out in the context of analysis of variance, whereas the analysis I carried out earlier is in line with examination of trend components as they enter into the analysis—an approach taken when the independent variable is composed of many distinct values (e.g., measures of mental ability, political attitudes). I elaborate on this approach in the context of nonexperimental research, discussed later in this chapter.

The Regression Equation

In my discussion of the previous analysis, I pointed out that to obtain a regression equation that includes only the significant components of the trend, the data have to be reanalyzed with the number of terms to be included in the regression equation. This was necessary because *b*'s change when variables (*powered vectors in the preceding analysis*) that are deleted are correlated with those remaining in the equation. In the case of orthogonal vectors, however, the *b*'s do not change when vectors are deleted. Furthermore, the intercept, *a,* is also not affected by deletion of vectors—when the vectors are orthogonal. Since the mean of each orthogonal vector is equal to zero (see the previous output), *a* is equal to the mean of the dependent variable. From the output given earlier, the mean of *Y* is 14.16667, which is also the value of *a* reported earlier. Clearly, each dependent variable score is expressed as a composite of the mean of the dependent variable and the contribution of components of the trend included in the regression equation.

To obtain the regression equation for any degree of the polynomial it is sufficient to read from the output the relevant *b*'s. The quadratic equation for the present data is therefore

$$Y' = 14.16667 + 1.55714(O1) - .36905(O2)$$

where O1 stands for the linear term and O2 for the quadratic. Note that when using this equation for prediction, the values inserted in it are the coded values corresponding to a given level and a given degree of the polynomial. Examine the input file given earlier (or equivalently the table of orthogonal polynomials in Appendix B) and notice, for example, that subjects who practiced for two minutes were assigned a -5 in the first vector (linear), and a $+5$ in the second vector (quadratic). For such subjects therefore,

$$Y' = 14.16667 + 1.55714(-5) + (-.369051)(5) = 4.54$$

For subjects practicing for eight minutes,

$$Y' = 14.16667 + 1.55714(1) + (-.36905)(-4) = 17.20$$

I calculated the same predicted values earlier, using the equation for the powered vectors and the original independent variable values.

In sum, then, when coding is not used, the regression equation needs to be recalculated with the degree of polynomial wanted. When orthogonal polynomials are used, on the other hand, no further calculations are required to get the regression equation at any degree polynomial wanted.

Factorial Designs

The use of orthogonal polynomials can be extended to designs with more than one continuous independent variable or to designs composed of continuous and categorical independent variables. When the independent variables are continuous, code each variable with orthogonal polynomial coefficients as if it is the only one in the design. Generate cross-product vectors by multiplying, in turn, the vectors of one variable by those of the other. The cross-product vectors represent the interaction. The approach is similar when the design includes continuous and categorical independent variables. The latter are coded in the usual manner (see Chapters 11 and 12), and the former are coded by orthogonal polynomial coefficients. Again, cross products of the vectors of variables represent the interactions. I give an example of such an analysis in Chapter 14.

You will find examples of trend analysis in factorial designs in, among other texts, Keppel (1991, pp. 266–270), Kirk (1982, pp. 379–387), Myers (1979, pp. 445–456), and Winer (1971, pp. 388–391 and 478–484). I suggest that you use a multiple regression program to analyze some of the numerical examples given in these, or other, texts. Comparing your results with those reported in the text and carefully studying the discussion of the results will enhance your understanding of such designs.

CURVILINEAR REGRESSION IN NONEXPERIMENTAL RESEARCH

Thus far, my presentation has been limited to experimental research. The method of studying trends, however, is equally applicable to data from nonexperimental research. When, for example, a researcher studies the regression of one attribute on another, it is imperative that the trend of the regression be determined. Failure to do so can lead to erroneous conclusions. For instance, using linear regression, a researcher may conclude that the regression of Y on X is weak, or even nonexistent, when in fact it is strong but curvilinear. Barnett (1983) concluded his cogent critique of misapplications of the linear model thus:

> I think we should press hard on the "functional form" issue whenever we suspect it has not been dealt with carefully. . . . If we . . . [do], we might bring closer the day when false linearity assumptions sit alongside omitted variables and inaccurate data on the "extremely dangerous" list, and thus the day when those researchers who refuse to deal seriously with the problem will have reached, as it were, the end of the line. (p. 65)

In what he referred to as a "light-hearted" example, Eysenck (1965) reasoned that the study of curvilinear relations may help resolve the contradiction "between two hypotheses which are held equally strong by popular imagination. One says that 'absence makes the heart grow fonder'. . . . Exactly the opposite is postulated by those who believe 'out of sight out of mind'" (p. 11).

Eysenck argued that regression of fondness on length of absence may be curvilinear, thus rendering both positions correct. According to this conception, fondness increases with increments in length of absence up to an optimal point, beyond which it decreases with increments in length of absence.

Also recognize that a relatively high r^2 does not constitute evidence that the regression is linear. In an instructive paper, Anscombe (1973) gave an example in which several fictitious data sets differed widely with respect to the type of relation between X and Y and yet the r^2's and the regression equations were identical. Although Anscombe did not calculate curvilinear regression for his data (the purpose of his paper was to show the importance of graphing data), I will point out that for one of his data sets (y_2 and x_1, Table, p. 19) $r^2_{yx} = .67$, whereas $R^2_{y.x, x^2} = 1.0!$[8]

A Numerical Example

A researcher who was interested in studying the regression of satisfaction with a given job on mental ability administered an intelligence test to a random sample of 40 employees. In addition, each employee was asked to rate his or her satisfaction with the job, using a 10-point scale (1 indicating very little satisfaction and 10 indicating a great deal of satisfaction). The data (illustrative) are presented in Table 13.6, where Y is job satisfaction and X is intelligence. I purposely use the labels Y and X to encourage you to substitute the variables I am using with ones with which

Table 13.6   Illustrative Data for Job Satisfaction (Y) and Intelligence (X); N = 40

Y	X	Y	X
2	90	9	104
2	90	10	105
3	91	10	105
4	92	9	107
4	93	9	107
5	94	10	110
5	94	9	110
6	95	8	112
5	96	9	112
6	96	10	115
5	97	8	117
5	98	8	118
6	98	7	120
7	100	7	120
6	100	7	121
7	102	6	124
8	102	6	124
9	103	6	125
9	103	5	127
10	104	5	127

NOTE: The third and fourth columns are, respectively, continuations of the first and the second columns.

[8]Other aspects of Anscombe's (1973) paper merit careful study.

you are more familiar or more comfortable (e.g., regression of problem-solving on anxiety, aggression on self-concept, attitudes on cognitive style).

In the examples I presented in preceding sections, the independent variable consisted of a small number of equally spaced values with an equal number of subjects at each. Consequently, I could fit the highest-degree polynomial possible or go to any level I wanted. Further, I could simplify calculations by using orthogonal polynomials. In nonexperimental research, attribute variables may consist of many distinct values, unequally spaced,[9] with unequal numbers of subjects at each level. The procedure, therefore, is to raise the independent variable successively to higher powers and to ascertain at each stage whether the proportion of variance incremented by a higher-degree polynomial is meaningful and statistically significant. Following is an SPSS input file for such an analysis, using the data in Table 13.6.

SPSS

Input

```
TITLE TABLE 13.6.
DATA LIST FREE/Y X.
COMPUTE X2=X**2.
COMPUTE X3=X**3.
BEGIN DATA
2  90
2  90                    [first two subjects]
.    .
5  127                   [last two subjects]
5  127
END DATA
LIST.
PLOT HSIZE=40/VSIZE=20/
   TITLE='TABLE 11.6'/HORIZONTAL='INTELLIGENCE'/
   VERTICAL='JOB SATISFACTION'/
   PLOT=Y WITH X.
REGRESSION VAR=Y TO X3/DES/STAT ALL/
   DEP=Y/ENTER X/ENTER X2/ENTER X3.
```

Commentary

Notice that first I use PLOT to plot the data, and then I use REGRESSION where I enter sequentially the linear, quadratic, and cubic terms. I generated the last two vectors by the COMPUTE statements.

---

[9]"Unequally spaced" does not mean that the measure used is not an interval scale, but rather that not all values within a given range are observed in a given sample. Consequently, the observed values are not equally spaced. Trend analysis relies heavily on the assumption that the independent variable measure forms an interval scale. When one knows of (or even suspects) serious departures from this assumption, trend analysis should not be used.

Output

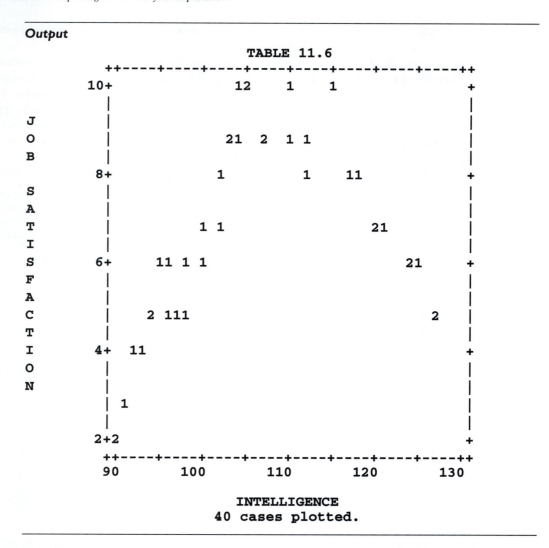

TABLE 11.6

INTELLIGENCE
40 cases plotted.

Commentary

The nonlinearity of the regression of Y on X is clearly evident from the plot, demonstrating the usefulness of plotting data. Other plots (e.g., residuals against predicted scores), which I discussed in Chapters 2 and 5, can also prove invaluable in detecting trends in the data.

Output

	Mean	Std Dev
Y	6.800	2.233
X	106.200	11.335
X2	11403.700	2458.893
X3	1238217.450	403520.967

N of Cases = 40

Correlation:

	Y	X	X2	X3
Y	1.000	.365	.325	.284
X	.365	1.000	.999	.996
X2	.325	.999	1.000	.999
X3	.284	.996	.999	1.000

Commentary

Notice the increasingly large standard deviations and the almost perfect correlations among the vectors representing the different terms. I discussed these points earlier.

Output

Equation Number 1   Dependent Variable..   Y
Variable(s) Entered on Step Number 1..   X

Multiple R	.36538	Analysis of Variance			
R Square	.13350		DF	Sum of Squares	Mean Square
Adjusted R Square	.11070	Regression	1	25.95249	25.95249
Standard Error	2.10543	Residual	38	168.44751	4.43283
		F = 5.85461		Signif F = .0204	

---------------------- Variables in the Equation ----------------------

Variable	B	SE B	T	Sig T
X	.071970	.029744	2.420	.0204
(Constant)	−.843246	3.176342		

Commentary

These are excerpts from the results of the linear regression of Y on X: $r_{yx}^2 = R_{y.x}^2 = .13350$; $F(1, 38) = 5.85, p < .05$. Had I terminated the analysis at this step, I would have concluded that the regression of job satisfaction on intelligence (one of the substantive examples I used earlier) is linear and that intelligence accounts for approximately 13% of the variance in satisfaction. Furthermore, as the sign of r_{yx} is positive, I would have concluded that the higher an employee's intelligence, the more he or she tends to be satisfied with the job. But let us see the results of the quadratic regression analysis.

Output

Variable(s) Entered on Step Number 2..   X2

Multiple R	.94415			Analysis of Variance			
R Square	.89141	R Square Change	.75791		DF	Sum of Squares	Mean Square
Adjusted R Square	.88554	F Change	258.24598	Regression	2	173.29029	86.64514
Standard Error	.75534	Signif F Change	.0000	Residual	37	21.10971	.57053
				F = 151.86707	Signif F = .0000		

```
-------------------------- Variables in the Equation --------------------------
```

Variable	B	SE B	T	Sig T
X	3.771150	.230438	16.365	.0000
X2	−.017070	.001062	−16.070	.0000
(Constant)	−199.033919	12.385468		

Block Number 3.   Method: Enter   X3

End Block Number 3   Tolerance = 1.00E-04 Limits reached.
No variables entered for this block.

Commentary

About 89% of the variance in job satisfaction is accounted for by both the linear and the quadratic terms; $F(2, 37)$ 151.87, $p < .05$. The interest at this step is in the dramatic increment in the proportion of variance accounted for due to the quadratic term: .75791; $F(1, 37) = 258.25$, $p < .05$. Recall that the test of the b for the highest-degree polynomial in the equation is equivalent to a test of the proportion of variance accounted for that is incremented by the highest-degree polynomial. Look at the output above and note that the b for X2 has a t ratio of −16.070 with 37 *df*, whose square (258.24) is, within rounding, equal to the F Change associated with the quadratic term. *For completeness of presentation, I also reproduced the* t *ratio for the linear term. I remind you, however, that it is irrelevant in the present context* (see the relevant discussion earlier in this chapter).

Finally, notice that the cubic term was not entered because its tolerance is lower than the default (.0001). Recall that earlier I forced the entry of higher-order terms by overriding this default. If you changed the criterion for tolerance you would find that the increment in proportion of variance due to the cubic term is .0005.

As I will explain, it is advisable to test the polynomial term beyond the first nonsignificant one. Although I do not present results of such an analysis, I will point out that the increment in proportion of variance due to the quartic term is neither meaningful nor statistically significant.

In behavioral research, particularly with attribute variables, it is rare to find significant trends beyond the quadratic. Moreover, the higher the degree of the polynomial the more it is affected by the reliability of the measure involved and the more difficult it is to interpret. When the reliability is not very high, trends may seem to appear when they do not exist, or trends that do exist may be overlooked. Unlike manipulated variables, attribute variables used in the behavioral sciences tend to have only moderate reliabilities. It is therefore recommended that analyses with such variables not be carried out beyond the quadratic term. Furthermore, results from analyses with variables whose measures are not highly reliable should be interpreted with caution. (For discussions of reliability see, for example, Nunnally, 1978, Chapters 6 and 7; Pedhazur & Schmelkin, 1991, Chapter 5.)

The Regression Equation

From the preceding output, the quadratic equation for the present data is

$$Y' = -199.03392 + 3.77115X - .01707X^2$$

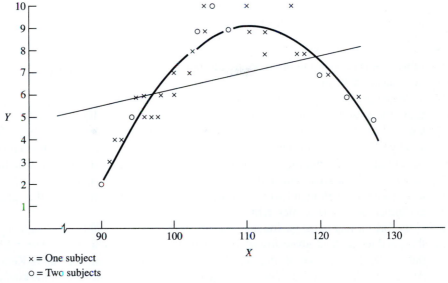

Figure 13.3

Using this equation, I can calculate predicted Y's for various X's, along the continuum of X. I can then use such predicted scores to plot a smoothed curve. I did this in Figure 13.3, along with the regression line for the linear trend (i.e., using the linear regression equation). Notice how the quadratic trend fits the data much better than the linear alone. Referring again to the substantive example I used earlier, I would conclude that subjects of relatively low or relatively high intelligence tend to be less satisfied with the job as compared with subjects of average intelligence. Accordingly, I would speculate that the type of job under study is moderately demanding intellectually and therefore people of average intelligence seem to be most satisfied with it.

MULTIPLE CURVILINEAR REGRESSION

As in experimental research, polynomial regression analysis with multiple independent variables may be applied also in nonexperimental research. The mechanics of the analysis are fairly simple, but the interpretation of the results is far from simple. For the purpose of the present discussion, I will use a second-degree polynomial equation with two independent variables, which takes the following form:

$$Y' = a + b_1 X + b_2 Z + b_3 XZ + b_4 X^2 + b_5 Z^2$$

where XZ is the cross product of X and Z. The analysis proceeds hierarchically. The first thing that one would generally determine is whether the regression of Y on X and Z is linear or curvilinear. In effect, one tests whether $\beta_3 = \beta_4 = \beta_5 = 0$ (note that these are parameters, *not* standardized regression coefficients). One can easily accomplish this by testing whether the increment in proportion of variance accounted for by the last three terms in the equation is statistically significant. That is,

$$F = \frac{(R^2_{y.x, z, xz, x^2, z^2} - R^2_{y.x, z})/(5 - 2)}{(1 - R^2_{y.x, z, xz, x^2, z^2})/(N - 5 - 1)}$$

with 3 and $N - 5 - 1$ *df.* If the increment is statistically not significant, one would conclude that a linear additive model best fits the data. That is,

$$Y' = a + b_1X + b_2Z$$

I discussed analysis and interpretation of multiple linear regression earlier in the text (especially in Chapters 5, 6, and 10).

When the increment in the proportion of variance due to XZ, X^2, and Z^2 is statistically significant, one would conclude that the regression is curvilinear. But because the test involved three terms, it is useful to test each of them singly or to test first whether $\beta_4 = \beta_5 = 0$—that is, whether X^2 and Z^2 add significantly to the proportion of variance accounted for by X, Z, and XZ. Assuming that this null hypothesis cannot be rejected, one can then test whether $\beta_3 = 0$—that is, whether XZ adds significantly to proportion of variance accounted for by X and Z. Other tests are also possible, though I will not discuss them except to point out that they proceed in the manner indicated here (i.e., hierarchically).

Before turning to the paramount issue of interpretation, I would like to caution you that some authors and researchers advocate and/or employ different approaches (e.g., Morris, Sherman, & Mansfield, 1986; for critiques of Morris et al., see Cronbach 1987; and Dunlap & Kemery, 1987, 1988). As long as a least-squares solution is used, only a hierarchical analysis of the kind outlined is valid.

Product Vectors: Interpretive Considerations

A spate of recent publications about product vectors has led to an increase in their use in research. As the mechanics of the analysis are relatively straightforward and can be easily mimicked, it is imperative that issues of interpretation are clearly understood. Before turning to such issues, though, it will be useful to (1) draw attention to a couple of analytic ones and (2) review briefly the approach most authors recommend researchers use when examining the results of analyses with product vectors.

What I said earlier about the likelihood of high correlations among powered vectors and the requirement that they be entered hierarchically applies also to product vectors. Not surprisingly, product vectors tend to be highly correlated with one or both of the constituent variables. Therefore, analyses that depart from the hierarchical approach outlined earlier (e.g., using the product vector without the constituent variables or entering it first) are bound to yield erroneous results (see "Research Examples," later in this chapter and in Chapter 14).

As in the case of powered vectors (see the preceding section), measurement errors have adverse effects on analyses with product vectors. For some discussions, see Bohrnstedt and Marwell (1977), Busemeyer and Jones (1983), and Dunlap and Kemery (1987, 1988).

Examining Results of Analyses with Product Vectors

Although, for convenience, I discuss the case of two independent variables, my comments apply also to more complex models. For two independent variables, X and Z, the model incorporating a product vector is

$$Y' = a + b_1X + b_2Z + b_3XZ \qquad (13.3)$$

To reiterate: first one tests whether the proportion of variance accounted for by the product vector (XZ), over and above what is accounted by X and Z, is statistically significant. This is accomplished in the manner I have applied repeatedly in this and preceding chapters (i.e., a test of the difference between two R^2's—one including the product vector and one including only the constituent variables). I hope that you recognize that, for the example under consideration, this is equivalent to a test of the regression coefficient for the product vector (b_3). In the event that you don't see why this is so, I suggest that you reread my earlier discussions (e.g., in Chapter 5 or 10) of the meaning of the test of a regression coefficient.

When the increment in the proportion of variance due to XZ is statistically significant, most authors recommend that the following reexpressions of (13.3) be used:

$$Y' = (a + b_2 Z) + (b_1 + b_3 Z)X \qquad (13.4a)$$

$$Y' = (a + b_1 X) + (b_2 + b_3 X)Z \qquad (13.4b)$$

where (13.4a) expresses the regression of Y on X for different values of Z, and (13.4b) expresses the regression of Y on Z for different levels of X.

To get a feel for the foregoing, assume that it is concluded that b_3 (the coefficient for the product vector) is statistically not different from zero. In other words, assume that the increment in the proportion of variance accounted for by XZ is statistically not significant. Under such circumstances (13.4a) and (13.4b) would be reduced to the additive model:

$$Y' = a + b_1 X + b_2 Z$$

where the effect of X on Y is b_1, regardless of the values of Z, and the effect of Z on Y is b_2, regardless of the values of X.

When b_3 is statistically significant, the effect of X (or the slope) is $b_1 + b_3$, where the latter indicates the expected change in Y associated with a unit change in Z. In other words, the effect of X depends on specific values of Z. A similar interpretation is made with respect to the effect of Z, which is said to depend on specific value of X. Darlington (1990), who among other authors calls such effects *conditional effects,* stressed this symmetry: "Interaction is symmetrical. The conditional effect or slope of X_2 changes with X_1 only if the conditional effect of slope X_1 changes with X_2" (p. 315), hence the term conditional regression analysis used by some authors (e.g., Denters & Van Puijenbroek, 1989). Other authors (e.g., Aiken & West, 1991, p. 12) use also the term *simple slope*—analogous to simple effects in the analysis of variance (see Chapter 12)—to refer to conditional effects.

Of other terms used to refer to conditional effects, the one used most often is *moderator effects.* Sharma, Durand, and Gur-Arie (1981), who pointed out that "a moderator variable has been defined as one which systematically modifies either the form and/or the strength of the relationship between a predictor and a criterion variable" (p. 291), also stated that "much confusion persists as to how they [moderator variables] are defined and identified" (p. 291). They proposed a typology of such variables (e.g., "pure and quasi moderator variables," p. 293) and reviewed analytic approaches for identifying them. Authors who use the term *moderator effect* refer to their analysis as *moderated multiple regression* (e.g., Dunlap & Kemery, 1988) or *moderated regression* (e.g., Stone & Hollenbeck, 1984, 1989).

As I stated earlier, my aim was to review briefly the suggested approach to examining the results of analyses with product vectors. You will find detailed discussions, including issues I did not address (e.g., centering the constituent variables, plotting conditional effects), along with numerical examples, in the references I gave earlier (particularly Aiken & West, 1991; Cohen, 1978; Cohen & Cohen, 1983; Darlington, 1990; Friedrich, 1982; Judd & McClelland, 1989). I turn now to my main concern in this section—the meaning attached to product vectors.

Product Vector = Interaction?

As you may have noticed, in the foregoing presentation I refrained from using the term *interaction* for the product vector. This position of mine is contrary to that held by most, if not all, authors who refer to *XZ* as the *interaction* between the *X* and *Z* (e.g., Agresti & Finlay, 1986, pp. 368–372; Aiken & West, 1991, Chapter 2; Allison, 1977; Arnold, 1982; Cohen, 1978; Cohen & Cohen, 1983, Chapter 8; Darlington, 1990, Chapter 13; Evans, 1991; Friedrich, 1982; Jaccard, Turrisi, & Wan, 1990; Judd & McClelland, 1989, Chapter 10; Pindyck & Rubinfeld, 1981, p. 110; Retherford & Choe, 1993, pp. 40–45).

I trust that my position does not come as a surprise to you, particularly if you recall that in Chapter 12 I stated conditions under which I deem it valid to use the term *interaction* for the product of two categorical variables. In that discussion, which you may wish to review at this point, I argued that whether or not a product vector is interpreted as an interaction is largely predicated on the research design. Specifically, I reasoned that in an experimental design, the product vector *does* represent the interaction between the constituent variables in the sense that it represents their joint effect on the dependent variable. In contrast, I recommended that the term *interaction not* be used for product vectors in nonexperimental research. Instead, I suggested that terms such as *multiplicative* or *joint relations* be used. Further, I cautioned against treating a nonexperimental design consisting of categorical variables as if it were a factorial experimental design. I found this practice particularly objectionable when one of the constituent variables could be construed as affecting the other (see my discussion of the example of a 2×2 design in which one of the variables was race and the other was education). As I will show, it is just such examples that are used by some of the previously cited authors when they argue in favor of interpreting the product vector as an interaction.

Except for the fact that in Chapter 12 I dealt with categorical variables, whereas in the present chapter I deal with continuous variables, the situations are alike and require the same orientation, notably the crucial distinction between experimental and nonexperimental research. Needless to say, acceptance of my stance is predicated on acceptance of my definition and explication of interaction in Chapter 12. Granted, authors may choose to define or use the term *interaction* more loosely. This still does not alter the fact that interaction cannot have the same meaning in experimental and nonexperimental research.

What all the preceding boils down to is that whereas the same analytic approach may be used in different designs, the interpretation of the results (interaction in the present context) depends very much on the type of design used. Moreover, as I stressed in earlier chapters, the analysis is meant to shed light on the viability of a specific model, hence the importance of a match between the analysis and the model.[10] For example, in my discussions of incremental partitioning of variance in Chapter 9, I showed that different models composed of the same variables afford different incremental partitioning of variance. Also, when the researcher treats a set of independent variables as exogenous, there is no meaningful way to do an incremental partitioning of variance (see in particular Figures 9.1 and 9.3 and the discussions related to them). Similarly, in Chapter 10, I showed that a model in which all the independent variables are treated as exogenous affords an estimation of direct effects only, whereas another model affords an estimation of direct as well as indirect effects of some of the same variables (see, for example, Figure 10.1 and the

---

[10]In the next two chapters, I illustrate the same in connection with attribute-treatment interactions and analysis of covariance designs.

discussion related to it). Decrying researchers' indifference to the role of a model in statistical analysis, Draper and Smith (1981) stated that "the question 'What model are you considering?' is often met with 'I am not considering one—I am using analysis of variance' " (p. 423).

I find it unsettling that matters concerning design type and model are not even alluded to in most, if not all, explications of analyses with product vectors, including those I referred to earlier. On the contrary, the examples given appear to create the impression that these issues are irrelevant. Following are but some examples.

In their very good explanation of an analysis with a product vector, Judd and McClelland (1989) state, "Whether or not there is an interaction between two variables in predicting a third is an issue totally independent of whether of not the two predictor variables are correlated or redundant with each other" (p. 248). As you will recall, very early in the book I stressed the importance of distinguishing between predictive and explanatory studies. Therefore, I am uneasy about the use of the terms *predicting* and *predictor variables* in the preceding. I doubt that Judd and McClelland meant to limit their presentation to pure prediction.[11] Be that as it may, I submit that when the aim is explanation, it matters very much whether or not the independent variables are correlated. Suffice it to remind you of my discussion in Chapter 12, where I stressed that an interaction is between two variables that are *not* correlated.

An example of what I believe is standing the issue of interaction on its head comes from Retherford and Choe (1993). After discussing interactions between correlated variables (pp. 40–45), they make a passing remark to the effect that *"it is also possible to have interaction without correlation"* [italics added] (p. 45).

Cohen and Cohen (1983) have been most influential in advocating the position that product vectors represent interactions. In fact, part of the title of Cohen's (1978) frequently cited paper reads "Partialed products *are* interactions." It is therefore noteworthy that even when Cohen and Cohen allude (in a footnote) to a model in which one constituent variable affects another, they persist in treating the product vector of the two variables as an interaction. Here is how they put it:

> If the content of the problem dictates that *U* [one of the constituent variables] is *causally* [italics added] prior (an "antecedent condition") and hence should be partialed from *V* [the other constituent variable] . . . then the model is fully hierarchical, and *U* is entered prior to *V*; one then has three steps, *U*, *V•U*, and the *interaction* [italics added] *UV•U,V.* (p. 308)

Before considering the implications of the preceding in the context of one of the examples Cohen and Cohen used, I would like to draw your attention to the point Keppel (1991) makes in the context of his detailed attempt to define interaction:

> One independent variable does *not* [italics added] influence the other independent variable—this makes no sense. . . . Independent variables influence the *dependent* variable, the behavior under study in an experiment. (p. 196)

Among their examples of "conditional relationships," Cohen and Cohen include the following: "the relationship between income (*Y*) and education (*U*) may vary as a function of race (*V*)" (p. 307). I would like to remind you that in Chapter 12 I used the very same example and argued

---

[11]It is noteworthy that in a recent paper McClelland and Judd (1993) do distinguish between experimental and nonexperimental research, but they do so to show that the failure of "nonexperimentalists conducting field studies" (p. 376) to find "interactions may not be due to sloppier procedures but to the field studies' much lower relative statistical power for detecting interactions and moderator effects" (p. 387).

that race affects education and, hence, it makes no sense to speak of an interaction between them. Without repeating my discussion, I would point out that when the researcher hypothesizes that one of the constituent variables affects the other (as Cohen and Cohen do in the earlier quotation), then a different analytic approach (not one in which a product vector is used) is called for. Referring to the example of race, education, and income, the researcher may, for example, study the direct and indirect (via education) effects of race on income and the direct effect of education on income. Alternatively, the researcher may hypothesize that race has no direct effect on income; that its effect is only indirect, via education. I gave examples of such models in Chapter 10, where I pointed out that I discuss them in detail in Chapter 18.

Without going far afield, I will draw your attention to some other examples authors I mentioned earlier use to illustrate conditional regression analysis. Agresti and Finlay (1986) used socioeconomic status (SES) and life events as independent variables and mental health as the dependent variable. In their description of life events, Agresti and Finlay said, among other things, that they "range from such severe personal disruptions as death in the family, a jail sentence . . . getting a new job" (p. 322; their conditional analysis is given on pp. 368–371). Could it be that SES affects some of the life events? Or, could some of the life events serve as indicators of SES?

In his illustration of the application of conditional regression, Friedrich (1982) used an example of the effects of energy consumption and democratic performance on income equality in 60 countries. I will not go into the theoretical rationale. Instead, I will only note that the correlation between energy consumption and democratic performance is .59 (see his Table 3, p. 815).

Here is how Aiken and West (1991) introduced their numerical example aimed at illustrating an analysis with a product vector:

> In our example we will predict the self-assurance of managers (criterion Y) based on two predictors, their length of time in managerial position (X) and their managerial ability (Z). The data we use are artificial: They were specifically constructed to include an interaction between X and Z. (p. 10)

As in the preceding example, I will not comment on the theoretical rationale. Instead, I will point out that the correlation between X and Z is .42 (see their Table 2.1 on p. 11).

Retherford and Choe (1993, pp. 41–45) explained the meaning of interaction in the context of a model of fertility as affected by education, income, and their interaction.

My final example is taken from Jaccard et al. (1990), who introduced it as follows:

> [S]uppose that an investigator was interested in understanding why some teenagers engage in sex without using birth control, while other teenagers tend to use birth control. A sample of 125 sexually active female teenagers is studied, and for each a measure of their intention to use birth control is obtained. . . . The researcher hypothesizes two general classes of factors that influence this intention. The first factor is the individual's personal feelings or attitude toward using birth control. . . . The second factor is the perceived peer pressure to use or not to use birth control. (p. 20)

Jaccard et al. constructed data to illustrate and explain the application of regression analysis with a product vector representing the "interaction" between personal feelings and perceived peer pressure. Far be it for me to fault them for using fictitious data. I do, however, question the data they came up with. In light of the variables used and in view of the fact that the study was presented as nonexperimental, I question the plausibility of there being *no* correlation between personal feeling about the use of birth control and perceived peer pressure to use birth control. In other words, Jaccard et al. ended up using (intentionally?) an unrealistic example—one whose data would be plausible in an experimental design, where the status of the product vector as representing an interaction is not debatable.

I believe you will benefit from analyzing Jaccard et al.'s data (their Table 2.1, p. 23) twice. First, replicate their analysis. You will note that the correlation between X_1 and X_2 is zero. But, as expected, the correlation between these constituent variables and their product is not zero (the correlation of each with the product vector is .671). It is for this reason that the analysis has to be carried out hierarchically, entering the product vector last, even in an orthogonal design. And it is this point that is appropriately stressed by, among others, Cohen and Cohen (1983):

> [T]he $u \times v$ interaction *'is carried by'* not 'is' the uv product. This is because, in general, uv will be linearly correlated with both u and v, often quite substantially so. Only when u and v have been linearly partialled from uv does it, in general, become the interaction IV we seek. (p. 305)

Second, use coefficients of orthogonal polynomials to represent the two independent variables. Generate the product of the two vectors, and reanalyze the data using the three vectors. Among other things, you will find (1) the constituent variables are *not* correlated with the product vector, (2) the squared zero-order correlation between the dependent variable and product vector is equal to the proportion of variance incremented by the product vector in the first analysis, and (3) the test of the b's for the product vector in both analyses is identical (i.e., $t = -15.556$, with 121 df).

RESEARCH EXAMPLES

In this section, I give examples of two types of studies. First, I review briefly two studies in which curvilinear regression was used. Second, I illustrate and comment on some misapplications of analyses with product vectors.

CURVILINEAR REGRESSION

Effect of Induced Muscular Tension on Heart Rate and on Learning

Wood and Hokanson (1965) tested an aspect of the theory of physiological activation, which states that subjects under moderate levels of tension will perform better than subjects under no tension. Under high levels of tension, however, the theory predicts a decrement in performance. Wood and Hokanson advanced the following two hypotheses. One, there is a positive linear relation between muscular tension and heart rate: increased muscular tension leads to increased heart rate. Two, there is a quadratic relation between muscular tension and performance on a simple learning task (a digit symbol task). Specifically, increased muscular tension leads to higher performance on a learning task up to an optimal point, beyond which further increase in such tension leads to a decline in performance on the task.

Subjects were assigned to five levels of induced muscular tension. Changes in heart rate and the learning of digit symbols were subjected to trend analyses. Both hypotheses were supported. Specifically, for heart rate only the linear trend was statistically significant, whereas for the digit symbols the quadratic trend was statistically significant.

Study Wood and Hokanson's Tables 1 and 2 and compare the results they reported for the trend analysis with those they reported for an analysis of variance in which muscular tension was, in effect, treated as a categorical variable with five categories. For digit symbols, for example, the authors reported $F(4, 76) = 4.54$, for the analysis of variance. For trend analysis, they reported $F < 1$ for the linear component, and $F(1, 76) = 16.09$ for the quadratic component. The F ratio for the cubic component was 0.00, and that for the quartic component was slightly larger than 1. Clearly, the trend for the digit symbol data was, as predicted, quadratic.

Group Size and Imitative Behavior

Milgram, Bickman, and Berkowitz (1969) studied the effect of the size of the group on the imitative behavior of passersby on a busy New York City sidewalk. Using groups ranging in size from 1 to 15, the researchers had them stop on a signal and look up for 60 seconds at a sixth-floor window across the street. Five randomly ordered trials were conducted for each group size. Motion pictures taken of the observation area were analyzed to determine the percentage of passersby who looked up but continued walking and the percentage who stopped and looked up.

The independent variable, then, was group size. Two dependent variables were used: looking up only and stopping and looking up. Milgram et al. first reported results of two one-way analyses of variance. For the percentage stopping, $F(5, 24) = 20.63, p < .001$. For the percentage looking up, $F(5, 24) = 16.28, p < .001$. In these two analyses, group size was treated as if it were a categorical variable. The authors then reported results of trend analyses:

> There is a significant linear trend ($F = 101.7, p < .01$) and a nonsignificant quadratic trend ($F = .42$) for the passersby who stopped. However, for the passersby who looked up, there are both significant linear ($F = 57.2, p < .01$) and quadratic ($F = 11.6, p < .01$) components. (p. 198)

The two trends are clearly evident from the authors' plots of the data. For the stopping behavior, there is a fairly constant increase from 4% of passersby who stopped alongside a single individual who was looking up, to 40% who stopped alongside a group of 15 people who were looking up. For the looking behavior, on the other hand, the percent of passersby increased steeply from 42 when a single individual was looking up, to 80 when five individuals were looking up. The curve then flattened, reflecting very small increases for groups larger than five.

In sum, the analyses in this study (identical to those with illustrative data in the beginning of this chapter) demonstrate that when the independent variable is continuous, trend analysis is more informative than a one-way analysis of variance.

PRODUCT VECTORS

Cognitive Style and School Achievement

Robinson and Gray (1974) used 11 measures of achievement (e.g., vocabulary, reading comprehension) as dependent variables for fifth-grade boys and girls. Of the five "independent variables," two were measures of mental ability (verbal and nonverbal IQ) and three were measures of cognitive style (categorical, descriptive, and relational). Before describing the analysis, I would like to point out that the correlations among the five aforementioned variables (indicators?) ranged from .58 to .78 (see Robinson & Gray, 1974, Table 2), casting serious doubt about treating them as distinct variables. This impression is strengthened, when one considers the reliabilities of the cognitive style measures (.78, .80, and .84; the reliabilities of the IQ measures were not reported).

The preceding reservation aside, I will describe now the method of analysis. Using all possible pairings among the five independent variables,[12] the authors generated 10 product terms (e.g., categorical by verbal IQ; verbal IQ by nonverbal IQ; categorical by relational). They then did 22 multiple regression analyses by regressing, in turn, each of the 11 measures of achievement on the 15 vectors (five variables and ten product terms) for boys and girls separately. "For each analysis, verbal and nonverbal IQ were forced into the equation, then the remaining 13 independent variables [*sic*][13] entered freely into the regression equation" (p. 797). In other words, after entering the two IQ measures, the remaining 13 vectors were subjected to a stepwise regression analysis (see Chapter 8 for a detailed discussion of the properties of this method of analysis). As you can see, this goes counter to all I said earlier in this chapter about analyses in which product vectors are also included.

It is instructive to summarize briefly the results of the entry of vectors after verbal and nonverbal IQ were forced into the analysis. Of 22 regression analyses, (1) no additional vectors were entered in 6, (2) one vector entered in each of 7 analyses (in all instances, it was a *product vector*), and (3) two vectors entered in each of the remaining 9 analyses. In all instances, a product vector entered *first,* followed by a constituent "variable."

I suggest that you examine the correlation matrix (their Table 2) and notice the relatively high correlations among the "independent variables" (you may even want to assess collinearity, using approaches I presented in Chapter 10). I hope that, in view of the relatively high correlations (not to mention correlations with product vectors that are not reported), the results I outlined above come as no surprise to you. Therefore, I will not comment on the meaningfulness of the "findings."

Finally, I believe you will benefit from rereading the following in connection with the study under consideration, as well as of those discussed later: (1) the use of stepwise regression analysis (Chapter 8), (2) the use of multiple indicators and the effects of collinearity in multiple regression analysis (Chapter 10), and (3) regression analysis with product vectors (the present chapter).

Product Vectors of Masculinity and Femininity

In recent years, a plethora of studies attempting to assess the effects of masculinity (M), femininity (F), and the interaction between them on a variety of dependent variables have been published. Such studies can be broadly classified into three categories. (1) Studies in which respondents were classified on the basis of median splits on M and F into one of four categories (i.e., masculine, feminine, androgynous, and undifferentiated). Using this classification, the data were treated as if they comprised a factorial design. (2) Studies in which attempts were made to examine interactions between the aforementioned sex-role categories and sex of the respondents. In these studies, too, the data were treated as if they comprised a factorial design. (3) Studies in which the product of masculinity and femininity (M × F) was used, along with M and F in multiple regression analysis. Here, I limit my comments to studies of the latter category. I comment on studies in the first two categories in the next chapter.

---

[12]Despite my earlier reservations, I refer to the indicators as independent variables as this is how they were treated by the authors in the analyses.

[13]Earlier in this chapter, I was critical of the practice of using the term *variable* when referring to a product vector.

Of the various scales alleged to measure sex roles, probably the most widely used is the Bem Sex Role Inventory (BSRI) (Bem, 1974). I said "alleged," as most such scales are of dubious validity. This is not the place to go into this important topic (for a critique of the BSRI, see Pedhazur & Tetenbaum, 1979; Pedhazur & Schmelkin, 1991, pp. 59–60; and references therein). Nevertheless, a couple of observations are in order. When I questioned, earlier in this chapter, the use of product vectors as representing interactions in nonexperimental research, I did so without even alluding to measurement problems. Needless to say, using measures of dubious validity exacerbates the problem, particularly when, as in the present case, the product vector is supposed to represent a new construct (androgyny). I recognize that the preceding may strike you as cryptic. Because of space consideration, this is unavoidable. If you want to get a better grasp of the controversy surrounding this and other scales, as well as sex-role research in general, you will have to read the literature (see the aforementioned references; also, additional references given in the following).

Sex Roles and Self-Disclosure

Drawing attention to findings that "gender differences in reported willingness to self-disclose depend on the intimacy of the subject's relationship with the target person," Stokes, Childs, and Fuehrer (1981) hypothesized "that this effect is mediated by sex roles and holds only for subjects who have adopted traditional sex roles as measured by the . . . BSRI" (p. 510).

For present purposes, I do not comment on differences between mediators and moderators, nor on relevant analytic approaches for each (for a discussion, see James & Brett, 1984). Further, my comments are limited to Stokes et al.'s analyses in which they used the product of masculinity and femininity as an interaction term. Here, then, is what they said of this aspect of their analyses and results:

> The remaining hypotheses . . . were tested with stepwise regression using BSRI masculinity (M) and femininity (F) scores and the interaction (M × F) to predict willingness to disclose to strangers, acquaintances, and intimates. For each of these three dependent measures, only one predictor variable [*sic*] met the .5 [*sic*] significance level required for entry into the stepwise regression. . . . For disclosure to intimates, the only predictor entered in the stepwise regression was M × F. (pp. 512–513)

I could stop here by noting that my comments on the analyses in the study I reviewed in the preceding section (i.e., cognitive style and school achievement) apply equally to the analyses in the present study. I do, however, wish to draw your attention to a couple of additional issues arising from a comment by Lubinski (1983) on Stokes et al., and a response by Stokes (1983).

Lubinski (1983) was critical of Stokes et al.'s incorrect application of multiple regression analysis, saying, among other things, that having "entered the product term *first,*" they "found it to be significant, and on that basis reported a significant interaction. Even though this result is actually uninterpretable, the authors conclude, 'the data show that the interaction of M × F predicts disclosure to intimates'" (p. 132).

From a purely analytic perspective, Lubinski is, of course, correct. While admitting to an "incorrect use of the word *interaction*" (p. 135), Stokes defended the original analysis saying, "Because we had a priori ideas about which predictors would be best for various target persons, stepwise regression seemed an appropriate statistical method to test our hypotheses. We used M, F, and their product (M × F) as predictors" (p. 134). This statement is, to say the least, not meaningful. As you will recall from Chapter 8, stepwise regression analysis is *not* designed to test "a priori ideas" or hypotheses about "which predictors would be best." Moreover, using a product vector without its constituent variables is not unlike using a quadratic component without the linear one (see the relevant discussion earlier in this chapter; see also my discussion of Jaccard et al.'s [1990] demonstration of an analysis with product vectors and my suggestions for reanalyses of their data to get a better understanding of the issues involved).

Finally, I would like to stress that even when the hierarchical requirement in the analysis with product vectors is adhered to as, for example, by Lubinski, Tellegen, and Butcher (1981, 1983), I still question the interpretation of the proportion of variance incremented by M × F, over and above M and F, as representing the interaction between M and F, let alone a new construct. As I stated earlier, I cannot go into these important matters here. As but one example of what is entailed, I recommend that you read Spence's (1983) critique of Lubinski et al.'s work on theoretical grounds, as well as the reply by Tellegen and Lubinski (1983).

Published Research of Analysis with Product Vectors: Commentary on the Review Process

I would like to conclude with yet another example of the inexplicable review process leading to publication in professional journals. Weigel, Wertlieb, and Feldstein (1989) published a paper in the *Journal of Personality and Social Psychology* in which they applied stepwise regression analysis to constituent variables and their products. Without going into the details of the study, I would like to quote a couple of the authors' statements concerning the analyses and the results. In a note to their Table 3, they stated, "Also allowed to compete in the stepwise procedure but not entering into the model as significant were age group, stress group" and about 20 other variables. Similar notes were given to Tables 4 and 5. Here now is some of what they said of their results:

> In both the domain-specific and cross-domain analyses, interaction terms proved to be more strongly related to behavior symptoms than the variables from which they were created. . . . Undesirable life events emerged as significant . . . , but neither of the . . . main effects . . . was retained. Instead, the products of each of these variables by undesirable life events emerged as significant predictors of total behavior symptoms. (p. 461)

In the hope that you recognize the errors in this approach, I will only note that problems attendant with the application of stepwise regression in explanatory research (see Chapter 8) were compounded by retaining product vectors without their constituent variables.

My sole purpose in presenting the preceding excerpts was to contrast them with excerpts from a paper by Hotard, McFatter, McWhirter, and Stegall (1989), which was published in the *same* journal and in the *same* year as the preceding paper. As in the case of the preceding paper, I will not describe the study itself.

Hotard et al. stated that it was their impression that the correct interpretation of regression equations containing product vectors was not widely understood among researchers. Hence, they "go into some detail in interpreting the equation contained in Table 2" (p. 323). Following are excerpts from their explanation:

> First, it is clear that there is a significant interaction in the equation. For the significance test for this term to be appropriate, it is necessary to have all the lower-order terms of the interaction in the equation . . .
>
> Consequently, even if the extraversion (E) or the social relationships (S) terms had not been significant, it would have been necessary to keep them in the equation to test and interpret the interaction term correctly.

Second, it is not generally appropriate in equations containing cross-product terms to interpret the nonproduct terms as main effects in an analysis of variance. (p. 323)

If you are wondering how editors could accept for publication two contradictory analytic approaches, not to mention accepting one that is clearly wrong, then I achieved my aim. Incidentally, the papers by Lubinski et al. (1981, 1983), in which they described the analytic approach along the lines outlined by Hotard et al. (1989), were also published in the same journal.

Finally, I would like to point out that what I said earlier about not interpreting product vectors as representing interactions in nonexperimental research applies also to Hotard et al.'s (1989) study. As but one example, consider their statement that they included "a personality variable, extraversion, which is closely tied to social relationships . . . as . . . [they] anticipated that social relationships might interact with this personality trait" (p. 321). As the authors did not report the correlation matrix, it is not clear what they meant by "closely tied." Whatever the relation, might it be because extraversion affects social relationships? Or, could social relationships be viewed as indicators of extraversion? As I explained in my introduction to the use of product vectors, I believe it inappropriate to speak of an interaction between two correlated variables or when one variable appears to affect the other.

CONCLUDING REMARKS

It is a sign of sophisticated theory when predictions or hypotheses derived from it are not limited to statements about differences between conditions, or treatments, but also specify the pattern of the differences. The methods I presented in this chapter provide the means for testing hypotheses about trends in the data. Among other things, I showed that when cruder analyses are applied to data for which trend analysis is appropriate, the consequences may be a failure to support the hypothesis being tested or, at the very least, a loss of information.

Of course, curvilinear regression analysis can also be used when a researcher has no hypotheses about the pattern of relations among the variables under study but wishes to explore what the pattern is. The discovery of trends may lead the researcher to reformulate theory and to conduct subsequent studies to test it.

Throughout the chapter, I stressed the effects of design type and the model on the interpretation of the results.

In sum, used appropriately, the methods I presented in this chapter can enhance the predictive and explanatory power of scientific inquiry.

STUDY SUGGESTIONS

1. Why is it not prudent to treat a continuous variable as if it were categorical?
2. Discuss hazards of extrapolation from the regression line.
3. Under what conditions is $\eta^2_{yx} = r^2_{yx}$?
4. In a study with a continuous independent variable consisting of eight distinct values, the following results were obtained: proportion of variance accounted for by the highest-degree polynomial possible = .36426; proportion of variance due to linear regression = .33267. The total number of subjects was 100. Calculate F ratios for the following:
   (a) Overall regression.
   (b) Linear regression.
   (c) Deviation from linearity.
5. When a continuous independent variable consists of six distinct values, what is the highest-degree polynomial that can be fitted to the data?

6. In a study with a continuous independent variable, a third-degree polynomial was fitted. Some of the results are $R^2_{y.x} = .15726$; $R^2_{y.x,x^2} = .28723$; $R^2_{y.x,x^2,x^3} = .31626$. The total number of subjects was 150. Calculate the F ratios for the following components:
   (a) Linear.
   (b) Quadratic.
   (c) Cubic.
7. Why should curvilinear regression analysis be carried out hierarchically (i.e., first X, then X^2, etc.)?
8. In a regression equation with polynomial terms, are the tests of the b's meaningful? Explain.
9. A continuous independent variable consists of seven distinct values equally spaced, with equal numbers of subjects at each value. Using an appropriate table, indicate the orthogonal polynomial coefficients for the following components:
   (a) Linear.
   (b) Quadratic.
   (c) Cubic.
10. A researcher studied the regression of risk taking on ego strength. A sample of 25 subjects was administered a measure of risk taking and one of ego strength. The data (illustrative) are as follows:

Risk Taking	Ego Strength
2	1
3	1
4	2
4	2

Risk Taking	Ego Strength
5	2
5	3
5	3
6	3
8	4
8	4
9	5
10	5
10	5
10	6
11	6
11	7
12	7
12	7
12	8
12	8
11	8
12	9
12	9
12	10
12	10

(a) What are the proportions of variance accounted for by the following components: (1) linear; (2) quadratic; (3) cubic?
(b) What are the F ratios for the following components: (1) linear; (2) quadratic; (3) cubic?
(c) What degree polynomial best fits the data?
(d) Plot the data and interpret the results.

ANSWERS

3. This is true when the regression is linear.
4. (a) $F = 7.53$, with 7 and 92 *df*
   (b) $F = 48.14$, with 1 and 92 *df*
   (c) $F = .76$, with 6 and 92 *df*
5. 5
6. (a) $F = 33.58$, with 1 and 146 *df*.
   (b) $F = 27.75$, with 1 and 146 *df*
   (c) $F = 6.20$, with 1 and 146 *df*
8. Only the test of the b for the highest-order polynomial is meaningful.
9. (a) linear: −3 −2 −1   0   1   2   3
   (b) quadratic: 5   0 −3 −4 −3   0   5
   (c) cubic: −1   1   1   0 −1 −1   1
10. (a) (1) linear $= .88542$; (2) quadratic $= .08520$; (3) cubic $= .00342$
    (b) (1) $F = 177.73$, with 1 and 23 *df*
        (2) $F = 63.79$, with 1 and 22 *df*
        (3) $F = 2.77$, with 1 and 21 *df*
    (c) quadratic

14

Continuous and Categorical Independent Variables—I: Attribute-Treatment Interaction; Comparing Regression Equations

In the preceding chapters, I treated separately analyses in designs consisting of either continuous or categorical independent variables. In this and the subsequent chapter, I present applications of multiple regression analysis in designs consisting of both continuous and categorical variables. Chapters 14 and 15 thus serve to integrate methods treated by some researchers as distinct and by others even as incompatible.

I begin with a discussion and an analysis of an experimental design in which one independent variable is continuous and another is categorical. Next, I discuss and illustrate the inadvisability of categorizing continuous independent variables. I then present designs consisting of (1) manipulated categorical and nonmanipulated continuous variables and (2) nonmanipulated categorical and continuous variables (i.e., nonexperimental designs). I follow this with a discussion and illustration of curvilinear regression analysis when one of the independent variables is continuous and another is categorical. I conclude the chapter with some research examples.

EFFECTS OF INCENTIVE AND STUDY TIME ON RETENTION

In an experiment on the effects of an incentive and time devoted to study on retention, subjects were randomly assigned to two groups, one receiving and the other not receiving an incentive. Within these groups, subjects were randomly assigned, in equal numbers, 5, 10, 15, or 20 minutes to study a passage specifically prepared for the experiment. At the end of the study period, a test of retention was administered. Note that one independent variable (no incentive—incentive) is categorical, whereas the other (study time) is continuous. As in factorial designs with categorical independent variables (see Chapter 12), the aim is to determine the separate effects of each variable and their interaction on the dependent variable (retention). Illustrative data from such an experiment are given in Table 14.1.

Table 14.1   Illustrative Data from a Retention Experiment with One Continuous and One Categorical Variable

Treatments	5	10	15	20	
		Study Time (in Minutes)			
	3	4	5	7	
No Incentive	4	5	6	8	
	5	6	8	9	$\bar{Y}_{\text{No Inc.}} = 5.83$
	7	9	8	10	
Incentive	8	10	11	11	
	9	11	12	13	$\bar{Y}_{\text{Inc.}} = 9.92$
$\bar{Y}$:	6.00	7.50	8.33	9.67	$\bar{Y}_t = 7.875$

To lay the groundwork for the discussion of the analysis, I plotted the data in Figure 14.1, where circles identify subjects in the incentive (I) group and crosses identify subjects in the no incentive (NI) group. The regression lines of retention on study time for the two groups are also shown in the figure. Two questions may be asked about these regression lines. The first question is whether the slopes (i.e., the *b*'s) are equal. Stated differently, are the two lines parallel? Equality of slopes means that the effect of the continuous variable (study time) is the same in both groups. When it is concluded that the *b*'s are equal, the second question addressed is: Are the intercepts (*a*'s) of the two regression lines equal? This question is addressed to the elevation of the regression lines. Equality of intercepts (after having concluded that the *b*'s are equal) means that a single regression line fits the data for both groups. When the *a*'s, but not the *b*'s, are different from each other, one can conclude that one group is superior to the other group along the continuum of the continuous variable.

Figure 14.1 shows that the regression lines are not parallel. Departure from parallelism may, however, be due to chance. This hypothesis is tested by testing the significance of the difference

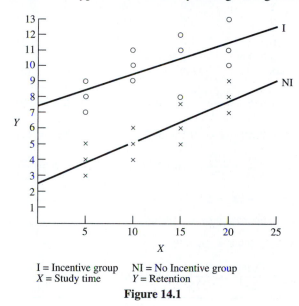

I = Incentive group   NI = No Incentive group
X = Study time   Y = Retention

Figure 14.1

between the b's. Failure to reject the null hypothesis that the b's are equal to each other indicates that the departure from parallelism is due to random fluctuations. Only under such circumstances is it meaningful to test the difference between the a's.

In Table 14.2, I summarize calculations of the regression equations for the two groups, from which you can see that the regression equation for the Incentive group is

$$Y_I' = 7.33330 + .20667X$$

and for the No Incentive group it is

$$Y_{NI}' = 2.49996 + .26667X$$

While the b's are quite alike, there is a marked difference between the a's. I now outline procedures for testing differences among regression coefficients and among intercepts, and apply them to the data in the example under consideration (Table 14.1).

Table 14.2   Calculation of Regression Statistics for Retention Experiment. Data from Table 14.1

	No Incentive			Incentive		
	Y	X	XY	Y	X	XY
	3	5	15	7	5	35
	4	5	20	8	5	40
	5	5	25	9	5	45
	4	10	40	9	10	90
	5	10	50	10	10	100
	6	10	60	11	10	110
	5	15	75	8	15	120
	6	15	90	11	15	165
	8	15	120	12	15	180
	7	20	140	10	20	200
	8	20	160	11	20	220
	9	20	180	13	20	260
Σ:	70	150	975	119	150	1565
M:	5.83333	12.50		9.91667	12.50	
SS:	446	2250		1215	2250	

$$\Sigma xy = 975 - \frac{(70)(150)}{12} = 100 \qquad\qquad \Sigma xy = 1565 - \frac{(119)(150)}{12} = 77.5$$

$$\Sigma x^2 = 2250 - (150)^2/12 = 375 \qquad\qquad \Sigma x^2 = 2250 - (150)^2/12 = 375$$

$$b = \frac{\Sigma xy}{\Sigma x^2} = \frac{100}{375} = .26667 \qquad\qquad b = \frac{\Sigma xy}{\Sigma x^2} = \frac{77.5}{375} = .20667$$

$$a = \bar{Y} - b\bar{X} = 5.83333 \qquad\qquad a = \bar{Y} - b\bar{X} = 9.91667$$

$$-(.26667)(12.5) = 2.49996 \qquad\qquad -(.20667)(12.5) = 7.33330$$

$$Y' = 2.49996 + .26667X \qquad\qquad Y' = 7.33330 + .20667X$$

$$SS_{reg} = \frac{(\Sigma xy)^2}{\Sigma x^2} = \frac{(100)^2}{375} = 26.66667 \qquad\qquad SS_{reg} = \frac{(\Sigma xy)^2}{\Sigma x^2} = \frac{(77.5)^2}{375} = 16.01667$$

Tests of Differences among Regression Coefficients

As I discussed in earlier chapters (particularly, Chapter 11), a test of significance can be conceived as an attempt to answer the question, Does additional information add significantly to the explanation of the dependent variable? Applied to the topic under consideration, the question is: Does the use of separate regression coefficients for each group yield a regression sum of squares that is significantly greater than the one obtained when a common regression coefficient is used?

A common regression coefficient for any number of groups may be calculated as follows:

$$b_c = \frac{\Sigma xy_1 + \Sigma xy_2 + \ldots + \Sigma xy_k}{\Sigma x_1^2 + \Sigma x_2^2 + \ldots + \Sigma x_k^2} \tag{14.1}$$

where b_c = common regression coefficient; Σxy_1 = sum of the products in group 1, and similarly for all other terms in the numerator; Σx_1^2 = sum of the squares in group 1, and similarly for all other terms in the denominator. Note that the numerator of (14.1) is the pooled sum of products within groups, and the denominator is the pooled sum of squares within groups. For the present example (see Table 14.2),

$$\text{No Incentive group: } \Sigma xy = 100.00; \Sigma x^2 = 375.00$$

$$\text{Incentive group: } \Sigma xy = 77.50; \Sigma x^2 = 375.00$$

$$b_c = \frac{100.00 + 77.50}{375 + 375} = .23667$$

Recall that the calculation of a regression coefficient is based on the principle of least squares: b is calculated so as to minimize the residual sum of squares. This, of course, results in maximizing the regression sum of squares. When regression lines are parallel, the b's are obviously identical. Consequently, the sum of the regression sums of squares obtained from using separate b's is the same as the regression sum of squares obtained from using a common b. When, however, regression lines are not parallel, the common b is not equal to the separate b's. As b for each group provides the best fit for the group data, the sum of the regression sums of squares obtained from using separate b's is larger than the regression sum of the squares obtained from using a common b. The discrepancy between the sum of the regression sums of squares from separate b's and the regression sum of squares from a common b is due to the departure from parallelism of the regression lines for the separate groups.

When the increment in the regression sum of squares due to the use of separate b's is statistically not significant, one can conclude that there are no statistically significant differences among the b's. In other words, a common b is tenable for all the groups. Note that such a conclusion is predicated on failure to reject the null hypothesis of no differences among the b's and is therefore tantamount to accepting it. To minimize type II error (i.e., failure to reject the null hypothesis when it should have been rejected, see Edwards, 1985, pp. 17–18; Hays, 1988, p. 261), it is suggested that a relatively large α (e.g., = .10 or even .25) be used for tests of significance of differences among b's.

In the calculations for Table 14.2, I used separate b's for each group. The regression sum of squares for the No Incentive group is 26.66667 and for the Incentive group is 16.01667. The sum of these regression sums of squares is 42.68334. The regression sum of squares due to a common b may be obtained as follows:

$$ss_{\text{reg}} \text{ for common } b = \frac{(\text{pooled } \Sigma xy)^2}{\text{pooled } \Sigma x^2} \tag{14.2}$$

For the present data,

$$\frac{(77.50 + 100.00)^2}{375 + 375} = \frac{177.50^2}{750.00} = 42.00833$$

The discrepancy between the sum of the regression sums of squares for the separate b's and the regression sum of squares for the common b is $42.68334 - 42.00833 = .67501$. It is this value that is tested for significance.

My aim in the foregoing presentation was to explain the meaning of a test of differences among b's. Although the procedure I presented can, of course, be used to do the calculations, I show now how to do the analysis in the context of procedures I presented in preceding chapters. Specifically, I will use REGRESSION of SPSS to analyze the data in Table 14.2, and will show, among other things, how to test the difference between the two b's.

SPSS

Input

```
TITLE ANALYSIS OF DATA OF TABLE 14.2.
DATA LIST/ Y,X,T 1-6.        [Y = Retention; X = Study Time;
                              T = Treatments]
VALUE LABELS T 1 'NO INCENTIVE' 2 'INCENTIVE'.
IF (T EQ 1) E=1.
IF (T EQ 2) E=−1.
COMPUTE XE=X*E.
BEGIN DATA
 3 5 1
 4 5 1
 5 5 1
 410 1
 510 1
 610 1
 515 1
 615 1
 815 1
 720 1
 820 1
 920 1
 7 5 2
 8 5 2
 9 5 2
 910 2
1010 2
1110 2
 815 2
1115 2
1215 2
1020 2
1120 2
```

```
1320  2
END DATA
LIST.
TEMPORARY.
SPLIT FILE BY T.
REGRESSION VAR Y X/DES/STAT ALL/DEP Y/ENTER.
REGRESSION VAR=Y,X,E,XE/DES/STAT=ALL/
  DEP=Y/ENTER X/ENTER E/ENTER XE.
```

Commentary

I trust that by now you are familiar with the basic input setup. Therefore, my comments will be brief. First, though, a reminder: italicized comments in brackets are *not* part of the input or the output (for explanation, see Chapter 4).

As in preceding chapters, I use the T vector and IF statements to generate a coded vector (*E*, for effect coding) for the categorical variable (treatments). Also, as in preceding chapters, I generate the interaction vector by multiplying *X* (study time) by *E* (treatments). See the data listing in the following output.

Although not necessary for the analysis, I show first how regression statistics for the separate groups may be obtained by using SPLIT FILE. I discussed this command in Chapter 12 (see "Multiple Comparisons"). Because I used the TEMPORARY command, SPLIT FILE applies only to the first REGRESSION (see SPSS Inc., 1993, p. 763). I then run a regression analysis in which I enter *X, E,* and *XE* sequentially.

Output

Y	X	T	E	XE	
3	5	1	1.00	5.00	*[No Incentive, first subject]*
.	.	.	.	.	
9	20	1	1.00	20.00	*[No Incentive, last subject]*
7	5	2	−1.00	−5.00	*[Incentive, first subject]*
.	.	.	.	.	
13	20	2	−1.00	−20.00	*[Incentive, last subject]*

	[No Incentive]			*[Incentive]*	
	Mean	Std Dev		Mean	Std Dev
Y	5.833	1.850	Y	9.917	1.782
X	12.500	5.839	X	12.500	5.839

N of Cases =   12   N of Cases =   12

Variable	B		Variable	B
X	.266667		X	.206667
(Constant)	2.500000		(Constant)	7.333333

Commentary

Here I have reproduced (1) excerpts from the listing of the data, generated by LIST, so that you can see the coded vector (*E*) and the product vector (*XE*) generated, respectively, by the IF and COMPUTE statements (see Input) and (2) excerpts from the separate regression analyses, which I placed alongside each other. Compare these results with those given in Table 14.2.

Output

Correlation:

	Y	X	E	XE
Y	1.000	.493	−.761	−.669
X	.493	1.000	.000	.000
E	−.761	.000	1.000	.913
XE	−.669	.000	.913	1.000

Step Number 3. .

---------------------- Variables in the Equation ----------------------

Variable	B	SE B	T	Sig T
X	.236667	.044647		
E	−2.416667	.611351		
XE	.030000	.044647	.672	.5093
(Constant)	4.916667	.611351		

Summary table
- - - - - - - - - - - -

Step	Variable	Rsq	RsqCh	FCh	SigCh
1	In: X	.2434	.2434	7.076	.014
2	In: E	.8229	.5795	68.712	.000
3	In: XE	.8268	.0039	.452	.509

Commentary

Examine the correlation matrix and notice that, as expected, the correlation between *X* and *E* is zero. Yet, the correlation between *E* and *XE* is .913. This should serve as a reminder of my discussion in Chapter 13 about correlations between a product vector and the constituent variables. Recall that because of this it is essential that the test of the product vector be based on the proportion of variance it increments over and above the proportion of variance accounted for by *X* and *E*. But, as I pointed out in Chapter 13, this is equivalent to a test of the *b* associated with *XE*. This information is available in the last step of the analysis, excerpts of which are given under Variables in the Equation. Clearly, the T ratio associated with the *b* for *XE* (.672) is statistically not significant (see Sig T). Accordingly, I conclude that the difference between the coefficients for the regression of Retention on Study Time in the two groups (NI and I) is statistically not significant.

I purposely did *not* reproduce the *t* ratios for *X* and *E,* as they are for tests of proportions of variance incremented by each when it is entered last (see Chapter 13 for detailed discussions of this point).

From the excerpts of the Summary table you can see that the increment in the proportion of variance due to XE is .0039 (RsqCh) and that the associated *F* ratio (FCh) is equal to the square of the *t* ratio reported in the preceding ($.672^2 = .453$). The *df* for the *t* ratio are 20, and those for the corresponding *F* ratio are 1 and 20.

I give other excerpts from this analysis later, after I explain the properties of the regression equation in which product vectors are included. From now on, I will use the term *overall regression equation* to refer to an equation that also includes product terms.

The Overall Regression Equation

I discussed regression equations that include product terms in preceding chapters. In Chapter 12, such equations included products of categorical variables, whereas in Chapter 13 they included products of continuous variables. In the present chapter, the overall regression equation includes products of a continuous variable by coded vectors representing a categorical variable. In such cases, the interpretation of the overall regression equation depends on the method of coding used to represent the categorical variable. In the numerical example under consideration, I used effect coding (see the preceding Input and Output). In the following I discuss properties of the overall regression equation when effect coding is used to represent the categorical variable. Later in this chapter, I discuss properties of such equations when dummy coding is used to represent the categorical variable.

From the output given earlier, the overall regression equation is

$$Y' = 4.916667 + .236667X - 2.416667E + .030000XE$$

where Y = retention; X = study time; E = treatments (no incentive, incentive); and XE = the interaction between X and E. The separate regression equations for the No Incentive and Incentive groups are (see Table 14.2 or output from SPLIT FILE)

$$Y'_{NI} = 2.49996 + .26667X$$

$$Y'_{I} = 7.33330 + .20667X$$

Now, the intercept, *a,* of the overall equation is equal to the average of the intercepts of the separate regression equations:

$$(2.49996 + 7.33330)/2 = 4.91663$$

The *b* for a coded vector in the overall regression equation is equal to the deviation of the intercept for the group identified in the vector (i.e., the group assigned 1) from the average of the intercepts. Consequently, the *a* for the group assigned 1 in a given vector is equal to the average of the intercepts, or the *a* of the overall regression equation, plus the *b* for this vector. In the present example, the No Incentive group was identified in *E* (see the Input and Output, given earlier). $b_E = -2.41667$. Hence, the intercept for the No Incentive group is

$$4.91667 + (-2.41667) = 2.5$$

which is the same as the corresponding value in the separate analyses reported earlier.

The intercept for the group assigned −1 in all the coded vectors is equal to the intercept of the overall regression equation minus the sum of the *b*'s for all the coded vectors in the overall regression equation. In the present example there is only one coded vector (*E*), whose coefficient is −2.41667. The Incentive group was assigned −1 in this vector. Therefore the intercept for this group is

$$4.91667 - (-2.41667) = 7.33334$$

Compare this with the results of the separate analyses.

Turning to the regression coefficients for the continuous variable and the product vector(s), the *b* for the continuous variable in the overall regression equation is equal to the average of the *b*'s of the separate regression equations:

$$(.26667 + .20667)/2 = .23667$$

Compare this with the *b* for *X* in the overall regression equation reported in the preceding.

The *b* for each product vector in the overall regression equation is equal to the deviation of the *b* for the group identified in the coded vector that was used to generate the product vector from the average of the *b*'s. In the present example, the product vector, *XE,* was generated by multiplying *X* by *E* in which the No Incentive group was identified. $b_{XE} = .03000$ (see the preceding). Hence, the *b* for the No Incentive group is

$$.23667 + .03000 = .26667$$

Compare this with the *b* obtained in the separate analysis of this group (Table 14.2 or the output given earlier).

The *b* for the group assigned −1 in all the coded vectors is equal to the average of the regression coefficients (i.e., the *b* for the continuous variable in the overall regression equation) minus the sum of the *b*'s for all the product vectors in the overall regression equation. In the present example, there is only one product vector, *XE,* whose coefficient is .03000. The *b* for the group assigned −1 (that is, the Incentive group) is therefore

$$.23667 - (.03000) = .20667$$

This is the same as the *b* I calculated earlier when I analyzed the data for the Incentive group (see Table 14.2 or output given earlier). I will now make several points.

First, in the present example the categorical variable consisted of two categories only. The same analytic approach is taken, and the overall regression equation is similarly interpreted, when the categorical variable consists of more than two categories. When this is the case, it is obviously necessary to generate a number of coded vectors equal to the number of categories minus one, or the number of degrees of freedom associated with the categorical variable. Each coded vector is, in turn, multiplied by the continuous variable.

Second, in the present example I used one continuous variable. The properties of the overall regression equation generalize to any number of continuous variables. When multiple continuous variables are used, product vectors are generated by multiplying the coded vectors of the categorical variable by each of the continuous variables. In Chapter 15, I give examples of analyses with categorical variables consisting of more than two categories and with multiple continuous variables.

Third, because there is only one product vector in the present example, it was possible to test the difference between the two *b*'s (for NI and I) by testing the *b* for the product vector. In fact, in view of the foregoing discussion of the properties of this *b,* you can see clearly what is being tested when only two groups are used. Recall that the b for the continuous variable in the overall regression equation is equal to the average of the b's for the two groups in their separate equations and that the b for the product term is a deviation of the b for one of the groups from the average of the two b's. Clearly, when the two b's from the separate equations are equal to each other, the b for the product vector term in the overall equation is zero. When, on the other hand, the separate b's are not equal to each other, the test of the b for the product vector is a test of the deviation of one of the b's from their average. But the deviation of the other b is the same, except for a reversal of its sign.

In designs with more than two groups, more than one product vector has to be generated. Under such circumstances, the test of the differences among the separate b's is done by testing the increment in the proportion of variance accounted for (or the regression sum of squares) by all the product vectors, over and above what the constituent variables account for.

The Common Regression Coefficient

Once one has concluded that the difference between the regression coefficients for the two groups is statistically not significant (see the preceding), a common regression coefficient may be used. Earlier, when I applied (14.1) to the data in Table 14.2, I found that $b_c = .23667$. Instead of applying (14.1), you may calculate the common regression coefficient by regressing the dependent variable on the original variables only, that is, by doing a multiple regression analysis without product vectors. The regression coefficient associated with the continuous variable in such an analysis *is the common regression coefficient.* In the present example, it is necessary to regress Y (retention) on X (study time) and E (treatments). The regression coefficient for X is b_c. As I will show, using the coded vector and the continuous variable without the product vector is tantamount to placing a restriction on the data of the two groups so that their regression equations will have two separate intercepts but the same regression coefficient. In other words, the regression lines are constrained to be parallel.

Anticipating the need for such an analysis, I entered the vectors sequentially. Hence the output for the second step includes the necessary results.

Output

---------------------- Variables in the Equation ----------------------

Variable	B	SE B	T	Sig T
X	.236667	.044060	5.371	.0000
E	−2.041667	.246302	−8.289	.0000
(Constant)	4.916667	.603314		

Commentary

The common regression coefficient is .236667, which is the same as the value reported earlier in the chapter. In the present example, b_c is equal to the average of the two b's. This will happen only when the Σx^2's (sums of squares for the continuous independent variable) for all the groups are equal to each other. In the present example,

$$\Sigma x_{NI}^2 = \Sigma x_I^2 = 375.00$$

(see the calculations in Table 14.2). To see why this is so, consider the following algebraic equivalent of (14.1):

$$b_c = \frac{\Sigma x_1^2 b_1 + \Sigma x_2^2 b_2 + \ldots + \Sigma x_k^2 b_k}{\Sigma x_1^2 + \Sigma x_2^2 + \ldots + \Sigma x_k^2}$$

From this equation you can see that b_c is a weighted average of the b's, in which each b is weighted by Σx^2 for its group. When all Σx^2's are equal to each other, the weighted average of the b's (i.e., b_c) is the same as the average of the b's.

To repeat: *the b for the continuous variable in the overall regression equation is equal to the average of the separate b's. The b for the continuous variable in the regression equation that does not include the product vector is the common b.*

Test of the Common Regression Coefficient

Having obtained b_c, it is necessary to determine whether it is statistically different from zero. In the context of the present example, this test addresses the question of whether the continuous variable, study time, has a statistically significant effect on the dependent variable, retention. The test of b_c is done in the usual manner. That is, dividing b_c by its standard error obtains a t ratio. This t ratio is reported above under Variables in the Equation as 5.371. The df for this t ratio are, as always, $N - k - 1$. In the present example, $N = 24$ (the number of subjects in both groups); $k = 2$ (E and X). Therefore the df for this t ratio are 21. These are, of course, the df associated with the mean square residual reported in the output of Step 2 (not reproduced here) for the regression of Y on X and E.

In view of the Sig T (see the previous output) one can conclude that study time has a statistically significant effect on retention. The expected change in the latter associated with a unit change in the former is .23667 (b_c) units.

Test of the Difference between Intercepts

The difference between intercepts is tested only after it is established that the b's do not differ significantly from each other.[1] Only then does it make sense to ask whether one of the treatments is more effective than the other along the continuum of the continuous variable. Testing the difference between intercepts amounts to testing the difference between the treatment effects of the categorical variable. One can accomplish this by testing the increment in the proportion of variance accounted for (or the regression sum of squares) by the coded vectors, over and above the proportion of variance accounted for by the continuous variable. This is a test between two R^2's I used frequently in preceding chapters.

Because the present example has only one coded vector, the same result may be obtained by testing the b for this coded vector. In the previous output, the t ratio for b_E is -8.289, with 21 df

---

[1]When the b's are significantly different from each other an interaction between the categorical and the continuous variable is indicated. I discuss this topic later in the chapter.

and $p < .01$. This, then, is a test of the difference between the two intercepts. One can conclude that the effect of No Incentive is significantly different from the effect of Incentive on Retention, or that there is a constant difference between No Incentive and Incentive along the continuum of Study Time. In E, No Incentive was assigned 1 (see Input and/or output listing given earlier). From the preceding output, $b_E = -2.041667$, which is the effect of No Incentive. The effect of Incentive is 2.041667. The difference between the two treatments is therefore

$$2.041667 - (-2.041667) = 4.08$$

As I explained in Chapter 11, when the categorical variable consists of more than two categories, it is represented by more than one coded vector. Under such circumstances, the test among the intercepts is done by testing the increment in the proportion of variance accounted for by the set of coded vectors representing the categorical variable (i.e., a test of the difference between two R^2's). When, based on this test, one can conclude that differences among intercepts are statistically significant, it is necessary to do multiple comparisons to determine which treatments, or categories, differ significantly from each other along the continuum of the continuous variable. I discuss and illustrate such tests in Chapter 15. To reiterate: when, as in the present example, the categorical variable consists of two categories, it is sufficient to test the b for the coded vector representing this variable to determine whether the two treatments, or the two intercepts, differ significantly from each other.

Separate Regression Equations

In the present example, the difference between the intercepts is statistically significant. Also, the difference between the b's is statistically not significant, and the common b is significantly different from zero. Accordingly, two separate regression equations in which the intercepts differ but the b's are the same are indicated. These can be easily derived following procedures I outlined earlier, except that instead of using the overall regression equation, you would use the equation in which a product vector(s) is *not* included. For the present example, this equation, reported at Step 2 of the output given earlier, is

$$Y' = 4.916667 + .236667X - 2.041667E$$

where $X =$ Study Time; and $E =$ No Incentive–Incentive, where No Incentive was assigned 1 (see the Input given earlier). Therefore the intercept for this group is

$$4.916667 + (-2.041667) = 2.875000$$

The Incentive group was assigned -1 in E. Therefore its intercept is

$$4.916667 - (-2.041667) = 6.958334$$

Using the common coefficient reported in the preceding (.236667), the two regression equations are

$$Y'_{NI} = 2.875000 + .236667X$$

$$Y'_I = 6.958334 + .236667X$$

where X is Study Time. Note that the difference between the two intercepts, $6.958334 - 2.875000 = 4.083334$, is (as I have noted) the difference between the effects of the two treatments of the categorical variable along the continuum of the continuous variable. In the context of the present example, this means that along the continuum of Study Time, subjects who were given an incentive are expected to have 4.083334 higher scores than subjects who were not given an incentive. This, of course, is the same as saying that there is no interaction between the categorical and the continuous variable.

A Single Regression Equation

For illustrative purposes, assume that the test of the difference between the intercepts in the present example is statistically not significant, but that the common regression coefficient (b_c) is statistically different from zero. If this were the case, one would have concluded that a single regression equation provides a good fit for the data of both groups. Such an equation is calculated by regressing Y on X (the continuous variable).

Note that by omitting the coded vector, no distinction is made between scores obtained under No Incentive and Incentive conditions. In other words, when this regression equation is calculated, both groups are treated as if they came from the same population. In light of the fact that I entered the vectors sequentially, all that is necessary to determine what such an equation would be is to read the equation reported at Step 1, that is, the step where I entered X. *Assuming that the difference between the intercepts is statistically not significant,* then the regression equation would be

$$Y' = 4.916667 + .236667X$$

where Y = Retention, and X = Study Time.

Recall, however, that *in the present example the difference between the intercepts is statistically significant.* Hence, two equations with separate intercepts and a common regression coefficient are required. I calculated and interpreted these equations in the preceding section.

Proportions of Variance Accounted For

As the design under consideration is orthogonal, it is possible to state unambiguously the proportion of variance accounted for by each variable.[2] From the output reported earlier in the Summary table,

$$R^2_{Y.X,E} = .8229$$

Study Time and No Incentive–Incentive account for about 82% of the variance in Retention. The proportion of variance due to Study Time is

$$R^2_{Y.X,E} - R^2_{Y.E} = R^2_{Y.X} \qquad (\text{because } r_{XE} = 0)$$

$$.8229 - .5795 = .2434$$

And the proportion of variance due to No Incentive–Inventive is

$$R^2_{Y.X,E} - R^2_{Y.X} = R^2_{Y.E}$$

$$.8229 - .2434 = .5795$$

These proportions of variance accounted for can be tested in the usual manner. I do this here to show the equivalence between these tests and the tests of the b's corresponding to them.

$$F_{ST} = \frac{.2434/1}{(1 - .8229)/(24 - 2 - 1)} = 28.86$$

[2]For an extensive discussion of orthogonal and nonorthogonal designs, see Chapter 12.

with 1 and 21 *df,* and

$$F_{NI-I} = \frac{.5795/1}{(1 - .8229)/(24 - 2 - 1)} = 68.71$$

with 1 and 21 *df.* These *F* ratios are equal to the corresponding squared *t* ratios for the tests of the *b*'s in the equation in which the product vector was *not* included (reported under Variables in the Equation in the Output given earlier).

Recapitulation

As I covered quite a bit of ground up to this point, a recapitulation will, I hope, be helpful. I will present the steps to be followed in the form of a set of questions. Depending on the nature of the answer to a given question, it may be necessary to go to another step or to terminate the analysis and summarize the results.

Create a vector *Y* that includes the measures of the dependent variable for all subjects. Create a coded vector(s) to represent group membership in the categories of the categorical variable. This is done in the usual manner, as I described extensively in Chapter 11. Create a vector(s) that includes the values of the continuous independent variable(s) for all subjects. Generate a new vector(s) by multiplying the vector(s) representing the categorical variable by the continuous variable(s). When more than one continuous variable is used, the vector(s) representing the categorical variable is multiplied, in turn, by each continuous variable. The product vectors represent the interaction terms.

To make the following presentation concise, I use an example of one categorical variable (*A*), which may comprise two or more categories and one continuous variable (*B*). As I explained in Chapter 11, the number of coded vectors used to represent the categorical variable equals the number of categories minus one. I use the letter *C* to represent the product(s) of the vector(s) representing the categorical variable(s) by the continuous variable.

1. *Is the proportion of variance accounted for meaningful?* Calculate $R^2_{y.abc}$. This indicates the proportion of variance accounted for by the main effects and the interaction. If $R^2_{y.abc}$ is too small to be meaningful in the context of your theoretical formulation and your knowledge of the findings in the field of study, terminate the analysis. Whether R^2 is statistically significant or not, if in your judgment its magnitude has little substantive meaning, there is no point in going further. If you deem $R^2_{y.abc}$ to be meaningful, go to step 2.

2. *Is there a statistically significant interaction?* Calculate $R^2_{y.ab}$. Test

$$F = \frac{(R^2_{y.abc} - R^2_{y.ab})/(k_1 - k_2)}{(1 - R^2_{y.abc})/(N - k_1 - 1)}$$

where k_1 is the number of vectors (the coded vectors, the continuous variable, and the product vectors) associated with $R^2_{y.abc}$; k_2 is the number of vectors (the coded vectors and the continuous variable) associated with $R^2_{y.ab}$. A statistically nonsignificant *F* ratio with $k_1 - k_2$ and $N - k_1 - 1$ *df* indicates that the interaction is statistically not significant. If the interaction is statistically not significant, go to step 3. If it is statistically significant, go to step 7.

3. *Is the common regression coefficient (b_c) statistically significant?* Calculate $R^2_{y.a}$. Test

$$F = \frac{(R^2_{y.ab} - R^2_{y.a})/(k_1 - k_2)}{(1 - R^2_{y.ab})/(N - k_1 - 1)}$$

where k_1 is the number of vectors (the coded vectors and the continuous variable) associated with $R^2_{y.ab}$; k_2 is the number of coded vectors associated with $R^2_{y.a}$. For uniformity of format, I presented this test, though it can be accomplished in a simpler manner. Remember that the b for the continuous variable in a regression equation in which product vectors are not included is b_c. Therefore, testing this b in the usual manner is equivalent to the preceding test. If this test is statistically not significant, go to step 4. If it is statistically significant, go to step 5.

4. *Are differences among treatments of the categorical variable statistically significant?* Calculate $R^2_{y.a}$. Test

$$F = \frac{R^2_{y.a}/k}{(1 - R^2_{y.a})/(N - k - 1)}$$

where k is the number of coded vectors used to represent the categorical variable. Because one has concluded (step 3) that b_c is statistically not significant, the design here is reduced to one with a categorical independent variable only. The analysis and interpretation of results proceed as in Chapter 11.

5. *Are differences among the intercepts statistically significant?* Calculate $R^2_{y.b}$. Test

$$F = \frac{(R^2_{y.ab} - R^2_{y.b})/(k_1 - k_2)}{(1 - R^2_{y.ab})/(N - k_1 - 1)}$$

where k_1 is the number of vectors (the coded vectors and the continuous variable) associated with $R^2_{y.ab}$; and $k_2 = 1$ (I use one continuous variable in the present context). If this test is statistically not significant, go to step 6. If this test is statistically significant, calculate separate regression equations in which the intercepts differ, but all have the same b (i.e., b_c). This can be done through the regression equation in which product vectors are *not* included. When the categorical variable consists of more than two categories, it is possible to do multiple comparisons among the intercepts—a topic I discuss in Chapter 15.

6. Having determined (step 5) that differences among the intercepts are statistically not significant, calculate a single regression equation for all subjects by regressing the dependent variable on the continuous variable. Interpret the results.

7. Having determined that the interaction is statistically significant (step 2), *calculate separate regression equations*. This can be done through the overall regression equation. *Establish regions of significance* (I show how to do this later in this chapter) and interpret the results.

CATEGORIZING CONTINUOUS VARIABLES

Social and behavioral scientists frequently partition continuous independent variables into dichotomies, trichotomies, and so on, and then analyze the data as if they came from distinct categories of an independent variable. Several broad classes of research in which this is practiced can be identified. The first class may be found in experiments in which continuous manipulated variables are treated as if they were categorical. Consider, for instance, the retention experiment I analyzed in preceding sections. Recall that one variable was categorical (No Incentive, Incentive), whereas the other was continuous (Study Time) with four levels. Instead of doing an analysis as in the preceding sections, some researchers would treat the continuous variable as if it consisted of four distinct categories and would analyze the data as comprising a 2×4 factorial analysis of variance.[3] I do such an analysis later and compare its results with those of my analysis in preceding sections.

The second class of research studies in which one frequently encounters categorization of a continuous variable is the so-called treatments-by-levels design. In such designs, the continuous variable is primarily a control variable. For example, a researcher may be interested in the difference between two methods of instruction. Because the subjects differ in intelligence, he or she may wish to control this variable. One way of doing this is to block or create groups with different levels of intelligence and randomly assign an equal number of subjects from each level to each treatment. One can then treat the levels as distinct categories and do a factorial analysis of variance. The purpose of introducing the levels into the design is to decrease the error term, which in the present example is accomplished by identifying the sum of squares due to intelligence, thereby removing it from the error term. A more sensitive F test for the main effect, methods of instruction, is thereby obtained. The reduction in the error term depends on the correlation between the continuous variable and the dependent variable. The larger the correlation, the greater the reduction in the error term will be.

The third class of studies in which researchers tend to categorize continuous variables is similar to the second class just described. But whereas categorization in the second class of studies is motivated primarily by the need for control, in this class of studies it is motivated by an interest in a possible interaction between the independent variables. This approach—referred to variously as Aptitude-Treatment Interaction (ATI), Attribute-Treatment Interaction (ATI), or Trait-Treatment Interaction (TTI)[4]—is important in the behavioral sciences, as it may help identify effects that will otherwise go unnoticed. Behavioral scientists and educators have frequently voiced concern that while lip service is paid to individual differences, little has been done to search for and identify optimal conditions of performance for different types of people.

If, for example, the variable of intelligence is included in a study of the effectiveness of different teaching methods because of an expectation of an interaction between it and teaching methods, the research is in the ATI framework. Note that the point of departure of the researcher is a search for the optimal methods of teaching subjects with different levels of intelligence. The analysis is the same as in the treatments-by-levels design, that is, a factorial analysis of variance. In both cases, the researcher studies the main effects and the interaction. The difference between the two approaches is in the conceptualization of the research: Does the researcher include the continuous variable primarily for control or for studying interaction?

Categorization of variables in the framework discussed is done in various areas. With achievement motivation, for example, researchers measure need achievement, dichotomize it into high and low need achievement, and treat it as a categorical variable. Similarly, researchers tend to partition variables like authoritarianism, dogmatism (e.g., Rickards & Slife, 1987), extraversion-introversion, field dependence-independence (e.g., Frank, 1984), and tolerance of ambiguity (e.g., Keinan, 1994).

Some of the conflicting results in the research literature of a given area may be due to the practice of categorization of continuous variables. For instance, assume that two researchers study independently the relation between dogmatism and susceptibility to a prestigious source.

---

[3]Whether the calculations are done by conventional methods or by methods I presented in Chapter 12, the results will, of course, be the same.

[4]For a comment on terminology, see "The Study of Interaction," later in this chapter.

Suppose, further, that the researchers follow identical procedures in their research designs, that is, they use the same type of prestigious source, the same type of suggestion, the same number of subjects, and so on. They administer the Dogmatism Scale (e.g., Rokeach, 1960) to their subjects, split them at the median and create a high Dogmatism and a low Dogmatism group. Subjects from each of these groups are then randomly assigned to a prestigious or a nonprestigious source. The result is a 2 × 2 factorial analysis of variance—two sources and two levels of dogmatism. Note, however, that the determination of "high" and "low" is entirely dependent on the type of subjects involved. True, when compared to members of one's group, it is appropriate to describe one as, say, high or low. But it is possible that, due to differences in samples, the highs of the first researcher are more like the lows of the second researcher. When the two studies are reported, it is likely that little specific information about the subjects is offered. Instead, reporting is generally limited to statements about high and low dogmatists, as if this was determined in an absolute manner rather than relative to the distribution of dogmatism of a given group that, in most instances, is not a probability sample.[5] Under such circumstances, one should not be surprised when the highs in one study behave more like the lows in the other study, thus leading to conflicting results in what are presumably similar studies.

A fourth class of studies in which continuous variables are categorized is in nonexperimental research. What I have in mind are studies in which more than one attribute (e.g., attitudes, aptitudes, personality variables) are categorized. *This is potentially the most misleading and harmful use of categorization as it casts the design in what appears to be a factorial analysis of variance, creating the illusion that it can yield the same information as is obtained in an experimental design.* Indeed, researchers who engage in such practices believe, erroneously, that having categorized two or more attributes they can study their main and joint effects (interactions) on a dependent variable of interest. Instead of discussing such misconceptions (for good discussions, see Humphreys, 1978; Humphreys & Fleishman, 1974), I would like to point out that what I said in Chapter 12 about multiple categorical independent variables in nonexperimental research and in Chapter 13 about products of continuous variables in nonexperimental research applies even with greater force in the situation under consideration.

The foregoing overriding concerns aside, two questions may be raised about the categorization of continuous variables: "On what basis does one categorize?" and "What effect does categorization have on the analysis?" I comment on each, beginning with the former.

Basis for Categorization

As categorization is an arbitrary operation, there can be no simple answer to the question of the basis for carrying it out. Often a median split is used, with those above the median labeled "high" and those below it labeled "low." Notice that subjects in each group are treated as if they had identical scores on what is essentially a continuous variable. Moreover, in a median split, a difference of one unit on the continuous variable may result in labeling a subject as high or low. To avoid this possibility, some researchers create a middle group, which they either include in or exclude from the analysis. Other variations on this theme are, of course, possible. The main point, however, is that categorization can have only adverse effects and should therefore be avoided.

---

[5]As I pointed out in Chapter 12, in most experiments, subjects who happen to be available (euphemistically referred to as samples of convenience) are used. For an introduction to sampling, see Pedhazur and Schmelkin (1991, Chapter 15) and the references therein.

Effects of Categorization

The answer to the second question—"What effects does categorization have on the analysis?"—is clear-cut. Categorization leads to loss of information and consequently to a less sensitive analysis (for a good discussion, see Cohen, 1983). Further, double median splits (see the following) may, in some situations, lead to a dramatic increase in the probability of Type I errors (Maxwell & Delaney, 1993).

As I noted earlier, all subjects in a category are treated alike even though they may have originally been quite different on the continuous variable. In the case of a median split, the continuum is transformed into a two-point scale. But if, as it stands to reason, the choice of the continuous variable was made because of its relation to the dependent variable of interest, then one would expect a difference in performance among subjects classified in a given category. It is this loss of information about differences among subjects, or the reduction in the variability of the continuous variable, that leads to a reduction in the sensitivity of the analysis, not to mention meaningfulness of results.

Double Median Splits

To highlight a serious deficiency often overlooked when categorizing continuous variables, I will use the simplest and rather prevalent case of dichotomizing two continuous variables (e.g., mental ability, motivation, attitudes, authoritarianism) at their respective medians. An area in which this is currently done routinely is sex-role research, where scores on masculinity (M) and femininity (F) are split at their respective medians thereby forming four categories, as depicted in Figure 14.2. The intersection of the vertical and horizontal lines indicates the medians on M and F. Scores above the point of intersection are above the median on M, and those below it are below the median on M. Similarly, scores to the right of the point of intersection are above the median on F, and those to the left of the point of intersection are below the median on F.

As indicated in the figure, this double median split is used to classify individuals into one of four types: (1) *masculine*: subjects above the median on M and below the median on F;

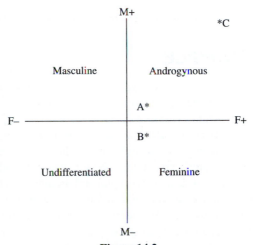

Figure 14.2

(2) *feminine*: subjects above the median on F and below the median on M; (3) *androgynous*: subjects above the median on both F and M; and (4) *Undifferentiated*: subjects below the median on both M and F. This is not the place to go into issues of construct validity of the measure used and the definition of the aforementioned classification based on it (for a critique, see Pedhazur & Tetenbaum, 1979). Instead, I would like to draw your attention to the three asterisks I inserted in the figure. They are meant to represent scores for individuals A, B, and C. Notice that although A and C are farther apart from each other (i.e., more dissimilar on M and F) than are A and B, A and C will be classified as androgynous, whereas B will be classified as feminine.

Despite this and other shortcomings of median splits, they are used frequently in published research. To illustrate how entrenched this practice is, I will cite but two instances.

One, in a manuscript Tetenbaum and I submitted to the *Journal of Personality and Social Psychology* (Pedhazur & Tetenbaum, 1979), we were critical of the use of median splits on the Bem Sex Role Inventory (BSRI). Following is what one of the referees had to say about our criticism: "Of course—so what else is new? What does this criticism have to do with the BSRI in particular? *It is simply a cost necessarily involved in the doing of research* [italics added]." Two things are implied in the preceding. (1) Median splits are used in other areas as well. Why, then, fault those who do this with the BSRI? The argument that everyone is doing it (whatever the "it") is used frequently as a response (excuse?) to criticism (see the following for another instance). (2) Median splits are the only means available for creating a typology. This is not the place to discuss the topic of classification about which a great deal has been written (for introductory treatments, see Aldenderfer & Blashfield, 1984; Bailey, 1994; Hudson et al., 1982; Lorr, 1983). All I will say is that the use of median splits is probably the crudest and least meaningful approach to the classification of people.

Two, responding to criticism of their use of double median splits, pursuant to which they applied the analysis of variance as if their data were obtained in a factorial design, Das and Kirby (1978) stated that they

> did not introduce median splits into the research literature in psychology. In fact, single median splits have been done routinely by psychologists. We divide people on the basis of age, intelligence, and high and low verbal ability. Double median splits such as the one we used in our 1977 article can be easily found in personality research. (p. 878)

To buttress their claim, they cited research examples in which double median splits were used.

A RESEARCH EXAMPLE

It will be instructive to use a research example that, in my opinion, embodies much of what is wrong with categorization of continuous variables and with attempts to study interactions in nonexperimental designs—topics I discussed in Chapters 12 and 13.

Wiggins and Holzmuller (1978) were interested in studying the effects of sex, sex roles, and the interaction between them on interpersonal behavior. For present purposes, I focus only on those aspects of their study relevant to the topic under consideration.

As a measure of sex roles, Wiggins and Holzmuller used the Bem Sex Role Inventory (BSRI; Bem, 1974) to which I alluded earlier in this chapter, as well as in Chapter 13. Especially pertinent for present purposes are the scoring procedures of the BSRI and classification strategies based on them. Specifically, in initial uses of the BSRI, classification into various categories (e.g., masculine, feminine) was based on a test (*t* ratio) of the difference between Masculinity and

Femininity scores for each individual. In response to criticism, this classification procedure was abandoned by virtually everyone, including the scale's author, in favor of the double median splits outlined in the preceding.[6] While acknowledging that this has taken place, Wiggins and Holzmuller (1978) decided to base their classification on the test of the difference between masculinity and femininity (i.e., the *t* ratio), saying:

> However, designs such as the present one that analyze *interactions* between sex role classification and other variables require the additional "near-stereotyped" groups yielded by the difference score method. (p. 43)

It is not my intention to comment on what is, in my opinion, a specious argument, as my aim in reviewing this study is to question the very design that allegedly necessitated tests of differences between masculinity and femininity. I mentioned the approach Wiggins and Holzmuller took because I need to refer to it when I explain their classification strategy and how they treated it in their design, analysis, and interpretation of the results.

Using tests of difference scores, then, Wiggins and Holzmuller created three categories: stereotyped, near-stereotyped, and androgynous. Subjects classified as stereotyped were either males whose Masculinity score was statistically significantly higher than their Femininity score (i.e., masculine males), or females whose Femininity score was statistically significantly higher than their Masculinity score (i.e., feminine females).[7] Classification into the Near-Stereotyped category followed the same strategy, except that *t* ratios for the test of the difference between the two measures were smaller than the critical value but larger than 1.01. Accordingly, subjects in this category were either "near masculine" or "near feminine" (see their Table 1, p. 43). Finally, subjects were classified as androgynous when the *t* ratio for the test of the difference between the two measures was equal to or smaller than 1.01.

I am ready now to discuss the design and analysis. To begin with, it is noteworthy that the authors used the subhead "*Experimental Design*" (p. 43) for the section in which they described their design.[8] Essentially they said that they used a 3×2 analysis of variance in which one factor was group (i.e., the three categories just described) and the other sex.

> Scores on the interpersonal adjective scales were entered separately as dependent variables. For each *interpersonal variable* [italics added], this permitted an evaluation of main effects for groups (stereotyped and androgynous groups *irrespective of gender* [italics added]), for gender (sex differences in responding *irrespective of groups* [italics added]), and for the interaction between these two factors. (p. 43)

---

[6]For more details, see Pedhazur and Tetenbaum (1979) and references therein.

[7]I do not comment on the validity of such tests of significance, as my sole aim is to describe what Wiggins and Holzmuller did. For a critique of such tests, see Strahan (1975).

[8]As an interesting aside, I would like to quote from a "Notice" (Hartlage, 1988) published in the *American Psychologist* (the official organ of the American Psychological Association).

> At the request of the Board of Directors, the following Comment is presented to the Membership:
> "In 1973 Hartlage and Lucus published a study in the *Journal of Learning Disabilities* . . . This field study, without random assignment of subjects or experimental manipulation, was correlational in nature. These data were reanalyzed and reported (Hartlage & Reynolds, 1981) in a manner that could be interpreted as their having been generated from an experimental paradigm, not a field study, thus possibly allowing a reader to draw different conclusions than might have been drawn if both studies had been read. This 1981 chapter has been cited subsequently . . . , thus perpetuating its misleading presentation." (p. 1092)

> Two things are noteworthy. (1) I believe that published statements such as this one are extremely rare. In my readings, I did not come across another one like it. I can only guess that it was published as a result of a complaint(s) received in the APA office. (2) *Wiggins and Holzmuller's study was published in an APA journal!*

The results were as follows: (1) "main effects" for the Group factor were statistically not significant; (2) seven of the eight tests for "main effects" for the Sex factor were statistically significant; and (3) six of the eight tests of "interactions" were statistically significant.

I invite you to consider the prudence of treating ratings on a set of interpersonal adjective scales (e.g., dominant-ambitious; arrogant-calculating; warm-agreeable) as if they constituted scores on eight distinct dependent variables. Also, I suggest that you examine the aforementioned adjective scales and others reported in Table 2 of Wiggins and Holzmuller (1978) along with the adjectives used in the BSRI (Bem, 1974. e.g., dominant, warm) and judge whether it is meaningful to treat the latter as measuring an independent variable and the former as measuring dependent variables.

To facilitate your examination of Wiggins and Holzmuller's design and analysis, I depicted the former in Figure 14.3. Using the percentages reported in their Table 1 (p. 43), I calculated the cell frequencies given in the figure. The first thing I will note is that Wiggins and Holzmuller do not even allude to the unequal cell frequencies. Therefore, needless to say, they make no mention of how they handled them in the analyses. This in itself would suffice to cast serious doubts about the validity of their pronouncements regarding effects of one variable "irrespective" of the other (see the previous quotation; see also the discussion of nonorthogonal designs in Chapter 12).

Nevertheless, the problem of unequal cell frequencies pales in comparison with what is, in my opinion, a major flaw of this study, which is why I singled it out for comment. To better understand what I have in mind, think of Figure 14.3 as an experimental design in which the columns represent three treatments and the rows represent, as in the study under consideration, sex. Assume that, following sound principles of experimental design, males and females, separately, were randomly assigned in equal numbers to the three treatments. Also, that there was no loss of subjects (i.e., the cell frequencies remained equal).

As I discussed in detail in Chapter 12, under these circumstances the design is orthogonal and it is therefore possible to speak unambiguously of the main effects of treatments and sex, as well as the interaction between them. That is, one may use language such as Wiggins and Holzmuller used in speaking of effects of treatments "irrespective" of sex and vice versa.[9] I remind you that, because of randomization, the three male groups may be viewed as equal to each other, and the three female groups may be viewed as equal to each other. They differ, of course, in the treatments to which they were exposed. I would like to stress here that each column of Figure 14.3 consists of a group of males and a group of females who were administered the *same* treatment. This may seem so obvious as to make you wonder why I even bother to state, let alone stress, it. I do this so that I may use it later as a contrast with Wiggins and Holzmuller's design.

	S	NS	AND	
M	8	21	33	62
F	42	33	39	114
	50	54	72	176

M = Male; F = Female.
S = Stereotyped; NS = Near Stereotyped;
AND = Androgynous.
See text for explanation.

Figure 14.3

[9]I would like, however, to remind you that in Chapter 12, I contended that when a classificatory variable (sex, in the present example) is used, interpretations of its main effect and an interaction between it and the treatments are not simple, even when the design is orthogonal.

Assume now that in the experimental design I have just described there was subject attrition, resulting in the unequal frequencies depicted in Figure 14.3. Even a *glance* only at the column labeled S should suffice to convince one of the folly of assuming that subject attrition was random. Consequently, attempts to adjust for the correlations between the terms of the design would be tantamount to shutting one's eyes to the more important issue of noncomparability of groups because of systematic attrition.

Now, instead of an experimental design, think of Figure 14.3 as a nonexperimental design. Assume, for example, that the variables are sex and stress. Overlooking, for present purposes, the inadvisability of categorizing continuous variables, assume that using scores on a measure of stress subjects were classified into high-, average-, and low-stress groups. Viewing Figure 14.3 in this context, the unequal cell frequencies would clearly indicate that sex and stress are correlated. Consequently, all I said about such designs in Chapter 12 (e.g., model specification, the questionable status of interaction) would also apply to this situation. But, analogous to my discussion of experimental research in the preceding paragraphs, I would like to stress here that each of the columns of Figure 14.3 would consist of males *and* females of the *same* stress level. For example, assume that S of Figure 14.3 stands for high stress. Then, whatever the criterion used to identify high stress, it stands to reason that it would be applied equally to males and females. Otherwise, one would have to question the meaning of placing them in the same category.

With the preceding examples as a backdrop, I will scrutinize Wiggins and Holzmuller's design and show that it is by no means of the garden variety nonexperimental designs with correlated independent variables I discussed in Chapter 13, but it is instead a hybrid that eludes meaningful description. To see what I mean, look at the column labeled S (i.e., stereotyped) in Figure 14.3. It consists of masculine males and feminine females (see the earlier description of Wiggins and Holzmuller's classification). Thus, using the label "stereotyped," males and females who are at opposite ends of whatever it is that is being measured are classified through semantic wizardry, so to speak, as belonging to the same category. Clearly, this differs from the situations I gave in the previous illustrations in connection with Figure 14.3.

Even if one were to argue that it is possible to come up with a conception that subsumes these radically different patterns of scores,[10] note that Wiggins and Holzmuller do not even hint that this issue exists. But let us consider the implications of Wiggins and Holzmuller's strategy. Not surprisingly, most people classified as masculine were males, and most of those classified as feminine were females. If this does not suffice to raise serious doubts in your mind regarding the validity of conceiving of gender and sex roles as two independent variables in a factorial design, perhaps the fact that Wiggins and Holzmuller excluded "sex-reversed" (p. 43) subjects (i.e., feminine males and masculine females) from the analysis will.

Let us consider briefly the implications of this strategy. Recall that the great virtue of a factorial design, that of affording estimation of main effects and interactions, stems from the fact that the factors are independent of each other. Referring to the illustrations I gave earlier in connection with Figure 14.3, the great virtue of the experimental setting is that the Sex factor is truly independent of the treatments. Complications arise when, because of subject attrition, the design becomes nonorthogonal (see Chapter 12).

---

[10]Doing this would require, among other things, the resolution of some very knotty measurement issues. It would be necessary, for instance, to support a contention that while the scores differ on the phenotypic level, they tap the same genotypic dimension. This is no mean task, even with more sophisticated strategies and with measures of less questionable validity than the BSRI (see Pedhazur & Tetenbaum, 1979).

Turning to the example of nonexperimental research I gave earlier, sex and stress are correlated, and this leads to the complications I discussed in Chapter 12 in connection with such designs. But, note the important difference between this example and Wiggins and Holzmuller's strategy. In this example, when a subject, *male or female,* is high on the Stress factor, he or she is placed in same column, say column *S* of Figure 14.3. But because the variables are correlated the design consists of unequal cell frequencies. This is not the case in Wiggins and Holzmuller's study, as is evidenced from their exclusion of "sex-reversed" subjects which, in effect, means a confounding of the two variables. Stated differently, this means that it is not sufficient for a subject to have one score statistically significantly higher than the other to be placed in the first column. The relevance (validity?) of the discrepancy between the two scores is predicated on the subject's gender. Is one, then, to conclude that, as long as the pattern of scores is *not* incompatible with gender, the same "trait" is being measured? If so, why the distinction between males and females in the design? Why not a one-way design consisting of stereotyped, near-stereotyped, and androgynous?

The preceding aside, let us now consider the implications that it *does* make a difference whether a subject is a stereotyped male or a stereotyped female. What would this mean for the estimation and tests of main effects for groups "irrespective of gender" (Wiggins & Holzmuller, 1978, p. 43)? Referring to Figure 14.3, this means comparing the columns while ignoring the rows. To get a feel for the answer to my question, it would suffice to examine the columns labeled *S* and *NS* of Figure 14.3. A contrast between these columns is one between 8 masculine males and 42 feminine females on the one hand, and 21 near-masculine males and 33 near-feminine females on the other hand.

I will not try to come up with an explanation of what this means. I believe I could not come up with a reasonable explanation even if I tried. I hope that you recognize the fatuousness of speaking of "main effects," no matter which of my alternative views of the classification strategy you take. Speaking of an interaction between the Sex and Groups factors verges, I regret to say, on the grotesque.

THE STUDY OF INTERACTION

I introduced the concept of interaction in Chapter 12, where I discussed it in detail for designs in which the independent variables are categorical. I addressed this topic again in Chapter 13, where my concern was with interactions between continuous variables. In this chapter, I consider interactions between continuous and categorical variables. Notwithstanding the type of variables, a test of an interaction addresses the question of whether a nonadditive model fits the data better than an additive one. When an interaction is statistically not significant, an additive model is sufficient to describe the data. This means that a subject's score on the dependent variable is conceived as a composite of several additive components. In the most general case, these are an intercept, treatment effects, and an error term. For the retention experiment I analyzed in the beginning of the chapter, the additive model is

$$Y = a + bX + bE + e \tag{14.3}$$

where X is the continuous variable (Study Time) and E is a vector representing treatments (No Incentive, Incentive).

When, on the other hand, the interaction is statistically significant, it means that terms reflecting the interaction ought to be part of the model. For the present example this may take the form

$$Y = a + bX + bE + bXE + e \qquad (14.4)$$

The difference between (14.3) and (14.4) is that in the latter I added a term that is the product of the values of the independent variables (XE). Earlier in this chapter, I showed that when, as in the present example, a single coded vector is sufficient to represent the categorical variable, a test of the coefficient for the product vector (b_{XE}) is a test of the interaction and is equivalent to a test of the increment in the proportion of variance accounted for by the product vector, over and above its constituent variables. Also, when one of the variables is categorical and the other is continuous, the test of an interaction addresses the question of whether the regression lines of the dependent variable on the continuous variable are parallel for all the categories of the categorical variable (two, in the retention experiment). In other words, a test of an interaction addresses the question of whether differences among regression coefficients from separate regression equations are statistically significant.

Attribute-Treatment Interaction

In the retention experiment, which I presented in the beginning of this chapter, both variables were manipulated. In many situations, a nonmanipulated continuous variable(s) is used in conjunction with a manipulated categorical variable(s). A prime example of such research is Attribute-Treatment Interaction (ATI), that is, research aimed at studying interactions between attributes (e.g., aptitudes, traits, attitudes) and treatments (e.g., teaching methods, therapies). Note that Cronbach and Snow (1977), who have been most influential in conceptualizing and promoting ATI research, used the term *aptitude* (instead of *attribute*), in the broad sense of "any characteristic of a person that forecasts his probability of success under a given treatment" (p. 6; see also Corno & Snow, 1986, p. 605; Snow, 1991). Some authors (e.g., Berliner & Cahen, 1973), nevertheless, viewed the term *aptitude* as too limiting, and recommended that *trait* be used instead, hence Trait-Treatment Interaction (TTI). Although it is probably true that most people think of aptitude in a narrow sense, I believe they also tend to think of trait as referring to personality characteristics only. Therefore, I prefer the term *attribute,* which I believe is more inclusive than the other two. Be that as it may, I agree that "the world will be as well served by any label, so long as the research itself goes forward" (Cronbach & Snow, 1977, p. 6).

Although the test of an interaction proceeds in the same manner when the continuous variable is manipulated or nonmanipulated, interpretation of the results is less ambiguous when the continuous variable is manipulated. The reason is that under such circumstances complete randomization is effected, and it is therefore plausible to assume that the continuous variable is not correlated with other variables that are subsumed under the error term—for example, *e* in (14.4). When a nonmanipulated continuous variable is used, subjects may be randomly assigned only to the treatments that make up the categorical variable. The purpose of such randomization is to equate the groups assigned to the different treatments, but this does not preclude the possibility that the continuous variable used in the study is correlated with other variables not included in the model. Consequently, when a continuous nonmanipulated variable is used, it is necessary to recognize that variables other than the one under consideration may be partly, even wholly, responsible for its interaction with a manipulated categorical variable. As always, the best guides for the interpretation of the results are theory and knowledge about the specific problem under study. And the best safeguard for avoiding flagrant misinterpretations is clear and critical thinking.[11]

Attributes versus Situations

Behavioral scientists, particularly psychologists, have been engaged in an ongoing person-situation debate revolving around the question of whether behavior is determined primarily by the situation or by a person's attributes (for a review, see Epstein & O'Brien, 1985). However, as was pointed out by some authors (e.g., Bowers, 1973; Ekenhammer, 1974), it is a person-situation interaction perspective that holds the greater promise for explaining behavior.

Bowers (1973), who offered an excellent review of "situationism in psychology," maintained that "we have been left with an almost religious allegiance to a main effects psychology that emphasizes the situational impact on behavior almost to the exclusion of person and interaction effects" (p. 325). Among other things, Bowers offered summaries of studies in which it was found that interactions between subjects' attributes and situations accounted for far greater proportions of variance of the dependent variable than did the main effects of either attributes or situations. An example of a research area in which such interactions were shown to predominate is conformity. Contrary to earlier conceptions of a conformist personality, it was found that certain types of people are prone to conform in certain types of situations (i.e., that there is an interaction between attributes and situations in their effects on conformity; for a review, see Moscovici, 1985). Similarly, recent formulations and research about leadership indicate that there is an interaction between type of leader, type of follower, and type of situation (for a review, see Hollander, 1985).

For a general thorough presentation of ATI, see Cronbach and Snow (1977). The first four chapters of their book consist of an excellent discussion of introductory and advanced topics in the design and analysis of ATI studies. The remainder of the book is devoted to a critical review of ATI research in various substantive areas (e.g., learning, personality).

Cronbach and Snow's formulations regarding ATI designs were initially contained in a widely circulated unpublished report whose recommendations were followed by many researchers. It is noteworthy that by the time they wrote the preface to their book, Cronbach and Snow found it necessary to "apologize to investigators misled by our unpublished report of 1969" (1977, p. ix). They stated that they were led to change their views as a result of more thorough study "during which we located many sources overlooked earlier, became aware of the critical relevance of statistical power" (p. ix). This in turn led them to change their interpretation and assessment of individual studies and even of "whole bodies of literature. We have now had to dismiss some published findings that we once trusted, and have occasionally unearthed positive evidence buried beneath an author's original negative conclusion" (p. ix).

The preceding is, needless to say, not meant as a criticism of Cronbach and Snow. Quite the contrary. Their statement is indeed "a sign of forward movement and of interest in our topic" (p. ix). My main purpose was to draw attention to Cronbach and Snow's lament: "Long after we had changed our views, the initial report was still influencing investigators" (p. ix).[12] The phenomenon of researchers continuing to use methods long after they were shown to be lacking and

[11]For a discussion that parallels the present one, see "Manipulated and Classificatory Variables" in Chapter 12.

[12]Cronbach (1992) has shown that a similar fate has befallen some of his other writings.

were supplanted by ones believed to be more appropriate for the task at hand is, unfortunately, not uncommon in behavioral research (the use of median splits, which I discussed in the preceding section, is another example).

That much is yet to be done to improve the state of ATI research is attested to by several relatively recent reviews (e.g., Berliner, 1983; Dance & Neufeld, 1988; Good & Stipek, 1983) in which the paucity of findings of interactions was attributed to, among other things, the use of inappropriate or deficient analytic approaches, inadequate definitions, measures of questionable validity, and unrealistic expectations of effects of weak and/or ambiguous treatments of short durations.

Because the following presentation is devoted solely to analytic issues, I do not dwell on the distinction between interactions with manipulated and nonmanipulated variables. Nor do I address issues of theory, research design, measurement, and the like. *I urge you, though, not to overlook these important issues in your own research or when reading research reports.*

Ordinal and Disordinal Interactions

I introduced the concepts of ordinal and disordinal interactions in Chapter 12 in connection with interactions between categorical variables. Although the overall conception is the same for interactions between continuous and categorical variables, the following presentation will show that the specifics of the definitions, graphic depictions, and tests of significance differ in the two settings. The differences stem from the fact that in the present setting the concern is with regression equations, regression lines, and comparisons among them, whereas in Chapter 12 the concern was with means, line segments connecting means, and comparisons of mean differences.

An ordinal interaction between a continuous and a categorical variable is indicated when non-parallel regression lines do not intersect within the research range of interest (see explanation that follows), whereas a disordinal interaction is indicated when regression lines intersect within the research range of interest. This distinction can be best understood when presented graphically. Figure 14.4 presents three illustrative situations of the regression of Y on X under two treatments (I and II). Depicted in (a) is a situation in which there is no interaction. The two regression lines are parallel. There is a constant difference between Treatments I and II along the continuum of X. In other words, the b's for the regression of Y on X under the two treatments are identical. Hence, the difference between the treatments is entirely accountable by the difference between the intercepts of the regression lines. In (b), while Treatment I is still superior to Treatment II along the X continuum, it is relatively more effective at the lower end of X than at the upper end. Note, however, that in no instance is Treatment II superior to Treatment I. This, then, is an ordinal interaction.

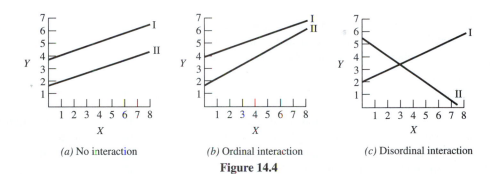

(a) No interaction   (b) Ordinal interaction   (c) Disordinal interaction

Figure 14.4

Finally, in (c) the regression lines cross, exemplifying a disordinal interaction. Treatment II is superior at the lower levels of X (up to 3), whereas Treatment I is superior at the upper levels of X (from 3 and up). At the value of $X = 3$, the two treatments seem to be equally effective.

Examine (b) in Figure 14.4 and notice that if the regression lines were extended, they would cross each other as in a disordinal interaction. The question therefore is: When is an interaction considered ordinal and when is it considered disordinal? The answer lies in the research range of interest.

The Research Range of Interest

The research range of interest is defined by the values of the continuous variable (X) of relevance to the purposes of the research. Recall that extrapolation from regression lines is hazardous (see Chapter 13). Therefore, values within the research range of interest should be included in the actual study. In the retention experiment I analyzed earlier in this chapter, the research range of interest was presumably from 5 to 20 minutes of study time. Or, using an example with a non-manipulated continuous variable, say IQ, the research range of interest might be from 90 to 120. In other words, it is for subjects within this range of intelligence that one wishes to make statements about the effectiveness of teaching methods or some other treatment.

The decision about whether an interaction is ordinal or disordinal is based on the point at which the regression lines intersect. If this point is outside the range of interest, the interaction is considered ordinal. If, on the other hand, the point of intersection is within the range of interest, then the interaction is considered disordinal. To illustrate, let us assume that for Figure 14.4 the researcher's range of interest is for X values from 1 to 8. It is evident that the regression lines in (b) do not intersect within the range of interest, whereas those in (c) intersect well within the range of interest (at $X = 3$).

Determining the Point of Intersection

Parallel regression lines indicate regression equations consisting of different intercepts and identical regression coefficients. Under such circumstances, a prediction of equal Y's for two treatments at a given value of X cannot occur. For example, assume that in a given research study consisting of two treatments (A and B) the regression lines are parallel. Assume further that the intercept for Treatment A is 7 whereas the intercept for Treatment B is 2, and that $b = .8$ for each of the regression lines. Thus, the two regression equations are

$$Y'_A = 7 + .8X$$

$$Y'_B = 2 + .8X$$

Notice that for any value of X, Y'_A will be 5 points higher than Y'_B (this is the difference between the intercepts, and it is constant along the X continuum).

Suppose, however, that the two equations are

$$Y'_A = 7 + .3X$$

$$Y'_B = 2 + .8X$$

Scrutiny of these equations reveals that for relatively small X values, Y'_A is larger than Y'_B. The reason is that the intercept plays a more important role relative to the regression coefficient in the prediction of Y. As X increases, the regression coefficients play an increasingly important role, offsetting the difference between the intercepts, until a balance is struck and $Y'_A = Y'_B$. Beyond that point, Y'_B is larger than Y'_A. Note that at the point of intersection the predicted Y for Treatment I is equal to the predicted Y for Treatment II. In view of the preceding, the point of intersection can be calculated as follows:

$$\text{Point of intersection } (X) = \frac{a_1 - a_2}{b_2 - b_1} \tag{14.5}$$

where the a's are intercepts and the b's are regression coefficients. In this example, $a_1 = 7, a_2 = 2$, $b_1 = .3$, and $b_2 = .8$. Hence,

$$X = \frac{7 - 2}{.8 - .3} = \frac{5}{.5} = 10$$

The point at which the lines intersect is at $X = 10$, as Figure 14.5 illustrates. If the range of interest in the research depicted in Figure 14.5 is, say, from 3 to 15, then the interaction is disordinal as the lines intersect within this range.

I now apply the regression equations, which are depicted in Figure 14.5, to several values of X to illustrate points I made in the preceding discussion. For $X = 10$,

$$Y'_A = 7 + (.3)(10) = 10$$

$$Y'_B = 2 + (.8)(10) = 10$$

The same value is predicted for subjects under treatments A or B. This is because the lines intersect at $X = 10$. For $X = 5$,

$$Y'_A = 7 + (.3)(5) = 8.5$$

$$Y'_B = 2 + (.8)(5) = 6$$

$X = 5$ is below the point of intersection, and the regression equation for Treatment A leads to a higher predicted value of Y than does the regression equation for Treatment B. The converse is true for X values above the point of intersection. For example, for $X = 12$,

$$Y'_A = 7 + (.3)(12) = 10.6$$

$$Y'_B = 2 + (.8)(12) = 11.6$$

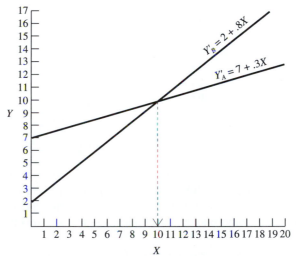

Figure 14.5

A Numerical Example

It has been maintained that students' satisfaction with the teaching styles of their teachers depends, among other variables, on the students' tolerance of ambiguity. Specifically, students whose tolerance of ambiguity is relatively low prefer teachers whose teaching style is largely directive, whereas students whose tolerance of ambiguity is relatively high prefer teachers whose style is largely nondirective. To test this hypothesis students were randomly assigned to "directive" and "nondirective" teachers.[13] At the beginning of the semester, students were administered a measure of tolerance of ambiguity on which the higher the score the greater the tolerance. At the end of the semester, students rated their satisfaction with their teacher on a 7-point scale, 1 indicating very little satisfaction, 7 indicating a great deal of satisfaction. This, then, is an example of an ATI or TTI study. Illustrative data for two classes, each consisting of twenty students, are given in Table 14.3.

Table 14.3 Tolerance of Ambiguity and Rating of Teachers, Illustrative Data

Nondirective		Directive	
Y	X	Y	X
2	5	7	5
1	7	7	7
2	10	7	9
2	15	6	13
3	17	5	12
3	20	6	16
3	25	5	18
4	23	5	21
4	27	5	22
5	30	4	27
6	35	4	26
5	37	3	32
5	40	3	35
5	42	2	40
6	45	3	45
6	47	2	47
6	50	2	49
7	55	1	53
7	60	2	58
6	62	1	63

NOTE: Y = ratings of teacher; X = tolerance of ambiguity.

SPSS

I trust that by now you need no guidance in setting up the input file for the analysis of the data in Table 14.3 using REGRESSION of SPSS or any multiple regression program you may be using. If you do need guidance, refer to the input and commentaries for the analysis of the data in Table 14.2, as the same layout may be used to analyze the data in Table 14.3. Therefore, I will report

[13]Henceforth, I will use the term directive and nondirective teachers to mean teachers using directive and nondirective teaching styles.

and comment on only brief excerpts of the output directly relevant to the topic under consideration. I suggest that you run the analysis and compare your results with those I report.

In analyzing the data in Table 14.2, I used only effect coding. For the present analysis, I used both dummy (D) and effect (E) coding. I suggest that you do the same. Of course, it is not necessary to use both coding methods. In the earlier analysis, I discussed properties of the overall regression equation with effect coding. In the present analysis, I used also dummy coding so that I may explain properties of the overall regression equation with this coding method.

Output

Summary tables

	[effect coding]						[dummy coding]				
Step	Variable	Rsq	RsqCh	FCh	SigCh	Step	Variable	Rsq	RsqCh	FCh	SigCh
1	In: X	.0033	.0033	.128	.723	1	In: X	.0033	.0033	.128	.723
2	In: E	.0158	.0125	.468	.498	2	In: D	.0158	.0125	.468	.498
3	In: XE	.9069	.8911	344.677	.000	3	In: XD	.9069	.8911	344.677	.000

Commentary

I placed the summary tables from the analyses with effect (E) and dummy (D) coding alongside each other to show that they are, as would be expected, identical. As I show later, the regression equations for the two analyses differ. Again, this is to be expected because of the different coding methods.

Note that $R^2_{Y.X,E,XE} = R^2_{Y.X,D,XD} = .9069$, and that the bulk of it is due to the increment accounted for by the interaction: .8911 (RsqCh). The test of this increment in the proportion of variance accounted for constitutes the test of the interaction. From FCh, note that $F(1, 36) = 344.677, p < .01$.

Output

-- Variables in the Equation --

Variable	B	SE B	T	Sig T	Variable	B	SE B	T	Sig T
X	−.004219	.005525			X	−.106796	.007699		
E	−2.999858	.197529			D	−5.999715	.395057		
XE	.102578	.005525	18.565	.0000	XD	.205155	.011050	18.565	.0000
(Constant)	4.193356	.197529			(Constant)	7.193213	.266724		

Commentary

Here, too, I placed the results of the two analyses alongside each other. Note that although the regression equations for the two coding methods differ, the T ratios for the b's associated with the product vectors (XE and XD) are identical. Further, the squared t ($18.565^2 = 344.659$) is, within rounding, equal to the F ratio for the test of the increment in the proportion of variance accounted for by the product vector, over and above its constituent variables (see the preceding).

I did not reproduce the T ratios for the other b's as they are irrelevant. All we want at this stage is to determine whether the interaction is statistically significant. Thus, based on either the F for the increment in the proportion of variance accounted for or the t for the b associated with the product vector, I conclude that the interaction is statistically significant. As I pointed out earlier, when the categorical variable consists of more than two categories, there is more than one product vector. Hence, the test for the interaction has to be carried out through the test of the increment in proportion of variance accounted for by the product vectors.

In sum, I conclude that the regressions of ratings of teachers on students' tolerance of ambiguity differ for directive and nondirective teachers. Consequently, it is necessary to calculate separate regression equations for the two groups.

Separate Regression Equations

Earlier, I showed how to obtain separate regression equations for the different treatments (groups) from the overall regression equation with effect coding. Therefore, I will make only minimal comments about this approach. Subsequently, I show how to obtain the separate regression equations from the overall regression equation with dummy coding.

Effect Coding. From the previous output, the overall regression equation is

$$Y' = 4.193356 - .004219X - 2.999858E + .102578XE$$

where Y = rating of teacher; X = student's tolerance of ambiguity; and E = effect coded vector. In the analysis, I assigned 1 to the group taught by the nondirective teacher and -1 to the group taught by the directive teacher.

As I explained earlier, the intercept, a, of the overall equation is equal to the average of the intercepts for the equations for the two treatments. In view of the codes I used, a for the equation whose group was taught by the nondirective teacher is

$$4.193356 + (-2.999858) = 1.193498$$

a for the equation whose group was taught by the directive teacher is

$$4.193356 - (-2.999858) = 7.193214$$

The average of the b's for the separate regression equations is $-.004219$ (b for X). The deviation of b for the group taught by the nondirective teacher from the average of the b's is .102578 (b for XE). Therefore, b for this group is

$$-.004219 + .102578 = .098359$$

b for the group taught by the directive teacher is

$$-.004219 - (.102578) = -.106797$$

Based on the preceding calculations, the regression equations for the two groups are

$$Y'_{ND} = 1.193498 + .098359X$$

$$Y'_D = 7.193214 - .106797X$$

where Y = rating of teacher; ND = nondirective; D = directive; and X = student's tolerance of ambiguity. The same regression equations would be obtained if they were calculated separately for each group, as in Table 14.2 (you may wish to do this as an exercise) or when using the SPLIT FILE command (see the Input for Table 14.2, presented earlier in this chapter).

Dummy Coding.   From the preceding output, the overall regression equation with dummy coding is

$$Y' = 7.193213 - .106796X - 5.999715D + .205155XD$$

where Y = rating of teacher; X = tolerance of ambiguity; and D = dummy vector. In the analysis, I assigned 1 to the group taught by the nondirective teacher and 0 to the group taught by the directive teacher. I show now how to obtain the separate regression equations from this overall regression equation.

The intercept, a, of the overall regression equation is equal to the intercept of the group assigned 0's in all the coded vectors.[14] Because I assigned 0 in D to the group taught by the directive teacher, a for this group is 7.193213.

Each b for a coded vector in the overall regression equation is equal to the deviation of a for the group identified in the vector in question (that is, the group assigned 1) from the a for the group assigned 0's in all the coded vectors. Therefore, to obtain a for a given group add a from the overall regression equation and b for the coded vector in which the group was identified. In the present example, there is only one dummy vector in which the group taught by a nondirective teacher was identified. b for this vector is -5.999715. a for the group taught by a nondirective teacher is therefore

$$7.193213 + (-5.999715) = 1.193498$$

The procedure for calculating the b's for the separate regression equations is analogous to that outlined for calculating the a's for the separate regression equations. Specifically, b for the continuous variable in the overall regression equation (b_X, in the present example) is equal to b for the continuous variable in the regression equation for the group assigned 0's throughout. In the present example, $b_X = -.106796$. This, then, is b for tolerance of ambiguity in the regression equation for the group taught by the directive teacher.

b for each product vector in the overall regression equation is equal to the deviation of b for the group identified in the coded vector that was used to generate the product vector from b for the group assigned 0's throughout. Recall that the latter is equal to b_X (b for the continuous variable in the overall regression equation). In the present example, X was multiplied by D to obtain XD. In D, the group taught by the nondirective teacher was identified. Accordingly, b_{XD} (.205155) is equal to the deviation of the b for the group taught by the nondirective teacher from b_X in the overall equation ($-.106796$). Therefore, b for the group taught by the nondirective teacher is

$$-.106796 + .205155 = .098359$$

The separate regression equations obtained from the overall regression equation with dummy coding are, of course, the same as those obtained from the overall regression equation with effect coding.

The Point of Intersection

Having calculated the separate regression equations, one can calculate the point where the two regression lines intersect. For convenience, I repeat the two regression equations:

$$Y'_{ND} = 1.193498 + .098359X$$

$$Y'_D = 7.193214 - .106797X$$

---

[14]I use the plural form, as what I say applies to categorical variables consisting of any number of categories.

where Y = rating of teacher; ND = nondirective; D = directive; and X = tolerance of ambiguity. Applying (14.5), the point of intersection is

$$X = \frac{1.193498 - 7.193214}{-.106797 - .098359} = 29.24$$

As the value of X at which the regression lines intersect is well within the range of scores of the continuous variable (the scores range from 5 to 63), the interaction is disordinal.

In Figure 14.6, I plotted the data in Table 14.3, along with the two regression lines, from which you can see that the regression of teacher ratings on tolerance of ambiguity is positive for the group taught by the nondirective teacher and negative for the group taught by the directive teacher. This, of course, is also evident from the regression coefficients of the separate regression equations. It appears, then, that students who are more tolerant of ambiguity prefer a nondirective teacher, whereas students who are less tolerant of ambiguity prefer a directive teacher.

In the previous example, the number of subjects in the groups was equal. The same approach applies to designs with unequal n's.

Regions of Significance: the Johnson-Neyman Procedure

Figure 14.6 reveals that students whose scores on tolerance of ambiguity are closer to the point where the regression lines intersect (29.24) differ less in their satisfaction with the teachers, as compared with students whose scores on tolerance are farther from the point of intersection. In

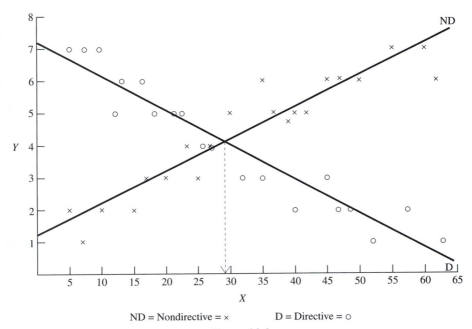

ND = Nondirective = ×   D = Directive = ○

Figure 14.6

other words, the differential effects of teaching styles are larger for students whose scores on tolerance of ambiguity are relatively high or low compared with students whose scores on tolerance of ambiguity are in the middle range.

Recall that when a statistically significant interaction is detected in a factorial design it is followed by tests of simple effects (see Chapter 12). Analogously, when a statistically significant interaction between a continuous and a categorical variable is detected, it is followed by calculation of regions of significance.

Johnson and Neyman (1936) developed a procedure for establishing regions of significance associated with a test of the difference between two treatments at any specific point on the X continuum. As Potthoff (1964) pointed out, such regions are nonsimultaneous in the sense that "it does *not* follow that one can state with 95 per cent confidence that there is a nonzero difference between the two groups simultaneously for *all* points in the region" (p. 241). Potthoff proposed an extension of the Johnson-Neyman procedure for establishing simultaneous regions. It is Potthoff's extension that I present and apply to the numerical example under consideration. After doing so, I comment on the calculation of nonsimultaneous regions of significance (for very good discussions of simultaneous and nonsimultaneous regions of significance and other issues concerning comparisons of regression equations, see Rogosa, 1980, 1981).

Simultaneous Regions of Significance

To establish regions of significance, it is necessary to solve for the X values in the following equation:

$$X = \frac{-B \pm \sqrt{B^2 - AC}}{A} \tag{14.6}$$

The terms of (14.6) for establishing *simultaneous* regions of significance, according to Potthoff's (1964) extension of the Johnson-Neyman's procedure, are defined as follows:

$$A = \frac{-2F_{\alpha(2, N-4)}}{N-4}(ss_{\text{res}})\left(\frac{1}{\Sigma x_1^2} + \frac{1}{\Sigma x_2^2}\right) + (b_1 - b_2)^2 \tag{14.7}$$

$$B = \frac{2F_{\alpha(2, N-4)}}{N-4}(ss_{\text{res}})\left(\frac{\overline{X}_1}{\Sigma x_1^2} + \frac{\overline{X}_2}{\Sigma x_2^2}\right) + (a_1 - a_2)(b_1 - b_2) \tag{14.8}$$

$$C = \frac{-2F_{\alpha(2, N-4)}}{N-4}(ss_{\text{res}})\left(\frac{N}{n_1 n_2} + \frac{\overline{X}_1^2}{\Sigma x_1^2} + \frac{\overline{X}_2^2}{\Sigma x_2^2}\right) + (a_1 - a_2)^2 \tag{14.9}$$

where $F_{\alpha(2, N-4)}$ = tabled F ratio with 2 and $N-4$ degrees of freedom at a selected α level; N = total number of subjects, or number of subjects in both groups; n_1, n_2 = number of subjects in groups 1 and 2, respectively; ss_{res} = residual sum of squares from the overall regression analysis, or, equivalently, the pooled residual sum of squares from separate regression analyses for each group; $\Sigma x_1^2, \Sigma x_2^2$ = sum of squares of the continuous independent variable (X) for groups 1 and 2, respectively; $\overline{X}_1, \overline{X}_2$ = means of groups 1 and 2, respectively, on the continuous independent variable, X; b_1, b_2 = regression coefficients of the regression equations for groups 1 and 2, respectively; and a_1, a_2 = intercepts of the regression equations for groups 1 and 2, respectively.

The values necessary for the application of the above formulas to the data of Table 14.3 are[15]

$$ss_{res} = 13.06758 \qquad n_1 = 20 \qquad n_2 = 20$$

$$\Sigma x_1^2 = 5776.80 \qquad \Sigma x_2^2 = 6123.80$$

$$\overline{X}_1 = 32.60 \qquad \overline{X}_2 = 29.90$$

$$a_1 = 1.19350 \qquad a_2 = 7.19321$$

$$b_1 = .09836 \qquad b_2 = -.10680$$

From Appendix B, the tabled F with 2 and 36 degrees of freedom at $\alpha = .05$ is 3.26.

$$A = \frac{-2(3.26)}{36} (13.06758)\left(\frac{1}{5776.80} + \frac{1}{6123.80}\right) + (.20516)^2 = .04129$$

$$B = \frac{2(3.26)}{36} (13.06758)\left(\frac{32.60}{5776.80} + \frac{29.90}{6123.80}\right) + (-5.99972)(.20516) = -1.20599$$

$$C = \frac{-2(3.26)}{36} (13.06758)\left(\frac{40}{400} + \frac{32.60^2}{5776.80} + \frac{29.90^2}{6123.80}\right) + (-5.99972)^2 = 34.97906$$

$$X = \frac{1.20599 \pm \sqrt{(-1.20599)^2 - (.04129)(34.97906)}}{.04129}$$

$$X_L = 26.77 \qquad X_U = 31.64$$

where X_L = lower boundary and X_U = upper boundary of the region of nonsignificance. Values of Y for subjects whose scores lie within the range of 26.77 and 31.64 on X are statistically not significantly different across treatments. There are two regions of significance, one for X scores above 31.64 and one for X scores below 26.77. In other words, there are statistically significant differences in the ratings of the two types of teachers by students whose scores on tolerance of ambiguity are above 31.64 or below 26.77. Specifically, students whose scores on tolerance of ambiguity are above 31.64 are more satisfied with the nondirective than the directive teacher, whereas students whose scores on tolerance of ambiguity are below 26.77 are more satisfied with the directive than the nondirective teacher.

In the present example, there are two regions of significance. Under certain circumstances, only one region of significance may exist (see Rogosa, 1980, 1981, for detailed discussions; see also, Serlin & Levin, 1980).

Nonsimultaneous Regions of Significance.   As I pointed out earlier, originally the Johnson-Neyman procedure was designed to test the difference between two treatments at a single point on the X continuum. Calculating nonsimultaneous regions of significance for such a test requires a minor modification of (14.7) through (14.9). Specifically, replace the tabled $2F_{\alpha(2, N-4)}$ with the tabled $F_{\alpha(1, N-4)}$. For the example I analyzed in the preceding, 2(3.26) would be replaced by 4.11, which is the tabled value of $F(1, 36)$ at $\alpha = .05$.

Calculation of Regions of Significance by Computer

None of the packages I use in this book have an option for calculating the regions of significance. I know of only one program, written for the IBM mainframe (Borich, Godbout, & Wunderlich,

---

[15]Note that the first two terms in (14.7) through (14.9) are the same, except that in (14.7) and (14.9) the sign is negative, whereas in (14.8) it is positive.

1976), that was designed to calculate nonsimultaneous regions of significance. I suspect that most readers will not have access to this program, if indeed it is still available at computing centers.

Thanks to the wide array of procedures for data manipulations and transformations available in current statistical packages, however, regions of significance can be calculated by utilizing relevant manipulations in conjunction with multiple regression programs. Examples of such uses for BMDP and SPSS (1975 version) are given in Karpman (1983), and examples for SAS and SPSS-X are given in Karpman (1986). I adapted Karpman's SPSS-X control statements, which were written for the mainframe, for use in the PC version, and also added some statements. I also made some changes in his SAS control statements. Still, the basic layout is Karpman's. For comparative purposes, I apply my adaptation of Karpman (1986) to the numerical example I analyzed earlier (i.e., Table 14.3).

SPSS

I remind you that the italicized statements in brackets are not part of the input file. Rather these comments are to help you see what is being accomplished. All page references are to SPSS Inc. (1993).

Input

```
. . . . [enter the data of Table 14.3 as in the preceding run]
END DATA
IF (T EQ 1) E=1.
IF (T EQ 2) E=−1.
COMPUTE X2=X**2.
COMPUTE XY=X*Y.
COMPUTE XE=X*E.
COMPUTE CON=1.
LIST.
SAVE OUTFILE=RAW.
SELECT IF (T EQ 1).                    [use subjects in group 1]
AGGREGATE OUTFILE=*/BREAK=T/MEAN1X MEAN1Y=MEAN (X Y)/
    N1=NU(X)/SUM1XY SUM1X SUM1Y SUM1X2=SUM (XY X Y X2).
                [See pp. 93–102, for AGGREGATE. Here I use it to generate
                means for X and Y and sums of, e.g., products of X and Y raw
                scores. OUTFILE=* replaces the active file.]
COMPUTE SSX1=SUM1X2−((SUM1X**2)/N1).            [compute Σx₁²]
COMPUTE B1=(SUM1XY−((SUM1X*SUM1Y)/N1))/SSX1.    [compute b₁]
COMPUTE A1=MEAN1Y−(MEAN1X*B1).                  [compute a₁]
[see Chapter 2, (2.2), (2.4), (2.7), and (2.8) for the preceding]
FORMATS B1 A1 (F10.5).                          [pp. 322–325]
SAVE OUTFILE=GROUP1/DROP T SUM1XY SUM1X SUM1Y SUM1X2.    [p. 710]
GET FILE=RAW.          [because the preceding AGGREGATE replaced it]
SELECT IF (T EQ 2).                [use subjects in group 2]
AGGREGATE OUTFILE=*/BREAK=T/MEAN2X MEAN2Y=MEAN (X Y)/
    N2=NU(X)/SUM2XY SUM2X SUM2Y SUM2X2=SUM (XY X Y X2).
```

```
COMPUTE SSX2=SUM2X2-((SUM2X**2)/N2).
COMPUTE B2=(SUM2XY-((SUM2X*SUM2Y)/N2))/SSX2.
COMPUTE A2=MEAN2Y-(MEAN2X*B2).
FORMATS B2 A2 (F10.5).
SAVE OUTFILE=GROUP2/DROP T SUM2XY SUM2X SUM2Y SUM2X2.
MATCH FILES FILE=GROUP1/FILE=GROUP2.                    [pp. 454-461]
SAVE OUTFILE=BOTH.
GET FILE=RAW.                [because the preceding AGGREGATE replaced it]
REGRESSION VARS=Y TO XE/DEP=Y/ENTER X E XE/SAVE=RESID(RESID)
  PRED(PRED).
PLOT HSIZE=40/VSIZE=20/
  PLOT=PRED WITH X BY T.
COMPUTE RESIDSQ=RESID**2.              [compute squared residuals]
AGGREGATE OUTFILE=RESID/BREAK=CON/SUMRESID=SUM(RESIDSQ).
    [sum squared residuals and put them in a file named RESID]
MATCH FILES FILE=BOTH/FILE=RESID/DROP CON.
FORMATS SUMRESID (F10.5).
LIST.
COMPUTE INTRSECT=(A1-A2)/(B2-B1).              [see (14.5)]
*SIMULTANEOUS REGIONS.
COMPUTE FCRIT=2*IDF.F(.95,2,N1+N2-4).    [2F_{\alpha(2, N-4)}, p. 144; see
                                          also, e.g., (14.7)]
LIST FCRIT.
COMPUTE TERM=(FCRIT/(N1+N2-4))*SUMRESID.
COMPUTE A=(-TERM)*((1/SSX1)+(1/SSX2))+(B1-B2)**2.        [(14.7)]
COMPUTE B=(TERM*((MEAN1X/SSX1)+(MEAN2X/SSX2)))+
          ((A1-A2)*(B1-B2)).                             [(14.8)]
COMPUTE C=(-TERM)*(((N1+N2)/(N1*N2))+((MEAN1X**2)/SSX1)+
          ((MEAN2X**2)/SSX2))+((A1-A2)**2).              [(14.9)]
COMPUTE LOWER=((B*-1)-(SQRT((B**2)-(A*C))))/A.    [lower region]
COMPUTE UPPER=((B*-1)+(SQRT((B**2)-(A*C))))/A.    [upper region]
FORMATS TERM A B C LOWER INTRSECT UPPER (F10.5).
LIST VAR= TERM A B C LOWER INTRSECT UPPER.
```

Output

A new (aggregated) active file has replaced the existing active file. It contains 8 variable(s) and 1 case(s).

Commentary

Much of the output consists of messages informing the user of what has been accomplished. As an example, I reproduced the message after the first AGGREGATE procedure.

Output

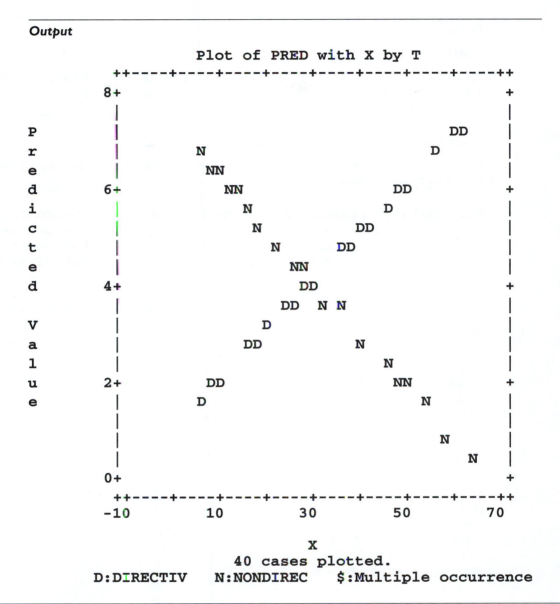

```
                 Plot of PRED with X by T
       ++----+----+----+----+----+----+----+----++
     8+                                              +
P     |
r     |            N                        D        |
e     |           NN                                 |
d   6+            NN                     DD           +
i     |            N                    D            |
c     |             N                 DD             |
t     |              N              DD               |
e     |             NN                               |
d   4+              DD                                +
      |             DD    N N                         |
V     |              D                               |
a     |            DD            N                   |
l     |                          N                   |
u   2+         DD                NN                   +
e     |         D                  N                 |
      |                                              |
      |                              N               |
      |                               N              |
    0+                                              +
       ++----+----+----+----+----+----+----+----++
       -10      10       30       50       70
                         X
                  40 cases plotted.
       D:DIRECTIV   N:NONDIREC   $:Multiple occurrence
```

Output

MEAN1X	MEAN1Y	N1	SSX1	B1	A1	MEAN2X	MEAN2Y	N2	SSX2	B2	A2	SUMRESID
32.60	4.40	20	5776.80	.09836	1.19350	29.90	4.00	20	6123.80	−.10680	7.19321	13.06758

Commentary

Compare this output with the summary data I gave prior to my application of (14.7) through (14.9).

Output

FCRIT 6.52

TERM	A	B	C	LOWER	INTRSECT	UPPER
2.36628	.04129	−1.20597	34.97918	26.78711	29.24474	31.62353

Commentary

FCRIT is 2*F for .05 level with 2 and 36 *df*. Compare the preceding with the results I obtained when I applied (14.7) through (14.9).

Karpman's (1986) Layout: Final Comment.   As the layout is applicable for the calculation of simultaneous regions of significance for any two groups, you may find it more efficient to read in the data from an external file. Also, for didactic purposes, I used two SPSS runs. Of course, I could have incorporated the preceding input statements in the earlier SPSS run.

SAS

Input

```
TITLE 'ATI, TABLE 14.3. REGIONS OF SIGNIFICANCE';
DATA T143;
  INPUT X 1 Y 2-3 T 4;
  CARDS;
2 51                    [first two subjects in group 1]
1 71
. . . .
2582                    [last two subjects in group 2]
1632
;
DATA A B;
  SET T143;
  IF T = 1 THEN OUTPUT A;
  ELSE OUTPUT B;
PROC SUMMARY DATA = A;
  VAR X;
  OUTPUT OUT = K1   MEAN = MU_X1   CSS = SSX1;
PROC REG DATA = A   OUTEST = EST1;
  MODEL Y = X;
  OUTPUT OUT = ONE   P = PRED;
DATA REG1;
  SET EST1;
  DROP _TYPE_;
PROC SUMMARY DATA = B;
  VAR X;
  OUTPUT OUT = K2   MEAN = MU_X2   CSS = SSX2;
```

```
PROC REG DATA = B   OUTEST = EST2;
   MODEL Y = X;
   OUTPUT OUT = TWO P = PRED;
DATA REG2;
   SET EST2;
   DROP _TYPE_;
DATA COMBINE;
   MERGE K1 (RENAME = (_FREQ_ = N1))
         K2 (RENAME = (_FREQ_ = N2))
REG1 (RENAME = (X = B1   INTERCEP = A1   _RMSE_ = SIGMA1))
REG2 (RENAME = (X = B2   INTERCEP = A2   _RMSE_ = SIGMA2));
      F = 2*FINV(.95, 2, N1 + N2 − 4);
      Q = F*((N1 − 2)*SIGMA1**2 + (N2 − 2)*SIGMA2**2 )/(N1 + N2 − 4);
      A = −Q*(1/SSX1 + 1/SSX2) + (B1 − B2)**2;
      B = Q*(MU_X1/SSX1 + MU_X2/SSX2) + (A1 − A2)*(B1 − B2);
      C = −Q*((N1 + N2)/(N1*N2) + MU_X1**2/SSX1 + MU_X2**2/SSX2) +
         (A1 − A2)**2;
   LOWER = (−B − SQRT(B**2 − A*C))/A;
   INTRSECT = (A2 − A1)/(B1 − B2);
   UPPER = (−B + SQRT(B**2 − A*C))/A;
PROC PRINT DATA = COMBINE;
   VAR B1 A2 B2 LOWER INTRSECT UPPER;
   ID A1;
   FORMAT A1 B1 A2 B2 11.4 LOWER INTRSECT UPPER 8.3;
TITLE 'REGRESSION COEFFICIENTS, POINT ESTIMATE OF THE INTERSECTION OF';
TITLE2 'TWO REGRESSION LINES & 95% CONFIDENCE INTERVALS';
TITLE3 ' _____Reg. Parameter Estimates_____ ____Pt of Int & 95% CI''s____';
DATA _LAST_;
   SET ONE TWO;
   IF T = 1 THEN GROUP = '*';
   ELSE GROUP = '+';
OPTIONS PS = 48;
PROC PLOT;
   PLOT PRED*X = GROUP;
   TITLE 'SCATTERPLOT OF INTERSECTING REGRESSION LINES';
   TITLE2 ' ';
   TITLE3 '(NOTE: Group 1 = " * "   Group 2 = " + " )';
   RUN;
```

Output

REGRESSION COEFFICIENTS, POINT ESTIMATE OF THE INTERSECTION OF
TWO REGRESSION LINES & 95% CONFIDENCE INTERVALS
_____Reg. Parameter Estimates_____   _____Pt of Int & 95% CI's_____

A1	B1	A2	B2	LOWER	INTRSECT	UPPER
1.1935	0.0984	7.1932	−0.1068	26.787	29.245	31.624

SCATTERPLOT OF INTERSECTING REGRESSION LINES
(NOTE: Group 1 = " * "   Group 2 = " + ")
Plot of PRED*X.   Symbol is value of GROUP.

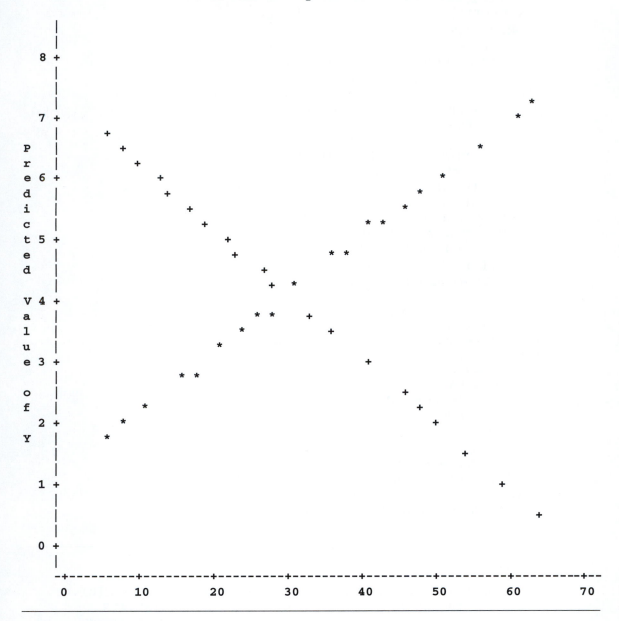

Commentary

If necessary, see relevant SAS manual(s) for an explanation of specific input statements. Compare the output with my earlier calculations and with the previous SPSS output.

Regions of Significance: Alternative Calculations

Instead of using (14.7) through (14.9) to calculate terms necessary for (14.6), you can take an alternative approach using regression coefficients and elements of the covariance matrix of the b's (**C**; for a discussion of this approach, see Rogosa, 1980).[16] In other words, elements of **C** can be used to calculate A, B, and C, which I obtained through (14.7) through (14.9).

$$A = b_{XD}^2 - 2F_{\alpha(2, N-4)}s_{XD}^2 \tag{14.10}$$

$$B = b_D b_{XD} - 2F_{\alpha(2, N-4)}s_{D,XD} \tag{14.11}$$

$$C = b_D^2 - 2F_{\alpha(2, N-4)}s_D^2 \tag{14.12}$$

where X = attribute; D = dummy coded vector; s_{XD}^2 = variance of b_{XD} (regression coefficient for the product term); $s_{D, XD}$ = covariance of b_D (regression coefficient for dummy coded vector) and b_{XD}; and s_D^2 = variance of b_D. For effect coding, see the following.

Output

<table>
<tr><th colspan="4" align="center">[Dummy coding]
Var-Covar Matrix of Regression Coefficients (B)
Below Diagonal: Covariance   Above: Correlation</th><th colspan="4" align="center">[Effect coding]
Var-Covar Matrix of Regression Coefficients (B)
Below Diagonal: Covariance   Above: Correlation</th></tr>
<tr><td></td><td align="center">X</td><td align="center">D</td><td align="center">XD</td><td></td><td align="center">X</td><td align="center">E</td><td align="center">XE</td></tr>
<tr><td>X</td><td>5.9275E-05</td><td>.58270</td><td>-.69672</td><td>X</td><td>3.0528E-05</td><td>-.06325</td><td>.02916</td></tr>
<tr><td>D</td><td>.00177</td><td>.15607</td><td>-.87521</td><td>E</td><td>-6.903E-05</td><td>.03902</td><td>-.87521</td></tr>
<tr><td>XD</td><td>-5.927E-05</td><td>-.00382</td><td>1.2211E-04</td><td>XE</td><td>8.9013E-07</td><td>-9.552E-04</td><td>3.0528E-05</td></tr>
</table>

Commentary

I obtained these matrices as a result of using STATISTICS=ALL in the first SPSS REGRESSION analysis of data in Table 14.3, given earlier in this chapter. When *not* using STATISTICS=ALL, call for BCOV on the STATISTICS subcommand (SPSS Inc., 1993, p. 628) to obtain **C**.

As indicated in the legend, values below the diagonal are covariances and those above the diagonal are correlations. Values on the diagonal are variances. For present purposes, we need values on and below the diagonal. Note also that some of the values are reported in scientific notation. For example, the variance of b_X is .000059275. For convenience, I repeat the regression equation with dummy coding:

$$Y' = 7.193213 - .106796X - 5.999715D + .205155XD$$

Using relevant b's and elements from **C**, I apply now (14.10) through (14.12):

$$A = (.205155)^2 - 2(3.26)(.000122) = .04129$$

$$B = (-5.999715)(.205155) - 2(3.26)(-.00382) = -1.20596$$

$$C = (-5.999715)^2 - 2(3.26)(.15607) = 34.97900$$

[16]I introduced **C** in Chapter 6 ("Variance/Covariance Matrix of the b's") and used it subsequently in Chapter 11 ("Multiple Comparisons via b's").

Compare with the results I obtained earlier or with those reported in the previous SPSS or SAS output.

Effect Coding. As expected, the regression equation and **C** for effect coding are not equal to those obtained for dummy coding (see the preceding output). Consequently, applying (14.10) through (14.12) to results with effect coding will yield different values for *A, B,* and *C* than those obtained through the use of (14.7) through (14.9) or through the analysis with dummy coding presented earlier. Note, however, that relevant values in the analysis with effect coding are proportional to their corresponding values in the analysis with dummy coding. Examine the two regression equations and notice that $b_E = (1/2)b_D$, and $b_{XE} = (1/2)b_{XD}$. Now examine the **C**'s from the two solutions and notice that relevant elements of **C** for effect coding equal 1/4 of their corresponding elements of **C** for dummy coding. As a result, the use of *A, B,* and *C* values obtained from an analysis with effect coding in (14.6) will yield the same regions of significance. I will now demonstrate this for the example under consideration. To apply (14.10) through (14.12) for effect coding, replace all the *D*'s with *E*'s.

For convenience, I repeat the regression equation with effect coding obtained earlier.

$$Y' = 4.193356 - .004219X - 2.999858E + .102578XE$$

Using relevant values from this equation and from **C** for effect coding reported earlier,

$$A = (.102578)^2 - 2(3.26)(.0000305) = .01032$$

$$B = (-2.999858)(.102578) - 2(3.26)(-.000955) = -.30149$$

$$C = (-2.999858)^2 - 2(3.26)(.03902) = 8.74474$$

Notice that each of the preceding is equal, within rounding, to 1/4 of its corresponding value for dummy coding. Applying (14.6),

$$X = \frac{-B \pm \sqrt{B^2 - AC}}{A}$$

$$X = \frac{.30149 \pm \sqrt{(-.30149)^2 - (.01032)(8.74474)}}{.01032}$$

$$X_L = 26.74 \qquad X_U = 31.69$$

C MATRIX FROM OTHER COMPUTER PROGRAMS

In what follows, I give input files for the three other packages I use in this book. In all instances, I read data from an external file (T143.DAT) that has the following layout: *Y* is in column 2, *X* is in columns 3 and 4, and *T* (treatments) is in column 6. My main aim here is to show how to obtain **C** from each of the programs so that its elements may be used in (14.10) through (14.12). Accordingly, I reproduce minimal output. For example, although the input file includes statements for analyses with both dummy and effect coding, I reproduce only minimal output from the former. If you are running any of the programs, compare your output with the SPSS output I reproduced earlier in this chapter.

BMDP

Input

/PROBLEM TITLE IS 'TABLE 14.3.   ATI, USING PROGRAM 2R'.
/INPUT VARIABLES ARE 3. FORMAT IS '3F2'.
 FILE IS 'T143.DAT'.
/VARIABLE NAMES ARE Y,X,T.
/TRANSFORM
 IF (T EQ 1) THEN D = 1.
 IF (T EQ 2) THEN D = 0.
 IF (T EQ 1) THEN E = 1.
 IF (T EQ 2) THEN E = −1.
 XD=X*D.
 XE=X*E.
/REGRESS DEPEND IS Y. INDEP=X,D,XD. SEQUENTIAL.
/REGRESS DEPEND IS Y. INDEP=X,E,XE. SEQUENTIAL.
/PRINT RREG.   *[print the correlation matrix of the* b's]
/END

Commentary

The preceding is input for BMDP 2R (Dixon, 1992, Vol. 1, pp. 387–425). As I commented on this program earlier in the text (e.g., Chapters 4 and 5), I comment here only on a couple of options relevant to the topic under consideration.

SEQUENTIAL. "SEQUENTIAL forces variables (or sets of variables) to enter the equation in order from the INDEPENDENT list" (Dixon, 1992, Vol. 1, p. 407).

RREG. This option results in the printing of the correlation matrix of the b's (see Dixon, 1992, Vol. 1, p. 418). When I reproduce this matrix, I show how to convert it to **C** (the covariance matrix of the b's).

Output

VARIABLES IN EQUATION FOR Y

VARIABLE		COEFFICIENT	STD. ERROR OF COEFF	F TO REMOVE
(Y-INTERCEPT		7.19321)		
X	2	−0.10680	0.0077	
D	4	−5.99971	0.3951	
XD	6	0.20516	0.0111	344.68

CORRELATION MATRIX OF REGRESSION COEFFICIENTS

	X	D	XD
X	1.0000		
D	0.5827	1.0000	
XD	−0.6967	−0.8752	1.0000

Commentary

Verify that the values of the CORRELATION MATRIX OF REGRESSION COEFFICIENTS are the same as those above the diagonal of SPSS Var/Cov matrix of the b's reported earlier.

To convert the above matrix into $\mathbf{C}$, replace each diagonal element with the square of the standard error of the b corresponding to it. For example, replace the first diagonal element (i.e., for the variance of b_X) with the squared standard error of b_X: $(.0077)^2 = .000059$. Notice that this is, within rounding, the same value as the corresponding element of $\mathbf{C}$ reported in the SPSS output given earlier. For each of the off-diagonal elements, multiply the correlation by the standard errors of the b's corresponding to it. For example, for the element in the second row and the first column (i.e., D and X):

$$(.5827)(.3951)(.0077) = .001773$$

Compare with the corresponding element in the SPSS output given earlier.

I suggest that you carry out the other transformations and compare your results with the SPSS output given earlier. Having obtained $\mathbf{C}$, you can use relevant elements from it and from the regression equation in (14.10) through (14.12) to calculate the terms necessary to apply (14.6) for the calculation of regions of significance.

MINITAB

Input

```
GMACRO
T143
ECHO
OUTFILE='T143.MIN';
   NOTERM.
NOTE TABLE 14.3. ATI
READ C1-C3;
   FILE 'T143.DAT';            [reading from external file]
   FORMAT (3F2).               [data in fields of 2 columns]
INDICATOR C3 C4-C5            [see Chapter 11 for explanation]
LET C6=C4-C5                  [subtract C5 from C4 to create effect coding]
LET C7=C2*C4                  [generate XD]
LET C8=C2*C6                  [generate XE]
NAME C1='Y'   C2='X'   C3='T'   C4='D'   C6='E'   C7='XD'   C8='XE'
PRINT C1-C8
```

REGRESS C1 3 C2 C4 C7;   *[regression with dummy coding]*
MSE K1;   *[put mean square error in K1]*
XPXINV M1.   *[put $(X'X)^{-1}$ in M1; see Chapter 6]*
MULTIPLY K1 M1 M2   *[M2 is C]*
NOTE FOLLOWING IS THE COVARIANCE MATRIX OF THE B'S FOR DUMMY CODING
PRINT M2
REGRESS C1 3 C2 C6 C8;   *[regression with effect coding]*
MSE K1;
XPXINV M1.
MULTIPLY K1 M1 M2
NOTE FOLLOWING IS THE COVARIANCE MATRIX OF THE B'S FOR EFFECT CODING
PRINT M2
ENDMACRO

Commentary

I remind you of my practice of running in batch mode. References in the italicized comments are to chapters in this book. I named the preceding input file T143.MAC and typed: %T143 at the MTB prompt. Note also that I designated an output file (see the first line of the input). If you require further explanation, see Chapter 4.

Output

The regression equation is
Y = 7.19 − 0.107 X − 6.00 D + 0.205 XD

Predictor	Coef	Stdev	t-ratio	p
Constant	7.1932	0.2667		
X	−0.106796	0.007699		
D	−5.9997	0.3951		
XD	0.20516	0.01105	18.57	0.000

MTB > NOTE FOLLOWING IS THE COVARIANCE MATRIX OF THE B'S FOR DUMMY CODING
MTB > PRINT M2
  MATRIX M2

0.071142	−0.001772	−0.071142	0.001772
−0.001772	0.000059	0.001772	−0.000059
−0.071142	0.001772	0.156070	−0.003821
0.001772	−0.000059	−0.003821	0.000122

Commentary

The first column and first row in the matrix above are associated with the intercept. I added the box around **C**. Compare this with the SPSS output given earlier.

SAS

Input

```
TITLE 'TABLE 14.3. ATI';
DATA BEGIN;
     INFILE 'T143.DAT';
INPUT Y 1–2 X 3–4 T 5–6;
IF T=1 THEN D=1; ELSE D=0;
IF T=1 THEN E=1; ELSE E=–1;
XD=X*D;
XE=X*E;
PROC PRINT;
PROC REG;
MODEL Y=X D XD/COVB;
MODEL Y=X E XE/COVB;
RUN;
```

Commentary

COVB. This is the option for printing **C.** If you require additional explanations about SAS, see Chapter 4, and subsequent chapters, where I used this program.

Output

Parameter Estimates

Variable	DF	Parameter Estimate	Standard Error	T for H0: Parameter=0	Prob > |T|
INTERCEP	1	7.193213	0.26672429		
X	1	–0.106796	0.00769903		
D	1	–5.999715	0.39505737		
XD	1	0.205155	0.01105036	18.565	0.0001

Covariance of Estimates

COVB	INTERCEP	X	D	XD
INTERCEP	0.0711418468	–0.001772322	–0.071141847	0.0017723223
X	–0.001772322	0.000059275	0.0017723223	–0.000059275
D	–0.071141847	0.0017723223	0.1560703288	–0.00382076
XD	0.0017723223	–0.000059275	–0.00382076	0.0001221105

Commentary

As in the case of MINITAB, SAS reports also variance and covariances associated with the INTERCEP(t). I enclosed **C** in the box. Compare this with the MINITAB and SPSS output.

Johnson-Neyman Procedure for Other Designs

The Johnson-Neyman procedure is not limited to a categorical variable with two categories or two groups, nor is it limited to one continuous independent variable. For illustrative applications to more than two categories or groups and more than one continuous variable, see Abelson (1953), Huitema (1980, Chapter 13), Johnson and Fay (1950), Johnson and Jackson (1959, pp. 438–441), Potthoff (1964), and Walker and Lev (1953, pp. 404–411).

COMPARING REGRESSION EQUATIONS IN NONEXPERIMENTAL RESEARCH

Thus far, my presentation has been limited to designs in which both the categorical and the continuous variables were manipulated or to ones in which only the categorical variable was manipulated (e.g., ATI designs). I now turn to designs in which neither the categorical nor the continuous variable is manipulated—that is, to nonexperimental designs. The analytic approach in such designs is identical to that in experimental designs. The difference between the two types of designs is in the interpretation of the results, which is generally more ambiguous and more complex in nonexperimental designs (see the following discussion).

When samples from different populations are combined in a regression analysis, it is assumed, wittingly or unwittingly, that the subjects came from the same population or that the separate regression equations for the different samples are identical. Often, researchers operate under a misconception that all that is necessary to take account of samples from different populations is to represent them by coded vectors in the analysis. As I showed earlier in this chapter, however, when product vectors of the categorical and the continuous variables are *not* included in the combined analysis, the separate regression equations for the groups under consideration are assumed to differ only in their intercepts. In other words, separate regression equations with identical regression coefficients but with different intercepts are fitted when product terms are not included in the combined regression analysis.

To show the possible deleterious consequences of ignoring a categorical variable or of not treating it appropriately in regression analysis, I return to the numerical example in Table 14.3. Recall that the example consisted of a continuous variable (tolerance of ambiguity) and a categorical manipulated variable (teaching styles). Assume, for present purposes, that the categorical variable is a classificatory one (e.g., male-female, Black-White). If one were to do an analysis in which this variable is ignored (i.e., regressing the dependent variable on the continuous variable only), the regression coefficient[17] for the data in Table 14.3 would be −.00626, and R^2 would be .00335—findings that are neither meaningful nor statistically significant.

If a coded vector representing the classificatory variable is also included in the analysis, then the regression coefficient associated with the continuous variable would be −.00721. Recall that this is the common regression coefficient (b_c).[18] For both the continuous and the classificatory variable, R^2 would be .01580, which is statistically not significant ($F < 1$). Using either of the analyses outlined above, a researcher would have to conclude that the results are not meaningful.

---

[17]Regression and correlation coefficients calculated across groups (as distinguished from ones calculated within or between groups) are called total coefficients. I discuss this topic in Chapter 15.

[18]Also called within groups, or pooled within groups, regression coefficient. See the preceding footnote.

Recall, however, that a strong interaction was found for the data in Table 14.3 and that its presence was detected by the inclusion of the product vector in the analysis. The b for one group was $-.10680$, whereas the b for the other group was $.09836$—hence, the very small b_c. Recall also that the inclusion of the product vector led to an $R^2 = .90693$, as compared with $R^2 = .01580$ in the analysis without the product vector.[19]

In short, when a categorical and a continuous variable are used in nonexperimental research, the analysis should proceed in exactly the same sequence as in experimental research.[20] But, as I have said, interpretation of the results differs in the two research settings. For example, a finding that regression equations differ from each other is interpreted as an interaction between the categorical and the continuous variable when the research is experimental. In nonexperimental research, on the other hand, such an interpretation may be misleading. Earlier in the text (particularly in Chapters 12 and 13), I recommended that the term interaction *not* be used in nonexperimental research. Instead of repeating my reasons for this recommendation, I will address unique problems in nonexperimental research.

Categorical variables may be narrow or broad in scope. Although this distinction obviously does not imply a dichotomy, I will attempt to clarify, by way of an example, what I mean by it. Consider an attitude or an interest question to which possible responses are as follows: yes, no; or yes, no, undecided. Either of these sets of responses can be represented as a categorical variable in a regression analysis (the first set would require one coded vector; the second set would require two vectors). Contrast this categorical variable with one that represents a broad classification (e.g., sex, race, religious affiliation, marital status, professional status), and my intended distinction between categorical variables that are broad or narrow in scope will, I hope, become clear. The main thing to bear in mind is that broad categorical variables are related to, subsume, or cause a host of other variables.

When regression equations are compared in nonexperimental research, the categorical variable is almost always a broad classificatory, or grouping, variable. Under such circumstances, the interpretation of differences between regression coefficients as indicating an interaction not only may be misleading but also may appear to provide answers when it should raise questions. This can, perhaps, be clarified by a relatively simple example. Suppose that the dependent variable is achievement and that two independent variables are used: sex and achievement motivation. Further, assume that the analysis was carried out in the proper sequence and that it was found that the regression of achievement on achievement motivation for males differs from that for females. Should these results be interpreted as an interaction between sex and achievement motivation, one may be led to believe that it explains the differential effects of achievement motivation on achievement among males and females. Issues of the absence of randomization and manipulation, and the attendant problems of specification errors notwithstanding (see Chapter 10), my focus here is on the categorical variable. Sex is a broad classificatory variable that, as I noted earlier, is related to, subsumes, or causes a host of variables. Therefore, to say that sex interacts with achievement motivation either says nothing or appears to say everything. Neither is, of course, the case. One need only mention the potential consequences due to different socialization practices for males and females (e.g., aspirations, motivation, self-concept) to realize the complexity of the situation.

In conclusion, my general arguments in earlier chapters against the use of the term *interaction* in nonexperimental research, apply also to the design I presented in this chapter. I gave the

---

[19]Later I return to the topic of this section (see "The Study of Bias").

[20]See "Recapitulation," earlier in this chapter, for a summary of the analytic sequence.

present discussion a special slant because I believe that the use of broad classificatory variables in the type of designs I presented in this chapter is generally more prone to misinterpretation and therefore requires extra vigilance.

The Study of Bias

The literature on test bias, selection bias, discriminatory practices in hiring and promotion, and the like, has grown steadily in recent years, primarily in response to civil rights legislation and to ever-increasing court cases in which plaintiffs challenge current practices in such diverse areas as selection for employment, admissions to colleges and professional schools, promotion on the job, or wages. It is not my intention to review this literature or to discuss the various definitions of test fairness that have been advanced (see, for example, Arvey & Faley, 1988; Berk, 1982; Bersoff, 1981; Cole, 1981; Cole & Moss, 1989; *Federal Register,* August 25, 1978, Part IV; Hunter, Schmidt, & Rauschenberger 1984; *Journal of Educational Measurement, 13,* Spring 1976; Linn, 1984; Petersen, 1980). My sole purpose here is to illustrate the central role played by the analytic approach I presented in this chapter in a definition of test bias advanced by Cleary (1968), which has enjoyed wide currency.

> A test is biased for members of a subgroup of the population if, in the prediction of the criterion for which the test was designed, consistent nonzero errors of prediction are made for members of the subgroup. In other words, the test is biased if the criterion score predicted from the common regression line is consistently too high or too low for members of the subgroup. (p. 115)

This definition is called the regression model, as what it amounts to is a comparison of regression equations for different subgroups. I illustrate this in Figure 14.7 for the case of two groups: *A* and *B*. The situations depicted in Figure 14.7 are but three of many possible patterns, but they will suffice to illustrate the definition of bias in the regression model. Consider first situation (a). Note that the regression lines for groups *A* and *B* are parallel and very close to each other. In other words, the regression coefficients are identical and the intercepts are very similar. It appears, then, that using a common regression line (or a common regression equation) in this situation will not result in bias toward members of either group.

Turn now to the situation depicted in (b) of Figure 14.7. Again, the regression lines are parallel. But this time they are widely apart. Using the common regression line under these circumstances will result in consistent overprediction for members of group *B* and consistent

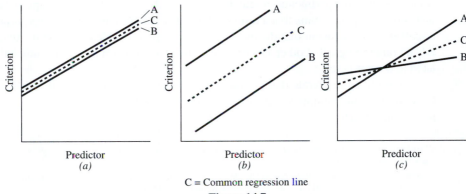

C = Common regression line

Figure 14.7

underprediction for members of group *A*. This, then, would constitute positive bias for group *B* and negative bias for group *A*.

Yet another situation is depicted in (c). This time the regression lines intersect, indicating that the regression coefficients for the two groups differ from each other. Using the common regression line results in positive bias for members of group *A* and negative bias for members of group *B* whose scores are below the point of intersection on the predictor. The reverse is true for subjects whose scores are above the point of intersection. As a cutting score on the predictor is used for selection, one can see that if, for instance, this score is above the point of intersection in (c), the use of a common regression line will consistently overpredict for members of group *B* and underpredict for members of group *A*, although the extent of over- and underprediction will vary depending on the specific score on the predictor. The farther the score is from the point of intersection, the larger the over- or underprediction.

Although Cleary's definition and my discussion of it were couched in terms of test bias, it applies generally to attempts to study bias through comparisons of regression equations. A notable case in point is the area of pay discrimination. For example, attempts to support claims of salary discrimination against women in academia are often presented in the form of comparisons of male and female regression of salary on years of experience, number of publications in refereed journals, years in rank, and the like.

In Chapter 10 (see "Social Science and Social Policy"), I pointed out that legal professionals found it necessary to become familiar with regression analysis, and I quoted from a lengthy opinion by Judge Higginbotham about uses and misuses of regression analysis in discrimination cases. Following are some additional examples.

Bloom and Killingsworth (1982), who reviewed some methodological issues concerning the use of regression analysis in wage discrimination cases, illustrated the diversity of judges' opinions regarding the use of regression analysis as evidence. In one case, "the judge remarked that the regression analysis presented in the testimony of the plaintiff's expert witness was 'simply not comprehensible to the Court'" (p. 320). A judge in another case "criticized the plaintiffs for *failing* to undertake a regression analysis" (p. 320).

In an introduction to their review of 29 court cases regarding salary discrimination, Barrett and Sansonetti (1988) pointed out that some courts "have readily accepted" (p. 503) regression analysis as evidence, whereas others "have questioned the power of regression analysis to explain promotion and pay discrimination in the real world" (p. 503). They then cited a Supreme Court ruling in which "regression analyses were accepted" (p. 503) in such cases.[21]

My earlier comments concerning problems in interpreting differences between regression equations in nonexperimental research apply equally to the use of this approach for detecting bias. For example, assume that a test of scholastic aptitude is used for decisions about admission to college. A conclusion that the use of a common regression equation constitutes bias implies, among other things, that other variables (e.g., mental ability, motivation, study habits) are not related to the predictor.

I would like to reiterate that my purpose in this section was *not* to discuss the very complex topic of bias and attempts to detect it, but only to show how multiple regression analysis is used in one approach to its definition and detection.[22]

---

[21]See Finkelstein (1980), for another review of judicial reception of results from multiple regression analyses in race and sex discrimination cases.

[22]For an approach to the study of bias from the perspective of multilevel analysis, see Kreft and de Leeuw (1994) and Lee and Smith (1990, 1991). For an introduction to multilevel analysis, see Chapter 16.

CURVILINEAR REGRESSION ANALYSIS

In the numerical examples I presented thus far it was clear from plots of the data (e.g., Figures 14.1 and 14.6) that the regression is linear. In many instances, however, the trend may not be apparent. Moreover, one should not rely on visual inspection alone, although the study of plotted data is always valuable. It is the application of tests for trends that enables one to ascertain the model that best fits a given set of data. In this section, I show curvilinear regression analysis in designs with one categorical and one continuous variable. First, I analyze an example in which the continuous variable is manipulated. I then give an example in which the continuous variable is an attribute.

Regression with Orthogonal Polynomials

I will apply curvilinear regression analysis to the data from the retention experiment I presented in the beginning of this chapter. Recall that the continuous variable (Study Time) consisted of four levels. Therefore, the highest-degree polynomial possible for these data is cubic (number of levels minus one). This may be done by raising the values of the continuous variable to the second and the third powers. Because the experiment also involved a categorical variable (No Incentive–Incentive), we must study the interactions on the linear, quadratic, and cubic levels. To do the entire analysis, it is necessary to have the following vectors for the independent variables: (1) No Incentive-Incentive (NI-I), (2) linear trend in Study Time (ST), (3) quadratic trend (ST^2), (4) cubic trend (ST^3), (5) NI-I by linear interaction (product of vectors 1 and 2), (6) NI-I by quadratic interaction (product of vectors 1 and 3), and (7) NI-I by cubic interaction (product of vectors 1 and 4).

Because the retention experiment consisted of equal cell frequencies and equal intervals for the continuous variable, it is possible to simplify the analysis by using orthogonal polynomials—a method I introduced in Chapter 13. I repeat the data from the experiment in Table 14.4, along with the necessary vectors to test for trends. As in earlier tables, I designate the dependent variable as *Y*. Vector *T* identifies the two treatments (NI-I). Vectors *L, Q,* and *C,* respectively, represent the linear, quadratic, and cubic components for ST. I took the coefficients for these vectors from a table of orthogonal polynomials (see Appendix B). I did not include product vectors necessary to represent the interaction between NI-I and ST in Table 14.4. Instead, I will, as in earlier analyses, generate them by the computer program (see the following input).

SAS

Input

```
TITLE 'TABLE 14.4, WITH ORTHOGONAL POLYNOMIALS';
DATA T144;
INPUT Y T L Q C;                [free format]
IF T=1 THEN E=1; ELSE E=-1;     [effect coded vector for NI-I]
ELIN=E*L;                       [generate E by Linear]
EQUAD=E*Q;                      [generate E by Quadratic]
ECUBIC=E*C;                     [generate E by Cubic]
```

```
CARDS;
 3  1 –3  1 –1
 4  1 –3  1 –1                    [first two subjects of Table 14.4]
 .   .    .    .    .
11  2   3  1   1                  [last two subjects of Table 14.4]
13  2   3  1   1
;
PROC PRINT;
PROC REG ALL;
MODEL Y=E L Q C ELIN EQUAD ECUBIC;
RUN;
```

Table 14.4   Data from the Retention Experiment (Table 14.2), Laid Out for Trend Analysis

Y	T	L	Q	C
3	1	–3	1	–1
4	1	–3	1	–1
5	1	–3	1	–1
4	1	–1	–1	3
5	1	–1	–1	3
6	1	–1	–1	3
5	1	1	–1	–3
6	1	1	–1	–3
8	1	1	–1	–3
7	1	3	1	1
8	1	3	1	1
9	1	3	1	1
7	2	–3	1	–1
8	2	–3	1	–1
9	2	–3	1	–1
9	2	–1	–1	3
10	2	–1	–1	3
11	2	–1	–1	3
8	2	1	–1	–3
11	2	1	–1	–3
12	2	1	–1	–3
10	2	3	1	1
11	2	3	1	1
13	2	3	1	1

Σy^2:   172.65

NOTE: Y = scores on retention originally given in Table 14.2; T = treatments, where 1 = No Incentive and 2 = Incentive; L = vector for linear component of Study Time; Q = vector for quadratic component of Study Time; C = vector for cubic component of Study Time. Blank lines separating sets of three scores are meant to indicate the different cells in Table 14.2.

Commentary

I introduced PROC REG of SAS in Chapter 4 and used it in subsequent chapters where I commented on both input and output. Therefore, I will not comment on the input, except to remind you that the italicized comments in the brackets are *not* part of it.

Output

Correlation

CORR	E	L	Q	C	ELIN	EQUAD	ECUBIC	Y
E	1.0000	0.0000	0.0000	0.0000	0.0000	0.0000	0.0000	−0.7613
L	0.0000	1.0000	0.0000	0.0000	0.0000	0.0000	0.0000	0.4933
Q	0.0000	0.0000	1.0000	0.0000	0.0000	0.0000	0.0000	−0.0155
C	0.0000	0.0000	0.0000	1.0000	0.0000	0.0000	0.0000	0.0486
ELIN	0.0000	0.0000	0.0000	0.0000	1.0000	0.0000	0.0000	0.0625
EQUAD	0.0000	0.0000	0.0000	0.0000	0.0000	1.0000	0.0000	0.0777
ECUBIC	0.0000	0.0000	0.0000	0.0000	0.0000	0.0000	1.0000	−0.0486
Y	−0.7613	0.4933	−0.0155	0.0486	0.0625	0.0777	−0.0486	1.0000

Analysis of Variance

Source	DF	Sum of Squares	Mean Square	F Value	Prob>F
Model	7	144.62500	20.66071	11.806	0.0001
Error	16	28.00000	1.75000		
C Total	23	172.62500			

Root MSE	1.32288	R-square	0.8378	
Dep Mean	7.87500	Adj R-sq	0.7668	

Parameter Estimates

Variable	DF	Parameter Estimate	Standard Error	T for H0: Parameter=0	Prob > |T|	Type I SS	Squared Semi-partial Corr Type I
INTERCEP	1	7.875000	0.27003086	29.163	0.0001	1488.375000	.
E	1	−2.041667	0.27003086	−7.561	0.0001	100.041667	0.57953174
L	1	0.591667	0.12076147	4.899	0.0002	42.008333	0.24335023
Q	1	−0.041667	0.27003086	−0.154	0.8793	0.041667	0.00024137
C	1	0.058333	0.12076147	0.483	0.6356	0.408333	0.00236544
ELIN	1	0.075000	0.12076147	0.621	0.5433	0.675000	0.00391021
EQUAD	1	0.208333	0.27003086	0.772	0.4516	1.041667	0.00603427
ECUBIC	1	−0.058333	0.12076147	−0.483	0.6356	0.408333	0.00236544

Commentary

Examine the correlation matrix and notice that, as expected, the vectors representing the independent variables and their interaction are not correlated. Hence, the overall R^2 (.8378) is equal to the sum of the squared zero-order correlations between the dependent variable (Y) and the vectors representing the independent variables and their interaction (as an exercise, you may wish to verify this).

In Chapter 5, I explained Type I and II SS (sum of squares) and Type I and II squared semipartial correlation in SAS (see also, SAS Institute Inc., 1990a, Vol. 1, pp. 115–117). For present purposes, I will only reiterate that Type I (SS or squared semipartial) refers to sequential values, that is, values attributed to a vector at the point of its entry into the analysis. In contrast, Type II refers to unique values, that is, values attributed to a vector when it is entered last in the analysis. As the vectors representing the independent variables and their interaction are orthogonal in the present example, the two types of SS and squared semipartial correlation are identical. For the same reason, each squared semipartial correlation reported here is equal to the square of its corresponding zero-order correlation. For example, $r_{YE}^2 = (-0.7613)^2 = .5796$, which is the same as the corresponding squared semipartial correlation reported earlier.

Examine the squared semipartial correlations and notice that (1) No Incentive–Incentive accounts for about 58% of the variance in Retention, (2) the linear component of Study Time accounts for about 24% of the variance in Retention, and (3) the remaining terms account for minuscule proportions of variance in Retention (altogether they account for about 1%).

Examine now the column labeled Parameter Estimate (i.e., the regression equation) and the T ratios corresponding to each term (i.e., T for H0) and notice that only NI-I and the linear term of ST are statistically significant. Incidentally, $df = 16$ for each t ratio (i.e., residual df, see output). Also, because of orthogonality, the test of each term of the regression equation is analogous to a test of the proportion of variance accounted for by the vector in question. For example, verify that the F for a test of .57953 is equal to the squared t ratio (i.e., -7.561^2). An even more direct way of seeing this is to test the SS. For example, the SS associated with L (linear component) is 42.008, which is, of course, equal to the product of the corresponding squared semipartial correlation and the total sum of squares: (.24335023)(172.62500) = 42.008333. Dividing this value by the mean squared residual reported earlier (1.75) yields $F(1, 16) = 24.005$, which is equal to the squared corresponding t ratio (4.899).

In sum, because of the special properties of the design under consideration, the analysis was uncomplicated, leading to the conclusion that only the effects of No Incentive–Incentive and the linear component of Study Time are statistically significant. Obviously, the approach I took in this analysis is not feasible when the continuous variable consists of many values, as is generally the case with attributes—a topic to which I now turn.

Curvilinear Regression with an Attribute

When the continuous variable is manipulated, the researcher is in a position to select values that are equally spaced and to randomly assign equal numbers of subjects to each level. Recall that this makes the use of orthogonal polynomials simple and straightforward. When the continuous variable is an attribute (e.g., IQ, motivation, anxiety, cognitive style), the values of the variable may not be equally spaced. Moreover, such variables tend to consist of many values with unequal numbers of subjects for the different values.[23] Nevertheless, deviation from linearity must

---

[23]For a discussion of the distinction between the two types of variables, the meaning of equally spaced values, and of equal n's at each level, see Chapter 13.

be studied and tested. In certain studies, a trend other than linear may be part of the hypothesis. In other words, based on theoretical formulations a researcher may hypothesize, say, a quadratic or a cubic trend. Obviously, such hypotheses ought to be tested.

The procedures for testing deviation from linearity, or specific trends, with attribute variables follow a sequence of steps. At each step, a decision needs to be made about the next appropriate one to be taken. I illustrate these procedures with a numerical example.

A Numerical Example

A set of illustrative scores on Y and X for two groups (T_1 and T_2) is given in Table 14.5. You may think of these data as having been obtained in experimental research where the categorical variable, T, represents two treatments, or a treatment and a control, and X represents an attribute. This, then, would be an example of an ATI design. If, instead, you choose to view the data as having been obtained in nonexperimental research, the categorical variable would represent two groups (e.g., male-female, Black-White). In this case, the purpose of the research would be to compare the regression equations of Y on X for the two groups. Recall that the analysis proceeds in the same manner, whether the design is experimental or nonexperimental. It is interpretations of the results that differ in the two research settings (see the discussion earlier in this chapter). For convenience, in the following analysis I will refer to the categorical variable as representing treatments.

Table 14.5   Illustrative Data for Curvilinear Regression Analysis

	T_1			T_2	
Y		X		Y	X
4		2		3	2
5		2		5	3
7		3		4	4
6		3		6	4
5		4		8	6
7		5		6	6
6		5		8	8
9		7		9	8
8		7		9	10
6		7		8	10
9		10		10	12
8		10		8	12
11		11		8	14
12		11		8	15
9		13		6	16
12		13		8	17
11		14		5	17
12		15		7	18
11		16		5	18
10		16		6	19

NOTE: T = Treatment; N = 20 in each group.

SAS

Input

```
TITLE 'TABLE 14.5. CURVILINEAR REGRESSION';
DATA T145;
INPUT Y 1-2 X 3-4 T 5-6;             [fixed format]
IF T=1 THEN E=1; ELSE E=-1;          [effect coded vector for T]
XE=X*E;                              [product of X and E]
X2=X**2;                             [X^2]
X2E=X2*E;                            [product of X^2 and E]
CARDS;
 4 2 1
 5 2 1                               [first two subjects in T1]
 .  .  .
 518 2                               [last two subjects in T2]
 619 2
;
PROC PRINT;
PROC REG;
MODEL Y=X E XE X2 X2E;
MODEL Y=X E XE;
MODEL Y=X E X2;
PROC REG;
MODEL Y=X E XE X2 X2E;
  CURVE: TEST X2, X2E;               [see commentary]
  INT: TEST XE, X2E;
PROC REG;BY T;                       [do separate analyses for T1 and T2]
MODEL Y=X X2;
MODEL Y=X;
RUN;
```

Commentary

Except for TEST, I used and explained all aspects of the input in earlier chapters. "The TEST statement tests hypotheses about the parameters estimated in the preceding MODEL statement" (SAS Institute Inc., 1990a, Vol. 2, p. 1384). Later I explain the use of TEST in connection with the relevant output. For now, I will only point out that TEST is analogous to the TEST keyword in SPSS REGRESSION, which I used and explained in Chapter 12. "An optional label is useful to identify each test with a name" (SAS Institute Inc., 1990a, Vol. 2, p. 1384). As examples, I used CURVE and INT(eraction).

In the present example I raised X to the second power only. Using the same strategy, analyses in which X is raised to higher-order powers can be carried out. As you can see, I call first for analyses in which data from both treatments are used. Subsequently, I do separate regression analyses within each treatment. Also, although I could have accomplished the task with a smaller number of models, I refrained from doing so for didactic reasons.

The analysis may proceed by different routes, depending on the specific questions one wishes to answer. I present the route I am taking here in the form of a set of questions and tests designed to answer them. As I will show, questions raised at a later stage of the analysis depend on the nature of the answers to earlier questions.

1. *Is the proportion of variance accounted for by the second-degree polynomial meaningful?* Calculate the overall R^2, that is, one in which Y is regressed on X, E, XE, X^2, and X^2E.

Output

Model: MODEL1
Dependent Variable: Y

Analysis of Variance

Source	DF	Sum of Squares	Mean Square	F Value	Prob>F
Model	5	172.02652	34.40530	26.986	0.0001
Error	34	43.34848	1.27496		
C Total	39	215.37500			

Root MSE	1.12914	R-square	0.7987
Dep Mean	7.62500	Adj R-sq	0.7691

Commentary

As I said several times earlier, meaningfulness depends on a researcher's judgment in a given research context. If the overall R^2 is deemed not meaningful, there is no point in continuing with the analysis. Instead, it is necessary to scrutinize and rethink all aspects of the study to decide about the steps to be taken (e.g., designing a new study, using other measures).

As I did not mention a substantive area concerning this numerical example, I will only note that the overall R^2 is high (.7987) and that it is therefore worthwhile to proceed to the next question.

2. *Is there a quadratic trend in the data?*

Output

Model: MODEL2   R-square   0.5836   *[X E XE]*

Analysis of Variance

Source	DF	Sum of Squares
Model	3	125.69724

Commentary

As indicated in the italicized comment in brackets, $R^2_{Y.X,E,XE} = .5836$. From output under MODEL1, overall $R^2 = .7987$. Test

$$F = \frac{(R^2_{Y.X,E,XE,X^2,X^2E} - R^2_{Y.X,E,XE})/(k_1 - k_2)}{(1 - R^2_{Y.X,E,XE,X^2,X^2E})/(N - k_1 - 1)}$$

$$= \frac{(.7987 - .5836)/(5 - 3)}{(1 - .7987)/(40 - 5 - 1)} = \frac{.2151/2}{.2013/34} = 18.17$$

with 2 and 34 *df, p* < .01. Note that in this test of the difference between two R^2's the first includes also the quadratic terms whereas the second does not include them. The difference between the two R^2's, then, indicates the increment in the proportion of variance accounted for by the quadratic terms. In the present example, this increment is .2151, which is statistically significant. Accordingly, one asks question 3. Before I do this, however, I comment on (1) alternative ways for obtaining the above result and (2) action taken when the quadratic terms are statistically not significant.

From MODEL1, $ss_{reg} = 172.02652$, $df = 5$; $MSR = 1.27496$

From MODEL2, $ss_{reg} = 125.69724$, $df = 3$

Test

$$F = \frac{(172.02652 - 125.69724)/(5 - 3)}{1.27496} = \frac{23.16464}{1.27496} = 18.17$$

with 2 and 34 *df.* Not surprisingly, this is the same as the *F* ratio I calculated earlier, when I used proportions of variance accounted for.

Output

Test: CURVE	Numerator:	23.1646	DF:	2	F value:	18.1690
Test: CURVE	Denominator:	1.274955	DF:	34	Prob>F:	0.0001

Commentary

This is an excerpt from the second PROC REG. Notice that the results are the same as those I calculated above.

I showed three alternative routes to the same results for two reasons: (1) so that you will be in a position to choose the one most suitable in the light of the software you are using and (2) to show what is accomplished by the TEST option. Clearly, if you are using SPSS or SAS, the simplest approach is to use TEST.

Turning now to the course of action when the *F* ratio for the quadratic terms is statistically not significant, the next set of questions would be addressed to models in which only *X, E,* and *XE* are included. Earlier in this chapter, I showed the sequence of testing different models with such terms and summarized it in the section entitled "Recapitulation." Briefly, test first whether there is a statistically significant linear interaction. If the interaction is statistically significant, use the Johnson-Neyman technique to establish regions of significance and interpret the results. If the linear interaction is statistically not significant, test the difference between the intercepts. If there is a statistically significant difference between the intercepts, two parallel lines fit the data. That is, one treatment is superior to the other along the continuum of the continuous variable. If the difference between the intercepts is statistically not significant, a single regression line fits the data adequately. In other words, there are no statistically significant differences between the treatments.

In the present example there is a statistically significant quadratic trend (see the previous discussion). Accordingly, I proceed to the next question.

3. *Is there an interaction between the categorical and continuous variable?* Stated differently: *Are the two regression curves parallel?*

Output

Model: MODEL3 R-square 0.7207 *[X E X²]*

<table>
<tr><td></td><td colspan="6">*[from the second PROC REG]*</td></tr>
<tr><td>Test: INT</td><td>Numerator:</td><td>8.4062</td><td>DF:</td><td>2</td><td>F value:</td><td>6.5934</td></tr>
<tr><td></td><td>Denominator:</td><td>1.274955</td><td>DF:</td><td>34</td><td>Prob>F:</td><td>0.0038</td></tr>
</table>

Commentary

The answer to question 3 is obtained by testing the difference between the overall R^2 (.7987) and R^2 for the regression of Y on X, E, and X^2 (.7207) in the manner I did under question 2. Instead of showing the calculations (I suggest that you do them as an exercise), I reproduced the results from the TEST for INT(eraction). Based on this test I conclude that the regression curves are not parallel, or that two separate regression equations, one for each treatment or group, are required.

Before turning to the separate regression equations, I comment on the steps to take when one has determined that the regression curves are parallel (i.e., when the above F ratio is statistically not significant). Under such circumstances, the appropriate question would be whether the intercepts of the two parallel curves differ from each other. This is accomplished by testing the difference between two R^2's: $R^2_{Y.X,X^2,E} - R^2_{Y.X,X^2}$. A statistically nonsignificant F ratio would indicate that a single quadratic equation, $Y' = a + bX + bX^2$, adequately fits the data for both treatments or both groups. In other words, there is no statistically significant difference between the treatments or the groups. If, on the other hand, the F ratio is statistically significant, two regression equations that differ in their intercepts only would be required. This, of course, means that there is a statistically significant difference between the treatments or groups along the continuum of the continuous variable.

In the present example, the interaction is statistically significant. As I pointed out earlier, this means that the regression of Y on X under one treatment or for one group differs from that under the other treatment or for the other group. Because the difference may take diverse forms, it is necessary to derive and examine the separate regression equations.

Separate Regression Equations

Earlier in this chapter, I showed how to use elements from the overall regression equation to calculate regression equations for separate groups. The same approach is applicable to situations in which the regression is curvilinear. Consequently, I apply it here without comments. If necessary, review the section entitled "The Overall Regression Equation," earlier in this chapter.

From the output (not reproduced here), the overall regression equation for the data of Table 14.5 is

$$Y' = 1.874199 + 1.140738X + 1.120435E - .266946XE - .042344X^2 + .019838X^2E$$

$$a_{T_1} = 1.874199 + 1.120435 = 2.994634$$

$$a_{T_2} = 1.874199 - 1.120435 = .753764$$

$$bX_{T_1} = 1.140738 - .266946 = .873792$$

$$bX_{T_2} = 1.140738 + .266946 = 1.407684$$

$$bX^2_{T_1} = -.042344 + .019838 = -.022506$$

$$bX^2_{T_2} = -.042344 - .019838 = -.062182$$

The separate regression equations are

$$Y'_{T_1} = 2.994634 + .873792X - .022506X^2$$

$$Y'_{T_2} = .753764 + 1.407684X - .062182X^2$$

It is necessary to examine each of these equations to determine whether the quadratic terms are required in both.

Output

-- T=1 --

Model: MODEL1 R-square 0.7987

Parameter Estimates

Variable	DF	Parameter Estimate	Standard Error	T for H0: Parameter=0	Prob > |T|
INTERCEP	1	2.994633	1.06467841	2.813	0.0120
X	1	0.873791	0.28413406	3.075	0.0069
X2	1	−0.022506	0.01562493	−1.440	0.1679

Model: MODEL2 R-square 0.7742

Parameter Estimates

Variable	DF	Parameter Estimate	Standard Error	T for H0: Parameter=0	Prob > |T|
INTERCEP	1	4.282291	0.59527938	7.194	0.0001
X	1	0.473300	0.06025539	7.855	0.0001

Commentary

The preceding are excerpts from the output for the regression analyses for T_1 (see PROC REG; BY T; in the input). Compare the quadratic equation with the one I calculated earlier for this treatment through the overall regression equation.

Examine the t ratio for X^2 and notice the $p > .05$ associated with it. Also, notice that the proportion of variance incremented by X^2 is rather small ($.7987 - .7742 = .02$). It appears, then, that a linear regression equation would suffice to fit the data for T_1. Because X and X^2 are correlated, it is necessary to recalculate the regression equation with X only. This I have done in MODEL2, from which it can be seen that the regression equation is

$$Y' = 4.282291 + .473300X$$

I turn now to the results of the separate analysis for T_2.

Output

```
---------------------------------------------- T=2 ------------------------------------------------------
```
Model: MODEL1 R-square 0.7238

Parameter Estimates

Variable	DF	Parameter Estimate	Standard Error	T for H0: Parameter=0	Prob > |T|
INTERCEP	1	0.753764	0.96600970	0.780	0.4460
X	1	1.407684	0.21153121	6.655	0.0001
X2	1	−0.062182	0.00968607	−6.420	0.0001

Commentary

Compare the quadratic equation with the one I calculated earlier through the overall regression equation.

In contrast with the analysis of the data for T_1, the quadratic term in T_2 is statistically significant: $t(17) = -6.42$, $p < .01$. Also, while $R^2_{Y.X,X^2} = .7238$ (see the preceding), the proportion of variance accounted for by the linear term (not shown in the output) is .05447. Thus, the increment in the proportion of variance due to the quadratic term is .6694. I suggest that you verify that $F(1, 17) = 41.22$ for the test of this increment, which is equal to the square of the t ratio for the test of the b for the quadratic term. In sum, the regression of Y on X is quadratic under T_2 and linear under T_1.[24]

Using the linear regression equation for T_1 and the quadratic equation for T_2, the two regression curves are depicted in Figure 14.8, which shows how each fits to its data.

Because more often than not researchers analyze their data as if the regression were linear, it will be instructive to conclude this section with a demonstration of the consequences of such an

---

[24]I give a substantive example of such a finding in the section entitled "Research Examples" (see "Involvement, Discrepancy of Information, and Attitude Change").

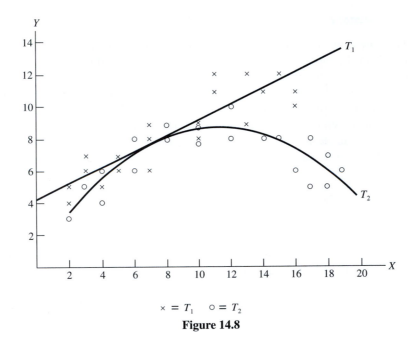

$$\times = T_1 \quad \circ = T_2$$

Figure 14.8

approach when applied to the data in Table 14.5. This time I analyze the data using X, E, and XE only. In other words, the regression of Y on X under both treatments is assumed to be linear.

Output

R-square 0.5836

Parameter Estimates

Variable	DF	Parameter Estimate	Standard Error	T for H0: Parameter=0	Prob > |T|
INTERCEP	1	5.147031	0.54269232	9.484	0.0001
X	1	0.274925	0.04960786	5.542	0.0001
E	1	−0.864740	0.54269232	−1.593	0.1198
XE	1	0.198375	0.04960786	3.999	0.0003

Commentary

Notice that b_{XE} is statistically significant: $t(36) = 3.999$, $p < .01$. Accordingly, separate regression equations are required for the two treatments. Using relevant values from the regression equation reported above, calculate the values for the separate regression equations:

$$a_{T_1} = 5.147031 - .864740 = 4.28229$$

$$a_{T_2} = 5.147031 + .864740 = 6.01177$$

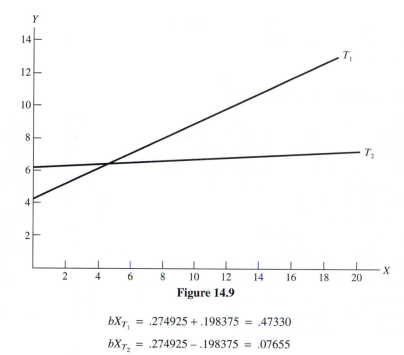

Figure 14.9

$$bX_{T_1} = .274925 + .198375 = .47330$$

$$bX_{T_2} = .274925 - .198375 = .07655$$

The separate regression equations are

$$Y'_{T_1} = 4.28229 + .47330X$$

$$Y'_{T_2} = 6.01177 + .07655X$$

The linear regression equation for T_1 is the same as the one I calculated earlier when I concluded that a first-degree polynomial is sufficient to fit the data for this treatment. Note, however, what happened to the regression equation for T_2. The test for the interaction (see preceding) indicated that there is a statistically significant difference between the two b's. Based on the magnitude of these b's, one would have to conclude that the effect of X under T_1 is much larger than its effect under T_2. Note that $R^2_{y.x} = .7742$ under T_1 and $R^2_{y.x} = .0544$ under T_2. Incidentally, because of the small sample size under each treatment, R^2 for T_2 is statistically not significant: $F(1, 18) = 1.04$. Nevertheless, for comparison with Figure 14.8, I drew the two regression lines in Figure 14.9.

Clearly, depending on which of the two analyses is used with the data in Table 14.5, one would reach strikingly different conclusions. The moral of this demonstration is obvious: Do not assume that the trend in your own or anyone else's data is linear! Also, always plot your data, and study the plot.

For a presentation of curvilinear regression analysis with more than one continuous independent variable, see Aiken and West (1991, Chapters 5 and 6).

RESEARCH EXAMPLES

In this section I summarize briefly several studies in which the methods I presented in this chapter were applied. Because my sole purpose is to illustrate applications of these methods, I do not comment on theory or design aspects of the studies (e.g., sampling, sample size, controls, adequacy of measuring instruments). When relevant, I give the authors' substantive conclusions without commenting on them. I suggest that you read the studies cited and draw your own conclusions.

Sex, Age, and the Perception of Violence

Moore (1966) used a stereoscope to present a viewer with pairs of pictures simultaneously. One eye was presented with a violent picture and the other eye was presented with a nonviolent picture. For example, one pair consisted of a mailman and a man who was stabbed. Under such conditions of binocular rivalry, binocular fusion takes place: the subject sees only one picture. Various researchers demonstrated that binocular fusion is affected by cultural and personality factors. Moore hypothesized that when presented with pairs of violent-nonviolent pictures in a binocular rivalry situation, males will see more violent pictures than will females. Moore further hypothesized that a positive relation exists between age and the perception of violent pictures, regardless of sex.

Subjects in the study were males and females from grades 3, 5, 7, 9, 11, and college freshmen. (Note that grade is a continuous independent variable with six levels.) As predicted, Moore found that males perceived more violent pictures than did females, regardless of the grade level. Furthermore, within each sex there was a statistically significant linear trend between grade (age) and the perception of violent pictures. Moore interpreted his findings in the context of differential socialization of sex roles across age.

Involvement, Discrepancy of Information, and Attitude Change

There is a good deal of evidence concerning the relation of attitude change to discrepancy of new information about the object of the attitude. For example, some studies showed that the more discrepant new information about an attitude object is from the attitude an individual holds, the more change there will be in his or her attitude toward the object. In other studies the individual's initial involvement with the object of the attitude was also taken into consideration. Thus, Freedman (1964) hypothesized that under low involvement the relation between the discrepancy of information and attitude change is monotonic. This means, essentially, that as the discrepancy between the information and the attitude held increases, there is a tendency toward an increase in attitude change. In any event, an increase in the discrepancy will not lead to a decrease in attitude change. With high involvement, however, Freedman hypothesized that the relation is nonmonotonic: with increased discrepancy between information and attitude there is an increase in attitude change up to an optimal point, beyond which increase in discrepancy leads to a decrease in attitude change, or what has been labeled a boomerang effect.

Freedman induced the conditions experimentally and demonstrated that in the low-involvement group the trend was linear, whereas in the high-involvement group the trend was quadratic. As predicted, in the high-involvement group, moderate discrepancy resulted in the greatest attitude change. Freedman maintained that the relation between discrepancy and attitude change is nonmonotonic also when the level of involvement is low. In other words, he claimed that in the low-involvement group too the trend is quadratic. Freedman attributed the linear trend in the low-involvement group to the range of discrepancy he used. He claimed that with greater discrepancy a quadratic trend would emerge in the low-involvement group as well. In Chapter 13, I discussed hazards of extrapolation. To test Freedman's notions, one would have to set up the appropriate experimental conditions.

Test Bias

Cleary (1968) was interested in determining whether the use of the Scholastic Aptitude Test (SAT) to predict grade-point average (GPA) in college is biased toward Blacks or Whites.[25] She used three integrated colleges. In each school, she regressed GPA on SAT (verbal and mathematical scores) and on SAT and high school rank (HSR, for two schools only) for the following groups: (1) all Black students; (2) a random sample of White students; (3) a sample of White students matched with the Black students on curriculum and class (for two schools only).

Cleary found that differences among regression coefficients in each school were small and statistically not significant. In two schools, the differences among the intercepts were also statistically not significant. In one school, the intercepts for the Whites were significantly larger than those for the Blacks. Cleary concluded:

> In the three schools studied . . . there was little evidence that the Scholastic Aptitude Test is biased as a predictor of college grades. In the two eastern schools, there were not significant differences in the regression lines for Negro and white students. In the one college in the southwest, the regression lines for Negro and white students were significantly different: the Negro students' scores were overpredicted by the use of the white common regression line. When high school grades or rank-in-class are used in addition to the SAT as predictors, the degree of positive bias for the Negro students increases. (p. 123)

Teaching Styles, Manifest Anxiety, and Achievement

This study by Dowaliby and Schumer (1973) is an example of an ATI design. College students were assigned to either a teacher-centered or a student-centered class in introductory psychology. Among other measures, the Taylor Manifest Anxiety scale was administered to the students. Two multiple-choice examinations served as measures of the criterion. Regressing each of these measures on manifest anxiety, the authors found a disordinal interaction between the latter and the two teaching styles. Students low on manifest anxiety achieved more under the student-centered condition than under the teacher-centered condition. The reverse was true for students high on manifest anxiety. The authors also reported regions of significance as established by the application of the Johnson-Neyman technique.

STUDY SUGGESTIONS

1. In a study of the regression of Y on X in three groups, some of the results were $\Sigma x_1y_1 = 72.56$; $\Sigma x_2y_2 = 80.63$; $\Sigma x_3y_3 = 90.06$; $\Sigma x_1^2 = 56.71$; $\Sigma x_2^2 = 68.09$; and $\Sigma x_3^2 = 75.42$. The subscripts refer to groups 1, 2, and 3 respectively. Using these data calculate the following:
   (a) The three separate b's.
   (b) The common b.
   (c) The regression sum of squares when the separate b's are used.
   (d) The regression sum of squares when the common b is used.

2. Distinguish between ordinal and disordinal interaction.
3. What is meant by "the research range of interest"?
4. In a study of two groups, A and B, the regression equations were

$$Y'_A = 22.56 + .23X$$
$$Y'_B = 15.32 + .76X$$

At what value of X do the two regression lines intersect?

---

[25]Earlier in this chapter, I gave Cleary's definition of test bias (see "The Study of Bias").

5. What is meant by "attribute-treatment interaction"? Give examples of research problems in which the study of ATI may be important.

6. Suppose that a researcher regresses Y on a continuous variable, X, and on a categorical variable, A, without using the product(s) of X and A. What is he assuming?

7. In an ATI study with three treatments, A_1, A_2, and A_3, and an attribute, X, effect coding was used to code the treatments as follows: in E1, subjects receiving treatment A_1 were identified (i.e., assigned 1's); in vector E2, subjects receiving treatment A_2 were identified; subjects receiving treatment A_3 were assigned -1's in both vectors. Product vectors were generated: XE1 and XE2. The overall regression equation was

$Y' = 20.35 + 2.37X + 5.72E1 - 3.70E2 + 1.12X E1 + .76X E2$

(a) What are the separate regression equations for the three groups?

(b) What vectors should be included in a regression analysis if one wishes to calculate the common regression coefficient (b_c)?

8. A researcher wished to determine whether the regression of achievement on achievement motivation is the same for males and females. For a sample of males ($N = 15$) and females ($N = 15$) she obtained measures of achievement and achievement motivation. Following are the data (illustrative):

Males

Achievement Motivation	Achievement
2	12
2	14
3	12
3	14
4	13
4	17
5	14
5	18
6	16
6	19
8	17
8	21
9	17
9	21
10	22

Females

Achievement Motivation	Achievement
1	12
1	14
3	13
3	15
4	16
5	15
6	14
6	16
7	14
7	17
8	15
8	17
10	16
10	18
11	18

What is(are) the following?

(a) Correlation between achievement motivation and achievement in each of the groups.

(b) Proportion of variance accounted for by sex, achievement motivation, and their product.

(c) Proportion of variance accounted for by the product of sex and achievement motivation.

(d) F ratio for the product vector.

(e) Overall regression equation for achievement motivation, sex, and the product vector (when males are assigned 1 and females -1 in the effect coded vector).

(f) Regression equations for the two groups.

(g) Point of intersection of the regression lines.

(h) Simultaneous regions of significance at the .05 level. Plot the regression lines and interpret the results.

ANSWERS

1. (a) $b_1 = 1.28$; $b_2 = 1.18$; $b_3 = 1.19$
   (b) $b_c = 1.21$
   (c) $ss_{reg} = 295.86$
   (d) $ss_{res} = 295.53$
4. $X = 13.66$
6. The researcher is assuming that the difference between the regression coefficient for Y on X in the separate groups is statistically not significant, or that the use of a common regression coefficient is tenable.
7. (a) $Y'_{A_1} = 26.07 + 3.49X$
      $Y'_{A_2} = 16.65 + 3.13X$
      $Y'_{A_3} = 18.33 + .49X$
   (b) X, E1, E2
8. (a) .836 for males, and .770 for females
   (b) .69101
   (c) .10357
   (d) 8.71471 with 1 and 26 *df*, $p < .01$
   (e) $Y' = 11.724326 + .730350X - 1.037579E + .301779XE$
   (f) $Y'_M = 10.686747 + 1.032129X$
      $Y'_F = 12.761905 + .428571X$
   (g) 3.44–see (14.5)
   (h) For (14.7): A = .08263; for (14.8): B = .37162; for (14.9): C = −7.25519

      The region of nonsignificance ranges from −14.89162 to 5.89640. Hence, males and females whose scores on achievement motivation are ≥ 6 differ significantly on achievement. (I obtained the preceding results by applying Karpman's layout for SPSS, as I showed earlier in this chapter.)

      Notice the relative similarity of the two correlations coefficients in the two groups [see (a)], as contrasted with the difference between the two b's [see (f)]. In the present example, the correlations are equal to their respective standardized regression coefficients (β's). For a discussion of properties of β's and b's, and recommendations when to use one or the other, see earlier chapters, particularly Chapter 10.

Continuous and Categorical Independent Variables—II: Analysis of Covariance

As you can see from its title, this chapter is a continuation Chapter 14. Analysis of covariance (ANCOVA) is used for two fundamentally different purposes: (1) statistical control of relevant variables that are not part of the model and (2) adjustment for initial differences among groups being compared. The application of ANCOVA for the first purpose is well founded, and may prove useful in diverse research areas. The application of ANCOVA for the second purpose, however, is highly questionable as it is fraught with serious flaws. I deal with each purpose separately.

ANCOVA FOR CONTROL

Viewed from a regression perspective, ANCOVA is not different from the methods I presented in the preceding chapter. The concern is still with comparisons of regression equations, except that in ANCOVA one or more variables (usually continuous) are introduced for the purpose of control. In Chapter 12, I showed how one can exercise direct control of relevant variables that are not part of the model under consideration by introducing them as factors in a factorial design. I noted that such control is designed to lead to a reduction of the error term, thereby increasing the precision of the analysis.

Assume, for example, an experiment aimed at assessing the effects of different instructional methods on academic achievement. Recall that it is essential that subjects be randomly assigned to treatments, thereby "equating" the groups on all other variables (for a discussion of the role of randomization in experiments, see Pedhazur & Schmelkin, 1991, pp. 216–223, and the references therein). Nevertheless, precision of the analysis in such designs is adversely affected when subjects vary on variables that, though not part of the model, are related to performance on the dependent variable. This is because variance due to such variables is relegated to the error term. Note carefully that it is precision, not the valid estimation of treatment effects, that is adversely affected by the failure to control relevant variables.

Relevant variables may be controlled for directly by introducing them into the design. When subjects in the preceding example vary in, say, mental ability—a variable known to be related to academic achievement—this source of variability may be controlled directly. For example, subjects may be grouped according to different levels of mental ability and then randomly assigned from each level to the different instructional methods. Mental ability is thus included as a factor, and the design is generally referred to as a treatments-by-levels design (Lindquist, 1953, Chapter 5). Or, subjects may be matched on mental ability and then randomly assigned to the instructional methods, thereby using what is referred to as a randomized blocks design (Edwards, 1985, Chapter 15). Other approaches for direct control of relevant variables are also possible.

Instead of controlling relevant variables directly, they can be controlled indirectly by statistical techniques. Basically, this is accomplished by partialing out of the dependent variable the variable(s) one wishes to control for. Referring again to the example, instead of introducing mental ability as a factor in the design, one would study the effects of the instructional methods after partialing out from the dependent variable the effect of mental ability. This, then, is an example of an ANCOVA in which mental ability is referred to as a covariate or a concomitant variable.[1]

Later, I will show that comparisons among treatments in ANCOVA are tantamount to comparisons among the intercepts of regression equations in which the dependent variable is regressed on the covariate(s). Note the similarity between ANCOVA and ATI designs (Chapter 14). In ATI designs an attribute (mental ability of the present example) is introduced because the researcher wishes to study how it interacts with treatments (instructional methods of the present example). In ANCOVA, on the other hand, the attribute is introduced for the purpose of controlling for it, thereby increasing the precision of the analysis.[2]

The similarity between ATI and ANCOVA is clearest when considering the action taken when results go counter to expectation. When in an ATI design there is no interaction between the attribute and the treatments (i.e., there are no statistically significant differences among the b's), the results are treated and interpreted as in ANCOVA. Conversely, when in ANCOVA there is an interaction between the covariate and the treatments, the results are interpreted as in ATI.

The Logic of Analysis of Covariance

Recall that a residualized variable is a variable from which whatever it shared with the predictor variable has been purged. As a result, the correlation between the residualized variable and the predictor is zero (see Chapter 7). Suppose now that when studying the effects of different teaching methods on academic achievement one wished to control for intelligence. One way to do this would be to residualize academic achievement on intelligence and analyze the residuals instead of the original achievement scores. If Y_{ij} is the achievement of individual i under treatment j, then Y'_{ij} is his or her predicted score (from intelligence). $Y_{ij} - Y'_{ij}$ is, of course, the residual. As I pointed out, the residuals thus obtained are not correlated with intelligence. Hence, tests of differences among treatments on the residuals constitute tests of achievement *after* controlling for

---

[1]See Feldt (1958), for comparisons among ANCOVA, treatments by levels, and randomized-blocks designs; see also Maxwell, Delaney, and Dill (1984).

[2]For good discussions of ANCOVA, its uses and assumptions, see Cochran (1957), Elashoff (1969), Huitema (1980), Porter and Raudenbush (1987), and Reichardt (1979).

intelligence (the covariate). This, then, is the logic behind the analysis of covariance, which can be summarized by the following equation:

$$Y_{ij} = \overline{Y} + T_j + b(X_{ij} - \overline{X}) + e_{ij} \tag{15.1}$$

where Y_{ij} = score of subject i under treatment j; $\overline{Y}$ = grand mean on the dependent variable; T_j = effect of treatment j; b = a common regression coefficient for Y on X (see the next section, "Homogeneity of Regression Coefficients"); X_{ij} = score on the covariate for subject i under treatment j; $\overline{X}$ = grand mean on the covariate; and e_{ij} = error associated with the score of subject i under treatment j. Equation (15.1) can be restated as

$$Y_{ij} - b(X_{ij} - \overline{X}) = \overline{Y} + T_j + e_{ij} \tag{15.2}$$

which clearly shows that after controlling for the covariate $[Y_{ij} - b(X_{ij} - \overline{X})]$, a score is conceived as composed of the grand mean, a treatment effect, and an error term. The right-hand side of (15.2) is an expression of the linear model I introduced in Chapter 11. When b is zero, that is, when the covariate is not related to the dependent variable, (15.2) is identical to (11.10).

Homogeneity of Regression Coefficients

Controlling for the covariate (X) in (15.1) involves the application of a *common* regression coefficient—see (14.1) and the discussion related to it—to the deviation of X from the grand mean of X. Hence, the validity of this procedure is predicated on the assumption that differences among the b's for the regression of Y on X in the different treatments are statistically not significant. The test of this assumption, referred to as homogeneity of regression coefficients, is done in the manner I showed in the preceding chapter (see "Tests of Differences among Regression Coefficients"). Briefly, one tests whether the use of separate regression coefficients adds meaningfully and significantly to the proportion of variance accounted for, as compared with the proportion of variance accounted for by the use of a common regression coefficient (b_c).

Having established that the use of b_c is appropriate, one can determine whether there are statistically significant differences among the treatment means after adjusting the scores on the dependent variable for possible differences on the covariate. As I will show, this is equivalent to a test of differences among intercepts, which I also presented in the preceding chapter.

Recall that tests among intercepts in ATI designs are done only after establishing that there are no statistically significant differences among the b's of the separate treatments (see Chapter 14). The same is true for ANCOVA. When the b's are found to be heterogeneous, ANCOVA should not be used. Instead, one can, as I showed in Chapter 14, study the pattern of regressions in the separate groups and establish regions of significance. Interpretation of results (e.g., whether differences among b's are interpreted as an interaction between the covariate and the treatments) depends on the specific research setting—a topic I discussed in detail in Chapter 14.

To clarify what is accomplished by ANCOVA, I presented it as an analysis of residuals. The foregoing discussion, however, should make clear that it is not necessary to calculate the residuals. Instead, calculations of ANCOVA follow the same pattern as in ATI designs, which I described in the preceding chapter.

A Numerical Example

As my concern in this section is with the use of ANCOVA for control rather than for adjustment, I constructed illustrative data to appear as if they were obtained in an experiment. Data for four

Table 15.1   Illustrative Data for ANCOVA with Four Treatments

	Treatments							
	A		B		C		D	
	Y	X	Y	X	Y	X	Y	X
	12	5	13	4	14	4	15	4
	15	5	16	4	16	4	16	5
	14	6	15	5	18	6	13	5
	14	7	16	6	20	6	15	6
	18	7	19	6	18	7	19	6
	18	8	17	8	19	8	17	7
	16	8	19	8	22	8	20	7
	14	9	23	9	21	9	18	9
	18	9	19	10	23	10	20	9
	19	10	22	10	20	10	21	11
M:	15.8	7.4	17.9	7.0	19.1	7.2	17.4	6.9
s:	2.35	1.71	3.11	2.31	2.73	2.20	2.36	2.18

treatments on a dependent variable, *Y,* and a covariate, *X,* are given in Table 15.1. From a purely analytic perspective, the approach I present in this section is applicable also in other settings (e.g., quasi-experimental, nonexperimental). *The interpretation of the results is, of course, very much dependent on the design and the setting.* Later in this chapter (see ANCOVA for Adjustment), I address issues concerning the interpretation of ANCOVA results in quasi-experimental and nonexperimental designs.

SPSS

Input

```
TITLE TABLE 15.1. ANCOVA WITH ONE COVARIATE.
DATA LIST/Y X T 1–6.
VALUE LABELS T 1 'A' 2 'B' 3 'C' 4 'D'.
COMPUTE E1=0.
COMPUTE E2=0.
COMPUTE E3=0.
IF (T EQ 1) E1=1.      [generate effect coded vectors]
IF (T EQ 4) E1=–1.
IF (T EQ 2) E2=1.
IF (T EQ 4) E2=–1.
IF (T EQ 3) E3=1.
IF (T EQ 4) E3=–1.
COMPUTE XE1=X*E1.      [products of covariate and coded vectors]
COMPUTE XE2=X*E2.
COMPUTE XE3=X*E3.
BEGIN DATA
12 5 1      [first subject in A]
 .   .   .
```

13 4 2   *[first subject in B]*

.   .   .

14 4 3   *[first subject in C]*

.   .   .

15 4 4   *[first subject in D]*

END DATA

LIST.

REGRESSION VAR=Y TO XE3/DES/STAT=ALL/

    DEP=Y/ENTER X/ENTER E1 TO E3/ENTER XE1 TO XE3/

    DEP=Y/ENTER E1 TO E3/   *[analysis without the covariate]*

    DEP=X/ENTER E1 TO E3.   *[covariate as dependent variable]*

Commentary

As in preceding chapters, I placed the scores for the four groups on the dependent variable, *Y*, and on the covariate, *X*, in single vectors. Also, I added a vector for group identification, T, so that I could use it to generate effect coded vectors (see COMPUTE and IF statements). My approach here is identical to the one I used repeatedly in Chapter 14, except that there the categorical variable consisted of two categories whereas here it consists of four categories. If necessary, refer to Chapter 14 for a more detailed explanation of the input.

    As you can see, I call for three regression analyses. *The first analysis is all that is necessary for ANCOVA.* I use results of the second and third analyses for specific purposes or to illustrate some specific points.

Output

Equation Number 1   Dependent Variable..   Y

Block Number 3.   Method: Enter   XE1   XE2   XE3

Multiple R	.83089		
R Square	.69038	R Square Change	.00313
Adjusted R Square	.62265	F Change	.10769
Standard Error	1.76482	Signif F Change	.9550

Commentary

As I stated earlier, ANCOVA should not be applied when the *b*'s are heterogeneous. Therefore, the first test addresses the question whether the *b*'s are homogeneous. As I showed in Chapter 14, to determine whether there are statistically significant differences among the *b*'s, test the increment in the proportion of variance accounted for by the product vectors, over and above the proportion of variance accounted for by the covariate and the effect coded vectors. This, then, is a test between two R^2's, which I introduced in Chapter 5 (see "Testing Increments in Proportion of Variance Accounted For") and used repeatedly in subsequent chapters. As I showed in preceding chapters, in SPSS this test is readily available in the form of a test of R Square Change. For present purposes, the R Square Change we need is that of the last step, when the product vectors were entered (i.e., Block Number 3), excerpts of which I reproduced here. Depending on the computer program you are using, you may first have to generate the two R^2's by specifying two models—one with and one without product vectors—and then apply (5.27).

Clearly, R Square Change due to the product vectors is minuscule (.00313) and statistically not significant ($F < 1$). Recall that the same test can be carried out using the increment in the regression sum of squares due to the product vectors. (I suggest that you run the analysis and use relevant values of the output to carry out this test.) In either case, the numerator *df* for the *F* ratio are $k_1 - k_2$ (3), where the former is equal to 7 (covariate, three effect coded vectors, and three product vectors), and the latter is equal to 4 (covariate and three effect coded vectors). The denominator *df* for the *F* ratio are $N - k_1 - 1$ (32).

In light of these results, I conclude that the use of a common *b* is appropriate for the present data. Before proceeding with the analysis, though, I show how to obtain separate regression equations for the various groups by using relevant values from the overall regression equation.

Separate Regression Equations

Although for the present data it is not necessary to derive separate regression equations for the various groups, I do it here to show that the method I described in Chapter 14 for the case of two groups generalizes to any number of groups. The overall regression equation (i.e., the one including the covariate, the effect coded vectors, and the product vectors) obtained in the last step is

$$Y' = 10.434604 + .999466X - 1.305816E1 - .263771E2 +$$
$$1.102093E3 - .097951XE1 + .104700XE2 + .050992XE3$$

As I described the properties of the overall regression equation in Chapter 14, I derive the separate regression equations without comment. If necessary, refer to Chapter 14 for a detailed explanation. The intercepts (*a*'s) for the separate regression equations are

$$a_A = 10.434604 + (-1.305816) \qquad\qquad = 9.13$$
$$a_B = 10.434604 + (-.263771) \qquad\qquad = 10.17$$
$$a_C = 10.434604 + (1.102093) \qquad\qquad = 11.54$$
$$a_D = 10.434604 - [(-1.305816) + (-.263771) + (1.102093)] = 10.90$$

The regression coefficients (*b*'s) for the separate regression equations are

$$b_A = .999466 + (-.097951) \qquad\qquad = .90$$
$$b_B = .999466 + (.104700) \qquad\qquad = 1.10$$
$$b_C = .999466 + (.050992) \qquad\qquad = 1.05$$
$$b_D = .999466 - [(-.097951) + (.104700) + (.050992)] = .94$$

The separate regression equations are

$$Y'_A = 9.13 + .90X$$
$$Y'_B = 10.17 + 1.10X$$
$$Y'_C = 11.54 + 1.05X$$
$$Y'_D = 10.90 + .94X$$

Incidentally, in Chapter 14 I showed how the separate regression equations may also be obtained in SPSS by using the SPLIT FILE command. To do this for the present example, add the following two lines to the end of the previous input file:

SPLIT FILE BY T.

REGRESSION VAR Y X/DES/DEP Y/ENTER.

Examine the *b*'s and notice that they are similar to each other. Moreover, as I showed earlier, the differences among them are statistically not significant. As a common *b* may be used, the next step is to test the differences among the intercepts. Before presenting this step, I reproduce an excerpt of the output from the first step in the analysis, when only the covariate was entered.

Output

Equation Number 1   Dependent Variable..   Y
Block Number 1.   Method: Enter   X

		Analysis of Variance			
Multiple R	.69656				
R Square	.48520		DF	Sum of Squares	Mean Square
Adjusted R Square	.47165	Regression	1	156.18514	156.18514
Standard Error	2.08828	Residual	38	165.71486	4.36092

F =   35.81475   Signif F =   .0000

------------------------------------- Variables in the Equation ---

Variable	B	SE B	Correl	T	Sig T
X	.980754	.163881	.696561	5.985	.0000
(Constant)	10.562125	1.213441			

Commentary

The results of this first step are for the regression of *Y* (the dependent variable) on *X* (the covariate). Notice that the data are treated as if they were obtained from a single group. R Square is, of course, the squared zero-order correlation of *Y* with *X* (see also Correl under Variables in the Equation). As I explain in the next chapter, this is referred to as a *total* correlation, to distinguish it from two other types of correlations (*within* and *between*). Similarly, *b* in this analysis is referred to as a *total* regression coefficient. Whether or not these results are interpreted depends on subsequent tests. For now, it will suffice to point out that if one determines that differences among the *b*'s as well as among the *a*'s of the separate groups are statistically not significant, it is valid to conclude that a single regression equation, consisting of estimates of total parameters, fits all the data.

Differences among Intercepts

As I showed in Chapter 14, a test of the difference among intercepts is done by comparing two models, one in which separate intercepts are fitted to each of the groups and one in which a common intercept is fitted to all of them. If the proportion of variance accounted for (or the regression sum of squares) in the model with separate intercepts does not differ significantly from that obtained when a common intercept is used, one can conclude that the latter model is appropriate to describe the data.

Output

Equation Number 1   Dependent Variable..   Y
Block Number 2.   Method: Enter   E1   E2   E3

				Analysis of Variance			
Multiple R	.82901						
R Square	.68726	R Square Change	.20206		DF	Sum of Squares	Mean Square
Adjusted R Square	.65151	F Change	7.53757	Regression	4	221.22741	55.30685
Standard Error	1.69598	Signif F Change	.0005	Residual	35	100.67259	2.87636

F = 19.22807   Signif F = .0000

------------------------------ Variables in the Equation ------------------------------

Variable	B	SE B	T	Sig T
X	1.013052	.133704	7.577	.0000
E1	−2.028589	.465917		
E2	.476631	.464765		
E3	1.474021	.464572		
(Constant)	10.332007	.989662		

Commentary

The preceding are excerpts from the output of the second step of the analysis (Block Number 2), when the effect coded vectors representing the treatments were entered. Recall that in the first step (Block Number 1; see the first step in the preceding output), the covariate was entered. Thus, R Square Change (.20206) is the increment in the proportion of variance accounted for after taking the covariate into account or after controlling for the covariate. As you can see, $F(3, 35) = 7.54$ and $p < .05$, leading to the rejection of the null hypothesis that there are no statistically significant differences among the intercepts. Accordingly, four separate regression equations consisting of a common b and separate intercepts are indicated. Before I do this, I will make several points.

1. Had the results of the test among the intercepts been statistically not significant, I would have concluded that, after controlling for the covariate, there are no statistically significant differences among the treatments. Under such circumstances, it would have been valid to use and interpret the results of the first step in the analysis, that is, the one in which only the covariate was entered (see the previous output).

2. $F(4, 35) = 19.23$ reported in the preceding is for a test of R^2 for both the covariate and the coded vectors representing the treatments. Later (see "Tests among Adjusted Means"), I use the Mean Square Residual (MSR) reported in the preceding.
3. As I pointed out in Chapter 14, the b associated with the continuous variable, X, in the equation in which product vectors are *not* included is the common b (b_c). In the present case, then, $b_c = 1.013052$. As always, this b is tested by dividing it by its standard error. From the computer output, $t(35) = 7.577, p < .05$, leading to the rejection of the null hypothesis that $b_c = 0$. I conclude that the covariate contributes significantly to the proportion of variance accounted for.
4. Although the output also includes t ratios for the b's associated with the coded vectors, I did not reproduce them as they are irrelevant. I did test the differences among the intercepts, and I found them to be statistically significant.

Having established (1) that a common b is tenable and (2) that there are statistically significant differences among the intercepts, I will use the regression equation reported at the second step of the analysis to calculate separate intercepts for the four treatment groups.

$$a_A = 10.332007 + (-2.028589) \qquad\qquad\qquad = 8.30$$

$$a_B = 10.332007 + (.476631) \qquad\qquad\qquad = 10.81$$

$$a_C = 10.332007 + (1.474021) \qquad\qquad\qquad = 11.81$$

$$a_D = 10.332007 - [(-2.028589) + (.476631) + (1.474021)] = 10.41$$

As with other statistics, I can now do pairwise comparisons between intercepts or comparisons between combinations of intercepts. Before doing this, though, it will be instructive to show what the conclusion would be if I analyzed the data in Table 15.1 without using the covariate. Subsequently, I introduce the concept of adjusted means and show how differences between them are tested.

Analysis without the Covariate

Examine the input file given earlier and notice that in the second analysis I called for the regression of Y on the effect coded vectors only. I introduced this type of analysis in Chapter 11, where I also showed its equivalence to a one-way, or a simple, analysis of variance. Following is an excerpt of the results from this analysis.

Output

Equation Number 2	Dependent Variable..	Y		
Block Number 1.	Method: Enter	E1	E2	E3

		Analysis of Variance			
Multiple R	.41747		DF	Sum of Squares	Mean Square
R Square	.17428				
Adjusted R Square	.10547	Regression	3	56.10000	18.70000
Standard Error	2.71723	Residual	36	265.80000	7.38333
		F = 2.53273		Signif F = .0723	

Commentary

Assuming $\alpha = .05$, I would conclude that the differences among the treatment means are statistically *not* significant—a conclusion that goes counter to the one I reached earlier, when I subjected the data to ANCOVA. In the present example, the proportion of variance accounted for by the treatments is slightly larger when analyzed in the context of ANCOVA (.20206) than ANOVA (.17428). Yet, this slight difference does not suffice to account for the difference in the results of the statistical tests. Rather, it is the considerable difference in the error terms in the two analyses—2.87636 in ANCOVA versus 7.38333 in the present analysis—that leads to the difference in the results of the statistical tests.

Another way of seeing this is to express the two error terms as proportions of variance not accounted for. From the output for ANCOVA of these data given earlier, R^2 of Y with the covariate and the coded vectors representing the treatments is .68726. Hence, .31274 $(1 - .68726)$ is attributed to error. By contrast, in the present analysis .82572 $(1 - .17428)$ is attributed to error. As an exercise, you may wish to test the proportion of variance accounted for by the coded vectors in the two analyses and verify that you obtain the same F ratios as in the two excerpts of the previous output. When doing the calculations, remember that the denominator *df* for the test of the proportion of variance incremented in the ANCOVA are 35 $(40 - 4 - 1)$, whereas for the present analysis they are 36 $(40 - 3 - 1)$.

I did the present analysis to show the benefits of using ANCOVA to remove from the error term a source of systematic variance due to the covariate, thereby increasing the precision of the analysis.

Adjusted Means

From Table 15.1, the means for the four treatment groups on the dependent variable are

$$\overline{Y}_A = 15.8 \qquad \overline{Y}_B = 17.9 \qquad \overline{Y}_C = 19.1 \qquad \overline{Y}_D = 17.4$$

These means reflect not only differences in treatment effects but also differences among the groups that are presumably due to their differences on the covariate. It is possible to adjust each of the means and study the differences among them after the effect of the covariate has been removed. For one covariate, the formula for adjusted means is

$$\overline{Y}_{j(\text{adj})} = \overline{Y}_j - b(\overline{X}_j - \overline{X}) \qquad (15.3)$$

where $\overline{Y}_{j(\text{adj})}$ = adjusted mean of treatment j; $\overline{Y}_j$ = mean of treatment j before the adjustment; b = common regression coefficient; $\overline{X}_j$ mean of the covariate for treatment j; and $\overline{X}$ = grand mean of the covariate.

To appreciate what is accomplished by (15.3), recall that the example I am using is meant to represent an experiment in which subjects were randomly assigned to the treatments. Assume, for the sake of illustration, that because of randomization all treatment groups ended up having identical means on the covariate. Under such circumstances, $\overline{X}_j = \overline{X}$ in (15.3), resulting in no adjustment for the means. This makes sense, as the groups are equal on the covariate. As I said earlier, the function of the covariate in experimental research is to identify a systematic source of variance and thereby reduce the error term. Although randomization will generally not result in equal group means on the covariate, differences among such means tend to be small, especially when relatively large numbers of subjects are used. Consequently, application of (15.3) generally results in relatively small mean adjustments.

When, on the other hand, intact groups are used (as in quasi-experimental or nonexperimental research), they may differ to a greater or lesser extent on the covariate. The greater the differences, the larger the adjustment will be. Later, I illustrate and discuss the nature of adjustments in such designs. For the example under consideration, the means on the covariate, though not identical, are similar. Hence, the adjusted means will not differ much from the unadjusted ones. From Table 15.1, the means for the four groups on the covariate are

$$\overline{X}_A = 7.4 \quad \overline{X}_B = 7.0 \quad \overline{X}_C = 7.2 \quad \overline{X}_D = 6.9$$

The grand mean on X is therefore 7.125. From the ANCOVA output given earlier, $b_c = 1.013052$. Applying (15.3), the adjusted means for the four groups are

$$\overline{Y}_{A(adj)} = 15.8 - (1.013)(7.4 - 7.125) = 15.52$$

$$\overline{Y}_{B(adj)} = 17.9 - (1.013)(7.0 - 7.125) = 18.02$$

$$\overline{Y}_{C(adj)} = 19.1 - (1.013)(7.2 - 7.125) = 19.02$$

$$\overline{Y}_{D(adj)} = 17.4 - (1.013)(6.9 - 7.125) = 17.63$$

The adjusted means are closer to each other than are the unadjusted means. This is because the means on the dependent variable for groups whose covariate means are smaller than the covariate grand mean are adjusted upward, whereas those for groups whose covariate means are larger than the covariate grand mean are adjusted downward. The more the covariate mean for a given group deviates from the covariate grand mean, the larger the adjustment. As expected, the adjustments in the present example are minor, reflecting the fact that in experimental research ANCOVA's primary function is control, *not* adjustment.

The adjustments are, of course, predicated on the covariate having a meaningful correlation with the dependent variable, which is reflected in b_c used in (15.3). As I pointed out earlier, $b_c = 0$ when the covariate is not related to the dependent variable, and no adjustment occurs when (15.3) is applied. It has been shown (Cochran, 1957; Feldt, 1958) that the use of a covariate whose correlation with the dependent variable is less than .3 does not lead to an appreciable increase in the precision of the analysis.

Tests among Adjusted Means

I discussed the topic of multiple comparisons among means in Chapter 11. Instead of repeating that discussion, I will point out that in ANCOVA the same type of comparisons (i.e., a priori and post hoc) are applied to adjusted means. The F ratio for a comparison between two adjusted means, say, A and B is

$$F = \frac{[\overline{Y}_{A(adj)} - \overline{Y}_{B(adj)}]^2}{MSR\left[\dfrac{1}{n_A} + \dfrac{1}{n_B} + \dfrac{(\overline{X}_A - \overline{X}_B)^2}{ss_{res(X)}}\right]} \tag{15.4}$$

where $\overline{Y}_{A(adj)}$ and $\overline{Y}_{B(adj)}$ = adjusted means for treatments A and B respectively; MSR = mean square residual from the ANCOVA; n_A, n_B = number of subjects in groups A and B, respectively; and $ss_{res(X)}$ = residual sum of squares of the covariate (X) when it is regressed on the treatments—that is, when X is used as a dependent variable and the coded vectors for the treatments are used as the independent variable. The *df* for the F ratio of (15.4) are 1 and $N - k - 2$, where k is the number of coded vectors for treatments. The reason the denominator *df* are

$N - k - 2$, and not $N - k - 1$, as in earlier chapters, is that an additional *df* is lost because of the use of a covariate. Note that $N - k - 2$ are the *df* associated with the residual sum of squares of the ANCOVA. As always, $\sqrt{F} = t$, with *df* associated with the denominator of *F*, which in the present case are $N - k - 2$. I will note several things about (15.4).

1. As I stated above, when the covariate mean is the same for all treatments, no adjustment of means takes place. Under such circumstances, the numerator of (15.4) consists of un-adjusted means, and the last term in the denominator vanishes. As a result, (15.4) is reduced to the conventional formula for a test of the difference between two means, except that the *MSR* is the one obtained in ANCOVA. Given a covariate that is meaning-fully correlated with the dependent variable, *MSR* from ANCOVA is smaller than *MSR* obtained without the use of a covariate (earlier, I illustrated this for the numerical ex-ample under consideration). This, of course, is the reason for using ANCOVA in the first place.

2. When subjects are randomly assigned to treatments, the numerator of the last term of the denominator (i.e., $\overline{X}_A - \overline{X}_B$) will generally be small because the means for the treatment groups on the covariate will tend to be similar, though not necessarily equal, to each other.

3. When ANCOVA is used with intact groups (e.g., as in quasi-experimental research) and differences among group covariate means are relatively large, the last term of the denom-inator of (15.4) will lead to a larger error term. The larger the difference between $\overline{X}_A$ and $\overline{X}_B$, the larger the error term will be. This has serious implications for testing differences between adjusted means when intact groups are used.

4. Examination of the denominator of (15.4) will reveal that the error term changes depend-ing on the specific covariate means for the groups whose adjusted means are being com-pared. Finney (1946) has therefore suggested the use of a general error term, as indicated in the following formula

$$F = \frac{[\overline{Y}_{A(\text{adj})} - \overline{Y}_{B(\text{adj})}]^2}{MSR\left(\dfrac{1}{n_A} + \dfrac{1}{n_B}\right)\left[1 + \dfrac{ss_{\text{reg}(X)}}{kss_{\text{res}(X)}}\right]} \tag{15.5}$$

where $ss_{\text{reg}(X)}$ = regression sum of squares of the covariate, *X*, when it is regressed on the treatments; k = number of coded vectors for treatments or the degrees of freedom for treatments. All other terms are as defined for (15.4).

For illustrative purposes, I apply (15.4) to test the difference between the adjusted means of groups *A* and *B* of the numerical example under consideration. Earlier, I reported the following values:

$$\overline{Y}_{A(\text{adj})} = 15.52 \qquad \overline{Y}_{B(\text{adj})} = 18.02 \qquad \overline{X}_A = 7.4 \qquad \overline{X}_B = 7.0$$

$$n_A = 10 \qquad n_B = 10 \qquad MSR = 2.87636$$

In addition, it is necessary to calculate the residual sum of squares of the covariate when it is re-gressed on the treatments. In the present example, this means doing a multiple regression analy-sis in which *X* is used as the dependent variable and the coded vectors (*E*1, *E*2, and *E*3) are used to represent the independent variable. In the input file for the analysis of the data in Table 15.1 (see the preceding) I called for such an analysis, an excerpt from which follows.

Output

Equation Number 3	Dependent Variable..	X	
Block Number 1.	Method: Enter E1 E2	E3	

		Analysis of Variance			
Multiple R	.09531		DF	Sum of Squares	Mean Square
R Square	.00908				
Adjusted R Square	−.07349	Regression	3	1.47500	.49167
Standard Error	2.11411	Residual	36	160.90000	4.46944

$$F = .11001 \qquad \text{Signif } F = .9537$$

Commentary

For present purposes, it would have sufficed to report that the residual sum of squares is 160.9. I included the preceding excerpt because I wanted to use this opportunity to dispel a mistaken notion not uncommon in presentations or applications of ANCOVA, namely that it is useless, or not necessary, when the differences among the means of the covariate are statistically not significant. Following are but two examples of such statements. (1) "Because the vocabulary scores of the field-dependent and field-independent students were comparable . . . , an analysis of variance, rather than an analysis of covariance, was performed" (Frank, 1984, p. 673). (2) In a paper aimed at instructing readers in the use of ANCOVA, Lovell, Franzen, and Golden suggested that analysis be carried out on the covariate, and stated; "if the results of this analysis are not significant, there is no need to control for the covariate in subsequent analyses" (quoted in Frigon & Laurencelle, 1993, p. 2).

Following misguided advice such as the preceding would lead one to reject ANCOVA for the very purpose for which it was developed (i.e., for increased control in experiments; see my earlier discussion of this point). Clearly, when subjects are randomly assigned to treatments, as is required in an experiment, the means for the various treatment groups on the covariate are expected to be similar to each other. Therefore, it is highly likely that the differences among them would be statistically not significant. As you can see from the preceding excerpt, this is true of the example under consideration. Yet, as I showed earlier, it is only because of the inclusion of the covariate that the differences among the treatment means were found to be statistically significant. See the earlier section, where based on an analysis of variance of these data one would conclude that differences among the treatment means are statistically not significant.

Returning now to the main purpose of this section, I apply (15.4) to test the difference between the adjusted means of *A* and *B*.

$$F = \frac{[15.52 - 18.02]^2}{2.87636 \left[\dfrac{1}{10} + \dfrac{1}{10} + \dfrac{(7.4 - 7.0)^2}{160.9} \right]} = 10.81$$

with 1 and 35 *df,* and $p < .05$.

I could, similarly, test differences between other pairs of means. Or I could use (15.5), instead, to avoid the calculation of different error terms for each comparison.

Until now, I dealt only with pairwise comparisons of adjusted means. But, as in the case of designs when a covariate is not used (see Chapter 11), linear combinations of adjusted means may be tested in ANCOVA. The formula for the *F* ratio is similar to (11.15), except that *MSR* in the denominator is from the ANCOVA, and the denominator includes an additional term as in (15.5) (see also Kirk, 1982, p. 736).

The reason I only briefly described the *F* ratio for the test of linear combinations of adjusted means, and the reason I do not illustrate its application to the numerical example under consideration, is that later I present a more direct approach for doing multiple comparisons in ANCOVA. Before I do this it is necessary that I discuss briefly the relation between the intercepts of the separate regression equations and the adjusted means.

Intercepts and Adjusted Means

Recall that with one independent variable, *X,* the intercept, *a,* is calculated as follows:

$$a = \overline{Y} - b\overline{X} \tag{15.6}$$

Compare this formula with the one for the calculation of an adjusted mean in ANCOVA, (15.3), which I repeat with a new number

$$\overline{Y}_{j(\text{adj})} = \overline{Y}_j - b(\overline{X}_j - \overline{X}) \tag{15.7}$$

where b = common regression coefficient; $\overline{X}_j$ mean of the covariate for treatment j; and $\overline{X}$ = grand mean of the covariate. Note that the intercept for each treatment group can be expressed as the adjusted mean minus a constant: $b\overline{X}$. For the present example, $b = 1.013052$ and $\overline{X} = 7.125$. The constant, then, is $(1.013052)(7.125) = 7.22$. In the preceding I calculated the adjusted mean for $A = 15.52$. Earlier, I showed that the intercept of the regression equation for this treatment is 8.30. Therefore,

$$15.52 - 8.30 = 7.22$$

The same is true for the difference between each adjusted mean and its corresponding intercept.

From the foregoing it follows that testing the difference between intercepts is the same as testing the difference between their corresponding adjusted means. For the test between the adjusted means of treatments *A* and *B* given in the preceding,

$$15.52 - 18.03 = -2.51 = 8.30 - 10.81$$

where the last two values are, respectively, the intercepts for treatments *A* and *B*, which I calculated earlier.

Look back now at the method of obtaining separate intercepts from the overall regression equation and notice that it comprises two components: (1) a constant that is equal to the average of all the intercepts, this being *a* from the equation consisting of the covariate and the coded vectors for treatments, and (2) the deviation of each intercept from the average of the intercepts, this being the *b* associated with a coded vector in which a given group was identified. Thus, the intercepts for treatment *A* and *B* are

$$a_A = a + b_A$$

$$a_B = a + b_B$$

where a = intercept of an equation consisting of the covariate and the coded vectors for treatments. In the present example it is the equation for X and vectors $E1$, $E2$, and $E3$. b_A is the regression coefficient for the coded vector in which treatment A was identified (i.e., assigned 1), and b_B is treated similarly.

Note that subtracting a_B from a_A is tantamount to subtracting b_B from b_A (because a is constant in both a_A and a_B). For the numerical example under consideration,

$$a_A - a_B = 8.30 - 10.81 = -2.51$$

$$b_A - b_B = -2.028589 - .476631 = -2.51$$

The same is true for the difference between any two b's for coded vectors that represent treatments.

The foregoing can be viewed from yet another perspective. Recall that an effect is defined as the deviation of a treatment mean from the grand mean of the dependent variable. This is true whether the design does not include a covariate (as in Chapter 11) or includes a covariate (as in the present chapter). In the latter case, however, the effect is defined as the deviation of the adjusted mean from the grand mean of the dependent variable. Using the adjusted means I calculated earlier and the grand mean of Y (17.55), the effects of the four treatments are

$$T_A = 15.52 - 17.55 = -2.03$$

$$T_B = 18.02 - 17.55 = .47$$

$$T_C = 19.02 - 17.55 = 1.47$$

$$T_D = 17.63 - 17.55 = .08$$

Not surprisingly, the first three values are, within rounding, the same as the b's for the respective coded vectors in the regression equation in which the product vectors are *not* included. For convenience, I repeat this equation:

$$Y' = 10.332007 + 1.013052X - 2.028589E1 + .476631E2 + 1.474021E3$$

where $E1$, $E2$, and $E3$ are the effect coded vectors representing, respectively, treatments A, B, and C of Table 15.1. Clearly, the b's represent the treatment effects after adjusting for the covariate. As always, the effect of the treatment assigned -1's in all the vectors is equal to minus the sum of the b's.

This somewhat lengthy detour was designed to demonstrate the equivalence of testing differences among b's, among intercepts, or among adjusted means. Consequently, the approach of testing differences among effects via differences among b's is applicable also in ANCOVA. It is to this approach that I now turn.

Multiple Comparisons among Adjusted Means via *b*'s

In Chapter 6, I introduced the variance/covariance matrix of the b's (**C**) and showed how to use elements from it to test differences between b's. In Chapter 11, I showed how to augment **C** to obtain **C*** and how to use elements of the latter in tests of comparisons among b's associated with coded vectors that represent a categorical variable. I also showed that doing this is equivalent to testing multiple comparisons among means. One reason I introduced this approach in earlier chapters was in anticipation of its use in ANCOVA.[3] As will become evident from the following presentation, this approach is more direct than the ones I presented earlier, and it involves minimal calculations. This is particularly true when the design includes multiple covariates (see later in this chapter).

---

[3]In Chapter 14, I used elements of **C** to calculate Johnson-Neyman regions of significance.

Output

Var-Covar Matrix of Regression Coefficients (B)
Below Diagonal: Covariance   Above: Correlation

	X	E1	E2	E3
X	.01788	−.07892	.03596	−.02158
E1	−.00492	.21708	−.33492	−.33051
E2	.00223	−.07252	.21601	−.33382
E3	−.00134	−.07154	−.07208	.21583

Commentary

The preceding is the variance/covariance matrix of the b's (C) for the numerical example of Table 15.1, which I obtained from SPSS output for the second regression analysis (see the input file given earlier).[4] Note that C includes also the variance of b_X (the covariate) and the covariances of this b with the b's of the coded vectors. As my interest here is in C for the coded vectors only, I inserted the box around the relevant segment of the matrix. Also, as indicated in the legend and as I explained in Chapters 11 and 14, *SPSS reports a hybrid matrix in which covariances are below the diagonal and correlations are above the diagonal.* Recall that the diagonal is composed of variances. Accordingly, C is

	E1	E2	E3
E1	.21708	−.07252	−.07154
E2	−.07252	.21601	−.07208
E3	−.07154	−.07208	.21583

where $E1$, $E2$, and $E3$ refer to effect coded vectors in which treatments A, B, and C of Table 15.1 were identified (see also IF statements in the input file given earlier in this chapter). For example, .21708 is the variance (squared standard error) of b_{E1} in which treatment A was identified (i.e., assigned 1). The covariance of b_{E1} and b_{E2} is −.07252. Other elements of C are treated similarly.[5]

Not included in C reported in the preceding is the variance of b for the treatment that was assigned −1's in the three vectors (treatment D, in the present example) and the covariance of this b with the remaining three b's. As I explained in Chapter 11, this information is obtained by augmenting C to obtain C^*. Recalling that the sum of each row and column of C^* is equal to zero, the missing elements are readily obtained (if necessary, see Chapter 11 for an explanation). C^* for the example under consideration is therefore

---

[4]In Chapter 14 (see "Other Computer Programs"), I showed that C may also be obtained from the other statistical packages I use in this book (i.e., BMDP, MINITAB, and SAS).

[5]If you are having difficulties with the presentation in this section, I suggest that you review discussions of C in earlier chapters, particularly those in Chapter 11.

	E1	E2	E3	D
E1	.21708	−.07252	−.07154	−.07302
E2	−.07252	.21601	−.07208	−.07141
E3	−.07154	−.07208	.21583	−.07221
D	−.07302	−.07141	−.07221	.21664

where I used D to refer to the treatment assigned −1 in all the vectors, and I inserted the vertical and horizontal lines to separate the values associated with it as a reminder that they are *not* part of the output.

I repeat the relevant b's for the effect coded vectors in the equation that includes also the covariate (see my earlier presentation).

$$b_{E1} = -2.028589 \qquad b_{E2} = .476631 \qquad b_{E3} = 1.474021$$

It is necessary now to obtain a b for the treatment that was assigned −1 in the three coded vectors (i.e., treatment D). This b, which I will label b_D as a reminder that it is not part of the output, is obtained in the usual manner: adding the b's for the effect coded vectors and reversing the sign. Using the values reported in the preceding:

$$b_D = -[(-2.028589) + (.476631) + (1.474021)] = .077937$$

We are ready now to test multiple comparisons among the four b's. To this end, I repeat a version of a formula for the F ratio I used in earlier chapters—see, in particular, (11.18) and the discussion following it—with a new number:

$$F = \frac{[a_1(b_1) + a_2(b_2) + \ldots + a_j(b_j)]^2}{\mathbf{a'C^*a}} \tag{15.8}$$

where $a_1, a_2, \ldots, a_j$ are coefficients by which b's are multiplied (I use a's instead of c's so as not to confuse them with elements of $\mathbf{C^*}$, the augmented $\mathbf{C}$); $\mathbf{a'}$ and $\mathbf{a}$ are the row and column vectors, respectively, of the coefficients of the linear combination; and $\mathbf{C^*}$ is the augmented variance/covariance matrix of the b's. As some of the a's of a given linear combination may be 0's, thus excluding the b's associated with them from consideration, it is convenient to exclude such a's from the numerator and the denominator of (15.8). Accordingly, I will use only that part of $\mathbf{C^*}$ whose elements correspond to nonzero a's in the denominator of (15.8).

I illustrate now the application of (15.8) to the numerical example under consideration. Assume, first, a test of the difference between b_{E1} (−2.028589) and b_{E2} (.476631):

$$F = \frac{[(1)(-2.028589) + (-1)(.476631)]^2}{[1 \quad -1] \begin{bmatrix} .21708 & -.07252 \\ -.07252 & .21601 \end{bmatrix} \begin{bmatrix} 1 \\ -1 \end{bmatrix}} = \frac{6.276127}{.57813} = 10.85$$

with 1 and 35 *df.* I obtained the same F ratio (within rounding) when I applied (15.4) to test the difference between the adjusted means of treatments A and B. This, then, shows the equivalence of testing differences between adjusted means and testing differences between b's associated with coded vectors that identify the groups whose adjusted means are being used.

Following are a couple of examples of tests of linear combinations of b's. For each test, I took relevant values from $\mathbf{C^*}$ (reported earlier) for the denominator. Test the average of b_{E1} (−2.028589) and b_{E2} (.476631) against b_{E3} (1.474021):

$$F = \frac{[(1)(-2.028589) + (1)(.476631) + (-2)(1.474021)]^2}{[1 \quad 1 \quad -2]\begin{bmatrix} .21708 & -.07252 & -.07154 \\ -.07252 & .21601 & -.07208 \\ -.07154 & -.07208 & .21583 \end{bmatrix}\begin{bmatrix} 1 \\ 1 \\ -2 \end{bmatrix}} = \frac{20.25}{1.72585} = 11.73$$

with 1 and 35 *df*. This is the same as testing the average of the adjusted means for treatments *A* and *B* against the adjusted mean of treatment *C*.

Test the difference between the average of b_{E1} (−2.028589) and b_{E3} (1.474021) against the average of b_{E2} (.476631) and b_D (.077937).

$$F = \frac{[(1)(-2.028589) + (-1)(.476631) + (1)(1.474021) + (-1)(.077937)]^2}{[1 \quad -1 \quad 1 \quad -1]\begin{bmatrix} .21708 & -.07252 & -.07154 & -.07302 \\ -.07252 & .21601 & -.07208 & -.07141 \\ -.07154 & -.07208 & .21583 & -.07221 \\ -.07302 & -.07141 & -.07221 & .21664 \end{bmatrix}\begin{bmatrix} 1 \\ -1 \\ 1 \\ -1 \end{bmatrix}} = \frac{1.23210}{1.15932} = 1.16$$

with 1 and 35 *df*. This is the same as testing the difference between the average of the adjusted means of treatments *A* and *C* with that of the average of the adjusted means of treatments *B* and *D*.

As I explained in Chapter 11, these tests may be used for any type of comparison (planned orthogonal, planned nonorthogonal, or post hoc). For example, assuming the above are Scheffé comparisons, then to be declared statistically significant the obtained *F* ratio would have to exceed $kF_{\alpha; k, N-k-2}$. In the preceding expression, *k* is the number of coded vectors for treatments; $F_{\alpha; k, N-k-2}$ is the tabled *F* value at a prespecified α with *k* and $N - k - 2$ *df* (the denominator *df* equal those for the residual sum of squares of the ANCOVA). For further details of tests among *b*'s, see Chapter 11.

Tabular Summary of ANCOVA

In Table 15.2, I report the major results of the ANCOVA, thus providing a succinct summary of the procedures followed in the analysis. Part I of the table consists of the ANCOVA results. In Part II, I report the original and adjusted means of the dependent variable.

RECAPITULATION

ANCOVA was initially developed in the context of experimental research to increase the precision of statistical analyses by controlling for sources of systematic variations.

Subsequently, ANCOVA also came into frequent use (mostly misuse) in attempts to "equate" intact groups in quasi-experimental and nonexperimental research (see the discussion later in this chapter).

ANCOVA is a special case of the general analytic approach in designs with categorical and continuous variables. Following is an outline of the sequence of steps in ANCOVA with one covariate.

1. Create a vector, *Y*, that includes the scores on the dependent variable for all subjects.
2. Create a vector, *X*, that includes the scores on the covariate for all subjects.

Table 15.2   Summary of ANCOVA for Data in Table 15.1

I:

Source	Proportion of Variance	ss	df	ms	F
$R^2_{y.x}$	.48520	156.18514	1	156.18514	
Treatments (after adjustment)					
$R^2_{y.x123} - R^2_{y.x}$	.20206	65.04227	3	21.68076	7.54
Error					
$(1 - R^2_{y.x123})$	.31274	100.67259	35	2.87636	
Total	1.00000	321.90000			

II:

	Treatments			
	A	B	C	D
Original means:	15.80	17.90	19.10	17.40
Adjusted means:	15.52	18.02	19.02	17.63

NOTE: Y = dependent variable; X = covariate; 1, 2, 3 = effect coded vectors for treatments.

3. Create coded vectors to represent group membership.
4. Multiply X by each of the coded vectors.
5. Test whether the increment in the proportion of variance accounted for by the product vectors is statistically significant. If yes, it means that the *b*'s are *not* homogeneous. Proceed with the analysis as in Chapter 14. If no, go to 6.
6. Test whether the increments in the proportion of variance accounted for by the coded vectors, over and above the variance accounted for by the covariate, is statistically significant. If no, calculate a single regression equation in which only the covariate is used. If yes, it means that the intercepts are significantly different from each other. Equivalently, this means that there are statistically significant differences among the adjusted means. Go to 7.
7. When the categorical variable consists of more than two categories, it is necessary to do multiple comparisons among adjusted means. Probably the simplest approach for doing this is via tests of differences among the *b*'s for the coded vectors. To this end, use elements of the augmented variance/covariance matrix of the *b*'s, $\mathbf{C}^*$.

ANCOVA WITH MULTIPLE COVARIATES

In this section, I discuss and illustrate ANCOVA with multiple covariates. Although for convenience I use two covariates, the approach I present generalizes to any number of covariates. Also, although my discussion is couched in ANCOVA terminology, the same overall analytic approach is applicable when the continuous variables are not viewed as covariates. For example, in an ATI design with two or more attributes, the analytic approach is the same as in the present section, although the focus is different. Thus, whereas in ANCOVA the continuous variables are used for control purposes, in ATI designs they are used to ascertain their possible interactions with treatments. The test of differences among regression coefficients, for instance, serves different

Table 15.3   Illustrative Data for ANCOVA with Four Treatments and Two Covariates

						Treatments					
	A			B			C			D	
Y	X	Z	Y	X	Z	Y	X	Z	Y	X	Z
12	5	10	13	4	10	14	4	8	15	4	16
15	5	10	16	4	10	16	4	14	16	5	10
14	6	9	15	5	15	18	6	11	13	5	13
14	7	13	16	6	12	20	6	11	15	6	7
18	7	15	19	6	16	18	7	16	19	6	15
18	8	17	17	8	16	19	8	20	17	7	20
16	8	17	19	8	18	22	8	19	20	7	16
14	9	15	23	9	15	21	9	19	18	9	21
18	9	14	19	10	19	23	10	12	20	9	15
19	10	18	22	10	18	20	10	16	21	11	21
M: 15.8	7.4	13.8	17.9	7.0	14.9	19.1	7.2	14.6	17.4	6.9	15.4
s: 2.35	1.71	3.22	3.11	2.31	3.25	2.73	2.20	4.06	2.63	2.18	4.60

NOTE: *Y* is the dependent variable; *X* and *Z* are covariates. Data for *Y* and *X* are from Table 15.1.

purposes in the two designs. In ANCOVA it is used to test whether the regression coefficients are homogeneous, whereas in ATI it is used to test whether the attributes and the treatments interact. Recall, however, that when in ANCOVA the *b*'s are not homogeneous, the interpretation is the same as in an ATI design—that is, that the covariates interact with the treatments.

A Numerical Example

Illustrative data for four treatments with two covariates (or two attributes) are given in Table 15.3. I constructed this table by adding values for *Z* (the second covariate) to the data in Table 15.1. As the present analysis is an extension of the one I presented in preceding sections, my comments here will be generally brief, except when a point is particularly germane to ANCOVA with more than one covariate. Moreover, I will not comment on results that parallel those I gave for the example with one covariate. Instead, I will state the results and conclusions.

SPSS

Input

```
TITLE TABLE 15.3. ANCOVA WITH TWO COVARIATES.
DATA LIST/Y X T Z 1-8.
VALUE LABELS T 1 'A' 2 'B' 3 'C' 4 'D'.
COMPUTE E1=0.
COMPUTE E2=0.
COMPUTE E3=0.
IF (T EQ 1) E1=1.        [generate effect coded vectors]
IF (T EQ 4) E1=-1.
IF (T EQ 2) E2=1.
IF (T EQ 4) E2=-1.
IF (T EQ 3) E3=1.
```

IF (T EQ 4) E3=−1.
COMPUTE XE1=X*E1.
COMPUTE XE2=X*E2.
COMPUTE XE3=X*E3.
COMPUTE ZE1=Z*E1.
COMPUTE ZE2=Z*E2.
COMPUTE ZE3=Z*E3.
BEGIN DATA
12 5 110   *[first subject in A]*
  .   .   .   .
13 4 210   *[first subject in B]*
  .   .   .   .
14 4 3 8   *[first subject in C]*
  .   .   .   .
15 4 416   *[first subject in D]*
END DATA
LIST.
REGRESSION VAR=Y TO ZE3/DES/STAT=ALL/
   DEP=Y/ENTER X Z/ENTER E1 TO E3/ENTER XE1 TO ZE3.

Commentary

Except for the addition of *Z,* the layout in this file is identical to that of the input file for the analysis of Table 15.1 presented earlier in this chapter. Having added *Z,* I generated product vectors for both *X* and *Z.* For additional explanation of the input, see the commentary on the input file for the analysis of Table 15.1.

Output

Equation Number 1   Dependent Variable..   Y
Block Number 3.   Method: Enter   XE1   XE2   XE3   ZE1   ZE2   ZE3

Multiple R	.84175		
R Square	.70854	R Square Change	.01923
Adjusted R Square	.59404	F Change	.30787
Standard Error	1.83049	Signif F Change	.9275

Commentary

As in the previous analysis, the contribution of the product vectors has to be examined first, hence the preceding excerpt from the output from Block Number 3, when the product vectors entered. As you can see, the small proportion of variance incremented by the six product vectors (.01923) is statistically not significant ($F < 1$). Incidentally, the *df* for the numerator of this *F* ratio are 6 (six product vectors) and those for the denominator are 28 ($40 - 11 - 1$: *df* for residual, not reproduced here). Clearly, the regression coefficients are homogeneous. Therefore, it is appropriate to use common *b*'s for the two covariates.

Output

Equation Number 1   Dependent Variable..   Y
Block Number 2.   Method: Enter   E1   E2   E3

				Analysis of Variance			
Multiple R	.83025				DF	Sum of Squares	Mean Square
R Square	.68932	R Square Change	.18945	Regression	5	221.89064	44.37813
Adjusted R Square	.64363	F Change	6.91086	Residual	34	100.00936	2.94145
Standard Error	1.71507	Signif F Change	.0009				

$$F = 15.08715 \qquad \text{Signif } F = .0000$$

-- Variables in the Equation --

Variable	B	SE B	T	Sig T
X	.953547	.184350	5.172	.0000
Z	.048355	.101834	.475	.6379
E1	−1.969914	.487093		
E2	.458313	.471575		
E3	1.482111	.470108		
(Constant)	10.046366	1.167670		

Commentary

The proportion of variance incremented by the treatments, over and above the covariates, is .18945, $F(3, 34) = 6.91$, $p < .05$. Thus, statistically significant differences exist among the intercepts or, equivalently, among the adjusted means. Parenthetically, $F(5, 34) = 15.09$ is for the test of the proportion of variance accounted for by the covariates *and* the treatments (.68932).

    The common b's for X and Z are, respectively, .953547 and .048355. Note that b_Z is statistically not significant ($t < 1$). Accordingly, Z would be removed from the equation. Doing this would bring us back to my earlier analysis (i.e., for the data of Table 15.1). Because my sole purpose here is to illustrate an analysis with two covariates, *I will ignore the fact that b_Z is statistically not significant.*

Separate Regression Equations

Using the regression equation given in the preceding, I will calculate the intercepts of the regression equations for the four treatments. Subsequently, I will report the separate equations for the four treatments.

$$a_A = 10.046366 + (-1.969914) \qquad\qquad = 8.076452$$

$$a_B = 10.046366 + (.458313) \qquad\qquad = 10.504679$$

$$a_C = 10.046366 + (1.482111) \qquad\qquad = 11.528477$$

$$a_D = 10.046366 - [(-1.969914) + (.458313) + (1.482111)] = 10.075856$$

As I established that the differences among the regression coefficients are statistically not significant, but those among the intercepts are statistically significant, regression equations with common b's but separate a's are indicated. They are

$$Y'_A = 8.076452 + .953547X + .048355Z$$

$$Y'_B = 10.504679 + .953547X + .048355Z$$

$$Y'_C = 11.528477 + .953547X + .048355Z$$

$$Y'_D = 10.075856 + .953547X + .048355Z$$

Adjusted Means

To calculate adjusted means, it is necessary to have the treatment means on all the variables and the grand means of the covariates. These are reported in Table 15.4. Using relevant values from this table and the common b's, I calculate the adjusted means:

$$\overline{Y}_{A(\text{adj})} = 15.8 - .953547(7.4 - 7.125) - .048355(13.8 - 14.675) = 15.58$$

$$\overline{Y}_{B(\text{adj})} = 17.9 - .953547(7.0 - 7.125) - .048355(14.9 - 14.675) = 18.01$$

$$\overline{Y}_{C(\text{adj})} = 19.1 - .953547(7.2 - 7.125) - .048355(14.6 - 14.675) = 19.03$$

$$\overline{Y}_{D(\text{adj})} = 17.4 - .953547(6.9 - 7.125) - .048355(15.4 - 14.675) = 17.58$$

As I explained earlier in this chapter, the difference between any two adjusted means is equal to the difference between the two intercepts corresponding to them. Therefore, testing differences between intercepts is tantamount to testing differences between adjusted means corresponding to them. But I also showed that the b's for the coded vectors representing treatments indicate the treatment effects after having adjusted for the covariates. Therefore, tests among such b's are tantamount to tests among corresponding adjusted means. As in the earlier analysis, I test differences among adjusted means via tests of differences among b's.

Multiple Comparisons via *b*'s

Earlier, I reported the b's for the three coded vectors for the data of Table 15.3:

$$b_{E1} = -1.969914 \qquad b_{E2} = .458313 \qquad b_{E3} = 1.482111$$

As always, the b for the treatment assigned -1's is:

$$b_D = -[(-1.969914) + (.458313) + (1.482111)] = .029490$$

Table 15.4   Treatments and Grand Means (M) for the Data in Table 15.3

| | Treatments | | | | |
	A	B	C	D	M
$\overline{Y}$:	15.8	17.9	19.1	17.4	17.550
$\overline{X}$:	7.4	7.0	7.2	6.9	7.125
$\overline{Z}$:	13.8	14.9	14.6	15.4	14.675

Recall that to test linear combinations of b's we need the augmented $\mathbf{C}$ (the covariance matrix of the b's). Following is $\mathbf{C}^*$

	E1	E2	E3	D
E1	.23726	−.07893	−.07105	−.08728
E2	−.07893	.22238	−.07436	−.06909
E3	−.07105	−.07436	.22100	−.07559
D	−.08728	−.06909	−.07559	.23196

I got the matrix enclosed by the vertical and horizontal lines from SPSS. Recall that SPSS reports correlations above the diagonal and covariances below the diagonal. In the above matrix, I replaced correlations with covariances. I calculated the values for D in the manner I showed several times earlier (recall that the sum of each row and each column is equal to zero).

Assume that I want to test the difference between the adjusted means for treatments A and B. First, I show the following equivalences:

$$\overline{Y}_{A(\text{adj})} - \overline{Y}_{B(\text{adj})} = 15.58 - 18.01 = -2.43$$

$$a_A - a_B = 8.07645 - 10.504679 = -2.43$$

$$b_{E1} - b_{E2} = -1.969914 - .458313 = -2.43$$

Using relevant values from $\mathbf{C}^*$, the test of the difference between b_{E1} and b_{E2} is

$$F = \frac{[(1)(-1.969914) + (-1)(.458313)]^2}{[1 \quad -1]\begin{bmatrix} .23726 & -.07893 \\ -.07893 & .22238 \end{bmatrix}\begin{bmatrix} 1 \\ -1 \end{bmatrix}} = \frac{5.896286}{.61750} = 9.55$$

with 1 and 34 df, $p < .05$.

It is instructive to show now how the same test is done when the conventional approach to the calculations of ANCOVA is used (see, for example, Kirk, 1982, p. 740). The F ratio for the comparison between adjusted means A and B is

$$F = \frac{[(1)\overline{Y}_{A(\text{adj})} + (-1)\overline{Y}_{B(\text{adj})}]^2}{MSR\left[\dfrac{2}{n} + \dfrac{\Sigma z^2(\overline{X}_A - \overline{X}_B)^2 - 2\Sigma xz(\overline{X}_A - \overline{X}_B)(\overline{Z}_A - \overline{Z}_B) + \Sigma x^2(\overline{Z}_A - \overline{Z}_B)^2}{\Sigma x^2 \Sigma z^2 - (\Sigma xz)^2}\right]} \tag{15.9}$$

where MSR = mean square residual from ANCOVA; Σz^2 = sum of squares of Z *within* treatments or, equivalently, residual sum of squares when Z is regressed on the three coded vectors; Σx^2 = sum of squares of X *within* treatments; Σxz = sum of the products of X and Z *within* treatments; and n = number of subjects in either of the treatments. The remaining terms in (15.9) should be clear.

Following are the values necessary for the application of (15.9):

$$\overline{Y}_{A(\text{adj})} = 15.58 \qquad\qquad \overline{Y}_{B(\text{adj})} = 18.01$$

$$\overline{X}_A = 7.4 \qquad\qquad \overline{X}_B = 7.0$$

$$\overline{Z}_A = 13.8 \qquad\qquad \overline{Z}_B = 14.9$$

$$MSR = 2.94145 \qquad\qquad n = 10$$

$$\Sigma z^2 = 527.3 \qquad \Sigma xz = 198.0 \qquad \Sigma x^2 = 160.9$$

$$F = \frac{[(1)(15.58) + (-1)(18.01)]^2}{2.94145\left[\dfrac{2}{10} + \dfrac{527.3(7.4 - 7.0)^2 - 2(198)(7.4 - 7.0)(13.8 - 14.9) + 160.9(13.8 - 14.9)^2}{(527.3)(160.9) - (198)^2}\right]} = 9.56$$

Earlier, I obtained the same F ratio, within rounding, when I tested the difference between b_{E1} and b_{E2}. But notice the much greater computational labor involved in the conventional approach. Consider, further, that much of what I did above will have to be recalculated for each comparison. Also, the calculations will become even more tedious when linear combinations of adjusted means are tested. Finally, if you imagine what an extension of (15.9) would look like had there been three covariates, then the advantage of doing multiple comparisons via the b's should become evident.

Here is another example. This time, I contrast the average of adjusted means for treatments A and B with that of C. Using the b's and relevant values of $\mathbf{C}^*$ reported earlier:

$$ F = \frac{[(1)(-1.969914) + (1)(.458313) + (-2)(1.482111)]^2}{[1 \quad 1 \quad -2] \begin{bmatrix} .23726 & -.07893 & -.07105 \\ -.07893 & .22238 & -.07436 \\ -.07105 & -.07436 & .22100 \end{bmatrix} \begin{bmatrix} 1 \\ 1 \\ -2 \end{bmatrix}} = 11.33 $$

with 1 and 34, $p < .05$.

You may wish to apply (15.9) to this comparison to convince yourself that the same F ratio is obtained through more complex calculations. If you do this, and assuming you use the coefficients 1, 1, and -2 for the comparison, then replace 2/10 in the denominator of (15.9) with 6/10—that is, $[(1)^2 + (1)^2 + (-2)^2]/10$.

In sum, to test any linear combination of adjusted means, test the linear combination of the b's for the coded vectors corresponding to the adjusted means in question. Tests of linear combinations of b's may be used for any type of multiple comparisons: planned orthogonal, planned nonorthogonal, or post hoc. My general discussion of this topic in Chapter 9 also applies to the present situation.

OTHER COMPUTER PROGRAMS

From the preceding sections it is clear, I hope, that any multiple regression program can be used to do ANCOVA. If you are running any of the other packages I am using in this book (i.e., BMDP, MINITAB, SAS), I trust that by now you are able to use their regression procedure(s) to replicate my analyses in the preceding sections. Study your output in conjunction with my commentaries on the SPSS output.

I assume that you are aware that the packages I am using have either special programs for ANCOVA (e.g., BMDP 1V) or enable one to do ANCOVA in procedures other than regression analysis (e.g., GLM of MINITAB, GLM of SAS, MANOVA of SPSS). I do not show how to use such procedures for ANCOVA as I believe they are susceptible to misapplications and misinterpretations. This is due, among other things, to unique labeling and options whose function may not be clear. In a review of popular statistical packages (including those just mentioned), Searle and Hudson (1982) concluded, "Computer output for the analysis of covariance is not all that it is made out to be by its labeling. Values with labels that appear to be the same can be quite different because they do in fact represent different calculations" (p. 744). Not much has changed since this observation was made.

As I showed in preceding sections, when ANCOVA is done through regression analysis the user can control the nature of the analysis and the resulting output. This is not to say that misinterpretations and misapplications cannot occur (unfortunately they do, as I show later in this chapter). There is no better safeguard against misuses of methods than knowledge and clear thinking.

Factorial ANCOVA

The examples I presented thus far concerned a single-factor ANCOVA with one or two covariates. ANCOVA is not limited to such designs. For instance, ANCOVA with one or multiple covariates may be part of a factorial design. The analytic approach in factorial ANCOVA is a direct extension of the approaches I presented in Chapter 12 and in the present one. Thus, the categorical variables of the factorial design are coded in the same manner as I showed in Chapter 12, that is, as if there were no covariates. The dependent variable is then regressed on the coded vectors (for main effects and interaction) and on the covariate(s).

As in the case of single-factor ANCOVA, it is necessary to test whether or not the regression coefficients are homogeneous. In a factorial design, homogeneity of regression coefficients refers to the regression of the dependent variable on the covariate(s) within the cells of the design. Analogous to a single-factor design, multiply the coded vectors (for main effects and the interaction) by the covariate(s). Test whether these product vectors add significantly to the proportion of variance accounted for, over and above that accounted for by the covariate(s), the main effects, and the interaction. A statistically nonsignificant F ratio indicates that it is valid to use a common b.

For a discussion of factorial ANCOVA and numerical examples, see Winer (1971, pp. 781–792). Winer uses the conventional ANCOVA approach to the analysis. You will benefit from analyzing his numerical example in the manner outlined here and comparing your results with those he reports.

ANCOVA FOR ADJUSTMENT

Until now, I dealt with the use of ANCOVA for control. Other uses, nay abuses, of ANCOVA abound in the social sciences. They all share a common goal, namely, an attempt to equate groups that are essentially nonequivalent, or to adjust for differences among preexisting groups on a covariate(s). Following are some broad areas in which ANCOVA is thus used.

One, when one or more manipulated variables are used with nonequivalent groups, ANCOVA is resorted to in an attempt to equate the groups, or to adjust for differences among them on relevant variables. Such designs, often referred to as quasi-experimental designs (Campbell & Stanley, 1963; Cook & Campbell, 1979; Pedhazur & Schmelkin, 1991, Chapter 13), are frequently encountered in social intervention programs. Some examples that come readily to mind are programs in compensatory education (e.g., Head Start), drug rehabilitation, birth control, and health care. A common characteristic of such programs is that most often subjects are *not* assigned to them randomly. On the contrary, it is those who are deemed most in need or most deserving that are assigned to such programs. Sometimes, a process of self-assignment, or self-selection, takes place, as when a program is made available to people who wish to participate in it. In either case, an attempt is made to assess the effectiveness of the program by comparing the group that received it with one that did not receive it. ANCOVA is used in an attempt to equate the groups on one or more relevant variables on which they may differ.

Two, in nonexperimental research, ANCOVA is often used to compare the performance of two or more groups on a given variable while controlling for one or more relevant variables. For example, when comparing academic achievement of subjects from different ethnic or religious groups, researchers use ANCOVA to control for relevant variables such as intelligence, motivation, or socioeconomic status. Or, when comparing the reading achievement of males and females, ANCOVA is used in an attempt to equate the groups on, say, motivation or study time.

Three, sometimes one wants to compare regression equations obtained in intact groups while controlling for relevant variables. For example, one may wish to compare the regression of achievement on locus of control among males and females while controlling for motivation. In such situations, too, the researcher will resort to a variant of ANCOVA

The preceding illustrations should give you an idea of the pervasiveness of ANCOVA in the social sciences. Unfortunately, applications of ANCOVA in quasi-experimental and nonexperimental research are by and large not valid. Before elaborating on problems and difficulties attendant with the use of ANCOVA in such settings, I present a numerical example.

A Numerical Example

For comparison with the first analysis in the preceding sections, I will use a numerical example of a quasi-experimental design with four treatments and a covariate. Recall that the absence of randomization is what distinguishes this design from an experiment. Alternatively, you can think of the data as having been obtained in nonexperimental research. Illustrative data for this example are given in Table 15.5. I generated the data by transforming the variables of Table 15.1. In all instances, the transformation consisted of the addition of a constant. For the specifics of the transformations, see the note that accompanies Table 15.5 or the IF statements I used in the input file to do the transformations.

SPSS

Input

```
TITLE TABLE 15.5. ANCOVA. QUASI-EXPERIMENTAL.
DATA LIST/Y X T 1-6.
VALUE LABELS T 1 'A' 2 'B' 3 'C' 4 'D'.
COMPUTE E1=0.
COMPUTE E2=0.
COMPUTE E3=0.
IF (T EQ 1) E1=1.        [generate effect coded vectors]
IF (T EQ 4) E1=−1.
IF (T EQ 2) E2=1.
IF (T EQ 4) E2=−1.
IF (T EQ 3) E3=1.
IF (T EQ 4) E3=−1.
IF (T EQ 1) Y=Y+2.       [this and the remaining IF statements are
IF (T EQ 1) X=X+1.       used for the transformations; see the text and
IF (T EQ 2) Y=Y+1.       Table 15.5]
IF (T EQ 2) X=X+2.
IF (T EQ 3) Y=Y+1.
IF (T EQ 3) X=X+3.
IF (T EQ 4) Y=Y+4.
IF (T EQ 4) X=X+4.
```

```
COMPUTE XE1=X*E1.
COMPUTE XE2=X*E2.
COMPUTE XE3=X*E3.
BEGIN DATA
12 5 1                      [first subject in A]
 . . .
13 4 2                      [first subject in B]
 . . .
14 4 3                      [first subject in C]
 . . .
15 4 4                      [first subject in D]
 . . .
END DATA
LIST.
REGRESSION VAR=Y TO XE3/DES/STAT=ALL/
  DEP=Y/ENTER E1 TO E3/
  DEP=X/ENTER E1 TO E3/
  DEP=Y/ENTER X/ENTER E1 TO E3/ENTER XE1 TO XE3.
PLOT HSIZE=40/VSIZE=20/PLOT=Y WITH X BY T.
```

Commentary

Except for some minor modification, this input file is the same as the one I used to analyze the data in Table 15.1, given earlier in this chapter. *Note that the data, too, are from Table 15.1.* I

Table 15.5   Illustrative Data for ANCOVA in a Quasi-Experiment

					Treatments				
	A		B		C		D		
	Y	X	Y	X	Y	X	Y	X
	14	6	14	6	15	7	19	8
	17	6	17	6	17	7	20	9
	16	7	16	7	19	9	17	9
	16	8	17	8	21	9	19	10
	20	8	20	8	19	10	23	10
	20	9	18	10	20	11	21	11
	18	9	20	10	23	11	24	11
	16	10	24	11	22	12	22	13
	20	10	20	12	24	13	24	13
	21	11	23	12	21	13	25	15
M:	17.8	8.4	18.9	9.0	20.1	10.2	21.4	10.9
s:	2.35	1.71	3.11	2.31	2.73	2.20	2.63	2.18

NOTE: As I explained in the text, I generated the data for this table by transforming (adding constants) the variables in Table 15.1. Following is a listing of the transformations by the treatment groups.

$$A: Y = Y + 2; X = X + 1. \quad B: Y = Y + 1; X = X + 2$$
$$C: Y = Y + 1; X = X + 3. \quad D: Y = Y + 4; X = X + 4$$

See also, IF statements in SPSS input file.

made the following modifications: (1) I added IF statements to transform the variables of Table 15.1, so as to generate the data for Table 15.5; (2) I reordered the regression analyses I called for (see the commentaries on the output); and (3) I added a PLOT procedure in which I call for plotting Y with X by the treatments (T).

Output

Equation Number 1	Dependent Variable..	Y	
Block Number 1.	Method: Enter	E1	E2	E3

		Analysis of Variance		
Multiple R	.46193			
R Square	.21338		DF	Sum of Squares	Mean Square
Adjusted R Square	.14782	Regression	3	72.10000	24.03333
Standard Error	2.71723	Residual	36	265.80000	7.38333

$F = 3.25508$ Signif $F = .0327$

Equation Number 2	Dependent Variable..	X	
Block Number 1.	Method: Enter	E1	E2	E3

		Analysis of Variance		
Multiple R	.43929			
R Square	.19298		DF	Sum of Squares	Mean Square
Adjusted R Square	.12573	Regression	3	38.47500	12.82500
Standard Error	2.11411	Residual	36	160.90000	4.46944

$F = 2.86948$ Signif $F = .0498$

Commentary

The preceding are excerpts from two analyses: (1) the regression of Y on the coded vectors and (2) the regression of X on the coded vectors. As you can see, the differences among the Y means (see Table 15.5) are statistically significant. Thus, had I carried out the first analysis only, I would have concluded that there are statistically significant difference among the effects of the four treatments.

The second regression analysis shows that there are also statistically significant differences among the covariate means. From output not reproduced here, the total correlation[6] between X and Y is high (.829). Keep in mind that I generated this example to illustrate the adjustment of means when the correlation between the covariate and the dependent variable is high and differences among the covariate means are relatively large. Based on the preceding results it is clear that, as a consequence of controlling for the covariate, differences among the Y adjusted means will be markedly smaller than those among the unadjusted means. It is to show what the results would be if data were analyzed without the covariate, and to draw attention to the mean differences on the covariate, that I ran the preceding analyses first. I turn now to ANCOVA output.

---

[6]The total correlation is one calculated across the four groups. That is, as if all subjects belonged to one group. I discuss total, between, and within correlations in the next chapter.

Table 15.6   Unadjusted and Adjusted Means for the Data in Table 15.5

| | Treatments | | | | |
	A	B	C	D	M
$\bar{Y}$:	17.80	18.90	20.10	21.40	19.550
$\bar{Y}_{adj}$:	19.04	19.53	19.52	20.11	19.550
$\bar{X}$:	8.40	9.00	10.20	10.90	9.625

NOTE: M = grand mean.

Output

Summary table

Step	Variable	Rsq	RsqCh	FCh	SigCh
1	In: X	.6877	.6877	83.695	.000
2	In: E3				
3	In: E2				
4	In: E1	.7021	.0143	.561	.645
5	In: XE2				
6	In: XE3				
7	In: XE1	.7050	.0030	.108	.955

Commentary

This excerpt of the summary table shows that the increment in the proportion of variance due to the product vectors (RsqCh = .003) is neither meaningful nor statistically significant, $F(3, 32) = .108$. Accordingly, I conclude that the b's are homogeneous.

   Turning to the second block, the increment due to the coded vectors, over and above the covariate, is negligible and statistically not significant, $F(3, 35) = .561$. When I entered the coded vectors only (see the preceding), they accounted for .21 of the variance, $F(3, 36) = 3.26$, and $p < .05$. By contrast, after taking the covariate into account, the differences among the treatment means are statistically not significant.

   The common b (I took it from the equation in which I entered X and E1 to E3, which I did not reproduce here) is 1.013052. Using this b and the means reported in Table 15.5, calculate adjusted means using (15.3). So that you may verify your calculations, I report the results in Table 15.6, along with the unadjusted means. Examine the unadjusted and the adjusted means and notice how much closer to each other the latter are than the former. This, of course, is what the adjustment is meant to accomplish. As I pointed out earlier, treatment means below the grand mean are adjusted upward, and those above the grand mean are adjusted downward.

Output

Block Number 1.   Method: Enter   X

Multiple R	.82930	Analysis of Variance			
R Square	.68774		DF	Sum of Squares	Mean Square
Adjusted R Square	.67953	Regression	1	232.38903	232.38903
Standard Error	1.66631	Residual	38	105.51097	2.77660

F =   83.69540   Signif F =   .0000

```
---------------------- Variables in the Equation ----------------------
Variable            B          SE B         T       Sig T

X                1.079624     .118011     9.149     .0000
(Constant)       9.158621    1.166010
```

Commentary

Having established that the differences among the intercepts (or, equivalently, the adjusted means) are statistically not significant, I conclude that a single regression equation fits the data of the four treatments. In other words, I treat all subjects as if they belonged to a single group. This is clearly seen from the following plot, where subjects are identified by the letter of the treatment to which they were exposed.

Output

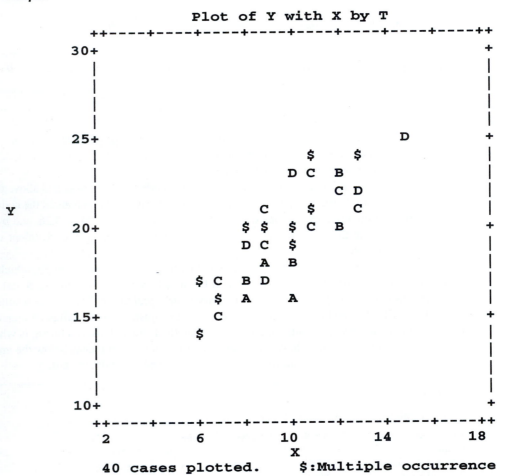

Plot of Y with X by T

40 cases plotted. $:Multiple occurrence

Commentary

On the surface, the preceding analysis appears straightforward, and may even have a certain allure. Perhaps this is why it is so frequently abused. Therefore, it is important to scrutinize the untenable assumptions on which it is based.

INTERPRETATIONAL PROBLEMS IN ANCOVA

Earlier I distinguished between the use of ANCOVA in experimental versus quasi-experimental and nonexperimental research. Recall that the use of ANCOVA in experimental research is aimed at identifying and removing extraneous variance, thereby increasing the precision of the analysis. In addition to the usual assumptions of ANCOVA (see Cochran, 1957; Elashoff, 1969; Reichardt, 1979), it is imperative that the treatments not affect the covariate, directly or indirectly; otherwise, adjustment for the covariate will result in removing not only extraneous variance but also variance due to the treatments.[7] The simplest way to ensure that this will not occur is to measure the covariate prior to the inception of the experiment. Following sound principles of research design, ANCOVA may serve a very useful purpose of control in experimental research.

The situation is radically different (some say hopeless) when ANCOVA is used in quasi-experimental or nonexperimental research to try to equate intact groups. The logical and statistical problems that arise in such situations are so serious that some authors argued that ANCOVA should not be used in them at all. Thus, Wolins (1982), who offers a penetrating discussion of the "absurd assumptions" (p. 13) that must be met when applying ANCOVA with intact groups, stated, "I have never seen it used appropriately for adjusting for group differences and I cannot imagine a social science investigation in which covariance could be legitimately applied for that purpose" (pp. 18–19). Anderson (1963) has, perhaps, best expressed the logical problem, saying, "One may well wonder what exactly it means to ask what the data would look like if they were not what they are" (p. 170).

Lord (1969), who argued cogently against the use of ANCOVA for adjustment when comparing intact groups, gave the following illuminating example. Suppose that a researcher is studying yields of black and white varieties of corn. Suppose, further, that the two are treated equally for several months, after which it is found that the white variety yielded much more grain than the black variety. But, as Lord pointed out, the average height of black plants at flowering time is 6 feet, whereas that of white plants is 7 feet. In this hypothetical situation, a researcher who uses ANCOVA to adjust for differences in the height of the plants is in effect asking the following question: "Would the black variety produce as much salable grain if conditions were adjusted so that it averaged 7 feet at flowering time?" (Lord, 1969, p. 336). Lord stated:

> I think it is quite clear that analysis of covariance is not going to provide us with a good answer to this question. In practice, the answer depends on what we do to secure black-variety plants averaging 7 feet in height. This could be done by destroying the shorter plants, by applying more fertilizer, or by stretching the plants at night while they are young, or by other means. *The answer depends on the means used.* (pp. 336–337)

---

[7]As I discuss later (see "Potential Errors and Misuses"), one of the most troubling and intractable problems in applying ANCOVA for adjustment is the likelihood of the variable(s) under study affecting, or being correlated with, the covariate(s).

The foregoing will serve as a broad frame of reference for viewing problems of using ANCOVA with intact groups. What follows is a brief, and hardly exhaustive, discussion of some specific problems regarding the use of ANCOVA in such situations.[8]

Specification Errors

Many problems attendant with attempts to equate nonequivalent groups through ANCOVA may be subsumed under the heading of specification errors. Recall that such errors refer to misspecified models.[9] In Chapter 10, I showed how specification errors lead to biased parameter estimates. In the present context, specification errors would result in, among other things, a biased estimate of the common regression coefficient for the covariate and, consequently, in an overadjustment or an underadjustment of treatment means. In either case, conclusions about differential effects of treatments, or differences between treatment and so-called control groups, would be erroneous.

The potential for specification errors in the application of ANCOVA with intact groups is so great that it is a virtual certainty in most instances. As one example, consider errors due to the omission of relevant variables. Recall that specification errors are committed whenever a variable in the equation (a covariate, in the present case) is correlated with variables that are not included in the equation and that are related to the dependent variable. It is not necessary to engage in great feats of imagination to realize that when one tries to equate intact groups on a given variable, they may differ on many other relevant variables. Indeed, as Meehl (1970) argued convincingly, the very act of equating groups on a variable may result in accentuating their differences on other variables. Attributing, under such circumstances, the so-called adjusted differences to treatments or to group membership (e.g., male-female) is erroneous and may often lead to strange conclusions.

Reichardt (1979) gave a very good example of the potential of arriving at wrong conclusions because some of the variables on which groups differ were left uncontrolled in an ANCOVA design. He described a situation in which a researcher was interested in assessing the effectiveness of driver education classes in promoting safe driving. In the absence of an experimental design, which would include random assignment to driver education and a control group, the researcher was faced with myriad variables that would have to be "controlled" for.

> Perhaps those who take a course in driver education are more motivated to be safe drivers, or are more fearful of accidents, or are more law-abiding and so feel more compelled to learn all the proper procedures, or are more interested in lowering their insurance costs (if completing the course provides a discount), than those who do not attend such classes. (Reichardt, 1979, p. 174)

Failure to control such variables may result in attributing observed differences in traffic violations between the groups to the fact that one of them was exposed to driver education, even when, in reality, the course may be useless. Even if it were possible to control for all the variables noted (not an easy task, to say the least), it is necessary to recognize that others may have been overlooked. As Reichardt pointed out, "Perhaps those who attend the course do so because they are unskilled at such tasks and realize that they need help. Or perhaps those who attend will

---

[8]Excellent discussions of ANCOVA will be found in Cochran (1957); Cronbach, Rogosa, Floden, and Price (1977); Elashoff (1969); Weisberg (1985); and Wolins (1982).

[9]Weisberg's (1985) discussion of ANCOVA is presented from this perspective.

end up driving more frequently than those who do not attend" (p. 175). In either case, it may turn out that the frequency of traffic violations or accidents is greater among those who have attended driver education courses. Failure to control for initial differences among the groups would, under such circumstances, lead to the conclusion that driver education courses are harmful!

Although this was a fictitious, but realistic, example, similar situations in which social intervention programs were alleged to be harmful have been noted. For extensive discussions of conditions that may lead to the conclusion that compensatory education is harmful, see Campbell and Boruch (1975), and Campbell and Erlebacher (1970); see also "Measurement Errors," later in this chapter.

Extrapolation Errors

When there are considerable differences on the covariate between, say, two groups so that there is little or no overlap between their distributions, the process of arriving at adjusted means involves two extrapolations. The regression line for the group that is lower on the covariate is extrapolated upward, whereas the regression line for the group higher on the covariate is extrapolated downward.[10] Smith's (1957) suggestion that it would be more appropriate to speak of "fictitious means" (p. 291) instead of corrected means in ANCOVA is particularly pertinent in situations of the kind I described here.

Differential Growth

Social scientists are frequently interested in assessing the effectiveness of a treatment in accelerating the growth of individuals on some dependent variable. In the absence of randomization, researchers attempt to adjust for pretreatment differences among nonequivalent groups. Although several methods of adjustment have been proposed, the one most commonly used is ANCOVA in which posttest measures of the dependent variable are adjusted for initial group differences on a pretest measure of the same variable. Recognize that when thus used one is assuming that the rate of growth of individuals in the nonequivalent groups is the same. When this assumption is not tenable, it is possible that observed differences among groups after adjusting for a pretest are due, in part or wholly, to differential growth of the groups rather than to the treatments. Bryk and Weisberg (1976, 1977) discussed this topic in detail and showed the type of growth patterns for which ANCOVA is appropriate and those for which it leads to overadjustment or underadjustment. In addition, they examined other proposed methods of adjustment for initial differences on a pretest, and offered an alternative approach for growth models. For additional discussions of this topic, see Bryk, Strenio, and Weisberg (1980); Campbell and Boruch (1975); Campbell and Erlebacher (1970); Kenny (1975; 1979, Chapter 11); Rogosa, Brandt, and Zimowski (1982).

Nonlinearity

Application of ANCOVA is most often based on the assumption that the regression of the dependent variable on the covariate is linear. In fact, I made this assumption implicitly in this chapter as I wanted to concentrate on the rationale of ANCOVA in the context of a relatively simple

---

[10]I discussed extrapolation errors in Chapter 13.

model. ANCOVA is, however, not limited to linear regression. Moreover, linearity should not be assumed. Methods of curvilinear regression analysis, which I presented in Chapters 13 and 14, are applicable also in ANCOVA designs. To repeat: do not assume that the regression is linear; study its shape, thereby avoiding erroneous assumptions and inappropriate analyses.

Measurement Errors

I discussed effects of errors in measuring the independent variables on regression statistics in earlier chapters. In Chapter 2, I showed that random measurement errors in the independent variable lead to an underestimation of the regression coefficient. It follows, therefore, that the consequence of using a fallible covariate in ANCOVA is an underadjustment for initial differences among groups. This may have far-reaching implications for conclusions about treatment effects. If, for example, the group given the treatment is lower on the covariate (this often happens in social intervention programs) than the control group, the underadjustment may even lead to the conclusion that not only was the treatment not beneficial but that it was actually harmful![11]

In Chapter 7, I showed that when the control variable is not perfectly reliable, the partial correlation is biased and may even differ in sign as compared with a partial correlation when the control variable is measured without error. In ANCOVA, the control variable is the covariate, and a partial regression coefficient is calculated instead. But the effects of measurement errors in the covariate are similar to those I indicated for the partial correlation.

In Chapter 10, I discussed problems of measurement errors with multiple independent variables, and noted that, unlike designs with one independent variable, measurement errors may result in either overestimation or underestimation of regression coefficients. The same bias would, of course, occur when the fallible variables are covariates.

As I noted in earlier chapters, all the foregoing considerations referred to random errors of measurement. Effects of other types of errors are more complicated, and little is known about them. But even if one were to consider the effects of random errors only, it is clear that they may lead to serious misinterpretations in ANCOVA. What, then, is the remedy? Unfortunately, there is no consensus among social scientists about the appropriate corrective measures in ANCOVA with fallible covariates. I cannot discuss here the different proposed solutions to deal with fallible covariates without going into complex issues regarding measurement models. My purpose was only to alert you to the problem in the hope that you will reach the obvious conclusions that (1) efforts should be directed to construct measures of the covariates that have very high reliabilities and (2) ignoring the problem, as is unfortunately done in most applications of ANCOVA, will not make it disappear. Detailed discussions of the effects of fallible covariates, and proposals for corrective measures, will be found in the following sources and in references therein: Campbell and Boruch (1975), Campbell and Erlebacher (1970), Cohen and Cohen (1983), Huitema (1980), Reichardt (1979), Weisberg (1985), and Wolins (1982).

In concluding this section I will note that the crux of the problems in the use and interpretation of ANCOVA with intact groups is that the researcher has no systematic control over the assignment of subjects to groups. Even when the assignment is not random but under the systematic control of the researcher, ANCOVA will lead to unbiased estimation of parameters. A case in point is a design in which the researcher assigns subjects to groups based on their status

---

[11]For very good discussions of this point, and numerical illustrations, see Campbell and Boruch (1975) and Campbell and Erlebacher (1970).

on the covariate. In certain studies it may be useful, for example, to assign subjects below a cut-off score on the covariate to a treatment and those above the cutoff score to another treatment or to a control group. Under such circumstances, the use of ANCOVA will lead to unbiased estimation of parameters. Incidentally, in such a design one should not correct for unreliability of the covariate. For further discussion of this topic, see Cain (1975), Overall and Woodward (1977a, 1977b), and Rubin (1977). See also discussions of Regression-Discontinuity Designs in Campbell and Stanley (1963); Cappelleri, Trochim, Stanley, and Reichardt (1991); Cook and Campbell (1979); Trochim (1984); Trochim, Cappelleri, and Reichardt (1991).

To repeat, then, problems in ANCOVA for adjustment stem from the use of preexisting groups about whose formation one has no control. It is the inherent inequality of preexisting groups, and the inherent impossibility of enumerating all the pertinent variables on which they differ, not to mention the task of controlling for them, that led some methodologists to conclude that attempts to equate such groups are doomed to fail. Lord (1967), for example, stated, "With the data usually available for such studies, there simply is no logical or statistical procedure that can be counted on to make the proper allowances for uncontrolled preexisting differences between groups" (p. 305). Similarly, Cochran and Rubin (1973) stated, "If randomization is absent, it is virtually impossible in many practical circumstances to be convinced that the estimates of the effects of treatments are in fact unbiased" (p. 417).

Although other methodologists may take a less pessimistic view of the use of ANCOVA with non-equivalent groups, all seem agreed that it is a "delicate instrument" (Elashoff, 1969) and "no miracle worker that can produce interpretable results from quasi-experimental designs" (Games, 1976, p. 54).

When Cronbach and Furby (1970) observed that the use of ANCOVA in studies in which assignment to groups was nonrandom "is now in bad repute" (p. 78), they seem to have been speaking of methodologists. Unfortunately, researchers seem to apply ANCOVA routinely, atheoretically, almost blindly. "Such blind applications of ANCOVA can result in substantial model misspecification and in considerably worse inferences than no adjustment whatsoever" (Bryk & Weisberg, 1977, p. 959).

One final note: In the foregoing discussion I dealt exclusively with the use of ANCOVA in quasi-experimental and nonexperimental research not because it is the only method used, or recommended for use, in such settings, but because it appears to be the one most commonly used.[12] Moreover, my discussion was not intended to convey the idea that research other than experimental holds no promise for the social sciences and should therefore be avoided. On the contrary, there are many good reasons for choosing to study certain phenomena in quasi-experimental or nonexperimental settings. Because of ethical considerations, economic or societal constraints, this type of research may be the only feasible one in various areas. But the conduct of such research, indeed all scientific research, requires sound theoretical thinking, constant vigilance, and a thorough understanding of the potential and limitations of the methods used.

Given the state of current methodology in the social sciences, the full potential of such studies will not be realized until more appropriate methods, suited to deal with the unique problems they pose, are developed.

> Attempting to develop such designs ought to be a top priority of evaluation methodologists. Until we have tried to develop alternatives based not on "approximations" to randomization, we should be cautious in discounting the value of uncontrolled studies. While statistical adjustments are certainly problematic, the potential contribution of uncontrolled studies has not really been tested. (Weisberg, 1979, p. 1163)

---

[12]For other approaches, see Cook and Campbell (1975), Kenny (1975, 1979, Chapter 11), and Rubin (1974).

POTENTIAL ERRORS AND MISUSES: SOME CAVEATS

Because of its somewhat greater complexity, the analytic approach I presented in this and the preceding chapter is frequently misapplied. In the hope of helping you avoid egregious errors in your work and alerting you to the need for extra vigilance when reading research reports in which this type of analysis was used, I make some general comments about errors and misapplications and then give some examples from the literature.

Earlier, I pointed out that a major problem in the application of ANCOVA for adjustment is the likelihood of the variable(s) under study affecting the covariate(s). Under such circumstances, adjustment through ANCOVA may amount to removing some or all the effect of the variable(s) under study. Unfortunately, such errors are committed, wittingly or unwittingly, with high frequency. Lieberson (1988) gave an example of an invidious use of such adjustments by an agency of the South African government in its attempt to demonstrate that the "huge gap" (p. 383) between Black and White income

> is due to nondiscriminatory factors. Controlling for racial differences in age (an approximation of experience), hours worked, education, and occupational status, it was found that about 70% of the black-white differential could be explained as not due to discrimination but to 'factors relating to productivity' (Department of Foreign Affairs, 1985, p. 481). But that is not all, they proceed to take into account the fact that quality of black education is lower because of the standards existing for different teachers, differences in student-teacher ratio, and gaps in the per capita money spent on students. By the time they get through it turns out that 91.5% of the gap (±4.5) is not discriminatory. (pp. 383–384)

Most other errors and misapplications of ANCOVA stem from the failure to recognize that a hierarchical analysis is required, and that the kind of action taken at a given step depends on conclusions reached in the step preceding it. Related to this is a lack of understanding of the properties of terms in regression equations obtained in a hierarchical analysis and their tests of significance, as is exemplified by what is probably the most common error, namely, testing all the b's in the overall regression equation.[13] Recalling that the test of a b is equivalent to a test of the proportion of variance incremented when the variable with which the b is associated is entered last (see, e.g., Chapter 10), it should be clear that such tests go counter to the requirement that the analysis be carried out hierarchically.

Recall that with effect coding, b_X (the b for the continuous variable) in the overall regression equation is the average of the b's of the separate regression equations and is, in most instances, not informative. Anyway, I doubt that researchers who test such b's routinely are aware of what they are testing. The situation is even murkier with dummy coding (see Chapter 14), as in this case b_X is equal to the b for the group assigned 0 in the dummy vector(s). Again, I doubt that researchers who test this b are aware of its meaning.

Turning to the meaning of a test of the b for the coded vector(s), E, in the overall regression equation, it should be clear that it is tantamount to testing the proportion of variance incremented by E when it is entered *after* X and XE. But this is tantamount to studying whether there is a main effect *after* having taken an interaction into account. Because E and XE are generally correlated, it follows that entering XE before E allows the former to appropriate whatever it shares with the

---

[13] I remind you that I am using the term *overall regression equation* to refer to the equation that includes *all* the terms of the design—that is, a coded vector(s) for the categorical variable(s), the attribute(s), *and* a product vector(s) of the categorical variable(s) with the attribute(s).

latter (see the numerical example that follows). The same is, of course, true of the test of the *b* for a dummy vector.

The situation I described in the preceding paragraphs is not unlike the one I discussed in Chapter 13 in connection with curvilinear regression analysis. Recall that such an analysis, too, has to be carried out hierarchically: linear first, then quadratic, then cubic, and so forth. As I showed in Chapter 13, because of the high correlations among the polynomial terms, wrong conclusions are reached (e.g., that the regression is quadratic, when it is linear) when the analysis is not done hierarchically. I also showed that, because of high collinearity, it may turn out that none of the *b*'s is statistically significant, when a simultaneous analysis is done. The same is true of ATI and ANCOVA designs. Against this backdrop, I give some examples of misconceptions and misapplications from the literature.

METHODOLOGICAL EXAMPLES

In this section, I give a couple of examples from methodological presentations aimed at instructing readers on how to compare regression equations. In the next section, I give several examples from substantive studies.

Simultaneous and Stepwise Regression Analyses

Gujarati (1970) attempted to show how to test differences among regression equations. Using an example of ANCOVA with four treatments and two covariates, he generated three dummy vectors and six vectors of products of the dummy coded vectors by the covariates. Recall that this is identical to the numerical example I analyzed earlier in this chapter (Table 15.3). Instead of doing a hierarchical analysis, along the lines of the one I showed earlier in this chapter, Gujarati instructed the reader to do a simultaneous analysis in which the *b*'s, *including those for the interaction vectors,* are tested. He made matters worse by stating:

> As a matter of fact, I ran equation (7) in a stepwise manner. In a stepwise regression program the *variable* [italics added] which contributes most to the explained sum of squares enters first, followed by the *variable* [italics added] whose contribution is next highest, and so on. (1970, p. 21)

In Chapter 11, I stressed the important distinction between a variable and coded vectors used to represent it. In Chapter 12, I discussed and illustrated deleterious consequences of overlooking this distinction. On these grounds alone Gujarati's recommendations and illustrative analysis are wrong. As to his use of stepwise regression analysis, I would like to remind you that in Chapter 8 I reasoned that, whatever its benefits, they are limited to predictive research. However, Gujarati's application of stepwise regression analysis is neither meaningful nor useful even for predictive purposes, *as each of the three dummy vectors, and each of the six product vectors (i.e., of the dummy vectors by the covariates), was treated as a distinct variable.* Not surprisingly, the results of his analysis are strange, to say the least. Retained in the final equation were the two covariates, one dummy vector (out of three) and one product vector (out of six).

Incidentally, as he pointed out, Gujarati borrowed the numerical example from Snedecor and Cochran (1967, p. 440), who used it to illustrate the application of ANCOVA for the case of four treatments and two covariates. In view of my description of Gujarati's analysis, you will probably not be surprised to learn that the conclusions he reached do not resemble those reached by

Snedecor and Cochran. I strongly recommend that you use these data and analyze them in the manner I presented in this chapter. Compare your results with those given in Snedecor and Cochran, and with those given by Gujarati.[14] I believe you will benefit greatly from this exercise.

I focused on Gujarati's paper because of the high likelihood that researchers will use it as a guide, as it is referred to frequently as a model to follow when analyzing data from the type of designs under consideration. A case in point is Trochim's (1984) statement in the context of his discussion of the analysis of the regression discontinuity design: "The recommended model . . . is suggested in the work of Chow (1960) and *consolidated in a more general model by Gujarti* [*sic.* Italics added] (1970)" (p. 122).

In some textbooks, the sole reference given in connection with the analysis of the design under consideration is to Gujarati's paper, whose popularity is probably due to the fact that it was published in *The American Statistician*. I will not speculate on how such a paper was approved for publication in such a journal. Instead, I will note that Cramer (1972) published a cogent critique of Gujarati's approach *in the same journal.* I can only surmise that authors who refer their readers to Gujarati's paper are unaware of Cramer's paper, which I strongly recommend that you read.

Wrong Testing Order

Bartlett, Bobko, Mosier, and Hannan (1978) instructed the reader on how to compare regression equations when studying test fairness. Essentially, they used a design like the one I used throughout Chapter 14, except that they focused on "validating an ability test (A) against a performance criterion (Y) and also . . . examining the effects of culture (C)" (p. 237).

Beginning with an overall equation of the kind I presented (i.e., comprised of A, C, and their product), they stated, "A significant weight for ability (b_a) indicates significant validity for the test over and above any cultural effect, regardless of the significance or non-significance of b_c[15] and b_{ac}" (p. 237). In view of my admonition against a simultaneous analysis (see the preceding), I will not comment on this preceding statement. Instead, I will point out that Bartlett et al. drew attention to the fact that the properties of the overall regression equation are affected by the specific coding scheme used, and they cautioned, "Therefore, interpretation of individual regression weights may lead to spurious conclusions" (p. 238). They then said, "A procedural strategy has been developed which allows for conclusions independent of the coding scheme" (p. 238).

Before I discuss their strategy, I will make a couple of points. First, the fact that elements of the overall regression equation have different meanings, depending on the coding scheme used, does not necessarily lead to spurious conclusions. All it means is that it is necessary to know the properties of the overall regression equation for a given coding scheme. For explanations of properties of regression equations with dummy and effect coding, see Chapter 14 and the present chapter. Second, the hierarchical analysis and tests of significance of its elements are *not* affected by the coding scheme, and such an analysis should be used if one is to arrive at relevant conclusions (e.g., retain separate equations with a common *b* and separate *a*'s; establish regions of significance).

---

[14]See also, Cramer's (1972) analysis of these data, using the approach I outlined in this chapter. As I point out later, Cramer was critical of Gujarati's paper.

[15]Note carefully that Bartlett et al.'s use of b_c refers to the regression coefficient for their categorical variable "culture," whereas my use of b_c throughout this and the preceding chapter refers to a *common regression coefficient*.

Turning to Bartlett et al.'s "suggested strategy" (p. 238), I will point out that it involves "an ordered step-up procedure" (p. 238). Specifically, as step 1, Bartlett et al. recommended that the regression of Y on A (their continuous variable) be calculated to determine "whether there is a significant overall relationship between ability and performance" (p. 238). As I pointed out several times earlier, such an analysis yields total statistics. In the next chapter, I show that such statistics are generally the least meaningful, as they are a mixture of within and between group statistics. For now, I will only remind you that in Chapter 14 I illustrated that, when the regression of Y on the continuous variable is positive in one group and negative in the other, the total regression coefficient can be neither meaningful nor statistically significant. That is why I stressed in the present chapter (see especially the analysis of the data in Table 15.5) that a total coefficient is tenable only after one has established that there are no statistically significant differences among the b's as well as among the a's.

I will not comment on Bartlett et al.'s alternative explanations when what they refer to as the overall relationship between ability is found to be statistically not significant. Instead, I will point out that they stated:

> From the point of view of fairness, when an overall relationship is demonstrated between ability and performance, differential prediction is still a possibility and should be investigated by the procedure suggested in Step 2. (p. 238)

Step 2 consists of adding a coded vector representing the categorical variable (culture in their example). According to Bartlett et al., "Adding the cultural term to ability term . . . provides a test for this hypothesis. If culture (b_c) does not add significantly to the prediction, the test can be recommended as fair by the Cleary (1968) definition and should be acceptable under any of the guidelines" (p. 239). I will make several points about this statement.

First, the authors made no mention of the fact that at their step 2 a common b is used for the ability variable. Recall that the validity of doing this is predicated on it having been established that the b's are homogeneous. At step 2 of Bartlett et al.'s "step-up" strategy, it is not possible to ascertain whether or not the b's are homogeneous.

Second, the intercepts obtained and tested in step 2 are based on the use of a common b. Obviously, then, when a common b is inappropriate, the calculations in step 2 are also inappropriate. As but one example, I will point out that separate intercepts may be obtained when a common b is *inappropriately* used, even though the intercepts may be identical in equations in which separate b's are *appropriately* used.

Third, when, despite it being inappropriate, a common b is used to calculate separate intercepts, it is, of course, possible to find the difference between the intercepts to be statistically not significant. This, according to Bartlett et al., would be interpreted as indicating test fairness, even when, unbeknownst to the researcher, the b's are heterogeneous.

Fourth, as I explained in Chapter 14, when the b's are heterogeneous, it is not meaningful to test differences among intercepts. Among other things, I pointed out that when the interaction is ordinal, the intercepts may be similar to each other or even identical. This, of course, would not constitute evidence of test fairness.

Recall that, following the approach I presented in Chapter 14 and in this chapter, one begins by testing differences among b's, that is, Bartlett et al.'s step 3, which they recommend almost as an afterthought, saying:

> However, if b_c is significant, Step 3 is recommended. (Even where b_c is nonsignificant, an improvement in prediction might be obtained by the inclusion of Step 3. However, considering the practical

problems of utilizing race as a predictor in differential prediction, *we suggest omitting Step 3, given that unfairness has not been detected in Step 2.*) [italics added] (p. 239)

In sum, then, following Bartlett et al.'s strategy, one may end up concluding that a test is fair for different racial or ethnic groups, even when the regression of *Y* on *A* is widely different in the different groups.

SUBSTANTIVE EXAMPLES

I remind you that when I comment on a substantive paper, I try to give as brief a description as possible of what it is about. Further, I single out specific aspects germane to the topic I discuss. As I suggested repeatedly, do not form an opinion about a paper I discuss without reading it carefully.

"Psychopathology as a Function of Neuroticism and a Hypnotically Implanted Aggressive Conflict"

Following is an excerpt from Smyth's (1982) abstract: "Hypnotically implanted paramnesias (false stories) designed to arouse an unacceptable aggressive impulse successfully generated psychopathology in experimental subjects who were high in neuroticism. Control subjects received a similar paramnesia that was designed to arouse an acceptable impulse" (p. 555).

Upon reading Smyth's paper, I decided to comment on it (Pedhazur, 1984) *not* because of the errors in the analysis, which are unfortunately not unique, but because of two statements he made. The first statement concerned his rationale for his analytic approach:

> Since conventional analyses of covariance (ANCOVAs) would ignore the possibility of the covariate (neuroticism) interacting with the experimental manipulations, ANCOVAs were performed by means of hierarchical multiple regression." (p. 558)

This is an example of a rather common misconception that the use of "conventional" ANCOVA precludes tests of homogeneity of regression coefficients. This misconception stems from the failure to recognize that application of "conventional" ANCOVA involves regression analysis. As Fisher (1958), who developed ANCOVA, pointed out, "it combines the advantages and reconciles the requirements of the two very widely applicable procedures known as regression analysis and analysis of variance" (p. 281). It is this notion that Fleiss (1986) alluded to when he referred to ANCOVA as "regression control" (p. 186).

Smyth's second statement, which concerned his results, was:

> Contrary to prediction (H1), significant main effects due to condition failed to materialize once the variance explained by the Neuroticism X Condition interaction was partialed out of the regression equation. (p. 559)

What the preceding amounts to is that Smyth entered the coded vector representing the groups (*E* or *D* in my numerical examples in Chapter 14) *after* the product vector (*XE* or *XD* in my numerical examples). Earlier, I pointed out that *E* and *XE* (or *D* and *XD*) tend to be correlated, often highly. I believe it will be instructive to illustrate this, and show how it leads to erroneous conclusions when the wrong testing order is used. For this purpose, I will reproduce the correlation matrix and two segments from the summary tables of two regression analyses of the data in Table 15.1—one with the correct testing order, the other with the order as in Smyth.

Output

Correlation:

	Y	X	E1	E2	E3	XE1	XE2	XE3
Y	1.000	.697	−.199	.062	.212	−.229	.081	.216
X	.697	1.000	.088	.018	.053	.046	.029	.052
E1	−.199	.088	1.000	.500	.500	.967	.475	.469
E2	.062	.018	.500	1.000	.500	.467	.956	.469
E3	.212	.053	.500	.500	1.000	.467	.475	.959
XE1	−.229	.046	.967	.467	.467	1.000	.483	.477
XE2	.081	.029	.475	.956	.475	.483	1.000	.486
XE3	.216	.052	.469	.469	.959	.477	.486	1.000

Commentary

The preceding is the correlation matrix for the data in Table 15.1, with effect coding (the E's) for the categorical variable and products of the effect coded vectors by the continuous variable (X). Note the high correlations, which I underlined, between each coded vector and its corresponding product vector.

Output

	Summary table [correct order of entry]						Summary table [wrong order of entry]				
Step	Variable	Rsq	RsqCh	FCh	SigCh	Step	Variable	Rsq	RsqCh	FCh	SigCh
1	In: X	.4852	.4852	35.815	.000	1	In: X	.4852	.4852	35.815	.000
2	In: E1					2	In: XE1				
3	In: E2					3	In: XE2				
4	In: E3	.6873	.2021	7.538	.001	4	In: XE3	.6844	.1992	7.366	.001
5	In: XE1					5	In: E1				
6	In: XE2					6	In: E2				
7	In: XE3	.6904	.0031	.108	.955	7	In: E3	.6904	.0059	.205	.892

Commentary

The preceding are excerpts from the summary tables of two hierarchical regression analyses of the data in Table 15.1, which I placed alongside each other for comparative purposes. As indicated in the italicized headings, the results on the left are based on the correct order of entry of the variables, whereas those on the right are based on a wrong order of entry. Examine first the left segment and notice that when the correct order of entry is used, the treatments are shown to account for about .20 (RsqCh) after controlling for the covariate (X) [$F(3, 35) = 7.538, p < .05$] whereas the interaction accounts for about .003 of the variance, $F < 1$. Now examine the right segment and notice the almost exactly opposite results when the wrong order of entry is used. This time, the interaction is shown to account for about .20 of the variance [$F(3, 35) = 7.366$,

$p < .05$], whereas the treatments are shown to account for about .006, $F < 1$. Of course, the dramatic impact the order of entry of the vectors has on the proportions of variance they account is due to the very high correlations among the effect coded vectors and the product vectors (see the previous output).[16]

The reason I bothered to single out Smyth's work is *not* to show that he committed errors. Rather, I did this because I wanted to alert you to the fact that, surprising as it may appear, serious errors and misconceptions, which I submit should be recognized as such even by a person with rudimentary knowledge in this area, may go undetected by referees and journal editors. Incidentally, as I showed in my comment on Smyth (Pedhazur, 1984), other elementary errors (e.g., the use of incorrect numbers of degrees of freedom) were also *not* detected during the review process.

To his credit, I would like to point out that in his response to my critique of his paper, Smyth (1984) forthrightly acknowledged his mistakes and offered results from a reanalysis of his data. Not surprisingly, the interactions that were originally detected because of the wrong hierarchical analysis have, by and large, disappeared. I say, by and large, because I do not wish to belabor the point, except to note, *again out of concern about the review process,* that unfortunately the response still contained some misconceptions (e.g., testing total coefficients), and a couple of discrepancies in the R^2's between the original paper and the response, which appear to be a result of transposing of a couple of figures in the latter. What is, however, particularly troubling about the review process is that, despite my criticism regarding incorrect numbers of degrees of freedom used in the original paper, Smyth's response, *which followed my critique in the same issue,* still contained some incorrect numbers of degrees of freedom.

Traits, Experience, and Academic Achievement

Wong and Csikszentmihalyi (1991) "examined the relationship of personality, experience while studying, and academic achievement" (p. 539). Following are excerpts from their description of their analyses:

> We encountered problems of collinearity in the process of identifying possible gender differences in the relationships between dependent and independent variables. Ideally, we would have combined boys and girls into one single data set and fit a model with interaction and main effects involving gender. However, because gender is a dummy variable, many of the interaction terms were highly correlated with the main effect terms and with one another. Moreover, the regression coefficients changed erratically when sex and its interaction terms were present in the model simultaneously. . . . Therefore, we conducted analyses separately for boys and girls. When significance tests of certain regression coefficients for the two groups showed different results (e.g., one is significant whereas one is not; one is significantly positive whereas the other is significantly negative), we assume that the two groups differed significantly from one another with respect to the effects of those independent variables. (pp. 551–553)

I trust that you recognize that the preceding statement betrays a lack of understanding of the method of comparing regression equations across groups. In view of my discussion of the hierarchical approach to the analysis and my earlier comments on Smyth (1982), I trust that you realize that the collinearity problems and the "erratic" behavior of the regression coefficients are a consequence of Wong and Csikszentmihalyi's inappropriate approach to the analysis.

---

[16]The present example consisted of four treatments. For a numerical example that parallels Smyth's design (i.e., one with two treatments), see my comment on his paper (Pedhazur, 1984).

Stress, Tolerance of Ambiguity, and Magical Thinking

In Chapter 10, I commented briefly on a study by Keinan (1994) in which he "investigated the relationship between psychological stress and magical thinking and the extent to which such a relationship may be moderated by individuals' tolerance of ambiguity" (p. 48). I return to this study to comment on some aspects of Keinan's analytic approach.

Keinan used two independent variables: (1) stress, which he defined as a categorical variable (high and low), and (2) tolerance of ambiguity, a continuous variable. When reporting the means and standard deviations of the dependent variable, however, Keinan used a median split to define high and low tolerance of ambiguity groups. As I discussed the inadvisability of categorizing continuous variables in general and the use of median splits in particular in Chapter 14 (see "Categorizing Continuous Variables"), I will not comment on this topic here.

Keinan had apparently intended to do a 2×2 analysis of variance (high-low stress by high-low tolerance of ambiguity). However, "A preliminary analysis revealed a small but significant correlation between the two independent variables . . . , indicating that the data were unsuitable for the analysis of variance" (p. 51). He therefore used multiple regression analysis in which he treated tolerance of ambiguity as a continuous variable. I will not comment on this topic either, as I discussed it in detail in Chapter 12 (see "Nonorthogonal Designs in Nonexperimental Research").

Keinan reported first results of an analysis of total scores on magical thinking (the dependent variable) and stated that the main effects of stress and tolerance of ambiguity, and their interaction, were statistically significant. Based on the *df* he reported, I surmise that he did a simultaneous analysis. Accordingly, his tests of the main effects are not valid.

Having found that the interaction was statistically significant, Keinan did not follow procedures I presented in this and the preceding chapter (e.g., developing separate equations, determining the nature of the interaction, calculating regions of significance). Instead, he reverted to his use of tolerance of ambiguity as a dichotomized variable and interpreted the interaction accordingly.

Keinan then stated that he did similar analyses on "items representing different types of magical thinking" (p. 51), and referred the reader to Table 2, saying, "As can be seen, for each type of magical thinking, significant main effects of stress conditions and tolerance of ambiguity, as well as a significant interaction between the two variables, were obtained" (p. 51).

In Chapter 10, I questioned Keinan's assertion that he was measuring different types of magical thinking on the grounds that the correlations among the subscales ranged from .73 to .93. Be that as it may, all that Keinan said by way of interpreting his results is that "[t]he directions of the main effects and interactions were identical to those found in the overall analyses of all the items of magical thinking" (p. 51).

Finally, I would like to point out that Table 2 to which Keinan referred the reader (see the preceding) consists of *t* ratios only. Nowhere did he report the means to which these *t*'s refer, not to mention standard deviations and effect sizes. I find this particularly surprising, as the paper appeared in a journal published by the American Psychological Association. The following statement is but one instance from the *Publication Manual of the American Psychological Association* about the reporting of results.

> When reporting inferential statistics (e.g., *t* tests, *F* tests, and chi-square), . . . [b]e sure to include descriptive statistics (e.g., means or medians); where means are reported, always include an associated measure of variability, such as standard deviations, variances, or mean square errors. (1994, pp. 15–16)

Lest you think that these are new guidelines that were not available to the author, the referees, and the editors, I would like to point out that similar ones were included in earlier editions of the manual (e.g., American Psychological Association, 1983, p. 27).

Concluding Comment

I would like to reiterate that my sole purpose for presenting examples of errors and misuses of the analytic approach was to impress upon you, once more, the importance of not accepting analyses and interpretations of results on faith, no matter how prestigious the source. As I said repeatedly, your best safeguard is to acquire the knowledge necessary to make an intelligent judgment.

CONCLUDING REMARKS

Collection and analysis of data in scientific research are guided by hypotheses derived from theoretical formulations. The closer the fit between the analytic method and the hypotheses being tested, the more is one in a position to draw appropriate and valid conclusions. The overriding theme of this and the preceding chapter was that certain analytic methods considered by some researchers as distinct or even incompatible are actually part of the multiple regression approach. To this end, I brought together in this and the preceding chapter methods I introduced separately in earlier chapters.

As I demonstrated in these two chapters, the basic approach I presented in earlier chapters generalizes to designs with continuous and categorical independent variables. That is, whatever the specifics of the design, the analytic aim is to bring all available and relevant information to bear on the explanation of the dependent variable.

From a broad analytic perspective, this chapter is a continuation of the preceding one. The two chapters differ, however, in their focus. In Chapter 14, I focused on ATI designs in experimental research and on comparisons of regression equations in nonexperimental research. In this chapter, I focused on ANCOVA. As I pointed out, ANCOVA was developed in the context of experimental design for the purpose of controlling for extraneous variables, thereby increasing the sensitivity of the analysis. I did, however, also point out that ANCOVA is used frequently with intact groups for the purpose of making adjustments for whatever relevant initial differences existed among them. I argued that the use of ANCOVA for the latter purpose is fraught with logical and analytic problems.

STUDY SUGGESTIONS

1. Distinguish between uses of ANCOVA for control and for adjustment.
2. Why is it important to ascertain whether the *b*'s are homogeneous before applying ANCOVA?
3. Discuss the similarities and differences between ATI and ANCOVA.
4. An educational researcher studied the effects of three methods of teaching on achievement in algebra. She

randomly assigned 25 students to each method. At the end of the semester she measured achievement on a standardized algebra test. To increase the sensitivity of her analysis, the researcher decided to use the students' IQ scores, which were on file, as a covariate. The data (illustrative) for the three groups are as follows:

Method A		Method B		Method C	
IQ	Algebra	IQ	Algebra	IQ	Algebra
91	47	91	47	90	48
90	43	92	43	90	44
93	46	94	47	93	49
95	44	96	44	95	46
95	48	97	48	94	49
97	44	99	45	96	47
97	46	98	46	95	47
97	49	97	50	96	51
98	45	99	45	98	47
99	48	101	50	98	52
100	50	101	51	99	53
102	46	103	46	101	48
102	49	103	50	103	51
102	51	103	52	101	52
104	47	105	48	103	48
104	51	104	52	103	54
105	52	106	53	104	51
106	50	107	51	105	53
108	48	109	49	107	51
108	51	109	50	107	52
108	53	109	55	107	56
109	54	110	55	108	57
111	51	112	52	110	53
111	54	113	55	110	57
111	55	112	56	110	58

Analyze the data, using effect coding for the methods, and assigning -1's to Method C. What is (are) the following:

(a) Separate regression equations for the three methods.

(b) Common b.

(c) F ratio for the test of homogeneity of regression coefficients.

(d) F ratio for the test of the common b.

(e) Proportion of variance accounted for by the teaching methods, over and above the covariate.

(f) F ratio for the differences among the teaching methods after covarying IQ.

(g) F ratio for the differences among the teaching methods without covarying IQ.

(h) Regression equation in which the product vectors are *not* included.

(i) Adjusted means for the three methods.

(j) Test of differences among the b's for the coded vectors in the equation obtained under (h) equivalent to.

(k) Variance/covariance matrix of the b's in the equation obtained under (h).

(l) Augmented variance/covariance matrix of the b's ($\mathbf{C}^*$).

(m) Using relevant elements of $\mathbf{C}^*$, test the differences between (1) b for Method A and b for Method B; (2) b for Method B and b for Method C; (3) b's for Methods A and B versus b for Method C.

ANSWERS

4. In the following, Y = Algebra; X = IQ; A, B, and C refer to the three teaching methods:

(a) $Y'_A = 5.849730 + .423027X$
$Y'_B = 3.235102 + .451020X$
$Y'_C = 3.519491 + .470080X$

(b) .447715

(c) $F = .11$, with 2 and 69 *df*

(d) $F = 121.42$, with 1 and 71 *df*

(e) .09186

(f) $F = 9.37$, with 2 and 71 *df*

(g) $F = 2.18$, with 2 and 72 *df*

(h) $Y' = 4.230019 + .447715X - .891547E1 - .655078E2$
(subjects in A were identified in E1; subjects in B were identified in E2)

(i) $\bar{Y}_{A(adj)} = 48.92$; $\bar{Y}_{B(adj)} = 49.16$; $\bar{Y}_{C(adj)} = 51.36$

(j) It is equivalent to a test of significance among adjusted means.

(k)

		E1	E2
	E1	.12746	−.06388
$\mathbf{C}$ =	E2	−.06388	.12905

(l)

$$
\mathbf{C^*} = \quad
\begin{array}{c|ccc}
 & E1 & E2 & C \\
\hline
E1 & .12746 & -.06388 & -.06358 \\
E2 & -.06388 & .12905 & -.06517 \\
\hline
C & -.06358 & -.06517 & -.12875 \\
\end{array}
$$

(m) (1) $F = .15$, with 1 and 71 df;

(2) $F = 12.49$, with 1 and 71 df;

(3) $F = 18.58$, with 1 and 71 df.

CHAPTER

16

Elements of Multilevel Analysis

As I begin writing this chapter, I am reminded of an anecdote told by Nobel laureate novelist Isaac Bashevis Singer. At a reception for Nobel laureates he found himself seated next to a physicist, whom he was about to ask, "What is new in physics?" Realizing that he didn't know what is old in physics, he refrained from asking the question. Considering the current status of multilevel analysis, much of what I say in this chapter is "old" for people versed in this subject. As the title indicates, this chapter is about *elements* of multilevel analysis. Essentially, I elaborate on concepts I introduced in Chapters 14 and 15 to show the need for multilevel analysis and introduce some of its basic ideas. Though it may sound trite, to understand the new in multilevel analysis, it is necessary to know the old—its basic building blocks, which are elements of the linear model I used in preceding chapters. If this chapter helps you read the literature expounding multilevel analysis (see the references in the section entitled "Hierarchical Linear Models" later in this chapter), then I will have accomplished my aim in writing it.

The essence of what I am trying to convey in this chapter is contained in Cronbach's (1976) opening statement to a report he issued two decades ago:

> If any fraction of the argument herein is correct, educational research—and a great deal of social science—is in serious trouble. The implications of my analysis can be put bluntly:
> 1. The majority of studies of educational effects—whether classroom experiments, or evaluations of programs, or surveys—have collected and analyzed data in ways that conceal more than they reveal. The established methods have generated false conclusions in many studies. (p. 1)

What Cronbach found fault with was the common practice of ignoring the hierarchical structure of the data from "research on classrooms and schools"; that is, the practice of merging data from students from different classes, schools, districts, states, and even countries when doing the analysis. In doing so, researchers acted as if class composition, class size, teacher attributes, school climate, administrative policies, and physical facilities, to name but some factors, had no bearing (or effect) on either the phenomenon studied (e.g., academic achievement) or on the manner in which student attributes (e.g., motivation, mental ability) interact with treatments in affecting it.

In an examination of an ATI study by Anderson (1941), in which 18 fourth-grade classes were used to study the effects of drill versus meaningful instruction on achievement in arithmetic, Cronbach and Webb (1975) reasoned that a high mean aptitude in a class may lead a teacher to crowd more material into the course, thereby resulting in either greater or lesser achievement for the class as a whole. Treatments may also have "comparative effects within a group" (Cronbach & Webb, 1975, p. 717). If, for example, "one method provides special opportunities or rewards for whoever is ablest within a class, the experience of a student with an IQ of 110 depends on whether the mean of his class is 100 or 120" (p. 717).[1]

Sociologists (e.g., Davis, 1966) similarly reasoned that an individual's standing in a group may affect his or her behavior. In certain research areas, this has come to be known as the frog-pond effect: being a large frog in a small pond or a small frog in a large pond (see also, Werts & Watley's, 1969, on "Big Fish–Little Pond or Little Fish–Big Pond"). Firebaugh (1980) gave a good discussion of the contrast between the frog-pond and contextual effects, which I discuss later in this chapter, and showed, among other things, why both should be investigated.

Though the aforementioned discussions focused on educational settings, the same reasoning applies whenever data have a hierarchical structure, that is, whenever units of a given level are nested in units of a higher level. Indeed, "once you know that hierarchies exist, you see them everywhere" (Kreft, De Leeuw, & Kim, 1990, p. 100). Thus, in studies of voting behavior, for example, individual voters are nested in electoral districts, which are nested in counties, which are nested in states (regions). For examples from industrial and organizational research, see Bryk and Raudenbush (1992, Chapter 5). In certain types of research, individuals constitute the higher level, as when each is measured repeatedly for the purpose of studying change (see Bryk & Raudenbush, 1992, Chapter 6).

Two issues have occupied early researchers and writers in this area: (1) problems inherent in cross-level inferences and (2) the appropriate unit of analysis and analytic approach. The two issues are not unrelated. Because the major questions have arisen in the context of cross-level inferences and because much of the analytic complexity can be illustrated within it, I address primarily this topic. As I discuss later in this chapter, in recent years concern with the appropriate unit of analysis has given way to the more meaningful multilevel analysis.

CROSS-LEVEL INFERENCES

When findings obtained from data collected on one level (e.g., individuals) are used to make inferences about another level (e.g., groups to which they belong), a cross-level inference is being made. For example, one might study the relation between mental ability and achievement using school data. That is, school means on mental ability and achievement are used to calculate, say, a correlation coefficient between these two variables. When, based on the correlation coefficient thus obtained, an inference is made about the relation between these variables on another level (say, individual students), a cross-level inference is being made. A similar example is when the relation between race and voting behavior is calculated using data obtained from individual voters, and an inference is made about the relation between these variables on the level of counties or states. In the first example, the cross-level inference is made from aggregates to individuals, whereas in the second example the inference is made from individuals to aggregates.

Cross-level inferences are also made from one type of aggregate to another, as when school data are used to make inferences to classrooms or vice versa. However, most discussions of cross-level inferences in the social sciences addressed inferences from the aggregate to the individual

---

[1]For a brief description of Cronbach and Webb's reanalysis of Anderson's data, see "Concluding Remarks" at the end of this chapter.

level. Although in the presentation that follows I address inferences from aggregates to individuals and vice versa, conceptually and analytically my discussion applies also to other kinds of cross-level inferences.

A question that probably comes first to mind is: Why not study the relation between the variables at the level of interest? The answer is that most often researchers use aggregate data because, for one reason or another, it is not feasible to collect data on individuals or to match data for individuals across variables. Research in sociology and political science is replete with examples in which data on census tracts, election districts, counties, states, countries, and the like were used because these were the only data available or obtainable in view of constraints regarding costs or confidentiality of information, to name but two reasons. Similarly, in many studies of educational effects, aggregates of some kind or another have been used. For example, because of problems caused by attempting to match measures obtained from individual teachers and the students they taught, measures of teacher variables were aggregated on a school basis. Or, because of feasibility problems, per-pupil expenditures were based on school districts (e.g., Armor, 1972; Coleman et al., 1966; Mayeske et al., 1972; Peaker, 1975).

Warnings of hazards of cross-level inferences have been sounded relatively early in the social sciences. An interesting example may be found in a comment by Thorndike (1939) on research reported by Burt (1925). In a study of juvenile delinquency, Burt reported correlations between juvenile delinquency rates and various indices of social conditions, using aggregate data from 29 metropolitan boroughs of London. Among other correlations, Burt reported a .67 correlation between poverty and juvenile delinquency and a .77 correlation between overcrowding and juvenile delinquency. Based on these correlations and others like them, Burt concluded:

> They indicate plainly that it is in the poor, overcrowded, insanitary households, where families are huge, where the children are dependent on charity and relief for their own maintenance, that juvenile delinquency is most rife. (p. 75)

It seems unnecessary to elaborate on the far-reaching implications of accepting such correlations as reflecting the signs and magnitudes of the relations between the variables when measured on the level of the family. Nor is it necessary to discuss how such cross-level inferences may serve to legitimize prejudices toward the poor. The important thing is that cross-level inferences may be, and most often are, fallacious and grossly misleading.

To show potential fallacies in making cross-level inferences, Thorndike (1939) constructed data on intelligence and number of persons per room for what were supposed to be 12 districts. When he calculated the correlation between the two variables in each of the 12 districts, it was zero. When, instead, he combined the data from all districts and calculated the correlation, it was .45. When he correlated averages of intelligence and persons per room from the 12 districts, the correlation was .90.

In the course of his demonstration, Thorndike drew attention to the fact that when data are available for more than one group (classroom, organization, company), it is possible to calculate three different correlation coefficients: (1) within groups, (2) between groups, and (3) total. I discuss these types of correlations in detail later, where I show that not only can they differ in magnitude, but their signs, too, may differ. Regrettably, Thorndike's statement, that had only incompetent scientists engaged in cross-level inferences there would have been no need to publish his note in a professional journal, is as timely today as it was over 50 years ago. Some examples of the apparent need to revisit the topic in professional journals are Knapp (1977); McIntyre (1990); Piantadosi, Byar, and Green (1988); and Sockloff (1975).

Although others voiced early warnings about the hazards of cross-level inferences (e.g., Lindquist, 1940, pp. 219–224; Walker, 1928), it was not until the publication of a paper by Robinson (1950) that social scientists, particularly sociologists and political scientists, were jolted into the awareness that cross-level inferences may be highly misleading. Using data on race (Black, White) and on illiteracy (illiterate, literate), Robinson demonstrated that the correlation between these two variables was .203 on the level of individuals. When, however, he calculated the correlation for the same data on the level of states, it was .773, and when he changed the level to census tracts (nine), the correlation between race and illiteracy was .946!

To further dramatize the problem, Robinson used data on national origin (native born, foreign born) and illiteracy. He reasoned that because of the lower educational background of foreign-born individuals (a plausible supposition, considering that the data were collected in 1930), the correlation between national origin and illiteracy was expected to be positive (i.e., when foreign born and illiterate were scored as 1's, whereas native born and literate were scored as 0's). Indeed, when he used individuals as the unit of analysis, he found a small positive correlation (.118) between the variables. But when he aggregated the data by census tracts, the correlation was −.619! Note that in this example the correlations differ not only in magnitude but also in sign.

Robinson used these examples to illustrate the fallacy of making inferences from correlations based on aggregate data—which he labeled ecological correlations—to individuals. This type of inference has come to be known as the ecological fallacy. Robinson's important contribution in alerting social scientists to the dangers of ecological fallacies is attested to, among other things, by the fact that almost every subsequent treatment of this topic in the social science literature views it as a point of departure in the discussion of cross-level inferences. Yet Robinson's classic paper suffers from what might be considered overstatements, as well as omissions. These are perhaps due to his zeal in conveying his very important message. Anyway, although Robinson's discussion of the ecological fallacy is sound and very well stated, his claim that the interest is always in individual correlations is not supportable. It is *not* true that "Ecological correlations are used simply because correlations between the properties of individuals are not available" (Robinson, 1950, p. 352). Frequently, one may be interested in ecological correlations for their own sake. Moreover, there are circumstances in which ecological correlations are either the only meaningful or the only ones that can be calculated. Thus, Menzel (1950) argued:

> It can hardly be said that a researcher correlating women's court cases with boys' court cases does so in order to imply that the very individuals who land in women's court are especially likely to land in boys' court also! (p. 674)

Among other examples, Menzel pointed out that one may be interested in the ecological correlation between the number of physicians per capita and infant mortality rate. "This correlation may be expected to be high and negative, and loses none of its significance for the fact that a corresponding individual correlation would be patently impossible" (p. 674). (See also Converse, 1969; Erbring, 1990; and Valkonen, 1969, for very good discussions of these issues.)

As I will show, a total correlation (i.e., a correlation based on individuals from more than one group) is a hybrid, so to speak, of between and within correlations. Accordingly, contrary to Robinson's assertion, this type of correlation is probably of least interest when the research involves more than one group.

Fallacies other than ecological ones have also been identified. For example, when based on correlations calculated on the individual level, inferences are made to the group level, individualistic fallacies may be committed (for a typology of fallacies, see Alker, 1969; see also Scheuch, 1966).

I will make two final points about Robinson's paper. First, he failed to distinguish between problems of data aggregation, model specification, and bias in parameter estimation (see, for example, Firebaugh, 1978; Hanushek, Jackson, & Kain, 1974; Scheuch, 1966; Smith, 1977). Second, Robinson's presentation is limited to correlations. Under certain circumstances, an ecological fallacy may be committed when correlations are used, but *not* when regression coefficients are used (see the following).

I now take a closer look at the three kinds of correlation coefficients and the corresponding regression coefficients that may be calculated when data are available for more than one group. First, I present the logic of the calculations. I then give a numerical example and discuss the relations among the three statistics.

Within, Between, and Total Statistics

When I introduced regression analysis for the first time in Chapter 2, I showed how the sum of squares of the dependent variable (Σy^2) may be partitioned into two components: regression and residual sums of squares. When I introduced the concept of regression of a continuous variable on a categorical variable in Chapter 11, I showed that the regression sum of squares is equivalent to the between-treatments or between-groups sum of squares, and that the residual sum of squares is equivalent to the within-treatments or within-groups sum of squares.[2] That is,

$$\Sigma(Y_{ij} - \overline{Y})^2 = \sum_j n_j(\overline{Y}_j - \overline{Y})^2 + \sum_j \sum_i (Y_{ij} - \overline{Y}_j)^2 \tag{16.1}$$

where Y_{ij} = score of individual i in group j; $\overline{Y}$ = grand mean of Y; $\overline{Y}_j$ = mean of group j; and n_j = number of people in group j. The term on the left of the equal sign is the total sum of squares, which I will designate as Σy_t^2 in the following presentation. The first term on the right of the equal sign is the between-groups sum of squares, or the regression sum of squares when Y is regressed on coded vectors representing group membership. Note that the deviation of each group mean from the grand mean is squared and weighted by the number of people in the group (n_j). These values for all treatment groups are added to yield the between-groups sum of squares, Σy_b^2. The second term on the right of the equal sign is the pooled within-groups sum of squares, or the residual sum of squares when Y is regressed on coded vectors representing group membership. Note that for each group, the deviation scores from the group mean are squared and added. These are then pooled to comprise the within-groups sum of squares, Σy_w^2.

When, in addition to Y scores, there are also X scores for individuals in different groups, the total sum of squares of X, Σx_t^2, may be partitioned in the same manner as that of Σy_t^2. That is,

$$\Sigma(X_{ij} - \overline{X})^2 = \sum_j n_j(\overline{X}_j - \overline{X})^2 + \sum_j \sum_i (X_{ij} - \overline{X}_j)^2 \tag{16.2}$$
$$\Sigma x_t^2 = \Sigma x_b^2 + \Sigma x_w^2$$

Similarly, the total sum of products, Σxy_t, is partitioned to between- and within-groups sums of products:

$$\Sigma(X_{ij} - \overline{X})(Y_{ij} - \overline{Y}) = \sum_j n_j(\overline{X}_j - \overline{X})(\overline{Y}_j - \overline{Y}) + \sum_j \sum_i (X_{ij} - \overline{X}_j)(Y_{ij} - \overline{Y}_j) \tag{16.3}$$
$$\Sigma xy_t = \Sigma xy_b + \Sigma xy_w$$

[2]See Chapter 11, particularly the discussion related to the analysis of the data in Tables 11.4 and 11.7.

Using the different sums of squares and sums of products, three correlation coefficients may be calculated:

$$r_t = \frac{\Sigma xy_t}{\sqrt{\Sigma x_t^2 \Sigma y_t^2}} \tag{16.4}$$

where r_t is the total correlation between X and Y. (Because it is clear that the correlations are between X and Y, I will not use subscripts to identify the variables.) Note that group membership is ignored when r_t is calculated. That is, all subjects are treated as if they belonged to a single group.

Using the between-groups values, one can calculate a between-groups correlation of X and Y:

$$r_b = \frac{\Sigma xy_b}{\sqrt{\Sigma x_b^2 \Sigma y_b^2}} \tag{16.5}$$

This is, in effect, a correlation between the means of the groups, except that the values are weighted by the number of people in the group. With equal numbers of subjects in all groups, one can obtain r_b by simply correlating their X and Y means.

Finally, a within-groups correlation coefficient can be calculated:

$$r_w = \frac{\Sigma xy_w}{\sqrt{\Sigma x_w^2 \Sigma y_w^2}} \tag{16.6}$$

Note that this is a *pooled within-groups correlation.* Obviously, it is possible to calculate the correlation of X and Y within each group by using the respective sum of products and the sums of squares. r_w, however, is calculated by using the pooled sums of products and sums of squares. To see the difference between the two types of the within correlations consider, for instance, the case of two groups. Assume that Σxy is the same in both groups, except that it is positive in one group and negative in the other. Accordingly, the correlation will be positive in one group and negative in the other. When these sums of products are pooled to calculate r_w, their sum will be equal to zero, and r_w will necessarily be zero. From the foregoing it follows that r_w *is meaningful only when separate correlations within groups do not differ significantly.*

Analogous to the three correlation coefficients, regression coefficients may be calculated. Recall, however, that whereas the correlation coefficient is symmetric, the regression coefficient is not. That is, although $r_{xy} = r_{yx}$, b_{yx} indicates the regression of Y on X and b_{xy} indicates the regression of X on Y. In the following presentation, I assume that Y is the dependent variable and will, for convenience, omit the yx subscripts. The three regression coefficients are calculated as follows:

$$b_t = \frac{\Sigma xy_t}{\Sigma x_t^2} \tag{16.7}$$

$$b_b = \frac{\Sigma xy_b}{\Sigma x_b^2} \tag{16.8}$$

$$b_w = \frac{\Sigma xy_w}{\Sigma x_w^2} \tag{16.9}$$

The pooled within-groups regression coefficient (b_w) is the same as the common regression coefficient (b_c), which I used in Chapters 14 and 15.

To clarify the calculations of the previous statistics, I will use a simple numerical example for two groups. Subsequently, I will discuss relations among the three statistics.

A Numerical Example

In Table 16.1, I give scores for subjects in two groups, I and II. In addition, I combined the scores for the two groups under T (Total). At the bottom of the table, I give values necessary to calculate the different statistics. The procedures for calculating these values should require no explanation as I introduced them in Chapter 2 and used them repeatedly in subsequent chapters. In any event, here are a couple of examples:

$$\Sigma x_1^2 = \Sigma X_1^2 - \frac{(\Sigma X_1)^2}{n} = 90 - \frac{(20)}{5} = 10$$

$$\Sigma xy_t = \Sigma XY_t - \frac{(\Sigma X_t)(\Sigma Y_t)}{N} = 340 - \frac{(55)(55)}{10} = 37.5$$

Using relevant values from the bottom of Table 16.1, I apply (16.4) through (16.9). The total correlation and regression coefficient are

$$r_t = \frac{\Sigma xy_t}{\sqrt{\Sigma x_t^2 \Sigma y_t^2}} = \frac{37.5}{\sqrt{(42.5)(82.5)}} = .63330$$

$$b_t = \frac{\Sigma xy_t}{\Sigma x_t^2} = \frac{37.5}{42.5} = .88235$$

Instead of continuing in this manner with the calculation of the other statistics, I present them in tabular format in Table 16.2. I took the values in the first three columns for the first three rows in Table 16.2 from the bottom of Table 16.1. Values in the fourth row (first three columns) are sums

Table 16.1 Illustrative Data for Two Groups

	I		II		T	
	X	Y	X	Y	X	Y
	5	1	8	6	5	1
	2	2	5	7	2	2
	4	3	7	8	4	3
	6	4	9	9	6	4
	3	5	6	10	3	5
					8	6
					5	7
					7	8
					9	9
					6	10
Σ:	20	15	35	40	55	55
M:	4	3	7	8	5.5	5.5
SS:	90	55	255	330	345	385
ss:	10	10	10	10	42.5	82.5
ΣXY:	60		280		340	
Σxy:	0		0		37.5	

NOTE: M = mean; SS = raw scores sum of squares (e.g., $\Sigma X_1^2 = 90$); ss = deviation sum of squares (e.g., $\Sigma y_t^2 = 82.5$); ΣXY = raw scores sum of products; and Σxy = deviation sum of products.

Table 16.2   Total, Within, and Between Statistics Based on Data from Table 16.1

Source	Σy^2	Σx^2	Σxy	r	b
Total	82.5	42.5	37.5	.63330	.88235
I	10.0	10.0	0	.00000	.00000
II	10.0	10.0	0	.00000	.00000
Within	20.0	20.0	0	.00000	.00000
Between	62.5	22.5	37.5	1.00000	1.66667

of values in the second and third rows. Values for the last row (first three columns) may be calculated directly, as indicated in the first term on the right of the equal sign in (16.1) through (16.3), or by subtraction. That is, Between equals Total minus Within. Thus, for example:

$$\Sigma y_b^2 = \Sigma y_t^2 - \Sigma y_w^2 = 82.5 - 20.0 = 62.5$$

I calculated the r's and the b's in Table 16.2 by using the values of the sums of squares and sum of products in their respective rows. For example,

$$r_b = \frac{37.5}{\sqrt{(62.5)(22.5)}} = 1.0$$

Before describing the relations among the statistics reported in Table 16.2, I discuss each of them separately. Turning first to the within-groups statistics, note that, for the present example, the correlation and the regression coefficient within each group are zero. Further, because $\Sigma xy = 0$ in both groups, $\Sigma xy_w = 0$, and r_w and b_w are necessarily zero. Thus, while $r_w = b_w = 0$, $r_t = .63330$ and $b_t = .88235$. Here, then, is an example of a difference between within and total statistics. It is instructive to note briefly how this has come about. Look back at the data in Table 16.1 and notice that subjects in group II tend to score higher on X and Y than do subjects in group I. When the scores for the two groups are combined, relatively high scores on X are paired with relatively high scores on Y, and relatively low scores on X are paired with relatively low scores on Y, resulting in a positive correlation and a positive regression coefficient. This demonstration should serve as a warning against the indiscriminate calculation of total statistics when data from more than one group are available.

When total statistics are calculated for the present example, a specification error is committed: a variable—group membership—that is related to, or affects, X and Y is omitted. Think, for instance, of group I as females and group II as males. It is evident that the correlation between X and Y is zero among males and among females. But because males tend to have higher scores than females on both X and Y, the variables are correlated when the scores for the groups are combined. To repeat, when the total statistics are calculated, a specification error is committed by the omission of the sex variable.

As a substantive example, assume that X is height and Y is achievement in mathematics. As males tend to be taller than females and also tend to score higher on mathematics tests, one would conclude, based on r_t, that there is a positive correlation between height and achievement in mathematics. But, as I have pointed out, the within-groups correlations of X and Y are zero. On the other hand, females tend to score higher on reading achievement than do males. Therefore, based on r_t of height and reading achievement scores, one would conclude that the two variables are negatively correlated.

It is worth noting that regressing Y on X and a vector representing group membership (e.g., effect coding) will indicate that b_c (i.e., the common, or the within, coefficient for X) is equal to zero, the intercept is 5.5, and the regression coefficient for the vector representing group membership is −2.5. Look back at the data in Table 16.1 and notice that $\overline{Y}_I = 3.0$, $\overline{Y}_{II} = 8.0$, $\overline{Y} = 5.5$. Consequently, the effect of group I is −2.5 (3.0 − 5.5) and that of group II is 2.5 (8.0 − 5.5), which is what the regression coefficient for the effect-coded vector for group membership would indicate.

In the foregoing, I described an ANCOVA in which I used X as the covariate. Because $b_c = 0$, the adjusted means for the two groups are, of course, equal to their original means. From the foregoing it also follows that the partial correlation between X and Y (partialing out group membership) is equal to zero. When group membership affects both X and Y, r_t is spurious.[3]

Turning now to the between-group statistics, note that $r_b = 1.0$. This is not surprising, as in the present example there are only two pairs of scores ($\overline{X}$ and $\overline{Y}$ for each group) and therefore, except when the means of the groups on one, or both, variables do not differ, the correlation is necessarily perfect. When the group means are equal on one of the variables, r_b is indeterminate as one of the vectors is a constant. A correlation coefficient is an index of a relation between two variables, *not* between a variable and a constant. Try to apply the formula for the correlation coefficient to data in which one vector is a variable and the other is a constant and you will find that you have to divide by zero—an unacceptable operation in mathematics.

Although the present example is artificial and small (involving two groups only), it illustrates the ecological fallacy that Robinson and others warned against. Using the correlation between group means to make inferences to the individual level, one would erroneously conclude that X and Y are perfectly correlated. With the individual as the unit of analysis, the correlation between X and Y (i.e., r_t) is .63330. But, as I noted earlier and as I discuss in greater detail later, r_t is generally not useful when more than one group is used. In the present example, the correlation between X and Y within each group is zero.

My preceding comments about the between-groups statistics were limited to the correlation coefficient. Concerning the regression coefficient (b_b), recall that it is a function of the correlation between X and Y and the ratio of the standard deviation of Y to that of X (i.e., $b = r_{xy}s_y/s_x$). Therefore, although for the case of two groups $r_b = |1.0|$,[4] b_b may take any value, depending on s_y/s_x. The same is true when more than two groups are involved. In such situations, r_b is, obviously, not necessarily 1.0. But the difference between r_b and b_b depends on the ratio of the two standard deviations.

Relations among the Different Statistics

To show the relations among total, between, and within statistics, it is necessary first to recall the meaning of η^2. In Chapter 11, I showed that η^2 is the ratio of the between-groups sum of squares to the total sum of squares, and that it is equal to R^2 for the regression of the dependent variable on coded vectors representing group membership. In other words, η^2, or R^2, is the proportion of

---

[3]In Chapter 15, I described a paper of mine (Pedhazur, 1984) in which I showed how the wrong testing order led to wrong conclusions in a published paper. As an illustration of how this occurred, I used the analysis of the data in Table 16.1.

[4]The absolute value of r is 1. The sign of r will be positive or negative, depending on the pattern of the means in the two groups. Suppose that in the numerical example under consideration $\overline{X}_{II}$ was smaller than $\overline{X}_I$, but the reverse was true for the Y means; then r_b would be −1.0.

variance of the dependent variable that is accounted for by group membership. In the context of the present discussion, two η^2's, or two R^2's, may be calculated: η_y^2 is the ratio of Σy_b^2 to Σy_t^2, and η_x^2 is the ratio of Σx_b^2 to Σx_t^2. Thus, it is possible to determine the proportion of variance of Y and of X accounted for by group membership. With this in mind, the three correlation coefficients may be expressed as follows:

$$r_t = r_w \sqrt{1 - \eta_x^2} \sqrt{1 - \eta_y^2} + r_b \eta_x \eta_y \tag{16.10}$$

$$r_w = \frac{r_t - r_b \eta_x \eta_y}{\sqrt{1 - \eta_x^2} \sqrt{1 - \eta_y^2}} \tag{16.11}$$

$$r_b = \frac{r_t - r_w \sqrt{1 - \eta_x^2} \sqrt{1 - \eta_y^2}}{\eta_x \eta_y} \tag{16.12}$$

Before I discuss these formulas, I will apply them to the numerical example in Table 16.1 in the hope of thereby clarifying their meaning. Except for the two η's, the terms necessary for the application of (16.10) through (16.12) are given in Table 16.2. Regressing Y in Table 16.1 for the combined scores (i.e., under T) on a coded vector representing group membership yields $R^2 = .75758$. Equivalently, using the between and total sums of squares for Y from Table 16.2,

$$\eta_y^2 = \frac{\Sigma y_b^2}{\Sigma y_t^2} = \frac{62.5}{82.5} = .75758$$

and similarly,

$$\eta_x^2 = \frac{\Sigma x_b^2}{\Sigma x_t^2} = \frac{22.5}{42.5} = .52941$$

Using these η's and the appropriate values from Table 16.2, I calculate the three correlation coefficients by applying (16.10) through (16.12):

$$r_t = .00 \sqrt{1 - .52941} \sqrt{1 - .75758} + (1.0)(.72761)(.87039) = .63330$$

$$r_w = \frac{.63330 - (1.0)(.72761)(.87039)}{\sqrt{1 - .52941} \sqrt{1 - .75758}} = .00$$

$$r_b = \frac{.63330 - .00 \sqrt{1 - .52941} \sqrt{1 - .75758}}{(.72761)(.87039)} = 1.0$$

Note that the interrelations among the three correlation coefficients are a function of the coefficients themselves and the two η's. Consider, for instance, the case of $\eta_y^2 = \eta_x^2 = .00$. This, of course, means that there are no differences among the means of X, nor are there differences among the means of Y. In other words, $\Sigma y_b^2 = \Sigma x_b^2 = .00$. All the variability is within groups. Consequently, $r_t = r_w$, and r_b is indeterminate.

Suppose now that $\eta_y^2 = \eta_x^2 = 1.0$. In this case, all the variability is between groups. Therefore, r_w is indeterminate and $r_t = r_b$.

The two extreme situations depicted here are rarely, if ever, encountered in actual research. Usually, something in between them takes place, depending on the composition of the groups studied. When, for example, the groups are relatively homogeneous, r_w tends to be relatively small and r_b tends to be relatively large. As a compromise, so to speak, the total correlation, r_t, takes on a value somewhere in between r_w and r_b. Because of these properties of r_t, it is generally a less useful index than r_w and r_b. A case can be made for using the pooled within-groups correlation, r_w, as an index of the relation between two variables within groups, *assuming that it was established that the correlations within the groups do not differ significantly from each other.* Similarly, it is conceivable that one might wish to study the relation between two variables on an aggregate level (e.g., using group measures) and will therefore calculate r_b. Note that in the situations I described, each correlation will be calculated for its own sake; not for cross-level inferences (i.e., using one correlation to make inferences about the other). A similar case cannot generally be made for r_t because it is a weighted combination of r_b and r_w and can therefore not be interpreted unambiguously, except when it is equal to r_b or r_w or when $r_t = r_b = r_w$. Note that when r_t or b_t is calculated, Y is regressed only on X—that is, coded vectors identifying groups are *not* included in the analysis. In Chapter 15, I showed that such an analysis is valid only after establishing that there are no statistically significant differences among the (1) b's (the b's are homogeneous) and (2) intercepts. In short, when r_t or b_t is calculated, one assumes that a single regression equation fits the data of all the groups.

In view of the foregoing, it is noteworthy that many studies designed to draw attention to, and illustrate, the ecological fallacy made comparisons between r_b and r_t. Perhaps this was motivated by the belief that the individual is the natural unit of the analysis (see, for example, Robinson, 1950). But this is based on the questionable assumption that individuals are not affected by the groups to which they belong (see the next section, "Group and Contextual Effects") or that groups are established by a random process.

As with the correlation coefficients, the three types of regression coefficients are also interrelated:

$$b_t = b_w + \eta_x^2(b_b - b_w) \tag{16.13}$$

Note that b_t is a function of b_w, b_b, and η_x^2. When, for example, $b_w = b_b$, then $b_t = b_w = b_b$. When $b_w = .00$, b_t is a function of b_b and η_x^2. This may be illustrated with the data in Table 16.2, where $b_b = 1.66667$, $b_w = .00$, $b_t = .88235$, and $\eta_x^2 = .52941$. Applying (16.13),

$$b_t = .00 + .52941(1.66667 - .00) = .88235$$

As with the correlation coefficients, b_w and b_b may be meaningfully used and interpreted for different purposes. The same is generally not true of b_t. "Insofar as relevant experiences are associated with groups there are two matters to consider: between-groups relations and within-groups relations. *The overall individual analysis combines these, to everyone's confusion* [italics added]" (Cronbach, 1976, p. 1.10).

There is an extensive literature on the relations among the indices I introduced in this section and the conditions under which cross-level inferences are biased or not (see, for example, Alker, 1969; Blalock, 1964; Duncan, Cuzzort, & Duncan, 1961; Firebaugh, 1978; Hammond, 1973; Hannan, 1971; Hannan & Burstein, 1974; Irwin & Lichtman, 1976; Kramer, 1983; Langbein & Lichtman, 1978; Przeworski, 1974; Smith, 1977). It is not possible, nor is it necessary, to review here these and other treatments of this topic. Instead, I will point out that although they may differ in their perspective, most focus on the process by which the groups under study were formed. I hope that a couple of examples will clarify this point. When, for example, the groups are formed by a random process, the within, between, and total statistics are expected, within random fluctuations, to be equal to each other. Consequently, cross-level inferences are expected to be not biased. When the groups are formed on the basis of individuals' scores on the independent variable (i.e., individuals who have similar scores on the independent variable are placed in the same group), r_b will be larger than r_t, but b_b will, within random fluctuations, be equal to b_t. Therefore, under such circumstances, using a between-groups correlation to make inferences about individuals will be biased. But using the between-groups *unstandardized* regression coefficient to make inferences about the *unstandardized* regression coefficient on the individual level will not be biased. Finally, when the groups are formed on the basis of individuals' scores on the dependent variable, or on the basis of a variable that is correlated both with the independent and the dependent variable, the correlations will differ from each other, as will the regression coefficients.[5]

The main problem is that when intact groups are studied, it is very difficult, often impossible, to unravel the processes by which they were formed. When, under such circumstances, data are available on the group level only, telling the direction and magnitude of the bias resulting from inferences made about individuals is generally not possible.

There is a fairly extensive literature in which analyses using the individual as the unit of analysis are contrasted with ones in which aggregates are used as the unit of analysis. This literature deserves careful study not only because it illustrates striking differences in the results one may obtain from the two analyses, but also because much of it contains discussions of methodological issues concerning the unit of analysis. For some examples, see Alexander and Griffin (1976); Bidwell and Kasarda (1975, 1976, 1980); Burstein (1976, 1978, 1980a, 1980b); Hannan, Freeman, and Meyer (1976); and Langbein (1977).

An important point to note when studying this literature is the distinction between R^2 when individuals are used as the unit of analysis and R^2 when aggregates are used as the unit of analysis. When individuals are used as the unit of analysis, R^2 indicates the proportion of the total variance accounted for by the independent variables. When, on the other hand, aggregates (e.g., classes, schools) are used as the unit of analysis, R^2 indicates the proportion of variance of the *between* aggregates that is accounted for by the independent variables. Consequently, when the variance between groups is relatively small, one should be careful not to be overly impressed even with a high R^2. For example, suppose that the variance between groups is .10. Then, $R^2 = .8$ obtained in an analysis with group data refers to an explanation of 80% of the variance between groups (i.e., of the 10%), *not* of the total variance. It is possible, then, to obtain high R^2's in analyses with aggregate data and yet explain only a minute proportion of the total variance. Typically, such are the findings in many studies of educational effects. Because most of the variance is within schools,[6] when the school is the unit of analysis, a small portion of the total variance is addressed, and R^2 is a fraction of this small portion that is being explained. The potential of wandering into a world of fantasy, under such circumstances, is very real.

I hope that the preceding discussion served its main purpose of alerting you to the potential hazards of cross-level inferences. Recall that the need to make such inferences usually arises when data on the unit of analysis that is of interest are not available or because the researcher is constrained (by administrative, economic, or other considerations) from using them. In many research settings, however, the researcher has access to data on more than one level (e.g., individuals as well as groups to which they belong), and therefore the issue of cross-level inferences does not, or should not, arise. Engaging in cross-level inferences when the data on the unit of interest are available is "obviously either poor research strategy or a regrettable adjustment to one's limited resources" (Scheuch, 1969, p. 136). Issues that come to the fore when data are available on more than one level concern methods of analysis and interpretation of results. It is to this topic that I now turn.

---

[5]For a very good discussion of these points, along with interesting numerical examples, see Blalock (1964); see also Langbein and Lichtman (1978).

[6]For example, Coleman et al. (1966) found that about 80% of the variance was within schools.

GROUP AND CONTEXTUAL EFFECTS

Social scientists, notably sociologists, social psychologists, and political scientists, have long been interested in the effects of social environments on the behavior of individuals. Among terms used to refer to such effects are *group, contextual, structural,* and *compositional.* There is no consensus about the definitions of these terms. Some researchers view them as referring to distinct types of social effects, whereas others use them interchangeably. As my treatment of this topic is limited to some analytic aspects, I will not attempt to define the aforementioned terms.[7] Later, I do distinguish between group and contextual effects from an analytic perspective. For now, however, it will be instructive to give a couple of research examples of contextual effects. As I use them for illustrative purposes only, I do not address the question of their validity.

The first example is from the Coleman Report (Coleman et al., 1966), which devoted a good deal of attention to the effects of student body composition and properties on the achievement of individual students. Among other conclusions, the authors of the report stated:

> Finally, it appears that a pupil's achievement is strongly related to the educational backgrounds and aspirations of other students in the school. . . . Analysis indicates . . . that children from a given family background, when put in schools of different social composition, will achieve at quite different levels. . . . If a minority pupil from a home without much educational strength is put with schoolmates with strong educational backgrounds, his achievement is likely to increase. (p. 22)[8]

The second example is from an analysis of voting behavior during the 1968 presidential election. Among other findings, Schoenberger and Segal (1971) reported a correlation of .55 between percent Black and a vote for Wallace for southern congressional districts. The authors stated:

> It would be a fallacy—ecological, logical, sociological and political—to infer from these data that blacks in the South provided a major source of Wallace support. Rather we suggest that our data demonstrate a contextual effect, viz., the greater the concentration of blacks in a congressional district, the greater the propensity of whites in the district to vote for Wallace. (p. 585)

There is a sizable literature on substantive findings regarding contextual, compositional, or structural effects that contains also some discussions of methodological approaches for detection of such effects (see, for example, Alexander & Eckland, 1975; Alwin & Otto, 1977; Blau, 1960; Bowers, 1968; Davis, 1966; Leiter, 1983; Markham, 1988; McDill, Rigsby, & Meyers, 1969; Meyer, 1970; Nelson, 1972a, 1972b; Rowan & Miracle, 1983; Sewell & Armer, 1966). More germane for this chapter are presentations devoted primarily to analytic issues. Among these are Alwin (1976), Blalock (1984), Boyd and Iversen (1979), Burstein (1978), Farkas (1974), Firebaugh (1979, 1980), Hauser (1970, 1971, 1974), Iversen (1991), Prysby (1976), Przeworski (1974), Sprague (1976), Stipak and Hensler (1982), Tannenbaum and Bachman (1964), and Valkonen (1969).[9] In the remainder of this section I will address analytic issues concerning the study of group and contextual effects, beginning with the former.

---

[7]For some attempts at defining these terms, see Burstein (1980a) and Karweit, Fennessey, and Daiger (1978).

[8]The pervasive impact of such statements is evident, among other things, from their use by Congress and the courts in legislation and rulings regarding school desegregation. For extensive documentation and discussions of these issues, see Grant (1973) and Young and Bress (1975).

[9]Issues I present in the present chapter are often discussed in the literature on analysis of contingency tables under the heading of Simpson's Paradox (Simpson, 1951). For some interesting examples, see Bickel, Hammel, and O'Connell (1975); Paik (1985); and Wagner (1982).

Group Effects

The analytic approach in the study of group effects is identical to that of ANCOVA (see Chapter 15). Conceptually, the covariate(s) is viewed as an attribute of individuals who belong to two or more groups. Assuming that the within-groups regression coefficients are homogeneous (see Chapter 15), one may test differences among groups after adjusting for, or partialing out, the effect of the attribute. In Chapter 15, I showed that this may be accomplished by using any one of three equivalent approaches, namely, testing differences among (1) adjusted means, (2) intercepts, or (3) regression coefficients for coded vectors representing group membership.

From the analytic perspective, detection of group effects poses no problems. This, however, does not mean that interpretation of results is free of problems and ambiguity. The problems are the same as those I discussed in connection with (1) ANCOVA in nonexperimental research (Chapter 15) and (2) comparisons among regression equations (Chapter 14), and I will therefore not repeat them here. These problems aside, when a group effect is detected, it is not possible to tell what it is about the group (i.e., what specific variables) that is responsible for the effect. Because of this limitation, advocates of contextual effects call for the use of specific group variables, instead of identification of overall group effects as is done when coded vectors are used to represent group membership.

Typology of Group Variables.   It is useful to distinguish among different types of variables or properties used to describe groups. Lazarsfeld and Menzel (1961), for instance, distinguished three types: (1) analytic properties based on the aggregation of data collected on members of the groups (e.g., mean intelligence, motivation, anxiety), (2) structural properties based on data of relations among group members (e.g., patterns of sociometric choices, group cliquishness), and (3) global properties of groups (e.g., forms of government of nations, educational policies of school districts). (See also Kendall & Lazarsfeld, 1955; Rosenberg, 1968.)

Contextual Effects

Most definitions, and most empirical studies, associate effects of group analytic variables with contextual effects. That is, a contextual effect is defined as the net effect of a group analytic variable after having controlled for the effect of the same variable on the individual level. For example, in research aimed at studying the contextual effect of socioeconomic status (SES) of region of residence on voting behavior, each individual has two scores: one's own SES score and the mean SES of the region in which one resides. Voting behavior is regressed on both the individuals' SES scores and the SES means for the regions. The partial regression coefficient for the vector of SES means is taken as the contextual effect of the regions' SES. Similarly, in a study of achievement one may use individuals' mental ability scores as well as the mean mental ability of their class (school, school district). Again, the partial regression coefficient for the mental ability means is taken as the contextual effect of the groups' mental abilities on achievement. I turn now to a numerical example to illustrate how the analysis is carried out and to examine some of its properties.

A Numerical Example

For comparative purposes, I will use the data from Table 15.5, which I analyzed through ANCOVA. In Table 16.3, I repeat the scores on Y and X for the four groups in Table 15.5. In addition, the means of the four groups on X are contained in the column labeled M.

Table 16.3   Illustrative Data for Contextual Analysis

	Y	X	M
	14	6	8.4
	17	6	8.4
	16	7	8.4
	16	8	8.4
A	20	8	8.4
	20	9	8.4
	18	9	8.4
	16	10	8.4
	20	10	8.4
	21	11	8.4
	14	6	9.0
	17	6	9.0
	16	7	9.0
	17	8	9.0
B	20	8	9.0
	18	10	9.0
	20	10	9.0
	24	11	9.0
	20	12	9.0
	23	12	9.0
	15	7	10.2
	17	7	10.2
	19	9	10.2
	21	9	10.2
C	19	10	10.2
	20	11	10.2
	23	11	10.2
	22	12	10.2
	24	13	10.2
	21	13	10.2
	19	8	10.9
	20	9	10.9
	17	9	10.9
	19	10	10.9
D	23	10	10.9
	21	11	10.9
	24	11	10.9
	22	13	10.9
	24	13	10.9
	25	15	10.9

NOTE: Data for *Y* and *X* are from Table 15.5. *M* = mean of *X* for respective group.

It will be instructive to cast the illustrative data in Table 16.3 in some substantive contexts. For example, Y may be achievement, X may be aspirations, and M the mean aspirations of the group (e.g., class, region) to which a given individual belongs; or Y may be productivity, X may be anxiety, and M the mean anxiety of the group to which a given individual belongs. Other examples come readily to mind, but these will suffice to give some substantive meaning to the analysis that follows.

As I stated earlier, the dependent variable, Y, is regressed on X and M. In what follows, I report results of such an analysis for the data in Table 16.3 and discuss them first with reference to R^2 and then to the regression equation. I conclude with some general observations about group and contextual effects.

Squared Multiple Correlation (R^2)

Using a multiple regression program, regress Y on X and M. You will find that $R^2_{Y.XM} = .69868$. When I analyzed the same data earlier through ANCOVA (i.e., using X as the covariate and three coded vectors to represent group membership), R^2 was .70206. I examine now the source of the discrepancy between these two R^2's. Look back at Table 16.3 and note that scores under M for each group are necessarily identical as the mean of the given group is assigned to all its members. Suppose now that instead of placing the four X means in a single vector, as I did in Table 16.3, I used them in separate vectors. Specifically, assume that instead of the single M vector, I generated three vectors as follows: vector A, consisting of the mean for group A and 0's for all other groups; vector B, consisting of the mean for group B and 0's for all other groups; and vector C, consisting of the mean for group C and 0's for all other groups. As a result of doing this, group D would be assigned 0's in all the vectors. What I have described is a method of coding group membership, but instead of 1 and 0 codes, say, the codes are group means and 0's. In Chapter 11, I stated that R^2 is the same regardless of the specific codes used to represent group membership. Consequently, if you were to regress Y of Table 16.3 on X and on three coded vectors in which the means of X are used as the codes, R^2 would be .70206 (i.e., the same as I obtained when I applied ANCOVA to these data).

It is now possible to state the condition under which R^2 obtained when the means are placed in a single vector (i.e., in contextual analysis) will be equal to R^2 obtained when the means are placed in separate vectors (i.e., when the data are analyzed as in ANCOVA). The two R^2's will be equal only when the means of the groups on X lie exactly on the regression plane. This is tantamount to saying that the squared correlation of the means of Y with the means of X is equal to 1.00. Whenever this is not the case, R^2 obtained in contextual analysis will be smaller than that obtained in ANCOVA of the same data.

The Regression Equation

The regression equation for the data in Table 16.3 is

$$Y' = 6.479012 + 1.013052X + .344973M$$

The first thing to note is that b_X (i.e., for individuals' scores) is the pooled within-groups regression coefficient (b_w or b_c). If you ran the ANCOVA for Table 15.5, I suggest that you review the output and notice that b_c is 1.013052. Recall that this b is used to calculate adjusted means when one has concluded that there are statistically significant differences among the intercepts (i.e., the adjusted means). Recall also that for the data in Table 15.5 I concluded that, after allowing for the covariate, the differences among the means were statistically not significant. As I show later, for the analysis of the data in Table 16.3, the contextual effect is statistically not significant; that is, there is no contextual effect.

An important difference between ANCOVA and contextual analysis can now be noted. In ANCOVA, the b's for the separate groups can be tested to determine whether the use of a common b is tenable. Recall that it is necessary to do this test before calculating adjusted means to see whether there are any group effects. In contextual analysis, on the other hand, it is not possible to test whether the separate regression coefficients are homogeneous. A common regression coefficient is all that one obtains and ends up using even when the separate regression coefficients are heterogeneous.

This shortcoming of contextual analysis aside, the focus in such an analysis is on the b for the vector of means. When this b is statistically significant, one can conclude that the group variable has an effect after the individual variable was partialed out—that is, a contextual effect was detected. It can be shown (e.g., Alwin, 1976; Firebaugh, 1978, 1979) that the b for the vector of means is equal to the difference between the between-groups regression coefficient (b_b) and the within-groups regression coefficients (b_w). Applying (16.8), $b_b = 1.358025$. For these data, then,

$$b_b - b_w = 1.358025 - 1.013052 = .344973$$

From this it is evident that when $b_b = b_w$, the regression coefficient for the vector of means (M in the present example) is zero and no contextual effect is indicated. Recall that a test of the b for the vector of means is equivalent to a test of the proportion of variance accounted for by this vector, over and above the vector of individuals' scores. It is possible to do such a test in the context of ANCOVA (see, for example, Myers, 1979, pp. 410–412; Schuessler, 1971, pp. 210–213). But, as these and other authors pointed out, the test is valid only when the within-groups regression coefficients are homogeneous and the regression of the Y means on the X means is linear. Here, then, is another weakness of contextual analysis; not only is it carried out as if the within-groups regression coefficients are homogeneous (see the preceding), but it is also assumed that the regression of the means of Y on the means of X is linear.[10] Because violations of both assumptions go undetected in contextual analysis, one cannot but deduce that such an analysis may lead to erroneous conclusions.

RUDIMENTARY MULTILEVEL ANALYSIS

Recognizing problems and pitfalls attendant with cross-level inferences (see earlier sections of this chapter), methodologists (e.g., Burstein, 1976; Burstein & Smith, 1977) attempted to provide guidelines for choice of the "appropriate" unit of analysis (e.g., individual, group) depending on the problem under investigation. However, some of the same methodologists (Burstein, 1980a, 1980b; Burstein, Linn, & Capell, 1978; Cronbach, 1976; Cronbach & Snow, 1977; Cronbach & Webb, 1975; Keesling, 1978; Snow, 1977) soon realized that a change in perspective was necessary. They reasoned that the issue was not one of choice of a unit of analysis but of the

---

[10]For a method of testing this assumption, see Schuessler (1971, pages 212–213). For a detailed discussion of the meaning of the test of the difference between b_b and b_w, see Smith (1957).

conceptualization and development of analytic approaches that will use the different types of information contained in the different levels or units frequently encountered in behavioral research.

It was about the same time that statistical theory and algorithms requisite for multilevel analysis were developed and incorporated in several computer programs: GENMOD (Mason, Anderson, & Hayat, 1988), HLM (Bryk, Raudenbush, Seltzer, & Congdon, 1989), ML3 (Prosser, Rasbash, & Goldstein, 1990), and VARCL (Longford, 1988). Models that can be analyzed by these programs are variously referred to as multilevel regression, multilevel linear models, hierarchical linear models, mixed-effects models, and random-effects models. In a thorough review and comparisons of the aforementioned programs, Kreft et al. (1990) showed that, though they differ in specific options and output, they yield essentially the same results.

Two things about Kreft et al.'s review are noteworthy. (1) Not surprisingly, even as they were working on it, the computer programs were undergoing corrections and revisions, calling to mind Wainer and Thissen's (1986) apt observation that "nowadays trying to get an up-to-date review of software or hardware is like trying to shovel the walk while it is still snowing" (p. 12). Therefore, it is important to keep in mind that "changes reported after November 15, 1989, have not been incorporated in our comparisons" (Kreft et al., p. 77). (2) Also not surprising, Kreft et al. "found a variety of bugs in the programs" (p. 100). Although more recent versions may still contain bugs, it goes without saying that you should use the latest version of whatever program you choose.[11]

You will find brief discussions of the conceptual and statistical advantages of multilevel analysis in the manuals for the respective computer programs. For more detailed discussions, see references given in the manuals and ones I give later in the chapter. For present purposes, I will discuss some contrasts between ordinary least squares and multilevel analysis to show advantages of the latter.

Ordinary Least Squares versus Multilevel Analysis

When ordinary least squares is applied to data of individuals from more than one group (i.e., when total statistics are estimated; see the preceding sections), it is assumed, willy-nilly, that group characteristics are irrelevant. Suffice it to mention contextual effects (see the preceding section) to appreciate the implausibility of this assumption. In contrast, multilevel analysis uses information from all available levels (e.g., students, classrooms, schools), making it possible to learn how variables at one level affect relations among variables at another level. Moreover, multilevel analysis affords estimation of variance between groups as distinct from variance within groups.

A least-squares solution ignores the fact that individuals belonging to a given group tend to be more alike than do individuals belonging to different groups. As a result, standard errors (e.g., of regression coefficients) are underestimated, resulting in increased Type I errors. Multilevel analysis, which is based on different estimation procedures, yields more realistic standard errors.

When based on small samples, ordinary least-squares estimates within units (e.g., regression equations within classrooms) are relatively unstable. By contrast, in multilevel analysis, data from all units are used and weighted according to their precision, thereby yielding more stable estimates.

---

[11]A recent review of five computer programs for multilevel analysis by Kreft, De Leeuw, and van der Leeden (1994) included release 2.1 of HLM. Later I will introduce HLM release 3.01.

Finally, multilevel analysis "allows specification of each variable at the conceptually appropriate level. Perhaps more important, the methods allow us to ask research questions which probably would otherwise have remained unasked" (Raudenbush & Willms, 1991a, p. xii).

HIERARCHICAL LINEAR MODELS (HLM)

Of the four computer programs I mentioned in the preceding section, I introduce only HLM$_3^2$ (Bryk, Raudenbush, & Congdon, 1994).[12] In their discussion of the design philosophy of HLM, Kreft et al. (1990) stated that

> it is the most popular program in the USA for at least two reasons: the easy-to-use interactive interface, and the output which includes significance tests, model testing, and other desirable properties. Another explanation is the educational character of the manual. It provides a theoretical background for multilevel modeling and an abundance of references for more study. The introduction explains why and how a hierarchical linear model is useful in many research situations. (p. 35)

Except for the absence of references in the manual because of a tie-in with a text (see the following), the preceding applies with even greater force to HLM$_3^2$. Two of its authors published a text devoted to hierarchical linear models in which HLM is prominently featured (Bryk & Raudenbush, 1992). As the authors of HLM$_3^2$ recommend, the program

> should be used in conjunction with the text, [as] the basic program structure, input specification, and output of results . . . closely coordinate with this textbook. This manual also cross-references the appropriate sections of the textbook for the reader interested in a full discussion of the details of parameter estimation and hypothesis testing. Many of the illustrative examples described in this manual are based on data distributed with the program and analyzed in the . . . text. (Bryk et al., 1994, p. 1)

For other explications of multilevel models and/or applications of such models, see Bock (1989); Cheung, Keeves, Sellin, and Tsoi (1990); Goldstein (1987); Hox and Kreft (1994); Jones, Johnston, and Pattie (1992); Kreft (1993a); Lee and Bryk (1989); Lee, Dedrick, and Smith (1991); Lee and Smith (1990, 1991); Mason, Wong, and Entwisle (1983); Nuttall, Goldstein, Prosser, and Rasbash (1989); Oosthoek and Van Den Eeden (1984); Pallas, Entwisle, Alexander, and Stluka (1994); Raudenbush (1988, 1993); Raudenbush and Bryk (1986, 1988); Raudenbush and Willms (1991b); Rowan, Raudenbush, and Kang (1991); Seltzer (1994); Willms (1986); Woodhouse and Goldstein (1988). In addition, you will find valuable information about recent developments and publications in the *Multilevel Modelling Newsletter,* published by the Department of Mathematics, Statistics & Computing, Institute of Education, University of London, 20 Bedford Way, London WC1H 0AL, England, e-mail:temsmya@ioe.ac.uk. The establishment of a World Wide Web site by the Multilevel Models project was announced in the June 1995 issue of the *Multilevel Modelling Newsletter.* Following are some services that it will provide:

- An introduction to multilevel models and some application fields.

---

[12]HLM$_3^2$ is a registered trademark of Scientific Software International, Inc., whom I would like to thank for furnishing me with a copy of the program. For information about HLM$_3^2$, contact Scientific Software, 1525 East 53rd Street, Suite 530, Chicago, IL 60615-4530. Telephone: 800-247-6113.

- Recent issues of the MM Newsletter and example data sets in compressed form for downloading.
- Links to other relevant Web sites. (p. 1)

The site address for public access is

http://www.ioe.ac.uk/multilevel

A Two-Level Model

Although in principle, models with any number of levels may be analyzed, two levels (e.g., students within classes, employees within organizations) were used in most applications. (HLM$\frac{2}{3}$ can also accommodate three-level models, as in a design of, say, students within classes and classes within schools.) In what follows, I briefly outline the analysis of a two-level model and then give a numerical example.

In line with my introductory remarks to this chapter, I would like to stress that my aim is *not* to give a formal statement of multilevel analysis but to describe it conceptually. To this end, it will be helpful to think of the analysis of a two-level model as a two-stage process. In the first stage, the dependent variable is regressed on level-1 independent variables within each unit (e.g., classes), yielding separate regression equations for each. In the second stage, coefficients (i.e., intercept and/or regression coefficients) estimated in the first stage are treated as dependent variables. Of interest at the second stage are sources of variability of coefficients estimated at the first stage. For example, when one finds that the regression coefficient for the regression of academic achievement on, say, mental ability varies in different classes (groups, settings, and the like), the question to address at the second stage is what characteristics of the classes (groups, settings, and the like) affect the coefficient. In other words, at the second stage, level-2 variables (e.g., teacher attributes, per pupil expenditure, group climate, mean mental ability) serve as the independent variables.

I hasten to point out that in a review of a book on applications of multilevel analysis, Kreft (1993b, pp. 125–127) cautioned against conceiving the analysis as a two-stage process and drew attention to misinterpretations to which this may lead. I strongly recommend that you read Kreft's insightful and instructive review.

A Numerical Example

In what follows, I use HLM$\frac{2}{3}$ version 3.01. Although the program can be executed in batch (see the manual, p. 3l; also the following)[13]—a mode I use throughout the book—I introduce HLM$\frac{2}{3}$ through its interactive mode for two reasons: (1) I wish to comment on some of its options, and (2) the batch format would, I think, be unintelligible to a novice. After I present and comment on the analysis in interactive mode, I give a file for running the same example in batch. In HLM$\frac{2}{3}$, two-level and three-level models are referred to, respectively, as HLM/2L and HLM/3L. *As I will be discussing and using only a two-level model, I will, for convenience, refer to it as HLM.*

To give you a glimpse at a multilevel analysis, I will use the simplest example possible consisting of one level-1 and one level-2 independent variable. For illustrative purposes, I will use a miniature example consisting of eight groups, each comprised of ten employees, as given in

---

[13]Unless otherwise stated, the page numbers I use hereafter refer to the manual (Bryk et al., 1994).

Table 16.4. Assume that the dependent variable, *Y,* is employee productivity (PRODUCT), and the independent variable, *X,* is job satisfaction (JOBSAT). Further, assume that the eight groups of employees are employed in similar settings (e.g., factory, office) and that cohesiveness of each group was rated on a 7-point scale, where 1 = very low cohesiveness and 7 = very high cohesiveness. These ratings are given in Table 16.5.

You may prefer to think of the data as having been obtained in an area of your interest. For example, the eight groups may represent eight classes taught by different teachers, where *Y* is,

Table 16.4   Illustrative Data and Estimates for Eight Groups

	1		*2*		*3*		*4*	
	Y	X	Y	X	Y	X	Y	X
	12	10	13	8	14	4	15	4
	15	10	16	8	16	4	16	5
	14	12	15	10	18	6	13	5
	14	14	16	12	20	6	15	6
	18	14	19	12	18	7	19	6
	18	16	17	16	19	8	17	7
	16	16	19	16	22	8	20	7
	14	18	23	18	21	9	18	9
	18	18	19	20	23	10	20	9
	19	20	22	20	20	10	21	11
M:	15.80	14.80	17.90	14.00	19.10	7.20	17.40	6.90
s:	2.35	3.42	3.11	4.62	2.73	2.20	2.63	2.18
r_{yx}:	.658		.821		.848		.781	
a:	9.129		10.171		11.537		10.902	
b:	.451		.552		1.050		.942	

	5		*6*		*7*		*8*	
	Y	X	Y	X	Y	X	Y	X
	14	6	14	6	15	7	19	8
	17	6	17	6	17	7	20	9
	16	7	16	7	19	9	17	9
	16	8	17	8	21	9	19	10
	20	8	20	8	19	10	23	10
	20	9	18	10	20	11	21	11
	18	9	20	10	23	11	24	11
	16	10	24	11	22	12	22	13
	20	10	20	12	24	13	24	13
	21	11	23	12	21	13	25	15
M:	17.80	8.40	18.90	9.00	20.10	10.20	21.40	10.90
s:	2.35	1.71	3.11	2.31	2.73	2.20	2.63	2.18
r_{yx}:	.658		.821		.848		.781	
a:	10.227		8.963		9.385		11.135	
b:	.902		1.104		1.050		.941	

NOTE: *1* through *8* are groups; *Y* = dependent variable (productivity, in my example); *X* = independent variable (job satisfaction, in my example); *M* = mean; *s* = standard deviation; *a* = intercept; and *b* = regression coefficient.

Table 16.5   Illustrative Ratings of Cohesiveness

ID	COHESIVE
1	3
2	2
3	3
4	2
5	4
6	5
7	6
8	7

NOTE: *ID* = group identification; *COHESIVE*: 1 = very low, 7 = very high.

say, academic achievement (ACH), and *X* is, say, student aptitude (APT). The level-2 variable may be a rating of teachers on, say, ability (commitment, motivation) using a 7-point scale, where 1 = very low and 7 = very high. Other examples come readily to mind.

Input Files

HLM requires two input files, a within-units file and a between-units file, which are used to generate an "SSM file" (Sufficient Statistics Matrices, p. 9). Thereafter, the SSM file (see the following) is used as input. The first piece of information in each input file must be an ID, which links the within-units data with those of the between-units. *"Note, all level-1 cases must be grouped together by their respective level-2 id"* (p. 14). A FORTRAN-STYLE format is used for input, where the ID is read in A (alphanumeric) format and the data are read in F format (see p. 16, for an explanation of acceptable formats).

In line with the preceding, I created two files for the example under consideration: (1) TAB164.W, consisting of a group ID and two level-1 variables (from Table 16.4), and (2) TAB165.B, consisting of a group ID and one level-2 variable (from Table 16.5). To show the layout of the within-units file, I will list the data for the first two cases from each of the eight groups. As the between-units file is very small, I will list it in its entirety.

TAB164.W

```
1 12 10    [col. 1 = group ID; col. 3–4 = PRODUCT; col. 6–7 = JOBSAT]
1 15 10    [first two subjects in group 1, Table 16.4]

.  .   .
2 13  8    [first two subjects in group 2]
2 16  8

.  .   .
3 14  4    [first two subjects in group 3]
3 16  4

.  .   .
4 15  4    [first two subjects in group 4]
4 16  5

.  .   .
```

```
5 14   6        [first two subjects in group 5]
5 17   6
.   .   .
6 14   6        [first two subjects in group 6]
6 17   6
.   .   .
7 15   7        [first two subjects in group 7]
7 17   7
.   .   .
8 19   8        [first two subjects in group 8]
8 20   9
```

TAB165.B

1 3	*[col. 1 = group ID; col. 3 = COHESIVE, Table 16.5]*
2 2	
3 3	
4 2	
5 4	
6 5	
7 6	
8 7	

Following are the input formats:
(A1,2F3.0) for TAB164.W; (A1,F2.0) for TAB165.B (see the following comments).

CONSTRUCTING AN SSM FILE

At the DOS prompt, I typed: **HLM2L**

Following are program prompts and my responses (capitalized and in bold for clarity). My comments are indented, italicized, and in brackets to distinguish them from the prompts.

Will you be starting with raw data? **Y**
[The answer is yes when a new data set is used, so that a SUFFICIENT STATISTICS MATRICES (SSM) file would be created. Below, I display excerpts of this file and comment on them.]

Is the input a v-known file? **N**

Are the input files SYSTAT.SYS files? **N**
[See p. 19.]

Input number of level-1 variables (not including the character ID): **2**

Input format of level-1 file (the first field must be the character ID) format: **(A1,2F3.0)**
[A1 indicates that the ID occupies the first column, and 2F3.0 indicates that each of the two variables occupies three columns, including a leading blank column, which I used for readability.]

Input name of level-1 file: **TAB164.W**

Is there missing data in the level-1 file? **N**
[See p. 10, for handling missing data.]

Input number of level-2 variables (not including the character ID): **1**

Input format of level-2 file (the first field must be the character ID) format: **(A1,F2.0)**

Input name of level-2 file: **TAB165.B**

Enter 8 character name for level-1 variable number 1? **PRODUCT**
Enter 8 character name for level-1 variable number 2? **JOBSAT**
Enter 8 character name for level-2 variable number 1? **COHESIVE**

Is there a level-1 weighting variable? **N**

Is there a level-2 weighting variable? **N**

Enter name of SSM file: **TAB164.SSM**

LEVEL-1 DESCRIPTIVE STATISTICS					
VARIABLE NAME	N	MEAN	SD	MINIMUM	MAXIMUM
PRODUCT	80	18.55	3.06	12.00	25.00
JOBSAT	80	10.18	3.82	4.00	20.00

Do you wish to save these descriptive statistics in a file? **Y**

LEVEL-2 DESCRIPTIVE STATISTICS					
VARIABLE NAME	N	MEAN	SD	MINIMUM	MAXIMUM
COHESIVE	8	4.00	1.85	2.00	7.00

80 level-1 records have been processed
8 level-2 records have been processed

Commentary

Because of my "Y" response, the above information is saved in a file named HLMSSM.STS. Whether or not you save these results, "it is important to review . . . [them] closely in order to assure that the data have been properly read into HLM/2L" (p. 18).

In addition, the program generates a log file: CREATESS.RSP, which can be used to learn what may have led to unreasonable results (see p. 18). If you wish to retain HLMSSM.STS and/or CREATESS.RSP, rename them as they are overwritten whenever a new SSM file is created.

It is always useful to examine the SSM file. Because this file is written in binary format, HLM provides a program (PRSSM2) to convert it to ASCII format (see p. 10). To convert my SSM file, I issued the following command at the DOS prompt:

PRSSM2 TAB164.SSM TAB164.SUM

Output

SSM file was made with version 3.01

There are 80 records at level-1
There are 8 records at level-2

There are 2 level-1 variables. Their names are:
PRODUCT   JOBSAT
There are 1 level-2 variables. Their names are:
COHESIVE
Level-1 grand means
18.549999 10.175000
Level-2 grand means
4.000000

10	*[number of subjects; unit 1]*
15.800000 14.800000	*[level-1 means; see Table 16.4]*
49.600000	*[sums of squares (diagonal);*
47.600000 105.600000	*cross products (off diagonal)]*
1 3.000000	*[unit ID, value of level-2 variable; see Table 16.5]*

. . . .

10	*[number of subjects; unit 8]*
21.400000 10.900000	*[level-1 means; see Table 16.4]*
62.400000	*[sums of squares (diagonal);*
40.400000 42.900000	*cross products (off diagonal)]*
8 7.000000	*[unit ID, value of level-2 variable; see Table 16.5]*

Commentary

The preceding are excerpts from the T164.SUM file (i.e., the converted T164.SSM file). As I indicated in the italicized comments, the two lines following the means of level-1 variables constitute a lower diagonal matrix of sum of squares and cross products of level-1 variables for the given unit. For example, for unit number 1, the sums of squares for PRODUCT and JOBSAT are, respectively, 49.6 and 105.60. The sum of cross products for PRODUCT and JOBSAT is 47.6. Using relevant values from this matrix, verify corresponding standard deviations and correlations reported in Table 16.4. For example, the standard deviation for PRODUCT is $\sqrt{(49.6)/9}$ = 2.348. The correlation between PRODUCT and JOBSAT is $47.6/\sqrt{(49.6)(105.6)}$ = .658.

Hereafter, the SSM file is used as input. To avoid some of the initial program prompts, one can type HLM2L and the name of the SSM file (HLM2L TAB164.SSM, for the present example). Before I do this, though, I comment on a default command file used to switch off, or set, specific features of the program. When the user does not include a command file name on the command line, the default command file supplied with HLM (COMFILE2.HLM) is used.

The contents of this file are listed on page 39. You can create your own command file, or edit COMFILE2.HLM, to switch off, or set, specific features (see Table 2.1, pp. 40–41, for keywords and options). Later, I give an example of such a file for running the numerical example I am analyzing here. HLM$\frac{2}{3}$ is supplied with several examples of such files.

I will now run HLM, using as input TAB164.SSM—the sufficient statistics file created in the first run. At the DOS prompt, I typed: **HLM2L TAB164.SSM**
Instead of creating a command file and specifying it on the command line, I edited the default command file (COMFILE2.HLM, see the preceding) changing the convergence criterion for stopping iterations from "0.000001" (see "stopval," p. 39) to 0.0001.

Following are the program prompts and my responses (capitalized and in bold for clarity). My comments are indented, italicized, and in brackets.

Output

Please specify a level-1 outcome variable
  The choices are:
  For PRODUCT enter 1   FOR JOBSAT enter 2
What is the outcome variable: **1**
   [I designate PRODUCT as the dependent variable.]

Do you wish to:
    Examine means,variances,chi-squared, etc.?   Enter 1
    Specify an HLM model?   Enter 2
    Define a new outcome variable?   Enter 3
    Exit?   Enter 4
What do you want to do? **2**
   [For an example and explanation of output when 1 is selected, see pp. 47–50.]

SPECIFYING AN HLM MODEL

Level-1 predictor variable specification

Which level-1 predictors do you wish to use?
  The choices are:
             FOR JOBSAT enter 2

level-1 predictor? (Enter 0 to end) **2**
   [Only JOBSAT (2) is available in the present example.]

Do you want to center any level-1 predictors? **Y**
(Enter 0 for no centering, enter 1 for group-mean, 2 for grand-mean)
How do you want to center   JOBSAT? **1**
   [In earlier chapters (e.g., 10 and 13) I explained the meaning and uses of centering, that is, subtracting the mean from each score. As you can see, in HLM you can choose to not center (0), center around the group mean (1), or center around the grand mean (2). When a variable is centered around the group mean, the within-unit intercept is the dependent-variable mean for the group in question (see the following output and commentaries). For a

discussion of the use of centering to enhance substantive interpretations, see Bryk and Raudenbush (1992, pp. 25–28).

There is no agreement about the value of centering for substantive interpretation. For a general good discussion of centering, see Iversen (1991, pp. 35–72). For an exchange on this topic in the context of multilevel analysis, see Longford (1989), Plewis (1989, 1990), and Raudenbush (1989a, 1989b). Plewis (1990) appears to convey accurately the general stance of the discussants: "In particular, we all agreed on the importance of linking model specification to the research question to [sic] hand, rather than seeing it [centering] as an unconnected technical problem which can always be solved in the same way" (p. 8). I used centering around the group mean to acquaint you with this option. As Kreft (1993b, p. 125) pointed out, centering is neither used nor recommended by authors of other multilevel-analysis programs. After drawing attention to studies in which only some of the variables were centered, Kreft asserted that arguments in favor of centering were not convincing. Finally, she expressed the belief that users of HLM may be inclined to use centering because the "standard question 'Do you want to center one or more variables?' . . . suggests that would be a good idea" (Kreft, 1993b, p. 125). For a detailed discussion of different forms of centering in HLM, see Kreft, de Leeuw, and Aiken (1995).]

Do you want to set the level-1 intercept to zero in this analysis? **N**
   [See p. 21.]

Level-2 predictor variable specification

Which level-2 variables do you wish to use?
The choices are:
   For COHESIVE enter 1

Which level-2 predictor to model INTRCPT1?
   Level-2 predictor? (Enter 0 to end) **1**

Which level-2 predictor to model JOBSAT slope?
   Level-2 predictor? (Enter 0 to end) **1**
   [In the present example only COHESIVE (1) is available. When more variables are available, some or all may be selected in the same manner. Selection is ended by typing a 0.]

Do you want to constrain the variances in any of the level-2 random effects to zero? **N**
   [See p. 22, for an explanation of the preceding prompts.]

Do you want to center any level-2 predictors? **N**

ADDITIONAL PROGRAM FEATURES

Select the level-2 variables that you might consider for inclusion as predictors in subsequent models.
   The choices are:
   For COHESIVE enter 1

Which level-2 variables to model INTRCPT1?
    Level-2 variable (Enter 0 to end) **0**
Which level-2 variables to model JOBSAT slope?
    Level-2 variable (Enter 0 to end) **0**
    [Responses in the present example are necessarily 0, as the only level-2 variable is
    COHESIVE, which I already used above.]

OUTPUT SPECIFICATIONS

How many iterations do you want to do? **100**
    [See p. 44.]

    Enter a problem title: **CHAPTER 16. TABLES 16.4 AND 16.5**
    Enter name of output file: **TAB164.OUT**
Computing . . . , please wait
Starting values computed. Iterations begun.

Output

```
*************************************************************
*                                                           *
*          H   H  L       M    M   22                        *
*          H   H  L       MM MM   2  2                       *
*          HHHHH  L       M  M M    2        Version 3.01    *
*          H   H  L       M    M   2                         *
*          H   H  LLLLL   M    M  2222                       *
*                                                           *
*************************************************************
```

    Problem Title: CHAPTER 16. TABLES 16.4 AND 16.5

    The data source for this run = TAB164.SSM
    Output file name   = TAB164.OUT
    The maximum number of level-2 units = 8
    The maximum number of iterations = 100
Weighting Specification

	Weighting?	Weight Variable Name	Normalized?
Level 1	no		no
Level 2	no		no

    The outcome variable is PRODUCT

    The model specified for the fixed effects was:

```
-----------------------------------------------------------

      Level-1                   Level-2
      Coefficients              Predictors
---------------------------    ---------------------

      INTRCPT1, B0             INTRCPT2, G00
                               COHESIVE, G01
*     JOBSAT slope, B1         INTRCPT2, G10
                               COHESIVE, G11
```

'*' - This level-1 predictor has been centered around its group mean.

Summary of the model specified (in equation format)
```
------------------------------------------------------------------
```

Level-1 Model

$$Y = B0 + B1*(JOBSAT) + R$$

Level-2 Model

$$B0 = G00 + G01*(COHESIVE) + U0$$
$$B1 = G10 + G11*(COHESIVE) + U1$$

Commentary

I believe that most of the preceding requires no comment. Accordingly, I will only give and explain notation used to represent the above equations in presentations of HLM.

Level-1 Model

$$Y_{ij} = \beta_{0j} + \beta_{1j}(JOBSAT)_{ij} + r_{ij}$$

where Y_{ij} = score of individual (employee, in the present example) i on the dependent variable (productivity, in the present example) in setting (group) j; β_{0j} = intercept of regression equation in setting j; β_{1j} = regression coefficient for independent variable (JOBSAT, in the present example) in setting j; $(JOBSAT)_{ij}$ = score on job satisfaction for employee i in setting j; and r_{ij} = random component for employee i in setting j.

Level-2 Model

$$\beta_{0j} = \gamma_{00} + \gamma_{01}(COHESIVE)_j + u_{0j}$$
$$\beta_{1j} = \gamma_{10} + \gamma_{11}(COHESIVE)_j + u_{1j}$$

In the preceding, γ's (gamma) are interpreted as intercept and regression coefficients, where level-1 parameters (β's) are treated, in turn, as dependent variables. The aim is to see whether level-2 variables (COHESIVE, in the present example) help explain variation of intercepts and regression coefficients across groups. u_{0j} and u_{1j} are random components for β_{0j} and β_{1j}, respectively, after controlling for level-2 variable(s) (COHESIVE, in the present example).

Output

Level-1 OLS regressions

```
-----------------------------
```

Level-2 Unit	INTRCPT1	JOBSAT slope
1	15.80000	0.45076
2	17.90000	0.55208
3	19.10000	1.05046
4	17.40000	0.94172
5	17.80000	0.90152
6	18.90000	1.10417
7	20.10000	1.05046
8	21.40000	0.94172

The average OLS level-1 coefficient for INTRCPT1 = 18.55000
The average OLS level-1 coefficient for   JOBSAT =   0.87411

Commentary

Reproduced here are ordinary least-squares (OLS) estimates of the regression equations for the separate groups. In Chapter 2—see (2.10) and the explanation related to it—I showed that when the independent variable is centered, the intercept is equal to the dependent-variable mean, and the regression coefficient is identical to that obtained when raw scores are used. Because JOBSAT was centered around the group mean (see the preceding), the intercepts in these equations are means of PRODUCT for the respective groups (see Table 16.4). Contrast the intercepts given in the preceding with those for noncentered data given in Table 16.4. Also, compare the regression coefficients reported in the preceding with those given in Table 16.4.

When the independent variable is centered around the group mean (as in the preceding), interpretation of the regression coefficient is made with respect to individuals' standing relative to the group mean. In other words, the regression coefficient indicates expected change in the dependent variable associated with a unit change relative to the mean (see Iversen, 1991, pp. 35–48, for a discussion of "relative" and "absolute" effects).

Output

The value of the likelihood function at iteration 1 = −1.701797E+02

.

.

.

The value of the likelihood function at iteration 20 = −1.701310E+02
Iterations stopped due to small change in likelihood function

Commentary

Reproduced here is the likelihood function at the first and the 20th iteration. As you can see, iterations were terminated early as convergence was reached (earlier I pointed out that I changed the criterion for stopping iterations in the command file). When the program terminates before reaching convergence, increase the limit for the number of iterations and run the analysis again.

Output

Sigma_squared = 3.04348
 [variance of level-1 random component r_{ij}; see the previous commentary on Summary of the model specified (in equation format)]

Tau
INTRCPT1	0.96021	0.11882
JOBSAT	0.11882	0.01731

 [variance/covariance matrix (T) of level-2 random components u_{0j} and u_{1j}; see the previous commentary on Summary of the model specified (in equation format)]

Tau (as correlations)
INTRCPT1	1.000	0.922
JOBSAT	0.922	1.000

Random level-1 coefficient	Reliability estimate
INTRCPT1, B0	0.759
JOBSAT, B1	0.254

Commentary

The diagonal of Tau is composed of variances (.96021 = variance of the intercept; .01731 = variance of the regression coefficient). Notice that the variance of the intercept is considerably larger than that of the regression coefficient.

The off-diagonal(s) element(s) of Tau is the covariance of the respective terms (intercept and regression coefficients, in the present example). For interpretive purposes, Tau is transformed into correlations, from which it can be seen that the correlation between the intercept and the regression coefficient is very high (.922). What this means is that larger intercepts (means, because of centering) tend to be associated with larger regression coefficients.

In light of the fact that in HLM estimated parameter variance is distinguished from estimated error, or sampling, variance, it is possible to arrive at overall reliability estimates of level-1 parameter estimates β_{0j} and β_{1j} (see Bryk & Raudenbush, 1992, p. 43). Recall that reliability estimates can range from 0 to 1 (see, e.g., Chapter 2). In the present example, the reliability of the estimate of β_{0j} (INTRCPT1, B0) is moderate (.759), whereas that of β_{1j} (JOBSAT, B1) is low (.254)—a pattern generally encountered in multilevel analysis (for an explanation, see Bryk & Raudenbush, 1992, pp. 43 and 69).

Output

The outcome variable is PRODUCT

Final estimation of fixed effects:

Fixed Effect	Coefficient	Standard Error	T-ratio	P-value
For INTRCPT1, B0				
INTRCPT2, G00	15.583333	1.000775	15.571	0.000
COHESIVE, G01	0.741667	0.229593	3.230	0.014
For JOBSAT slope, B1				
INTRCPT2, G10	0.419130	0.210822	1.988	0.064
COHESIVE, G11	0.098795	0.053514	1.846	0.077

Commentary

G(amma) coefficients are interpreted as in ordinary regression analysis. Thus, the expected change in the within-unit intercept (B0)—which because of centering is mean PRODUCT (see the preceding)—associated with a unit change in COHESIVE is .741667, $t = 3.228, p < .05$. By contrast, G(amma) for the regression coefficient (B1) is .098795 and statistically not significant at $\alpha = .05$. This is primarily due to the very small "sample" sizes and the fact that, except for the first two coefficients (.451 and .552), the remaining coefficients range from about .9 to about 1.1 (see output above or Table 16.4). This example should serve as a reminder of the importance of using appropriate sample sizes and of studying the OLS estimates.

Output

Final estimation of variance components:

Random Effect	Standard Deviation	Variance Component	df	Chi-square	P-value
INTRCPT1, U0	0.97991	0.96021	6	25.03164	0.001
JOBSAT slope, U1	0.13157	0.01731	6	6.85721	0.334
level-1, R	1.74456	3.04348			

Statistics for current covariance components model

Deviance =   340.26171
Number of estimated parameters =   4

Commentary

Based on the statistically significant Chi-square associated with variance of INTRCPT1, the null hypothesis would be rejected, leading to the conclusion that after controlling for COHESIVE, variation among means remains to be explained. By contrast, based on the P-value (.334) for the Chi-square associated with the variance of JOBSAT slope, the null hypothesis cannot be rejected. That is, no variance remains to be explained.

Often it is of interest to do multiparameter tests of variance-covariance components. This is accomplished by testing the difference between two models: one of which (restricted) is nested within the other (full). The restricted model is obtained by constraining parameters of the full model (e.g., hypothesizing that they are equal to zero). The difference between the two models is tested by the likelihood ratio test for which Deviance statistics (an example of which is reported in the above output) are used (see pp. 52 and 54–55; also, Bryk & Raudenbush, 1992, p. 56 and 74–76). In Chapter 17, I explain the likelihood ratio test and illustrate its application in logistic regression analysis (see also, Chapters 18 and 19).

Batch Processing

Earlier, I said that I would give a command file for executing HLM in batch mode, using the numerical example I analyzed earlier. Following is a listing of the file, which I named T164.HLM, along with brief comments on it.

```
LEVEL1:PRODUCT=INTRCPT1+JOBSAT,1+RANDOM
        [1 following JOBSAT specifies centering around group mean]
LEVEL2:INTRCPT1=INTRCPT2+COHESIVE+RANDOM
LEVEL2:JOBSAT=INTRCPT2+COHESIVE+RANDOM/
NUMIT:100
LEV1OLS:10
RESFIL:N
HYPOTH:N
STOPVAL:.0001
CONSTRAIN:N
FIXTAU:3
OUTPUT:T164BAT.OUT
TITLE: CHAPTER 16, TABLES 16.4 AND 16.5
```

Commentary

For an explanation of running HLM in batch mode, accompanied by several examples, see pages 38–47. For an explanation of keywords and options I used in the above file, see Table 2.1, pages 40–41. I comment only on HYPOTH:N. As is stated in Table 2.1, "during batch execution, hypoth:n should be selected in order to suppress screen prompt" (p. 40). I would like to point out that screen prompts are *not* suppressed even when HYPOTH:N is specified when, as in the present example, the use of exploratory analysis for assessing the possible inclusion of level-2 variables in subsequent models is inapplicable (the example consists of only one level-2 variable; see my comment on the relevant prompt in the input for the interactive processing). After some experimentation, I found out that by terminating either of the LEVEL2 lines in the preceding file with a forward slash (/), the screen prompt is indeed suppressed. Note that such a slash is used to separate the level-2 variables in the model from ones to be used in exploratory analysis (see, e.g., p. 42).

To run my example in batch mode, I typed the following at the DOS prompt:
HLM2L TAB164.SSM T164.HLM
TAB164.SSM is the sufficient statistics matrices file I generated earlier and used in the interactive mode, and T164.HLM is the above listed command file.

CAVEATS

I conclude this section with some caveats that, though briefly stated, merit your serious consideration.

Don't Attempt Multilevel Modeling without Further Study

My presentation was but a brief sketch of multilevel analysis. To understand the research literature or to carry out multilevel analysis, it is imperative that you first study the topic thoroughly.

The Plausibility of the Model Is Paramount

I hope that you recognize by now that when the model is questionable, nothing else matters. Think clearly and critically about the model. Applying multilevel analysis to an implausible model is bound to lead to confusion.

Use Computer Programs and Read Research Reports Judiciously

Computer programs seem to undergo continuous revision. When written in an evolving field like multilevel analysis, different versions of the same program may yield radically different results. Among other things, this may be due to the use of different algorithms and to ubiquitous bugs that have become accepted as a fact of computing life. Following are a couple of instances. (1) In the discussion of an illustrative example in the HLM 2.2 manual (Bryk et al., 1989), the reader is told, "the results reported here are somewhat different from those in Strenio et al. The program employed in that paper resulted in an underestimate of the within-unit error variance" (p. 12). (2) In a discussion of results of an analysis in the HLM$\frac{2}{3}$ manual, the reader is told, *"These results are slightly more precise than those reported in Table 4.5, p. 72 of Hierarchical Linear Models, because they are based on the more efficient computing routines used in Version 3"* (Bryk et al., 1994, p. 27).

Perusal of the multilevel-modeling literature reveals discrepancies between results reported by the same authors of more than one paper in which they seem to have tested the same models using the same data. See, for example, discrepancies between Lee and Smith (1990) and Lee and Smith (1991). As but one instance, I will point out that there are discrepancies in results reported in their Table 3 (p. 71 of the former and p. 240 of the latter). Although ascertaining the source of the discrepancies is not possible, it is likely that different versions of HLM were used in the preparation of the two reports. It is noteworthy that in a comment on Lee and Smith (1991), Woodhouse (1992) stated:

> By the time I reached Table 3 in Chapter 15 (p240) [*sic*], which contains a suspiciously large estimate for a quadratic effect of years of experience and variance estimates which do not appear to agree with

those in Table 4 on the next page, I gave up trying to understand the implications and assumed that these too were mistakes. (p. 2)[14]

Finally, try not to be influenced by computer programs in what results of your investigation you report and how you report them. Evidently, this is easier said than done, as is attested by Kreft's (1993b) observation in her review of a compilation of studies from a multilevel perspective: "the choice of software packages has an influence on the emphases and intentions in the authors' reports" (p. 128).

Measurement Considerations

Early in this book (Chapter 2), I drew attention to adverse effects of measurement errors on regression estimates. In subsequent chapters, I elaborated on this topic and also introduced issues concerning the use of multiple indicators (e.g., Chapters 9 and 10; see also Chapter 19). Unfortunately, as Burstein, Kim, and Delandshere (1989) pointed out: "Most of the specific analytical models for multilevel analysis are silent about measurement problems of any kind. They typically operate as if one had perfectly measured the latent variables of interest" (p. 250). Further, "none of the widely heralded analytical alternatives allows for multiple indicators" (p. 250). This is particularly troubling when one realizes that "taking seriously the possibility of profound effects due to aspects of . . . organizational (group) levels opens up a virtual Pandora's box of measurement and statistical dilemmas" (Sirotnik & Burstein, 1985, p. 171). As but one instance, Sirotnik and Burstein argued cogently that "there is simply no logical reason to suppose that the 'something' being measured at the group level is the same thing that is being measured at the individual level" (p. 176; see also Sirotnik, 1980).

It is noteworthy that an announcement about "future plans for the multilevel models project," published in *Multilevel Modelling Newsletter,* 1990, *2*(1), included the following statement:

> The present methods involve the assumption that the explanatory variables are measured without error. This assumption is often violated leading to bias in parameter estimates. While the basic theory for measurement error in the level 1 explanatory variables has been developed . . . , *it has not been implemented or applied. It also needs extending to deal with measurement error in higher level explanatory variables* [italics added]. (p. 4)

For some attempts to come to grips with measurement issues and latent variables in the context of multilevel analysis, see McDonald (1994); Muthén (1990, 1991, 1994); and Yang, Woodhouse, Goldstein, Pan, and Rasbash (1992).

CONCLUDING REMARKS

I began this chapter by discussing pitfalls inherent in cross-level inferences, following which I introduced the notion of within, between, and total statistics and explained relations among them. I then pointed out that awareness that the three types of statistics may yield different

---

[14]Without going into Lee and Smith's model specification, I would like to draw your attention to their questionable interpretation of a simultaneous analysis that includes linear and quadratic terms of years of teaching experience, as is exemplified by the following statement: "The strongest effect on salary is experience . . . and the negative effect of the quadratic term is also quite strong" (1991, p. 239). For detailed discussions of polynomial regression, see Chapter 13 of this book.

results led to attempts to answer the question about the appropriate unit of analysis. However, it was soon realized that preoccupation with this question was imprudent, as the choice of one level to the exclusion of another may result in either masking certain effects or in showing effects when none existed. Accordingly, efforts were directed to the development of analytic approaches commensurate with the multilevel models called for in studies involving more than one level. I then presented a rudimentary introduction to multilevel analysis.

The potential benefits of multilevel modeling are undeniable, not the least of them being the shedding of new light on findings or dethroning "verities" arrived at through unilevel modeling. An early example is given in Cronbach and Webb's (1975) reanalysis of an ATI study by Anderson (1941). Briefly, Anderson used 18 fourth-grade classes in a study of the effects of drill versus meaningful instruction on achievement in arithmetic. Using the individual as the unit of analysis, Anderson reported an interaction between the methods of instruction and student ability. Cronbach and Webb (1975) reanalyzed Anderson's data separately within and between classes. Without going into the details of their analyses, I will note that they concluded that Anderson's data did not support the hypothesis of an interaction between the teaching methods and student ability. As Cronbach (1992) put it, "Reanalysis reduced the findings to rubble" (p. 397).

Regrettably, many behavioral science fields of study do not even evidence an awareness of problems that may arise in studies involving more than one level, let alone familiarity with recent developments in multilevel modeling. In some fields where there is an awareness of the problems, approaches to dealing with them are outmoded, inadequate, or wrong. Following are a couple of examples.

In a critique of a published study, Ahlgren (1990) stated, "Although there is sometimes room for argument about whether students or classes are the appropriate unit of analysis" (p. 712), it is clear that in the study in question the class should have been used. I will not comment on the vestigial question of the appropriate unit of analysis. Instead, I will point out that in a response, the author (Lawrenz, 1990) stated that because she was "looking for possible perceptual differences within a class," she "could not use the class mean as the unit of analysis" (p. 713). Without going into details or other aspects of the author's response, it will suffice to point out that in carrying out a total analysis (i.e., analyzing scores of individuals from different classes and different schools), she could not address the question she sought to answer.

The second example comes from a study whose expressed aim was "reconsidering the unit of analysis" (Cranton & Smith, 1990, p. 207). Briefly, Cranton and Smith were interested in studying the structure of students' ratings of instruction. They asserted that "it is now generally accepted that class mean ratings should be used . . . however, it has not yet been demonstrated empirically that this unit of analysis yields a different structure" (p. 207). Accordingly, they carried out three factor analyses "using individual ratings, class means, and deviations from class means" (p. 207). Based on their analyses they concluded that "the underlying structure of class means is different from the structure yielded by the other units of analysis" (p. 207).

Without going far afield, I will comment briefly on what I believe are the most egregious errors and misconceptions of this study.

First, probably most surprising is that the authors did not give a single reference to the extensive methodological literature addressed to analytic questions when data from more than one level are available, including recent development in comparisons of factor structures from different groups. The literature on these topics seems to have gone unnoticed not only by the authors but also by the referees and the editors. Witness the statement by the editor of the special section on instruction in higher education of which Cranton and Smith's (1990) paper was a part:

> Although researchers have repeatedly debated whether individual ratings, class means, or deviations from class means are the appropriate unit . . . further empirical evidence is warranted. Cranton and Smith contribute to this debate in support of class means as the appropriate unit of analysis. (Perry, 1990, p. 185)

Second, even a modicum understanding of relations among total, between, and within correlations—see (16.10) through (16.12) and the discussion related to them—should suffice to realize that the approach taken by Cranton and Smith is neither original nor meaningful.

Third, it is important to recognize that correlations based on "deviations from class means" (p. 207) are *pooled within class correlations.* As I stressed earlier in this chapter, this type of correlation may be used only when it has been established that the correlations do not differ significantly across classes. To get a glimpse at the deleterious consequences of ignoring this issue, I refer you to a numerical example in Chapter 14. Recall that I used the illustrative data in Table 14.3 to show how students' tolerance of ambiguity interacted with teaching styles (nondirective and directive) in their effects on ratings of the teachers. For present purposes, I suggest that you reanalyze the data to obtain the correlation of tolerance of ambiguity and teacher ratings within each group as well as the pooled within-groups correlation.[15] You may wish to do the analysis using Tables 16.1 and 16.2 as guides or you may choose to do it by computer. In any case, if you did the analysis, you would find that the correlation between tolerance of ambiguity and ratings is .943 in the class taught by a nondirective teacher and −.959 in the class taught by a directive teacher. In light of these correlations, it is not surprising that the pooled within class correlation is very low: −.067. Clearly, it would be highly misleading to use this correlation, let alone interpret it substantively.

Without even alluding to the possibility that the within class correlations may vary, Cranton and Smith used the pooled within groups correlations for their within groups factor analysis. I suggest that you think of their approach in light of my demonstration in the preceding paragraph. Think also of their use of total correlations. You may find it useful to review earlier sections of this chapter.

Fourth, earlier I discussed difficulties arising from the fact that individuals who belong to the same group are more alike than those who belong to different groups. Matters are even more complicated in the case of Cranton and Smith's study, in light of the fact that students may have contributed multiple ratings and teachers may have been rated more than once. "It is possible that one instructor was rated a maximum of six times and that one student contributed 15 ratings to the data base" (Cranton & Smith, 1990, p. 208).

The special section that included Cranton and Smith's paper included also a paper by Abbott, Wulff, Nyquist, Ropp, and Hess (1990) in which the individual was the unit of analysis. Specifically, students' scores in classes "selected from a wide range of academic departments" were combined in the analysis (p. 202). Remarkably, the editor of the special section made no comment on the unit-of-analysis used—a topic that occupied Cranton and Smith and on which he commented (see the preceding).

I hope that these examples served as reminders of the importance of being knowledgeable and vigilant when reading the research literature. Only when researchers, referees, and editors of professional journals adopt such an orientation can we hope to make progress toward achieving cumulative knowledge in the social sciences.

---

[15]As I explained earlier in this chapter, the between groups correlation is perfect when there are only two groups. The total correlation (i.e., using the individual student as the unit of analysis) for these data is −.058.

STUDY SUGGESTIONS

1. Here are illustrative data on X and Y for three groups:

X	Y	X	Y	X	Y
1	5	4	9	6	10
2	5	5	8	7	10
3	6	6	8	8	13
4	6	7	10	9	11
5	9	8	11	10	12
6	8	9	11	11	13

(a) Calculate Σx^2, Σy^2, and Σxy for (1) total (i.e., treating all the data as if they were obtained in a single group), (2) within each group, (3) pooled within groups, (4) between groups.

(b) Use information from (a) to calculate r_{xy} and b_{yx} for (1) total, (2) within each group, (3) pooled within groups, (4) between groups. Display the results as in Table 16.2.

(c) Using information from (a), calculate η_x^2 and η_y^2.

(d) Using information from (b) and (c), apply (16.10) through (16.13).

2. Using the data given in Study Suggestion 1, do a contextual analysis in which Y is the dependent variable.

(a) What is $R_{y.x\bar{x}}^2$?

(b) What is the regression equation?

(c) What does $b_{yx.\bar{x}}$ represent?

(d) What does $b_{y\bar{x}.x}$ represent?

(e) What is the F ratio for $b_{y\bar{x}.x}$?

(f) What conclusions would a researcher doing contextual analysis reach based on the results obtained in (e)?

3. If you have access to HLM, do the following analysis. As the level-1 data, use those of my illustrative application of multilevel analysis (i.e., data in Table 16.4). For level-2 data, use, in addition to COHESIVE (data in Table 16.5), the means of JOBSAT for the eight groups. In short, except for using two level-2 variables, do an analysis similar to the one I did in the chapter. Interpret the results.

4. As I stated in the chapter, my presentation of multilevel analysis was rudimentary. I believe you will benefit from analyzing my example, as well as the one in Study Suggestion 3, following Bryk and Raudenbush's (1992) detailed analyses in their Chapter 4.

ANSWERS

1.

Source	Σx^2	Σy^2	Σxy	r	b
Total	128.5	108.5	109.5	.92736	.85214
I	17.5	13.5	13.5	.87831	.77143
II	17.5	9.5	10.5	.81435	.60000
III	17.5	9.5	9.5	.73679	.54286
Within	52.5	32.5	33.5	.81100	.63810
Between	76.0	76.0	76.0	1.00000	1.00000

(c) $\eta_x^2 = .59114$ $\eta_y^2 = .70046$

2. (a) $R_{y.x\bar{x}}^2 = .89748$

(b) $Y' = 3.00000 + .63810X + .36190\,\bar{X}$

(c) $b_{yx.\bar{x}}$ is the common b or b_w; compare with results under number 1.

(d) $b_{y\bar{x}.x}$ is the deviation of b_b from b_w.

$b_b = 1.00000$; $b_w = .63810$ (see under number 1).

$b_{y\bar{x}.x} = 1.00000 - .63810 = .36190$

(e) $F = 5.48$, with 1 and 15 df, $p < .05$

(f) The researcher would conclude that there is a contextual effect.

3.

Output

Sigma_squared =   2.90723

Tau
INTRCPT1	0.98183	0.03066
JOBSAT	0.03066	0.00138

Tau (as correlations)
INTRCPT1	1.000	0.833
JOBSAT	0.833	1.000

Random level-1 coefficient	Reliability estimate
INTRCPT1, B0	0.772
JOBSAT, B1	0.031

The outcome variable is PRODUCT

Final estimation of fixed effects:

Fixed Effect	Coefficient	Standard Error	T-ratio	P-value
For INTRCPT1, B0				
INTRCPT2, G00	17.101805	1.818457	9.405	0.001
MEANSAT, G01	−0.145192	0.144990	−1.001	0.185
COHESIVE, G02	0.731382	0.230498	3.173	0.017
For JOBSAT slope, B1				
INTRCPT2, G10	1.347020	0.412131	3.268	0.016
MEANSAT, G11	−0.068359	0.027163	−2.517	0.032
COHESIVE, G12	0.057385	0.048318	1.188	0.149

Final estimation of variance components:

Random Effect	Standard Deviation	Variance Component	df	Chi-square	P-value
INTRCPT1, U0	0.99087	0.98183	5	21.81532	0.001
JOBSAT slope, U1	0.03714	0.00138	5	0.62456	>.500
level-1, R	1.70506	2.90723			

Commentary

Level-1 regression equations are the same as those I reported in the chapter.

Using $\alpha = .05$, COHESIVE has a positive effect on the intercept (B0), whereas MEANSAT (mean job satisfaction) has a negative effect on the regression coefficient (B1).

The null hypothesis with respect to variance component for the intercept is rejected.

17

Categorical Dependent Variable: Logistic Regression

In all the designs I presented in preceding chapters, the dependent variable was continuous, whereas the independent variables were continuous and/or categorical. In this chapter, I address designs in which the dependent variable is categorical. As in preceding chapters, the independent variables may be continuous and/or categorical.

Although categorical variables can consist of any number of categories, my presentation is limited to designs with a dichotomous (binary) dependent variable.[1] The ubiquity of such variables in social and behavioral research is exemplified by a yes or no response to diverse questions about behavior (e.g., voted in a given election), ownership (e.g., of a personal computer), educational attainment (e.g., graduated from college), status (e.g., employed), to name but some. Among other binary response modes are agree-disagree, success-failure, presence-absence, and pro-con.

If a "yes" response is coded 1 and a "no" is coded 0, then ΣY is equal to the number of 1's. Dividing ΣY by N yields a mean that is equal to the proportion of 1's (i.e., proportion responding yes) symbolized as P. The proportion responding no (assuming no missing data) is equal to $1 - P$ (also symbolized as Q). The variance of a dichotomous variable is equal to $P(1 - P)$ or PQ. Considering these properties of a dichotomous variable, assumptions of linear regression analysis (see Chapter 2) are false.[2] In particular, note the following:

1. Contrary to the assumption of linear regression analysis, the population means of the Y's at each level of X are *not* on a straight line. In other words, the relation between the Y means and X is nonlinear.
2. It can be shown (e.g., Hanushek & Jackson, 1977, p. 181; Neter et al., 1989, p. 581) that the variance of errors for a given value of the independent variable, X_i, is $P_i(1 - P_i)$. Consequently, the assumption of homoscedasticity is untenable.
3. The errors are not normally distributed.

---

[1]For analyses of designs in which the dependent variable consists of more than two categories (called polytomous or polychotomous variables), see Aldrich and Nelson (1984, pp. 65–77), Fox (1984, pp. 311–320), Hosmer and Lemeshow (1989, Chapter 8), and Menard (1995, Chapter 5).

[2]To parallel the discussion of assumptions of simple linear regression in Chapter 2, I comment on the case of a single independent variable.

In light of the preceding, the application of linear regression analysis when the dependent variable is dichotomous would have undesirable consequences, among which are the following: (1) predicted values greater than 1 and smaller than 0 may occur (such values are inappropriate inasmuch as proportions are bounded between 0 and 1), and (2) the magnitude of the effects of independent variables may be greatly underestimated.

Among suggested models for data with a dichotomous dependent variable are linear probability, logistic, and probit (for an introduction, see Aldrich & Nelson, 1984). I present only logistic regression, as it is the most versatile.[3] As I will show, after transforming the dependent variable, logistic regression analysis parallels least-squares regression analysis. Accordingly, topics I presented in preceding chapters (e.g., hierarchical and stepwise regression analysis, coding categorical independent variables, generating vectors representing interactions) are equally applicable in logistic regression.

I begin with the simplest design possible—one dichotomous independent variable—in the context of which I introduce basic concepts of logistic regression. I then turn to an example with an independent variable consisting of more than two categories and show that coding methods I introduced in Chapter 11 are also applicable in designs with a dichotomous dependent variable and have analogous properties to those I described in Chapter 11. I then present a design with two dichotomous independent variables and address the issue of interaction. Next, I present a design with a continuous independent variable and then one with a continuous and a dichotomous independent variable.

ONE DICHOTOMOUS INDEPENDENT VARIABLE

When the design consists of a dichotomous independent variable and a dichotomous dependent variable, the data may be conveniently displayed in a 2×2, or a fourfold, table as in Figure 17.1.[4] You are probably familiar with such tables from introductory statistics courses and from reading research literature. In any case, notice that in Figure 17.1, *a* represents the number of people who have a "score"[5] of 1 on both *X* and *Y*, *b* represents the number of people who have a score of 0 on *X* and a score of 1 on *Y*, and so forth for the remaining cells.

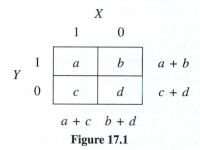

Figure 17.1

[3]In Chapter 20, I present discriminant analysis—an alternative approach limited to designs in which all the independent variables are continuous.

[4]The alternative of creating *X* and *Y* vectors each comprising, say, 1's and 0's would be extremely unwieldy for relatively large samples.

[5]The quotation marks are meant to remind you that the 1's and 0's are arbitrary codes. Nevertheless, it seems "natural" to assign 1 to, say, exposure to a treatment and 0 to nonexposure; or 1 to "yes" and 0 to "no." Henceforth, I will use the term score without quotation marks.

Assume that in Figure 17.1 an experiment is depicted such that subjects were randomly assigned to the two categories of X (e.g., 1 = treatment, 0 = control; 1 = drug, 0 = placebo), and Y is the dependent variable (e.g., 1 = success, 0 = failure; 1 = disease, 0 = no disease). Under such circumstances, it is of interest to compare the proportion of successes, say, in the treatment group with those in the control group. Referring to Figure 17.1, this is a comparison between $a/(a + c)$ and $b/(b + d)$.

Instead of an experiment, Figure 17.1 may represent a quasi-experiment or a nonexperiment. Examples of the former abound in medical research, where X represents an exposure factor (e.g., smoking versus nonsmoking) and the dependent variable represents the presence or absence of a disease (e.g., lung cancer). An example of a nonexperimental study would be a contrast between males and females in their support for a woman's right to an abortion.

Earlier in the text (especially in Chapters 8 through 13), I pointed out that although the same analytic approaches may be used in different types of designs, validity of interpretation of the results depends largely on the design. As the same is true of designs I present in this chapter, I will not repeat earlier discussions of this important topic. Recall, however, the role of randomization, sampling, and manipulation to recognize the importance of keeping in mind the design characteristics, especially when interpreting results and drawing conclusions from them.

A substantive example of a 2×2 design will be instructive when I introduce some basic ideas of logistic regression analysis. Accordingly, assume that X is gender (1 = male; 0 = female) and Y is admission to a mechanical engineering program (1 = yes; 0 = no). Often, it is meaningful to cast the problem in terms of odds. Thus, one might ask what are the odds of a male and a female being admitted to the program.[6] Referring to Figure 17.1 and letters therein, these are, respectively, a/c and b/d.[7] Dividing the odds for males by those for females, an odds ratio is obtained:

$$\text{OR} = \frac{a/c}{b/d} = \frac{ad}{bc} \tag{17.1}$$

where OR = odds ratio and the letters refer to frequencies of cells depicted in Figure 17.1. Notice that OR = 1 means that the odds for males and females are identical. Stated differently, OR = 1 means that there is no relation between gender and admission to the program. OR > 1 means that the odds for males being admitted are greater than those for females, and the converse is true when OR < 1. As will become evident, OR plays an important role in the interpretation of logistic regression results.

Odds or ORs can range from 0 to $+\infty$, with 1 indicating no difference. Because of this asymmetry, the same odds, but in the opposite direction, may appear different. For example, odds of 5.0 (i.e., 5/1) of losing could be expressed as odds of .2 of winning (i.e., 1/5). By taking the natural logarithm (ln) of the odds (or OR), symmetry is achieved, with 0 indicating no difference (ln 1 = 0) and the possible range being from $-\infty$ to $+\infty$. Thus, for the previous example, ln 5.0 = 1.609, and ln .2 = −1.609, that is, the same odds, albeit in the opposite direction.

Instead of expressing odds as the ratio of two frequencies (as in the preceding), it is more common to do so with probabilities. Thus, odds of admission to the program, say, can be expressed as

$$\text{odds} = \frac{P}{1 - P} \tag{17.2}$$

---

[6]"The word *odds* refers to a single entity, but tradition and formal English dictate that the word be treated as plural noun" (Selvin, 1991, p. 344).

[7]As my aim here is limited to the introduction of basic ideas, I overlook design issues (e.g., sampling, control for variables that may play a role in the admissions process). I examine such issues later in this chapter.

where P is the probability of being admitted, and $1 - P$ is the probability of not being admitted. In logistic regression, a logistic transformation of the odds (referred to as logit) serves as the dependent variable. That is,

$$\log(\text{odds}) = \text{logit}(P) = \ln\left(\frac{P}{1-P}\right) \tag{17.3}$$

where $\ln$ = natural logarithm. Accordingly, a simple logistic regression equation with independent variable X takes the following form:

$$\text{logit}(P) = a + bX \tag{17.4}$$

As in least-squares regression, it is assumed that the relation between the logit (P) and X is linear. Also, when one suspects or determines that the relation is curvilinear, an equation incorporating polynomial terms (e.g., quadratic) can be fitted. Analogous to simple linear regression (see Chapter 2), b is interpreted as the expected change of logit(P) associated with a unit change in X. When b is positive, increases in X are associated with increases in logits. When b is negative, increases in X are associated with decreases in logits.

Most people would probably find it easier to attach substantive meaning to odds rather than logits. Odds can be readily obtained by taking antilogs. Thus, for one independent variable,

$$\frac{P}{1-P} = e^{a + bX} = e^a(e^b)^X \tag{17.5}$$

where e is the base of the natural logarithm (many pocket calculators have an e^x button). The second expression of (17.5) shows that changes in X lead to a multiplicative effect of e^b on the odds.

Finally, algebraic manipulation of preceding formulas yields a formula for the calculation of the probability of an event (admission to the program, in the previous example):

$$P = \frac{e^{a + bX}}{1 + e^{a + bX}} \tag{17.6}$$

Equivalently,

$$P = \frac{1}{1 + e^{-(a + bX)}} \tag{17.7}$$

I am afraid that by now you may be confused and frustrated, especially if this subject matter is new to you. If so, be patient. I believe that a numerical example, to which I now turn, will help clarify the concepts I presented thus far. Moreover, I will use numerical examples to present extensions to multiple logistic regression and to more complex designs.

A Numerical Example

Table 17.1 presents illustrative data for a study of admissions of males and females to a mechanical engineering program. Of course, in actual research much larger samples are required. Moreover, following good research practice, sample size should be determined in light of, among other things, preferred effect size and power of the statistical test of significance (see Cohen, 1988, for thorough discussions). I am using extremely small numbers of cases as I intend to extend this example, later in this chapter, by adding a continuous variable. At that point, it will be necessary to present the data in vectors (instead of the format I use in Table 17.1), requiring multiple pages for large numbers of cases.

Table 17.1   Illustrative Data for an Admissions Study

Admit	Gender M	F	Totals
Yes	7	3	10
No	3	7	10
Totals	10	10	

As you can see from Table 17.1, seven out of ten male applicants to the program were admitted, whereas three out of ten females were admitted. Applying (17.1): OR = [(7)(7)]/[(3)(3)] = 49/9 = 5.44. Thus, the odds of being admitted to the program, rather than being denied, are about 5.44 times greater (more favorable) for males than they are for females. Alternatively, applying (17.2),

$$\text{odds(M)} = .7/.3 = 2.33333$$

$$\text{odds(F)} = .3/.7 = .42857$$

$$\text{OR} = 2.33333/.42857 = 5.44$$

As in linear regression analysis, we are interested in estimating the parameters of the logistic regression equation, bearing in mind that in the latter the dependent variable is logit(P)—see (17.4). Recall that parameter estimation in linear regression is aimed at minimizing the sum of the squared residuals (i.e., the principle of least squares; see Chapter 2). In logistic regression, the aim is to estimate parameters most likely to have given rise to the sample data. Hence, the name maximum likelihood (ML) for the estimation procedure. For introductions to the theory and practice of ML estimation, see Aldrich and Nelson (1984, pp. 49–54); Bollen (1989, e.g., pp. 107–111); Eliason (1993); King (1989, Chapter 4); Kleinbaum, Kupper, and Muller (1988, Chapter 21); and Selvin (1991, Appendix E). I believe that Mulaik's (1972) intuitive explication of ML will help you surmise what it entails:

> The idea of a maximum-likelihood estimator is this: We assume that we know the *general form* of the population distribution from which a sample is drawn. For example, we might assume the population distribution is a multivariate normal distribution. But what we do not know are the population parameters which give this distribution a particular form among all possible multivariate normal distributions. For example, we do not know the population means and the variances and covariances for the variables. But if we did know the values of these parameters for the population, we could determine the density of a sample-observation vector from this population having certain specified values for each of the variables. In the absence of such knowledge, however, we can take arbitrary values and treat them *as if* they were the population parameters and then ask ourselves what is the *likelihood* . . . of observing certain values for the variables on a single observation drawn from such a population. If we have more than one observation, then we can ask what is the joint likelihood of obtaining such a sample of observation vectors? . . . Finally we can ask: What values for the population parameters make the sample observations have the greatest joint likelihood? When we answer this question, we will take such values to be the *maximum-likelihood estimators* of the population parameters. (p. 162)

ML estimation resorts to iterative algorithms requiring the use of a computer for their application. It is the ready availability of software in which such algorithms are used that has made methods such as logistic regression and structural equation modeling (see Chapters 18 and 19) popular among applied researchers. Of the four packages I introduced in this book, BMDP, SAS, and SPSS have logistic regression programs (for information about logistic macros for

MINITAB, see *MUG*, October, 1993, p. 10). As in preceding chapters, I will use one program for a detailed presentation of output and commentaries. Following that, I will present input and brief excerpts of output for the other two programs.

SPSS

Input

TITLE TABLE 17.1: A CATEGORICAL INDEPENDENT VARIABLE.
DATA LIST FREE/GENDER,ADMIT,FREQ.
VALUE LABELS GENDER 1 'MALE' 2 'FEMALE'/ADMIT 1 'YES' 0 'NO'.
WEIGHT BY FREQ.
BEGIN DATA
1   1   7
1   0   3
2   1   3
2   0   7
END DATA
LIST.
LOGISTIC REGRESSION ADMIT WITH GENDER/CATEGORICAL=GENDER/
    CONTRAST(GENDER)=INDICATOR/ID=GENDER/PRINT ALL/CASEWISE.

Commentary

Except for entering the data in grouped format (see the explanation that follows), the general layout of the logistic regression program is very similar to that of the multiple regression program. Accordingly, I will comment primarily on keywords and subcommands specific to the logistic regression program. See Chapter 4 for an introduction to SPSS and conventions I follow in presenting input, output, and commentaries.

As in the multiple regression program, the logistic regression program has options for variable selection (e.g., stepwise). Earlier in the text (especially in Chapters 8 through 10), I discussed variable selection procedures in detail and stressed that they are appropriate only when one's aim is limited to prediction. As the same is true of variable selection in logistic regression, I will not repeat my earlier discussions of this topic. Further, as my concern in this chapter is with explanation, I will not use variable selection procedures.

Using WEIGHT BY FREQuency obviates the need of repeating the same pattern of responses. Had I not used this option, I would have had to enter the data—composed of 1's and 0's—in 20 rows (subjects) by two columns (GENDER and ADMIT). To appreciate the great convenience of the grouped data format, not to mention the lesser likelihood of errors in data entry, note that regardless of the sample sizes only four lines (as in the preceding) are necessary for a 2×2 design. This convenience generalizes to more complex designs, as long as all the independent variables are categorical (see the examples that follow).

The dependent variable is dichotomous. As I stated earlier, the independent variables can be categorical and/or continuous. As in multiple regression analysis, each categorical variable is represented by a set of $g - 1$ coded vectors, where g is the number of categories (see Chapter 11).

Further, as in multiple regression analysis, various coding schemes can be used (e.g., dummy, effect). Unlike the multiple regression program, however, in the logistic regression program it is *not* necessary to actually enter the coded vectors or to generate them by, say, COMPUTE and/or IF statements (see examples in earlier chapters). Instead, one can identify the categorical variables (as in the preceding input) and let the program generate the type of coded vectors one specifies (see the following).

An important aspect of identifying the categorical variables in the logistic regression program—regardless of whether they are generated by the program, by the user (e.g., with IF statements), or actually entered—is that the program appropriately treats coded vectors representing each categorical variable as a set. Thus, when it encounters a command to enter or remove a categorical variable, it enters or removes all the coded vectors representing it. Variables not identified as categorical are treated as continuous. Thus, coded vectors representing a categorical variable that are *not* identified as such are treated as distinct variables. Recall that this is how such vectors are treated in the multiple regression program, which does not include an option to identify categorical variables. Earlier in the text (e.g., Chapters 12 and 15), I illustrated deleterious consequences of doing stepwise regression analysis in designs consisting of categorical variables that are represented by multiple coded vectors. As you may recall, I stressed that it is the user's responsibility to bear in mind the distinction between variables and sets of coded vectors representing variables. When using a variable selection procedure in the logistic regression program (e.g., stepwise), the program enters or removes the set of coded vectors representing a given categorical variable thus sparing the user the aberration of output composed of fractions of variables.

By default, the logistic regression program uses effect coding with the last category assigned −1's (I introduced the same approach in Chapter 11 and used it in subsequent chapters). If one wants another coding method it is specified through the CONTRAST keyword. Among coding schemes, dummy coding (see Chapter 11)—labeled INDicator variables[8] in the logistic regression program—can be specified. By default, the program assigns 0's to the last category or group in all the coded vectors, thus treating it as a control or comparison group. In the previous input, I used CONTRAST(GENDER)=INDICATOR. As the females are the second group, they will be assigned 0's in the single vector representing gender, whereas the males will be assigned 1's.

To assign the 0's to a group other than the last one, the sequence number of the group in question is inserted in parentheses after the keyword INDicator. To assign 0's to males, in the present example, IND(1) would be specified.

ID is used to specify a variable whose values or value labels will be used to identify subjects (cases) in the CASEWISE listing. I specified GENDER. In the absence of an ID subcommand, subjects are identified by their case number.

CASEWISE can be used to generate various diagnostics analogous to those available in the multiple regression program, which I introduced in Chapters 3 and 4 (e.g., Cook's D, leverage, dfbeta). For discussions of such diagnostics in logistic regression, see Hosmer and Lemeshow (1989, pp. 149–170); Hosmer, Taber, and Lemeshow (1991); and Pregibon (1981).

---

[8]Many texts and computer program manuals (e.g., SPSS and SAS) refer to coded vectors as indictor *variables* or dummy *variables*. I believe such nomenclature is imprudent, as inexperienced users may misinterpret it to mean that each vector is a distinct variable. Also, I believe that restricting the use of the term *indicator* to refer to a measure of a latent variable, as is done in structural equation modeling (see Chapters 18 and 19), would be useful.

Output

	Value	Parameter Coding (1)
GENDER		
MALE	1.00	1.000
FEMALE	2.00	.000

Commentary

Under Value are reported the original values for each categorical independent variable. In the present example, there is only one categorical variable (GENDER). As GENDER consists of two categories, a single coded vector (1) was generated to represent it. Under Parameter Coding are reported the codes assigned to the categories of GENDER: MALE = 1, FEMALE = 0.

Output

−2 Log Likelihood   27.725887
* Constant is included in the model.

Commentary

As indicated in this excerpt, at this stage only the constant (a) is included in the model. What this means is that the likelihood, or probability, of being admitted to the program is calculated without considering any information available about the subjects (their gender, in the present example). Examine Table 17.1 and notice that ten applicants were admitted and ten were denied admission. Using this information only, the probability of being admitted is .5 (10/20) and, of course, the probability of being denied admission is also .5 (1 − .5). As the observations are independent of each other, the overall likelihood is the product of all the probabilities: $.5^{20}$ = .00000095. As likelihood values tend to be very small, it is customary to use the natural log (ln) of the likelihood (−13.862944, in the present example) and to multiply it by −2, yielding the value reported in the preceding.

I will make several observations about the transformed value (often presented as −2LL). (1) It takes positive values. (2) *It is a measure of lack of fit*: the smaller the value, the better the fit of the model to the data. When the fit is perfect (likelihood = 1), −2LL = 0 (ln 1 = 0). (3) Considered by itself, "it does not in general have any well-defined distribution" (Kleinbaum, Kupper, & Morgenstern, 1982, p. 431). In my commentary on the output of the next step, I show how it is used for hypothesis testing.

Output

Beginning Block Number 1. Method: Enter
Variable(s) Entered on Step Number
1..   GENDER

Estimation terminated at iteration number 3 because parameter estimates changed by less than .001

Iteration History:

Iteration	Log Likelihood	Constant	GENDER(1)
1	−12.222013	−.80000000	1.6000000
2	−12.217286	−.84686800	1.6937360
3	−12.217286	−.84729782	1.6945956

−2 Log Likelihood	24.435		
	Chi-Square	df	Significance
Model Chi-Square	3.291	1	0696
Improvement	3.291	1	.0696

Commentary

By default, the number of iterations is 20. However, they are terminated when parameter estimates change by less than .001 (the default). The number of iterations and/or the value for termination can be changed (see CRITERIA).

−2LL = 24.435 is for the model that includes a constant (*a*) and a coefficient for GENDER (*b*). Notice that the model in which only *a* is included (the preceding step) is actually one in which *b* for gender was constrained to equal zero. When a model is obtained by constraining one or more of the parameters of another model, it is said to be *nested* in it. The nested model is referred to as the reduced model, whereas the one in which it is nested is referred to as the full model. Clearly, these designations are relative. In the example under consideration, the model of the preceding step is nested in the model of the current step, as it was obtained by constraining *b* for gender to be equal to zero.[9] Thus, the model of the preceding step is reduced, whereas the model of the current step is full. The difference between −2LL for two models, one of which is nested in the other, has an approximate chi-square (χ^2) distribution in *large* samples. That is,

$$\chi^2 = -2LL_R - (-2LL_F) = -2 \ln(\text{likelihood}_R/\text{likelihood}_F) \tag{17.8}$$

where R = reduced and F = full. Some authors use 0 (null hypothesis) instead of reduced and 1 (alternative hypothesis) instead of full. Because of its format, (17.8) is referred to as the *likelihood ratio test*. It plays a prominent role in various analytic techniques (see Chapters 18 and 19).

The *df* (degrees of freedom) associated with the χ^2 are equal to the difference in the number of the parameters in the two models. In the present example, one parameter (*a*) is estimated in the reduced model, whereas two parameters (*a* and *b*) are estimated in the full one. Therefore, *df* = 1. For the present example, $\chi^2 = 27.726 - 24.435 = 3.291$ with 1 *df* (see Model Chi-Square) is a test of the null hypothesis that the *b* for gender is 0. *For illustrative purposes only*, overlook the fact that the data are fictitious and "sample" sizes are very small. Further, assume that I selected $\alpha = .10$. Accordingly, I would conclude that the difference in the odds of admission to the program for males and females is statistically significant.

[9]Other types of constraints may be applied. For example, two coefficients may be constrained to be equal to each other.

In addition to the Model Chi-Square, the previous output includes a line labeled Improvement, which is analogous to a test of the increment in the proportion of variance accounted for by a variable(s) at its point of entry in a multiple regression analysis. In the present example, there is only one independent variable. Hence Model Chi-Square is the same as Improvement. "The improvement chi-square test is comparable to the *F*-change test in multiple regression" (Norušis/SPSS Inc., 1993b, p. 11).

Output

--- Variables in the Equation ---

Variable	B	S.E.	Wald	df	Sig	Exp(B)
GENDER(1)	1.6946	.9759	3.0152	1	.0825	5.4444
Constant	−.8473	.6901	1.5076	1	.2195	

Commentary

Recall that in the present example, males were assigned a 1, whereas females were assigned a 0. Hence, a unit change in gender indicates the difference, in logit(*P*), between males in females. To express this difference as an odds ratio, exponentiate *b* for gender: $e^{1.6946}$ = 5.4444, which is the value reported in the column labeled Exp(B).[10] This demonstrates the advantage of using dummy coding when the aim is to contrast one or more groups with a control (or reference) group.[11]

As in multiple regression analysis, a test of the coefficient for a dummy vector constitutes a test of the difference between the group assigned 1 and the group assigned 0. In the excerpt of the output under consideration, S.E. is the standard error of the corresponding coefficient. Some authors (e.g., Aldrich & Nelson, 1984, p. 55; Darlington, 1990, p. 455) interpret the ratio of the coefficient to its standard error as *t*, with *df* equal to the number of subjects minus the number of estimated parameters, and use it for testing the coefficient or for setting confidence intervals (see BMDP output in the next section). Other authors (e.g., Liao, 1994, p. 15; Neter et al., 1989, p. 602) interpret the ratio of the coefficient to its standard error as *z* and use it for the same purposes. With large samples, as is required for such tests, there is little difference between the two orientations.

When the categorical variable is represented by a single vector, Wald's test is equal to the squared ratio of the coefficient to its standard error. For the present example, $(1.6946/.9759)^2$ = 3.0152. Under such circumstances, *t* is equal to the square root of Wald's test. Hauck and Donner (1977) showed that Wald's test "behaves in an aberrant manner" (p. 851). Among other things, its statistical power decreases when the value of the coefficient is relatively large. It is therefore recommended that the likelihood ratio test, which I calculated earlier, be used instead.

---

[10]Earlier in this chapter, I obtained this value when I applied (17.1).

[11]In the next numerical example, I use more than two groups.

Output

Classification Table for ADMIT

		Predicted		Percent Correct
		NO	YES	
		N	Y	
Observed		+---------+---------+		
NO	N	| 7 | 3 |		70.00%
		+---------+---------+		
YES	Y	| 3 | 7 |		70.00%
		+---------+---------+		
			Overall	70.00%

	Observed			
ID	ADMIT	Pred	PGroup	Resid
MALE	S Y	.7000	Y	.3000
MALE	S N **	.7000	Y	−.7000
FEMALE	S Y **	.3000	N	.7000
FEMALE	S N	.3000	N	−.3000

S=Selected U=Unselected cases

** = Misclassified cases

Commentary

The Classification Table is reported earlier in the output. I placed it here so as to present it together with results from the CASEWISE subcommand.

As I pointed out earlier—see (17.6) and (17.7) and discussion related to them—the regression equation can be used to estimate the probability of an event (admission to the program, in the example under consideration). Using the regression equation reported earlier, and applying (17.7),

$$P_M = \frac{1}{1 + e^{-(-.8473 + 1.6946)}} = \frac{1}{1 + .42857} = .70$$

and

$$P_F = \frac{1}{1 + e^{-(-.8473)}} = \frac{1}{1 + 2.33334} = .30$$

These are the pred(icted) values reported in the preceding. By default, $P > .5$ is used to predict that an applicant will be admitted to the program (will say yes, or whatever the event may be), whereas $P < .5$ is used to predict that the applicant will be denied admission. Thus, under PGroup (predicted group) those whose predicted score is .7 are predicted to be admitted (Y), whereas those whose predicted score is .3 are predicted to be denied admission (N).

Analogous to comparisons of observed and predicted scores in regression analysis, it is informative to compare predicted group membership with observed ones (i.e., actual admission status). Notice that this is done both in the Classification Table and in the listing under CASEWISE output, where ** indicates misclassification. Based on the regression equation, males are predicted to be admitted but only seven out of the ten were admitted. Similarly, females are predicted to be denied admission but three out of ten were admitted. The Classification Table indicates how well the model fits the data. In the present case, using the regression equation, 70% of the subjects were correctly classified. However, analogous to shrinkage of R^2 in least-squares regression (see Chapter 8), predicted probabilities based on an equation derived from the same data tend to be inflated.[12]

Some authors assert that comparisons of predicted probabilities are more informative than odds and odds ratios, whereas others argue that the opposite is the case (for a recent exchange on this topic, see DeMaris, 1993; Roncek, 1991, 1993). As the two approaches are not mutually exclusive, both may be used in the interpretation of results, provided their properties are kept in mind. It is particularly important to note that the estimate of the intercept (a) is valid only in longitudinal designs. In other designs (e.g., cross-sectional, case-control), the estimate of a is affected by the sampling scheme and has to be adjusted if predicted probabilities are to be used (see Afifi & Clark, 1990, pp. 332–335, for a discussion and an illustrative application; for a discussion of different types of designs and sampling schemes related to them, see Kleinbaum et al., 1982, Chapters 4 and 5).

As shown earlier, the estimate of an odds ratio does not entail the use of a (see commentary on e^b in the preceding). Thus, estimated odds ratios are valid in designs where predicted probabilities are not valid without an adjustment of a. Later in this chapter (see "One Continuous Independent Variable"), I discuss other issues concerning the use of odds ratios and predicted probabilities.

When the default cutoff point (.5) is used for classification, consequences of false positive and false negative errors are deemed as being alike. Clearly, there are situations when this is not the case (e.g., prediction of heart disease, recidivism, success in a costly program). Under such circumstances, the user can specify a different cutoff point.

Before turning to logistic regression programs in other packages, I would like to point out that when all the independent variables are categorical, other programs in SPSS (and in the other packages I discuss later) can be used to do logistic regression analysis. Notable examples are programs for log-linear analysis and analysis of contingency tables (e.g., LOGLINEAR in SPSS, 4F in BMDP, CATMOD in SAS). For very good presentations of log-linear models and illustrations of their use for logistic regression analysis, see Alba (1988) and Swafford (1980).

OTHER COMPUTER PROGRAMS

In what follows, I present input and brief excerpts from the output of a logistic regression analysis of the data in Table 17.1 using programs from BMDP and SAS. For orientations to these packages and the conventions I follow in presenting input, output, and commentaries, see Chapter 4. As I suggested several times earlier, when you are running a program from a package for which I present only brief commentaries, study your output in conjunction with output of the program on which I commented in detail (for the present example, see SPSS output and commentaries in the preceding section).

---

[12]Later in this chapter, I discuss indices of fit.

BMDP

Input

```
/PROBLEM TITLE IS 'TABLE 17.1, USING LR'.
/INPUT VARIABLES ARE 3. FORMAT IS FREE.
/VARIABLE NAMES ARE GENDER,ADMIT,FREQ.
/GROUP CODES(ADMIT)=1,0.    NAMES(ADMIT) =YES,NO.
 CODES(GENDER)=1,0.    NAMES(GENDER)=MALE,FEMALE.
/REGRESS COUNT IS FREQ.
 DEPEND IS ADMIT.
 MODEL=GENDER. METHOD=MLR.    [MLR = maximum likelihood ratio]
/END
1  1   7
1  0   3
0  1   3
0  0   7
/END
```

Commentary

The preceding is the input file for LR: a program for stepwise logistic regression with a dichotomous dependent variable. BMDP also has a program for polychotomous stepwise logistic regression (PR). As I stated earlier, when all the independent variables are categorical, other BMDP programs (notably 4F) can be used for logistic regression analysis.

The general layout of LR is similar to that of 2R (stepwise regression), which I introduced in Chapter 4 and used in subsequent chapters. Here, I comment only on statements specific to LR. When a MODEL statement is included, all the specified variables are entered in the first step, and none is removed. In other words, a stepwise analysis is *not* carried out. I use this option in all the LR runs in this chapter. As in SPSS (see the preceding section), I enter grouped data.

Output

VARIABLE NO.	NAME	CODE	GROUP INDEX	CATEGORY NAME
1	GENDER	1.000	1	MALE
		0.000	2	FEMALE
2	ADMIT	1.000	1	YES
		0.000	2	NO

VARIABLE NO.	N A M E	GROUP INDEX	FREQ	DESIGN VARIABLES (1)
1	GENDER	1	10	0
		2	10	1

Commentary

By default, variables *not* declared as INTERVAL (continuous) are treated as categorical. Also, dummy coding—referred to in LR as PARTial—with the first category as the control group (i.e., assigned 0's in all the vectors) is used by default (see DESIGN VARIABLES in the output). Unlike SPSS, there is no option for designating another category as the control or reference group. Instead, the data have to be sorted so that the category in question is the first one.

Two other coding schemes: MARGinal (called effect coding in this book) and ORTHOGonal can be applied by specifying DVAR and the method of choice. To apply effect coding, say, specfy DVAR=MARG (see the next numerical example).

Output

LOG LIKELIHOOD =   −12.217

TERM	COEFFICIENT	STANDARD ERROR	COEF/SE	EXP(COEF)	95% C.I. OF EXP(COEF) LOWER-BND	UPPER-BND
GENDER	−1.695	0.976	−1.74	0.184	0.236E-01	1.43
CONSTANT	0.8473	0.690	1.23	2.33	0.547	9.94

STATISTICS TO ENTER OR REMOVE TERMS

TERM	APPROX. CHI-SQ. REMOVE	D.F.	P-VALUE	LOG LIKELIHOOD
GENDER	3.29	1	0.0696	−13.8629
GENDER	IS IN			MAY NOT BE REMOVED.
CONSTANT	1.65	1	0.1996	−13.0401
CONSTANT	IS IN			MAY NOT BE REMOVED.

Commentary

The first log likelihood (−12.217) is the same as the value of the last iteration in the SPSS output. Recall that it is multiplied by −2 to yield −2LL for the model under consideration. Compare with SPSS output.

The regression equation differs from the one reported in the SPSS output, as different groups are used as controls in the two programs. In SPSS, the last group (female) served as the control (default), whereas in LR the first group (male) served as the control (default). Accordingly, in the present output EXP(COEF) for gender is for the odds ratio of females to males. As I explained earlier, to calculate the odds ratio for males to females, take the reciprocal of EXP(B): $1/.184 = 5.435$, which is, within rounding, equal to the value reported in the SPSS output.

Finally, notice that the CHI-SQ (3.29) is the same as the one reported in SPSS for the Model and Improvement. See the commentary on the SPSS output.

SAS

Input

```
TITLE 'TABLE 17.1.   DUMMY CODING';
DATA T171D;
   INPUT GENDER ADMIT N;
CARDS;
1   7   10
0   3   10
PROC PRINT;
PROC LOGISTIC;
MODEL ADMIT/N=GENDER;
RUN;
```

Commentary

As I stated earlier, when all the independent variables are categorical, other PROC's (notably CATMOD) can be used for logistic regression.

As in the BMDP and SPSS programs, PROC LOGISTIC can be used for variable selection (e.g., stepwise). The default is no variable selection. ADMIT/N follows the "*events/trials syntax,* . . . only applicable to binary response data" (SAS Institute Inc., 1990a, Vol. 2, p. 1079). Notice that with this syntax only two lines are necessary for a 2 × 2 design. According to the first line, seven out of ten subjects whose gender is 1 (male) were admitted. According to the second line, three out of ten females (coded 0) were admitted. You can also use input with a WEIGHT statement (as in BMDP and SPSS). "The model will be fitted correctly, but *certain printed statistics will not be correct* [italics added]" (SAS Institute Inc., 1990a, Vol. 2, p. 1086).

Unlike the BMDP and SPSS programs, PROC LOGISTIC has no option for specifying a coding scheme for categorical independent variables. Consequently, it has to be entered or generated (e.g., using IF statements; see Chapter 11). Notice that in the present example I entered dummy codes for gender. In the next example, I show how to enter effect coding for a categorical variable with more than two categories.

Output

Criterion	Intercept Only	Intercept and Covariates	Chi-Square for Covariates
−2 LOG L	27.726	24.435	3.291 with 1 DF (p=0.0696)

Analysis of Maximum Likelihood Estimates

Variable	DF	Parameter Estimate	Standard Error	Wald Chi-Square	Pr > Chi-Square
INTERCPT	1	−0.8473	0.6901	1.5076	0.2195
GENDER	1	1.6946	0.9759	3.0152	0.0825

Commentary

Compare the preceding with SPSS output. To reiterate, I reproduced only brief excerpts of the output. Further, PROC LOGISTIC has various options that I did not use (e.g., influence statistics).

ONE INDEPENDENT VARIABLE WITH MULTIPLE CATEGORIES

In this section, I present a design in which the independent variable consists of more than two categories. Although I give an example of a variable with three categories, the same approach generalizes to any number of categories. Table 17.2 gives illustrative data for a study consisting of two different training programs, T1 and T2, and a control group. Alternatively, you can think of the study as nonexperimental, where the independent variable is, say, ethnicity (i.e., three ethnic groups).

I begin with an SPSS run, using both dummy and effect coding, and then give input files and excerpts of output for LR of BMDP and PROC LOGISTIC of SAS.

SPSS

Input

TITLE TABLE 17.2 TWO TREATMENTS AND A CONTROL.
DATA LIST FREE/TREAT, DEP, FREQ.
VALUE LABELS TREAT 1 'T1' 2 'T2' 3 'CONT'/DEP 1 'SUCCESS'
  0 'FAILURE'.
WEIGHT BY FREQ.
BEGIN DATA
1 1 30
1 0 20
2 1 40
2 0 10
3 1 10
3 0 40
END DATA
LIST.
TITLE DUMMY CODING, USING DEFAULT CATEGORY.
LOGISTIC REGRESSION DEP WITH TREAT/CATEGORICAL=TREAT/
  CONTRAST(TREAT) =IND/ID=TREAT/CASEWISE.
TITLE EFFECT CODING, USING DEFAULT CATEGORY.
LOGISTIC REGRESSION DEP WITH TREAT/CATEGORICAL=TREAT/
  ID=TREAT/CASEWISE/PRINT CORR.

Commentary

As I stated earlier, I carry out two analyses: (1) with dummy coding (IND), where the last category serves as the control (default), and (2) with effect coding, where the last category is assigned -1 in both vectors (default). In the second run, I call for the printing of CORR $=$ correlation matrix of parameter estimates (see commentary on the relevant output).

Table 17.2 Illustrative Data for Training Programs

Dependent Variable	Training			Totals
	T1	*T2*	*Control*	
Success	30	40	10	80
Failure	20	10	40	70
Totals	50	50	50	150

Output

	Value	Freq	Parameter Coding	
			(1)	(2)
TREAT				
T1	1.00	2	1.000	.000
T2	2.00	2	.000	1.000
CONT	3.00	2	.000	.000

Dependent Variable.. DEP
Beginning Block Number 0. Initial Log Likelihood Function

−2 Log Likelihood 207.27699
* Constant is included in the model.

Beginning Block Number 1. Method: Enter
Variable(s) Entered on Step Number
1.. TREAT
Estimation terminated at iteration number 3 because
Log Likelihood decreased by less than .01 percent.

		Chi-Square	df	Significance
−2 Log Likelihood	167.382			
Goodness of Fit	149.998			
Model Chi-Square		39.895	2	.0000
Improvement		39.895	2	.0000

Commentary

Except for the fact that two dummy vectors were generated to represent the three categories of the independent variable, the output is very similar to the one for the data in Table 17.1. If necessary, refer to the commentaries on that output. As I pointed out earlier, in LOGISTIC REGRESSION all vectors representing a categorical variable are entered (removed) as a set. Thus, the Model Chi-Square has 2 *df*. As there is only one independent variable, Improvement is the same as Model (see the commentary on the output for Table 17.1).

Output

-- Variables in the Equation --

Variable	B	S.E.	Wald	df	Sig	Exp(B)
TREAT			31.8757	2	.0000	
TREAT(1)	1.7917	.4564	15.4096	1	.0001	5.9998
TREAT(2)	2.7725	.5000	30.7483	1	.0000	15.9992
Constant	−1.3863	.3536	15.3742	1	.0001	

Commentary

Numbers in the parentheses refer to coded vectors (not categories). For example, TREAT(1) refers to the first coded vector in which T1 was identified (i.e., assigned 1; see the preceding output). Recalling that in the present example the third group is a control group, each Exp(B) is interpretable as the odds ratio of the given treatment to the control. Thus, the odds of success for subjects in T1 and T2 are, respectively, about 6 and 16 times greater than for those in the control group. This can be readily verified from Table 17.2, using (17.1):

$$(1) \ [(30)(40)]/[(10)(20)] \ = \ 6.0$$

$$(2) \ [(40)(40)]/[(10)(10)] \ = \ 16.0$$

As I explained earlier, dividing a coefficient by its standard error yields a t with $df = N - q$, where $N =$ number of subjects, and $q =$ number of parameters. In the present example, $df = 147$. Alternatively, you can obtain the t ratios by taking the square roots of the Wald values corresponding to the coefficients in question. Thus, for b_{T1}, $t = 3.93$; for b_{T2}, $t = 5.55$.

Output

Classification Table for DEP

		Predicted		
		FAILURE	SUCCESS	Percent Correct
		F	S	
Observed				
FAILURE	F	40	30	57.14%
SUCCESS	S	10	70	87.50%
			Overall	73.33%

ID	Observed DEP	Pred	PGroup	Resid
T1	S S	.6000	S	.4000
T1	S F **	.6000	S	−.6000

T2	S S	.8000	S	.2000
T2	S F **	.8000	S	−.8000
CONT	S S **	.2000	F	.8000
CONT	S F	.2000	F	−.2000

S=Selected U=Unselected cases
** = Misclassified cases

Commentary

Using .5 as the cutoff point (default), percent of correct success predictions is considerably greater than percent correct failure predictions.[13] Use (17.6) or (17.7) with relevant values from the regression equation reported earlier to verify the predicted values (Pred) in the preceding output.

Output

	Parameter Value	Freq	Coding (1)	(2)
TREAT				
T1	1.00	2	1.000	.000
T2	2.00	2	.000	1.000
CONT	3.00	2	−1.000	−1.000

------------------------------------- Variables in the Equation -------------------------------------

Variable	B	S.E.	Wald	df	Sig	Exp(B)
TREAT			31.8757	2	.0000	
TREAT(1)	.2703	.2546	1.1273	1	.2883	1.3104
TREAT(2)	1.2511	.2805	19.8886	1	.0000	3.4942
Constant	.1352	.1924	.4932	1	.4825	

Commentary

The preceding are excerpts of output from the analysis with effect coding. As model testing results are the same, whatever the coding method, I did not reproduce them here (see the output for the analysis with dummy coding).

---

[13]Recall, however, that these estimates are inflated. See the commentary on the output for the analysis of Table 17.1.

Turning to the regression coefficients, it is important to bear in mind that, as in effect coding with a continuous dependent variable (see Chapter 11), they refer to deviations from the overall mean, which in the case of logistic regression is the average of logits. Hence, "exponentiation of the estimated coefficient expresses the odds relative to an 'average' odds, the geometric mean. Whether this is in fact useful will depend on being able to 'place a meaningful interpretation on the 'average' odds'" (Hosmer & Lemeshow, 1989, p. 52). Unless you have good reason not to, you should ignore Exp(B) in regression equations for effect coding.

The case under consideration should serve as a reminder of the importance of being familiar with the defaults of computer programs you are using. Regrettably, as Lemeshow and Hosmer (1984, p. 151) point out, many users pay no attention to such matters and end up with erroneous interpretations of results. A word of caution, in the event you intend to read Lemeshow and Hosmer's (1984) paper: it contains a minor error (see Dullberg's, 1985, comment) and some ambiguities, which Fleiss (1985) helped clarify. See also Lemeshow and Hosmer's (1985) reply.

When the design does not include a control or reference group, effect coding is probably more useful than dummy coding, as its properties are analogous to those for designs with a continuous dependent variable (see Chapters 11 and 12). In what follows I describe briefly the properties of effect coding in logistic regression. If necessary, refer to Chapter 11 for a general discussion of coding schemes.

As in designs with continuous dependent variables, the effect of the category assigned -1 in all the coded vectors (control, in the present example) is equal to minus the sum of the b's for the coded vectors. Thus, $b_C = -(.2703 + 1.2511) = -1.5214$.[14] Also, a contrast between two b's can, among other things, be used to ascertain the relevant odds ratio. For comparative purposes, I contrast first each treatment with that of the control group.

$$b_{T1} - b_C = .2703 - (-1.5214) \quad = 1.7917$$

$$b_{T2} - b_C = 1.2511 - (-1.5214) = 2.7725$$

Notice that these are the same values as those I obtained when I used dummy coding. Of course, exponentiation of these values yields the same odds ratios reported under Exp(B) in the output for the analysis with dummy coding.

As another example, assume that it is of interest to contrast the two treatments:

$$b_{T2} - b_{T1} = 1.2511 - .2703 = .9808$$

$e^{.9808} = 2.67$. Thus, the odds of success for subjects in T2 are about 2.67 greater than those for subjects in T1. This can be verified by applying (17.1) to the relevant data in Table 17.2:[15]

$$[(40)(20)]/[(30)(10)] = 2.67$$

In Chapter 6—see (6.11) and the presentation related to it—I introduced the covariance matrix of the b's (**C**) and showed how to use its elements to calculate the standard error of the difference between two b's. In Chapter 11, I expanded on this topic in the context of comparisons between b's for effect coding. I show now that the same approach applies to effect coding in logistic regression analysis.

---

[14]As I explained in Chapter 11, I use b with an appropriate subscript for this category although its value is *not* part of the regression equation.

[15]To obtain a ratio > 1, which lends itself to a more intuitive interpretation, I interchanged the first two columns in Table 17.2. Alternatively, calculate the odds ratio without interchanging the columns (.375) and take its reciprocal (2.67).

Output

Correlation Matrix:

	Constant	TREAT(1)	TREAT(2)
Constant	1.00000	−.18898	.08575
TREAT(1)	−.18898	1.00000	−.45374
TREAT(2)	.08575	−.45374	1.00000

Commentary

Recall (see Chapter 11) that REGRESSION of SPSS reports the correlation *and* the covariance matrices of the estimated parameters. In contrast, LOGISTIC REGRESSION reports only the correlation matrix of the estimated parameters, as in the preceding. I will not speculate as to the reason for the difference between the two programs. In BMDP the situation is reversed: in the regression program (2R) only the correlation matrix of the estimated parameters can be obtained, whereas in the logistic regression program (LR) both the correlation and the covariance matrices can be obtained (see the following output). When I reported output of 2R in Chapter 14, I showed how to convert the correlation matrix to a covariance matrix. The same procedure has to be applied here to relevant elements of the correlation matrix reported above.

As the interest here is in elements of the correlation matrix corresponding to the coefficients for the treatments, I ignore the elements relevant to the Constant (first row and first column). To construct the relevant **C**, replace each diagonal element with the square of the standard error of the *b* corresponding to it. From output reported under Variables in the Equation, the standard errors of the *b*'s for TREAT(1) and TREAT(2), respectively, are .2546 and .2805. Thus, the diagonal elements of **C** are .06482 and .07868.

Multiply each off-diagonal element (i.e., correlation) by the standard errors of the *b*'s corresponding to it. In the present example, there is only one such element (the matrix is symmetric). Thus, $(−.45374)(.2546)(.2805) = −.03240$. Hence,

$$\mathbf{C} = \begin{bmatrix} .06482 & −.03240 \\ −.03240 & .07868 \end{bmatrix}$$

As I explained in Chapter 11, it is now necessary to augment **C** by adding the missing elements related to the coefficient for the group assigned −1 in all the vectors (control group, in the present example). A missing element in a row (or column) of **C** is equal to $−\Sigma c_i$ (or $−\Sigma c_j$), where i is row i of **C** and j is column j of **C**. Note that what this means is that the sum of each row (and column) of the augmented matrix (**C***) is equal to zero. For the present example,

$$\mathbf{C^*} = \begin{bmatrix} .06482 & −.03240 & −.03242 \\ −.03240 & .07868 & −.04628 \\ −.03242 & −.04628 & .07870 \end{bmatrix}$$

where I inserted dashes so that elements added to **C** could be seen clearly.

As I showed in Chapter 6—see (6.12) and the discussion related to it—the variance of estimate of the difference between two *b*'s is

$$s^2_{b_i − b_j} = c_{ii} + c_{jj} − 2c_{ij} \tag{17.9}$$

where $s^2_{b_i - bj}$ = variance of estimate of the difference between b_i and b_j; c_{ii} = diagonal element of $\mathbf{C}^*$ for i, and similarly for c_{jj}; and c_{ij} = are off-diagonal elements of $\mathbf{C}^*$ corresponding to ij. Of course, the square root of the variance of estimate is the standard error.

Using relevant elements from $\mathbf{C}^*$,

$$s_{b_{T1} - b_c} = \sqrt{(.06482) + (.07870) - 2(-.03242)} = .4565$$

which is, within rounding, the same as the value of the standard error of b_{T1} in the output for the analysis with dummy coding (see the preceding). As I showed earlier, the difference between the two coefficients is the same as the coefficient for b_{T1} with dummy coding. Consequently, the t ratio for the test of this difference will also be the same as the one in the analysis with dummy coding. Using relevant values from $\mathbf{C}^*$, verify that $s_{b_{T2} - b_c} = .50$, which is the same as the standard error for b_{T2} in the regression equation for dummy coding (see the preceding).

Finally, earlier I showed that $b_{T2} - b_{T1} = .9808$. Suppose one wishes to test this difference. Using relevant values from $\mathbf{C}^*$ in the preceding, the standard error of this difference is

$$s_{b_{T2} - b_{T1}} = \sqrt{(.06482) + (.07868) - 2(-.03240)} = .4564$$

$t = .9808/.4564 = 2.15$, with 147 *df*.

BMDP

Input

/PROBLEM TITLE IS 'TABLE 17.2.   DUMMY CODING, DEFAULT CATEGORY'.
/INPUT VARIABLES ARE 3. FORMAT IS FREE. FILE IS 'T172.DAT'.
/VARIABLE NAMES ARE TREAT,DEP,FREQ.
/GROUP CODES(DEP)=1,0.   NAMES(DEP)=SUCCESS,FAILURE.
 CODES(TREAT)=1,2,3.   NAMES(TREAT)=T1,T2,CONT.
/REGRESS COUNT IS FREQ.
 DEPEND IS DEP.
 MODEL=TREAT.   METHOD=MLR.
/PRINT COVA.
/END
/PROBLEM TITLE IS 'TABLE 17.2.   EFFECT CODING, DEFAULT CATEGORY'.
/INPUT
/VARIABLE
/GROUP
/REGRESS COUNT IS FREQ.
 DEPEND IS DEP.
 MODEL=TREAT.   METHOD=MLR.   DVAR=MARG.
/PRINT COVA.
/END

Commentary

I am using a BMDP format for processing multiple problems (for an explanation, see the BMDP manual or Chapter 5 of this book). As I explained in connection with my analysis of Table 17.1, by default BMDP (1) treats independent variables as categorical and (2) uses dummy coding. To use effect coding in the second problem, I specified DVAR=MARG. By default, the first category is assigned −1 in all the vectors. The correlation matrix of the parameter estimates is printed by default. PRINT COVA results in the printing of the covariance matrix of the parameter estimates.

Output

VARIABLE NO.	N A M E	GROUP INDEX	FREQ	DESIGN VARIABLES (1)	(2)
1	TREAT	1	50	0	0
		2	50	1	0
		3	50	0	1

TERM	COEFFICIENT	STANDARD ERROR	COEF/SE	EXP(COEF)
TREAT (1)	0.9808	0.456	2.15	2.67
(2)	−1.792	0.456	−3.93	0.167
CONSTANT	0.4055	0.289	1.40	1.50

Commentary

Recall that in BMDP the default category is the first, whereas in SPSS it is the last. Examine the above output and notice that in TREAT(1) T2 of Table 17.2 was identified (assigned 1), and in TREAT(2) the control group was identified. Therefore, although the test of the model is the same in the two outputs, the regression equations are not. Thus, the first coefficient (.9808) refers to the difference between T2 and T1. Earlier I obtained this coefficient and its associated statistics by subtracting the *b* of T1 from the *b* of T2, using the coefficients from the regression equation for effect coding.

The second coefficient (−1.792) refers to the difference between the control group and T1 of Table 17.2. The same value, but with the opposite sign, was reported in the SPSS output for dummy coding (see also my earlier calculations using the coefficients from the regression equation with effect coding). The change in sign is due to the change in the reference category (T1 here; Control in SPSS). Notice, however, that the reciprocal of EXP(COEF) for the coefficient reported here (.167) is 5.98, which is the same as the value reported in SPSS.

I trust that the preceding underscores what I said earlier about the importance of knowing the defaults of the programs you are using. See also the following commentary on the regression equation with effect coding.

Output

VARIABLE NO.	N A M E	GROUP INDEX	FREQ	DESIGN VARIABLES (1)	(2)
1	TREAT	1	50	−1	−1
		2	50	1	0
		3	50	0	1

TERM		COEFFICIENT	STANDARD ERROR	COEF/SE	EXP(COEF)
TREAT	(1)	1.251	0.281	4.46	3.49
	(2)	−1.521	0.281	−5.42	0.218
CONSTANT		0.1352	0.192	0.702	1.14

Commentary

Examine the DESIGN VARIABLES and notice that the first category (T1 of Table 17.2) is assigned −1 in both vectors. Recall that in SPSS the last category is assigned −1 by default. Consequently, the regression equation reported here differs from the one obtained in SPSS. Nevertheless, I show that contrasts between categories yield the same results as those in SPSS. First, though, I calculate b for T1:

$$-(1.251 - 1.521) = .27.$$

For comparative purposes, I carry out the same contrasts I did earlier using the b's for the equation with effect coding obtained from SPSS.

$$b_{T2} - b_{T1} = 1.251 - .27 = .981$$

$$b_{T2} - b_C = 1.251 - (-1.521) = 2.772$$

$$b_{T1} - b_C = .27 - (-1.521) = 1.791$$

The preceding are, within rounding, the same as the values I obtained earlier when I used results from the SPSS analysis with effect coding.

Output

CORRELATION MATRIX OF COEFFICIENTS

	TREAT(1)	TREAT(2)	CONSTANT
TREAT(1)	1.000		
TREAT(2)	−0.588	1.000	
CONSTANT	0.086	0.086	1.000

COVARIANCE MATRIX OF COEFFICIENTS

	TREAT(1)	TREAT(2)	CONSTANT
TREAT(1)	0.07870		
TREAT(2)	−0.04630	0.07870	
CONSTANT	0.00463	0.00463	0.03704

Commentary

For convenience, I placed the two matrices side by side. Keep in mind that TREAT(1) refers to T2 of Table 17.2, and TREAT(2) refers to Control of Table 17.2. Hence, the correlation between the two is *not* equal to the correlation reported in the SPSS output.

As an exercise, use relevant information to convert the correlation matrix to the covariance matrix reported alongside it. If necessary, refer to my explanation in connection with the preceding SPSS output. Calculate the augmented covariance matrix ($\mathbf{C^*}$) and compare it with this one.

$$\mathbf{C^*} = \begin{bmatrix} .0787 & -.0463 & -.0324 \\ -.0463 & .0787 & -.0324 \\ \hline -.0324 & -.0324 & .0648 \end{bmatrix}$$

Notice that, except for the rearrangement of the terms (i.e., placing T2 first and Control second), this matrix is the same as the augmented matrix I derived from the SPSS output for the analysis with effect coding. Of course, standard errors of differences between pairs of b's would be the same as those I obtained earlier. You may wish to calculate them as an exercise.

SAS

Input

```
TITLE 'TABLE 17.2. DUMMY CODING';
DATA T172D;
   INPUT T1 T2 R N;
CARDS;
1  0   30   50
0  1   40   50
0  0   10   50
PROC PRINT;
PROC LOGISTIC;
MODEL R/N=T1 T2/CORRB COVB;
DATA T172E;
   INPUT T1 T2 R N;
CARDS;
 1   0   30   50
 0   1   40   50
-1  -1   10   50
TITLE 'TABLE 17.2. EFFECT CODING';
PROC PRINT;
PROC LOGISTIC;
MODEL R/N=T1 T2/CORRB COVB;
RUN;
```

Commentary

Earlier, I explained the general format of the SAS input (see the SAS analysis of Table 17.1). Therefore, I will only point out that for each of the analyses reported here I entered two coded vectors to represent the independent variable. As was my practice in other chapters (e.g., Chapter 11), I assigned 0 to the last category under dummy coding, and −1 under effect coding. As I pointed out earlier, these are also the defaults used in SPSS. Thus, excerpts of the results reported in the following are the same as SPSS output, which I reproduced and commented on earlier. The options CORRB and COVB call for, respectively, the correlation and covariance matrices of the parameter estimates.

Output

TABLE 17.2. DUMMY CODING

Variable	Parameter Estimate	Standard Error	Wald Chi-Square	Pr > Chi-Square
INTERCPT	−1.3863	0.3536	15.3747	0.0001
T1	1.7918	0.4564	15.4101	0.0001
T2	2.7726	0.5000	30.7494	0.0001

TABLE 17.2. EFFECT CODING

Variable	Parameter Estimate	Standard Error	Wald Chi-Square	Pr > Chi-Square
INTERCPT	0.1352	0.1924	0.4932	0.4825
T1	0.2703	0.2546	1.1273	0.2883
T2	1.2511	0.2805	19.8894	0.0001

	Estimated Correlation Matrix				Estimated Covariance Matrix		
Variable	INTERCPT	T1	T2	Variable	INTERCPT	T1	T2
INTERCPT	1.00000	−0.18898	0.08575	INTERCPT	0.0370366465	−0.009258869	0.0046294295
T1	−0.18898	1.00000	−0.45374	T1	−0.009258869	0.0648144243	−0.032407207
T2	0.08575	−0.45374	1.00000	T2	0.0046294295	−0.032407207	0.0787027225

Commentary

For convenience, I placed the two matrices alongside each other. As I stated earlier, this output is the same as the one I obtained from SPSS. Recall, however, that SPSS reports only the correlation matrix. Except for the fact that SAS reports calculations to a larger number of decimal places, the relevant segment of the covariance matrix is the same as the one I obtained when I converted the correlation matrix reported in SPSS. As an exercise, you may wish to augment the covariance matrix and compare your results with those I gave earlier.

FACTORIAL DESIGNS

In this section, I turn to factorial designs. Although I discuss and analyze a design with two factors, each at two levels, the same approach generalizes to more complex designs. From time to time, I will refer you to Chapter 12, as the ideas and approaches to the analysis of factorial designs I introduced there apply also to designs with a categorical dependent variable. I strongly suggest that you reread relevant sections of Chapter 12 whenever you wish further clarification of topics I allude to or mention briefly in the present chapter (e.g., coding independent variables, the meaning of interaction, orthogonal and nonorthogonal designs, factorial designs in experimental and nonexperimental research).

Reverse Discrimination: A Research Example

Instead of using fictitious data, I will analyze one aspect of a published study, as it affords the opportunity to illustrate a recurring theme in this book, namely the importance of critically reading research reports and the merit of reanalyzing the data reported in them.

Dutton and Lake (1973) conducted an ingenious experiment aimed at testing

> the notion that "reverse discrimination," defined as more favorable behavior by whites toward minority group members than toward other whites, may result from whites' observations of "threatening cues of prejudice in their own behavior." (p. 94)

Briefly, Dutton and Lake randomly assigned white males and females to two conditions: High Threat and Low Threat. Under the High Threat condition, subjects were given cues designed to lead them to believe that they are prejudiced toward minority group members. Under the Low Threat condition, no such cues were given. After treatment administration, subjects were told that the study was over and were instructed to go to an office in another building where they would be paid the amount promised for participation.

All subjects were paid the same amount in change. Upon leaving the building, each subject was approached, according to a random scheme, by either a Black or a White panhandler, who asked whether he or she could spare some change for food. The design is thus a $2 \times 2 \times 2$: (1) Threat (High or Low), (2) Race of Panhandler (Black or White), and (3) Subject's Gender (Male or Female). In their main analysis, Dutton and Lake used the amount of donation in cents as the measure of the dependent variable, and proceeded in a manner I described in Chapter 12.

Without going into details, I will point out that having found that the second-order interaction was statistically not significant, they examined the three first-order interactions. Of these, only Race of Panhandler by Threat was statistically significant. Accordingly, Dutton and Lake proceeded to examine simple main effects and found, as hypothesized, that donations to a Black panhandler were larger under High Threat than under Low Threat (recall that those exposed to High Threat were led to believe that they are prejudiced toward minority group members). By contrast, and again as hypothesized, donations to a White panhandler under the two threat conditions were about the same.

In Chapter 12, I stressed that in the presence of an interaction it is generally not meaningful to interpret main effects. Dutton and Lake's results are a case in point. Only the Threat main effect was statistically significant. Interpreting this result at face value (Dutton and Lake did not), would lead to a conclusion that donations are larger under High Threat than they are under Low Threat, regardless of Race of Panhandler. However, in view of the interaction and the simple effects described in the preceding paragraph, this conclusion would be inappropriate and misleading.

I believe you will benefit from reading Dutton and Lake's discussion of the theoretical rationale for their hypotheses and interpretation of the results. In any case, I will say no more about this analysis. Instead, I turn to my main concern: Dutton and Lake's other analysis in which a "chi-square test was performed on the percentages of subjects donating to black and white panhandlers in the high- and low-threat conditions, collapsing over sex of subjects" (p. 99). The authors reported:

> This test was not significant at .05 level ($df = 1$), yielding a value of 1.6. However, given that the n per cell was relatively small ($n = 20$) and that no great discrepancy in percentage of donors between conditions for the white panhandler was expected, this lack of significance is not surprising. (p. 99)

In a reanalysis of the data, I will show that the analysis as well as some of the reasoning for the failure to reject the null hypothesis are flawed. For the reanalysis, I transformed the percentages of subjects donating, reported in the Total row of Table 1 (Dutton & Lake, 1973, p. 98), to frequencies of donations. Further, I added frequencies of no donation. The data are reported in Table 17.3.

Examine Part I of Table 17.3 and note that, not counting the two categories of the dependent variable, the design is a 2×2. Accordingly, three parameters can be estimated: (1) main effect of Threat, (2) main effect of Race of Panhandler, and (3) interaction between Threat and Race of Panhandler. From the preceding it follows that there are 3 *df* in the design (*not* 1 as stated by Dutton and Lake). Before analyzing the data in Part I of Table 17.3, it will be instructive to conjecture how Dutton and Lake arrived at their results. I believe that Dutton and Lake ignored the No

Table 17.3   Frequencies of Donations: Data from Dutton and Lake (1973)

I.	*Black Panhandler*		*White Panhandler*	
	High Threat	*Low Threat*	*High Threat*	*Low Threat*
Yes	17	9	10	13
No	3	11	10	7
Totals	20	20	20	20

II.	*High Threat*	*Low Threat*	*Totals*
Black Panhandler	17 a	9 b	26 $a + b$
White Panhandler	10 c	13 d	23 $c + d$
Totals	27 $a + c$	22 $b + d$	49 N

NOTE: See text for explanation.

Donations category, thereby creating a 2×2 table as displayed in Part II of Table 17.3. Assuming this is the case, they probably applied a formula for the 2×2 chi-square test with Yates' correction for continuity (e.g., Hays, 1988, p. 780) as follows:

$$\chi^2 = \frac{N(|ad - bc| - N/2)^2}{}$$

with 1 *df.*

Using relevant values from Part II of Table 17.3,

$$\chi^2 = \frac{49(|(17)(13) - (9)(10)| - 49/2)^2}{} = 1.56$$

with 1 *df.*

Be that as it may, I now present input for the analysis of Part I of Table 17.3, followed by excerpts of the output and commentaries.

SPSS

Input

TITLE TABLE 17.3, PART I.
SUBTITLE DUTTON AND LAKE (1973), REVERSE DISCRIMINATION.
DATA LIST FREE/RACE,THREAT,DONATE,FREQ.
WEIGHT BY FREQ.
VALUE LABELS RACE 1 'BLACK' 2 'WHITE'
  /THREAT 1 'HIGH' 2 'LOW'
  /DONATE 1 'YES' 0 'NO'.
BEGIN DATA

```
1  1  1  17
1  1  0  3
1  2  1  9
1  2  0  11
2  1  1  10
2  1  0  10
2  2  1  13
2  2  0  7
END DATA
LIST.
LOGISTIC REGRESSION DONATE/CATEGORICAL=RACE,THREAT/
   ENTER RACE/ENTER THREAT/ENTER RACE BY THREAT/
   PRINT ALL.
SPLIT FILE BY RACE.
LOGISTIC REGRESSION DONATE WITH THREAT/
   CATEGORICAL=THREAT/CONTRAST(THREAT)=IND.
```

Commentary

As most of this input is very similar to inputs I used earlier in this chapter, my comments will be brief.

I declared RACE and THREAT as categorical. By default, effect coding with the second category assigned −1 will be used for each factor.

When the keyword BY is used to connect two or more factors, interactions among them are calculated.[16]

I enter the main effects and the interaction between them in three steps.

Following the overall analysis, I split the file by Race and do analyses of Donate with Threat. For comparative purposes, I use dummy coding in these analyses (see the commentaries on relevant output).

Output

	Value	Freq	Parameter Coding (1)
THREAT			
HIGH	1.00	4	1.000
LOW	2.00	4	−1.000
RACE			
BLACK	1.00	4	1.000
WHITE	2.00	4	−1.000

Interactions:

INT_1   RACE(1) by THREAT(1)

Dependent Variable..   DONATE

---

[16]By contrast, in LOGISTIC of SAS the BY statement is used to carry out analyses in separate groups or strata. This should serve as a reminder of the importance of being thoroughly familiar with the computer program you are using.

Beginning Block Number 0.   Initial Log Likelihood Function
−2 Log Likelihood   106.81867
* Constant is included in the model.

Beginning Block Number 1.   Method: Enter
Variable(s) Entered on Step Number
1..   RACE
−2 Log Likelihood   106.344

	Chi-Square	df	Significance
Improvement	.475	1	.4909

Beginning Block Number 2.   Method: Enter
Variable(s) Entered on Step Number
1..   THREAT

	Chi-Square	df	Significance
Improvement	1.329	1	.2490

Beginning Block Number 3.   Method: Enter
Variable(s) Entered on Step Number
1..   RACE * THREAT

	Chi-Square	df	Significance
Improvement	6.957	1	.0083

Commentary

Assuming that $\alpha = .05$ was selected, only the interaction is statistically significant. In any case, as I explained in Chapter 12, the interaction is scrutinized first to determine whether tests of main effects or simple effects should be pursued. In the presence of a statistically significant interaction, tests of simple effects are called for. In the present example, it is probably most meaningful to compare effects of High and Low Threat within each level of Race of Panhandler. As I showed in Chapter 12, one way of doing this is to carry out separate analyses within levels of a given factor. For the present example, I call for the regression of DONATE on THREAT separately for Black and White Panhandler (see SPLIT FILE and the commands following it in the input file). After reporting output from these analyses, I show how some of the same results can be obtained from the overall regression equation.[17]

Output

RACE: 1.00   BLACK

	Value	Freq	Parameter Coding (1)
THREAT			
HIGH	1.00	2	1.000
LOW	2.00	2	.000

Dependent Variable..   DONATE

[17]As in earlier chapters (e.g., Chapter 12), by overall regression equation I mean the equation that includes all the terms of the design (i.e., main effects and interaction).

Beginning Block Number 0.   Initial Log Likelihood Function
−2 Log Likelihood   51.795731
* Constant is included in the model.

Beginning Block Number 1.   Method: Enter
Variable(s) Entered on Step Number
1..   THREAT

	Chi-Square	df	Significance
Model Chi-Square	7.362	1	.0067

---------------------------------------Variables in the Equation --

Variable	B	S.E.	Wald	df	Sig	Exp(B)
THREAT(1)	1.9349	.7708	6.3019	1	.0121	6.9233
Constant	−.2007	.4495	.1993	1	.6553	

Commentary

As indicated in the beginning of this segment, this output is from the analysis of Donate with Threat for Black Panhandler. I trust that you will have no difficulties interpreting these results. Notice, first, that Model Chi-Square is statistically significant. Examine Exp(B) and notice that the odds of donating under High Threat are about 6.9 greater than under Low Threat. This can be easily verified by applying (17.1) to relevant values from Table 17.3,

$$OR = [(17)(11)]/[(9)(3)] = 6.9$$

Output

| RACE: | 2.00 | WHITE | |

	Value	Freq	Parameter Coding (1)
THREAT			
HIGH	1.00	2	1.000
LOW	2.00	2	.000

Dependent Variable..   DONATE

Beginning Block Number 0.   Initial Log Likelihood Function
−2 Log Likelihood   54.548369
* Constant is included in the model.

Beginning Block Number 1.   Method: Enter
Variable(s) Entered on Step Number
1..   THREAT

	Chi-Square	df	Significance
Model Chi-Square	.925	1	.3363

```
--------------------------------------- Variables in the Equation ---------------------------------------
```

Variable	B	S.E.	Wald	df	Sig	Exp(B)
THREAT(1)	−.6190	.6479	.9127	1	.3394	.5385
Constant	.6190	.4688	1.7433	1	.1867	

Commentary

As you can see, for White Panhandler the Model Chi-Square is statistically not significant. This matter aside, notice that Exp(B) is a fraction. Recalling that High Threat was assigned 1, this means that the odds of donating under High Threat are smaller than under Low Threat. Earlier, I suggested that when an odds ratio is a fraction, it is preferable to use its reciprocal for interpretive purposes. Thus, $1/.5385 = 1.86$, meaning that the odds of donating under *Low Threat* are 1.86 greater than under High Threat. But, as I pointed out above, *the coefficient is statistically not significant.* In other words, the null hypothesis that there is no difference in the odds of donating under High and Low Threat cannot be rejected. As an exercise, you may want to calculate the odds ratio using relevant elements from Table 17.3 (if necessary, see my calculations for Black Panhandler).

Notice that the results of the tests of simple effects are consistent with Dutton and Lake's expectations for donations to Black and White Panhandlers under the two threat conditions, calling into question their reasoning that their failure to detect statistical significance was, in part, due the fact that "no great discrepancy in percentage of donors between conditions for the white panhandler was expected" (Dutton & Lake, p. 99). In the present example, tests of simple effects indicate that there are statistically significant differences in the effect of Threat at one level (Black Panhandler) but not at the other level (White Panhandler).

Finally, as I explained in Chapter 12, when carrying out tests of simple effects, α levels have to be adjusted. Earlier I assumed that $\alpha = .05$ was selected. Therefore, for the previous tests of simple effects $\alpha/2 = .025$ would be used (see Chapter 12).

Output

```
--------- Variables in the Equation ---------
```

Variable	B
RACE(1)	.2286
THREAT(1)	.3290
RACE(1) by THREAT(1)	.6385
Constant	.5381

Commentary

This excerpt of output is from the last step of the overall analysis. Following procedures I explained in Chapter 12 (see "Simple Effects from Overall Regression Equation"), I display the various effects in Table 17.4 in a format similar to that of Table 12.8. As in Table 12.8, I attach

Table 17.4   Main Effects and Interaction for Data in Table 17.3

	Black Panhandler	*White Panhandler*	*Threat Effects*
High Threat	$.6385 = b_{T1R1}$	$-.6385$	$.3290 = b_{T1}$
Low Threat	$-.6385$	$.6385$	$-.3290$
Race Effects	$.2286 = b_{R1}$	$-.2286$	

subscripts only to terms obtained from the regression equation. As I used effect coding, I obtained the remaining terms in view of the constraint that the sum of any given set of effects equals zero. If you are having difficulties with this presentation, I suggest that you read the explanations in the aforementioned section of Chapter 12.

Turning first to the comparison under Black Panhandler, notice from Table 17.4 that the effects are

High Threat: .3290 and   .6385

Low Threat: −.3290 and −.6385

The difference between High Threat and Low Threat under Black Panhandler is therefore

$$[(.3290) + (.6385)] - [(-.3290) + (-.6385)] = 1.935$$

This is, within rounding, the *b* for Threat in the separate analysis with dummy coding for Black Panhandler (see the preceding output). Of course, $e^{1.935} = 6.9$ is the odds ratio I obtained and interpreted earlier.

Parenthetically, had I used effect coding in the separate analyses, I would have obtained *b* = .9675 for Threat under Black Panhandler. Notice that this is equal to the sum of the two effects under High Threat (i.e., .3290 + .6385). Also, as I explained earlier, in such an analysis I would have concluded that *b* = −.9675 for Low Threat. Finally, the difference between these two *b*'s would have yielded the same results as in the preceding (1.935).

Turning to the comparison under White Panhandler, the effects are

High Threat: .3290 and −.6385

Low Threat: −.3290 and   .6385

The difference between High Threat and Low Threat is

$$[(.3290) + (-.6385)] - [(-.3290) + (.6385)] = -.619$$

which is equal to the *b* for Threat in the analysis with dummy coding for White Panhandler (see the preceding output).

Finally, using relevant values from the covariance matrix of the *b*'s of the overall analysis (not reported here), standard errors of the tests of simple effects, analogous to those reported under the separate analyses carried out through the SPLIT FILE command, can be obtained.

The Meaning of Interaction: A Reminder

Earlier in the text (see, in particular, Chapters 12 through 15), I discussed the concept of interaction. What follows is meant to remind you of some major issues I raised. I strongly suggest that you reread relevant sections in the aforementioned chapters, especially those dealing with the distinction between experimental and nonexperimental research and its relevance to the definition, estimation, and interpretation of interaction.

In Chapter 12, I stressed that the meaning of an interaction as the joint effect of two or more independent variables is unambiguous only in the context of orthogonal experimental designs. I then drew attention to the controversy surrounding analytic approaches in nonorthogonal experimental designs. Following that, I asserted that the term *interaction* in nonexperimental designs is inappropriate, as in such designs "independent" variables not only tend to be correlated, but the correlations may even be a consequence of one or more of the "independent" variables affecting other "independent" variables. In sum, I suggested that the term *interaction not* be used in nonexperimental designs.

As I showed in Chapters 12 and 13, the mechanics of including interactions in a model are simple, requiring only that one generate products of the vectors representing the variables in question. As a result, I contended, interaction terms are often used in multiple regression analysis without regard to matters of theory and research design. The situation is even worse in the methodological and research literature on logistic regression analysis, where product vectors are used routinely to represent interactions without questioning their validity and meaning in designs other than experimental ones.

In epidemiologic literature, several authors (e.g., Koopman, 1981; Kupper & Hogan, 1978; Rothman, Greenland, & Walker, 1980; Walker & Rothman, 1982; Walter & Holford, 1978) attempted to come to grips with the meaning of interaction in logistic regression. Yet, "not enough thought has been given to an understanding of what cross-product terms in such models [logistic regression] really mean with regard to measuring interaction" (Kleinbaum et al., 1982, p. 412). Not much has changed since the time the preceding statement was made, as is exemplified by the following.

Afifi and Clark (1984) stated, "[I]t is sometimes useful to incorporate *interactions* of two or more variables in the logistic regression model. Interactions are *simply* [italics added] represented as the products of variables in the model" (p. 294). They then gave an example of an interaction between age and income in a model aimed at explaining depression. Suffice it to point out that age and income tend to be correlated to cast doubt about the meaning of an interaction between them. In any case, Afifi and Clark did not even allude to potential problems in the interpretation of product vectors as an interaction. Using the same example in the second edition of their book, Afifi and Clark (1990, p. 338) instructed the reader on how to incorporate an interaction between age, sex, and income in a program for stepwise logistic regression analysis.

In a similar vein, Norušis/SPSS Inc. (1993b) tell the user of the LOGISTIC REGRESSION program, "Just as in linear regression, you can include terms in the model that are products of single terms. . . . Interaction terms for categorical variables can also be computed. They are created as products of the values of the new variables" (p. 14).[18] The user is only cautioned to "make sure that the interaction terms created are those of interest" (p. 14). After a brief explanation, it is suggested that the program's default coding (effect) be used.

Kahn and Sempos (1989) described a study of myocardial infarction in which blood pressure and age were used as independent variables. They stated, "If the association of blood pressure and risk is different at different ages . . . , we say there is an *interaction* between age and

---

[18]In Chapter 11, I pointed out that various authors and software manuals refer to multiple coded vectors representing a categorical variable as *variables*. I suggested that this nomenclature be avoided, as it may lead to misinterpretations, particularly among inexperienced users and readers. The statement here is a case in point, where the reference to "new variables" is actually to coded vectors representing categorical variables.

blood pressure in relation to risk of disease" (p. 107). It is noteworthy that they preferred the term *interaction* to *effect modification,* asserting that the latter "implies a real effect requiring data beyond those of the *associations* [italics added] we are discussing" (p. 107). As further justification for their preference of the term *interaction,* Kahn and Sempos pointed out that it "is a quite common term in the statistical epidemiologic literature" (p. 107). As in the sources I cited earlier, Kahn and Sempos did not allude to implications of independent variables being correlated (see their discussion of the correlation between age and blood pressure on p. 105 and the illustrative data in their Table 5–4, p. 106).

ONE CONTINUOUS INDEPENDENT VARIABLE

Thus far, my presentation was limited to categorical independent variables. As I stated in the beginning of this chapter, both categorical and continuous independent variables can be part of a logistic model. In this section, I give an example with a continuous independent variable.

A Numerical Example

Table 17.5 presents data for a continuous independent variable, X, and a categorical dependent variable, Y. Assume, as for the data in Table 17.1, that Y is admission to a mechanical engineering program (1 = yes; 0 = no). Whereas in Table 17.1 the independent variable was categorical (gender), here it is continuous, say, mechanical aptitude. Although this is an example of a non-experimental study, the same analytic approach would be taken in an experimental study (e.g., Y = mastery of a task, X = number of hours in training). Of course, interpretation of results is affected by the characteristics of the design.

SPSS

Input

TITLE TABLE 17.5. A CONTINUOUS INDEPENDENT VARIABLE.
DATA LIST FREE/APTITUDE,ADMIT.
VALUE LABELS ADMIT 1 'YES' 0 'NO'.
BEGIN DATA
8   1
7   0   *[first two subjects]*

.   .
3   0   *[last two subjects]*
2   0
END DATA
LIST.
LOGISTIC REGRESSION ADMIT WITH APTITUDE/ID=APTITUDE/
    PRINT ALL/CASEWISE.

Table 17.5   Illustrative Data with a Continuous Independent Variable

X	Y	X	Y
8	1	4	0
7	0	7	1
5	1	3	1
3	0	2	0
3	0	4	0
5	1	2	0
7	1	3	0
8	1	4	1
5	1	3	0
5	1	2	0

NOTE: X = mechanical aptitude and Y = admission to program (1 = yes, 0 = no). The second set of two columns is a continuation of the first set.

Commentary

The structure of this input is the same as that in the examples in preceding sections, except that here I enter the data by subjects whereas in the preceding examples I took advantage of the grouped data format. Recall that the program treats as continuous any independent variables not identified as categorical (see the commentary that accompanies the input for the analysis of Table 17.1). Thus, APTITUDE will be treated as continuous.

Output

Beginning Block Number 0.   Initial Log Likelihood Function
−2 Log Likelihood   27.725887
* Constant is included in the model.

Beginning Block Number 1.   Method: Enter
Variable(s) Entered on Step Number
1..   APTITUDE
  −2 Log Likelihood   18.606

	Chi-Square	df	Significance
Improvement	9.120	1	.0025

Classification Table for ADMIT

		Predicted		Percent Correct
		NO	YES	
		N	Y	
Observed				
NO	N	9	1	90.00%
YES	Y	2	8	80.00%
			Overall	85.00%

--Variables in the Equation --

Variable	B	S.E.	Wald	df	Sig
APTITUDE	.9455	.4229	4.9991	1	.0254
Constant	−4.0951	1.8340	4.9857	1	.0256

ID	Observed ADMIT		Pred	PGroup	Resid
8.00	S	Y	.9698	Y	.0302
7.00	S	N **	.9258	Y	−.9258
5.00	S	Y	.6530	Y	.3470
3.00	S	N	.2212	N	−.2212
.	.	.	.	.	.
4.00	S	N	.4223	N	−.4223
.	.	.	.	.	.
2.00	S	N	.0994	N	−.0994

Commentary

These excerpts of output are similar to those I reproduced, and commented on, in earlier sections. Here, I comment only on the regression equation, as it consists of a continuous independent variable, whereas in earlier examples the independent variables were categorical.

As in the earlier examples, this regression equation can be used to predict an applicant's probability of being admitted to the program. *For illustrative purposes, I am ignoring here matters of design and sampling. Recall that in certain designs the estimated intercept has to be adjusted* (see the commentary on the analysis of Table 17.1). Notice from Table 17.5, or from the first line of data in the input file, that the first applicant's aptitude score is 8. Using the regression equation, and applying (17.7),

$$P = \frac{1}{1 + e^{-[-4.0951 + (.9455)(8)]}} = .9698$$

which is the value reported for the first applicant. Predicted scores for other applicants are similarly calculated.

As I stated in the beginning of this chapter—see (17.4) and the discussion related to it—analogous to linear regression, b is interpreted as the expected change in logit(P) associated with a unit change in X. However, this is *not* true for estimated probabilities. Unlike linear regression, where the rate of change is constant (equal to b), the rate of change of predicted probabilities varies, depending on the location of the starting point on X. This can be readily verified from the preceding output. For example, examine the probabilities associated with scores of 7 and 8, and notice that a unit increment in X is associated with a .044 (.9698 − .9258) increment in the probability of admission to the program. In contrast, increments in probabilities associated with a unit change from 4 to 5, and from 2 to 3, respectively, are .2307 and .1268. From the foregoing it follows that, unlike linear regression, a predicted change in probability associated with an increment of k units in X is *not* equal to k times the predicted change in probability associated with a unit change in X.

I will now examine the odds for admission to the program. Using (17.2), for applicants whose aptitude score is 8 the odds are

$$.9698/(1 - .9698) = 32.11$$

In a similar manner, verify that the odds for admission for applicants whose aptitude score is 7 are 12.48. Notice that, as I explained earlier, a unit increment in aptitude multiplies the odds by 2.57, which is equal to e^b (i.e., $e^{.9455} = 2.57$). This can perhaps be seen more clearly by applying (17.5). For applicants whose aptitude score is 8,

$$\text{Odds} = P/(1 - P) = e^{(-4.0951)}(e^{.9455})^8 = 32.10$$

For those whose aptitude score is 7,

$$\text{Odds} = P/(1 - P) = e^{(-4.0951)}(e^{.9455})^7 = 12.47$$

Thus, the odds ratio for applicants whose aptitude score is 8 to those whose aptitude score is 7 is about 2.57. In other words, the odds of admission to the program are about 2.57 greater for applicants whose score is 8 than for those whose score is 7.

As another example, for applicants whose aptitude score is 4,

$$\text{Odds} = e^{(-4.0951)}(e^{.9455})^4 = .73$$

Thus, the odds ratio for applicants whose score is 8 to those whose score is 4 is 43.97 (32.10/.73).

The odds ratio can be more directly calculated using the following formula:

$$\text{OR} = e^{b(X_i - X_j)} \tag{17.10}$$

where OR is the odds ratio; X_i and X_j are two scores of interest. For the preceding example,

$$\text{OR} = e^{(.9455)(8 - 4)} = e^{(.9455)(4)} = 43.90$$

which is, within rounding, the ratio I calculated earlier. Two things will be noted about (17.10). One, it does *not* contain the intercept (a). Hence, as I pointed out earlier, estimates of odds ratios are valid in all sampling designs, whereas predicted probabilities may not be. Two, although I expressed it in a format suitable for a single independent variable, generalizations to multiple independent variables are straightforward.

The preceding presentation shows that the relative simplicity of the interpretation of b's for categorical independent variables (see earlier sections in this chapter) does not generalize to b's for continuous independent variables. How, then, are such b's to be interpreted? Generally speaking, what are deemed meaningful values on the independent variable(s) should be used to calculate odds ratios. Some authors (e.g., Roncek, 1991) recommend that predicted probabilities be used instead (see DeMaris, 1993, and Roncek, 1993, for an exchange on the merits of comparing probabilities or odds). Alba (1988), who suggested that converting odds ratios into "percentage differences" may be helpful in getting an "intuitive grasp," fittingly added that "such differences are not a substitute for the odds ratios themselves" (p. 267).

Referring to the example I analyzed earlier, and assuming a different range of scores than the one I used for illustrative purposes, a researcher may wish to compare scores at intervals of, say, 10 points. As another example, consider an attempt to ascertain the effects of different dosages of a drug on some ailment. It stands to reason that comparisons would be made among dosages deemed meaningful for the drug and the ailment in question. For a good discussion of the interpretation of b's for continuous variables and some interesting recommendations, see Darlington (1990, pp. 447–448).

TWO INDEPENDENT VARIABLES: ONE CONTINUOUS AND ONE CATEGORICAL

Earlier—see (Table 17.3) and the discussion related to it—I discussed and illustrated an extension of simple logistic regression to multiple logistic regression with two categorical independent variables. I turn now to an example of a design with one continuous and one categorical independent variable. For more extensive examples, see references given earlier in this chapter (e.g., Aldrich & Nelson, 1984; Hosmer & Lemeshow, 1989; Neter et al., 1989).

A Numerical Example

For this example, whose data I give in Table 17.6, I merged the data from Tables 17.1 and 17.5. In both tables the dependent variable was admission to a mechanical engineering program. But whereas in Table 17.1 the independent variable was gender, in Table 17.5 it was mechanical aptitude. *Solely for illustrative purposes,* I use these data to show (1) a general application of multiple logistic regression, where one independent variable "happens" to be categorical and the other continuous, and (2) analysis of covariance (ANCOVA).

SPSS

Input

TITLE TABLE 17.6   TWO INDEPENDENT VARIABLES.
DATA LIST FREE FILE='T176.DAT'/APTITUDE GENDER ADMIT.
VALUE LABELS GENDER 1 'MALE' 2 'FEMALE'/ADMIT 1 'Y' 0 'N'.
LIST.
LOGISTIC REGRESSION ADMIT WITH APTITUDE GENDER/
   CATEGORICAL=GENDER/CONTRAST(GENDER)=INDICATOR/
   ENTER GENDER/ENTER APTITUDE.
TITLE TABLE 17.6.   ANCOVA.   DUMMY CODING.
LOGISTIC REGRESSION ADMIT WITH APTITUDE GENDER/
   CATEGORICAL=GENDER/CONTRAST(GENDER)=INDICATOR/
   ENTER APTITUDE/ENTER GENDER/ENTER APTITUDE BY GENDER.
TITLE TABLE 17.6.   ANCOVA.   EFFECT CODING.
LOGISTIC REGRESSION ADMIT WITH APTITUDE GENDER/
   CATEGORICAL=GENDER/
   ENTER APTITUDE/ENTER GENDER/ENTER APTITUDE BY GENDER.

Commentary

As you can see from the second line, I am reading in the data from an external file with a free format. For greater clarity, I carry out three separate analyses, although a smaller number would have sufficed. I elaborate on the specific purposes of each analysis in the context of my commentaries on output generated by it.

Table 17.6   Illustrative Data with Two Independent Variables

X_1	X_2	Y	X_1	X_2	Y
8	1	1	4	2	0
7	1	0	7	2	1
5	1	1	3	2	1
3	1	0	2	2	0
3	1	0	4	2	0
5	1	1	2	2	0
7	1	1	3	2	0
8	1	1	4	2	1
5	1	1	3	2	0
5	1	1	2	2	0

NOTE: X_1 = mechanical aptitude; X_2 = gender (1 = male, 2 = female) and Y = admission to program (1 = Yes, 0 = no). The second set of three columns is a continuation of the first set.

Output

Beginning Block Number 1.   Method: Enter
Variable(s) Entered on Step Number
1..   GENDER

	Chi-Square	df	Significance
Improvement	3.291	1	.0696

-- Variables in the Equation ---

Variable	B	S.E.	Wald	df	Sig	Exp(B)
GENDER(1)	1.6946	.9759	3.0152	1	.0825	5.4444
Constant	−.8473	.6901	1.5076	1	.2195	

Commentary

Examine the input and notice that in the first analysis, I enter GENDER first, followed by APTI-TUDE. By doing this, I do *not* mean to imply that my aim is to carry out a hierarchical analysis where variables are accorded priority of entry into the analysis because of their role in the design (e.g., when control variables are entered first; see my commentary on the output from the second analysis, which follows; see also Chapters 9, 14, and 15 for discussions of hierarchical regression analysis). I entered GENDER first for two reasons: (1) to show that, as expected, the results are identical to those I obtained from the analysis of Table 17.1, where I entered the data in grouped format (in the analysis of Table 17.1, I reproduced larger segments of output and gave detailed commentaries; therefore, I do not comment on these results); and (2) to use the log-likelihood test—see (17.8) and the discussion related to it—to test the contribution of APTITUDE.

Output

Beginning Block Number 2.   Method: Enter
Variable(s) Entered on Step Number
1..   APTITUDE

	Chi-Square	df	Significance
Improvement	5.870	1	.0154

Classification Table for ADMIT

		Predicted		Percent Correct
		NO	YES	
		N	Y	
Observed		+---------+---------+		
NO	N	9	1	90.00%
		+---------+---------+		
YES	Y	2	8	80.00%
		+---------+---------+		
			Overall	85.00%

------------------------------------- Variables in the Equation --

Variable	B	S.E.	Wald	df	Sig	Exp(B)
GENDER(1)	.2672	1.3009	.0422	1	.8373	1.3063
APTITUDE	.8983	.4714	3.6312	1	.0567	2.4553
Constant	−4.0287	1.8384	4.8025	1	.0284	

Commentary

Assuming that $\alpha = .05$ was selected, Improvement due to APTITUDE is statistically significant. Overall, 85% of the cases are correctly classified.[19] However, notice from the regression equation that the coefficient for GENDER is clearly statistically not significant. A researcher obtaining such results would be well advised to delete GENDER and reestimate the equation. It is not necessary to do this here, as I carried out such an analysis when I used the data in Table 17.5. I will only point out that when I used only APTITUDE, the percent of correctly classified cases was the same (85%) as reported in the present analysis, where I used both GENDER and APTITUDE. For other results and commentaries, see the preceding section.

Finally, when an equation is reestimated after one or more variables were deleted upon examining the results, it is important to replicate the study before accepting the results as evidence in support of a given hypothesis.

---

[19]Remember that earlier in this chapter I pointed out that values in such tables are inflated.

ANCOVA AND INTERACTION: BRIEF REMINDERS

As I have pointed out, the next two analyses are meant to illustrate the application of logistic regression for ANCOVA. Before turning to the results of these analyses, though, I believe it imperative to remind you of important issues related to ANCOVA and to the concept of interaction, which I discussed earlier in the text (especially in Chapters 12 through 15). *What follows are merely reminders. I strongly urge you to reread relevant sections of the aforementioned chapters.*

In Chapter 15, I stressed the importance of distinguishing between the use of ANCOVA for control and for adjustment, and I showed that whereas application of ANCOVA for control in experimental designs is nonproblematic and can prove to be very useful, its application for adjustment is fraught with serious logical and methodological problems. I believe it particularly important to stress this issue here, as it seems to me that in much of the literature on logistic regression analysis it is hardly acknowledged. Notable examples are case-control studies in epidemiology where ANCOVA is routinely applied for adjustment. Typically, researchers are interested in the effect of a risk(s) factor(s) (e.g., smoking, exposure to a pollutant) on, say, lung cancer, after "adjusting" for differences between cases (diseased) and controls (not diseased) on "relevant" variables (e.g., age, socioeconomic status). As far as I can tell, this is generally done without explicit or implicit reservations.

In Chapters 12 through 15, I elaborated on the concept of interaction and discussed, among other things, problems attendant with attempts to estimate and interpret it in nonexprimental designs. Accordingly, I recommended that in designs like the one considered here terms such as *comparisons of regression equations* and *homogeneity of regression coefficients* be used instead of the term *interaction*. No such distinctions are made in SPSS or other computer programs I know of. Although, *for convenience, I will refer to output where the interaction term was entered or tested, I urge you to keep the preceding comments in mind.*

Output

TITLE TABLE 17.6.   ANCOVA.   DUMMY CODING.
Beginning Block Number 1.   Method: Enter
Variable(s) Entered on Step Number
1..   APTITUDE

	Chi-Square	df	Significance
Improvement	9.120	1	.0025

Beginning Block Number 2.   Method: Enter
Variable(s) Entered on Step Number
1..   GENDER

	Chi-Square	df	Significance
Improvement	.042	1	.8384

Beginning Block Number 3.   Method: Enter
Variable(s) Entered on Step Number
1..   APTITUDE * GENDER

	Chi-Square	df	Significance
Improvement	.236	1	.6272

Commentary

As I explained in Chapter 15, in ANCOVA the various components have to be entered in the following hierarchy: (1) control variable(s); (2) coded vector(s) representing treatments (risk factors, groups, or the like); and (3) interaction term(s). The results are examined in the reverse order, beginning with the interaction, which in the present example is represented by the product of APTITUDE and GENDER. If it is statistically not significant it is concluded that the regression coefficients are homogeneous, thus satisfying a major assumption of ANCOVA (see Chapter 15, where I also discuss action to be taken when the interaction is statistically significant).

As you can see from the previous output, the interaction is statistically not significant. The next step, therefore, is to determine whether improvement due to the vector(s) representing risk factor(s) (treatments, groups) is statistically significant. In the present example, this boils down to a question of whether GENDER, when entered after APTITUDE (covariate), leads to a statistically significant improvement. From the result reported at the second step, it is clear that the null hypothesis that GENDER does not improve the model cannot be rejected. Consequently, one would proceed to examine the results of the first step, consisting of APTITUDE only. I reported, and interpreted, results of an analysis with APTITUDE only when I analyzed the data in Table 17.5.

Reservations about the use of ANCOVA in nonexperimental research aside (see the preceding), it is interesting to contrast the present findings of the second step with those from the analysis in which I used only GENDER as an independent variable. When I did an analysis with GENDER only—see my analysis of Table 17.1 and the discussion related to it—I pointed out that using a relatively liberal $\alpha = .10$, one would conclude that there is evidence of discrimination against females in admissions to a mechanical engineering program. No evidence of discrimination exists after adjusting for male and female differences in mechanical aptitude. It is this seemingly facile "equating" of groups differing on one or more "relevant" variables that appeals to many researchers. I would, however, remind you that in Chapter 15 I raised serious doubts about the validity of this approach. Also, *keep in mind that the data, which I devised for illustrative purposes, may have no resemblance to reality.*

Output

[Dummy Coding]

-------------------------- Variables in the Equation --------------------------

Variable	B	S.E.	Wald	df	Sig	Exp(B)
APTITUDE	.8983	.4714	3.6312	1	.0567	2.4553
GENDER(1)	.2672	1.3009	.0422	1	.8373	1.3063
Constant	−4.0287	1.8384	4.8025	1	.0284	

[Effect Coding]

------------------- Variables in the Equation -------------------

Variable	B	S.E.	Wald	df	Sig
APTITUDE	.8983	.4714	3.6312	1	.0567
GENDER(1)	.1336	.6504	.0422	1	.8373
Constant	−3.8951	2.0396	3.6470	1	.0562

Commentary

For comparative purposes, I placed the regression equations (without the product term) for dummy and effect coding alongside each other. To show how the coefficient for GENDER is interpreted, *I overlook the fact that improvement due to GENDER is statistically not significant.* Turning first to the results for dummy coding, and recalling that males were identified (assigned 1) in the vector representing GENDER, one would conclude, based on Exp(B), that after adjusting for differences in APTITUDE, the odds of admission to the engineering program are 1.3 greater for males than for females. Without "adjustment" for differences in APTITUDE, the odds ratio was 5.4—see my analysis of Table 17.1 and the discussion related to it. To repeat: *I engaged in the preceding interpretation solely for illustrative purposes.* As I pointed out earlier, after "adjusting" for differences in APTITUDE, the coefficient for GENDER is statistically not significant.

Turning to the output for effect coding, recall that the *b* for the group assigned −1 in all the coded vectors is equal to the negative sum of the *b*'s for the coded vectors. In the present example, there is only one effect-coded vector in which males were identified. The coefficient for this vector is .1336. Therefore, the coefficient for females is −.1336. The difference between the two coefficients is .2672, which is equal to the coefficient for the dummy-coded vector for GENDER. Of course, $e^{.2672}$ yields the same odds ratio as in the preceding.

In designs with two groups, it is simplest and most efficient to use dummy coding. However, as I demonstrated in Chapter 15, in designs with more than two groups it is more advantageous to use effect coding, especially when one wishes to test multiple comparisons among adjusted means (a priori or post hoc) via tests of differences among *b*'s.

I conclude this section by showing that, as in multiple regression analysis (see Chapters 14 and 15), regression equations for separate groups (treatments, risk factors) can be obtained from the overall regression equation. For this purpose, I use the overall equation with effect coding.

Output

------------ Variables in the Equation ------------

Variable	B
APTITUDE	.9855
GENDER(1)	1.1338
APTITUDE by GENDER(1)	−.2542
Constant	−4.0888

Commentary

Recall that males were identified (assigned 1) in the effect-coded vector GENDER(1) and that females were assigned −1. Following procedures I described in Chapters 14 and 15, *a* and *b*, respectively, for males are −2.9550 [(−4.0888) + 1.1338] and .7313 [.9855 + (−.2542)]. The respective values for females are −5.2226 [(−4.0888) + (−1.1338)] and 1.2397 (.9855 + .2542). I suggest that, as an exercise, you analyze the data for males and females separately and verify these results. One way to do this is through the use of the SPLIT FILE command (for an example, see the input for the analysis of the data in Table 17.3).

ASSESSMENT OF FIT

Considering that R^2 is used by many as an index of fit in linear regression analysis, it is not surprising that a number of indices of fit "in the spirit of R^2" (Aldrich & Nelson, 1984, p. 57) were proposed for logistic regression analysis. Aldrich and Nelson describe several so-called "pseudo-R^2 measures" (pp. 57–59). Hagle and Mitchell (1992), who examined several pseudo-R^2 indices through simulation techniques, concluded that two "perform quite well, comparing favorably with OLS [ordinary least squares] R^2. The choice between them may simply be a matter of availability and ease of use" (p. 762). They did, however, acknowledge that "[s]ome regression analysts find the R^2 statistic to be of little utility. Others use it extensively while evaluating model performance" (p. 762). In Chapter 9 (see "The Notion of Variance Partitioning"), I pointed out that even authors who advocate the use of R^2 as an index of fit concede that it is of little utility for ascertaining the effects of independent variables on the dependent variable.

Other proposed indices of fit relate to discrepancies between observed and expected frequencies. The Pearson Chi-square is an example of such an index. Researchers who use it take large values of p associated with it as an indication of a "good" fit. However, as Hosmer et al. (1991) pointed out, the Pearson Chi-square does "not have an easily interpreted distribution under the assumptions . . . typical of most practical applications of logistic regression" (p. 1632). They therefore advised against the use of p values for Chi-square reported in computer outputs for assessment of fit, and they went on to say, "About all we can do in the way of assessing fit is to compare their [Chi-square] values with the degrees of freedom" (p. 1632). That is, a small ratio of Chi-square to *df* is taken as in indication of "good" fit. Naturally, there is no agreement as to the meaning of "small."[20] Drawing attention to the limitations of indices of fit, Hosmer et al. (1991) stressed the importance of relying on diagnostics analogous to those used in linear regression analysis (e.g., leverage, Cook's *D*).

Clearly, assessment of fit in logistic regression "is not straightforward" (Selvin, 1991, p. 233). The moral is that you should not put too much faith in any single fit index. More important, you would do well to heed Hosmer et al.'s (1991) exhortation to place greater emphasis on regression diagnostics (see their paper for an illustrative application).

RESEARCH EXAMPLES

In his instructive paper on applications of log-linear and logit models, Swafford (1980) found it necessary to caution that "a high proportion of sociological articles based on these techniques contains statistical or methodological errors" (p. 684). He even devoted a section to eight common errors, which he annotated with examples from the literature. Several years later, Alba (1988) introduced his paper on the interpretation of log-linear parameters thus: "The confusion that still envelops parameter interpretation is attested to by the frequency of articles on this topic . . . Noteworthy is that these articles frequently devote considerable space to correcting errors of their predecessors" (p. 258). In the preface to their book on logistic regression, Hosmer and Lemeshow (1989) noted that upon reviewing papers published in a variety of journals "it became clear that the quality of the use of the method is not on the same level as analyses using linear regression" (p. vii). Considering the questionable quality of many applications of linear regression, this is a serious indictment.

The increasing availability of user-friendly computer programs for log-linear and logistic regression has probably exacerbated the situation. Many published papers, including methodological

---

[20]As I discuss in Chapters 18 and 19, the same problem arises when Chi-Square is used as a index of fit in structural equation modeling.

ones aimed at instructing readers in the use and interpretation of logistic regression, betray a lack of understanding of its properties. In what follows, I present some recent examples of misapplications of or misconceptions about logistic regression. I begin with a relatively extended examination of a recent paper because it embodies many common errors. I then comment briefly on misinterpretation of odds ratios. In all instances, I do *not* review or summarize the papers I cite nor deal exhaustively with their analyses. Instead, I focus on *some* specific issues, while ignoring others, not to mention broader important topics (e.g., theory, design characteristics). I include brief descriptions of, or quotations from, the papers I cite to give you an idea what they are about. Obviously, these are not substitutes for reading the papers themselves.

Misinterpretation of Parameter Estimates

Chinn, Waggoner, Anderson, Schommer, and Wilkinson (1993) reported on a study designed "to identify the factors that converge moment by moment to influence what happens at each step of the oral reading episode" (p. 362). Before commenting on Chinn et al.'s interpretation of results from logistic regression analyses, I will describe the tortuous route by which they arrived at them. They stated that they "used a hierarchical approach to entering variables" (p. 371) and listed the order in which blocks of variables were entered. I will not comment on this topic for two reasons. One, earlier in the text (especially in Chapters 9 and 15), I delineated specific purposes for which hierarchical regression analysis is suited and the kind of inferences it affords. Two, Chinn et al. did not adhere to the hierarchy they specified. Following are some of their statements in support of my assertion.

> As a first step, models that explored all relevant relationships were examined. Then, factors that were not reliable and *did not enter into reliable interactions were deleted* [italics added] and the analysis was rerun. The tables present models that have been reduced in this manner. (p. 371)

Although the topic of interaction is complex and controversial (see earlier in this chapter), I believe that all parties to the debate would agree that it makes no sense to delete variables because they do not interact with other variables.

> Because of the large number of variables, overfitting was a constant danger. To illustrate, consider what typically happened when both individual comprehension and individual fluency were entered into the equation. For all the dependent variables we examined, individual comprehension was a better predictor of the dependent variable than individual fluency, so that individual comprehension entered the equation first. Then when individual fluency entered, it entered with the sign opposite of the sign with which it would have entered had it entered first. We took this to be a mark of overfitting the equation, yielding results that are quite misleading. Hence, as a general rule, whenever a variable entered the equation with a sign opposite the sign with which it would have entered at an earlier stage in the analysis, we deleted the variable from the equation. (p. 371)

Although the reference to overfitting may have a nice ring for some, a more plausible explanation for the "contradictory" results can be found in the authors' statement that "several of the predictor variables . . . were highly intercorrelated, sometimes because of logical or conceptual dependencies among the variables" (p. 371). Put simply, some of the high intercorrelations were among multiple indicators of variables. In Chapter 8, I illustrated deleterious consequences of using multiple indicators in a stepwise regression analysis—see (Table 8.2) and the discussion related to it. In Chapter 10, I discussed collinearity and illustrated through several numerical examples havoc it may wreak. Further, I presented several approaches to the diagnosis of collinearity and reviewed some suggested remedies. Here, I will only make two points. One, multiple indicators should not be avoided. On the contrary, as I show in Chapter 19, they play an important role in models with latent variables. Two, the indiscriminate deletion of variables (or indicators) is not a viable solution to collinearity problems, especially when, as in the research under consideration, the aim is explanation.

The most egregious error the authors have committed was in interpreting the results as if they were obtained in a multiple regression analysis. (As I explain later, their interpretations are incorrect even for the case of multiple regression analysis.) Their misconception was betrayed when they stated, "The output from logistic regression analysis is analogous to the output from ordinary least squares regression analysis. Instead of F values, however, the test distribution in logistic regression is a χ^2 distribution" (p. 371).

Except for occasional vague references to likelihood (e.g., "feedback . . . was negatively associated to the likelihood of hesitations" p. 375), Chinn et al. interpreted b's as relations or associations (e.g., "High-meaning-change errors were negatively associated with individual comprehension and with grade and positively with the density of hard words on each page" p. 373). Making matters worse, they assessed the relative importance of variables by comparing the b's associated with them. Following are but a couple of examples of their conclusions based on comparisons among b's: "It is noteworthy that the density of hard words on a page was a better predictor . . . than any other measure of difficulty" (p. 373). "The proportion of hard words on a page was a much better predictor . . . than any of the measures of general story difficulty" (p. 375).

Early in this book (Chapter 5), I pointed out that it is inappropriate to compare b's (unstandardized regression coefficients) associated with different variables as their sizes are affected by the scales used to measure the variables. Among other things, I stressed that a relatively large b may be substantively not meaningful, whereas a relatively small one may be substantively meaningful. Further, I pointed out that this is why authors who wish to speak of relative importance of variables resort to standardized regression coefficients. These are the issues that I had in mind when I said earlier that Chinn et al.'s interpretations are incorrect even for multiple regression analysis.

Chinn et al. also erred in their interpretations of terms in equations that included products of variables. For example, referring to their Table 5 they said, "Notice . . . that whereas there were no main effects of individual comprehension or meaning change, these two factors did interact reliably" (p. 376). Complexities attendant with interpreting product vectors in nonorthogonal designs as interactions aside (see earlier in this chapter), it appears that in arriving at statements such as the preceding Chinn et al. used results from simultaneous analyses. Earlier in the text (especially in Chapter 10), I discussed the difference between simultaneous and hierarchical analyses. Among other things, I pointed out that in nonorthogonal designs a hierarchical approach is called for when testing an interaction and that it is inappropriate to test or interpret b's for "main effects" in an equation that includes also an interaction term (see my critique of the Philadelphia School District Studies; I discussed this topic in greater detail in Chapter 13).

In conclusion, I trust that, in view of what I said about this study, you will not be surprised to learn that no mention was made in it of terms central to logistic regression (e.g., logits, odds ratios, predicted probabilities). Incidentally, except for a reference to the SAS program they used, the authors made no reference to the literature on logistic regression.

Misinterpretation of Odds Ratios

The odds ratio is one of the most frequently misinterpreted terms in logistic regression. Broadly, odds ratios are incorrectly interpreted as probabilities. Following are some examples. In a study of values of Canadians and Americans, Baer, Grabb, and Johnston (1990) applied logistic regression, among other analyses. Here is an example of how they interpreted odds ratios: "English Canadians are 1.345 *times as likely* [italics added] as Americans to agree with the statement that they have no say, while Quebeckers are 1.920 *times as likely* [italics added] to agree" (p. 707; see Roncek, 1991, for a detailed critique of Baer et al.).

In a paper aimed at showing how to use logistic regression in testing HIV positive, Yarandi and Simpson (1991) interpreted one odds ratio correctly, saying, "for a male, the odds in favor of being HIV positive are 7.56 times as large than for a female" (p. 373). Shortly after that, however, they interpreted another odds ratio thus: "In comparison, an individual using intravenous drugs is 2.60 *times as likely* [italics added] to test HIV positive as an intravenous drug free individual" (p. 373).

In a paper aimed at introducing the case-control design as "an appropriate strategy for nursing research," Polivka and Nickel (1992) stated, "The OR [odds ratio] was calculated as 4.1 . . . indicating that case mothers were 4.1 *times as likely* [italics added] to report a history of premature births as control mothers" (p. 253).

CONCLUDING REMARKS

I trust that in the course of studying this chapter you recognized that my introductory remarks about the relevance of many topics I introduced in earlier chapters (e.g., coding categorical independent variables, hierarchical and simultaneous analyses, stepwise regression analysis) to logistic regression analysis were borne out. Perhaps you may have even been frustrated by my frequent references to earlier chapters. This, however, was unavoidable, as the amount of repetitions that would have otherwise been required would have probably led to even greater frustration, not to mention the amount of space that would have been required. Anyway, I urge you to keep consulting relevant discussions in earlier chapters when you reread this chapter.

I hope that my introduction to logistic regression served to illustrate its value as well as the potential for misapplying it or misinterpreting results it yields. I recommend that you study references I gave throughout the chapter before you launch your own study. Of course, be vigilant and think critically when reading the research literature.

STUDY SUGGESTIONS

1. Assume that the following illustrative data were obtained in an experiment in which the independent variable, *X,* consisted of exposure to a message—attributed to either a leading economist or a labor leader—about the effects of NAFTA (North American Free Trade Agreement) on the U.S. economy. The dependent variable, *Y,* was the perception of whether the message was unbiased (scored as 1) or biased (scored as 0).

	Source of Message	
	Economist	*Labor Leader*
Unbiased	38	20
Biased	12	30

(a) What are the odds of perceiving the message as unbiased when it is attributed to (1) a leading economist and (2) a labor leader?

(b) What is the odds ratio? Interpret it.

2. Analyze the data given under Study Suggestion 1 with a computer program for logistic regression. Using dummy coding for the categorical independent variable, assign 0 to the second category (labor leader).

(a) What is the regression equation?

(b) What is −2LL (log likelihood) for a model consisting of an intercept only?

(c) What is −2LL for a model consisting of an intercept and X?

(d) What is the difference between the −2LL of (a) and (b)? How is it interpreted?

(e) Show how you would use the regression coefficient for X to estimate the odds ratio.

(f) Using the regression equation, estimate the probability of perceiving the message as unbiased when it is attributed to (1) a leading economist and (2) a labor leader.

(g) Transform the probabilities obtained under (f) into odds.

3. To the example of Study Suggestions 1 and 2, I added another category—politician. Following are the illustrative data:

	Source of Message		
		Labor	
	Economist	*Leader*	*Politician*
Unbiased	38	20	11
Biased	12	30	39

Using a computer program, do a logistic regression with effect coding, assigning −1 to the last category (Politician). Call for the printing of the covariance matrix of the b's, $\mathbf{C}$. If you are using a program that reports only the correlation matrix of the b's (e.g., SPSS), follow procedures I explained in this chapter and in Chapter 11 to transform it to a covariance matrix.

(a) What is the regression equation?

(b) Does the inclusion of the source of the message lead to a statistically significant improvement of the model, over a model composed of the intercept only?

(c) Using relevant information from the regression equation, calculate the effect of the last category (i.e., Politician).

(d) Using information from (a) and (c), calculate the odds ratios of (1) Economist to Labor Leader, (2) Economist to Politician, and (3) Labor Leader to Politician.

(e) Assume that dummy coding was used and the Politician category was assigned 0. Use relevant information from (a) and (c) to arrive at the regression coefficients for the vectors in which Economist and Labor Leader categories were identified (i.e., assigned 1's).

(f) From the computer output, what is $\mathbf{C}$ (the covariance matrix of the b's) for the coded vectors?

(g) Augment $\mathbf{C}$ reported under (f) to obtain $\mathbf{C}^*$.

(h) Using relevant information from $\mathbf{C}^*$, test the difference between (1) b for Economist and b for Politician, and (2) b for Labor Leader and b for Politician. As I explained in the chapter, I use the term "b" for the category assigned −1 (Politician, in the present example), although it is *not* part of the regression equation.

(i) If you were to run the analysis with dummy coding, assigning 0 to Politician, to what results would those obtained under (h) be equal?

4. Assume that in the example in Study Suggestion 3, males and females were randomly assigned in equal numbers to the various treatments (source of message). The data are as follows:

	Source of Message					
	Economist		*Labor Leader*		*Politician*	
Gender	Male	Female	Male	Female	Male	Female
Unbiased	18	20	12	8	6	5
Biased	7	5	13	17	19	20

(a) Is the interaction between source of message and gender statistically significant?

(b) Is the effect of gender statistically significant?

(c) Interpret the results.

5. Assume that the following illustrative data were obtained in an experiment in which subjects were randomly assigned to one of two categories of T (e.g., training programs, drugs). Prior to the experiment, subjects were measured on a continuous variable, X (e.g., motivation, depression). The dependent variable, Y, consisted of two categories: Yes (e.g., successful

completion of a task) scored as 1; No (e.g., failure to complete a task) scored as 0.

T1	T_1 X	Y	T2	T_2 X	Y
1	10	0	2	10	1
1	10	0	2	11	1
1	11	0	2	11	1
1	12	0	2	12	1
1	12	0	2	12	1
1	13	0	2	13	1
1	14	0	2	15	1
1	15	1	2	15	0
1	16	1	2	16	0
1	16	0	2	16	0
1	17	1	2	17	1
1	18	1	2	18	0
1	19	1	2	18	0
1	19	1	2	19	0
1	20	1	2	19	0

Analyze the data and interpret the results.

ANSWERS

1. (a) (1) 3.16667; (2) .66667
   (b) 4.75. The odds of perceiving the message as unbiased is about 4.75 greater when it is attributed to a leading economist rather than to a labor leader.
2. (a) $-.4055 + 1.5581X$
   (b) $-2LL = 136.0584$ (intercept only)
   (c) $-2LL = 122.409$ (intercept and X)
   (d) Difference between the two $-2LL = 13.649$ is distributed as a Chi-Square with 1 df for a test of model improvement due to X.
   (e) $e^{1.5581} = 4.75$, as in 1(b)
   (f) (1) .76, (2) .40; see (17.6) or (17.7)
   (g) (1) .76/.24 = 3.16667; (2) .40/.60 = .66667; compare with 1(a)
3. (a) $-.1728 + 1.3255$(Economist) $-.2326$(Labor Leader)
   (b) Yes. Chi-Square for Improvement = 31.883, 2 df, $p < .0001$
   (c) $-1.0929 = -(1.3255 - .2326)$
   (d) (1) 4.75 $[1.3255 - (-.2326) = 1.5581; e^{1.5581} = 4.75]$
       (2) 11.23 $[1.3255 - (-1.0929) = 2.4184; e^{2.4184} = 11.23]$
       (3) 2.36 $[-.2326 - (-1.0929) = .8603; e^{.8603} = 2.36]$
       As expected, the odds ratio for Economist to Labor Leader is the same as the one obtained under study suggestion 1(b).
   (e) 2.4184(Economist) $+ .8603$(Labor Leader). Exponents of these coefficients are reported under (d): (2) and (3).
   (f) .07092   −.02993
        −.02993   .06217
   (g)

	Econ.	Labor	Polit.
Economist	.07092	−.02993	−.04099
Labor Leader	−.02993	.06217	−.03224
Politician	−.04099	−.03224	.07323

(h) (1) $t = 5.09$, with 147 *df*

(2) $t = 1.92$, with 147 *df*

(i) Square roots of Wald tests for the two coefficients associated with the dummy vectors

4. (a) No; Chi-Square for Improvement (over main effects) = 1.594, with 2 *df*, $p = .4507$

(b) No; Chi-Square for Improvement (over source) = .303, with 1 *df*, $p = .5819$

(c) Retain the model that includes only source of message. See Study Suggestion 3.

5. Beginning Block Number 3.   Method: Enter

Variable(s) Entered on Step Number

1..   T * X

	Chi-Square	df	Significance
Improvement	26.668	1	.0000

Variable	B
X	.2221
T(1)	−19.0966
X by T(1)	1.2489
Constant	−3.3423

As I suggested in the chapter (see also Chapters 14 and 15), I entered the variables and their interaction in the following sequence: (1) X, (2) T, and (3) X BY T. The excerpts of output given here are from the last step. As you can see, the interaction is statistically significant. Hence, separate regression equations are called for. As I showed in the chapter (see also Chapters 14 and 15), the overall regression equation can be used to derive the separate equations within the treatments. As I used effect coding, the separate equations are

$$T1: a [-3.3423 + (-19.0966)] = -22.4389$$
$$b (.2221 + 1.2489) = 1.471$$
$$T2: a [-3.3423 - (-19.0966)] = 15.7543$$
$$b (.2221 - 1.2489) = -1.0268$$

Notice that the sign of *b* is positive under T1 and negative under T2.

You may wish to run the data with the SPLIT FILE command to obtain separate analyses for each treatment (see this chapter for an example). In any case, you would interpret each equation as shown in the chapter for a design with a continuous independent variable.

18

Structural Equation Models with Observed Variables: Path Analysis

The topics of this and the next chapter are discussed under a variety of headings, among which are causal models, latent variable models, models with unobserved variables, analysis of covariance structures, structural modeling. Some authors even use names of popular computer programs for the analysis of such models (e.g., LISREL or EQS modeling). The term most commonly used, though, is *structural equation models* (SEM).

For historical and pedagogic reasons, I use the perspective of path analysis to introduce basic concepts and approaches of SEM. Doing this will, among other things, serve as a bridge between multiple regression and SEM. As I show later, multiple regression analysis can be viewed as a special case of path analysis, which is a special case of SEM.

As causal thinking plays a central role in the analysis of SEM, I begin with brief discussions of causation and the role of theory. I then present elements of path analysis and illustrate its application to the analysis of correlations among a set of variables. Following that, I show how to do this for covariances among a set of variables. I then introduce two computer programs for the analysis of SEM, in the context of which I discuss tests of models and assessment of fit. I conclude the chapter with comments on some research applications.

CAUSATION

The concept of causation is controversial among philosophers and scientists alike. I do not intend to review the controversy;[1] instead, I will give you a glimpse at it through some quotations from varied sources. Following that, I will (1) make some general comments about causal thinking and the role it plays (or should play) in the research design and (2) comment on the paramount role of theory in the conceptualization, estimation, and testing of causal models.

---

[1]Following are but some references to discussions of causation and its role in scientific research: Blalock (1964, 1985); Bullock, Harlow, and Mulaik (1994); Cook and Campbell (1979); Feigl and Brodbeck (1953); Grünbaum (1952); Hanson (1958, 1969, 1971); Harré and Madden (1975); Holland (1986); Kempthorne (1978); Lerner (1965); Mackie (1965, 1974); Margenau (1950); Mulaik (1987, 1993); Mulaik and James (1995); Scriven (1971, 1975); Simon (1957, 1968); Wallace (1972, 1974); White (1990); and Wold (1956). Among symposia on causation are *Issues in Criminology,* 1968, *3,* 129–194; *Journal of Educational Statistics,* 1987, *12,* 101–223; *The Journal of Philosophy,* 1967, *64,* 691–725; *Synthese,* 1986, *67,* 157–379; 1986, *68,* 1–180; and Clogg (1988, pp. 347–493).

[C]ausation is a mystical condition that is approachable, but not attainable. (Biddle, Slavings, & Anderson, 1985, p. 92)

The causal principle is, in short, neither a panacea nor a myth; it is a general hypothesis subsumed under the universal principle of determinacy, and having an approximate validity in its proper domain. (Bunge, 1979, p. 353)

The concept of cause is generally considered to be the most important one for the development of science. Our conception of causality has been continually changed with the progress of science; but most people would say still that a scientific explanation must be given in causal terms. Indeed, they would identify the causal with the scientific explanation. (Hutten, 1962, p. 87)

[T]he interesting fact remains that at present all branches of science that have reached a satisfactory state of precision espouse causality as a principle of their methodology. (Margenau, 1950, p. 412)

It would be very healthy if more researchers abandon thinking of and using terms such as *cause* and *effect*. (Muthen, 1987, p. 180)

[T]he reason why physics has ceased to look for causes is that, in fact, there are no such things. The law of causality, I believe, . . . is a relic of a bygone age, surviving, like the monarchy, only because it is erroneously supposed to do no harm. (Russell, 1929, p. 180)

Cause is the most valuable concept in the methodology of the applied sciences. (Scriven, 1968, p. 79)

The purpose of scientific theory is to understand causation. (Stolzenberg & Land, 1983, p. 613)

Let's drop that word *cause* and bring educational research out of the middle ages. (Travers, 1981, p. 32)

According to Kemeny (1959), "The search for causal laws is deeply tied up with our subconscious tendency to recreate the universe in our own image" (p. 48). Indeed, it is only through our human perspective that we perceive the universe and engender meaning on our environment. "Any attempt rigorously to eliminate our human perspective from our picture of the world must lead to absurdity" (Polanyi, 1964, p. 3). As Protagoras put it, "Man is the measure of all things, of things that are, that they are, of things that are not, that they are not" (Quoted by Mackay, 1977, p. 125).

Philosophical skepticism notwithstanding, preoccupation with causes and causation is in response to strongly felt needs to understand ourselves and our environment. "A change in the environment gains its meaning from the source to which it is attributed" (Heider, 1944, p. 372). No wonder ancient and modern authors exulted in causal explanations. "In the fifth century B.C., the philosopher Democritus maintained that he would rather uncover a single causal connection than sit on the throne of Persia" (Boruch, 1982, *36,* p. 1). And Virgil declared, "Happy is he who gets to know the reasons of things" (Quoted by Mackay, 1977, p. 154).

Causal Thinking

Even in the work of researchers who reject the term *causation,* one encounters terms that indicate or imply causal thinking. A case in point is a statement by Nash, Hulsey, Sexton, Harralson, and Lambert (1993), who strenuously objected to a critique of their work, saying that nowhere did they use "the words *cause, causal antecedent,* or *causality*" (p. 289). Instead, they maintained, their study was concerned with mediators and mediation. In earlier chapters (see, e.g., Chapter 7, Figure 7.2, and the discussion related to it; see also "Causal Assumptions"), I discussed the idea of mediation and the implication of causality that it carries. Indirect effect—a topic I discuss in detail in this chapter—means the effect of a variable on another variable through the mediation of one or more intervening variables.[2]

Other examples abound. Thus, when researchers speak of effects of child-rearing practices on personality, reinforcement on subsequent behavior, or attitudes on perception, they imply causation. The same is true of terms used in, say, political science (e.g., *influence, power, decision making*).

In observations on the "Panel on the Economics of Educational Reform," Passell (1994a) asserted, "What virtually all economists seem to agree on is that there has been scandalously little attention paid to measuring cause and effect." And in a paper entitled "'Truth' Is Stranger Than Prediction, More Questionable Than Causal Inference," King (1991b) asserted that the reason "for asking model specification questions is to improve causal inference, a goal that I believe to be at the heart of most of what we are and should be doing in quantitative political science" (p. 1049).

The tendency to imply causation, even when refraining from using the term, is reflected also in some of the methods employed by behavioral scientists. For example, proportions of variance are attributed to certain independent variables; a presumed cause is partialed from two variables to ascertain whether the relation between them is spurious. "Thus, the difference between true and spurious correlations resolves into a difference between causal and noncausal connections" (Brodbeck, 1963, p. 73).[3]

In an address to the Royal Statistical Society, Cochran (1965) stated:

> I hope that I shall not be asked to explain exactly what is meant by cause and effect, since writers on the philosophy of science seem unanimously to discard the concept sooner or later as more confusing than helpful in complex situations. But to illustrate situations in which the concept is clear enough, the ultimate goal in applied studies may be to be able to predict the consequences of a new social programme, or of an experience that individual subjects may undergo, or of changes in the subject's living habits. Even in theoretical studies designed mainly to increase our understanding of people's behaviour, the idea of cause and effect is useful in the simpler situations. (p. 237)

Nagel (1965) summed up the status of the concept of causation, saying, "Though the *term* may be absent the *idea* for which it stands continues to have wide currency" (p. 11). Drawing attention to the frequency of causal statements in behavioral as well as physical sciences, Nagel concluded, "In short, the idea of cause is not as outmoded in modern science as is sometimes alleged" (p. 11). That this is so is not surprising as the scientist's question of why a certain event has occurred carries with it an implication of causality. Moreover, a behavioral scientist who wishes to bring about change in human behavior must be able to identify factors affecting the behavior or, more plainly, the causes of the behavior. In short, scientists, *qua* scientists, seem to have a need to resort to causal thinking, though on philosophical grounds they may have reservations about the concept of causation.

Causation and the Research Design

Scientists who accept the notion of causal analysis disagree about the conditions required for its valid application—the major one being whether or not manipulation of the cause(s) is necessary.

---

[2] For discussions of mediation and how to estimate it, see James and Brett (1984), Judd and Kenny (1981), Mackinnon and Dwyer (1993).

[3] See Chapter 7 for a discussion of spurious correlations. Also see Blalock (1968), Brodbeck (1963), and Simon (1957, particularly Chapters 1 through 3).

This is, perhaps, best encapsulated in the motto "NO CAUSATION WITHOUT MANIPULATION" (Holland, 1986, p. 959). Einstein seemed to have this in mind when he proclaimed that one of the "two great achievements" on which the "development of Western Science is based," is "the discovery of the possibility to find out causal relationship by *systematic experiment* [italics added]" (Quoted by Mackay, 1977, p. 51).

Kempthorne (1978), who argued strongly that causation can be studied only through manipulation, went so far as to brand the philosopher Bertrand Russell as being "very stupid" for his failure to give the "slightest recognition to the idea of experimentation" (p. 8) in his discussions of causation. Kempthorne further expressed his amazement

> that top minds of the world have written at length on causation and have written material which is useless, at best. It would seem that the notion of experimentally varying forces and observing the results, which is the basis of all good science, is given essentially no place. (p. 8)

The insistence on manipulation stems from one of the basic requirements for supporting the idea of causation: responsiveness. That is, manipulation should be shown, or at least alleged, to have elicited a response.

Blalock (1964), Mulaik (1993), and Pratt and Schlaifer (1984a), among others, argued that the foregoing conceptions are too restrictive, and outlined conditions under which causal statements are supportable in nonexperimental designs. See Berk (1988) for a good discussion of the two orientations. See also comments following Pratt and Schlaifer (1984a) and their rejoinder (1984b).

In Chapters 7, 9, and 10, I discussed distinctions between experimental and nonexperimental designs and the general advantages of the former for the interpretation of effects of variables. I did, however, also discuss why in many areas of social and behavioral research conducting experiments is either not desirable or impossible, and I explored the implications of doing nonexperimental research. As the points I made in those chapters apply also to designs I consider here, I will not repeat them. You may find it worthwhile to reread the relevant sections in those chapters (e.g., "Effects in Experimental and Nonexperimental Research" in Chapter 10).

THE ROLE OF THEORY

The role of theory in the formulation of causal models was most forcefully expressed by Hanson:

> Causes are connected with effects; but this is because our theories connect them, not because the world is held together by cosmic glue. The world *may* be glued together by imponderables, but that is irrelevant for understanding causal explanation. The notions behind "the cause *x*" and "the effect *y*" are intelligible only against a pattern of theory, namely one which puts guarantees on inferences from *x* to *y*. Such guarantees distinguish truly causal sequences from mere coincidence. (1958, p. 64)

It is a model of causation among variables under study that determines, among other things, the type of data to be collected and the method of analysis. "When theory does not play a selective role, our data-gathering activities belong in the realm of journalism rather than science" (Kulka, 1989, p. 794).

Broadly, analysis is designed to shed light on the question of whether or not the causal model is consistent with the data. If the model is inconsistent with the data, doubt is cast about the theory from which the model was derived. This, of course, is predicated on the assumption that the study was validly designed and executed. Consistency of the model with the data, however, does not constitute proof of a theory; at best it lends support to it. Or, following Popper's (1959, 1968) conception that all research can accomplish is falsification of theory, it would be concluded that the theory survived the test in that it was not disconfirmed.

It is possible for competing causal models to be consistent with the same data. Consider, for example, the following competing models: (1) $X \rightarrow Y \rightarrow Z$; (2) $X \leftarrow Y \rightarrow Z$. According to the first model, X affects Y, which in turn affects Z. The second model, on the other hand, indicates that Y affects both X and Z. As I will show, both models may be consistent with correlations among the three variables. The decision as to which of them is more tenable rests not on the data but on the theory from which the causal model was generated in the first place. *When, in what follows, I speak of a theory or a causal model being consistent with the data, I mean that the theory withstood the test; that it was not disconfirmed.*

Further, bear in mind that "all models are wrong, but some are useful" (G. E. P. Box; quoted by Snee & Marquardt, 1984, p. 83). King (1991b), similarly, argued that "the idea of a 'true *model*' makes no sense. . . . Instead, a model is necessarily (and preferably) an abstraction and thus a drastic simplification, one that if successful will enable one to study only the essential elements of reality" (p. 1048; see also Zeger, 1991).

Failure to simplify, to pare down, a model may lead to infinite regress, even despair. Warning against explanations that "may frequently deteriorate into an endless search for the 'ultimate,' or 'first,' cause," Krech and Crutchfield (1948) reasoned:

> If it is said that Mr. Arbuthnot seeks membership in the country club because he sees it as a goal of social approval, it is then asked why he seeks that goal. If it is answered that this goal has arisen because of a need for personal security, it is then asked why that feeling of insecurity arose. If it is answered that the feeling of personal insecurity has arisen because of a socially embarrassing speech defect that Mr. Arbuthnot has acquired, it is then asked why that speech defect. The answer may be that the speech defect was a defense against a precocious younger brother. Thus, at this stage, we are to understand that Mr. Arbuthnot seeks membership in the country club because his younger brother was precocious! But why stop here? The analysis can go as far as the ingenuity of the theorist will carry him, without ever really reaching the ultimate, or first, cause. (p. 34)

The unsettling, even destructive, effects of an ever-receding search for prior causes was captured in one of Bertolt Brecht's (1961) anecdotes of Mr. Keuner:

A Man of Purpose

> Mr K put the following questions:
> 'Every morning my neighbour plays music on his gramophone. Why does he play music? I hear that it is because he does exercises. Why does he do exercises? Because he needs to be strong, I hear. Why does he need to be strong? Because he has to get the better of his enemies in the town, he says. Why must he get the better of his enemies? Because he wants to eat, I hear.'
> Having learnt that his neighbour played music in order to do exercises, did exercises in order to be strong, wanted to be strong in order to kill his enemies, killed his enemies in order to eat, he put the question: 'Why does he eat?' (pp. 121–122)

PATH ANALYSIS

Path analysis was developed by Sewall Wright as a method for studying direct and indirect effects of variables hypothesized as causes of variables treated as effects. It is important to stress from the outset that, being a method, path analysis is intended *not* to discover causes but to shed light on the tenability of the causal models a researcher formulates based on knowledge and theoretical considerations. In Wright's words:

> The method of path coefficients is not intended to accomplish the impossible task of deducing causal relations from the values of the correlation coefficients. It is intended to combine the quantitative information given by the correlations with such a qualitative information as may be at hand on causal relations to give a quantitative interpretation. (Wright, 1934, p. 193)

My aim in this chapter is to introduce basic principles and illustrative applications of path analysis. For more detailed treatments, see Blalock (1985), Bollen (1989), Duncan (1975), Heise (1975), Li (1975), and Wright (1934, 1954, 1960, 1968).

Path Diagram

The path diagram, although not essential for numerical analysis, is very useful for displaying graphically the hypothesized pattern of causal relations among a set of variables. In a causal model, a distinction is made between exogenous and endogenous variables. An *exogenous variable* is one whose variation is assumed to be determined by causes outside the hypothesized model. Therefore, no attempt is made to explain the variability of an exogenous variable or its relations with other exogenous variables. An *endogenous variable,* on the other hand, is one whose variation is explained by exogenous or other endogenous variables in the model.

I will use Figure 18.1 to illustrate the distinction between the two kinds of variables and conventions used in depicting relations among them. Variables 1 and 2 in Figure 18.1 are exogenous. The correlation between exogenous variables is depicted by a curved (or straight) double-headed arrow, thus indicating that the researcher does not conceive of one variable being a cause of the other. Consequently, a relation between exogenous variables (r_{12}, in the present case) remains unanalyzed.

Variables 3 and 4 in Figure 18.1 are endogenous. Paths, in the form of arrows, are drawn from the variables taken as causes (independent) to variables taken as effects (dependent). The two paths leading from variables 1 and 2 to variable 3 denote that variables 1 and 2 affect variable 3. The same is true for the three paths leading from variables 1, 2, and 3 to variable 4.

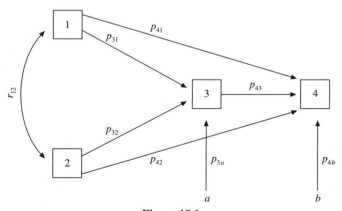

Figure 18.1

My presentation in this chapter is limited to models in which the causal flow (usually displayed as going from left to right) is unidirectional. In such models—called recursive models—no allowance is made for reciprocal causation between variables, either directly or through a causal loop. For example, if variable 2 in Figure 18.1 is taken as a cause of variable 3, then the possibility of variable 3 being a cause of variable 2, directly or indirectly, is ruled out.

In recursive models, an endogenous variable treated as dependent on one set of variables may also be conceived as an independent variable with respect to another endogenous variable(s). Variable 3, for instance, is taken as dependent on variables 1 and 2 and as one of the independent variables with respect to variable 4. Note that in this example the causal flow is still unidirectional. Because it is almost never possible to account for the total variance of a variable, residuals are introduced to represent effects of variables not included in the model. In Figure 18.1, *a* and *b* are residuals, analogous to the residual, *e,* in regression analysis (see, for example, Chapters 2 and 3).

Assumptions

Among assumptions underlying the application of path analysis *as presented in this chapter* are the following:

1. Relations among variables in the model are linear, additive, and causal. Consequently, curvilinear, multiplicative, or interaction relations are excluded.
2. Each residual is not correlated with the variables that precede it in the model. Thus, for example, in Figure 18.1 it is assumed that *a* is not correlated with variables 1 and 2 and that *b* is not correlated with variables 1, 2, and 3. It can be shown that this implies that the residuals are not correlated among themselves. For the model depicted in Figure 18.1 this means that *a* and *b* are not correlated. Hence, the absence of a double-headed arrow between them.

   The implication of the preceding statements is that all relevant variables are included in the model being tested. Variables not included and subsumed under residuals are assumed to be not correlated with the relevant variables. Each endogenous variable is conceived of as a linear combination of exogenous and/or endogenous variables in the model and a residual. Exogenous variables are treated as given. Moreover, when exogenous variables are correlated among themselves, these correlations are treated as given and remain unanalyzed.
3. There is a one-way causal flow in the system—that is, reciprocal causation between variables is ruled out.
4. The variables are measured on an interval scale.
5. The variables are measured without error.

I will show that, given these assumptions, the method of path analysis reduces to the solution of one or more multiple linear regression analyses. Therefore, what I said earlier in this book about the consequences of violating the assumptions of multiple regression analysis (e.g., specification errors and measurement errors; see, in particular, Chapter 10) applies also to path analysis of recursive models.

Clearly, some of the preceding assumptions (notably that all relevant variables are included in the model and that measures are error free) are untenable. For discussions of the implications of weakening or violating these assumptions, see Bohrnstedt and Carter (1971), Duncan (1975),

Heise (1969, 1975), and Kenny (1979). I return to these problems later in this chapter and the next one. For pedagogic purposes, however, I ignore them here so that I may introduce basic ideas of path analysis without overwhelming you.

Path Coefficients

Wright (1934) defined a path coefficient as

> [t]he fraction of the standard deviation of the dependent variable (with the appropriate sign) for which the designated factor is directly responsible, in the sense of the fraction which would be found if this factor varies to the same extent as in the observed data while all others (including the residual factors . . .) are constant. (p. 162)

More succinctly, a path coefficient indicates the direct effect of a variable hypothesized as a cause of a variable taken as an effect.

The symbol for a path coefficient is a p with two subscripts, the first indicating the effect (or the dependent variable), and the second indicating the cause (the independent variable). For example, p_{32} in Figure 18.1 indicates the direct effect of variable 2 on variable 3.

Calculation of Path Coefficients

Each endogenous (dependent) variable in a causal model can be represented by an equation consisting of the variables on which it is hypothesized to be dependent and a residual representing variables not included in the model. For each independent variable in the equation there is a path coefficient indicating the amount of expected change in the dependent variable as a result of a unit change in the independent variable. Recall that exogenous variables are assumed to be dependent on variables not included in the model and are therefore represented by a residual term only. The letter e or u with an appropriate subscript is used to represent residuals. As an illustration, I will give the equations for the four-variable model depicted in Figure 18.2.

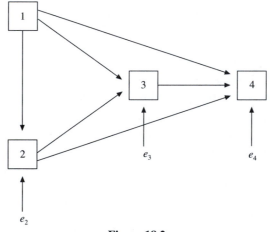

Figure 18.2

Expressing all variables in standard scores (z), the equations are

$$z_1 = e_1 \tag{18.1a}$$

$$z_2 = p_{21}z_1 + e_2 \tag{18.1b}$$

$$z_3 = p_{31}z_1 + p_{32}z_2 + e_3 \tag{18.1c}$$

$$z_4 = p_{41}z_1 + p_{42}z_2 + p_{43}z_3 + e_4 \tag{18.1d}$$

where the e's (variables not included in the model) are also expressed in standard scores. Being exogenous, variable 1 is represented by a residual (e_1) only, which stands for variables outside the system affecting it. Variable 2 is shown to be dependent on variable 1 and on e_2, which stands for variables outside the system affecting variable 2. Similar interpretations apply to the other equations. A set of equations such as (18.1) is referred to as a recursive system. It is a system of equations in which at least half of the path coefficients are equal to zero. Consequently, a recursive system can be organized in a lower triangular form, as the upper half of the matrix is assumed to consist of path coefficients that are equal to zero. For example, (18.1a) implies

$$z_1 = e_1 + 0_{12}z_2 + 0_{13}z_3 + 0_{14}z_4$$

Similarly, for the other equations in (18.1).

As I pointed out above, it is assumed that each of the residuals in (18.1) is not correlated with the variables in the equation in which it appears, nor with any of the variables preceding it in the model. These assumptions imply that the residuals are not correlated among themselves. Under such conditions, the solution for the path coefficients takes the form of an ordinary least squares solution for the β's (standardized regression coefficients) that I presented earlier (e.g., Chapters 5 and 6).

I now demonstrate the procedure for calculating path coefficients for the model of Figure 18.2. I begin with p_{21}—the path coefficient for the effect of variable 1 on variable 2. Recall that

$$r_{12} = \frac{1}{N}\Sigma z_1 z_2$$

Substituting (18.1b) for z_2,

$$r_{12} = \frac{1}{N}\Sigma z_1(p_{21}z_1 + e_2)$$

$$= p_{21}\frac{\Sigma z_1 z_1}{N} + \frac{\Sigma z_1 e_2}{N}$$

The term $\Sigma z_1 z_1/N = \Sigma z_1^2/N = 1$ (the variance of standard scores equals one) and the covariance between variable 1 and e_2 is assumed to be zero (see the preceding). Hence,

$$r_{12} = p_{21} \tag{18.2}$$

Recall that in simple regression β is equal to the correlation coefficient. Accordingly, $r_{12} = \beta_{21} = p_{21}$. Thus, the path coefficient from variable 1 to variable 2 is equal to β_{21}, which can be estimated from the data by calculating r_{12}.

A path coefficient is equal to a zero-order correlation whenever a variable is conceived to be dependent on a single cause and a residual. (Note that this is the case for variable 2 in Figure 18.2.) The same principle still applies when a variable is conceived to be dependent on more than one cause, provided the causes are independent. For example, in Figure 18.3 variables X and Z are conceived as independent causes of Y. Therefore, $p_{yx} = r_{yx}$ and $p_{yz} = r_{yz}$.

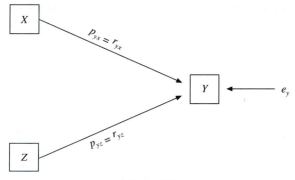

Figure 18.3

Returning to Figure 18.2, note that the path coefficient from e_2 to variable 2 cannot be calculated directly as e_2 represents unmeasured variables, or variables not included in the system. In view of the assumption that e_2 is not correlated with variable 1, and recalling that all the variables are expressed in standard score form, the solution for the residual path coefficient (from e_2) is straightforward. I said earlier that when causes are independent of each other, the effect of each cause (or its path coefficient) is equal to its zero-order correlation with the endogenous variable. Now, e_2 represents causes of variable 2 that are independent of variable 1. Therefore, the path coefficient from e_2 to variable 2 is equal to the correlation between e_2 and variable 2. Recalling that e_2 represents the residual, it can be shown (see, for example, Nunnally, 1978, p. 129) that the correlation of variable 2 with its residual (e_2) is equal to $\sqrt{1 - r_{12}^2}$, which is also the path coefficient from e_2 to variable 2. Note also that the variance of variable 2 accounted for by variable 1 is equal to r_{12}^2, and that accounted for by e_2 is equal to $1 - r_{12}^2$, which are the squares of the path coefficients (or β's) for variable 1 and e_2, respectively.

Following the same reasoning, one may show that in a recursive system the path coefficient from unmeasured variables (or a residual path coefficient) to an endogenous variable, j, is equal to $\sqrt{1 - R_{j.12...i}^2}$, where $R_{j.12...i}^2$ is the squared multiple correlation of endogenous variable j with variables 1, 2, ..., i that affect it. In the case of variable 2 of Figure 18.2, the preceding expression reduces to $\sqrt{1 - R_{2.1}^2} = \sqrt{1 - r_{21}^2}$.

Turning now to variable 3 of Figure 18.2, note that this variable is affected by variables 1 and 2, which are not independent of each other. In fact, variable 2 is conceived to be dependent on variable 1 (in addition, it is dependent on e_2). I now show how the coefficients for the two paths leading to variable 3—p_{31} and p_{32}—are calculated. Because of the assumptions about the residuals, or e's (see the preceding), it is possible to drop these terms from all the equations that follow, thereby simplifying the presentation.

$$r_{13} = \frac{1}{N}\Sigma z_1 z_3$$

Substituting (18.lc) for z_3

$$r_{13} = \frac{1}{N}\Sigma z_1(p_{31}z_1 + p_{32}z_2)$$

$$= p_{31}\frac{\Sigma z_1^2}{N} + p_{32}\frac{\Sigma z_1 z_2}{N}$$

$$r_{13} = p_{31} + p_{32}r_{12} \tag{18.3a}$$

Equation (18.3a) consists of two unknowns (p_{31} and p_{32}) and therefore cannot be solved (r_{12} and r_{13} are, of course, obtainable from the data). It is possible, however, to construct another equation with the same unknowns thereby making a solution possible. To obtain the second equation,

$$r_{23} = \frac{1}{N}\Sigma z_2 z_3$$

Again substituting (18.1c) for z_3,

$$r_{23} = \frac{1}{N}\Sigma z_2(p_{31}z_1 + p_{32}z_2)$$

$$= p_{31}\frac{\Sigma z_2 z_1}{N} + p_{32}\frac{\Sigma z_2^2}{N}$$

$$r_{23} = p_{31}r_{12} + p_{32} \tag{18.3b}$$

We thus have two equations involving the path coefficients leading to variable 3:

$$r_{13} = p_{31} + p_{32}r_{12} \tag{18.3a}$$

$$r_{23} = p_{31}r_{12} + p_{32} \tag{18.3b}$$

Equations (18.3) are similar to the normal equations I used in earlier chapters for the solution of β's.[4] To show that this is so, I rewrite the preceding equations:

$$\beta_{31.2} + \beta_{32.1}r_{12} = r_{13} \tag{18.4a}$$

$$\beta_{31.2}r_{12} + \beta_{32.1} = r_{23} \tag{18.4b}$$

Except for the fact that path coefficients are written without the dot notation, (18.3) and (18.4) are obviously identical. Thus, the solution for path coefficients is the same as that for β's—that is, it is arrived at by applying a least-squares solution to the regression of variable 3 on variables 1 and 2. Each path coefficient is equal to the β for the same variable. Thus, $p_{31} = \beta_{31.2}$ and $p_{32} = \beta_{32.1}$. Note that $p_{31} \neq p_{13}$. As I pointed out earlier, p_{31} indicates the effect of variable 1 on variable 3, whereas p_{13} indicates the effect of variable 3 on variable 1. In the type of models I present in this chapter (i.e., recursive models) it is not possible to have both p_{31} and p_{13}. The same is true for other path coefficients. Path coefficients calculated are those that reflect the causal model formulated by the researcher. If, as in the present example, the model indicates that variable 1 affects variable 3, then p_{31} is calculated.

In line with what I said earlier, the path coefficient from e_3 to variable 3 is equal to $\sqrt{1 - R_{3.12}^2}$.

Turning now to variable 4 of Figure 18.2, note that it is necessary to calculate three path coefficients for the effects of variables 1, 2, and 3 on variable 4. Therefore, three equations are constructed in the manner illustrated earlier. For example, the first equation is constructed as follows:

$$r_{14} = \frac{1}{N}\Sigma z_1 z_4$$

---

[4]See Chapter 5, particularly the discussion in connection with (5.15); also see the discussion in connection with (6.15) in Chapter 6.

Substituting (18.1d) for z_4,

$$r_{14} = \frac{1}{N}\Sigma z_1(p_{41}z_1 + p_{42}z_2 + p_{43}z_3)$$

$$= p_{41}\frac{\Sigma z_1^2}{N} + p_{42}\frac{\Sigma z_1 z_2}{N} + p_{43}\frac{\Sigma z_1 z_3}{N}$$

$$r_{14} = p_{41} + p_{42}r_{12} + p_{43}r_{13} \tag{18.5a}$$

The other two equations, which are similarly constructed, are

$$r_{24} = p_{41}r_{12} + p_{42} + p_{43}r_{23} \tag{18.5b}$$

$$r_{34} = p_{41}r_{13} + p_{42}r_{23} + p_{43} \tag{18.5c}$$

Again, we have a set of normal equations (18.5), which are solved in the manner illustrated in earlier chapters.

In sum, then, when variables in a causal model are expressed in standard scores (z), and the assumptions, which I discussed earlier, are reasonably met, path coefficients turn out to be standardized regression coefficients (β's) obtained in multiple regression analysis. There is, however, an important difference between the two analytic approaches. In multiple regression, a dependent variable is regressed in a single analysis on all the independent variables under consideration. In path analysis, on the other hand, more than one regression analysis may be called for. At each stage, an endogenous variable is regressed on the variables that are hypothesized to affect it. The β's thus calculated are the path coefficients for the paths leading from the particular set of independent variables to the dependent variable under consideration. The model in Figure 18.2 requires three regression analyses for the calculation of all the path coefficients. The path from 1 to 2 (p_{21}) is calculated by regressing 2 on 1, as is indicated by (18.2). p_{31} and p_{32} are obtained by regressing variable 3 on variables 1 and 2, as indicated by (18.3). p_{41}, p_{42}, and p_{43} are obtained by regressing variable 4 on variables 1, 2, and 3, as indicated by (18.5). The path coefficient from e_4 to variable 4 is equal to $\sqrt{1 - R_{4.123}^2}$.

One of the advantages of path analysis is that it affords the decomposition of correlations among variables, thereby enhancing the interpretation of relations as well as the pattern of the effects of one variable on another. It is to these topics that I now turn.

Decomposing Correlations

Given a causal model, it is possible to decompose the correlation between an exogenous and an endogenous variable, or between two endogenous variables, into different components. For example, in Figure 18.4(a) variables 1 and 2 are exogenous, whereas variable 3 is endogenous. As I pointed out earlier, correlations among exogenous variables are treated as given and can therefore not be decomposed. But what about the correlation between 1 and 3? Note from Figure 18.4(a) that r_{13} consists of two parts: (1) the direct effect of 1 on 3, indicated by the path coefficient from 1 to 3 (p_{31}), and (2) that part of r_{13} that is due to the correlation of 1 with another cause of 3, namely 2, which is indicated by $r_{12}p_{32}$. Equivalently, the part of r_{13} that is due to correlated causes may be expressed as $r_{13} - p_{31}$ (as $r_{13} = p_{31} + r_{12}p_{32}$). From the perspective of causal explanation, the part of r_{13} that is due to correlated causes is left unanalyzed. Unless the researcher can state the cause, or causes, for the correlation between 1 and 2, which implies a

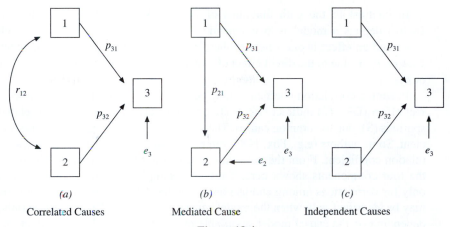

(a)   (b)   (c)

Correlated Causes   Mediated Cause   Independent Causes

Figure 18.4

different causal model, there is no meaningful method of interpreting in causal terms the component of r_{13} that is due to correlated causes. This is why it is treated as unanalyzed.

The decomposition of r_{23} of Figure 18.4(a) is similar to that of r_{13}. That is, p_{32} indicates the direct effect of 2 on 3, and $r_{12}p_{31} = r_{23} - p_{32}$ is the unanalyzed component due to correlated causes (i.e., 1 and 2).

Consider now model (b) of Figure 18.4, where variable 1 is exogenous and variables 2 and 3 are endogenous. Note that variable 1 has a direct effect on variable 3 (indicated by p_{31}). In addition, variable 1 affects variable 2, which in turn affects variable 3. This latter route indicates the indirect effect of variable 1 on variable 3 as mediated by variable 2 (i.e., $p_{21}p_{32}$). r_{13} can therefore be decomposed into two parts: (1) the direct effect of 1 on 3 and (2) the indirect effect of 1 on 3 via 2. The sum of the direct and indirect effects has been labeled the total effect of one variable on another (e.g., Alwin & Hauser, 1975; Duncan, 1975; Finney, 1972). Some authors (e.g., Fox, 1980; Lewis-Beck & Mohr, 1976) have suggested that the sum of the direct and indirect effects be labeled the effect coefficient of the variable taken as the cause on the effect variable.

In Figure 18.4(b) the total effect, or the effect coefficient, of variable 1 on variable 3 is equal to r_{13}. Contrast this with Figure 18.4(a), where variable 1 has no indirect effect on 3. Although one may refer to the direct effect of 1 on 3 as the total effect (e.g., Alwin & Hauser, 1975, p. 46), some authors (e.g., Duncan, 1975, p. 41; MacDonald, 1979, p. 295) argue against such usage when speaking of correlated exogenous variables. The reason is that it is not possible to determine whether the part of the correlation between a given exogenous and an endogenous variable attributed to the correlation of the exogenous variable with other exogenous variables is due partly, or wholly, to some unspecified indirect effect. One may clarify this point by contrasting models (a) and (b) of Figure 18.4. In (a), variables 1 and 2 are treated as exogenous, and it is therefore not possible to tell whether either of them has an indirect effect on variable 3. In (b), on the other hand, only variable 1 is treated as exogenous, and it is possible to ascertain its indirect effect on variable 3, via variable 2.

Turning now to the decomposition of r_{23} of Figure 18.4(b), note that the direct effect of 2 on 3 is equal to p_{32}. The remainder of the correlation between 2 and 3 is spurious, due to the fact that they share a common cause—namely, variable 1. The spurious part of r_{23} is indicated by $p_{31}p_{21}$, or $r_{23} - p_{32}$.

In contrast to the path diagrams of Figure 18.4(a) and 18.4(b), the diagram of Figure 18.4(c) depicts a model with independent causes. In such a case, the correlation between a cause and an effect is due solely to the direct effect of the former on the latter. Thus in Figure 18.4(c), r_{13} is due to the direct effect of 1 on 3, or p_{31}, and r_{23} is due to the direct effect of 2 on 3, or p_{32}.

In sum, a correlation coefficient may be decomposed into the following components: (1) direct effect (DE); (2) indirect effects (IE); (3) unanalyzed (U), due to correlated causes; and (4) spurious (S), due to common causes. The sum of DE and IE is the total effect, or the effect coefficient. Some authors (e.g., Fox, 1980) refer to the sum of U and S as the noncausal part of the correlation coefficient. From the preceding discussion it follows that not all correlations consist of the four components shown here. Thus, for example, spurious components may be identified only for correlations among endogenous variables. Unanalyzed components, on the other hand, may be identified only when the model consists of correlated exogenous variables. Furthermore, depending on the causal model, a variable may have only an indirect effect on another variable (see the numerical examples presented later in the chapter).

With the foregoing considerations in mind, I turn to more detailed treatments of the decomposition of correlations. I do this for the four-variable model depicted in Figure 18.2. For convenience, I repeat the necessary equations that I developed in the previous section in connection with this model.

$$r_{12} = p_{21} \tag{18.2}$$

$$r_{13} = p_{31} + p_{32}r_{12} \tag{18.3a}$$

$$r_{23} = p_{31}r_{12} + p_{32} \tag{18.3b}$$

$$r_{14} = p_{41} + p_{42}r_{12} + p_{43}r_{13} \tag{18.5a}$$

$$r_{24} = p_{41}r_{12} + p_{42} + p_{43}r_{23} \tag{18.5b}$$

$$r_{34} = p_{41}r_{13} + p_{42}r_{23} + p_{43} \tag{18.5c}$$

Look back at Figure 18.2 and note that, except for the residual (e_2), which is assumed not to be correlated with variable 1, variable 2 is affected by variable 1 only. Therefore r_{12} is due solely to the direct effect of variable 1 on variable 2 as is indicated in (18.2).

Consider now the correlation between variables 1 and 3. Since $r_{12} = p_{21}$, see (18.2), it is possible to substitute p_{21} for r_{12} in (18.3a), obtaining

$$r_{13} = p_{31} + p_{32}p_{21} \tag{18.3a'}$$
$$\phantom{r_{13} = } \text{DE} \quad\ \text{IE}$$

It can now be seen that r_{13} is composed of two components: the direct effect (DE) of variable 1 on 3, indicated by p_{31}; and the indirect effect (IE) of 1 on 3, via 2, indicated by $p_{32}p_{21}$ (see Figure 18.2 for these direct and indirect paths).

Substituting p_{21} for r_{12} in (18.3b),

$$r_{23} = p_{31}p_{21} + p_{32} \tag{18.3b'}$$
$$\phantom{r_{23} = } \text{S} \qquad \text{DE}$$

The decomposition of the correlation between variables 2 and 3 indicates that it is composed of two components: the direct effect of 2 on 3 (p_{32}) and a spurious (S) component ($p_{31}p_{21}$), which is due to a common cause affecting the two variables (variable 1).

I decompose now the correlation between variables 1 and 4. In (18.5a) I substitute p_{21} for r_{12}. In addition, I substitute the right-hand term of (18.3a′) for r_{13}. Making these substitutions:

$$r_{14} = p_{41} + p_{42}p_{21} + p_{43}(p_{31} + p_{32}p_{21})$$

$$= p_{41} + \underbrace{p_{42}p_{21} + p_{43}p_{31} + p_{43}p_{32}p_{21}}_{} \qquad (18.5a')$$

$$\text{DE} \qquad\qquad \text{IE}$$

It is evident that the correlation between variables 1 and 4 is composed of a direct effect (p_{41}) and several indirect effects as follows: $1 \rightarrow 2 \rightarrow 4$; $1 \rightarrow 3 \rightarrow 4$; $1 \rightarrow 2 \rightarrow 3 \rightarrow 4$.

Now, I decompose the correlation between variables 2 and 4. In (18.5b) I substitute p_{21} for r_{12}, and (18.3b′) for r_{23}:

$$r_{24} = p_{41}p_{21} + p_{42} + p_{43}(p_{31}p_{21} + p_{32})$$

$$= p_{41}p_{21} + p_{42} + p_{43}p_{31}p_{21} + p_{43}p_{32}$$

Rearranging the terms:

$$r_{24} = p_{42} + p_{43}p_{32} + \underbrace{p_{41}p_{21} + p_{43}p_{31}p_{21}}_{} \qquad (18.5b')$$

$$\text{DE} \quad \text{IE} \qquad\qquad \text{S}$$

Clearly, variable 2 affects 4 directly, as well as indirectly via variable 3. In addition, part of r_{24} is spurious, as indicated above.

Finally, in (18.5c) I substitute (18.3a′) for r_{13} and (18.3b′) for r_{23}, and rearrange the terms to obtain the decomposition of r_{34}.

$$r_{34} = p_{43} + \underbrace{p_{41}p_{31} + p_{41}p_{21}p_{32} + p_{42}p_{21}p_{31} + p_{42}p_{32}}_{} \qquad (18.5c')$$

$$\text{DE} \qquad\qquad\qquad \text{S}$$

Variable 3 has only a direct effect on variable 4. The remainder of the correlation between 3 and 4 is spurious, due to common causes (i.e., variables 1 and 2) as indicated above.

Using the four variables under consideration, it will be instructive to note how the decomposition of the correlation coefficients would be affected if causal models that differ from the one depicted in Figure 18.2 were posited. Assume, first, that the model is as depicted in Figure 18.5. Note that this time variables 1 and 2 are treated as exogenous. Consequently, unlike the model of Figure 18.2, the correlation between 1 and 2 is unanalyzed.

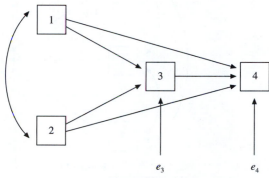

Figure 18.5

Following the procedures outlined earlier, decomposition of the correlations among the variables in Figure 18.5 is as follows.

$$r_{13} = \underset{\text{DE}}{p_{31}} + \underset{\text{U}}{p_{32}r_{12}} \tag{18.6}$$

$$r_{23} = \underset{\text{DE}}{p_{32}} + \underset{\text{U}}{p_{31}r_{12}} \tag{18.7}$$

$$r_{14} = \underset{\text{DE}}{p_{41}} + \underset{\text{IE}}{p_{43}p_{31}} + \underset{\text{U}}{p_{42}r_{12} + p_{43}p_{32}r_{12}} \tag{18.8}$$

$$r_{24} = \underset{\text{DE}}{p_{42}} + \underset{\text{IE}}{p_{43}p_{32}} + \underset{\text{U}}{p_{41}r_{12} + p_{43}p_{31}r_{12}} \tag{18.9}$$

$$r_{34} = \underset{\text{DE}}{p_{43}} + \underset{\text{S}}{p_{41}p_{31} + p_{41}p_{32}r_{12} + p_{42}p_{32} + p_{42}p_{31}r_{12}} \tag{18.10}$$

Note that although some of elements of r_{34} involve r_{12}, they still make up part of the spurious component because variables 1 and 2 are common, though correlated, causes of 3 and 4.

Careful study of the equations for the two causal models (Figures 18.2 and 18.5) reveals that for a given endogenous variable, the direct effects are the same. Thus, for example, the direct effects of variables 1, 2, and 3 on 4 are the same in both models. The two models differ in the degree to which remaining terms are elaborated. Contrast, for instance, (18.5a′) with (18.8). Both refer to the correlation between variable 1 and 4. However, in (18.5a′) r_{14} is decomposed into direct and indirect effects of 1 on 4, whereas in (18.8) part of the correlation that involves r_{12} (the correlated causes) is unanalyzed. Similarly, r_{13} of Figure 18.2 is decomposed into a direct and indirect effect, (18.3a′), whereas r_{13} of Figure 18.5 is decomposed into a direct effect and a component that is unanalyzed—see (18.6).

In short, the more elaborate the causal model, the less ambiguous is the decomposition of correlations. This important point will perhaps become clearer as I turn to yet another causal model for the four variables under consideration as depicted in Figure 18.6. This time variables 1, 2, and 3 are treated as exogenous.

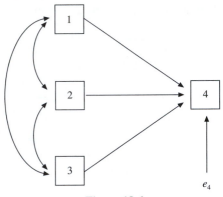

Figure 18.6

Consequently, the equations for this model are

$$r_{14} = p_{41} + p_{42}r_{12} + p_{43}r_{13} \tag{18.11a$'$}$$

$$r_{24} = p_{42} + p_{41}r_{12} + p_{43}r_{23} \tag{18.11b$'$}$$

$$r_{34} = p_{43} + p_{41}r_{13} + p_{42}r_{23} \tag{18.11c$'$}$$

Note that the first term in the right-hand side of (18.11) indicates the direct effect of each exogenous variable on the endogenous variable (4). In this respect, the three models are alike. Unlike the preceding models, however, all the remaining terms in (18.11) are unanalyzed because they involve correlated exogenous variables. Because the model of Figure 18.6 is the least elaborate of the three, it affords the least decomposition of the correlations into unambiguous components. To further note what is taking place in the decomposition of the correlations for different models, compare Equations (18.5) with (18.11). Note that, except for the rearrangement of the terms, the two sets of equations are identical. But because (18.5) refers to a more elaborate model (Figure 18.2), it was possible to further decompose the elements—see (18.5a$'$), (18.5b$'$) and (18.c$'$). A similar decomposition was not possible for the model of Figure 18.6.

It is very important to note that the analyses of the three models I have discussed are based on the same data. That is, the correlations among the four variables are used to calculate the different components. It should therefore be clear that *the choice among these and other possible models cannot and should not be made on the basis of the data.* As I said earlier, the causal model reflects the theoretical formulation regarding the relations among the variables under consideration. The absence of such a model precludes any decomposition of the correlations. In other words, when a causal model is not posited, it is not possible to speak of direct and indirect effects, or about spurious and unanalyzed components.

Finally, note that when a dependent variable is regressed on a set of independent variables, and the β's are interpreted as indices of the effects of each of the independent variables on the dependent variable, a path analytic model is being used, wittingly or unwittingly. That is, all the independent variables are treated as exogenous (as in Figure 18.6). This is the most rudimentary causal model possible, indicating that the researcher is either unwilling or unable to explicate the causes of the relations among the exogenous variables. Consequently, all that I said in earlier chapters about the interpretation of a regression equation (see, in particular, Chapter 10) applies equally to models such as that depicted in Figure 18.6. For example, when collinearity is high, the researcher is forced to conclude that most or all the variables have little direct effect on the dependent variable and that the correlation of each independent variable with the dependent variable is largely due to the operation of correlated causes. This may be a reflection of the researcher's lack of knowledge about the phenomenon under study.

NUMERICAL EXAMPLES

In this section, I present several numerical examples for the sole purpose of illustrating the calculations of path coefficients, the decomposition of correlation coefficients, and the use of path coefficients to reproduce the correlation matrix. In subsequent sections, I introduce tests of causal models and indices of fit for such models.

THREE-VARIABLE MODELS

Suppose that a researcher postulated a three-variable causal model as depicted in Figure 18.7. That is, variable 1 affects variables 2 and 3, and variable 2 affects variable 3. Suppose that the correlations are $r_{12} = .50$; $r_{23} = .50$; and $r_{13} = .25$.

The equations of the model of Figure 18.7 are

$$z_1 = e_1$$

$$z_2 = p_{21}z_1 + e_2$$

$$z_3 = p_{31}z_1 + p_{32}z_2 + e_3$$

Following procedures I outlined in the preceding section, calculate the path coefficients:

$$p_{21} = \beta_{21} = r_{21} = .50$$

To obtain the path coefficients from variables 1 and 2 to 3, regress the latter on the two former variables to calculate $\beta_{31.2} = p_{31}$ and $\beta_{32.1} = p_{32}$. In Chapter 5—see (5.15)—I introduced formulas for the calculation of β's when the model consists of two independent variables.

$$\beta_{31.2} = \frac{r_{31} - r_{32}r_{12}}{1 - r_{12}^2} = \frac{(.25) - (.50)(.50)}{1 - .50^2} = \frac{.25 - .25}{1 - .25} = \frac{0}{.75} = 0$$

$$\beta_{32.1} = \frac{r_{32} - r_{31}r_{12}}{1 - r_{12}^2} = \frac{(.50) - (.25)(.50)}{1 - .50^2} = \frac{.50 - .125}{1 - .25} = \frac{.375}{.75} = .50$$

Thus, $p_{31} = .00$ and $p_{32} = .50$.

The path coefficient from e_2 to variable 2 is equal to $\sqrt{1 - r_{12}^2} = \sqrt{1 - .50^2} = .866$. As I explained in the preceding section, the path coefficient from e_3 to variable 3 is equal to $\sqrt{1 - R_{3.12}^2}$. Using (5.20),

$$R_{3.12}^2 = \frac{r_{31}^2 + r_{32}^2 - 2r_{31}r_{32}r_{12}}{1 - r_{12}^2} = \frac{(.25)^2 + (.50)^2 - 2(.25)(.50)(.50)}{1 - .50^2} = .25$$

The path coefficient from e_3 is therefore $\sqrt{1 - .25} = .866$

I now show how the path coefficients I calculated in the preceding may be used to reproduce the correlation coefficients among the variables. This also illustrates the decomposition of each of the correlation coefficients. As in the preceding section, I will use the following abbreviations to identify the different components of the correlation coefficient: DE = direct effect, IE = indirect effect, U = unanalyzed, and S = spurious.

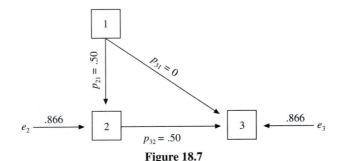

Figure 18.7

I will use the equations of the model of Figure 18.7 (see the preceding) without comment, as I have already discussed the procedures and the assumptions upon which they are based. Reproducing:

$$r_{12} = \frac{1}{N}\Sigma z_1 z_2 = \frac{1}{N}\Sigma z_1(p_{21}z_1) = \underset{\text{DE}}{p_{21}} = .50$$

As there are no intervening variables between variable 1 and variable 2, the former can have only a direct effect, which is also the total effect, on the latter.

Turning now to r_{13} and using the relevant equations of the model of Figure 18.7 (see the preceding),

$$r_{13} = \frac{1}{N}\Sigma z_1 z_3 = \frac{1}{N}\Sigma z_1(p_{31}z_1 + p_{32}z_2) = p_{31} + p_{32}r_{12}$$

As $r_{12} = p_{21}$,

$$r_{13} = p_{31} + p_{32}p_{21} = \underset{\text{DE}}{.00} + \underset{\text{IE}}{(.50)(.50)} = .25$$

Note that using the appropriate path coefficients r_{13} is reproduced. Note also the separate components of r_{13}: Variable 1 has no direct effect on variable 3; the indirect effect of variable 1 on 3 is .25, which is also the total effect of 1 on 3.

Turning to r_{23},

$$r_{23} = \frac{1}{N}\Sigma z_2 z_3 = \frac{1}{N}\Sigma z_2 (p_{31}z_1 + p_{32}z_2) = p_{31}r_{12} + p_{32}$$

As $r_{12} = p_{21}$,

$$r_{23} = p_{31}p_{21} + p_{32} = \underset{\text{S}}{(.00)(.50)} + \underset{\text{DE}}{(.50)} = .50$$

The correlation between 2 and 3 is reproduced by the use of the path coefficients. Also, the direct effect of 2 on 3 is .50, which is the total effect of 2 on 3. Note that in the present example r_{23} has no spurious component.

Just-Identified Models

In the preceding, I showed how path coefficients can be used to reproduce correlations among the variables or, more succinctly, the correlation matrix (**R**). As I explain in the following, the use of path coefficients to reproduce **R** plays an important role in assessing the validity of a given causal model. *It is therefore very important to recognize that in a just-identified, or exactly iden-tified, causal model (see the following) **R** can be reproduced, no matter how questionable, even bizarre, the model may be on substantive or logical grounds.* Later I discuss identification. For now, it will suffice to point out that a recursive model is just identified when all the variables are interconnected either by curved lines (among the exogenous variables) or by paths (from exoge-nous and endogenous variables to other endogenous variables), and the assumptions about the residuals are tenable (see the earlier section). Such a model is referred to as fully recursive.

A just-identified model is one in which the number of equations is equal to the number of pa-rameters to be estimated, thereby affording a unique solution for each of them. Figure 18.7 is an example of a just-identified model.

To show numerically that as long as the model is just-identified, **R** can be reproduced, I changed the model of Figure 18.7 to the one depicted in Figure 18.8. Recall that $r_{12} = .50$, $r_{23} = .50$, and $r_{13} = .25$.

Following procedures I used in the preceding, I calculate the path coefficients for the model of Figure 18.8:

$$p_{23} = \beta_{23.1} = \frac{r_{23} - r_{21}r_{13}}{1 - r_{13}^2} = \frac{(.50) - (.50)(.25)}{1 - .25^2} = \frac{.375}{.9375} = .40$$

$$p_{13} = \beta_{13} = r_{13} = .25$$

$$p_{21} = \beta_{21.3} = \frac{r_{21} - r_{23}r_{13}}{1 - r_{13}^2} = \frac{(.50) - (.50)(.25)}{1 - .25^2} = \frac{.375}{.9375} = .40$$

$$e_1 = \sqrt{1 - r_{13}^2} = \sqrt{1 - .25^2} = .968$$

$$R_{2.13}^2 = \frac{r_{21}^2 + r_{23}^2 - 2r_{21}r_{23}r_{13}}{1 - r_{13}^2} = \frac{(.50)^2 + (.50)^2 - 2(.50)(.50)(.25)}{1 - .25^2} = \frac{.375}{.9375} = .40$$

$$e_2 = \sqrt{1 - R_{2.13}^2} = \sqrt{1 - .40} = .775$$

I now use the preceding results to reproduce **R**. The equations for the model of Figure 18.8 are

$$z_3 = e_3$$

$$z_1 = p_{13}z_3 + e_1$$

$$z_2 = p_{23}z_3 + p_{21}z_1 + e_2$$

Hence,

$$r_{13} = \frac{1}{N}\Sigma z_3 z_1 = \frac{1}{N}\Sigma z_3(p_{13}z_3) = p_{13} = .25$$
$$\qquad\qquad\qquad\qquad\qquad\qquad\quad \text{DE}$$

The direct effect, which is also the total effect, of variable 3 on 1 is .25.

$$r_{23} = \frac{1}{N}\Sigma z_3 z_2 = \frac{1}{N}\Sigma z_3(p_{23}z_3 + p_{21}z_1) = p_{23} + p_{21}r_{13}$$

As $r_{13} = p_{13}$,

$$r_{23} = p_{23} + p_{21}p_{13} = .40 + (.40)(.25) = .50$$
$$\qquad\qquad\quad \text{DE} \qquad \text{IE}$$

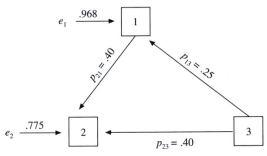

Figure 18.8

The direct effect of 3 on 2 is .4. The indirect effect of 3 on 2 is .1[(.40)(.25)]. The total effect (DE + IE) of 3 on 2 is .5, which is equal to r_{23}.

$$r_{12} = \frac{1}{N}\Sigma z_1 z_2 = \frac{1}{N}\Sigma z_1 (p_{23}z_3 + p_{21}z_1) = p_{23}r_{13} + p_{21}$$

As $r_{13} = p_{13}$,

$$r_{12} = p_{23}p_{13} + p_{21} = (.40)(.25) + .40 = .50$$
$$\phantom{r_{12} = p_{23}p_{13} + p_{21} = } \text{S} \qquad \text{DE}$$

Note that the direct effect of 1 on 2 is .40, which is also the total effect of 1 on 2. Further, part of the correlation between 1 and 2 is spurious (.1) as these two variables share a common cause, variable 3.

Although the models of Figures 18.7 and 18.8 are radically different, the path coefficients obtained in each afforded the reproduction of **R**. This is because both models are just identified. Path coefficients for any other just-identified model for the three variables under consideration will be equally effective in reproducing **R**. Thus, the fact that **R** can be reproduced in just-identified models has no bearing on the assessment of the validity of a specific model. It is only for overidentified models, to which I now turn, that reproduction of **R** may be used for assessment of their validity.

Overidentified Models

Consider the model depicted in Figure 18.9, according to which variable 1 affects variable 2, which in turn affects variable 3. The absence of a path from variable 1 to variable 3 indicates that it is hypothesized that the former has no direct effect on the latter. Figure 18.9 is an example of an overidentified model. Essentially, this means that the model contains more information than is necessary to estimate the path coefficients. Specifically, there are three known elements (the correlations among the three variables) and only two unknowns (the two path coefficients). In the present case, one can construct three equations for two unknowns, hence the overidentification.

Assume that the correlations among the variables of Figure 18.9 are the same as those in the earlier models (i.e., $r_{12} = .50$, $r_{23} = .50$, $r_{13} = .25$). Accordingly,

$$p_{21} = \beta_{21} = r_{12} = .50$$

$$p_{32} = \beta_{32} = r_{23} = .50$$

$$e_2 = \sqrt{1 - r_{12}^2} = \sqrt{1 - .50^2} = .866$$

$$e_3 = \sqrt{1 - r_{23}^2} = \sqrt{1 - .50^2} = .866$$

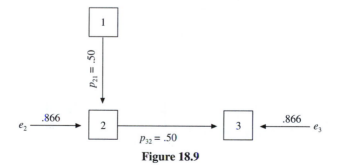

Figure 18.9

Now, the equations for the model of Figure 18.9 are

$$z_1 = e_1$$

$$z_2 = p_{21}z_1 + e_2$$

$$z_3 = p_{32}z_2 + e_3$$

Using the path coefficients I calculated above, I reproduce the correlation between 1 and 3:

$$r_{13} = \frac{1}{N}\Sigma z_1 z_3 = \frac{1}{N}\Sigma z_1(p_{32}z_2) = p_{32}r_{12}$$

As $r_{12} = p_{21}$,

$$r_{13} = p_{32}p_{21} = (.50)(.50) = .25$$
$$\text{IE}$$

The fact that r_{13} could be reproduced, using the calculated path coefficients, shows that the postulated model of Figure 18.9 is consistent with the data. Specifically, this means that a model in which 1 affects 3 only indirectly is consistent with the data.

Two points need to be made regarding the preceding statement. One, although in this example r_{13} was exactly reproduced, this will generally not happen. But, as I explain later, a close approximation of r_{13} may serve as evidence of consistency of the model with the data. Two, different over-identified causal models may be equally effective in reproducing **R**. To reiterate: *consistency of a causal model with a set of data is no proof of the validity of the model.* I discuss this issue later in this chapter (see "Testing Causal Models"). At this stage I will only demonstrate that path coefficients for a causal model that differs from the one depicted in Figure 18.9 are equally effective in reproducing r_{13}.

Consider the model depicted in Figure 18.10, according to which variable 2 is a common cause of variables 1 and 3. For this model, $p_{12} = r_{12} = .50$, and $p_{32} = r_{23} = .50$. The equations for this model are

$$z_2 = e_2$$

$$z_1 = p_{12}z_2 + e_1$$

$$z_3 = p_{32}z_2 + e_3$$

Hence,

$$r_{13} = \frac{1}{N}\Sigma z_1 z_3 = \frac{1}{N}\Sigma z_1(p_{32}z_2) = p_{32}r_{12}$$

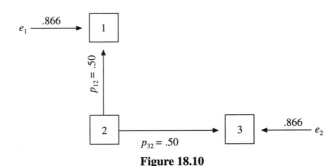

Figure 18.10

As $r_{12} = p_{12}$,

$$r_{13} = p_{32}p_{12} = (.50)(.50) = .25$$
$$S$$

Thus, r_{13} was exactly reproduced in the models of Figures 18.9 and 18.10. But these models are radically different from each other. According to Figure 18.9, r_{13} is due to the indirect effect of 1 on 3, via 2. According to Figure 18.10, on the other hand, r_{13} is spurious. To repeat: from the perspective of reproducing r_{13} both models are consistent with the data.

I turn now to yet another overidentified causal model for the three variables under consideration. This time, I hypothesize that variable 3 affects variable 1, which in turn affects variable 2. In other words, I hypothesize that 3 affects 2 indirectly but not directly. This model is depicted in Figure 18.11.

The equations for this model are

$$z_3 = e_3$$
$$z_2 = p_{21}z_1 + e_2$$
$$z_1 = p_{13}z_3 + e_1$$

Therefore,

$$p_{13} = r_{13} = .25 \qquad p_{21} = r_{21} = .50$$

Attempting now to reproduce r_{23},

$$r_{23} = \frac{1}{N}\Sigma z_3 z_2 = \frac{1}{N}\Sigma z_3(p_{21}z_1) = p_{21}r_{13}$$

As $r_{13} = p_{13}$,

$$r_{23} = p_{21}p_{13} = (.50)(.25) = .125$$
$$IE$$

The large discrepancy between the original r_{23} (.50) and the reproduced one (.125) leads to the conclusion that the model of Figure 18.11 does not fit the data. One possibility is that 3 affects 2 directly as well as indirectly. As I said earlier, I discuss testing causal models later in this chapter. At this stage, my sole purpose was to demonstrate that the use of path coefficients to reproduce r_{23} fell far short of the mark.

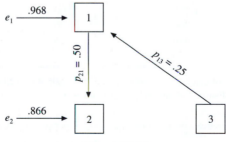

Figure 18.11

A FOUR-VARIABLE MODEL

I turn now to a four-variable model. This time, however, I give the variables substantive meaning in the hope of thereby enhancing your understanding of the use of causal models in behavioral research.

An Example from Educational Research

I first presented the causal model of Figure 18.12 in Chapter 9 (see Figure 9.4), where I used it to illustrate incremental partitioning of variance. Subsequently, I used the illustrative data connected with this model in Chapter 9 to illustrate the application of commonality analysis. I used the same data again in Chapter 10 in connection with the study of the effects of independent variables on a dependent variable. I use the same model and the same data here so that I may compare path analysis with the analytic methods I presented earlier. For convenience, I repeat the correlations among the variables in the upper half matrix of Table 18.1.

Assume that the causal model for the variables in this example is the one depicted in Figure 18.12. Note that SES and IQ are treated as exogenous variables; SES and IQ are hypothesized to affect AM (achievement motivation); SES, IQ, and AM are hypothesized to affect GPA.[5] As it will be necessary to make frequent reference to these variables in the form of subscripts, I will identify them by the numbers attached to them in Figure 18.12. That is, 1 = SES, 2 = IQ, 3 = AM, and 4 = GPA.

To calculate the path coefficients for the causal model of Figure 18.12 it is necessary to regress (1) variable 3 on variables 1 and 2 to obtain $\beta_{31.2} = p_{31}$ and $\beta_{32.1} = p_{32}$ and (2) variable 4 on variables 1, 2, and 3 to obtain $\beta_{41.23} = p_{41}$, $\beta_{42.13} = p_{42}$, $\beta_{43.12} = p_{43}$.

In the interest of space, I do not show the calculations of the β's for the present problem and for subsequent ones. Instead, I report results and apply them in path analysis.[6] From the regression of variable 3 on 1 and 2, I got $\beta_{31.2} = p_{31} = .398$ and $\beta_{32.1} = p_{32} = .041$. From the regression of variable 4 on variables 1, 2, and 3, I got $\beta_{41.23} = p_{41} = .009$, $\beta_{42.13} = p_{42} = .501$, and $\beta_{43.12} = p_{43} = .416$. The path from e_3 to variable 3 is $\sqrt{1 - R^2_{3.12}} = \sqrt{1 - .1696} = .911$, and the path from e_4 to variable 4 is $\sqrt{1 - R^2_{4.123}} = \sqrt{1 - .49647} = .710$.

Table 18.1   Original and Reproduced Correlations for a Four-Variable Model; N = 300

	1 SES	2 IQ	3 AM	4 GPA
1	1.000	.300	.410	.330
2	.300	1.000	.160	.570
3	.410	.123	1.000	.500
4	.323	.555	.482	1.000

NOTE: The original correlations are reported in the upper half of the matrix. The reproduced correlations are reported in the lower half of the matrix. See the explanation in the text.

[5]I do not discuss theoretical considerations that would generate this model, as my sole purpose is to illustrate the analysis of such a model.

[6]You may wish to do the calculations as an exercise. In earlier chapters (e.g., Chapter 7), I showed how to use correlation matrices as input in multiple regression analysis procedures of BMDP, SAS, and SPSS.

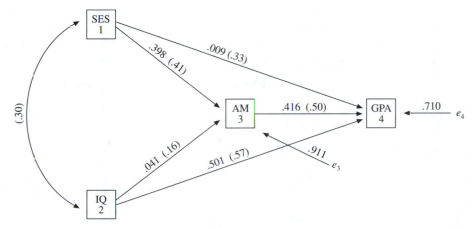

Figure 18.12

The equations for the endogenous variables of Figure 18.12 are

$$z_3 = p_{31}z_1 + p_{32}z_2 + e_3$$

$$z_4 = p_{41}z_1 + p_{42}z_2 + p_{43}z_3 + e_4$$

I will now decompose the correlations of Table 18.1. Recalling that correlations among exogenous variables remain unanalyzed, r_{12} is unanalyzed. Beginning with r_{13},

$$r_{13} = \frac{1}{N}\Sigma z_1 z_3 = \frac{1}{N}\Sigma z_1 (p_{31}z_1 + p_{32}z_2)$$

$$= p_{31} + p_{32}r_{12} = .398 + (.041)(.30) = .41$$
$$ \text{DE} \qquad \text{U}$$

r_{13} is decomposed into two components: direct effect of SES on AM (.398) and a component that is unanalyzed (.012) because SES is correlated with another exogenous variable—IQ.

$$r_{23} = \frac{1}{N}\Sigma z_2 z_3 = \frac{1}{N}\Sigma z_2 (p_{31}z_1 + p_{32}z_2)$$

$$= p_{31}r_{12} + p_{32} = (.398)(.30) + .041 = .16$$
$$ \text{U} \qquad\qquad \text{DE}$$

The direct effect of IQ on AM is relatively small (.041), whereas .119 of the correlation between IQ and AM remains unanalyzed because IQ is correlated with the exogenous variable SES.

$$r_{14} = \frac{1}{N}\Sigma z_1 z_4 = \frac{1}{N}\Sigma z_1 (p_{41}z_1 + p_{42}z_2 + p_{43}z_3)$$

$$= p_{41} + p_{42}r_{12} + p_{43}r_{13}$$

As $r_{13} = p_{31}r_{12}$ (see the preceding),

$$r_{14} = p_{41} + p_{42}r_{12} + p_{43}(p_{31} + p_{32}r_{12})$$

$$= p_{41} + p_{42}r_{12} + p_{43}p_{31} + p_{43}p_{32}r_{12}$$

$$= .009 + (.501)(.30) + (.416)(.398) + (.416)(.041)(.30) = .33$$
$$ \text{DE} \qquad \text{U} \qquad\quad \text{IE} \qquad\qquad \text{U}$$

Note that the direct effect of SES on GPA is virtually zero (.009). The indirect effect of SES on GPA, via AM, is .166. Therefore, the total effect of SES on GPA, or the effect coefficient for SES, is .175 (i.e., DE + IE). The remainder of the correlation between SES and GPA (.155) is unanalyzed, as its components include correlated exogenous variables (r_{12}).

$$r_{24} = \frac{1}{N}\Sigma z_2 z_4 = \frac{1}{N}\Sigma z_2 (p_{41} z_1 + p_{42} z_2 + p_{43} z_3)$$

$$= p_{41} r_{12} + p_{42} + p_{43} r_{23}$$

As $r_{23} = p_{31} r_{12} + p_{32}$ (see the preceding),

$$r_{24} = p_{41} r_{12} + p_{42} + p_{43}(p_{31} r_{12} + p_{32})$$

$$= \underset{}{p_{41} r_{12}} \quad + \quad p_{42} \quad + \quad p_{43} p_{31} r_{12} \quad + \quad p_{43} p_{32}$$

$$= \underset{U}{(.009)(.30)} + \underset{DE}{(.501)} + \underset{U}{(.416)(.398)(.30)} + \underset{IE}{(.416)(.041)} = .57$$

The bulk of the correlation between IQ and GPA is due to the direct effect of the former on the latter (.501). The indirect effect of IQ on GPA, via AM, is .017. The effect coefficient of IQ on GPA is therefore .518 (DE + IE). The remainder of the correlation between IQ and GPA (.052) is unanalyzed.

$$r_{34} = \frac{1}{N}\Sigma z_3 z_4 = \frac{1}{N}\Sigma z_3 (p_{41} z_1 + p_{42} z_2 + p_{43} z_3)$$

$$= p_{41} r_{13} + p_{42} r_{23} + p_{43}$$

As $r_{13} = p_{31} + p_{32} r_{12}$, and $r_{23} = p_{31} r_{12} + p_{32}$

$$r_{34} = p_{41}(p_{31} + p_{32} r_{12}) + p_{42}(p_{31} r_{12} + p_{32}) + p_{43}$$

$$= \underset{}{p_{41} p_{31}} \quad + \quad p_{41} p_{32} r_{12} \quad + \quad p_{42} p_{31} r_{12} \quad + \quad p_{42} p_{32} \quad + \quad p_{43}$$

$$= \underset{S}{(.009)(.398)} + \underset{S}{(.009)(.041)(.30)} + \underset{S}{(.501)(.398)(.30)} + \underset{S}{(.501)(.041)} + \underset{DE}{(.416)} = .50$$

The direct effect of AM on GPA is .416. The remainder of the correlation between these variables (.084) is spurious, due to their common causes (SES and IQ).

The preceding demonstration shows that by using path analysis one can learn not only about effects (direct and indirect) of one variable on another but also about spurious and unanalyzed components of relations between variables. When one wishes to determine the effect of a variable on a given endogenous variable, it is the total effect (or the effect coefficient) that should be used. Using the direct effect only for such purposes may be misleading as, being a β, it is calculated while controlling for all the variables that affect the endogenous variable in question. That is, variables that mediate the effect of a variable on an endogenous variable are also controlled when the direct effect of the former on the latter is calculated. For instance, when the direct effect of SES on GPA is calculated in the model of Figure 18.12, AM is also controlled. But when one wishes to determine the effect of SES on GPA, its indirect effects should also be taken into account. In the example under consideration, SES affects GPA indirectly via AM.

It follows, then, that when one wishes to study differential effects of several variables on an endogenous variable, it is their total effects (or effect coefficients) that should be compared. In the example under consideration, the effect coefficients of SES, IQ, and AM on GPA are .175,

.518, and .416, respectively. Accordingly, one may conclude that IQ has the largest effect on GPA, followed by AM, and SES. Moreover, the effect of SES on GPA is relatively smaller than the effect of either of the other two variables.[7]

Only effect coefficients that impinge on the same endogenous variable may be compared (for a detailed discussion, see Schoenberg, 1972). Also, the comparisons I made in the preceding were possible because all the variables were expressed in standard score form. Although this is a decided advantage of standard scores, there are also serious disadvantages in using such scores (see "Path Regression Coefficients," later in this chapter).

It will be instructive to compare the results of the present analysis with results I obtained when I used other analytic approaches with the same data. In the interest of space, I will make such comparisons only about the effect of SES on GPA. In Chapter 9, I used the model depicted in Figure 18.12 to illustrate the method of incremental partitioning of variance (see Figure 9.4 and the discussion related to it). Because I treated SES and IQ as exogenous variables, I argued in Chapter 9 that there was no way of partitioning the variance of GPA that the two of them account for in combination. All I could say is that SES and IQ account for .35268 of the variance in GPA. Recall also that I reasoned that because incremental partitioning of variance yields asymmetric indices, it is inappropriate to compare among them to learn about the relative importance of variables (see Figure 9.3 and the discussion related to it).

The next time I used the data in Table 18.1 in Chapter 9 was to illustrate the application of commonality analysis, where I found that the uniqueness associated with SES was .00006. Without repeating my discussion of commonality analysis (see Chapter 9), I will only note here that if uniqueness were used as a criterion for the importance of a variable, one would have to conclude that SES is not important in explaining GPA.

I used the data in Table 18.1 again in Chapter 10, when I discussed interpretation of β's, and found that when GPA was regressed on SES, IQ, and AM, β for SES was .00919. Interpreting this β as an index of an effect, one would have to conclude that SES has practically no effect on GPA. Earlier in the present chapter, I noted that (1) when one variable is treated as endogenous and all the others are treated as exogenous (i.e., a single-stage path model), the path coefficients are the same as their corresponding β's obtained in a multiple regression analysis; and (2) the direct effect of an exogenous variable in a multistage path analysis is the same as the direct effect of the same variable in a single-stage path analysis. In fact, in my analysis of the model of Figure 18.12 I found that the direct effect of SES on GPA was .009. Thus, using only the direct effect as an index of the effect of SES on GPA, the conclusion would be the same whether one uses multiple regression analysis (as in Chapter 10) or path analysis. But in multiple regression analysis, all the independent variables are used as exogenous by default, so to speak. If, on the other hand, one hypothesizes that the causal model is as depicted in Figure 18.12, then it is revealed that although the direct effect of SES on GPA is practically zero, it has an indirect effect on GPA (see the preceding analysis).

The preceding brief discussion should serve as a contrast between path analysis and the analytic methods I presented in Chapters 9 and 10. I suggest that you reread relevant sections of the aforementioned chapters to enhance your understanding of the different analytic approaches I contrasted in the foregoing.

The model of Figure 18.12 is just identified. It is possible, however, that an overidentified model is consistent with the data in Table 18.1. I will now examine one such model.

---

[7]For a discussion of the usefulness of interpretation of effect coefficients see Lewis-Beck and Mohr (1976).

An Overidentified Model

In my analysis of the model depicted in Figure 18.12, the direct effect of SES on GPA was practically zero (.009). Also, the direct effect of IQ on AM was small (.041). Suppose that I deleted these two paths. In other words, suppose that I hypothesized that these two paths are equal to zero. Of course, there is a difference between hypothesizing *a priori* that the two coefficients are equal to zero and arriving at such a "hypothesis" *post hoc,* based on an examination of the results. I address this topic later (see "Theory Trimming or Model Revision"). Figure 18.13 depicts this overidentified model.

Calculation of path coefficients in an overidentified model proceeds as in a just-identified model (for a discussion, see Goldberger, 1970). For the model of Figure 18.13, I regressed (1) variable 3 on variable 1 to get $p_{31} = \beta_{31} = r_{13} = .41$ and (2) variable 4 on variables 2 and 3 to get $p_{42} = \beta_{42.3} = .503$ and $p_{43} = \beta_{43.2} = .420$.

Does this model fit the data? Although it is possible to apply a statistical test in an attempt to answer this question (see the following), the approach I take here is to note whether **R** can be reproduced or closely approximated. The equations for the model of Figure 18.13 are

$$z_3 = p_{31}z_1 + e_3$$

$$z_4 = p_{42}z_2 + p_{43}z_3 + e_4$$

Following procedures I outlined earlier, I calculate the reproduced correlations, r_{ij}^*:

$$r_{13}^* = p_{31} = .41$$

$$r_{23}^* = \frac{1}{N}\Sigma z_2 z_3 = \frac{1}{N}\Sigma z_2(p_{31}z_1) = p_{31}r_{12} = (.41)(.30) = .123$$

Originally, $r_{23} = .160$.

$$r_{14}^* = \frac{1}{N}\Sigma z_1 z_4 = \frac{1}{N}\Sigma z_1(p_{42}z_2 + p_{43}z_3) = p_{42}r_{12} + p_{43}r_{13}$$

Substituting p_{31} for r_{13},

$$r_{14}^* = p_{42}r_{12} + p_{43}p_{31} = (.503)(.30) + (.420)(.410) = .323$$

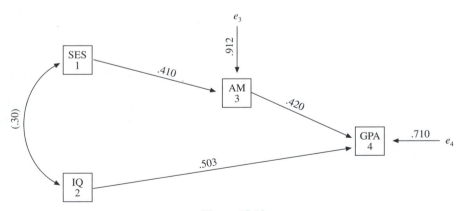

Figure 18.13

Originally, $r_{14} = .330$.

$$r_{24}^* = \frac{1}{N}\Sigma z_2 z_4 = \frac{1}{N}\Sigma z_2(p_{42}z_2 + p_{43}z_3) = p_{42} + p_{43}r_{23}$$

Substituting $p_{31}r_{12}$ for r_{23}.

$$r_{24}^* = p_{42} + p_{43}p_{31}r_{12} = (.503) + (.420)(.410)(.30) = .555$$

Originally, $r_{24} = .57$.

$$r_{34}^* = \frac{1}{N}\Sigma z_3 z_4 = \frac{1}{N}\Sigma z_3(p_{42}z_2 + p_{43}z_3) = p_{42}r_{23} + p_{43}$$

Substituting $p_{31}r_{12}$ for r_{23},

$$r_{34}^* = p_{42}p_{31}r_{12} + p_{43} = (.503)(.410)(.30) + (.420) = .482$$

Originally, $r_{34} = .50$.

The discrepancies between the original and the reproduced correlations are relatively small. (To make it easier to compare original and reproduced correlations, I placed the former in the upper half and the latter in the lower half of the matrix of Table 18.1.) I turn now to a more complex example in the context of which I elaborate on various definitions of indirect effects and their calculations.

SPECIFIC INDIRECT EFFECTS

In the numerical examples I analyzed thus far, there was only one indirect effect from any given independent variable to any given dependent variable. For instance, the model of Figure 18.12 showed only one indirect effect of SES on GPA (i.e., SES $\rightarrow$ AM $\rightarrow$ GPA). In more complex models, a variable may affect another variable indirectly through multiple paths. Thus, in the model of Figure 18.2—see also (18.5a$'$)—variable 1 affects variable 4 indirectly through three compound paths: $1 \rightarrow 2 \rightarrow 4$; $1 \rightarrow 3 \rightarrow 4$; $1 \rightarrow 2 \rightarrow 3 \rightarrow 4$. It stands to reason that indirect effects through certain paths may be more meaningful and/or stronger than others. Hence, the interest in specific indirect effects. Varying definitions of specific indirect effects were advanced. I comment on a couple of them in the context of the numerical example to which I now turn.

A Numerical Example

The model depicted in Figure 18.14 and the data in Table 18.2 are from Duncan, Featherman, and Duncan (1972, p. 38, for the 35–44 age group).[8] In the figure, I included the path coefficients, which I estimated by regressing (1) Y_1 on X_1, X_2, and X_3; (2) Y_2 on X_1, X_2, X_3, and Y_1; and (3) Y_3 on X_1, X_2, X_3, Y_1, and Y_2. Following Duncan et al., I use X's to identify exogenous variables and Y's to identify endogenous variables. Because my sole purpose here is to illustrate calculations of specific indirect effects, I will not comment on substantive aspects of the model, nor on the findings. I strongly recommend that you read Duncan et al.'s (1972) penetrating discussions of the models they analyze in their book.

---

[8]For the present analysis, I use only the correlation matrix. When I reanalyze this example later to illustrate calculations of path regression coefficients, I use also the standard deviations.

Table 18.2   Correlation Matrix for Nonblack Men, 35–44 Age Group

	X_1	X_2	X_3	Y_1	Y_2	Y_3
X_1	1.0000	.5300	−.2871	.4048	.3194	.2332
X_2	.5300	1.0000	−.2476	.4341	.3899	.2587
X_3	−.2871	−.2476	1.0000	−.3311	−.2751	−.1752
Y_1	.4048	.4341	−.3311	1.0000	.6426	.3759
Y_2	.3194	.3899	−.2751	.6426	1.0000	.4418
Y_3	.2332	.2587	−.1752	.3759	.4418	1.0000
s:	3.72	23.14	2.88	3.20	24.71	5.36

NOTE: Data taken from O. D. Duncan, D. L. Featherman, and B. Duncan, *Socioeconomic Background and Achievement*, p. 38. Copyright 1972 by Seminar Press. Reprinted by permission. *s* = standard deviations; X_1 = father's education; X_2 = father's occupation; X_3 = number of siblings; Y_1 = education; Y_2 = occupation; and Y_3 = income.

I selected this example because it was analyzed by various authors. Alwin and Hauser (1975) used it to illustrate the application of their approach to the calculation of indirect effects and effect coefficients in fully recursive models. Fox (1985) used it to illustrate his proposed approach to the calculation of specific indirect effects. Sobel (1986, 1987) used it to illustrate calculations of standard errors of indirect effects. I believe you will benefit from studying the aforementioned references as well as Bollen (1987, 1989) in connection with the following discussion.

Before I present a general approach for calculating specific indirect effects, I will use Figure 18.14 to illustrate the value of studying specific indirect effects as well as the implications of dif-

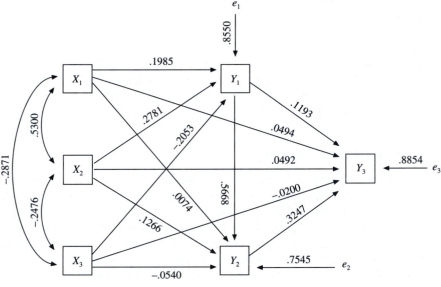

Figure 18.14

ferent definitions of such effects. I will do this by focusing on indirect effects of X_1 on Y_3. Examine Figure 18.14 and notice that, in addition to a direct effect, X_1 affects Y_3 indirectly as follows:

$$(1)\ X_1 \to Y_1 \to Y_3\ =\ (.1985)(.1193) \qquad\qquad =\ .0237$$

$$(2)\ X_1 \to Y_1 \to Y_2 \to Y_3\ =\ (.1985)(.5668)(.3247)\ =\ .0365$$

$$(3)\ X_1 \to Y_2 \to Y_3\ =\ (.0074)(.3247) \qquad\qquad =\ .0024$$

In the preceding calculations, I used the path coefficients I reported in Figure 18.14. The total indirect effect of X_1 on Y_3 is equal to the sum of the above three components: .0626. Recalling that these components are composed of products of standardized regression coefficients, it is clear that (3) is virtually zero—a potentially important finding that is obscured when only the total indirect effect is reported.

As I pointed out earlier, varying definitions of specific indirect effects were proposed. Bollen (1987), who reviewed several definitions, pointed out that according to one proposed by Fox (1985), specific indirect effects refer to "*all* paths coming into or going out of a particular variable" (Bollen, 1987, p. 52). He therefore named them "*inclusive specific effects*" (p. 52). According to this definition, the specific indirect effect of X_1 on Y_3 via Y_1 is equal to .0602 (.0237 + .0365). Thus, one would conclude that the total indirect effect of X_1 on Y_3 (.0626; see the preceding) is virtually all due to this specific indirect effect. Notice, however, that being composed of more than one element, inclusive specific effects are not sufficiently specific, so to speak. In the case under consideration, indirect effects (1) and (2), calculated in the preceding, are combined, thereby obscuring the sizes of each. According to a different definition of specific indirect effects proposed by Greene, which Bollen (1987) named "*exclusive specific effects*" (p. 51), the specific indirect effect of X_1 on Y_3 via Y_1 is limited to (1), that is, .0237. Clearly, different definitions of specific indirect effects may lead to different conclusions about the model being investigated.

In his review of several definitions of specific indirect effects, Bollen (1987) pointed out that they "share one limitation. They are oriented toward *variables* rather than *paths*" (p. 55). Bollen's recommendation that the study of specific indirect effects be path oriented has merit in being potentially less ambiguous than the variable-oriented approach. Further, adopting such an orientation would eliminate conflicting conclusions due to different definitions of specific indirect effects. The three compound paths I discussed above serve as a simple example of the virtue of such an orientation.

Calculations of specific indirect effects are relatively simple in the example under consideration. In more complex models, however, they may become unwieldy and, hence, error prone. Several authors, notably Greene (1977), Fox (1985), and Bollen (1987, 1989) proposed approaches to the calculation of specific indirect effects that do not rely on tracing paths between a given independent variable and a given dependent variable, as I did in the preceding. Before I introduce and apply a general approach to the calculation of specific indirect effects for the model of Figure 18.14, I will make several points.

1. The approaches proposed by the above-mentioned authors require the use of matrix algebra. If necessary, review relevant sections in Chapter 6 and Appendix A, particularly those that examine inversion, multiplication, and subtraction of matrices.
2. Although proposed approaches can be used for both recursive (one-way causation) and nonrecursive models, my presentation is limited to the former.
3. In the following presentation, I use Bollen's approach, though I do not use his SEM notation as I present such notation only later in this and the next chapter.
4. For illustrative purposes, I show how to calculate inclusive specific effects (see the preceding) with Bollen's approach. Note, however, that his is a general approach applicable to other definitions of specific indirect effects as well as to his recommended path-oriented

approach to specific indirect effects (as discussed earlier). I strongly recommend that you study Bollen's (1987) presentation.

5. As earlier, I use X's to identify exogenous variables and Y's to identify endogenous variables.

6. I use $\mathbf{D}_{yx}$ for the matrix of direct effects of exogenous variables on endogenous variables[9] and $\mathbf{D}_{yy}$ for the matrix of direct effects of endogenous variables on endogenous variables. It is, of course, possible to calculate the values in these two matrices by using matrix algebra. However, as I pointed out earlier, I calculated them by regressing in turn each endogenous variable on the variables affecting it. The β's I thus obtained are the indices of the direct effects, or the path coefficients.

7. I do not discuss the derivation of Bollen's approach, as my sole purpose is to show how its use facilitates the calculation of specific indirect effects in complex models.

For the data in Table 18.2 and the model depicted in Figure 18.14,

$$\mathbf{D}_{yy} = \begin{bmatrix} 0 & 0 & 0 \\ .5668 & 0 & 0 \\ .1193 & .3247 & 0 \end{bmatrix}$$

$$\mathbf{D}_{yx} = \begin{bmatrix} .1985 & .2781 & -.2053 \\ .0074 & .1266 & -.0540 \\ .0494 & .0492 & -.0200 \end{bmatrix}$$

I took the values for the above matrices from Figure 18.14. Included in $\mathbf{D}_{yx}$ are the direct effects of exogenous variables (columns) on endogenous variables (rows). The first row is composed of the direct effects of the three X's on Y_1: .1985 is the direct effect of X_1, .2781 is the direct effect of X_2, and −.2053 is the direct effect of X_3. The second and third rows consist of direct effects of exogenous variables on Y_2 and Y_3, respectively.

Included in $\mathbf{D}_{yy}$ are effects of endogenous variables on endogenous variables. Each row and column of such a matrix refers to one of the endogenous variables. The first row and column refer to Y_1, the second to Y_2, and so on. Thus, .5668 is the direct effect of Y_1 on Y_2, .1193 is the direct effect of Y_1 on Y_3, and .3247 is the direct effect of Y_2 on Y_3. Recall that the model under consideration is recursive. In such models, $\mathbf{D}_{yy}$ can be ordered so that only the elements below its principal diagonal can have nonzero values. (In nonrecursive models, this matrix is composed of some nonzero elements both above and below the diagonal.)

Using matrix algebra, total effects of X's on Y's are calculated as follows:[10]

$$\mathbf{T}_{yx} = (\mathbf{I} - \mathbf{D}_{yy})^{-1}\mathbf{D}_{yx} \tag{18.12}$$

where $\mathbf{T}_{yx}$ = total effects of X's (exogenous variables) on Y's (endogenous variables), and $\mathbf{I}$ = identity matrix whose dimensions are equal to those of $\mathbf{D}_{yy}$ (3 by 3, in the present example); I defined $\mathbf{D}_{yy}$ and $\mathbf{D}_{yx}$ in the preceding. The superscript −1 signifies the inverse of a matrix. In the present case, it refers to the inverse of the matrix resulting from the subtraction of $\mathbf{D}_{yy}$ from an identity matrix.

Total indirect effects of X's on Y's are calculated as follows:

$$\mathbf{I}_{yx} = \mathbf{T}_{yx} - \mathbf{D}_{yx} \tag{18.13}$$

---

[9]As I explained in Chapter 6 and in Appendix A, matrices are presented by bold uppercase letters, and vectors are presented by bold lowercase letters.

[10]See Bollen (1987) for the formulas I use. As I explained earlier, however, I do *not* use his notation.

where $\mathbf{I}_{yx}$ = total indirect effects of X's on Y's; $\mathbf{T}_{yx}$ = total effects of X's on Y's—see (18.12); and $\mathbf{D}_{yx}$ = direct effects of X's on Y's (see the preceding). Equation (18.13) is based on the notion that total effects are equal to the sum of direct and indirect effects (see earlier sections of this chapter).

Referring to the same model I analyze here, Bollen (1987) explains his approach thus:

> Suppose that we want to know the inclusive specific indirect effects of **x** [a vector of X's] on **y** [a vector of Y's] through y_1 (see Figure 3) [Bollen's p. 51, or my Figure 18.14]. These include all the paths that traverse y_1. The standard indirect effects with the original coefficient matrices provide the effects through y_1 and through the other variables in the model. If we can find the decomposition resulting if paths through y_1 are eliminated, we will know the decomposition of effects due *not* to y_1 but only to the remaining variables. Subtracting the second from the first gives only those specific indirect effects through y_1, the quantity desired. . . . To remove the influence of y_1, all the paths coming into or leaving y_1 are set to zero. . . . Recalculate the indirect effects with these modified matrices. . . . [S]ubtract the modified indirect effects from the original effects to obtain inclusive specific effects. (pp. 56–57)

I will calculate the inclusive specific effects that Bollen noted using PROC IML of SAS. To this end, I will set the elements in the first row of $\mathbf{D}_{yx}$ and the first column of $\mathbf{D}_{yy}$ to zeros and then carry out the calculations as Bollen described in the quotation. In the input, I will refer to the modified matrices as DYXR1 (row 1 set to zeros) and DYYC1 (column 1 set to zeros).

SAS

Input

```
TITLE 'TABLE 18.2. SPECIFIC INDIRECT EFFECTS';
TITLE2 'AS IN BOLLEN (1987, p. 56-57)';
PROC IML;
RESET PRINT;                              [print all results]
DYX={.1985     0.2781     -0.2053,        [direct effects: X's on Y's]
     .0074     0.1266     -0.0540,
     .0494     0.0492     -0.0200};
DYY={0         0          0,              [direct effects: Y's on Y's]
     .5668     0          0,
     .1193     .3247      0};
I=I(3);                                   [3 × 3 identity matrix]
TYX=INV(I-DYY)*DYX;                       [calculate total effects: X's on Y's]
IYX=TYX-DYX;                              [calculate total indirect effects: X's on Y's]
DYYC1=DYY;
DYYC1[,1]=0;                              [column 1 of DYY set to zeros]
DYXR1=DYX;
DYXR1[1,]=0;                              [row 1 of DYX set to zeros]
I1=INV(I-DYYC1)*DYXR1-DYXR1;
IY1=IYX-I1;                               [calculate inclusive specific indirect effects]
DIFF=IYX-IY1;                             [see commentary on the output]
```

Commentary

I remind you that the commentaries in italics are *not* part of the input file. I trust that they will suffice to give you an idea of the matrix operations. Of course, you should consult the SAS manual for explanations of IML commands.

Output

I	3 rows		3 cols	*[identity matrix]*
	1	0	0	
	0	1	0	
	0	0	1	

TYX   3 rows   3 cols   *[total effects: X's on Y's]*

	$[X_1]$	$[X_2]$	$[X_3]$	*[see (18.12)]*
$[Y_1]$	0.1985	0.2781	−0.2053	
$[Y_2]$	0.1199098	0.2842271	−0.170364	
$[Y_3]$	0.1120158	0.1746659	0.099809	

IYX   3 rows   3 cols   *[total indirect effects: X's on Y's]*

	$[X_1]$	$[X_2]$	$[X_3]$	*[see (18.13)]*
$[Y_1]$	0	0	0	
$[Y_2]$	0.1125098	0.1576271	−0.116364	
$[Y_3]$	0.0626158	0.1254659	−0.079809	

DYYC1   3 rows   3 cols   *[modified D_{yy}, zeros in column 1]*

	$[Y_1]$	$[Y_2]$	$[Y_3]$	
$[Y_1]$	0	0	0	
$[Y_2]$	0	0	0	
$[Y_3]$	0	0.3247	0	

DYXR1   3 rows   3 cols   *[modified D_{yx}, zeros in row 1]*

	$[X_1]$	$[X_2]$	$[X_3]$	
$[Y_1]$	0	0	0	
$[Y_2]$	0.0074	0.1266	−0.054	
$[Y_3]$	0.0494	0.0492	−0.02	

IY1   3 rows   3 cols   *[inclusive specific indirect effects:*

	$[X_1]$	$[X_2]$	$[X_3]$	*via Y_1]*
$[Y_1]$	0	0	0	
$[Y_2]$	0.1125098	0.1576271	−0.116364	
$[Y_3]$	0.060213	0.0843588	−0.062276	

DIFF   3 rows   3 cols   *[difference between total and*

				specific indirect effects]
	0	0	0	
	0	0	0	
	0.0024028	0.041107	−0.017534	

Commentary

The preceding are excerpts from the output. I believe that the comments in italics, along with the column and row labels that I inserted in each matrix, will clarify what is accomplished by each command. When examining this output, refer to the respective commands in the input file. In what follows, I comment only on the last two matrices.

As indicated by my comment, the penultimate matrix (IY1) consists of the inclusive specific indirect effects of the X's on the Y's via Y_1. It is this matrix that I sought through the matrix operations. I will now use relevant values from $\mathbf{D}_{yx}$ and $\mathbf{D}_{yy}$ (see the input or Figure 18.14) to show what each element of this matrix consists of).

	X_1	X_2	X_3
Y_2	.11251	.15763	−.11636
	(.1985)(.5668)	(.2781)(.5668)	(−.2053)(.5668)
Y_3	.06021	.08436	−.06228
	(.1985)(.1193)	(.2781)(.1193)	(−.2053)(.1193)
	+	+	+
	(.1985)(.5668)(.3247)	(.2781)(.5668)(.3247)	(−.2053)(.5668)(.3247)

Examine Figure 18.14 and notice that the X's have no indirect effects on Y_1. Hence, the zeros corresponding to this row in matrices of indirect effects in the preceding output.

Examine now the paths from the X's to Y_2 via Y_1 and notice that in each case there is one compound path, for example, $X_1 \rightarrow Y_1 \rightarrow Y_2$ (shown in my calculations, underneath the indirect effects as the product of two coefficients). These indirect effects, then, are equal to the total indirect effects (compare them with the first row of $\mathbf{I}_{yx}$ in the output).

Examine now the paths from the X's to Y_3 via Y_1 and notice that in each case there are two compound paths. For example, $X_1 \rightarrow Y_1 \rightarrow Y_3$; $X_1 \rightarrow Y_1 \rightarrow Y_2 \rightarrow Y_3$. See my calculation, where the first line underneath the specific indirect effect refers to the first compound path, and the second line refers to the second compound path (see my explanations and illustrative calculations in the section preceding the SAS Input).

Finally, I obtained the last matrix in the output (DIFF) by subtracting the matrix of specific indirect effects (the penultimate matrix) from the matrix of the total indirect effects $\mathbf{I}_{yx}$ (second matrix in the output). The values in the third row of this matrix represent the indirect effects of the X's on Y_3 *not* mediated by Y_1. In the present example, these are the indirect effects via Y_2. The indirect effect of the X's on Y_3 via Y_2 are

$$X_1 = (.0074)(.3247) = .0024$$

$$X_2 = (.1266)(.3247) = .0411$$

$$X_3 = (−.054)(.3247) = −.0175$$

Compare the preceding results with the values reported in the output for last matrix. As you can see, the indirect effect of X_1 on Y_3, via Y_2, is virtually zero. By contrast, about 30% of the total indirect effect of X_2 on Y_3 is mediated by Y_2.

PATH REGRESSION COEFFICIENTS

My presentation thus far has been limited to analyses of correlations. That is, all the variables were standardized (transformed to z scores). As I showed earlier, under such circumstances path coefficients are standardized regression coefficients (β's). Accordingly, advantages and disadvantages of β's, which I discussed in detail earlier in the text (especially in Chapter 10), apply also to path coefficients. Briefly, I pointed out that the major advantage of β's is that they are scale-free and can therefore be compared across different variables. But I also pointed out that the major drawback of β's is that they are population-specific and therefore should not be used for comparisons or generalizations across populations. It is for this and other reasons that various authors (e.g., Blalock, 1968; Duncan, 1975, Chapter 4; Namboodiri, Carter, & Blalock, 1975, pp. 468–475; Tukey, 1954; Turner & Stevens, 1959) argued against the use of β's in path analysis.[11] As Duncan (1975) put it:

> It would probably be salutary if research workers relinquished the habit of expressing variables in standard form. The main reason for this recommendation is that standardization tends to obscure the distinction between the structural coefficients of the model and the several variances and covariances that describe the joint distribution of the variables in a certain population. (p. 51)

In response to criticism of the use of β's in path analysis, Wright (1960) contended that the issue was not one of a choice between two alternative conceptions (i.e., between β's and *b*'s).

> It has always seemed to me that these should be looked upon as two aspects of a single theory corresponding to different modes of interpretation which, taken together, often give a deeper understanding of a situation than either can give by itself. (p. 189)

This is a reasonable position particularly in view of the fact that many measures used in behavioral research lack interpretable units. Needless to say, the ultimate solution lies in the development of measures that have meaningful units so that the *b*'s associated with them could be meaningfully interpreted. In the absence of such measures, one may be forced to resort to β's, despite their obvious shortcomings.[12] I would like to make a couple of recommendations about this topic.

One, both standardized and unstandardized coefficients should be reported so that a reader who wishes to interpret one or the other, or both, would be in a position to do so. When only path coefficients (β's) are reported, standard deviations for all the variables should be reported as well so that *b*'s could be calculated (see the following).

Two, although within a given causal model β's may be used to compare effects of different variables, *b*'s should be used when comparing models across different groups. Good discussions of model comparisons across groups, along with numerical examples, may be found in Schoenberg (1972) and Specht and Warren (1975).

To distinguish between standardized and unstandardized coefficients, Wright (1960) suggested that the former be called *path coefficients* and the latter *path regression coefficients*. Duncan (1975, p. 53) used the term *structural coefficients* for unstandardized coefficients. The specific label notwithstanding, in recursive models of the type I am considering in this chapter, path regression coefficients are partial regression coefficients (*b*'s). Consequently, they are calculated by the method of least squares I used repeatedly earlier in the text (e.g., Chapters 5 and 10). To illustrate calculations of path regression coefficients, I will reanalyze a couple of numerical examples from preceding sections.

---

[11]I return to this topic when I discuss tests of causal models.

[12]See Chapter 10 for a detailed discussion of this point.

Numerical Examples

To calculate path regression coefficients, either raw data or a correlation matrix *and* standard deviations are required. When a correlation matrix and standard deviations are used, they are converted to a covariance matrix, which is then used in the analysis. (This is done automatically when a correlation matrix and standard deviations are read as input into a regression program.) Each endogenous variable is regressed on the exogenous and endogenous variables that are hypothesized to affect it. The regression coefficients thus calculated are the path regression coefficients.

Alternatively, having calculated path coefficients, path regression coefficients can be calculated by applying a formula I introduced in Chapter 5—see (5.16)—which I repeat here:

$$b_j = \beta_j \frac{s_y}{s_j} \tag{18.14}$$

where b = unstandardized regression coefficient for variable j affecting variable y; β = standardized regression coefficient; and s_y and s_j = standard deviations of y and j, respectively. It is this approach that I will use here.

For my first example, I return to the four-variable model in Figure 18.12, which I repeat here as Figure 18.15. The path coefficients for this model, which I calculated earlier, are given in parentheses in Figure 18.15. To transform these coefficients into b's, standard deviations for the four variables are required. Assume that these are as follows:

$$SES = 2.10 \quad IQ = 15.00 \quad AM = 3.25 \quad GPA = 1.25$$

Using these standard deviations and the path coefficients reported in Figure 18.15, I apply (18.14).

$$b_{31.2} = .398 \frac{3.25}{2.10} = .6160$$

$$b_{32.1} = .041 \frac{3.25}{15.00} = .0089$$

$$b_{41.23} = .009 \frac{1.25}{2.10} = .0054$$

$$b_{42.13} = .501 \frac{1.25}{15.00} = .0417$$

$$b_{43.12} = .416 \frac{1.25}{3.25} = .1600$$

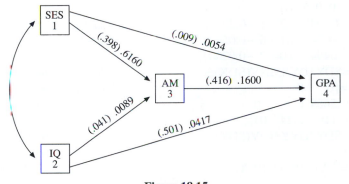

Figure 18.15

Path regression coefficients are interpreted as unstandardized regression coefficients (see Chapter 10, for detailed discussions of standardized and unstandardized coefficients). Thus, for example, the path regression coefficient from SES to AM (.6160) is interpreted as the expected change in AM associated with a unit change in SES, while partialing out the effect of IQ. The remaining path regression coefficients are similarly interpreted. As I noted earlier and in Chapter 10, meaningful interpretation of b's is predicated on using measures whose units can be interpreted meaningfully.

As with path coefficients, path regression coefficients refer to direct effects of one variable on another. Total, total indirect, and specific indirect effects are calculated in the manner I showed earlier. For example, the direct effect of SES on GPA is .0054, whereas its indirect effect, via AM, is .0986 [(.6160)(.1600)].

Matrix Approach

The matrix approach I introduced earlier for the calculation of total, total indirect, and specific indirect effects is applicable also when using path regression coefficients. As I will show, the matrix approach obviates the need of repeated application of (18.14) to convert β's to b's. Earlier, I used the matrix approach to calculate various effects using path coefficients from Figure 18.14 (the correlation matrix from Table 18.2). Here, I will use those path coefficients along with the standard deviations reported in Table 18.2 to calculate path regression coefficients and effects analogous to those I calculated earlier, based on the path coefficients.

SAS

Input

```
TITLE 'TABLE 18.2. PATH REGRESSION COEFFICIENTS, ETC.';
PROC IML;
RESET PRINT;                          [print all results]
SDX={3.72 0 0,                        [standard deviations of X's; see commentary]
     0 23.14 0,
     0 0 2.88};
SDY={3.20 0 0,                        [standard deviations of Y's; see commentary]
     0 24.71 0,
     0 0 5.36};
DYX={.1985 0.2781 −0.2053,            [direct effects: X's on Y's;
     .0074 0.1266 −0.0540,            see Figure 18.14]
     .0494 0.0492 −0.0200};
PYX=SDY*DYX*INV(SDX);                 [calculate path regressions: X's on Y's]
DYY={0    0    0,                     [direct effects: Y's on Y's;
     .5668 0    0,                    see Figure 18.14]
     .1193 .3247 0};
PYY=SDY*DYY*INV(SDY);                 [calculate path regressions: Y's on Y's]
I=I(3);                              [3 × 3 identity matrix]
TYX=INV(I-PYY)*PYX;                   [calculate total effects: X's on Y's]
```

IYX=TYX-PYX;   *[calculate total indirect effects: X's on Y's]*
DYYC1=PYY;
DYYC1[,1]=0;   *[column 1 of PYY set to zeros]*
DYXR1=PYX;
DYXR1[1,]=0;   *[row 1 of PYX set to zeros]*
I1=INV(I-DYYC1)*DYXR1-DYXR1;
IY1=IYX-I1;   *[calculate inclusive specific indirect effects]*

Commentary

I remind you that italicized comments are *not* part of the input or the output given in the following.

Notice that I placed the standard deviations of X's and Y's (SDX and SDY) in two diagonal matrices—that is, square matrices whose off-diagonal elements are zeros (see Appendix A).

I convert the path coefficients (β's) of X's on Y's to b's by premultiplying the matrix of these β's (DYX) by the matrix of the standard deviations of the Y's (SDY), and postmultiplying the resulting matrix by the inverse of the matrix of the standard deviations of the X's (SDX; see the PYX statement in the input). Similarly, I convert the β's of Y's on Y's to b's by premultiplying the matrix of these β's (DYY) by SDY and postmultiplying the resulting matrix by the inverse of SDY (see the PYY statement in the input). These matrix operations yield the same results as repeated applications of (18.14). You may wish to verify this by applying (18.14) to some of the β's.

Except for some name changes (e.g., PYX instead of DYX), the rest of the input statements are the same as those I used in the earlier application of the matrix approach.

Output

PYX   3 rows   3 cols   *[path regression coefficients]*

	[X₁]	*[X₂]*	*[X₃]*
[Y₁]	0.1707527	0.0384581	−0.228111
[Y₂]	0.0491543	0.1351895	−0.463313
[Y₃]	0.0711785	0.0113964	−0.037222

PYY   3 rows   3 cols   *[path regression coefficients]*

	[Y₁]	*[Y₂]*	*[Y₃]*
[Y₁]	0	0	0
[Y₂]	4.3767588	0	0
[Y₃]	0.1998275	0.0704327	0

TYX   3 rows   3 cols   *[total effects: X's on Y's]*
                                         [see (18.12)]

	[X₁]	*[X₂]*	*[X₃]*
[Y₁]	0.1707527	0.0384581	−0.228111
[Y₂]	0.7964976	0.3035113	−1.4617
[Y₃]	0.1613991	0.0404585	−0.185757

IYX   3 rows   3 cols   *[total indirect effects: X's on Y's]*
        [X₁]   *[X₂]*   *[X₃]*   *[see (18.13)]*

	$[X_1]$	$[X_2]$	$[X_3]$
$[Y_1]$	0	0	0
$[Y_2]$	0.7473433	0.1683217	−0.998387
$[Y_3]$	0.0902206	0.0290621	−0.148534

IY1   3 rows   3 cols   *[inclusive specific indirect effect:*
        [X₁]   *[X₂]*   *[X₃]*   *via Y₁]*

	$[X_1]$	$[X_2]$	$[X_3]$
$[Y_1]$	0	0	0
$[Y_2]$	0.7473433	0.1683217	−0.998387
$[Y_3]$	0.0867585	0.0195403	−0.115902

Commentary

Interpretations of these results parallel those of my earlier analysis in which I used path coefficients, except that the size of any given effect (direct or indirect) is affected by the units of the measures used. Moreover, the meaning of results depends very much on the meaning of the units in which the variables are measured. To give you a glimpse at the complexities that arise, I will use the following indirect effect $X_1 \rightarrow Y_1 \rightarrow Y_2 \rightarrow Y_3$ as an example. Numerically, it is simple to determine that it is $[(.1707527)(4.3767588)(.0704327)] = .0526374$. Of course, one can declaim glibly that it is the effect of father's education on son's income via son's education and occupation. But what does this mean substantively? What does it mean to say that it is the product of the effect of father's education on son's education by the effect of son's education on son's occupation by the effect of the latter on son's income? This does not just sound complicated, it is extremely complicated. At this stage, I will not elaborate further. My aim here was to alert you that hard thinking is called for when interpreting results of SEM. As I discuss in later sections and in Chapter 19, this depends largely on the theoretical rationale underlying model specification.

Decomposition of Covariances

Earlier, I showed how to use path coefficients to decompose correlations among variables in a causal model. I also showed how to use path coefficients from an overidentified model in an attempt to reproduce the correlation matrix. These approaches may be similarly used with path regression coefficients, except that it is the covariances among the variables that are decomposed or reproduced. Detailed descriptions of applications of these procedures in models with path regression coefficients are given in Duncan (1975, Chapter 4) and in Fox (1980).

TESTING CAUSAL MODELS

Broadly speaking, tests of a causal model are aimed at ascertaining whether it is consistent with the pattern of relations among the variables under consideration. Both global tests (of the model as a whole) and specific tests (of specific elements of the model) are available. Before turning to these topics, though, I comment briefly on the issue of identification.

Identification

Identification is a complex topic that has received extensive treatments, particularly from econometricians (e.g., Fisher, 1966; Goldberger, 1991, Chapter 33; Johnston, 1972, pp. 352–372; Koopmans, 1949; for simpler good discussions in the context of social research see Duncan, 1975, Chapters 6 and 7; Heise, 1975, Chapter 5; Namboodiri, Carter, & Blalock, 1975, Chapters 11 and 12; O'Brien, 1994). Here, I attempt a brief intuitive overview of this topic.

Causal models may be just (or exactly) identified, overidentified, or underidentified. As I pointed out in the preceding section, unique parameter estimates can be obtained in a just-identified model. It is, however, necessary to recognize that a model is just identified because of assumptions, or restrictions, imposed by the researcher. Thus, for example, a fully recursive model is just identified as a result of (1) conceiving the causal flow as unidirectional, that is, ruling out reciprocal causation or feedback among the variables; (2) specifying direct paths from each variable to variables conceived as following it in the causal flow; (3) assuming that each residual term is not correlated with variables preceding it in the model (see earlier discussion of this point).

An overidentified model, as the name implies, consists of more equations than are necessary for parameter estimation. Consequently, more than one estimate may be obtained for certain parameters. Overidentification, too, is a consequence of restrictions, or constraints, imposed by the researcher on some elements of the causal model. Such constraints reflect not statistical assumptions but the researcher's hypotheses about the causal model. One of the most common overidentifying constraints is the postulation that a path coefficient(s) is equal to zero. In other words, it is hypothesized that a variable has no direct effect on a given endogenous variable, although it may affect it indirectly (see, for example, Figures 18.9 and 18.11). Another example of a constraint is the setting of two path coefficients to be equal to each other.

An underidentified model is one that contains insufficient information for a determinate solution of parameter estimates. Stated differently, in an underidentified model an infinite number of solutions may be obtained. This is why some authors (e.g., Namboodiri, Carter, & Blalock, 1975, p. 503) refer to underidentified models as being "hopeless." "Underidentification is a theoretical rather than a statistical problem" (Heise, 1975, p. 152) that the researcher can attempt to resolve by imposing appropriate constraints that will render the model just identified or overidentified. Examples of underidentification may be found in factor analytic models, which with given restrictions become identifiable (see, for example, Duncan, 1972; Turner & Stevens, 1959). Finally, it is more useful to consider the question of identification with reference to parameter estimation than to the model as a whole. The reason is that in a given model some parameters may be overidentified, whereas others may be underidentified (see Bielby & Hauser, 1977, p. 149).

As I will discuss, the validity of a causal model is assessed in light of its efficacy to reproduce, or closely approximate, the covariance (or correlation) matrix of the variables under study. In preceding sections I showed how path coefficients may be used to reproduce the correlation matrix. Also, I pointed out that when the model is just identified, the correlation (or covariance) matrix may be reproduced no matter how untenable or unreasonable the model is on logical and/or theoretical grounds. In other words, a just-identified model may always be shown to fit the data perfectly. Consequently, though elements of a just-identified model can be tested, the model as a whole is not testable.

It is important to recognize that when testing a model, or some of its components, it is assumed to be correctly specified. Earlier in the text (especially in Chapter 10), I discussed model specification in the context of regression analysis. Among other things, I discussed specification errors and pointed out that probably the gravest and most intractable is omission of relevant variables. The same is true with even greater force for the type of models I discuss in this and the next chapter.

In the next chapter, I discuss model testing in greater detail. For present purposes it would suffice to point out that two broad approaches are taken when analyzing models of the kind I present in this chapter: (1) theory trimming and (2) tests of overidentified models. Later, I discuss the second approach. Here, I discuss briefly the first approach.

Theory Trimming or Model Revision

Some researchers have suggested (e.g., Duncan, 1975, p. 49; Heise, 1969) that, having estimated parameters of a just-identified model, path coefficients that do not meet criteria of statistical significance and/or meaningfulness be deleted from the model—hence the name *theory trimming* (Heise, 1969) to characterize this approach. More recently, this approach has been characterized as model revision or respecification. I discuss criteria for deletion of paths based on statistical tests of significance and meaningfulness, beginning with the former.

Statistical Tests.   Recall that in recursive models the path coefficients are β's and path regression coefficients are b's. Therefore, testing a given β (or b) is tantamount to testing the path (or path regression) coefficient corresponding to it. Earlier in this book (e.g., Chapters 5 and 10), I showed how each b can be tested for significance, using a t or an F ratio. Following the theory trimming approach, path coefficients whose t ratios are smaller than the tabled t at a prespecified level of significance are deleted.

In earlier chapters (see, in particular, Chapter 10), I pointed out that when more than one b in a given equation is statistically not significant, the deletion of one of them from the equation may lead not only to changes in the magnitudes of the remaining b's but also to changes in the results of their tests of statistical significance (see discussions and illustrations in Chapter 10). When one wishes to test simultaneously more than one path coefficient in a given equation, the F test I introduced early in the book—see (5.27) and the discussion related to it—can be used.

Thus far, I discussed deletion of path coefficients from within a single regression equation. But, as I illustrated earlier, in a multistage causal model more than one regression equation is calculated. Testing path coefficients from different stages of a model is tantamount to testing b's in more than one regression equation based on the same data.

Clearly, tests of the significance of path coefficients do not constitute a test of the model as a whole. It is possible, for example, for tests of given path coefficients in separate equations to indicate that some or all of them are statistically not significant (hence, that they may be deleted), and yet an overall test of the model may be statistically significant, leading to the conclusion that it does not fit the data (see overall tests of models, later in this chapter).

Meaningfulness.   Turning now to the criterion of meaningfulness, recall that when the sample size is relatively large, even substantively meaningless regression coefficients may be statistically significant. Consequently, many researchers prefer to use a criterion of meaningfulness for the deletion of paths, even when their coefficients are statistically significant. As I pointed out in earlier chapters, meaningfulness depends, among other things, on the specific area studied, economic considerations, and the consequences of decisions made based on the results. In the absence of guidelines, researchers tend to choose an arbitrary criterion of meaningfulness for the deletion of path coefficients (e.g., those smaller than .05). As questionable as such a decision may be with respect to path coefficients (i.e., standardized coefficient), a choice of an arbitrary criterion for the meaningfulness of path regression coefficients is obviously even more so.

The theory trimming approach suffers from the very serious shortcoming of being applied post hoc (see Chapter 11 for a discussion of post hoc hypothesis testing and some of its short-comings). As Peirce (1932) pointed out, "if we look over the phenomena to find agreement with theory, it is a mere question of ingenuity and industry how many we shall find" (p. 496; see also Merton, 1968, pp. 147–149, for a good discussion and examples of post hoc theorizing). McPherson (1976) argued cogently against theory trimming. Without going into the details of his specific points, I will note that his major theme is that "the data cannot tell the researcher which hypothesis to test; at best the data may tell when a particular hypothesis is supported or unsupported, when *a priori* grounds exist for testing it" (p. 99).

COMPUTER PROGRAMS

In this and the next chapter, I will use the two most comprehensive and most popular computer programs for the analysis of SEM: LISREL (Jöreskog & Sörbom, 1989, 1993a, 1993b)[13] and EQS (Bentler, 1992a; Bentler & Wu, 1993).[14] First, I introduce LISREL and use it to analyze a couple of examples I analyzed earlier. I then do the same for EQS. In the next chapter I will use either or both programs.[15]

LISREL: AN ORIENTATION

Following is an excerpt from my introduction to LISREL (LInear Structural RELations) version IV in the second edition of this book:

> Users of LISREL IV encounter difficulties in the formulation of the equations to represent their models and in translating the equations into appropriate computer instructions. Commenting on such difficulties, a colleague said: "My students climb the wall!" It is not at all surprising that Kenny (1979), who provides a very good introduction to LISREL, states: "When I run LISREL I presume I have made an error. I check and recheck my results" (p. 183). (p. 638)

Here is some of what Schmelkin and I (Pedhazur & Schmelkin, 1991) said when we introduced LISREL 7:

> LISREL requires a basic understanding of matrices, as it is in this form that the model to be tested has to be specified. . . . It will be necessary to present the matrices used in LISREL on an expository level

---

[13]LISREL is a registered trademark of Scientific Software, Inc., whom I would like to thank for furnishing me with a review copy of this program. For information about LISREL and related programs, contact Scientific Software, 1525 East 53rd Street, Suite 530, Chicago, IL 60615-4530. Telephone: (800) 247-6113.

[14]EQS is a registered trademark of BMDP Statistical Software, Inc., whom I would like to thank for furnishing me with a review copy of this program. For information about EQS, contact BMDP, 12121 Wilshire Boulevard, Suite 300, Los Angeles, CA 90025. Telephone: (310) 207-8800.

[15]Among other programs for the analysis of SEM are PROC CALIS of SAS (SAS Inc., 1990a, Vol. 1) and AMOS (Arbuckle, 1991, 1992). For information about AMOS contact James Arbuckle, Psychology Department, Temple University, Philadelphia, PA 19122. Telephone: (215)204-1572. For a review of AMOS, see Rigdon (1994b). For a comparative review of AMOS, EQS, and LISREL for Windows, see Hox (1995).

to help you understand the input and output for this program. Further, because LISREL uses Greek notation, you will have to become familiar with some letters of the Greek alphabet. (p. 633)

With the release of Version 8, which I will be using,[16] matters have changed drastically. The major change is the introduction of the SIMPLIS command language (Jöreskog & Sörbom, 1993a), which is truly simple to use. The LISREL command language of earlier versions was retained in Version 8. Either command language can be used, "but the two languages cannot be mixed in the same input file" (Jöreskog & Sörbom, 1993a, p. ii). "Beginning users of LISREL and users who often make mistakes when they specify the LISREL model will benefit greatly from using the SIMPLIS language, as this is much easier to learn and reduces the possibilities for mistakes to a minimum" (Jöreskog & Sörbom, 1993a, p. ii). As I strongly agree with the preceding statement, I will use only the SIMPLIS command language in this and the next chapter. For an introduction to the LISREL command language, see Pedhazur and Schmelkin (1991, Chapters 23 and 24). For detailed presentations of the LISREL command language, see Jöreskog and Sörbom (1989).

From the perspective of application, SIMPLIS and LISREL command languages differ broadly in two ways:

1. LISREL command language contains some options not available in SIMPLIS command language (see Jöreskog & Sörbom, 1993a, p. 118). Most users will probably not need these options.
2. LISREL command language has additional output options (e.g., standardized solution, decomposition of effects) not available in SIMPLIS command language. However, as I will show, LISREL output can be obtained when using SIMPLIS command language input.

In sum, using SIMPLIS command language, you can get practically everything that is available through LISREL command language. Yet, you will need to become familiar with LISREL format and notation, at least with its output, as it is used in most of the literature on this topic. "Understanding the LISREL output may also serve as a first step to learn the LISREL input language" (Jöreskog & Sörbom, 1993a, p. 133). With this in mind, I will comment, from time to time, on LISREL notation and output.

LISREL can be executed either from a DOS prompt or from Windows. In both instances, the program runs under DOS. Some menus in the Windows interface may be helpful, particularly in the initial stages of learning to run this program. The input files I present can be run from either a DOS prompt or from Windows.

A very versatile and easy-to-use facility for drawing path diagrams, as well for model revision followed by reestimation (introduced in LISREL 8), is explained in detail in Jöreskog and Sörbom (1993a, Chapter 3). Again, all the facilities of path diagrams are available whether the program is executed from DOS or Windows. In Chapter 19, I give several path diagrams generated through LISREL.

Of seven estimation procedures available in LISREL (Jöreskog & Sörbom, 1993a, p. 116), I use only the default: maximum likelihood (ML). In Chapter 17, I made a general comment about ML and gave references to more formal and detailed treatments. A ML solution is arrived at through an iterative procedure that requires starting values. "Since these starting values are

---

[16]Specifically, I am using version 8.03 for the PC. In the presentations that follow I will refrain from using the version number.

normally generated by LISREL 8, for most problems there is no need for users to specify starting values" (Jöreskog & Sörbom, 1993a, p. 174).

In what follows, I will analyze first the same just-identified model I analyzed earlier through multiple regression analysis. I hope that your familiarity with the example will facilitate your learning about SIMPLIS and its output. Pursuant to the analysis of the just-identified model, I will analyze the overidentified model, which I analyzed earlier. In the context of commentaries on the output from this analysis, I will introduce elementary ideas about testing models and evaluating their fit. I will then introduce EQS and apply it to the same examples I analyzed through LISREL.

A Just-Identified Model

Earlier, I used the causal model depicted in Figure 18.12 to analyze the data in Table 18.1. Briefly, I treated socioeconomic status (SES) and intelligence (IQ) as two correlated exogenous variables. I hypothesized that SES and IQ affect achievement motivation (AM), and that SES, IQ, and AM affect achievement as measured by grade-point average (GPA). Following is a SIMPLIS input file for the LISREL analysis of this model.[17]

LISREL

Input

! TABLE 18.1 AND FIGURE 18.12. SIMPLIS OUTPUT.
! INPUT CORRELATION MATRIX & STANDARD DEV. FREE FORMAT.
OBSERVED VARIABLES: SES IQ AM GPA
CORRELATION MATRIX:
1.00
.30 1.00
.41   .16 1.00
.33   .57   .50 1.00
STANDARD DEVIATIONS:
2.10 15.00 3.25 1.25
SAMPLE SIZE 300
EQUATIONS
AM = SES IQ
GPA = SES IQ AM
NUMBER OF DECIMALS = 3
PATH DIAGRAM
END OF PROBLEM
! TABLE 18.1 AND FIGURE 18.12. LISREL OUTPUT.
OBSERVED VARIABLES: SES IQ AM GPA
SAMPLE SIZE 300
EQUATIONS

---

[17]As I stated earlier, I use SIMPLIS for all the input files in this book. Therefore, in subsequent runs I will refrain from stating this.

AM = SES IQ
GPA = SES IQ AM
NUMBER OF DECIMALS = 3
LISREL OUTPUT: SS EF
END OF PROBLEM

Commentary

For detailed explanations of SIMPLIS input files, see Jöreskog and Sörbom (1993a, Chapter 6). In what follows, I comment briefly on the preceding input file.

Both uppercase and lowercase letters can be used in LISREL. Note, however, that "labels are case sensitive; upper case or lower case can be used without restriction but one must use the same name to refer to the same variable each time" (Jöreskog & Sörbom, 1993a, p. 164). Following my practice in running other programs, I use uppercase letters only.

Although a title line(s) is not required, the advantage of using one is obvious. Use detailed titles so that you may see at a glance what your analysis was about. The program reads multiple lines as part of the title until it encounters "a physical line beginning with the words Observed Variables or Labels, which is the first command line in a SIMPLIS input file" (Jöreskog & Sörbom, 1993a, p. 162). To avoid conflict with command lines, "begin every title line with !" (Jöreskog & Sörbom, 1993a, p. 163).

Except for references to source of data and the model (e.g., Table 18.1 and Figure 18.12) I will use title lines to alert you to specific issues. Here I use them to tell you about the (1) output format (SIMPLIS in the first analysis, LISREL in the second; see the title for the second problem, after the first END OF PROBLEM line); (2) type of input I am using (summary data in the form of a correlation matrix and standard deviations); (3) input format (free). Other forms of data (e.g., raw data) and other input formats (e.g., fixed) can be used (Jöreskog & Sörbom, 1993a, pp. 165–170).

The data can be part of the input file, as in the preceding, or in an external file. An external file is particularly recommended for raw data.

"After the title lines, if any, a header line must follow with the words Observed Variables or Labels. The reason for the qualification Observed is that LISREL deals also with variables that are unobserved, or so-called latent variables, whose names must also be defined" (Jöreskog & Sörbom, 1993a, p. 163). I introduce latent variables in the next chapter.

The header EQUATIONS (RELATIONSHIPS, RELATIONS) is optional. Following that, the model equations are stated, where the dependent variable is placed to the left of the equal sign, and the independent variables are placed to the right of the equal sign. "The variable names are separated by spaces or + signs" (Jöreskog & Sörbom, 1993a, p. 171). Alternatively, relations (equations) can be specified in the form of paths (Jöreskog & Sörbom, 1993a, e.g., pp. 9 and 172).

For a description of options, see Jöreskog and Sörbom (1993a, pp. 178–180). "Each option can either be spelled out directly on a separate line or be put as a two-character keyword on an options line" (Jöreskog & Sörbom, 1993a, p. 178). As you can see, I use here the first approach, specifying that output be reported to three decimal places (default is two). In a later run, I use the second approach to specify options.

END OF PROBLEM. "This is optional but recommended, especially when several problems are stacked together in the same input file" (Jöreskog & Sörbom, 1993a, p. 184). Contrary to the preceding statement, the END OF PROBLEM line is *not* optional when running stacked problems. I found this out when I, inadvertently, omitted this line. Not only was the run aborted but also the program gave the following diagnostics, which will, surely, baffle many a user:

W_A_R_N_I_N_G: Matrix to be analyzed is not positive definite
F_A_T_A_L   E_R_R_O_R: Matrix to be analyzed is not positive definite.

The previous input is an example of stacked problems, which I used to generate both types of output (SIMPLIS and LISREL). The default output (SIMPLIS) will be printed for the first run. In the second run, I called for LISREL output (see the penultimate line) and specified two options: SS = Print standardized solution and EF = Print total and indirect effects, their standard errors, and *t*-values (Jöreskog & Sörbom, 1993a, p. 184).

Finally, I will point out that (1) when the same data are used in stacked problems, it is not necessary to repeat them; (2) the control statements for the two problems are identical, except that the second includes also a LISREL OUTPUT line.

Running LISREL

I named the input file T181.SPL. At the DOS prompt, I typed:
LISREL8E T181.SPL T181.OUT

The preceding will be executed from any working directory, as long as the directory in which the program resides is on the path. The "E" stands for the DOS EXTENDER version. If you type only LISREL8E, you will be prompted for the names of input and output files.

Following Jöreskog and Sörbom, I use SPL as an extension for input files containing SIMPLIS command language. For convenience, I created the following batch file so that all I have to type is LIS and the name of the input file (without the extension).

LIS.BAT (batch file name):
LISREL8E %1.SPL %1.OUT

Output

COVARIANCE MATRIX TO BE ANALYZED

	AM	GPA	SES	IQ
	--------	--------	--------	--------
AM	10.563			
GPA	2.031	1.563		
SES	2.798	0.866	4.410	
IQ	7.800	10.687	9.450	225.000

Commentary

Using the correlation matrix and the standard deviations the program generates the covariance matrix, whose diagonal elements are variances and off-diagonal elements are covariances. For example, the variance of AM (10.563) is the square of its standard deviation (3.25²). The same is true for the other variances. The covariance between any two variables is equal to the product of the correlation between them and their respective standard deviations. For example, the covariance between AM and GPA is equal to (.50)(3.25)(1.25) = (2.031). The same is true for the other covariances.

Notice that the variables in the covariance matrix are *not* listed in the order in which I read them in. The reason is that LISREL requires that the variables be ordered according to the causal model, beginning with the endogenous variables. In the model under consideration, AM and GPA are endogenous, and the former affects the latter. The variables are reordered accordingly. When SIMPLIS input is used the reordering is done automatically, as in the preceding. When LISREL input is used, the data have to be entered in the requisite order or reordered through the SE Line (Jöreskog & Sörbom, 1989, p. 62). Here, then, is an example of the simpler input format used in SIMPLIS.

Output

LISREL ESTIMATES (MAXIMUM LIKELIHOOD)

| *[SIMPLIS output. Path regressions]* | *[LISREL output]* |

[LISREL output]

STANDARDIZED SOLUTION

BETA

AM = 0.616*SES + 0.00881*IQ,
   (0.0858)   (0.0120)
   7.177   0.734
  Errorvar.= 8.771, R^2 = 0.170
      (0.720)
      12.186

	AM	GPA
	--------	--------
AM	– –	– –
GPA	0.416	– –

GAMMA

GPA = 0.160*AM + 0.00547*SES + 0.0417*IQ,
   (0.0174)   (0.0278)   (0.00360)
   9.209   0.197   11.589
  Errorvar.= 0.787, R^2 = 0.496
      (0.0646)
      12.186

	SES	IQ
	--------	--------
AM	0.398	0.041
GPA	0.009	0.501

Commentary

As indicated by the italicized comments, which are *not* part of the output, the excerpt on the left is from SIMPLIS output, whereas that on the right is from LISREL output. For ease of examination, I placed the two excerpts alongside each other. *The parameter estimates from the SIMPLIS output are unstandardized coefficients (i.e., path regression coefficients) whereas those from the LISREL output are standardized (i.e., path coefficients). LISREL output includes also an unstandardized solution, which I did not reproduce as it is identical to the SIMPLIS output, except that it is printed in matrix format.*

Compare the values from the two outputs with those I calculated in earlier sections. The easiest way to do this it by examining the values in Figure 18.15, where I inserted both path regressions and path coefficients. I will now make several points about the two types of output.

First, SIMPLIS output is reported as equations, each of which includes all the variables (exogenous and endogenous) affecting a given endogenous variable. LISREL output, on the other hand, is reported as matrices, each consisting of different kinds of information (see the next point).

Second, in LISREL output, effects of endogenous variables on endogenous variables are reported in the BETA (B) matrix. In the present example, this matrix consists of only one value (.416)—the effect of AM on GPA. The effects of exogenous variables (columns) on endogenous variables (rows) are reported in the GAMMA (Γ) matrix. For the present example, the first row is composed of effects of SES and IQ on AM (.398 and .041, respectively), whereas the second row is composed of effects of the same exogenous variables on GPA (.009 and .501, respectively). Compare the values in these two matrices with the path coefficients I calculated earlier.

Third, examine the SIMPLIS output and notice the two values under each parameter estimate. The value in parenthesis is the standard error of the parameter estimate. Dividing the parameter estimate by its standard error yields a *t*-value, which is the value reported under the standard error. For instance, 7.177 is the *t*-value for the test of the coefficient for SES. Examine now the LISREL output and notice the absence of standard errors and *t* ratios. The reason is that standard errors of standardized parameters may, under certain circumstances, be incorrect (Bollen, 1989; Cudeck, 1989; Jöreskog & Sörbom, 1989, p. 47). Standard errors and *t*-values *are* reported in the LISREL matrices of unstandardized coefficients (not reproduced in the output).

Fourth, in SIMPLIS output, the residual or error variance (Errorvar.) is reported for each dependent variable. For example, the error variance of AM is 8.771. Dividing the error variance by the variance of the dependent variable yields the proportion of its variance due to residuals or error. For example, for AM: $8.771/10.563 = .830$, and $1 - .830 = .170$ is R^2 of AM with SES and IQ (see output, following Errorvar.). In LISREL output, residual variances are given in the PSI (Ψ) matrix, following which the squared multiple correlations are reported.

Output

GOODNESS OF FIT STATISTICS

CHI-SQUARE WITH 0 DEGREE OF FREEDOM $= 0.0$ ($P = 1.000$)

The Model is Saturated, the Fit is Perfect !

Commentary

As I pointed out earlier in this chapter, a just-identified (saturated) model fits the data perfectly. I discuss the CHI-SQUARE test in my commentary on the output for the analysis of the overidentified model.

Output

[LISREL output]

TOTAL AND INDIRECT EFFECTS				STANDARDIZED TOTAL AND INDIRECT EFFECTS		
TOTAL EFFECTS OF X ON Y				STANDARDIZED TOTAL EFFECTS OF X ON Y		
	SES	IQ			SES	IQ
	---------	---------			--------	--------
AM	0.616	0.009		AM	0.398	0.041
	(0.086)	(0.012)		GPA	0.175	0.518
	7.177	0.734				

GPA	0.104	0.043
	(0.029)	(0.004)
	3.570	10.576

INDIRECT EFFECTS OF X ON Y

	SES	IQ
	---------	---------
AM	– –	– –
GPA	0.099	0.001
	(0.017)	(0.002)
	5.661	0.731

STANDARDIZED INDIRECT EFFECTS OF X ON Y

	SES	IQ
	--------	--------
AM	– –	– –
GPA	0.166	0.017

TOTAL EFFECTS OF Y ON Y

	AM	GPA
	---------	---------
AM	– –	– –
GPA	0.160	– –
	(0.017)	
	9.209	

STANDARDIZED TOTAL EFFECTS OF Y ON Y

	AM	GPA
	--------	--------
AM	– –	– –
GPA	0.416	– –

Commentary

As I pointed out earlier, decomposition of effects (direct and indirect) is *not* available in SIMPLIS output. To get this information in LISREL output, specify EF on the LISREL OUTPUT line (see input for second problem). For ease of comparisons, I placed the results of the unstandardized solution (left segment) and the standardized solution (right segment) alongside each other. As in the earlier excerpt of output, only unstandardized parameter estimates have standard errors and *t*-values attached to them.

Recall that the total effect is equal to the direct plus the sum of indirect effects of an independent variable on a dependent variable. Compare these results with those I calculated earlier in this chapter.

When I distinguished between total and specific indirect effects earlier in this chapter, I pointed out that LISREL reports only the former. I showed earlier how to calculate specific indirect effects through matrix operations.

An Overidentified Model

Earlier, I used the model depicted in Figure 18.13 and the data in Table 18.1 to illustrate the analysis of an overidentified model. I now carry out the same analysis through LISREL.

LISREL

Input

! TABLE 18.1 AND FIGURE 18.13. SIMPLIS OUTPUT.
! OVERIDENTIFIED MODEL.

. . . .

EQUATIONS
AM = SES
GPA = IQ AM
OPTIONS: ND=3 RS

. . . .

! TABLE 18.1 AND FIGURE 18.13. LISREL OUTPUT.
! OVERIDENTIFIED MODEL.

. . . .

EQUATIONS
AM = SES
GPA = IQ AM
OPTIONS: ND=3
LISREL OUTPUT: SS EF RS

. . . .

Commentary

Dots indicate omitted lines that are identical to those of the input file for the just-identified model given earlier. You can run these two problems together with the two for the just-identified model. If you do this, the data need to be included only for the first problem. As in the case of the just-identified model, I use the second run (LISREL output) to get a standardized solution, which is not available in SIMPLIS output (for an explanation, see my commentary on the analysis of the just-identified model, presented earlier in this section).

In my commentary on the earlier run, I pointed out that there are two approaches for specifying options in SIMPLIS: (1) placing each option on a separate line or (2) placing keywords on an option line. Earlier, I used the first approach. Here I use the second.

Examine first the OPTIONS line in the first excerpt of input (the one in which SIMPLIS OUTPUT is specified in the title), and note that I specified two options:

ND=3 calls for printing output to three decimal places.

RS specifies that all residuals be printed. By default, residuals are printed only in summary form (Jöreskog & Sörbom, 1993a, p. 179).

Examine now the second excerpt of input and note that, unlike the first excerpt, I specified only ND=3 on the OPTIONS line. I omitted RS for two reasons. One is obvious: to avoid redundant output. The other reason is to alert you that it is also possible to specify RS on the LISREL OUTPUT line. *Note, however, that although this is shown in an example on p. 144 of Jöreskog and Sörbom (1993a), it is not listed among "all the keywords"* [italics added] *(Jöreskog &*

Sörbom, 1993a. p. 184) for the LISREL OUTPUT line. *Further, contrary to the statement that "MR [is] Equivalent to RS and VA"* [italics added] (Jöreskog & Sörbom, 1993a, p. 184), *residuals in summary form are printed when MR is specified.*

Output

| [SIMPLIS output. Path regressions] | [LISREL output] |
| LISREL ESTIMATES (MAXIMUM LIKELIHOOD) | STANDARDIZED SOLUTION |

AM = 0.635*SES,
   (0.0819)
    7.747
  Errorvar.= 8.787, R^2 = 0.168
     (0.721)
     12.186

GPA = 0.161*AM + 0.0419*IQ,
   (0.0160)   (0.00346)
   10.111   12.120
  Errorvar.= 0.787, R^2 = 0.488
     (0.0646)
     12.186

BETA

	AM	GPA
	------	------
AM	– –	– –
GPA	0.423	– –

GAMMA

	SES	IQ
	------	------
AM	0.410	– –
GPA	– –	0.507

Commentary

Compare the preceding with my results of the same analyses through multiple regression.

Output

GOODNESS OF FIT STATISTICS

CHI-SQUARE WITH 2 DEGREES OF FREEDOM = 0.580 (P = 0.748)
ESTIMATED NON-CENTRALITY PARAMETER (NCP) = 0.0
90 PERCENT CONFIDENCE INTERVAL FOR NCP = (0.0 ; 3.728)

MINIMUM FIT FUNCTION VALUE = 0.00195
POPULATION DISCREPANCY FUNCTION VALUE (F0) = 0.0
90 PERCENT CONFIDENCE INTERVAL FOR F0 = (0.0 ; 0.0126)
ROOT MEAN SQUARE ERROR OF APPROXIMATION (RMSEA) = 0.0
90 PERCENT CONFIDENCE INTERVAL FOR RMSEA = (0.0 ; 0.0792)
P-VALUE FOR TEST OF CLOSE FIT (RMSEA < 0.05) = 0.867

EXPECTED CROSS-VALIDATION INDEX (ECVI) = 0.0558
90 PERCENT CONFIDENCE INTERVAL FOR ECVI = (0.0606 ; 0.0732)
ECVI FOR SATURATED MODEL = 0.0673
ECVI FOR INDEPENDENCE MODEL = 1.00

CHI-SQUARE FOR INDEPENDENCE MODEL WITH 6 DEGREES OF FREEDOM = 288.919
INDEPENDENCE AIC = 296.919
MODEL AIC = 16.580
SATURATED AIC = 20.000

$$\text{INDEPENDENCE CAIC} = 315.734$$
$$\text{MODEL CAIC} = 54.210$$
$$\text{SATURATED CAIC} = 67.038$$

$$\text{ROOT MEAN SQUARE RESIDUAL (RMR)} = 0.578$$
$$\text{STANDARDIZED RMR} = 0.0151$$
$$\text{GOODNESS OF FIT INDEX (GFI)} = 0.999$$
$$\text{ADJUSTED GOODNESS OF FIT INDEX (AGFI)} = 0.995$$
$$\text{PARSIMONY GOODNESS OF FIT INDEX (PGFI)} = 0.200$$

$$\text{NORMED FIT INDEX (NFI)} = 0.998$$
$$\text{NON-NORMED FIT INDEX (NNFI)} = 1.015$$
$$\text{PARSIMONY NORMED FIT INDEX (PNFI)} = 0.333$$
$$\text{COMPARATIVE FIT INDEX (CFI)} = 1.000$$
$$\text{INCREMENTAL FIT INDEX (IFI)} = 1.005$$
$$\text{RELATIVE FIT INDEX (RFI)} = 0.994$$

$$\text{CRITICAL N (CN)} = 4748.850$$

Commentary

To give you an idea of the embarrassment of riches in this area, I reproduced here, for one time only, all the information reported under the GOODNESS OF FIT STATISTICS. As Loehlin (1992) pointed out:

> This area is in a state of flux. There have been numerous articles in the past few years criticizing existing indices and proposing new ones. The only strong recommendation that seems justified at present is to treat the indications of any one such index with caution. (p. 71)

Instead of reviewing this complex topic, I will list some sources of thorough reviews. Bollen (1989, pp. 256–289) gives a very good review of approaches to model evaluation. For more recent thorough treatments of this topic, see the book edited by Bollen and Long (1993a). See also Chou and Bentler (1995) and Hu and Bentler (1995). In the aforementioned references and others, various classifications of approaches to model evaluations have been proposed, among which are "overall model fit measures" (Bollen, 1989, pp. 256–281) versus "components fit measures" (Bollen, 1989, pp. 281–289; also called "focused measures of goodness of fit" [Herting & Costner, 1985, p. 333] and "detailed assessment of fit" [Jöreskog & Sörbom, 1993a, pp. 126–128]), and "those that simply describe goodness of fit, and those that involve considerations of parsimony—i.e., that take into account the number of unknowns used to achieve the fit" (Loehlin, 1992, p. 71; for a simulation study of parsimony-based fit indices, see Williams & Holahan, 1994). For a very good discussion of parsimony of a model and how it relates to various fit indices, see Mulaik et al. (1989; see also the next chapter). Tanaka (1993) organized his exhaustive review of fit indices along six dimensions.

In what follows, I comment briefly on *several* indices reproduced in the output, which are also among those I will reproduce in subsequent runs.[18] My choice of indices to report is *not* meant to

---

[18]When I introduce EQS in the next section, I comment on some additional indices reported here, as they were developed by Bentler (the author of EQS) and his associate.

imply that they are the "best." Rather, I chose them because they are probably easier to comprehend. For convenience, I will repeat one or more indices from the previous output and comment on them.

CHI-SQUARE WITH 2 DEGREES OF FREEDOM = 0.580 (P = 0.748)

As you probably know, in customary applications of the χ^2 test the researcher wishes to reject the null hypothesis so as to claim support for its alternative. When it is thus applied, the larger the χ^2, the "better." In the present context, on the other hand, the researcher does *not* wish to reject the null hypothesis. Accordingly, the smaller the χ^2, the better the fit of the model. This is why Jöreskog and Sörbom (1993a) refer to its use in the present context as a "badness-of-fit measure" (p. 122), instead of the term *goodness-of-fit* used in its customary application. Recall that in the output for the just-identified model presented earlier in this section, χ^2 was equal to zero and p was equal to 1.00, indicating a perfect fit.

In the present example, the χ^2 test addresses the two overidentifying restrictions, namely that two coefficients (from SES to GPA and from IQ to AM) are equal to zero. Stated differently, the test addresses the question whether this overidentified model differs significantly from one that fits the data perfectly. As the p value for χ^2 far exceeds conventional α levels, the null hypothesis is not rejected, leading to the conclusion that the overidentified model is consistent with the data.

I believe it safe to assume that you are familiar with the basic logic of statistical tests of significance and that you therefore appreciate the logical problems attendant with this approach. As you probably recall, the null hypothesis cannot be confirmed. One can either reject it or fail to reject it.

As discussions of hypothesis testing stress, failure to reject the null hypothesis should *not* be construed as support for it. Although it is customary to deem failure to reject the null hypothesis as an indication that the model is consistent with the data, it is important to keep in mind that alternative, even widely diverse, models may be consistent with the same data (earlier, I gave examples of such occurrences). Moreover, the validity of the χ^2 test is predicated on the viability of several assumptions, notable among which are that the (1) observed variables follow a multivariate normal distribution, (2) "model holds exactly in the population" (Jöreskog & Sörbom, 1993a, p. 123), (3) "sample size is sufficiently large" (Jöreskog & Sörbom, 1993a, p. 122), and (4) covariance matrix (as opposed to a correlation matrix) is analyzed. The χ^2 test is "very sensitive to departures from multivariate normality of the observed variables" (Jöreskog & Sörbom, 1989, p. 43; see also Bentler, 1982, p. 421) and to departure from the assumption that the model holds exactly in the population. As to sample size, lack of agreement about the meaning of "sufficiently large" aside, when the sample size is large, the likelihood of rejecting the null hypothesis is high, hence an overidentified model may be rejected even when on substantive grounds it is deemed consistent with the data. Conversely, when the sample size is small, the likelihood of rejecting the null hypothesis is small, hence a model may be deemed consistent with the data even when this is not so. For discussions of the logic of statistical tests of significance and how they are affected by sample size, effect size, Type I, and Type II errors, see Pedhazur and Schmelkin (1991, Chapter 9, and the references therein). For discussions of sample size in SEM, see Anderson and Gerbing (1984), Boomsma (1987), Kaplan (1995), Saris and Satorra (1993), Tanaka (1987).

In the preceding, I frequently referred to samples. As is well known, however, the use of probability sampling from defined populations is extremely rare in social and behavioral research. As Jöreskog (1993) pointed out:

Most empirical research employing structural equation models does not even report what the population is and how the sample was selected. . . . Without a clear definition of population and sampling scheme, it is difficult to attach meaning to such often-used terms as *significance level, p value, power, t value* and *standard error.* (p. 301)

Not surprisingly, Jöreskog and Sörbom (1989) asserted that "χ^2 is not valid in most empirical applications" (p. 43) and suggested that

In practice it is more useful to regard chi-square as a *measure* of fit rather than as a *test statistic.* In this view, chi-square is a measure of overall fit of the model to the data. It measures the distance (difference, discrepancy, deviance) between the sample covariance (correlation) matrix and the fitted covariance (correlation) matrix. (p. 122)

Further, they suggested that "the degrees of freedom serve as a standard by which to judge whether χ^2 is large or small" (Jöreskog & Sörbom, 1989, p. 43). As is wont to happen in such cases, various rules of thumb for what is deemed a small χ^2/df, hence a good fit, were advanced. Wheaton (1987) appropriately questioned the validity and usefulness of such ratios for assessment of fit.

Finally, Jöreskog and Sörbom developed PRELIS[19]—a companion program to LISREL—designed for, among other things, studying distributions of observed variables, data screening and transformations, and calculating measures of association among non-normally distributed or ordinal variables (see, Jöreskog & Sörbom, 1989, pp. 19–20, for a description of PRELIS; and see Jöreskog & Sörbom, 1993c, for PRELIS 2).

ROOT MEAN SQUARE RESIDUAL (RMR) = 0.578
STANDARDIZED RMR = 0.0151
GOODNESS OF FIT INDEX (GFI) = 0.999
ADJUSTED GOODNESS OF FIT INDEX (AGFI) = 0.995

Analogous to regression analysis, a residual is the difference between an observed value (variance, covariance, correlation) and its corresponding reproduced (predicted) value (see FITTED RESIDUALS in next section). ROOT MEAN SQUARE RESIDUAL (RMR) is a kind of average of the fitted residuals. Values of RMR based on the covariance matrix may be difficult to interpret as their sizes are affected by the units of the measures of the observed variables. In contrast, STANDARDIZED RMR is easier to interpret as it is based on standardized units, as when the correlation matrix is analyzed. As the formula for RMR shows (e.g., Jöreskog & Sörbom, 1989, p. 44), when a correlation matrix is analyzed, values of RMR may range from 0 (perfect fit) to 1 (null model, according to which all the correlations are zero; in other word, no model at all). For the present example, then, the STANDARDIZED RMR is small (.0151), indicating a good fit.

To avert problems attendant with the interpretation of RMR (see the preceding), Jöreskog and Sörbom (1993a, p. 123) proposed the GOODNESS OF FIT INDEX (GFI), which is a standardized overall measure of fit based on properties of the observed and reproduced values of the covariance (correlation) matrix. In the calculation of the GFI, no account is taken of the number of

---

[19]PRELIS is a registered trademark of Scientific Software, Inc., whom I would like to thank for furnishing me with a review copy of this program.

the model parameters. As I explained and illustrated earlier, the fit of a model improves with increases in the number of its parameters. Therefore, Jöreskog and Sörbom (1993a, p. 123) proposed the ADJUSTED GOODNESS OF FIT INDEX (AGFI), which is adjusted for the number of the model degrees of freedom.

> Both of these measures should be between zero [total lack of fit] and one [perfect fit], although it is theoretically possible for them to become negative. This should not happen, of course, since it means that the model fits worse than no model at all. (Jöreskog & Sörbom, 1993a, p. 123)

Tanaka (1993, pp. 19–20), who showed an analogy relation between GFI and R^2, and between AGFI and adjusted (or shrunken) R^2—see (8.3) and discussion related to it—also noted that "the absence of any rationale for the GFI and AGFI made interpretations difficult" (p. 15). It is probably for this reason that Jöreskog and Sörbom refrained from proposing criteria for "good" fit based on GFI and AGFI. Actually, they hardly referred to these indices when they interpreted results of various examples they presented in the manual (Jöreskog & Sörbom, 1989). Wheaton (1987) found the lowest level of GFI to be .717 for his null model, and he found that "large differences in fit produce rather small changes in GFI" (p. 140). The preceding did not stop other authors from proposing criteria for fit indices. For example, Cole (1987) suggested that values greater than .9 and .8 for GFI and AGFI, respectively, "usually indicate a satisfactory fit" (p. 586).

The indices I have discussed are for overall model fit. Even when the overall index indicates a good fit, however, individual components may fit poorly. Regardless of the type of overall fit indices used, fit of individual components should always be examined. It is to this topic that I now turn.

Output

FITTED COVARIANCE MATRIX

	AM	GPA	SES	IQ
AM	10.563			
GPA	1.956	1.538		
SES	2.798	0.848	4.410	
IQ	5.996	10.396	9.450	225.000

CORRELATION MATRIX OF Y AND X

	AM	GPA	SES	IQ
AM	1.000			
GPA	0.485	1.000		
SES	0.410	0.325	1.000	
IQ	0.123	0.559	0.300	1.000

FITTED RESIDUALS

	AM	GPA	SES	IQ
AM	– –			
GPA	0.076	0.024		
SES	– –	0.019	– –	
IQ	1.804	0.291	– –	– –

SUMMARY STATISTICS FOR FITTED RESIDUALS

SMALLEST FITTED RESIDUAL = 0.000

MEDIAN FITTED RESIDUAL = 0.009

LARGEST FITTED RESIDUAL = 1.804

STANDARDIZED RESIDUALS

	AM	GPA	SES	IQ
AM	– –			
GPA	0.623	0.449		
SES	– –	0.135	– –	
IQ	0.658	0.304	– –	– –

SUMMARY STATISTICS FOR STANDARDIZED RESIDUALS
SMALLEST STANDARDIZED RESIDUAL =   0.000
MEDIAN STANDARDIZED RESIDUAL =   0.068
LARGEST STANDARDIZED RESIDUAL =   0.658

Commentary

Analogous to predicted values in regression analysis, entries in the fitted covariance matrix are predicted values based on parameter estimates. This is also true for the correlation matrix, which I placed alongside the covariance matrix for ease of comparison. For instance, the observed covariance between IQ and AM is 7.800 (see COVARIANCE MATRIX TO BE ANALYZED in the output for analysis of the just-identified model, earlier in this section). From the previous output, the fitted covariance between these two variables is 5.996. The residual—reported in the FITTED RESIDUALS matrix—is therefore 1.804 (7.800 − 5.996). Similarly, the correlation between IQ and AM is .160, whereas the reproduced (predicted) correlation between these variables is .123 (compare this result with the relevant values in Table 18.1 and with my earlier calculations).

When studying fitted residuals, the aim is to search for instances in which the model underestimates (large positive residual) or overestimates (large negative residual) the covariance between a given pair of variables. This information may serve as clues for model revision. I remind you, however, of my earlier discussion of pitfalls in post hoc model revision (see "Theory Trimming or Model Revision"; also see "Model Revision" in Chapter 19).

The size of residuals is affected by the units of the measures of the observed variables, making it difficult to tell whether they are large. Therefore, LISREL reports also standardized residuals:

> In principle, each standardized residual can be interpreted as a standard normal deviate and considered "large" if it exceeds the value of 2.58 in absolute value. When interpreting the standardized residuals statistically, one must bear in mind, however, that they are correlated from cell to cell. (Jöreskog & Sörbom, 1989, p. 32)

Examine the standardized residuals reported in the preceding and notice that they would be considered very small, even if a more lenient criterion were used.

EQS: AN ORIENTATION

Bentler (1987) attributed the paucity of SEM applications in certain areas to "unnecessarily complicated" (p. 65) matrix language used in presentations of, and software for, SEM. To make SEM more accessible to researchers, Bentler developed EQS (pronounced "X")—a computer program that uses the simpler equations language.[20] Documentation for EQS 4.02—the version I will be using—consists of (1) a manual for Version 3.0 (Bentler, 1992a) and (2) a user's guide for EQS/Windows (Bentler & Wu, 1993). The manual for Version 3.0 "should be consulted for detailed descriptions of the various technical features of the program" (Bentler & Wu, 1993, p. 1). The *EQS/Windows user's guide* deals mainly with the Windows interface and specific features (e.g., data screening and transformations, building EQS input files in Windows, plotting). Two books on using EQS are Byrne (1994) and Dunn, Everitt, and Pickles (1993).

As with LISREL, EQS runs under DOS. That is, whether the input file is created with an ASCII editor or in EQS/Windows, the program is executed under DOS. Thus, an input file created with an ASCII editor can be run by invoking EQS from the DOS prompt (see the following) or it can be opened in EQS/Windows and run from there. When the latter is done, the program exits Windows, runs EQS under DOS, and returns to Windows. As I did for LISREL, I will list input files and show how to run them from the DOS prompt. If you prefer, you can open such files, or create them, in EQS/Windows (see Bentler & Wu, 1993, for details).

I remind you that my brief introductions to, and comments on, programs I use are *not* meant to supplant their documentation. The importance of studying program manuals can be illustrated with reference to EQS. Suppose you decided to run EQS under DOS and therefore paid attention only to the EQS manual (Bentler, 1992a). As a result, you would not learn that the instructions for creating path diagrams are obsolete. Only if you also read the *EQS/Windows user's guide* (Bentler & Wu, 1993) would you learn that "there is a major upgrade in the /DIAGRAM section on EQS. *This description should replace all the discussions on the subject of diagram in EQS, the Structural Equations Program Manual* (i.e., page 71–72 [*sic*] and page 99)" (p. 159).

On-Line Help

How you get on-line help in EQS depends on the mode in which you run the program. If you run from the DOS prompt, invoke help before running EQS. Do this by issuing the command EQSHELP at the DOS prompt. This loads help as a Terminate-and-Stay-Resident (TSR) program, which you can invoke any time by pressing ALT-H (to unload help, type EQSHELP/U at the DOS prompt). In Windows, you can get help by pressing F1.

Variable Types

Four types of variables may be used in EQS. Following are their codes, names, and meanings as presented in Bentler (1992a, p. 53). Hereafter, I will refer to Bentler (1992a) as the EQS manual or just the manual.

Code	Name	Meaning
V	Variable	Measured variable
F	Factor	Latent variable
E	Error	Residual of measured variable
D	Disturbance	Residual of latent variable

---

[20]As I showed in the preceding section, the same can be accomplished in LISREL by using the SIMPLIS language.

The model is specified in the form of regression-like equations, each consisting of a dependent variable (on the left of the equal sign), and one or more independent variables (on the right of the equal sign).

> Independent variables are defined in EQS as those measured variables or latent variables that are never structurally regressed on any other variables in the system. . . . Dependent variables are those that are structurally regressed on at least one other variable in a model. It is possible for a dependent variable to also be a predictor of other variables in a model. However, this does not mean it is an independent variable in the sense used by EQS. If a variable is ever structurally regressed on any other variable in the model, i.e., if it appears at least once on the left-hand side of one equation . . . , then it is a dependent variable, regardless of its relationships to other variables in the system. . . . Only V and F variables can be dependent variables, i.e., on the left side of an equation. E and D must never be on the left side of an equation. As residuals, they are always independent variables. (pp. 53–54)

You can readily see this usage in EQS in path diagrams. Variables to which one or more unidirectional arrows point are considered dependent variables, whereas those to which no unidirectional arrows point are considered independent variables. I will illustrate this with reference to the models depicted earlier in Figures 18.2 and 18.5. In the former, variables 2, 3, and 4 are dependent, whereas variable 1 and the residuals (e_2, e_3, and e_4) are independent variables. By contrast, in Figure 18.5 only variables 3 and 4 are dependent.

All four types of variables are not required to be used in any given model. For instance, the models I present and analyze in this chapter consist of V and E variables only.

I discuss other aspects of EQS in my commentaries on numerical examples, to which I now turn. As I stated earlier, I will use EQS to analyze the same examples I analyzed earlier through LISREL. I believe you will gain a better understanding of features of both programs by comparing their respective outputs.

A Just-Identified Model

I begin with an analysis of the just-identified model depicted in Figure 18.12 (data in Table 18.1), which I analyzed earlier through regression and LISREL.

EQS

Input

```
/TITLE
 TABLE 18.1 AND FIGURE 18.12. A JUST-IDENTIFIED MODEL.
/SPECIFICATIONS
 CASES=300; VARIABLES=4; MA=CORRELATION;
/LABELS
 V1=SES; V2=IQ; V3=AM; V4=GPA;
/EQUATIONS
 V3 = .5*V1 + .05*V2 + E3;
 V4 = .01*V1 + .05*V2 + .2*V3 + E4;
/VARIANCES
 V1 TO V2=*;
 E3 TO E4=*;
```

```
/COVARIANCES
 V1,V2=*;
/MATRIX
1.00
 .30  1.00
 .41   .16  1.00
 .33   .57   .50  1.00
/STANDARD DEVIATIONS
2.10  15.00  3.25  1.25
/PRINT
 EFFECT=YES;
/END
```

Commentary

The control language of EQS is organized in sections or paragraphs, consisting of one or more sentences. Each paragraph is indicated by a keyword that is preceded by a slash (e.g., /TITLE). A keyword, which can be abbreviated to its first three letters, occupies a separate line.

Uppercase or lowercase letters can be used. Nevertheless, "currently there are parts of EQS/ Windows interface that require capital letters, so you might as well use capital letters consistently" (Bentler & Wu, 1993, p. 128).

Sentences in a paragraph are separated by semicolons and may be presented in any order. Blanks and/or separate lines can be used to facilitate readability and examination of the input. I recommend that you follow Bentler's advice and "develop a standard practice that makes it easy to review the program input, e.g., starting keywords in column 1, and beginning statements below the keyword, indented a few characters" (Manual, pp. 43–44).

/TITle. The title, which is optional, may consist of multiple lines. All lines are printed only once. The first line of the title is printed as a header on all output pages. Use detailed titles so that you could, even with the passage of time, tell at a glance what an analysis was about.

/SPEcification. For a listing of specification keywords, along with their meanings, see page 46 of the manual. The default method of estimation is Maximum Likelihood (ML), and the default input is a covariance matrix.

As you can see, I am reading in a correlation matrix, followed by standard deviations. My use of MA=CORRELATION deserves special attention, as it goes counter to what is stated in the manual. Following an input file similar to the one I am using, the EQS manual states, "EQS will create the covariance matrix from the correlations and the standard deviations without any further instruction, and the analysis will be done on the covariance matrix" (Manual, p. 22). *This is not so. The program will generate the covariance matrix and analyze it only if MA=COR is specified. In the absence of this specification, the correlation matrix will be analyzed.* I informed BMDP of this bug. It is possible that it has been fixed in the version of the program you are using (as I pointed out earlier, I am using Version 4.02).

/LABels. EQS names input variables sequentially as V1, V2, and so on. Substantive labels, consisting of up to eight characters, may be assigned to V and F variables only (see the preceding for the four types of variables used in EQS). I assigned labels to the four V variables. As I stated earlier, I do not use F variables in the examples of this chapter. For more details about labels, see the EQS manual (pp. 52–53).

/EQUations. As I stated earlier, the model is specified in the form of equations. "One and only one equation is required for each dependent variable. The dependent variables may be either observed or latent, and parameters within the equations may be specified as either fixed or free" (Manual, p. 53). An asterisk is used to indicate that a parameter is free (i.e., to be estimated). In the preceding input, coefficients for V1, V2, and V3 are free, as are the variances of V1, V2, E3, E4, and the covariance between V1 and V2 (see VARIANCES and COVARIANCES, below).

As I explained earlier, ML estimates are arrived at through an iterative process whose convergence can be accelerated by a judicious use of start values. "Start values are not needed for most jobs" (Manual, p. 55). When none are supplied, "the typical default start value is 1.0*" (Manual, p. 55).

> However, it is probably good practice to provide start values because EQS's start values may be inadequate in some models and thus the program may not converge. More importantly, providing start values helps clarify which coefficients are expected to be large positive or large negative. The final results then can be informative about one's expectations. (Manual, p. 55)

Start values depend on the specific model and the scales of the measures used. For general guidelines for choosing start values, see the EQS manual (p. 55). For illustrative purposes, I use start values for the coefficients for the V variables but not for the variances and the covariances.

Note that the coefficients for the errors are fixed (no asterisks). By default, they are set equal to 1.0.

/VARiances. Independent variables must have variances, which can be fixed or free. "*Dependent variables are not allowed to have variances as parameters, whether fixed or free*" (Manual, p. 56).

/COVariances. Independent variables may have covariances. When a COV is not specified, it is assumed to be fixed at zero. "*Dependent variables cannot have covariances*" (Manual, p. 57).

/MATRIX. "Raw data is always assumed to reside in a separate file" (Manual, p. 44). Input in this section can be a covariance matrix or a correlation matrix, which may be followed by standard deviations, as in my input file. In addition, means may also be included.

Of various input formats possible (see Manual, pp. 65–67), I use a free format, according to which the lower triangular matrix is read in by rows with the first row consisting of one element, the second of two, and so forth. A semicolon (;) is *not* used to indicate the end of rows in matrix input. The same is true of rows of standard deviations and means.

When a model consists of a subset of the input variables, EQS selects the relevant variables based on the model equations.

/PRINT. This paragraph is used for specifying additional output (see Manual, pp. 72–74). EFFECT=YES means print effect decomposition (i.e., direct and indirect effects), which I explained earlier in this chapter.

Running EQS

Following Bentler (1992a), I use EQS as an extension for input files. Thus, I named the above input file T181.EQS. At the DOS prompt, I typed:

EQS IN=T181.EQS

By default, EQS will name the output file T181.LOG. If you prefer another name and/or extension, add **OUT=[file name]** to the command line. Alternatively, you can type only **EQS** at the

DOS prompt. You will then be prompted for the names of the input and output files. Of course, you can create a batch file so that all you would have to type at the DOS prompt is its name and the name of the input file (without the extension). For an example of such a file, see "Running LISREL" in the preceding section.

Output

COVARIANCE MATRIX TO BE ANALYZED: 4 VARIABLES
(SELECTED FROM 4 VARIABLES), BASED ON 300 CASES.

		SES V 1	IQ V 2	AM V 3	GPA V 4
SES	V 1	4.410			
IQ	V 2	9.450	225.000		
AM	V 3	2.798	7.800	10.563	
GPA	V 4	0.866	10.687	2.031	1.563

BENTLER-WEEKS STRUCTURAL REPRESENTATION:

NUMBER OF DEPENDENT VARIABLES = 2
DEPENDENT V'S: 3   4

NUMBER OF INDEPENDENT VARIABLES = 4
INDEPENDENT V'S: 1   2
INDEPENDENT E'S: 3   4

DETERMINANT OF INPUT MATRIX IS   0.62310E+04

PARAMETER ESTIMATES APPEAR IN ORDER,
NO SPECIAL PROBLEMS WERE ENCOUNTERED DURING OPTIMIZATION.

Commentary

EQS first lists the input file, which I did not reproduce. Using the correlation matrix and the standard deviations, EQS created the covariance matrix to be analyzed. Compare this matrix with the one given earlier in the LISREL output, where I also commented on it.

Under the BENTLER-WEEKS STRUCTURAL REPRESENTATION is a summary of the number and types of variables used in the model. For an explanation, see "Variables Types," earlier in this section.

In Chapters 6, 10, and 11, I discussed the determinant of a matrix (see also, Appendix A). Here, I will only remind you that a matrix whose determinant is zero is said to be singular. Under such circumstances, an ML solution is not possible; EQS will abort, giving diagnostics to the effect that there is a problem with the input matrix.

Finally, note the message that the parameter estimates appear in order and no special problems were encountered during optimization.

Output

CHI-SQUARE = 0.000 BASED ON 0 DEGREES OF FREEDOM
NONPOSITIVE DEGREES OF FREEDOM. PROBABILITY COMPUTATIONS ARE
UNDEFINED.
BENTLER-BONETT NORMED FIT INDEX= 1.000
NON-NORMED FIT INDEX WILL NOT BE COMPUTED BECAUSE A DEGREES OF
FREEDOM IS ZERO.

Commentary

Recall that the model under consideration is just-identified. Hence, zero degrees of freedom and a perfect fit (see earlier sections for discussions of this topic). I comment on fit indices reported in EQS later, when I analyze an overidentified model.

Output

MEASUREMENT EQUATIONS WITH STANDARD ERRORS AND TEST STATISTICS

AM	=V3	=	.616*V1	+	.009*V2	+	1.000 E3	
			.085		.012			
			7.201		.736			
GPA	=V4	=	.160*V3	+	.005*V1	+	.042*V2	+	1.000 E4
			.017		.028		.004	
			9.240		.197		11.628	

DECOMPOSITION OF EFFECTS WITH STANDARDIZED VALUES
PARAMETER TOTAL EFFECTS

AM	=V3	=	.398*V1	+	.041*V2	+	.911 E3
GPA	=V4	=	.416*V3	+	.175*V1	+	.518*V2	+	.379 E3
			.710 E4				

PARAMETER INDIRECT EFFECTS

GPA	=V4	=	.166*V1	+	.017*V2	+	.379 E3

STANDARDIZED SOLUTION:

AM	=V3	=	.398*V1	+	.041*V2	+	.911 E3	
GPA	=V4	=	.416*V3	+	.009*V1	+	.501*V2	+	.710 E4

Commentary

In the interest of space, I reproduced here only excerpts of the output. Although they differ in layout, the results are the same as those of LISREL's. I suggest that you study these excerpts, or output you may have generated with EQS, together with LISREL's output and my comments on it. You may also find it helpful to review my analysis of the same example through multiple regression, presented earlier in this chapter.

An Overidentified Model

I now turn to an analysis of the overidentified model depicted in Figure 18.13, which I analyzed in earlier sections by regression and LISREL.

EQS

Input

```
. . . . . . . . . . . . . . . . . . . . . . . . . .
/EQU
 V3 = .5*V1 + E3;
 V4 = .05*V2 + .2*V3 + E4;

. . . . . . . . . . . . . . . . . . . . . . . . . .
/PRINT
 DIG=4;
/END
```

Commentary

Unlike LISREL, EQS does not accept stacked jobs. Therefore, each model has to be run separately. Dotted lines indicate omitted statements that are identical to those in the input for the just-identified model in the preceding.

Earlier, I explained why I modified the just-identified model, rendering it overidentified. Therefore, all I will do here is point out that I deleted V2 from the first equation, and V1 from the second equation, thus constraining to zero the effect of (1) IQ on AM and (2) SES on GPA. I suggest that you modify the TITLE to the effect that an overidentified model is being analyzed.

As you can see from the preceding run, by default EQS reports results to three decimals. In this file *I specified DIGits=4, not because I wanted results to four decimals but because this is also how one specifies that optional fit indices be reported* (i.e., in addition to those reported by default; see the following commentary on fit indices). This option is not documented in the manual, as it was added in Version 4.02. The strange manner in which it is specified will undoubtedly be changed in a future release of EQS.

Output

RESIDUAL COVARIANCE MATRIX (S-SIGMA) :

		SES V 1	IQ V 2	AM V 3	GPA V 4
SES	V 1	0.0000			
IQ	V 2	0.0000	0.0000		
AM	V 3	0.0000	1.8038	0.0000	
GPA	V 4	0.0187	0.2913	0.0756	0.0244

AVERAGE ABSOLUTE COVARIANCE RESIDUALS = 0.2214
AVERAGE OFF-DIAGONAL ABSOLUTE COVARIANCE RESIDUALS = 0.3649

Commentary

As I explained in my commentary on the LISREL output for the same problem, this matrix consists of differences between observed (S) and predicted (SIGMA) variances and covariances. Except for differences in rounding and layout, the values in this matrix are the same as those reported in LISREL. Notice that EQS reports two averages of absolute values of residuals. "Usually, the off-diagonal elements are more critical to the goodness-of-fit chi-square statistic" (Manual, p. 90).

Output

STANDARDIZED RESIDUAL MATRIX:

			SES V 1	IQ V 2	AM V 3	GPA V 4
SES	V	1	0.0000			
IQ	V	2	0.0000	0.0000		
AM	V	3	0.0000	0.0370	0.0000	
GPA	V	4	0.0071	0.0155	0.0186	0.0156

AVERAGE ABSOLUTE STANDARDIZED RESIDUALS = 0.0094
AVERAGE OFF-DIAGONAL ABSOLUTE STANDARDIZED RESIDUALS = 0.0130

Commentary

LISREL and EQS use the term STANDARDIZED RESIDUAL *differently*. In LISREL it means the ratio of the residual to its standard error (see Jöreskog & Sörbom, 1989, pp. 31–32; also see my commentary on the LISREL output). By contrast, in EQS *standardized residual* means the difference between an observed and a predicted correlation (see Manual, p. 90). To see clearly the difference between the two uses, I suggest that you analyze the same model with both programs using only the correlation matrix. If you did so, you would find that (1) EQS reports the same values under RESIDUALS and STANDARDIZED RESIDUALS, (2) LISREL reports under the heading FITTED RESIDUALS the same values EQS reports under STANDARDIZED RESIDUALS, and (3) the STANDARDIZED RESIDUALS in LISREL are the same as those reported when the covariance matrix is analyzed.

Clearly, interpretation of standardized residuals in the two programs is different. Earlier, I discussed their interpretation in LISREL. In EQS you would judge whether discrepancies between the observed and reproduced correlations are "large" to warrant some action (e.g., revise the model, transform the data, delete outliers).

Output

INDEPENDENCE MODEL CHI-SQUARE = 288.919 ON 6 DEGREES OF FREEDOM

INDEPENDENCE AIC = 276.91854   INDEPENDENCE CAIC = 248.69584
MODEL AIC = −3.41992   MODEL CAIC = −12.82749

CHI-SQUARE =   0.580 BASED ON   2 DEGREES OF FREEDOM
PROBABILITY VALUE FOR THE CHI-SQUARE STATISTIC IS   0.74823
THE NORMAL THEORY RLS CHI-SQUARE FOR THIS ML SOLUTION IS   0.580.

BENTLER-BONETT NORMED   FIT INDEX=   0.998
BENTLER-BONETT NONNORMED FIT INDEX=   1.015
COMPARATIVE FIT INDEX   =   1.000

BOLLEN (IFI)   FIT INDEX=   1.005
McDonald (MFI)   FIT INDEX=   1.002
LISREL GFI   FIT INDEX=   0.999
LISREL AGFI   FIT INDEX=   0.995
ROOT MEAN SQUARED RESIDUAL   =   0.578
STANDARDIZED RMR   =   0.004

Commentary

By default, EQS reports the information above the dashed line, *which I inserted.* To get the information listed below the dashed line, you have to specify DIG=4 in the PRINT paragraph (see the
preceding input). In my commentary on LISREL output in the preceding section, I commented
on some of the indices below the dashed line and gave general references to discussions of fit indices. Here, I will comment on indices above the dashed line.

Notice that EQS reports two CHI-SQUARE values. The first is a test of the null hypothesis
that the covariances (correlations) among the observed variables are all zero (i.e., independence
model). The second, which is the same as that reported in LISREL, is a test of the overidentified
model. Below, I show how the two CHI-SQUARES enter in calculation of fit indices reported
above the dashed line.

Analogous to increments in R^2, (see, e.g., Chapter 9), the fit indices above the dashed line are
aimed at assessing incremental fit of models. Basically, the incremental fit of a substantive model
of interest is assessed against a baseline model. You can readily see this from the manner in
which BENTLER-BONETT NORMED FIT INDEX (NFI) is calculated:

$$\text{NFI} = \frac{\chi_b^2 - \chi_s^2}{\chi_b^2} \tag{18.15}$$

where b = baseline model and s = substantive model. Bentler and Bonett (1980), who developed this index used the term *null* (instead of baseline), which they defined as "the most restrictive theoretically defensible model" (p. 600), that is, independence model (see the preceding).[21]
Using the two CHI-SQUARES reported previously,

$$\text{NFI} = (288.919 - .580)/.580 = .998$$

which is the value reported in the preceding.

Except for an adjustment for degrees of freedom, BENTLER-BONETT NONNORMED FIT
INDEX (NNFI) is similar to NFI. For the calculation of NNFI, see the EQS manual (p. 93),

---

[21]In using the term *baseline,* I am following Sobel and Bohrnstedt (1985), who were critical of this approach (see the following) and pointed out that "baseline is more general and includes null as a special case" (p. 157).

which points out that, unlike NFI, this index "can be outside the 0–1 range" (p. 93). The present example is a case in point.

Bentler (1990) proposed a COMPARATIVE FIT INDEX (CFI), which "has the advantage of the NNFI in reflecting fit relatively well at all sample sizes, especially, in avoiding the underestimation of fit sometimes found in true models with NFI" (Manual, p. 93). According to Bentler (1992b), "the NNFI is not as good as the CFI in measuring the quality of model fit" (p. 401; see Goffin, 1993, for a comparison of CFI with another recently proposed index of fit).

Criteria for "Good" Fit

Addressing the issue of criteria for "good" fit, Bentler and Bonett (1980) stated:

> Since the scale of the fit indices is not necessarily easy to interpret (e.g., the indices are not squared multiple correlations), experience will be required to establish values of the indices that are associated with various degrees of meaningfulness of results. In our experience, models with overall fit indices of less than .9 can usually be improved substantially. (p. 600)

This statement was apparently taken by various authors to mean that Bentler and Bonett suggested .9 "as a threshold" (Wheaton, 1987, p. 133; see also Schmitt & Stults, 1986, p. 14). Judd, Jessor, and Donovan (1986) even referred to it as "the 'magic' .90 level" (p. 166).

As is wont to happen, the .9 criterion is interpreted variously by various authors, even by Bentler himself. In the manual, Bentler stated that "values of NFI greater than .9 are *desirable* [italics added]" (p. 93), whereas in another discussion (Bentler, 1992b) he spoke of "*excellent* [italics added] models having NFI values above .9 or so" (p. 401). Referring to Bentler (1992b), Byrne (1994) characterized "a value greater than .90 [as] indicating an *acceptable* [italics added] fit to the data" (p. 55). And Dunn et al. (1993) stated, "Experience shows that these indices need to have values above 0.9 before the corresponding model can even be considered *moderately adequate* [italics added]" (p. 73).

Of course, my aim in the foregoing was not to confuse you, though it probably has done just that. Unfortunately, matters become even more complicated when the choice of a baseline model is considered.

Choice of Baseline Model

Routine use of the "nullest" of null models (i.e., independence model; see the preceding) is prone to lead to misconceptions and misinterpretations. Thus, Fornell (1983) cautioned:

> Without the requirement of strong theoretical justification for the null model, the Bentler and Bonett test makes it even easier for any given model to pass the test: simply specify the "worst possible model" as the null hypothesis and then test your model against it. In most cases, your favorite model will stand up to the test. (p. 447)

Sobel and Bohrnstedt (1985) asserted that the baseline models used by Bentler and Bonett "are inappropriate in all but the purely exploratory case" (p. 153). In confirmatory studies, they maintained, the baseline model should reflect knowledge of and theory about the phenomenon studied. To illustrate their reasoning, Sobel and Bohrnstedt reanalyzed a model analyzed by Bentler and Bonett using a different baseline model that they believed to be "more defensible in the research context and relevant theoretical consideration" and reported results that led them to "a conclusion that is in sharp contrast to that of Bentler and Bonett (1980)" (p. 175).

Fit Indices: Summary Statement

Cautioning against undue reliance on and indiscriminate use of fit indices, especially as a means for model revision, Matsueda and Bielby (1986) correctly observed that this is tantamount to "transforming a powerful modeling and testing method into the data-dredging, exploratory approach it was meant to supplant" (p. 155). In a similar vein, Sobel and Bohrnstedt (1985) asserted that "scientific progress could be impeded if fit coefficients (even appropriate ones) are used as the primary criterion for judging the adequacy of a model" (p. 158).

Although there is no agreement about the value of fit indices, there seems to be unanimity that (1) no single fit index should be relied upon; (2) evaluation of individual fit component (e.g., study of residuals, see the preceding) be an integral part of model evaluation; and, above all, (3) just as model formulation should be theory driven, so must theory and substantive considerations play a prominent role in its evaluation. As Bollen and Long (1993b) put it in their incisive overview of this topic, "In the final analysis, assessing model fit in SEMs is like other areas of assessing goodness of fit. The test statistics and fit indices are very beneficial, but they are no replacement for sound judgment and substantive expertise" (p. 8).

Output

MEASUREMENT EQUATIONS WITH STANDARD ERRORS AND TEST STATISTICS

AM	=V3	=	.6345*V1	+	1.0000 E3
			.0816		
			7.7729		

GPA	=V4	=	.1614*V3	+	.0419*V2	+	1.0000 E4
			.0159		.0034		
			10.1454		12.1600		

STANDARDIZED SOLUTION:

| AM | =V3 | = | .4100*V1 | + | .9121 E3 | | |
| GPA | =V4 | = | .4229*V3 | + | .5068*V2 | + | .7152 E4 |

Commentary

Study the preceding together with relevant LISREL output, and my commentaries on it, in the preceding section.

RESEARCH EXAMPLES

Writing over a decade ago, Saris and Stronkhorst (1984) stated, "A secondary analysis of data reported in journals specializing in many research areas shows that the majority of the models presented as final causal theories should not have been accepted" (p. V; see also Saris, Den Ronden, & Satorra, 1987). The number of poorly conceived and executed SEM studies has increased dramatically since then, largely due to the user-friendly software that has become widely available.

My aim in this section is to alert you to some egregious errors in the hope of helping you (1) avoid them in your research and (2) read the research literature more critically. When appropriate, I group several studies under a common heading. My comments vary in length, depending on what I deem necessary to illustrate specific points I am trying to make.

As in other chapters, I neither summarize nor review studies on which I comment. Instead, I give the briefest description possible of what they are about. Moreover, in most instances I use studies to illustrate a single topic or issue. Accordingly, I pay no attention to how other issues, no matter their importance and relevance, were dealt with. To learn more about a study, and to be in a position to evaluate it, you would have to read it.

MISCONCEPTION ABOUT CAUSATION

In the beginning of this chapter, I commented on the controversy surrounding the idea of causation. I do not intend to repeat that presentation. Instead, I will give an example that all parties to the debate would, I believe, deem a misconception, even caricature, of the idea of causation.

In a report of a study aimed at determining implications of marital noncohabitation (e.g., whether it is prone to lead to divorce), Rindfuss and Stephen (1990) stated, "A common sociological assumption is that if one event occurs before another and if they are related to one another, then the first causes the second" (p. 265). Apparently, the authors (referees and editors too?) believed the assumption so common as to not require even a single reference.

METHODS IN SEARCH OF SUBSTANCE

As I stressed repeatedly, an analysis is meant to help determine whether a model is consistent with the data. In this section, I give examples where analyses were expected to do the opposite: generate models. Glenn (1989) probably had such misconceptions in mind when he remarked that "all too often students get the impression that the way to truth is through the mating of a good computer program with a good data set" (p. 136).

Anxiety, Coping Strategies, and Performance

Krohne and Schaffner (1983) reported on a study of the effects of anxiety and coping strategies on performance on a grammar test. For present purposes, I will only cite the authors' assertion that they used "path analysis . . . primarily as an instrument for generating hypotheses and only secondarily to test hypotheses" (p. 166).

Spatial Vision

Sekuler, Wilson, and Owsley (1984) were interested in answering "two related questions: how many different mechanisms are needed to account for the properties of human spatial vision? What are the characteristics of those mechanisms?" (p. 689). Following are excerpts of the authors' description of their use of LISREL.

> Successive runs of the LISREL program required LISREL to given [*sic*] the best possible account of the matrix of correlations, using either one, two, three, or four intervening endogenous variables,

hereafter referred to as "filters.". . . *LISREL was free to incorporate in its models* [italics added] corre-lations between the filters. . . . For each model, then, the ultimate loading pattern of any or all filters was determined by LISREL *with minimal interference by us. . . . Because we were particularly concerned that we not bias the outcome, we took another, more neutral tack, allowing LISREL to both generate and test the models* [italics added]. (p. 692)

I will not comment on the preceding, except to say that it is a strange conception of the researcher's role (rather its absence) in formulation and tests of models.

I felt it particularly important to draw attention to this study as it is one of two referred to in a survey of graduate training in statistics, methodology, and measurement in psychology in North America. Here is how the authors of the survey referred to it: "Few of the analytic techniques included in the survey, such as structural equation models, are currently represented in experimental journals (but see, e.g., Geiselman, Woodward & Beatty, 1982; Sekuler, Wilson, & Owsley, 1984)" (Aiken, West, Sechrest, & Reno, 1990, p. 728). Interpretation of results (e.g., fit indices) in the first named study is also seriously flawed.

Reference to these studies, without comment, is particularly troubling considering the status of the authors of the survey and the prestigious forum in which it appeared.

Sexual Preferences

In a study conducted under the auspices of the Kinsey Institute for sex research, Bell, Weinberg, and Hammersmith (1981) sought to explain the development of sexual preferences in men and women. It is noteworthy that not only did the study receive wide coverage in the mass media, but some writers and reviewers (e.g., Brody, 1981; Gagnon, 1981) exhibited greater circumspection and restraint than its authors in interpreting the alleged results.

Using responses to about 200 questions, the authors performed various analyses aimed at selecting sets of variables to be included in a large number of causal models they examined. Before I comment on these analyses, I would like to point out that the authors treated each question as a distinct variable, even though many of the questions were clearly multiple indicators of some latent variables. In various chapters (e.g., 8 through 10), I discussed serious problems that arise when multiple indicators of a latent variable are treated as if they were distinct variables in a multiple regression analysis (for a presentation in the context of SEM, see Chapter 19). Keep this comment in mind when you read the following presentation, where, for convenience, I use the authors' nomenclature.

The gist of their dubious analytic approach is perhaps captured by the authors' references to variables that "survived" variable-screening procedures. For instance, when they instructed the reader in the meaning of path analysis and in their approach to the selection of variables, they made reference to a hypothetical causal model, saying, "In this diagram [i.e., their illustrative model], Close Relationship with Father has presumably *survived a variable-screening process and thus earned a place in the model* [italics added]" (Bell, et al., 1981, Vol. 1, p. 34). Of course, a variable "earns a place" in a causal model not by surviving some screening procedure, but because of its role in a theoretical formulation.

The authors reported that "many variables were eliminated" (p. 33) in the course of repeated variable-screening operations. Without going into the details, I will note and comment briefly on some operations and criteria they used for variable selection.

According to one criterion, variables whose zero-order correlations with the dependent variable (sexual preference) were statistically not significant were discarded. I trust that at this stage it is not necessary to comment on this erroneous approach (if necessary, see earlier chapters, e.g., 9 and 10).

According to another criterion, a variable was discarded if homosexuals and heterosexuals did not differ significantly on it. This is inappropriate, as the authors' aim was to compare patterns of causality among variables for homosexuals and heterosexuals. Whether or not homosexuals and heterosexuals differ on a given variable does not imply if, and how, it is related to other variables in each group. Thus, the two groups may not differ in their Identification with Father, say, but this variable may have a positive relation with some variable(s) among homosexuals and a negative relation (or no relation) with the same variable(s) among heterosexuals. The converse of the preceding is, of course, also possible. That is, although the two groups may differ on a given variable, its relations with other variables may be the same in each group.

As if the preceding were not trouble enough, the authors carried out a series of multiple regression analyses, each time eliminating variables based on tests of statistical significance. Here is what they said about this process:

> After one or more variables were eliminated from the model, the effects of the surviving variables were recalculated without them, and again variables with no significant connection to adult sexual preference were dropped. This screening process was repeated several times until we were left with a manageable number of variables for inclusion in the path analysis. (Bell et al., 1981, Vol. 1, p. 33)

In view of the foregoing it is pointless to comment on the many path-analyses Bell et al. carried out.

Mood and Rheumatoid Arthritis Pain

Affleck, Tennen, Urrows, and Higgins (1992) were interested in the effects of several variables (see the following) on chronic pain and chronic mood. Using data from 54 (N.B.) subjects, they first carried out two hierarchical regression analyses,

> one predicting chronic pain . . . and the other chronic mood. For the pain equation, disease activity, disability, neuroticism, depression, pain coping, and pain catastrophizing were entered as a block, followed by chronic mood. The equation predicting mood was identical, except that age (the only demographic variable related to mood) was included in the first block, and chronic pain was entered last. (p. 122)

The authors then reported, in addition to "R^2 change," "Final β" (see their Tables 2 and 3, p. 124). Among other things, they stated, "Because of the moderately high colinearity [*sic*] of depression and neuroticism ($r = .60$), regression coefficients were calculated for each excluding the other. Neither alone predicted pain when other variables were taken into account" (p. 122). I discussed collinearity in earlier chapters (especially, Chapter 10). Therefore, I will not comment on the preceding, except to say that (1) the approach taken by the authors is wrong (if necessary, review relevant sections in Chapter 10) and (2) evidently the authors were not concerned about a similar correlation (.56) between depression and catastrophizing. As serious as the preceding misconceptions are, they pale in comparison to the ones I turn to now.

To begin with, I would like to remind you of the distinction between hierarchical and simultaneous regression analysis. Without repeating what I said about these topics earlier (see, especially, Chapters 9 and 10), I would like to stress that the two analyses are *not* interchangeable. They address different questions and reflect, wittingly or unwittingly, different models. For present purposes, it will suffice to point out that if the final β's the authors reported (see the preceding) are from simultaneous analyses in which all the variables were included, then the information they provide goes counter to that yielded by the hierarchical analyses.

As an illustration of the havoc that might be wreaked when methods are unleashed in search of a model, I will focus on the role of neuroticism. Apparently, based on results from simultaneous regression analyses, the authors stated, "On balance, our findings do not accord neuroticism a *primary* role in pain reports in this sample. Neuroticism did not predict pain over and above the ability of clinical and biological indicators of joint inflammation to do so" (p. 124). But according to Figure 1 (p. 124), where path models were displayed, neuroticism was the only exogenous variable!

The authors introduced their path analyses thus:

> We hypothesized that a person's typical responses to increasing pain might mediate neuroticism's association with chronic mood and chronic pain. A path analysis was performed on a mediational model that takes (a) mood to be a function of pain, (b) pain to be a function of pain responses, and (c) pain responses to be a function of neuroticism. (p. 122)

If the path models are tenable from a theoretical perspective (an issue I will not address), then the earlier regression analyses go counter to it.

Finally, even a cursory examination of Figure 1 should reveal problems with the reported results. For instance, according to model (A), neuroticism is the only variable affecting pain coping and pain catastrophizing (see also the preceding quotation for the authors' description of their path analysis). Recalling that the authors analyzed a correlation matrix, the path coefficients from neuroticism to the two pain responses should be equal to the corresponding zero-order correlations (see earlier sections of this chapter). Now, from Table 1, the correlations between neuroticism and pain coping, and neuroticism and pain catastrophizing are, respectively, −.28 and .52. But the corresponding path coefficients reported in Figure 1 are, respectively, .53 and .63.

CLEARLY WRONG RESULTS

Early on (i.e., Chapter 2), I recommended that whenever you examine results of a study (your own or that of others) you should question whether they make sense, thereby increasing the likelihood of detecting results that are clearly wrong or inadmissible (examples of the latter are negative variances, correlations greater than $|1.00|$). All too often it seems that authors (referees and editors) fail to even glance at results with this question in mind.

Military Service, Combat Exposure, and Posttraumatic Stress Disorder

"The purpose of this study was to examine whether appraisals of desirable and undesirable effects of military service mediated the effect of combat stress on posttraumatic stress disorder (PTSD) symptoms in later life" (Aldwin, Levenson, & Spiro, 1994, p. 34).

For illustrative purposes, I comment only on Aldwin et al.'s results for their first path model (their Figure 2, p. 39), according to which (1) Combat Exposure Affects Undesirable Effects of Military Service, Desirable Effects of Military Service, and PTSD; and (2) both Undesirable Effects of Military Service and Desirable Effects of Military Service Affect PTSD. In a summary of effects (direct, indirect, and total; their Table 4, p. 41), Aldwin et al. reported, in addition to a direct effect, an indirect effect for Undesirable Effects of Military Service. This is inconsistent with their path diagram, according to which there is no such indirect effect. Further, according to their Figure 2, the direct effect of Undesirable Effects of Military Service on PTSD is .30, whereas in Table 4 it is reported to be 6.361. As but one other example, according to Figure 2, the direct effect of Desirable Effects of Military Service on PTSD is −.14, but in Table 4 it is reported to be −2.056.

I suspect that discrepancies such as the preceding came about as a result of misuse of a computer program and/or misunderstanding of its output. I say this based on the authors' comments about the computer program they used and what they perceived to be some of its requirements. Thus, they stated:

> We used the GEMINI program . . . to construct [*sic*] the path models used in this study. . . . The GEMINI program requires that the variables be entered in a theoretically determined order. Thus, combat exposure, undesirable experiences, and desirable experiences were entered first, second, and third, respectively. (p. 38)

Though I am not familiar with GEMINI, I suspect that the authors misconstrued whatever was stated in the manual about a requirement of order of entry of variables. Anyway, from the authors' statement about the order in which they entered the variables, I surmise that the program yielded an indirect effect for undesirable experiences, though, as I pointed out earlier, according to Figure 2, the authors hypothesized no such effect.

As to the discrepancies in the magnitudes of the direct effects, I suggest that you replicate Aldwin et al.'s analyses using (1) correlations only and (2) correlations and standard deviations. If you did this, you would find the results of the first analysis to be similar, though not identical, to those Aldwin et al. reported in Figure 2. The results of the second analysis, however, would be nowhere near those reported in Table 4.

Personality Traits, Cognitive Factors, and Accidents

"The purpose of this research was to construct and test a causal model of the accident process" (Hansen, 1989) in industrial settings. For present purposes, I will only point out that after giving an erroneous characterization of Root Mean Square Residual (RMR; see p. 85), Hansen reported RMR values that even a cursory inspection should have sufficed to recognize as being in error. I remind you that earlier in this chapter I explained RMR and pointed out that when a correlation matrix is analyzed, its values may range from 0 (perfect fit) to 1 (a null model; see the discussion of RMR under LISREL, earlier in this chapter).

Having analyzed a correlation matrix, Hansen reported for one of his models (Figure 2, p. 86) $\chi^2 = 3.85$ ($df = 3$), GFI = .943, and RMR = .777 (see p. 85). In light of the χ^2 and GFI, the size of the RMR should have been viewed with suspicion. Anyway, that the results are wrong should have been obvious when an RMR = 1.82 was reported for another model (see p. 86). If you replicated Hansen's analyses, you would find that RMR values for the first and second models, respectively, are .0145 and .0255.

Finally, I would like to point out that Hansen lavished laudatory comments on his research, as is exemplified by the following: "This study broke new ground in accident research by postulating and testing a causal model of the accident process" (p. 86). He added, "Overall, this study is of pivotal importance in that it establishes a new direction for accident research by developing and validating a causal model of the accident process and by using a methodology and analytical technique not previously used" (p. 89). Evidently, the referees and editors agreed!

STUDY SUGGESTIONS

1. Distinguish between exogenous and endogenous variables.
2. What is a recursive model? Give examples.
3. Distinguish between exactly identified and overidentified models. What is a serious limitation of an exactly identified model?
4. What is meant by theory trimming? Discuss potential problems in such an approach.
5. Distinguish between path coefficients and path regression coefficients.
6. What is an effect coefficient?
7. In studies of authoritarianism it has been found that the *F* scale (a measure of authoritarianism) is correlated negatively with mental ability and years of education. Assume that the following causal model is hypothesized:

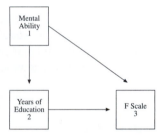

Suppose that the correlations for these variables are $r_{12} = .6$; $r_{13} = -.5$; $r_{23} = -.6$. The subscripts refer to the variable numbers in the figure. Using the information provided, do a path analysis.

(a) What is the direct effect of mental ability on years of education?
(b) What is the direct effect of mental ability on authoritarianism?
(c) What is the direct effect of years of education on authoritarianism?
(d) What is the indirect effect of mental ability on authoritarianism?
(e) Decompose r_{13} and r_{23}.
(f) What are the effect coefficients of mental ability and years of education on authoritarianism?
(g) What are the coefficients for the residual paths to years of education and to authoritarianism?

8. I used the following illustrative correlation matrix ($N = 150$) in Study Suggestions for Chapters 8, 9, and 10.

1 Race	2 IQ	3 School Quality	4 Self-Concept	5 Level of Aspiration	6 Verbal Achievement
1.00	.30	.25	.30	.30	.25
.30	1.00	.20	.20	.30	.60
.25	.20	1.00	.20	.30	.30
.30	.20	.20	1.00	.40	.30
.30	.30	.30	.40	1.00	.40
.25	.60	.30	.30	.40	1.00

The causal model depicted in the following figure is the same as the one I used in Chapter 9 for incremental partitioning of variance.

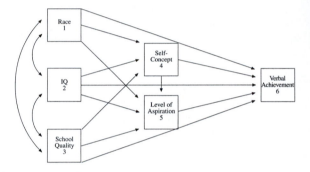

Using a program of your choice (e.g., EQS, LISREL, or a multiple regression program), do a path analysis according to the model depicted in the figure.

(a) What are the direct effects of variables 1, 2, and 3 on variable 4?
(b) What are the direct effects of variables 1, 2, 3, and 4 on 5?
(c) What are the direct effects of variables 1, 2, 3, 4, and 5 on 6?
(d) What are the following: (1) total effects of exogenous variables on endogenous variables; (2) total indirect effects of exogenous variables on endogenous variables; (3) total effects of endogenous variables on endogenous variables; (4) total indirect effects of endogenous variables on endogenous variables?
(e) What are the coefficients for the residual paths to variables 4, 5, and 6?
(f) Use the matrix approach I introduced in the chapter to calculate inclusive specific (indirect) effects of 1, 2, and 3 on 5 and 6, via 4.

Delete the paths from variable 2 to 4, and from 1 to 6.

(g) What are the path coefficients for the revised model?
(h) What is the overall fit of the revised model?
(i) What is the largest standardized residual in the revised model?

Interpret the results. Also, compare the results with those given in study suggestions of earlier chapters, where I subjected the data to incremental partitioning of variance (Chapter 9) and to a multiple regression analysis (Chapter 10).

ANSWERS

3. An exactly identified model cannot be tested.
5. Path coefficients are standardized. Path regression coefficients are unstandardized.
6. An effect coefficient is equal to the sum of the direct and indirect effects of a variable on a given endogenous variable.
7. (a) $p_{21} = .6$
   (b) $p_{31} = -.219$
   (c) $p_{32} = -.469$
   (d) IE $= -.281$
   (e) $r_{13} = -.5 = \underset{\text{DE}}{-.219} + \underset{\text{IE}}{(-.281)}$

   $r_{23} = -.6 = \underset{\text{DE}}{-.469} + \underset{\text{S}}{(-.131)}$
   (f) $EC_1 = -.5$; $EC_2 = -.469$
   (g) $p_{2e} = .80$; $p_{3e} = .78$
8. (a) $p_{41} = .239$; $p_{42} = .104$; $p_{43} = .119$
   (b) $p_{51} = .116$; $p_{52} = .171$; $p_{53} = .178$; $p_{54} = .296$
   (c) $p_{61} = -.019$; $p_{62} = .506$; $p_{63} = .130$; $p_{64} = .110$; $p_{65} = .171$
   (d)   *[LISREL output]*

(1)   TOTAL EFFECTS OF X ON Y

	RACE	IQ	QUAL
SELF	0.239	0.104	0.119
	(0.083)	(0.082)	(0.081)
	2.867	1.269	1.472
ASP	0.186	0.201	0.213
	(0.080)	(0.079)	(0.078)
	2.322	2.542	2.729
ACH	0.039	0.552	0.180
	(0.069)	(0.068)	(0.067)
	0.572	8.109	2.678

(2)   INDIRECT EFFECTS OF X ON Y

	RACE	IQ	QUAL
SELF	– –	– –	– –
ASP	0.071	0.031	0.035
	(0.031)	(0.026)	(0.026)
	2.309	1.207	1.377
ACH	0.058	0.046	0.050
	(0.026)	(0.023)	(0.024)
	2.251	1.978	2.100

(3)   TOTAL EFFECTS OF Y ON Y

	SELF	ASP	ACH
	---------	---------	---------
SELF	– –	– –	– –
ASP	0.296	– –	– –
	(0.076)		
	3.896		
ACH	0.160	0.171	– –
	(0.067)	(0.072)	
	2.389	2.373	

(4)   INDIRECT EFFECTS OF Y ON Y

	SELF	ASP	ACH
	---------	---------	---------
SELF	– –	– –	– –
ASP	– –	– –	– –
ACH	0.050	– –	– –
	(0.025)		
	2.027		

(e)

	SELF	ASP	ACH
	---------	---------	---------
	.940	.862	.749

(f)   *[SAS output]*

IY1   3 rows   3 cols

	[RACE]	[IQ]	[QUAL]
	0	0	0
[ASP]	0.070744	0.030784	0.035224
[ACH]	0.0383872	0.0167041	0.0191133

[see chapter for explanation]

(g) $p_{41} = .267; p_{42} = 0; p_{43} = .133$
   $p_{51} = .116; p_{52} = .171; p_{53} = .178; p_{54} = .296$
   $p_{61} = 0; p_{62} = .503; p_{63} = .128; p_{64} = .107; p_{65} = .168$

(h)   *[LISREL output]*

CHI-SQUARE WITH 2 DEGREES OF FREEDOM = 1.711 (P = 0.425)
ROOT MEAN SQUARE RESIDUAL (RMR) = 0.0251
STANDARDIZED RMR = 0.0252
GOODNESS OF FIT INDEX (GFI) = 0.996
ADJUSTED GOODNESS OF FIT INDEX (AGFI) = 0.960
NORMED FIT INDEX (NFI) = 0.990
NON-NORMED FIT INDEX (NNFI) = 1.014
COMPARATIVE FIT INDEX (CFI) = 1.000

(i) 1.178 *[SELF and IQ]*

CHAPTER

19

Structural Equation Models with Latent Variables

In the preceding chapter, I introduced basic ideas of SEM in the context of path analysis. As I pointed out, path analysis, which is a special case of SEM, is based on a set of restrictive assumptions, some of which are that the (1) variables are measured without error, (2) residuals are not correlated, and (3) causal flow is unidirectional (i.e., the recursive model). The first assumption, in particular, is rarely, if ever, met in applied settings, especially in nonexperimental research.

It is a truism that measures are fallible. Many measures used in social and behavioral research have moderate reliabilities. Moreover, classical approaches to reliability (e.g., Nunnally, 1978; Pedhazur & Schmelkin, 1991, Chapter 5) treat errors as being random. However, many sources of error are nonrandom (systematic), hence affecting validity, not reliability, of measures.

Social and behavioral research is replete with unobservable (latent) variables (e.g., motivation, anxiety, intelligence, attitudes). It is unrealistic to expect single indicators to capture validly and reliably such complex constructs. Instead, multiple indicators are necessary to capture the essence of such variables. In path analysis, as in regression analysis, multiple indicators of latent variables are treated as if they were distinct variables. Accordingly, what I said earlier in the text (especially in Chapter 10) about deleterious consequences of using multiple indicators in regression analysis applies also to path analysis.

Often, it is unreasonable to assume, as is done in path analysis, that residuals from different equations are not correlated. For example, such an assumption is untenable in longitudinal research when subjects are measured at several points in time on the same variables.

Finally, the formulation of recursive models (i.e., models with unidirectional causation) is unrealistic in many research areas. Moreover, interest in reciprocal causation may be the focus of the research. In studies of academic achievement, for instance, it seems sound to suggest that parents' or teachers' expectations affect students' achievement and, in turn, are affected by students' achievement. Similarly, one may suggest that students' motivation affects their academic achievement and is affected by it.

In this chapter, I extend my presentation of SEM to models with multiple indicators of latent variables. As a result, I address two major components: (1) measurement equations, also called measurement model or submodel, and (2) structural equations, also called structural model or submodel. As in Chapter 18, I will give only an elementary intuitive introduction. Although the very simple models I will present cannot convey the full flavor of SEM, I believe they are suited for grasping its basic principles. Specifically, my presentation is limited to recursive models in a single sample. At the conclusion of this chapter, I will comment on more complex models and more advanced topics and give relevant references.

As in Chapter 18, I will use both LISREL and EQS and will show how models with latent variables are handled in each. Recall that though in both programs models can be expressed in equation format, certain aspects of the results can be obtained in LISREL only by calling for LISREL output. Therefore, although I will use LISREL's SIMPLIS language, I will also explain notation and matrices used in LISREL to help you understand its output. This is particularly important, as almost all published reports of LISREL applications use LISREL notation and output format.

I begin by introducing notation and matrix formats for measurement and structural equations in LISREL. Following that, I cast a path analysis example from Chapter 18 in LISREL notation to make explicit measurement assumptions used implicitly in applications of path analysis. I then show how to incorporate in the analysis, reliability estimates for variables represented by single indicators. Next, I turn to models with multiple indicators of latent variables. As in Chapter 18, I present some research examples to alert you to egregious errors. I conclude the chapter with comments, along with selected references, about topics I did not address.

LISREL

In what follows, I present notation and matrix forms of structural and measurement equations as used in LISREL.

Structural Equations

Structural equations express relations among exogenous and endogenous variables. Most often, these variables are constructs and are therefore unobserved. Unobserved variables—also called latent or true—have a central role in social and behavioral sciences (e.g., intelligence, motivation, attitudes, ambition, anxiety, aspirations, cognitive styles). In LISREL, latent dependent, or endogenous, variables are designated as η (eta), whereas latent independent, or exogenous, variables are designated as ξ (xi). In matrix form, the structural equations are as follows:

$$\eta = \mathbf{B}\eta + \Gamma\xi + \zeta \tag{19.1}$$

where η (eta) is an m by 1 vector of latent endogenous variables; ξ (xi) is an n by 1 vector of latent exogenous variables; $\mathbf{B}$ (beta) is an m by m matrix of coefficients of the effects of endogenous on endogenous variables (η's); Γ (gamma) is an m by n matrix of coefficients of effects of exogenous variables (ξ's) on endogenous variables (η's); and ζ (zeta) is an m by 1 vector of residuals, or errors in equations. It is assumed that the means of all the variables are equal to zero, that is, the variables are expressed in deviation scores. Also, it is assumed that ζ and ξ are uncorrelated and that "$\mathbf{B}$ has zeros in the diagonal and $\mathbf{I} - \mathbf{B}$ is non-singular" (Jöreskog & Sörbom, 1989, p. 4).[1]

---

[1] $\mathbf{I}$ is an identity matrix whose dimensions are the same as those of $\mathbf{B}$. In Chapters 10 and 11 I explained the properties of a singular matrix. See also Appendix A.

Measurement Equations

Measurement equations express relations between unobserved and observed, or latent and manifest, variables. Two equations describe such relations:

$$\mathbf{y} = \Lambda_y \boldsymbol{\eta} + \boldsymbol{\epsilon} \tag{19.2}$$

where $\mathbf{y}$ is a p by 1 vector of measures of dependent variables; Λ (lambda) is a p by m matrix of coefficients, or loadings, of $\mathbf{y}$ on the latent dependent variables ($\boldsymbol{\eta}$); and $\boldsymbol{\epsilon}$ (epsilon) is a p by 1 vector of errors of measurement of $\mathbf{y}$. It is assumed that $\boldsymbol{\eta}$ and $\boldsymbol{\epsilon}$ are uncorrelated.

$$\mathbf{x} = \Lambda_x \boldsymbol{\xi} + \boldsymbol{\delta} \tag{19.3}$$

where $\mathbf{x}$ is a q by 1 vector of measures of independent variables; Λ (lambda) is a q by n matrix of coefficients, or loadings, of $\mathbf{x}$ on the latent independent variables ($\boldsymbol{\xi}$); and $\boldsymbol{\delta}$ (delta) is a q by 1 vector of errors of measurement of $\mathbf{x}$. It is assumed that $\boldsymbol{\xi}$ and $\boldsymbol{\delta}$ are uncorrelated. Further, it is assumed that "ζ, ϵ, and δ are mutually uncorrelated" (Jöreskog & Sörbom, 1989, p. 4).

To clarify the terms in (19.1) through (19.3), I will present a relatively simple model—first graphically and then in matrix form. To highlight the differences between the type of models I deal with here and those I presented in Chapter 18, I will present a model that parallels one I presented in Chapter 18. Specifically, the model in Figure 19.1 parallels that of Figure 18.13.

In SEM literature it is customary to use squares or rectangles to represent observed variables and circles or ellipses to represent unobserved variables. The model of Figure 19.1 consists of two latent exogenous variables (ξ_1 and ξ_2) and two latent endogenous variables (η_1 and η_2). Assume that ξ_1 is socioeconomic status (SES) and that ξ_2 is intelligence (IQ). SES is measured by three indicators (X_1 X_2, and X_3) and IQ is measured by two indicators (X_4 and X_5). Assume,

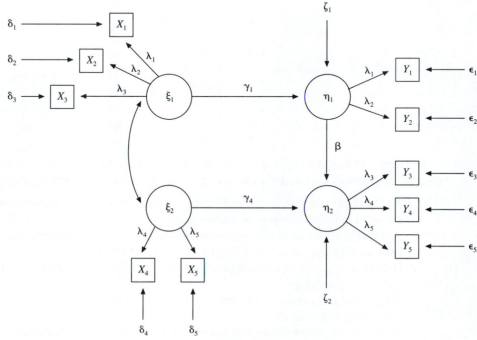

Figure 19.1

further, that η_1 is achievement motivation (AM) and is measured by two indicators (Y_1 and Y_2). η_2 is achievement (ACH) and is measured by three indicators (Y_3, Y_4, and Y_5).

According to the model in Figure 19.1, SES and IQ are correlated. SES affects AM directly, and it affects ACH indirectly via AM. IQ affects ACH directly. To repeat: this model is the same as that in Figure 18.13, except that in the latter I used a single measure for each construct. Thus, in the preceding chapter I assumed *unrealistically* that the constructs and the scales used to measure them are identities, whereas in the present chapter I treat the constructs as unobserved variables, each of which is measured by two or more fallible measures.

Whereas the model of Figure 19.1 is recursive, LISREL accommodates also nonrecursive models. For example, in Figure 19.1, I could have indicated that not only does η_1 affect η_2, but also that the latter affects the former. Furthermore, whereas errors in Figure 19.1 are depicted as being not correlated among themselves, LISREL can accommodate models with correlated errors.

The matrices for the structural equations of Figure 19.1 are

$$\underset{\boldsymbol{\eta}}{\begin{bmatrix} \eta_1 \\ \eta_2 \end{bmatrix}} = \underset{\mathbf{B}}{\begin{bmatrix} 0 & 0 \\ \beta & 0 \end{bmatrix}} \underset{\boldsymbol{\eta}}{\begin{bmatrix} \eta_1 \\ \eta_2 \end{bmatrix}} + \underset{\boldsymbol{\Gamma}}{\begin{bmatrix} \gamma_1 & 0 \\ 0 & \gamma_4 \end{bmatrix}} \underset{\boldsymbol{\xi}}{\begin{bmatrix} \xi_1 \\ \xi_2 \end{bmatrix}} + \underset{\boldsymbol{\zeta}}{\begin{bmatrix} \zeta_1 \\ \zeta_2 \end{bmatrix}}$$

The matrices for the measurement equations of Figure 19.1 are

$$\underset{\mathbf{x}}{\begin{bmatrix} x_1 \\ x_2 \\ x_3 \\ x_4 \\ x_5 \end{bmatrix}} = \underset{\boldsymbol{\Lambda}_x}{\begin{bmatrix} \lambda_1 & 0 \\ \lambda_2 & 0 \\ \lambda_3 & 0 \\ 0 & \lambda_4 \\ 0 & \lambda_5 \end{bmatrix}} \underset{\boldsymbol{\xi}}{\begin{bmatrix} \xi_1 \\ \xi_2 \end{bmatrix}} + \underset{\boldsymbol{\delta}}{\begin{bmatrix} \delta_1 \\ \delta_2 \\ \delta_3 \\ \delta_4 \\ \delta_5 \end{bmatrix}}$$

$$\underset{\mathbf{y}}{\begin{bmatrix} y_1 \\ y_2 \\ y_3 \\ y_4 \\ y_5 \end{bmatrix}} = \underset{\boldsymbol{\Lambda}_y}{\begin{bmatrix} \lambda_1 & 0 \\ \lambda_2 & 0 \\ 0 & \lambda_3 \\ 0 & \lambda_4 \\ 0 & \lambda_5 \end{bmatrix}} \underset{\boldsymbol{\eta}}{\begin{bmatrix} \eta_1 \\ \eta_2 \end{bmatrix}} + \underset{\boldsymbol{\epsilon}}{\begin{bmatrix} \epsilon_1 \\ \epsilon_2 \\ \epsilon_3 \\ \epsilon_4 \\ \epsilon_5 \end{bmatrix}}$$

Jöreskog and Sörbom (1989, p. 5) showed that, based on the assumptions stated earlier, the covariance matrix of the observed variables (Σ) is a function of the following eight matrices:

1. $\boldsymbol{\Lambda}_y$ (lambda) is a matrix of coefficients, or loadings, relating indicators of endogenous variables to latent endogenous variables (η).
2. $\boldsymbol{\Lambda}_x$ (lambda) is a matrix of coefficients, or loadings, relating indicators of exogenous variables to latent exogenous variables (ξ).
3. $\mathbf{B}$ (beta) is a matrix of coefficients of the effects of latent endogenous variables on latent endogenous variables.
4. $\boldsymbol{\Gamma}$ (gamma) is a matrix of coefficients of the effects of latent exogenous variables on latent endogenous variables.
5. $\boldsymbol{\Phi}$ (phi) is a variance-covariance matrix of the latent exogenous variables (ξ).
6. $\boldsymbol{\Psi}$ (psi) is a variance-covariance matrix of the residuals (ζ) or errors in equations.

7. Θ_ϵ (theta) is a variance-covariance matrix of measurement errors of *y*'s.
8. Θ_δ (theta) is a variance-covariance matrix of measurement errors of *x*'s.

Estimation

Elements of the above noted matrices may be of three kinds:

- *fixed parameters* that have been assigned given values,
- *constrained parameters* that are unknown but equal to one or more other parameters, and
- *free parameters* that are unknown and not constrained to be equal to any other parameter. (Jöreskog & Sörbom, 1989, p. 5)

With a covariance matrix among the observed variables as input, LISREL is used to arrive at estimates of elements in all or some of the eight matrices listed, depending on the model. For instance, an extensive literature is limited to measurement models. Among topics addressed in this literature are reliability and validity of measures, separation of method, and trait variance. In most instances, studies of measurement models in SEM take the form of confirmatory factor analysis. Though I comment on measurement issues, I do not address measurement as a separate topic, nor do I discuss confirmatory factor analysis. For introductions to measurement models and confirmatory factor analysis, see Jackson and Borgatta (1981), Long (1983), McDonald (1985), and Pedhazur and Schmelkin (1991, Chapter 23). See also my comment on the "Two-Step Approach in SEM," later in this chapter.

Path Model: Depiction with LISREL Notation

In Chapter 18, Figure 18.12, I presented a four-variable model, which I analyzed in detail using regression analysis, LISREL, and EQS. Briefly, I treated socioeconomic status (SES) and intelligence (IQ) as two correlated exogenous variables. I hypothesized that SES and IQ affect achievement motivation (AM), and that SES, IQ, and AM affect achievement as measured by grade-point average (GPA). Following conventions of drawing causal models in LISREL (see the preceding), I depict this causal model in Figure 19.2. For illustrative purposes, I use the results I obtained from the analysis of the correlation matrix (i.e., path coefficients).

The difference between Figure 19.2 and Figure 18.12 is that in the former latent variables (enclosed in circles) are distinguished from manifest variables (enclosed in squares). Note that I labeled variable 4 of Figure 18.12 Achievement (ACH) to distinguish it from its indicator, GPA. Examine Figure 19.2 and notice that each indicator is treated as a perfectly reliable and valid measure of the variable that it presumably measures. I indicate this in Figure 19.2 by coefficients that are equal to 1.00 emanating from each latent variable to its indicator and by .00 errors associated with the indicators. Needless to say, these assumptions are most unrealistic when one considers the type of variables studied and the kind of measures generally used to tap them. The virtue of the diagram in Figure 19.2 is that it brings to light these untenable assumptions. In Figure 18.12, on the other hand, the same assumptions are in the background, so to speak, and therefore the likelihood of overlooking them is much greater than when the model is depicted as in Figure 19.2. I suggest that you study the notation in Figure 19.2 in conjunction with the LISREL notation and matrices I presented earlier.

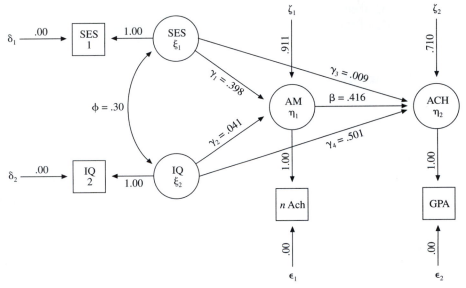

Figure 19.2

MEASUREMENT ERRORS

Earlier in the text (particularly in Chapters 2 and 10), I discussed adverse effects of measurement errors on regression analysis. Also, I gave references to general presentations of measurement and its relation to various aspects of research. As in other areas, the posture regarding measurement among researchers applying SEM varies widely, from utter disregard to lip service to concern coupled with attempts to take appropriate actions at various stages of the research (e.g., scale construction and validation, reliability estimation, analysis, interpretation of results).

Recall that a major assumption of path analysis is that the variables are measured without error (see the preceding discussion and Chapter 18). Regrettably, many, if not most, researchers act as if this is indeed the case for their data. I say this because most do not even allude to measurement errors when they report results of path analysis. Some researchers state flatly that they assumed that their measures were perfectly reliable. Then there are those who report reliabilities of measures they use but do nothing about them at the analysis and interpretation stages. Moreover, many researchers (editors and referees too?) seem unaware that reliability of a measure is sample specific. I say this because they do *not* report reliability estimates based on responses of their subjects but rather ones given in the manuals for the measures they use or ones reported by other researchers using the same measures.

When single indicators are used for some or all the variables in a model, it is possible to incorporate estimates of their reliabilities in the analysis.[2] As you probably know, various approaches to reliability estimation exist (e.g., test-retest, internal consistency). I cannot address this topic here (for an introduction and references, see Pedhazur & Schmelkin, 1991, Chapter 5; for reliability studies in the context of SEM, see Bohrnstedt, Mohler, & Müller, 1987). *In what follows I use the term* reliability, *and its notation,* r_{tt}, *generically.* Of course, in actual applications

---

[2]Later, I address the issue of measurement errors in designs with multiple indicators. See Bollen (1989, Chapters 5 and 6) for thorough treatments of measurement errors in models with single and multiple indicators.

Table 19.1   Correlations, Standard Deviations, and Reliabilities for a Four-Variable Model; N = 300

	1 *SES*	*2* *IQ*	*3* *AM*	*4* *GPA*
1	1.00	.30	.41	.33
2	.30	1.00	.16	.57
3	.41	.16	1.00	.50
4	.33	.57	.50	1.00
s:	2.10	15.00	3.25	1.25
r_{tt}:	.70	.85	.80	.70

NOTE: s = standard deviation and r_{tt} = reliability.

the type of reliability estimate used is important. Nevertheless, as Jöreskog and Sörbom (1993a) asserted, "an arbitrary [reliability] value . . . is a better assumption than the equally arbitrary value of 1.00" (p. 37) when no reliability estimate is used in the analysis.

A Numerical Example

For comparative purposes, I return to an example I analyzed thoroughly in Chapter 18, namely the model depicted in Figure 18.12 for which I used the data in Table 18.1. As I pointed out earlier, by default my analyses in Chapter 18 were based on the *unrealistic* assumption that all the measures have perfect reliabilities. In Table 19.1, I repeated the correlations reported in Table 18.1, as well as the standard deviations I used when I calculated path regression coefficients (unstandardized coefficients) for these data. In addition, I included in Table 19.1 illustrative reliability estimates for the four measures in question.

I will use LISREL to analyze the data in Table 19.1 (specifically, the correlations and the reliability estimates) according to the model of Figure 18.12 (see also Figure 19.2, whose results are based on the assumption that the measures of the observed variables are perfectly reliable). Later, I comment on using also the standard deviations in Table 19.1 to obtain path regression coefficients.

LISREL

Input

! TABLE 19.1.   INPUT CORRELATION MATRIX ONLY.
! RELIABILITIES: SES = .7, IQ = .85, AM = .8, GPA = .7
OBSERVED VARIABLES: SES IQ AM GPA
CORRELATION MATRIX:
1.00
 .30 1.00
 .41   .16 1.00
 .33   .57 .50 1.00
SAMPLE SIZE 300

```
LATENT VARIABLES: SESL IQL AML ACH
RELATIONS
SES = 1*SESL
IQ = 1*IQL
AM = 1*AML
GPA = 1*ACH
SET ERROR VARIANCE OF SES TO .3
SET ERROR VARIANCE OF IQ TO .15
SET ERROR VARIANCE OF AM TO .2
SET ERROR VARIANCE OF GPA TO .3
AML = SESL IQL
ACH = SESL IQL AML
OPTIONS: ND=3
```

Commentary

For an orientation to LISREL, see Chapter 18. As most of the input is similar to the one I used in Chapter 18 (see input for model of Figure 18.12), I will comment only on statements concerning LATENT VARIABLES and ERROR VARIANCE, beginning with the former.

For convenience, I named latent variables, except for ACH, by attaching an "L" (for latent) to the name of each observed variable. Normally, names of latent variables refer to constructs (e.g., mental ability, aggression, motivation, self-concept), whereas names of observed variables refer to the operationalism of constructs (e.g., measures, observations, manipulations).

As latent variables are unobservable, it is necessary to assign them units of measurement. One way of doing this "is to fix a non-zero coefficient (usually one) in the relationship for one of its observed indicators. This defines the unit for each latent variable in relation to one of the observed variables, a so-called *reference variable*" (Jöreskog & Sörbom, 1993a, p. 173) or *reference indicator*. As a result, coefficients associated with latent variables are interpreted in units of the measures of their corresponding reference indicators. In this section, I use reference indicators to scale the latent variables. Later, I introduce another approach.

As the present example consists of single indicators, I use each as the reference indicator for the latent variable it presumably measures. For instance, SES = 1*SESL means fixing the coefficient of SESL to 1.0. The same procedure is used for the other three equations relating latent to observed variables. Notice that after stating relations between latent and observed variables, I use the former in statements of relations among variables, analogous to those I used for observed variables in the preceding chapter. For instance, analogous to AM = SES IQ in the preceding chapter, I use here AML = SESL IQL.

Random error variance is defined as one minus the reliability of the measure used (for explanations and references, see Pedhazur & Schmelkin, 1991, Chapter 5). For instance, error variance for SES = 1 − .7 = .3, where .7 is the reliability of the SES measure. The same procedure is used for the other measures. Thus, in contrast to my analysis of the same model in Chapter 18, where I made no mention of measurement errors, in the present analysis I set error variances equal to $1 - r_{tt}$ of the measures in question.

Measurement errors for all indicators need not be incorporated in an analysis. When no correction is to be made for measurement errors of a given indicator, its error variance is set equal to zero. For example, if no correction is to be made for measurement errors in GPA, then the relevant statement in the preceding input would be changed to SET ERROR VARIANCE OF GPA TO 0 (for an example, see Jöreskog & Sörbom, 1993a, p. 36). If in the present example the error variance for each indicator were set equal to zero, the results of the analysis would be identical to those I obtained in Chapter 18 for the same model (see "A Just-Identified Model").

Finally, as I explained in Chapter 18, of seven estimation procedures available in LISREL, I use only the default: maximum likelihood.

Output

LISREL ESTIMATES (MAXIMUM LIKELIHOOD)
AML $= 0.595$*SESL $- 0.0218$*IQL, Errorvar. $= 0.560$, $R^2 = 0.301$
ACH $= 0.565$*AML $- 0.119$*SESL $+ 0.606$*IQL, Errorvar. $= 0.111$, $R^2 = 0.841$

Commentary

When I analyzed the data in Table 18.1 in Chapter 18 for a just-identified model (Figure 18.12), I reported both path regression coefficients (unstandardized) and path coefficients (standardized). As the previous estimates are based on an analysis of the correlation matrix,[3] you should compare them to the corresponding path coefficients in Chapter 18, or the values reported in Figure 19.2, to see consequences of correcting for measurement errors in the present analysis of the same model. Thus, for example, the effect of SES on AM in the analysis of these data in Chapter 18 (with no corrections for measurement errors) was .398. In the present analysis, the corresponding value is .595. As another example, the effect of IQ on GPA in the earlier analysis was .501, whereas in the present analysis it is .606. Similar differences can be observed in the R^2's in the two analyses. In the earlier analysis, R^2's for AM and GPA, respectively, were .170 and .496. The corresponding values in the present analysis are .301 and .841. I suggest that you study the LISREL outputs from the analyses of the same model in Chapter 18 (with no measurement errors) and the present chapter (with measurement errors). Among other things, note also the difference in error variances in the two analyses.

Path Regression Coefficients

As in Chapter 18, it is possible to obtain path regression coefficients by analyzing the covariance matrix. To do this for the present data, make the following changes in the previous input file: (1) add the standard deviations (see input files in Chapter 18 on how this may be done) and (2) change the error variances to reflect the fact that a covariance matrix is analyzed. To do this, multiply the variance of each observed variable by one minus the reliability of its measure. For example, the standard deviation and reliability of SES are, respectively, 2.10 and .7. Therefore, the error variance for SES is $(1 - .7)(2.10^2) = 1.323$. The remaining error variances are treated similarly. In sum, replace the values in the four error variance statements with the following:

[3]Later I comment on an analysis of the covariance matrix.

SET ERROR VARIANCE OF SES TO 1.323

SET ERROR VARIANCE OF IQ TO 33.75

SET ERROR VARIANCE OF AM TO 2.112

SET ERROR VARIANCE OF GPA TO .469

Compare your results with my results in Chapter 18, where I analyzed the covariance matrix without corrections for measurement errors.

I turn now to an analysis of the same data (Table 19.1) and the same model (Figure 18.12) using EQS.

EQS

Input

```
/TIT
TABLE 19.1. A JUST-IDENTIFIED MODEL, AS IN FIGURE 18.12.
  RELIABILITIES: SES = .7; IQ = .85; AM = .8; GPA = .7
/SPE
CAS=300; VAR=4;
/LAB
V1=SES; V2=IQ; V3=AM; V4=GPA;
/EQU
V1=F1 + E1;
V2=F2 + E2;
V3=F3 + E3;
V4=F4 + E4;
F3 = .4*F1 + .05*F2 + D3;
F4 = .05*F1 + .5*F2 + .4*F3 + D4;
/VAR
F1 TO F2=*;
E1=.3;E2=.15;E3=.2;E4=.3;
D3 TO D4=*;
/COV
F1,F2=*;
/MAT
1.00
 .30 1.00
 .41  .16 1.00
 .33  .57  .50 1.00
/END
```

Commentary

For an orientation to EQS, see Chapter 18, where I also commented on an input file similar to the preceding for an analysis of the model in Figure 18.12. Here, I comment only on statements concerning latent variables and error variances.

As I pointed out in Chapter 18, in EQS latent variables are designated as F's (factors), and residuals of latent variables as D's (disturbances). Also, asterisks (*) indicate free parameters. A number preceding an * is a start value. Parameters without * are fixed. When not preceded by a number, fixed parameters are set to 1.0. Thus in the first four equations in the previous input, 1.0 will be used as the coefficient for the four latent variables (F's) as well as for the four error terms (E's).[4]

As in my LISREL run for the same model and data, I designated each observed variable as a reference indicator for the latent variable it presumably measures. Also, as in my LISREL run, I fixed measurement error variances to $1 - r_{tt}$ for each of the measures (see E's without * in the /VAR paragraph).

The * for the other terms in the /VAR paragraph and in the /COV paragraph mean that the variances of the F's and the D's, and the covariance of the F's are free.

Output

```
F3    =F3  =  .595*F1  +  −.022*F2  +  1.000 D3
F4    =F4  =  .565*F3  +  −.119*F1  +   .606*F2  +  1.000 D4
```

Commentary

Compare the preceding with results I reported earlier from the LISREL analysis, where I also commented on them. As I suggested earlier, if you run both programs, compare their results and notice that they are alike, though they are presented in different formats. For instance, what is reported in LISREL as Errorvar. (i.e., 0.560 and 0.111, see the preceding) is reported in EQS under D for the VARIANCE OF INDEPENDENT VARIABLES (not reproduced here).

Path Regression Coefficients

As in the LISREL run, path regression coefficients can be obtained in EQS by analyzing the covariance matrix. In Chapter 18, I gave an input file for the analysis of a covariance matrix. To analyze the covariance matrix for the data in Table 19.1, incorporating reliability estimates, make the following additions or modifications to the previous input file. (1) Add a paragraph of standard deviations (see the input file in Chapter 18). (2) Modify the line of measurement error variances in the /VAR paragraph to reflect the fact that a covariance matrix is analyzed. Specifically, replace the line consisting of the E's with the following:

---

[4]In the event you are running both LISREL and EQS, keep in mind that they differ in their approach to the designation of free and fixed parameters. In LISREL parameters *without* an asterisk (*) are free, whereas those preceded by an * are fixed. To distinguish between values for fixed parameters and start values, the latter are placed in parentheses (see Jöreskog & Sörbom, 1993a, p. 174). For example, in LISREL 1.5*SES means that the coefficient for SES is fixed at 1.5, whereas (1.5)*SES means that 1.5 is to be used as a start value in the estimation of the coefficient for SES.

E1=1.323; E2=33.75; E3=2.112; E4=.469;

For an explanation, see my earlier comments on the LISREL input. (3) Use some appropriate start values (e.g., *3 and *190 for the variances of F1 and F2, respectively, in the /VAR paragraph). In the absence of some appropriate start values the program will fail to converge. (See Chapter 18 for an explanation of the use of start values in EQS). (4) As I pointed out in Chapter 18, because of a bug in Version 4.02, which I am using, the covariance matrix will *not* be analyzed unless MA=COR is stated in the /SPE paragraph. It is, of course, possible that the bug has been fixed in the version of EQS you are using.

A Final Comment

The results I reported in the preceding are based on the analysis of the correlation matrix. Therefore, I did not report tests of statistical significance of the path coefficients (see Chapter 18 for an explanation). My sole purpose was to introduce the idea of incorporating measurement errors in the analysis and to illustrate how this affects results.

DESIGNS WITH MULTIPLE INDICATORS

Thus far, I presented designs with single indicators. I trust that you recognize that when studying constructs and relations among them it is imperative to use multiple indicators. Earlier in the text (particularly in Chapters 9 and 10) I discussed and illustrated deleterious consequences of using multiple indicators of independent variables in regression analysis (recall that this is because in regression analysis multiple indicators are treated as if they were distinct variables).

The inappropriateness of multiple regression analysis for designs with multiple indicators is particularly apparent when they are used for the dependent variable. Probably the most common approach taken in such circumstances is doing separate regression analyses in which each indicator of the dependent variable is treated, in turn, as a distinct dependent variable (see "Research Examples," later in this chapter). I trust that the weaknesses of this approach are obvious and will therefore not comment on them. A second approach that researchers often take is to combine scores on multiple indicators of the dependent variable into a composite score, which then serves as the score on the dependent variable in a regression analysis. I will not comment on this approach either, except to point out that often composite scores are arrived at with little reason.

As I pointed out earlier, multiple indicators of latent variables are an integral part of the measurement submodel of SEM. A major advantage of using multiple indicators in SEM is that they afford the study of relations among latent variables uncontaminated by errors of measurement in the indicators. This is predicated, among other things, on judicious choices of indicators, or manifest variables.

How Many Indicators?

The great diversity of latent variables in social and behavioral sciences precludes the possibility of prescribing a number of necessary indicators.

> Since the LVs [latent variables] are in practice abstractions that presumably underlie MVs [manifest variables], a poor choice of MVs will create doubt as to whether a theory's constructs are in fact embedded in a model. Choosing the right number of indicators for each LV is something of an art: in principle, the more the better; in practice, too many indicators make it difficult if not impossible to fit a model to data. (Bentler, 1980, p. 425)

In another context, Bentler (1987) stated, "Ideally, three or more indicators of a factor would be used in a study so as to better anchor the factor in its indicators" (p. 66). It is, of course, preferable to use a relatively small number of "good" indicators than to delude oneself with a relatively large number of "poor" ones.

Multi-Item Measures as Indicators

Often, researchers use measures composed of multiple items as indicators of latent variables. Thus, several multi-item measures may be used as indicators of, say, mental ability, self-concept, or conservatism. When this is done in an SEM analysis, psychometric properties of the measures (e.g., internal consistency, unidimensionality) are, willy-nilly, assumed to be satisfactory. Depending, among other things, on the scope of the measures, their properties can be studied in separate analyses (e.g., confirmatory factor analysis)[5] or as the measurement submodel of the causal model under consideration (see "Two-Step Approach," under "Miscellaneous Topics," later in this chapter).

A Numerical Example

Earlier in this chapter, I introduced a model with multiple indicators of four latent variables (see Figure 19.1 and the discussion related to it). Briefly, the model consisted of two exogenous latent variables—socioeconomic status (SES) and intelligence (IQ)—and two endogenous latent variables—achievement motivation (AM) and academic achievement (ACH). I will analyze this model using the illustrative data in Table 19.2. As I stated in the footnote to Table 19.2 (also in Figure 19.1), X_1, X_2, and X_3 are indicators of SES (e.g., parental income, years of education); X_4 and X_5 are indicators of IQ (e.g., Stanford-Binet, Wechsler); Y_1 and Y_2 are indicators of AM (e.g., ratings by teacher and counselor); and Y_3, Y_4, and Y_5 are indicators of ACH (e.g., measures of reading, spelling, arithmetic).

LISREL

Input

! TABLE 19.2. MULTIPLE INDICATORS	!TABLE 19.2. MULTIPLE INDICATORS
! REFERENCE INDICATORS	! NO REFERENCE INDICATORS
! SES = X1, X2, X3; IQ = X3, X4;	! SES = X1, X2, X3; IQ = X3, X4;
! AM = Y1, Y2; ACH = Y3, Y4, Y5	! AM = Y1, Y2; ACH = Y3, Y4, Y5
OBSERVED VARIABLES: X1-X5 Y1-Y5	OBSERVED VARIABLES: X1-X5 Y1-Y5
LATENT VARIABLES: SES IQ AM ACH	LATENT VARIABLES: SES IQ AM ACH

---

[5]Earlier in this chapter, I gave references to confirmatory factor analysis.

CORRELATION MATRIX:
1.00
.47   1.00
.41   .45   1.00
.28   .29   .35   1.00
.25   .25   .34   .65   1.00
.41   .40   .35   .16   .20   1.00
.37   .36   .30   .18   .15   .45   1.00
.34   .32   .37   .47   .50   .40   .38   1.00
.36   .34   .31   .45   .48   .42   .35   .62   1.00
.35   .36   .38   .52   .50   .45   .40   .65   .68   1.00
STANDARD DEVIATIONS:
2.10   1.76   2.22   15.00   16.30   6.85   10.14   12.25   15.32   18.92

SAMPLE SIZE 300	SAMPLE SIZE 300
RELATIONS	RELATIONS
X1 = 1*SES	X1 X2 X3 = SES
X2 X3 = SES	X4 X5 = IQ
X4 = 1*IQ	Y1 Y2 = AM
X5 = IQ	Y3 Y4 Y5 = ACH
Y1 = 1*AM	AM = SES
Y2 = AM	ACH = IQ AM
Y3 = 1*ACH	OPTIONS: ND=3 RS
Y4 Y5 = ACH	END OF PROBLEM
AM = SES	
ACH = IQ AM	
OPTIONS: ND=3 RS	
PATH DIAGRAM UL=4,4	
END OF PROBLEM	

Table 19.2   Correlations and Standard Deviations, for a Model with Multiple Indicators, as in Figure 19.1; N = 300

	X_1	X_2	X_3	X_4	X_5	Y_1	Y_2	Y_3	Y_4	Y_5
X_1	1.00	.47	.41	.28	.25	.41	.37	.34	.36	.35
X_2	.47	1.00	.45	.29	.25	.40	.36	.32	.34	.36
X_3	.41	.45	1.00	.35	.34	.35	.30	.37	.31	.38
X_4	.28	.29	.35	1.00	.65	.16	.18	.47	.45	.52
X_5	.25	.25	.34	.65	1.00	.20	.15	.50	.48	.50
Y_1	.41	.40	.35	.16	.20	1.00	.45	.40	.42	.45
Y_2	.37	.36	.30	.18	.15	.45	1.00	.38	.35	.40
Y_3	.34	.32	.37	.47	.50	.40	.38	1.00	.62	.65
Y_4	.36	.34	.31	.45	.48	.42	.35	.62	1.00	.68
Y_5	.35	.36	.38	.52	.50	.45	.40	.65	.68	1.00
s:	2.10	1.76	2.22	15.00	16.30	6.85	10.14	12.25	15.32	18.92

NOTE: s = standard deviation; X_1, X_2, and X_3 are indicators of SES; X_4 and X_5 are indicators of IQ; Y_1 and Y_2 are indicators of AM; Y_3, Y_4, and Y_5 are indicators of ACH.

Commentary

The preceding input consists of two problems, which I placed alongside each other for ease of comparisons. As you can see from the second line of the titles, I use reference indicators for the problem on the left of the broken line, but not for the one on the right of the line. To run these problems stacked, place the statements on the right after the END OF PROBLEM statement of the input on the left. Note that it is not necessary to repeat the correlation matrix and the standard deviations for the second problem. In sum, the difference between the two problems is that in the one on the left I use reference indicators, whereas in the one on the right I do not use reference indicators.

Earlier, I explained that reference indicators are used to scale latent variables. Thus, in the input on the left SES is scaled to units of X1 (see 1*SES), IQ is scaled to units of X4, AM is scaled to units of Y1, and ACH is scaled to units of Y3. Reference indicators are particularly useful when the units of the measure used to scale the latent variables are substantively interpretable, as this affords meaningful statements about the magnitude of effects of latent variables.

When the units of the measures of the indicators are not readily interpretable, Jöreskog and Sörbom (1993a), among others, recommend that the researcher "assume that . . . [the latent variables] are standardized so that they have unit variances in the population. This means that the unit of measurement of each latent variable equals its population standard deviation" (p. 173). However, as in regression analysis (see, for example, Chapter 10), the use of standardized coefficients only appears to solve the problem. Only through the development and use of better measures can one come to grips with it.

When, as in the input on the right, reference indicators are not specified, LISREL automatically standardizes the latent variables (see the following output and commentaries).

As the rest of the input statements are similar to ones I used in earlier runs, I will not comment on them. If necessary, refer to commentaries on inputs for earlier runs in this and the preceding chapter.

Finally, in the input on the left I called for a path diagram. See the line before the first END OF PROBLEM. I give the diagram at the end of the output, where I also explain UL and comment on other options for generating path diagrams.

Output

COVARIANCE MATRIX TO BE ANALYZED

	Y1	Y2	Y3	Y4	Y5	X1	X2	X3	X4	X5
Y1	46.922									
Y2	31.257	102.820								
Y3	33.565	47.202	150.063							
Y4	44.076	54.371	116.355	234.702						
Y5	58.321	76.740	150.651	197.101	357.966					
X1	5.898	7.879	8.747	11.582	13.906	4.410				
X2	4.822	6.425	6.899	9.167	11.988	1.737	3.098			
X3	5.322	6.753	10.062	10.543	15.961	1.911	1.758	4.928		
X4	16.440	27.378	86.363	103.410	147.576	8.820	7.656	11.655	225.000	
X5	22.331	24.792	99.838	119.864	154.198	8.558	7.172	12.303	158.925	265.690

Commentary

As I explained earlier, LISREL uses the correlation matrix and the standard deviations to construct the covariance matrix. Also, it reorders the indicators so that those reflecting endogenous variables are listed first.

Output

| *[reference indicators]* | *[no reference indicators]* |
| LISREL ESTIMATES (MAXIMUM LIKELIHOOD) | LISREL ESTIMATES (MAXIMUM LIKELIHOOD) |

Y1 = 1.000*AM, Errorvar.= 21.382, R^2 = 0.544	Y1 = 5.054*AM, Errorvar.= 21.382, R^2 = 0.544
Y2 = 1.290*AM, Errorvar.= 60.351, R^2 = 0.413	Y2 = 6.517*AM, Errorvar.= 60.351, R^2 = 0.413
Y3 = 1.000*ACH, Errorvar.= 58.802, R^2 = 0.611	Y3 = 9.608*ACH, Errorvar.= 58.802, R^2 = 0.611
Y4 = 1.271*ACH, Errorvar.= 87.241, R^2 = 0.631	Y4 = 12.213*ACH, Errorvar.= 87.242, R^2 = 0.631
Y5 = 1.678*ACH, Errorvar.= 101.142, R^2 = 0.720	Y5 = 16.118*ACH, Errorvar.= 101.142, R^2 = 0.720
X1 = 1.000*SES, Errorvar.= 2.403, R^2 = 0.455	X1 = 1.417*SES, Errorvar.= 2.403, R^2 = 0.455
X2 = 0.861*SES, Errorvar.= 1.610, R^2 = 0.480	X2 = 1.219*SES, Errorvar.= 1.610, R^2 = 0.480
X3 = 1.009*SES, Errorvar.= 2.886, R^2 = 0.414	X3 = 1.429*SES, Errorvar.= 2.886, R^2 = 0.414
X4 = 1.000*IQ, Errorvar.= 78.228, R^2 = 0.652	X4 = 12.115*IQ, Errorvar.= 78.228, R^2 = 0.652
X5 = 1.088*IQ, Errorvar.= 91.820, R^2 = 0.654	X5 = 13.186*IQ, Errorvar.= 91.820, R^2 = 0.654

AM = 2.677*SES, Errorvar.= 11.159, R^2 = 0.563	AM = 0.750*SES, Errorvar.= 0.437, R^2 = 0.563
(0.343) (2.752)	(0.123)
7.805 4.054	6.100

ACH = 0.972*AM + 0.444*IQ, Errorvar.= 19.375,	ACH = 0.511*AM + 0.560*IQ, Errorvar.= 0.210,
(0.140) (0.0534) (4.685)	(0.100) (0.0895)
6.966 8.310 4.136	5.099 6.253
R^2 = 0.790	R^2 = 0.790

Commentary

As is indicated in the italicized headings, which are not part of the output, the output on the left is for the problem with reference indicators, whereas that on the right is for the one without reference indicators (see the commentary on the input). I will make several points about these excerpts.

Except for the fixed coefficients for the reference indicators (1's in the output on the left), LISREL reports standard errors and *t*-values for parameter estimates. "Parameters whose *t*-values are larger than two in magnitude are normally judged to be different from zero" (Jöreskog & Sörbom, 1989, p. 89). For illustrative purposes, I reproduced *t*-values for only the coefficients of the structural equations.

Error variances and R^2's for the measurement equations (i.e., for indicators) are identical in both outputs, as are the R^2's for the structural equations. Error variances for the structural equations in the two outputs differ, as those on the right are standardized.

R^2's associated with indicators are interpreted as reliability coefficients. Had the results reported earlier been from an analysis of real data (recall that my data are fictitious), I would have concluded that the reliabilities are low to moderate. For interpretation of reliability coefficients, see the section entitled "Measurement Errors" and the references therein.

Recall that the structural model included two endogenous latent variables (AM and ACH), hence two equations for latent variables. As I pointed out in the preceding, coefficients in the equations on the left are expressed in units of the measures of the reference indicators. Coefficients in the equations on the right are standardized. Assuming that the data were real, and using the standardized coefficients, I would have probably concluded that they reflect strong direct effects. Further, I would have assumed that the direct effects of IQ and AM on ACH are about the same. Later, I discuss total and indirect effects.

Output

	COVARIANCE MATRIX OF LATENT VARIABLES						COVARIANCE MATRIX OF LATENT VARIABLES			
	AM	ACH	SES	IQ			AM	ACH	SES	IQ
	--------	--------	-------	----------			-------	-------	-------	-------
AM	25.540					AM	1.000			
ACH	35.053	92.316				ACH	0.722	1.000		
SES	5.373	9.043	2.007			SES	0.750	0.664	1.000	
IQ	23.037	87.553	8.606	146.772		IQ	0.376	0.752	0.501	1.000

Commentary

The covariance matrix of the latent variables is in output on the left, with the endogenous ones listed first. For instance, the covariance of AM and ACH is 35.053. When latent variables are standardized (output on the right), the covariance matrix is a correlation matrix. Using relevant values from the matrix on the left, correlations reported in the matrix on the right can be calculated. For instance, the correlation of AM and ACH is $35.053/\sqrt{(25.540)(92.316)} = .722$. The other values in the output on the right are treated similarly. If necessary, review the relevant sections in Chapter 2 on variance, covariance, and correlation.

Output

GOODNESS OF FIT STATISTICS

CHI-SQUARE WITH 31 DEGREES OF FREEDOM = 25.769 (P = 0.732)

ROOT MEAN SQUARE RESIDUAL (RMR) = 2.376
STANDARDIZED RMR = 0.0267
GOODNESS OF FIT INDEX (GFI) = 0.983
ADJUSTED GOODNESS OF FIT INDEX (AGFI) = 0.970

NORMED FIT INDEX (NFI) = 0.978
NON-NORMED FIT INDEX (NNFI) = 1.007
COMPARATIVE FIT INDEX (CFI) = 1.000

Commentary

I discussed the evaluation of overidentified models in Chapter 18, where I also showed that LISREL reports many more fit indices than those I reproduced here. The indices I did reproduce make it clear that the model fits the data very well. If necessary, review my explanations of the preceding indices in Chapter 18.

SUMMARY STATISTICS FOR STANDARDIZED RESIDUALS
SMALLEST STANDARDIZED RESIDUAL = −1.854
MEDIAN STANDARDIZED RESIDUAL = −0.213
LARGEST STANDARDIZED RESIDUAL =   2.442

Commentary

As I explained in Chapter 18, in addition to overall fit, it is important to examine the fit of individual components. To this end, it is useful to examine the fitted covariance matrix, the fitted residuals, and the standardized residuals. Because of space considerations, I did not reproduce these matrices. Instead, I reproduced the statistics for standardized residuals from which you can surmise that the standardized residuals tend to be small. If you ran this example, examine the standardized residual matrix and notice that most of its elements are indeed small. Again, I remind you that my data are fictitious. Therefore, view my comments as illustrative.

LISREL Output

In Chapter 18 I pointed out that when using the SIMPLIS language it is possible to call for LISREL output, which provides for options (e.g., direct and indirect effects) not available in the SIMPLIS output. Accomplish this by adding a LISREL OUTPUT line. For a list of the options that may be specified on this line, see Jöreskog and Sörbom (1993a, p. 184).

Earlier I showed that when reference indicators of latent variables are not used, the latent variables are standardized. Using a LISREL OUTPUT line with the relevant option, one can obtain a standardized solution when using reference indicators. Two kinds of standardized solutions are available in LISREL:

> SS (Standardized Solution), in which the latent variables are scaled to have variances equal to one and the *observed variables are still in the original metric* and SC (for Standardized Completely), in which both the observed and latent variables are standardized. (Jöreskog & Sörbom, 1993a, p. 152)

For illustrative purposes, I added the line "LISREL OUTPUT: EF SS" (without quotation marks) to the input file in which I used reference indicators (see the preceding). I used the first option (EF) to get total, direct, and indirect effects. In what follows I will give brief excerpts of the output.

Output

STANDARDIZED SOLUTION

BETA

	AM	ACH			SES	IQ
AM	– –	– –		AM	0.750	– –
ACH	0.511	– –		ACH	– –	0.560

GAMMA

TOTAL AND INDIRECT EFFECTS

TOTAL EFFECTS OF KSI ON ETA			STANDARDIZED TOTAL EFFECTS OF KSI ON ETA		
	SES	IQ		SES	IQ
	-------	----------		-------	-------
AM	2.677	– –	AM	0.750	– –
	(0.343)		ACH	0.384	0.560
	7.805				
ACH	2.602	0.444			
	(0.433)	(0.053)			
	6.007	8.310			

INDIRECT EFFECTS OF KSI ON ETA			STANDARDIZED INDIRECT EFFECTS OF KSI ON ETA		
	SES	IQ		SES	IQ
	-------	----------		-------	-------
AM	– –	– –	AM	– –	– –
			ACH	0.384	– –
ACH	2.602	– –			
	(0.433)				
	6.007				

TOTAL EFFECTS OF ETA ON ETA			STANDARDIZED TOTAL EFFECTS OF ETA ON ETA		
	AM	ACH		AM	ACH
	-------	----------		-------	-------
AM	– –	– –	AM	– –	– –
			ACH	0.511	– –
ACH	0.972	– –			
	(0.140)				
	6.966				

Commentary

Except for differences in layout (see the explanation in Chapter 18), most of the output is the same as that of SIMPLIS, which I reported earlier. Therefore, I reproduced here only excerpts of output not available in SIMPLIS. Dashes indicate zero values. For ease of comparisons, I rearranged some of the output.

As I pointed out in the preceding, when SS is specified on the LISREL OUTPUT line, only the latent variables are standardized. BETA contains effects of endogenous (ETA) on endogenous variables. The present example has only one such effect, that of AM on ACH. In the

GAMMA matrix are reported effects of exogenous (KSI) variables (columns) on endogenous variables (rows). For instance, the effect of SES on AM is .750.[6] Compare the values reported in BETA and GAMMA with those given earlier in the output for the problem in which I did not use reference indicators (the output on the right). As I explained earlier, when reference indicators are not used, LISREL standardizes the latent variables.

I explained the meaning of total and indirect effects in Chapter 18. Recall that these terms are obtained when EF is specified on the LISREL OUTPUT line. To facilitate comparisons, I placed the unstandardized total and indirect effects (output on the left) alongside the standardized ones. Notice that the present analysis has only one indirect effect, namely that of SES on ACH (via AM). Further, according to the model being analyzed (see Figure 19.1; also see the following path diagram), SES has no direct effect on ACH. Therefore, its total effect is equal to its indirect effect. For the standardized solution this is equal to (.750)(.511), whereas for the unstandardized solution it is equal to (2.677)(.972). By contrast, the total effect of AM on ACH is equal to its direct effect (the former has no indirect effect on the latter). The same is true of the total effect of IQ on ACH.

Output

! TABLE 19.2   MULTIPLE INDICATOR MODEL
LISREL Estimates

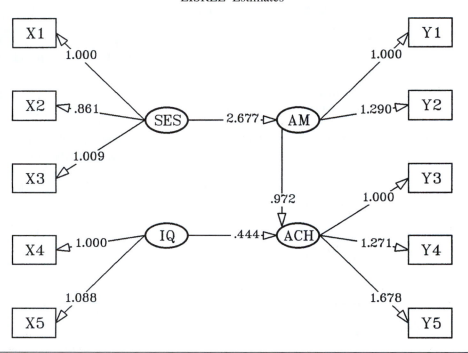

Commentary

The preceding was generated because of the line PATH DIAGRAM, which I included in the input with the reference indicators (the output on the left). Compare the results reported in the diagram with those given in the previous output.

[6]See Chapter 18 for an explanation of LISREL output.

When running LISREL from the DOS prompt, as I have done, the path diagram is displayed at the completion of the analysis, at which point it can be printed by pressing the letter P. This is how I printed the diagram given here. For an explanation of path diagrams, see Jöreskog and Sörbom (1993a, Chapter 3). See pages 105–106 for an explanation of printing options. UL, which I have used (see the input), is explained on page 106.

Pressing F1 while the path diagram is on the screen brings up the help menu, which displays different keys and their functions (e.g., to depict the measurement model for **x**, the structural model, *t*-values). These are also given in Jöreskog and Sörbom (1993a, pp. 108–109), which also explains how to modify the model and reestimate it. To exit from the path diagram, press Q (see the help menu or p. 109). As explained on pages 106–107, the path diagram, which is saved on disk, can be accessed by PATHDIAG.

When running LISREL under Windows, the path diagram is displayed at the completion of the analysis, at which point it can be (1) printed, (2) saved to the clipboard, (3) saved to a file. Choosing either (2) or (3) enables one to import the diagram into, say, a word processor, thereby having greater control on its printing (e.g., adding a caption, incorporating it in the text). To exit the path diagram when in Windows, use the exit menu or press Ctrl+Q.

EQS

Input

```
/TIT
 TABLE 19.2.   MULTIPLE INDICATOR MODEL
 SES = X1, X2, X3;  IQ = X3, X4;  AM = Y1, Y2;  ACH = Y3, Y4, Y5
/SPE
 CAS=300; VAR=10; MA = COR;
/LAB
 V1=X1; V2=X2; V3=X3; V4=X4; V5=X5;
 V6=Y1; V7=Y2; V8=Y3; V9=Y4; V10=Y5;
 F1=SES; F2=IQ; F3 = AM; F4=ACH;
/EQU
 V1   =   F1 + E1;
 V2   = *F1 + E2;
 V3   = *F1 + E3;
 V4   =      F2 + E4;
 V5   =     *F2 + E5;
 V6   =          F3 + E6;
 V7   =         *F3 + E7;
 V8   =               F4 + E8;
 V9   =              *F4 + E9;
 V10  =              *F4 + E10;
 F3   = *F1 + D3;
 F4 =        *F2 + *F3 + D4;
/VAR
 F1=100*;
 F2=20*;
```

```
D3,D4=20*;
E1 TO E10=5*;
/COV
F1,F2=4*;
/MAT
1.00
 .47  1.00
 .41   .45  1.00
 .28   .29   .35  1.00
 .25   .25   .34   .65  1.00
 .41   .40   .35   .16   .20  1.00
 .37   .36   .30   .18   .15   .45  1.00
 .34   .32   .37   .47   .50   .40   .38  1.00
 .36   .34   .31   .45   .48   .42   .35   .62  1.00
 .35   .36   .38   .52   .50   .45   .40   .65   .68  1.00
/STA
2.10  1.76  2.22  15.00  16.30  6.85  10.14  12.25  15.32  18.92
/PRINT
EFFECT=YES;
/END
```

Commentary

For an orientation to EQS, see Chapter 18. Here, I will comment briefly on some aspects of the input.

As I explained in Chapter 18, in EQS latent variables are designated as F's and residuals of latent variables are designated as D's.

Recall that in EQS the absence of an asterisk (*) means that the coefficient is fixed (by default to 1.0). Examine the measurement equations and notice that I used the same reference indicators as those I used in LISREL (e.g., V1=X1 is the reference indicator for F1=SES). By default, EQS prints also a completely standardized solution (i.e., of both the manifest and latent variables).

Following Bentler's (1992a) recommendation, I added blanks to make the structure of the model "more visible" (p. 55).

Notice that I used start values (see Chapter 18) for the variances and covariances.

Finally, I called for the printing of total and indirect effects (i.e., EFFECT=YES in the PRINT paragraph).

Output

CHI-SQUARE = 25.769 BASED ON 31 DEGREES OF FREEDOM
PROBABILITY VALUE FOR THE CHI-SQUARE STATISTIC IS 0.73232

BENTLER-BONETT NORMED   FIT INDEX=   0.978
BENTLER-BONETT NONNORMED FIT INDEX=   1.007
COMPARATIVE FIT INDEX   =   1.000

MAXIMUM LIKELIHOOD SOLUTION (NORMAL DISTRIBUTION THEORY)
MEASUREMENT EQUATIONS

X1	=V1	=	1.000 F1	+	1.000 E1
X2	=V2	=	.861*F1	+	1.000 E2
X3	=V3	=	1.009*F1	+	1.000 E3
X4	=V4	=	1.000 F2	+	1.000 E4
X5	=V5	=	1.088*F2	+	1.000 E5
Y1	=V6	=	1.000 F3	+	1.000 E6
Y2	=V7	=	1.290*F3	+	1.000 E7
Y3	=V8	=	1.000 F4	+	1.000 E8
Y4	=V9	=	1.271*F4	+	1.000 E9
Y5	=V10	=	1.678*F4	+	1.000 E10

CONSTRUCT EQUATIONS WITH STANDARD ERRORS AND TEST STATISTICS

    AM   =F3 = 2.677*F1 + 1.000 D3
                  .343
                 7.805

    ACH =F4 =   .972*F3 +   .444*F2 + 1.000 D4
                  .140   .053
                 6.966   8.309

VARIANCES OF INDEPENDENT VARIABLES

                    F   D
                    --   ---
I F1 – SES   2.007*I D3 – AM   11.159*I
I   .349 I   2.752 I
I   5.754 I   4.054 I
I   I   I
I F2 – 1Q   146.772*I D4 – ACH   19.375*I
I   19.844 I   4.685 I
I   7.396 I   4.135 I
I   I   I

COVARIANCES AMONG INDEPENDENT VARIABLES

                 F

I F2 – 1Q   8.606*I
I F1 – SES   1.538 I
I   5.596 I
I   I

DECOMPOSITION OF EFFECTS WITH NONSTANDARDIZED VALUES
PARAMETER TOTAL EFFECTS

AM   =F3 =   2.677*F1 +   1.000 D3

ACH   =F4 =   .972*F3 +   2.602 F1 + .444*F2 + .972 D3
                1.000 D4

DECOMPOSITION OF EFFECTS WITH NONSTANDARDIZED VALUES
PARAMETER INDIRECT EFFECTS

ACH   =F4 =   2.602 F1 +   .972 D3
               .715   .254
              3.637   3.821

DECOMPOSITION OF EFFECTS WITH STANDARDIZED VALUES
PARAMETER TOTAL EFFECTS

AM   =F3 =   .750*F1 +   .661 D3
ACH   =F4 =   .511*F3 +   .384 F1 +   .560*F2

DECOMPOSITION OF EFFECTS WITH STANDARDIZED VALUES
PARAMETER INDIRECT EFFECTS

ACH   =F4 =   .384 F1 +   .338 D3

Commentary

The preceding are excerpts of the EQS output, some of which I reorganized. Notwithstanding differences in layout, these results are the same as those of the LISREL output, which I reproduced and commented on earlier. If you have access to both programs, run the example on both and study the outputs along with my commentaries on the LISREL output. If you have access to only one of the programs, or to another SEM program, compare your output with that of LISREL (given earlier) and refer to my commentaries on it whenever necessary.

SEM IN PRACTICE

In a discussion of tests of SEM, Jöreskog and Sörbom (1993a) distinguished among the following research situations:

SC In a *strictly confirmatory* situation the researcher has formulated one single model and has obtained empirical data to test it. The model should be accepted or rejected.

AM The researcher has specified several *alternative models* or *competing models* and on the basis of an analysis of a single set of empirical data, one of the models should be selected.

MG *The researcher has specified a tentative initial model* [italics added]. If the initial model does not fit the given data, the model should be modified and tested again using the same data. Several models may be tested in this process. The goal may be to find a model which not only fits the data well from a statistical point of view, but also has the property that every parameter of the model can be given a substantively meaningful interpretation. The re-specification of each model may be theory-driven or data-driven. Although a model may be tested in each round, the whole approach is *model generating* rather than model testing.

> In practice, the **MG** situation is by far the most common. The **SC** situation is very rare because few researchers are contented with just rejecting a given model without suggesting an alternative model. The **AM** situation is also rare because researchers seldom specify the alternative models a priori. (p. 115)

Bentler (1987) asserted, "In practice, most initially specified models do not fit the data, and it becomes essential to make adjustments by adding new parameters, dropping insignificant ones, etc." (p. 77).

Although the preceding statements reflect accurately current practice in SEM applications in social and behavioral sciences, they were not meant to imply that this is an ideal state, nor that SEM can be applied in the absence of a model. On the contrary, the point of departure in both statements is that an initial model, tentative though it may be, is postulated. Indeed, *"In exploratory situations with many variables and weak or non-existing substantive theory, LISREL is probably not a useful tool"* [italics added] (Jöreskog & Sörbom, 1989, p. 225).

Also, the importance of testing alternative models cannot be overstated. As Geoffrey Rose put it, "You cannot exclude the explanation you have not considered" (quoted by Datta, 1993, p. 345). Chamberlin (1890/1965) and Platt (1964) who, among others, elaborated on the role of alternative hypotheses in the progress of science, did so in the context of research in advanced sciences, notably physics. Admittedly, the state of theory and measurement in social and behavioral sciences, to name but two major factors, makes the formulation of alternative *plausible* models much more difficult and tenuous. Yet, it appears that most researchers do not even consider this possibility. For instance, in a review of 72 articles in which SEM was applied, Breckler (1990) found that "only 1 acknowledged the existence of a specific equivalent model. . . . However, in the majority of instances, plausible theoretically compelling alternative models could be formulated" (p. 266).

Testing Alternative Models

Obviously, formulation of meaningful alternative models is inconceivable without theory. Yet, I cannot in this book engage in theoretical formulations. Accordingly, in what follows *I discuss only mechanics of testing alternative models.* Moreover, I do so in the context of a miniature numerical example.

A Numerical Example

Earlier, I used the model depicted in Figure 19.1 and the data in Table 19.2 to illustrate the application of SEM to a model with multiple indicators. Assume that I formulated a priori an

! FIGURE 19.3   DATA FROM TABLE 19.2
LISREL Estimates

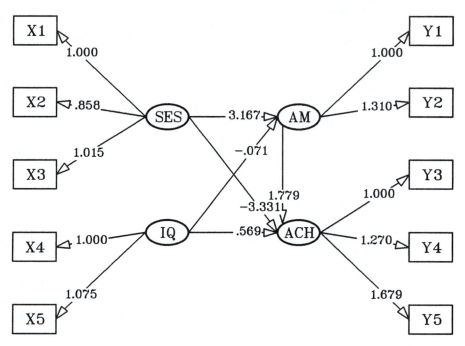

alternative model as depicted in Figure 19.3. Notice that the difference between Figures 19.1 and 19.3 is that in the latter the structural model includes two additional paths: (1) from SES to ACH and (2) from IQ to AM.

As you may note from the title of Figure 19.3, I generated it through LISREL. In my commentary on the analysis in Table 19.2 data, according to the model depicted in Figure 19.1, I commented on PATH DIAGRAM of LISREL. In the following I describe the input file I used for the present run and give excerpts of output. I will follow the same practice when I introduce additional revised models. Later, I comment on the negative coefficient from SES to ACH.

In Chapter 17, I introduced the idea of nested models. Briefly, a nested model is a subset, or a special case, of a more comprehensive model. In other words, a nested model is arrived at by constraining one or more parameters of a more comprehensive model (e.g., setting coefficients equal to zero or to each other). Examine the model of Figure 19.1 and notice that it is nested in Figure 19.3, as it is arrived at by setting two coefficients in the latter (the effect of SES on ACH and that of IQ on AM) equal to zero.

To test the difference between the two models it is necessary to analyze both. As I already analyzed the model in Figure 19.1, I now analyze the model in Figure 19.3. To this end, I made the following changes in the equations for the latent variables in the LISREL input file I used earlier in this chapter to analyze the data in Table 19.2 according to Figure 19.1. Specifically, I added IQ to the equation for AM, and I added SES to the equation for ACH. Thus, the two equations read:

AM = SES IQ
ACH = SES IQ AM

The rest of the input is unchanged. As I pointed out earlier, Figure 19.3 was generated through this run.

Output

GOODNESS OF FIT STATISTICS

CHI-SQUARE WITH 29 DEGREES OF FREEDOM = 18.657 (P = 0.930)

ROOT MEAN SQUARE RESIDUAL (RMR) = 1.754
STANDARDIZED RMR = 0.0214
GOODNESS OF FIT INDEX (GFI) = 0.988

ADJUSTED GOODNESS OF FIT INDEX (AGFI) = 0.977

NORMED FIT INDEX (NFI) = 0.984
NON-NORMED FIT INDEX (NNFI) = 1.014
COMPARATIVE FIT INDEX (CFI) = 1.000

Commentary

Having two additional parameters, the model in Figure 19.3 is expected to have a better overall fit than that in Figure 19.1. The question, though, is whether the improvement in fit warrants retention of the comprehensive model over the more parsimonious one of Figure 19.1 (I discuss model parsimony later). As always, criteria of meaningfulness and/or statistical significance can be used in an attempt to answer this question.

The likelihood ratio (LR) test (also called Chi-square difference test), which I introduced in Chapter 17, is used to test the difference between two models, one of which is nested in the other. Specifically, the difference between the Chi-squares (χ^2) for the two models is distributed as a χ^2 with degrees of freedom (*df*) equal to the difference between the *df* for the two models. From the analysis of the model in Figure 19.1 (see the output given earlier), $\chi^2 = 25.769$, with 31 *df*. Therefore, for the test of the difference between the models, $\chi^2 = 7.112$ (25.769 − 18.657), with 2 (31 − 29) *df*, which can be checked against a tabled χ^2 value for 2 *df* at a prespecified α (alpha). Assuming that I specified $\alpha = .01$, the tabled value is 9.210 (see the χ^2 Table in Appendix B). Thus, the fit of the more comprehensive model is statistically not significantly different from that of the nested model. Accordingly, I would retain the latter model.

As I pointed out in Chapter 18, the validity of the χ^2 test is predicated on a set of restrictive assumptions that are rarely met in practice (see, in particular, my comments about the distributional and sampling assumptions). Further, the validity of the LR test is based on the assumption that the more comprehensive model "has been tested by a valid chi-square test . . . and found to fit the data and to be interpretable in a meaningful way" (Jöreskog & Sörbom, 1993a, p. 119). It is for these reasons that Jöreskog and Sörbom suggested that χ^2 be used as a measure of fit, rather than a test statistic (see Chapter 18). For nested models, they note the following:

A large drop in χ^2, compared to the difference in degrees of freedom, indicates that the changes made in the model represent a real improvement. On the other hand, a drop in χ^2 close to the difference in the number of degrees of freedom indicates that the improvement in fit is obtained by "capitalizing on chance," and the added parameters may not have real significance and meaning. (Jöreskog & Sörbom, 1989, p. 44)

As I pointed out in Chapter 18, it is recommended that multiple fit indices be used for model evaluation. Earlier I reproduced the same indices as those I included earlier in the output for the analysis of the model of Figure 19.1 (for an explanation of these indices, see Chapter 18). Compare the two sets of indices and notice that they are very similar, lending support to a decision to retain the more parsimonious model.

Finally, I would like to remind you that, in addition to overall fit, it is important to study the fit of individual components (see Chapter 18). Also, as I will show, the *t*-values for the coefficients from SES to ACH and from IQ to AM are < 2.0.

MODEL REVISION

Broadly, a model is revised or respecified to (1) increase parsimony or (2) improve overall fit. I will discuss and illustrate each in turn. Before doing this, though, I would like to stress that when, as in most applications, the model is revised post hoc, based on an examination of the results, the analysis is exploratory. Accordingly, it is imperative to cross-validate the revised model with fresh data or in a newly designed study. For a discussion of this topic, see "Theory Trimming or Model Revision" in Chapter 18. See also Chapter 8 for a discussion of cross-validation in the context of regression analysis.

INCREASING PARSIMONY

You are probably familiar with the idea of Occam's razor, which in scientific research has come to mean that theories should be as simple, or parsimonious, as possible (for a review in the context of SEM, see Mulaik et al., 1989, pp. 437–439). As Bentler and Mooijaart (1989) put it, "models with fewer unknown parameters may be considered as standing a better chance of being scientifically replicable and explainable" (p. 315).

A number of indices of fit aimed at reflecting on the parsimony of a model have been developed and proposed for use in model selection. Some such indices have been incorporated in EQS (Bentler, 1992a, p. 92) and, particularly, in LISREL (Jöreskog & Sörbom, 1993a, Chapter 4). This is a complex topic that I will not go into. For reviews, see the references I gave here and in Chapter 18 (in my commentaries on fit indices). See also McDonald and Marsh (1990), who questioned the usefulness of parsimony indices for model selection and who discussed "problems attending the definition of parsimonious fit indices" (p. 247).

A Numerical Example

To illustrate a post hoc approach to increasing parsimony, I will use the same numerical examples I used under "Testing Alternative Models." This time, though, assume that I started with the model depicted in Figure 19.3 and carried out the analysis, as in the preceding.

Output

$$AM = 3.167*SES - 0.0710*IQ, \text{ Errorvar.}= 7.420 , \quad R^2 = 0.689$$
$$\quad (0.454) \qquad (0.0403) \qquad\qquad (2.905)$$
$$\quad 6.978 \qquad -1.761 \qquad\qquad 2.555$$

$$ACH = 1.779*AM - 3.331*SES + 0.569*IQ, \text{ Errorvar.}= 9.363 , \quad R^2 = 0.897$$
$$\quad (0.597) \qquad (2.179) \qquad (0.0996) \qquad\qquad (8.647)$$
$$\quad 2.980 \qquad -1.529 \qquad 5.716 \qquad\qquad 1.083$$

Commentary

Examine the two equations and notice that the *t*-value for the IQ coefficient in the first equation and that for SES in the second equation is < 2.0. Following common practice, one would delete the two coefficients and estimate the parameters of the revised model. Before I do this, though, I would like to remind you that such decisions should not be made solely on statistical grounds. Thus, assuming, for instance, that the researcher deemed the effect of SES on ACH (second equation) substantial, then its negative sign should have raised doubts about the validity of the model, as it goes counter to the extensive literature on this topic. Again, *I remind you that my model is illustrative and the data are fictitious. My discussion and speculations are meant to illustrate a process one should engage in when revising a model post hoc.*

As my aim here is to illustrate common practice in SEM applications (not to condone it), I would, based on tests of significance, revise the model by deleting the paths from IQ to AM and from SES to ACH. This would bring me back to the model of Figure 19.1. I would then reanalyze the data in Table 19.2 according to the revised model (I did this earlier) and would attempt to ascertain whether the revised model does not differ much from the original one. In essence, I would do the same comparisons as those I did earlier for tests of alternative models, and would reach the same conclusions. Clearly, however, there is a vast difference between the two approaches. Here, my model revision would be post hoc, and therefore the tests and the comparisons between the two models would be exploratory (see the preceding). In contrast, in the earlier analyses I compared two models that I hypothesized a priori.

IMPROVING FIT

Because the fit of most initial models is deemed unsatisfactory (see Jöreskog & Sörbom's, and Bentler's statements in the beginning of this section), "model modification . . . has been an inevitable process in the application of covariance structure analysis" (Chou & Bentler, 1993, p. 97). Broadly, model modification, under such circumstances, consists of freeing fixed parameters with the aim of improving the fit of the model. In most instances, parameters are freed sequentially, one at a time, until the researcher is satisfied with the fit of the revised model. Before explaining how researchers go about deciding which fixed parameters to free, I will make several comments.

First, I would like to remind you that in Chapter 18 (see "Fit Indices: Summary Statement") I cautioned against undue reliance on, and indiscriminate use of, fit indices for model modification.

Second, in Chapter 18 and in this chapter I pointed out that post-hoc model modification constitutes exploratory analysis, and I stressed the importance of replication. As Steiger (1990) put it, "*An ounce of replication is worth a ton of inferential statistics*" (p. 176). Yet, judging by published research in a variety of journals, replications of models that were revised post hoc are conspicuous in their absence.

Third, I would like to remind you that I introduced the idea of specification errors in Chapter 2 and discussed it in various subsequent chapters (especially Chapter 10). In the context of SEM, I commented briefly on this topic in Chapter 18 and earlier in the present chapter. Among other things, I pointed out that when testing a model one assumes that it is correctly specified. I mention this topic here, as I believe it unfortunate that model modification aimed at improving fit is frequently discussed under the heading of specification searches (e.g., Kaplan, 1988; Long, 1983, pp. 68–77; MacCallum, 1986; MacCallum, Roznowski, & Necowitz, 1992), lending an aura of theory formulation to a process driven primarily, if not solely, by a desire to improve model fit. Not surprisingly, revised models, arrived at as a result of attempts to improve fit, are frequently grossly misspecified. A notable case in point can be seen in models whose fit is improved by adding correlated errors (see the following).

Fourth, the practice of model revision for the sake of improving model fit is controversial (see the previously cited references; also see Kaplan's, 1990a, proposed strategy, reactions to it by several authors, and Kaplan's rejoinder, 1990b).

Fifth, reviews of studies in which model revision was practiced are notable in their criticisms and gloomy in their assessments and conclusions (see, in particular, Breckler, 1990; MacCallum, 1986; MacCallum et al., 1992).

Finally, ready availability in SEM software of diagnostic indices that can greatly facilitate model revision for improvement of fit has led to a proliferation of mindless revision of models.

MODIFICATION INDEX

A modification index (MI) suggests by how much chi-square is expected to decrease if a given fixed parameter is freed and the revised model is estimated. Specifically,

> the modification index is approximately equal to the difference in chi-square between two models in which one parameter is fixed or constrained in one model and free in the other, all other parameters being estimated in both models. The largest modification index shows the parameter that improves the fit most when set free. (Jöreskog & Sörbom, 1993a, p. 127)

Before illustrating how MI's are obtained in LISREL, I would like to hasten and add that Jöreskog and Sörbom (1993a) stressed that a fixed parameter be freed based on MI only "*if this parameter can be interpreted substantively*" (p. 128). Nevertheless, I believe Steiger (1990) correctly characterized current practice of model revision when he ventured a guess that the percentage of researchers who will be unable to "think up a *theoretical justification* for freeing a parameter . . . is 'near zero'" (p. 175; see also, Steiger, 1988, and "Theory Trimming or Model Revision" in Chapter 18 of this book). Worse yet is the absence of a substantive justification for model revision in much of published research (for reviews, see Breckler, 1990; MacCallum et al., 1992; see also the research examples presented later in this chapter).

A Numerical Example

To illustrate how researchers use MI for model revision, I return to the data in Table 19.2, which I analyzed earlier according to the models in Figures 19.1 and 19.3. This time, I will assume that

! FIGURE 19.4   DATA FROM TABLE 19.2
LISREL Estimates

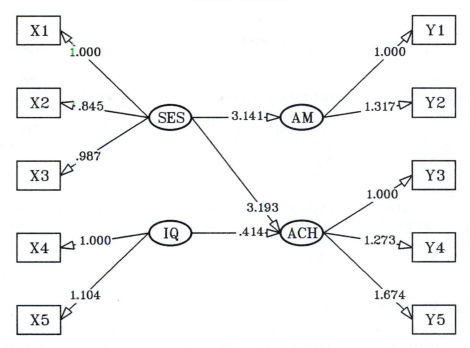

the researcher started out with the model depicted in Figure 19.4. Contrast Figures 19.1 and 19.4 and notice that they differ only in the structural models. Specifically, according to Figure 19.1, SES affects ACH only indirectly (via AM), whereas according to Figure 19.4, SES affects ACH directly only. Thus, according to Figure 19.4, the relation (covariance, correlation) between the endogenous variables (AM and ACH) is due to the effects of the correlated exogenous variables (SES and IQ). Notice that SES is a common cause of the endogenous variables.

As in other examples, I will not give a theoretical rationale for this model. Also, *keep in mind that my data are fictitious. In short, I use the analysis for purely illustrative purposes.*

As I explained earlier, I generated Figure 19.4 through LISREL. To estimate the parameters of this model through LISREL, I made the following modifications in the input file I used earlier in this chapter, when I analyzed the data in Table 19.2 according to the model depicted in Figure 19.1.

AM = SES
ACH = IQ SES

The remaining statements in the input file are unchanged.

Output

AM = 3.141*SES, Errorvar.= 4.945 , R^2 = 0.792
      (0.365)   (2.535)
       8.604   1.951

$$\text{ACH} = 3.193*\text{SES} + 0.414*\text{IQ}, \text{Errorvar.} = 25.546, \quad R^2 = 0.720$$
$$(0.516) \qquad (0.0571) \qquad\qquad (5.082)$$
$$6.185 \qquad\quad 7.257 \qquad\qquad\quad 5.027$$

CHI-SQUARE WITH 31 DEGREES OF FREEDOM = 52.337 (P = 0.00966)

GOODNESS OF FIT INDEX (GFI) = 0.965
ADJUSTED GOODNESS OF FIT INDEX (AGFI) = 0.938

THE MODIFICATION INDICES SUGGEST TO ADD THE

PATH TO	FROM	DECREASE IN CHI-SQUARE	NEW ESTIMATE
X3	IQ	8.1	0.04
ACH	AM	31.5	2.74

THE MODIFICATION INDICES SUGGEST TO ADD AN ERROR COVARIANCE

BETWEEN	AND	DECREASE IN CHI-SQUARE	NEW ESTIMATE
ACH	AM	31.5	13.55
X4	Y1	8.1	−10.00

Commentary

As is well known, despite repeated attempts to dethrone the statistical test of significance, it reigns supreme in social and behavioral research even when, as is most commonly the case, probability sampling is not used.[7] In Chapter 18, I discussed specific shortcomings of the chi-square (χ^2) test. Nevertheless, it is a safe bet that, based on the χ^2 reported in the preceding, many researchers would reject the model; even if based on other fit indices, two of which I reproduced here, the searcher may conclude that the model fits the data fairly well (see Chapter 18, and the references therein, for discussions of the use of fit indices for model evaluation). Anyway, for present purposes, I will assume that, based on an examination of the results (notably the χ^2), the researcher decides to revise the model. Under such circumstance, it is highly likely that he or she would use MODIFICATION INDICES (MI) as guides. In SIMPLIS, "only modification indices larger than 7.882, which is the 99.5 percentile of the chi-square distribution with one degree of freedom" (Jöreskog & Sörbom, 1993a, p. 93) are reported.[8]

Examine the modification indices reported in the preceding and notice that in the first segment it is suggested that the largest expected drop in χ^2 (MI = 31.5) would occur as a result of freeing the parameter for the path from AM to ACH. Note, however, that the same drop in χ^2 is expected if the model were modified to include a correlation between the errors of AM and ACH. I discuss correlated errors later. For now, I just wanted to show that even in a miniature example as the one under consideration the researcher cannot shirk the responsibility of making a decision.

---

[7]In Chapter 2, I commented on, and gave references to, the controversy surrounding the use of statistical tests of significance.

[8]In LISREL output, on the other hand, modification indices are reported for all fixed parameters, when *MI is specified on the LISREL OUTPUT line.* The reason I italicized the preceding is that MI is *not* listed among "all keywords" (Jöreskog & Sörbom, 1993a, p. 184) that can be used on the LISREL OUTPUT line. This is, obviously, an inadvertent omission, as in the examples of LISREL output lines (Jöreskog & Sörbom, 1993a, Chapter 5), MI *is* used (e.g., p. 133).

It goes without saying that theory should be the ultimate guide for model revision. Assuming that the researcher examines the results from a substantive perspective (earlier I pointed out that many, if not most, do not), then it is highly likely that the researcher would revise the model to include an effect of AM on ACH. This revised model is depicted in Figure 19.5, which I generated through LISREL.

To estimate the parameters of this model, I added AM to the structural equation in which ACH is the dependent variable. Thus, I revised the second structural equation given earlier to read

---

ACH = IQ SES AM

All other input statements are unchanged.

Output

AM = 2.724*SES, Errorvar.= 8.842 , R^2 = 0.629
   (0.341)   (2.811)
    7.990   3.146

ACH = 1.503*AM − 2.025*SES + 0.486*IQ, Errorvar.= 12.421, R^2 = 0.867
   (0.409)   (1.273)   (0.0588)   (6.674)
    3.678   −1.591   8.278   1.861

CHI-SQUARE WITH 30 DEGREES OF FREEDOM = 21.978 (P = 0.855)

GOODNESS OF FIT INDEX (GFI) = 0.985
ADJUSTED GOODNESS OF FIT INDEX (AGFI) = 0.973

! FIGURE 19.5   DATA FROM TABLE 19.2
LISREL Estimates

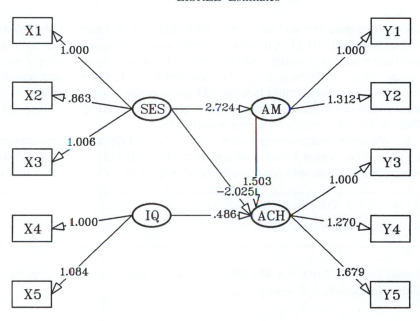

Commentary

Notice that as a result of adding a path from AM to ACH, the χ^2 indeed dropped by more than 30 points. Had the two models been formulated a priori, and assuming that $\alpha = .01$ was specified, one would have concluded that the fit of this model is significantly better than the earlier one ($\chi^2 = 30.36$, with 1 *df, p < .01*). In the present example, the model was revised post hoc. Nevertheless, based on published research, it is safe to assume that most researchers would take the P = .855 associated with the previous χ^2 as an indication that the null hypothesis cannot be rejected and, hence, that the revised model fits the data.

To illustrate the importance of scrutinizing all aspects of the revised model, I would like to draw your attention to the second structural equation (see also Figure 19.5). Note that SES is said to have a *negative* effect on ACH. I commented on such a "finding" in an earlier analysis. As my sole purpose here is to give an example of potential problems that may arise when models are revised, *I am ignoring the fact that the* t *ratio for this coefficient is < 2.* Thus, as a result of model revision, a positive effect of SES on ACH (as estimated for the model of Figure 19.4) has turned into a negative effect in the model of Figure 19.5. Researchers who, appropriately, scrutinize all their results would have to come to grips with the idea that SES has a negative effect on ACH, as it goes counter to the extensive literature in this area. Some would probably revise the model again by deleting the direct effect of SES on ACH. In other words, they would hypothesize (post hoc) that SES affects ACH only indirectly, via AM. Assuming that the model were thus revised, then it would bring us back to the model in Figure 19.1, which I analyzed and commented on earlier. If you replicated my earlier analysis, using SIMPLIS, I suggest that you examine the output and notice that no modification indices are reported, as none exceed the criterion of 7.882 (see the preceding explanation).

I turn now to a description and illustration of a diagnostic index given in EQS, which serves a similar purpose to that of the modification index in LISREL.

EQS

Analogous to modification indices in LISREL, EQS reports Lagrange Multipliers (LM) (Bentler, 1992a, Chapter 6). "The LM test is very useful for evaluating whether, *from a statistical point of view* [italics added], a model could be improved substantially by freeing a previously fixed parameter" (Bentler, 1992a, p. 128). LM is invoked by the LMTEST paragraph. EQS provides for a variety of options to control how the LM test is applied, to which matrices, and to which elements within these matrices. Default output is given when no options are specified (see Bentler, 1992a, p. 133; also see the following output).

For illustrative and comparative purposes, I will use EQS to evaluate parameters of the model in Figure 19.4, which I evaluated earlier through LISREL. As in the LISREL input file, I changed the two structural equations in the EQS input file I used earlier to read as follows:

```
F3   =   *F1 + D3;

F4   =       *F1 + *F2 + D4;
```

where F1=SES, F2=IQ, F3=AM, F4=ACH (see the input file presented earlier in this chapter). Further, I added the following paragraph:

/LMTEST

All other input statements are unchanged.

Output

CHI-SQUARE = 52.337 BASED ON 31 DEGREES OF FREEDOM
PROBABILITY VALUE FOR THE CHI-SQUARE STATISTIC IS 0.00966

BENTLER-BONETT NORMED   FIT INDEX= 0.956
BENTLER-BONETT NONNORMED FIT INDEX= 0.973
COMPARATIVE FIT INDEX   = 0.981

AM =F3 =   3.141*F1   +   1.000 D3
                .365
               8.603

ACH =F4 =   3.193*F1   +   .414*F2   +   1.000 D4
                 .516   .057
                6.185   7.257

Commentary

Except for the fit indices, which are different from those I reproduced from the LISREL output, these results are the same as those of LISREL. As in the LISREL analysis, I assume that, based on the χ^2 test, the researcher decides to revise the model. Further, I assume that he or she would consult LM for this purpose.

Output

LAGRANGE MULTIPLIER TEST (FOR ADDING PARAMETERS)

ORDERED UNIVARIATE TEST STATISTICS:

NO	CODE		PARAMETER	CHI-SQUARE	PROBABILITY	PARAMETER CHANGE
1	2	22	F4,F3	31.538	0.000	2.739
2	2	10	D4,D3	31.538	0.000	13.551
3	2	12	V3,F2	8.079	0.004	0.038
4	2	22	F3,F4	5.888	0.015	0.160
.	.	.		.	.	.
39	2	12	V7,F1	0.000	1.000	0.000
40	2	0	V6,F3	0.000	1.000	0.000

Commentary

Reproduced here are LM tests in descending order of their associated χ^2 values and numbered sequentially in the NO column (in the interest of space, I omitted lines 5–38). This output indicates that freeing F4,F3, that is, allowing for an effect of AM (F3) on ACH (F4) is expected to result in a drop of 31.538 in the χ^2. Compare this result with LISREL's output presented earlier, where the same value was reported for the corresponding MI. Also, as in LISREL, the second line indicates that freeing the correlation between the errors of F3 (AM) and F4 (ACH) is expected to result in a reduction in χ^2 identical to that expected from the addition of a path from AM to ACH. I will not comment on this aspect of the results and their implications for model revision, as I have done this in connection with the LISREL output. Instead, I will comment briefly on the layout of the output and on some other options available in EQS.

Turning to the CODE, the first digit indicates the type of LM test used. The default (used here, and signified by the number 2) means that "they will be considered together in the multivariate test" (Bentler, 1992a, p. 142). The remaining two digits of the code generally identify the matrix to which the element in question belongs. Thus, 22 (e.g., line 1) refers to values in the FF matrix of latent dependent variable, whereas 10 (e.g., line 2) refers to values in the DD matrix of errors in latent variable. For a detailed description and explanation of numeric identification of matrices in EQS, see Bentler (1992a, pp. 136–138).

As I pointed out earlier, EQS provides for various options to apply the LM test according to theoretical considerations regarding the model being fitted. For example, one may specify elements that should not be included in the LM test, that is, elements that should remain fixed. As another example, a hierarchy according to which the LM test is to be applied may be specified. Nevertheless, my reservations about the use of modification indices for model modification in LISREL apply equally to the use LM for the same purpose.

As is the case with MI in LISREL, the univariate tests reported here are not independent of each other. Hence, it is not possible to tell what effect freeing of one parameter will have on LM for the remaining ones. In an attempt to address this difficulty, EQS offers also a multivariate test, which is applied in a forward stepwise fashion. At each step, the element entered is the one expected to lead to the greatest expected reduction of the chi-square, after taking into account the contribution of the element(s) in the preceding steps. For more details, see Bentler (1992a, pp. 141–143), who gives an example in which "the univariate LM statistics are highly misleading" (p. 143).

The multivariate test in EQS reduces the drudgery of freeing one parameter at a time and repeating the analysis. However, the likelihood of this fostering indiscriminate applications of the LM test and thoughtless revision of models is, in my opinion, high.

Finally, in addition to the LM test, EQS provides for a "Wald test" which "is designed to determine whether sets of parameters that were treated as free in the model could in fact be simultaneously set to zero without substantial loss to model fit" (Bentler, 1992a, p. 68). I will not discuss the Wald test (see Bentler, 1992a, pp. 128–133, for a discussion), except to point out that it is meant to do the converse of what the LM test does. The distinction between the two approaches is very much like that between forward selection and backward elimination procedures in multiple regression analysis, which I presented in Chapter 9.

RESEARCH EXAMPLES USING MODIFICATION INDICES

In what follows, I give examples from the research literature in which modification indices were used for model modification, with no allusion to theoretical considerations. To give you an idea what each study was about, I state *briefly* its authors' aims (often in their own words). *I do not address other aspects of the studies I cite.* To learn more about a given study, you will have to read it.

(1) Randhawa, Beamer, and Lundberg (1993) examined "the role of self-efficacy as a mediator between attitudes and achievement in mathematics" (p. 41). Using LISREL, they reported, among other things, a statistically significant χ^2 ($p < .05$) and concluded "that the specified model did not fit the data well" (p. 44). They then stated, "For this model, the modification index of one of the manifest observed [*sic*] variables, the daily subscale, was 25.32" (p. 44). Accordingly, they revised the model by adding a path from "M-Achievement" ("mathematics achievement") to "Daily"—one of the indicators of "M-Efficacy" ("mathematics self-efficacy"). But, *according to their model (see their Figure 1, p. 44), M-Efficacy affects M-Achievement.* As you can see from the quotation I gave, the authors' aim was to examine the role of M-Efficacy as a mediator of the effect of attitudes on M-Achievement. *Based on a modification index, however, they posited that the latent dependent variable M-Achievement affects a subscale of a measure of the latent variable M-efficacy, which is said to affect M-Achievement.*

(2) Using LISREL, Sujan, Weitz, and Kumar (1994) tested a causal model that focused "on prescriptions for learning within the personal selling domain" (p. 39). After reporting and discussing various aspects of their results, which I will not go into, they added two paths "In an attempt to improve the model [*sic*]" (p. 50). They stated, "*The modification indices suggested these changes* [italics added]" (p. 50).[9]

(3) Brown and Peterson (1994) investigated "whether exertion of effort influences job satisfaction only through the mediation of performance or whether it has a direct effect on satisfaction that is not contingent on performance" (p. 70). After reporting results of a first analysis, the authors stated:

> In spite of the adequate fit of the hypothesized model, modifications were undertaken to provide a more accurate and parsimonious representation of the data. . . . LISREL modification indices suggested the existence of a direct relationship between competitiveness [a variable hypothesized to affect effort; see their Figure 1, p. 73] and sales performance that was not mediated by effort. . . . No other additions to the model were suggested by the modification indices. (pp. 75–76)

As the authors do not state what they mean by "a more accurate . . . representation," I cannot comment on it. As to a "more parsimonious representation," a model becomes *less* parsimonious when parameters are added to it (see "Increasing Parsimony," earlier in this chapter). Finally, I would like to draw your attention to the work of MacCallum et al. (1992), which led them to suggest that "when an initial model fits well, it is probably unwise to modify it to achieve even better fit because the modifications may simply be fitting small idiosyncratic characteristics of the sample" (p. 501).

(4) Hull and Mendolia (1991) used SEM to "test the hypothesis that expectancies mediate the influence of attributions on depressions" (p. 85). After concluding that the initial "model failed to fit the data" (p. 87), they stated, "Modification indexes suggested that the fit of the model can be improved by allowing four errors to correlate. This model provided a relatively good fit to the data" (p. 87). I discuss correlated errors in the next section. Here, I just wanted to illustrate the fairly common practice of relying on modification indices when adding correlated errors to improve the fit of a model.

---

[9]I return to this study in the section entitled "Correlated Errors."

(5) Wyatt and Newcomb (1990) stated that they "used path analyses to examine whether the various circumstances of child sexual abuse contributed directly to adult problems or affected these later outcomes through intervening conditions reflected in the mediator variables" (p. 759). Having concluded that their initial model did not fit the data, Wyatt and Newcomb engaged in model modification. First they added parameters based on modification indices. Then they deleted parameters that were statistically not significant. I will comment briefly on each approach.

"On the basis of selected modification indices (Bentler & Chou, 1986), two paths were added from circumstances of abuse variables to the outcome variable" (Wyatt & Newcomb, 1990, p. 762). Before commenting on this statement, I would like to take this opportunity to comment on the fairly common practice of not giving page references when paraphrasing or citing a source as, say, recommending a specific action (e.g., an analytic approach) or supporting a specific point of view. Regrettably, this is reinforced by policies of editorial boards of various journals and by prescriptions in some style manuals (e.g., American Psychological Association, 1994, p. 97) that do not require page references under such circumstances. Not only does this make it difficult, often impossible (when the reference is to a book), to locate the place where the topic in question was discussed, but it also makes it difficult to tell the purpose for which the reference was given. The example under consideration is a case in point. I, for one, could not tell whether the reference to Bentler and Chou was meant to (1) tell the reader that it contains more information about modification indices or (2) imply that, in their use of modification indices, the authors were following recommendations made by Bentler and Chou. Other purposes come readily to mind.

I could not get hold of Bentler and Chou's paper, which was presented at a convention, and therefore cannot tell why it was cited. I believe, however, that it will be useful to give you an idea of Bentler and Chou's thinking about model modification, as expressed in a paper they published about the same time (1987) as the one cited in the preceding, and its bearing on some of Wyatt and Newcomb's actions.

> If the data are examined, and structural hypotheses are formed after . . . data snooping, the statistical theory may become incorrect because one may then be capitalizing on chance associations in the data. The effects of capitalizing on chance are particularly acute in small samples, as is shown by MacCallum (1986). (p. 96; see the following for Wyatt & Newcomb's reference to MacCullum's paper, and my comment)

Note that Wyatt and Newcomb used 11 variables with 111 women.

"It is essential that constraints to be added or dropped should be based on theory" (Bentler & Chou, 1987, p. 107). Wyatt and Newcomb gave no theoretical rationale for adding parameters or for setting parameters equal to zero (see the following).

"[T]he practice of substituting correlation for covariance matrices in analysis is only rarely justified, since the associated statistics will usually be inappropriate" (Bentler & Chou, 1987, p. 90). Although Wyatt and Newcomb report variances for their variables (see their Table 3, p. 762), they analyzed the correlation matrix.

As to deletion of paths, Wyatt and Newcomb (1990) stated, "Only significant paths and correlations were retained in the final model. This method of overfitting and then deleting nonsignificant parameters was suggested by MacCallum (1986) as the best way to determine the true model" (p. 762).

Here, too, Wyatt and Newcomb gave no page number. Before I quote some of MacCallum's suggestions regarding specification searches (model modification), I would like to quote him on sample size: "The results . . . demonstrate the drastic effect of sample size on the success of specification searches, with all searches failing when sample size was set at 100 observations" (MacCallum, 1986, p. 118; as I pointed out above, Wyatt & Newcomb used 111 subjects with 11 variables).

Following are MacCallum's (1986) recommendations for model modification:

> These findings suggest that empirical investigators can do several things to enhance the likelihood of success in specification searches. These include (a) careful formulation of the initial model, so as to maximize correspondence between it and the true model; (b) use of as large a sample as possible; (c) use of a restrictive search strategy, wherein no model modifications are made without rigorous substantive justification; and (d) a willingness to continue a search beyond the point of finding a model with a nonsignificant chi-square. (p. 118)

I suspect that Wyatt and Newcomb had (d) in mind when they referred to MacCallum. Anyway, MacCallum (1986) spoke of "willingness to continue" when he discussed the use of modification indices for adding variables to improve fit (see his discussion section on p. 118). By contrast, Wyatt and Newcomb referred to him as recommending overfitting and deleting nonsignificant parameters "as the best way to determine the true model" (p. 762).

I believe it important to point out that MacCallum, appropriately, recommended that parameters be added or deleted one a time "during a search, because a single change in the model can affect other parts of the solution" (p. 109).[10] Based on univariate statistical tests of significance, Wyatt and Newcomb deleted all the nonsignificant coefficients simultaneously. Earlier, I drew attention to the Wald test, which "is designed to determine whether sets of parameters that were treated as free in a model could in fact be simultaneously set to zero without substantial loss in model fit" (Bentler, 1992, p. 68).

In conclusion, I would like to make two additional points. One, Wyatt and Newcomb's model included also correlated errors (see their Figure 2, p. 764; I discuss correlated errors in the next section). Two, I quoted from Bentler and Chou (1987) and from MacCallum (1986) in some length in the hope of thereby encouraging you to study these important papers.

CORRELATED ERRORS

Probably the least reasonable form of model modification is the addition of correlated errors to improve fit. Two kinds of correlated errors can be identified: (1) those between error terms of indicators of latent variables (i.e., measurement errors) and (2) those between error terms of latent variables (i.e., residuals). As Jöreskog and Sörbom (1993a) pointed out, correlated measurement errors may be justified in very limited situations, as "when error terms correlate for the same variable over time" (p. 113). In general, however,

> if the error terms for two or more indicators correlate, it means that the indicators measure *something else* or *something in addition* to the construct they are supposed to measure. If this is the case, the meaning of the construct and its dimensions may be different from what is intended. (p. 113)

Particularly pernicious are correlated errors of latent variables aimed at improving fit, as they create an illusion of an explanation. As Gerbing and Anderson (1984) put it, "While the use of

---

[10]I made the same point when I discussed deletion of regression coefficients that are statistically not significant (see, for example, Chapter 8).

correlated errors improves the fit by accounting for . . . unwanted covariation, it does so at a correspondent loss of the meaning and substantive conclusions which can be drawn from the model" (p. 574).

Whatever type of correlated errors is used, "*every correlation between error terms must be justified and interpreted substantively* [italics added]" (Jöreskog & Sörbom, 1993a, p. 113). Even a superficial examination of the research literature reveals that, barring the occasional post hoc lame speculation about why errors are correlated, most researchers give no substantive interpretations for them. In what follows, I give some examples that illustrate this.

RESEARCH EXAMPLES USING CORRELATED ERRORS

As with the research examples I gave earlier concerning the use of modification indices, I give the briefest description possible of the studies I comment on. Moreover, except for the matter of correlated errors, *I do not address other aspects of the studies I cite.*

(1) DeBaryshe, Patterson, and Capaldi (1993) tested "a model for conduct-related school failure in young adolescent boys. In this model, family characteristics and child antisocial behavior serve as predictors of school adjustment and academic performance" (p. 795).

According to one aspect of their model (see their Figure 1, p. 801), (a) parent achievement affects ineffective discipline and antisocial behavior and (b) ineffective discipline and antisocial behavior are not linked by a path (i.e., neither affects the other). The authors stated, "We included a nondirectional association between discipline and antisocial behavior by estimating the correlation between the disturbance terms for these two constructs" (p. 799).

Although the authors also estimated "12 correlated residuals indicators [*sic*]" (p. 799), I address only the correlation between the residuals of the two previously mentioned latent variables. After noting that there were "moderate to strong associations between the latent variables," the authors stated, "Ineffective discipline and antisocial behavior were strongly related ($\Psi_{31} = .66$)" (p. 800).[11] I will make a couple of observations about this statement.

First, $\Psi = .66$ is *not* the correlation between ineffective discipline and antisocial behavior but between their residuals (see the explanation of LISREL output presented earlier in this chapter). According to their Table 5 (p. 801), the estimated correlation between these two constructs is .86.

Second, other aspects of the model aside, the large correlation between the residuals indicates a failure of the model to account for the estimated correlation between ineffective discipline and antisocial behavior. I suggest that you examine DeBaryshe et al.'s Figure 1 (1993, p. 801) and notice that the standardized effects of parental achievement on ineffective discipline and antisocial behavior are, respectively, −.58 and −.35. Multiplying these coefficients yields an estimated correlation of .20, which falls far short of the estimated correlation between the two constructs (.86; see the preceding comment).

Here, then, is an example of what I said earlier, namely that correlated residuals do not constitute an explanation. Moreover, when (as in the present case) a correlation between residuals leads to a noticeable improvement in model fit, it is highly likely that model misspecification would be overlooked.

(2) Earlier, when I commented on Sujan et al.'s (1994) use of modification indices to improve fit (see "Research Examples Using Modification Indices"), I pointed out that they also used

---

[11]The correlation is between the residuals of η_1 and η_2 (see their figure). The subscript 31 is probably a typographical error.

correlated errors (see their Figure B1, p. 48). For present purposes, visualize a model in which two endogenous variables—those representing learning orientation and performance orientation (each measured by a single indicator)—are (a) affected by two correlated exogenous variables, (b) not connected by a path (i.e., neither is hypothesized to be affecting the other), (c) correlated (.39; see Table A1 in Sujan et al., p. 47). Sujan et al. stated, "The error for each construct [*sic*] was set to one minus the composite reliability" (p. 48).

In view of the foregoing, for a model to be deemed fitting the data, it would have, among other things, to account, within random fluctuations, for the correlation between the two endogenous variables under consideration. Now, after concluding that the fit of the model is acceptable, Sujan et al., stated, "Within the context of a significant positive correlation between learning and performance orientations ($\Psi = .27$), learning orientation has a significant positive influence on working both smart . . . and hard . . . supporting" (p. 49) two of their hypotheses. They then made a similar statement about the effect of performance orientation.

To begin with, $\Psi = .27$ is a correlation between residuals (see the explanation of LISREL output presented earlier in this chapter). As the endogenous variables under consideration were measured by single indicators (see the preceding), it is a correlation between errors of the two indicators. Assuming that the reliability estimates used to adjust for measurement errors (see the previous quotation) were appropriate, then the correlation between the errors indicates a failure on the part of the model to account for the correlation between the two endogenous variables under consideration. Stated differently, this is an indication of model misspecification. I will not speculate about the nature and origin of the misspecification. Instead, I would like to state that Sujan et al.'s interpretation of the results, as exemplified by the quotation beginning with "within the context" constitutes no explanation. Other than ignoring the problem, I don't know what it means.

Sujan et al. treated similarly (i.e., used correlated errors and gave a similar "interpretation") two other endogenous variables, which according to their model are affected by the endogenous variables I commented on in the preceding (see their figure B1, p. 48).

(3) Berndt and Miller (1990) used SEM to study the effects of "expectancies and values" on "achievement" (p. 319). Using LISREL, they analyzed a model with multiple indicators of the variables under consideration. After concluding that the model "did not fit the data well" (p. 322), they stated, "The fit of the model was substantially improved by allowing for nonzero covariances (or correlated errors) for 7 of the 55 elements in the matrix of measurement error covariances" (p. 322). Though they did not state their criteria for "allowing" errors to be correlated, it is highly likely that they did this based on modification indices.

(4) Conger et al. (1993) "investigated the mediational role of family processes in linking economic problems to both the prosocial and problematic adjustment of early adolescents. Specifically, . . . [they] expected that parental moods and behaviors would provide the bridge between family economic hardship and adjustments of . . . early adolescents" (p. 206).

According to their model (see their Figure 1, p. 207), family economic pressure is the sole construct affecting father's depressed mood and mother's depressed mood. As the two depression constructs are not linked in the model, it follows that they are correlated because they share the common cause: family economic pressure. Here, now, is the authors' statement about the results for this part of their model.

> Based on the expectation that they would be significantly related . . . , residuals for the same reporter indicators were allowed to correlate across the two depression constructs. Once these correlations and the influence of economic pressure were partialed out, there was still a significant residual correlation

(.48) between mothers' and fathers' depression. Because of the high collinearity between the two depression constructs, estimation of path coefficients would be quite unstable with both of them entered into the same model; therefore, we use them separately in later analyses. (p. 211)

Being overlooked, or explained away, in the preceding is the failure of family economic pressure to account for the correlation between the depression constructs, suggesting that the model is misspecified. Doing two separate analyses evades this problem, much like when separate regression analyses are done on several correlated dependent variables.

(5) Flay et al. (1994) studied "[d]ifferential effects of parental smoking and friends' smoking on adolescent initiation and escalation of smoking" (p. 248). A portion of their model (Figure 1, p. 252) consisted of two correlated exogenous variables: "Friends' Smoking" and "Parental Smoking" (p. 252), and four mediating variables. In their discussion of the structural model, the authors stated, *without elaboration,* "We also hypothesize that the disturbance terms of some of the mediating constructs will be correlated" (p. 251). Instead of commenting, I refer you to my introductory remarks to this section, where I also drew attention to Jöreskog and Sörbom's exhortation that correlated residuals ought to be justified substantively.

Recapitulation

Post hoc model revision aimed at improving fit poses very serious threats to valid interpretations and conclusions of SEM. The miniature examples I have given here cannot do justice to the complexities that may arise. Nonetheless, I hope they served to alert you to the hazards of relying blindly on modification indices for model revision. Also, as my sole aim in this, and the preceding, section was to caution you against undue reliance on the modification index (MI) or correlated errors for model revision and improvement of fit, I paid no attention to important issues related to these topics (e.g., sample size and the power of statistical tests of significance, sampling fluctuations, model misspecification). I strongly recommend that you study MacCallum (1986) and MacCallum et al. (1992) on these and related issues. See also, Saris, Satorra, and Sörbom (1987), who concluded their cogent discussion saying, "MI cannot be used as simply as it usually is. At the least, one should expect that the use of this index can lead to incorrect conclusions in many instances" (p. 118).

Borrowing a phrase from Steiger (1988, p. 286), model revision for the sole purpose of fit improvement would be more appropriately characterized as model fiddling. I believe that Browne (1982) captured the essence of this activity when he branded results it yields as "wastebasket parameters" (p. 101).

CORRELATED ENDOGENOUS VARIABLES

In the preceding section, I discussed correlated errors and pointed out that, more often than not, they are indicative of model misspecification. However, I also pointed out that under certain limited circumstances correlated errors are valid and meaningful. In this section I discuss inadmissible correlations in a causal model, namely those between endogenous variables. Stated succinctly, a causal model is supposed to account for such correlations (covariances), *not* postulate them. This can, perhaps, be grasped best through the simple model depicted in Figure 19.6. Though this model consists of four variables, my concern in this section is with the correlation between Y and Z, which *I display solely for this discussion.* Such a correlation *must not be*

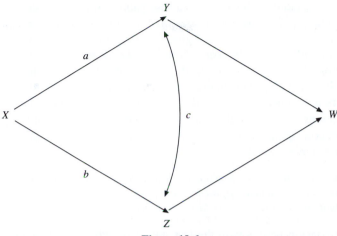

Figure 19.6

displayed as part of the model. This is not to say that the correlation may not exist. Rather, that a model that fits the data well is expected to account for it.

For ease of discussing this point, and research examples on which I will comment, I attached the letters a and b to the effects of X on Y and Z, respectively, and the letter c to the correlation between Y and Z. In addition, I will assume that (1) all variables are observed (i.e., except for the inadmissible correlation between Y and Z, Figure 19.6 is a path-analytic model of the kind I introduced in Chapter 18) and (2) a correlation matrix is analyzed. What I will say, however, applies also to the analysis of covariance matrices with multiple indicators of latent variables.

Referring to the variables in Figure 19.6, assume that

$$r_{xy} = .2 \qquad r_{xz} = .4 \qquad r_{yz} = .6$$

Based on my above assumptions, it follows that the effect of X on Y (a, in Figure 19.6) is .2, and that of X on Z (b, in Figure 19.6) is .4. Accordingly, the reproduced correlation between Y and Z (c, in Figure 19.6) is .08 [(.2)(.4)].[12] Clearly, the model fails to account for the correlation between Y and Z. Faced with this predicament, a researcher would probably attempt to revise the model.[13] I will not repeat my earlier discussion of model revision. Moreover, not having used a substantive example for the model under consideration, I cannot conjecture how it would be revised (e.g., adding relevant variables that have been omitted; hypothesizing that Y affects Z). Clearly, however, inserting a correlation between Y and Z, as I did in Figure 19.6, is *not* a valid option. Yet, as I will show, researchers do just that.

RESEARCH EXAMPLES USING CORRELATED ENDOGENOUS VARIABLES

Surprisingly, causal models that include correlated endogenous variables are not as rare as one might have expected. I say "surprisingly" because researchers who advance such models, and

---

[12]If necessary, review relevant sections in Chapter 18 for an explanation of how to calculate effects and reproduced correlations.

[13]As I pointed out earlier, I limit my discussion to the part of the model involving variables X, Y, and Z.

referees and editors who accept them for publication, do not seem to realize that they call attention to the failure of the model to account for correlations between endogenous variables.

As I did in earlier sections, I give the briefest description possible of the studies I comment on, and I *address only the issue of correlated endogenous variables.* In my commentaries, I will refer from time to time to Figure 19.6 and the notation I used in it.

(1) Peterson (1982) challenged the idea advanced by other researchers that "income is largely a function of either the direct influence of one's class background or the influence of one's years of schooling" (p. 24). To this end, he advanced a model similar to my Figure 19.6 in which family SES corresponds to my *X,* education to my *Y,* and verbal ability to my *Z.* Elaborating on his model, Peterson stated:

> Income is treated as a function of socioeconomic status, education, and ability. *It is further assumed that education and ability are in part a function of family SES. No assumptions are made as to whether ability is causally prior to education or vice versa* [italics added]. (p. 26)

My concern here is with the last statement, which Peterson depicted as a correlation in his model (similar to *c* in my Figure 19.6). Peterson used the same model to analyze several data sets (e.g., White males, Black males). For present purposes, I comment on his first analysis (White males), which he depicted as Figure 1 (p. 26). Using my notation in Figure 19.6, above, Peterson reported

$$a = .29 \qquad b = .11 \qquad c = .60$$

Even a cursory look at the two effects (*a* and *b*) reveals that, as in my previous example, the model fails to account for the correlation between education and verbal ability. Anyway, multiplying *a* by *b* yields a predicted correlation of .03, whereas the estimated correlation is .60. Results of Peterson's analyses for the other data sets are virtually the same.

I started with Peterson's work for several reasons. (a) He addressed an important and controversial topic. (b) He used a strident tone in criticizing researchers who advanced opposing views. Not only did he assert that "their analysis has serious technical flaws" (p. 25) but also referring to some of their observations he stated, "These canards are now treated as sage observations of contemporary society. They are handy shells in the armory used by those generals and lieutenants who feel compelled to search and destroy the Great Society and its social reform policies" (p. 32). (c) He presented his work under prestigious auspices on the occasion of the 50th anniversary of the Social Science Research Building at the University of Chicago.

(2) Ryff and Essex (1992) stated, "The objective of this study was to investigate how life experience (e.g., in community relocation) and the way it is construed by an individual relates to mental health" (p. 507). Among other things, they reported results for a couple of models for which they claimed to show direct effects of "Push/Pull Discrepancy" (analogous to *X* in my Figure 19.6) on "Personal Growth" (analogous to *W* in my Figure 19.6), as well as its indirect effects via "Social Self-Assessment" and "Behavioral Self-Perception" (analogous, respectively to my *Y* and *Z* [see their Figure 1, p. 512]). Using my notation in my Figure 19.6, their *a* = .09, *b* = .20, and *c* = .52. Here, too, is a clear case of a model's failure to account for the correlation between the two mediating variables.

(3) LeBlanc (1993) presented "an analytical framework . . . that facilitates the examination of key factors which shape HIV-related knowledge among adults in the U.S." (p. 23). In a path model, the author showed six variables (e.g., education, age) affecting two sources of information:

television and newspapers (see his Figure 1, p. 31). As in the preceding examples, television and newspapers were conceived as mediating variables that do not affect each other. LeBlanc inserted the correlation between these variables (−.56) in his model (similar to my *c* in Figure 19.6). An examination of the effects of the six variables on Television and Newspapers (see path coefficients in LeBlanc's Figure 1) should suffice to reveal that the model fails to account for the correlation between the two mediating variables. If you are having difficulties seeing this, I suggest that you analyze LeBlanc's data according to his model in Figure 1. If you did this, you would find that the predicted correlation between television and newspapers is virtually zero. As I pointed out earlier, the observed correlation between these variables in −.56.

(4) Bornholt, Goodnow, and Cooney (1994) studied the effects of gender stereotypes on adolescents' perceptions of their achievement in English and mathematics. My concern here is limited to their covariance structure analyses, which they reported on pages 685–688.

I would like to begin by pointing out that, despite several attempts, I could not decipher the analyses Bornholt et al. carried out. I found their reporting woefully inadequate and their presentation and interpretation confusing. Essentially, they studied perceptions by male and female students of five latent variables: task difficulty, effort, current performance, natural talent, and future performance. Referring to two models involving the aforementioned variables (one for achievement in mathematics and one for achievement in English), the authors stated:

> Similar patterns of interrelations among aspects of general perceptions of achievement in mathematics and English are described in Figure 3. The fit of a unitary factor model to the data was poor, with average residuals for mathematics, for example, at 0.12. The five correlated factor model was preferred. Low average residuals around .03 or .04 indicated a good fit of each model to the data. (p. 685)

Before I comment on specifics of the preceding statement, and others concerning Bornholt et al.'s analyses, I would like to point out that the reference to the average residuals is *all that they reported in the way of evaluating the fit of their models.*

From the quotation it appears that the authors carried out two sets of confirmatory factor-analyses on the data for mathematics and English achievement. In the first set, they used a single factor, whereas in the second set they used five correlated factors. Though they did not explain their choice of the number of factors, their analyses seemed to address measurement models. In the next section (see "Miscellaneous Topics"), I comment on confirmatory factor analysis and the two-step approach, according to which one should begin with an evaluation of the measurement model and analyze the structural model only after concluding that the measurement model is satisfactory.

For present purposes, though, it is important to note that Figure 3 to which the authors referred consisted of structural, *not* measurement, models. Specifically, in each model, task difficulty and effort were conceived as exogenous variables; current performance and natural talent were conceived as endogenous variables, affected by task difficulty and effort and mediating their effect on future performance. I trust that you can see that the meager results of the factor analyses the authors reported (see again the quotation) and their interpretations have no direct bearing on their structural models.

Before I comment on the structural models in their Figure 3 and the authors' interpretations of them, I would like to point out that the authors reported correlation matrices among the five latent variables for males and females for mathematics and English achievement (see their Table 2, p. 686). I assume that the preceding are the results from their analyses with five factors. Referring to these correlation matrices, the authors stated, "Most important, the patterns of interrelations among general perceptions were quite similar when considered for males and females" (p. 686).

In the next section ("Miscellaneous Topics"), I draw attention to multisample comparisons and point out that these should be applied to covariance, *not* correlation, matrices. For now, I would point out that multisample comparisons should involve more than just an examination of the correlation matrices, which is what the authors seem to have done. The foregoing aside, even a cursory look at the correlation matrices reported in the authors' Table 2 casts doubt about the authors' claims. Following are but a few examples of correlations for males and females, respectively. Between (a) Current and Talent: .62 and .85; (b) Current and Task: −.51 and −.74; (c) Future and Effort: −.08 and −.21.

It seems that based on examination of correlations such as the preceding the authors decided to combine males and females in their structural equation analyses. The structural models depicted in their Figure 3, p. 687, seem to be based on responses of male and female combined. I will now comment on several issues concerning these structural models.

Earlier, I pointed out that, according to the authors' Figure 3, task difficulty and effort (exogenous variables) affect natural talent and current performance (endogenous mediating variables). In Figure 3, the latter are connected with a double-headed arrow on which a value was inserted (.78 for the English achievement model and .67 for the mathematics achievement model). Here is *all* the authors said about this segment of their model: "Perceived Talent and Current Performance, are represented as correlated aspects of achievement" (p. 685). As the authors did not report the correlation matrices for the combined male and female samples, I can only surmise that the previous values are correlations among two endogenous latent variables affected by the two exogenous variables. Earlier I pointed out that such correlations are inadmissible in a structural model. All I will say here is that an examination of the coefficients for the effects of the two exogenous variables on the endogenous variables under consideration reveals that they fall far short from accounting for the reported correlation between the latter.

Here now is how the authors interpreted their results for the causal models depicted in their Figure 3:

> In general, the concept of natural talent played a central role in students' perceptions of achievement. General perceptions of current and future performance were closely related to one another, and both were associated with perceived natural talent. Perceived effort and perceived task difficulty were also positively associated with each other, and were negatively associated with perceived natural talent. (pp. 686–687)

From the preceding one would not gather that, except for the correlation between perceived effort and perceived task difficulty (exogenous variables), the "relations" the authors speak of are coefficients of effects. Further, according to their models the exogenous variables affect perceived future performance (the ultimate endogenous variable) only indirectly, via perceived current performance and perceived natural talent. Yet, the authors do not even allude to this issue. Regrettably, this is consistent with the absence of any tests and fit indices.

I cannot refrain from expressing my astonishment that the paper under consideration was published in a leading journal. As indicated at the end of the paper, it was revised after its submission and before final acceptance, presumably in response to comments and/or suggestions by referees and/or editors.

MISCELLANEOUS TOPICS

My aim in Chapter 18 and the present chapter was to give an elementary introduction to SEM. For a thorough treatment of SEM, I recommend highly Bollen's (1989) text. To avoid repetitious references, I will point out here that Bollen discusses all the topics that I will now mention. For an extensive annotated bibliography of theoretical and technical contributions to SEM, see Austin and Calderón (1996).

In the present section, I would like to acquaint you with some major topics I did not address or even allude to. After brief remarks on a given topic, I will give selected references for relevant discussions and/or applications. *Though I will not refer to manuals for EQS and LISREL, you should consult them as they give illustrative applications of, commentaries on, and references to topics I introduce.*

Confirmatory Factor Analysis

As you may know, factor analysis is used to study structure underlying a set of correlated variables or items. You may also know of the distinction between exploratory and confirmatory factor analysis. The latter plays a paramount role in measurement models in SEM. For example, confirmatory factor analysis is used to study validity of claims that given indicators reflect several dimensions of a construct or several interrelated constructs. Stated differently, confirmatory factor analysis is used to study relations between constructs and their indicators, as well as relations among constructs. Among other things, confirmatory factor analysis is also used to test different measurement models and to identify trait and method variance in mutlitrait-multimethod matrices. For an introduction to confirmatory factor analysis and illustrative applications, see Pedhazur and Schmelkin (1991, Chapter 23, and references therein).

Two-Step Approach to SEM

According to the two-step approach, the validity of the measurement model is to be established before proceeding to the second step of evaluating the structural model. As Jöreskog and Sörbom (1993a) put it:

> The testing of the structural model, i.e., the testing of the initially specified theory, may be meaningless unless it is first established that the measurement model holds. If the chosen indicators for a construct do not measure that construct, the specified theory must be modified before it can be tested. Therefore, the measurement model should be tested before the structural relations are tested. (p. 113)

Essentially, the measurement model is evaluated through confirmatory factor analysis. For a review of the two-step approach, see Anderson and Gerbing (1988). Fornell and Yi (1992a), who questioned the validity of the two-step approach, asserted, "A fundamental assumption of any two-step approach is that measurement and substantive theory can be taken apart and treated separately" (p. 296). See Anderson and Gerbing (1992) for a comment on Fornell and Yi, and Fornell and Yi's (1992b) reply.

Reflective versus Formative Indicators

My discussions and illustrations of the role of indicators were limited to what are called reflective indicators, that is, indicators that presumably reflect a given construct or are said to be caused by it (e.g., items reflecting mental ability, anxiety, frustration). Other terms used for such indicators are "reflectors" (e.g., Costner, 1969) or "effect indicators" (e.g., Blalock, 1971). By contrast, formative indicators—also called "producers" (Costner, 1969) or "cause indicators" (Blalock, 1971)—are conceived as causes of a variable. For example, it is customary to use indicators such as income, education, or type of job as reflective of socioeconomic status. However, as Bollen and Lennox (1991, p. 306) argued cogently, it would be more appropriate to treat them as formative indicators.

> Most researchers in the social sciences assume that indicators are effect indicators. Cause indicators are neglected despite their appropriateness in many instances. . . . Establishing causal priority is necessary to determine if an indicator is a cause or an effect of a latent variable. (Bollen, 1989, p. 65)

In addition to the preceding references, you will find good discussions and examples of the distinction between the two types of indicators in Alwin (1988, pp. 36–41) and MacCallum and Browne (1993).

Nonrecursive Models

My presentation was limited to recursive models. As I pointed out in Chapter 18, a recursive model is one in which the causal flow is unidirectional. In nonrecursive models, endogenous variables may have reciprocal effects on each other either directly or through a loop. For introductions to nonrecursive models, see Berry (1984), Duncan (1975, Chapter 7), and Fox (1984, Chapter 4).

Missing Data

In Chapter 11, I commented briefly on threats to the validity of results arising from subject attrition, nonresponse, and the like (see "Unequal Sample Sizes"). These and related issues are addressed under the general heading of missing data or missing values. The handling of missing data is a very complex and controversial topic, as it hinges on the often intractable mechanisms that have led to it. For reviews of the literature and methods of handling missing data in statistical analysis, see Anderson, Basilevsky, and Hum (1983); Dodge (1985); Little and Rubin (1987, 1989); and Madow, Nisselson, and Olkin (1983).

The basic elements used in the application of SEM are covariances (or correlations) among indicators. The two most common approaches to missing data for such purposes are (1) pairwise deletion and (2) listwise deletion. In pairwise deletion, a covariance is calculated based on the subjects for whom data are available on the given pair of indicators under consideration. Consequently, different subjects are deleted, depending on the specific pair of indicators under consideration. In listwise deletion, on the other hand, subjects for whom data are missing are deleted from the analysis altogether. Under listwise deletion, then, the number of subjects becomes the one for whom data are available on all the indicators.

Long (1983), who discussed difficulties that may arise in pairwise deletion, suggested that it "be used only if there are a small number of missing observations scattered evenly across the variables and cases" (p. 63; see also Bentler & Chou, 1987, p. 100). For a more general critique of pairwise and listwise deletion in SEM, and a proposed alternative approach, see Muthén, Kaplan, and Hollis (1987); also see Allison (1987); Brown (1994); and Rovine (1994).

Multisample Comparisons

Analogous to comparisons of regression equations across samples (see Chapters 14 and 15), researchers are often interested in comparing measurement and structural models across samples. Both EQS (e.g., Bentler, 1992a, Chapters 7 through 9) and LISREL (e.g., Jöreskog & Sörbom, 1993a, Chapter 2) are well suited to handle various facets of such comparisons.

Following is but a small selection from the extensive literature addressed to methodological and/or substantive aspects of this topic: Alwin (1988); Alwin and Jackson (1979, 1981); Byrne (1989; 1991; 1994, Part 3); Byrne and Shavelson (1987); Cole and Maxwell (1985); Dunn et al. (1993, Chapter 7); Marsh (1985, 1994a); Marsh and Grayson (1990); Rindskopf and Everson (1984); Rock, Werts, and Flaugher (1978); Schoenberg (1982); and Wong (1994).

Multilevel SEM

I introduced multilevel analysis in Chapter 16. Several papers addressing multilevel SEM have appeared recently. Among them are McDonald (1994) and Muthén (1991, 1994).

Longitudinal Research

My presentation of SEM was limited to cross-sectional research, that is, research based on data collected at a single point in time. By contrast, in longitudinal research subjects are observed repeatedly over time. Some authors contend that longitudinal research is a prerequisite for studying causation. As Lieberson (1985) put it, "*longitudinal data provide the only fully appropriate 'test' of a causal proposition's validity*" (p. 180). For general observations on longitudinal research, its status in social and behavioral research, and general references as well as specific ones concerning applications of SEM, see Pedhazur and Schmelkin (1991, pp. 315–317). Following are some additional recent references of SEM applications in longitudinal research. A book devoted to recent advances in longitudinal research, edited by Collins and Horn (1991), contains several chapters on SEM applications. See also Farrell (1994), Jöreskog (1979), Marsh (1993, 1994b), Marsh and Grayson (1994), Rogosa (1979), von Eye and Clogg (1994), Willett and Sayer (1994).

CONCLUDING REMARKS

Several times earlier, I cautioned against being dazzled by complex analytic approaches to the extent of forgetting that they are means that, when applied perspicaciously, may help shed light on the ends of theory. Judging from the research literature in SEM, reiterating, even belaboring, the obvious is imperative: to evaluate a model, you have to have one. As I have shown, some researchers expect the analytic approach to "uncover" the model(s). Among researchers who do recognize the prerequisite to formulate a model(s), many do not seem to appreciate the inherent difficulties, and the hard thinking required, in formulating one worth evaluating and testing. As a result, the research literature is replete with caricatures of models.

Writing more than 30 years ago, McNemar (1960) stated, "Among things that worry me about model building is the apparent ease by which a student who has had only freshman college mathematics can build models. One suspects that such building rests on a foundation of mathematical quicksand and psychological bog" (p. 300). Various authors have since then drawn attention to deficiencies in the formulation and evaluation of models. Notable among them are Breckler (1990), Cliff (1983), and Steiger (1988, 1990). In addition, the summer 1987 issue of the *Journal of Educational Statistics* consists of a thorough critique of path analysis by Freedman (1987a), responses from more than ten leading exponents, and his rejoinder (Freedman, 1987b). It is noteworthy that in his response to Freedman, Cliff (1987b) expressed the opinion that his (1983) statement and those of others "seem to have had little effect on the volume of . . . naive applications of path analysis" (p. 158).

I believe that you will benefit from careful study of the foregoing references. In addition, you can learn of recent concerns and developments in SEM from reading such journals as *Multivariate Behavioral Research* and *Structural Equation Modeling,* and from interchanges on the SEMNET forum on the Internet (for a description of SEMNET, how to join, and the like, see Rigdon, 1994a).

STUDY SUGGESTIONS

1. Distinguish between measurement and structural equation models.

2. Suppose that I formulated the following causal model, according to which socioeconomic status (SES) affects locus of control (LOC) and aspirations (ASP). In addition, LOC affects ASP.

Note that for each latent variable I use two indicators. Suppose that the correlation matrix among the indicators, and the standard deviations are as follows in the table on the right ($N = 300$).

	Y_1	Y_2	Y_3	Y_4	X_1	X_2
Y_1	1.00					
Y_2	.70	1.00				
Y_3	.60	.60	1.00			
Y_4	.58	.52	.80	1.00		
X_1	.30	.32	.20	.25	1.00	
X_2	.33	.30	.30	.30	.50	1.00
s:	3.67	2.16	1.32	1.73	2.62	2.13

NOTE: s = standard deviation; Y_1 and Y_2 are indicators of LOC; Y_3 and Y_4 are indicators of ASP; X_1 and X_2 are indicators of SES.

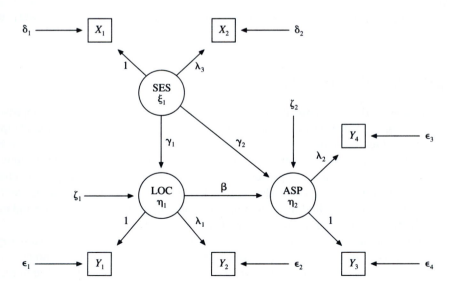

Analyze the preceding data, using EQS and/or LISREL, or any other suitable program to which you may have access.

3. In LISREL, to what do the following refer?
   (a) η; (b) ξ; (c) **B**; (d) Γ.

4. Many researchers who apply path analysis do not report reliabilities of their measures. Among those who do report reliabilities, only a small minority do any-

thing about them. In other words, despite having reliability estimates, they do the path analysis as if their measures were perfectly reliable. I suggest that you peruse literature in your area(s) of interest for such papers, reanalyze the data, allowing for the reported reliabilities (for guidance, see my analysis in Table 19.1), and compare your results with those reported in the original papers.

ANSWERS

2. Following are excerpts from LISREL output, using SIMPLIS and LISREL output:

SIMPLIS Output

COVARIANCE MATRIX TO BE ANALYZED

	Y1	Y2	Y3	Y4	X1	X2
Y1	13.469					
Y2	5.549	4.666				
Y3	2.907	1.711	1.742			
Y4	3.682	1.943	1.827	2.993		
X1	2.885	1.811	0.692	1.133	6.864	
X2	2.580	1.380	0.843	1.105	2.790	4.537

Number of Iterations = 7

LISREL ESTIMATES (MAXIMUM LIKELIHOOD)

$Y1 = 1.000*LOC$, Errorvar.= 3.724 , $R^2 = 0.724$
    (0.592)
    6.290

$Y2 = 0.569*LOC$, Errorvar.= 1.506 , $R^2 = 0.677$
    (0.0402)   (0.206)
    14.175   7.325

$Y3 = 1.000*ASP$, Errorvar.= 0.242 , $R^2 = 0.861$
    (0.0688)
    3.518

$Y4 = 1.218*ASP$, Errorvar.= 0.768 , $R^2 = 0.743$
    (0.0714)   (0.116)
    17.056   6.614

$X1 = 1.000*SES$, Errorvar.= 3.713 , $R^2 = 0.459$
    (0.584)
    6.362

$X2 = 0.885*SES$, Errorvar.= 2.066 , $R^2 = 0.545$
    (0.149)   (0.426)
    5.928   4.853

$LOC = 0.924*SES$, Errorvar.= 7.057 , $R^2 = 0.276$
    (0.157)   (1.001)
    5.885   7.050

ASP = 0.301*LOC + 0.00470*SES, Errorvar.= 0.612 , R^2 = 0.592
    (0.0301)   (0.0505)   (0.0921)
    9.993   0.0930   6.642

GOODNESS OF FIT STATISTICS

CHI-SQUARE WITH 6 DEGREES OF FREEDOM = 13.976 (P = 0.0299)

ROOT MEAN SQUARE RESIDUAL (RMR) = 0.0756
STANDARDIZED RMR = 0.0190
GOODNESS OF FIT INDEX (GFI) = 0.985
ADJUSTED GOODNESS OF FIT INDEX (AGFI) = 0.949

LISREL Output

TOTAL AND INDIRECT EFFECTS

TOTAL EFFECTS OF KSI ON ETA

	SES

LOC	0.924
	(0.157)
	5.885
ASP	0.282
	(0.056)
	5.039

INDIRECT EFFECTS OF KSI ON ETA

	SES

LOC	--
ASP	0.278
	(0.054)
	5.164

TOTAL EFFECTS OF ETA ON ETA

	LOC	ASP
	---------	--------
LOC	--	--
ASP	0.301	--
	(0.030)	
	9.993	

STANDARDIZED SOLUTION
GAMMA

	SES

LOC	0.525
ASP	0.007

STANDARDIZED TOTAL EFFECTS OF KSI ON ETA

	SES

LOC	0.525
ASP	0.409

STANDARDIZED INDIRECT EFFECTS OF KSI ON ETA

	SES

LOC	– –
ASP	0.402

Notice, among other things, that the direct effect of SES on ASP is statistically not significant ($t = .093$), whereas its indirect effect is statistically significant ($t = 5.164$). From the excerpts of the standardized solution you can see that the (1) direct effect of SES on ASP is virtually zero (.007), (2) total effect of SES on ASP = .409, and (3) indirect effect of SES on ASP = .402. In sum, SES affects ASP only indirectly, via LOC.

EQS OUTPUT

CHI-SQUARE =   13.976 BASED ON   6 DEGREES OF FREEDOM
PROBABILITY VALUE FOR THE CHI-SQUARE STATISTIC IS   0.02991

BENTLER-BONETT NORMED   FIT INDEX=   0.983
BENTLER-BONETT NONNORMED FIT INDEX=   0.976
COMPARATIVE FIT INDEX   =   0.990

CONSTRUCT EQUATIONS WITH STANDARD ERRORS AND TEST STATISTICS

```
LOC    =F1 =      .924*F3    +     1.000 D1
                  .157
                  5.886


ASP    =F2 =      .300*F1    +     .005*F3    + 1.000 D2
                  .030             .050
                  9.993            .094
```

DECOMPOSITION OF EFFECTS WITH STANDARDIZED VALUES

PARAMETER TOTAL EFFECTS

```
LOC    =F1 =    .525*F3    +    .851 D1
ASP    =F2 =    .766*F1    +    .409*F3    +    .652 D1    +    .639 D2
```

PARAMETER INDIRECT EFFECTS

```
ASP    =F2 =    .402*F3    +    .652 D1
```

I included the preceding brief excerpts from EQS output for comparative purposes.

3. (a) η is a vector of latent endogenous variables.
   (b) ξ is a vector of latent exogenous variables.
   (c) **B** is a matrix of coefficients of effects of endogenous variables on endogenous variables.
   (d) Γ is a matrix of coefficients of effects of exogenous variables on endogenous variables.

Regression and Discriminant Analysis

In Parts 1 and 2 of this book, I showed how multiple regression analysis may be used to analyze data obtained in diverse experimental and nonexperimental designs. Whereas in Part 1 I discussed designs in which the independent variables are continuous, in Part 2 I discussed designs in which the independent variables are categorical, or categorical and continuous. Although the designs I presented in Parts 1 and 2 may consist of multiple independent variables, they can include only one dependent variable.

In social and behavioral research, as well as in other areas, one is often interested in explaining, or predicting, multifaceted phenomena. Consider, for instance, the multifaceted phenomenon of academic achievement. Although researchers use students' grade point average as a dependent variable, this is very often done not because it is believed that this index captures the complex phenomenon of academic achievement, but because it is a single, easily obtainable index. Clearly, more insight can be gained by studying effects of different teaching styles, say, on achievement in reading, spelling, composition, arithmetic, or science, to name but a few.

As another example, suppose that an experiment on changing attitudes has been done in which three appeals, A_1, A_2, and A_3 were used with prejudiced individuals. A_1 was a democratic appeal or argument in which prejudice was depicted as being inconsistent with democracy. A_2 was a fair-play appeal: the American notion of fair play demands equal treatment for all. A_3 was a religious appeal: prejudice is a violation of the ethics of the major religions.[1] Now, if one wanted to determine which of the three appeals is most effective in changing prejudicial attitudes toward Blacks, say, and if a single measure of such attitudes were used, the analysis would proceed as shown in Chapter 11. Suppose, however, that the researcher's conception of prejudice is broader in that it refers to such attitudes toward minority groups, say, Blacks, Hispanics, or Mexican Americans. One may attempt to use a single measure of such attitudes, but the validity of doing this is predicated on the assumption that attitudes toward the three groups are unidimensional; otherwise one may be adding apples and oranges.

The preceding examples referred to experimental research. Similar problems arise very often in nonexperimental research. For example, one may wish to study how males and females differ in their conceptions of sex roles or how members of various ethnic groups differ in their conceptions of human nature. Or one may wish to study differences among preexisting groups in cognitive and affective domains. When the phenomenon being studied is multidimensional, one cannot encapsulate it in a single score without thereby distorting it or even stripping it entirely of its meaning.

---

[1] I took this idea from an actual experiment by Citron, Chein, and Harding (1950).

Thus far, my discussion has been limited to situations in which one wishes to study differences among groups on multiple dependent variables. Another common research situation is one in which one wishes to study relations between two *sets* of variables within a single group. For instance, one may have five measures of cognitive variables and four measures of affective variables on a sample of schoolchildren, and the purpose may be to study relations between these two sets of variables. As I show in Chapter 21, problems of this kind are handled by canonical analysis.

In reading the foregoing, you may have wondered what would be wrong if one were to analyze each of a set of dependent variables separately, using methods I presented in Parts 1 and 2. Or what would be wrong if one were to calculate zero-order correlations for all possible pairings of variables in situations of the kind I described in the last example. Actually, most researchers do just that. Without going into the details, I will note first that the use of multiple univariate tests on the same data affects the preselected α level (see, e.g., Bock, 1975, pp. 20–22; Harris, 1985, p. 6). More important, however, is that studying each dependent variable separately or calculating zero-order correlations only ignores the very essence and richness of multifaceted phenomenon being studied. Much of the social world is multivariate in nature, and studying it piecemeal does not hold promise of understanding it. As Harris (1985) so aptly put it:

> If researchers were sufficiently narrowminded or theories and measurement techniques so well developed or nature so simple as to dictate a single independent variable and a single outcome measure as appropriate in each study, there would be no need for multivariate statistical techniques. (p. 5)

In short, when the phenomenon studied is multivariate, resorting to analytic methods commensurate with it is necessary. It goes without saying that it is not possible to give an exhaustive treatment of multivariate analysis in a couple of chapters. Among excellent books on multivariate analysis are Bernstein (1987), Bock (1975), Chatfield and Collins (1980), Cliff (1987a), Finn (1974), Green (1978), Harris (1985), Marascuilo and Levin (1983), Maxwell (1977), Overall and Klett (1972), Stevens (1996), and Tatsuoka (1988). My objectives here are very limited. In this chapter, I introduce discriminant analysis (DA). Among other things, I discuss its relation to regression analysis. In the next chapter, I introduce multivariate analysis of variance (MANOVA) and canonical analysis (CA). Among other things, I discuss relations among DA, MANOVA, and CA. I hope that my introductions will stimulate you to pursue the study of multivariate analysis and that they will facilitate your efforts in doing so.

Because DA for *two* groups can also be calculated through multiple regression analysis, I begin this chapter with a demonstration of how this is done. I then apply DA to the same data. Although the DA equations I present apply to designs with any number of groups, I apply them in this chapter to two groups only so that the results may be compared with those I obtained from the analysis of the same data through multiple regression (I use the same equations in Chapter 21 for the analysis of a numerical example with more than two groups). I show that for two groups the two approaches lead to overall identical results, although some intermediate ones differ from one approach to the other. I then introduce programs for DA from SPSS and SAS and use them for the analysis of the same numerical example.

MULTIPLE REGRESSION ANALYSIS

Assume that the data reported in Table 20.1 were obtained from two groups in nonexperimental or experimental settings. Thus, for example, A_1 and A_2 may represent any two preexisting groups

Table 20.1   Illustrative Data on Two Dependent Variables for Two Groups

	A_1		A_2	
	X_1	X_2	X_1	X_2
	8	3	4	2
	7	4	3	1
	5	5	3	2
	3	4	2	2
	3	2	2	5
$\overline{X}$:	5.2	3.6	2.8	2.4

(e.g., males and females; Blacks and Whites). The dependent variables could be, say, X_1 = Masculinity, X_2 = Femininity;[2] X_1 = Locus of Control, X_2 = Anxiety. Alternatively, A_1 and A_2 may be two treatments, or a treatment group and a control group, and the dependent variables may be reading and arithmetic. Although, to minimize calculations, I use only two dependent variables, *the approach I present applies equally to any number of dependent variables, provided they have been obtained from two groups.* For convenience, I use only five subjects per group and single-digit scores. The lack of realism of the numerical example will, I believe, be offset by the ease with which all the calculations can be carried out by hand.

Table 20.2 displays the data in Table 20.1 in a format suitable for multiple regression analysis. At the bottom of the table, I included results from intermediate calculations. Note that I presented the two dependent variables, X_1 and X_2, as two column vectors. In addition, I included a coded vector, Y, to represent group membership. Any coding method will do. In the present example, I used dummy coding: 1's for members of group A_1 and 0's for members of group A_2. For the purpose of the analysis, the roles of the independent and the dependent variables are reversed. That is, the coded vector representing group membership is treated as the dependent variable, whereas the actual dependent variables are treated as independent variables.

I could, of course, use a computer program for multiple regression analysis to calculate the regression of Y on X_1 and X_2. As I pointed out, however, I use a small numerical example so that all the calculations can be done easily by hand. I presented and discussed formulas for multiple regression analysis with two independent variables in Chapter 5. Therefore, although I use these formulas here, I do not comment on them. When necessary, refer to Chapter 5 for explanations. I turn first to the calculation of the squared multiple correlation of Y on X_1 and X_2. To avoid cumbersome subscripts, I will refer to X_1 as variable 1 and to X_2 as variable 2.

$$R^2_{y.12} = \frac{r^2_{y1} + r^2_{y2} - 2r_{y1}r_{y2}r_{12}}{1 - r^2_{12}}$$

Using relevant values from the bottom of Table 20.2,

$$R^2_{y.12} = \frac{(.61559)^2 + (.44721)^2 - 2(.61559)(.44721)(.22942)}{1 - (.22942)^2} = .47778$$

This R^2 can be tested for significance in the usual manner:

$$F = \frac{R^2_{y.12}/k}{(1 - R^2_{y.12})/(N - k - 1)} = \frac{.47778/2}{(1 - .47778)/(10 - 2 - 1)} = 3.20$$

[2]Because the roles of the independent and the dependent variables are reversed for the purpose of the analysis (see the following), I use X's to represent the dependent variables so as to be consistent with the notation I used in earlier chapters. Also, this notation is consistent with the one used in presentations of DA in the literature.

Table 20.2   Data in Table 20.1, Displayed for Multiple Regression Analysis

	X_1	X_2	Y
	8	3	1
	7	4	1
A_1	5	5	1
	3	4	1
	3	2	1
	4	2	0
	3	1	0
A_2	3	2	0
	2	2	0
	2	5	0
Σ:	40	30	5
M:	4	3	.5
ss:	38	18	2.5
s:	2.0548	1.4142	.5270

$$\Sigma x_1 y = 6 \qquad \Sigma x_2 y = 3 \qquad \Sigma x_1 x_2 = 6$$
$$r_{x_1 y} = .61559 \qquad r_{x_2 y} = .44721 \qquad r_{x_1 x_2} = .22942$$

NOTE: Y = coded vector for group membership; M = mean; ss = deviation sum of squares; s = standard deviation; $\Sigma x_1 y$ = sum of cross-product deviations between X_1 and Y, and the other terms are treated similarly; $r_{x_1 y}$ = correlation between X_1 and Y, and the other terms are treated similarly.

with 2 and 7 *df*, $p > .05$. Assuming that I selected $\alpha = .05$, I would conclude that the two groups do not differ significantly on the two dependent variables when they are analyzed simultaneously. Obviously, the failure to reject the null hypothesis is, in part, due to the small number of subjects I used. As the data are illustrative and as my sole purpose here is to show the identity of multiple regression analysis and discriminant analysis, when they are applied to data from two groups, I will not be concerned with the failure to reject the null hypothesis.

I turn now to the calculation of the standardized regression coefficients:

$$\beta_1 = \frac{r_{y1} - r_{y2}r_{12}}{1 - r_{12}^2} = \frac{.61559 - (.44721)(.22942)}{1 - (.22942)^2} = .54149$$

$$\beta_2 = \frac{r_{y2} - r_{y1}r_{12}}{1 - r_{12}^2} = \frac{.44721 - (.61559)(.22942)}{1 - (.22942)^2} = .32298$$

Using these results and the standard deviations reported at the bottom of Table 20.2, the unstandardized regression coefficients are

$$b_1 = \beta_1 \left(\frac{s_y}{s_1} \right) = .54149 \left(\frac{.5270}{2.0548} \right) = .13888$$

$$b_2 = \beta_2 \left(\frac{s_y}{s_2} \right) = .32298 \left(\frac{.5270}{1.4142} \right) = .12036$$

The intercept is equal to

$$a = \overline{Y} - b_1\overline{X}_1 - b_2\overline{X}_2$$
$$= .5 - (.13888)(4) - (.12036)(3) = -.41660$$

The regression equation is

$$Y' = -.41660 + .13888X_1 + .12036X_2$$

This equation can be used and interpreted in the usual manner. For example, one may use subjects' scores on the X's to predict Y's, which in the present case refers to group membership. Roughly speaking, if the predicted score is closer to 1, the subject may be classified as "belonging" to group A_1. If, on the other hand, the predicted score is closer to 0, the subject may be classified as "belonging" to group A_2. The b's may be tested for statistical significance in the usual manner. Also, one may use the β's in an attempt to assess the relative importance of the dependent variables. I will not discuss these issues here because I do this later, in the context of discriminant analysis (DA). Before presenting DA, though, I turn to a brief discussion of structure coefficients.

Structure Coefficients

Recall that in multiple regression analysis the independent variables, or predictors, are differentially weighted (the weights are the b's or the β's) so that the correlation between the composite scores thus obtained and the dependent variable, or the criterion, is maximized (see Chapter 5 for a detailed discussion). Using the regression equation and scores on the independent variables one can, of course, calculate each person's score on the composite. These are actually predicted scores, which I used frequently in earlier chapters. Having calculated composite scores for subjects, I can calculate correlations between each original independent variable and the vector of composite scores. Such correlations are called *structure coefficients, structure correlations,* or *loadings,* as they are interpreted as factor loadings in factor analysis. The square of a structure coefficient indicates the proportion of variance shared by the variable with which it is associated and the vector of composite scores.

My description of how structure coefficients may be calculated was meant to give you an idea what they are about. A much simpler way to calculate them is through the following formula:

$$s_i = \frac{r_{yi}}{R_{y.12\ldots k}} \tag{20.1}$$

where s_i = structure coefficient for independent variable X_i; r_{yi} = the correlation between the dependent variable, Y, and X_i; and $R_{y.12\ldots k}$ = the multiple correlation of Y with the k independent variables. In short, to obtain structure coefficients, divide the zero-order correlation of each independent variable with the dependent variable by the multiple correlation of the dependent variable with all the independent variables.

For the numerical example under consideration, I calculated earlier,

$$r_{y1} = .61559 \qquad r_{y2} = .44721 \qquad R^2_{y.12} = .47778$$

Therefore,

$$R_{y.12} = \sqrt{.47778} = .69122$$

and

$$s_1 = \frac{.61559}{.69122} = .89058$$

$$s_2 = \frac{.44721}{.69122} = .64699$$

I discuss the interpretation of structure coefficients later and in Chapter 21 in the context of discriminant analysis and canonical analysis. For now, I will only point out that structure coefficients are useful in discriminant analysis, for example, for describing or interpreting dimensions that have been found to discriminate among groups (see the following and Chapter 21). Because my purpose in the preceding section was to show that, with two groups, multiple regression analysis can be used to obtain the same results as those obtained when a discriminant analysis is applied, I also showed how structure coefficients may be obtained in the context of multiple regression analysis.

Some authors (e.g., Thompson & Borrello, 1985; Thorndike, 1978, pp. 151–156 and 170–172) recommend that structure coefficients be used also for interpretive purposes in general applications of multiple regression analysis. The reason I have not done so in this book is that I think such coefficients do not enhance the interpretation of results of multiple regression analysis. This becomes evident when the manner in which structure coefficients is calculated in regression analysis is considered. As (20.1) shows, such coefficients are simply zero-order correlations of independent variables with the dependent variable divided by a constant, namely, the multiple correlation coefficient. Hence, the zero-order correlations provide the same information.

Moreover, because one may obtain large structure coefficients even when the results are meaningless, their use in such instances may lead to misinterpretations. This is best shown by a numerical example. Assume that the following were obtained in a study:

$$r_{y1} = .02 \qquad r_{y2} = .01 \qquad r_{12} = .60$$

where Y is the dependent variable, and 1 and 2 are the independent variables. Using these data, calculate $R^2_{y.12} = .00041$. Clearly, the correlations between the independent variables and the dependent variable are not meaningful; nor is the squared multiple correlation. But calculate now the structure coefficients:

$$R_{y.12} = \sqrt{.00041} = .02025$$

Applying (20.1),

$$s_1 = \frac{.02}{.02025} = .988$$

$$s_2 = \frac{.01}{.02025} = .494$$

These are impressive coefficients, particularly the first one. True, they are the correlations between the independent variables and the vector of the composite scores obtained by the application of the regression equation. But what is not apparent from an examination of these coefficients is that they were obtained from meaningless results.

The foregoing should not be taken to mean that potential problems with the use of structure coefficients are limited to multiple regression analysis. Similar problems occur in discriminant analysis and canonical analysis. But, as I discuss in the next section and in Chapter 21, structure coefficients are calculated only for what are considered meaningful discriminant functions or canonical variates. One could therefore argue that the same be done in multiple regression analysis—that is, that structure coefficients be calculated only after the squared multiple correlation has been deemed meaningful. There is, of course, nothing wrong with such an approach, except that, as I pointed out earlier, essentially the same information is available from the zero-order correlations of the independent variables with the dependent variable. I turn now to a presentation of discriminant analysis.

DISCRIMINANT ANALYSIS (DA)

DA was developed by Fisher (1936) for classifying objects into one of two clearly defined groups. Shortly thereafter, DA was generalized to classification into any number of groups and was labeled multiple discriminant analysis (MDA). For some time, DA was used exclusively for taxonomic problems in various disciplines (e.g., botany, biology, geology, clinical psychology, vocational guidance). In recent years, DA has come into use as a method of studying group differences on several variables simultaneously. Because of some common features of DA and multivariate analysis of variance (MANOVA) some researchers treat the two as interchangeable methods for studying group differences on multiple variables. More often, however, it is suggested that DA be used pursuant to MANOVA to identify the dimensions along which the groups differ.[3]

The two purposes for which DA is used have been labeled *predictive discriminant analysis* (PDA) and *descriptive discriminant analysis* (DDA), respectively (see Green, 1979, for a good discussion of the two kinds of functions and suggested nomenclature). My presentation in this and the next chapter is limited to DDA. You will find good introductions to DA in Klecka (1980) and Tatsuoka (1970, 1976). More advanced discussions are given in the books on multivariate analysis I cited earlier.

Sophisticated classification methods, of which DA is but one, are available, and are presented, among others, by Bailey (1994); Hudson et al. (1982); Rulon, Tiedeman, Tatsuoka, and Langmuir (1967); Tatsuoka (1974, 1975); and Van Ryzin (1977). Additional discussions will be found in books on multivariate analysis cited earlier (see, in particular, Overall & Klett, 1972). For an excellent thorough treatment of PDA and DDA, including detailed discussions and illustrations of computer programs, see Huberty (1994).

Before I give a formal presentation of DA, I will discuss the idea of sums of squares and cross products (SSCP) matrices.

SSCP

Recall that in univariate analysis of variance, the total sum of squares of the dependent variable is partitioned into two components: (1) pooled within-groups sum of squares and (2) between-groups sum of squares.[4] For multiple dependent variables, within and between sums of squares can, of course, be calculated for each. In addition, the total sum of cross products between any two variables can be partitioned into (1) pooled within-groups sum of products and (2) between-groups sum of products. For multiple dependent variables it is convenient to assemble the sums of squares and cross products in the following three matrices: $\mathbf{W}$ = pooled within-groups

---

[3]I discuss this topic in Chapter 21.

[4]See Chapter 11, where I also showed that when coded vectors are used to represent group membership, the residual sum of squares is equal to the within-groups sum of squares, and the regression sum of squares is equal to the between-groups sum of squares.

SSCP; **B** = between-groups SSCP; **T** = total SSCP. To clarify these notions, I will use two dependent variables. Accordingly, the elements of the above matrices are

$$\mathbf{W} = \begin{bmatrix} ss_{w_1} & scp_w \\ scp_w & ss_{w_2} \end{bmatrix}$$

where ss_{w_1} = pooled sum of squares within groups for variable 1; ss_{w_2} = pooled sum of squares within groups for variable 2; and scp_w = pooled within-groups sum of products of variables 1 and 2.

$$\mathbf{B} = \begin{bmatrix} ss_{b_1} & scp_b \\ scp_b & ss_{b_2} \end{bmatrix}$$

where ss_{b_1} and ss_{b_2} are the between-groups sums of squares for variables 1 and 2, respectively; and scp_b is the between-groups sum of cross products of variables 1 and 2.

$$\mathbf{T} = \begin{bmatrix} ss_1 & scp_t \\ scp_t & ss_2 \end{bmatrix}$$

where ss_1 and ss_2 are the total sums of squares for variables 1 and 2, respectively; and scp_t is the total sum of cross products of variables 1 and 2. Note that elements of **T** are calculated as if all the subjects belonged to a single group.

A Numerical Example

I will calculate SSCP matrices for the illustrative data in Table 20.1. Later, I will use these matrices in DA. For convenience, I repeat the data used in Table 20.1 in Table 20.3, along with some intermediate results, which I will use to calculate the elements of the SSCP matrices.

Table 20.3   Illustrative Data on Two Dependent Variables for Two Groups

	A_1		A_2			
	X_1	X_2	X_1	X_2		
	8	3	4	2		
	7	4	3	1		
	5	5	3	2		
	3	4	2	2		
	3	2	2	5		
ΣX:	26	18	14	12	$\Sigma X_{t_1} = 40$	$\Sigma X_{t_2} = 30$
ΣX^2:	156	70	42	38	$\Sigma X_{t_1}^2 = 198$	$\Sigma X_{t_2}^2 = 108$
$\overline{X}$:	5.2	3.6	2.8	2.4		
CP:		95		31	$CP_t = 126$	

NOTE: The data are repeated from Table 20.1. The sums of squares (ΣX^2) and the sums of cross products (CP) are in raw scores.

Using relevant values from the bottom of Table 20.3, I calculate the elements of the pooled within-groups SSCP matrix (**W**):

$$ss_{w_1} = \left[156 - \frac{(26)^2}{5}\right] + \left[42 - \frac{(14)^2}{5}\right] = 23.6$$

$$ss_{w_2} = \left[70 - \frac{(18)^2}{5}\right] + \left[38 - \frac{(12)^2}{5}\right] = 14.4$$

$$scp_w = \left[95 - \frac{(26)(18)}{5}\right] + \left[31 - \frac{(14)(12)}{5}\right] = -1.2$$

$$\mathbf{W} = \begin{bmatrix} 23.6 & -1.2 \\ -1.2 & 14.4 \end{bmatrix}$$

Calculating the elements of the between-groups SSCP matrix (**B**):

$$ss_{b_1} = \left[\frac{(26)^2}{5} + \frac{(14)^2}{5}\right] - \frac{(40)^2}{10} = 14.4$$

$$ss_{b_2} = \left[\frac{(18)^2}{5} + \frac{(12)^2}{5}\right] - \frac{(30)^2}{10} = 3.6$$

$$scp_b = \left[\frac{(26)(18)}{5} + \frac{(14)(12)}{5}\right] - \frac{(40)(30)}{10} = 7.2$$

$$\mathbf{B} = \begin{bmatrix} 14.4 & 7.2 \\ 7.2 & 3.6 \end{bmatrix}$$

Because $\mathbf{T} = \mathbf{W} + \mathbf{B}$, the elements of the total SSCP matrix (**T**) are

$$\mathbf{T} = \underset{\mathbf{W}}{\begin{bmatrix} 23.6 & -1.2 \\ -1.2 & 14.4 \end{bmatrix}} + \underset{\mathbf{B}}{\begin{bmatrix} 14.4 & 7.2 \\ 7.2 & 3.6 \end{bmatrix}} = \begin{bmatrix} 38.0 & 6.0 \\ 6.0 & 18.0 \end{bmatrix}$$

For completeness of presentation, however, I calculate the elements of **T** directly.

$$ss_{t_1} = 198 - \frac{(40)^2}{10} = 38.0$$

$$ss_{t_2} = 108 - \frac{(30)^2}{10} = 18.0$$

$$scp_t = (95 + 31) - \frac{(40)(30)}{10} = 6.0$$

In conclusion, I would like to point out that normally **W**, **B**, and **T** are obtained through matrix operations on raw score matrices. This is how computer programs are written. In the present case, I felt that it would be simpler to avoid the matrix operations. Also, as I showed earlier, only two of the three matrices have to be calculated. The third may be obtained by addition or subtraction, whatever the case may be. In the preceding I obtained **T** by adding **W** and **B**. If, instead, I calculated **T** and **W**, then **B** = **T** − **W**. I now resume my discussion of DA.

Elements of DA

Although the presentation of DA for two groups may be simplified (see, for example, Green, 1978, Chapter 4; Lindeman, Merenda, & Gold, 1980, Chapter 6), I believe it will be more instructive to present the general case—that is, for any number of groups. Although in the presentation that follows I apply the equations to DA with two groups, *the same equations are applicable to DA with any number of groups* (see Chapter 21). Calculating DA, particularly the eigenvalues (see the following), can become very complicated. Consequently, DA is generally calculated through a computer program (I discuss computer programs later in the chapter). Because the present example is small, doing all the calculations by hand is easy, and doing so affords a better grasp of the elements of DA.

The idea of DA is to find a set of weights, **v**, by which to weight each individual's scores so that the ratio of **B** (between-groups SSCP) to **W** (pooled within-groups SSCP) is maximized. As a result, discrimination among the groups is maximized. This may be expressed as follows:

$$\lambda = \frac{\mathbf{v'Bv}}{\mathbf{v'Wv}} \tag{20.2}$$

where **v'** and **v** are a row and column vectors of weights, respectively; and λ (lambda) is referred to as the discriminant criterion.

A solution of λ is obtained by solving the following determinantal equation:

$$|\mathbf{W^{-1}B} - \lambda\mathbf{I}| = 0 \tag{20.3}$$

where $\mathbf{W^{-1}}$ is the inverse of **W**, and **I** is an identity matrix. λ is referred to as the largest eigenvalue, or characteristic root, of the matrix, whose determinant is set equal to zero—that is, Equation (20.3). With two groups, only one eigenvalue may be obtained.[5] Before I show how (20.3) is solved, I spell it out, using the matrices I calculated in the preceding section.

$$\left| \begin{bmatrix} 23.6 & -1.2 \\ -1.2 & 14.4 \end{bmatrix}^{-1} \begin{bmatrix} 14.4 & 7.2 \\ 7.2 & 3.6 \end{bmatrix} - \lambda \begin{bmatrix} 1 & 0 \\ 0 & 1 \end{bmatrix} \right| = 0$$

$$\qquad\quad \mathbf{W} \qquad\qquad\quad \mathbf{B} \qquad\qquad \mathbf{I}$$

First, I will calculate the inverse of **W**. In Chapter 6 and in Appendix A, I explain how to invert a 2 × 2 matrix. Here, I invert **W** without comment. The determinant of **W** is

$$\begin{vmatrix} 23.6 & -1.2 \\ -1.2 & 14.4 \end{vmatrix} = (23.6)(14.4) - (-1.2)(-1.2) = 338.4$$

$$\mathbf{W^{-1}} = \begin{bmatrix} 23.6 & -1.2 \\ -1.2 & 14.4 \end{bmatrix}^{-1} = \begin{bmatrix} \dfrac{14.4}{338.4} & \dfrac{1.2}{338.4} \\[2mm] \dfrac{1.2}{338.4} & \dfrac{23.6}{338.4} \end{bmatrix} = \begin{bmatrix} .04255 & .00355 \\ .00355 & .06974 \end{bmatrix}$$

[5]For solutions with more than two groups, see Chapter 21.

Multiplying $\mathbf{W}^{-1}$ by $\mathbf{B}$,

$$\underbrace{\begin{bmatrix} .04255 & .00355 \\ .00355 & .06974 \end{bmatrix}}_{\mathbf{W}^{-1}} \underbrace{\begin{bmatrix} 14.4 & 7.2 \\ 7.2 & 3.6 \end{bmatrix}}_{\mathbf{B}} = \begin{bmatrix} .63828 & .31914 \\ .55325 & .27662 \end{bmatrix}$$

It is now necessary to solve the following:

$$\begin{vmatrix} .63828 - \lambda & .31914 \\ .55325 & .27662 - \lambda \end{vmatrix} = 0$$

To this end, a value of λ is sought so that the determinant of the matrix will be equal to zero. Therefore,

$$(.63828 - \lambda)(.27662 - \lambda) - (.31914)(.55325) = 0$$

$$.17656 - .63828\lambda - .27662\lambda + \lambda^2 - .17656 = 0$$

$$\lambda^2 - .91490\lambda = 0$$

Solving the quadratic equation,

$$\lambda = \frac{-b \pm \sqrt{b^2 - 4ac}}{2a}$$

where for the present example,

$$a = 1 \qquad b = -.91490 \qquad c = 0$$

$$\lambda = \frac{.91490 \pm \sqrt{(-.91490)^2 - (4)(1)(0)}}{2} = .91490$$

Having calculated λ, the weights, $\mathbf{v}$, are calculated by solving the following:

$$(\mathbf{W}^{-1}\mathbf{B} - \lambda\mathbf{I})\mathbf{v} = 0 \tag{20.4}$$

The terms in the parentheses are those used in the determinantal equation (20.3). $\mathbf{v}$ is referred to as the eigenvector, or the characteristic vector. Using the value of λ and the values of the product $\mathbf{W}^{-1}\mathbf{B}$ I obtained earlier, (20.4) for the present example is

$$\begin{bmatrix} .63828 - .91490 & .31914 \\ .55325 & .27662 - .91490 \end{bmatrix} \begin{bmatrix} v_1 \\ v_2 \end{bmatrix} = \begin{bmatrix} 0 \\ 0 \end{bmatrix}$$

$$\begin{bmatrix} -.27662 & .31914 \\ .55325 & -.63828 \end{bmatrix} \begin{bmatrix} v_1 \\ v_2 \end{bmatrix} = \begin{bmatrix} 0 \\ 0 \end{bmatrix}$$

This set of homogeneous equations is easily solved by forming the adjoint of the preceding matrix, which is[6]

$$\begin{bmatrix} -.63828 & -.31914 \\ -.55325 & -.27662 \end{bmatrix}$$

---

[6]For a discussion of the adjoint of a 2×2 matrix, see Appendix A.

Note that the ratio of the first element to the second element in the first column is equal to the ratio of the first element to the second element in the second column. That is,

$$\frac{-.63828}{-.55325} = \frac{-.31914}{-.27662} = 1.15$$

As the solution of homogeneous equations yields coefficients that have a constant proportionality, one may choose the first or the second column as the values of the eigenvector. For that matter, multiplying the adjoint by any constant results in an equally proportional set of weights. How, then, does one decide which weights to use? Before I address this issue, I will show the equivalence of the results I obtained here and those I obtained earlier in the regression analysis of the same data.

When I analyzed the same data through multiple regression analysis, with a dummy vector representing group membership as the dependent variable, I obtained the following regression coefficients:

$$b_1 = .13888 \qquad b_2 = .12036$$

The ratio of b_1 to b_2 is

$$\frac{.13888}{.12036} = 1.15$$

which is the same as that I obtained earlier.

Of the various approaches used to resolve the indeterminancy of the weights obtained in DA, I will present two: (1) raw, or unstandardized, coefficients and (2) standardized coefficients.

Raw Coefficients

The pooled within-groups variance of discriminant scores[7] can be expressed as follows:

$$\text{Var}(y) = \mathbf{v'Cv} \tag{20.5}$$

where $\mathbf{v'}$ and $\mathbf{v}$ are row and column eigenvectors, respectively; and $\mathbf{C}$ is the pooled within-groups covariance matrix defined as

$$\mathbf{C} = \frac{\mathbf{W}}{N - g} \tag{20.6}$$

where $\mathbf{W}$ = pooled within-groups SSCP; N = total number of subjects; and g = number of groups.

Now, raw coefficients are calculated by setting the constraint that the pooled within-groups variance of the discriminant scores be equal to 1.00. That is, $\mathbf{v'Cv} = 1.00$. This is accomplished by dividing each element of the eigenvector by $\sqrt{\mathbf{v'Cv}}$. That is,

$$v_i^* = \frac{v_i}{\sqrt{\mathbf{v'Cv}}} \tag{20.7}$$

where v_i^* = ith raw coefficient; v_i = ith element of the eigenvector; and $\mathbf{v'Cv}$ is as defined for (20.5).

---

[7]Discriminant scores are obtained by applying the discriminant function to subjects' scores. Later I calculate such scores for the subjects in the numerical example under consideration.

To clarify the foregoing formulations, I will apply them to the numerical example under consideration. I repeat **W**, which I calculated earlier.

$$\mathbf{W} = \begin{bmatrix} 23.6 & -1.2 \\ -1.2 & 14.4 \end{bmatrix}$$

Applying (20.6), with $N - g = 8$,

$$\mathbf{C} = \frac{1}{8} \begin{bmatrix} 23.6 & -1.2 \\ -1.2 & 14.4 \end{bmatrix} = \begin{bmatrix} 2.95 & -.15 \\ -.15 & 1.80 \end{bmatrix}$$

To find $\mathbf{v'Cv}$, either the first or the second column of the adjoint of the matrix obtained previously may be selected as **v**. Alternatively, one may use the b's obtained from the multiple regression analysis of the same data. For illustrative purposes, I will use the elements of the first column of the adjoint of the matrix: $-.63828$ and $-.55325$. As multiplication of these elements by a constant will not affect their proportionality, it will be convenient to multiply them by -1 so as to change their signs. Applying (20.5),

$$\mathbf{v'Cv} = [.63828 \quad .55325] \begin{bmatrix} 2.95 & -.15 \\ -.15 & 1.8 \end{bmatrix} \begin{bmatrix} .63828 \\ .55325 \end{bmatrix} = 1.64685$$

$$\qquad\qquad\quad \mathbf{v'} \qquad\qquad\quad \mathbf{C} \qquad\quad \mathbf{v}$$

I now use (20.7) to calculate the raw coefficients:

$$v_1^* = \frac{.63828}{\sqrt{1.64685}} = .49738$$

$$v_2^* = \frac{.55325}{\sqrt{1.64685}} = .43112$$

I show now that $\mathbf{v'*Cv*} = 1.00$

$$[.49738 \quad .43112] \begin{bmatrix} 2.95 & -.15 \\ -.15 & 1.80 \end{bmatrix} \begin{bmatrix} .49738 \\ .43112 \end{bmatrix} = 1.00$$

It will be instructive to show that you can obtain the same raw coefficients by using the b's from the multiple regression analysis of the same data. The two b's are .13888 and .12036 (see my calculations earlier in this chapter). Applying (20.5),

$$[.13888 \quad .12036] \begin{bmatrix} 2.95 & -.15 \\ -.15 & 1.80 \end{bmatrix} \begin{bmatrix} .13888 \\ .12036 \end{bmatrix} = .07796$$

$$\qquad\qquad \mathbf{b'} \qquad\qquad\quad \mathbf{C} \qquad\quad \mathbf{b}$$

Calculating the raw coefficients,

$$v_1^* = \frac{.13888}{\sqrt{.07796}} = .49740$$

$$v_2^* = \frac{.12036}{\sqrt{.07796}} = .43107$$

These values are, within rounding, the same as those I obtained previously.

Using the raw coefficients and the means of the dependent variables, a constant, c, is obtained as follows:

$$c = -(v_1^* \overline{X}_1 + v_2^* \overline{X}_2 + \ldots + v_k^* \overline{X}_k) \qquad (20.8)$$

For the numerical example under consideration, $\overline{X}_1 = 4$ and $\overline{X}_2 = 3$. Using the raw coefficients I obtained earlier,

$$c = -[(.49740)(4) + (.43107)(3)] = -3.28281$$

It is now possible to write the discriminant function:

$$Y = -3.28281 + .49740X_1 + .43107X_2$$

As I show later, this function is used to calculate discriminant scores based on raw scores. At this stage, I will only point out that the raw coefficients are difficult to interpret, particularly when one wishes to determine the relative importance of the dependent variables. This is because the magnitude of a raw coefficient depends, among other things, on the properties and units of the scale used to measure the variable with which it is associated. I drew attention to the same problem when I discussed unstandardized regression coefficients (see, in particular, Chapter 10). As in multiple regression analysis, researchers using DA often resort to standardized coefficients when they wish to study the relative importance of variables.

Standardized Coefficients

Standardized coefficients in DA are readily obtainable, as is indicated in the following:

$$\beta_i = v_i^* \sqrt{c_{ii}} \qquad (20.9)$$

where β_i = standardized coefficient[8] associated with variable i; v_i^* = raw coefficient for variable i; and c_{ii} = diagonal element of the pooled within-groups covariance matrix (**C**) associated with variable i. Note that c_{ii} is the pooled within-groups variance of variable i. In short, to convert a raw coefficient to a standardized one, all that is necessary is to multiply the former by the pooled within-groups standard deviation of the variable with which it is associated.[9]

I will now calculate standardized coefficients for the numerical example under consideration. For this example, I found $v_1^* = .49740$ and $v_2^* = .43107$. Also,

$$\mathbf{C} = \begin{bmatrix} 2.95 & -.15 \\ -.15 & 1.80 \end{bmatrix}$$

Applying (20.9),

$$\beta_1 = (.49740)\sqrt{2.95} = .85431$$

$$\beta_2 = (.43107)\sqrt{1.80} = .57834$$

---

[8]There is no consensus regarding the symbols used for raw and standardized coefficients. Because the standardized coefficients are interpreted in a manner analogous to β's in multiple regression analysis, I use the same symbol here.

[9]Commenting on a paper dealing with standardized discriminant coefficients by Mueller and Cozad (1988), Nordlund and Nagel (1991) argued that it is more "consistent and parsimonious" (p. 101) to calculate standardized coefficients by using the total covariance matrix. For a response, see Mueller and Cozad (1993). Without going far afield, I will note that a case may be made for either approach and that a similar question arises when calculating structure coefficients. My comments on the latter (see the following) apply broadly also to standardized coefficients.

These coefficients, which are applied to subjects' standard scores (z's), are interpreted in a manner analogous to β's in multiple regression analysis. Accordingly, one may use their relative magnitudes as indices of the relative contribution, or importance, of the dependent variables to the discrimination between the groups. Based on this criterion, one would conclude that in the numerical example I analyzed previously, variable 1 makes a greater contribution to the discrimination between the groups than does variable 2.

It is important, however, to note that standardized coefficients in DA suffer from the same shortcomings as their counterparts in multiple regression analysis (see Chapter 10 for a detailed discussion of this point). Briefly, the standardized coefficients lack stability because they are affected by the variability of the variables with which they are associated, as can be clearly seen from (20.9) and by the intercorrelations among the variables. Because of the shortcomings of standardized coefficients, an alternative approach to the interpretation of the discriminant function, that of structure coefficients, has been recommended. It is to this topic that I turn now.

Structure Coefficients

Earlier in this chapter, I introduced the idea of a structure coefficient in the context of multiple regression analysis, where I pointed out that it is a correlation between an independent variable and the predicted scores. As I will show, the discriminant function may be used to predict a discriminant score for each subject. Having done this, one may correlate such scores with each of the original variables. Such correlations, too, are referred to as *structure coefficients*[10] or loadings because, as I noted earlier, they are interpreted as factor loadings in factor analysis. The square of a structure coefficient indicates the proportion of variance of the variable with which it is associated that is accounted for by the given discriminant function. (As I discuss later, with more than two groups, one may obtain more than one discriminant function and may calculate structure coefficients for each.)

Structure coefficients are primarily useful for determining the nature of the function(s) or the dimension(s) on which the groups are discriminated. Some authors also use the relative magnitudes of structure coefficients as an indication of the relative importance of variables on a given function or dimension. I will address these issues after showing how structure coefficients are calculated in DA.

As in multiple regression analysis, structure coefficients in DA may be obtained without having to calculate the correlation between the original variables and discriminant scores. One can accomplish this as follows:

$$\mathbf{s} = \mathbf{R}_t \boldsymbol{\beta}_t \tag{20.10}$$

where $\mathbf{s}$ = vector of structure coefficients for a given discriminant function; $\mathbf{R}_t$ = total correlation matrix (i.e., the correlations are calculated by treating all the subjects as if they belonged to a single group), hence the subscript t to distinguish it from the pooled within-groups correlation matrix (see the following); and $\boldsymbol{\beta}_t$ = vector of standardized coefficients, based on the total number of subjects (see the following). From the preceding, it should be clear that structure coefficients may also be calculated by using the pooled within-groups statistics. Actually, as I discuss later, some authors advocate that this be done, instead of using the total statistics. For now, I will

---

[10]For obvious reasons, some authors (e.g., Huberty, 1994) use the term "*structure r's*" (p. 209).

only point out that in what follows I present calculations based on total statistics, or "total struc-ture coefficients" (Klecka, 1980, p. 32).

In the preceding section I showed how to calculate raw coefficients, v^*, subject to the con-straint that the pooled within-groups variance of the discriminant scores be equal to 1.00. I then showed how to use v^* to calculate standardized discriminant function coefficients (see the sec-tions entitled "Raw Coefficients" and "Standardized Coefficients"). The same procedure is fol-lowed in calculating β_t, except that the total covariance matrix, C_t, is used, instead of the pooled within-groups covariance matrix, C_w, which I used in the aforementioned sections.

For the numerical example under consideration, I calculated earlier the total SSCP matrix:

$$\mathbf{T} = \begin{bmatrix} 38.0 & 6.0 \\ \\ 6.0 & 18.0 \end{bmatrix}$$

The total number of subjects is 10. Therefore, to obtain the total covariance matrix, I multiply $\mathbf{T}$ by the reciprocal of 9 (i.e., $N-1$).

$$\mathbf{C}_t = \frac{1}{9} \begin{bmatrix} 38.0 & 6.0 \\ \\ 6.0 & 18.0 \end{bmatrix} = \begin{bmatrix} 4.22222 & .66667 \\ \\ .66667 & 2.00000 \end{bmatrix}$$

Analogous to (20.5), I use the coefficients, $\mathbf{v}$, which I obtained earlier from the adjoint of the determinantal matrix, to calculate $\mathbf{v}^*$ so that the variance of the scores for the total sample is equal to 1.00. For the present example,

$$\mathbf{v'C}_t\mathbf{v} = [.63828 \quad .55325] \begin{bmatrix} 4.22222 & .66667 \\ \\ .66667 & 2.00000 \end{bmatrix} \begin{bmatrix} .63828 \\ \\ .55325 \end{bmatrix} = 2.80315$$

$$\qquad\qquad \mathbf{v'} \qquad\qquad\qquad \mathbf{C} \qquad\qquad\quad \mathbf{v}$$

Applying now (20.7),

$$v_1^* = \frac{.63828}{\sqrt{2.80315}} = .38123$$

$$v_2^* = \frac{.55325}{\sqrt{2.80315}} = .33044$$

Note that the ratio of these coefficients is the same as that of the raw coefficients I obtained earlier when I used the pooled within-groups covariance matrix (i.e., .38123/.33044 = 1.15).

Now, using v^*, β_t is calculated through (20.9), except that instead of multiplying each v_i^* by the square root of relevant elements from the pooled within-groups covariance matrix, as I did in earlier applications, relevant elements from the total covariance matrix are used. For the present example,

$$\beta_1 = .38123\sqrt{4.22222} = .78335$$

$$\beta_2 = .33044\sqrt{2.00000} = .46731$$

The ratio of the β's based on the total covariance matrix is *not* equal to the ratio of the β's I calculated earlier, when I used elements from the pooled within-groups covariance matrix. Specifically, the ratio of β_1 to β_2 I calculated here is 1.68 (.78335/.46731), whereas the ratio of the corresponding β's I calculated earlier was 1.48 (.85431/.57834). Note, however, that the ratio of the β's I calculated here is equal to the ratio of the β's I obtained in the beginning of this chapter, when I analyzed the same numerical example through multiple regression with a coded vector as the dependent variable (i.e., $.54149/.32298 = 1.68$).

To calculate the structure coefficients, **s**, it is necessary to obtain also $\mathbf{R}_t$, the total correlation matrix. In the present case, this entails calculation of the correlation between X_1 and X_2. Actually, I reported this correlation in Table 20.2 (i.e., $r_{x_1 x_2} = .22942$). For completeness of presentation, however, I will show how to do this by using $\mathbf{C}_t$, the total covariance matrix. In this matrix, 4.22222 is the variance of X_1 and 2.00000 is the variance of X_2. Therefore, $\sqrt{4.22222}$ and $\sqrt{2.00000}$ are the standard deviations of X_1 and X_2, respectively (see the preceding). In $\mathbf{C}_t$ the covariance between X_1 and X_2 is .66667. Dividing a covariance by the product of the standard deviations of the variables in question yields the correlation coefficient between them—see (2.40). Therefore,

$$
\mathbf{R}_t = \begin{bmatrix} \dfrac{4.22222}{\sqrt{(4.22222)(4.22222)}} & \dfrac{.66667}{\sqrt{(4.22222)(2.00000)}} \\[3mm] \dfrac{.66667}{\sqrt{(4.22222)(2.00000)}} & \dfrac{2.00000}{\sqrt{(2.00000)(2.00000)}} \end{bmatrix} = \begin{bmatrix} 1.00000 & .22942 \\ .22942 & 1.00000 \end{bmatrix}
$$

Of course, calculation of the diagonal elements of $\mathbf{R}_t$ was not necessary, as they are 1's. Again, for completeness of presentation, I carried out all the calculations. Also, using matrix notation, it is possible to present the calculation of $\mathbf{R}_t$ more succinctly. I used the preceding format, as I felt that following it would be easier.

I am ready now to calculate structure coefficients, **s**. Using $\boldsymbol{\beta}_t$ and $\mathbf{R}_t$, which I calculated earlier, I apply (20.10):

$$
\mathbf{s} = \underbrace{\begin{bmatrix} 1.00000 & .22942 \\ .22942 & 1.00000 \end{bmatrix}}_{\mathbf{R}_t} \underbrace{\begin{bmatrix} .78335 \\ .46731 \end{bmatrix}}_{\boldsymbol{\beta}_t} = \begin{bmatrix} .89056 \\ .64703 \end{bmatrix}
$$

I said earlier that structure coefficients are correlations of original variables with discriminant function scores. In the following, I calculate discriminant scores (see Table 20.4). If you were to calculate the correlation between X_1 and the discriminant scores in Table 20.4 *across* the groups, you would find that it is .89056. Similarly, the correlation between X_2 and the discriminant scores is .64703. Earlier, I obtained the same coefficient (within rounding) when I analyzed the data through multiple regression.

As a rule of thumb, structure coefficients $\geq .30$ are treated as meaningful.[11] Based on this criterion, one would conclude that both variables have meaningful structure coefficients. With two variables only, it is difficult to convey the flavor of the interpretation of structure coefficients. Generally, one would use a larger number of variables in DA. Under such circumstances, one would use the meaningful structure coefficients, particularly the high ones, in attempts to interpret the discriminant function. Assume, for example, that eight variables are used in a DA and that only three have meaningful loadings. One would then examine these variables and attempt to name the function as is done in factor analysis. If it turns out that the three variables with the

---

[11]Drawing attention to problems attendant with the rules of thumb, Dalgleish (1994) suggested approaches to tests of the significance of structure coefficients.

meaningful structure coefficients refer to, say, different aspects of socioeconomic status, one would conclude that the function that discriminates between the groups primarily reflects their differences in socioeconomic status. Of course, the interpretation is not always as obvious. As in factor analysis, one might encounter structures that are difficult to interpret or that elude interpretation altogether. The naming of a function is a creative act—an attempt to capture the flavor of the dimension that underlies a set of variables even when they appear to be diverse.

The square of the first structure coefficient, $.890569^2 = .79310$, indicates that about 79% of the variance of X_1 is accounted for by the discriminant function. The square of the second structure coefficient, $.64703^2 = .41865$, indicates that about 42% of the variance of X_2 is accounted for by the discriminant function. Based on the preceding, one would conclude that X_1 is more important than X_2. Although in the present example one would reach the same conclusion based on the β's, which I calculated earlier ($\beta_1 = .85431$; $\beta_2 = .57834$), this will not always be so. It is possible for the two criteria to lead to radically different conclusions. Which of the two indices (i.e., β's or structure coefficients) is preferable? This depends on the purpose of the interpretation, as each addresses a different question. Reminding the reader that the β's are *partial* coefficients, Tatsuoka (1973) stated, "This is fine when the purpose is to gauge the contribution of each variable in the company of all others, but it is inappropriate when we wish to give substantive interpretations to the . . . discriminant functions" (p. 280). It is for the latter purpose that structure coefficients are useful. In short, "Both approaches are useful, provided we keep their different objectives clearly in mind" (Tatsuoka, 1973, p. 280).

Lest you think that there is unanimity on this topic, I will point out that Harris (1985), for example, rejected the use of structure coefficients:

> Thus, we might as well omit Manova altogether if we're going to interpret loadings rather than discriminant function coefficients. We have repeatedly seen the very misleading results of interpreting loadings rather than score coefficients in analyses in which we can directly observe our variables; it therefore seems unlikely that loadings will suddenly become more informative than weights when we go to latent variables (factors) that are not directly observable. (p. 319; see also, Harris, 1993, pp. 288–289)

Neither standardized coefficients nor structure coefficients are unambiguous indices of relative importance of the variables with which they are associated. "As in multiple regression analysis, the notion of variable contribution in discriminant analysis is an evasive one" (Huberty, 1975a, p. 63).

Total versus Within-Groups Structure Coefficients.

Some authors (e.g., Cooley & Lohnes, 1971, p. 248; Green, 1978, p. 309; Thorndike, 1978, p. 219) advocated, or used without elaboration, total structure coefficients, whereas others (e.g., Bernstein, 1988, p. 259; Huberty, 1994, p. 209; Marascuilo & Levin, 1983, p. 318) advocated, or used without elaboration, within-groups structure coefficients. While noting that some authors use total structure coefficients, Huberty (1994) maintained, "it seems most reasonable to focus on within-group" (p. 209) structure coefficients. These differences in orientation relate, of course, to the fact that three types of statistics (within, between, and total) can be calculated in designs consisting of multiple groups (see detailed discussions in Chapter 16).

Addressing this topic, Klecka (1980) asserted that total structure coefficients "are useful for identifying the kind of information carried by the functions which is useful for discriminating *between* groups" (p. 32). He went on to say, "Sometimes, however, we are interested in knowing how the functions are related to the variables *within* the groups. This information can be obtained from the pooled within-groups correlations—called 'within-group structures coefficients'"

(p. 32). I agree. It is noteworthy that, consistent with Klecka's interpretation, total structure coefficients are obtained when in (1) multiple regression analysis a coded vector is used to represent two groups (see earlier in this chapter) or (2) canonical correlation analysis multiple coded vectors are used to represent more than two groups (see Chapter 21).

On a practical level, though, the choice between the two types of coefficients will, generally, make little difference. Referring to his numerical example, Klecka (1980) pointed out that the within-groups structure coefficients "are smaller than the total structure coefficients but the ranking from the largest absolute magnitude to the smallest are similar (although not identical). This is a typical result but not a necessary condition" (p. 32).[12] Huberty (1975b) perhaps summed it up best, saying, "In terms of labeling the functions, the resulting interpretations based on . . . [total or within coefficients] will be about the same. Such interpretations are, at best, *a very crude approximation* [italics added] to any identifiable psychological dimensions" (p. 552).

Discriminant Scores and Centroids

The discriminant function can be used to calculate discriminant scores for each subject in the groups under study. Earlier, I said that I do not address the use of DA for classification (i.e., PDA). Therefore, I will only point out in passing that discriminant scores may be calculated for subjects who were not members of the groups under study. Such scores may be used to decide which of the existing groups each subject most resembles.[13]

Earlier, I calculated the discriminant function for the numerical example under consideration:

$$Y = -3.28281 + .49740X_1 + .43107X_2$$

I now use this function to calculate discriminant scores for the subjects in the numerical example I analyzed previously.

The scores for the first subject in group A_1 are $X_1 = 8$ and $X_2 = 3$ (see Table 20.3). Accordingly, this subject's discriminant score is

$$Y = -3.28281 + (.49740)(8) + (.43107)(3) = 1.9896$$

I calculated similarly discriminant scores for all subjects and reported them in Table 20.4. Earlier, I suggested that you calculate the correlations of these scores with X_1 and X_2 of Table 20.3 to verify that they are equal to total structure coefficients, which I calculated by applying (20.10).

At the bottom of Table 20.4 are mean discriminant scores—referred to as centroids—for groups A_1 (.8555) and A_2 (−.8555). As the mean of these centroids is zero, you can readily see that subjects whose discriminant scores are positive "belong" to group A_1, whereas those whose discriminant scores are negative "belong" to group A_2. Based on this criterion, you can see that the last two subjects in group A_1 resemble more those of group A_2 (they have negative scores, as do all the subjects in group A_2). This kind of misclassification may indicate the separation of the groups. The stronger the separation, the smaller the number of such misclassifications.

Frequently, one is not interested in individual discriminant scores. Under such circumstances, one may calculate group centroids by inserting group means on the dependent variables in the discriminant function. In the present example, the means of the groups are (see Table 20.3)

$$A_1: \overline{X}_1 = 5.2 \qquad \overline{X}_2 = 3.6$$
$$A_2: \overline{X}_1 = 2.8 \qquad \overline{X}_2 = 2.4$$

---

[12]In Chapter 21, I give a numerical example in which the within and the total structure coefficients are quite disparate.
[13]Earlier, I gave references to PDA.

Table 20.4 **Discriminant Scores for the Data in Table 20.3**

	A_1	A_2
	1.9896	−.4311
	1.9233	−1.3595
	1.3595	−.9285
	−.0663	−1.4259
	−.9285	−.1327
Σ:	4.2776	−4.2777
$\overline{Y}$:	.8555	−.8555
ΣY^2:	10.3723	4.9470

Calculating centroids,

$$\overline{Y}_{A_1} = -3.28281 + (.49740)(5.2) + (.43107)(3.6) = .8555$$

$$\overline{Y}_{A_2} = -3.28281 + (.49740)(2.8) + (.43107)(2.4) = -.8555$$

Compare these results with the values reported in Table 20.4.

One other aspect of the results reported in Table 20.4 is worth noting. At the bottom of the table are the sums and the sums of squares of the discriminant scores. Using these values, I calculate the pooled within-groups deviation sum of squares:

$$\left[10.3723 - \frac{(4.2776)^2}{5} \right] + \left[4.9470 - \frac{(-4.2777)^2}{5} \right] = 8.00$$

Dividing this pooled sum of squares by its degrees of freedom (i.e., $N - g = 10 - 2 = 8$) yields a pooled within-groups variance equal to 1.00. This confirms what I said earlier, namely that the raw coefficients are calculated subject to the restriction that the pooled within-groups variance of the discriminant scores be equal to 1.00—see (20.5)–(20.7) and the discussion related to them.

Measures of Association

As in univariate analysis, it is desirable to have a measure of association between the independent and the dependent variables in multivariate analysis. Of several such measures proposed (see, for example, Haase, 1991; Huberty, 1972, 1994, pp. 194–196; Shaffer & Gillo, 1974; Smith, I. L., 1972; Stevens, 1972; Tatsuoka, 1988, p. 97), I present only one related to Wilks' Λ (lambda), which is defined as

$$\Lambda = \frac{|\mathbf{W}|}{|\mathbf{T}|} \tag{20.11}$$

where $\mathbf{W}$ = pooled within-groups SSCP and $\mathbf{T}$ = total SSCP. Note that Λ is a ratio of the determinants of these two matrices.[14]

Before I describe the measure of association that is related to Λ, it will be instructive to show how Λ can be expressed for the case of univariate analysis. Recall that in univariate analysis of

---

[14]Λ plays an important role in multivariate analysis, and is therefore discussed in detail in books on this topic. For a particularly good introduction, see Rulon and Brooks (1968).

variance the total sum of squares (ss_t) is partitioned into between-groups sum of squares (ss_b) and within-groups sum of squares (ss_w). Accordingly, in univariate analysis,

$$\Lambda = \frac{ss_w}{ss_t} \tag{20.12}$$

Because $ss_t = ss_b + ss_w$, Λ can also be written

$$\Lambda = \frac{ss_t - ss_b}{ss_t} = 1 - \frac{ss_b}{ss_t} \tag{20.13}$$

and, from the preceding,

$$\frac{ss_b}{ss_t} = 1 - \Lambda \tag{20.14}$$

As is well known—see (11.5)—the ratio of ss_b to ss_t is defined as η^2: proportion of variance of the dependent variable accounted for by the independent variable, or group membership. Clearly, (1) Λ indicates the proportion of variance of the dependent variable *not* accounted for by the independent variable, or the proportion of error variance and (2) Λ may vary from zero to one. When $\Lambda = 0$ it means that $ss_b = ss_t$ and that the proportion of error variance is equal to zero. When, on the other hand, $\Lambda = 1$, it means that $ss_b = 0$ ($ss_w = ss_t$) and that the proportion of error variance is equal to one. In other words, the independent variable does not account for any proportion of the variance of the dependent variable.

In Chapter 11, I showed that when the dependent variable is regressed on coded vectors that represent a categorical independent variable, the following equivalences hold:

$$ss_w = ss_{res} \qquad ss_b = ss_{reg} \qquad \eta^2 = R^2$$

where ss_{res} = residual sum of squares; ss_{reg} = regression sum of squares; and R^2 = squared multiple correlation of the dependent variable with the coded vectors. Accordingly, Λ can be expressed as follows:

$$\Lambda = \frac{ss_{res}}{ss_t} = 1 - \frac{ss_{reg}}{ss_t} = 1 - R^2 \tag{20.15}$$

and

$$R^2 = 1 - \Lambda \tag{20.16}$$

From the foregoing, $1 - \Lambda$ in multivariate analysis may be conceived as a generalization of η^2 or R^2 of univariate analysis. When in multivariate analysis $\Lambda = 1$, it means that there is no association between the independent and the dependent variables. When, on the other hand, $\Lambda = 0$, it means that there is a perfect association between the independent and the dependent variables.

I will now show that for the special case of a DA with two groups, $1 - \Lambda$ is equal to R^2 of a coded vector representing group membership with the dependent variables.

To calculate Λ for the numerical example I analyzed earlier, it is necessary first to calculate the determinants of **W** and **T**. These matrices, which I calculated earlier for the data of Table 20.3, are

$$\mathbf{W} = \begin{bmatrix} 23.6 & -1.2 \\ -1.2 & 14.4 \end{bmatrix}$$

$$\mathbf{T} = \begin{bmatrix} 38.0 & 6.0 \\ 6.0 & 18.0 \end{bmatrix}$$

The determinants of these matrices are

$$|\mathbf{W}| = (23.6)(14.4) - (-1.2)(-1.2) = 338.4$$

$$|\mathbf{T}| = (38.0)(18.0) - (6.0)(6.0) = 648.0$$

Applying (20.11),

$$\Lambda = \frac{|\mathbf{W}|}{|\mathbf{T}|} = \frac{338.4}{648.0} = .52222$$

and

$$1 - \Lambda = 1 - .52222 = .47778$$

The last value is identical to R^2 that I obtained in the beginning of this chapter, when I regressed a coded vector representing membership in groups A_1 and A_2 on the two dependent variables. (Recall that, for analytic purposes only, the roles of the independent and the dependent variables are reversed.)

Throughout this section, I demonstrated that DA with two groups, regardless of the number of the dependent variables, can be done via a multiple regression analysis in which a coded vector representing group membership is regressed on the dependent variables. As I will show, the same holds true for tests of significance. Before I turn to this topic, it will be useful to show how to obtain Λ by using other statistics calculated in the course of calculating DA. In Chapter 21, I extend this approach to multiple DA and to MANOVA with multiple groups.

In the beginning of this section—see (20.3) and the discussion related to it—I showed how to solve for the eigenvalue, λ, in the following determinantal equation:

$$|\mathbf{W}^{-1}\mathbf{B} - \lambda\mathbf{I}| = 0$$

In the case of two groups,

$$\Lambda = \frac{1}{1 + \lambda} \tag{20.17}$$

For the data in Table 20.3, I found earlier that $\lambda = .91490$. Therefore,

$$\Lambda = \frac{1}{1 + .91490} = .52222$$

which is the same as the value I obtained when I applied (20.11). Also,

$$1 - \frac{1}{1 + \lambda} = R^2 = 1 - .52222 = .47778$$

Another expression using λ is

$$1 - \Lambda = R^2 = \frac{\lambda}{1 + \lambda} \tag{20.18}$$

For the present numerical example,

$$\frac{.91490}{1 + .91490} = .47778 = 1 - \Lambda = R^2$$

A Note on Multiple Discriminant Analysis

As I stated earlier, the equations I used for DA with two groups are applicable for DA with any number of groups. With more than two groups, more than one discriminant function is calculated. The number of discriminant functions that can be calculated is equal to the number of groups minus one, or to the number of dependent variables, whichever is smaller. Thus, with three groups, say, only two discriminant functions can be calculated, regardless of the number of dependent variables. If, on the other hand, there are six groups but only three dependent variables, the number of discriminant functions that can be calculated is three (the number of the dependent variables). In Chapter 21, I give an example of DA for more than two groups.

In the beginning of this chapter I showed that for two groups, DA can be calculated by multiple regression analysis in which the groups are represented by a coded vector. With more than two groups, it is necessary to use more than one coded vector (see Chapter 11). As I show in Chapter 21, canonical analysis with coded vectors may be used to calculate DA for any number of groups.

TESTS OF SIGNIFICANCE

In Chapter 21, I present the test of Λ for the general case of any number of groups and any number of dependent variables. Here, I present a special case of this test for the situation in which only two groups are studied on any number of dependent variables. It is

$$F = \frac{(1 - \Lambda)/t}{\Lambda/(N - t - 1)} \tag{20.19}$$

where t is the number of dependent variables and N is the total number of subjects. The *df* for this F ratio are t and $N - t - 1$. Although I use different symbols in (20.19), it is identical in form to the test of R^2 I used earlier in this chapter when I regressed a coded vector representing group membership on the dependent variables. This can be seen clearly when you recall that $1 - \Lambda = R^2$—see (20.16) and the discussion related to it. Also, because the roles of the independent and the dependent variables are reversed when DA is done via multiple regression analysis, k (used in the formula for testing R^2) is equal to t of (20.19). I use t, instead of k, for consistency with the notation in the general formula for the test of Λ (see Chapter 21).

Earlier, I found $\Lambda = .52222$ for the data in Table 20.3. Applying (20.19),

$$F = \frac{(1 - .52222)/2}{.52222/(10 - 2 - 1)} = 3.20$$

with 2 and 7 *df, p > .*05. Not surprisingly, I obtained identical results when I did a DA of the same data via multiple regression analysis (see "Multiple Regression Analysis," earlier in this chapter).

I noted earlier that a test of Λ addresses differences among groups on all the variables taken simultaneously. When the null hypothesis is rejected, it is of interest to identify specific variables on which the groups differ meaningfully. This brings us back to the study of standardized coefficients and structure coefficients (see earlier sections).

One may also wish to test whether differences among groups on single dependent variables, or on subsets of such variables, are statistically significant. I discuss this topic in Chapter 21 for the case of more than two groups. With two groups only, such tests may be carried out via multiple regression analysis. That is, tests of b's may be used for single variables and tests of differences between two R^2's for subsets of variables. As I discussed the use and interpretation of such tests in earlier parts of the book (see, in particular, Chapters 8–10), I will not discuss these topics here.

As in multiple regression analysis, one may use variable-selection procedures in multivariate analysis. For instance, it is possible to do a stepwise DA. In Chapter 6, I discussed uses and limitations of variable-selection procedures in multiple regression analysis. The points I made there regarding the appropriateness of variable-selection procedures in predictive versus explanatory research apply equally to the use of such procedures in multivariate analysis. In designs with two groups, variable-selection procedures may be applied via multiple regression analysis in which the dependent variable is a coded vector representing group membership.

Finally, as with other statistics, validity of the methods I presented in this chapter is based on assumptions. These are discussed in detail in the books on multivariate analysis I cited in the beginning of this chapter. I suggest that you read such discussions and that you pay special attention to the assumptions that the (1) data follow a multivariate normal distribution and (2) within-groups covariance matrices are homogeneous. In the references I cited earlier, you will also find discussions of (1) tests of homogeneity of within-groups covariance matrices and (2) consequences of failure to meet the aforementioned assumptions.

COMPUTER PROGRAMS

Excellent computer programs for multivariate analysis are available. The packages I use in this book contain one or more procedures for DA. Also, programs I discuss in Chapter 21 have an option for DA (see Huberty, 1994, Appendix B, for detailed discussion of programs and outputs in BMDP, SAS, and SPSS). I will now analyze the data in Table 20.3, using SAS and SPSS, beginning with the latter.

SPSS

___

Input

```
TITLE TABLE 20.3.   TWO GROUP DISCRIMINANT ANALYSIS.
DATA LIST FREE/X1,X2,TREAT.
BEGIN DATA
   8   3   1
   7   4   1
   5   5   1
   3   4   1
   3   2   1
   4   2   2
   3   1   2
   3   2   2
   2   2   2
   2   5   2
END DATA
LIST.
DISCRIMINANT GROUPS=TREAT(1,2)/VARIABLES=X1,X2/
   STATISTICS=ALL.
```

___

Commentary

For an introduction to SPSS, see Chapter 4. As you can see, the general layout is similar to SPSS inputs I used and commented on in earlier chapters. Therefore, I comment only on the DIS-CRIMINANT procedure. See Norušis/SPSS Inc. (1994), Chapter 1, for a general discussion of DA in SPSS, and see pages 278–296 for syntax. Unless otherwise stated, the page references I give in the following discussion apply to this source. Several variable-selection methods can be specified (see p. 284). When none is specified, "DISCRIMINANT enters all the variables into the discriminant equation (the DIRECT method), provided that they are not so highly correlated that multicollinearity problems arise" (p. 280). I will be using only the direct method, and will, therefore, not comment on the others. For a discussion of collinearity see Chapter 10, where I also discussed tolerance, which is also used in DISCRIMINANT (default .001; see p. 284) to exclude variables that are highly collinear.

As a minimum, DISCRIMINANT requires a GROUP and a VARIABLE subcommand, which "must precede all other subcommands and may be entered in any order" (p. 280). For illustrative purposes, I named the independent (grouping) variable TREAT(ments). Of course, any name will do. The numbers in parentheses are the minimum and maximum values of TREAT (group membership; see the last column of data in the previous input). Consecutive integers are required for group identification. Had the study consisted of, say, five groups, I would have used integers 1 through 5 to identify them, and would have inserted "1,5" (without quotation marks) in the parentheses. Under VARIABLES, I specify the two dependent variables. As I pointed out in Chapter 4, I use STATISTICS=ALL even when I report only excerpts of the output (see pp. 289–290 for a description of the STATISTICS subcommand).

Output

Group means

TREAT	X1	X2
1	5.20000	3.60000
2	2.80000	2.40000
Total	4.00000	3.00000

Group standard deviations

TREAT	X1	X2
1	2.28035	1.14018
2	.83666	1.51658
Total	2.05480	1.41421

Pooled within-groups covariance matrix with 8 degrees of freedom

	X1	X2
X1	2.9500	
X2	−.1500	1.8000

Total covariance matrix with 9 degrees of freedom

	X1	X2
X1	4.2222	
X2	.6667	2.0000

Eigenvalue	Canonical Correlation	Wilks' Lambda
.91489	.6912147	.5222222

Standardized canonical discriminant function coefficients

	Func 1
X1	.85430
X2	.57835

Structure matrix:

Pooled within-groups correlations between discriminating
variables and canonical discriminant functions
(Variables ordered by size of correlation within function)

	Func 1
X1	.81666
X2	.52274

Unstandardized canonical discriminant function coefficients

	Func 1
X1	.4973955
X2	.4310761
(Constant)	−3.2828103

Canonical discriminant functions evaluated at group means
(group centroids)

Group	Func 1
1	.85552
2	−.85552

Commentary

Compare the preceding excerpts with the results of my calculations in Tables 20.1 through 20.3 and in the text. Among other things, this will help you become familiar with SPSS layout and terminology. *Note that SPSS reports within-group structure coefficients, whereas I reported total structure coefficients.* See my discussion of this topic, earlier in the chapter.

SAS

Input

```
TITLE 'TABLE 20.3.   TWO GROUP DISCRIMINANT ANALYSIS.   CANDISC.';
DATA T203;
INPUT  X1  X2  TREAT;
CARDS;
    8   3   1
    7   4   1
    5   5   1
    3   4   1
    3   2   1
    4   2   2
    3   1   2
    3   2   2
    2   2   2
    2   5   2
;
PROC PRINT;
PROC CANDISC ALL;
   CLASS TREAT;
RUN;
```

Commentary

For an introduction to SAS procedures for DA, see SAS Institute Inc. (1990a, Volume 1, Chapter 5). As you may note from the title, I use CANDISC, which is described in Chapter 16. "Canonical discriminant analysis is equivalent to canonical correlation analysis between the quantitative variables and a set of dummy variables coded from the class variable" (p. 389). In Chapter 21, I elaborate on this conception.

"ALL activates all of the printing options" (p. 390). The CLASS statement, which is required, is analogous to the GROUPS subcommand in SPSS. See the input data where the third column contains class identification, which I labeled TREAT.

Output

Pooled Within-Class SSCP Matrix

Variable	X1	X2
X1	23.60000000	−1.20000000
X2	−1.20000000	14.40000000

Total-Sample SSCP Matrix

Variable	X1	X2
X1	38.00000000	6.00000000
X2	6.00000000	18.00000000

Pooled Within-Class Covariance Matrix   DF = 8

Variable	X1	X2
X1	2.950000000	−0.150000000
X2	−0.150000000	1.800000000

Total-Sample Covariance Matrix   DF = 9

Variable	X1	X2
X1	4.222222222	0.666666667
X2	0.666666667	2.000000000

Multivariate Statistics and Exact F Statistics

Statistic	Value	F	Num DF	Den DF	Pr >
Wilks' Lambda	0.52222222	3.2021	2	7	0.1029

Total Canonical Structure

	CAN1
X1	0.890587
X2	0.646997

Pooled Within Canonical Structure

	CAN1
X1	0.816657
X2	0.522739

Pooled Within-Class Standardized Canonical Coefficients

CAN1

X1	0.8543048136
X2	0.5783492693

Raw Canonical Coefficients

CAN1

X1	0.4973954926
X2	0.4310760936

Class Means on Canonical Variables

TREAT	CAN1
1	0.8555202473
2	−.8555202473

Commentary

Compare the preceding excerpts with corresponding excerpts of output from SPSS given earlier, and note that the results are the same. Unlike SPSS, however, *SAS reports both total and within-group structure coefficients.*

STUDY SUGGESTIONS

1. In a study with two groups and five dependent variables, how many discriminant functions can one obtain?

2. What is the meaning of a structure coefficient?

3. When Λ (lambda) is calculated for two groups only, what term is it equal to if the data for the two groups are subjected to a multiple regression analysis in which the dependent variable is a coded vector representing group membership?

4. What is the ratio of the determinant of the within-groups SSCP to the determinant of the total SSCP equal to?

5. A researcher studied the differences between males ($N = 180$) and females ($N = 150$) on six dependent variables. Λ was found to be .62342. What is the F ratio for the test of Λ?

6. The following example is a facet of a study encountered in research on attribution theory (e.g., Weiner, 1974). Subjects were randomly assigned to perform a task under either a Success or a Failure condition. That is, subjects under the former condition met with success while performing the task, whereas those under the latter condition met with failure. Subsequently, the subjects were asked to rate the degree to which their performance was due to their ability and to the difficulty of the task in which they engaged. Following are data (illustrative), where higher ratings indicate greater attribution to ability and to task difficulty.

Success		Failure	
Ability	Difficulty	Ability	Difficulty
6	5	3	6
7	6	3	6
3	4	2	7
5	5	1	5
6	5	1	7
6	4	5	6
7	6	4	5
7	7	3	6

(a) Do a multiple regression analysis, regressing the treatments, represented as a dummy variable, on the two dependent variables.

(b) Do a discriminant analysis of the same data. Compare the results with those you obtained under (a). Interpret the results.

I use a miniature example so that you may do all the calculations by hand. You may find it useful to analyze the data also by computer and to compare the output with your hand calculations.

ANSWERS

1. Only one function can be obtained, regardless of the number of dependent variables.
2. It is the correlation of an original variable with the discriminant function scores.
3. $1 - R^2$
4. Λ
5. $F = 32.52$, with 6 and 323 df.
6. (a) $R^2 = .68762$

$F = 14.31$, with 2 and 13 df.

$Y' = .64316 + 18069(AB) - .16398(DIF)$

$\qquad (4.67, p < .001)(-1.94, p > .05)$

The numbers in the parentheses are t ratios for each b.

Structure coefficients: .93173(AB); −.48783(DIF)

$\beta_{(AB)} = .73081 \qquad \beta_{(DIF)} = -.30402$

(b)

$$W = \begin{bmatrix} 26.375 & 5.250 \\ 5.250 & 11.500 \end{bmatrix}$$

$$B = \begin{bmatrix} 39.0625 & -9.3750 \\ -9.3750 & 2.2500 \end{bmatrix}$$

$$T = \begin{bmatrix} 65.4375 & -4.1250 \\ -4.1250 & 13.7500 \end{bmatrix}$$

$\lambda = 2.20127$

$Y = .57789 + .72936(AB) - .66191(DIF)$

Centroids: Success $= 1.38784$; Failure $= -1.38784$

Standardized coefficients: 1.00109(AB); −.59991(DIF)

Total structure coefficients: .93175(AB); −.48778(DIF)

$\Lambda = .31238$. $F = 14.31$, with 2 and 13 df.

Ratings of ability make a greater contribution to the discrimination between the treatment groups than do ratings of task difficulty. Subjects exposed to Success attribute their performance to a greater extent to their ability than do subjects exposed to Failure. The converse is true, though to a much smaller extent, concerning the ratings of the difficulty of the task. That is, subjects exposed to Failure perceive the task as being more difficult than do subjects exposed to Success. Following are the means of the two groups:

	Ability	Difficulty
Success	5.875	5.250
Failure	2.750	6.000

Note that in the regression analysis of the same data, (a), the regression coefficient for task difficulty is statistically not significant at the .05 level. This is, of course, due in part to the small group sizes. The mean difference in the ratings of this variable is meaningful when assessed in relation to the pooled within-groups standard deviation.

21

Canonical and Discriminant Analysis, and Multivariate Analysis of Variance

In Chapter 20, I introduced basic ideas of multivariate analysis and focused on the simultaneous analysis of multiple dependent variables for the case of two groups. In this chapter, I apply these ideas to relations between multiple independent and multiple dependent variables or, more generally, between two *sets* of variables or measures. Situations of this kind abound in behavioral and social research, as is evidenced when one seeks relations between (1) mental abilities and academic achievement in several subject areas; (2) attitudes and values; (3) personality characteristics and cognitive styles; (4) measures of adjustment of husbands and those of their wives; (5) pretests and posttests in achievement, personality, and the like. The list could be extended indefinitely to encompass diverse phenomena from various research disciplines and orientations. Examples of potential and actual studies of relations between sets of variables in psychology, education, political science, sociology, communication, and marketing are given, among other sources, in Darlington, Weinberg, and Walberg (1973); Hair, Anderson, Tatham, and Black (1992); Hand and Taylor (1987); Nesselroade and Cattell (1988); and Tatsuoka (1988).

It is for studying relations between two sets of variables that Hotelling (1936) developed the method of canonical analysis (CA). With only one dependent variable, or one criterion, CA reduces to multiple regression (MR). Thus, CA may be conceived as an extension of MR or, alternatively, MR may be conceived as subsumed under CA.

The generality of CA can be further noted when one realizes that it is not limited, as one might have been led to believe from the previous examples, to continuous variables. CA is applicable also in designs consisting of categorical variables. For instance, one set could consist of coded vectors representing a categorical variable (e.g., treatments, groups), and the other set may consist of multiple dependent variables. This is an extension of the approach I presented in Chapter 20, where I showed that for the case of *two* groups, MR can be used to obtain results identical to those of discriminant analysis (DA). Recall that I accomplished this by regressing a coded vector representing group membership on the dependent variables. With more than two groups, more than one coded vector is necessary to represent group membership. Therefore, MR can no longer be used in lieu of DA or MANOVA. But, as I have stated, CA can be used in such situations. Not surprisingly, Cliff (1987a) stated, "A statistician faced with exile and allowed to take along only a single computer program would slyly take one for doing cancor [canonical correlation], since this program can be persuaded to do all the other analyses" (pp. 453–454). In sum, CA is a most general analytic approach that subsumes MR, DA, and MANOVA.

Although the conceptual step from MR to CA is not a large one, the computational step may be very large. Except for the simplest of problems, CA is so complex as to make solutions with only the aid of calculators forbidding. Consequently, intelligent and critical reliance on computer analysis is essential even with moderately complex CA problems. In fact, because of the unavailability of computer facilities, CA lay dormant, so to speak, for several decades since its development, except for some relatively simple applications mostly for illustrative purposes. Nowadays the availability of various computer programs (see the following) renders solutions of even extremely complex CA problems easily obtainable. In view of the great capacity and speed of present-day computers, it is one's theoretical formulations and one's ability to comprehend and interpret the results that set limits on the complexity of CA problems that may be attempted.

Fortunately, as with MR, all the ingredients of the calculations and all aspects of the interpretation of CA can be done with relative ease without a computer in designs consisting of only two variables in each set. Gaining an understanding of CA through the use of such simple problems enables you to then proceed, with the aid of a computer, to more complex ones. Accordingly, after an overview, I will calculate and interpret CA via two small numerical examples. The first example represents the general application of CA in studying relations between two sets of continuous variables. The second example is a special application of CA namely, when one set consists of continuous variables and the other set consists of coded vectors representing a categorical variable. Through this example, I show how CA can be used to calculate MANOVA or DA for more than two groups.

In the process of presenting the two examples, I show all the calculations. Except for being more complex, the same kind of calculations are carried out in CA with more than two variables in each set. But, as I have stated, it is best to do this with the aid of a computer. To acquaint you with computer programs for CA, I analyze the numerical examples that I present also by computer.

I conclude the chapter with brief comments on miscellaneous topics that I have not covered.

CA: AN OVERVIEW

As I stated several times earlier, CA is designed to study relations between two sets of variables, p and q, where $p \geq 2$ could be a set of independent variables, and $q \geq 2$ could be a set of dependent variables. Alternatively, p could be predictors and q criteria. When the preceding designations do not apply (that is, when one's aim is to study relations between two sets of variables without designating one as independent or predictors, and the other as dependent or criteria), the p variables are referred to as "variables on the left," or Set 1, and the q variables are referred to as "variables on the right," or Set 2. In what follows, I use X's to represent variables on the left and Y's to represent variables on the right.

The basic idea of CA is that of forming two linear combinations, one of the X_p variables and one of the Y_q variables, by differentially weighting them to obtain the maximum possible correlation between the two linear combinations. The correlation between the two linear combinations, also referred to as *canonical variates,* is the canonical correlation, R_c. The square of the canonical correlation, R_c^2, is an estimate of the variance shared by the two canonical variates. It is very important to keep in mind that R_c^2 is *not* an estimate of the variance shared between X_p and Y_q, but of the linear combinations of these variables.[1]

From the foregoing characterization of CA, its analogy with MR should be apparent. As I pointed out earlier, when p or q consists of one variable, we are back to MR. Recall that the multiple correlation coefficient is the maximum correlation that one can obtain between the dependent variable, Y, and a linear combination of the independent variables, the X's—see (5.18) and the discussion related to it. Like MR, CA seeks a set of weights that will maximize a correlation coefficient. But unlike MR, in which only the X's are weighted, in CA both the X's and the Y's are differentially weighted. Moreover, after having obtained the maximum R_c in CA, additional R_c's are calculated, subject to the restriction that each succeeding pair of canonical variates of the X's and the Y's not be correlated with all the pairs of canonical variates preceding it. In short, the first pair of linear combinations is the one that yields the largest R_c possible in a given data set. The second R_c is then based on linear combinations of X's and Y's that are not correlated with the first pair and that yield the second largest R_c possible in the given data—and the same is true for succeeding R_c's. The maximum number of R_c's that can be extracted is equal to the number of variables in the smaller set, when $p \neq q$. When, for instance, $p = 5$ and $q = 7$, five R_c's can be calculated. This is not to say that all obtainable R_c's are necessarily meaningful or statistically significant. I discuss these topics later. At this stage I will only reiterate that CA extracts the R_c's in a descending order of magnitude, subject to the restriction I noted above.

Data Matrices for CA

The basic data matrix for CA is depicted in Table 21.1. Note that this is a matrix of N (subjects, cases) by $p + q$ (or $X_p + Y_q$) variables. As usual, the first subscript of each X or Y stands for rows (subjects, cases) and the second subscript stands for columns (variables, tests, items, and so on). Note the broken vertical line: it partitions the matrix into X_p and Y_q variables, or p variables on the left and q variables on the right. Table 21.1 shows clearly that MR is a special case of CA. In the former, one variable, Y, is partitioned from the rest, the X's, whereas in the latter, the matrix is partitioned into two sets of variables, X_p and Y_q, where $p \geq 2$ and $q \geq 2$.

Instead of consisting of raw scores, as in Table 21.1, the data matrix may consist of deviation or standard scores. The variables of the data matrix are intercorrelated and a correlation matrix, **R**, is formed. I show such a matrix, which is also partitioned, in Table 21.2, where I use broken lines to indicate the partitioning.

Table 21.1   Basic Data Matrix for CA

Cases	X					Y			
1	X_{11}	X_{12}	. . .	X_{1p}		Y_{11}	Y_{12}	. . .	Y_{1q}
2	X_{21}	X_{22}	. . .	X_{2p}		Y_{21}	Y_{22}	. . .	Y_{2q}
.	.	.		.		.	.		.
.	.	.	. . .	.		.	.	. . .	.
.	.	.		.		.	.		.
N	X_{N1}	X_{N2}	. . .	X_{Np}		Y_{N1}	Y_{N2}	. . .	Y_{Nq}

NOTE: N = number of cases; p = number of X variables; q = number of Y variables.

---

[1]See discussion of redundancy, presented later in this chapter.

Table 21.2   Partitioned Correlation Matrix for CA

		X						Y				
		1	2	.	.	.	p	1	2	.	.	q
	1											
	2											
	.											
X	.			$\mathbf{R}_{xx}$						$\mathbf{R}_{xy}$		
	.											
	p											
	1											
	2											
	.											
Y	.			$\mathbf{R}_{yx}$						$\mathbf{R}_{yy}$		
	.											
	q											

NOTE: p = number of X variables; q = number of Y variables.

The four partitions of the matrix can be succinctly stated thus:

$$\mathbf{R} = \begin{bmatrix} \mathbf{R}_{xx} & \mathbf{R}_{xy} \\ \mathbf{R}_{yx} & \mathbf{R}_{yy} \end{bmatrix}$$

where $\mathbf{R}$ = supermatrix of correlations among all the variables;[2] $\mathbf{R}_{xx}$ = correlation matrix of the X_p variables; $\mathbf{R}_{yy}$ = correlation matrix of the Y_q variables; $\mathbf{R}_{xy}$ = correlation matrix of the X_p with the Y_q variables; and $\mathbf{R}_{yx}$ = transpose of $\mathbf{R}_{xy}$. The preceding four matrices are used in the solution of the CA problem.

CA WITH CONTINUOUS VARIABLES

In this section, I present CA for designs in which both sets of variables are continuous. It is for the analysis of data obtained in such designs that CA was initially developed. Later in this chapter, I present an adaptation of CA to designs in which one set of variables is continuous and the other is categorical. I will show the calculations and interpretations of CA when both sets of variables are continuous through a numerical example in which $p = q = 2$, to which I now turn.

A Numerical Example

Table 21.3 presents a correlation matrix for illustrative data on two X and two Y variables. As I pointed out earlier, the X's may be independent variables and the Y's dependent variables, or the

---

[2]For a discussion of supermatrices, see Horst (1963, Chapter 5).

Table 21.3   Correlation Matrix for Canonical Analysis; N = 300

| | | $\mathbf{R}_{xx}$ | | | $\mathbf{R}_{xy}$ | |
		X_1	X_2		Y_1	Y_2
	X_1	1.00	.60	|	.45	.48
	X_2	.60	1.00	|	.40	.38
$\mathbf{R} =$				|		
		$\mathbf{R}_{yx}$		|	$\mathbf{R}_{yy}$	
	Y_1	.45	.40	|	1.00	.70
	Y_2	.48	.38	|	.70	1.00

X's may be predictors and the Y's criteria. Most generally, the X's are the variables on the left, or the first set; the Y's are the variables on the right, or the second set. Earlier, I gave examples of potential applications of CA in various substantive areas. Therefore, I will not attempt to attach substantive meanings to the variables under consideration.

Canonical Correlations

I said earlier that the number of canonical correlations obtainable in a given set of data is equal to the number of variables in the smaller of the two sets of variables. In the present example, $p = q = 2$. Therefore, two canonical correlations may be obtained. The canonical correlations are equal to the square roots of the eigenvalues, or characteristic roots, of the following determinantal equation:

$$\left| \mathbf{R}_{yy}^{-1} \mathbf{R}_{yx} \mathbf{R}_{xx}^{-1} \mathbf{R}_{xy} - \lambda \mathbf{I} \right| = 0 \tag{21.1}$$

where $\mathbf{R}_{yy}^{-1}$ = inverse of $\mathbf{R}_{yy}$; $\mathbf{R}_{xx}^{-1}$ = inverse of $\mathbf{R}_{xx}$; and $\mathbf{I}$ = identity matrix. In Chapter 20, I solved a problem similar to the one in (21.1)—see (20.3) and the calculations related to it.

First, I will calculate the two inverses. Using data from Table 21.3, the determinant of $\mathbf{R}_{yy}$ is:

$$\left| \mathbf{R}_{yy} \right| = \begin{vmatrix} 1.00 & .70 \\ .70 & 1.00 \end{vmatrix} = .51$$

and

$$\mathbf{R}_{yy}^{-1} = \frac{1}{.51} \begin{bmatrix} 1.00 & -.70 \\ -.70 & 1.00 \end{bmatrix} = \begin{bmatrix} 1.96078 & -1.37255 \\ -1.37255 & 1.96078 \end{bmatrix}$$

The determinant of $\mathbf{R}_{xx}$ is

$$\left| \mathbf{R}_{xx} \right| = \begin{vmatrix} 1.00 & .60 \\ .60 & 1.00 \end{vmatrix} = .64$$

and

$$\mathbf{R}_{xx}^{-1} = \frac{1}{.64} \begin{bmatrix} 1.00 & -.60 \\ -.60 & 1.00 \end{bmatrix} = \begin{bmatrix} 1.56250 & -.93750 \\ -.93750 & 1.56250 \end{bmatrix}$$

I now carry out the matrix operations in the sequence indicated in (21.1):

$$\mathbf{R}_{yy}^{-1}\mathbf{R}_{yx} = \begin{bmatrix} 1.96078 & -1.37255 \\ -1.37255 & 1.96078 \end{bmatrix} \begin{bmatrix} .45 & .40 \\ .48 & .38 \end{bmatrix} = \begin{bmatrix} .22353 & .26274 \\ .32353 & .19608 \end{bmatrix}$$

$$\mathbf{R}_{yy}^{-1}\mathbf{R}_{yx}\mathbf{R}_{xx}^{-1} = \begin{bmatrix} .22353 & .26274 \\ .32353 & .19608 \end{bmatrix} \begin{bmatrix} 1.56250 & -.93750 \\ -.93750 & 1.56250 \end{bmatrix} = \begin{bmatrix} .10295 & .20097 \\ .32169 & .00307 \end{bmatrix}$$

$$\mathbf{R}_{yy}^{-1}\mathbf{R}_{yx}\mathbf{R}_{xx}^{-1}\mathbf{R}_{xy} = \begin{bmatrix} .10295 & .20097 \\ .32169 & .00307 \end{bmatrix} \begin{bmatrix} .45 & .48 \\ .40 & .38 \end{bmatrix} = \begin{bmatrix} .12672 & .12578 \\ .14599 & .15558 \end{bmatrix}$$

It is now necessary to solve the following:

$$\begin{vmatrix} .12672 - \lambda & .12578 \\ .14599 & .15558 - \lambda \end{vmatrix} = 0$$

$$(.12672 - \lambda)(.15558 - \lambda) - (.14599)(.12578) = 0$$

$$.01972 - .15558\lambda - .12672\lambda + \lambda^2 - .01836 = 0$$

$$\lambda^2 - .28230\lambda + .00136 = 0$$

Solving this quadratic equation,

$$\lambda = \frac{-b \pm \sqrt{b^2 - 4ac}}{2a}$$

where $a = 1$, $b = -.28230$, and $c = .00136$:

$$\lambda_1 = \frac{.28230 + \sqrt{(-.28230)^2 - (4)(1)(.00136)}}{2} = .27740$$

$$\lambda_2 = \frac{.28230 - \sqrt{(-.28230)^2 - (4)(1)(.00136)}}{2} = .00490$$

Note that the sum of the λ's $(.27740 + .00490 = .2823)$ is equal to the trace (the sum of the elements of the principal diagonal) of the matrix used to solve for λ's. In other words, it is the trace of the matrix whose determinant is set equal to zero. Look back at this matrix and note that the two elements in its principal diagonal are .12672 and 15558. Their sum (.2823) is equal to the sum of the λ's, or roots, I calculated above. This could serve as a check on the calculations of the λ's.

Taking the positive square roots of the λ's,

$$R_{c1} = \sqrt{\lambda_1} = \sqrt{.27740} = .52669$$
$$R_{c2} = \sqrt{\lambda_2} = \sqrt{.00490} = .07000$$

Recall that R_c^2 indicates the proportion of variance shared by a pair of canonical variates to which it corresponds. Accordingly, the first pair of canonical variates share about 28% of the variance

$(R_{c1}^2 = \lambda_1)$, and the second pair share about .5% of the variance $(R_{c2}^2 = \lambda_2)$. Later, I show how to test canonical correlations for statistical significance. But, as with other statistics, the criterion of meaningfulness is more important. Some authors (e.g., Cooley & Lohnes, 1971, p. 176; Thorndike, 1978, p. 183) have suggested that, as a rule of thumb, $R_c^2 < .10$ (i.e., less than 10% of shared variance) be treated as not meaningful. In any case, the second R_c in the present example is certainly not meaningful. Nevertheless, I retain it for completeness of presentation.

Canonical Weights

I said earlier that R_c is a correlation between a linear combination of X's and a linear combination of Y's. I show now how the weights used to form such linear combinations—referred to as canonical weights—are calculated. Canonical weights are calculated for each R_c that is retained for interpretation of the results. Thus, for example, in a given problem seven R_c's may be obtainable, but using a criterion of meaningfulness or statistical significance (see the following), one may decide to retain the first two only. Under such circumstances, the canonical weights associated with the first two R_c's are of interest.

To differentiate between canonical weights to be used with the X's (variables on the left) and the Y's (variables on the right), I will use the letter a for the former and the letter b for the latter. Thus **A** is a matrix of canonical weights for the X's, and $\mathbf{a}_j$ is the jth column vector of such coefficients associated with the jth R_c. Similarly, **B** is a matrix of canonical weights for the Y's, and $\mathbf{b}_j$ is the jth column vector of such coefficients.

I will now calculate **B**, using relevant results I calculated in the preceding section. To obtain $\mathbf{b}_1$ (the canonical weights associated with R_{c1}), it is necessary first to obtain the eigenvector, $\mathbf{v}_1$, or the characteristic vector, associated with λ. Earlier, I calculated $\lambda_1 = .27740$. Following procedures I explained in Chapter 20, I form the following homogeneous equations:

$$\begin{bmatrix} .12672 - .27740 & .12578 \\ .14599 & .15558 - .27740 \end{bmatrix} \begin{bmatrix} v_1 \\ v_2 \end{bmatrix} = \begin{bmatrix} 0 \\ 0 \end{bmatrix}$$

$$\begin{bmatrix} -.15068 & .12578 \\ .14599 & -.12182 \end{bmatrix} \begin{bmatrix} v_1 \\ v_2 \end{bmatrix} = \begin{bmatrix} 0 \\ 0 \end{bmatrix}$$

A solution for these equations is obtained by forming the adjoint of the preceding matrix:[3]

$$\begin{bmatrix} -.12182 & -.12578 \\ -.14599 & -.15068 \end{bmatrix}$$

Accordingly,

$$\mathbf{v}_1' = [-.12182 \quad -.14599]$$

or, alternatively,

$$\mathbf{v}_1' = [-.12578 \quad -.15068]$$

Recall that there is a constant proportionality between the elements of each column and that it therefore makes no difference which of the two columns is taken as **v**. Also, it is convenient to

---

[3]For a discussion of the adjoint of a 2×2 matrix, see Appendix A.

change the signs of $\mathbf{v}$, because both are negative. Using the values of the first column of the adjoint,

$$\mathbf{v}_1' = [.12182 \quad .14599]$$

Now, β_j is calculated subject to the restriction that the variance of the scores on the *j*th canonical variate is equal to one. The preceding can be stated as follows:

$$\beta_j' \mathbf{R}_{yy} \beta_j = 1.00 \tag{21.2}$$

To accomplish this, I apply

$$\beta_j = \frac{1}{\sqrt{\mathbf{v}_j' \mathbf{R}_{yy} \mathbf{v}_j}} \mathbf{v}_j \tag{21.3}$$

where $\mathbf{v}_j$ is the *j*th eigenvector; $\mathbf{v}_j'$ is the transpose of $\mathbf{v}_j$; and $\mathbf{R}_{yy}$ is the correlation matrix of the *Y*'s. For the present example,

$$\underset{\mathbf{v}_1'}{\underbrace{[.12182 \quad .14599]}} \underset{\mathbf{R}_{yy}}{\underbrace{\begin{bmatrix} 1.00 & .70 \\ .70 & 1.00 \end{bmatrix}}} \underset{\mathbf{v}_1}{\underbrace{\begin{bmatrix} .12182 \\ .14559 \end{bmatrix}}} = .06105$$

$$\sqrt{\mathbf{v}_1' \mathbf{R}_{yy} \mathbf{v}_1} = \sqrt{.06105} = .24708$$

$$\beta_1 = \frac{1}{.24708} \begin{bmatrix} .12182 \\ .14559 \end{bmatrix} = \begin{bmatrix} .49304 \\ .59086 \end{bmatrix}$$

Two canonical weights for Y_1 and Y_2, respectively, are .49304 and .59086. I will note two things about these weights. One, they are standardized coefficients and are therefore applied to standard scores (*z*) on Y_1 and Y_2. Two, they are associated with the first canonical correlation R_{c1}. Before I calculate the weights for the second function, I will show that β_1 satisfies the condition stated in (21.2):

$$\underset{\beta_1'}{\underbrace{[.49304 \quad .59086]}} \underset{\mathbf{R}_{yy}}{\underbrace{\begin{bmatrix} 1.00 & .70 \\ .70 & 1.00 \end{bmatrix}}} \underset{\beta_1}{\underbrace{\begin{bmatrix} .49304 \\ .59086 \end{bmatrix}}} = 1.00$$

I turn now to the calculation of β_2—the canonical weights for *Y*'s associated with the second canonical correlation. The procedure is the same as that used in calculating β_1, except that now $\mathbf{v}_2$, the eigenvector associated with λ_2, is obtained. Earlier, I calculated $\lambda_2 = .00490$. Therefore,

$$\begin{bmatrix} .12672 - .00490 & .12578 \\ .14599 & .15558 - .00490 \end{bmatrix} \begin{bmatrix} v_1 \\ v_2 \end{bmatrix} = \begin{bmatrix} 0 \\ 0 \end{bmatrix}$$

$$\begin{bmatrix} .12182 & .12578 \\ .14599 & .15068 \end{bmatrix} \begin{bmatrix} v_1 \\ v_2 \end{bmatrix} = \begin{bmatrix} 0 \\ 0 \end{bmatrix}$$

The adjoint of the preceding matrix is

$$\begin{bmatrix} .15068 & -.12578 \\ -.14599 & .12182 \end{bmatrix}$$

and $\mathbf{v}_2' = [.15068 \quad -.14599]$, or $[-.12578 \quad .12182]$

$$\mathbf{v}_2' \mathbf{R}_{yy} \mathbf{v}_2 = \underset{\mathbf{v}_2'}{[.15068 \quad -.14599]} \underset{\mathbf{R}_{yy}}{\begin{bmatrix} 1.00 & .70 \\ .70 & 1.00 \end{bmatrix}} \underset{\mathbf{v}_2}{\begin{bmatrix} .15068 \\ -.14559 \end{bmatrix}} = .01322$$

$$\sqrt{\mathbf{v}_2' \mathbf{R}_{yy} \mathbf{v}_2} = \sqrt{.01322} = .11498$$

Applying (21.3),

$$\boldsymbol{\beta}_2 = \frac{1}{.11498} \begin{bmatrix} .15068 \\ -.14559 \end{bmatrix} = \begin{bmatrix} 1.31049 \\ -1.26970 \end{bmatrix}$$

The matrix of the canonical weights for the Y's is

$$\mathbf{B} = \begin{bmatrix} .49304 & 1.31049 \\ .59086 & -1.26970 \end{bmatrix}$$

Before I address issues of interpretation of these results, I will calculate the canonical weights for the X's. I will note first that I could do this by following the procedure I used in the preceding to calculate $\mathbf{B}$, except that I would begin with the following equation:

$$\left| \mathbf{R}_{xx}^{-1} \mathbf{R}_{xy} \mathbf{R}_{yy}^{-1} \mathbf{R}_{yx} - \lambda \mathbf{I} \right| = 0 \tag{21.4}$$

The λ's obtained from the solution of (21.4) will be the same as those I obtained when I solved (21.1). In other words, I could insert in (21.4) the λ's I calculated earlier to obtain their associated eigenvectors and then calculate $\mathbf{A}$ in a manner analogous to the calculation of $\mathbf{B}$. But since $\mathbf{B}$ is already available, I may take a simpler approach to the calculation of $\mathbf{A}$; that is,

$$\mathbf{A} = \mathbf{R}_{xx}^{-1} \mathbf{R}_{xy} \mathbf{B} \mathbf{D}^{-1/2} \tag{21.5}$$

where $\mathbf{R}_{xx}^{-1}$ = inverse of the correlation matrix of the X's; $\mathbf{R}_{xy}$ = correlation matrix of the X's with the Y's; $\mathbf{B}$ = canonical weights for the Y's; and $\mathbf{D}^{-1/2}$ = diagonal matrix whose elements are the reciprocals of the square roots of the λ's. For the present example, (21.5) translates into

$$\mathbf{A} = \underset{\mathbf{R}_{xx}^{-1}}{\begin{bmatrix} 1.56250 & -.93750 \\ -.93750 & 1.56250 \end{bmatrix}} \underset{\mathbf{R}_{xy}}{\begin{bmatrix} .45 & .48 \\ .40 & .38 \end{bmatrix}} \underset{\mathbf{B}}{\begin{bmatrix} .49304 & 1.31049 \\ .59086 & -1.26970 \end{bmatrix}} \underset{\mathbf{D}^{-1/2}}{\begin{bmatrix} \dfrac{1}{\sqrt{.27740}} & 0 \\ 0 & \dfrac{1}{\sqrt{.00490}} \end{bmatrix}}$$

Upon carrying out the matrix operations, one finds that

$$\mathbf{A} = \begin{bmatrix} .74889 & -.99914 \\ .35141 & 1.19534 \end{bmatrix}$$

These, then, are the standardized weights for the X's.

Applying the standardized canonical weights to the subjects' standard scores (z) on the X's and the Y's results in canonical variate scores for each subject. These are the linear combinations I referred to earlier, when I introduced the concept of the canonical correlation.

In the present example it is, of course, not possible to calculate canonical variate scores because I used data in the form of a correlation matrix. It will be useful, however, to note that had subjects' scores been available and had canonical variate scores been calculated for them, then the correlation between the canonical variate scores on the first function would have been equal to the value of the first canonical correlation (i.e., $R_{c1} = .52669$; see the preceding). Similarly, the correlation between the canonical variate scores on the second function would have been equal to the second canonical correlation (i.e., $R_{c2} = .07$; see the preceding).

Standardized canonical weights are interpreted in a manner analogous to the interpretation of standardized regression coefficients (β's) in multiple regression analysis. Accordingly, some researchers use them as indices of the relative importance, or contribution, of the variables with which they are associated. Consider the weights obtained for the first canonical correlation. They are .49304 and .59086 for Y_1 and Y_2, respectively, and .74889 and .35141 for X_1 and X_2, respectively. Based on these results one would probably conclude that Y_1 and Y_2 are about of equal importance, whereas X_1 is more important than X_2. It is, however, important to note that, being standardized coefficients, canonical weights suffer from the same shortcomings as those of standardized regression coefficients (β's).[4] It is for this reason that some authors (e.g., Cooley & Lohnes, 1971, 1976; Meredith, 1964; Thorndike & Weiss, 1973) prefer to use structure coefficients for interpretive purposes. It is to this topic that I now turn.

Structure Coefficients

I introduced structure coefficients in connection with discriminant analysis (Chapter 20), where I pointed out that they are correlations between original variables and the discriminant function. In canonical analysis, structure coefficients (also referred to as loadings) are similarly defined: they are correlations between original variables and the canonical variates. In other words, a structure coefficient is the correlation between a given original variable and the canonical variate scores (see the preceding) on a given function. As in discriminant analysis, to obtain the structure coefficients it is not necessary to carry out the calculations indicated in the preceding sentence. Having calculated standardized canonical weights, structure coefficients are readily obtainable. Structure coefficients for the X's are calculated as follows:

$$\mathbf{S}_x = \mathbf{R}_{xx}\mathbf{A} \tag{21.6}$$

where $\mathbf{S}_x$ = matrix of structure coefficients for the X's; $\mathbf{R}_{xx}$ = correlation matrix of the X's; and $\mathbf{A}$ = standardized canonical weights for the X's. For the present example,

$$\underset{\mathbf{R}_{xx}}{\mathbf{S}_x = \begin{bmatrix} 1.00 & .60 \\ .60 & 1.00 \end{bmatrix}} \underset{\mathbf{A}}{\begin{bmatrix} .74889 & -.99914 \\ .35141 & 1.19534 \end{bmatrix}} = \begin{bmatrix} .95974 & -.28194 \\ .80074 & .59586 \end{bmatrix}$$

The correlation between X_1 and the first canonical variate (i.e., the structure coefficient) is .96, and that between X_2 and the first canonical variate is .80. Similarly, the structure coefficients for X_1 and X_2 with the second canonical variate are $-.28$ and .60, respectively. Before I discuss interpretations, I will calculate the structure coefficients for the Y's. The formula for doing this is analogous to (21.6):

$$\mathbf{S}_y = \mathbf{R}_{yy}\mathbf{B} \tag{21.7}$$

---

[4]For detailed discussions of shortcomings of β's, see Chapter 10.

where S_y = matrix of structure coefficients for the Y's; R_{yy} = correlation matrix of the Y's; and B = standardized canonical weights for the Y's. For the present example,

$$S_y = \begin{bmatrix} 1.00 & .70 \\ .70 & 1.00 \end{bmatrix} \begin{bmatrix} .49304 & 1.31049 \\ .59086 & -1.26970 \end{bmatrix} = \begin{bmatrix} .90664 & .42170 \\ .93600 & -.35236 \end{bmatrix}$$

$$\underset{R_{yy}}{} \qquad \underset{B}{}$$

As a rule of thumb, structure coefficients $\geq .30$ are treated as meaningful. Using this criterion, one would conclude that both X_1 and X_2 have meaningful loadings on the first canonical variate, but that only X_2 has a meaningful loading on the second canonical variate. On the other hand, both Y's have meaningful structure coefficients on both canonical variates. *It is, however, important to recall that the second canonical correlation was not meaningful and that I retained it solely for completeness of presentation. Normally, one would not calculate structure coefficients for canonical correlations that are considered not meaningful.*

I cannot show here how the structure coefficients are interpreted substantively because I gave no substantive meaning to the variables I used in the numerical example. Moreover, my example consists of only two variables in each set. Generally, one would use a larger number of variables in canonical analysis. Under such circumstances the variables with the larger structure coefficients on a given canonical variate are used much as factor loadings in factor analysis. That is, they provide a means of identifying the dimension on which they load. Assume, for example, that in a given canonical analysis 10 X variables have been used and only 3 of them have meaningful loadings on the first canonical variate. One would then examine these variables and attempt to name the first canonical variate in a manner similar to that done in factor analysis. If, for example, it turns out that the three X's with the high structure coefficients deal with different aspects of verbal performance, one might conclude that the first canonical variate is one that primarily reflects verbal ability. Needless to say, the interpretation is not always as obvious as in the example I just gave. As in factor analysis, one may encounter difficulties interpreting canonical variates based on the high structure coefficients associated with them. Sometimes the difficulties may be overcome by rotating the canonical variates, much as one rotates factors in factor analysis. This is a topic I cannot address here (see, for example, Cliff & Krus, 1976; Hall, 1969; Krus, Reynolds, & Krus, 1976; Reynolds & Jackosfsky, 1981). What I said about interpretation of canonical variates with high structure coefficients for the X's applies equally to the interpretation of canonical variates with high structure coefficients for the Y's.

In Chapter 20, I said that the square of a structure coefficient, or a loading, indicates the proportion of variance of the variable with which it is associated that is accounted for by the discriminant function. Structure coefficients in canonical analysis are similarly interpreted. Accordingly, the first canonical variate accounts for about 92% of the variance of X_1 ($.95974^2 \times 100$) and for about 64% ($.80074^2 \times 100$) of the variance of X_2. Similarly, the first canonical variate accounts for about 82% and 88% of the variance of Y_1 and Y_2, respectively.

The sum of the squared structure coefficients of a set of variables (i.e., X's or Y's) on a given canonical variate indicates the amount of variance of the set that is accounted for, or extracted, by the canonical variate. Dividing the amount of variance extracted by the number of variables in the set (i.e., p for the X's and q for the Y's) yields the proportion of its total variance that is extracted by the canonical variate.

Recalling that premultiplying a column vector by its transpose is the same as squaring and summing its elements (see Appendix A), the foregoing can be stated as follows:

$$PV_{x_j} = \frac{s'_{x_j} s_{x_j}}{p} \tag{21.8}$$

where PV_{x_j} is the proportion of the total variance of the X's extracted by canonical variate j; and $\mathbf{s}_{x_j}$ and $\mathbf{s}'_{x_j}$, respectively, are a column vector of structure coefficients of the X's on canonical variate j and its transpose; and p is the number of X variables. Similarly,

$$PV_{y_j} = \frac{\mathbf{s}'_{y_j}\mathbf{s}_{y_j}}{q} \tag{21.9}$$

where PV_{y_j} is the proportion of the total variance of the Y's that is extracted by canonical variate j; $\mathbf{s}_{y_j}$ and $\mathbf{s}'_{y_j}$, respectively, are a column vector of structure coefficients of the Y's on canonical variate j and its transpose; and q is the number of Y variables.

The matrix of structure coefficients for the X's (**A**) for the numerical example I analyzed above is

$$\mathbf{A} = \begin{bmatrix} .95974 & -.28194 \\ .80074 & .59586 \end{bmatrix}$$

Applying, successively, (21.8) to each column of **A**,

$$PV_{x_1} = \frac{1}{2}[.95974 \quad .80074]\begin{bmatrix} .95974 \\ .80074 \end{bmatrix} = .78114$$

Thus, about 78% of the total variance of the X's is extracted by the first canonical variate.

$$PV_{x_2} = \frac{1}{2}[-.28194 \quad .59586]\begin{bmatrix} -.28194 \\ .59586 \end{bmatrix} = .21727$$

About 22% of the total variance of the X's is extracted by the second canonical variate.

The matrix of structure coefficients for the Y's (**B**) for the numerical example I analyzed above is

$$\mathbf{B} = \begin{bmatrix} .90664 & .42170 \\ .93600 & -.35236 \end{bmatrix}$$

Applying, successively, (21.9) to each column of **B**,

$$PV_{y_1} = \frac{1}{2}[.90664 \quad .93600]\begin{bmatrix} .90664 \\ .93600 \end{bmatrix} = .84905$$

Thus, about 85% of the total variance of the Y's is extracted by the first canonical variate.

$$PV_{y_2} = \frac{1}{2}[.42170 \quad -.35236]\begin{bmatrix} .42170 \\ -.35236 \end{bmatrix} = .15099$$

About 15% of the total variance of the Y's is extracted by the second canonical variate.

Note that the sum of the proportions of variance of the X's extracted by the two canonical variates is 1.00 (.78114 + .21727), as is the sum of the proportions of variance of the Y's extracted by the two canonical variates (.84905 + .15099 = 1.00). In general, the sum of the proportions of variance of the set with the smaller number of variables that is extracted by all the canonical variates is 1.00 (or 100%). In the present example, both sets consist of two variables. Therefore, the sum of the proportions of variance extracted by the two canonical variates in each set is 1.00.

Recall that when the two sets consist of different numbers of variables, the maximum number of canonical variates obtainable is equal to the number of variables in the smaller set. Under such circumstances the maximum number of canonical variates cannot extract all of the variance of the variables in the larger set. Depending on the number of variables in each set, and on the patterns of relations among them, 100% of the variance of the variables of the smaller set may be extracted, whereas only a small fraction of the percent of the variance of the variables in the larger set may be extracted.

As I show in the next section, the PV's play an important role in a redundancy index. Before I turn to this topic I would like to stress that canonical weights and structure coefficients should be interpreted with caution, particularly when they have not been cross-validated. As in multiple regression analysis (see Chapter 8), cross-validation is of utmost importance in canonical analysis. For a very good discussion of cross-validation in canonical analysis, see Thorndike (1978), who stated, "It might be argued that cross-validation is more important for canonical analysis because there are two sets of weights, each of which will make maximum use of sample-specific covariation, rather than just one" (p. 180).

Redundancy

Using the idea of proportion of variance extracted by a canonical variate, Stewart and Love (1968) and Miller (1969) have, independently, proposed a redundancy index, which for the X variables is defined as follows:

$$Rd_{x_j} = PV_{x_j} R_{c_j}^2 \qquad (21.10)$$

where Rd_{x_j} is the redundancy of the X's given the jth canonical variate of Y; PV_{x_j} is the proportion of the total variance of the X's extracted by the jth canonical variate of the X's—see (21.8); $R_{c_j}^2$ is the square of the jth canonical correlation. Basically, the redundancy of X_j is the product of the proportion of the variance of the X's the jth canonical variate of X extracts (PV_{x_j}) by the variance that the jth canonical variate of X's shares with the jth canonical variate of Y's $(R_{c_j}^2)$. This could perhaps be clarified recalling that a canonical variate is a linear combination of variables and that R_c^2 is the squared correlation between two linear combinations: one for the X's and one for the Y's. Now, the redundancy of X_j is the proportion of the variance of the X's that is redundant with (or predicted from, or explained by) the jth linear combination of the Y's.

I hope the foregoing will become clearer through illustrative calculations. In the example I analyzed in the preceding, I found that $PV_{x_1} = .78114$ and $PV_{x_2} = .21727$. Also, $R_{c_1}^2 = .27740$ and $R_{c_2}^2 = .00490$. Applying (21.10),

$$Rd_{x_1} = (.78114)(.27740) = .21669$$

This means that about 22% of the total variance of the X's is predictable from the first canonical variate (linear combination) of the Y's. Also,

$$Rd_{x_2} = (.21727)(.00490) = .00106$$

About .1% of the total variance of the X's is predictable from the second canonical variate (linear combination) of the Y's.

The total redundancy of X, given all the linear combinations of the Y's is simply the sum of the separate redundancies; that is,

$$\overline{Rd}_x = \Sigma Rd_{x_j} \qquad (21.11)$$

where $\overline{Rd_x}$ is the total redundancy and ΣRd_{x_j} is the sum of the separate redundancies. For the present example,

$$\overline{Rd_x} = .21669 + .00106 = .21775$$

Before I show how to calculate redundancies of Y, and before I elaborate on the meaning of these indices, I believe it will be useful to examine the concept of redundancy from yet another perspective—namely, multiple regression analysis. For this purpose, I repeat the zero-order correlations between X's and Y's reported in Table 21.3:

$$r_{x_1y_1} = .45 \qquad r_{x_1y_2} = .48 \qquad r_{x_2y_1} = .40 \qquad r_{x_2y_2} = .38 \qquad r_{y_1y_2} = .70$$

Using these correlations, I will calculate two R^2's:

$$R^2_{x_1 \cdot y_1 y_2} = \frac{(.45)^2 + (.48)^2 - 2(.45)(.48)(.70)}{1 - (.70)^2} = .25588$$

The proportion of variance of X_1 that is predictable from all the variables in the other set (Y_1 and Y_2 in the present case) is .25588.

$$R^2_{x_2 \cdot y_1 y_2} = \frac{(.40)^2 + (.38)^2 - 2(.40)(.38)(.70)}{1 - (.70)^2} = .17961$$

The proportion of variance of X_2 that is predictable from all the variables in the other set (the Y's) is .17961.

The average of the R^2's I calculated in the preceding is:

$$\frac{.25588 + .17961}{2} = .21775$$

Notice that this is the same as the the $\overline{Rd_x}$ I calculated earlier. The total redundancy of X given Y, then, is equal to the average of the squared multiple correlations of each of the X's with all the Y's. In other words, redundancy "is synonymous with average predictability" (Cramer & Nicewander, 1979, p. 43).

I turn now to a definition and calculation of redundancies of Y given the X's. Analogous to Rd_{x_j}

$$Rd_{y_j} = PV_{y_j} R^2_{c_j} \tag{21.12}$$

where Rd_{y_j} is the redundancy of the Y's given the jth canonical variate of X; PV_{y_j} is the proportion of the total variance of the Y's extracted by the jth canonical variate of the Y's—see (21.9); and $R^2_{c_j}$ is the square of the jth canonical correlation.

Using the following values, which I calculated earlier, I will calculate the redundancies of Y.

$$PV_{y_1} = .84905 \qquad PV_{y_2} = .15099 \qquad R^2_{c_1} = .27740 \qquad R^2_{c_2} = .00490$$

Applying (21.12),

$$Rd_{y_1} = (.84905)(.27740) = .23553$$

About 24% of the total variance of the Y's is redundant with (or predictable from) the first linear combination (canonical variate) of the X's. Also,

$$Rd_{y_2} = (.15099)(.00490) = .00074$$

About .07% of the total variance of the Y's is redundant with the second canonical variate of the X's. Now,

$$\overline{Rd_y} = \Sigma Rd_{y_j} \tag{21.13}$$

where $\overline{Rd_y}$ is the total redundancy of Y and ΣRd_{y_j} is the sum of the separate redundancies. For the present example,

$$\overline{Rd_y} = (.23553) + (.00074) = .23627$$

The total redundancy of Y given the X's is about 24%. In a manner analogous to that I showed for the total redundancy of X, it can be shown that the total redundancy of Y is equal to the average of the squared multiple correlations of each of the Y's with all the variables in the other set (the two X's, in the present example).

Note carefully that redundancy is an asymmetric index; that is, $Rd_{y_j} \neq Rd_{x_j}$ or $\overline{Rd_y} \neq \overline{Rd_x}$. One can see that this is so by examining the formulas for the calculation of Rd_{x_j} and Rd_{y_j}—(21.10) and (21.12), respectively. Both equations contain a common term (i.e., $R_{c_j}^2$). But each uses the proportion of variance extracted (PV) by its canonical variate. These PV's are not necessarily equal to each other.

Speaking of the total redundancy, Stewart and Love (1968) pointed out that it should be viewed "as a summary index. In general it is not to be viewed as an analytic tool" (p. 162). This does not diminish its utility in, among other things, serving as a safeguard against wandering into a world of fantasy. An elaboration of the preceding statement will, I hope, help explain the substantive meaning of redundancy and shed further light on R_c^2.

When I introduced R_c^2, I stressed that it is an estimate of the shared variance of two linear combinations of variables; *not* of the variance of the variables themselves. From my discussion of redundancy it should be clear that even when R_c^2 is high, the redundancy of Y, X, or both may be very low. This may best be clarified by a numerical example. Assume that the first canonical correlation between two sets of variables, X and Y, is relatively high, say .80. Therefore, the shared variance of the first pair of linear combinations of the X's and the Y's is .64. Such a value of proportions of variance shared or accounted for would be considered meaningful, even very impressive, in many research areas.

Assume now that PV_{y_1} (proportion of variance extracted by the first linear combination of the Y's) is .10, and that $PV_{x_1} = .07$. Accordingly, $Rd_{y_1} = .064$ (.64 × .10), and $Rd_{x_1} = .045$ (.64 × .07). The predictable variance of the Y's from the linear combination of the X's is about 6%, and the predictable variance of the X's from the linear combinations of the Y's is about 4%. Without a substantive example, it is nevertheless safe to say that in many areas of social and behavioral research results as the preceding would be considered not impressive, perhaps not meaningful. Be that as it may, my point is that sole reliance on R_c^2 poses a real threat of wandering into a world of fantasy in which impressive figures that may have little to do with the variability of the variables themselves are cherished and heralded as meaningful scientific findings. I conclude with several remarks about the uses of the redundancy index.[5]

One, redundancy indices would generally be calculated only for meaningful or statistically significant canonical variates.

Two, although in my numerical examples redundancies of X and Y were quite similar to each other, this is not necessarily the case. Redundancies for the two sets of variables may be radically different from each other.

Three, depending on the research design, redundancies may be meaningfully calculated for only one of the two sets of variables. For instance, when the X's are treated as predictors and the

---

[5]Good discussions and numerical examples of the use of the redundancy index are given in Cooley and Lohnes (1971, 1976) and in Stewart and Love (1968).

Y's are treated as criteria, it is meaningful to calculate redundancies only for the latter because the interest is in determining the proportion of variance of the criteria that is predictable from the predictors—not vice versa. In experimental research, one would, similarly, calculate redundancies for only the dependent variables.

Four, in my discussions of the interpretation of the redundancy index I used terms such as *variance redundant with, predictable from,* or *explained by* interchangeably. Needless to say, these are not equivalent terms. Because I did not use substantive examples, it was not possible to select the most appropriate term. In actual applications, the choice should generally be clear. Thus, for example, the term *variance predictable from* is appropriate in predictive research, whereas the stronger term *variance explained by* is more appropriate in explanatory research.[6]

Finally, as Cramer and Nicewander (1979) pointed out, the redundancy index is not a measure of multivariate association. After discussing several such measures, Cramer and Nicewander raised the question of whether a single measure can provide satisfactory information about the relation between two sets of variables, and concluded, "In our view the answer to this question generally is, 'No.'" (p. 53)[7]

Tests of Significance

As I discuss later in this chapter, several different approaches have been proposed for statistical tests of significance in multivariate analysis. Here, I present Bartlett's (1947) test of Wilks' Λ (lambda), which is the most widely used test of significance in canonical analysis.

In Chapter 20, I presented Wilks' Λ as a ratio of the determinants of two matrices (the Within-Groups SSCP to the Total SSCP)—see (20.11) and the discussion related to it. Instead of presenting an analogous expression of Λ in the context of canonical analysis (see Tatsuoka, 1988, p. 247), I will show how to calculate Λ by using R_c^2.

$$\Lambda = (1 - R_{c_1}^2)(1 - R_{c_2}^2) \ldots (1 - R_{c_j}^2) \tag{21.14}$$

where Λ = Wilks' lambda, and $R_{c_1}^2$ = the square of the first canonical correlation, $R_{c_2}^2$ = the square of the second canonical correlation, and so on up to the square of the *j*th canonical correlation.

In the numerical example I analyzed earlier I found $R_{c_1}^2 = .27740$ and $R_{c_2}^2 = .00490$. Applying (21.14),

$$\Lambda = (1 - .27740)(1 - .00490) = .71906$$

Bartlett (1947) proposed the following test of significance of Λ:

$$\chi^2 = -[N - 1 - .5(p + q + 1)]\log_e \Lambda \tag{21.15}$$

where N = number of subjects; p = number of variables on the left; q = number of variables on the right; $\log_e$ = natural logarithm. The degrees of freedom associated with this χ^2 are pq. For the present example, $\log_e .71906 = -.32981; p = q = 2; N = 300$ (see Table 21.3). Applying (21.15),

$$\chi^2 = -[300 - 1 - .5 (2 + 2 + 1)](-.32981)$$

$$= -(299 - 2.5)(-.32981) = (-296.5)(-.32981) = 97.79$$

with $pq = 4$ degrees of freedom, $p < .001$.

---

[6]See earlier chapters (particularly Chapters 8–10) for discussions of differences between predictive and explanatory research.

[7]For a discussion of measures of association in the context of canonical analysis, see Darlington et al. (1973).

The test I just performed refers to all the R_c^2's; that is, it is an overall test of the null hypothesis that all the R_c^2's are equal to zero. In the present example it refers to the two R_c^2's. It is, however, desirable to determine which R_c^2's obtainable from a given set of data are statistically significant. This is accomplished by applying (21.15) sequentially as follows.

First, the overall Λ is tested (as in the preceding). If the null hypothesis is rejected, one can conclude that at least the first R_c^2 is statistically significant, and a Λ' based on the remaining R_c^2's is tested for significance, using (21.15). Λ' is calculated as was Λ—that is, using (21.14)—except that $R_{c_1}^2$ is removed from the equation. If Λ' is statistically significant, one can conclude that the first two R_c^2's are statistically significant. Equation (21.14) is then applied to calculate Λ'' based on the remaining R_c^2's. Λ'' is then tested for significance, using (21.15). The procedure is continued until a given Λ is found to be statistically not significant at a prespecified α, at which point it is concluded that the R_c^2's preceding this step are statistically significant, whereas the remaining ones are not. The df for the χ^2 test of Λ' (i.e., after removing the first R_c^2) are $(p-1)(q-1)$; for the χ^2 test of Λ'' (after removing the first two R_c^2's) are $(p-2)(q-2)$, and so on.[8]

I now apply this procedure to the numerical example under consideration. Earlier, I found that Λ is statistically significant. Therefore I remove $R_{c_1}^2$ and use (21.14) to calculate Λ'. Recalling that $R_{c_2}^2 = .00490$,

$$\Lambda' = (1 - .00490) = .9951$$

$$\log_e .9951 = -.00491$$

applying (21.15),

$$\chi^2 = -[300 - 1 - .5(2 + 2 + 1)](-.00491)$$

$$= (-296.5)(-.00491) = 1.46$$

with 1 df, $(p-1)(q-1)$, $p > .05$.

I conclude that $R_{c_2}^2$ is statistically not significant. In the present example, there are only two R_c^2's. Had there been more than two, and had Λ' been statistically not significant, I would have concluded that all but the first R_c^2 are statistically not significant.

Having retained the statistically significant R_c^2's, one would proceed and interpret only the statistics (e.g., canonical weights, structure coefficients) that are associated with them. *For illustrative purposes, I calculated earlier canonical weights and structure coefficients for both functions, though the second was clearly not meaningful.* Recall that I suggested earlier that the main criterion for retaining R_c^2 be meaningfulness. Also, I pointed out that some authors suggested that $R_c^2 < .10$ be treated as not meaningful.

Finally, it is convenient to give a summary of the results in tabular form. Table 21.4 summarizes the numerical example I analyzed in this section. Again, for completeness of presentation, I give results associated with both R_c^2's, though the second one is not meaningful.

COMPUTER PROGRAMS

Of the four packages I am using in this book, BMDP and SAS have specific procedures for canonical analysis, which I will use in this section to analyze the numerical example in Table 21.3. As I analyzed this example by hand and commented on the results in detail, my comments

---

[8]Harris (1985, pp. 172–173) questioned the validity of the testing sequence I outlined. I cannot deal here with the issues Harris raised.

Table 21.4   Summary of Canonical Analysis for the Data in Table 21.3

		Root 1		Root 2			Root 1		Root 2	
	Variables	β	s	β	s	Variables	β	s	β	s
	X_1	.75	.96	−1.00	−.28	Y_1	.49	.91	1.31	.42
	X_2	.35	.80	1.20	.60	Y_2	.59	.94	−1.27	−.35
PV:			.78		.22			.85		.15
Rd:			.22		.00			.24		.00
$\overline{Rd}$:				.22					.24	
$R^2_{c_1}$ = .2774		$R^2_{c_2}$ = .0049								

NOTE: β = standardized coefficient; s = structure coefficient; PV = proportion of variance extracted; Rd = redundancy; $\overline{Rd}$ = total redundancy.

on the outputs will be brief, intended primarily to refer you to relevant sections in which I discussed a given topic. Following my practice in earlier chapters, I will reproduce excerpts of the outputs, while retaining the basic layout so that you may compare your output with the excerpts I reproduce. To become more familiar with the output and nomenclature of a given program, I suggest that you study it in conjunction with my discussion of the same results I obtained earlier through hand calculations.

BMDP

Input

```
/PROBLEM TITLE IS 'TABLE 21.3.   CANONICAL ANALYSIS WITH 6M'.
/INPUT VARIABLES ARE 4.   TYPE=CORR.   SHAPE=LOWER.
   FORMAT IS '(4F4.2)'.   CASES ARE 300.
/VARIABLE NAMES ARE X1, X2, Y1, Y2.
/CANONICAL FIRST ARE X1, X2.   SECOND ARE Y1, Y2.
/PRINT MATRICES=LOAD, COEF.
/END
 100
  60 100
  45   40 100
  48   38   70 100
```

Commentary

For a general introduction to BMDP, see Chapter 4. As indicated in the TITLE, I am using program 6M (Dixon, 1992, Vol. 2., pp. 921–932; page references given in the following discussions relate to this volume).

    TYPE = CORR. This indicates that a correlation matrix is to be read as input.

    SHAPE = LOWER. Reading a lower triangular correlation matrix.

    FORMAT. "The format should describe the longest row, and each row should begin a new record" (p. 929). Thus the first row consists of one element (the diagonal, which is equal to 1.00). The second row consists of two elements, and so forth.

CANONICAL. FIRST refers to the first set of variables, or variables on the left. SECOND refers to the second set of variables, or variables on the right.

PRINT. By default, correlations and loadings are printed. "When any matrix is specified, only those matrices specified are printed" (p. 930). I requested loadings and coefficients (see the following output).

Output

EIGENVALUE	CANONICAL CORRELATION	NUMBER OF EIGENVALUES	BARTLETT'S TEST FOR REMAINING EIGENVALUES		
			CHI-SQUARE	D.F.	TAIL PROB.
			97.79	4	0.0000
0.27742	0.52671	1	1.45	1	0.2289
0.00487	0.06979				

Commentary

See "Tests of Significance," where I calculated the same values and explained that the first CHI-SQUARE refers to the test of all (two in the present example) the canonical correlations, whereas the second refers to the second canonical correlation.

Output

COEFFICIENTS FOR CANONICAL VARIABLES FOR FIRST SET OF VARIABLES

		CNVRF1	CNVRF2
		1	2
X1	1	0.748834	−1.000873
X2	2	0.351398	1.199591

COEFFICIENTS FOR CANONICAL VARIABLES FOR SECOND SET OF VARIABLES

		CNVRS1	CNVRS2
		1	2
Y1	3	0.493090	1.310590
Y2	4	0.590785	−1.269550

Commentary

See "Canonical Weights," where I identified matrices similar to the preceding as **A** and **B**, respectively.

Output

CANONICAL VARIABLE LOADINGS

(CORRELATIONS OF CANONICAL VARIABLES WITH ORIGINAL VARIABLES)
FOR FIRST SET OF VARIABLES

		CNVRF1 1	CNVRF2 2
X1	1	0.960	−0.281
X2	2	0.801	0.599

CANONICAL VARIABLE LOADINGS

(CORRELATIONS OF CANONICAL VARIABLES WITH ORIGINAL VARIABLES)
FOR SECOND SET OF VARIABLES

		CNVRS1 1	CNVRS2 2
Y1	3	0.907	0.422
Y2	4	0.936	−0.352

Commentary

The preceding are the structure coefficients. Compare with my calculations of $\mathbf{S}_x$ and $\mathbf{S}_y$, respectively.

Output

CANON. VAR.	AVERAGE SQUARED LOADING FOR EACH CANONICAL VARIABLE (1ST SET)	AV. SQ. LOADING TIMES SQUARED CANON. CORREL. (1ST SET)	AVERAGE SQUARED LOADING FOR EACH CANONICAL VARIABLE (2ND SET)	AV. SQ. LOADING TIMES SQUARED CANON. CORREL. (2ND SET)	SQUARED CANON. CORREL.
1	0.78105	0.21668	0.84900	0.23553	0.27742
2	0.21895	0.00107	0.15100	0.00074	0.00487

THE AVERAGE SQUARED LOADING MULTIPLIED BY THE SQUARED CANONICAL
CORRELATION IS THE AVERAGE SQUARED CORRELATION OF A
VARIABLE IN ONE SET WITH THE CANONICAL VARIABLE FROM
THE OTHER SET.   IT IS SOMETIMES CALLED A REDUNDANCY INDEX.

Commentary

I retained BMDP's comment so that you may compare it with my explanations of the same results
(within rounding). See my calculations of *PV*'s (under "Structure Coefficients" and "Redundancy").

SAS

Input

TITLE 'TABLE 21.3.   CANONICAL CORRELATION';
DATA T213(TYPE=CORR);
    INPUT _TYPE_ $ _NAME_ $ X1 X2 Y1 Y2;
    CARDS;

N	.	300	300	300	300
CORR	X1	1.00	.60	.45	.48
CORR	X2	.60	1.00	.40	.38
CORR	Y1	.45	.40	1.00	.70
CORR	Y2	.48	.38	.70	1.00

;
PROC PRINT;
PROC CANCORR ALL;
  VAR X1 X2;
  WITH Y1 Y2;
RUN;

Commentary

For an introduction to SAS, see Chapter 4. In Chapter 7 (see the SAS analysis of Table 7.3), I explained the input of a correlation matrix. PROC PRINT will result in the printing of the correlation matrix.

   For a description of CANCORR, see SAS Institute Inc. (1990a, Vol. 1, Chapter 15). Although
I call for *all* the statistics, I will reproduce only some.

   VAR refer to the variables on the left. WITH refers to variables on the right.

Output

   Canonical Correlation Analysis

	Canonical Correlation	Squared Canonical Correlation
1	0.526708	0.277421
2	0.069787	0.004870

Test of H0: The canonical correlations in the
current row and all that follow are zero

	Likelihood Ratio	Approx F	Num DF	Den DF	Pr > F
1	0.71905944	26.5337	4	592	0.0001
2	0.99512978	1.4535	1	297	0.2289

Commentary

The likelihood ratios in the preceding are the lambdas (Λ) I reported earlier—see (21.14) and the discussion related to it. From the caption you can see that the first test refers to all the canonical correlations, whereas the second test refers to the second canonical correlation. I tested the same values, using Bartlett's test—see (21.15) and the discussion related to it. Later, I discuss the type of test reported here by SAS.

Output

Canonical Correlation Analysis

Raw Canonical Coefficients for the 'VAR' Variables

	V1	V2
X1	0.7488340317	−1.000873415
X2	0.3513983131	1.1995912744

Raw Canonical Coefficients for the 'WITH' Variables

	W1	W2
Y1	0.4930902005	1.3105900838
Y2	0.5907853879	−1.269549896

Commentary

See "Canonical Weights," where I identified matrices similar to the preceding as **A** and **B**, respectively.

Output

Canonical Structure

Correlations Between the 'VAR' Variables and Their Canonical Variables

	V1	V2
X1	0.9597	−0.2811
X2	0.8007	0.5991

Correlations Between the 'WITH' Variables and Their Canonical Variables

	W1	W2
Y1	0.9066	0.4219
Y2	0.9359	−0.3521

Commentary

The preceding are the structure coefficients. VAR refers to the variables on the left, and WITH refers to the variables on the right. Compare with my calculations of S_x and S_y, respectively. Compare also with BMDP output.

Output

Canonical Redundancy Analysis
Raw Variance of the 'VAR' Variables
Explained by

	Their Own Canonical Variables			The Opposite Canonical Variables	
	Proportion	Cumulative Proportion	Canonical R-Squared	Proportion	Cumulative Proportion
1	0.7810	0.7810	0.2774	0.2167	0.2167
2	0.2190	1.0000	0.0049	0.0011	0.2177

Raw Variance of the 'WITH' Variables
Explained by

	Their Own Canonical Variables			The Opposite Canonical Variables	
	Proportion	Cumulative Proportion	Canonical R-Squared	Proportion	Cumulative Proportion
1	0.8490	0.8490	0.2774	0.2355	0.2355
2	0.1510	1.0000	0.0049	0.0007	0.2363

Commentary

In the preceding, the values reported under "Their Own" are what I reported under *PV,* whereas those reported under "The Opposite" are the redundancy coefficients. The last value under "Cumulative Proportion" is the total redundancy—see (21.11) and (21.13) and the calculations related to them.

CANONICAL ANALYSIS WITH A CATEGORICAL INDEPENDENT VARIABLE

Thus far, I analyzed and discussed an example in which both sets of variables are continuous. I turn now to a design in which the dependent variables are continuous, and the independent variable is categorical and represented by coded vectors. Such designs are prevalent in experimental and nonexperimental research. In the former, the categorical variable consists of more than two treatments (e.g., teaching methods, modes of communication, drugs), whereas in the latter, it consists of more than two preexisting groups (e.g., national, racial, religious, political).[9]

As in univariate analysis, multivariate analysis is carried out in the same manner, irrespective of whether the data are from experimental or nonexperimental research. Of course, interpretation of the results is greatly determined by the type of research setting in which they were obtained.[10]

Conventionally, the type of design I described is analyzed either through MANOVA or DA. Some researchers begin with MANOVA and apply DA when the results of the former are statistically significant.

In this section, I show that designs in which the dependent variables, or criteria, are continuous, and the independent variable, or predictor, is categorical are a special case of CA. For convenience, I will use a numerical example consisting of two dependent variables and a categorical variable consisting of three categories. What I say about application of CA and the interpretation of results, though, applies to designs with any number of continuous variables and any number of categories of one or more categorical variables. Later, I analyze the same example through MANOVA and DA.

A Numerical Example

Assume that a researcher wishes to study how Conservatives (A_1), Republicans (A_2), and Democrats (A_3) differ in their expectations regarding government spending on social welfare programs (Y_1) and on defense (Y_2). Table 21.5 illustrates data for such a design.

Table 21.5   Illustrative Data for Three Groups and Two Dependent Variables

	A_1		A_2		A_3	
	Y_1	Y_2	Y_1	Y_2	Y_1	Y_2
	3	7	4	5	5	5
	4	7	4	6	6	5
	5	8	5	7	6	6
	5	9	6	7	7	7
	6	10	6	8	7	8
Σ:	23	41	25	33	31	31
$\bar{Y}$:	4.6	8.2	5.0	6.6	6.2	6.2

---

[9]When there are only two treatments, or two groups, the analysis proceeds as in Chapter 20.

[10]My discussions of this issue in earlier chapters are equally applicable here.

Before proceeding with the analysis, I will make several points about this example. One, though admittedly contrived, I will use it to illustrate the interpretation of results of the kind of analysis I present in this section. Two, to encourage you to think of other variables from your own areas of interest, I will use the terms groups (A_1, A_2, and A_3) and variables (Y_1 and Y_2) throughout the analyses. Only when I interpret results will I refer to the substantive variables I mentioned previously. In general, you may think of A_1, A_2, and A_3 as representing any three pre-existing groups or any three treatments of your choice. Similarly, you may view Y_1 and Y_2 as any two criteria or dependent variables. Three, although I will do the analysis by computer, I use only two dependent variables and a very small number of subjects to encourage you to replicate the analysis through hand calculations. I believe you will benefit from such an exercise. When necessary, use my hand calculations in the preceding section as a guide.

I turn now to CA of the data in Table 21.5. As in designs consisting of one dependent variable and a categorical independent variable (see Chapter 11), I placed the scores of all the subjects on the two dependent variables in two vectors, Y_1 and Y_2. I coded the categorical variable in the usual manner. That is, I created two coded vectors to represent the three groups or treatments. For illustrative purposes, I used dummy coding. I display the data in Table 21.5 in this format in Table 21.6.

The procedure I outlined would be followed, whatever the number of the dependent variables or categories of the independent variable. For example, if the design consisted of eight dependent variables, Y's, and five treatments, X's, then one would generate eight Y vectors of dependent variables for all the subjects and four coded vectors to represent the five categories of the independent variable.

Having generated the vectors as in Table 21.6, CA is carried out in the same manner as I did earlier in the chapter, when the design consisted of two sets of continuous variables. As I have stated, I will carry out the calculations by computer. As with the earlier example, I will use both BMDP and SAS, beginning with the former.

Table 21.6 Data from Table 21.5 Displayed for Canonical Analysis

	X_1	X_2	Y_1	Y_2
	1	0	3	7
	1	0	4	7
A_1	1	0	5	8
	1	0	5	9
	1	0	6	10
	0	1	4	5
	0	1	4	6
A_2	0	1	5	7
	0	1	6	7
	0	1	6	8
	0	0	5	5
	0	0	6	5
A_3	0	0	6	6
	0	0	7	7
	0	0	7	8

NOTE: X_1 and X_2 are dummy coded vectors for groups; Y_1 and Y_2 are dependent variables.

BMDP

Input

```
/PROBLEM TITLE IS 'TABLE 21.6.   CANONICAL ANALYSIS WITH 6M'.
/INPUT VARIABLES ARE 4.   FORMAT IS FREE.
/VARIABLE NAMES ARE X1, X2, Y1, Y2.
/CANONICAL FIRST ARE X1, X2.   SECOND ARE Y1, Y2.
/PRINT MATRICES=LOAD, COEF.
/END
1 0 3 7      [first two subjects in group 1]
1 0 4 7

.  .  .  .
0 1 4 5      [first two subjects in group 2]
0 1 4 6

.  .  .  .
0 0 5 5      [first two subjects in group 3]
0 0 6 5

.  .  .  .
```

Commentary

This input is very similar to the one I used earlier to analyze the data in Table 21.3. The only difference between the two inputs is that in the former I entered a correlation matrix, whereas here I enter raw data in free format. Of course, I could have generated the coded vectors through the computer instead of reading them as input (see Chapter 11). With larger samples, which would normally be used, this would be preferable not only as a labor-saving device, but also because it is less prone to input errors. Because my example is very small, I felt it would be helpful to display the coded vectors and enter them as input.

Output

EIGENVALUE	CANONICAL CORRELATION	NUMBER OF EIGENVALUES	BARTLETT'S TEST FOR REMAINING EIGENVALUES		
			CHI-SQUARE	D.F.	TAIL PROB.
			26.88	4	0.0000
0.89794	0.94760	1	0.64	1	0.4241
0.05404	0.23246				

Commentary

I described the preceding test under "Tests of Significance," earlier in this chapter—see (21.14) and (21.15) and the discussions related to them. Notice that the second canonical correlation is statistically not significant at conventional alpha levels (e.g., .05). Earlier I pointed out that it has been suggested that $R_c^2 < .10$ be deemed not meaningful. On these grounds, the second canonical correlation would be disregarded even if it were statistically significant. As the interest in the present example is in the statistics associated with the dependent variables, and in the interest of space, I will reproduce only results associated with the *Y*'s. Moreover, in light of the results of the tests of significance, I will reproduce statistics for only the first canonical variate.

Output

COEFFICIENTS FOR CANONICAL VARIABLES FOR SECOND SET OF VARIABLES

		CNVRS1			(THESE ARE THE COEFFICIENTS FOR THE STANDARDIZED VARIABLES)		CNVRS1
		1					1
Y1	3	−0.700551			Y1	3	−0.815
Y2	4	0.560308			Y2	4	0.820

Commentary

In the interest of space, I moved the standardized coefficients alongside the raw coefficients (those on the left). Based on the standardized coefficients, it appears that both variables contribute equally to the separation among the three groups. The signs of these coefficients indicate that in forming the linear combination of the two variables, Y_1 is weighted negatively and Y_2 is weighted positively. Or, referring to the substantive example I gave in the beginning of this section, expectations regarding government spending on social welfare programs are weighted negatively, whereas expectations regarding defense spending are weighted positively.

Output

CANONICAL VARIABLE LOADINGS

(CORRELATIONS OF CANONICAL VARIABLES WITH ORIGINAL VARIABLES)
FOR SECOND SET OF VARIABLES

		CNVRS1
		1
Y1	3	−0.608
Y2	4	0.615

Commentary

The preceding are structure coefficients for the Y's on the first canonical variate—see (21.7) and the discussion related to it. Thus, the correlation between Y_1 and the scores on the first canonical variate is $-.61$, and that of Y_2 with the scores on the first canonical variate is $.62$. Based on the criterion that a structure coefficient of $\geq .3$ be considered meaningful, both dependent variables have equally meaningful loadings on the first canonical variate.

I said earlier that structure coefficients are interpreted as loadings in factor analysis. When, in factor analysis, some variables have high positive loadings on a factor and other variables have high negative loadings on it, the factor is said to be bipolar. In the present example, the first canonical variate is bipolar. When I introduced this numerical example, I said that Y_1 is expectations regarding government spending on social welfare programs, and Y_2 is expectations regarding defense spending. The structure coefficients show that the three groups are separated on a single dimension that may be named social welfare versus defense. Groups that have high expectations regarding defense spending tend to have lower expectations regarding spending on social welfare programs, and vice versa.

Generally, more than two dependent variables are used. Under such circumstances, the variables with high structure coefficients on a given canonical variate serve to identify it. Thus, when more than one canonical correlation is meaningful, it is possible to study the number and the nature of the dimensions that separate the groups.

Output

CANON. VAR.	AVERAGE SQUARED LOADING FOR EACH CANONICAL VARIABLE (2ND SET)	AV. SQ. LOADING TIMES SQUARED CANON. CORREL. (2ND SET)	SQUARED CANON. CORREL.
1	0.37413	0.33595	0.89794

Commentary

Again, I reproduced only the values associated with the dependent variables (Y's). The value reported in the first column shows that about 37% of the total variance of the Y's is extracted by the first canonical variate—see (21.9) and the discussion related to it. The value in the second column shows that about 34% of the total variance of the Y's is explained by the first linear combination of the X's—see "Redundancy" and (21.12), earlier in this chapter. Recalling that in the present example the Y's are the dependent variables and the X's represent three groups, or three treatments, one can conclude that the differences among the groups explain about 34% of the total variance of the dependent variables. Referring to the substantive example I gave earlier, this means that about 34% of the variability in expectations regarding government spending is due to the differences among Conservatives, Republicans, and Democrats.

SAS

Input

TITLE 'TABLE 21.6. CANONICAL CORRELATION';
DATA T216;
  INPUT X1 X2 Y1 Y2;
  CARDS;
1 0 3 7   *[first two subjects in group 1]*
1 0 4 7
. . . .
0 1 4 5   *[first two subjects in group 2]*
0 1 4 6
. . . .
0 0 5 5   *[first two subjects in group 3]*
0 0 6 5
. . . .
;
PROC CANCORR ALL;
  VAR X1 X2;
  WITH Y1 Y2;
RUN;

Commentary

The only difference between this input and the one I gave earlier for the analysis of Table 21.3 is that here I am reading in raw data, whereas in the earlier run I read in a correlation matrix. If necessary, refer to my comments on the analysis of Table 21.3 for an explanation of the input. As I explained in my comment on the BMDP input for the analysis of Table 21.6, because my example is very small I include the dummy vectors as part of the input instead of generating them by the computer program.

Output

Canonical Correlation Analysis

	Canonical Correlation	Squared Canonical Correlation
1	0.947599	0.897944
2	0.232456	0.054036

	Likelihood Ratio	Approx F	Num DF	Den DF	Pr > F
1	0.09654135	12.2013	4	22	0.0001
2	0.94596400	0.6855	1	12	0.4239

Commentary

As I stated in my commentary on SAS output for the analysis of Table 21.3, I explain the preceding type of test later in this chapter. In any case, the conclusions from these tests are the same as from Bartlett's test reported in BMDP, namely, only the first canonical correlation is statistically significant.

Output

Raw Canonical Coefficients for the 'WITH' Variables		Standardized Canonical Coefficients for the 'WITH' Variables	
	W1		W1
Y1	−0.700551114	Y1	−0.8147
Y2	0.560307754	Y2	0.8202

Correlations Between the 'WITH' Variables
and Their Canonical Variables

	W1
Y1	−0.6082
Y2	0.6151

Canonical Redundancy Analysis
Standardized Variance of the 'WITH' Variables
Explained by

	Their Own Canonical Variables			The Opposite Canonical Variables	
	Proportion	Cumulative Proportion	Canonical R-Squared	Proportion	Cumulative Proportion
1	0.3741	0.3741	0.8979	0.3359	0.3359

Commentary

As I explained in the commentary on BMDP output for the same analysis (see the preceding), I reproduce only the values for the dependent variables for the first canonical variate. Except for minor differences in layout and nomenclature, the results are identical to those of the BMDP run. If necessary, study these results in conjunction with the BMDP output and my commentaries on it.

MULTIVARIATE ANALYSIS OF VARIANCE (MANOVA)

MANOVA is an extension of univariate analysis of variance designed to test simultaneously differences among groups on multiple dependent variables. I introduce MANOVA in the context of an analysis of the data in Table 21.5, which I analyzed in the preceding section via CA. In this section, I carry out the analysis by hand, in the hope of thereby helping you better understand elements of MANOVA. (Later in this chapter, I will use computer programs to analyze the same data.) In the course of the presentation, I will compare results from MANOVA with those I obtained earlier via CA. For convenience, I repeat the data in Table 21.5 in Table 21.7.

Table 21.7   Illustrative Data for Three Groups and Two Dependent Variables

	A_1		A_2		A_3	
	Y_1	Y_2	Y_1	Y_2	Y_1	Y_2
	3	7	4	5	5	5
	4	7	4	6	6	5
	5	8	5	7	6	6
	5	9	6	7	7	7
	6	10	6	8	7	8
Σ:	23	41	25	33	31	31
$\bar{Y}$:	4.6	8.2	5.0	6.6	6.2	6.2

SSCP

Following procedures I explained in Chapter 20, I calculated the following sums of squares and cross products (SCCP) matrices: **B** (between groups), **W** (pooled within groups), and **T** (total).

$$\begin{bmatrix} 6.93333 & -7.20000 \\ -7.20000 & 11.20000 \end{bmatrix} \quad \begin{bmatrix} 12.00 & 13.20 \\ 13.20 & 18.80 \end{bmatrix} \quad \begin{bmatrix} 18.93333 & 6.00000 \\ 6.00000 & 30.00000 \end{bmatrix}$$
$$\mathbf{B} \qquad\qquad\qquad \mathbf{W} \qquad\qquad\qquad \mathbf{T}$$

If necessary, refer to SSCP in Chapter 20 for an explanation on how to calculate such matrices.

Wilks' Lambda

In Chapter 20, I showed that Wilks' lambda (Λ) can be calculated as follows:

$$\Lambda = \frac{|\mathbf{W}|}{|\mathbf{T}|} \tag{21.16}$$

where $|\mathbf{W}|$ = determinant of the pooled within-groups SSCP; and $|\mathbf{T}|$ = determinant of the total SSCP. I now calculate these determinants.

$$|\mathbf{W}| = \begin{vmatrix} 12.00 & 13.20 \\ 13.20 & 18.80 \end{vmatrix} = (12.00)(18.00) - (13.20)^2 = 51.36$$

$$|\mathbf{T}| = \begin{vmatrix} 18.93333 & 6.00000 \\ 6.00000 & 30.00000 \end{vmatrix} = (18.93333)(30.00000) - (6.00000)^2 = 531.9999$$

Applying (21.16),

$$\Lambda = \frac{51.36}{531.9999} = .09654$$

I obtained the same value of Λ when I analyzed these data via CA in the preceding section.

Tests of Significance

I could, of course, use now Bartlett's test of Λ. But I have already done this in the preceding section ($\chi^2 = 26.88$, with 4 df). Instead, I will present an approach for testing Λ proposed by Rao (1952, pp. 258–264).

$$F = \frac{1 - \Lambda^{1/s}}{\Lambda^{1/s}} \left[\frac{ms - v}{t(k-1)} \right] \tag{21.17}$$

where t = number of dependent variables; and k = number of treatments or groups;

$$m = \frac{2N - t - k - 2}{2}$$

$$s = \sqrt{\frac{t^2(k-1)^2 - 4}{t^2 + (k-1)^2 - 5}}$$

$$v = \frac{t(k-1) - 2}{2}$$

N in this definition of m is the total number of subjects.

The F ratio has $t(k-1)$ and $ms - v$ degrees of freedom for the numerator and the denominator, respectively.

For the present example, $N = 15$, $t = 2$, and $k = 3$. Therefore,

$$m = \frac{(2)(15) - 2 - 3 - 2}{2} = 11.5$$

$$s = \sqrt{\frac{(2)^2(3-1)^2 - 4}{(2)^2 + (3-1)^2 - 5}} = \sqrt{\frac{12}{3}} = 2$$

$$v = \frac{(2)(3-1) - 2}{2} = 1$$

Applying (21.17),

$$F = \frac{1 - .09654^{1/2}}{.09654^{1/2}} \left[\frac{(11.5)(2) - 1}{2(3-1)} \right] = \frac{1 - \sqrt{.09654}}{\sqrt{.09654}} (5.50) = 12.20$$

with 4 $[t(k-1)]$ and 22 $(ms - v)$ degrees of freedom, $p < .001$. The differences among the three groups on the two dependent variables, when these are analyzed simultaneously, are statistically significant (see the following for different conclusions, when I subject these data to univariate analyses). For the substantive example I presented earlier, this means that Conservatives, Republicans, and Democrats differ significantly in their expectations regarding government spending. Had A_1, A_2, and A_3 been treatments, one would have concluded that they have differential effects on the dependent variables.

Table 21.8   Exact F Tests of Λ for Special Cases

k (Groups)	t (Variables)	F	Degrees of Freedom (v_1, v_2)
Any number	2	$\dfrac{1-\sqrt{\Lambda}}{\sqrt{\Lambda}}\left[\dfrac{N-k-1}{k-1}\right]$	$2(k-1),\ 2(N-k-1)$
2	Any number	$\dfrac{1-\Lambda}{\Lambda}\left[\dfrac{N-t-1}{t}\right]$	$t,\ N-t-1$
3	Any number	$\dfrac{1-\sqrt{\Lambda}}{\sqrt{\Lambda}}\left[\dfrac{N-t-2}{t}\right]$	$2t,\ 2(N-t-2)$

NOTE: v_1 = degrees of freedom for numerator; v_2 = degrees of freedom for denominator.

Generally, F of (21.17) is approximately distributed, except for some special cases when it is exact. The special cases are given in Table 21.8, from which you may note that (21.17) is greatly simplified for them. Also, the numerical example under consideration is an instance of the last category in Table 21.8. For a very good discussion of (21.17), see Rulon and Brooks (1968, pp. 72–76).

Other Test Criteria

Unlike univariate analysis of variance, more than one criterion is currently used for tests of significance in multivariate analysis. Though it is possible for the different test criteria not to agree, they generally yield similar tests of significance results. My aim here is not to review merits and demerits of available criteria for tests of significance in multivariate analysis, but rather to introduce two criteria, in addition to Λ, that are obtainable from the canonical analysis without further calculations.[11]

The first criterion, proposed by Roy (1957), is referred to as Roy's largest root criterion as it uses the largest root, λ, obtained in CA, or the largest R_c^2. When I analyzed the numerical example under consideration via CA, I found that the largest $\lambda = R_c^2 = .89793$. It is this root that is tested for significance. Heck (1960) provided charts for the significance of the largest characteristic root. Pillai (1960) provided tables for the significance of the largest root. The tables and/or the charts are reproduced in various books on multivariate analysis (e.g., Harris, 1985; Marascuilo & Levin, 1983; Morrison, 1976; Timm, 1975). The charts and the tables are entered with three values: s, m, and n. For CA, s = number of nonzero roots; $m = .5(q - p - 1)$, where $q \geq p$; $n = .5(N - p - q - 2)$.

For the numerical example I analyzed in the preceding section via CA,

$$s = 2$$

$$m = .5(2 - 2 - 1) = -.5$$

$$n = .5(15 - 2 - 2 - 2) = 4.5$$

It is with these values that one enters Heck's charts, for example. If the value of the largest root exceeds the value given in the chart, the result is statistically significant at the level indicated in that chart.

[11]For a review and a discussion of different test criteria in multivariate analysis, see Olson (1976).

A second criterion for multivariate analysis is the sum of the roots, which is equal to the trace (the sum of the elements in the principal diagonal) of the matrix used to solve for λ's in CA. In other words, it is the trace of the matrix whose determinant is set equal to zero. Look back at this matrix in the section on CA and note that the two elements in its principal diagonal are .47218 and .47979. Their sum (.95197) is equal to the sum of the roots extracted (.89793 + .05404). Pillai (1960) provided tables for testing the sum of the roots. The tables are entered with values of s, m, and n, as previously defined.

As I show later, various computer programs report results from the tests noted, along with their associated probabilities.

Multiple Comparisons among Groups, and Contributions of Variables

An overall test of significance in MANOVA addresses the null hypothesis that the mean vectors of the groups are equal. When in a design consisting of more than two groups the null hypothesis is rejected, it is necessary to determine which pairs, or combinations, of groups differ significantly from each other. As I showed in Chapter 11, in univariate analysis this is accomplished by doing multiple comparisons among the means. I also showed that, depending on one's hypotheses, such comparisons may be a priori (orthogonal and nonorthogonal) or post hoc. In MANOVA, too, methods of multiple comparisons among groups are available. You will find detailed discussions of this topic in texts on multivariate analysis (see, in particular, Bock, 1975; Finn, 1974; Marascuilo & Levin, 1983; Morrison, 1976; Stevens, 1996; Timm, 1975; see also Huberty & Smith, 1982; Huberty & Wisenbaker, 1992; Swaminathan, 1989). I return to this topic when I use computer programs to analyze the data of the current example.

From a statistically significant comparison in multivariate analysis it is not possible to tell which of the multiple dependent variables contribute mostly to the difference between the groups being compared. Among approaches recommended for the study of the contribution of specific variables to the separation between groups are discriminant analysis (see the following) and simultaneous confidence intervals. These and other methods are discussed in the references cited above. Wilkinson (1975), who gave a good discussion and a numerical example of different approaches to multiple comparisons in MANOVA, concluded, "Except in the rarest cases of known independent or known equicorrelated responses, no one of these measures sufficiently describes the relation between treatment and response" (p. 412). In short, the relatively neat situation of multiple comparisons in univariate analysis (see Chapters 11 and 12) occurs rarely in MANOVA.

Univariate F Ratios

Some authors (e.g., Hummel & Sligo, 1971) suggested that an overall statistically significant result in MANOVA be followed by calculation of univariate F ratios for each dependent variable. This suggestion is ill advised as it ignores the correlations among the dependent variables, thereby subverting the very purpose of doing MANOVA in the first place. For instance, MANOVA may indicate that there are statistically significant differences among groups, whereas separate analyses of each dependent variable may indicate that differences among the groups are statistically not significant.[12] I expressly constructed the numerical example under consideration to show such an occurrence.

Statistics necessary for the calculation of the two univariate F ratios for the example under consideration are available in the principal diagonals of the **B** (between-groups or between-treatments SSCP) and **W** (within-groups or within-treatments SSCP) given earlier. Specifically, the between-groups sums of squares for Y_1 and Y_2, respectively, are 6.93333 and 11.20000. The within-groups sums of squares for Y_1 and Y_2, respectively, are 12.00 and 18.80. Recall that mean squares between groups and within groups are obtained by dividing sums of squares by their degrees of freedom, and that the F ratio is a ratio of the mean square between groups to the mean square within groups. In the present example, the number of groups is three, and therefore the degrees of freedom for the mean square between groups are two. The degrees of freedom for the mean square within groups are 12 [$g(n_j - 1)$, where g = number of groups or treatments and n_j = number of subjects in group j].

Testing first the differences among the three groups on Y_1,

$$F = \frac{6.93333/2}{12.00/12} = 3.47$$

with 2 and 12 *df*, $p > .05$. Assuming $\alpha = .05$, the mean differences among the three groups on Y_1 are statistically not significant.

The F ratio for Y_2 is

$$F = \frac{11.20/2}{18.80/12} = 3.57$$

with 2 and 12 *df*, $p > .05$. The mean differences among the three groups on Y_2 are statistically not significant. Thus, the results of the univariate F tests contradict the results of CA and MANOVA of the same data that there are statistically significant differences among the three groups. How can such a result happen? Following C. C. Li (1964, Chapter 30), I demonstrate this graphically.

In Figure 21.1, I plotted the paired scores of the dependent variables, Y_1 and Y_2. I show pairs of A_1 with open circles, those of A_2 with black circles, and those of A_3 with crosses. I also plotted the means of the three groups, which I show with circled asterisks. Notice that the plotted points overlap a good deal if viewed horizontally or vertically. Visualize the projections of all the plotted points on the variable-1 axis first, and notice the substantial overlap. Also, notice the projection of the three Y_1 means on the variable-1 axis (circled asterisks): 4.6, 5.0, 6.2. Now visualize the projections on the variable-2 axis of all the points. Again, there is considerable overlap. Examine now the plotted means' projections on the variable-2 axis: 8.2, 6.6, 6.2. Note when considering variable 1 alone, there is little difference between the means of A_1, the lowest mean, and A_2, but both are different from A_3, the highest mean. When considering variable 2 alone, on the other hand, the mean of A_1, now the highest mean, is quite different from the means of A_2 and A_3—and the latter is now the lowest mean.

If, instead of regarding the plotted points one-dimensionally, we regard them two-dimensionally in the 1-2 plane, the picture changes radically. There are clear separations between the plotted points and the plotted means of A_1, A_2, and A_3. See the straight lines separating the clusters of plotted points. Considering the two dependent variables together, then, the groups are separated in the two-dimensional space, and the multivariate analysis faithfully reflects the separation.

---

[12]For clear discussions and demonstrations of this point, see Li, C. C. (1964, pp. 405–410), and Tatsuoka (1971, pp. 22–24).

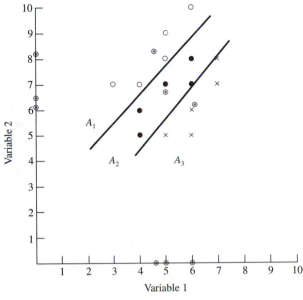

Figure 21.1

Although, as I stated earlier, the present example was contrived to demonstrate that MANOVA and univariate analyses of the same data may lead to contradictory conclusions, this is not necessarily a rare occurrence in actual research. This can particularly happen in larger designs, consisting of more than two dependent variables and more than one independent variable. Under such circumstances the possibilities and complexities increase enormously, and it is only by resorting to multivariate analyses that one may hope to begin to unravel them. The promise held by the application of multivariate analysis to the study of complex phenomena should, I hope, be evident from my almost trivial example (for a good discussion of my numerical example, see Stevens, 1996, pp. 165–167).

I pointed out earlier that overall results and tests of significance in CA (canonical analysis) with coded vectors representing a categorical independent variable, MANOVA (multivariate analysis of variance), and DA (discriminant analysis) are identical. But, as I also noted, various authors (e.g., Borgen & Seling, 1978; Tatsuoka, 1988) suggested that an overall statistically significant finding in MANOVA be followed by a DA for the purpose of shedding light on the nature of the dimensions on which the groups differ. I elaborate on these points by applying DA to the same numerical example that I analyzed by CA and MANOVA.

DISCRIMINANT ANALYSIS

I introduced DA in Chapter 20, where I stated that although I used an example with two groups, the same approach is applicable with more than two groups, except that, unlike the case of two groups, more than one discriminant function can be calculated. In general, the number of discriminant functions obtainable in a set of data is equal to the number of groups minus one, or the number of dependent variables, whichever is smaller. Thus, with three groups, for instance, only two discriminant functions may be derived, regardless of the number of dependent variables. On the other hand, given 10 groups and 4 dependent variables, for instance, only 4 discriminant functions may be derived. (This is not to say that all the obtainable discriminant functions are meaningful and/or statistically significant.) The numerical example I analyzed in the preceding sections (see Table 21.7), and which I will now analyze via DA, consisted of 3 groups and 2 dependent variables. Therefore, a maximum of 2 discriminant functions may be derived.

Because the general approach in DA is the same as that I presented in Chapter 20, my comments on calculations will be kept to a minimum. While doing the calculations, I will refer to equations I introduced in Chapter 20, thereby facilitating your consulting, whenever necessary, my detailed discussions of them.

I showed in Chapter 20—see (20.3) and the discussion related to it—that DA begins with the solution of the roots, λ, of the following determinantal equation:

$$|\mathbf{W}^{-1}\mathbf{B} - \lambda\mathbf{I}| = 0 \qquad (21.18)$$

where $\mathbf{W}^{-1}$ is the inverse of the pooled within-groups SSCP; $\mathbf{B}$ is the between-groups SSCP; λ are the eigenvalues, or characteristic roots; and $\mathbf{I}$ is an identity matrix. Earlier, I calculated $\mathbf{W}$ and $\mathbf{B}$. They are

$$\mathbf{W} = \begin{bmatrix} 12.00 & 13.20 \\ 13.20 & 18.80 \end{bmatrix}$$

$$\mathbf{B} = \begin{bmatrix} 6.93333 & -7.20000 \\ -7.20000 & 11.20000 \end{bmatrix}$$

The determinant of $\mathbf{W}$ is

$$|\mathbf{W}| = (12.00)(18.80) - (13.20)^2 = 51.36$$

The inverse of $\mathbf{W}$ is

$$\mathbf{W}^{-1} = \frac{1}{51.36} \begin{bmatrix} 18.80 & -13.20 \\ -13.20 & 12.00 \end{bmatrix} = \begin{bmatrix} .36604 & -.25701 \\ -.25701 & .23364 \end{bmatrix}$$

$$\mathbf{W}^{-1}\mathbf{B} = \begin{bmatrix} .36604 & -.25701 \\ -.25701 & .23364 \end{bmatrix} = \begin{bmatrix} 6.93333 & -7.20000 \\ -7.20000 & 11.20000 \end{bmatrix} = \begin{bmatrix} 4.38835 & -5.51400 \\ -3.46414 & 4.46724 \end{bmatrix}$$

$$\begin{vmatrix} 4.38835 - \lambda & -5.51400 \\ -3.46414 & 4.46724 - \lambda \end{vmatrix} = 0$$

Thus:

$$(4.38835 - \lambda)(4.46724 - \lambda) - (-5.51400)(-3.46414) = 0$$

$$19.60381 - 4.46724\lambda - 4.38835\lambda + \lambda^2 - 19.10127 = 0$$

$$\lambda^2 - 8.85559\lambda + .50254 = 0$$

from which

$$\lambda_1 = \frac{8.85559 + \sqrt{(-8.85559)^2 - (4)(1)(.50254)}}{2} = 8.79847$$

$$\lambda_2 = \frac{8.85559 - \sqrt{(-8.85559)^2 - (4)(1)(.50254)}}{2} = .05712$$

Index of Discriminatory Power

Having calculated the two roots, the proportion of discriminatory power of each of the discriminant functions associated with them can be calculated. In general,

$$P_j = \frac{\lambda_j}{\Sigma \lambda} \tag{21.19}$$

where P_j = proportion of discriminatory power of the discriminant function associated with the jth root; and $\Sigma \lambda$ = sum of the roots.

For the present example,

$$P_1 = \frac{8.79847}{8.79847 + .05712} = .99355$$

$$P_2 = \frac{.05712}{8.79847 + .05712} = .00645$$

Thus, 99.35% of the discriminatory power is due to the first discriminant function, whereas that associated with the second function is only about .65%. It is important to keep in mind that P_j indicates the discriminatory power of the jth function in relation to the other functions—*not* the proportion of variance of the dependent variables accounted by the jth function. In other words, P_j is an index of the proportion of the discriminatory power of the jth function of whatever the total amount of discriminatory power all the functions may possess. Therefore, a large P_j does not necessarily mean that the discriminant function associated with it yields a meaningful discrimination among the groups. Nevertheless, P_j is a useful descriptive index, providing at a glance an indication of the relative power of each discriminant function. As shown in the present numerical example, P_2 is so small as to lead to the conclusion that the second function is useless.

Tests of Significance

Using the roots of the determinantal equation (21.18), Wilks' Λ is calculated as follows:

$$\Lambda = \frac{1}{(1 + \lambda_1)(1 + \lambda_2) \dots (1 + \lambda_j)} \tag{21.20}$$

For the present example,

$$\Lambda = \frac{1}{(1 + 8.79847)(1 + .05712)} = .09654$$

This is, within rounding, the same as the value I obtained in the analysis of these data via CA. As in CA, the first root can be removed to obtain Λ':

$$\Lambda' = \frac{1}{1 + .05712} = .94597$$

Again, I obtained the same value of Λ' when I analyzed these data via CA. Earlier, I showed how Bartlett's χ^2 can be used to test the discriminatory power of all the functions as well as to determine the number of functions that are statistically significant.

Alternatively, instead of calculating Λ, Bartlett's χ^2 may be applied directly to the roots obtained in DA. This takes the following form:

$$\chi^2 = [N - 1 - .5(p + k)]\Sigma\log_e(1 + \lambda_j) \tag{21.21}$$

where N = total number of subjects; p = number of dependent variables; k = number of treatments, or groups; and $\log_e$ = natural logarithm. The degrees of freedom associated with the χ^2 are $p(k - 1)$.

For the present example,

$$\chi^2 = [15 - 1 - .5(2 + 3)][\log_e 9.79847 + \log_e 1.05712]$$

$$= (11.5)(2.28223 + .05555) = 26.88$$

with 4 *df, p* < .001. I obtained the same result when I analyzed these data via CA.

Removing the first root amounts to removing the logarithm associated with it (i.e., 2.28223) from the last expression in the preceding. Therefore, for the remaining root,

$$\chi^2 = (11.5)(.05555) = .64$$

with 1 [$(p - 1)(k - 2)$] *df, p* > .05. Again, I obtained the same result when I analyzed these data via CA.

The foregoing shows that the other test criteria I discussed in the section entitled MANOVA are easily obtainable from DA. Thus, Roy's largest root, or $R^2_{c_j}$ is

$$\frac{\lambda_1}{1 + \lambda_1} = \frac{8.79847}{9.79847} = .89794$$

Pillai's trace is similarly obtained:

$$\frac{\lambda_1}{1 + \lambda_1} + \frac{\lambda_2}{1 + \lambda_2} = \frac{8.79847}{9.79847} + \frac{.05712}{1.05712} = .95198$$

Compare these results with those I obtained in the sections of CA and MANOVA of the same data.

Discriminant Functions

I will now calculate the first discriminant function. Because I explained how to do this in Chapter 20, I will keep my comments to a minimum. I hope that my application of formulas I introduced in Chapter 20, some of which I will repeat without explanation, will suffice to help you grasp the meaning of their terms. When in doubt, consult Chapter 20 for detailed explanations.

Subtracting the first root, 8.79847, from the elements of the principal diagonal of $\mathbf{W}^{-1}\mathbf{B}$, calculated in the preceding, I form the following:

$$\begin{bmatrix} 4.38835 - 8.79847 & -5.51400 \\ -3.46414 & 4.46724 - 8.79847 \end{bmatrix} \begin{bmatrix} v_1 \\ v_2 \end{bmatrix} = \begin{bmatrix} 0 \\ 0 \end{bmatrix}$$

$$\begin{bmatrix} -4.41012 & -5.51400 \\ -3.46414 & -4.33123 \end{bmatrix} \begin{bmatrix} v_1 \\ v_2 \end{bmatrix} = \begin{bmatrix} 0 \\ 0 \end{bmatrix}$$

Forming the adjoint of the preceding matrix:

$$\begin{bmatrix} -4.33123 & 5.51400 \\ 3.46414 & -4.41012 \end{bmatrix}$$

$$\mathbf{v}' = [-4.33123 \quad 3.46414] \text{ or } [5.51400 \quad -4.41012]$$

I calculate now $\mathbf{C}_w$—the pooled within-groups covariance matrix.

$$\mathbf{C}_w = \frac{1}{12}\begin{bmatrix} 12.0 & 13.2 \\ 13.2 & 18.8 \end{bmatrix} = \begin{bmatrix} 1.00000 & 1.10000 \\ 1.10000 & 1.56667 \end{bmatrix}$$

Applying (20.5),

$$\mathbf{v}'\mathbf{C}\mathbf{v} = \underbrace{[-4.33123 \quad 3.46414]}_{\mathbf{v}'} \underbrace{\begin{bmatrix} 1.00000 & 1.10000 \\ 1.10000 & 1.56667 \end{bmatrix}}_{\mathbf{C}} \underbrace{\begin{bmatrix} -4.33123 \\ 3.46414 \end{bmatrix}}_{\mathbf{v}} = 4.55124$$

Using (20.7), $v_i^* = v_i/\sqrt{\mathbf{v}'\mathbf{C}\mathbf{v}}$, I calculate the raw coefficients:

$$v_1^* = \frac{-4.33123}{\sqrt{4.55124}} = -2.03024$$

$$v_2^* = \frac{3.46414}{\sqrt{4.55124}} = 1.62379$$

When I analyzed these data earlier in this chapter via CA, I found that the raw coefficients on the first canonical variate were $-.70055$ and $.56032$ for Y_1 and Y_2, respectively. Note that the ratio of these coefficients is the same as the ratio of the ones I obtained here. That is,

$$\frac{-.70055}{.56032} = \frac{-2.03024}{1.62379} = -1.25$$

Using the treatment means from Table 21.7, I calculate grand means for Y_1 and Y_2:

	A_1	A_2	A_3
$\overline{Y}_1$:	4.6	5.0	6.2
$\overline{Y}_2$:	8.2	6.6	6.2

$$\overline{Y}_1 = \frac{4.6 + 5.0 + 6.2}{3} = 5.26667$$

$$\overline{Y}_2 = \frac{8.2 + 6.6 + 6.2}{3} = 7.00000$$

Using (20.8), $c = -(v_1^*\overline{Y}_1 + v_2^*\overline{Y}_2)$, I calculate the constant, c, for the first discriminant function.

$$c = -[(-2.03024)(5.26667) + (1.62379)(7.00000)] = -.67393$$

The first discriminant function is

$$X_1 = -.67393 - 2.03024Y_1 + 1.62379Y_2$$

Examine this function and notice that subjects whose scores are relatively high on Y_2 and relatively low on Y_1 have relatively high positive discriminant scores. Conversely, subjects whose scores are relatively high on Y_1 and relatively low on Y_2 have relatively high negative discriminant scores (see the comment in the next section, "Group Centroids").

As I discussed in Chapter 20, some researchers use standardized coefficients to determine the relative importance of variables in a given function. Applying (20.9), $\beta_i = v_i^* \sqrt{c_{ii}}$, the standardized coefficients for the first function are

$$\beta_1 = -2.03024\sqrt{1.00000} = -2.03024$$

$$\beta_2 = 1.62379\sqrt{1.56667} = 2.03244$$

Using the magnitude of β as a criterion of the relative importance of the variable with which it is associated, one would conclude that in the present example Y_1 and Y_2 are virtually of equal importance.

Following the procedures I used earlier, the second function may be calculated. For completeness of presentation, I will report the second function, without showing the calculations:

$$X_2 = -5.60054 + .52025Y_1 + .40865Y_2$$

The standardized coefficients for the second function are

$$\beta_1 = .52025 \qquad \beta_2 = .51149$$

Recall, however, that the second function is not meaningful (see the section entitled "Index of Discriminatory Power"), *nor is it statistically significant,* and is therefore not interpreted.

Group Centroids

Using the group means and the discriminant functions, given above, I will calculate group centroids. For the first function,

$$X_{1(A_1)} = -.67393 - 2.03024(4.6) + 1.62379(8.2) = 3.30$$

$$X_{1(A_2)} = -.67393 - 2.03024(5.0) + 1.62379(6.6) = -.11$$

$$X_{1(A_3)} = -.67393 - 2.03024(6.2) + 1.62379(6.2) = -3.19$$

The centroids for the three groups are almost equally spaced on the first discriminant variate, with A_1 and A_3 at the two extremes and A_2 occupying the intermediate position. Referring to the substantive example I gave when I introduced these data, one would conclude that Conservatives, Republicans, and Democrats are about equally separated in their expectations of government spending on the dimension of defense versus social welfare programs. Specifically, the Conservatives' relatively high centroid indicates that their expectations regarding defense spending are relatively high, whereas their expectations regarding spending on social welfare are relatively low. The converse is true of the Democrats, whereas the Republicans occupy an intermediate position on the dimension under consideration.

To help interpret the results from DA, it is very useful to plot the group centroids. Before doing this, I calculate group centroids on the second discriminant variate. Using the second function and the group means, given previously, the centroids are

$$X_{2(A_1)} = -5.60054 + .52025(4.6) + .40865(8.2) = .14$$

$$X_{2(A_2)} = -5.60054 + .52025(5.0) + .40865(6.6) = -.30$$

$$X_{2(A_3)} = -5.60054 + .52025(6.2) + .40865(6.2) = .16$$

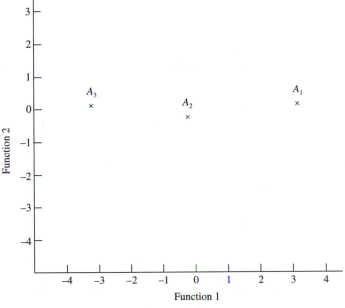

Figure 21.2

A plot of the centroids is given in Figure 21.2, where the abscissa represents the first discriminant variate and the ordinate represents the second. Notice how clearly the three groups are separated by the first function, whereas the second function hardly separates them. That is, the centroids are almost on a straight line. This, of course, is not surprising in view of what we know about the second discriminant function.

For illustrative purposes, Figure 21.3 presents another plot on two discriminant variates for three groups. Note carefully that this plot *does not* refer to the numerical example I analyzed earlier. Suppose that such a plot was obtained in a study with three preexisting groups or with three treatments. It can be seen at a glance that the first function discriminates between A_1 and A_2 on the one hand, and A_3, on the other hand. The second function discriminates between A_2, on the one hand, and A_1 and A_3, on the other hand. Using structure coefficients associated with the two functions, one would determine the dimension on which A_1 and A_2 are discriminated from A_3, and that on which A_2 is discriminated from A_1 and A_3. Later, I use SPSS to generate a plot similar to Figure 21.2.

Structure Coefficients

Following procedures discussed in detail in Chapter 20, I will calculate structure coefficients for the first discriminant variate. Recall that I suggested that total structure coefficients be used. First, I will calculate the total covariance matrix, $\mathbf{C}_t$. Taking the total SSCP matrix, which I calculated earlier, and recalling that $N = 15$,

$$\mathbf{C}_t = \frac{1}{14} \begin{bmatrix} 18.93333 & 6.00000 \\ 6.00000 & 30.00000 \end{bmatrix} = \begin{bmatrix} 1.35238 & .42857 \\ .42857 & 2.14286 \end{bmatrix}$$

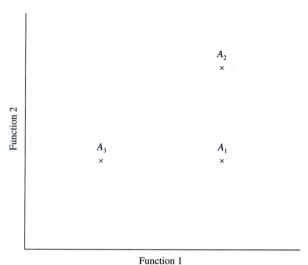

Function 1

Figure 21.3

Using the first eigenvector, $\mathbf{v}'$, which I calculated earlier, I now calculate

$$\underset{\mathbf{v}'}{\mathbf{v}'\mathbf{C}_t\mathbf{v}} = [-4.33123 \quad 3.46414] \underset{\mathbf{C}_t}{\begin{bmatrix} 1.35238 & .42857 \\ .42857 & 2.14286 \end{bmatrix}} \underset{\mathbf{v}}{\begin{bmatrix} -4.33123 \\ 3.46414 \end{bmatrix}} = 38.22442$$

Applying (20.7), $v_i^* = v_i/\sqrt{\mathbf{v}'\mathbf{C}\mathbf{v}}$,

$$v_1^* = \frac{-4.33123}{\sqrt{38.22442}} = -.70055$$

$$v_2^* = \frac{3.46414}{\sqrt{38.22442}} = .56031$$

These raw coefficients, $\mathbf{v}^*$, are identical to those I obtained earlier when I analyzed these data via CA. Using (20.9), $\beta_i = v_i^*\sqrt{c_{ii}}$, I now calculate the standardized coefficients,

$$\beta_1 = -.70055\sqrt{1.35238} = -.81468$$

$$\beta_2 = .56031\sqrt{2.14286} = .82021$$

As I explained in Chapter 20, these standardized coefficients are based on the total covariance matrix, $\mathbf{C}_t$; hence, it is the diagonal elements of this matrix that are used in their calculation. Again, I obtained the same values when I analyzed these data via CA.

Finally, to obtain the structure coefficients, $\mathbf{s}$, I will first calculate the total correlation matrix, $\mathbf{R}_t$, using $\mathbf{C}_t$, and then apply (20.10): $\mathbf{s} = \mathbf{R}_t\boldsymbol{\beta}_t$.

$$\mathbf{R}_t = \begin{bmatrix} \dfrac{1.35238}{\sqrt{(1.35238)(1.35238)}} & \dfrac{.42857}{\sqrt{(1.35238)(2.14286)}} \\[4mm] \dfrac{.42857}{\sqrt{(1.35238)(2.14286)}} & \dfrac{2.14286}{\sqrt{(2.14286)(2.14286)}} \end{bmatrix} = \begin{bmatrix} 1.00000 & .25175 \\ .25175 & 1.00000 \end{bmatrix}$$

Table 21.9   Summary of DA for the Data in Table 21.7

Function	Variables	Raw	β	s	Group	Centroids
1	Y_1	−2.03	−2.03	−.61	A_1	3.30
	Y_2	1.62	2.03	.62	A_2	−.11
					A_3	−3.19
2	Y_1	.52	.52	.79	A_1	.14
	Y_2	.41	.51	.79	A_2	−.30
					A_3	.16

$$\lambda_1 = 8.80 \quad P_1 = .99; \quad \lambda_2 = .06 \quad P_2 = .01$$

NOTE: Raw = raw coefficient; β = standardized coefficient; s = structure coefficient; λ = eigenvalue; P = proportion of discriminatory power.

$$\mathbf{s} = \begin{bmatrix} 1.00000 & .25175 \\ .25175 & 1.00000 \end{bmatrix} \begin{bmatrix} -.81468 \\ .82021 \end{bmatrix} = \begin{bmatrix} -.60819 \\ .61511 \end{bmatrix}$$

These are equal to the structure coefficients I obtained when I applied CA to these data. Because I discussed their interpretation in the CA section, I will not discuss them here. Instead, I will note that had I applied only DA to the numerical example under consideration, I would have used these coefficients to interpret the dimension on which the groups are separated in the manner I did earlier. I will note in passing that in the present example, the within groups structure coefficients are quite different from the total structure coefficients given above (see my comment on the SPSS and SAS DA outputs that follow).

I will not show the calculation of the structure coefficients associated with the second function (you may wish to do this as an exercise). They are $s_1 = .79$ and $s_2 = .79$. *Again, I remind you that the second function is not meaningful.*

I summarize the results of the DA in Table 21.9.

COMPUTER PROGRAMS

In this section, I will use procedures from SPSS and SAS to analyze the example I analyzed by hand in preceding sections (Table 21.7). I will reproduce only short excerpts of the outputs, and I will comment on them briefly. I suggest that you study the outputs in conjunction with my hand calculations and my detailed commentaries on them.

SPSS

Input

TITLE TABLE 21.7.   MANOVA AND DA.
DATA LIST FREE/Y1 Y2 G.
BEGIN DATA
3 7 1   *[first two subjects in group 1]*
4 7 1
. . .

```
4 5 2        [first two subjects in group 2]
4 6 2

.  .  .
5 5 3        [first two subjects in group 3]
6 5 3

.  .  .
END DATA
LIST.
MANOVA Y1 Y2 BY G(1,3)/PRINT CELLINFO PARAMETERS/DESIGN/
   CONTRAST(G)=SPECIAL(1 1 1 1 −1 0 1 1 −2)/
   DESIGN G(1)G(2).
DISCRIMINANT GROUPS=G(1,3)/VARIABLES=Y1 Y2/
   STATISTICS=ALL/PLOT COMBINED.
```

Commentary

For an orientation to SPSS, see Chapter 4. See Norušis/SPSS Inc. (1993b), Chapter 3 for a general discussion of MANOVA in SPSS, and see pages 391–432 for syntax. Unless otherwise stated, page references I give in the following discussion apply to this source. I introduced MANOVA in Chapter 12, where I used it for univariate analysis. Nevertheless, I will refer you to this chapter, as my comments on input and output are applicable, in a general sense, also to multivariate analysis.

DATA LIST. Notice that I named the categorical variable G, which is meant to stand for pre-existing or treatment groups.

MANOVA. As I explained in Chapter 12, the dependent variables must be listed first and be separated from the factor name(s) by the keyword BY. Numbers in parentheses are minimum and maximum values of G.

PRINT. Although I will not reproduce the information generated by it, I called, as an example, for default printing of CELLINFO ("basic information about each cell in the design," p. 402) and PARAMETERS ("the estimated parameters themselves, along with standard errors, *t* tests, and confidence intervals," p. 404).

CONTRAST. See pages 398–400 for various contrasts available in MANOVA. In Chapter 12, I introduced and discussed this subcommand and used SPECIAL contrasts in univariate analysis. I included such contrasts here in anticipation of my brief discussion of multiple comparisons (see my commentary on the output generated by the second DESIGN subcommand).

DISCRIMINANT. I explained and used this procedure in Chapter 20. Although MANOVA contains a DISCRIM subcommand (see p. 429), I apply the DISCRIMINANT procedure instead, as I wish to illustrate the use of its PLOT subcommand (see my commentary on the relevant output).

Output

$$***Analysis \ of \ Variance--Design \ 1****$$

EFFECT .. G
Multivariate Tests of Significance (S = 2, M = −1/2, N = $4\frac{1}{2}$)

Test Name	Value	Approx. F	Hypoth. DF	Error DF	Sig. of F
Pillais	.95198	5.45016	4.00	24.00	.003
Hotellings	8.85566	22.13915	4.00	20.00	.000
Wilks	.09654	12.20133	4.00	22.00	.000
Roys	.89794				

Note.. F statistic for WILKS' Lambda is exact.

Commentary

The preceding is an excerpt from the output of the overall analysis (first DESIGN subcommand). For a description of the preceding tests, see page 83. Except for Hotellings, I calculated the same test criteria. Compare my test of Wilks' Λ with the preceding. Note that, except for "Roys," the program provides *p* values, making it unnecessary to resort to the tables and charts I described earlier.

Based on results such as these, I concluded earlier that there are statistically significant differences among the three groups. As in the case of univariate analysis, multiple comparisons among groups can be carried out.

Output

$$***\text{A n a l y s i s   o f   V a r i a n c e} \text{ -- Design } 2****$$

EFFECT .. G(2)
Multivariate Tests of Significance (S $= 1, M = 0, N = 4\frac{1}{2}$)

Test Name	Value	Exact F	Hypoth. DF	Error DF	Sig. of F
Pillais	.86471	35.15317	2.00	11.00	.000
Hotellings	6.39148	35.15317	2.00	11.00	.000
Wilks	.13529	35.15317	2.00	11.00	.000
Roys	.86471				

EFFECT .. G(1)
Multivariate Tests of Significance (S $= 1, M = 0, N = 4\frac{1}{2}$)

Test Name	Value	Exact F	Hypoth. DF	Error DF	Sig. of F
Pillais	.71133	13.55296	2.00	11.00	.001
Hotellings	2.46417	13.55296	2.00	11.00	.001
Wilks	.28867	13.55296	2.00	11.00	.001
Roys	.71133				

Commentary

In Chapter 11, I explained and illustrated the application of planned (orthogonal or nonorthogonal) and post hoc comparisons among means. Among other things, I pointed out that (1) various multiple comparisons procedures have been proposed for specific purposes, and (2) there is no consensus about their use. As you may well imagine, the situation is more complex in MANOVA. I do not intend to review the various proposals that have been made in this regard (for an excellent discussion, see Stevens, 1996, Chapter 5).

My sole purpose here is to illustrate how MANOVA can be used to carry out planned comparisons. To this end, I am using two orthogonal comparisons: (1) between G1 and G2 and (2) between G1+G2 and G3. For a detailed discussion of such comparisons, see Chapter 11, where I pointed out, among other things, that (1) they are formulated a priori, based on theoretical considerations and expectations, and (2) the overall test is of little or no interest when such comparisons are used.

As you may note from the heading of the previous excerpts of the output, they refer to the second DESIGN statement. As I explained in Chapter 12, SPECIAL contrasts are entered in parentheses as a matrix whose number of rows and columns equal the number of levels of the factor. Also, (1) "the first row represents the mean effect of the factor and is generally a vector of 1's" (p. 400), and (2) the matrix can be placed in a single line (see the input).

As a result of my specifications in the second DESIGN [i.e., G(1)G(2)], each contrast is tested separately. Examine the previous output and notice that both comparisons are statistically significant at, say, .01 level (notice that the results of the second comparison are printed first). As I explained in Chapter 20 and earlier in this chapter, discriminant analyses can be used to determine the nature of the dimension underlying the discrimination between groups (or combination of groups) reflected in a given contrast. Some authors (e.g., Stevens, 1996, Chapter 5) suggest following statistically significant comparisons with univariate analyses to identify variables on which the groups being compared differ.

Output

Canonical Discriminant Functions

Function	Eigenvalue	Percent of Variance	Cumulative Percent	Canonical Correlation	:	After Function	Wilks' Lambda	Chi-square	df	Significance
					:	0	.0965414	26.88451	4	.0000
1*	8.79854	99.35	99.35	.9475990	:	1	.9459640	.63883	1	.4241
2*	.05712	.65	100.00	.2324565	:					

* marks the 2 canonical discriminant functions remaining in the analysis.

Commentary

Compare the preceding output, which was generated by the DISCRIMINANT procedure of SPSS, with my hand calculations, where I got the same results and explained them.

Output

Standardized canonical discriminant function coefficients

	Func 1	Func 2
Y1	−2.03024	.52025
Y2	2.03246	.51149

Structure matrix:
Pooled within-groups correlations between discriminating
variables and canonical discriminant functions
  (Variables ordered by size of correlation within function)

	Func 1	Func 2
Y1	−.24405	.96976*
Y2	.24823	.96870*

* denotes largest absolute correlation between each variable and any discriminant function.

Commentary

As indicted here, and as I explained earlier, SPSS reports within-groups structure coefficients. Commenting on the possibility of calculating total coefficients, Norušis/SPSS Inc. (1994) pointed out that while total coefficients will be larger than within-groups coefficients, "Variables with high total correlations will also have high pooled within-groups correlations" (p. 19). As illustrated in the example under consideration, this will not always be the case. Focusing on the results for Func 1 (recall that Func 2 is *not* meaningful), note that there is a considerable difference between the within and the total structure coefficients (−.61 and .62 for Y1 and Y2, respectively), which I calculated earlier. Assuming that you adopt the convention that structure coefficients ≥ .30 be viewed as meaningful, you would reach opposite conclusions, depending on which coefficients you interpret (i.e., within-groups or total).

Clearly, if you are using SPSS and wish to obtain total structure coefficients, you will have to do some hand calculations (see my presentation in earlier sections). As I will show, SAS reports within, between, and total structure coefficients.

Output

Unstandardized canonical discriminant function coefficients

	Func 1	Func 2
Y1	−2.0302384	.5202454
Y2	1.6238049	.4086514
(Constant)	−.6740453	−5.6005186

Canonical discriminant functions evaluated at group means (group centroids)

Group	Func 1	Func 2
1	3.30206	.14355
2	−.10813	−.30219
3	−3.19393	.15864

Commentary

Except for the structure coefficients (see my previous commentary), I obtained the same results as reported in this and the preceding excerpts (see Table 21.9 for a summary of the results of my calculations). Although I reproduced statistics for both functions, I remind you again that the second function is *not* meaningful.

Output

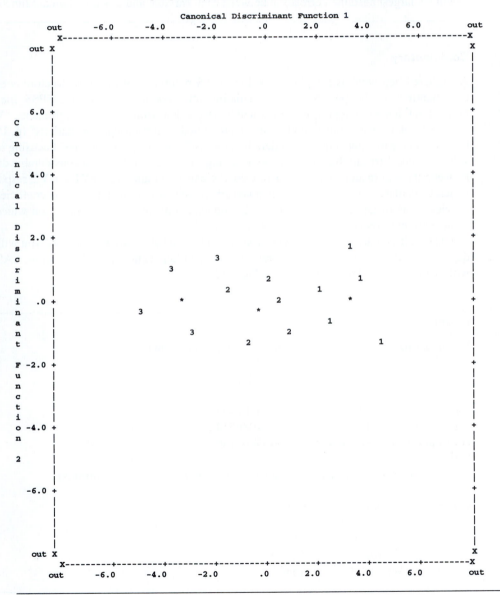

All-groups Scatterplot - * Indicates a group centroid

Commentary

The preceding is one of several plots available in the DISCRIMINANT procedure (see Norušis/ SPSS Inc., 1994, p. 292). Compare this plot with Figure 21.2, where I plotted only the centroids.

SAS

Input

```
TITLE 'TABLE 21.7.   PROC GLM WITH ORTHOGONAL CONTRASTS';
DATA T217;
INPUT Y1 Y2 G;
CARDS;
3 7 1       [first two subjects in group 1]
4 7 1
.  .  .
4 5 2       [first two subjects in group 2]
4 6 2
.  .  .
5 5 3       [first two subjects in group 3]
6 5 3
.  .  .
;
PROC PRINT;
PROC GLM;
CLASS G;
MODEL Y1 Y2=G;
CONTRAST 'G1 VS. G2' G 1 –1 0;
CONTRAST 'G1+G2 VS. G3' G 1 1 –2;
MANOVA H=G/CANONICAL;
RUN;
```

Commentary

For an orientation to SAS, see Chapter 4. For a description of GLM, see SAS Inc. (1990a, Vol. 2, Chapter 24; page references I give in the following discussion apply to this source). I introduced and applied GLM in Chapters 11 and 12, where I used contrasts similar to the preceding in univariate analyses. My comments on such contrasts are also applicable, in a general sense, to multivariate analysis.

CLASS. This refers to the independent variable(s). As in SPSS, I use the label G to refer to preexisting groups or treatments.

MODEL. For a description of the MODEL statement and its options, see pages 917–920. For present purposes, I will only point out that the dependent variables appear on the left of the equal sign, and the independent variables appear on the right.

CONTRAST. For a description of CONTRAST statement, see pages 905–906. Note that I am using the same orthogonal contrasts I used in SPSS. When, as in this example, both

CONTRAST and MANOVA statements are used, "the MANOVA statement must appear after the CONTRAST statement" (p. 910).

MANOVA. For a description of the MANOVA statement and its options, which appear after the slash (/), see pages 910–912.

Output

General Linear Models Procedure
Multivariate Analysis of Variance
Canonical Analysis

	Canonical Correlation	Squared Canonical Correlation
1	0.947599	0.897944
2	0.232456	0.054036

	Eigenvalue	Difference	Proportion	Cumulative
1	8.7985	8.7414	0.9935	0.9935
2	0.0571	.	0.0065	1.0000

Test of H0: The canonical correlations in the
current row and all that follow are zero

	Likelihood Ratio	Approx F	Num DF	Den DF	Pr > F
1	0.09654135	12.2013	4	22	0.0001
2	0.94596400	0.6855	1	12	0.4239

Commentary

Compare the preceding with my hand calculations and with the previous SPSS output.

Output

Total Canonical Structure

	CAN1	CAN2
Y1	−0.6082	0.7938
Y2	0.6151	0.7884

Within Canonical Structure

	CAN1	CAN2
Y1	−0.2441	0.9698
Y2	0.2482	0.9687

Commentary

As I pointed out in my commentary on SPSS output, SAS reports total, within, and between (not reproduced here) structure coefficients. Notice that the within-groups coefficients are the same as those reported in SPSS. The total structure coefficients are the same as those I calculated earlier by hand. Thus, results yielded by SAS afford the greatest flexibility in choosing the structure coefficients deemed most appropriate or relevant.

Output

Standardized Canonical Coefficients

	CAN1	CAN2
Y1	−2.3610	0.6050
Y2	2.3770	0.5982

Raw Canonical Coefficients

	CAN1	CAN2
Y1	−2.030238435	0.5202453854
Y2	1.6238049083	0.4086513642

Manova Test Criteria and F Approximations for the Hypothesis of no Overall G Effect

$$S=2 \quad M=-0.5 \quad N=4.5$$

Statistic	Value	F	Num DF	Den DF	Pr > F
Wilks' Lambda	0.09654135	12.2013	4	22	0.0001
Pillai's Trace	0.95197995	5.4502	4	24	0.0029
Hotelling-Lawley Trace	8.85565940	22.1391	4	20	0.0001
Roy's Greatest Root	8.79853671	52.7912	2	12	0.0001

NOTE: F Statistic for Roy's Greatest Root is an upper bound.
NOTE: F Statistic for Wilks' Lambda is exact.

Commentary

Compare the preceding results with my hand calculations and SPSS output. Notice that SPSS reports Roy as .89794, whereas SAS reports 8.79853671. Earlier, under "Tests of Significance," I showed that

$$\frac{\lambda_1}{1 + \lambda_1} = \frac{8.79847}{9.79847} = .89794$$

See Huberty (1994, p. 187) for an explanation of different ways Roy's criterion is reported in different computer programs.

Output

Manova Test Criteria and Exact F Statistics for the Hypothesis of no Overall G1 VS. G2 Effect

S=1   M=0   N=4.5

Statistic	Value	F	Num DF	Den DF	Pr > F
Wilks' Lambda	0.28866906	13.5530	2	11	0.0011
Pillai's Trace	0.71133094	13.5530	2	11	0.0011
Hotelling-Lawley Trace	2.46417445	13.5530	2	11	0.0011
Roy's Greatest Root	2.46417445	13.5530	2	11	0.0011

Manova Test Criteria and Exact F Statistics for the Hypothesis of no Overall G1+G2 VS. G3 Effect

S=1   M=0   N=4.5

Statistic	Value	F	Num DF	Den DF	Pr > F
Wilks' Lambda	0.13529081	35.1532	2	11	0.0001
Pillai's Trace	0.86470919	35.1532	2	11	0.0001
Hotelling-Lawley Trace	6.39148494	35.1532	2	11	0.0001
Roy's Greatest Root	6.39148494	35.1532	2	11	0.0001

Commentary

As indicated by the titles, the preceding are tests of the two orthogonal comparisons. Compare them with SPSS output, where I commented on the same results.

MISCELLANEOUS TOPICS

As I pointed out in my introductory remarks to Chapter 20, my aim in that chapter and the present one was to give a rudimentary introduction to multivariate analysis. Consequently, my presentation was limited to designs with one categorical independent variable. Moreover, I did not even allude to various important topics. In the present section, I will comment briefly on miscellaneous topics. Typically, my presentation will consist of a brief statement about a given topic and some relevant references.

Designs with Multiple Independent Variables

The approaches I presented in Chapters 20 and 21 can be extended to designs with multiple (1) categorical independent variables, as in factorial designs; (2) continuous independent variables, as in multivariate regression analysis; and (3) categorical and continuous independent variables as in multivariate analysis of covariance. You will find detailed discussions of such designs in the texts I cited in this and the preceding chapter. MANOVA can also be applied to the special case of repeated measures designs (for detailed discussions of this topic, see Hand & Taylor, 1987; O'Brien & Kaiser, 1985). In the present chapter, I applied canonical analysis to a design with one categorical independent variable. For application of canonical analysis to factorial designs, see Pruzek (1971).

Effect Size, Power, and Sample Size

As in univariate analysis, various proposals have been advanced for assessment of effect size, calculation of power, and sample size. You will find good discussions of one or more of these topics in Cohen (1988, Chapter 10); Cole, Maxwell, Arvey, and Salas (1994); Haase (1991); Huberty and Smith (1982); Marascuilo, Busk, and Serlin (1988); Raudenbush, Becker, and Kalaian (1988); Stevens (1992, pp. 172–182); and Strahan (1982).

Canonical Analysis of Contingency Tables

There is a vast literature on various approaches to the analysis of contingency tables, which I will not cite. Instead, I will only point out that among approaches suggested is the use of canonical analysis. For discussions of this topic see Gilula and Haberman (1986); Holland, Levi, and Watson (1980); Isaac and Milligan (1983); and Knapp (1978).

Discriminant Analysis and Logistic Regression

As I showed in Chapter 17, logistic regression is used in designs with a categorical dependent variable. Among various authors who compared discriminant analysis and logistic regression are Cleary and Angel (1984), Cox and Snell (1989), Darlington (1990), Harrell and Lee (1985), Press and Wilson (1978), and Sapra (1991). Broadly, the aforementioned authors pointed out that, being based on more restrictive assumptions, discriminant analysis is less robust than logistic regression.[13] Darlington (1990) has, perhaps, made this point most forcefully by devoting a chapter to logistic regression, while only commenting briefly on the limitations of discriminant analysis, and asserting that it "is in the process of being replaced in most modern practice by logistic regression" (p. 458).

Multivariate Analysis and Structural Equation Models

I presented structural equation models (SEM) in Part 3, where I showed, among other things, how they afford (1) distinctions between latent variables and their indicators and (2) identification of measurement errors, thereby preventing them from contaminating relations among latent variables. Not surprisingly, various authors have shown how multivariate analysis can be

---

[13]My dear friend James Gibbons had been working on a detailed review and treatment of comparisons between linear discriminant function and logistic regression. On the day of his untimely death, he called to ask whether I would be willing to distribute his work in progress to interested readers. Of course, I consented. Jim's work consists of (1) a Readme file, (2) an extensive document, (3) SAS input for comparisons he discussed in the document, (4) SAS output, and (5) six data sets from the literature and associated SAS input files. For a copy, please send a diskette along with a self-addressed stamped mailer to: Elazar Pedhazur, 3530 Mystic Pointe Dr., Apt. 505, Aventura, FL 33180.

subsumed under SEM, some advocating the latter as an alternative to the former. You will find discussions of these topics in Bagozzi, Fornell, and Larcker (1981); Bagozzi and Yi (1989); Bagozzi, Yi, and Singh (1991); Bray and Maxwell (1985, pp. 57–68); Cole, Maxwell, Arvey, and Salas (1993); and Kühnel (1988).

STUDY SUGGESTIONS

1. Suppose that you wish to study relations between a set of personality measures and a set of achievement measures. If you obtain scores on six personality measures and four achievement measures from a group of subjects, how many canonical correlations can you calculate?

2. In a canonical analysis with three variables in Set 1 and four variables in Set 2, the following results were obtained: $R_{c_1}^2 = .432$, $R_{c_2}^2 = .213$, $R_{c_3}^2 = .145$. The structure coefficients were as follows:

Set 1			Set 2		
.876	.521	.237	.220	.839	.430
.072	.972	.473	.836	.127	.376
−.736	.163	.406	.511	.647	.483
			.764	.256	.331

The number of subjects was 350.
(a) Calculate the overall Λ.
(b) What is the χ^2 associated with Λ?
(c) What is the total redundancy of (1) Set 1 given Set 2; (2) Set 2 given Set 1?

3. A researcher wishes to study the differences among five groups on ten dependent variables. Assuming that the data are subjected to canonical analysis, answer the following:
(a) How many coded vectors are required?
(b) How many canonical correlations may be obtained in such an analysis?
(c) Would the overall results obtained in such an analysis differ from those that would be obtained if the data were analyzed via MANOVA?

4. A researcher was interested in studying how lower-class, middle-class, and upper-class adolescents differed in their perceptions of the degree to which they controlled their destiny and in their career aspirations. The researcher administered a measure of locus of control and a measure of career aspirations to samples from the three populations. The data (illustrative) follow, where higher scores indicate greater feelings of control and higher career aspirations.
(a) Do a canonical analysis in which one set of variables consists of the measures of locus of control and career aspirations and the other set consists of coded vectors representing group membership.
(b) Do a discriminant analysis of the same data. Plot the centroids.
(c) Do a MANOVA of the same data.
Interpret and compare the results obtained under (a)–(c).

Lower-Class		Middle-Class		Upper-Class	
Locus of Control	Career Aspirations	Locus of Control	Career Aspirations	Locus of Control	Career Aspirations
2	2	3	5	3	6
3	4	5	5	4	6
4	5	5	4	5	6
4	3	6	6	5	6
3	5	5	6	5	5
5	4	4	7	6	7
4	4	7	7	5	6
5	5	6	6	5	7

ANSWERS

1. 4
2. (a) $\Lambda = .382$
   (b) $\chi^2 = 332.01$, with 12 *df*.
   (c) $\overline{Rd}_1 = .299$; $\overline{Rd}_2 = .260$
3. (a) 4
   (b) 4
   (c) No

4.

BMDP Canonical Analysis (6M) Output (excerpts)

EIGENVALUE	CANONICAL CORRELATION	NUMBER OF EIGENVALUES	BARTLETT'S TEST FOR REMAINING EIGENVALUES		
			CHI-SQUARE	D.F.	TAIL PROB.
			16.92	4	0.0020
0.53109	0.72876	1	1.40	1	0.2370
0.06593	0.25677				

COEFFICIENTS FOR CANONICAL VARIABLES FOR FIRST SET OF VARIABLES

		CNVRF1 1	CNVRF2 2
LOC	1	0.079567	1.031812
ASP	2	0.724811	−0.594293

STANDARDIZED COEFFICIENTS FOR CANONICAL VARIABLES FOR FIRST SET OF VARIABLES

(THESE ARE THE COEFFICIENTS FOR THE STANDARDIZED VARIABLES)

		CNVRF1 1	CNVRF2 2
LOC	1	0.094	1.216
ASP	2	0.943	−0.773

CANONICAL VARIABLE LOADINGS

(CORRELATIONS OF CANONICAL VARIABLES WITH ORIGINAL VARIABLES)
FOR FIRST SET OF VARIABLES

		CNVRF1 1	CNVRF2 2
LOC	1	0.634	0.773
ASP	2	0.997	−0.077

CANON. VAR.	AVERAGE SQUARED LOADING FOR EACH CANONICAL VARIABLE (1ST SET)	AV. SQ. LOADING TIMES SQUARED CANON. CORREL. (1ST SET)	SQUARED CANON. CORREL.
1	0.69805	0.37073	0.53109
2	0.30195	0.01991	0.06593

SPSS Output (excerpts)

–> MANOVA LOC ASP BY G(1,3)/PRINT CELLINFO PARAMETERS/DISCRIM.

Multivariate Tests of Significance (S = 2, M = −1/2, N = 9)

Test Name	Value	Approx. F	Hypoth. DF	Error DF	Sig. of F
Pillais	.59702	4.46819	4.00	42.00	.004
Hotellings	1.20320	5.71520	4.00	38.00	.001
Wilks	.43799	5.11009	4.00	40.00	.002
Roys	.53109				

Note.. F statistic for WILKS' Lambda is exact.

–> DISCRIMINANT GROUPS=G(1,3)/VARIABLES=LOC ASP/
–>   STATISTICS=ALL/PLOT COMBINED.

Canonical Discriminant Functions

Function	Eigenvalue	Percent of Variance	Cumulative Percent	Canonical Correlation	:	After Function	Wilks' Lambda	Chi-square	df	Significance
					:	0	.4379918	16.92388	4	.0020
1*	1.13261	94.13	94.13	.7287606	:	1	.9340676	1.39823	1	.2370
2*	.07059	5.87	100.00	.2567731	:					

* Marks the 2 canonical discriminant functions remaining in the analysis.

Canonical discriminant functions evaluated at group means (group centroids)

Group	Func 1	Func 2
1	−1.39430	−.04866
2	.52833	.32578
3	.86597	−.27711

SAS Output (excerpts)

PROC CANCORR ALL;

Test of H0: The canonical correlations in the
current row and all that follow are zero

	Likelihood Ratio	Approx F	Num DF	Den DF	Pr > F
1	0.43799178	5.1101	4	40	0.0020
2	0.93406757	1.4823	1	21	0.2369

Multivariate Statistics and F Approximations

S=2   M=−0.5   N=9

Statistic	Value	F	Num DF	Den DF	Pr > F
Wilks' Lambda	0.43799178	5.1101	4	40	0.0020
Pillai's Trace	0.59702440	4.4682	4	42	0.0042
Hotelling-Lawley Trace	1.20320073	5.7152	4	38	0.0011
Roy's Greatest Root	1.13261437	11.8925	2	21	0.0004

Raw Canonical Coefficients for the 'WITH' Variables

	W1	W2
LOC	0.0795667248	1.0318116455
ASP	0.7248112399	−0.594293297

Standardized Canonical Coefficients for the 'WITH' Variables

	W1	W2
LOC	0.0938	1.2163
ASP	0.9433	−0.7735

Correlations Between the 'WITH' Variables and Their Canonical Variables

	W1	W2
LOC	0.6340	0.7733
ASP	0.9970	−0.0769

PROC GLM;
  CLASS G;
  MODEL LOC ASP=G;
  MANOVA H=G/CANONICAL;

General Linear Models Procedure
Multivariate Analysis of Variance
Canonical Analysis

Test of H0: The canonical correlations in the
current row and all that follow are zero

	Likelihood Ratio	Approx F	Num DF	Den DF	Pr > F
1	0.43799178	5.1101	4	40	0.0020
2	0.93406757	1.4823	1	21	0.2369

Total Canonical Structure

	CAN1	CAN2
LOC	0.6340	0.7733
ASP	0.9970	−0.0769

Within Canonical Structure

	CAN1	CAN2
LOC	0.5023	0.8647
ASP	0.9941	−0.1082

Commentary

In the preceding, LOC = locus of control and ASP = career aspirations. Notice, among other things, that

1. the second canonical correlation is neither meaningful nor statistically significant;
2. only the first lambda is statistically significant;
3. ASP makes a much greater contribution to the discrimination among the groups than does LOC; and
4. from the centroids it is evident that the discrimination is primarily between lower-class adolescents, on the one hand, and middle- and upper-class adolescents, on the other hand.

Matrix Algebra: An Introduction

Matrix algebra is one of the most useful and powerful branches of mathematics for conceptualizing and analyzing psychological, sociological, and educational research data. As research becomes more and more multivariate, the need for a compact method of expressing data becomes greater. Certain problems require that sets of equations and subscripted variables be written. In many cases the use of matrix algebra simplifies and, when familiar, clarifies the mathematics and statistics. In addition, matrix algebra notation and thinking fit in nicely with the conceptualization of computer programming and use.

In this chapter I provide a brief introduction to matrix algebra. The emphasis is on those aspects that are related to subject matter covered in this book. Thus many matrix algebra techniques, important and useful in other contexts, are omitted. In addition, I neglect certain important derivations and proofs. Although the material presented here should suffice to enable you to follow the applications of matrix algebra in this book, I strongly suggest that you expand your knowledge of this topic by studying one or more of the following texts: Dorf (1969), Green (1976), Hohn (1964), Horst (1963), and Searle (1966). In addition, you will find good introductions to matrix algebra in the books on multivariate analysis cited in Chapters 20 and 21.

BASIC DEFINITIONS

A *matrix* is an n-by-k rectangle of numbers or symbols that stand for numbers. The order of the matrix is n by k. It is customary to designate the rows first and the columns second. That is, n is the number of rows of the matrix and k the number of columns. A 2-by-3 matrix called **A** might be

$$\mathbf{A} = \begin{matrix} & 1 & 2 & 3 \\ 1 & \\ 2 & \end{matrix} \begin{bmatrix} 4 & 7 & 5 \\ 6 & 6 & 3 \end{bmatrix}$$

Elements of a matrix are identified by reference to the row and column that they occupy. Thus, a_{11} refers to the element of the first row and first column of **A**, which in the preceding example is 4. Similarly, a_{23} is the element of the second row and third column of **A**, which in the above example is 3. In general, then a_{ij} refers to the element in row i and column j.

The *transpose* of a matrix is obtained simply by exchanging rows and columns. In the present case, the transpose of **A**, written **A′**, is

$$\mathbf{A}' = \begin{bmatrix} 4 & 6 \\ 7 & 6 \\ 5 & 3 \end{bmatrix}$$

If $n = k$, the matrix is square. A square matrix can be symmetric or asymmetric. A *symmetric* matrix has the same elements above the principal diagonal as below the diagonal except that they are transposed. The principal diagonal is the set of elements from the upper left corner to the lower right corner. Symmetric matrices are frequently encountered in multiple regression analysis and in multivariate analysis. The following is an example of a correlation matrix, which is symmetric:

$$\mathbf{R} = \begin{bmatrix} 1.00 & .70 & .30 \\ .70 & 1.00 & .40 \\ .30 & .40 & 1.00 \end{bmatrix}$$

Diagonal elements refer to correlations of variables with themselves, hence the 1's. Each off-diagonal element refers to a correlation between two variables and is identified by row and column numbers. Thus, $r_{12} = r_{21} = .70$; $r_{23} = r_{32} = .40$. Other elements are treated similarly.

A *column vector* is an n-by-1 array of numbers. For example,

$$\mathbf{b} = \begin{bmatrix} 8.0 \\ 1.3 \\ -2.0 \end{bmatrix}$$

A *row vector* is a 1-by-n array of numbers:

$$\mathbf{b}' = [8.0 \quad 1.3 \quad -2.0]$$

b′ is the *transpose* of **b**. Note that vectors are designated by lowercase boldface letters and that a prime is used to indicate a row vector.

A *diagonal* matrix is frequently encountered in statistical work. It is a square matrix in which some values other than zero are in the principal diagonal of the matrix and all the off-diagonal elements are zeros. Here is a diagonal matrix:

$$\begin{bmatrix} 2.759 & 0 & 0 \\ 0 & 1.643 & 0 \\ 0 & 0 & .879 \end{bmatrix}$$

A particularly important form of a diagonal matrix is an *identity* matrix, **I**, which has 1's in the principal diagonal:

$$\mathbf{I} = \begin{bmatrix} 1 & 0 & 0 \\ 0 & 1 & 0 \\ 0 & 0 & 1 \end{bmatrix}$$

MATRIX OPERATIONS

The power of matrix algebra becomes apparent when we explore the operations that are possible. The major operations are addition, subtraction, multiplication, and inversion. A large number of statistical operations can be done by knowing the basic rules of matrix algebra. Some matrix operations are now defined and illustrated.

Addition and Subtraction

Two or more vectors can be added or subtracted provided they are of the same dimensionality. That is, they have the same number of elements. The following two vectors are added:

$$\begin{bmatrix} 4 \\ 3 \\ 5 \end{bmatrix} + \begin{bmatrix} 7 \\ 7 \\ 4 \end{bmatrix} = \begin{bmatrix} 11 \\ 10 \\ 9 \end{bmatrix}$$
$$\mathbf{a} \qquad \mathbf{b} \qquad \mathbf{c}$$

Similarly, matrices of the same dimensionality may be added or subtracted. The following two 3-by-2 matrices are added:

$$\begin{bmatrix} 6 & 4 \\ 5 & 6 \\ 9 & 5 \end{bmatrix} + \begin{bmatrix} 7 & 4 \\ 7 & 4 \\ 1 & 3 \end{bmatrix} = \begin{bmatrix} 13 & 8 \\ 12 & 10 \\ 10 & 8 \end{bmatrix}$$
$$\mathbf{A} \qquad\quad \mathbf{B} \qquad\quad \mathbf{C}$$

Now, **B** is subtracted from **A**:

$$\begin{bmatrix} 6 & 4 \\ 5 & 6 \\ 9 & 5 \end{bmatrix} - \begin{bmatrix} 7 & 4 \\ 7 & 4 \\ 1 & 3 \end{bmatrix} = \begin{bmatrix} -1 & 0 \\ -2 & 2 \\ 8 & 2 \end{bmatrix}$$
$$\mathbf{A} \qquad\quad \mathbf{B} \qquad\quad \mathbf{C}$$

Multiplication

To obtain the product of a row vector by a column vector, corresponding elements of each are multiplied and then added. For example, multiplication of $\mathbf{a}'$ by $\mathbf{b}$, each consisting of three elements, is

$$\begin{bmatrix} a_1 & a_2 & a_3 \end{bmatrix} \begin{bmatrix} b_1 \\ b_2 \\ b_3 \end{bmatrix} = a_1 b_1 + a_2 b_2 + a_3 b_3$$
$$\mathbf{a}' \qquad\quad \mathbf{b}$$

Note that the product of a row by a column is a single number called a *scalar.* This is why the product of a row by a column is referred to as the scalar product of vectors.

Here is a numerical example:

$$\begin{bmatrix} 4 & 1 & 3 \end{bmatrix} \begin{bmatrix} 1 \\ 2 \\ 5 \end{bmatrix} = (4)(1) + (1)(2) + (3)(5) = 21$$

Scalar products of vectors are very frequently used in statistical analysis. For example, to obtain the sum of the elements of a column vector it is premultiplied by a unit row vector of the same dimensionality. Thus,

$$\Sigma X: \quad \begin{bmatrix} 1 & 1 & 1 & 1 & 1 \end{bmatrix} \begin{bmatrix} 1 \\ 4 \\ 1 \\ 3 \\ 7 \end{bmatrix} = 16$$

One can obtain the sum of the squares of a column vector by premultiplying the vector by its transpose.

$$\Sigma X^2: \quad [1 \quad 4 \quad 1 \quad 3 \quad 7] \begin{bmatrix} 1 \\ 4 \\ 1 \\ 3 \\ 7 \end{bmatrix} = 76$$

Similarly, one can obtain the sum of the products of X and Y by multiplying the row of X by the column of Y or the row of Y by the column of X.

$$\Sigma XY: \quad [1 \quad 4 \quad 1 \quad 3 \quad 7] \begin{bmatrix} 3 \\ -5 \\ 7 \\ 2 \\ -1 \end{bmatrix} = -11$$

Instead of multiplying a row vector by a column vector, one may multiply a column vector by a row vector. The two operations are entirely different from each other. In the preceding, I showed that the former results in a scalar. The latter operation, on the other hand, results in a matrix. This is why it is referred to as the matrix product of vectors. For example,

$$\begin{bmatrix} 3 \\ -5 \\ 7 \\ 2 \\ -1 \end{bmatrix} [1 \quad 4 \quad 1 \quad 3 \quad 7] = \begin{bmatrix} 3 & 12 & 3 & 9 & 21 \\ -5 & -20 & -5 & -15 & -35 \\ 7 & 28 & 7 & 21 & 49 \\ 2 & 8 & 2 & 6 & 14 \\ -1 & -4 & -1 & -3 & -7 \end{bmatrix}$$

Note that each element of the column is multiplied, in turn, by each element of the row to obtain one element of the matrix. The products of the first element of the column by the row elements become the first row of the matrix. Those of the second element of the column by the row become the second row of the matrix, and so forth. Thus, the matrix product of a column vector of k elements and a row of vector of k elements is a $k \times k$ matrix.

Matrix multiplication is done by multiplying rows by columns. An illustration is easier than verbal explanation. Suppose we want to multiply two matrices, **A** and **B**, to produce the product matrix, **C**:

$$\begin{bmatrix} 3 & 1 \\ 5 & 1 \\ 2 & 4 \end{bmatrix} \times \begin{bmatrix} 4 & 1 & 4 \\ 5 & 6 & 2 \end{bmatrix} = \begin{bmatrix} 17 & 9 & 14 \\ 25 & 11 & 22 \\ 28 & 26 & 16 \end{bmatrix}$$

$$\quad\quad \mathbf{A} \quad\quad\quad\quad \mathbf{B} \quad\quad\quad\quad \mathbf{C}$$

Following the rule of scalar product of vectors, we multiply and add as follows (follow the arrows):

$$(3)(4) + (1)(5) = 17 \quad\quad (3)(1) + (1)(6) = 9 \quad\quad (3)(4) + (1)(2) = 14$$

$$(5)(4) + (1)(5) = 25 \quad\quad (5)(1) + (1)(6) = 11 \quad\quad (5)(4) + (1)(2) = 22$$

$$(2)(4) + (4)(5) = 28 \quad\quad (2)(1) + (4)(6) = 26 \quad\quad (2)(4) + (4)(2) = 16$$

From the foregoing illustration it may be discerned that in order to multiply two matrices it is necessary that the number of columns of the first matrix be equal to the number of rows of the second matrix. This is referred to as the *conformability* condition. Thus, for example, an n-by-k matrix can be multiplied by a k-by-m matrix because the number of columns of the first (k) is equal to the number of rows of the second (k). In this context, the k's are referred to as the "interior" dimensions; n and m are referred to as the "exterior" dimensions.

Two matrices are conformable when they have the same "interior" dimensions. There are no restrictions on the "exterior" dimensions when two matrices are multiplied. It is useful to note that the "exterior" dimensions of two matrices being multiplied become the dimensions of the product matrix. For example, when a 3-by-2 matrix is multiplied by a 2-by-5 matrix, a 3-by-5 matrix is obtained:

$$(\text{3-by-2}) \times (\text{2-by-5}) = (\text{3-by-5})$$

In general,

$$(n\text{-by-}k) \times (k\text{-by-}m) = (n\text{-by-}m)$$

A special case of matrix multiplication often encountered in statistical work is the multiplication of a matrix by its transpose to obtain a matrix of raw score, or deviation, Sums of Squares and Cross Products (SSCP). Assume that there are n subjects for whom measures on k variables are available. In other words, assume that the data matrix, **X**, is an n-by-k. To obtain the raw score SSCP calculate **X′X**. Here is a numerical example:

$$
k\begin{bmatrix} 1 & 4 & 1 & 3 & 7 \\ 2 & 3 & 3 & 4 & 6 \\ 2 & 5 & 1 & 3 & 5 \end{bmatrix}
n\begin{bmatrix} 1 & 2 & 2 \\ 4 & 3 & 5 \\ 1 & 3 & 1 \\ 3 & 4 & 3 \\ 7 & 6 & 5 \end{bmatrix}
= \begin{bmatrix} 76 & 71 & 67 \\ 71 & 74 & 64 \\ 67 & 64 & 64 \end{bmatrix}
$$

$$\quad\quad\quad \mathbf{X'} \quad\quad\quad\quad\quad \mathbf{X} \quad\quad\quad\quad \mathbf{X'X}$$

In statistical symbols, **X′X** is

$$\Sigma X_i X_j = \begin{bmatrix} \Sigma X_1^2 & \Sigma X_1 X_2 & \Sigma X_1 X_3 \\ \Sigma X_2 X_1 & \Sigma X_2^2 & \Sigma X_2 X_3 \\ \Sigma X_3 X_1 & \Sigma X_3 X_2 & \Sigma X_3^2 \end{bmatrix}$$

Using similar operations, one may obtain deviation SSCP matrices. Such matrices are used frequently in this book (see, in particular, Chapters 6, 20, and 21).

A matrix can be multiplied by a scalar: each element of the matrix is multiplied by the scalar. Suppose, for example, we want to calculate the mean of each of the elements of a matrix of sums of scores. Let $N = 10$. The operation is

$$\frac{1}{10} \begin{bmatrix} 20 & 48 \\ 30 & 40 \\ 35 & 39 \end{bmatrix} = \begin{bmatrix} 2.0 & 4.8 \\ 3.0 & 4.0 \\ 3.5 & 3.9 \end{bmatrix}$$

Each element of the matrix is multiplied by the scalar $\frac{1}{10}$.

A matrix can be multiplied by a vector. The first of the following examples is premultiplication by a vector, the second is postmultiplication:

$$[6 \quad 5 \quad 2] \begin{bmatrix} 7 & 3 \\ 7 & 2 \\ 4 & 1 \end{bmatrix} = [85 \quad 30]$$

$$\begin{bmatrix} 7 & 7 & 4 \\ 3 & 2 & 1 \end{bmatrix} \begin{bmatrix} 6 \\ 5 \\ 2 \end{bmatrix} = \begin{bmatrix} 85 \\ 30 \end{bmatrix}$$

Note that in the latter example, (2-by-3) × (3-by-1) becomes (2-by-1). This sort of multiplication of a matrix by a vector is done frequently in multiple regression analysis (see, for example, Chapter 6).

Thus far, I said nothing about the operation of division in matrix algebra. In order to show how this is done it is necessary first to discuss some other concepts, to which I now turn.

DETERMINANTS

A *determinant* is a certain numerical value associated with a square matrix. The determinant of a matrix is indicated by vertical lines instead of brackets. For example, the determinant of a matrix **B** is written

$$\det \mathbf{B} = |\mathbf{B}| = \begin{vmatrix} 4 & 2 \\ 1 & 5 \end{vmatrix}$$
$$\mathbf{B}$$

The calculation of the determinant of a 2×2 matrix is very simple: it is the product of the elements of the principal diagonal minus the product of the remaining two elements. For the above matrix,

$$|\mathbf{B}| = \begin{vmatrix} 4 & 2 \\ 1 & 5 \end{vmatrix} = (4)(5) - (1)(2) = 20 - 2 = 18$$

or, symbolically,

$$|\mathbf{B}| = \begin{vmatrix} b_{11} & b_{12} \\ b_{21} & b_{22} \end{vmatrix} = b_{11}b_{22} - b_{12}b_{21}$$

The calculation of determinants for larger matrices is quite tedious and will not be shown here (see references cited in the beginning of the chapter). In any event, matrix operations are most often done with the aid of a computer (see Chapter 6). My purpose here is solely to indicate the role played by determinants in some applications of statistical analysis.

Applications of Determinants

To give the flavor of the place and usefulness of determinants in statistical analysis, I turn first to two simple correlation examples. Suppose we have two correlation coefficients, r_{y1} and r_{y2}, calculated between a dependent variable, Y, and two variables, 1 and 2. The correlations are $r_{y1} = .80$ and $r_{y2} = .20$. I set up two matrices that express the two relations, but I do this immediately in the form of determinants, whose numerical values I calculate:

$$\begin{vmatrix} & 1 & y \\ 1.00 & .80 \\ .80 & 1.00 \end{vmatrix} = (1.00)(1.00) - (.80)(.80) = .36$$

and

$$\begin{vmatrix} & 2 & y \\ 1.00 & .20 \\ .20 & 1.00 \end{vmatrix} = (1.00)(1.00) - (.20)(.20) = .96$$

The two determinants are .36 and .96.

Now, to determine the percentage of variance shared by y and 1 and by y and 2, square the r's:

$$r_{y1}^2 = (.80)^2 = .64$$

$$r_{y2}^2 = (.20)^2 = .04$$

Subtract each of these from 1.00: $1.00 - .64 = .36$, and $1.00 - .04 = .96$. These are the determinants just calculated. They are $1 - r^2$, or the proportions of the variance not accounted for.

As an extension of the foregoing demonstration, it may be shown how the squared multiple correlation, R^2, can be calculated with determinants:

$$R_{y.12...k}^2 = 1 - \frac{|\mathbf{R}|}{|\mathbf{R}_x|}$$

where $|\mathbf{R}|$ is the determinant of the correlation matrix of all the variables, that is, the independent variables as well as the dependent variable, and $|\mathbf{R}_x|$ is the determinant of the correlation matrix of the independent variables. As the foregoing shows, the ratio of the two determinants indicates the proportion of variance of the dependent variable, Y, *not* accounted by the independent variables, X's. (See Study Suggestions 6 and 7 at the end of this appendix.)

The ratio of two determinants is also frequently used in multivariate analyses (see the sections of Chapters 20 and 21 dealing with Wilks' Λ).

Another important use of determinants is related to the concept of linear dependencies, to which I now turn.

Linear Dependence

Linear dependence means that one or more vectors of a matrix, rows or columns, are a linear combination of other vectors of the matrix. The vectors $\mathbf{a}' = \begin{bmatrix} 3 & 1 & 4 \end{bmatrix}$ and $\mathbf{b}' = \begin{bmatrix} 6 & 2 & 8 \end{bmatrix}$ are dependent since $2\mathbf{a}' = \mathbf{b}'$. If one vector is a function of another in this manner, the coefficient of correlation between them is 1.00. Dependence in a matrix can be defined by reference to its determinant. If the determinant of the matrix is zero it means that the matrix contains at least one linear dependency. Such a matrix is referred to as being *singular*. For example, calculate the determinant of the following matrix:

$$\begin{vmatrix} 3 & 1 \\ 6 & 2 \end{vmatrix} = (3)(2) - (1)(6) = 0$$

The matrix is singular, that is, it contains a linear dependency. Note that the values of the second row are twice the values of the first row.

A matrix whose determinant is not equal to zero is referred to as being *nonsingular.* The notions of singularity and nonsingularity of matrices play very important roles in statistical analysis. For example, in Chapter 10 issues regarding collinearity are discussed in reference to the determinant of the correlation matrix of the independent variables. As I will show, a singular matrix has no inverse.

I turn now to the operation of division in matrix algebra, which I present in the context of the discussion of matrix inversion.

MATRIX INVERSE

Recall that the division of one number into another amounts to multiplying the dividend by the reciprocal of the divisor:

$$\frac{a}{b} = \frac{1}{b} a$$

For example, $12/4 = 12(1/4) = (12)(.25) = 3$. Analogously, in matrix algebra, instead of dividing a matrix **A** by another matrix **B** to obtain matrix **C**, we multiply **A** by the *inverse* of **B** to obtain **C**. The inverse of **B** is written $\mathbf{B}^{-1}$. Suppose, in ordinary algebra, we had $ab = c$, and we wanted to find b. We would write

$$b = \frac{c}{a}$$

In matrix algebra, we write

$$\mathbf{B} = \mathbf{A}^{-1}\mathbf{C}$$

(Note that **C** is premultiplied by $\mathbf{A}^{-1}$ and not postmultiplied. In general, $\mathbf{A}^{-1}\mathbf{C} \neq \mathbf{C}\mathbf{A}^{-1}$.)

The formal definition of the inverse of a square matrix is: Given **A** and **B**, two square matrices, if $\mathbf{AB} = \mathbf{I}$, then **A** is the inverse of **B**.

Generally, the calculation of the inverse of a matrix is very laborious and, therefore, error prone. This is why it is best to use a computer program for such purposes (see the following). Fortunately, however, the calculation of the inverse of a 2×2 matrix is very simple, and is shown here because (1) it affords an illustration of the basic approach to the calculation of the inverse, (2) it affords the opportunity of showing the role played by the determinant in the calculation of the inverse, and (3) inverses of 2×2 matrices are frequently calculated in some chapters of this book (see, in particular, Chapters 6, 20, and 21).

In order to show how the inverse of a 2×2 matrix is calculated it is necessary first to discuss briefly the *adjoint* of such a matrix. I show this in reference to the following matrix:

$$\mathbf{A} = \begin{bmatrix} a & b \\ c & d \end{bmatrix}$$

The adjoint of **A** is

$$\text{adj } \mathbf{A} = \begin{bmatrix} d & -b \\ -c & a \end{bmatrix}$$

Thus, to obtain the adjoint of a 2×2 matrix, interchange the elements of its principal diagonal (*a* and *d* in the above example) and change the signs of the other two elements (*b* and *c* in the above example).[1]

Now the inverse of a matrix **A** is

$$\mathbf{A}^{-1} = \frac{\text{adj } \mathbf{A}}{|\mathbf{A}|} = \frac{1}{|\mathbf{A}|} \text{ adj } \mathbf{A}$$

where $|\mathbf{A}|$ is the determinant of **A**.

I calculate now the inverse of the following matrix, **A**:

$$\mathbf{A} = \begin{bmatrix} 6 & 2 \\ 8 & 4 \end{bmatrix}$$

First, I calculate the determinant of **A**:

$$|\mathbf{A}| = \begin{vmatrix} 6 & 2 \\ 8 & 4 \end{vmatrix} = (6)(4) - (2)(8) = 8$$

Second, I form the adjoint of **A**:

$$\text{adj } \mathbf{A} = \begin{bmatrix} 4 & -2 \\ -8 & 6 \end{bmatrix}$$

Third, I multiply the adj **A** by the reciprocal of $|\mathbf{A}|$ to obtain the inverse of **A**:

$$\mathbf{A}^{-1} = \frac{1}{|\mathbf{A}|} \text{ adj } \mathbf{A} = \frac{1}{8} \begin{bmatrix} 4 & -2 \\ -8 & 6 \end{bmatrix} = \begin{bmatrix} .50 & -.25 \\ -1.00 & .75 \end{bmatrix}$$

Earlier, I said that $\mathbf{A}^{-1}\mathbf{A} = \mathbf{I}$. For the present example,

$$\mathbf{A}^{-1}\mathbf{A} = \underset{\mathbf{A}^{-1}}{\begin{bmatrix} .50 & -.25 \\ -1.00 & .75 \end{bmatrix}} \underset{\mathbf{A}}{\begin{bmatrix} 6 & 2 \\ 8 & 4 \end{bmatrix}} = \underset{\mathbf{I}}{\begin{bmatrix} 1.00 & 0 \\ 0 & 1.00 \end{bmatrix}}$$

Also, a matrix whose determinant is zero is singular. From the foregoing demonstration of the calculation of the inverse it should be clear that a singular matrix has no inverse. Although one does not generally encounter singular matrices in social science research, an unwary researcher may introduce singularity in the treatment of the data. For example, suppose that a test battery consisting of five subtests is used to predict a given criterion. If, under such circumstances, the researcher uses not only the scores on the five subtests but also a total score, obtained as the sum of the five subscores, he or she has introduced a linear dependency (see the preceding), thereby rendering the matrix singular. Similarly, when one uses scores on two scales as well as the differences between them in the same matrix. Other situations when one should be on guard not to introduce linear dependencies in a matrix occur when coded vectors are used to represent categorical variables (see Chapter 11).

---

[1]For a general definition of the adjoint of a matrix, see references cited in the beginning of this appendix. Adjoints of 2×2 matrices are used frequently in Chapters 20 and 21.

CONCLUSION

I realize that this brief introduction to matrix algebra cannot serve to demonstrate its great power and elegance. To do this, it would be necessary to use matrices whose dimensions are larger than the ones I used here for simplicity of presentation. To begin to appreciate the power of matrix algebra, I suggest that you think of the large data matrices frequently encountered in behavioral research. Using matrix algebra, one can manipulate and operate upon large matrices with relative ease, when ordinary algebra will simply not do. For example, when in multiple regression analysis only two independent variables are used, it is relatively easy to do the calculations by ordinary algebra (see Chapter 5). But with increasing numbers of independent variables, the use of matrix algebra for the calculation of multiple regression analysis becomes a must. Also, as I amply demonstrated in Parts 3 and 4 of this book, matrix algebra is the language of structural equation models and multivariate analysis. In short, to understand and be able to intelligently apply these methods it is essential that you develop a working knowledge of matrix algebra. Therefore, I strongly suggest that you do some or all the calculations of the matrix operations presented in the various chapters, particularly those in Chapter 6 and in Parts 3 and 4 of the book. Furthermore, I suggest that you learn to use computer programs when you have to manipulate relatively large matrices. In Chapter 6, I introduce matrix procedures from Minitab, SAS, and SPSS.

STUDY SUGGESTIONS

1. You will find it useful to work through some of the rules of matrix algebra. Use of the rules occurs again and again in multiple regression, factor analysis, discriminant analysis, canonical correlation, and multivariate analysis of variance. The most important of the rules are as follows:

(1) $\mathbf{ABC} = (\mathbf{AB})\mathbf{C} = \mathbf{A}(\mathbf{BC})$

This is the *associative rule* of matrix multiplication. It simply indicates that the multiplication of three (or more) matrices can be done by pairing and multiplying the first two matrices and then multiplying the product by the remaining matrix, or by pairing and multiplying the second two and then multiplying the product by the first matrix. Or we can regard the rule in the following way:

$$\mathbf{AB} = \mathbf{D}, \text{ then } \mathbf{DC}$$
$$\mathbf{BC} = \mathbf{E}, \text{ then } \mathbf{AE}$$

(2) $\mathbf{A} + \mathbf{B} = \mathbf{B} + \mathbf{A}$

That is, the order of addition makes no difference. And the associative rule applies:

$$\mathbf{A} + \mathbf{B} + \mathbf{C} = (\mathbf{A} + \mathbf{B}) + \mathbf{C}$$
$$= \mathbf{A} + (\mathbf{B} + \mathbf{C})$$

(3) $\mathbf{A}(\mathbf{B} + \mathbf{C}) = \mathbf{AB} + \mathbf{AC}$

This is the *distributive rule* of ordinary algebra.

(4) $(\mathbf{AB})' = \mathbf{B}'\mathbf{A}'$

The transpose of the product of two matrices is equal to the transpose of their product in reverse order.

(5) $(\mathbf{AB})^{-1} = \mathbf{B}^{-1}\mathbf{A}^{-1}$

This rule is the same as that in (4), except that it is applied to matrix inverses.

(6) $\mathbf{AA}^{-1} = \mathbf{A}^{-1}\mathbf{A} = \mathbf{I}$

This rule can be used as a proof that the calculation of the inverse of a matrix is correct.

(7) $\mathbf{AB} \neq \mathbf{BA}$

This is actually not a rule. I included it to emphasize that the order of the multiplication of matrices is important.

Here are three matrices, **A**, **B**, and **C**.

$$\begin{pmatrix} 2 & 3 \\ 1 & 2 \end{pmatrix} \quad \begin{pmatrix} 3 & 4 \\ 0 & 1 \end{pmatrix} \quad \begin{pmatrix} 0 & 2 \\ 5 & 3 \end{pmatrix}$$
$$\mathbf{A} \qquad\quad \mathbf{B} \qquad\quad \mathbf{C}$$

(a) Demonstrate the associative rule by multiplying:

$$\mathbf{A} \times \mathbf{B}; \text{ then } \mathbf{AB} \times \mathbf{C}$$
$$\mathbf{B} \times \mathbf{C}; \text{ then } \mathbf{A} \times \mathbf{BC}$$

(b) Demonstrate the distributive rule using **A**, **B**, and **C** of (a).

(c) Using **B** and **C**, above, show that **BC** ≠ **CB**.

2. What are the dimensions of the matrix that will result from multiplying a 3-by-6 matrix **A** by a 6-by-2 matrix **B**?

3. Given:

$$\mathbf{A} = \begin{bmatrix} 1.26 & -.73 \\ 2.12 & 1.34 \\ 4.61 & -.31 \end{bmatrix} \quad \mathbf{B} = \begin{bmatrix} 4.11 & 1.12 \\ -2.30 & -.36 \end{bmatrix}$$

What is **AB**?

4. When it is said that a matrix is singular, what does it imply about its determinant?

5. Calculate the inverse of the following matrix:

$$\begin{bmatrix} 15 & -3 \\ 6 & 12 \end{bmatrix}$$

6. In a study of Holtzman and Brown (1968), the correlations among measures of study habits and attitudes, scholastic aptitude, and grade-point averages were reported as follows:

	SHA	*SA*	*GPA*
SHA	1.00	.32	.55
SA	.32	1.00	.61
GPA	.55	.61	1.00

The determinant of this matrix is .4377. Calculate R^2 for GPA with SHA and SA. (*Hint:* You need to calculate the determinant of the matrix of the independent variables, and then use the two determinants for the calculation of R^2.)

7. Liddle (1958) reported the following correlations among intellectual ability, leadership ability, and withdrawn maladjustment:

	IA	*LA*	*WM*
IA	1.00	.37	-.28
LA	.37	1.00	-.61
WM	-.28	-.61	1.00

The determinant of this matrix is .5390. Calculate the following:

(a) The proportion of variance of WM *not* accounted for by IA and LA.

(b) R^2 of WM with IA and LA.

(c) Using matrix algebra, the regression equation of WM on IA and LA. (See Chapter 6 for matrix equation.)

8. I strongly suggest that you study one or more of the references cited in the beginning of this appendix.

ANSWERS

1. (a)

$$\mathbf{ABC} = \begin{bmatrix} 55 & 45 \\ 30 & 24 \end{bmatrix}$$

(b)

$$\mathbf{A(B + C)} = \begin{bmatrix} 21 & 24 \\ 13 & 14 \end{bmatrix}$$

(c)

$$\mathbf{BC} = \begin{bmatrix} 20 & 18 \\ 5 & 3 \end{bmatrix} \quad \mathbf{CB} = \begin{bmatrix} 0 & 2 \\ 15 & 23 \end{bmatrix}$$

2. 3-by-2

3.

$$\mathbf{AB} = \begin{bmatrix} 6.8576 & 1.6740 \\ 5.6312 & 1.8920 \\ 19.6601 & 5.2748 \end{bmatrix}$$

4. The determinant is zero.

5.

$$\begin{bmatrix} .06061 & .01515 \\ -.03030 & .07576 \end{bmatrix}$$

6. The determinant of the matrix of the independent variables is .8976.

$$R^2 = 1 - \frac{.4377}{.8976} = .5124$$

7. (a) .62449
   (b) .37551
   (c)

$$\beta = \mathbf{R}^{-1}\mathbf{r} = \begin{bmatrix} -.06291 \\ -.58672 \end{bmatrix}$$

B

Tables of F, Chi Squared Distributions, and Orthogonal Polynomials

The 5 (Roman Type) and 1 (Boldface Type) Percent Points for the Distribution of F*

n_1 degrees of freedom (for greater mean square)

n_2	1	2	3	4	5	6	7	8	9	10	11	12	14	16	20	24	30	40	50	75	100	200	500	∞
1	161 / **4,052**	200 / **4,999**	216 / **5,403**	225 / **5,625**	230 / **5,764**	234 / **5,859**	237 / **5,928**	239 / **5,981**	241 / **6,022**	242 / **6,056**	243 / **6,082**	244 / **6,106**	245 / **6,142**	246 / **6,169**	248 / **6,208**	249 / **6,234**	250 / **6,258**	251 / **6,286**	252 / **6,302**	253 / **6,323**	253 / **6,334**	254 / **6,352**	254 / **6,361**	254 / **6,366**
2	18.51 / **98.49**	19.00 / **99.00**	19.16 / **99.17**	19.25 / **99.25**	19.30 / **99.30**	19.33 / **99.33**	19.36 / **99.34**	19.37 / **99.36**	19.38 / **99.38**	19.39 / **99.40**	19.40 / **99.41**	19.41 / **99.42**	19.42 / **99.43**	19.43 / **99.44**	19.44 / **99.45**	19.45 / **99.46**	19.46 / **99.47**	19.47 / **99.48**	19.47 / **99.48**	19.48 / **99.49**	19.49 / **99.49**	19.49 / **99.49**	19.50 / **99.50**	19.50 / **99.50**
3	10.13 / **34.12**	9.55 / **30.82**	9.28 / **29.46**	9.12 / **28.71**	9.01 / **28.24**	8.94 / **27.91**	8.88 / **27.67**	8.84 / **27.49**	8.81 / **27.34**	8.78 / **27.23**	8.76 / **27.13**	8.74 / **27.05**	8.71 / **26.92**	8.69 / **26.83**	8.66 / **26.69**	8.64 / **26.60**	8.62 / **26.50**	8.60 / **26.41**	8.58 / **26.35**	8.57 / **26.27**	8.56 / **26.23**	8.54 / **26.18**	8.54 / **26.14**	8.53 / **26.12**
4	7.71 / **21.20**	6.94 / **18.00**	6.59 / **16.69**	6.39 / **15.98**	6.26 / **15.52**	6.16 / **15.21**	6.09 / **14.98**	6.04 / **14.80**	6.00 / **14.66**	5.96 / **14.54**	5.93 / **14.45**	5.91 / **14.37**	5.87 / **14.24**	5.84 / **14.15**	5.80 / **14.02**	5.77 / **13.93**	5.74 / **13.83**	5.71 / **13.74**	5.70 / **13.69**	5.68 / **13.61**	5.66 / **13.57**	5.65 / **13.52**	5.64 / **13.48**	5.63 / **13.46**
5	6.61 / **16.26**	5.79 / **13.27**	5.41 / **12.06**	5.19 / **11.39**	5.05 / **10.97**	4.95 / **10.67**	4.88 / **10.45**	4.82 / **10.27**	4.78 / **10.15**	4.74 / **10.05**	4.70 / **9.96**	4.68 / **9.89**	4.64 / **9.77**	4.60 / **9.68**	4.56 / **9.55**	4.53 / **9.47**	4.50 / **9.38**	4.46 / **9.29**	4.44 / **9.24**	4.42 / **9.17**	4.40 / **9.13**	4.38 / **9.07**	4.37 / **9.04**	4.36 / **9.02**
6	5.99 / **13.74**	5.14 / **10.92**	4.76 / **9.78**	4.53 / **9.15**	4.39 / **8.75**	4.28 / **8.47**	4.21 / **8.26**	4.15 / **8.10**	4.10 / **7.98**	4.06 / **7.87**	4.03 / **7.79**	4.00 / **7.72**	3.96 / **7.60**	3.92 / **7.52**	3.87 / **7.39**	3.84 / **7.31**	3.81 / **7.23**	3.77 / **7.14**	3.75 / **7.09**	3.72 / **7.02**	3.71 / **6.99**	3.69 / **6.94**	3.68 / **6.90**	3.67 / **6.88**
7	5.59 / **12.25**	4.74 / **9.55**	4.35 / **8.45**	4.12 / **7.85**	3.97 / **7.46**	3.87 / **7.19**	3.79 / **7.00**	3.73 / **6.84**	3.68 / **6.71**	3.63 / **6.62**	3.60 / **6.54**	3.57 / **6.47**	3.52 / **6.35**	3.49 / **6.27**	3.44 / **6.15**	3.41 / **6.07**	3.38 / **5.98**	3.34 / **5.90**	3.32 / **5.85**	3.29 / **5.78**	3.28 / **5.75**	3.25 / **5.70**	3.24 / **5.67**	3.23 / **5.65**
8	5.32 / **11.26**	4.46 / **8.65**	4.07 / **7.59**	3.84 / **7.01**	3.69 / **6.63**	3.58 / **6.37**	3.50 / **6.19**	3.44 / **6.03**	3.39 / **5.91**	3.34 / **5.82**	3.31 / **5.74**	3.28 / **5.67**	3.23 / **5.56**	3.20 / **5.48**	3.15 / **5.36**	3.12 / **5.28**	3.08 / **5.20**	3.05 / **5.11**	3.03 / **5.06**	3.00 / **5.00**	2.98 / **4.96**	2.96 / **4.91**	2.94 / **4.88**	2.93 / **4.86**
9	5.12 / **10.56**	4.26 / **8.02**	3.86 / **6.99**	3.63 / **6.42**	3.48 / **6.06**	3.37 / **5.80**	3.29 / **5.62**	3.23 / **5.47**	3.18 / **5.35**	3.13 / **5.26**	3.10 / **5.18**	3.07 / **5.11**	3.02 / **5.00**	2.98 / **4.92**	2.93 / **4.80**	2.90 / **4.73**	2.86 / **4.64**	2.82 / **4.56**	2.80 / **4.51**	2.77 / **4.45**	2.76 / **4.41**	2.73 / **4.36**	2.72 / **4.33**	2.71 / **4.31**
10	4.96 / **10.04**	4.10 / **7.56**	3.71 / **6.55**	3.48 / **5.99**	3.33 / **5.64**	3.22 / **5.39**	3.14 / **5.21**	3.07 / **5.06**	3.02 / **4.95**	2.97 / **4.85**	2.94 / **4.78**	2.91 / **4.71**	2.86 / **4.60**	2.82 / **4.52**	2.77 / **4.41**	2.74 / **4.33**	2.70 / **4.25**	2.67 / **4.17**	2.64 / **4.12**	2.61 / **4.05**	2.59 / **4.01**	2.56 / **3.96**	2.55 / **3.93**	2.54 / **3.91**
11	4.84 / **9.65**	3.98 / **7.20**	3.59 / **6.22**	3.36 / **5.67**	3.20 / **5.32**	3.09 / **5.07**	3.01 / **4.88**	2.95 / **4.74**	2.90 / **4.63**	2.86 / **4.54**	2.82 / **4.46**	2.79 / **4.40**	2.74 / **4.29**	2.70 / **4.21**	2.65 / **4.10**	2.61 / **4.02**	2.57 / **3.94**	2.53 / **3.86**	2.50 / **3.80**	2.47 / **3.74**	2.45 / **3.70**	2.42 / **3.66**	2.41 / **3.62**	2.40 / **3.60**
12	4.75 / **9.33**	3.88 / **6.93**	3.49 / **5.95**	3.26 / **5.41**	3.11 / **5.06**	3.00 / **4.82**	2.92 / **4.65**	2.85 / **4.50**	2.80 / **4.39**	2.76 / **4.30**	2.72 / **4.22**	2.69 / **4.16**	2.64 / **4.05**	2.60 / **3.98**	2.54 / **3.86**	2.50 / **3.78**	2.46 / **3.70**	2.42 / **3.61**	2.40 / **3.56**	2.36 / **3.49**	2.35 / **3.46**	2.32 / **3.41**	2.31 / **3.38**	2.30 / **3.36**
13	4.67 / **9.07**	3.80 / **6.70**	3.41 / **5.74**	3.18 / **5.20**	3.02 / **4.86**	2.92 / **4.62**	2.84 / **4.44**	2.77 / **4.30**	2.72 / **4.19**	2.67 / **4.10**	2.63 / **4.02**	2.60 / **3.96**	2.55 / **3.85**	2.51 / **3.78**	2.46 / **3.67**	2.42 / **3.59**	2.38 / **3.51**	2.34 / **3.42**	2.32 / **3.37**	2.28 / **3.30**	2.26 / **3.27**	2.24 / **3.21**	2.22 / **3.18**	2.21 / **3.16**

*Reproduced from Snedecor: *Statistical Methods*, Iowa State College Press, Ames, Iowa, by permission of the author and publisher.

The 5 (Roman Type) and 1 (Boldface Type) Percent Points for the Distribution of F*—Continued

n_1 degrees of freedom (for greater mean square)

n_2	1	2	3	4	5	6	7	8	9	10	11	12	14	16	20	24	30	40	50	75	100	200	500	∞
14	4.60 **8.86**	3.74 **6.51**	3.34 **5.56**	3.11 **5.03**	2.96 **4.69**	2.85 **4.46**	2.77 **4.28**	2.70 **4.14**	2.65 **4.03**	2.60 **3.94**	2.56 **3.86**	2.53 **3.80**	2.48 **3.70**	2.44 **3.62**	2.39 **3.51**	2.35 **3.43**	2.31 **3.34**	2.27 **3.26**	2.24 **3.21**	2.21 **3.14**	2.19 **3.11**	2.16 **3.06**	2.14 **3.02**	2.13 **3.00**
15	4.54 **8.68**	3.68 **6.36**	3.29 **5.42**	3.06 **4.89**	2.90 **4.56**	2.79 **4.32**	2.70 **4.14**	2.64 **4.00**	2.59 **3.89**	2.55 **3.80**	2.51 **3.73**	2.48 **3.67**	2.43 **3.56**	2.39 **3.48**	2.33 **3.36**	2.29 **3.29**	2.25 **3.20**	2.21 **3.12**	2.18 **3.07**	2.15 **3.00**	2.12 **2.97**	2.10 **2.92**	2.08 **2.89**	2.07 **2.87**
16	4.49 **8.53**	3.63 **6.23**	3.24 **5.29**	3.01 **4.77**	2.85 **4.44**	2.74 **4.20**	2.66 **4.03**	2.59 **3.89**	2.54 **3.78**	2.49 **3.69**	2.45 **3.61**	2.42 **3.55**	2.37 **3.45**	2.33 **3.37**	2.28 **3.25**	2.24 **3.18**	2.20 **3.10**	2.16 **3.01**	2.13 **2.96**	2.09 **2.89**	2.07 **2.86**	2.04 **2.80**	2.02 **2.77**	2.01 **2.75**
17	4.45 **8.40**	3.59 **6.11**	3.20 **5.18**	2.96 **4.67**	2.81 **4.34**	2.70 **4.10**	2.62 **3.93**	2.55 **3.79**	2.50 **3.68**	2.45 **3.59**	2.41 **3.52**	2.38 **3.45**	2.33 **3.35**	2.29 **3.27**	2.23 **3.16**	2.19 **3.08**	2.15 **3.00**	2.11 **2.92**	2.08 **2.86**	2.04 **2.79**	2.02 **2.76**	1.99 **2.70**	1.97 **2.67**	1.96 **2.65**
18	4.41 **8.28**	3.55 **6.01**	3.16 **5.09**	2.93 **4.58**	2.77 **4.25**	2.66 **4.01**	2.58 **3.85**	2.51 **3.71**	2.46 **3.60**	2.41 **3.51**	2.37 **3.44**	2.34 **3.37**	2.29 **3.27**	2.25 **3.19**	2.19 **3.07**	2.15 **3.00**	2.11 **2.91**	2.07 **2.83**	2.04 **2.78**	2.00 **2.71**	1.98 **2.68**	1.95 **2.62**	1.93 **2.59**	1.92 **2.57**
19	4.38 **8.18**	3.52 **5.93**	3.13 **5.01**	2.90 **4.50**	2.74 **4.17**	2.63 **3.94**	2.55 **3.77**	2.48 **3.63**	2.43 **3.52**	2.38 **3.43**	2.34 **3.36**	2.31 **3.30**	2.26 **3.19**	2.21 **3.12**	2.15 **3.00**	2.11 **2.92**	2.07 **2.84**	2.02 **2.76**	2.00 **2.70**	1.96 **2.63**	1.94 **2.60**	1.91 **2.54**	1.90 **2.51**	1.88 **2.49**
20	4.35 **8.10**	3.49 **5.85**	3.10 **4.94**	2.87 **4.43**	2.71 **4.10**	2.60 **3.87**	2.52 **3.71**	2.45 **3.56**	2.40 **3.45**	2.35 **3.37**	2.31 **3.30**	2.28 **3.23**	2.23 **3.13**	2.18 **3.05**	2.12 **2.94**	2.08 **2.86**	2.04 **2.77**	1.99 **2.69**	1.96 **2.63**	1.92 **2.56**	1.90 **2.53**	1.87 **2.47**	1.85 **2.44**	1.84 **2.42**
21	4.32 **8.02**	3.47 **5.78**	3.07 **4.87**	2.84 **4.37**	2.68 **4.04**	2.57 **3.81**	2.49 **3.65**	2.42 **3.51**	2.37 **3.40**	2.32 **3.31**	2.28 **3.24**	2.25 **3.17**	2.20 **3.07**	2.15 **2.99**	2.09 **2.88**	2.05 **2.80**	2.00 **2.72**	1.96 **2.63**	1.93 **2.58**	1.89 **2.51**	1.87 **2.47**	1.84 **2.42**	1.82 **2.38**	1.81 **2.36**
22	4.30 **7.94**	3.44 **5.72**	3.05 **4.82**	2.82 **4.31**	2.66 **3.99**	2.55 **3.76**	2.47 **3.59**	2.40 **3.45**	2.35 **3.35**	2.30 **3.26**	2.26 **3.18**	2.23 **3.12**	2.18 **3.02**	2.13 **2.94**	2.07 **2.83**	2.03 **2.75**	1.98 **2.67**	1.93 **2.58**	1.91 **2.53**	1.87 **2.46**	1.84 **2.42**	1.81 **2.37**	1.80 **2.33**	1.78 **2.31**
23	4.28 **7.88**	3.42 **5.66**	3.03 **4.76**	2.80 **4.26**	2.64 **3.94**	2.53 **3.71**	2.45 **3.54**	2.38 **3.41**	2.32 **3.30**	2.28 **3.21**	2.24 **3.14**	2.20 **3.07**	2.14 **2.97**	2.10 **2.89**	2.04 **2.78**	2.00 **2.70**	1.96 **2.62**	1.91 **2.53**	1.88 **2.48**	1.84 **2.41**	1.82 **2.37**	1.79 **2.32**	1.77 **2.28**	1.76 **2.26**
24	4.26 **7.82**	3.40 **5.61**	3.01 **4.72**	2.78 **4.22**	2.62 **3.90**	2.51 **3.67**	2.43 **3.50**	2.36 **3.36**	2.30 **3.25**	2.26 **3.17**	2.22 **3.09**	2.18 **3.03**	2.13 **2.93**	2.09 **2.85**	2.02 **2.74**	1.98 **2.66**	1.94 **2.58**	1.89 **2.49**	1.86 **2.44**	1.82 **2.36**	1.80 **2.33**	1.76 **2.27**	1.74 **2.23**	1.73 **2.21**
25	4.24 **7.77**	3.38 **5.57**	2.99 **4.68**	2.76 **4.18**	2.60 **3.86**	2.49 **3.63**	2.41 **3.46**	2.34 **3.32**	2.28 **3.21**	2.24 **3.13**	2.20 **3.05**	2.16 **2.99**	2.11 **2.89**	2.06 **2.81**	2.00 **2.70**	1.96 **2.62**	1.92 **2.54**	1.87 **2.45**	1.84 **2.40**	1.80 **2.32**	1.77 **2.29**	1.74 **2.23**	1.72 **2.19**	1.71 **2.17**
26	4.22 **7.72**	3.37 **5.53**	2.98 **4.64**	2.74 **4.14**	2.59 **3.82**	2.47 **3.59**	2.39 **3.42**	2.32 **3.29**	2.27 **3.17**	2.22 **3.09**	2.18 **3.02**	2.15 **2.96**	2.10 **2.86**	2.05 **2.77**	1.99 **2.66**	1.95 **2.58**	1.90 **2.50**	1.85 **2.41**	1.82 **2.36**	1.78 **2.28**	1.76 **2.25**	1.72 **2.19**	1.70 **2.15**	1.69 **2.13**

*Reproduced from Snedecor: *Statistical Methods*, Iowa State College Press, Ames, Iowa, by permission of the author and publisher.

The 5 (Roman Type) and 1 (Boldface Type) Percent Points for the Distribution of F*—Continued

n_1 degrees of freedom (for greater mean square)

n_2	1	2	3	4	5	6	7	8	9	10	11	12	14	16	20	24	30	40	50	75	100	200	500	∞
27	4.21 / 7.68	3.35 / 5.49	2.96 / 4.60	2.73 / 4.11	2.57 / 3.79	2.46 / 3.56	2.37 / 3.39	2.30 / 3.26	2.25 / 3.14	2.20 / 3.06	2.16 / 2.98	2.13 / 2.93	2.08 / 2.83	2.03 / 2.74	1.97 / 2.63	1.93 / 2.55	1.88 / 2.47	1.84 / 2.38	1.80 / 2.33	1.76 / 2.25	1.74 / 2.21	1.71 / 2.16	1.68 / 2.12	1.67 / 2.10
28	4.20 / 7.64	3.34 / 5.45	2.95 / 4.57	2.71 / 4.07	2.56 / 3.76	2.44 / 3.53	2.36 / 3.36	2.29 / 3.23	2.24 / 3.11	2.19 / 3.03	2.15 / 2.95	2.12 / 2.90	2.06 / 2.80	2.02 / 2.71	1.96 / 2.60	1.91 / 2.52	1.87 / 2.44	1.81 / 2.35	1.78 / 2.30	1.75 / 2.22	1.72 / 2.18	1.69 / 2.13	1.67 / 2.09	1.65 / 2.06
29	4.18 / 7.60	3.33 / 5.42	2.93 / 4.54	2.70 / 4.04	2.54 / 3.73	2.43 / 3.50	2.35 / 3.33	2.28 / 3.20	2.22 / 3.08	2.18 / 3.00	2.14 / 2.92	2.10 / 2.87	2.05 / 2.77	2.00 / 2.68	1.94 / 2.57	1.90 / 2.49	1.85 / 2.41	1.80 / 2.32	1.77 / 2.27	1.73 / 2.19	1.71 / 2.15	1.68 / 2.10	1.65 / 2.06	1.64 / 2.03
30	4.17 / 7.56	3.32 / 5.39	2.92 / 4.51	2.69 / 4.02	2.53 / 3.70	2.42 / 3.47	2.34 / 3.30	2.27 / 3.17	2.21 / 3.06	2.16 / 2.98	2.12 / 2.90	2.09 / 2.84	2.04 / 2.74	1.99 / 2.66	1.93 / 2.55	1.89 / 2.47	1.84 / 2.38	1.79 / 2.29	1.76 / 2.24	1.72 / 2.16	1.69 / 2.13	1.66 / 2.07	1.64 / 2.03	1.62 / 2.01
32	4.15 / 7.50	3.30 / 5.34	2.90 / 4.46	2.67 / 3.97	2.51 / 3.66	2.40 / 3.42	2.32 / 3.25	2.25 / 3.12	2.19 / 3.01	2.14 / 2.94	2.10 / 2.86	2.07 / 2.80	2.02 / 2.70	1.97 / 2.62	1.91 / 2.51	1.86 / 2.42	1.82 / 2.34	1.76 / 2.25	1.74 / 2.20	1.69 / 2.12	1.67 / 2.08	1.64 / 2.02	1.61 / 1.98	1.59 / 1.96
34	4.13 / 7.44	3.28 / 5.29	2.88 / 4.42	2.65 / 3.93	2.49 / 3.61	2.38 / 3.38	2.30 / 3.21	2.23 / 3.08	2.17 / 2.97	2.12 / 2.89	2.08 / 2.82	2.05 / 2.76	2.00 / 2.66	1.95 / 2.58	1.89 / 2.47	1.84 / 2.38	1.80 / 2.30	1.74 / 2.21	1.71 / 2.15	1.67 / 2.08	1.64 / 2.04	1.61 / 1.98	1.59 / 1.94	1.57 / 1.91
36	4.11 / 7.39	3.26 / 5.25	2.86 / 4.38	2.63 / 3.89	2.48 / 3.58	2.36 / 3.35	2.28 / 3.18	2.21 / 3.04	2.15 / 2.94	2.10 / 2.86	2.06 / 2.78	2.03 / 2.72	1.98 / 2.62	1.93 / 2.54	1.87 / 2.43	1.82 / 2.35	1.78 / 2.26	1.72 / 2.17	1.69 / 2.12	1.65 / 2.04	1.62 / 2.00	1.59 / 1.94	1.56 / 1.90	1.55 / 1.87
38	4.10 / 7.35	3.25 / 5.21	2.85 / 4.34	2.62 / 3.86	2.46 / 3.54	2.35 / 3.32	2.26 / 3.15	2.19 / 3.02	2.14 / 2.91	2.09 / 2.82	2.05 / 2.75	2.02 / 2.69	1.96 / 2.59	1.92 / 2.51	1.85 / 2.40	1.80 / 2.32	1.76 / 2.22	1.71 / 2.14	1.67 / 2.08	1.63 / 2.00	1.60 / 1.97	1.57 / 1.90	1.54 / 1.86	1.53 / 1.84
40	4.08 / 7.31	3.23 / 5.18	2.84 / 4.31	2.61 / 3.83	2.45 / 3.51	2.34 / 3.29	2.25 / 3.12	2.18 / 2.99	2.12 / 2.88	2.07 / 2.80	2.04 / 2.73	2.00 / 2.66	1.95 / 2.56	1.90 / 2.49	1.84 / 2.37	1.79 / 2.29	1.74 / 2.20	1.69 / 2.11	1.66 / 2.05	1.61 / 1.97	1.59 / 1.94	1.55 / 1.88	1.53 / 1.84	1.51 / 1.81
42	4.07 / 7.27	3.22 / 5.15	2.83 / 4.29	2.59 / 3.80	2.44 / 3.49	2.32 / 3.26	2.24 / 3.10	2.17 / 2.96	2.11 / 2.86	2.06 / 2.77	2.02 / 2.70	1.99 / 2.64	1.94 / 2.54	1.89 / 2.46	1.82 / 2.35	1.78 / 2.26	1.73 / 2.17	1.68 / 2.08	1.64 / 2.02	1.60 / 1.94	1.57 / 1.91	1.54 / 1.85	1.51 / 1.80	1.49 / 1.78
44	4.06 / 7.24	3.21 / 5.12	2.82 / 4.26	2.58 / 3.78	2.43 / 3.46	2.31 / 3.24	2.23 / 3.07	2.16 / 2.94	2.10 / 2.84	2.05 / 2.75	2.01 / 2.68	1.98 / 2.62	1.92 / 2.52	1.88 / 2.44	1.81 / 2.32	1.76 / 2.24	1.72 / 2.15	1.66 / 2.06	1.63 / 2.00	1.58 / 1.92	1.56 / 1.88	1.52 / 1.82	1.50 / 1.78	1.48 / 1.75
46	4.05 / 7.21	3.20 / 5.10	2.81 / 4.24	2.57 / 3.76	2.42 / 3.44	2.30 / 3.22	2.22 / 3.05	2.14 / 2.92	2.09 / 2.82	2.04 / 2.73	2.00 / 2.66	1.97 / 2.60	1.91 / 2.50	1.87 / 2.42	1.80 / 2.30	1.75 / 2.22	1.71 / 2.13	1.65 / 2.04	1.62 / 1.98	1.57 / 1.90	1.54 / 1.86	1.51 / 1.80	1.48 / 1.76	1.46 / 1.72
48	4.04 / 7.19	3.19 / 5.08	2.80 / 4.22	2.56 / 3.74	2.41 / 3.42	2.30 / 3.20	2.21 / 3.04	2.14 / 2.90	2.08 / 2.80	2.03 / 2.71	1.99 / 2.64	1.96 / 2.58	1.90 / 2.48	1.86 / 2.40	1.79 / 2.28	1.74 / 2.20	1.70 / 2.11	1.64 / 2.02	1.61 / 1.96	1.56 / 1.88	1.53 / 1.84	1.50 / 1.78	1.47 / 1.73	1.45 / 1.70

*Reproduced from Snedecor: *Statistical Methods*, Iowa State College Press, Ames, Iowa, by permission of the author and publisher.

The 5 (Roman Type) and 1 (Boldface Type) Percent Points for the Distribution of F*—Concluded

n_1 degrees of freedom (for greater mean square)

n_2	1	2	3	4	5	6	7	8	9	10	11	12	14	16	20	24	30	40	50	75	100	200	500	∞
50	4.03 / **7.17**	3.18 / **5.06**	2.79 / **4.20**	2.56 / **3.72**	2.40 / **3.41**	2.29 / **3.18**	2.20 / **3.02**	2.13 / **2.88**	2.07 / **2.78**	2.02 / **2.70**	1.98 / **2.62**	1.95 / **2.56**	1.90 / **2.46**	1.85 / **2.39**	1.78 / **2.26**	1.74 / **2.18**	1.69 / **2.10**	1.63 / **2.00**	1.60 / **1.94**	1.55 / **1.86**	1.52 / **1.82**	1.48 / **1.76**	1.46 / **1.71**	1.44 / **1.68**
55	4.02 / **7.12**	3.17 / **5.01**	2.78 / **4.16**	2.54 / **3.68**	2.38 / **3.37**	2.27 / **3.15**	2.18 / **2.98**	2.11 / **2.85**	2.05 / **2.75**	2.00 / **2.66**	1.97 / **2.59**	1.93 / **2.53**	1.88 / **2.43**	1.83 / **2.35**	1.76 / **2.23**	1.72 / **2.15**	1.67 / **2.06**	1.61 / **1.96**	1.58 / **1.90**	1.52 / **1.82**	1.50 / **1.78**	1.46 / **1.71**	1.43 / **1.66**	1.41 / **1.64**
60	4.00 / **7.08**	3.15 / **4.98**	2.76 / **4.13**	2.52 / **3.65**	2.37 / **3.34**	2.25 / **3.12**	2.17 / **2.95**	2.10 / **2.82**	2.04 / **2.72**	1.99 / **2.63**	1.95 / **2.56**	1.92 / **2.50**	1.86 / **2.40**	1.81 / **2.32**	1.75 / **2.20**	1.70 / **2.12**	1.65 / **2.03**	1.59 / **1.93**	1.56 / **1.87**	1.50 / **1.79**	1.48 / **1.74**	1.44 / **1.68**	1.41 / **1.63**	1.39 / **1.60**
65	3.99 / **7.04**	3.14 / **4.95**	2.75 / **4.10**	2.51 / **3.62**	2.36 / **3.31**	2.24 / **3.09**	2.15 / **2.93**	2.08 / **2.79**	2.02 / **2.70**	1.98 / **2.61**	1.94 / **2.54**	1.90 / **2.47**	1.85 / **2.37**	1.80 / **2.30**	1.73 / **2.18**	1.68 / **2.09**	1.63 / **2.00**	1.57 / **1.90**	1.54 / **1.84**	1.49 / **1.76**	1.46 / **1.71**	1.42 / **1.64**	1.39 / **1.60**	1.37 / **1.56**
70	3.98 / **7.01**	3.13 / **4.92**	2.74 / **4.08**	2.50 / **3.60**	2.35 / **3.29**	2.23 / **3.07**	2.14 / **2.91**	2.07 / **2.77**	2.01 / **2.67**	1.97 / **2.59**	1.93 / **2.51**	1.89 / **2.45**	1.84 / **2.35**	1.79 / **2.28**	1.72 / **2.15**	1.67 / **2.07**	1.62 / **1.98**	1.56 / **1.88**	1.53 / **1.82**	1.47 / **1.74**	1.45 / **1.69**	1.40 / **1.62**	1.37 / **1.56**	1.35 / **1.53**
80	3.96 / **6.96**	3.11 / **4.88**	2.72 / **4.04**	2.48 / **3.56**	2.33 / **3.25**	2.21 / **3.04**	2.12 / **2.87**	2.05 / **2.74**	1.99 / **2.64**	1.95 / **2.55**	1.91 / **2.48**	1.88 / **2.41**	1.82 / **2.32**	1.77 / **2.24**	1.70 / **2.11**	1.65 / **2.03**	1.60 / **1.94**	1.54 / **1.84**	1.51 / **1.78**	1.45 / **1.70**	1.42 / **1.65**	1.38 / **1.57**	1.35 / **1.52**	1.32 / **1.49**
100	3.94 / **6.90**	3.09 / **4.82**	2.70 / **3.98**	2.46 / **3.51**	2.30 / **3.20**	2.19 / **2.99**	2.10 / **2.82**	2.03 / **2.69**	1.97 / **2.59**	1.92 / **2.51**	1.88 / **2.43**	1.85 / **2.36**	1.79 / **2.26**	1.75 / **2.19**	1.68 / **2.06**	1.63 / **1.98**	1.57 / **1.89**	1.51 / **1.79**	1.48 / **1.73**	1.42 / **1.64**	1.39 / **1.59**	1.34 / **1.51**	1.30 / **1.46**	1.28 / **1.43**
125	3.92 / **6.84**	3.07 / **4.78**	2.68 / **3.94**	2.44 / **3.47**	2.29 / **3.17**	2.17 / **2.95**	2.08 / **2.79**	2.01 / **2.65**	1.95 / **2.56**	1.90 / **2.47**	1.86 / **2.40**	1.83 / **2.33**	1.77 / **2.23**	1.72 / **2.15**	1.65 / **2.03**	1.60 / **1.94**	1.55 / **1.85**	1.49 / **1.75**	1.45 / **1.68**	1.39 / **1.59**	1.36 / **1.54**	1.31 / **1.46**	1.27 / **1.40**	1.25 / **1.37**
150	3.91 / **6.81**	3.06 / **4.75**	2.67 / **3.91**	2.43 / **3.44**	2.27 / **3.14**	2.16 / **2.92**	2.07 / **2.76**	2.00 / **2.62**	1.94 / **2.53**	1.89 / **2.44**	1.85 / **2.37**	1.82 / **2.30**	1.76 / **2.20**	1.71 / **2.12**	1.64 / **2.00**	1.59 / **1.91**	1.54 / **1.83**	1.47 / **1.72**	1.44 / **1.66**	1.37 / **1.56**	1.34 / **1.51**	1.29 / **1.43**	1.25 / **1.37**	1.22 / **1.33**
200	3.89 / **6.76**	3.04 / **4.71**	2.65 / **3.88**	2.41 / **3.41**	2.26 / **3.11**	2.14 / **2.90**	2.05 / **2.73**	1.98 / **2.60**	1.92 / **2.50**	1.87 / **2.41**	1.83 / **2.34**	1.80 / **2.28**	1.74 / **2.17**	1.69 / **2.09**	1.62 / **1.97**	1.57 / **1.88**	1.52 / **1.79**	1.45 / **1.69**	1.42 / **1.62**	1.35 / **1.53**	1.32 / **1.48**	1.26 / **1.39**	1.22 / **1.33**	1.19 / **1.28**
400	3.86 / **6.70**	3.02 / **4.66**	2.62 / **3.83**	2.39 / **3.36**	2.23 / **3.06**	2.12 / **2.85**	2.03 / **2.69**	1.96 / **2.55**	1.90 / **2.46**	1.85 / **2.37**	1.81 / **2.29**	1.78 / **2.23**	1.72 / **2.12**	1.67 / **2.04**	1.60 / **1.92**	1.54 / **1.84**	1.49 / **1.74**	1.42 / **1.64**	1.38 / **1.57**	1.32 / **1.47**	1.28 / **1.42**	1.22 / **1.32**	1.16 / **1.24**	1.13 / **1.19**
1000	3.85 / **6.66**	3.00 / **4.62**	2.61 / **3.80**	2.38 / **3.34**	2.22 / **3.04**	2.10 / **2.82**	2.02 / **2.66**	1.95 / **2.53**	1.89 / **2.43**	1.84 / **2.34**	1.80 / **2.26**	1.76 / **2.20**	1.70 / **2.09**	1.65 / **2.01**	1.58 / **1.89**	1.53 / **1.81**	1.47 / **1.71**	1.41 / **1.61**	1.36 / **1.54**	1.30 / **1.44**	1.26 / **1.38**	1.19 / **1.28**	1.13 / **1.19**	1.08 / **1.11**
∞	3.84 / **6.64**	2.99 / **4.60**	2.60 / **3.78**	2.37 / **3.32**	2.21 / **3.02**	2.09 / **2.80**	2.01 / **2.64**	1.94 / **2.51**	1.88 / **2.41**	1.83 / **2.32**	1.79 / **2.24**	1.75 / **2.18**	1.69 / **2.07**	1.64 / **1.99**	1.57 / **1.87**	1.52 / **1.79**	1.46 / **1.69**	1.40 / **1.59**	1.35 / **1.52**	1.28 / **1.41**	1.24 / **1.36**	1.17 / **1.25**	1.11 / **1.15**	1.00 / **1.00**

*Reproduced from Snedecor: *Statistical Methods*, Iowa State College Press, Ames, Iowa, by permission of the author and publisher.

Table of χ^2*

Degrees of Freedom df	P = .99	.98	.95	.90	.80	.70	.50	.30	.20	.10	.05	.02	.01
1	.000157	.000628	.00393	.0158	.0642	.148	.455	1.074	1.642	2.706	3.841	5.412	6.635
2	.0201	.0404	.103	.211	.446	.713	1.386	2.408	3.219	4.605	5.991	7.824	9.210
3	.115	.185	.352	.584	1.005	1.424	2.366	3.665	4.642	6.251	7.815	9.837	11.341
4	.297	.429	.711	1.064	1.649	2.195	3.357	4.878	5.989	7.779	9.488	11.668	13.277
5	.554	.752	1.145	1.610	2.343	3.000	4.351	6.064	7.289	9.236	11.070	13.388	15.086
6	.872	1.134	1.635	2.204	3.070	3.828	5.348	7.231	8.558	10.645	12.592	15.033	16.812
7	1.239	1.564	2.167	2.833	3.822	4.671	6.346	8.383	9.803	12.017	14.067	16.622	18.475
8	1.646	2.032	2.733	3.490	4.594	5.527	7.344	9.524	11.030	13.362	15.507	18.168	20.090
9	2.088	2.532	3.325	4.168	5.380	6.393	8.343	10.656	12.242	14.684	16.919	19.679	21.666
10	2.558	3.059	3.940	4.865	6.179	7.267	9.342	11.781	13.442	15.987	18.307	21.161	23.209
11	3.053	3.609	4.575	5.578	6.989	8.148	10.341	12.899	14.631	17.275	19.675	22.618	24.725
12	3.571	4.178	5.226	6.304	7.807	9.034	11.340	14.011	15.812	18.549	21.026	24.054	26.217
13	4.107	4.765	5.892	7.042	8.634	9.926	12.340	15.119	16.985	19.812	22.362	25.472	27.688
14	4.660	5.368	6.571	7.790	9.467	10.821	13.339	16.222	18.151	21.064	23.685	26.873	29.141
15	5.229	5.985	7.261	8.547	10.307	11.721	14.339	17.322	19.311	22.307	24.996	28.259	30.578
16	5.812	6.614	7.962	9.312	11.152	12.624	15.338	18.418	20.465	23.542	26.296	29.633	32.000
17	6.408	7.255	8.672	10.085	12.002	13.531	16.338	19.511	21.615	24.769	27.587	30.995	33.409
18	7.015	7.906	9.390	10.865	12.857	14.440	17.338	20.601	22.760	25.989	28.869	32.346	34.805
19	7.633	8.567	10.117	11.651	13.716	15.352	18.338	21.689	23.900	27.204	30.144	33.687	36.191
20	8.260	9.237	10.851	12.443	14.578	16.266	19.337	22.775	25.038	28.412	31.410	35.020	37.566
21	8.897	9.915	11.591	13.240	15.445	17.182	20.337	23.858	26.171	29.615	32.671	36.343	38.932
22	9.542	10.600	12.338	14.041	16.314	18.101	21.337	24.939	27.301	30.813	33.924	37.659	40.289
23	10.196	11.293	13.091	14.848	17.187	19.021	22.337	26.018	28.429	32.007	35.172	38.968	41.638
24	10.856	11.992	13.848	15.659	18.062	19.943	23.337	27.096	29.553	33.196	36.415	40.270	42.980
25	11.524	12.697	14.611	16.473	18.940	20.867	24.337	28.172	30.675	34.382	37.652	41.566	44.314
26	12.198	13.409	15.379	17.292	19.820	21.792	25.336	29.246	31.795	35.563	38.885	42.856	45.642
27	12.879	14.125	16.151	18.114	20.703	22.719	26.336	30.319	32.912	36.741	40.113	44.140	46.963
28	13.565	14.847	16.928	18.939	21.588	23.647	27.336	31.391	34.027	37.916	41.337	45.419	48.278
29	14.256	15.574	17.708	19.768	22.475	24.577	28.336	32.461	35.139	39.087	42.557	46.693	49.588
30	14.953	16.306	18.493	20.599	23.364	25.508	29.336	33.530	36.250	40.256	43.773	47.962	50.892

*Reprinted from Table III of Fisher: *Statistical Methods for Research Workers*, Oliver & Boyd Ltd., Edinburgh, by permission of the author and publishers.

For larger values of df, the expression $\sqrt{2\chi^2} - \sqrt{2(df)} - 1$ may be used as a normal deviate with unit standard error.

Coefficients of Orthogonal Polynomials

Polynomial	$X = 1$	2	3	4	5	6	7	8	9	10
Linear	−1	0	1							
Quadratic	1	−2	1							
Linear	−3	−1	1	3						
Quadratic	1	−1	−1	1						
Cubic	−1	3	−3	1						
Linear	−2	−1	0	1	2					
Quadratic	2	−1	−2	−1	2					
Cubic	−1	2	0	−2	1					
Quartic	1	−4	6	−4	1					
Linear	−5	−3	−1	1	3	5				
Quadratic	5	−1	−4	−4	−1	5				
Cubic	−5	7	4	−4	−7	5				
Quartic	1	−3	2	2	−3	1				
Linear	−3	−2	−1	0	1	2	3			
Quadratic	5	0	−3	−4	−3	0	5			
Cubic	−1	1	1	0	−1	−1	1			
Quartic	3	−7	1	6	1	−7	3			
Linear	−7	−5	−3	−1	1	3	5	7		
Quadratic	7	1	−3	−5	−5	−3	1	7		
Cubic	−7	5	7	3	−3	−7	−5	7		
Quartic	7	−13	−3	9	9	−3	−13	7		
Quintic	−7	23	−17	−15	15	17	−23	7		
Linear	−4	−3	−2	−1	0	1	2	3	4	
Quadratic	28	7	−8	−17	−20	−17	−8	7	28	
Cubic	−14	7	13	9	0	−9	−13	−7	14	
Quartic	14	−21	−11	9	18	9	−11	−21	14	
Quintic	−4	11	−4	−9	0	9	4	−11	4	
Linear	−9	−7	−5	−3	−1	1	3	5	7	9
Quadratic	6	2	−1	−3	−4	−4	−3	−1	2	6
Cubic	−42	14	35	31	12	−12	−31	−35	−14	42
Quartic	18	−22	−17	3	18	18	3	−17	−22	18
Quintic	−6	14	−1	−11	−6	6	11	1	−14	6

This table is adapted with permission from B. J. Winer: *Statistical Principles in Experimental Design* (New York: McGraw Hill, 1962).

References

Abbott, R. D., Wulff, D. H., Nyquist, J. D., Ropp, V. A., & Hess, C. W. (1990). Satisfaction with processes of collecting student opinions about instruction: The student perspective. *Journal of Educational Psychology, 82,* 201–206.

Abelson, R. P. (1953). A note on the Neyman-Johnson technique. *Psychometrika, 18,* 213–218.

Abelson, R. P. (1985). A variance explanation paradox: When a little is a lot. *Psychological Bulletin, 97,* 129–133.

Abelson, R. P. (1995). *Statistics as principled argument.* Hillsdale, NJ: Lawrence Erlbaum Associates.

Achen, C. H. (1982). *Interpreting and using regression.* Thousand Oaks, CA: Sage.

Achen, C. H. (1991). What does "explained variance" explain?: Reply. In J. A. Stimson (Ed.), *Political analysis: Vol. 2, 1990* (pp. 173–184). Ann Arbor: The University of Michigan.

Affleck, G., Tennen, H., Urrows, S., & Higgins, P. (1992). Neuroticism and the pain-mood relation in rheumatoid arthritis: Insights from a prospective daily study. *Journal of Consulting and Clinical Psychology, 60,* 119–126.

Afifi, A. A., & Clark, V. (1984). *Computer-aided multivariate analysis.* New York: Van Nostrand Reinhold.

Afifi, A. A., & Clark, V. (1990). *Computer-aided multivariate analysis* (2nd ed.). New York: Van Nostrand Reinhold.

Agresti, A., & Finlay, B. (1986). *Statistical methods for the social sciences* (2nd ed.). San Francisco: Dellen.

Ahlgren, A. (1990). Commentary on "Gender effects of student perception of the classroom psychological environment." *Journal of Research in Science Teaching, 27,* 711–712.

Aiken, L. S., & West, S. G. (1991). *Multiple regression: Testing and interpreting interactions.* Thousand Oaks, CA: Sage.

Aiken, L. S., West, S. G., Sechrest, L., & Reno R. R. (1990). Graduate training in statistics, methodology, and measurement in psychology: A survey of PhD programs in North America. *American Psychologist, 45,* 721–734.

Alba, R. D. (1988). Interpreting the parameters of log-linear models. In S. Long (Ed.), *Common problems/proper solutions: Avoiding error in quantitative research* (pp. 258–287). Thousand Oaks, CA: Sage.

Aldenderfer, M. S., & Blashfield, R. K. (1984). *Cluster analysis.* Thousand Oaks, CA: Sage.

Aldrich, J. H., & Nelson, F. D. (1984). *Linear probability, logit, and probit models.* Thousand Oaks, CA: Sage.

Aldwin, C. M., Levenson, M. R., & Spiro, A. (1994). Vulnerability and resilience to combat experience: Can stress have lifelong effects? *Psychology and Aging, 9,* 34–44.

Alexander, K., & Eckland, B. (1975). Contextual effects in the high school attainment process. *American Sociological Review, 40,* 402–416.

Alexander, K. L., & Griffin, L. J. (1976). School district effects on academic achievement: A reconsideration. *American Sociological Review, 41,* 144–151.

Alker, H. R. (1969). A typology of ecological fallacies. In M. Dogan & S. Rokkan (Eds.), *Social ecology* (pp. 69–86). Cambridge, MA: M.I.T. Press.

Allison, P. D. (1977). Testing for interaction in multiple regression. *American Journal of Sociology, 83,* 144–153.

Allison, P. D. (1987). Estimation of linear models with incomplete data. In C. C. Clogg (Ed.), *Sociological methodology 1987* (pp. 71–103). Washington, DC: American Sociological Association.

Altman, L. K. (1991, November 5). Researchers in furor over AIDS say they can't reproduce results. *The New York Times* (National Edition), p. B6.

Alwin, D. F. (1976). Assessing school effects: Some identities. *Sociology of Education, 49,* 294–303.

Alwin, D. F. (1988). Measurement and the interpretation of effects in structural equation models. In J. S. Long (Ed.), *Common problems/Proper solutions: Avoiding error in quantitative research* (pp. 15–45). Thousand Oaks, CA: Sage.

Alwin, D. F., & Hauser, R. M. (1975). The decomposition of effects in path analysis. *American Sociological Review, 40,* 37–47.

Alwin, D. F., & Jackson, D. J. (1979). Measurement models for response errors in surveys: Issues and applications. In K. F. Schuessler (Ed.), *Sociological methodology 1980* (pp. 68–119). San Francisco: Jossey-Bass.

Alwin, D. F., & Jackson, D. J. (1981). Applications of simultaneous factor analysis to issues of factorial invariance. In D. J. Jackson & E. F. Borgatta (Eds.), *Factor analysis and measurement in sociological research: A multi-dimensional perspective* (pp. 242–279). Thousand Oaks, CA: Sage.

Alwin, D. F., & Otto, L. B. (1977). High school context effects on aspirations. *Sociology of Education, 50,* 259–273.

American Psychological Association. (1983). *Publication manual of the American Psychological Association* (3rd ed.). Washington, DC: Author.

American Psychological Association. (1994). *Publication manual of the American Psychological Association* (4th ed.). Washington, DC: Author.

Anderson, A. B., Basilevsky, A., & Hum, D. P. J. (1983). Missing data: A review of the literature. In P. H. Rossi, J. D. Wright, & A. B. Anderson (Eds.), *Handbook of survey research* (pp. 415–494). New York: Academic Press.

Anderson, G. L. (1941). *A comparison of the outcomes of instruction under two theories of learning.* Unpublished doctoral dissertation, University of Minnesota.

Anderson, J. C., & Gerbing, D. W. (1984). The effect of sampling error on convergence, improper solutions, and goodness-of-fit indices for maximum likelihood confirmatory factor analysis. *Psychometrika, 49,* 155–173.

Anderson, J. C., & Gerbing, D. W. (1988). Structural equation modeling in practice: A review and recommended two-step approach. *Psychological Bulletin, 103,* 411–423.

Anderson, J. C., & Gerbing, D. W. (1992). Assumptions and comparative strengths of the two-step approach: Comment on Fornell and Yi. *Sociological Methods & Research, 20,* 321–333.

Anderson, N. H. (1963). Comparison of different populations: Resistance to extinction and transfer. *Psychological Review, 70,* 162–179.

Anderson, N. H., & Shanteau, J. (1977). Weak inference with linear models. *Psychological Bulletin, 84,* 1155–1170.

Andrews, D. F. (1978). Comment. *Journal of the American Statistical Association, 73,* 85.

Angier, N. (1993a, January 2). Supreme Court is set to determine what science juries should hear. *The New York Times* (National Edition), pp. 1 and 7.

Angier, N. (1993b, June 30). Court ruling on scientific evidence: A just burden. *The New York Times* (National Edition), p. A8.

Anscombe, F. J. (1973). Graphs in statistical analysis. *The American Statistician, 27*(1), 17–21.

Appelbaum, M. I., & Cramer, E. M. (1974). Some problems in the nonorthogonal analysis of variance. *Psychological Bulletin, 81,* 335–343.

Arbuckle, J. (1991). *Getting started with AMOS under MSDOS.* Temple University, Philadelphia: Author.

Arbuckle, J. (1992). *Getting started with AmosDraw under Windows.* Temple University, Philadelphia: Author.

Armor, D. J. (1972). School and family effects on black and white achievement: A reexamination of the USOE data. In F. Mosteller & D. P. Moynihan (Eds.), *On equality of educational opportunity* (pp. 168–229). New York: Vintage Books.

Arnold, H. J. (1982). Moderator variables: A clarification of conceptual, analytic, and psychometric issues. *Organizational Behavior and Human Performance, 29,* 143–174.

Arvey, R. D., & Faley, R. H. (1988). *Fairness in selecting employees* (2nd ed.). Reading, MA: Addison-Wesley.

Astin, A. W. (1968). Undergraduate achievement and institutional excellence. *Science, 161,* 661–668.

Astin, A. W. (1970). The methodology of research on college impact, part one. *Sociology of Education, 43,* 223–254.

Astin, A. W., & Panos, R. J. (1969). *The educational and vocational development of college students.* Washington, DC: American Council on Education.

Atkinson, A. C. (1985). *Plots, transformations, and regression: An introduction to graphical methods of diagnostic regression analysis.* Oxford, United Kingdom: Clarendon.

Austin, J. T., & Calderón, R. F. (1996). Theoretical and technical contributions to structural equation modeling: An updated bibliography. *Structural Equation Modeling, 3,* 105–175.

Baer, D., Grabb, E., & Johnston, W. A. (1990). The values of Canadians and Americans: A critical analysis and reassessment. *Social Forces, 68,* 693–713.

Bagozzi, R. P., Fornell, C., & Larcker, D. F. (1981). Canonical correlation analysis as a special case of a structural relations model. *Multivariate Behavioral Research, 16,* 437–454.

Bagozzi, R. P., & Yi, Y. (1989). On the use of structural equation models in experimental designs. *Journal of Marketing Research, 26,* 271–284.

Bagozzi, R. P., Yi, Y., & Singh, S. (1991). On the use of structural equation models in experimental designs: Two extensions. *International Journal of Research in Marketing, 8,* 125–140.

Bailey, K. D. (1994). *Typologies and taxonomies: An introduction to classification techniques.* Thousand Oaks, CA: Sage.

Bales, J. (1986). 2 new editors discuss their journals. *The APA Monitor, 17*(2), 14.

Barcikowski, R. S. (Ed.). (1983a). *Computer packages and research design. Volume 1: BMDP.* New York: University Press of America.

Barcikowski, R. S. (Ed.). (1983b). *Computer packages and research design. Volume 2: SAS.* New York: University Press of America.

Barcikowski, R. S. (Ed.). (1983c). *Computer packages and research design. Volume 3: SPSS and SPSSX.* New York: University Press of America.

Barnett, A. (1983). Misapplications reviews: The linear model and some of its friends. *Interfaces, 13*(1), 61–65.

Barrett, G. V., & Sansonetti, D. M. (1988). Issues concerning the use of regression analysis in salary discrimination cases. *Personnel Psychology, 41,* 503–516.

Bartlett, C. J., Bobko, P., Mosier, S. B., & Hannan, R. (1978). Testing for fairness with a moderated multiple regression strategy: An alternative to differential analysis. *Personnel Psychology, 31,* 233–241.

Bartlett, M. S. (1947). Multivariate analysis. *Journal of the Royal Statistical Society,* Series B, *9,* 176–197.

Beaton, A. E. (1969a). Scaling criterion of questionnaire items. *Socio-Economic Planning Sciences, 2,* 355–362.

Beaton, A. E. (1969b). Some mathematical and empirical properties of criterion scaled variables. In G. W. Mayeske et al., *A study of our nation's schools* (pp. 338–343). Washington, DC: U.S. Office of Education.

Beaton, A. E. (1973). *Commonality*. Unpublished manuscript.

Becker, T. E. (1992). Foci and bases of commitment: Are they distinctions worth making? *Academy of Management Journal, 35,* 232–244.

Bell, A. P., Weinberg, M. S., & Hammersmith, S. K. (1981). *Sexual preference: Its development in men and women* (2 Vols.). Bloomington, IN: Indiana University Press.

Belsley, D. A. (1984a). Demeaning conditioning diagnostics through centering. *The American Statistician, 38,* 73–77.

Belsley, D. A. (1984b). Reply. *The American Statistician, 38,* 90–93.

Belsley, D. A. (1991). *Conditioning diagnostics: Collinearity and weak data in regression.* New York: Wiley.

Belsley, D. A., Kuh, E., & Welsch, R. E. (1980). *Regression diagnostics: Identifying influential data and sources of collinearity.* New York: Wiley.

Bem, S. L. (1974). The measurement of psychological androgyny. *Journal of Consulting and Clinical Psychology, 42,* 155–162.

Bentler, P. M. (1980). Multivariate analysis with latent variables: Causal modeling. *Annual Review of Psychology, 31,* 419–456.

Bentler, P. M. (1982). Confirmatory factor analysis via noniterative estimation: A fast, inexpensive method. *Journal of Marketing Research, 19,* 417–424.

Bentler, P. M. (1987). Drug use and personality in adolescence and young adulthood: Structural models with nonnormal variables. *Child Development, 58,* 65–79.

Bentler, P. M. (1990). Comparative fit indexes in structural models. *Psychological Bulletin, 107,* 238–246.

Bentler, P. M. (1992a). *EQS: Structural equations program manual.* Los Angeles: BMDP Statistical Software.

Bentler, P. M. (1992b). On the fit of models to covariances and methodology to the *Bulletin. Psychological Bulletin, 112,* 400–404.

Bentler, P. M., & Bonett, D. G. (1980). Significance tests and goodness of fit in the analysis of covariance structures. *Psychological Bulletin, 88,* 588–606.

Bentler, P. M., & Chou, C.-P. (1987). Practical issues in structural modeling. *Sociological Methods & Research, 16,* 78–117.

Bentler, P. M., & Mooijaart, A. (1989). Choice of structural model via parsimony: A rationale based on precision. *Psychological Bulletin, 106,* 315–317.

Bentler, P. M., & Wu, J. C. (1993). *EQS/Windows user's guide.* Los Angeles: BMDP Statistical Software.

Berk, K. N. (1987). Effective microcomputer statistical software. *The American Statistician, 41,* 222–228.

Berk, K. N., & Francis, I. S. (1978). A review of the manuals for BMDP and SPSS. *Journal of the American Statistical Association, 73,* 65–71.

Berk, R. A. (Ed.). (1982). *Handbook of methods for detecting test bias.* Baltimore: Johns Hopkins University Press.

Berk, R. A. (1983). Applications of the general linear model to survey data. In P. H. Rossi, J. D. Wright, & A. B. Anderson (Eds.), *Handbook of survey research* (pp. 495–546). New York: Academic Press.

Berk, R. A. (1988). Causal inference for sociological data. In N. J. Smelser (Ed.), *Handbook of sociology* (pp. 155–172). Thousand Oaks, CA: Sage.

Berliner, D. C. (1983). Developing conceptions of classroom environments: Some light on the T in classroom studies of ATI. *Educational Psychologist, 18,* 1–13.

Berliner, D. C., & Cahen, L. S. (1973). Trait-Treatment Interaction and learning. In F. N. Kerlinger (Ed.), *Review of research in education 1* (pp. 58–94). Itasca, IL: F. E. Peacock.

Berndt, T. J., & Miller, K. E. (1990). Expectancies, values, and achievement in junior high school. *Journal of Educational Psychology, 82,* 319–326.

Bernstein, I. H. (1988). *Applied multivariate analysis.* New York: Springer–Verlag.

Berry, W. D. (1984). *Nonrecursive causal models.* Thousand Oaks, CA: Sage.

Bersoff, D. N. (1981). Testing and the law. *American Psychologist, 36,* 1047–1056.

Bibby, J. (1977). The general linear model—A cautionary tale. In C. A. O'Muircheartaigh & C. Payne (Eds.), *The analysis of survey data* (Vol. 2, pp. 35–79). New York: Wiley.

Bickel, P. J., Hammel, E. A., & O'Connell, J. W. (1975). Sex bias in graduate admissions: Data from Berkeley. *Science, 187,* 398–404.

Biddle, B. J., Slavings, R. L., & Anderson, D. S. (1985). Methodological observations on applied behavioral science. *The Journal of Applied Behavioral Science, 21,* 79–93.

Bidwell, C. E., & Kasarda, J. D. (1975). School district organization and student achievement. *American Sociological Review, 40,* 55–70.

Bidwell, C. E., & Kasarda, J. D. (1976). Reply to Hannan, Freeman and Meyer, and Alexander and Griffin. *American Sociological Review, 41,* 152–159.

Bidwell, C. E., & Kasarda, J. D. (1980). Problems of multilevel measurement: The case of school and schooling. In K. H. Roberts & L. Burstein (Eds.), *Issues in aggregation* (pp. 53–64). San Francisco: Jossey-Bass.

Bielby, W. T., & Hauser, R. M. (1977). Structural equation models. *Annual Review of Sociology, 3,* 137–161.

Bielby, W. T., & Kluegel, J. R. (1977). Statistical inference and statistical power in applications of the general linear model. In D. R. Heise (Ed.), *Sociological methodology 1977* (pp. 283–312). San Francisco: Jossey-Bass.

Binder, A. (1959). Considerations of the place of assumptions in correlational analysis. *American Psychologist, 14,* 504–510.

Blalock, H. M. (1964). *Causal inferences in nonexperimental research.* Chapel Hill, NC: University of North Carolina Press.

Blalock, H. M. (1968). Theory building and causal inference. In H. M. Blalock & A. B. Blalock (Eds.), *Methodology in social research* (pp. 155–198). New York: McGraw-Hill.

Blalock, H. M. (1971). Causal models involving unmeasured variables in stimulus-response situations. In H. M. Blalock (Ed.), *Causal models in the social sciences* (pp. 335–347). Chicago: Aldine.

Blalock, H. M. (1972). *Social statistics* (2nd ed.). New York: McGraw-Hill.

Blalock, H. M. (1984). Contextual-effects models: Theoretical and methodological issues. *Annual Review of Sociology, 10,* 353–372.

Blalock, H. M. (Ed.). (1985). *Causal models in the social sciences* (2nd ed.). Chicago: Aldine.

Blalock, H. M. (1989). The real and unrealized contributions of quantitative sociology. *American Sociological Review, 54,* 447–460.

Blalock, H. M., Wells, C. S., & Carter, L. F. (1970). Statistical estimation with measurement error. In E. F. Borgatta & G. W. Bohrnstedt (Eds.), *Sociological methodology 1970* (pp. 75–103). San Francisco: Jossey-Bass.

Blau, P. (1960). Structural effects. *American Sociological Review, 25,* 178–193.

Bloom, D. E., & Killingsworth, M. R. (1982). Pay discrimination research and litigation: The use of regression. *Industrial Relations, 21,* 318–339.

BMDP Statistical Software, Inc. (1992). *BMDP user's digest: Quick reference for the BMDP programs.* Los Angeles: Author.

BMDP Statistical Software, Inc. (1993). *BMDP/PC User's guide Release 7.* Los Angeles: Author.

Bock, R. D. (1975). *Multivariate statistical methods in behavioral research.* New York: McGraw-Hill.

Bock, R. D. (Ed.). (1989). *Multilevel analysis of educational data.* San Diego, CA: Academic Press.

Boffey, P. M. (1986, April 22). Major study points to faulty research at two universities. *The New York Times,* pp. C1, C11.

Bohrnstedt, G. W. (1969). Observations on the measurement of change. In E. F. Borgatta & G. W. Bohrnstedt (Eds.), *Sociological methodology 1969* (pp. 113–133). San Francisco: Jossey-Bass.

Bohrnstedt, G. W. (1983). Measurement. In P. H. Rossi, J. D. Wright, & A. B. Anderson (Eds.), *Handbook of survey research* (pp. 69–121). New York: Academic Press.

Bohrnstedt, G. W., & Carter, T. M. (1971). Robustness in regression analysis. In H. L. Costner (Ed.), *Sociological methodology 1971* (pp. 118–146). San Francisco: Jossey-Bass.

Bohrnstedt, G. W., & Marwell, G. (1977). The reliability of products of two random variables. In K. Schuessler (Ed.), *Sociological methodology 1978* (pp. 254–273). San Francisco: Jossey-Bass.

Bohrnstedt, G. W., Mohler, P. P., & Müller, W. (Eds.). (1987). An empirical study of the reliability and stability of survey research items [Special issue]. *Sociological Methods & Research, 15*(3).

Boik, R. J. (1979). Interactions, partial interactions, and interaction contrasts in the analysis of variance. *Psychological Bulletin, 86,* 1084–1089.

Bollen, K. A. (1987). Total, direct, and indirect effects in structural equation models. In C. C. Clogg (Ed.), *Sociological methodology 1987* (pp. 37–69). Washington, DC: American Sociological Association.

Bollen, K. A. (1989). *Structural equations with latent variables.* New York: Wiley.

Bollen, K. A., & Jackman, R. W. (1985). Regression diagnostics: An expository treatment of outliers and influential cases. *Sociological Methods & Research, 13,* 510–542.

Bollen, K., & Lennox, R. (1991). Conventional wisdom on measurement: A structural equation perspective. *Psychological Bulletin, 110,* 305–314.

Bollen, K. A., & Long, J. S. (Eds.). (1993a). *Testing structural equation models.* Thousand Oaks, CA: Sage.

Bollen, K. A., & Long, J. S. (1993b). Introduction. In K. A. Bollen & J. S. Long (Eds.), *Testing structural equation models* (pp. 1–9). Thousand Oaks, CA: Sage.

Boomsma, A. (1987). The robustness of maximum likelihood estimation in structural equation models. In P. Cuttance & R. Ecob (Eds.), *Structural modeling by example: Applications in educational, sociological, and behavioral research* (pp. 160–188). New York: Cambridge University Press.

Borgen, F. H., & Seling, M. J. (1978). Use of discriminant analysis following MANOVA: Multivariate statistics for multivariate purposes. *Journal of Applied Psychology, 63,* 689–697.

Borich, G. D., Godbout, R. C., & Wunderlich, K. W. (1976). *The analysis of aptitude-treatment interactions: Computer programs and calculations.* Chicago: International Educational Services.

Bornholt, L. J., Goodnow, J. J., & Cooney, G. H. (1994). Influences of gender stereotypes on adolescents' perceptions of their own achievement. *American Educational Research Journal, 31,* 675–692.

Boruch, R. F. (1982). Experimental tests in education: Recommendations from the Holtzman Report. *The American Statistician, 36,* 1–8.

Bowers, K. S. (1973). Situationism is psychology: An analysis and a critique. *Psychological Review, 80,* 307–336.

Bowers, W. J. (1968). Normative constraints on deviant behavior in the college context. *Sociometry, 31,* 370–385.

Bowles, S., & Levin, H. M. (1968). The determinants of scholastic achievement: An appraisal of some recent evidence. *Journal of Human Resources, 3,* 3–24.

Box, G. E. P. (1966). Use and abuse of regression. *Technometrics, 8,* 625–629.

Boyd, L. H., & Iverson, G. R. (1979). *Contextual analysis: Concepts and statistical techniques.* Belmont, CA: Wadsworth.

Bradley, R. A., & Strivastava, S. S. (1979). Correlation in polynomial regression. *The American Statistician, 33,* 11–14.

Braithwaite, R. B. (1953). *Scientific explanation.* Cambridge, England: Cambridge University Press.

Bray, J. H., & Maxwell, S. E. (1985). *Multivariate analysis of variance.* Thousand Oaks, CA: Sage.

Brecht, B. (1961). *Tales from the calendar* (Y. Kapp, Trans.). London: Methuen.

Breckler, S. J. (1990). Applications of covariance structure modeling in psychology: Cause for concern? *Psychological Bulletin, 107,* 260–273.

Brewer, M. B., Campbell, D. T., & Crano, W. D. (1970). Testing a single-factor model as an alternative to the misuse of partial correlations in hypothesis-testing research. *Sociometry, 33,* 1–11.

Brodbeck, M. (1963). Logic and scientific method in research on teaching. In N. L. Gage (Ed.), *Handbook of research on teaching* (pp. 44–93). Chicago: Rand McNally.

Brodbeck, M. (Ed.). (1968). *Readings in the philosophy of the social sciences.* New York: Macmillan.

Brody, J. E. (1973, October 29). New heart study absolves coffee. *The New York Times,* p. 6.

Brody, J. E. (1981, August 23). Kinsey study finds homosexuals show early predisposition. *The New York Times,* pp. 1, 30.

Brown, R. L. (1994). Efficacy of the indirect approach for estimating structural equation models with missing data: A comparison of five methods. *Structural Equation Modeling, 1,* 287–316.

Brown, S. P., & Peterson, R. A. (1994). The effect of effort on sales performance and job satisfaction. *Journal of Marketing, 58,* 70–80.

Browne, M. W. (1982). Covariance structures. In D. M. Hawkins (Ed.), *Topics in applied multivariate analysis* (pp. 72–141). Cambridge, England: Cambridge University Press.

Bruce, P. C. (1991). *Resampling stats: User guide.* Arlington, VA: Resampling Stats, 612 N. Jackson St., 22201.

Bryk, A. S., & Raudenbush, S. W. (1992). *Hierarchical linear models: Applications and data analysis methods.* Thousand Oaks, CA: Sage.

Bryk, A. S., Raudenbush, S. W., & Congdon, R. T. (1994). *HLM$_3^2$: Hierarchical linear modeling with HLM/2L and HLM/3L programs.* Chicago: Scientific Software.

Bryk, A. S., Raudenbush, S. W., Seltzer, M., & Congdon, R. T. (1989). *An introduction to HLM: Computer program and users' guide.* Chicago: Scientific Software.

Bryk, A. S., Strenio, J. F., & Weisberg, H. I. (1980). A method for estimating treatment effects when individuals are growing. *Journal of Educational Statistics, 5,* 5–34.

Bryk, A. S., & Weisberg, H. I. (1976). Value-added analysis: A dynamic approach to the estimation of treatment effects. *Journal of Educational Statistics, 1,* 127–155.

Bryk, A. S., & Weisberg, H. I. (1977). Use of the nonequivalent control group design when subjects are growing. *Psychological Bulletin, 84,* 950–962.

Bullock, H. E., Harlow, L. L., & Mulaik, S. A. (1994). Causation issues in structural equation modeling research. *Structural Equation Modeling, 1,* 253–267.

Bunge, M. (1979). *Causality and modern science* (3rd ed.). New York: Dover Publications.

Buri, J. R., Louiselle, P. A., Misukanis, T. M., & Mueller, R. A. (1988). Effects of parental authoritarianism and authoritativeness on self-esteem. *Personality and Social Psychology Bulletin, 14,* 271–282.

Burke, C. J. (1953). A brief note on one-tailed tests. *Psychological Bulletin, 50,* 384–387.

Burks, B. S. (1926a). On the inadequacy of the partial and multiple correlation technique. Part I. *Journal of Educational Psychology, 17,* 532–540.

Burks, B. S. (1926b). On the inadequacy of the partial and multiple correlation technique. Part II. *Journal of Educational Psychology, 17,* 625–630.

Burks, B. S. (1928). Statistical hazards in nature-nurture investigations. In M. Whipple (Ed.), *National society for the study of education: 27th yearbook* (Part 1, pp. 9–33). Bloomington, IL: Public School Publishing Company.

Burstein, L. (1976). The choice of unit of analysis in the investigation of school effects: IEA in New Zealand. *New Zealand Journal of Educational studies, 11,* 11–24.

Burstein, L. (1978). Assessing differences between grouped and individual-level regression coefficients. *Sociological Methods and Research, 7,* 5–28.

Burstein, L. (1980a). Analyzing multilevel educational data: The choice of an analytical model rather than a unit of analysis. In E. L. Baker & E. S. Quellmalz (Eds.), *Educational testing and evaluation: Design, analysis, and policy* (pp. 77–94). Thousand Oaks, CA: Sage.

Burstein, L. (1980b). The analysis of multilevel data in educational research and evaluation. In D. Berliner (Ed.), *Review of research in education, 8* (pp. 158–233). Washington, DC: American Educational Research Association.

Burstein, L., Kim, K. S., & Delandshere, G. (1989). Multilevel investigations of systematically varying slopes: Issues, alternatives, and consequences. In R. D. Bock (Ed.), *Multilevel analysis of educational data* (pp. 233–276). San Diego, CA: Academic Press.

Burstein, L., Linn, R. L., & Capell, F. J. (1978). Analyzing multilevel data in the presence of heterogeneous within-class regressions. *Journal of Educational Statistics, 3,* 347–383.

Burstein, L., & Smith, I. D. (1977). Choosing the appropriate unit for investigating school effects. *The Australian Journal of Education, 21,* 65–79.

Burt, C. (1921). *Mental and scholastic tests.* London: P. S. King and Son.

Burt, C. (1925). *The young delinquent.* New York: D. Appleton.

Burt, C. (1962). *Mental and scholastic tests* (4th ed.). London: Staples Press.

Busemeyer, J. R., & Jones, L. E. (1983). Analysis of multiplicative combination rules when the causal variables are measured with error. *Psychological Bulletin, 93,* 549–562.

Byrne, B. M. (1989). Multigroup comparisons and the assumption of equivalent construct validity across groups: Methodological and substantive issues. *Multivariate Behavioral Research, 24,* 503–523.

Byrne, B. M. (1991). The Maslach Burnout Inventory: Validating factorial structure and invariance across intermediate, secondary, and university educators. *Multivariate Behavioral Research, 26,* 583–605.

Byrne, B. M. (1994). *Structural equation modeling with EQS and EQS/Windows: Basic concepts, applications, and programming.* Thousand Oaks, CA: Sage.

Byrne, B. M., & Shavelson, R. J. (1987). Adolescent self-concept: Testing the assumption of equivalent structure across gender. *American Educational Research Journal, 24,* 365–385.

Cain, G. G. (1975). Regression and selection models to improve nonexperimental comparisons. In C. A. Bennett & A. A. Lumsdaine (Eds.), *Evaluation and experiment: Some critical issues in assessing social programs* (pp. 297–317). New York: Academic Press.

Cain, G. G., & Watts, H. W. (1968). The controversy about the Coleman Report: Comment. *Journal of Human Resources, 3,* 389–392.

Cain, G. G., & Watts, H. W. (1970). Problems in making policy inferences from the Coleman Report. *American Sociological Review, 35,* 228–242.

Campbell, D. T., & Boruch, R. F. (1975). Making the case for randomized assignment to treatments by considering the alternatives: Six ways in which quasi-experimental evaluations in compensatory education tend to underestimate effects. In C. A. Bennett & A. A. Lumsdaine (Eds.), *Evaluation and experiment: Some critical issues in assessing social programs* (pp. 195–296). New York: Academic Press.

Campbell, D. T., & Erlebacher, A. (1970). How regression artifacts in quasi-experimental evaluations can mistakenly make compensatory education look harmful. In J. Hellmuth (Ed.), *Disadvantaged child. Compensatory education: A national debate* (Vol. 3, pp. 185–210). New York: Bruner/Mazel.

Campbell, D. T., & Stanley, J. C. (1963). Experimental and quasi-experimental designs for research on teaching. In N. L. Gage (Ed.), *Handbook of research on teaching* (pp. 171–246). Chicago: Rand McNally.

Cappelleri, J. C., Trochim, W. M. K., Stanley, T. D., & Reichardt, C. S. (1991). Random measurement error does not bias the treatment effect estimate in the regression-discontinuity design: I. The case of no interaction. *Evaluation Review, 15,* 395–419.

Carlson, J. E., & Timm, N. H. (1974). Analysis of nonorthogonal fixed-effects designs. *Psychological Bulletin, 81,* 563–570.

Carroll, J. B. (1975). *The teaching of French as a foreign language in eight countries.* New York: Wiley.

Carver, R. P. (1978). The case against statistical significance testing. *Harvard Educational Review, 48,* 378–399.

Casti, J. L. (1990). *Searching for certainty: What scientists can know about the future.* New York: William Morrow.

Cattell, R. B., & Butcher, H. J. (1968). *The prediction of achievement and creativity.* Indianapolis: Bobbs-Merrill.

Cattin, P. (1980). Estimation of the predictive power of a regression model. *Journal of Applied Psychology, 65,* 407–414.

Chamberlin, T. C. (1965). The method of multiple working hypotheses. *Science, 148,* 754–759. (Original work published 1890)

Chang, J. (1992, January 22). Will women runners overtake men? *The New York Times* (National Edition), Letters, p. A14.

Chatfield, C. (1988). *Problem solving: A statistician's guide.* New York: Chapman and Hall.

Chatfield, C. (1991). Avoiding statistical pitfalls. *Statistical Science, 6,* 240–268.

Chatfield, C., & Collins, A. J. (1980). *Introduction to multivariate analysis.* London: Chapman Hall.

Chatterjee, S., & Hadi, A. S. (1986a). Influential observations, high leverage points, and outliers in linear regression. *Statistical Science, 1,* 379–393.

Chatterjee, S., & Hadi, A. S. (1986b). Rejoinder. *Statistical Science, 1,* 415–416.

Chatterjee, S., & Price, B. (1977). *Regression analysis by example.* New York: Wiley.

Chen, M. M. (1984). Partitioning variance in regression analyses for developing policy impact models: The case of the Federal Medicaid Program. *Management Science, 30,* 25–36.

Cherry, K. E., & Park, D. C. (1993). Individual difference and contextual variables influence spatial memory in younger and older adults. *Psychology of Aging, 8,* 517–526.

Cheung, K. C., Keeves, J. P., Sellin, N., & Tsoi, S. C. (1990). The analysis of multilevel data in educational research: Studies of problems and their solutions [Monograph]. *International Journal of Educational Research* (pp. 215–319).

Chinn, C. A., Waggoner, M. A., Anderson, R. C., Schommer, M., & Wilkinson, I. A. G. (1993). Situated actions during reading lessons: A microanalysis of oral reading error episodes. *American Educational Research Journal, 30,* 361–392.

Chou, C.-P., & Bentler, P. M. (1993). Invariant standardized estimated parameter change for model modification in covariance structure analysis. *Multivariate Behavioral Research, 28,* 97–110.

Chou, C.-P., & Bentler, P. M. (1995). Estimates and tests in structural equation modeling. In R. H. Hoyle (Ed.), *Structural equation modeling: Concepts, issues, and applications* (pp. 37–53). Thousand Oaks, CA: Sage.

Cicchetti, D. V. (1991). The reliability of peer review for manuscript and grant submissions: A cross-disciplinary investigation. *Behavioral and Brain Sciences, 14,* 119–135.

Citron, A., Chein, I., & Harding, J. (1950). Anti-minority remarks: A problem for action research. *Journal of Abnormal and Social Psychology, 45,* 99–126.

Cizek, G. J. (1995). Crunchy granola and the hegemony of the narrative. *Educational Researcher, 24*(2), 26–28.

Cleary, P. D., & Angel, R. (1984). The analysis of relationships involving dichotomous dependent variables. *Journal of Health and Social Behavior, 25,* 334–348.

Cleary, T. A. (1968). Test bias: Prediction of grades of Negro and white students in integrated colleges. *Journal of Educational Measurement, 5,* 115–124.

Clemans, W. V. (1965). An analytical and empirical examination of some properties of ipsative measures. *Psychometrika, Monograph Supplement* (No. 14).

Cleveland, W. S., & McGill, R. (1984). The many faces of a scatterplot. *Journal of the American Statistical Association, 79,* 807–822.

Cliff, N. (1983). Some cautions concerning the application of causal modeling methods. *Multivariate Behavioral Research, 18,* 115–126.

Cliff, N. (1987a). *Analyzing multivariate data.* San Diego, CA: Harcourt Brace Jovanovich.

Cliff, N. (1987b). Comments on Professor Freedman's paper. *Journal of Educational Statistics, 12,* 158–160.

Cliff, N., & Krus, D. J. (1976). Interpretation of canonical analysis: Rotated vs. unrotated solutions. *Psychometrika, 41,* 35–42.

Clogg, C. C. (Ed.). (1988). *Sociological methodology 1988* (pp. 347–493). Washington, DC: American Sociological Association.

Cochran, W. G. (1957). Analysis of covariance: Its nature and uses. *Biometrics, 13,* 261–281.

Cochran, W. G. (1965). The planning of observational studies of human populations. *Journal of the Royal Statistical Society,* Series A, *128,* 234–255.

Cochran, W. G. (1968). Errors of measurement in statistics. *Technometrics, 10,* 637–666.

Cochran, W. G. (1970). Some effects of errors of measurement on multiple correlation. *Journal of the American Statistical Association, 65,* 22–34.

Cochran, W. G., & Cox, G. M. (1950). *Experimental designs.* New York: Wiley.

Cochran, W. G., & Rubin, D. B. (1973). Controlling bias in observational studies: A review. *Sankhya, The Indian Journal of Statistics,* Series A, *35,* 417–446.

Cody, R. P., & Smith, J. K. (1991). *Applied statistics and the SAS programming language* (3rd ed.). New York: North-Holland.

Cohen, J. (1965). Some statistical issues in psychological research. In B. B. Wolman (Ed.), *Handbook of clinical psychology* (pp. 95–121). New York: McGraw-Hill.

Cohen, J. (1968). Multiple regresson as a general data-analytic system. *Psychological Bulletin, 70,* 426–443.

Cohen, J. (1973). Eta-squared and partial eta-squared in fixed factor ANOVA designs. *Educational and Psychological Measurement, 33,* 107–112.

Cohen, J. (1978). Partialed products *are* interactions; partialed vectors *are* curve components. *Psychological Bulletin, 85,* 858–866.

Cohen, J. (1983). The cost of dichotomization. *Applied Psychological Measurement, 7,* 249–253.

Cohen, J. (1988). *Statistical power analysis for the behavioral sciences* (2nd ed.). Hillsdale, NJ: Lawrence Erlbaum Associates.

Cohen, J. (1992). A power primer. *Psychological Bulletin, 112,* 155–159.

Cohen, J. (1994). The earth is round ($p < .05$). *American Psychologist, 49,* 997–1003.

Cohen, J., & Cohen, P. (1983). *Applied multiple regression/correlation analysis for the behavioral sciences* (2nd. ed.). Hillsdale, NJ: Lawrence Erlbaum Associates.

Cole, D. A. (1987). Utility of confirmatory factor analysis in test validation research. *Journal of Consulting and Clinical Psychology, 55,* 584–594.

Cole, D. A., & Maxwell, S. E. (1985). Multitrait-multimethod comparisons across populations: A confirmatory factor analytic approach. *Multivariate Behavioral Research, 20,* 389–417.

Cole, D. A., Maxwell, S. E., Arvey, R., & Salas, E. (1993). Multivariate group comparisons of variable systems: MANOVA and structural equation modeling. *Psychological Bulletin, 114,* 174–184.

Cole, D. A., Maxwell, S. E., Arvey, R., & Salas, E. (1994). How the power of MANOVA can both increase and decrease as a function of the intercorrelations among the dependent variables. *Psychological Bulletin, 115,* 465–474.

Cole, N. S. (1981). Bias in testing. *American Psychologist, 36,* 1067–1077.

Cole, N. S., & Moss, P. A. (1989). Bias in test use. In R. L. Linn (Ed.), *Educational measurement* (3rd ed., pp. 201–219). New York: Macmillan.

Coleman, J. S. (1968). Equality of educational opportunity: Reply to Bowles and Levin. *Journal of Human Resources, 3,* 237–246.

Coleman, J. S. (1970). Reply to Cain and Watts. *American Sociological Review, 35,* 242–249.

Coleman, J. S. (1972). The evaluation of *Equality of educational opportunity.* In F. Mosteller & D. P. Moynihan (Eds.), *On equality of educational opportunity* (pp. 146–167). New York: Vintage Books.

Coleman, J. S. (1975a). Methods and results in the IEA studies of effects of school on learning. *Review of Educational Research, 45,* 335–386.

Coleman, J. S. (1975b). Social research advocacy: A response to Young and Bress. *Phi Delta Kappan, 55,* 166–169.

Coleman, J. S. (1976). Regression analysis for the comparison of school and home effects. *Social Science Research, 5,* 1–20.

Coleman, J. S., Campbell, E. Q., Hobson, C. J., McPartland, J., Mood, A. M., Weinfeld, F. D., & York, R. L. (1966). *Equality of educational opportunity.* Washington, DC: U.S. Government Printing Office.

Coleman, J. S., & Karweit, N. L. (1972). *Information systems and performance measures in schools.* Englewood Cliffs, NJ: Educational Technology Publications.

Collins, L. M., & Horn, J. L. (Eds.). (1991). *Best methods for the analysis of change: Recent advances, unanswered questions, future directions.* Washington, DC: American Psychological Association.

Comber, L. C., & Keeves, J. P. (1973). *Science education in nineteen countries.* New York: Wiley.

Conger, A. J. (1974). A revised definition for suppressor variables: A guide to their identification and interpretation. *Educational and Psychological Measurement, 34,* 35–46.

Conger, R. D., Conger, K. J., Elder, G. H., Lorenz, F. O., Simons, R. L., & Whitbeck, L. B. (1993). Family economic stress and adjustment of early adolescent girls. *Developmental Psychology, 29,* 206–219.

Conrad, H. (1950). Information which should be provided by test publishers and testing agencies on the validity and use of their test. *Proceedings, 1949 Invitational Conference on Testing Problems* (pp. 63–68). Princeton, NJ: Educational Testing Service.

Converse, P. E. (1969). Survey research in the decoding of patterns in ecological data. In M. Dogan & S. Rokkan (Eds.), *Social ecology* (pp. 459–485). Cambridge, MA: M.I.T Press.

Cook, R. D. (1977). Detection of influential observation in linear regression. *Technometrics, 19,* 15–18.

Cook, R. D. (1979). Influential observations in linear regression. *Journal of the American Statistical Association, 74,* 169–174.

Cook, R. D., & Weisberg, S. (1982). *Residuals and influence in regression.* New York: Chapman and Hall.

Cook, T. D., & Campbell, D. T. (1979). *Quasi-experimentation: Design & analysis issues for field settings.* Chicago: Rand McNally.

Cooley, W. W., & Lohnes, P. R. (1971). *Multivariate data analysis.* New York: Wiley.

Cooley, W. W., & Lohnes, P. R. (1976). *Evaluation research in education.* New York: Wiley.

Corno, L., & Snow, R. E. (1986). Adapting teaching to individual differences among learners. In M. C. Wittrock (Ed.), *Handbook of research on teaching* (3rd ed., pp. 605–629). New York: Macmillan.

Costner, H. L. (1969). Theory, deduction, and rules of correspondence. *American Journal of Sociology, 75,* 245–263.

Cotter, K. L., & Raju, N. S. (1982). An evaluation of formula-based population squared cross-validity estimates and factor score estimates in prediction. *Educational and Psychological Measurement, 42,* 493–519.

Cox, D. R. (1958). *Planning of experiments.* New York: Wiley.

Cox, D. R., & Snell, E. J. (1989). *Analysis of binary data* (2nd ed.). New York: Chapman and Hall.

Cramer, E. M. (1972). Significance tests and tests of models in multiple regression. *The American Statistician, 26*(4), 26–30.

Cramer, E. M., & Appelbaum, M. I. (1980). Nonorthogonal analysis of variance—once again. *Psychological Bulletin, 87,* 51–57.

Cramer, E. M., & Nicewander, W. A. (1979). Some symmetric, invariant measures of multivariate association. *Psychometrika, 44,* 43–54.

Crandall, R. (1991). What should be done to improve reviewing? *Behavioral and Brain Sciences, 14,* 143.

Cranton, P., & Smith, R. A. (1990). Reconsidering the unit of analysis: A model of student rating of instruction. *Journal of Educational Psychology, 82,* 207–212.

Creager, J. A. (1971). Orthogonal and nonorthogonal methods for partitioning regression variance. *American Educational Research Journal, 8,* 671–676.

Cronbach, L. J. (1971). Test validation. In R. L. Thorndike (Ed.), *Educational measurement* (2nd ed. pp. 443–507). Washington, DC: American Council on Education.

Cronbach, L. J. (1976). *Research on classrooms and schools: Formulation of questions, design, and analysis* (Occasional paper). Stanford, CA: Stanford Evaluation Consortium, Stanford University.

Cronbach, L. J. (1987). Statistical tests for moderator variables: Flaws in analyses recently proposed. *Psychological Bulletin, 102,* 414–417.

Cronbach, L. J. (1992). Four *Psychological Bulletin* articles in perspective. *Psychological Bulletin, 112,* 389–392.

Cronbach, L. J., & Furby, L. (1970). How we should measure "change"—or should we? *Psychological Bulletin, 74,* 68–80.

Cronbach, L. J., & Gleser, G. C. (1965). *Psychological tests and personnel decisions* (2nd ed.). Urbana, IL: University of Illinois Press.

Cronbach, L. J., Rogosa, D. R., Floden, R. E., & Price, G. G. (1977). *Analysis of covariance in nonrandomized experiments: Parameters affecting bias* (Occasional paper). Stanford, CA: Stanford Evaluation Consortium, Stanford University.

Cronbach, L. J., & Snow, R. E. (1977). *Aptitudes and instructional methods: A handbook for research on interactions.* New York: Irvington.

Cronbach, L. J., & Webb, N. (1975). Between-class and within-class effects in a reported aptitude × treatment interaction: Reanalysis of a study by G. L. Anderson. *Journal of Educational Psychology, 67,* 717–724.

Crow, E. L. (1991). Response to Rosenthal's comment "How are we doing in soft psychology?" (1991). *American Psychologist, 46,* 1083.

Cudeck, R. (1989). Analysis of correlation matrices using covariance structure models. *Psychological Bulletin, 105,* 317–327.

Cummings, L. L., & Frost, P. J. (Eds.). (1985). *Publishing in the organizational sciences.* Homewood, IL: Richard D. Irwin.

Cunningham, A. E., & Stanovich, K. E. (1991). Tracking the unique effects of print exposure in children: Associations with vocabulary, general knowledge, and spelling. *Journal of Educational Psychology, 83,* 264–274.

Cureton, E. E. (1951). Validity. In E. F. Lindquist (Ed.), *Educational measurement* (pp. 621–692). Washington, DC: American Council on Education.

Dalgleish, L. I. (1994). Discriminant analysis: Statistical inference using the jackknife and bootstrap procedures. *Psychological Bulletin, 116,* 498–508.

Dallal, G. E. (1988). Statistical microcomputing—like it is. *The American Statistician, 42,* 212–216.

Dance, K. A., & Neufeld, W. J. (1988). Aptitude-treatment interaction research in clinical setting: A review of attempts to dispel the "patient uniformity" myth. *Psychological Bulletin, 104,* 192–213.

Daniel, C., & Wood, F. S. (1980). *Fitting equations to data* (2nd ed.). New York: Wiley.

Dar, R., Serlin, R. C., & Omer, H. (1994). Misuse of statistical tests in three decades of psychotherapy research. *Journal of Consulting and Clinical Psychology, 62,* 75–82.

Darlington, R. B. (1968). Multiple regression in psychological research and practice. *Psychological Bulletin, 69,* 161–182.

Darlington, R. B. (1990). *Regression and linear models.* New York: McGraw-Hill.

Darlington, R. B., Weinberg, S. L., & Walberg, H. J. (1973). Canonical variate analysis and related techniques. *Review of Educational Research, 43,* 433–454.

Das, J. P., & Kirby, J. R. (1978). The case of the wrong exemplar: A reply to Humphreys. *Journal of Educational Psychology, 70,* 877–879.

Datta, M. (1993). You cannot exclude the explanation you have not considered. *The Lancet, 342,* 345–347.

Datta, S. K., & Nugent, J. B. (1986). Adversary activities and per capita income growth. *World Development, 14,* 1457–1461.

Davis, D. J. (1969). Flexibility and power in comparisons among means. *Psychological Bulletin, 71,* 441–444.

Davis, J. A. (1966). The campus as a frog pond: An application of the theory of relative deprivation to career decisions of college men. *American Journal of Sociology, 72,* 17–31.

DeBaryshe, B. D., Patterson, G. R., & Capaldi, D. M. (1993). A performance model for academic achievement in early adolescent boys. *Developmental Psychology, 29,* 795–804.

Deegan, J. (1974). Specification error in causal models. *Social Science Research, 3,* 235–259.

DeGroot, A. D. (1969). *Methodology: Foundations of inference and research in the behavioral sciences.* The Hague: Mouton.

DeMaris, A. (1993). Odds versus probabilities in logit equations: A reply to Roncek. *Social Forces, 71,* 1057–1065.

Denters, B., & Van Puijenbroek, R. A. G. (1989). Conditional regression analysis: Problems, solutions and an application. *Quality and Quantity, 23,* 83–108.

Diaconis, P., & Efron, B. (1983). Computer-intensive methods in statistics. *Scientific American, 248*(5), 116–130.

Dixon, W. J. (Ed.). (1992). *BMDP statistical software manual: Release 7* (Vols. 1–2). Berkeley, CA: University of California Press.

Doby, J. T. (1967). Explanation and prediction. In J. T. Doby (Ed.), *An introduction to social research* (2nd ed., pp. 50–62). New York: Appleton-Century-Crofts.

Dodge, Y. (1985). *Analysis of experiments with missing data.* New York: Wiley.

Dorf, R. C. (1969). *Matrix algebra: A programmed introduction.* New York: Wiley.

Dorfman, D. D. (1978). The Cyril Burt question: New findings. *Science, 201,* 1177–1186.

Dowaliby, F. J., & Schumer, H. (1973). Teacher-centered versus student-centered mode of college classroom instruction as related to manifest anxiety. *Journal of Educational Psychology, 64,* 125–132.

Draper, N., & Smith, H. (1981). *Applied regression analysis* (2nd ed.). New York: Wiley.

Drasgow, F., & Dorans, N. J. (1982). Robustness of estimators of the squared multiple correlation and squared cross-validity coefficient to violations of multivariate normality. *Applied Psychological Measurement, 6,* 185–200.

Drasgow, F., Dorans, N. J., & Tucker, L. R. (1979). Estimators of the squared cross-validity coefficient: A Monte Carlo investigation. *Applied Psychological Measurement, 3,* 387–399.

DuBois, P. H. (1957). *Multivariate correlational analysis.* New York: Harper & Brothers.

Dullberg, C. (1985). Another view. *American Journal of Epidemiology, 121,* 477–478.

Duncan, O. D. (1970). Partials, partitions, and paths. In E. F. Borgatta & G. W. Bohrnstedt (Eds.), *Sociological methodology 1970* (pp. 38–47). San Francisco: Jossey-Bass.

Duncan, O. D. (1972). Unmeasured variables in linear models for panel analysis. In H. L. Costner (Ed.), *Sociological methodology 1972* (pp. 36–82). San Francisco: Jossey-Bass.

Duncan, O. D. (1975). *Introduction to structural equation models.* New York: Academic Press.

Duncan, O. D., Cuzzort, R. P., & Duncan B. (1961). *Statistical geography: Problems in the analysis of areal data.* New York: Free Press.

Duncan, O. D., Featherman, D. L., & Duncan, B. (1972). *Socioeconomic background and achievement.* New York: Seminar Press.

Dunlap, W. P., & Kemery, E. R. (1987). Failure to detect moderating effects: Is multicollinearity the problem? *Psychological Bulletin, 102,* 418–420.

Dunlap, W. P., & Kemery, E. R. (1988). Effects of predictor intercorrelations and reliabilities on moderated regression analysis. *Organizational Behavior and Human Decision Processes, 41,* 248–258.

Dunn, G., Everitt, B., & Pickles, A. (1993). *Modelling covariances and latent variables using EQS.* New York: Chapman & Hall.

Dunn, O. J. (1961). Multiple comparisons among means. *Journal of the American Statistical Association, 56,* 52–64.

Dunnett, C. W. (1955). A multiple comparison procedure for comparing several treatments with a control. *Journal of the American Statistical Association, 50,* 1096–1121.

du Toit, S. H. C., Steyn, A. G. W., & Stumpf, R. H. (1986). *Graphical exploratory data analysis.* New York: Springer-Verlag.

Dutton, D, G., & Lake, R. A. (1973). Threat of own prejudice and reverse discrimination in interracial situations. *Journal of Personality and Social Psychology, 28,* 94–100.

Edwards, A. L. (1964). *Expected values of discrete random variables and elementary statistics.* New York: Wiley.

Edwards, A. L. (1979). *Multiple regression and the analysis of variance and covariance.* San Francisco: W. H. Freeman.

Edwards, A. L. (1985). *Experimental design in psychological research* (5th ed.). New York: Harper & Row.

Efron, B., & Gong, G. (1983). A leisurely look at the bootstrap, the jackknife, and cross-validation. *The American Statistician, 37,* 36–48.

Ehrenberg, A. S. C. (1990). The unimportance of relative importance. *The American Statistician, 44,* 260.

Ekenhammer, B. (1974). Interactionism in personality from a historical perspective. *Psychological Bulletin, 81,* 1026–1048.

Elashoff, J. D. (1969). Analysis of covariance: A delicate instrument. *American Educational Research Journal, 6,* 383–401.

Eliason, S. R. (1993). *Maximum likelihood estimation: Logic and practice.* Thousand Oaks, CA: Sage.

Elliott, T. R., Witty, T. E., Herrick, S., & Hoffman, J. T. (1991). Negotiating reality after physical loss: Hope, depression, and disability. *Journal of Personality and Social Psychology, 61,* 608–613.

Epstein, S., & O'Brien, E. J. (1985). The person-situation debate in historical and current perspective. *Psychological Bulletin, 98,* 513–537.

Erbring, L. (1990). Individuals writ large: An epilogue on the "Ecological Fallacy." In J. A. Stimson (Ed.), *Political analysis* (Vol. 1, 1989, pp. 235–269). Ann Arbor, MI: The University of Michigan Press.

Erickson, F. (1986). Qualitative methods in research on teaching. In M. C. Wittrock (Ed.). *Handbook of research on teaching* (3rd ed., pp. 119–161). New York: Macmillan.

Evans, M. G. (1991). The problem of analyzing multiplicative composites: Interactions revisited. *American Psychologist, 46,* 6–15.

Eysenck, H. J. (1965). *Fact and fiction in psychology.* New York: Penguin.

Ezekiel, M., & Fox, K. A. (1959). *Methods of correlation and regression analysis* (3rd ed.). New York: Wiley.

Failla, S., & Jones, L. C. (1991). Families of children with developmental disabilities: An examination of family hardiness. *Research in Nursing & Health, 14,* 41–50.

Farkas, G. (1974). Specification, residuals and contextual effects. *Sociological Methods & Research, 2,* 333–363.

Farrell, A. D. (1994). Structural equation modeling with longitudinal data: Strategies for examining group differences and reciprocal relationships. *Journal of Consulting and Clinical Psychology, 62,* 477–487.

Feigl, H., & Brodbeck, M. (Eds.). (1953). *Readings in the philosophy of science.* New York: Appleton-Century-Crofts.

Feldt, L. S. (1958). A comparison of the precision of three experimental designs employing a concomitant variable. *Psychometrika, 23,* 335–354.

Finkelstein, M. O. (1980). The judicial reception of multiple regression studies in race and sex discrimination cases. *Columbia Law Review, 80,* 737–754.

Finn, J. D. (1974). *A general model for multivariate analysis.* New York: Holt, Rinehart and Winston.

Finney, D. J. (1946). Standard errors of yields adjusted for regression on an independent measurement. *Biometrics Bulletin, 2,* 557–572.

Finney, D. J. (1982). The questioning statistician. *Statistics in Medicine, 1,* 5–13.

Finney, J. M. (1972). Indirect effects in path analysis. *Sociological Methods & Research, 1,* 175–186.

Firebaugh, G. (1978). A rule for inferring individual-level relationships from aggregate data. *American Sociological Review, 43,* 557–572.

Firebaugh, G. (1979). Assessing group effects. *Sociological Methods & Research, 7,* 384–395.

Firebaugh, G. (1980). Group contexts and frog ponds. In K. H. Roberts & L. Burstein (Eds.), *Issues in aggregation* (pp. 43–52). San Francisco: Jossey-Bass.

Fisher, F. M. (1966). *The identification problem in econometrics.* New York: McGraw-Hill.

Fisher, F. M. (1980). Multiple regression in legal proceedings. *Columbia Law Review, 80,* 702–736.

Fisher, R. A. (1926). The arrangement of field experiments. *Journal of the Ministry of Agriculture of Great Britain, 33,* 503–513.

Fisher, R. A. (1936). The use of multiple measurements in taxonomic problems. *Annals of Eugenics, 7,* 179–188.

Fisher, R. A. (1958). *Statistical methods for research workers* (13th ed.). New York: Hafner.

Fisher, R. A. (1966). *The design of experiments* (8th ed.). New York: Hafner.

Fisher, R. A., & Yates, F. (1963). *Statistical tables for biological, agricultural and medical research* (6th ed.). New York: Hafner.

Flay, B. R., Hu, F. B., Siddiqui, O., Day, L. E., Hedeker, D., Petraitis, J., Richardson, J., & Sussman, S. (1994). Differential influence of parental smoking and friends' smoking on adolescent initiation and escalation of smoking. *Journal of Health and Social Behavior, 35,* 248–265.

Fleiss, J. L. (1985). Re: "Estimating odds ratios with categorically scaled covariates in multiple logistic regression analysis. *American Journal of Epidemiology, 121,* 476–477.

Fleiss, J. L. (1986). *The design and analysis of clinical experiments.* New York: Wiley.

Fleiss, J. L., & Shrout, P. E. (1977). The effects of measurement errors on some multivariate procedures. *American Journal of Public Health, 67,* 1188–1191.

Fornell, C. (1983). Issues in the application of covariance structure analysis: A comment. *Journal of Consumer Research, 9,* 443–450.

Fornell, C., & Yi, Y. (1992a). Assumptions of the two-step approach to latent variable modeling. *Sociological Methods & Research, 20,* 291–320.

Fornell, C., & Yi, Y. (1992b). Assumptions of the two-step approach: Reply to Anderson and Gerbing. *Sociological Methods & Research, 20,* 334–339.

Fox, J. (1980). Effect analysis in structural equation models. *Sociological Methods & Research, 9,* 3–28.

Fox, J. (1984). *Linear statistical models and related methods: With applications to social research.* New York: Wiley.

Fox, J. (1985). Effect analysis in structural-equation models II. *Sociological Methods & Research, 14,* 81–95.

Fox, J. (1991). *Regression diagnostics.* Thousand Oaks, CA: Sage.

Fox, K. A. (1968). *Intermediate economic statistics.* New York: Wiley.

Frank, B. M. (1984). Effect of field independence-dependence and study technique on learning from a lecture. *American Educational Research Journal, 21,* 669–678.

Freedman, D. A. (1987a). As others see us: A case study in path analysis. *Journal of Educational Statistics, 12,* 101–128.

Freedman, D. A. (1987b). A rejoinder on models, metaphors, and fables. *Journal of Educational Statistics, 12,* 206–223.

Freedman, J. L. (1964). Involvement, discrepancy, and change. *Journal of Abnormal and Social Psychology, 69,* 290–295.

Friedlander, F. (1964). Type I and Type II bias. *American Psychologist, 19,* 198–199.

Friedrich, R. J. (1982). In defense of multiplicative terms in multiple regression equations. *American Journal of Political Science, 26,* 797–833.

Frigon, J., & Laurencelle, L. (1993). Analysis of covariance: A proposed algorithm. *Educational and Psychological Measurement, 53,* 1–18.

Gagnon, J. H. (1981, December 13). Searching for the childhood of Eros [Review of *Sexual preference: Its development in men and women*]. *The New York Times Book Review,* pp. 10, 37.

Games, P. A. (1971). Multiple comparisons of means. *American Educational Research Journal, 8,* 531–565.

Games, P. A. (1973). Type IV errors revisited. *Psychological Bulletin, 80,* 304–307.

Games, P. A. (1976). Limitations of analysis of covariance on intact group quasi-experimental designs. *Journal of Experimental Education, 44,* 51–54.

Gatsonis, C., & Sampson, A. R. (1989). Multiple correlation: Exact power and sample calculations. *Psychological Bulletin, 106,* 516–524.

Gerbing, D. W., & Anderson, J. C. (1984). On the meaning of within-factor correlated measurement errors. *Journal of Consumer Research, 11,* 572–580.

Gilula, Z., & Haberman, S. J. (1986). Canonical analysis of contingency tables by maximum likelihood. *Journal of the American Statistical Association, 81,* 780–788.

Glantz, S. A. (1980). Biostatistics: How to detect, correct and prevent errors in the medical literature. *Circulation, 61,* 1–7.

Glenn, N. D. (1989). What we know, what we say we know: Discrepancies between warranted and unwarranted conclusions. In H. Eulau (Ed.), *Crossroads of social science: The ICPSR 25th anniversary volume* (pp. 119–140). New York: Agathon Press.

Glick, N. (1991). Comment. *Statistical Science, 6,* 258–262.

Gocka, E. F. (1973). Stepwise regression for mixed mode predictor variables. *Educational and Psychological Measurement, 33,* 319–325.

Goffin, R. D. (1993). A comparison of two new indices for the assessment of fit of structural equation models. *Multivariate Behavioral Research, 28,* 205–214.

Goldberger, A. S. (1970). On Boudon's method of linear causal analysis. *American Sociological Review, 35,* 97–101.

Goldberger, A. S. (1991). *A course in econometrics.* Cambridge, MA: Harvard University Press.

Goldstein, H. (1987). *Multilevel models in educational and social research.* New York: Oxford University Press.

Goldstein, R. (1991). Editor's notes. *The American Statistician, 45,* 304–305.

Goldstein, R. (1992). Editor's notes. *The American Statistician, 46,* 319–320.

Good, T. L., & Stipek, D. J. (1983). Individual differences in the classroom: A psychological perspective. In G. D. Fenstermacher & J. I. Goodlad (Eds.), *Individual differences and the common curriculum* (Part I, pp. 9–43). Chicago: National Society for the Study of Education (Eighty-second Yearbook). Distributed by the University of Chicago Press.

Goodwin, I. (1971, July 19). Prof fired after finding sex great for scholars. *New York Post,* p. 36.

Gordon, R. A. (1968). Issues in multiple regression. *American Journal of Sociology, 73,* 592–616.

Gorsuch, R. L. (1983). *Factor analysis* (2nd ed.). Hillsdale, NJ: Lawrence Erlbaum Associates.

Grant, G. (1973). Shaping social policy: The politics of the Coleman Report. *Teachers College Record, 75,* 17–54.

Graybill, F. A. (1961). *An introduction to linear statistical models* (Vol. 1). New York: McGraw-Hill.

Green, B. F. (1979). The two kinds of linear discriminant functions and their relationship. *Journal of Educational Statistics, 4,* 247–263.

Green, P. E. (1976). *Mathematical tools for applied multivariate analysis.* New York: Academic Press.

Green, P. E. (1978). *Analyzing multivariate data.* Hinsdale, IL: The Dryden Press.

Green, S. B. (1991). How many subjects does it take to do a regression analysis? *Multivariate Behavioral Research, 26,* 499–510.

Greene, V. L. (1977). An algorithm for total and indirect causal effects. *Political Methodology, 4,* 369–381.

Greenhouse, L. (1993, June 29). Justices put judges in charge of deciding reliability of scientific testimony. *The New York Times* (National Edition), p. A10.

Grünbaum, A. (1952). Causality and the science of human behavior. *The American Scientist, 40,* 665–676.

Guilford, J. P. (1954). *Psychometric methods* (2nd ed.). New York: McGraw-Hill.

Guilford, J. P., & Fruchter, B. (1978). *Fundamental statistics in psychology and education* (5th ed.). New York: McGraw-Hill.

Gujarati, D. (1970). Use of dummy variables in testing for equality between sets of coefficients in linear regressions: A generalization. *The American Statistician, 24*(5), 18–22.

Guttman, L. (1985). The illogic of statistical inference for cumulative science. *Applied Stochastic Models and Data Analysis, 1,* 3–10.

Haase, R. F. (1991). Computational formulas for multivariate strength of association from approximate F and χ^2 tests. *Multivariate Behavioral Research, 26,* 227–245.

Haberman, C. (1993, March 31). Justices struggle to clarify rule on science data. *The New York Times* (National Edition), pp. A1, A9.

Hagle, T. M., & Mitchell, G. E. (1992). Goodness-of-fit for probit and logit. *American Journal of Political Science, 36,* 762–784.

Hair, J. F., Anderson, R. E., Tatham, R. L., & Black, W. C. (Eds.). (1992). *Multivariate data analysis with readings* (3rd ed.). New York: Macmillan.

Hall, C. E. (1969). Rotation of canonical variates in multivariate analysis of variance. *Journal of Experimental Education, 38,* 31–38.

Hammond, J. L. (1973). Two sources of error in ecological correlations. *American Sociological Review, 38,* 764–777.

Hand, D. J., & Taylor, C. C. (1987). *Multivariate analysis of variance and repeated measures: A practical approach for behavioural scientists.* New York: Chapman and Hall.

Hannah, T. E., & Morrissey, C. (1987). Correlates of psychological hardiness in Canadian adolescents. *The Journal of Social Psychology, 127,* 339–344.

Hannan, M. T. (1971). *Problems of aggregation and disaggregation in sociological research.* Lexington, MA: Lexington Books.

Hannan, M. T., & Burstein, L. (1974). Estimation from grouped observations. *American Sociological Review, 39,* 374–392.

Hannan, M. T., Freeman, J. H., & Meyer, J. W. (1976). Specification of models for organizational effectiveness. *American Sociological Review, 41,* 136–143.

Hansen, C. P. (1989). A causal model of the relationship among accidents, biodata, personality, and cognitive factors. *Journal of Applied Psychology, 74,* 81–90.

Hanson, N. R. (1958). *Patterns of discovery: An inquiry into the conceptual foundations of science.* New York: Cambridge University Press.

Hanson, N. R. (1969). *Perception and discovery: An introduction to scientific inquiry.* San Francisco: Freeman, Cooper & Company.

Hanson, N. R. (1971). *Observation and explanation: A guide to philosophy of science.* New York: Harper & Row.

Hanushek, E. A., & Jackson, J. E. (1977). *Statistical methods for social scientists.* New York: Academic Press.

Hanushek, E. A., Jackson, J. E., & Kain, J. F. (1974). Model specification, use of aggregate data, and the ecological correlation fallacy. *Political Methodology, 1,* 89–107.

Hanushek, E. A., & Kain, J. F. (1972). On the value of *Equality of educational opportunity* as a guide to public policy. In F. Mosteller & D. P. Moynihan (Eds.), *On equality of educational opportunity* (pp. 116–145). New York: Vintage Books.

Hargens, L. L. (1976). A note on standardized coefficients as structural parameters. *Sociological Methods & Research, 5,* 247–256.

Harman, H. H. (1976). *Modern factor analysis* (3rd ed.). Chicago: University of Chicago Press.

Härnqvist, K. (1975). The international study of educational achievement. In F. N. Kerlinger (Ed.), *Review of research in education 3* (pp. 85–109). Itasca, IL: F. E. Peacock.

Harré, R., & Madden, E. H. (1975). *Causal powers: A theory of natural necessity.* Totowa, NJ: Rowman and Littlefield.

Harrell, F. E., & Lee, K. L. (1985). A comparison of the discriminant analysis and logistic regression under multivariate normality. In P. K. Sen (Ed.), *Biostatistics: Statistics in biomedical, public health and environmental sciences* (pp. 333–343). New York: North-Holland.

Harris, C. W. (Ed.). (1963). *Problems in measuring change.* Madison, WI: University of Wisconsin Press.

Harris, R. J. (1985). *A primer of multivariate statistics* (2nd ed.). Orlando, FL: Academic Press.

Harris, R. J. (1993). Multivariate analysis of variance. In L. K. Edwards (Ed.), *Applied analysis of variance in behavioral sciences* (pp. 255–296). New York: Marcel Dekker.

Hartlage, L. C. (1988). Notice. *American Psychologist, 43,* 1092.

Hauck, W. W., & Donner, A. (1977). Wald's test as applied to hypotheses in logit analysis. *Journal of the American Statistical Association, 72,* 851–853.

Hauser, R. M. (1970). Context and consex: A cautionary tale. *American Journal of Sociology, 75,* 645–664.

Hauser, R. M. (1971). *Socioeconomic background and educational performance.* Rose Monograph Series. Washington, DC: American Sociological Association.

Hauser, R. M. (1974). Contextual analysis revisited. *Sociological Methods & Research, 2,* 365–375.

Hays, W. L. (1988). *Statistics* (4th. ed.). New York: Holt, Rinehart and Winston.

Hechinger, F. M. (1979, November 5). Frail Sociology. *The New York Times,* p. A18.

Heck, D. L. (1960). Charts for some upper percentage points of the distribution of the largest characteristic root. *Annals of Mathematical Statistics, 31,* 625–642.

Heider, F. (1944). Social perception and phenomenal causality. *Psychological Review, 51,* 358–374.

Heim, J., & Perl, L. (1974). *The educational production function: Implications for educational manpower policy.* Ithaca, NY: Institute of Public Employment (Monograph 4), New York State School of Industrial and Labor Relations, Cornell University.

Heise, D. R. (1969). Problems in path analysis and causal inference. In E. F. Borgatta & G. W. Bohrnstedt (Eds.), *Sociological methodology 1969* (pp. 38–73). San Francisco: Jossey-Bass.

Heise, D. R. (1975). *Causal analysis.* New York: Wiley.

Hempel, C. G. (1952). *Fundamentals of concept formation in empirical science.* Chicago: University of Chicago Press.

Hempel, C. G. (1965). *Aspects of scientific explanation and other essays in the philosophy of science.* New York: The Free Press.

Herting, J. R., & Costner, H. L. (1985). Respecification in multiple indicator models. In H. M. Blalock (Ed.), *Causal models in the social sciences* (pp. 321–393). Chicago: Aldine.

Herzberg, P. A. (1969). The parameters of cross-validation. *Psychometrika Monograph, 34*(2, Pt. 2).

Hill, M. D. (1988). Class, kinship density, and conjugal role segregation. *Journal of Marriage and the Family, 50,* 731–741.

Himmelfarb, S. (1975). What do you do when the control group doesn't fit into the factorial design. *Psychological Bulletin, 82,* 363–368.

Hoaglin, D. C. (1992). Diagnostics. In D. C. Hoaglin & D. S. Moore (Eds.), *Perspectives on contemporary statistics* (pp. 123–144). Washington, DC: Mathematical Association of America.

Hoaglin, D. C., & Welsch, R. E. (1978). The hat matrix in regression and ANOVA. *The American Statistician, 32,* 17–22.

Hobfoll, S. E., Shoham, S. B., & Ritter, C. (1991). Women's satisfaction with social support and their receipt of aid. *Journal of Personality and Social Psychology, 61,* 332–341.

Hochberg, Y., & Tamhane, A. C. (1987). *Multiple comparison procedures.* New York: Wiley.

Hocking, R. R. (1974). Misspecification in regression. *The American Statistician, 28,* 39–40.

Hocking, R. R. (1976). The analysis and selection of variables in linear regression. *Biometrics, 32,* 1–49.

Hodson, F. R. (1973). Scientific archaeology [Review of *Models in archaeology*]. *Nature, 242,* 350.

Hoffmann, S. (1960). Contemporary theories of international relations. In S. Hoffmann (Ed.), *Contemporary theory in international relations* (pp. 29–54). Englewood Cliffs, NJ: Prentice-Hall.

Hohn, F. E. (1964). *Elementary matrix algebra* (2nd ed.). New York: Macmillan.

Holland, P. W. (1986). Statistics and causal inference. *Journal of the American Statistical Association, 81,* 945–960.

Holland, T. R., Levi, M., & Watson, C. G. (1980). Canonical correlation in the analysis of a contingency table. *Psychological Bulletin, 87,* 334–336.

Hollander, E. P. (1985). Leadership and power. In G. Lindzey & E. Aronson (Eds.), *Handbook of social psychology* (3rd ed., Vol. 2, pp. 485–538). New York: Random House.

Holling, H. (1983). Suppressor structures in the general linear model. *Educational and Psychological Measurement, 43,* 1–9.

Holzinger, K. L., & Freeman, F. N. (1925). The interpretation of Burt's regression equation. *Journal of Educational Psychology, 16,* 577–582.

Honan, W. H. (1995, May 4). Professor writing of aliens is under inquiry at Harvard. *The New York Times* (National Edition), p. A9.

Horel, A. E., & Kennard, R. W. (1970a). Ridge regression: Biased estimation for nonorthogonal problems. *Technometrics, 12,* 55–67.

Horel, A. E., & Kennard, R. W. (1970b). Ridge regression: Applications to nonorthogonal problems. *Technometrics, 12,* 69–82.

Hornbeck, F. W. (1973). Factorial analyses of variance with appended control groups. *Behavioral Science, 18,* 213–220.

Horst, P. (1941). The role of prediction variables which are independent of the criterion. In P. Horst (Ed.), The prediction of personal adjustment. *Social Research Bulletin, 48,* 431–436.

Horst, P. (1963). *Matrix algebra for social scientists.* New York: Holt, Rinehart and Winston.

Horst, P. (1966). *Psychological measurement and prediction.* Belmont, CA: Wadsworth.

Hosmer, D. W., & Lemeshow, S. (1989). *Applied logistic regression.* New York: Wiley.

Hosmer, D. W., Taber, S., & Lemeshow, S. (1991). The importance of assessing the fit of logistic models: A case study. *American Journal of Public Health, 81,* 1630–1635.

Hotard, S. R., McFatter, R. M., McWhirter, R. M., & Stegall, M. E. (1989). Interactive effects of extraversion, neuroticism, and social relationships on subjective well-being. *Journal of Personality and Social Psychology, 57,* 321–331.

Hotelling, H. (1936). Relations between two sets of variables. *Biometrika, 28,* 321–377.

Howe, H. (1976). Education research—the promise and the problem. *Educational Researcher, 5*(6), 2–7.

Hox, J. J. (1995). AMOS, EQS, and LISREL for Windows: A comparative review. *Structural Equation Modeling, 2,* 79–91.

Hox, J. J., & Kreft, I. G. G. (Eds.). (1994). Multilevel analysis methods [Special issue]. *Sociological Methods & Research, 1994, 22*(3).

Hu, L.-T., & Bentler, P. M. (1995). Evaluating model fit. In R. H. Hoyle (Ed.), *Structural equation modeling: Concepts, issues, and applications* (pp. 76–99). Thousand Oaks, CA: Sage.

Huberty, C. J. (1972). Multivariate indices of strength of association. *Multivariate Behavioral Research, 7,* 523–526.

Huberty, C. J. (1975a). The stability of three indices of relative contribution in discriminant analysis. *Journal of Experimental Education, 44,* 59–64.

Huberty, C. J. (1975b). Discriminant analysis. *Review of Educational Research, 45,* 543–598.

Huberty, C. J. (1987). On statistical testing. *Educational Researcher, 16*(8), 4–9.

Huberty, C. J. (1989). Problems with stepwise methods—better alternatives. In B. Thompson (Ed.), *Advances in social science methodology: A research annual* (Vol. 1, pp. 43–70). Greenwich, CT: JAI Press.

Huberty, C. J. (1994). *Applied discriminant analysis.* New York: Wiley.

Huberty, C. J., & Mourad, S. A. (1980). Estimation in multiple correlation/prediction. *Educational and Psychological Measurement, 40,* 101–112.

Huberty, C. J., & Smith, J. D. (1982). The study of effects in MANOVA. *Multivariate Behavioral Research, 17,* 417–432.

Huberty, C. J., & Wisenbaker, J. M. (1992). Variable importance in multivariate group comparisons. *Journal of Educational Statistics, 17,* 75–91.

Hudson, H. C., and others (1982). *Classifying social data: New applications of analytic methods for social science research.* San Francisco: Jossey-Bass.

Huitema, B. E. (1980). *The analysis of covariance and alternatives.* New York: Wiley.

Hull, J. G., & Mendolia, M. (1991). Modeling the relations of attributional style, expectancies, and depression. *Journal of Personality and Social Psychology, 61,* 85–97.

Hummel, T. J., & Sligo, J. R. (1971). Empirical comparison of univariate and multivariate analysis of variance procedures. *Psychological Bulletin, 76,* 49–57.

Humphreys, L. G. (1978). Doing research the hard way: Substituting analysis of variance for a problem in correlational analysis. *Journal of Educational Psychology, 70,* 873–876.

Humphreys, L. G., & Fleishman, A. (1974). Pseudo-orthogonal and other analysis of variance designs involving individual-differences variables. *Journal of Educational Psychology, 66,* 464–472.

Hunter, J. E., Schmidt, F. L., & Rauschenberger, J. (1984). Methodological, statistical, and ethical issues in the study of bias in psychological tests. In C. R. Reynolds & R. T. Brown (Eds.), *Perspectives on bias in mental testing* (pp. 41–99). New York: Plenum.

Husén, T. (1987). Policy impact of IEA research. *Comparative Education Review, 31,* 29–46.

Hutten, E. H. (1962). *The origins of science: An inquiry into the foundations of western thought.* London: George Allen and Unwin.

Huynh, H. (1982). A comparison of four approaches to robust regression. *Psychological Bulletin, 92,* 505–512.

Igra, A. (1979). On forming variable set composites to summarize a block recursive model. *Social Science Research, 8,* 253–264.

Inkeles, A. (1977). The international evaluation of educational achievement. *Proceedings of the National Academy of Education, 4,* 139–200.

Irwin, L., & Lichtman, A. J. (1976). Across the great divide: Inferring individual level behavior from aggregate data. *Political Methodology, 3,* 411–439.

Isaac, P. D., & Milligan, G. W. (1983). A comment on the use of canonical correlation in the analysis of contingency tables. *Psychological Bulletin, 93,* 378–381.

Iversen, G. R. (1991). *Contextual analysis.* Thousand Oaks, CA: Sage.

Jaccard, J., Turrisi, R., & Wan, C. K. (1990). *Interaction effects in multiple regression.* Thousand Oaks, CA: Sage.

Jackson, D. J., & Borgatta, E. F. (Eds.). (1981). *Factor analysis and measurement in sociological research: A multidimensional perspective.* Thousand Oaks, CA: Sage.

James, L. R., & Brett, J. M. (1984). Mediators, moderators, and tests for mediation. *Journal of Applied Psychology, 69,* 307–321.

Jencks, C., and others (1972). *Inequality: A reassessment of the effect of family and schooling in America.* New York: Basic Books.

Jencks, C., and others (1979). *Who gets ahead?.* New York: Basic Books.

Jensen, A. R. (1972). Sir Cyril Burt. *Psychometrika, 37,* 115–117.

Johnson, A. F. (1985). Beneath the technological fix: Outliers and probability statements. *Journal of Chronic Diseases, 38,* 957–961.

Johnson, D. R., & Benin, M. H. (1984). Ethnic culture or methodological artifacts? A comment on Mirowsky and Ross. *American Journal of Sociology, 89,* 1189–1194.

Johnson, P. O., & Fay, L. C. (1950). The Johnson-Neyman technique, its theory and application. *Psychometrika, 15,* 349–367.

Johnson, P. O., & Jackson, R. W. B. (1959). *Modern statistical methods: Descriptive and inductive.* Chicago: Rand McNally.

Johnson, P. O., & Neyman, J. (1936). Tests of certain linear hypotheses and their applications to some educational problems. *Statistical Research Memoirs, 1,* 57–93.

Johnston, J. (1972). *Econometric methods* (2nd ed.). New York: McGraw-Hill.

Jones, K., Johnston, R. J., & Pattie, C. J. (1992). People, places, and regions: Exploring the use of multi-level modelling in the analysis of electoral data. *British Journal of Political Science, 22,* 343–380.

Jöreskog, K. G. (1979). *Statistical estimation of structural models in longitudinal-developmental investigations.* In J. R. Nesselroade & P. B. Baltes (Eds.), *Longitudinal research in the study of behavior and development* (pp. 303–351). New York: Academic Press.

Jöreskog, K. G. (1993). Testing structural equation models. In K. A. Bollen & J. S. Long (Eds.), *Testing structural equation models* (pp. 294–316). Thousand Oaks, CA: Sage.

Jöreskog, K. G., & Sörbom, D. (1989). *LISREL 7: A guide to the program and applications* (2nd ed.). Chicago: SPSS.

Jöreskog, K. G., & Sörbom, D. (1993a). *LISREL 8: Structural equation modeling with the SIMPLIS command language.* Hillsdale, NJ: Lawrence Erlbaum Associates.

Jöreskog, K. G., & Sörbom, D. (1993b). *LISREL 8 user's reference guide.* Chicago: Scientific Software.

Jöreskog, K. G., & Sörbom, D. (1993c). *New features in PRELIS 2.* Chicago: Scientific Software.

Judd, C. M., Jessor, R., & Donovan, J. E. (1986). Structural equation models and personality research. *Journal of Personality, 54,* 149–198.

Judd, C. M., & Kenny, D. A. (1981). Process analysis: Estimating mediation in treatment evaluations. *Evaluation Review, 5,* 602–619.

Judd, C. M., & McClelland, G. H. (1989). *Data analysis: A model-comparison approach.* San Diego, CA: Harcourt Brace Jovanovich.

Kahn, H. A., & Sempos, C. T. (1989). *Statistical methods in epidemiology.* New York: Oxford University Press.

Kahneman, D. (1965). Control of spurious association and the reliability of the control variable. *Psychological Bulletin, 64,* 326–329.

Kaiser, H. F. (1960). Directional statistical decisions. *Psychological Review, 67,* 160–167.

Kamin, L. (1974). *The science and politics of IQ.* Potomac, MD: Lawrence Erlbaum Associates.

Kaplan, A. (1964). *The conduct of inquiry: Methodology for behavioral science.* San Francisco: Chandler.

Kaplan, D. (1988). The impact of specification error on the estimation, testing, and improvement of structural equation models. *Multivariate Behavioral Research, 23,* 69–86.

Kaplan, D. (1989). Model modification in covariance structure analysis: Application of the expected parameter change statistic. *Multivariate Behavioral Research, 24,* 285–305.

Kaplan, D. (1990a). Evaluating and modifying covariance structure models: A review and recommendation. *Multivariate Behavioral Research, 25,* 137–155.

Kaplan, D. (1990b). A rejoinder on evaluating and modifying covariance structure models. *Multivariate Behavioral Research, 25,* 197–204.

Kaplan, D. (1995). Statistical power in structural equation modeling. In R. H. Hoyle (Ed.), *Structural equation modeling: Concepts, issues, and applications* (pp. 100–117). Thousand Oaks, CA: Sage.

Karpman, M. B. (1983). The Johnson-Neyman technique using SPSS or BMDP. *Educational and Psychological Measurement, 43,* 137–147.

Karpman, M. B. (1986). Comparing two non-parallel regression lines with the parametric alternative to the analysis of covariance using SPSS-X or SAS—the Johnson-Neyman technique. *Educational and Psychological Measurement, 46,* 639–644.

Karweit, N. L., Fennessey, J., & Daiger, D. C. (1978). *Examining the credibility of offsetting contextual effects.* Report No. 250. Center for Social Organization of Schools. The Johns Hopkins University, Baltimore.

Kean, M. H., Summers, A. A., Raivetz, M. J., & Farber, I. J. (1979). *What works in reading? The results of a joint School District/Federal Reserve Bank empirical study in Philadelphia.* Philadelphia: Office of Research and Evaluation, The School District of Philadelphia.

Keesling, J. W. (1978, March). *Some explorations in multilevel analysis.* Paper presented at the annual meeting of the American Educational Research Association, Toronto.

Keinan, G. (1994). Effects of stress and tolerance of ambiguity on magical thinking. *Journal of Personality and Social Psychology, 67,* 48–55.

Kemeny, J. G. (1959). *A philosopher looks at science.* Princeton, NJ: Van Nostrand.

Kemeny, J. G., Snell, J. L., & Thompson, G. L. (1966). *Introduction to finite mathematics* (2nd ed.). Englewood Cliffs, NJ: Prentice-Hall.

Kempthorne, O. (1978). Logical, epistemological and statistical aspects of nature-nurture data interpretation. *Biometrics, 34,* 1–23.

Kendall, M. G. (1951). Regression, structure and functional relationship. *Biometrika, 38,* 11–25.

Kendall, P. L., & Lazarsfeld, P. F. (1955). The relation between individual and group characteristics in "The American soldier." In P. F. Lazarsfeld & M. Rosenberg (Eds.), *The language of social research* (pp. 290–296). New York: The Free Press.

Kennedy, J. J. (1970). The eta coefficient in complex ANOVA designs. *Educational and Psychological Measurement, 30,* 885–889.

Kenny, D. A. (1975). A quasi-experimental approach to assessing treatment effects in the nonequivalent control group design. *Psychological Bulletin, 82,* 345–362.

Kenny, D. A. (1979). *Correlation and causality.* New York: Wiley.

Keppel, G. (1991). *Design & analysis: A researcher's handbook* (3rd ed.). Englewood Cliffs, NJ: Prentice-Hall.

Keppel, G., & Zedeck, S. (1989). *Data analysis for research designs: Analysis of variance and multiple regression/correlation approaches.* New York: W. H. Freeman.

Keren, G., & Lewis, C. (1979). Partial omega squared for ANOVA designs. *Educational and Psychological Measurement, 39,* 119–128.

Kerlinger, F. N., & Pedhazur, E. J. (1973). *Multiple regression in behavioral research.* New York: Holt, Rinehart, and Winston.

Kerlinger, F. N. (1986). *Foundations of behavioral research* (3rd ed.). New York: Holt, Rinehart and Winston.

Khamis, H. J. (1991). Manual computations—a tool for reinforcing concepts and techniques. *The American Statistician, 45,* 294–299.

Kim, J. O., & Mueller, C. W. (1976). Standardized and unstandardized coefficients in causal analysis. *Sociological Methods & Research, 4,* 423–438.

King, G. (1986). How not to lie with statistics: Avoiding common mistakes in quantitative political science. *American Journal of Political Science, 30,* 666–687.

King, G. (1989). *Unifying political methodology: The likelihood theory of statistical inference.* New York: Cambridge University Press.

King, G. (1991a). Stochastic variation: A comment on Lewis-Beck and Skalaban's "the *R*-squared". In J. A. Stimson (Ed.), *Political analysis: Vol. 2, 1990* (pp. 185–200). Ann Arbor, MI: The University of Michigan.

King, G. (1991b). "Truth" is stranger than prediction, more questionable than causal inference. *American Journal of Political Science, 35,* 1047–1053.

Kirk, R. E. (1982). *Experimental design: Procedures for the behavioral sciences* (2nd ed.). Belmont, CA: Brook/Cole.

Kish, L. (1959). Some statistical problems in research design. *American Sociological Review, 24,* 328–338.

Kish, L. (1975). Representation, randomization, and control. In H. M. Blalock, A. Aganbegian, F. M Borodkin, R. Boudon, & V. Capecchi (Eds.), *Quantitative sociology. International perspectives on mathematical and statistical modeling* (pp. 261–284). New York: Academic Press.

Klecka, W. R. (1980). *Discriminant analysis.* Thousand Oaks, CA: Sage.

Kleinbaum, D. G., Kupper, L. L., & Morgenstern, H. (1982). *Epidemiologic research*: *Principles and quantitative methods.* New York: Van Nostrand Reinhold.

Kleinbaum, D. G., Kupper, L. L., & Muller, K. E. (1988). *Applied regression analysis and other multivariable methods* (2nd ed.). Boston: PWS-Kent.

Kmenta, J. (1971). *Elements of econometrics.* New York: Macmillan.

Knapp, T. R. (1977). The unit-of-analysis problem in applications of simple correlation analysis to educational research. *Journal of Educational Statistics, 2,* 171–186.

Knapp, T. R. (1978). Canonical correlation analysis: A general parametric significance-testing system. *Psychological Bulletin, 85,* 410–416.

Konovsky, M. A., Folger, R., & Cropanzano, R. (1987). Relative effects of procedural and distributive justice on employee attitudes. *Representative Research in Social Psychology, 17,* 15–24.

Koopman, J. S. (1981). Interaction between discrete causes. *American Journal of Epidemiology, 113,* 716–724.

Koopmans, T. C. (1949). Identification problems in economic model construction. *Econometrica, 17,* 125–143.

Kramer, G. H. (1983). The ecological fallacy revisited: Aggregate- versus individual-level findings on economics and elections, and sociotropic voting. *American Political Science Review, 77,* 92–111.

Krech, D., & Crutchfield, R. S. (1948). *Theory and problems of social psychology.* New York: McGraw-Hill.

Kreft, I. G. G. (1993a). Using multilevel analysis to study school effectiveness: A study of Dutch secondary schools. *Sociology of Education, 66,* 104–129.

Kreft, I. G. G. (1993b). [Review of *Schools, classrooms and pupils, international studies of schooling from a multilevel perspective*]. *Journal of Educational Statistics, 18,* 119–128.

Kreft, I., & De Leeuw, J. (1994). The gender gap in earnings: A two-way nested multiple regression analysis with random effects. *Sociological Methods & Research, 22,* 319–341.

Kreft, I., De Leeuw, J., & Aiken, L. S. (1995). The effect of different forms of centering in hierarchical linear models. *Multivariate Behavioral Research, 30,* 1–21.

Kreft, I., De Leeuw, J., & Kim, K. S. (1990). *Comparing four different statistical packages for hierarchical linear regression, GENMOD, HLM, ML2, and VARCL.* CSE Technical Report 311, UCLA Center for Research on Evaluation, Standards and Student Testing.

Kreft, I., De Leeuw, J., & van der Leeden, R. (1994). Review of five multilevel analysis programs: BMDP-5V, GENMOD, HLM, ML3, VARCL. *The American Statistician, 48,* 324–335.

Krohne, H. W., & Schaffner, P. (1983). Anxiety, coping strategies, and performance. In S. B. Anderson & J. S. Helmick (Eds.), *On educational testing* (pp. 150–174). San Francisco: Jossey-Bass.

Krus, D. J., Reynolds, T. J., & Krus, P. H. (1976). Rotation in canonical variate analysis. *Educational and Psychological Measurement, 36,* 725–730.

Kruskal, W. (1988). Miracles and statistics: The casual assumption of independence. *Journal of the American Statistical Association, 83,* 929–940.

Kühnel, S. M. (1988). Testing MANOVA designs with LISREL. *Multivariate Behavioral Research, 16,* 504–523.

Kulka, A. (1989). Nonempirical issues in psychology. *American Psychologist, 44,* 785–794.

Kupper, L. L., & Hogan, M. D. (1978). Interaction in epidemiologic studies. *American Journal of Epidemiology, 108,* 447–453.

Langbein, L. I. (1977). Schools or students: Aggregation problems in the study of student achievement. In M. Guttentag (Ed.), *Evaluation studies: Review annual 2* (pp. 270–298). Thousand Oaks, CA: Sage.

Langbein, L. I., & Lichtman, A. J. (1978). *Ecological inference.* Thousand Oaks, CA: Sage.

LaTour, S. A. (1981a). Effect-size estimation: A commentary on Wolf and Bassler. *Decision Sciences, 12,* 136–141.

LaTour, S. A. (1981b). Variance explained: It measures neither importance nor effect size. *Decision Sciences, 12,* 150–160.

Lauter, D. (1984, December 10). Making a case with statistics. *The National Law Journal,* pp. 1, 10.

Lawrenz, F. (1990). Author's response. *Journal of Research in Science Teaching, 27,* 714–715.

Lazarsfeld, P. F., & Menzel, H. (1961). On the relation between individual and collective properties. In A. Etzioni (Ed.), *Complex organizations* (pp. 422–440). New York: Holt, Rinehart and Winston.

Leamer, E. E. (1985). Sensitivity analyses would help. *The American economic review, 75,* 308–313.

LeBlanc, A. J. (1993). Examining HIV-related knowledge among adults in the U.S. *Journal of Health and Social Behavior, 34,* 23–36.

Lee, V. E., & Bryk, A. S. (1989). A multilevel model of the social distribution of high school achievement. *Sociology of Education, 62,* 172–192.

Lee, V. E., Dedrick, R. F., & Smith, J. B. (1991). The effect of the social organization of schools on teachers' efficacy and satisfaction. *Sociology of Education, 64,* 190–208.

Lee, V. E., & Smith, J. B. (1990). Gender equity in teachers' salaries: A multilevel approach. *Educational Evaluation and Policy Analysis, 12,* 57–81.

Lee, V. E., & Smith, J. B. (1991). Sex discrimination in teachers' salary. In S. W. Raudenbush & J. D. Willms (Eds.), *Schools, classrooms, and pupils: International studies of schooling from a multilevel perspective* (pp. 225–247). San Diego, CA: Academic Press.

Leiter, J. (1983). Classroom composition and achievement gains. *Sociology of Education, 56,* 126–132.

Lemeshow, S., & Hosmer, D. W. (1984). Estimating odds ratios with categorically scaled covariates in multiple logistic regression analysis. *American Journal of Epidemiology, 119,* 147–151.

Lemeshow, S., & Hosmer, D. W. (1985). The authors reply. *American Journal of Epidemiology, 121,* 478.

Lerner, D. (Ed.). (1965). *Cause and effect.* New York: The Free Press.

Levin, J. R., & Marascuilo, L. A. (1972). Type IV errors and interactions. *Psychological Bulletin, 78,* 368–374.

Levin, J. R., & Marascuilo, L. A. (1973). Type IV errors and Games. *Psychological Bulletin, 80,* 308–309.

Levin, J. R., Serlin, R. C., & Seaman, M. A. (1994). A controlled, powerful multiple-comparison strategy for several situations. *Psychological Bulletin, 115,* 153–159.

Levine, A. (1991). *A guide to SPSS for analysis of variance.* Hillsdale, NJ: Lawrence Erlbaum Associates.

Lewis-Beck, M. S. (1980). *Applied regression: An introduction.* Thousand Oaks, CA: Sage.

Lewis-Beck, M. S., & Mohr, L. B. (1976). Evaluating effects of independent variables. *Political Methodology, 3,* 27–47.

Lewis-Beck, M. S., & Skalaban, A. (1991). The *R*-squared: Some straight talk. In J. A. Stimson (Ed.), *Political analysis: Vol. 2, 1990* (pp. 153–171). Ann Arbor, MI: The University of Michigan.

Li, C. C. (1964). *Introduction to experimental statistics.* New York: McGraw-Hill.

Li, C. C. (1975). *Path analysis: A primer.* Pacific Grove, CA: Boxwood Press.

Li, J. C. R. (1964). *Statistical inference* (rev. ed. Vols. I–II). Ann Arbor, MI: Edwards Brothers.

Liao, T. F. (1994). *Interpreting probability models: Logit, probit, and other generalized linear models.* Thousand Oaks, CA: Sage.

Lieberson, S. (1985). *Making it count: The improvement of social research and theory.* Berkeley, CA: University of California Press.

Lieberson, S. (1988). Asking too much, expecting too little. *Sociological Perspectives, 31,* 379–397.

Lindeman, R. H., Merenda, P. F., & Gold, R. Z. (1980). *Introduction to bivariate and multivariate analysis.* Glenview, IL: Scott, Foresman.

Lindquist, E. F. (1940). *Statistical analysis in educational research.* Boston: Houghton Mifflin.

Lindquist, E. F. (1953). *Design and analysis of experiments in psychology and education.* Boston: Houghton Mifflin.

Linn, R. L. (1984). Selection bias: Multiple meanings. *Journal of Educational Measurement, 21,* 33–47.

Linn, R. L., & Werts, C. E. (1969). Assumptions in making causal inferences from part correlations, partial correlations, and partial regression coefficients. *Psychological Bulletin, 72,* 307–310.

Linn, R. L., & Werts, C. E. (1973). Errors of inference due to errors of measurement. *Educational and Psychological Measurement, 33,* 531–543.

Linn, R. L., Werts, C. E., & Tucker, L. R. (1971). The interpretation of regression coefficients in a school effects model. *Educational and Psychological Measurement, 31,* 85–93.

Little, R. J. A., & Rubin, D. B. (1987). *Statistical analysis with missing data.* New York: Wiley.

Little, R. J. A., & Rubin, D. B. (1989). The analysis of social science data with missing values. *Sociological Methods & Research, 18,* 292–326.

Liu, K. (1988). Measurement error and its impact on partial correlation and multiple linear regression analysis. *American Journal of Epidemiology, 127,* 864–874.

Lock, R. H. (1993). A comparison of five student versions of statistics packages. *The American Statistician, 47,* 136–145.

Loehlin, J. C. (1992). *Latent variable models: An introduction to factor, path, and structural analysis* (2nd ed.). Hillsdale, NJ: Lawrence Erlbaum Associates.

Lohnes, P. R., & Cooley, W. W. (1978, March). *Regarding criticisms of commonality analysis.* Paper presented at the annual meeting of the American Educational Research Association, Toronto, Canada.

Long, J. S. (1983). *Confirmatory factor analysis.* Thousands Oaks, CA: Sage.

Longford, N. T. (1988). *VARCAL: Software for variance component analysis of data with hierarchically nested effects (maximum likelihood).* Manual. Princeton, NJ: Educational Testing Service.

Longford, N. T. (1989). To center or not to center. *Multilevel Modelling Newsletter, 1*(3) 7, 11.

Lord, F. M. (1963). Elementary models for measuring change. In C. W. Harris (Ed.), *Problems in measuring change* (pp. 21–38). Madison, WI: University of Wisconsin Press.

Lord, F. M. (1967). A paradox in the interpretation of group comparisons. *Psychological Bulletin, 68,* 304–305.

Lord, F. M. (1969). Statistical adjustments when comparing preexisting groups. *Psychological Bulletin, 72,* 336–337.

Lord, F. M. (1974). Significance test for a partial correlation corrected for attenuation. *Educational and Psychological Measurement, 34,* 211–220.

Lord, F. M., & Novick, M. R. (1968). *Statistical theories of mental test scores.* Reading, MA: Addison-Wesley.

Lorr, M. (1983). *Cluster analysis for social scientists: Techniques for analyzing and simplifying complex blocks of data.* San Francisco: Jossey-Bass.

Lubin, A. (1961). The interpretation of significant interaction. *Educational and Psychological Measurement, 21,* 807–817.

Lubinski, D. (1983). The androgyny dimension: A comment on Stokes, Childs, and Fuehrer. *Journal of Counseling Psychology, 30,* 130–133.

Lubinski, D., Tellegen, A., & Butcher, J. N. (1981). The relationship between androgyny and subjective indicators of emotional well-being. *Journal of Personality and Social Psychology, 40,* 722–730.

Lubinski, D., Tellegen, A., & Butcher, J. N. (1983). Masculinity, femininity, and androgyny viewed and assessed as distinct concepts. *Journal of Personality and Social Psychology, 44,* 428–439.

Lunneborg, C. E. (1985). Estimating the correlation coefficient: The bootstrap approach. *Psychological Bulletin, 98,* 209–215.

Lunneborg, C. E. (1987). *Bootstrap applications for the behavioral sciences (Vol. 1).* Seattle: University of Washington, Author.

Lunneborg, C. E., & Abbott, R. D. (1983). *Elementary multivariate analysis for the behavioral sciences: Applications of basic structure.* New York: North-Holland.

Luskin, R. C. (1991). Abusus non tollit usum: Standardized coefficients, correlations, and R^2s. *American Journal of Political Science, 35,* 1032–1046.

Luzzo, D. A. (1993). Value of career-decision-making self-efficacy in predicting career-decision-making attitudes and skills. *Journal of Counseling Psychology, 40,* 194–199.

MacCallum, R. (1986). Specification searches in covariance structure modeling. *Psychological Bulletin, 100,* 107–120.

MacCallum, R. C., & Browne, M. W. (1993). The use of causal indicators in covariance structure models: Some practical issues. *Psychological Bulletin, 114,* 533–541.

MacCallum, R. C., Roznowski, M., & Necowitz, L. B. (1992). Model modifications in covariance structure analysis: The problem of capitalizing on chance. *Psychological Bulletin, 111,* 490–504.

Macdonald, K. I. (1977). Path analysis. In C. A. O'Muircheartaigh & C. Payne (Eds.), *The analysis of survey data* (Vol. 2, pp. 81–104). New York: Wiley.

MacDonald, K. I. (1979). Interpretation of residual paths and decomposition of variance. *Sociological Methods & Research, 7,* 289–304.

MacEwen, K. E., & Barling, J. (1991). Effects of maternal employment experiences on children's behavior via mood, cognitive difficulties, and parenting behavior. *Journal of Marriage and the Family, 53,* 635–644.

Mackay, A. L. (1977). *The harvest of a quiet eye: A selection of scientific quotations.* Bristol, Great Britain: The Institute of Physics.

Mackie, J. L. (1965). Causes and conditions. *American Philosophical Quarterly, 2,* 245–264.

Mackie, J. L. (1974). *The cement of the universe: A study of causation.* London: Oxford University Press.

Mackinnon, D. P., & Dwyer, J. H. (1993). Estimating mediated effects in prevention studies. *Evaluation Review, 17,* 144–158.

Madaus, G. F., Kellaghan, T., Rakow, E. A., & King, D. J. (1979). The sensitivity of measures of school effectiveness. *Harvard Educational Review, 49,* 207–230.

Madow, W. G., Nisselson, H., & Olkin, I. (Eds.). (1983). *Incomplete data in sample surveys* (Vols. 1–3). New York: Academic Press.

Maeroff, G. I. (1975, February 2). Factors traced in pupil success. *The New York Times,* p. B27.

Mahoney, M. J. (1977). Publication prejudices: An experimental study of confirmatory bias in the peer review system. *Cognitive Therapy and Research, 1,* 161–175.

Mallinckrodt, B. (1992). Childhood emotional bonds with parents, development of adult social competencies, and availability of social support. *Journal of Counseling Psychology, 39,* 453–461.

Mandel, J. (1982). Use of singular value decomposition in regression analysis. *The American Statistician, 36,* 15–24.

Manes, S. (1988, December 27). Of course it's true: My PC says so. *PC Magazine,* 85–86.

Marascuilo, L. A., Busk, P. L., & Serlin, R. C. (1988). Large sample multivariate procedures for comparing and combining effect sizes within a single study. *Journal of Experimental Education, 57,* 69–85.

Marascuilo, L. A., & Levin, J. R. (1970). Appropriate post hoc comparisons for interactions and nested hypotheses in analysis of variance designs: The elimination of Type IV errors. *American Educational Research Journal, 7,* 397–421.

Marascuilo, L. A., & Levin, J. R. (1976). A note on the simultaneous investigation of interaction and nested hypotheses in two-factor analysis of variance. *American Educational Research Journal, 13,* 61–65.

Marascuilo, L. A., & Levin, J. R. (1983). *Multivariate statistics in the social sciences: A researcher's guide.* Monterey, CA: Brooks/Cole.

Margenau, H. (1950). *The nature of physical reality: A philosophy of modern physics.* New York: McGraw-Hill.

Marini, M. M., & Singer, B. (1988). Causality in the social sciences. In C. C. Clogg (Ed.), *Sociological methodology 1988* (pp. 347–409). Washington, DC: American Sociological Association.

Markham, S. E. (1988). Pay-for-performance dilemma revisited: Empirical example of the importance of group effects. *Journal of Applied Psychology, 73,* 172–180.

Markoff, J. (1991, November 5). So who's talking: Human or machine? *The New York Times,* pp. B5, B8.

Marquardt, D. W. (1980). Comment. *Journal of the American Statistical Association, 75,* 87–91.

Marquardt, D. W., & Snee, R. D. (1975). Ridge regression in practice. *The American Statistician, 29,* 3–20.

Marsh, H. W. (1985). The structure of masculinity/femininity: An application of factor analysis to higher-order factor structures and factorial invariance. *Multivariate Behavioral Research, 20,* 427–449.

Marsh, H. W. (1993). Stability of individual differences in multiwave panel studies: Comparison of simplex models and one-factor models. *Journal of Educational Measurement, 30,* 157–183.

Marsh, H. W. (1994a). Confirmatory factor analysis models of factorial invariance: A multifaceted approach. *Structural Equation Modeling, 1,* 5–34.

Marsh, H. W. (1994b). Longitudinal confirmatory factor analysis: Common, time-specific, item-specific, and residual-error components of variance. *Structural Equation Modeling, 1,* 116–145.

Marsh, H. W., & Grayson, D. (1990). Public/Catholic differences in High School and Beyond data: A multigroup structural equation modeling approach to testing mean differences. *Journal of Educational Statistics, 15,* 199–235.

Marsh, H. W., & Grayson, D. (1994). Longitudinal stability of latent means and individual differences: A unified approach. *Structural Equation Modeling, 1,* 317–359.

Marshall, E. (1993). Supreme Court to weigh science. *Science, 259,* 588–590.

Mason, R., & Brown, W. G. (1975). Multicollinearity problems and ridge regression in sociological models. *Social Science Research, 4,* 135–149.

Mason, R. L., Gunst, R. F., & Hess, J. L. (1989). *Statistical design and analysis of experiments: With applications to engineering and science.* New York: Wiley.

Mason, W. M., Anderson, A. F., & Hayat, N. (1988). *Manual for GENMOD.* Ann Arbor, MI: Population Studies Center, University of Michigan.

Mason, W. M., Wong, G. Y., & Entwisle, B. (1983). Contextual analysis through the multilevel linear model. In S. Leinhardt (Ed.), *Sociological methodology 1983–1984* (pp. 72–103). San Francisco: Jossey-Bass.

Matsueda, R. L., & Bielby, W. T. (1986). Statistical power in covariance structure models. In N. B. Tuma (Ed.), *Sociological methodology, 1986* (pp. 120–158). Washington, DC: American Sociological Association.

Mauro, R. (1990). Understanding L.O.V.E. (left out variables error): A method for estimating the effects of omitted variables. *Psychological Bulletin, 108,* 314–329.

Maxwell, A. E. (1975). Limitations on the use of multiple linear regression model. *British Journal of Mathematical and Statistical Psychology, 28,* 51–62.

Maxwell, A. E. (1977). *Multivariate analysis in behavioral research.* London: Chapman and Hall.

Maxwell, S. E., Camp, C. J., & Arvey, R. D. (1981). Measures of strength of association: A comparative examination. *Journal of Applied Psychology, 66,* 525–534.

Maxwell, S. E., & Delaney, H. D. (1990). *Designing experiments and analyzing data: A model comparison perspective.* Belmont, CA: Wadsworth.

Maxwell, S. E., & Delaney, H. D. (1993). Bivariate median splits and spurious statistical significance. *Psychological Bulletin, 113,* 181–190.

Maxwell, S. E., Delaney, H. D., & Dill, C. A. (1984). Another look at ANCOVA versus blocking. *Psychological Bulletin, 95,* 136–147.

Mayeske, G. W. (1970). Teacher attributes and school achievement. In *Do teachers make a difference?* Washington, DC: U.S. Office of Education.

Mayeske, G. W., & Beaton, A. E. (1975). *Special studies of our nation's students.* Washington, DC: U.S. Government Printing Office.

Mayeske, G. W., Cohen, W. M., Wisler, C. E., Okada, T., Beaton, A. E., Proshek, J. M., Weinfeld, F. D., & Tabler, K. A. (1969). *A study of our nation's schools.* Washington, DC: U.S. Department of Health, Education, and Welfare, Office of Education.

Mayeske, G. W., Cohen, W. M., Wisler, C. E., Okada, T., Beaton, A. E., Proshek, J. M., Weinfeld, F. D., & Tabler, K. A. (1972). *A study of our nation's schools.* Washington, DC: U.S. Government Printing Office.

Mayeske, G. W., Okada, T., & Beaton, A. E. (1973a). *A study of the attitude toward life of our nation's students.* Washington, DC: U.S. Government Printing Office.

Mayeske, G. W., Okada, T., Beaton, A. E., Cohen, W. M., & Wisler, C. E. (1973b). *A study of the achievement of our nation's students.* Washington, DC: U.S. Government Printing Office.

McClelland, G. H., & Judd, C. M. (1993). Statistical difficulties of detecting interactions and moderator effects. *Psychological Bulletin, 114,* 376–390.

McDill, E. L., Rigsby, L. C., & Meyers, E. D. (1969). Educational climate of high schools: Their effects and sources. *American Journal of Sociology, 74,* 567–586.

McDonald, R. P. (1985). *Factor analysis and related methods.* Hillsdale, NJ: Lawrence Erlbaum Associates.

McDonald, R. P. (1994). The bilevel reticular action model for path analysis with latent variables. *Sociological Methods & Research, 22,* 399–413.

McDonald, R. P., & Marsh, H. W. (1990). Choosing a multivariate model: Noncentrality and goodness of fit. *Psychological Bulletin, 107,* 247–255.

McFatter, R. M. (1979). The use of structural equation models in interpreting regression equations including suppressor and enhancer variables. *Applied Psychological Measurement, 3,* 123–135.

McGraw, K. O. (1991). Problems with the BESD: A comment on Rosenthal's "How are we doing in soft psychology." *American Psychologist, 46,* 1084–1086.

McIntyre, R. M. (1990). Spurious estimation of validity coefficients in composite samples: Some methodological considerations. *Journal of Applied Psychology, 75,* 91–94.

McIntyre, S. H., Montgomery, D. B., Srinivasan, V., & Weitz, B. A. (1983). Evaluating the statistical significance of models developed by stepwise regression. *Journal of Marketing Research, 20,* 1–11.

McNemar, Q. (1960). At random: Sense and nonsense. *American Psychologist, 15,* 295–300.

McNemar, Q. (1962). *Psychological statistics* (3rd ed.). New York: Wiley.

McNemar, Q. (1969). *Psychological statistics* (4th ed.). New York: Wiley.

McPherson, J. M. (1976). Theory trimming. *Social Science Research, 5,* 95–105.

Meehl, P. E. (1956). Wanted—a good cookbook. *American Psychologist, 11,* 263–272

Meehl, P. E. (1970). Nuisance variables and the ex post facto design. In M. Radner & S. Winokur (Eds.), *Minnesota studies in the philosophy of science* (Vol. 4, pp. 373–402). Minneapolis: University of Minnesota Press.

Menard, S. (1995). *Applied logistic regression analysis.* Thousand Oaks, CA: Sage.

Menzel, H. (1950). Comment on Robinson's "Ecological correlations and the behavior of individuals." *American Sociological Review, 15,* 674.

Meredith, W. (1964). Canonical correlation with fallible data. *Psychometrika, 29,* 55–65.

Merton, R. K. (1968). *Social theory and social structure* (enlarged ed.). New York: The Free Press.

Meyer, D. L. (1991). Misinterpretation of interaction effects: A reply to Rosnow and Rosenthal. *Psychological Bulletin, 110,* 571–573.

Meyer, J. W. (1970). High school effects on college intentions. *American Journal of Sociology, 76,* 59–70.

Michelson, S. (1970). The association of teacher resources with children's characteristics. In *Do teachers make a difference?* (pp. 120–168). Washington, DC: U.S. Office of Education.

Milgram, S., Bickman, L., & Berkowitz, L. (1969). Note on the drawing power of crowds of different size. *Journal of Personality and Social Psychology, 13,* 79–82.

Miller, J. K. (1969). *The development and application of bi-multivariate correlation: A measure of statistical association between multivariate measurement sets.* Unpublished doctoral dissertation, State University of New York at Buffalo.

Miller, R. G. (1966). *Simultaneous statistical inference.* New York: McGraw-Hill.

Minitab Inc. (1994a). *MINITAB reference manual: Release 10 for Windows.* State College, PA: Author.

Minitab Inc. (1994b). *MINITAB user's guide: Release 10 for Windows.* State College, PA: Author.

Minitab Inc. (1995a). *MINITAB reference manual: Release 10 Xtra for Windows and Macintosh.* State College, PA: Author.

Minitab Inc. (1995b). *MINITAB user's guide: Release 10 Xtra for Windows and Macintosh.* State College, PA: Author.

Mirowsky, J., & Ross, C. E. (1980). Minority status, ethnic culture, and distress: A comparison of Blacks, Whites, and Mexican Americans. *American Journal of Sociology, 86,* 479–495.

Mirowsky, J., & Ross, C. E. (1984). Meaningful comparison versus statistical manipulation: A reply to Johnson and Benin. *American Journal of Sociology, 89,* 1194–1200.

Mood, A. M. (1969). Macro-analysis of the American educational system. *Operations Research, 17,* 770–784.

Mood, A. M. (1970). Do teachers make a difference? In *Do teachers make a difference?* (pp. 1–24). Washington, DC: U.S. Office of Education.

Mood, A. M. (1971). Partitioning variance in multiple regression analyses as a tool for developing learning models. *American Educational Research Journal, 8,* 191–202.

Mood, A. M. (1973). Foreword to G. W. Mayeske et al., *A study of the attitude toward life of our nation's students* (pp. iii–iv). Washington, DC: U.S. Government Printing Office.

Mooney, C. Z., & Duval, R. D. (1993). *Bootstrapping: A nonparametric approach to statistical inference.* Thousand Oaks, CA: Sage.

Moore, M. (1966). Aggression themes in a binocular rivalry situation. *Journal of Personality and Social Psychology, 3,* 685–688.

Morris, J. H., Sherman, J. D., & Mansfield, E. R. (1986). Failures to detect moderating effects with ordinary least squares-moderated multiple regression: Some reasons and a remedy. *Psychological Bulletin, 99,* 282–288.

Morrison, D. E., & Henkel, R. E. (Eds.). (1970). *The significance test controversy.* Chicago: Aldine.

Morrison, D. F. (1976). *Multivariate statistical methods* (2nd ed.). New York: McGraw-Hill.

Moscovici, S. (1985). Social influence and conformity. In G. Lindzey & E. Aronson (Eds.), *Handbook of social psychology* (3rd ed., Vol. 2, pp. 347–412). New York: Random House.

Mosier, C. I. (1951). Batteries and profiles. In E. F. Lindquist (Ed.), *Educational measurement* (pp. 764–808). Washington, DC: American Council on Education.

Mosteller, F., & Moynihan, D. P. (1972). A pathbreaking report. In F. Mosteller & D. P. Moynihan (Eds.), *On equality of educational opportunity* (pp. 3–66). New York: Vintage Books.

Mueller, R. O., & Cozad, J. B. (1988). Standardized discriminant coefficients: Which variance estimate is appropriate? *Journal of Educational Statistics, 13,* 313–318.

Mueller, R. O., & Cozad, J. B. (1993). Standardized discriminant coefficients: A rejoinder. *Journal of Educational Statistics, 18,* 108–114.

Mulaik, S. A. (1972). *The foundations of factor analysis.* New York: McGraw-Hill.

Mulaik, S. A. (1987). Toward a conception of causality applicable to experimentation and causal modeling. *Child Development, 58,* 18–32.

Mulaik, S. A. (1993). Objectivity and multivariate statistics. *Multivariate Behavioral Research, 28,* 171–203.

Mulaik, S. A., & James, L. R. (1995). Objectivity and reasoning in science and structural equation modeling. In R. H. Hoyle (Ed.), *Structural equation modeling: Concepts, issues, and applications* (pp. 118–137). Thousand Oaks, CA: Sage.

Mulaik, S. A., James, L. R., Van Alstine, J., Bennett, N., Lind, S., & Stilwell, C. D. (1989). Evaluation of goodness-of-fit indices for structural equation models. *Psychological Bulletin, 105,* 430–445.

Muller, M. E. (1978). A review of the manuals for BMDP and SPSS. *Journal of the American Statistical Association, 73,* 71–80.

Murray, L. W., & Dosser, D. A. (1987). How significant is a significant difference? Problems with the measurement of the magnitude of effect. *Journal of Counseling Psychology, 34,* 68–72.

Muthén, B. O. (1987). Response to Freedman's critique of path analysis: Improve credibility by better methodological training. *Journal of Educational Statistics, 12,* 178–184.

Muthén, B. O. (1990). Multilevel covariance structure work. *Multilevel Modelling Newsletter, 2*(3), 3, 11.

Muthén, B. O. (1991). Multilevel factor analysis of class and student achievement components. *Journal of Educational Measurement, 28,* 338–354.

Muthén, B. O. (1994). Multilevel covariance structure analysis. *Sociological Methods & Research, 22,* 376–397.

Muthén, B. O., Kaplan, D., & Hollis, M. (1987). On structural equation modeling with data that are not missing completely at random. *Psychometrika, 52,* 431–462.

Myers, J. L. (1979). *Fundamentals of experimental design* (3rd ed.). Boston: Allyn and Bacon.

Myers, R. H. (1990). *Classical and modern regression with applications* (2nd ed.). Boston: PWS-Kent.

Nagel, E. (1965). Types of causal explanation in science. In D. Lerner (Ed.), *Cause and effect* (pp. 11–26). New York: The Free Press.

Namboodiri, N. K. (Ed.). (1978). *Survey sampling and measurement.* San Diego, CA: Academic Press.

Namboodiri, N. K., Carter, L. F., & Blalock, H. M. (1975). *Applied multivariate analysis and experimental designs.* New York: McGraw-Hill.

Nash, J. C. (1992). Statistical shareware: Illustrations from regression techniques. *The American Statistician, 46,* 312–318.

Nash, M. R., Hulsey, T. L., Sexton, M. C., Harralson, T. L., & Lambert, W. (1993). Reply to comment by Briere and Elliott. *Journal of Consulting and Clinical Psychology, 61,* 289–290.

Nelson, J. I. (1972a). High school context and college plans: The impact of social structure on aspirations. *American Sociological Review, 37,* 143–148.

Nelson, J. I. (1972b). Reply to Armer and Sewell. *American Sociological Review, 37,* 639–640.

Nesselroade, J. R., & Cattell, R. B. (Eds.). (1988). *Handbook of multivariate experimental psychology* (2nd ed.). New York: Plenum.

Neter, J., Wasserman, W., & Kutner, M. H. (1989). *Applied linear regression models* (2nd ed.). Homewood, IL: Irwin.

Newton, R. G., & Spurrell, D. J. (1967a). A development of multiple regression analysis of routine data. *Applied Statistics, 16,* 51–64.

Newton, R. G., & Spurrell, D. J. (1967b). Examples of the use of elements for clarifying regression analyses. *Applied Statistics, 16,* 165–172.

Nordlund, D. J., & Nagel, R. (1991). Standardized discriminant coefficients revisited. *Journal of Educational Statistics, 16,* 101–108.

Noreen, E. W. (1989). *Computer intensive methods for testing hypotheses: An introduction.* New York: Wiley.

Norman, D. A. (1988). *The psychology of everyday things.* New York: Basic Books.

Norušis, M. J., & SPSS Inc. (1993a). *SPSS base system user's guide: Release 6.0.* Chicago: Author.

Norušis, M. J., & SPSS Inc. (1993b). *SPSS for Windows advanced statistics: Release 6.0.* Chicago: Author.

Norušis, M. J., & SPSS Inc. (1994). *SPSS professional statistics: Release 6.1.* Chicago: Author.

Nunnally, J. (1960). The place of statistics in psychology. *Educational and Psychological Measurement, 20,* 641–650.

Nunnally, J. (1967). *Psychometric theory.* New York: McGraw-Hill.

Nunnally, J. (1978). *Psychometric theory* (2nd ed.). New York: McGraw-Hill.

Nuttall, D. L., Goldstein, H., Prosser, R., & Rasbash, J. (1989). Differential school effectiveness. *International Journal of Educational Research, 13,* 769–776.

Oberst, M. T. (1995). Our naked emperor. *Research in Nursing and Health, 18,* 1–2.

O'Brien, R. G., & Kaiser, M. K. (1985). MANOVA method for analyzing repeated measures designs: An extensive primer. *Psychological Bulletin, 97,* 316–333.

O'Brien, R. M. (1994). Identification of simple measurement models with multiple latent variables and correlated errors. In P. V. Marsden (Ed.), *Sociological methodology 1994* (pp. 137–170). Cambridge, MA: Basil Blackwell.

O'Grady, K. E. (1982). Measures of explained variance: Cautions and limitations. *Psychological Bulletin, 92,* 766–777.

O'Grady, K. E., & Medoff, D. R. (1988). Categorical variables in multiple regression: Some cautions. *Multivariate Behavioral Research, 23,* 243–260.

Olson, C. L. (1976). On choosing a test statistic in multivariate analysis of variance. *Psychological Bulletin, 83,* 579–586.

Oosthoek, H., & Van Den Eeden, P. (Eds.). (1984). *Education from the multi-level perspective: Models, methodology and empirical findings.* New York: Gordon and Breach.

Overall, J. E., & Klett, C. J. (1972). *Applied multivariate analysis.* New York: McGraw-Hill.

Overall, J. E., Spiegel, D. K., & Cohen, J. (1975). Equivalence of orthogonal and nonorthogonal analysis of variance. *Psychological Bulletin, 82,* 182–186.

Overall, J. E., & Woodward, J. A. (1977a). Common misconceptions concerning the analysis of covariance. *Multivariate Behavioral Research, 12,* 171–186.

Overall, J. E., & Woodward, J. A. (1977b). Nonrandom assignment and the analysis of covariance. *Psychological Bulletin, 84,* 588–594.

Pagel, M. D., & Lunneborg, C. E. (1985). Empirical evaluation of ridge regression. *Psychological Bulletin, 97,* 342–355.

Paik, M. (1985). A graphic representation of a three-way contingency table: Simpson's paradox and correlation. *The American Statistician, 39,* 53–54.

Pallas, A. M., Entwisle, D. R., Alexander, K. L., & Stluka, M. F. (1994). Ability-group effects: Instructional, social, or institutional? *Sociology of Education, 67,* 27–46.

Parsons, C. K., & Liden, R. C. (1984). Interviewer perceptions of applicant qualifications: A multivariate field study of demographic characteristics and nonverbal cues. *Journal of Applied Psychology, 69,* 557–568.

Passell, P. (1994a, October 13). Economic Scene. *The New York Times* (National Edition), p. C2.

Passell, P. (1994b, October 27). It's a grim message: Dummies fail more often [Review of *The bell curve: Intelligence and class substructure in American life*]. *The New York Times* (National Edition), p. B3.

Peaker, G. F. (1975). *An empirical study of education in twenty-one countries: A technical report.* New York: Wiley.

Pederson, J. K., & DeGuire, D. J. (1982). SATs: The scores that came out of the cold. *Phi Delta Kappan, 64,* 68–69.

Pedhazur, E. J. (1975). Analytic methods in studies of school effects. In F. N. Kerlinger (Ed.), *Review of research in education 3* (pp. 243–286). Itasca, IL: Peacock.

Pedhazur, E. J. (1982). *Multiple regression in behavioral research: Explanation and prediction* (2nd ed.). New York: Holt, Rinehart and Winston.

Pedhazur, E. J. (1984). Sense and nonsense in hierarchical regression analysis: Comment on Smyth. *Journal of Personality and Social Psychology, 46,* 479–482.

Pedhazur, E. J., & Schmelkin, L. P. (1991). *Measurement, design, and analysis: An integrated approach.* Hillsdale, NJ: Lawrence Erlbaum Associates.

Pedhazur, E. J., & Tetenbaum, T. J. (1979). Bem sex role inventory: A theoretical and methodological critique. *Journal of Personality and Social Psychology, 37,* 996–1016.

Peirce, C. S. (1932). *Collected papers of Charles Sanders Peirce* (Vol. 2, C. Hartshorne & P. Weiss, Eds.). Cambridge, MA: Harvard University Press.

Perlmutter, J., & Myers, J. L. (1973). A comparison of two procedures for testing multiple contrasts. *Psychological Bulletin, 79,* 181–184.

Perry, R. P. (1990). Introduction to the special section. *Journal of Educational Psychology, 82,* 183–188.

Petersen, N. S. (1980). Bias in the selection rule—Bias in the test. In L. J. Th. van der Kemp, W. F. Langerak, & D. N. M. de Gruijter (Eds.), *Psychometrics for educational debates* (pp. 103–122). New York: Wiley.

Peterson, P. E. (1982). Effects of credentials, connections, and competence on income. In W. H. Kruskal (Ed.), *The social sciences: Their nature and uses* (pp. 21–33). Chicago: Chicago University Press.

Piantadosi, S., Byar, D. P., & Green, S. B. (1988). The ecological fallacy. *American Journal of Epidemiology, 127,* 893–903.

Picard, R. R., & Berk, K. N. (1990). Data splitting. *The American Statistician, 44,* 140–147.

Pickles, A. (1992). [Review of *SPSS/PC+: Version 4.0*]. *Applied Statistics, 41,* 438–441.

Pillai, K. C. S. (1960). *Statistical tables for test of multivariate hypotheses.* Manila, Philippines: University of the Phillippines.

Pillemer, D. B. (1991). One- versus two-tailed hypothesis tests in contemporary educational research. *Educational Researcher, 20*(9), 13–17.

Pindyck, R. S., & Rubinfeld, D. L. (1981). *Econometric models and economic forecasts* (2nd ed.). New York: McGraw-Hill.

Platt, J. R. (1964). Strong inference. *Science, 146,* 347–353.

Plewis, I. (1989). Comment on "centering" predictors in multilevel analysis. *Multilevel Modelling Newsletter, 1*(3) 6, 11.

Plewis, I. (1990). Centering: A postscript (?). *Multilevel Modelling Newsletter, 2*(1), 8.

Polanyi, M. (1964). *Personal knowledge: Towards a post-critical philosophy.* New York: Harper Torchbooks.

Polivka, B. J., & Nickel, J. T. (1992). Case-control design: An appropriate strategy for nursing research. *Nursing Research, 41,* 250–253.

Popper, K. R. (1959). *The logic of scientific discovery.* New York: Basic Books.

Popper, K. R. (1968). *Conjectures and refutations: The growth of scientific knowledge.* New York: Harper Torchbooks.

Porter, A. C., & Raudenbush, S. W. (1987). Analysis of covariance: Its model and use in psychological research. *Journal of Counseling Psychology, 34,* 383–392.

Potthoff, R. F. (1964). On the Johnson-Neyman technique and some extensions thereof. *Psychometrika, 29,* 241–256.

Pratt, J. W., & Schlaifer, R. (1984a). On the nature of discovery of structure. *Journal of the American Statistical Association, 79,* 9–21.

Pratt, J. W., & Schlaifer, R. (1984b). Rejoinder. *Journal of the American Statistical Association, 79,* 29–33.

Preece, D. A. (1987). Good statistical practice. *The Statistician, 36,* 397–408.

Pregibon, D. (1981). Logistic regression diagnostics. *The Annals of Statistics, 9,* 705–724.

Press, S. J. (1972). *Applied multivariate analysis.* New York: Holt, Rinehart and Winston.

Press, S. J., & Wilson, S. (1978). Choosing between logistic regression and discriminant analysis. *Journal of the American Statistical Association, 73,* 699–705.

Price, B. (1977). Ridge regression: Application to nonexperimental data. *Psychological Bulletin, 84,* 759–766.

Pridham, K. F., Lytton, D., Chang, A. S., & Rutledge, D. (1991). Early postpartum transition: Progress in maternal identity and role attainment. *Research in Nursing & Health, 14,* 21–31.

Prosser, J., Rasbash, J., & Goldstein, H. (1990). *ML3: Software for three-level analysis users' guide.* London: Institute of Education, University of London.

Pruzek, R. M. (1971). Methods and problems in the analysis of multivariate data. *Review of Educational Research, 41,* 163–190.

Prysby, C. L. (1976). Community partisanship and individual voting behavior: Methodological problems of contextual analysis. *Political Methodology, 3,* 183–198.

Przeworski, A. (1974). Contextual models for political behavior. *Political Methodology, 1,* 27–60.

Purves, A. C. (1973). *Literature education in ten countries.* New York: Wiley.

Purves, A. C. (1987). The evolution of the IEA: A memoir. *Comparative Education Review, 31,* 10–28.

Purves, A. C., & Levine, D. U. (Eds.). (1975). *Educational policy and international assessment.* Berkeley, CA: McCutchan.

Pyant, C. T., & Yanico, B. J. (1991). Relationship of racial identity and gender-role attitudes to Black women's psychological well-being. *Journal of Counseling Psychology, 38,* 315–322.

Randhawa, B. S., Beamer, J. E., & Lundberg, I. (1993). Role of mathematics self-efficacy in the structural model of mathematics achievement. *Journal of Educational Psychology, 85,* 41–48.

Rao, C. R. (1952). *Advanced statistical methods in biometric research.* New York: Wiley.

Rao, P. (1971). Some notes on misspecification in multiple regressions. *The American Statistician, 25,* 37–39.

Rao, P., & Miller, R. L. (1971). *Applied econometrics.* Belmont, CA: Wadsworth.

Raudenbush, S. W. (1988). Educational applications of hierarchical models: A review. *Journal of Educational Statistics, 13,* 85–116.

Raudenbush, S. (1989a). "Centering" predictors in multilevel analysis: Choices and consequences. *Multilevel Modelling Newsletter, 1*(2), 10–12.

Raudenbush, S. (1989b). A response to Longford and Plewis. *Multilevel Modelling Newsletter, 1*(3), 8–11.

Raudenbush, S. W. (1993). Hierarchical linear models and experimental design. In L. K. Edwards (Ed.), *Applied analysis of variance in behavioral science* (pp. 459–496). New York: Marcel Dekker.

Raudenbush, S. W., Becker, B. J., & Kalaian, H. (1988). Modeling multivariate effect sizes. *Psychological Bulletin, 103,* 111–120.

Raudenbush, S. W., & Bryk, A. S. (1986). A hierarchical model for studying school effects. *Sociology of Education, 59,* 1–17.

Raudenbush, S. W., & Bryk, A. S. (1988). Methodological advances in analyzing the effects of schools and classrooms on student learning. In E. Z. Rothkopf (Ed.), *Review of research in education* (Vol. 15, pp. 423–475). Washington, DC: American Educational Research Association.

Raudenbush, S. W., & Willms, J. D. (1991a). Preface. In S. W. Raudenbush & J. D. Willms (Eds.), *Schools, classrooms, and pupils: International studies of schooling from a multilevel perspective* (pp. xi–xii). San Diego, CA: Academic Press.

Raudenbush, S. W., & Willms, J. D. (Eds.). (1991b). *Schools, classrooms, and pupils: International studies of schooling from a multilevel perspective.* San Diego, CA: Academic Press.

Reichardt, C. S. (1979). The statistical analysis of data from nonequivalent group designs. In T. D. Cook & D. T. Campbell (Eds.), *Quasi-experimentation: Design & analysis issues for field settings* (pp. 147–205). Chicago: Rand McNally.

Reinhold, R. (1973, November 18). Study questions belief that home is more vital to pupil achievement than the school. *The New York Times*, p. B49.

Retherford, R. D., & Choe, M. K. (1993). *Statistical models for causal analysis.* New York: Wiley.

Reynolds, T. J., & Jackosfsky, E. F. (1981). Interpreting canonical analysis: The use of orthogonal transformations. *Educational and Psychological Measurement, 41,* 661–671.

Rickards, J. P., & Slife, B. D. (1987). Interaction of Dogmatism and rhetorical structure in text recall. *American Educational Research Journal, 24,* 635–641.

Rigdon, E. E. (1994a). SEMNET: Structural equation modeling discussion network. *Structural Equation Modeling, 1,* 190–192.

Rigdon, E. E. (1994b). Amos and AmosDraw [a review]. *Structural Equation Modeling, 1,* 196–201.

Rindfuss, R. R., & Stephen, E. H. (1990). Marital noncohabitation: Separation does not make the heart grow fonder. *Journal of Marriage and the Family, 52,* 259–270.

Rindskopf, D., & Everson, H. (1984). A comparison of models for detecting discrimination: An example from medical school admissions. *Applied Psychological Measurement, 8,* 89–106.

Rist, R. C. (1980). Blitzkrieg ethnography: On the transformation of a method into a movement. *Educational Researcher, 9*(2), 8–10.

Robinson, J. E., & Gray, J. L. (1974). Cognitive styles as a variable in school learning. *Journal of Educational Psychology, 66,* 793–799.

Robinson, W. S. (1950). Ecological correlations and the behavior of individuals. *American Sociological Review, 15,* 351–357.

Rock, D. A., Werts, C. E., & Flaugher, R. L. (1978). The use of analysis of covariance structures for comparing the psychometric properties of multiple variables across populations. *Multivariate Behavioral Research, 13,* 403–418.

Rogosa, D. (1979). Causal models in longitudinal research: Rationale, formulation, and interpretation. In J. R. Nesselroade & P. B. Baltes (Eds.), *Longitudinal research in the study of behavior and development* (pp. 263–302). New York: Academic Press.

Rogosa, D. (1980). Comparing nonparallel regression lines. *Psychological Bulletin, 88,* 307–321.

Rogosa, D. (1981). On the relationship between the Johnson-Neyman region of significance and statistical tests of parallel within-group regressions. *Educational and Psychological Measurement, 41,* 73–84.

Rogosa, D., Brandt, D., & Zimowski, M. (1982). A growth curve approach to the measurement of change. *Psychological Bulletin, 92,* 726–746.

Rokeach, M. (1960). *The open and closed mind.* New York: Basic Books.

Roncek, D. W. (1991). Using logit coefficients to obtain the effects of independent variables on changes in probabilities. *Social Forces, 70,* 509–518.

Roncek, D. W. (1993). When will they ever learn that first derivatives identify effects of continuous independent variables or "officer, you can't give me a ticket, I wasn't speeding for an entire hour." *Social Forces, 71,* 1067–1078.

Ronis, D. L. (1981). Comparing the magnitude of effects in ANOVA designs. *Educational and Psychological Measurement, 41,* 993–1000.

Rosenberg, M. (1968). *The logic of survey analysis.* New York: Basic Books.

Rosenthal, R. (1990). How are we doing in soft psychology? *American Psychologist, 45,* 775–776.

Rosenthal, R. (1991). Effect sizes: Pearson's correlation, its display via the BESD, and alternative indices. *American Psychologist, 46,* 1086–1087.

Rosenthal, R., & Rosnow, R. L. (1985). *Contrast analysis. Focused comparisons in the analysis of variance.* New York: Cambridge University Press.

Rosenthal, R., & Rubin, D. B. (1979). A note on percent of variance explained as a measure of importance of effects. *Journal of Applied Social Psychology, 9,* 395–396.

Rosnow, R. L., & Rosenthal, R. (1988). Focused tests of significance and effect size estimation in counseling psychology. *Journal of Counseling Psychology, 35,* 203–208.

Rosnow, R. L., & Rosenthal, R. (1989). Definition and interpretation of interaction effects. *Psychological Bulletin, 105,* 143–146.

Rosnow, R. L., & Rosenthal, R. (1991). If you're looking at the cell means, you're not looking at *only* the interaction (unless all main effects are zero). *Psychological Bulletin, 110,* 574–576.

Rothman, K. J., Greenland, S., & Walker, A. M. (1980). Concepts of interaction. *American Journal of Epidemiology, 112,* 467–470.

Rousseeuw, P. J., & Leroy, A. M. (1987). *Robust regression and outlier detection.* New York: Wiley.

Rovine, M. J. (1994). Latent variables models and missing data analysis. In A. von Eye & C. C. Clogg (Eds.), *Latent variables analysis: Applications for developmental research* (pp. 181–225). Thousand Oaks, CA: Sage.

Rowan, B., & Miracle, A. W. (1983). Systems of ability grouping and the stratification of achievement in elementary schools. *Sociology of Education, 56,* 133–144.

Rowan, B., Raudenbush, S. W., & Kang, S. J. (1991). Organizational design in high schools: A multilevel analysis. *American Journal of Education, 99,* 238–266.

Roy, S. N. (1957). *Some aspects of multivariate analysis.* New York: Wiley.

Rozeboom, W. W. (1960). The fallacy of the null-hypothesis significance test. *Psychological Bulletin, 57,* 416–428.

Rozeboom, W. W. (1978). Estimation of cross-validated multiple correlation: A clarification. *Psychological Bulletin, 85,* 1348–1351.

Rozeboom, W. W. (1979). Ridge regression: Bonanza or beguilement? *Psychological Bulletin, 86,* 242–249.

Rubin, D. B. (1974). Estimating causal effects of treatments in randomized and nonrandomized studies. *Journal of Educational Psychology, 66,* 688–701.

Rubin, D. B. (1977). Assignment to treatment group on the basis of a covariate. *Journal of Educational Statistics, 2,* 1–26.

Rulon, P. J., & Brooks, W. D. (1968). On statistical tests of group differences. In D. K. Whitla (Ed.), *Handbook of measurement and assessment in behavioral sciences* (pp. 60–99). Reading, MA: Addison-Wesley.

Rulon, P. J., Tiedeman, D. V., Tatsuoka, M. M., & Langmuir, C. R. (1967). *Multivariate statistics for personnel classification.* New York: Wiley.

Russell, B. (1929). *Mysticism and logic.* London: George Allen & Unwin.

Ryan, B. F., Joiner, B. L., & Ryan, T. A. (1985). *Minitab handbook* (2nd ed.). Boston: PWS-Kent.

Ryan, T. A. (1959a). Multiple comparisons in psychological research. *Psychological Bulletin, 56,* 26–47.

Ryan, T. A. (1959b). Comments on nonorthogonal components. *Psychological Bulletin, 56,* 394–396.

Ryff, C. D., & Essex, M. J. (1992). The interpretation of life experience and well-being: The sample case of relocation. *Psychology of Aging, 7,* 507–517.

Salthouse, T. A. (1993). Speed mediation of adult age differences in cognition. *Developmental Psychology, 29,* 722–738.

Sapra, S. K. (1991). A connection between the logit model, normal discriminant analysis, and multivariate normal mixtures. *The American Statistician, 45,* 265–268.

Saris, W. E., Den Ronden, J., & Satorra, A. (1987). Testing structural equation models. In P. Cuttance & R. Ecob (Eds.), *Structural modeling by example: Applications in educational, sociological, and behavioral research* (pp. 202–220). New York: Cambridge University Press.

Saris, W. E., & Satorra, A. (1993). Power evaluations in structural equation models. In K. A. Bollen & J. S. Long (Eds.), *Testing structural equations models* (pp. 181–204). Thousand Oaks, CA: Sage.

Saris, W. E., Satorra, A., & Sörbom, D. (1987). The detection and correction of specification errors in structural equation models. In C. C. Clogg (Ed.), *Sociological methodology 1987* (pp. 105–129). San Francisco: Jossey-Bass.

Saris, W. E., & Stronkhorst, L. H. (1984). *Causal modelling in nonexperimental research: An introduction to the LISREL approach.* Amsterdam, The Netherlands: Sociometric Research Foundation.

SAS Institute Inc. (1990a). *SAS/STAT user's guide, version 6, fourth edition* (Vols. 1–2). Cary, NC: Author.

SAS Institute Inc. (1990b). *SAS/IML: Usage and reference, version 6, first edition.* Cary, NC: Author.

SAS Institute Inc. (1993). *SAS companion for the Microsoft Windows environment: Version 6, first edition.* Cary, NC: Author.

Scheffé, H. (1959). *The analysis of variance.* New York: Wiley.

Scheffler, I. (1957). Explanation, prediction, and abstraction. *British Journal of Philosophy of Science, 7,* 293–309.

Scheuch, E. K. (1966). Cross-national comparisons using aggregate data: Some substantive and methodological problems. In R. L. Merritt & S. Rokkan (Eds.), *Comparing nations* (pp. 131–167). New Haven, CT: Yale University Press.

Scheuch, E. K. (1969). Social context and individual behavior. In M. Dogan & S. Rokkan (Eds.), *Social ecology* (pp. 133–155). Cambridge, MA: M.I.T. Press.

Schmidt, P., & Muller, E. N. (1978). The problem of multicollinearity in a multistage causal alienation model: A comparison of ordinary least squares, maximum-likelihood and ridge estimators. *Quality and Quantity, 12,* 267–297.

Schmitt, N., Coyle, B. W., & Rauschenberger, J. (1977). A Monte Carlo evaluation of three formula estimates of cross-validated multiple correlation. *Psychological Bulletin, 84,* 751–758.

Schmitt, N., & Stults, D. M. (1986). Methodology review: Analysis of multitrait-multimethod matrices. *Applied Psychological Measurement, 10,* 1–22.

Schoenberg, R. (1972). Strategies for meaningful comparison. In H. L. Costner (Ed.), *Sociological methodology 1972* (pp. 1–35). San Francisco: Jossey-Bass.

Schoenberg, R. (1982). Multiple indicator models: Estimation of unconstrained construct means and their standard errors. *Sociological Methods & Research, 10,* 421–433.

Schoenberger, R. A., & Segal, D. R. (1971). The ecology of dissent: The southern Wallace vote in 1968. *Midwest Journal of Political Science, 15,* 583–586.

Schuessler, K. (1971). *Analyzing social data.* Boston: Houghton Mifflin.

Schumm, W. R., Southerly, W. T., & Figley, C. R. (1980). Stumbling block or stepping stone: Path analysis in family studies. *Journal of Marriage and the Family, 42,* 251–262.

Schwille, J. R. (1975). Predictors of between-student differences in civic education cognitive achievement. In J. V. Torney, A. N. Oppenheim, & R. F. Farnen, *Civic education in ten countries* (pp. 124–158). New York: Wiley.

Scriven, M. (1959). Explanation and prediction in evolutionary theory. *Science, 130,* 447–482.

Scriven, M. (1968). In defense of all causes. *Issues in Criminology, 4,* 79–81.

Scriven, M. (1971). The logic of cause. *Theory and decision, 2,* 49–66.

Scriven, M. (1975). Causation as explanation. *Noùs, 9,* 3–16.

Seaman, M. A., Levin, J. R., & Serlin, R. C. (1991). New developments in pairwise multiple comparisons: Some powerful and practicable procedures. *Psychological Bulletin, 110,* 577–586.

Searle, S. R. (1966). *Matrix algebra for the biological sciences (including applications in statistics).* New York: Wiley.

Searle, S. R. (1971). *Linear models.* New York: Wiley.

Searle, S. R. (1989). Statistical computing packages: Some words of caution. *The American Statistician, 43,* 189–190.

Searle, S. R., & Hudson, G. F. S. (1982). Some distinctive features of output from statistical computing packages for analysis of covariance. *Biometrics, 38,* 737–745.

Sechrest, L. (1963). Incremental validity: A recommendation. *Educational and Psychological Measurement, 23,* 153–158.

Sechrest, L., & Yeaton, W. H. (1982). Magnitudes of experimental effects in social science research. *Evaluation Review, 6,* 579–600.

Sekuler, R., Wilson, H. R., & Owsley, C. (1984). Structural modeling of spatial vision. *Vision Research, 24,* 689–700.

Seligman, D. (1992, June 15). Ask Mr. statistician. *Fortune, 159.*

Seltzer, M. H. (1994). Studying variation in program success: A multilevel modeling approach. *Evaluation Review, 18,* 342–361.

Selvin, H. C., & Stuart, A. (1966). Data-dredging procedures in survey analysis. *The American Statistician, 20*(3), 20–23.

Selvin, S. (1991). *Statistical analysis of epidemiologic data.* New York: Oxford University Press.

Serlin, R. C., & Levin, J. R. (1980). Identifying regions of significance in aptitude-by-treatment-interaction research. *American Educational Research Journal, 17,* 389–399.

Sewell, W. H., & Armer, J. M. (1966). Neighborhood context and college plans. *American Sociological Review, 31,* 159–169.

Shaffer, J. P., & Gillo, M. W. (1974). A multivariate extension of the correlation ratio. *Educational and Psychological Measurement, 34,* 521–524.

Shapiro, M. F., & Charrow, J. D. (1985). Scientific misconduct in investigational drug trials. *The New England Journal of Medicine, 312,* 731–736.

Sharma, S., Durand, R. M., & Gur-Arie, O. (1981). Identification and analysis of moderator variables. *Journal of Marketing Research, 18,* 291–300.

Shaw, B. (1930). Preface on doctors. *Collected works: Plays* (Vol. 12, pp. 3–80). New York: Wm. H. Wise.

Simon, H. A. (1957). *Models of man.* New York: Wiley.

Simon, H. A. (1968). Causation. In D. L. Sills (Ed.), *International encyclopedia of the social sciences* (Vol. 2, pp. 350–356). New York: Macmillan.

Simon, J. L. (1991). *Resampling: Probability and statistics a radically different way.* Arlington, VA: Resampling Stats, 612 N. Jackson St., 22201.

Simpson, E. H. (1951). The interpretation of interaction in contingency tables. *Journal of the Royal Statistical Association,* Series B, *13,* 238–141.

Simpson, G., & Buckhalt, J. A. (1988). Estimating general intelligence functioning in adolescents with the PPVT-R and PIAT using a multiple regression approach. *Educational and Psychological Measurement, 48,* 1097–1103.

Sirotnik, K. A. (1980). Psychometric implications of the unit-of-analysis problem (with examples from the measurement of organizational climate). *Journal of Educational Measurement, 17,* 245–282.

Sirotnik, K. A., & Burstein, L. (1985). Measurement and statistical issues in multilevel research on schooling. *Educational Administration Quarterly, 21,* 169–185.

Sjoberg, G., & Nett, R. (1968). *Methodology for social research.* New York: Harper & Row.

Smith, H. F. (1957). Interpretation of adjusted treatment means and regressions in analysis of covariance. *Biometrics, 13,* 282–308.

Smith, I. L. (1972). The eta coefficient in MANOVA. *Multivariate Behavioral Research, 7,* 361–372.

Smith, K. W. (1977). Another look at the clustering perspective on aggregation problems. *Sociological Methods & Research, 5,* 289–315.

Smith, K. W., & Sasaki, M. S. (1979). Decreasing multicollinearity. *Sociological Methods & Research, 8,* 35–56.

Smith, M. S. (1972). *Equality of educational opportunity:* The basic findings reconsidered. In F. Mosteller & D. P. Moynihan (Eds.), *On equality of educational opportunity* (pp. 230–342). New York: Vintage Books.

Smith, R. J., Arnkoff, D. B., & Wright, T. L. (1990). Test anxiety and academic competence: A comparison of alternative models. *Journal of Counseling Psychology, 37,* 313–321.

Smith, R. L., Ager, J. W., & Williams, D. L. (1992). Suppressor variables in multiple regression/correlation. *Educational and Psychological Measurement, 52,* 1729.

Smyth, L. D. (1982). Psychopathology as a function of neuroticism and a hypnotically implanted aggressive conflict. *Journal of Personality and Social Psychology, 43,* 555–564.

Smyth, L. D. (1984). A correction to the hierarchical regression analysis used by Smyth: A comment on Pedhazur. *Journal of Personality and Social Psychology, 46,* 483–484.

Snedecor, G. W., & Cochran, W. G. (1967). *Statistical methods* (6th ed.). Ames, IA: The Iowa State University Press.

Snee, R. D., & Marquardt, D. W. (1984). Comment: Collinearity diagnostics depend on the domain of prediction, the model, and the data. *The American Statistician, 38,* 83–87.

Snell, E. J. (1987). *Applied statistics: A handbook for BMDP analyses.* New York: Chapman and Hall.

Snow, R. E. (1977). Research on aptitude for learning: A progress report. In L. E. Shulman (Ed.), *Review of research in education 4* (pp. 50–105). Itasca, IL: F. E. Peacock.

Snow, R. E. (1991). The concept of aptitude. In R. E. Snow & D. E. Wiley (Eds.), *Improving inquiry in social science: A volume in honor of L. J. Cronbach* (pp. 249–284). Hillsdale, NJ: Lawrence Erlbaum Associates.

Sobel, M. E. (1986). Some new results on indirect effects and their standard errors in covariance structure models. In N. B. Tuma (Ed.), *Sociological methodology 1986* (pp. 159–186). San Francisco: Jossey-Bass.

Sobel, M. E. (1987). Direct and indirect effects in linear structural equation models. *Sociological Methods & Research, 16,* 155–176.

Sobel, M. E., & Bohrnstedt, G. W. (1985). Use of null models in evaluating the fit of covariance structure models. In N. Tuma (Ed.), *Sociological Methodology 1985* (pp. 152–178). San Francisco: Jossey-Bass.

Sockloff, A. L. (1975). Behavior of the product-moment correlation coefficient when two heterogeneous subgroups are pooled. *Educational and Psychological Measurement, 35,* 267–276.

Specht, D. A., & Warren, R. D. (1975). Comparing causal models. In D. R. Heise (Ed.), *Sociological methodology 1976* (pp. 46–82). San Francisco: Jossey-Bass.

Spence, J. T. (1983). Comment on Lubinski, Tellegen, and Butcher's "masculinity, femininity, and androgyny viewed and assessed as distinct concepts." *Journal of Personality and Social Psychology, 44,* 440–446.

Spencer, N. J., Hartnett, J., & Mahoney, J. (1985). Problems with reviews in the standard editorial practice. *Journal of Social Behavior and Personality, 1,* 21–36.

Sprague, J. (1976). Estimating a Boudon-type contextual model: Some practical and theoretical problems. *Political Methodology, 3,* 333–353.

SPSS Inc. (1993). *SPSS base system syntax reference guide: Release 6.0.* Chicago: Author.

Steiger, J. H. (1988). Aspects of person-machine communication in structural modeling of correlations and covariances. *Multivariate Behavioral Research, 23,* 281–290.

Steiger, J. H. (1990). Structural model evaluation and modification: An interval estimation approach. *Multivariate Behavioral Research, 25,* 173–180.

Stevens, J. (1996). *Applied multivariate statistics for the social sciences* (3rd ed.). Mahwah, NJ: Lawrence Erlbaum Associates.

Stevens, J. P. (1972). Global measures of association in multivariate analysis of variance. *Multivariate Behavioral Research, 7,* 373–378.

Stewart, D., & Love, W. (1968). A general canonical correlation index. *Psychological Bulletin, 70,* 160–163.

Stimson, J. A., Carmines, E. G., & Zeller, R. A. (1978). Interpreting polynomial regression. *Multivariate Behavioral Research, 6,* 515–524.

Stine, R. (1990). An introduction to bootstrap methods. *Sociological Methods & Research, 18,* 243–291.

Stipak, B., & Hensler, C. (1982). Statistical inference in contextual analysis. *American Journal of Political Science, 26,* 151–175.

Stokes, J. (1983). Androgyny as an interactive concept: A reply to Lubinski. *Journal of Counseling Psychology, 30,* 134–136.

Stokes, J., Childs, L., & Fuehrer, A. (1981). Gender and sex roles as predictors of self-disclosure. *Journal of Counseling Psychology, 28,* 510–514.

Stolzenberg, R. M. (1979). The measurement and decomposition of causal effects in nonlinear and nonadditive models. In K. F. Schuessler (Ed.), *Sociological methodology 1980* (pp. 459–488). San Francisco: Jossey-Bass.

Stolzenberg, R. M., & Land, K. C. (1983). Causal modeling in survey research. In P. H. Rossi, J. D. Wright, & A. B. Anderson (Eds.), *Handbook of survey research* (pp. 613–675). New York: Academic Press.

Stone, E. F., & Hollenbeck, J. R. (1984). Some issues associated with the use of moderated regression. *Organizational Behavior and Human Performance, 34,* 195–213.

Stone, E. F., & Hollenbeck, J. R. (1989). Clarifying some controversial issues surrounding statistical procedures for detecting moderator variables: Empirical evidence and related matters. *Journal of Applied Psychology, 74,* 3–10.

Stoto, M. A., & Emerson, J. D. (1983). Power transformations for data analysis. In S. Leinhardt (Ed.), *Sociological methodology 1983–1984* (pp. 126–168). San Francisco: Jossey-Bass.

Strahan, R. F. (1975). Remarks on Bem's measurement of psychological androgyny: Alternative methods and supplementary analysis. *Journal of Consulting and Clinical Psychology, 43,* 568–571.

Strahan, R. F. (1982). Multivariate analysis and the problem of type I error. *Journal of Consulting Psychology, 29,* 175–179.

Strahan, R. F. (1991). Remarks on the binomial effect size display. *American Psychologist, 46,* 1083–1084.

Strube, M. J. (1988). Some comments on the use of magnitude-of-effect estimates. *Journal of Counseling Psychology, 35,* 342–345.

Sujan, H., Weitz, B. A., & Kumar, N. (1994). Learning orientation, working smart, and effective selling. *Journal of Marketing, 58,* 39–52.

Summers, A. A., & Wolfe, B. L. (1974, December). *Equality of educational opportunity: A production function approach.* Paper presented at the meeting of the Econometric Society.

Summers, A. A., & Wolfe, B. L. (1975). Which school resources help learning? Efficiency and equity in Philadelphia public schools. *Federal Reserve Bank of Philadelphia Business Review,* February Issue.

Summers, A. A., & Wolfe, B. L. (1977). Do schools make a difference? *American Economic Review, 67,* 639–652.

Swafford, M. (1980). Three parametric techniques for contingency table analysis: A nontechnical commentary. *American Sociological Review, 45,* 664–690.

Swaminathan, H. (1989). Interpreting the results of multivariate analysis of variance. In B. Thompson (Ed.), *Advances in social science methodology* (Vol. 1, pp. 205–232). Greenwich, CT: JAI Press.

Tanaka, J. S. (1987). "How big is big enough?": Sample size and goodness of fit in structural equation models with latent variables. *Child Development, 58,* 134–146.

Tanaka, J. S. (1993). Multifaceted conceptions of fit in structural equation models. In K. A. Bollen & J. S. Long (Eds.), *Testing structural equation models* (pp. 10–39). Thousand Oaks, CA: Sage.

Tannenbaum, A. S., & Bachman, J. G. (1964). Structural versus individual effects. *American Journal of Sociology, 69,* 585–595.

Tatsuoka, M. M. (1970). *Discriminant analysis.* Champaign, IL: Institute for Personality and Ability Testing.

Tatsuoka, M. M. (1971). *Significance tests: Univariate and multivariate.* Champaign, IL: Institute for Personality and Ability Testing.

Tatsuoka, M. M. (1973). Multivariate analysis in educational research. In F. N. Kerlinger (Ed.), *Review of research in education 1* (pp. 273–319). Itasca, IL: Peacock.

Tatsuoka, M. M. (1974). *Classification procedures: Profile similarity.* Champaign, IL: Institute for Personality and Ability Testing.

Tatsuoka, M. M. (1975). Classification procedures. In D. J. Amick & H. J. Walberg (Eds.), *Introductory multivariate analysis: For educational, psychological, and social research* (pp. 257–284). Berkeley, CA: McCuthan.

Tatsuoka, M. M. (1976). Discriminant analysis. In P. M. Bentler, D. J. Lettieri, & G. A. Austin (Eds.), *Data analysis strategies and designs for substance abuse research* (pp. 201–220). Washington, DC: U.S. Government Printing Office.

Tatsuoka, M. M. (1988). *Multivariate analysis: Techniques for educational and psychological research* (2nd ed.). New York: Macmillan.

Tellegen, A., & Lubinski, D. (1983). Some methodological comments on labels, traits, interaction, and types in the study of "femininity" and "masculinity": Reply to Spence. *Journal of Personality and Social Psychology, 44,* 447–455.

Terman, L. M. (Ed.). (1926). *Genetic studies of genius* (Vol. 1, 2nd ed.). Stanford, CA: Stanford University Press.

Thisted, R. A. (1979). Teaching statistical computing using computer packages. *The American Statistician, 33,* 27–30.

Thisted, R. A., & Velleman, P. F. (1992). Computers and modern statistics. In D. C. Hoaglin & D. S. Moore (Eds.), *Perspectives on contemporary statistics* (pp. 41–53). Washington, DC: Mathematical Association of America.

Thomas, D. H. (1978). The awful truth about statistics in archaeology. *American Antiquity, 43,* 231–244.

Thomas, S. P., & Williams, R. L. (1991). Perceived stress, trait anger, modes of anger expression, and health status of college men and women. *Nursing Research, 40,* 303–307.

Thompson, B. (1989). Editorial: Why won't stepwise methods die? *Measurement and Evaluation in Counseling and Development, 21,* 146–148.

Thompson, B. (Ed.). (1993). Statistical significance testing in contemporary practice: Some proposed alternatives with comments from journal editors [special issue]. *Journal of Experimental Education, 61*(4).

Thompson, B., & Borrello, G. M. (1985). The importance of structure coefficients in regression research. *Educational and Psychological Measurement, 45,* 203–209.

Thorndike, E. L. (1939). On the fallacy of imputing the correlations found for groups to the individuals or smaller groups composing them. *American Journal of Psychology, 52,* 122–124.

Thorndike, R. L. (1949). *Personnel selection: Test and measurement techniques.* New York: Wiley.

Thorndike, R. L. (1973). *Reading comprehension in fifteen countries.* New York: Wiley.

Thorndike, R. M. (1978). *Correlational procedures for research.* New York: Gardner Press.

Thorndike, R. M., Cunningham, G. K., Thorndike, R. L., & Hagen, E. P. (1991). *Measurement and evaluation in psychology and education* (5th ed.). New York: Macmillan.

Thorndike, R. M., & Weiss, D. J. (1973). A study of the stability of canonical correlations and canonical components. *Educational and Psychological Measurement, 33,* 123–134.

Timm, N. H. (1975). *Multivariate analysis with applications in education and psychology.* Monterey, CA: Brooks/Cole.

Tokar, D. M., & Swanson, J. L. (1991). An investigation of the validity of Helms's (1984) model of White racial identity development. *Journal of Counseling Psychology, 3,* 296–301.

Toothaker, L. E. (1991). *Multiple comparisons for researchers.* Thousand Oaks, CA: Sage.

Torney, J. V., Oppenheim, A. N., & Farnen, R. F. (1975). *Civic education in ten countries.* New York: Wiley.

Travers, R. M. W. (1981). Letter to the editor. *Educational Researcher, 10*(6), 32.

Trochim, W. M. K. (1984). *Research design for program evaluation: The regression-discontinuity approach.* Thousand Oaks, CA: Sage.

Trochim, W. M. K., Cappelleri, J. C., & Reichardt, C. S. (1991). Random measurement error does not bias the treatment effect estimate in the regression-discontinuity design: II. When an interaction effect is present. *Evaluation Review, 15,* 571–604.

Tuckman, B. W. (1990). A proposal for improving the quality of published educational research. *Educational Researcher, 19*(9), 22–24.

Tukey, J. W. (1954). Causation, regression, and path analysis. In O. Kempthorne, T. A. Bancroft, J. W. Gowen, & J. D. Lush (Eds.), *Statistics and mathematics in biology* (pp. 35–66). Ames, IA: Iowa State College Press.

Tukey, J. W. (1969). Analyzing data: Sanctification or detective work? *American Psychologist, 24,* 83–91.

Turner, M. E., & Stevens, C. D. (1959). The regression analysis of causal paths. *Biometrics, 15,* 236–258.

Twain, M. (1911). *Life on the Mississippi.* New York: Harper & Brothers.

Tzelgov, J., & Henik, A. (1981). On the differences between Conger's and Velicer's definitions of suppressor. *Educational and Psychological Measurement, 41,* 1027–1031.

Tzelgov, J., & Henik, A. (1991). Suppression situations in psychological research: Definitions, implications, and applications. *Psychological Bulletin, 109,* 524–536.

Ulam, S. M. (1976). *Adventures of a mathematician.* New York: Scribner's.

Valkonen, T. (1969). Individual and structural effects in ecological research. In M. Dogan & S. Rokkan (Eds.), *Social ecology* (pp. 53–68). Cambridge, MA: M.I.T. Press.

Van Ryzin, J. (Ed.). (1977). *Classification and clustering.* New York: Academic Press.

Velicer, W. F. (1978). Suppressor variables and the semipartial correlation coefficient. *Educational and Psychological Measurement, 38,* 953–958.

Velleman, P. F., & Welsch, R. E. (1981). Efficient computing of regression diagnostics. *The American Statistician, 35,* 234–242.

von Eye, A., & Clogg, C. C. (Eds.). (1994). *Latent variables analysis: Applications for developmental research.* Thousand Oaks, CA: Sage.

Wagner, C. H. (1982). Simpson's paradox in real life. *The American Statistician, 36,* 46–48.

Wainer, H. (1972). A practical note on one-tailed tests. *American Psychologist, 27,* 775–776.

Wainer, H., & Thissen, D. (1986). *Plotting in the modern world.* Princeton, NJ: Educational Testing Service.

Walker, A. M., & Rothman, K. J. (1982). Models of varying parametric form in case-referent studies. *American Journal of Epidemiology, 115,* 129–137.

Walker, H. M. (1928). A note on the correlation of averages. *Journal of Educational Psychology, 19,* 636–642.

Walker, H. M. (1940). Degrees of freedom. *Journal of Educational Psychology, 31,* 253–269.

Walker, H. M., & Lev, J. (1953). *Statistical inference.* New York: Henry Holt.

Wallace, W. A. (1972, 1974). *Causality and scientific explanation* (2 Vols.). Ann Arbor, MI: University of Michigan Press.

Walter, S. D., & Holford, T. R. (1978). Additive, multiplicative, and other models for disease risks. *American Journal of Epidemiology, 108,* 341–346.

Ward, J. H. (1969). Partitioning variance and contribution or importance of a variable: A visit to a graduate seminar. *American Educational Research Journal, 6,* 467–474.

Warren, W. G. (1971). Correlation or regression: Bias or precision. *Applied Statistics, 20,* 148–164.

Weigel, C., Wertlieb, D., & Feldstein, M. (1989). Perceptions of control, competence, and contingency as influences on the stress-behavior relation in school-age children. *Journal of Personality and Social Psychology, 56,* 456–464.

Weiner, B. (1974). *Achievement motivation and attribution theory.* Morristown, NJ: General Learning Press.

Weisberg, H. I. (1979). Statistical adjustments and uncontrolled studies. *Psychological Bulletin, 86,* 1149–1164.

Weisberg, S. (1980). *Applied linear regression.* New York: Wiley.

Weisberg, S. (1985). *Applied linear regression* (2nd ed.). New York: Wiley.

Welsch, R. E. (1986). Comment. *Statistical Science, 1,* 403–405.

Werts, C. E., & Linn, R. L. (1969). Analyzing school effects: How to use the same data to support different hypotheses. *American Educational Research Journal, 6,* 439–447.

Werts, C. E., & Watley, D. J. (1968). Analyzing college effects: Correlation vs. regression. *American Educational Research Journal, 5,* 585–598.

Werts, C. E., & Watley, D. J. (1969). A student's dilemma: Big fish—little pond or little fish—big pond. *Journal of Counseling Psychology, 16,* 14–19.

Wheaton, B. (1987). Assessment of fit in overidentified models with latent variables. *Sociological Methods & Research, 16,* 118–154.

Wherry, R. J. (1975). Underprediction from overfitting: 45 years of shrinkage. *Personnel Psychology, 28,* 1–18.

White, P. A. (1990). Ideas about causation in philosophy and psychology. *Psychological Bulletin, 108,* 3–18.

Wiggins, J. S., & Holzmuller, A. (1978). Psychological androgyny and interpersonal behavior. *Journal of Consulting and Clinical Psychology, 46,* 40–52.

Wilkinson, L. (1975). Response variable hypotheses in the multivariate analysis of variance. *Psychological Bulletin, 82,* 408–412.

Wilkinson, L. (1979). Tests of significance in stepwise regression. *Psychological Bulletin, 86,* 168–174.

Willett, J. B. (1988). Questions and answers in the measurement of change. In E. Z. Rothkopf (Ed.), *Review of research in education* (Vol. 15, pp. 345–422). Washington, DC: American Educational Research Association.

Willett, J. B., & Sayer, A. G. (1994). Using covariance structure analysis to detect correlates and predictors of individual change over time. *Psychological Bulletin, 116,* 363–381.

Williams, E. J. (1959). *Regression analysis.* New York: Wiley.

Williams, L. J., & Holahan, P. J. (1994). Parsimony-based fit indices for multiple-indicator models: Do they work? *Structural Equation Modeling, 1,* 161–189.

Willms, J. D. (1986). Social class segregation and its relationship to pupils' examination results in Scotland. *American Sociological Review, 51,* 224–241.

Winer, B. J. (1971). *Statistical principles in experimental design* (2nd ed.). New York: McGraw-Hill.

Wisler, C. E. (1969). Partitioning the explained variance in regression analysis. In G. W. Mayeske et al., *A study of our nation's schools* (pp. 344–360). Washington, DC: U.S. Department of Health, Education, and Welfare, Office of Education.

Wold, H. (1956). Causal inference from observational data: A review of ends and means. *Journal of the Royal Statistical Society* (Series A), *119,* 28–61.

Wold, H., & Juréen, L. (1953). *Demand analysis.* New York: Wiley.

Wolf, F. M., & Cornell, R. G. (1986). Interpreting behavioral, biomedical, and psychological relationships in chronic disease from 2 × 2 tables using correlation. *Journal of Chronic Disease, 39,* 605–608.

Wolins, L. (1982). *Research mistakes in the social and behavioral sciences.* Ames, IA: Iowa State University Press.

Wong, Mei-ha, M., & Csikszentmihalyi, M. (1991). Motivation and academic achievement: The effects of personality traits and the quality of experience. *Journal of Personality, 59,* 539–574.

Wong Sin-Kwok, R. (1994). Model selection and use of association models to detect group differences. *Sociological Methods & Research, 22,* 460–491.

Wood, C. G., & Hokanson, J. E. (1965). Effects of induced muscular tension on performance and the inverted U function. *Journal of Personality and Social Psychology, 1,* 506–510.

Woodhouse, G. (1992). [Review of *Schools, classrooms, and pupils: International studies of schooling from a multilevel perspective*]. *Multilevel Modelling Newsletter, 4*(3), 2–4.

Woodhouse, G., & Goldstein, H. (1988). Educational performance indicators and LEA league tables. *Oxford Review of Education, 14,* 301–320.

Wright, G. C. (1976). Linear models for evaluating conditional relationships. *American Journal of Political Science, 20,* 349–373.

Wright, S. (1934). The method of path coefficients. *Annals of Mathematical Statistics, 5,* 161–215.

Wright, S. (1954). The interpretation of multivariate systems. In O. Kempthorne, T. A. Bancroft, J. W. Gowen, & J. D. Lush (Eds.), *Statistics and mathematics in biology* (pp. 11–33). Ames, IA: Iowa State College Press.

Wright, S. (1960). Path coefficients and path regressions: Alternative or complementary concepts? *Biometrics, 16,* 189–202.

Wright, S. (1968). *Genetics and biometric foundations* (Vol. 1). Chicago: University of Chicago Press.

Wyatt, G. E., & Newcomb, M. (1990). Internal and external mediators of women's sexual abuse in childhood. *Journal of Consulting and Clinical Psychology, 58,* 758–767.

Yang, M., Woodhouse, G., Goldstein, H., Pan, H., & Rasbash, J. (1992). Adjusting for measurement unreliability in multilevel modelling. *Multilevel Modelling Newsletter, 4*(2), 7–9.

Yarandi, H. N., & Simpson, S. H. (1991). The logistic regression model and the odds of testing HIV positive. *Nursing Research, 40,* 372–373.

Yates, F. (1968). Theory and practice in statistics. *Journal of the Royal Statistical Society,* Series A, *131,* 463–475.

Young, B. W., & Bress, G. B. (1975). Coleman's retreat and the politics of good intentions. *Phi Delta Kappan, 55,* 159–166.

Zeger, S. L. (1991). Statistical reasoning in epidemiology. *American Journal of Epidemiology, 134,* 1062–1066.

Zeisel, H. (1985). *Say it with figures* (6th ed.). New York: Harper & Row.

Zeller, R. A., & Carmines, E. G. (1980). *Measurement in the social sciences: The link between theory and data.* Cambridge: Cambridge University Press.

Zellner, A. (1992). Statistics, science and public policy. *Journal of the American Statistical Association, 87,* 1–6.

NAME INDEX

SUBJECT INDEX